Miss Ann Mackenzie

THE NEW STANDARD DICTIONARY

A Completely New Dictionary of the living language, designed on the most modern lines--the spelling, pronunciation and meaning of over 30,000 words with synonyms and antonyms and classified supplements

THE LITERARY PRESS
GLASGOW

GENERAL EDITOR: G. F. MAINE

CONTENTS

Printed in Great Britain at the Press of the Publishers

HOW TO USE THIS DICTIONARY

A modern dictionary is much more than a collection of words which go to form a vocabulary. It is a vital organism which must grow continuously if it is to keep pace with new notations and adapt itself to current needs. It must include not only words which have become indispensable because of tradition and usage, and new words which have been minted for the requirements of modern scientific and cultural progress, but also those terse and colourful idioms which add spice to conversation, and some of which have become permanent features in our language.

The aim of the editors has been to supply, in a book of reasonable length, a really comprehensive vocabulary in which the user will find all that he requires: all, that is, other than words which are too technical or too archaic for everyday use. This has been made possible only by methods of compilation and setting which have achieved miracles of space-saving, and this without any sacrifice of clarity or content. No other dictionary of similar dimensions contains so full and varied a vocabulary. Furthermore its keynote is simplicity. Special care has been taken to present the meaning of words clearly and precisely, a fact which makes this dictionary an indispensable reference book in home, school or office.

The pronunciation of most words is indicated simply by placing an accent (′) immediately after the accented syllable. The division of words into syllables in English is more or less arbitrary and advantage has been taken of this to show differences of pronunciation in the vowels. Where the accent comes after the vowel this is usually pronounced long, but where the accent follows a consonant, the vowel of that syllable is to be taken as short; thus, **sa′vour** with a long *a*, but **sav′age** with a short *a*; **crit′ical** with a short vowel, **cri′sis** with a long one. Words of one syllable are not shown with an accent, and the silent *e* (e.g. at the end of words such as *bite*, *abate*, etc.) is ignored. For most words this indication of the stress will be found enough, but wherever the spelling is misleading, or there is some peculiarity of pronunciation, this is explained in a bracket immediately after the word (e.g. **enough′** (e-nuf′), **laugh** (lāf), **rose** (-z)). The notation used for the phonetic re-spelling of words or parts of words is as follows:—

ā m*a*te.	a p*a*t.	ė there.
ē mete.	e pet.	ȧ f*a*ther.
ī m*i*te.	i p*i*t.	e̱ her.
ō mote.	o pot.	aw *aw*l.
ū m*u*te.	u n*u*t.	oi *oi*l.
o͞o boot.	oo foot.	ow *ow*l.

th	*th*in (a voiceless sound.)	y	*y*et.
TH	*th*ine (a voiced sound).	g	*g*et.
zh	lei*s*ure, a*z*ure.	j	*j*am, *g*entleman.
ch	*ch*ur*ch*.	hw	*wh*en.
ng	si*ng*.	s	*s*i*s*ter.

The French nasalised *n* is denoted thus : bõn.

ACKNOWLEDGMENTS

The compilation of a modern dictionary necessarily requires the work of experts in many subjects, and grateful thanks are due to the helpers who have taken part in an exacting task ; to the following especially :

Professor Abel Coetzee, M.A., D.Litt., D.Lit. et Phil., George Mac Raness, Litt.D., and Anne Scott, M.A.

ABBREVIATIONS
USED IN THIS BOOK

a	. adjective	*pl.*	. plural
abbrev.	. abbreviation	*p.p.*	. past participle
adv.	. adverb	*prep.*	. preposition
Ant.	. Antonym	*pres.*	. present
comp.	. comparative	*pres. p.*	. present participle
conj.	. conjunction	*pron.*	. pronoun
esp.	. especially	*p.t.*	. past tense
f., fem.	. feminine	*sing.*	. singular
fig.	. figuratively	*sl.*	. slang
ind.	. indicative	*sup.*	. superlative
interj.	. interjection	*Syn.*	. Synonym
m.	. masculine	*v. aux.*	. auxiliary verb
n., ns.	. noun, nouns	*v.i.*	. intransitive verb
v. refl.	. reflexive verb	lit.	. literally
v.t.	. transitive verb	obs.	. obsolete
		orig.	. originally
apoth.	. apothecaries' weight	pert.	. pertaining
avoir.	. avoirdupois weight	prob.	. probably
corrupt.	. corruption	q.v.	. which see
cp.	. compare	R.C.	. Roman Catholic
dial.	. dialect	S.	. South
dim.	. diminutive	Sp.	. Spanish
e.g.	. for instance	U.S.,	} United States of
fr.	. from	U.S.A.	} America
gen.	. generally	v.i.	. see below
i.e.	. that is	v.s.	. see above

DICTIONARY

OF THE ENGLISH LANGUAGE

A

a, an *a.* one; any.—*prefix,* without; as *apathy, anarchy.* [surprised.
aback' *adv.* backwards.—**taken aback,**
ab'acus *n.* a flat piece at the top of a column; a frame with parallel wires on which slide beads for counting.
abaft' *adv.* and *prep.* behind.
aban'don *v.t.* to give up altogether.—**aban'doned** *p.p.* and *a.* given up, *esp.* to evil.—**aban'donment** *n.*
Syn. to yield, surrender, cede, relinquish, renounce. *Ant.* to keep, retain, adhere to, cherish.
abase' *v.t.* to lower, humiliate.—**abase'ment** *n.* (**abas'ing** *pres. p.*)
abash' *v.t.* to make ashamed.
abate' *v.t.* to lessen.—*v.i.* to become less. —**abate'ment** *n.* reduction.
ab'atis, ab'attis *n.* a barricade of felled trees for defence.
abattoir' *n.* slaughter-house.
ab'be (ab-ā) *n.* a cleric in minor orders; an ecclesiastic without charge.
abb'ot *n.* the head of a monastery.—**abb'ess** *n. fem.*—**abb'ey** *n.* a monastery. —**abb'acy** *n.* the office of abbot.
abbre'viate *v.t.* to shorten.—**abbrevia'tion** *n.* a shortened form.
ab'dicate *v.t.* to give up formally.—*v.i.* to give up power.—**abdica'tion** *n.*
abdo'men *n.* belly.—**abdom'inal** *a.*
abduct' *v.t.* to carry off.—**abduc'tion** *n.*
abeam' *adv.* abreast (*nautical*).
abed' *adv.* in bed.
abberra'tion *n.* wandering, *esp.* mental disorder; (*opt.*) divergence.—**aber'rant** *a.*
abet' *v.t.* to help in something bad.—**abett'er, abett'or** *n.* (**abet'ted** *p.t./pr.p.*) **abet'ment** *n.* act of abetting.
abey'ance *n.* condition of not being in use or action.—suspension; disuse.
abhor' *v.t.* to dislike very strongly, loathe.—**abhor'rence** *n.*—**abhor'rent** *a.*
abide' *v.i.* to stay, reside.—*v.t.* to endure (**abode'** *p.t.* and *p.p.*—**abi'ding** *pres.p.*).
ab'ject *a.* mean, despicable; miserable.—**ab'jectly** *adv.*
abjure' *v.t.* to give up by oath, renounce. —**abjura'tion** *n.* (**abju'ring** *pres.p.*).
ab'lative *a.* and *n.* a Latin case of nouns, primarily meaning "away from."
ablaze' *a.* burning; on fire; glowing.
a'ble *a.* capable, having power.—**a'bly** *adv.*—**abil'ity** *n.*—**able-bod'ied** *adj.*
ablep'sy *n.* want of sight; blindness.
ablu'tion *n.* washing; clensing the body.
ab'negate *v.t.* to give up, renounce.—**abnega'tion** *n.* rejection; self-sacrifice.
abnorm'al *a.* irregular; not usual.—**abnorm'ally** *adv.*—**abnormal'ity** *n.*
aboard' *adv.* on a ship, train or plane.—*prep.* on board of.
abode' *n.* home; dwelling.—*p.t.* and *p.p.* of **abide.**
abol'ish *v.t.* to do away with.—**aboli'tion** *n.*—**aboli'tionist** *n.* one who wishes to abolish an evil, e.g. slavery.
abom'inate *v.t.* to detest.—**abom'inable** *a.*—**abom'inably** *adv.*—**abomina'tion** *n.*
aborig'ines (-ji-nēz) *n.pl.* the original inhabitants of a country.—**aborig'inal** *a.*
abort' *v.i.* to miscarry.—**abor'tion** *n.* something misshapen or unnatural.—**abort'ive** *a.*—**abort'ively** *adv.*
abound' *v.i.* to be plentiful.
about' *adv.* on all sides; nearly; out, astir.—*prep.* round; near; dealing with.
above' *adv.* in a higher place; overhead. —*prep.* on top of; more than; higher in rank.—**above'-board** *a.* honest.
abrade' *v.t.* to rub off, scrape away.—**abra'sion** *n.* a place worn or rubbed.
abreac'tion *n.* in psycho-analysis, elimination of a morbid complex by association with the original cause.
abreast' *adv.* side by side.
abridge' *v.t.* to cut short, abbreviate.—**abridg'ment** *n.* (**abridg'ing** *pres.p.*).
abroad' *adv.* out of house or country; at large.—**to spread abroad.**
ab'rogate *v.t.* to cancel.—**abroga'tion** *n.*
abrupt' *a.* hasty; steep; sudden; blunt. —**abrupt'ness** *n.*—**abrupt'ly** *adv.*
ab'scess (-ses) *n.* a collection of pus.
abscind' (sind) *v.t.* to cut off; to rend apart.—**abscis'sion** *n.*
abscond'(-sk-) *v.i.* to withdraw, decamp.
ab'sent *a.* away; not attentive.—**absent** *v.t.* to keep away.—**ab'sent-mind'ed** *a.*—**ab'sence** *n.*—**ab'sently** *adv.* —**absentee'** *n.* one who habitually stays away.—**absentee'ism** *n.* the practice of a landlord living away from his estate or of workers absenting themselves from work without permission.
absinthe' *n.* wormwood; liqueur flavoured with wormwood.
absolve' *v.t.* to free from, pardon.—

absolu'tion *n.*—**ab'solute** *a.* not limited, unconditional; entire, pure (as *absolute alcohol*).—**ab'soluteness** *n.* **ab'solutely** *adv.*
absorb' *v.t.* to drink in.—**absorp'tion** *n.* —**absorb'ent** *n.* and *a.*—**absorp'tive** *a.*
abstain' *v.i.* to keep from, refrain, *esp.* from strong drink.—**abstain'er** *n.*—**absten'tion** *n.*—**ab'stinence** *n.* an abstaining.—**ab'stinent** *a.* abstemius.
abste'mious *a.* sparing in food or *esp.* drink.—**abste'miousness** *n.*—**abste'miously** *adv.*
absterge' *v.t.* to clean by wiping.—**abster'gent** *a.*—**abster'sion** *n.*
ab'stract *a.* separate; existing only in the mind; not concrete.—*n.* a summary, abridgment.—**abstract'** *v.t.* to draw from, remove.—**abstrac'tion** *n.* **abstract'ed** *a.* absent-minded.—**abstract'ly** *adv.*
abstruse' *n.* hard to understand, profound.—**abstruse'ly** *adv.*
absurd' *a.* silly, contrary to reason.—**absurd'ity** *n.*—**absurd'ly** *adv.*
abun'dance *n.* great plenty.—**abun'dant** *a.*—**abun'dantly** *adv.*
abuse' (-būz) *v.t.* to misuse; address in rude language.—**abuse'** (-būs) *n.*—**abu'sive** *a.*—**abu'sively** *adv.*
abut' *v.i.* to border on.—**abut'ment** *n.* a support, *esp.* for the end of a bridge.
abyss' *n.* a very deep gulf or pit.—**abys'mal** (-z-) *a.*—**abys'mally** *adv.*
aca'cia (a-kā'sha) *n.* a genus of thorny gum-yielding tree.
acad'emy *n.* a higher school; a society to advance arts or sciences.—**academi'cian** *n.*—**academ'ic, academ'ical** *a.* of an academy; theoretical.—**academ'ically** *adv.*
acan'thus *n.* a prickly plant; an architectural ornament like its leaf (**acan'thuses, -thi** *pl.*)
accede' (aks-) *v.i.* to enter on an office; agree, consent.—**acces'sion** *n.*
accel'erate (aks-) *v.t.* and *i.* to quicken motion, increase speed.—**accelera'tion** *n.*—**accel'erative** *a.*—**accel'erator** *n.* mechanism to increase speed, *esp.* in motoring. *Syn.* speed up, quicken, expedite, despatch. *Ant.* retard, check, linger.
ac'cent (aks-) *n.* a stress of the voice; a mark to show such stress; a manner of speech peculiar to a district or individual.—**accent'** *v.t.*—**accent'uate** *v.t.* —**accentua'tion** *n.*—**accent'ual** *a.*
accept' (aks-) *v.t.* to take, receive; admit; agree to.—**accept'able** *a.*—**accept'ably** *adv.*—**acceptabil'ity**—**accept'ance**—**accepta'tion**—**accept'er** *ns.*
ac'cess (aks-) *n.* admission; entrance; attack.—**access'ible** *a.* easy to approach. —**accessibil'ity** *n.*—**access'ibly** *adv.*—**access'ary** *n.* a helper, *esp.* in a crime.—**access'ory** *n.* something helping or additional.—*a.* contributing.
ac'cidence (aks-) *n.* the part of grammar dealing with changes in the form of words, e.g. plurals, etc.
ac'cident (aks-) *n.* something happening by chance; a mishap, a quality not essential, **accident'al** *a.* **accident'ally** *adv.*
acclaim' *v.t.* to applaud, receive with applause, **acclama'tion** *n.* **acclam'atory** *a.*
accli'matize *v.t.* to accustom to a new climate.—**acclimatiza'tion** *n.*
acclivi'ty *n.* an upward slope.
accolade' *n.* part of the ceremony of conferring knighthood, a light stroke with a sword.
accomm'odate *v.t.* to fit; harmonise; supply.—**accommo'dating** *a.* obliging.—**accommoda'tion** *n.* lodgings; a loan.
accom'pany *v.t.* to go with; join with (**accom'panied** *p.t.* and *p.p.*—**accom'panying** *pres. p.*).—**accom'paniment** *n.* something which accompanies *esp.* in music.—**accom'panist** *n.* one who plays an accompaniment.
accom'plice *n.* a companion *esp.* in evil deeds.
accom'plish *v.t.* to carry out; finish.—**accom'plished** *a.* complete, perfect.—**accom'plishment** *n.* completion; a personal ability.
Syn. to achieve, effect, execute, fulfil, realise, perfect. *Ant.* fail in, leave unfinished or incomplete, spoil.
accord' *v.t.* to compose, settle.—*v.i.* to agree.—*n.* agreement, harmony.—**accord'ant** *a.*—**accord'ance** *n.*—**accord'ing** *adv.*—**accord'ingly** *adv.* as the circumstances suggest; therefore.
accord'ion *n.* a wind instrument worked by a bellows in the hands.
accost' *v.t.* to speak to, approach.
account' *v.t.* to reckon, judge.—*v.i.* to give a reason; make a statement of money.—*n.* a statement of monies; a report, description.—**account'able** *a.* responsible.—**accountabil'ity** *n.*—**account'ant** *n.* one skilled in accounts.
accou'tre (-ōō'-) *v.t.* to equip.—**accou'trements** *n. pl.* equipment, *esp.* military.
accred'it *v.t.* to recommend; vouch for.
accre'tion *n.* something added on.
accrue' (-ōō') *v.i.* to result; come as an addition (**accru'ing** *pres.p.*—**accrued'** *p.t.* and *p.p.*)
accu'mulate *v.t.* to amass.—*v.i.* to grow into a mass, increase.—**accumula'tion** *n.* —**accu'mulator** *n.* an electrical battery.
acc'urate *a.* exact, correct; precise.—**acc'urately** *adv.*—**acc'uracy** *n.* exactness.
accurs'ed, accurst' *a.* under a curse, ill-fated, hateful.
accuse' *v.t.* to charge with wrong-doing; blame.—**accu'ser** *n.*—**accusa'tion** *n.*—**accu'satory** *a.*—**accu'sative** *n.* a Latin case indicating the direct object.
accus'tom *v.t.* to make used to.—**accus'tomed** *a.* familiar; usual.
ace *n.* the one at dice, cards, dominoes; *sl.* airman who has shot down 5 or more

enemy planes; one expert, highly skilled in any achievement, as a *flying ace.*
acen'tric (-sen'-) *a.* not central.
acer'bate *v.t.* to make bitter; to exasperate; *a.* embittered; severe.
acerb'ity *n.* sourness; bitterness.
acetan'ilide (as-et-an'-il-īd) *n.* a white, crystalline odourless drug which reduces pain and fever.
ace'tic *a.* derived from or having the nature of vinegar.—**ac'etous** (as'-) *a.*
ac'etone (as'-) *n.* an inflammable gas.
acet'ylene *n.* an illuminating gas, made from calcium carbide and water.
ache (āk) *n.* a continuous pain.—*v.i.* to be in pain.—**ach'ing** *a.* (**ach'ed** *p.t./p.p.*).
achieve' *v.t.* to finish, accomplish.—**achieve'ment** *n.* something accomplished.
achromat'ic *a.* free from or not showing colour, as of a lens.
ac'id *a.* sharp, sour.—*n.* a sour substance, one of a class of compounds which combine with bases (alkalis, oxides, etc.) to form salts.—**acid'ify** *v.t.* (-**ified** *p.t.* and *p.p.*—**ifying** *pres.p.*)—**acid'ity** *n.*—**acido'sis** *n.* a state of acidity in the blood.—**acid'ulous** *a.*—**acid'ulate** *v.t.* to make slightly acid.—**acid test,** conclusive test.
ack-ack' *n. sl.* anti-aircraft guns or gun-fire.
ack emm'a *n.* signallers' name for A.M. of time and air mechanic.
acknowl'edge (ak-nol'ij) *v.t.* to admit, own, recognise.—**acknowl'edgment** *n.*
ac'me *n.* highest point, culmination; point of perfection.
acne (ak'ni) *n.* skin disease, eruption of inflamed pimples due to defective functioning of skin and sweat glands.
ac'olyte *n.* an attendant on a priest.
ac'onite *n.* a poisonous plant; wolf's bane, or monks' hood.
a'corn (āk-) *n.* the fruit of the oak.
acous'tic *a.* pertaining to hearing.—**acous'tics** *n.pl.* the science of sounds.—**acous'ticon** *n.* an appliance to aid hearing.
acquaint' *v.t.* to make to know, inform.—**acquaint'ance** *n.* personal knowledge; a person known.—**acquaint'anceship** *n.*
acquiesce' *v.i.* to agree in silence; consent.—**acquies'cence** *n.*—**acquies'cent** *a.*
acquire' *v.t.* to gain, get.—**acquire'ment** *n.*—**acquisi'tion** *n.* act of getting; a material gain.—**acquis'itive** *a.* desirous of gaining.—**acquis'itiveness** *n.*
acquit' *v.t.* to settle, discharge, as a debt; declare innocent.—**acquitt'al** *n.* act of declaring innocent in a court.—**acquitt'ance** *n.* discharge of a debt.
a'cre (-ker) a measure of land, 4840 square yards; *pl.* lands, estates.—**a'creage** *n.* area in acres.
ac'rid *a.* bitter and hot; irritating.—**acrid'ity** *n.*—**ac'ridness** *n.*
ac'rimony *n.* bitterness of feelings or language.—**acrimo'nious** *a.* sharp.
Syn. harshness, animosity, asperity. *Ant.* love, concord, sympathy.
ac'robat *n.* a rope-dancer; tumbler, gymnast.—**acrobat'ic** *a.*
across' *adv.* and *prep.* cross-wise; from one side to the other; on the other side.
acros'tic *n.* a poem in which the first and or last letters of the lines in order, spell a word or words.
act *n.* a thing done, a deed; process of doing; law; section of a play.—*v.t.* to perform, as in a play.—*v.i.* to exert force; work, as a mechanism; behave.—**Act of God** (*leg.*) *n.* the workings of the forces of Nature causing unavoidable, disastrous effects, e.g. earthquakes.—**act'ing** *n.* performance of a part; working.—**ac'tion** *n.* activity; operation; gesture; a battle; a lawsuit.—**ac'tionable** *a.* subject to a lawsuit.—**act'ive** *a.* **act'ively** *adv.*—**activ'ity** *n.* **act'or** *n.* (*fem.* **act'ress**).
ac'tinism *n.* the chemical action of the sun's rays.—**actin'ic** *a.*—**actinother'apy** *n.* treatment of disease by light, *esp.* sunshine.
actin'ium *n.* a radio-active substance found in pitchblende.
acti'vate *v.t.* to stimulate; to make chemically active.—**activa'tor** *n.* a catalyst.
ac'tual *a.* real; existing in the present.—**actual'ity** *n.*—**ac'tually** *adv.* in fact.
ac'tuary *n.* a registrar, one who makes calculations for insurance companies.
ac'tuate *v.t.* to move; impel; urge on.
acu'men *n.* sharpness of wit; shrewdness; quickness of perception.
acute' *a.* sharp; sensitive; severe (pain); critical.—**acute'ly** *adv.*—**acute'ness** *n.*
Syn. sagacious, subtle, penetrating. *Ant.* obtuse, dull, stupid.
adage *n.* an old saying, a proverb.
ad'a'gio *a.* and *adv.* (*music*) slowly.
adamant *n.* a very hard stone; diamond.—*a.* very hard.—**adaman'tine** *a.*
Adam's ap'ple *n.* the projecting part of a man's throat; the thyroid cartilage.
adapt *v.t.* to fit; to alter.—**adapta'tion** *n.*—**adapt'able** *a.*—**adaptabil'ity** *n.*
add *v.t.* and *i.* to join; to put something on.—**addi'tion** *n.*—**additional** *a.*—**adden'dum** (-*a. pl.*) something to be added.
add'er *n.* a small poisonous snake.
add'ict *n.* one given up to something, usually an evil, e.g. a *drug-addict.*—**addict'ed** *a.* given over to.—**addic'tion** *n.*
ad'dle *v.t.* and *i.* to make or become rotten; empty.—(**addle-headed**) *a.*
address' *v.t.* to speak to; direct; dispatch.—*n.* skill; a speech; the direction on a letter.—**addressee'** *n.* person addressed.—**address'es** *n.pl.* courtship.
Adress'ograph *n.* a machine for addressing envelopes. (Trade Name.)
adduce' *v.t.* to bring forward as proof; allege.—**addu'cible** *a.*—**adduc'tion** *n.*
ad'enoids *n.pl.* small growths at the back of the nose which impede breathing.
adept' *a.* skilled.—*n.* an expert.

ader'min *n.* a constituent of the vitamin B complex, deficiency in which results in skin eruptions.
ad'equate *a.* sufficient, suitable.—**ad'equacy** *n.*-**ad'equately** *adv.* as required.
adhere' *v.i.* to stick to.—**adhe'rent** *n.* and *a.*—**adhe'sion** *n.* —**adhe'sive** *a.*
adieu' (a-dū') *interj.* farewell.—*n.* act of taking leave (**adieus'**, **adieux'** *pl.*).
ad'ipose *a.* fatty.—**adipos'ity** *n.*
ad'it *n.* a horizontal entrance into a pit.
adja'cent *a.* lying close to, contiguous. —**adja'cency** *n.*
ad'jective *n.* a word added to a noun to show quality, etc.—**adjecti'val** *a.*
adjoin *v.t.* and *i.* to add; to be next to. —**adjoin'ng** *a.* neighbouring.
adjourn' (a-jern') *v.t.* and *i.* to put off, postpone, as a meeting.-**adjourn'ment** *n.*
adjudge' *v.t.* to decide; award. (**adjudg'ing** *pres.p.*).—**adjudg(e)ment** *n.*
adju'dicate *v.t.* and *i*, to try, judge; to sit in judgment.—**adjudica'tion** *n.*—**adju'dicator** *n.*
ad'junct *a.* joined, added.—*n.* a person or thing added.
adjure' *v.t.* to beg, entreat.—**adjura'tion** *n.*
adjust' *v.t.* to set right; make exact or suitable.—**adjust'ment** *n.*—**adjust'able** *a.*
ad'jutant *n.* a military officer who assists a superior officer.—**ad'jutancy** *n.*
ad-lib' *v.i.* (*music*) to improvise; to insert extemporary variations.
admin'ister *v.t.* to manage, dispense, as justice, etc.; supply.—**administra'tion** *n.*—**admin'istrative** *a.*—**admin'istrator** *n.* (*fem.*) **administra'trix.**
ad'miral *n.* a naval officer of highest rank at sea.—**Ad'miralty** *n.* the board which controls the navy.
admire' *v.t.* to look on with wonder and pleasure; respect highly.—**ad'mirable** *a.* —**ad'mirably** *adv.*—**admira'tion** *n.*—**admi'rer** *n.*—**admi'ringly** *adv.*
admit' *v.t.* to let in; accept as true.—**admiss'ible** *a.*—**admis'sion** *n.*—**admitt'ance** *n.* **admissibil'ity** *n.* **admiss'ibly** *adv.*
Syn. to permit, suffer, tolerate, receive, acknowledge. *Ant.* refuse, reject, deny, repudiate; keep out, exclude.
admix'ture *n.* act of mixing; a blend, alloy, or compound.
admon'ish *v.t.* to warn; reprove gently; advise.—**admoni'tion** *n.*—**admon'itory** *a.*
ado' (a-dōō') *n.* fuss (**ados'**, **adoes'** (*pl.*).
ado'be (-bi) *n.* sun-dried brick.
adoles'cent *a.* growing to manhood.—*n.* a youth.—**adoles'cence** *n.*
adopt' *v.t.* to take into relationship, *esp.* as one's child; to take up, as a principle, a resolution.—**adop'tion** *n.*—**adopt'ive** *a.*
adore' *v.t.* and *i.* to worship; love intensely.—**ado'rable** *a.*—**adora'tion** *n.*
adorn' *v.t.* to beautify, embellish.—**adorn'ment** *n.* ornament.
adre'nalin *n.* extract of the adrenal glands, a powerful astringent.—**adrenal glands**, the suprarenal glands, two ductless glands near the kidneys.
adrift' *a.* and *adv.* floating free.
adroit' *a.* skilful, expert, clever.—**adroit'ly** *adv.*—**adroit'ness** *n.*
adula'tion *n.* excessive flattery.—**ad'ulatory** *a.*—**ad'ulate** *v.t.* praise too highly.—**ad'ulator** *n.*
adult' *a.* mature.—*n.* grown-up person.
adul'terate *v.t.* to corrupt; make impure by mixture.—**adul'terated** *a.*—**adul'terant** *n.*—**adul'teration** *n.*—**adul'terator** *n.* (**adul'terating** *pres. p.*).
adul'tery *n.* sexual intercourse of two persons, either of whom is married to a third.—**adul'terer** *n.m.*—**adul'teress** *n.f.* —**adul'terous** *a.* illicit.
ad'umbrate *v.t.* to outline.—**adumbra'tion** *n.*—**adum'brant, adum'brative** *a.*
advance' *v.t.* to bring forward; promote; encourage; pay beforehand; in motoring, to time spark earlier in engine cycle.—*v.i.* to go forward; improve in rank or value.—*n.*—**advance'ment** *n.*
advan'tage *n.* gain; superiority.—**advanta'geous** *a.*—**advanta'geously** *adv.*
ad'vent *n.* a coming, the coming of Christ; the four weeks before Christmas. —**advent'ual** *a.* **adven'tist** *n.*
adventi'tious (-shus) *a.* accidental.
adven'ture *n.* enterprise; risk; bold exploit; a commercial speculation.—*v.t.* and *i.* to risk; take a risk.—**adven'turer** *n.m.*—**adven'turess** *n.f.* one who lives on his wits.—**adven'turous** *a.*—**adven'turously** *adv.*—**adven'turousness** *n.*
ad'verb *n.* a word added to a verb, adjective, or other adverb to modify the meaning.—**adverb'ial** *a.* **adverb'ially** *adv.*
ad'verse *a.* opposed to; hostile; contrary to desire.—**ad'versely** *adv.*—**ad'versary** *n.* enemy.—**advers'ity** *n.* distress, misfortune.—**advers'ative** *a.*
advert' *v.i.* to turn attention to; refer.—**advert'ence** *n.*—**advert'ency** *n.*—**advert'ent** *a.*—**advert'ently** *adv.*
ad'vertise *v.t.* to make known, *esp.* in newspapers, etc.—**ad'vertiser** *n.*—**advert'isement** *n.*—**ad'vertising** *a.*
Syn. to announce, publish, proclaim, promulgate, apprise. *Ant.* conceal, withdraw, withhold.
advice' *n.* opinion given; counsel; information, news (*esp.* in *pl.*).
advise' *v.t.* to give an opinion to; recommend a line of conduct; inform.—**advi'sable** *a.* expedient.—**advised'** (-zd) *a.* considered, as in *well-advised.*—**advi'sedly** *adv.*—**advi'ser** *n.*—**advi'sory** *a.*
ad'vocate *n.* defender; one who pleads another's cause.—*v.t.* to recommend.—**ad'vocacy** *n.*—**advoca'tion** *n.*
advow'son *n.* the right of presentation to a church benefice.—**advow'ee** *n.*
adze (adz) *n.* a carpenter's tool, with a curved steel blade set at right angles to wooden handle.

ae'gis *n.* a shield given by Zeus to Minerva; anything that protects.
aeo'lian *a.* acted on by the wind, as Æolian harp.
ae'on *n.* a period of time; eternity.
a'erate *v.t.* to expose to air; charge with gas.—**a'erator** *n.*—**aera'tion** *n.*
aer'ial *a.* belonging to the air.—*n.* a wire to send out or receive radio signals. —**ae'rial torpe'do** *n.* a powerful bomb discharged from aircraft.
a'erie, a'ery, ey'ry *n.* the nest of a bird of prey.
a'ero- *prefix,* having to do with air or aircraft.—**aerobat'ics** *n.* a series of breath-taking manœuvres carried out by aircraft.—**a'erobomb** *n.*—**a'ero-cam'era** *n.*—**a'erodart** *n.*—**a'erodrome** *n.* an aircraft station.—**aerodynam'ics** *n.*—**a'erofoil** *n.* any plane of an aeroplane.—**a'erogram** *n.* wireless message.—**aero-hy'droplane** *n.*—**a'erolite** *n.* a meteoric stone.—**a'eromotor** *n.*—**a'eronaut** *n.* an "air-sailor."—**aerol'ogy** *n.*—**aerom'etry** *n.*—**aeroneuro'sis** *n.* a psychoneurosis occurring among aviators, characterised by nausea, insomnia, etc.—**aeroneurotic.** —**ae'rophone** *n.* instrument for amplifying sound waves.—**a'erophyte** *n.* a plant which feeds on air.—**a'eroplane** *n.* a heavier-than-air flying machine.—**a'erostat** *n.* a balloon.—**aerosta'tion** *n.* the art of raising balloons.—**aero-stat'ics** *n.*—**ae'rotropic** *n.* seeking air.
Aer'tex (ār'-) *n.* a loosely woven fabric giving some degree of insulation against heat and cold (Trade Name).
æsthet'ic (ēs-) *a.* relating to the principles of beauty and taste, and of art.—**æsthet'ics** *n.*—**æs'thete** *n.* one who affects an extravagant love of art. —**æsthet'icism** *n.*—**æsthet'ically** *adv.*
ae'ther, *see* **ether.**
aetiol'ogy *n.* the study of causes, *esp.* of a disease.—**ætiolo'gical** *a.*
afar' *adv.* from, at, or to, a distance.
af'able *a.* easy to speak to, polite and friendly.—**af'ably** *adv.*—**affabil'ity** *n.*
affair' *n.* a business operation; any small matter; *pl.* matters in general.
affect' *v.t.* to act upon; move the feelings; make a show of, make pretence; assume; have a liking for.—**affecta'tion** *n.* show, pretence.—**affect'ed** *a.* making a pretence.—**affect'edly** *adv.*—**affec'tion** *n.* fondness, love.—**affec'tionate** *a.*—**affec'tionately** *adv.*—**affect'ing** *a.* moving the feelings, pathetic.—**affect'ingly** *adv.*
aff'erent *a.* bringing to, *esp.* of nerves which carry sensation to the brain.
affi'ance *v.t.* to betroth; (**affi'anced** *p.t.* and *p.p.*) engaged to marry.
affida'vit *n.* a written statement on oath signed before a witness.
affil'iate *v.t.* to adopt; to attach, as a society to a federation, etc.; to attribute to, father on.—**affilia'tion** *n.*
affin'ity *n.* relationship; resemblance; attraction, *esp.* chemical attraction.—**affin'itive** *a.*—(**affin'ities** *pl.*).
affirm' *v.t.* to assert positively; to maintain a statement.—*v.i.* to declare solemnly.—**affirma'tion** *n.*—**affirm'ative** *a.*—*n.*—**affirm'atively** *adv.*
affix' *v.t.* to fasten to, attach.—**aff'ix** *n.* an addition, *esp.* as a suffix or prefix.
affla'tus *n.* breathing or blowing upon; inspiration, as of poet, orator; religious inspiration, *the divine afflatus.*
afflict' *v.t.* to give pain or grief; vex.—**afflic'tion** *n.*—**afflict'ive** *a.*
aff'luent *a.* wealthy.—*n.* a tributary stream.—**aff'luence** *n.* wealth.
afford' *v.t.* to be able to buy; yield.
affor'est *v.t.* to turn land into forest.—**afforesta'tion** *n.* plant with trees.
affray' *n.* a fight in public; brawl.
affright' *v.t.* to terrify—*n.* fear, terror. *Syn.* to alarm, intimidate, daunt, dismay. *Ant.* calm, quiet, pacify, soothe, encourage, hearten.
affront' *v.t.* insult openly; meet face to face.—*n.* an insult.—**affront'ed** *adj.*
afield' *adv.* in or on the field.
afire' *adv.* on fire.
aflame' *adv.* burning; ardent; passionate.
afloat' *adv.* floating; at sea; flooded.
afoot' *adv.* on foot; astir; in preparation; in operation.
afore' *prep.* and *adv.* before. Usually in compounds, as **afore'said, afore'thought.**
afraid' *a.* in fear; timid.
afresh' *adv.* again, anew.
Afric'ander, Afrika'ner, *n.* S. African of European descent (white man).—**Afrikaans',** *n.* S. African language derived from 17th cent. Dutch; one of the official languages of the Union of S. Africa.
aft (âft) *adv.* towards or near the stern of a ship.
af'ter (âft-) *adv.* behind; later.—*prep.* like or in imitation of; behind; later than.—*a.* behind; later; farther aft.
af'ter (âft-) as prefix makes compounds, as **af'terbirth** *n.* membrane expelled after a birth.—**af'terclap** *n.*—**af'tercrop** *n.*—**af'terdamp** *n.* gas left after an explosion in a coal-mine.—**af'terglow** *n.* light after sunset.—**af'termath** *n.* second mowing of grass; results, consequences.—**afternoon'** *n.*—**af'terthought** *n.*
af'terwards (âft-) **af'terward** *adv.* later.
a'ga (ä'-) *n.* Turkish civil or military officer of high rank.
again' *adv.* once more; back, in return; [besides.
against' *prep.* opposite; in opposition to; in contact with; in exchange for.
a'gar-a'gar *n.* a substance prepared from seaweed, in which bacteria are cultivated.
ag'ate *n.* a precious stone.
age *n.* the length of time a person or

thing has existed; a period of time; periods of history; maturity; a long time.—*v.t.* to make old.—*v.i.* to grow old. —**a'ged** *a.* old.—*n.pl.* old people.—**age'-'less** *a.*—**age'long** *a.*—**of age**, recognised by law as grown up (usually 21 years).

agen'da *n.pl.* things to be done; the programme of a business meeting.

a'gent *n.* a person or thing producing an effect; cause; natural force; person authorised to act for another.—**a'gency** *n.*

agglom'erate *v.t.* and *i.* to gather into a mass.—**agglom'erate, agglom'erated** *a.* —**agglom'erate** *n.* rock consisting of volcanic fragments.—**agglomera'tion** *n.* —**agglom'erative** *a.*

agglu'tinate *v.t.* unite with glue or other sticky substance; form words into compounds—*a.* united, as by glue.—**agglutina'tion** *n.*—**agglutinative** *a.*

agg'randize *v.t.* to make greater in size, power, or rank.—**aggran'dizement** *n.*

agg'ravate *v.t.* to make worse.—**aggrava'tion** *n.*—**agg'ravating** *a.*

Syn. to exaggerate, magnify, exasperate, irritate. *Ant.* allay, alleviate, soothe, placate, minimise, diminish.

agg'regate *v.t.* to gather into a mass.—*n.* mass, sum total.—**aggrega'tion** *n.*—**agg'regative** *a.*

aggres'sion *n.* an unprovoked attack. —**aggress'ive** *a.*—**aggress'iveness** *n.*—**aggress'or** *n.*—**aggress'** *v.*

aggrieve' *v.t.* to pain or injure (**aggrieving** *pres. p.*).—**aggrieved'** *adj.* hurt in the feelings.

aghast' *a.* struck with horror.

ag'ile (-j-) *a.* quick, active, nimble.—**ag'ilely** *adv.*—**agil'ity** *n.*

ag'itate (-j-) *v.t.* to keep in motion, excite.—**agita'tion** *n.*—**ag'itator** *n.*

agnos'tic *n.* one who holds that we know nothing of things outside the material world.—**agnos'ticism** *n.*

ago' *adv.* past; gone by ; since.

agog' *a.* and *adv.* eager; highly excited.

ag'ony *n.* extreme suffering; death struggle.—**ag'onize** *v.i.*—**ag'onizing** *a.*

agra'rian *a.* relating to land or its management.—**agra'rianism** *n.* a political movement designed to change the conditions of land ownership.

agree' *v.i.* to be of one mind; consent; harmonise, determine; suit (**agreed'** *p.t.* and *p.p.*—**agree'ing** *pres.p.*)—**agree'able** *a.*—**agree'ably** *adv.*—**agree'ment** *n.*—**agree'ableness** *n.*—**agreeabil'ity** *n.*

ag'riculture *n.* the art or practice of cultivating the ground.—**agricul'tural** *a.* —**agricul'turist** *n.* a farmer.

agrimo'tor *n.* a motor vehicle or tractor used for agricultural purposes.

agron'omy *n.* the science of land culture and crops.—**agron'omist** *n.* one who studies agronomy.

aground' *adv.* stranded; touching bottom (of a ship).

a'gue *n.* a fever with shivering; quaking.

ahead' *adv.* in front of; forward; advance.

ahoy' *interj.* a shout used at sea.

aid *v.t.* to help.—*n.* help.

Syn. to assist, succour, support, relieve. *Ant.* hinder, obstruct, embarrass.

aide-de-camp(ā-de-kon') *n.* officer who attends a general (**aides-de-camp** *pl.*).

aigrette' *n.* a tuft of feathers; a spray of jewellery; a small heron.

aiguille' (ā-gwēl') *n.* in geology, a sharp, slender peak; a drill used in blasting rocks.

ail *v.t.* to trouble, disturb.—*v.i.* to be ill. —**ail'ing** *a.*—**ail'ment** *n.* illness.

ai'leron (ā'-) *n.* a part of the wing of an aeroplane that serves to balance and steer the machine.

aim *v.t.* and *i.* to direct effort towards, try to; to give direction to a weapon; strike or throw.—*n.* a direction; endeavour; object, purpose.—**aim'less** *a.* without object.

air *n.* the mixture of gases we breathe; breeze; a tune; a manner; affected manner.—*pl.* affected manners.—*v.t.* to expose; to dry or warm.—**air'y** *a.*—**air'ily** *adv.*—**air-iness** *n.*—**air'ing** *n.* a trip into the open.—**air'less** *a.*

air- used as prefix makes compounds denoting things in, of, or having to do with the air, as **air'-balloon** *n.*—**air'-base** *n.*—**air'bath** *n.*—**air'bed** *n.*—**air'-borne troops**, troops transported by air, and dropped by parachute or in gliders behind the enemy lines.—**air'brake** *n.* —**air'brush** *n.* a mechanical paint sprayer in which paint is forced through the nozzle at high pressure in a fine spray.—**air'cell** *n.*—**air'-cham'ber** *n.* —**air'chief-mar'shal** *n.*—**air'comm'odore** *n.*—**aircondi'tion** *v.t.* to maintain a constant stream of warm, clean fresh air in a building.—**aircondi'tioner** *n.* a mechanical machine used to air-condition a building.—**air'craft** *n.*—**air'-craftman** *n.* the lowest rank in the Royal Air Force; R.A.F. " A.C. plonk " *sl.*—**air'-cushion** *n.* a pillow which can be inflated.—**air'-duct** *n.*—**air'field** *n.*—**air'-force** *n.* the strength of a country in aircraft.—**air'-funnel** *n.* **air'-gas** *n.*—**air'-gun** *n.* a gun discharged by force of compressed air.—**air'-hole** *n.* —**air'-line** *n.* a bee-line; an aircraft route.—**air-liner** *n.*—**air'-lock** *n.*—**air'-man** *n.*—**air'mail** *n.* mails carried by aircraft.—**air-map** *n.* a map drawn so that the distance between each point represents the distance by air; an aerial navigation chart.—**air'-mechanic** *n.* an artificer working on aircraft.—**air'-pilot** *n.* one who steers and controls an aeroplane.—**air'-pock'et** *n.* a part of the air where an aeroplane drops suddenly. —**air'-port** *n.* a station for passenger aircraft.—**air'-power** *n.*—**air'-pump** *n.* a machine to extract or supply air. —**air'-raid** *n.* an attack by aircraft.—**air'-scout'** *n.*—**air'-screw** *n.* the propeller of any aircraft.—**air'-shaft** *n.*—**air'ship** *n.*—**air'stone** *n.* a meteorite.—**air'stop** *n.* a helicopter passenger station.—**air'strip** *n.* a clearing used as a landing ground for aircraft in an area otherwise unsuitable for use by aircraft, e.g. jungle.—**air'tight** *a.* not allowing the passage of air.—**air'-trap** *n.* —**air'-valve** *n.*—**air vice-mar'shal** *n.* **air'way** *n.* a regular aircraft route.—**air'worthy** *a.* fit for service in the air.—**airwor'thiness** *n.*

air'craft-car'rier *n.* a warship fitted with hangars and flight-decks for aircraft to take off and land.

Aire'dale *n.* a large terrier dog; U.S.A. *sl.* sailor serving in aircraft carrier.

aisle (īl) *n.* the wing of a church; a walk between seats in a church.

ait *n.* a small flat island in a river.

aitch'bone *n.* the bone of the rump; the cut of beef over this bone.

ajar' *adv.* partly open, as a door.

akim'bo *adv.* with arm bent and hand on hip only in phrase **arms** *a.*

akin' *a.* related by blood, or by character; alike; connected with.

alabam'ine (ēn) *n.* a rare element of the halogen group.

al'abaster *n.* a soft, white, semi-transparent stone resembling marble.

alack' *interj.* a cry of sorrow.

alac'rity *n.* quickness, briskness.

alarm' *n.* notice of danger; sudden fright; call to arms.—*v.t.* to warn of danger; frighten.—**alarm'ing** *a.*—**alarm'ist** *n.* one given to prophesying danger, panic-monger.

alarum (alarm') *n.* alarm, now mainly used in **alarum-clock,** a clock which rings a bell at a set time.

alas' *interj.* a cry of grief.

alb *n.* vestment.

al'batross *n.* a large, long-winged sea-bird, remarkable for its flying powers.

albi'no (-ē'-) *n.* a person or animal with unusually white skin and hair, and pink eyes (**albi'nos** *pl,*)—**al'binism** *n.*

al'bum *n.* a book of blank leaves, for portraits, stamps, autographs, etc.

albu'men *n.* a constituent of animal and vegetable matter, found nearly pure in white of egg.—**albu'minous** *a.*

alcal'de (kal'-di) *n.* a Spanish judge or mayor.

al'chemy *n.* the earlier stage of chemistry, in which the main aims were turning base metals into gold and finding an elixir of life.—**al'chemist** *n.*

al'cohol *n.* a liquid made in fermenting sugar, etc., and forming the intoxicating part of fermented drinks.—**alcohol'ic** *a.*—**al'coholism** *n.* a disease, alcohol poisoning.—**al'coholise** *v.t.*—**alcoholisa'tion** *n.*

al'cove *n.* a recess.

al'der (awl-) *n.* a tree of the birch family.

al'derman (awl-) *n.* city or town councillor not elected, but appointed for a period.—**alderman'ic** *a.*

ale *n.* fermented malt liquor; beer made from malt and hops.—**ale'-house** *n.*

alert' *a.* watchful, brisk.—*n.* a sudden attack or surprise, a warning given by watchers, e.g., an air-raid warning.—**alert'ness** *n.* *Syn.* active, smart, quick. *Ant.* sluggish, somnolent, lazy.

alfal'fa *n.* a fodder plant, lucerne.

alfres'co *n.* and *a.* in the open air.—**alfresco meal,** a picnic.

al'gebra *n.* a method of calculating, using letters to represent the numbers and signs to show relations between them.—**algebra'ic, algebra'ical** *a.*—**algebra'ist** *n.* an expert in algebra.

a'lias (ā-li-as) *adv.* otherwise.—*n.* an assumed name (**a'liases** *pl.*).

al'ibi *n.* plea that a person was elsewhere when an act occurred (**alibis** *pl.*).

a'lien *a.* foreign; different in nature; adverse.—*n.* a foreigner.—**a'lienate** *v.t.* to transfer; estrange.—**a'lienable** *a.* capable of being transferred, as property not entailed.—**alienabil'ity** *n.*—**aliena'tion** *n.*—**a'lienism** *n.*—**a'lienist** *n.* a specialist in mental diseases.

alight' *v.i.* to get down; to settle, come to earth (as a bird).

alight' *a.* on fire; lighted up; radiant.

align', aline' *v.t.* to bring into line.—**align'ment, aline'ment** *n.* in a straight line; ground plan of railway or road.

alike', *a.* like, similar.

al'iment *n.* food.—*v.t.* to feed; support. —**aliment'ary** *a.*—**alimenta'tion** *n.*

al'imony *n.* an income allowed to a wife legally separated from her husband.

alipha'tic (al-i-fat'-ik) *a.* (*chem.*) denoting the class of organic compounds of which the fats are typical.

al'iquot *a.* such part of a number as will divide it without remainder.

alive' *a.* living; in life or activity.

al'kali *n.* substance which combines with acid forming a salt (**al'kalis** (-līz), **-lies** (-līz) *pl.*).—**al'kaline** *a.*—**alkalin'ity** *n.*—**al'kaloid** *n.* and *a.*—**al'kalise** *v.t.*

all (awl) *a.* the whole of, every one of.—*adv.* wholly, entirely.—*n.* the whole.—**all-in** *a.* and *adv.* all inclusive, all embracing; *sl.* tired out, exhausted.—**all-in policy,** an insurance policy covering all risks.—**all-in wrestling,** wrestling in which all forms of holds are permitted except biting and eye gouging.—**all round,** versatile; from every point of view; complete.—**all clear,** continuous note of single pitch sounded by a siren during World War 2, denoting that an alert period had ended.

Al'lah *n.* Arabic name for the Supreme Being; the Absolute.
allay' *v.t.* to lighten, relieve, lessen. *Syn.* to soothe, tranquillise. *Ant.* irritate, arouse, inflame.
allege' *v.t.* and *i.* to plead, bring forward as an argument; assert.—**allega'tion** *n.* statement or assertion.
alle'giance *n.* the duty of a subject to his sovereign; loyalty.
all'egory *n.* a story with a meaning other than the literal one.—**allego'rical** *a.* figurative—**allego'rically** *adv.*—**all'egorise** *v.t.*—**all'egorist** *n.*
alle'gro (-lā'-) *adv.* (*music*) briskly.—**allegret'to** *a.* not so quick as allegro.
al'lergy *n.* in hypersensitive individuals, a pathological condition of repugnance to certain substances, etc.—**aller'gic** *a.* affected with allergy.
alle'viate *v.t.* to make light, ease, lessen.—**allevia'tion** *n.*—**alle'viator** *n.*
all'ey *n.* a narrow passage; an enclosure for playing skittles (**alleys** *pl.*).
all'ey *n.* a fine marble (in the game).
alli'ance *n.* state of being allied; union of families by marriage, of states by treaty; the parties allied.
all'igator *n.* an animal of the crocodile family found in America.
allitera'tion *n.* the beginning of two or more words in close succession with the same sound, as e.g. *Sing a Song of Sixpence.*—**allit'erative** *a.*—**allit'erate** *v.i.*
all'ocate *v.t.* to place; to assign as a share.—**alloca'tion** *n.* (**al'locating** *pres.p.*)
all'ocution *n.* a formal speech or address.—**all'ocute** *v.i.*
allomor'phism *n.* the power of changing form without change of composition.
allop'athy *n.* the orthodox practice of medicine; opposite of *homeopathy.*
allot' *v.t.* to give out; distribute as shares.—**allot'ment** *n.* distribution; a small plot of land for vegetable growing.
allot'ropy *n.* the property of some elements of existing in more than one form, as e.g. carbon in the form of diamond, and charcoal.—**allotrop'ic** *a.*—**allot'ropism** *n.*
allow' *v.t.* to acknowledge; permit.—**allow'able** *a.*—**allow'ance** *n.*—**allow'ably** *adv.* *Syn.* to grant, concede, admit, tolerate. *Ant.* disallow, refuse, reject.
alloy' *n.* a mixture of two or more metals.—*v.t.* to mix metals.—**alloy'age** *n.*
all'spice (awl-) *n.* pimento or Jamaica pepper, supposed to combine the flavours of various spices.
allude' *v.i.* to mention lightly.—**allu'sion** *n.*—**allu'sive** *a.* (**allu'ding** *pr.p.*).
allure' *v.t.* to entice; to tempt; to fascinate.—**allu'ring** *a.*—**allur'ingly** *adv.*—**allure'ment** *n.*
allu'vial (-ōōv'-) *a.* deposited by rivers.—**allu'vium** *n.* water-borne matter deposited on lower lands (*allu'viums, -via pl.*).—**allu'vion** *n.* land so formed.
ally' *v.t.* to join by treaty, marriage, or friendship (**allied'** *p.t.* and *p.p.*—**ally'ing** *pres. p.*).—**allied'** *a.*—**all'y** *n.* a confederate; a state or sovereign bound to another by treaty (**allies** *pl.*).
al'manac (awl'-) *n.* a table of days, weeks, and months, etc.
almighty (awl-mi'ti) *a.* having all power.—**The Almighty** *n.* God.
alm'ond (ahm'-) *n.* the kernel of the fruit of a tree related to the peach; that tree.—**alm'ond blossom.**—**almond oil**
al'most (awl'-) *adv.* nearly, all but.
alms (àmz) *n.* gifts to the poor.—**alm'oner** *n.* a distributor of alms; a member of a hospital staff.—**alm'onry** *n.* place of distribution of alms.—**alms'-house** *n.* a house endowed for poor persons to live in.
al'oe *n.* a genus of plants.—**aloes** *pl.* a bitter drug made from the plant.
aloft' *adv.* on high; overhead.
alone' *a.* single, solitary.-*adv.* separately.
along' *adv.* lengthwise; together (with).
aloof' *adv.* at a distance, withdrawn; apart.—**aloof'ness** *n.*
aloud' *adv.* with loud voice.
alp *n.* a high mountain; *pl.* **Alps**, *esp.* the mountains in Switzerland.—**al'pine** *a.*—**al'pinist** *n.* a mountain climber.
alpac'a *n.* the Peruvian sheep; cloth made from its wool, or containing such.
al'penstock *n.* a long, stout staff, shod with iron.
al'pha *n.* the first letter of the Greek alphabet, used to denote *first*; (*astr.*) the chief star of a constellation; (*chem.*) the first of two or more isomerous modifications of a compound; (*nat. hist.*) the first sub-species; **Al'pha and Om'ega,** the first and the last; **Al'pha particles,** positively charged particles given off by radio-active substances; **al'pha rays,** streams of alpha particles.
al'phabet *n.* the set of letters used in writing a language.—**alphabet'ic, alphabet'ical** *a.*—**alphabet'ically** *adv.*
alread'y (awl-red'i) *adv.* previously.
Alsa'tian (al-sā'shan) *n.* a large dog of a breed like a wolf; a native of Alsace.
al'so (awl'-) *adv.* further, too.
al'tar (awl'-) *n.* a raised place, a stone, etc., on which sacrifice may be offered; in a Christian church, the table on which the priest consecrates the eucharist.
al'ter (awl'-) *v.t.* to make different.—*v.i.* to become different.—**al'terable** *a.*—**alterabil'ity** *n.*—**al'terably** *adv.*—**altera'tion** *n.*—**al'terative** *a.*
alterca'tion (awl-) *n.* dispute, wrangling.—**al'tercate** *v.i.*—**al'tercative** *a.*
al'ternate *v.t.* to cause to occur by turns.—*v.i.* to happen by turns.—**alter'nate** *a.*—**alter'nately** *adv.*—**altera'tion** *n.*—**alter'native** *a.* and *n.*—**alter'natively** *adv.*

alterna'tor (-nā'-) *n.* an electric generator for producing alternating current.—**alternating current,** an electrical current flowing in a circuit first in one direction then in the opposite.
althorn *n.* horn of the same range as the French horn and used in brass bands.
although' (awl-THō') *conj.* admitting that, notwithstanding that.
altim'eter *n.* an instrument for measuring heights, *esp.* above sea level.
al'titude *n.* height; distance above sea level. *Syn.* eminence, elevation, loftiness. *Ant.* depression, depth, lowness.
al'to *n.* music, the male voice of highest pitch: part written for it (**al'tos** (-tōz) *pl.*).
altogeth'er (awl-) *adv.* entirely.
al'truism *n.* the principle of living and acting for the good of others.—**altruis'tic** *a.*—**altruis'tically** *adv.*
al'um *n.* a mineral salt, double sulphate of aluminium and potassium.
alumin'ium *n.* a very light untarnishable metal resembling silver.
alum'nus *n.* a pupil; a graduate of a college (**alum'ni** *pl.*).
al'ways (awl'-) *adv.* at all times; for ever.—also **alway.** [at once; greatly.
amain' *adv.* with full force, vehemently;
amal'gam *n.* a compound of mercury and another metal.—**amal'gamate** *v.t.* to mix mercury with another metal; compound.—*v.i.* to unite; blend; *esp.* to unite two companies, societies, etc.—**amalgama'tion** *n.* (**amal'gamating** *pr.p.*).
amanuen'sis *n.* one who writes to dictation; secretary (**amanuen'ses** *pl.*).
am'aranth *n.* another name for plant, love-lies-bleeding; an imaginary flower that never fades; a purple colour.
amass' *v.t.* to collect in quantity; to heap together.—**amass'able** *a.*
am'ateur (-ter) *n.* one who carries on an art, study, game, etc., for the love of it, not for money.—**am'ateur, amateur'ish** *a.* not like the work of a professional.—**amateur'ishly** *adv.*—**amateur'ism** *n.*
am'atol *n.* explosive consisting of ammonium nitrate and trinitro-toluene.
am'atory *a.* relating to or causing love.
amaze' *v.t.* to surprise greatly, cause wonder, astound.—**amaze'ment** *n.*—**ama'zing** *a.*—**ama'zingly** *adv.*—**amaze'ment** *n.* great astonishment.
am'azon *n.* a female warrior; a masculine woman.—**amazo'nian** *a.*
ambass'ador *n.* a representative of the highest rank sent by one state to another.—**ambass'adress** *n. fem.*—**ambassado'rial** *a.*—**ambass'adorship** *n.*—**am'bassage** now usually **em-bassage** *n.*
am'ber *n.* a yellowish fossil resin.—*a.* made of, or coloured like, amber.
am'bergris *n.* a gray, fragrant substance, found on the seashore, and in the spermaceti whale.
ambidex'ter, ambidex'trous *a.* able to use both hands with equal ease.—**ambidexter'ity** *n.*
ambig'uous *a.* of double meaning, doubtful.—**ambig'uously** *adv.*—**ambigu'ity** *n.* (**ambigu'ities** *pl.*).
am'bit *n.* a circuit; space round.
ambi'tion (-bish'un) *n.* desire of power, fame, honour; the object of that desire.—**ambi'tious** *a.*—**ambi'tiously** *adv.*—**ambi'tiousness** *n.*—**ambition'less** *adj.*
ambiv'alence, -ency *n.* in psycho-analysis the simultaneous operation of two irreconcilable wishes.
am'ble *v.i.* of a horse, to move at an easy pace.—*n.* this motion.—**am'bler** *n.*
ambro'sia *n.* the food of the gods, anything delicious.—**ambro'sial** *a.*
am'bulance *n.* a carriage for the sick or wounded; a movable hospital.
ambuscade' *n.* a hiding to attack by surprise; a concealed force.
am'bush *n.* a lying in wait.—*v.t.*
ame'liorate *v.t.* and *i.* to make better.—**ameliora'tion** *n.*—**ame'liorative** *a.*
amen' (á-, â-) *interj.* surely, so let it be; **Amen'** *n.* god of ancient Egypt.
ame'nable *a.* easy to be led or controlled; subject to.—**amenabil'ity, ame'nableness** *n.*—**ame'nably** *adv.*
amend' *v.i.* to grow better—*v.t.* to make better, alter in detail, as a bill in parliament, etc.—**amend'ment** *n.*—**amends'** *n.pl.* reparation.—**to make amends,** to atone, compensate.
ame'nity *n.* pleasantness; *pl.* civilities.
amer'icium (-ish'-i-um) *n.* a radio-active element of the halogen family.
am'ethyst *n.* a precious stone.
a'miable *a.* friendly, kindly.—**a'miably** *adv.*—**amiabil'ity, a'miableness** *n.s.* *Syn.* lovely, lovable, charming, pleasing. *Ant.* offensive, revolting, hateful.
am'icable *a.* friendly, peaceable.—**am'icably** *adv.*—**amicabil'ity** *n.*
amice *n.* vestment worn at mass.
Am'idol *n.* a compound of phenol used in photography in developing bromide plates (Trade Name).
amid', amidst' *prep.* among.
amid'ships *adv.* half-way between stem and stern of a ship.
amiss' *a.* wrong.—*adv.* faultily.
am'ity *n.* friendship.
ammo'nia *n.* a pungent alkaline gas.—**ammo'niac, ammo'niacal** *a.* **ammo'niated** *a.*—**ammo'nium** *n.* the hypothetical base of ammonia.
ammuni'tion *n.* collective name for military stores; firearms, shells, explosives, etc.
amne'sia *n.* loss of memory.
am'nesty *n.* a general pardon.
amœ'ba *n.* the simplest microscopic animal (**amœbas, -bæ** *pl.*).
amok' *see* **amuck.**
among' (-mu-) **amongst'** *prep.* mixed with, of the number of, making part of.

am'orous *a.* easily moved to love; in love.—**am'orously** *adv.*—**am'orousness** *n.*
amorph'ous *a.* shapeless; uncrystallised.—**amorph'ism** *n.*
amount' *v.i.* to come to, be equal to.—*n.* sum total, the whole.
amour' (-ōō-) *n.* a love intrigue.—**amour propre** *n.* self-esteem.
am'pere *n.* unit of current of electricity.
amphet'amine (fet'-ạ-mēn) *n.* a stimulant and inhalant; benzedrine.
amphib'ious *a.* living both on land and in water.—**amphib'ian** *n.* an animal of the class Amphibia; an aeroplane that can rise from or descend on either land or water; a tank which can move on land or water (**amphib'ia** *pl.*).
amphithe'atre *n.* a building with tiers of seats round an open arena.
am'ple *a.* big enough, full, spacious.—**am'ply** *adv.*—**am'pleness** *n.*—**am'plify** *v.t.* to make bigger, louder, etc. (**am'plified** *p.t.* and *p.p.*—**am'plifying** *pres. p.*).—**am'plifier** *n.* a device for increasing volume of sound, as in radio reception.—**amplifica'tion** *n.*—**am'plitude** *n.* spaciousness, width.—**amplifica'tory** *a.*—**am'plifier** *n.* [for a hypodermic dose.
am'poule (am'pōōl) *n.* small container
am'putate *v.t.* to cut off (a limb, etc.).—**amputa'tion** *n.* (**am'putating** *pres. p.*).
amuck', amok' *adv.* (only in phrase, *to run amuck*) in murderous frenzy.
am'ulet *n.* something worn as a charm.
amuse' *v.t.* to divert; occupy pleasantly; excite a sense of fun.—**amu'sing** *a.*—**amu'singly** *adv.*—**amu'sement** *n.*
am'yl *n.* hypothetical radicle thought to exist in many chemical compounds.
ana- *prefix,* through, back, up; as *anatomy, analyse.*—*suffix,* as Americana, Australiana, etc.
anabap'tist *n.* one who holds that baptism should be adult only.
anab'o'lism (izm) *n.* in physiology, the building up which alternates with breaking down (catabolism) in the chemical routine (metabolism) of the living organism.
an'abranch *n.* in Australia, a tributary of a river which rejoins the main stream forming an island between the two water-courses.
anac'hronism (-k-) *n.* a mistake of time, by which something is put in the wrong period.—**anac'hronise** *v.t.*—**anachronis'tic** *a.*
anacolu'thon *n.* break in the structure or grammatical sequence of a sentence.
anacon'da *n.* a large snake, which kills by constriction; a boa in South America; a python in Ceylon.
anæ'mia *n.* lack of blood.—**anæ'mic** *a.*
anæsthet'ic *a.* causing insensibility.—*n.* a drug that does this.—**anæsthe'sia** *n.* state of insensibility.—**anæsthet'ically** *adv.*—**anæ'sthetise** *v.t.*—**anæ'sthetist** *n.* one who administers anæsthetics.
an'agram *n.* a word or sentence made by rearranging the letters of another word or sentence; e.g. *ant* from *tan.*—**anagrammat'ic,** *a.*—**anagramm'atise** *v.t.*
analge'sic (je'-zik) *n.* anodyne; *a.* producing analgesia.—**analge'sia** *n.* painlessness; insensibility to pain.
anal'ogy *n.* agreement, likeness in respects; correspondence.—**analo'gical** *a.*—**analo'gically** *adv.*—**anal'ogise** *v.t.*—**anal'ogist** *n.*—**anal'ogous** *a.* similar.—**anal'ogously** *adv.* (**anal'ogies** *pl.*).
anal'ysis *n.* a separation or breaking up of anything into its component parts (**anal'yses** *pl.*).—**an'alyse** *v.t.*—**an'alyst** *n.*—**analyt'ic'-al** *a.*—**analyt'ically** *adv.*
an'aphylaxis (-fil-ak-sis) *n.* making an animal more susceptible to small doses of serum by first giving it large doses.
an'archy *n.* lack of government; lawlessness.—**anarc'hic, -al,** *a.*—**anarch'ically** *adv.*—**an'archism** *n.*—**an'archist** *n.*
anath'ema *n.* a solemn curse; anything accursed (**-mas,** *pl.*).—**anath'ematize** *v.t.*
anat'omy *n.* the dissection of a body; the science of the structure of the body.—**anatom'ical** *a.*—**anatom'ically** *adv.*—**anat'omise** *v.t.*—**anat'omist** *n.*
an'cestor *n.* a forefather (**an'cestress** *fem.*).—**ances'tral** *a.*—**an'cestry** *n.* (**an'cestries** *pl.*).
anc'hor (-k-) *n.* an implement for chaining a ship to the bottom of the sea.—*v.t.* to fasten by an anchor.—*v.i.* to cast anchor.—**anc'horage** *n.*
anc'horite, anc'horet (-k-) *n.* one who has retired from the world, *esp.* for religion; a hermit.
ancho'vy (-ch-) *n.* a small fish of the herring family (**ancho'vies** *pl.*).
an'cient (ān'shent) *a.* old; belonging to a former age; time-worn.—*n.* an old man; one who lived in an earlier age (*esp.* in *pl.*).—**an'ciently** *adv.*
an'cillary *a.* subordinate, subservient.
Anco'na *n.* a breed of domestic fowl, usually speckled black and white.
Andalu'sian *n.* a native of Andalusia, a breed of fowls, blue in colour.
andan'te *adv.* (*music*) moderately slow.
an'diron *n.* an iron bar or bracket for supporting logs in a wood fire.
an'drogen (drō-jen) *n.* a compound producing male characteristics.
andros'terine (-tẹr-ēn) *n.* the male sex hormone.
an'ecdote *n.* a very short story dealing with a single incident.—**an'ecdotal** *a.*—**an'ecdotage** *n.* a collection of anecdotes; garrulous old age.
anelec'tric (-lek'-) *a.* non-electric;—*n.* a body that does not become electric; a conductor of electricity.
anem'ograph *n.* an instrument for recording automatically the force and direction of the wind.

anemom'eter *n.* an instrument to measure the strength of wind.—**anemomet'ric** *a.*—**anemom'etry** *n.*

anem'one (-ni) *n.* wind-flower.—**sea-anem'one** *n.* plant-like sea animal.

anent' *prep.* in respect of, or regard to; as to; about.

an'eroid *a.* Barometer which works without the use of mercury or other liquid.

an'eurism, an'eurysm *n.* a swelling out of a part of an artery.

anew' *adv.* afresh, again.

an'gel (ānj-) *n.* a divine messenger; a ministering or attendant spirit; a person with the qualities of such a spirit.—**angel'ic** *a.*—**angel'ically** *adv.*

angel'ica *n.* aromatic plant.

an'gelus *n.* in the R.C. church a devotional service in memory of the incarnation, said at morning, noon, and sunset; **an'gelus-bell,** the signal to say the angelus.

an'ger (ang'ger) *n.* wrath; a strong emotion including a sense of injury and a desire to retaliate.—*v.t.* to rouse this emotion in.—**an'gry** *a.*—**an'grily** *adv.*

angi'na *n.* inflammation of the throat.—**angi'na pectoris,** spasm of the chest.

an'gle (ang'gl) *v.i.* to fish.—*n.* a hook.—**an'gler** *n.*—**an'gling** *n.*

an'gle (ang'gl) *n.* a corner; the meeting of two lines; a point of view.—**an'gular** *a.*—**angular'ity** *n.* angularness.

An'glican (ang'gli-) *a.* of the Church of England.—**An'glicanism** *n.*

an'glicise (ang'gli-) *v.t.* to express in English.—**an'glicanism** *n.* an English idiom or peculiarity (**an'glicising** *pres.p.*).

An'glo- (ang'glō) *prefix,* English; as *Anglo-American, Anglo-Catholic, Anglo-Indian, Anglo-Saxon,* etc.—**anglopho'bia** *n.* dislike of England.

ango'ra *n.* a goat, cat or rabbit with long white fine fur; cloth or wool made from the hair of the goat or rabbit.

an'guish (ang'gw-) *n.* great pain, mental or bodily. *Syn.* agony, suffering, pang. *Ant.* pleasure, happiness, ecstasy.

anhy'drous *a.* free from water.

an'iline *n.* a product of coal-tar which yields dyestuffs.

animadvert' *v.i.* to criticise, pass censure.—**animadver'sion** *n.*

an'imal *n.* a being having life, feeling, and the power of voluntary motion; a beast.–*a.*—**an'imalism** *n.*–**an'imally** *adv.*

animal'cule *n.* a microscopic animal. —**animal'cular** *a.*

an'imate *v.t.* to give life to; actuate.—**an'imated** *a.* lively.—**anima'tion** *n.*—**an'imator** *n.* one who executes the drawings photographed to form a cartoon of the Donald Duck type.

an'imism *n.* primitive religion, a belief that natural effects are due to spirits, that inanimate things have spirits.

animos'ity *n.* hatred, enmity.–**an'imus** *n.* actuating spirit; enmity (**an'imi** *pl.*).

an'ion *n.* an electro-negative ion.

an'ise *n.* a plant with aromatic seeds used for flavouring and in medicines.—**an'iseed** *n.*—**anisette'** *n.* an aromatic liqueur flavoured with oil of anise seeds.

an'ker *n.* an old liquid measure of about 10 gallons.

an'kle (ang'kl) *n.* the joint between the foot and the leg.—**ank'let** *n.* an ornament or ring for the ankle.

ann'a *n.* an Indian coin, the sixteenth part of a rupee.

ann'als *n.pl.* records of events set down year by year.—**ann'alist** *n.*

anneal' *v.t.* to toughen metal or glass by heating and slow cooling.–**anneal'ing** *n.*

annex' *v.t.* to add; take possession of, *esp.* territory.—**ann'exe** *n.* something added; a supplementary building.—**annexa'tion** *n.*

Syn. to affix, unite, bind to, join. *Ant.* separate, disunite, sever.

anni'hilate *v.t.* to reduce to nothing, destroy.—**annihila'tion** *n.*—**anni'hilator** *n.*—**anni'hilative** *a.* (**anni'hilating** *pr.p.*).

anniver'sary *a.* yearly.—*n.* the day on which an event happened or is celebrated.

ann'otate *v.t.* to make notes upon.—**annota'tion** *n.*—**ann'otator** *n.* (**ann'otated** *pres. p.*).

announce' *v.t.* to make known, proclaim.—**announce'ment** *n.*—**announ'cer** *n.* a broadcasting official who announces items in the programme, introduces speakers, etc. (**announ'cing** *pres.p.*).

annoy' *v.t.* to trouble, vex; tease.—**annoy'ance** *n.* **annoy'ing** *adj.*

ann'ual *a.* yearly.—*n.* a plant which lives only a year; a book published every year.—**ann'ually** *adv.*

annu'ity *n.* a sum paid every year.—**annu'itant** *n.* one who receives such (**annu'ities** *pl.*).

annul' *v.t.* to reduce to nothing, abolish. —**annul'ment** *n.* (**annull'ing** *pres. p.* **anulled'** *p.t.* and *p.p.*).

ann'ular *a.* ring-shaped.—**ann'ulated** *a.* formed in rings.—**annula'tion** *n.*—**ann'ulet** *n.* a ring or fillet.

annuncia'tion *n.* an announcing; the angel's announcement to the Virgin.

an'ode *n.* in electricity, the positive pole, or point of entry of a current.—**anode rays,** wireless, rays from heated anode (plate) of a thermionic valve.

an'odyne *a.* relieving pain.—*n.* a drug.

anoint' *v.t.* to smear with oil or ointment; to consecrate with oil.—**anoint'ment** *n.*—**the Anointed** *n.* the Messiah.

anom'alous *a.* irregular.—**anom'aly** *n.* something showing irregularity.

anon' *adv.* in a short time, quickly.

anon'ymous *a.* nameless; *esp.* without an author's name (often written **anon**). —**anonym'ity** *n.*—**anon'ymously** *adv.*

anoph'eles (an-off'-el-ez) *n.* the only genus of mosquitoes carrying the parasite of malaria.

anoth'er (-u-) *pron.* one other, a different one, *a.* different.

An'schluss (-shloos) *n.* a combining; annexation, *esp.* the Nazi annexation of Austria in 1939.

an'swer (ȧn'sẹr) *v.t.* to reply to; pay, meet; satisfy.—*v.i.* to reply; succeed.—*n.*—**an'swerable** *a.*—**an'swerer** *n.*

ant' *n.* a small social insect.—**ant'-eater** *n.* a S. American animal which feeds on ants.—**ant'-hill** *n.* the mound raised by ants in building their home.

ant- *prefix,* for **anti-** before a vowel, *see* words in **anti-.**

anta'cid *n.* a substance which neutralises an acid; an alkali.

antag'onist *n.* an opponent.—**antag'onism** *n.* hostility.—**antag'onise** *v.t.*—**antagonis'tic** *a.*—**antagonis'tically** *adv.*

antarc'tic *a.* of the south polar regions.

an'te *n.* a player's stake in poker.—*v.t.* to put up a stake.

ante- *prefix,* found in compound words as **antece'dent** *a.* or *n.* going before.—**an'techamber** *n.*—**an'techapel** *n.*—**antedate'** *v.t.*—**antedilu'vian** *a.* before the flood.—**antemerid'ian** *a.*—**antemun'dane** *a.*—**antena'tal** *a.* before birth.—**anteni'cene** *a.*—**antenup'tial** *a.*—**antepenult'** *n.*—**antepenul'timate** *a.*—**an'teroom** *n.*

an'telope *n.* a deer-like ruminant animal, remarkable for grace and speed.

antenn'a *n.* an insect's feeler (**antenn'æ** *pl.*); in wireless, an aerial.

ante'rior *a.* before or previous.
Syn. antecedent, prior, precedent, previous. *Ant.* succeeding, following, subsequent, later.

an'them *n.* a piece of Scripture set to music; a piece of sacred music.

an'ther *n.* the top of the pollen-bearing stamen in a flower.

anthol'ogy *n.* a collection of choice poems, literary extracts, etc.—**anthol'ogist** *n.* a maker of such (**anthol'ogies** *pl.*).

an'thracite *n.* a hard coal burning almost without flame or smoke.

an'thrax *n.* a carbuncle; a malignant disease in cattle, communicable to man.

an'thropoid *a.* like man.—*n.* an ape resembling man.

anthropol'ogy *n.* the scientific study of mankind.—**anthropolog'ical** *a.*—**anthropol'ogist** *n.*

anthropomorph'ism *n.* the ascription of human form and qualities to deities.—**anthropomorp'hic** *adj.*

anti- *prefix,* against; **ant-** before a vowel. Makes compounds as **anti-air'craft** *a.*—**an'ti-body** *n.* a substance in, or introduced into, blood serum which is antagonistic to a toxin or poison injurious to the animal organisation.—**anticath'olic** *a.*—**an'tichrist** *n.*—**anticli'max** *n.*—**anticli'nal** *a.*—**anticy'clone** *n.*—**an'tidote** *n.* a counter poison.—**antilog'arithm** *n.*—**antimacas'sar** *n.* a cover to protect chairs from *macassar oil.*—**an'timasque** *n.*—**antimonarc'hical** *a.*—**antiphlogis'tic** *a.*—**an'tipope** *n.* a pope elected in opposition to the one regularly chosen.—**antirachit'ic** *a.*—**antiscorbu'tic** *n.*—**antisemit'ic** *a.*—**antisep'tic** *a.* and *n.*—**antispasmod'ic** *a.* and *n.*—**antitox'in** *n.*—**an'titrade** *n.*—etc.

an'tic *a.* odd, fanciful, grotesque.—*n.* a grotesque figure or movement.

anti'cipate (-tis'-) *v.t.* to be beforehand; forestall; foresee; enjoy in advance; expect.—**anticipa'tion** *n.*—**anti'cipative,** **anti'cipatory** *a.*

an'tigen (-ti-jen) *n.* an agent which helps the development of the antibodies in the system.—**antigen'ic** *a.*

an'timony *n.* a brittle metal.

antipast'o (ȧn-tē-) *n.* Italian hors d'oeuvres, usually consisting of celery, anchovies, olives, etc.

antip'athy *n.* dislike.—**antipathet'ic** *a.*
Syn. hatred, enmity. *Ant.* liking, sympathy, esteem, affinity.

antip'odes *n.pl.* a region of the globe exactly opposite ours.—**antip'odal** *a.*

antique' (-ēk') *a.* ancient; old-fashioned.—*n.* a relic of former times.—**antiq'uity** *n.* former times.—**an'tiquary, antiqua'rian** *n.*—**an'tiquated** *a.*

antirrhi'num (-rī-) *n.* snap-dragon.

antith'esis *n.* contrast; direct opposite (**antith'eses** *pl.*).—**antithet'ical** *a.*—**antithet'ically** *adv.*

ant'ler *n.* a deer's horn.—**ant'lered** *a.*

an'tonym *n.* word opposed in meaning to another, e.g. *cold* is an antonym of *hot.*

an'trum *n.* a cave; (*anat.*) natural hollow in upper jaw-bone connected with the nose; the maxillary sinus.

a'nus (ā'-) *n.* lower opening of bowels.

an'vil *n.* an iron block on which a smith hammers metal.

anx'ious (angk'shus) *a.* troubled, uneasy.—**anx'iously** *adv.*—**anxi'ety** *n.*

an'y (en'i) *a.* and *pron.* one indefinitely; some.—**an'ybody** *n.*—**an'ything** *n.*—**an'yhow, an'yway, an'ywhere** *adv.*

An'zac *a.* of the Australian-New Zealand Army Corps in the War of 1914-18.—*n.* a soldier of that corps.

aort'a *n.* the great artery which rises from the left ventricle of the heart.

apace' *adv.* at a quick pace; swiftly.

apache' (-ȧsh) *n.* a desperado, *esp.* a Parisian one (**apaches'** (a-pȧsh') *pl.*).

apart' *adv.* separately; aside; at a distance.

apart'ment *n.* a room; *pl.* lodgings, [rooms rented. U.S. a flat.

ap'athy *n.* want of feelings; indifference.—**apathet'ic** *a.*—**apathet'ically** *adv.*

ape *n.* a monkey; a monkey with no tail; an imitator.—*v.t.* to imitate.—**a'pish** *a.*—**a'pishly** *adv.*

apercu' (-sū') *n.* a rapid survey of a subject; a brief outline.

ape'rient *a.* opening; mildly laxative. —*n.* any such medicine.

aper'itif (ap-ăr-it-ēf) *n.* an alcoholic drink taken before meals.

ap'erture *n.* an opening; a gap.

a'pex (ā-) *n.* top or peak of anything (**a'pexes, a'pices** *pl.*).

apha'sia *n.* loss of power of speech.

aphe'lion *n.* the point of a planet's orbit farthest from the sun (**aphe'lia, -lions** *pl.*)

a'phis (ā'-) *n.* small parasitic insect on roots, leaves, etc., of plants.

aph'orism *n.* a maxim, a pithy saying. —**aphoris'tic** *a.*—**aph'orist** *n.*

aphrodis'iac *a.* exciting to sexual intercourse.—*n.* that which so excites.

a'piary (ā-) *n.* a place where bees are kept.—**a'piarist** *n.* a bee-keeper.—**apia'rian, a'pian** *a.*—**a'piculture** *n.*

apiece' *adv.* for each, to each.

aplomb' *n.* self-possession, coolness.

apoc'alypse *n.* the Revelation of St. John; any revelation.—**apocalyp'tic** *a.* —**apocalyp'tically** *adv.*

apoc'rypha *n.* a religious writing of doubtful authenticity, or excluded from the Canon; *esp.* the Apocrypha of the Old Testament.—**apoc'ryphal** *a.*

apod'osis *n.* in grammar, the consequent clause in a conditional sentence, as distinct from the *protasis*, or *if* clause (**apod'oses** *pl.*).

ap'ogee *n.* the point of the sun or moon's orbit farthest from the earth.

ap'ologue *n.* a moral fable or parable.

apol'ogy *n.* something spoken in defence; acknowledgement of an offence and expression of regret; a poor substitute (with *for*).—**apol'ogise** *v.i.*—**apol'ogist** *n.*—**apologet'ic** *a.*—**apologet'ically** *adv.*—**apologet'ics** *n.* the branch of theology charged with the *defence* of Christianity.—**apolo'gia** *n.* a written or spoken defence.

ap'ophthegm, ap'othegm (-o-them) *n.* a terse saying.

ap'oplexy *n.* sudden stroke, causing loss of sense and motion.—**apoplec'tic** *a.*

apos'tasy *n.* abandonment of one's religion or other faith.—**apos'tate** *n.*

apos'tle (-sl) *n.* one sent to preach the Gospel, *esp.* one of the first disciples of Jesus; the chief champion of any new system. — **apos'tleship** *n.* — **apostol'ic, apostol'ical** *a.*—**apostoli'city** *n.*

apos'trophe *n.* a turning away from the subject of a speech to address some person present or absent; a mark (') showing the omission of a letter or letters in a word.—**apos'trophise** *v.t.*

apoth'ecary *n.* old name for druggist.

ap'othegm *see* **apophthegm.**

apotheo'sis *n.* deification, the act of raising any person or thing into a god (**apotheo'ses,** *pl.*).

appal'(-awl') *v.t.* to dismay.—**appall'ing** *a.* *Syn.* overwhelm, daunt, scare, frighten. *Ant.* assure, reassure, encourage.

app'anage, ap'anage *n.* an allowance for bread and other victuals; lands assigned by a prince for the maintenance of his younger sons.

appara'tus *n.* equipment for performing any experiment or operation (**appara'tus, -tuses** *pl.*).

appar'el (-a-) *v.t.* to clothe.—*n.* clothing.

appa'rent *a.* seeming; obvious.—**appa'rently** *adv.* **appa'rentness** *n.*

appari'tion (-ish'un) *n.* an appearance, *esp.* of a ghost or other odd thing.

appeal *v.i.* to call upon, make earnest request; refer to, have recourse to; refer to a higher court.—*n.* a request, reference, supplication.—**appeal'ing** *a.*—**appeal'ingly** *adv.*—**appeal'able** *a.*—**appell'ant** *n.* one who appeals to a higher court.—**appell'ate** *a.*

appear' *v.i.* to become visible; to come before; to seem.—**appear'ance** *n.*

appease' *v.t.* to pacify, quiet, allay.—**appease'able** *a.*—**appease'ment** *n.*

appell'ant *see* **appeal.**

appella'tion *n.* a name.-**appell'ative** *a.*

append' *v.t.* to join on, add.—**append'age** *n.*—**appendix** *n.* (**appendices, -ixes** *pl.*).—**appendici'tis** *n.* inflammation of the vermiform appendix.—**appendicec'tomy,** operation to remove appendix.

apperceive' *v.t.* in psychology, to understand a perception by adding it to the ideas already possessed.

appertain' *v.i.* to belong, relate to.

app'etite *n.* desire, inclination, *esp.* for food.—**appet'itive** *a.*—**app'etiser** *n.*—**app'etising** *a.*—**app'etisingly** *adv.*

applaud' *v.t.* to praise by handclapping; to praise loudly, commend.—**applaud'er** *n.*—**applaud'ing** *a.*—**applaud'ingly** *adv.*—**applause'** *n.*

ap'ple *n.* a familiar round, firm, fleshy fruit; the tree bearing it.

appli'qué (a-plē-kā) *n.* ornaments, embroidery, etc., secured to the surface of material.—*v.t.* to secure such.

apply' *v.t.* to lay or place on; administer; devote, employ (**applied'** *p.t.* and *p.p.*—**apply'ing** *pres. p.*).—**appli'ance** *n.*—**app'licable** *a.*—**applicabil'ity** *n.*—**app'licably** *adv.*-**app'licant** *n.*-**applica'tion** *n.*

appoint' *v.t.* to fix, settle; name to an office; equip.—**appoint'ment** *n.* choice for a position; promise to meet at a given time.—**appoint'ed** *adj.*

app'ort (ap'or) *n.* in spiritualism, the alleged moving of material objects without material agency, *esp.* at seances.

appor'tion *v.t.* to divide out in shares. —**appor'tionment** *n.*

app'osite *a.* suitable, apt.—**app'ositely** *adv.*—**app'ositeness** *n.*—**apposi'tion** *n.* proximity; the placing of one word beside another in explanation.-**appos'itive** *a.*

appraise' *v.t.* to set a price or value on. —**apprais'able** *a.*—**appraise'ment** *n.*—**apprais'al** *n.*—**apprais'er** *n.*

appre'ciate (-shi-) *v.t.* to estimate justly;—*v.i.* to rise in price.—**appre'ciable** *a.*—**appre'ciably** *adv.*—**apprecia'tion** *n.*—**appre'ciative** *a.*—**appre'ciator** *n.*

apprehend' *v.t.* to take hold of; seize by authority; fear.—**apprehen'sible** *a.*—**apprehensibil'ity** *n.*—**apprehen'sion** *n.* —**apprehen'sive** *a.*—**apprehen'siveness** *n.*

appren'tice *n.* one bound to a master to learn an art or trade; a novice.—*v.t.* to bind as an apprentice.—**appren'ticeship** *n.* the time for which he serves.

apprise' *v.t.* to inform, to give notice.

approach' *v.i.* to draw near; come near in quality, condition, etc.—*v.t.* to come near to, a stroke in golf.—**approach'able** *a.*—**approachabil'ity** *n.*

approba'tion *n.* sanction, approval.

appro'priate *v.t.* to take to oneself.—*a.* suitable, fitting.—**appro'priately** *adv.* —**appro'priateness** *n.*—**appropria'tion** *n.* parliamentary vote of money.—**appro'priator** *n.*—**appro'priative** *a.*

Syn. to claim, annex, assume, usurp, arrogate. *Ant.* to give up, surrender.

approve' (-ōōv) *v.t.* to think well of, commend.—**approv'al** *n.*—**approv'er** *n.*

approx'imate *a.* nearly resembling; nearing correctness.—*v.t.* to bring close. —*v.i.* to come near.—**approx'imately** *adv.* —**approxima'tion** *n.*—**approx'imative** *a.*

appurt'enance *n.* a thing which appertains to; an accessory.

a'pricot (ā-) *n.* an orange-coloured stone-fruit.—*a.* apricot-coloured.

A'pril (ā-) *n.* the fourth month.

a priori (ā-pri-or-i) denoting knowledge gained independently of experience.

a'pron (ā-) *n.* a cloth, piece of leather, etc., worn in front to protect the clothes, or as part of an official dress.

apropos' (-pō') *adv.* or *a.* to the purpose.

apse *n.* an arched recess at the eastern end of a church.—**ap'sidal** *a.*

apsy'chic (a-si'kik) *a.* not controlled by, or connected with, mind.

apt *a.* suitable; quick-witted; likely.—**apt'ly** *adv.*—**apt'ness** *n.*—**apt'itude** *n.*

ap'teryx (-te-riks) *n.* a genus of birds in N. Zealand with rudimentary wings and no tail; kiwi.

a'quacade (ak'-wa-kād) *n.* a spectacular display of swimming and diving.—**a'qua-fortis** *n.* nitric acid.—**aqua regia** *n.* (*chem*). a mixture of nitric and hydrochloric acids in which gold can be dissolved.

aquamarine' *n.* a precious stone, the beryl.—*a.* sea-coloured.

aq'uaplane (ak'wa-) *n.* a plank or boat towed by a fast motor-boat.—*v.i.* to ride on an aquaplane.—**aquapla'ning** *n.*

aqua'rium *n.* a tank for keeping fish or other water animals, plants, etc. (**aqua'riums, aqua'ria** *pl.*).

Aqua'rius *n.* 11th sign of the Zodiac symbolised by a water-bearer, operative July 22–Aug. 21.

aquat'ic *a.* living or growing in water, or having to do with water.—**aquat'ics** *n.pl.* water-sports.

aq'uatint *n.* engraving and etching produced by aquafortis on copper.

aq'ueduct *n.* an artificial channel for water, *esp.* a bridge to carry water across a valley, etc.

a'queous *a.* watery.

aq'uiline *a.* relating to an eagle; hooked like an eagle's beak.

Ar'ab (a-) *n.* a native of Arabia; an Arabian horse.—**Ar'abic** *n.* the language of the Arabs.—**street arab**, a neglected, homeless child.

arabesque' *n.* a painted or carved ornament of Arabian design.—*a.*

ar'able (a-) *a.* fit for tillage or ploughing. *Syn.* cultivable, agricultural. *Ant.* barren, uncultivable.

Ar'alac *n.* a plastic fibre made from casein (protected trade name).

arb'iter *n.* a judge, umpire.—**arb'itress** *fem.*—**arbit'rament** *n.*—**arb'itrate** *v.i.* to act as umpire, to decide a dispute.—*v.t.* to submit a dispute to an umpire.—**arbitra'tion** *n.*—**arb'itrator** *n.*—**arbit'rary** *a.* not bound by rules, despotic.—**arb'itrarily** *adv.*

arbo'real, arbo'reous *a.* relating to trees.—**arbore'tum** *n.* a place for cultivating trees (**-tums, -ta** *pl.*).—**arboricul'ture** *n.*—**arboricul'tural** *a.*

arb'our *n.* a garden seat enclosed by branches, plants; a shaded walk.

arc *n.* part of a circle or other curve; luminous discharge between two terminals.—**arc-lamp** *n.*—**arc-light** *n.*

arcade' *n.* a row of arches on pillars; a covered walk, often lined with shops.

arca'num *n.* a secret (**arca'na** *pl.*).

arch *n.* a curved structure in building. —*v.t.* to give, or make into an arch.—**arch'ed** *a.*—**arch'way** *n.*

arch *a.* chief; roguish, sly.—**arch'ly** *adv.* —**arch'ness** *n.*—**arch-** *prefix* chief, e.g. **arch-an'gel** (-k-) *n.*—**archbishop** *n.*—**archdeacon** *n.*—**archduke** *n.*—**arch-en'emy** *n.*—**arch-her'etic** *n.*

archæol'ogy (-k-) *n.* the study of ancient times from remains of art, implements, etc.—**archæolo'gical** *a.*—**archæol'ogist** *n.*

archa'ic (-k-) *a.* old, primitive.—**archa'ically** *adv.*—**archa'ism** *n.* an obsolete word or phrase.

arch'er *n.* one who shoots with a bow and arrow; a bowman.—**arch'ery** *n.*

arc'hetype (-k-) *n.* an original pattern or model.—**arc'hetypal** *a.*

archiepis'copal (-k-) *a.* relating to an archbishop.—**archiepis'copate** *n.*

archipel'ago *n.* a sea full of small islands; a group of islands (**archipel'agoes** *pl.*).—**archipela'gic** *a.*
arc'hitect (-k-) *n.* one who designs buildings; any maker or contriver.—**architecton'ic** *a.*—**arc'hitecture** *n.* the art of building.—**architec'tural** *a.*
arc'hives (-kivz) *n.pl.* the place where government records are kept; public records.—**arc'hival** *a.*—**arc'hivist** *n.*
arc'tic *a.* of northern polar regions; extremely cold.—*n.*
ard'ent *a.* fiery; passionate, enthusiastic.—**ard'ently** *adv.*—**ard'our, ard'ency** *n.* *Syn.* intense, fierce, zealous, earnest. *Ant.* indifferent, cool, calm.
ard'uous *a.* laborious, hard to accomplish.—**ard'uously** *adv.*—**ard'uousness** *n.*
are (ār, ȧr) *n.* a unit of square measure containing 100 square metres.
ar'ea (er-) *n.* an open space; a sunken yard round a house; the superficial contents of a figure; extent, scope.
are'na *n.* the space in an amphitheatre (*esp.* Roman); a place of public contest; a battlefield (**are'nas, are'næ** *pl.*).
arêt'e (a-rāt') *n.* a sharp rising ridge on a mountain, a knife-edge.
ar'gent *n.* silver.—*a.* silvery-white, *esp.* in heraldry.
arg'on *n.* a gas forming part of the air.
arg'osy *n.* richly-laden ship (/**-gosies** *pl.*)
arg'ot (-ō) *n.* slang.
arg'ue *v.i.* to prove; offer reasons; dispute.—*v.t.* prove by reasoning; discuss.—**arg'uable** *a.*—**arg'uer** *n.*—**arg'ument** *n.*—**argumenta'tion** *n.* **argument'ative** *a.*
a'ria (ȧ'-) *n.* an air, song in opera, etc.
ar'id *a.* parched; dry; empty; uninteresting.—**arid'ity** *n.*
A'ries (ȧ'-re-āys) *n.* 1st sign of the Zodiac, symbolised by a ram. Operative Mar. 21st—Apl. 21st.
aright' *adv.* rightly, correctly.
arise' *v.i.* to come up; spring up; ascend; develop (**arose'** *p.t.*—**aris'en** *p.p.*—**ari'sing** *pres.p.*).
aristoc'racy *n.* government by the best in birth or fortune; the nobility or chief persons of a state; upper classes generally.—**ar'istocrat** *n.*—**aristocrat'ic** *a.*—**aristocrat'ically** *adv.*
arith'metic *n.* the science of numbers; the art of reckoning by figures.—**arithmet'ical** *a.*—**arithmet'ically** *adv.*—**arithmeti'cian** *n.* one skilled in arithmetic.
ark *n.* a box, chest; Noah's vessel.
arm *n.* the limb extending from the shoulder to the wrist; anything projecting from the main body, as a branch of the sea, etc.—*v.t.* to give an arm to.—**arm'chair** *n.*—**arm'ful** *n.* (**arm'fuls** *pl.*).—**arm'hole** *n.*—**arm'let** *n.*, etc.
arm *n.* a weapon.—*pl.* weapons; war; military profession.—*v.t.* to supply with weapons.—*v.i.* take up arms.—**armed'** *a.*—**arm'ament** *n.* armed equipment.
arma'da (-ȧd-) *n.* a fleet of armed ships.
armadill'o *n.* a small S. American animal protected by bands of bony plates (**armadill'os** *pl.*).
arm'ature *n.* apparatus for defence; a piece of iron across the ends of a magnet; the revolving part of a dynamo or motor.
arm'istice *n.* a truce between armies, a suspension of fighting.
arm'our *n.* defensive covering; plating of warships.—**arm'ourer,** a maker of arms *n.*—**arm'oury, arm'ory,** arms store *n.*—**armo'rial** *a.* of heraldic arms.
arm'y *n.* a large body of men armed for warfare; a host; a great number.
arn'ica *n.* a genus of the compositæ. A tincture of *arnica montana* is used for sprains and bruises.
aro'ma *n.* a sweet smell; a peculiar charm.—**aromat'ic** *a.*—**aro'matise** *v.t.*
arose' *p.t.* of **arise.**
around' *adv.* on every side; in a circle.—*prep.* on all sides of.
arouse' *v.t.* awaken (**arous'ing** *pr.p.*).
arpe'ggio (-j-) *n.* notes of a chord sounded in quick succession (*-ios pl.*).
a'rrack (a'rak) *n.* an Eastern spirit distilled from rice and molasses.
arraign' (-ān') *v.t.* to accuse, indict, put on trial.—**arraign'er** *n.*—**arraign'ment** *n.*
arrange' *v.t.* to set in order; settle, adjust; plan.—*v.i.* to make agreement.—**arrange'ment** *n.* *Syn.* to adapt, dispose, determine. *Ant.* derange, disarrange, misplace, muddle, dislocate.
ar'rant *a.* downright, notorious.
ar'ras *n.* tapestry, made first at Arras.
array' *v.t.* to set in order; dress.—*n.*
arrear' *n.* anything unpaid or undone (*pl.*) behindhand; **in arrears,** in debt.
arrest' *v.t.* to stop; catch the attention; apprehend by legal authority.—*n.* seizure by warrant; making prisoner.
arrive' *v.i.* to reach a destination; (with *at*) to attain an object. **-arri-val** *n.*
ar'rogate *v.t.* to claim as one's own;—**ar'rogance** *n.* aggressive conceit.—**ar'rogant** *a.* (**ar'rogating** *pres.p.*—**ar'rogated** *p.t.* and *p.p.*).
ar'row *n.* a pointed weapon to be shot with a bow.—**ar'rowy** *a.*—**ar'row-head** *n.*
ar'rowroot *n.* a West-Indian plant; its easily digested nutritious starch.
ars'enal *n.* a magazine of stores for warfare, guns, ammunition, etc.
ars'enic *n.* a soft, gray metal; its oxide, a powerful poison.—**ars'enate** *n.*—**arsen'ical** *a.*—**arse'nious** *a.*
ars'on *n.* the crime of fire-raising.
art *n.* skill; human skill as opposed to nature; skill applied to music, painting, poetry, etc.; any of the subjects of this skill; a system of rules; a profession or craft; contrivance, cunning, trick; *pl.* certain branches of learning, languages, history, etc., as distinct from natural science.—**art'ful** *a.*—**art'fully** *adv.*—**art'-**

fulness *n.*—**art'less** *a.*—**art'lessly** *adv.*—**art'lessness** *n.*—**art'ist** *n.* one who practises a fine art, *esp.* painting; one who makes his craft a fine art.—**artis'tic** *a.*—**artis'tically** *adv.*—**art'istry** *n.*—**art'iste** *n.* a professional singer or other entertainer.—**art silk,** *see* **artificial silk.**

art second person singular present indicative of **be** (our Father which art).

ar'terioscler'osis (ar-ter-e-o-skler-o'-sis) *n.* hardening of the arteries.

art'ery *n.* a vessel carrying blood from the heart; any main channel of communications (**ar'teries** *pl.*).—**arte'rial** *a.* main, important, as *arterial road.*

arte'sian *a.* of a well bored for water which rises by itself.—**wells** *n.pl.*

arthri'tis *n.* inflammation of a joint; gout.—**arthrit'ic** *a.*

art'ichoke *n.* a thistle-like, perennial, edible plant.—**Jerusalem artichoke,** a sunflower with tubers like the potato.

art'icle *n.* a clause, head, paragraph, section; a literary composition in a journal, etc.; rule or condition; a commodity or object.—*v.t.* to indict; to bind as an apprentice.

artic'ulate *v.t.* to joint; utter distinctly. —*v.t.* to speak.—*a.* jointed; of speech, clear, distinct.—**artic'ulately** *adv.*—**articula'tion** *n.*—**artic'ulateness** *n.*

art'ifice *n.* a contrivance, trick; cunning, skill.—**artif'icer** *n.* a craftsman.—**artifi'cial** *a.*—**artifi'cially** *adv.*—**artificial'ity** *n.*—**artificial silk,** synthetic yarn resembling natural silk in appearance.

artill'ery *n.* cannon or large rifled guns; the troops who use them.

artisan' *n.* a craftsman, mechanic.

Ar'yan (er-) *a.* relating to the Indo-European nations and languages.

as *adv., conj.* in that degree, so far, since, because, when, while, in like manner.

asafœ'tida *n.* a medicinal resin, with an offensive smell.

asbes'tos *n.* a fibrous mineral which does not burn.

ascend' *v.i.* to climb, mount up; rise; go back in time.—*v.t.* to walk, climb, mount up.—**ascen'sion** *n.*—**ascent'** *n.* rise.—**ascend'ancy** *n.* control, domination.—**ascend'ant** *a.* rising.

ascertain' *v.t.* and *i.* to get to know. —**ascertain'able** *a.*—**ascertain'ment** *n.*

ascet'ic *n.* a strict hermit; one who shuns pleasures for the sake of conscience or religion.–*a.* rigidly abstinent, austere. —**ascet'ically** *adv.*—**ascet'icism** *n.*

ascor'bic acid vitamin C, lack of which results in scurvy.

ascribe' *v.t.* to attribute, assign.—**ascri'bable** *a.* (**ascri'bing** *pres.p.*—**ascribed'** *p.t.* and *p.p.*).—**ascrip'tion** *n.*

asep'tic (ā-) not liable to decay, or to blood-poisoning.—**asep'sis** *n.*

asex'ual *a.* without sex; produced by other than sexual processes.

ash *n.* a familiar timber tree; its wood. —**ash'es** *pl.*—**ash'en** *a.* of this tree; pale.

ash *n.* the residue of anything burnt; *pl.* a dead body.—**ash'y** *a.*—**the Ashes** *n. pl.* symbol of victory in cricket test-match series between England and Australia.

ashamed' (-āmd') *a.* filled with shame.

ash'lar *n.* a hewn stone for building.

ashore' *adv.* on shore; run aground.

aside' *adv.* to, or on one side; privately. —*n.* words spoken in an undertone.

as'inine *a.* of or like an ass.—**asinin'ity** *n.*

ask *v.t.* to request, require, invite; entreat for.—*v.i.* to make inquiry.

askance', **askant'** *adv.* sideways, with a side look or meaning.—**to look askance,** to look at with suspicion.

askar'i (-kȧr'-) *n.* a native soldier serving a European power in E. Africa.

askew' *adv.* aside, awry, crookedly.

aslant' (-ȧnt) *adv.* obliquely.

asleep' *a.* and *adv.* sleeping; at rest. *Syn.* dead, dormant, benumbed, inactive. *Ant.* awake, unwearied, indefatigable, industrious, diligent.

asp *n.* a small venomous snake.

aspar'agus *n.* a kitchen-garden plant whose young shoots are eaten.

as'pect *n.* look, view, appearance.

as'pen *n.* the trembling poplar tree.—*a.* of the aspen; tremulous.

asper'ity *n.* roughness; harshness.

asperse' *v.t.* to besprinkle; to calumniate.—**asper'sion** *n.* (**aspersed'** *p.t./p.p.*).

as'phalt, asphal'tum *n.* a black, hard bituminous substance, used for paving, etc.—**asphal-tic** *a.*

as'phodel (-fōd-) *n.* a flower similar to the lily; (*myth.*) a flower said to cover the Elysian fields.

asphyx'ia *n.* suffocation.—**asphyx'iate** *v.t.*—**asphyx'iated** *a.*—**asphyxia'tion** *n.*

as'pic *n.* the asp; a jelly containing meat, eggs, fish, etc.

aspire' *v.i.* to desire eagerly; aim at high things; tower up.—**as'pirant** *n.* one who aspires; a candidate.—**aspira'tion** *n.*—**aspi'ring** *a.*—**aspi'ringly** *adv.*—**as'pirate** *v.t.* to pronounce with "h."

as'pirin *n.* a drug used to relieve rheumatic and neuralgic pains.

ass *n.* a donkey; a stupid fellow.

ass'agai, ass'egai *n.* a slender spear used by South African tribes.

assail' *v.t.* attack, assault.—**assail'ant** *n.*

assass'in *n.* one who kills by treacherous violence, usually for reward.—**assass'inate** *v.t.*—**assassina'tion** *n.*

assault' *n.* a sudden attack; an attack of any kind.—*v.* to storm.—*v.t.* to make an attack on.—**assault'er** *n.*

assay' *v.t.* to test the proportions of metals in an alloy or ore; a test of the fineness of a metal, etc.—**assay'er** *n.*—**assay'ing** *n.* making an assay.

assem'ble *v.i.* to bring together;

collect; put together, as machinery.—*v.i.* to meet together.—**assem'blage** *n.*—**assem'bly** *n.* (**assem'bled** *p.t.* and *p.p.*).
assent' *v.i.* to concur, agree.—*n.* acquiescence, agreement.
assert' *v.t.* to declare strongly, insist upon.—**asser'tion** *n.* a declaration.—**assert'ive** *a.*—**assert'ively** *adv.*
assess' *v.t.* to fix the amount (of a tax or fine); to tax or fine; to fix the value, *esp.* for taxation.—**assess'able** *a.*—**assess'ment** *n.*—**assess'or** *n.* (he **assess'es**).
ass'ets *n.pl.* property available to pay debts; the estate of an insolvent debtor. —*sing*, a thing of value.
assev'erate *v.t.* and *i.* to assert positively, solemnly.—**assevera'tion** *n.*
assid'uous *a.* persevering.—**assid'uously** *adv.*—**assidu'ity** *n.* close attention.
assign' (-in') *v.t.* to allot; transfer; ascribe.-**assign'able** *a.*-**assigna'tion** (-ig-nā'-) *n.* tryst.—**assignee'** (-i-nē'), **assign'** *n.*—**assign'or** *n.*—**assign'ment** *n.* transfer of title or interest; allotted task.
assim'ilate *v.t.* make similar; convert into like substance, absorb into the system.—**assim'ilable** *a.*—**assimila'tion** *n.*-**assim'ilative** *a.* (**assim'ilated,** *p.t.*/*p.p.*)
assist' *v.t.* to help.—*v.i.* to be present.—**assistance** *n.*—**assist'ant** *n.* and *a.*
assize' *n. pl.* sittings of a court held in counties periodically for civil and criminal cases, tried by a judge of the High Court and a jury (*pl.* **assi'zes**).
asso'ciate *v.t.* to join with, unite.—*v.i.* to combine.—*n.* a companion, partner, friend.—*a.*—**associa'tion** *n.*
ass'onance *n.* likeness in sound; in rhyming syllables correspondence of the accented vowels but not of the consonants.—**ass'onant** *a.*
assort' *v.t.* to classify.—*v.i.* to match, agree with.—**assort'ed** *a.*—**assort'ment** *n.*
assuage' (-sw-) *v.t.* to soften.—**assuage'ment** *n.* (**assuaged'** *p.t.* and *p.p.*).
assume' *v.t.* to take for granted; put on; arrogate; pretend.—*v.i.* to be arrogant. —**assump'tive** *a.*—**assump'tion** *n.*
assure' *v.t.* to make safe; to insure; tell positively; give confidence.—**assur'ed** *a.* —**assur'edly** *adv.*—**assur'ance** *n.*
astat'ic *a.* in physics, having no tendency to take a fixed position.—**astatic coil,** in wireless, an inductance with a limited external field.
as'ter *n.* a plant with star-like flowers; in N. America, the Michaelmas daisy.
as'terisk *n.* a star (*) used in printing,
astern' *adv.* behind; **to go astern,** to reverse engines; to move backwards.
as'teroid *n.* a small planet.
asth'ma (-sm-) *n.* disease of nervous system entailing difficulty of breathing. —**asthmat'ic** *a.*—**asthmat'ically** *adv.*
astig'matism *n.* a defect of the eye in which the rays are not brought to a focus at one point.—**astigmat'ic** *a.*
astir' *adv.* on the move; out; excited.
aston'ish, astound' *v.t.* to amaze; surprise greatly.—**aston'ishing** *a.*—**aston'ishment** *n.*—he **aston'ishes.**
as'trakhan *n.* lambskin with curled wool, from the Caspian region.
as'tral *a.* of the stars, starry.
astray' *adv.* out of the right way.
astride' *adv.* with the legs apart.
astrin'gent *a.* binding, contracting.—*n.* a binding medicine.—**astrin'gency** *n.*
astrol'ogy *n.* art of prediction by the stars.—**astrol'oger** *n.*—**astrolo'gical** *a.*
astron'omy *n.* the scientific study of the heavenly bodies.—**astron'omer** *n.*—**astronom'ical** *a.*
astro'physics *n.* study of the physical structure of the planets and stars.
astute' *a.* cunning, shrewd.—**astute'ly** *adv.*—**astute'ness** *n.*
Syn. wily, sly, subtle, keen. *Ant.* dull, slow-witted, apathetic, stupid.
asun'der *adv.* apart, in pieces.
asy'lum *n.* a refuge, a sanctuary; a home for the care of the unfortunate, *esp.* the insane (**asy'lums, -la,** *pl.*).
at *prep.* near to, by, in; engaged on; in the direction of.
at'abrine (-a-brēn) *n.* one of the synthetic drugs now replacing quinine in the treatment of malaria.
at'avism *n.* appearance of ancestral, not parental, characteristics in an animal or plant.—**atavis'tic** *a.*
a'taxia *n.* (*med.*) disease of the nerves and muscles resulting in faulty bodily co-ordination.
atelier' (-el-vā) *n.* workshop, studio.
a'theism (ā'-) *n.* disbelief in the existence of a God.—**a'theist** *n.*—**atheis'tic, atheis'tical** *a.*
athirst' *a.* thirsty.
ath'lete *n.* one trained to physical exercises, feats or contests of strength.—**athlet'ic** *a.*—**athlet'ics** *n.pl.* sports of running, wrestling, etc.—**athlet'icism** *n.* —**athlet'ically** *adv.*
athwart' *prep.* across.—*adv.* across, *esp.* obliquely; transversely.
Atlan'tic Char'ter, document drawn up by Franklin Roosevelt and Winston Churchill on 4th Aug., 1941, listing the post-war aims of the U.S.A. and Britain.
at'las *n.* a volume of maps (**at'lases** *pl.*).
at'mosphere *n.* the mass of gas surrounding a heavenly body, *esp.* the earth.—**atmospher'ic** *a.*—**atmospher'ical** *a.*—**atmospher'ics** *n.pl.* noises in wireless reception due to electrical disturbances.
atoll' *n.* a ring-shaped coral island.
at'om *n.* the smallest particle of matter which enters into chemical combination; anything very small.—**atom'ic** *a.*—**atom-bomb, atomic bomb** *n.* an explosive weapon of immense power, developed in U.S.A. by European and American scientists during World War 2, and first

dropped on Hiroshima, Japan, on 6th August, 1945. The bomb derives its power from the nuclear disintegration of atoms of elements of high atomic mass, e.g. uranium.—**atom'ic age,** name given to the period in the development of civilisation begun by the first public demonstration of the potentialities of atomic energy. It connotes the influence of modern atomic research on the moral and physical life of the people.—**atom'ic diplo'macy,** power diplomacy supported by the threat of the atomic bomb.—**atom'ic en'ergy,** power released by the nuclear fission of the atom.

atone' *v.i.* to give satisfaction or make reparation.—**atone'ment** *n.* **The Atone'ment,** Christ's crucifixion. **Day of Atone'ment,** Jewish fast.

atrabil'ious, atrabil'iar *a.* melancholy; bad-tempered.

atro'cious (-shus) *a.* extremely cruel or wicked.—**atro'ciously** *adv.*—**atro'city** *n.*

at'rophy *n.* wasting away in a living body.—*v.i.* to waste away, become useless(**at'rophied** *p.t.* and *p.p.*—**at'rophying** *pres. p.*).—**at'rophied** *a.*

attach' *v.t.* to fasten, connect.—*v.i.* to adhere.—**attach'ment** *n.*—**attach'able** *a.*

attach'e (a-tash'ā) *n.* a member of an ambassador's suite (**attach'es** (-āz) *pl.*). **attach'e-case** *n.* a small handcase for carrying papers, etc.

attack' *v.t.* to fall upon violently; assault, assail, criticise harshly; affect (of a disease).—*n.* an assault, seizure.

attain' *v.t.* to arrive at, reach, gain by effort, achieve.—**attain'able** *a.*—**attainabil'ity** *n.*—**attain'ment** *n.* esp. a personal accomplishment.

attain'der *n.* loss of rights through conviction of high treason.—**attaint'** *v.t.* to convict; deprive of rights.

att'ar *n.* fragrant oil made from roses.

attempt' *v.t.* to try, endeavour, make an effort or attack on.—*n.*

attend' *v.t.* to wait upon, wait for.—*v.i.* to give the mind (to).—**attend'ance** *n.*—**attend'ant** *n.*—**atten'tion** *n.*—**atten'tive** *a.*—**atten'tively** *adv.*—**atten'tiveness** *n.*

Syn. to serve, heed, mind, regard, listen, escort. *Ant.* to ignore, disregard, slight, be inattentive.

atten'uate *v.t.* to make thin, weaken, reduce.—*v.i.* to become weak or slender. —**atten'uated** *a.*—**attenua'tion** *n.*

attest' *v.t.* to bear witness to.—**attesta'tion** *n.* a testimony, *esp.* signed.

att'ic *n.* a low story above the cornice of a building; a room in the roof.

attire' *v.t.* to dress, array.—*n.* dress.

att'itude *n.* posture, behaviour, relation of persons expressing thought, feeling, etc.—**attitu'dinise** *v.i.*

attor'ney (-tẹr-) *n.* a solicitor; one appointed to act for another (**-neys** *pl.*).

attract' *v.t.* to draw towards, literally or figuratively; entice; cause to approach.—**attrac'tion** *n.*—**attract'ive** *a.*—**attract'ively** *adv.*—**attract'iveness** *n.*

attrib'ute *v.t.* to ascribe, assign, refer to.—**att'ribute** *n.* a quality or characteristic.—**attrib'utable** *a.*—**attribu'tion** *n.*—**attrib'utive** *a.* (**attrib'uted** *p.t.* and *p.p.*).

attri'tion (-ish'un) *n.* rubbing away.

attune' *v.t.* to put in tune (**attu'ning** *pres. p.*—**attuned'** *p.t.* and *p.p.*).

au'burn *a.* reddish brown.

auc'tion *n.* a public sale of property to the highest bidder.—**auctioneer'** *n.*—**auc'tion-bridge** *n.* a card game.

auda'cious *a.* bold, daring.—**auda'city** *n.*

au'dible *a.* able to be heard.—**audibly** *adv.*—**audibil'ity** *n.*

au'dience *n.* act of hearing; formal interview; an assembly of hearers.

au'dit *n.* a formal examination of accounts.—*v.t.* to examine (accounts).

audi'tion *n.* sense of hearing; a hearing. —**audito'rium** *n.* a place for hearing, a hall (**audito'riums, -ria** *pl.*).—**aud'itory** *a.*

au'dion (aw'-) *n.* in wireless telephony, an instrument for amplifying sound.

au'ger *n.* a carpenter's boring tool.

aught *n.* anything.—*adv.* to any extent.

augment' *v.t.* and *i.* to increase, enlarge. —**aug'ment** *n.* increase.—**augmenta'tion** *n.*—**augment'ative** *a.*—**augmen'table** *a.*

au'gur *n.* among the Romans one who predicted the future. *v.* to foretell.—**au'gury** *n.* an omen.

august' *a.* majestic, dignified.—**Au'gust** *n.* the eighth month of the year.

auk *n.* a northern sea-bird with short wings used only as paddles.

aunt (ȧnt) *n.* sister of one's father or mother; wife of one's uncle.

au'ra (aw'-) *n.* a subtle emanation from the body; atmosphere; character; a peculiar sensation, as of a current of air rising to the head, preceding an attack of epilepsy or hysteria; a gentle breeze.

au'ral *a.* of the ear.—**au'rally** *adv.*

aure'ola, aur'eole *n.* gold colour or illumination painted round the head of holy persons in Christian art; a halo.

au'ricle *n.* the outside ear; *pl.* the upper cavities of the heart.—**auric'ular** *a.* of the ear; known by ear, told in the ear, *esp.* of confession.

au'riferous *a.* bearing or yielding gold.

au'rist *n.* an ear-doctor.

auro'ra *n.* lights in the atmosphere to be seen radiating from the regions of the poles (**auro'ras** *pl.*).—**aurora borealis** the northern and **aurora australis** the southern.—*n.* the dawn.—**aurori'al** *a.*

ausculta'tion *n.* listening to the heart and lungs with a stethoscope.—**auscul'ta'tor** *n.*—**auscul'tatory** *a.*

aus'pice *n.* an omen drawn from the observation of birds (usually in *pl.* **aus'pices**).—**auspi'cious** *a.* of good omen, favourable.—**auspi'ciously** *adv.*

austere' *a.* harsh, severe, strict.—**austere'ly** *adv.*—**auster'ity** *n.*
Syn. rigid, rough, unrelenting, stern. *Ant.* kindly, engaging, tender, sweet.
aus'tral *a.* southern.—**australa'sian** *a.* and *n.* pert. to Australia.
authen'tic *a.* genuine, true, trustworthy.—**authen'tically** *adv.*—**authen'ticate** *v.t.*—**authentica'tion** *n.*—**authenti'city** *n.* genuineness.
au'thor *n.* an originator; the writer of a book.–**au'thoress** *fem.*–**au'thorship** *n.*
author'ity *n.* legal power or right; delegated power; influence; permission; a book, person, etc., settling a question, entitled to be believed; a body or board in control, *esp.* in *pl.*—**author'itative** *a.*—**author'itatively** *adv.*—**au'thorize** *v.t.* (**au-th'orizing,** *pres. p.*).—**authoriza'tion** *n.*
au'to- *prefix,* self; as in *autograph,* etc.
au'to-anal'ysis *n.* psycho-analysis, self-applied.
autobiog'raphy *n.* the biography of a person written by himself.—**autobiog'rapher** *n.*—**autobiograph'ical** *a.*—**autobiograph'ically** *adv.*
au'tocrat *n.* absolute ruler.—**autoc'racy** *n.*—**autocrat'ic** *a.*—**autocrat'ically** *adv.*
au'to-da-fe *n.* public judgment and punishment by the Inquisition in Spain and Portugal, *esp.* the burning of heretics (**autos-da-fe** *pl.*).
au'to-er'otism *n.* in psycho-analysis self-love, with satisfaction of desire.
autogi'ro (-jī'-) *n.* aeroplane using horizontal airscrew for vertical ascent and descent (**autogi'ros** *pl*). Also **-gyro.**
au'tograph *n.* one's own handwriting; a signature.—**autograph'ic** *a.*
au'to-intox'ication *n.* (*med.*) poisoning of the body's tissues by absorption of poisons from bodily waste.
autoject'or *n.* instrument for reviving animals which have been apparently dead for several minutes.
autom'aton *n.* a self-acting machine, *esp.* one simulating a human being; *fig.* person acting by routine, without intelligence (**autom'ata, -tons,** *pl.*).—**automat'ic** *a.* self-acting; mechanical.—**automat'ically** *adv.*—**autom'atism** *n.*
automo'bile *n.* a motor-car.—**automo'bilism** *n.*—**automo'bilist** *n.*
auton'omy *n.* right of self-government. —**auton'omous** *a.*
autop'sy *n.* post-mortem examination.
au'to-sugges'tion *n.* a process of influencing the mind (towards health, etc.), done by the subject himself.
auto'truck *n.* an automobile designed to carry freight.
au'tovac *n.* in motoring, a vacuum device to raise petrol from a low tank to one from which it will run by gravity to the carburettor.
au'tumn *n.* the third season of the year. —**autum'nal** *a.*—**autum'nally** *adv.*
auxil'iary *a.* helping, subsidiary.—*n.* a helper; something subsidiary, as troops; a verb used to form tenses of other verbs.
avail' *v.i.* to be of value, of use.—*v.t.* to benefit, help;] **to avail oneself of,** to make use of.—*n.* benefit.—**avail'able** *a.*—**availabil'ity** *n.*—**of no avail,** in vain.
Syn. of *n.* advantage, profit, utility. *Ant.* uselessness, futility, inutility.
av'alanche *n.* a mass of snow and ice sliding down a mountain.
av'arice *n.* greed for wealth.–**avari'cious** *a.* covetous, grasping.—**avari'ciously** *adv.*
avast' *interj.* enough ! stop !
avatar' *n.* descent of a Hindu god in visible form; incarnation.
avaunt' *interj.* away, begone.
avenge' *v.t.* to take vengeance on behalf of (a person) or on account of (a thing). —**aven'ger** *n.* (**aven'ging** *pres. p.*).
av'enue *n.* an approach; a walk bordered with trees.
aver' *v.t.* to declare true; assert, affirm. —**aver'ment** *n.* (**aver'ring** *pres. p.* **averred'** *p.t.* and *p.p.*).
av'erage *n.* the mean value or quantity. —*a.* medium, ordinary.—*v.t.* to calculate a mean.—*v.i.* exist in, form a mean.
avert' *v.t.* to turn away, ward off.—**averse'** *a.* disinclined.—**aver'sion** *n.* dislike; person or thing disliked.
a'viary *n.* a place for keeping birds.
avia'tion (ā-) *n.* the art of flying by mechanical means.—**a'viator** *n.*
av'id *a.* eager, greedy.—**avid'ity** *n.*
avoca'tion *n.* employment, business.
av'ocet *n.* bird of the snipe group.
avoid' *v.t.* to keep clear of, escape.—**avoid'able** *a.*—**avoid'ance** *n.*
avoirdupois' (av-er-dū-poiz') *n.* or *a.* the British system of weights.
avow' *v.t.* to own, acknowledge, to declare openly.—**avow'al** *n.*—**avow'able** *a.*—**avowed'** *a.*—**avow'edly** *adv.*
Syn. to confess, aver, profess, recognise, admit. *Ant.* deny, conceal, refute.
await' *v.t.* to wait or stay for.
awake', awa'ken *v.t.* to rouse from sleep; stir up.—*v.i.* to cease from sleep; bestir oneself (**awoke'** or **awaked'** (-wakt) *p.t.* and *p.p.*—**awa'king** *pres. p.*).—*a.* not sleeping.—**awa'kening** *n.*
award' *v.t.* to adjudge.—*n.* judgment.
aware' *a.* informed, knowing, conscious. **aware'ness** *n.* state of being aware.
awash' *adv.* level with the surface of water; washed by the waves.
away' *adv.* absent, apart, at a distance.
awe *n.* dread mingled with reverence.—**awe'some** *a.*—**aw'ful** *a.*—**aw'fully** *adv.*
awhile' *adv.* for a short time.
awk'ward *a.* clumsy, ungainly; difficult to deal with; embarrassed.—**awk'wardly** *adv.*—**awk'wardness** *n.*
awl *n.* a pointed tool for boring holes.
awn'ing *n.* a covering of canvas, etc., to shelter from the sun.

awry' (a-rī') *adv.* crookedly, perversely. —*a.* crooked, distorted; wrong.
axe *n.* a tool for hewing or chopping.
ax'iom *n.* a self-evident truth; a received principle.—**axiomat'ic** *a.*
ax'is *n.* a straight line round which a body revolves; a line or column about which parts are arranged; an alliance between countries, e.g. *Rome-Berlin Axis* between Italy and Germany (ax'es *pl.*).—**ax'ial** *a.*—**ax'ially** *adv.*
ax'le (ak'sl), **ax'le-tree** *n.* the rod on which a wheel turns.
ay, aye *adv.* ever *affir*; yes.—*naut.* [Ay, ay, sir!
a'yah (ī'ya) *n.* Indian nurse.
aye *adv.* yes.—*n.* an affirmative answer or vote; *pl.* those voting for a motion.
aza'lea *n.* a genus of shrubby plants.
az'ure (a'zhur, ā'zhur) *a.* clear blue, sky-coloured.—*n.* a delicate blue.

B

baas *n.* in South Africa, the master or "boss," always a white man; manager, overseer; crack, champion.
babb'itt *n.* a soft anti-friction alloy used to line machine bearings.
bab'ble *v.i.* to speak like a baby; talk idly.—*v.t.* to utter idly.—*n.*—**bab'bling, bab'blement** *n.*—**bab'bler** *n.*
babe *n.* an infant, a child.—**ba'by** *n.*—**ba'byish** *a.*—**ba'byhood** *n.*
ba'bel *n.* a confusion of sounds; a scene of confusion or tumult.
baboon' *n.* a species of large monkey, with long face and dog-like tusks.
ba'by *n. see* **babe**; S. Africa, machine for sifting diamonds from excavated soil.
bacc'arat (-rȧ) *n.* a game of cards.
bacc'hanal (-ka-) *n.* a worshipper of Bacchus; dance, revelry; drunken orgy. —**bacchana'lian** *a.*
bach'elor *n.* an unmarried man; one who has taken his first degree at a university; a young knight.—**bach'elorship, bach'elorhood** *n.*
bacill'us *n.* a microbe, a minute organism causing disease (**bacill'i** *pl.*).—**bacill'iform** *a.* rod-shaped.
back *n.* the hinder part.—*a.* situated behind.—*v.t.* to support; to make recede. —*v.i.* to move away, to the rear.—*adv.* to the rear; to a former condition; in return. **back-bench'er** *n.* a member of Parliament sitting in one of the back benches; a rank-and-file member.—**back'bite** *v.t.* to slander an absent person.—**back'biter** *n.*—**back'biting** *n.*—**back'blocks** *n.pl.* the interior of Australia.—**back'bone** *n.* spinal column.—**back-chat** *n.* and *v.t. sl.* answering impertinently.—**back'cloth** *n.* painted cloth at the back of a theatre or film stage, being a principal part of the scenery.—**back'er** *n.* one who supports another, *esp.* in a contest.—**backfire'** *v.i.* to ignite wrongly, as a gas-burner, etc.—*n.* in internal combustion engines, explosion in cylinder occurring before piston has reached top of stroke.—**backgamm'on** *n.* a game played with draughtsmen and dice.—**back'ground** *n.* space at the back; space behind the chief figures of a picture, etc.—**back'-hand** *n.* a stroke with the hand turned backward; writing that slopes to the left.—**back'ing** *n.* support.—**back-mar'ker** *n.* in a race, a man who starts from scratch.—**back'-slanging** *n.* in Australia, the custom of seeking hospitality at settlers' houses when travelling in the interior.—**back'slide** *v.i.* to fall back in faith or morals.—**back'stays** *n.pl.* ropes to strengthen the mast of a ship.—**back'wards, back'ward** *adv.* to the rear, from a better to a worse state.—**back'ward** *a.*—**back'wardness** *n.*
ba'con *n.* cured pig's flesh.
bacte'rium *n.* microbe, a disease-germ. —**bacte'ria** *pl.*—**bacte'rial** *a.*—**bacteriol'ogy** *n.*—**bacteriol'ogist.** *n.*—**bac'tericide** *n.* an agent which destroys bacteria.
bad *a.* not good, evil; faulty (**worse** *comp.*—**worst** *sup.*).—**bad'ly** *adv.*—**bad'ness** *n.* *Syn.* vile, unwholesome, vicious, sinful, corrupt, hurtful. *Ant.* good, virtuous, moral, wholesome.
bade' *p.t.* of **bid.**
badge *n.* a mark or sign.
badg'er *n.* a burrowing night animal.—*v.t.* to hunt eagerly, to worry.
bad'inage (-ȧzh) *n.* playful talk, chaff.
bad'minton *n.* a game like lawn-tennis, but played with shuttlecocks.
baf'fle *v.t.* to check, frustrate.—**baffle'-board** *n.* also **baffle** (*radio*) a piece of board placed in front of a loud-speaker to improve sound reproduction.
bag *n.* a sack, pouch; a measure of quantity—(*pl.*) trousers.—*v.i.* to swell out.—*v.t.* to put in a bag; to kill, seize, as game, etc.—**bagg'ing** *n.* cloth.—**bagg'y** *a.*—**bag'man** *n.* commercial traveller.
bagatelle' *n.* a trifle; a game played with nine balls and cue on a board.
bagg'age *n.* luggage, *esp.* of an army; a saucy or worthless woman.
bag'pipe *n.* a musical wind-instrument, consisting of a leather wind-bag and pipes.—**bag'piper** *n.* usually **piper**.
bag'uette, baguet (bag-et') *n.* a precious stone cut into an elongated lozenge shape; the shape itself.
bail *n.* (*law*) security given for a person's reappearance in court; one giving such security.—*v.t.* to release on security.
bail *n.* a pole separating horses in a stable; a crosspiece on the top of the wicket at cricket.
bail, bale *v.t.* to empty out water from a boat.—**bail out** *v.i.* to drop from aircraft by parachute.

bail'iff *n.* a sheriff's officer.—**baili'wick** *n.* the jurisdiction of a bailiff.
bairn' *n.* an infant.
bait *n.* food to entice animals; any lure or enticement; refreshment on a journey.—*v.t.* to set a lure; to feed and water; to annoy, persecute.—*v.i.* to take refreshment on a journey.
baize *n.* coarse woollen cloth.
ba'ka-bomb *n.* a rocket bomb piloted by a Japanese suicide pilot.
bake *v.t.* to cook or harden by dry heat.—*v.i.* to make bread; to become scorched.—**ba'king** *n.*—**ba'ker** *n.*—**ba'kery, bake'house** *n.* (**baked** *p.t.* and *p.p.*).
bake'lite *n.* a hard, strong synthetic resin, used as insulating material, and in coloured ware (trade name).
balalai'ka (-li'-) *n.* an old Slavic musical instrument, resembling a guitar.
bal'ance *n.* a pair of scales; equilibrium; surplus.—*v.t.* bring to equilibrium; adjust.—*v.i.* to have equal weight; to be in equilibrium.—**balance-sheet** *n.* tabular statement of assets and liabilities.—**bal'ance-wheel** *n.* the regulating wheel of a watch.—**balance of power,** equality of military power between or among nations; the ability of a small group to decide issues by siding with one of two larger factions, neither of which has a majority (**bal'ancing** *pres. p.*).
bal'cony *n.* a platform projecting from the wall of a building; a gallery.
bald (bawld) *a.* hairless; plain, meagre.—**bald'ly** *adv.*—**bald'ness** *n.*—**bald'head** *n.*
bal'derdash (bawl-) *n.* senseless talk.
bal'dric (bawl-) *n.* a shoulder-belt.
bale *n.* bundle, package.—*v.t.* to make into bundles.—**bale out,** *v.i. sl.* evacuate in order to save one's life, *esp.* to escape from a plane by parachute.
bale *v.t. see* **bail.**
bale *n.* evil, mischief, woe.—**bale'ful** *a.*—**bale'fully** *adv.*—**bale'fulness** *n.*
balk, baulk (bawk) *n.* a strip of land left unploughed; a squared timber; a hindrance.—*v.t.* to thwart, hinder.—*v.i.* to swerve, pull up.
ball (bawl) *n.* anything round; a globe, sphere; bullet.—*v.i.* to clog.
ball (bawl) *n.* an assembly for dancing.
ball'ad *n.* a simple song; a narrative poem in short stanzas.
ballade' (-ȧd') *n.* a form of poem.
ball'ast *n.* material put in a ship to give steadiness; earth or gravel laid between rails and sleepers on a railway line.—*v.t.* to load thus.
ball'et (-ā) *n.* a theatrical dance.—**balletomane'** *n.* one with an extravagant enthusiasm for ballet.
ballis'tics *n.* the science that deals with the motion of projectiles.
balloon' *n.* a large bag filled with gas to make it rise in the air.—*v.i.* to go up in a balloon; to puff out.—**balloon'ist** *n.*
ball'ot *n.* a method of voting secretly by putting balls or tickets into a box.—*v.i.* to vote by this method.—**ball'ot-box** *n.*
balm (bȧm) *n.* an aromatic substance; a healing or soothing ointment.—**balm'y** *a.* mild.—**balm'iness** *n.*
bal'sam (bawl'-) *n.* a resinous aromatic substance.—**balsam'ic** *a.*
bal'uster *n.* a short pillar used as a support to the rail of a staircase, etc.—**balustrade'** *n.* a row of short pillars surmounted by a rail.
bamboo' *n.* a large Indian reed, with hard, hollow stem (*pl.* **bamboos'**).
bam'boozle *v.t.* hoax, deceive, mystify.
ban *n.* a denunciation; proclamation.—*v.t.* to curse, forbid, outlaw.—**banns** *n.pl.* proclamation of marriage.
Syn. censure, prohibition, outlawry, interdict. *Ant.* permission, grant, sanction, licence, approval.
ba'nal *a.* commonplace.—**banal'ity** *n.*
bana'na (-nȧ'-) *n.* a tropical or subtropical tree; its fruit.—**bana'na oil** *n.* a synthetic organic compound which can be used as a solvent, etc.
band *n.* a strip used to bind; a bond.—**ban'dage** *n.* a strip of cloth used for binding up wounds.
band *n.* a company; a company of musicians.—*v.t.* and *i.* to join into a band.—**band'master** *n.*—**bands'man** *n.*—**band'stand** *n.*
bandann'a *n.* a patterned, brightly coloured handkerchief.
band'box *n.* a light box for hats, etc.
ban'dit *n.* an outlaw; robber, highwayman (**bandits', banditti** *pl.*).
ban'dolier', ban'doleer' (-ēr') *n.* a shoulder-belt with pockets for cartridges.
ban'dy *n.* a game like hockey.—*v.t.* to toss from one to another (**band'ied** *p.t.* and *p.p.*—**ban'dying** *pres. p.*).—**ban'dy, ban'dy-legged** *a.* having crooked legs.
bane *n.* ruin; poison.—**bane'ful** *a.*—**bane'fully** *adv.*—**bane'fulness** *n.*
bang *n.* a heavy blow; a sudden loud noise, an explosion.—*v.t.* to beat; strike violently, slam.
ban'gle (bang'gl) *n.* a ring worn on arm or leg, bracelet.
ban'ish *v.t.* to exile.—**ban'ishment** *n.*
Syn. to expatriate, transport, expel. *Ant.* to welcome, invite, summon.
ban'ister *n.* corrupt of **baluster.**
ban'jo *n.* a musical instrument, having a body like a flat drum, a long neck and strings played with the fingers (**ban'jos** *pl.*).—**ban'joist** *n.*
bank *n.* a ridge of earth; margin of a river, lake, etc.; rising ground in the sea.—*v.t.* and *i.* to enclose with a ridge; to pile up; of an aeroplane, to tilt inwards in turning.—**bank'er** *n.* in Australia, a river swollen to the top of its banks.
bank *n.* an establishment for keeping, lending, exchanging, etc., money.—*v.t.*

to put in a bank.—*v.i.* to keep or deal with a bank.—**bank'er** *n.*—**bank'ing** *n.*
bank'rupt *n.* one who cannot pay his debts.—**bank'ruptcy** *n.* insolvency.
bann'er *n.* a flag bearing a device.
banns *n.* *see* **ban.**
banq'uet (bang'kwet) *n.* a feast, rich entertainment.—*v.i.* to feast.—*v.t.* to treat with a feast.—**banq'ueter** *n.*
ban'shee *n.* Irish female spirit whose wail is said to be a warning of death.
ban'tam *n.* a dwarf variety of domestic fowl; a very light boxing weight.
ban'ter *v.t.* to make fun of.—*n.*
ban'tling *n.* a child; brat.
banzai' (ban-zī) *Japanese exclamation.* Ten thousand years! Health!: in World War 2, Attack! Charge!—*a.* desperate; suicidal.
baptize' (-īz') *v.t.* to immerse in, or sprinkle with water ceremoniously; to christen.—**bap'tism** *n.*—**bap'tist** *n.* a believer in baptism by immersion only. —**baptis'mal** (-z-) *a.*—**baptis'mally** *adv.*
bar *n.* a rod of any substance; an obstacle; a bank of sand at the mouth of a river; a rail in a law-court; a body of lawyers; a counter in a public-house; meteorological unit of atmospheric pressure, equal to 1 dyne per square centimetre.—*v.t.* to make fast; obstruct; except.—*prep.* except.—**barr'ing** *prep.* excepting.—**bar'maid** *n.*
barb *n.* the curved jag on the point of a spear, fish-hook, etc.—*v.t.* to furnish with such jags.—**barb'ed wire** *n.*
barb'arous *a.* savage, uncivilised.—**barba'rian** (-ē-) *n.*–**barbar'ic** *a.*–**barbar'ity** *n.*—**barb'arism** *n.*—**barb'arously** *adv.*
Syn. rude, wild, cruel, brutal, ferocious, untutored, ignorant. *Ant.* civilised, tame, gentle, cultured, kind, humane.
barb'er *n.* one who shaves beards and cuts hair; in S. Africa, an edible fish.
bar'becue (bah'-) *n.* wooden framework on which meat is smoked or dried; any large animal broiled or roasted whole; hence a function in the open air, at which animals are cooked whole.
bar'berry *n.* a yellow-flowered shrub.
barb'ital *n.* a hypnotic drug in the form of a white powder.
bar'bitone *n.* veronal.
barbitu'rate *n.* chemical compound often used in hypnotic methods which, in excess, may be dangerous to health.
bard *n.* a poet, minstrel.—**bard'ic** *a.*
bare *a.* uncovered; naked; scanty.—*v.t.* to make bare.—**bare'ly** *adv.* scarcely. —**bare'ness** *n.*—**bare'faced** *a.* impudent.
barg'ain (-gin) *n.* a contract or agreement; a favourable purchase.—*v.i.* to make a bargain; to chaffer.
barge *n.* a flat-bottomed freight boat; a state or pleasure boat; a naval pinnace.—**barge'man, bargee'** *n.*
bar'itone *n.* male voice between tenor and bass, singer with such voice—*a.*
ba'rium (-ē-) *n.* a metal.–**barium meal** *n.*
bark *n.* the rind of a tree.—*v.t.* to strip the bark from; to rub off (skin).
bark, barque *n.* a three-masted vessel with fore and main masts square-rigged and mizzen mast fore-and-aft rigged.
bark *v.i.* to utter a sharp cry, *esp.* of a dog; in S. Africa, to watch the camp-fire at night when camping in the open veld. —*n.* the cry of a dog.—**bark'er** *n.* an announcer outside a show, store, etc.
barl'ey *n.* a cereal used for food and for making malt liquors and spirits.—**barl'ey-corn** *n.*—**barl'ey-sugar** *n.* a sweetmeat made with barley.
barm *n.* yeast.
barm'y (*sl.*) *adj.* mad, foolish.
barn *n.* a building to store grain, hay, etc., a stable.—**barn-dance** *n.*—**barn'-stormer** *n.* third-rate actor.
barn'acle *n.* a shellfish which sticks to rocks and bottoms of ships.—**barn'acle-goose** *n.* a species of wild goose.
barom'eter *n.* an instrument to measure the weight or pressure of the atmosphere.—**baromet'ric** *a.*—**bar'ograph** *n.* a recording barometer.
bar'on *n.* a peer of the lowest rank; foreign nobleman.—**bar'oness** *fem.*—**bar'onage** *n.*—**baro'nial** *a.*—**bar'ony** *n.*—**bar'on of beef** a joint of two sirloins.
bar'onet *n.* the lowest hereditary title in the United Kingdom.—**bar'onetcy** *n.*
baroque' (-k) *a.* extravagantly ornamented (in art).
barouche' (-ōōsh') *n.* a four-wheeled carriage with folding top.
barque *n.* **barq'uentine,** *see* **bark.**
barr'ack *n.* usu. in *pl.* a building for soldiers; a huge bare building.
barr'ack *v.t.* and *i.* (of spectators) to jeer at players, *esp.* on a cricket field.
barr'age (-ázh) *n.* a dam built across a river; a curtain of shellfire to cover an attack, etc.—**barr'age bal'loon** *n.* in World War 2, lighter than air balloons moored above merchant ships, cities, etc., as protection against air attack.
barr'atry *n.* fraudulent breach of duty by the master of a ship; vexatious encouragement of law suits.
barr'el *n.* a round wooden vessel, made of curved staves bound with hoops; capacity of such vessel; anything long and hollow, as tube of a gun, etc.—*v.t.* to put in a barrel.—**barr'elled** *a.*
barr'en *a.* unfruitful.—**barr'enness** *n.*
Syn. unproductive, unfertile, unprolific, scanty, empty. *Ant.* prolific, plentiful, rich, plenteous, abundant, fecund.
bar'rette *n.* an ornamental hair clasp.
barricade' *n.* an improvised fortification.—*v.t.* to obstruct, fortify.
barr'ier *n.* a fence, obstruction.
barr'ister *n.* an advocate in the higher law courts.

barr'ow *n.* a small wheeled hand-cart.
barr'ow *n.* a burial mound.
bart'er *v.i.* to traffic by exchange of things.—*v.t.* to give (one thing) in exchange for another.—*n.*
bar'ytone *n. see* **baritone.**
bas'alt (-sawlt) *n.* a dark-coloured, hard, igneous rock.—**basalt'ic** *a.*
base *n.* a bottom, foundation; starting-point; fixed point.—*v.t.* to found, establish.—**base'less** *a.*—**base'ment** *n.* lowest story of a building.
base *a.* low; despicable.—**base'ly** *adv.*—**base'ness** *n.*—**base'born** *a.*
Syn. vile, ignoble, plebeian, vulgar, contemptible, worthless. *Ant.* high, praiseworthy, eminent, honourable, exalted.
base'-ball *n.* an American game, developed from rounders.
bash *v.t.* to smash in (he **bash'es**).
bash'ful *a.* shy, modest, wanting confidence.—**bash'fully** *adv.*—**bash'fulness** *n.*
ba'sic *a.* fundamental.—**basic English,** an English vocabulary devised by C. K. Ogden consisting of 850 words, apart from technical and scientific words, which are adequate to convey all ideas and meanings.
bas'il (baz'-) *n.* an aromatic plant; slope of the cutting edge of a tool; roughly tanned and undressed sheepskin leather.
basil'ica *n.* church built with double colonnade and apse.
bas'ilisk (-z-) *n.* a fabulous small fire-breathing dragon.
ba'sin *n.* a deep circular dish; a dock for ships; the land drained by a river.
ba'sis *n.* foundation (**ba'ses** (-sēz) *pl.*).
bask (-â-) *v.i.* to lie in warmth and sunshine; to revel in.
bask'et (bâsk'-) *n.* a vessel made of plaited twigs, rushes, etc.—**bas'ket-ball** *n.* team game played with large ball.
bas-relief' *n.* sculpture in low relief.
bass (bā-) *n.* the lowest part in music; man's lowest voice; one having such a voice.—*a.* low in the scale, deep.
bass (bas) *n.* the sea perch.
bassinet' *n.* a baby-carriage or cradle.
bassoon' *n.* a wood-wind instrument.
bast *n.* the inner bark of trees; fibre, matting manufactured from it.
bast'ard *n.* a child of unmarried parents.—*a.* illegitimate; not genuine, spurious.—**bast'ardy** *n.*
baste *v.t.* to beat with a stick.—**ba'sting** *n.*
baste *v.t.* to pour melted fat over roasting meat (**bas'ted** *p.t.* and *p.p.*).
baste *v.t.* to sew together loosely.
bastina'do *n.* a beating with a stick, *esp.* on the soles of the feet (**-does** (dōz) *pl.*).—*v.t.* to beat so (**-doed** (dōd) *p.t.* and *p.p.*—**doing** (-dō-ing) *pres. p.*).
bas'tion *n.* a projecting part of a fortification, *esp.* a corner tower.
bat *n.* a flat club, *esp.* as used in cricket.—*v.i.* to use the bat in cricket.—**bats'-man** *n.*—**batt'ing** *n.* (**bat'ted** *p.t.*/*p.p.*).
bat *n.* a mouse-like flying animal.
batch *n.* quantity of bread baked at one time; any quantity or number; a set.
bate *v.* same as **abate.**
bath (bâth) *n.* water to plunge the body in; act of, vessel for bathing.—*v.t.* to wash.—**bath-bun** *n.*—**bath-chair** *n.*
bathe (-th) *v.t.* and *i.* to wash (**bathed** (bath d) *p.t.* and *p.p.*—**ba'thing** (bā'th-ing) *pres. p.*).—**ba'ther** *n.*—**ba'thing** *n.*
ba'thos (-th) *n.* a ludicrous descent from the elevated to the mean.
ba'tik (bâ'tēk) *n.* a process of dyeing with several colours; a fabric so treated; a design so produced.
bat'man *n.* an officer's servant.
bat'on *n.* staff, *esp.* of a policeman, a conductor, or marshal.
batra'chian (-trā'ki-) *n.* an animal of the frog order.
battal'ion (-yon) *n.* a division of a regiment of infantry, about 1,000 strong.
ba'tten *n.* long, narrow board used for making floors, etc.—*v.t.* to fasten or strengthen with battens.
batt'er *v.t.* to strike continuously.—*n.* ingredients beaten up with liquid into a paste.—**battering ram** *n.*
batt'ery *n.* a number of guns or cannon; the place where they are mounted; a division of artillery; (*law*) assault by beating; a set of electric cells.
bat'tle *n.* a fight between armies.—*v.i.*—**battle fatigue** *n.* a type of psychoneurosis caused by the stress of modern warfare.
battle-cruiser *n.* warship, the armament of which approximates to that of a battleship, with speed of a cruiser.
bat'tledore *n.* a bat for striking a shuttlecock.
bat'tlement *n.* an indented parapet.
bau'ble *n.* a jester's stick; a trifle.
baulk *see* **balk.**
bawd *n.* a procurer; prostitute; keeper of a brothel.
bawl *v.i.* to shout.—*n.* a shout.
bay *a.* reddish-brown ; a *bay* horse.
bay *n.* a wide inlet of the sea.
bay *n.* space between columns; recess.—**bay'-window** *n.* window built out.
bay *n.* the laurel-tree; *pl.* an honorary crown of victory or achievement.
bay *n.* bark; cry of hounds in pursuit.—*v.i.* to bark.—*v.t.* to bark at.—**at bay,** cornered, awaiting assault.
bay'onet *n.* a stabbing weapon fixed to a rifle.—*v.t.* to stab with a bayonet (**-eted** *p.t.* and *p.p.*—**eting** *pres. p.*).
bazaar' (-zâr') *n.* an Eastern market; a shop; a sale *esp.* for charity.
bazoo'ka *n.* a trick musical instrument consisting of two pieces of pipe with a funnel in the end; a portable rocket gun.
be *v.i.* to live; exist; to have a state or

quality (I **am**, thou **art**, he **is**; we, you, they **are** *pres. ind.*—**was**, *pl.* **were** *p.t.*—**been** *p.p.*—**being** *pres. p.*).

beach *n.* the shore of the sea.—*v.t.* to run a boat on the shore.—**beach'head** *n.* consolidated position on a beach, in the face of the enemy.

beac'on *n.* a signal-fire; a sea-mark.—**radio beac'on** *n.* apparatus that transmits signals for direction-finding.

bead *n.* a little ball, etc., *e.g.* of stone or glass, pierced for stringing; a narrow moulding.—**bead'y** *a.*—**bead'ed** *a.*—**bead'ing** *n.* pattern on wood-work.

bea'dle *n.* a mace-bearer; a parish officer; a Scottish church officer.

bea'gle *n.* a small hound.

beak *n.* the bill of a bird; anything pointed or projecting; *sl.* a magistrate; a schoolmaster.

beak'er *n.* a large drinking-cup; a glass vessel with lip used by chemists.

beam *n.* a long squared piece of wood; the bar of a balance; a shaft of light.—*v.t.* to emit in rays.—*v.i.* to shine.—*a.* (of wireless transmission) in a controlled direction.—*n.* (*radio*) path of parallel radio carrier waves transmitted by and received on directional aerials, as a guide to navigators.

bean *n.* any of various kinds of leguminous plants and their seeds.

bear (bėr) *v.t.* to carry; support; produce, as crops or young; press (upon) (**bore** *p.t.*—**born** *p.p.* (produced), **borne** *p.p.* (carried).—**bear'ing** *pres. p.*).

bear (bėr) *n.* heavy, partly-carnivorous quadruped; a rough fellow; a speculator for a fall in stocks.—**bear'skin** *n.* tall fur head-dress worn by Guards.

beard *n.* the hair on the chin; a similar growth in plants.—*v.t.* to defy.

beast *n.* an animal; a four-footed animal; a brutal man.—**beast'ish** *a*—**beast'ly** *a.*—**beast'liness** *n.*

beat *v.t.* to strike repeatedly; to overcome.—*v.i.* to throb; to sail against the wind (**beat** *p.t.*—**beat** or **beat'en** *p.p.*).—*n.* a stroke; a pulsation; a regularly-trodden course; policeman's round; accent in music.

beat'ify (bē-at'-) *v.t.* to make happy; to pronounce in eternal happiness (**beat'ified** *p.t.* and *p.p.*—**beat'ifying** *pres. p.*).—**beatif'ic** *a.*—**beatifica'tion** *n.*—**beat'itude** *n.* extreme happiness.

beaune (bōn) *n.* a red wine of Burgundy.

beau'ty (bū'-) *n.* loveliness; a beautiful person or thing.—**beau'tiful** *a.*—**beau'teous** *a.*—**beau'tifully** *adv.*—**beau'tify** *v.t.* (-**tified** *p.t./p.p.*—**tifying** *pr./p.*)—**beauti'cian** *n.* one skilled in the craft of making beautiful by the use of cosmetics, massage, etc.—**beauty cul'ture,** face treatment, massage, etc.—**beauty par'lour,** establishment for such treatment. *Syn.* of "beautify," to adorn, deck, embellish, decorate, grace. *Ant.* to mar, tarnish, sully, blemish.

bea'ver *n.* an amphibious rodent quadruped; its fur; a hat made of the fur; a quick snack or drink; the front lower guard of a helmet.

becalm' (-kåm') *v.t.* to make calm; deprive of wind.—**becalm'ed** *a.*

became' *p.t.* of **become.**

because' *adv.* and *conj.* by reason of.

bêche'-de-mer (bāsh'de-mār) *n.* trepang, a fóod-fish prized by the Chinese.

beck *n.* a sign, gesture, nod; a brook.

beck'on *v.i.* to make a silent signal.—*v.t.* to call by a nod or sign.

become' (-kum') *v.i.* to come to be.—*v.t.* to suit (**became'** *p.t.*—**become'** *p.p.*—**becom'ing** *pres. p.*).—**becom'ing** *a.*

becreep *v.t.* in S. Africa, to stalk, as in hunting.—**becreep'ing cap** *n.* a large fur cap meant to resemble the back of an animal worn only when hunting game.

bed *n.* a place to sleep on; the bottom of a river; a layer, a garden plot.—*v.t.* to lay in a bed; to plant.—**bedd'ing** *n.*—**bed'ridden** *a.*—**bed'rock** *n.*—**bed'room** *n.*—**bed'spread** *n.* a top cover on a bed.—**bed'stead** *n.* the frame of a bed.

bedeck' *v.t.* to adorn, decorate, festoon

bedi'zen (-i'zn or -ī'zn) *v.t.* to dress gaudily.—**bedi'zened** *a.*

bed'lam *n.* a lunatic asylum; a place of uproar.—**bed'lamite** *n.*

bed'ouin (-oo-in) *n.* nomadic race of arabs; a member of such.—*a.* nomadic.

bee *n.* an insect that makes honey.—**bee'hive** *n.*—**bee'line** *n.* shortest route.—**bees'wax** *n.* wax used for polishing.

beech *n.* a tree bearing small nuts.—**beech'en** *a.*—**beech'mast** *n.* beech nuts.

beef *n.* the flesh of an ox, or cow; ox, etc., intended for slaughter; vigour, force (**beeves** *pl.*).—**beef'y** *a.* fleshy, stolid.—**beef-steak** (-stāk) *n.* a cut of beef.—**beef'wood** *n.* in Australia, the hard red wood of the casuarina tree.

beef'eater *n.* a yeoman of the guard; a warder of the Tower of London; in S. Africa, a bird resembling a starling.

beer *n.* fermented alcoholic liquor made from malt and hops.—**beer'house** *n.*—**beer'y** *a.* of or affected by beer.

beet *n.* a plant with an edible root, used for salads and for extraction of sugar.

bee'tle *n.* a coleopterous insect.—**bee'tle-browed** *a.* with prominent brows.

bee'tle *n.* a heavy wooden mallet.

befall' (-awl') *v.i.* to happen.—*v.t.* to happen to (**befell'** *p.t.*—**befall'en** *p.p.*).

befit' *v.t.* to be suitable to.—**befitt'ing** *a.*—**befitt'ingly** *adv.* (**befit'ted** *p.t.* and *p.p.*).

before' *prep.* in front of; in presence of; in preference to; earlier than.—*adv.* ahead; earlier; in front.—*conj.* sooner than.—**before'hand** *adv.* before.

befoul' (-owl') *v.t.* to make dirty.

befriend' (-rend') *v.t.* help.

beg *v.t.* to beseech, entreat.—*v.i.* to ask for or live on alms.—**begg'ar** *n.*—**begg'ary** *n.*—**begg'arly** *a.*—**to beg the question** to take for granted what ought to have been proved (**beg'ging** *pres. p.* **beg'ged** *p.t.* and *p.p.*).

beget' *v.t.* to produce, generate (**begot'**, **begat'** *p.t.*—**begott'en**, **begot'** *p.p.*—**begett'ing** *pres. p.*).—**begett'er** *n.*

begin' *v.i.* to commence.—*v.t.* to enter on, originate (**began'** *p.t.*—**begun'** *p.p.*—**beginn'ing** *pres. p.*).—**beginn'ing** *n.*—**beginn'er** *n.* learner.—**begone'** *interj.* Away! depart!

begrudge' *v.t.* to envy anyone the possession of; give unwillingly.

beguile' (-gīl') *v.t.* to cheat; while away.—**beguile'ment** *n.*—**beguil'er** *n.*

be'gum (bā'-) *n.* Moslem princess or lady of rank.

behalf' (-hâf') *n.* favour, benefit (in phrases such as *on behalf of*).

behave' *v.i.* to bear, conduct (*esp.* oneself).—**beha'viour** (-yer) *n.*—**behav'iourism** *n.* school of psychology relating all human behaviour to stimulus-response reactions, and denies the existence of consciousness, sensation or will.

behead' *v.t.* to cut off the head.

behest' *n.* charge, command.

behind' (-hī-) *prep.* in the rear of.—*adv.* in the rear.—**behind'hand** *adv.*; *a.* in arrears, late.

behold' (-hō-) *v.t.* to watch, see (**beheld'** *p.t.*—**beheld'** **behold'en** *p.p.*).—**behold'en** *a.* bound in gratitude.—**behold'er** *n.*

behoof' *n.* use, benefit.—**behove'** *v.i.* to be fit, necessary (only impersonal).

beige (bāzh) *n.* woollen cloth made of undyed wool; hence the colour of unbleached wool.

be'ing *n.* existence; that which exists, an animal.—*pres. p.* of **be.**

bela'bour *v.t.* to beat soundly.

bela'ted *a.* overtaken by night; late.

belay' *v.t.* to fasten a running rope by coiling it round a cleat.

belch *v.i.* to void wind by the mouth.—*v.t.* to eject violently.—*n.* emission of wind, smoke from funnel, etc.

bel'dam *n.* old woman, *esp.* an ugly one.

beleag'uer (-er) *v.t.* to besiege.

bel'fry *n.* a bell-tower (**bel'fries,** *pl.*).

belie' (-lī') *v.t.* to falsify; speak falsely of (**belied'** *p.t.* and *p.p.*—**bely'ing** *pres. p.*).

believe' *v.t.* to regard as true.—*v.i.* to have faith.—**belief'** *n.*—**believ'er** *n.*—**believ'ing** *a.*—**believ'able** *a.*

Syn. to credit, think, suppose, trust in, understand. *Ant.* to suspect, doubt, distrust, question, dispute.

Belish'a Bea'con, traffic sign indicating a pedestrian crossing.

belit'tle *v.t.* to make light of; deprecate; to make small.—**belit'tlement** *n.*

bell *n.* a hollow metal vessel to give a ringing sound when struck; anything shaped like a bell.—**bell'-boy** *n.* a page-boy in a hotel.—**bell-topp'er** *n.* in Australia, a silk hat.

belladon'na *n.* deadly night-shade, a poisonous plant; medicine or drug prepared from this.

bell'icose *a.* war-like.—**bellicos'ity** *n.*

belli'gerent (-ij'-) *a.* waging war.—*n.* a nation or person taking part in war.

bell'ow *v.i.* to roar like a bull.—*n.*

bell'ows *n.* an instrument for making a blast or current of air.

bell'wether *n.* a sheep, with a bell on its neck, which leads the flock.

bell'y *n.* the part of the body which contains the bowels; the stomach.—*v.t.* and *i.* to swell out, bulge (**bell'ied** *p.t.* and *p.p.*—**bell'ying** *pres. p.*).

belong' *v.i.* to be the property or attribute of; to be connected with.—**belong'ings** *n. pl.* possessions.

belov'ed (-luv'-) *a.* much loved.

below' (-ō') *adv.* beneath.—*prep.* lower than, under; inferior to.

belt *n.* a band; girdle.—*v.t.* to furnish, or mark, with a band.

bemoan' *v.t.* to bewail, to lament for.

bemuse' *v.t.* to stupefy.—**bemused'** *a.*

bench *n.* a long seat; a seat or body of judges, etc.—*v.t.*—**bench'er** *n.* a senior member of an inn of court.

bend *v.t.* to curve or bow.—*v.i.* to take a curved shape (**bent** *p.t.* and *p.p.*).—*n.* a curve (**bend'ed** *p.p.*—**bent** *p.t.* and *p.p.*).

beneath' *prep.* lower than.—*adv.* in a lower place or position.

ben'edick *n.* confirmed bachelor who suddenly marries; a newly married man.

benedic'tion *n.* an invocation of the divine blessing.

ben'efit *n.* advantage, profit, good.—*v.t.* to do good to.—*v.i.* to receive good (**-fited** *p.t.* and *p.p.*—**fiting** *pres. p.*).—**benefac'tion** *n.*—**ben'efactor** *n.*—**ben'efactress** *fem.*—**benef'icent** *a.*—**benef'icently** *adv.*—**benef'icence** *n.*—**benefi'cial** *a.*—**benefi'cially** *adv.*—**ben'efice** *n.* an ecclesiastical living.—**benefi'ciary** *n.*

benev'olent *a.* kindly, charitable.—**benev'olently** *adv.*—**benev'olence** *n.*

ben'galine (-gạ-lēn) *n.* a fine-ribbed dress material.

benight'ed (-nīt'-) *a.* overtaken by night; in mental or moral darkness.

benign' (-in') *a.* kindly, gentle.—**benign'ly** *adv.*—**benig'nant** *a.*—**benig'nantly** *adv.*-**beity** *n.***nig'n**-**benig'nancy** *n.*

Syn. gracious, generous, liberal, propitious, favourable. *Ant.* unsympathetic, hard, cruel, severe.

bent *n.* turn of mind; a wiry grass.

benumb' (-m) *v.t.* to deaden, stupefy.

ben'zedrine (-dreen) *n.* trade name for amphetamine.

ben'zene *n.* a hydrocarbon obtained from coal-tar.—**ben'zine** (-ēn) *n.* a dis-tillate of American petroleum.—**ben'zol** *n.* benzene.—**ben'zoline** *n.* impure benzene or benzine.—**ben'zoin** *n.* an aromatic gum.

bequeath' (-th) *v.t.* to leave by will.—**bequest'** *n.* act of bequeathing; a legacy.

bereave' *v.t.* to rob of (**-reaved'** (-rēvd) or **-reft** *p.t.* and *p.p.*).—**bereave'ment** *n.*

ber'et (-rā, -ret) *n.* a soft, round, close-fitting cap.

be'ri-be'ri *n.* (*med.*) an Eastern disease due to lack of vitamin B.

berr'y *n.* small stoneless fruit (**-ries** *pl.*).

berg' *n.* an iceberg; in S. Africa, a mountain.

berth *n.* a ship's anchoring place; a place to sleep in a ship; a situation.—*v.t.*

ber'yl *n.* a green precious stone.

beseech' *v.t.* to entreat, implore (**besought'** *p.t./p.p.*) (**besought'** *p.t./p.p.*).

beset' *v.t.* to assail, invest (**beset'** *p.t.* and *p.p.*—**besett'ing** *pres. p.*).

beside' *prep.* by the side of, alongside, near; distinct from.—**besides'** *adv.* and *prep.* in addition, otherwise.—**beside oneself,** out of one's senses.

besiege' *v.t.* to beset with armed forces.

be'som (bēz-) *n.* a broom of twigs.

besought' *p.t.* and *p.p.* of **beseech.**

bespeak' *v.t.* to engage beforehand (**bespoke'** *p.t.*—**bespo'ken** *p.p.*).

Bess'emer *n.* and *a.* process of making steel by passing air through molten iron.

best *a., adv.* superlative of **good** or **well.**—*v.t.* to defeat.—**best-man** *n.* groomsman.—**best-sell'er** *n.* a book which sells in abnormally large numbers.

bes'tial *a.* like a beast.—**bestial'ity** *n.*
Syn. brutish, brutal, carnal, sensual, vile. *Ant.* humane, considerate, intellectual, spiritual, pure, immaculate.

bestir' *v.t.* to rouse to lively action.

bestow' *v.t.* to give, confer; put away.—**bestow'al** *n.*

bestride' *v.t.* to sit or stand over with legs apart (**bestrode'** *p.t.*—**bestridd'en** *p.p.*—**bestrid'ing** *pres. p.*).

bet *n.* a wager.—*v.t.* and *i.* to wager (**bet** or **bett'ed** *p.t./p.p.*—**bett'ing** *pr. p.*).

beta rays *n.* stream of electrons from radium and other radioactive substances.

be'tel (bē'tl) *n.* a species of pepper, the leaves of which are chewed by the inhabitants of India.—**betel-nut,** the nut of the areca palm.

betide' *v.i.* to happen.

betimes' *adv.* early, in good time.

betok'en *v.t.* to signify by some sign; to presage; to foreshadow.

betray' *v.t.* to give up treacherously; show signs of.—**betray'al** *n.*—**betray'er** *n.*

betroth' (-ōth') *v.t.* to bind to marry.—**betroth'al** *n.*—**betrothed'** *n.* and *a.*

bett'er *a.* and *adv.* comparative of **good** and **well.**—*v.t.* and *i.* to improve.

between', betwixt' *prep.* in the middle of two, of space, time, etc.; in the middle or intermediate space.—*adv.* midway.

bev'el *n.* a slant, diagonal surface; a tool for setting off angles (**-elled** *p.t./pp.a.*).

bev'erage *n.* a liquor for drinking.

bev'y *n.* a flock of birds, *esp.* quails; a company, *esp.* of ladies (**bev'ies** *pl.*).

bewail' *v.t.* to lament, to weep for.

beware' *v.i.* to be on one's guard.

bewil'der *v.t.* to puzzle, lead astray.—**bewil'derment** *n.*—**bewil'dering** *a.*—**bewil'deringly** *adv.*

bewitch' *v.t.* affect by witchraft; charm.—**bewitch'ing** *a.*—**bewitch'ingly** *adv.*

bey' *n.* Turkish governor.

beyond' *adv.* farther away.—*prep.* on farther side of; later than; out of reach.

bezique' *n.* game of cards for two or four persons usually played with two packs of cards; a hand at this game containing queen of spades and knave of diamonds.

Bha'rat (ba') *n.* since 1949, an alternative name for India.

bi-, bin-, bis-, *prefix,* twice, double, as in *biennial, bicarbonate, binocular,*

bi'as *n.* a one-sided inclination; bent; swaying impulse (**bi'ases** *pl.*).—*v.t.* to influence, affect (**bi'ased** or **bi'assed** *p.t.* and *p.p.*—**bi'asing** or **bi'assing** *pres. p.*).—**bi'ased** *a.* prejudiced.

bib *n.* a cloth put under a child's chin.

bi'ble *n.* the sacred writings of the Christian Church.—**bib'lical** *a.*

bibliog'raphy *n.* history and description of books.—**bibliograph'ical** *a.*—**bibliog'rapher** *n.*—**bib'liophile biblioph'ilist** *n.* book-lover.

bib'ulous *a.* given to drinking.

bi'ceps *n.* a two-headed muscle, *esp.* the muscle of the upper arm.

bi'chloride (-klor-īd) *n.* a compound containing two atoms of chlorine and one other atom.

bick'er *v.i.* to brawl.—**bick'ering** *n.*

bi'cycle *n.* a vehicle with two wheels one in front of the other.—**bi'cyclist** *n.*

bid *v.t.* to offer; command (**bade** *p.t.*—**bidd'en** *p.p.*—**bidd'ing** *pr. p.*).—*n.* an offer, *esp.* of a price.—**bidd'er** *n.*—**bidd'ing** *n.* *Syn.* to call, invite, summon, order. *Ant.* forbid, prohibit, disallow.

bide *v.i.* to remain.—*v.t.* to await.

bienn'ial (bī-en'-) *a.* happening every two years; lasting two years.—*n.* a plant which lives two years.—**'-ially** *adv.*

bier *n.* a frame of wood for bearing the dead to the grave.

bifo'cal (bī-fō-kal) *a.* with two foci, used *esp.* of glasses in two segments for seeing both near and distant objects.

big *a.* large; pregnant; haughty; beastful (**bigg'er** *comp.*—**bigg'est** *sup.*).—**big'ness** *n.*—**big-time** *a.* famous, important, successful.—*n.* state of success, importance, etc.

big'amy *n.* the crime of having two husbands or two wives at once.—**big'amist** *n.*—**big'amous** *a.*

bight (bīt) *n.* the loop of a rope; a bay.

big'ot *n.* one blindly and obstinately devoted to a party or creed.—**big'oted** *a.* —**big'otry** *n.* blind zeal.

bi'jou *n.* jewel, trinket; *a.* small, neat.

bilat'eral (bī-) *a.* two-sided.

bil'berry *n.* the whortleberry.

bile *n.* the fluid secreted by the liver; anger, bitter temper or feeling.—**bil'ious** *a.*—**bil'iousness** *n.*

bilge *n.* the bottom of a ship's hull; the foulness collecting there.—*v.i.* to spring a leak.—**bilge'water** *n.*

biling'ual (bī-) *a.* having or written in two languages.—**biling'ualism** *n.*

bill *n.* a tool for pruning; an old weapon.

bill *n.* a bird's beak.—*v.i.* to join bills, as doves; to caress.

bill *n.* a note of charges; the draft of an Act of Parliament; an advertisement; a commercial document.-*v.t.* to announce by advertisement.

bill'abong, bil'abong *n.* in Australia, a backwater; a branch from a stream, often returning to it, sometimes ending in weeds, sand, etc.

bill'et *n.* a note; civilian quarters for troops; a resting place.—*v.t.* to quarter, as troops; a job; a piece of wood.

bill'iards (-ly-) *n.* a game played on a table with balls and cues.

bill'ion *n.* a million millions (in U.S.A. and France, a thousand millions).

bill'ow *n.* a great swelling wave.—*v.i.*

bill'y, bill'y-can *n.* in Australia, a round tin can with a lid, used as a kettle. —**billy goat** *n.* a he-goat.

bil'tong *n.* in S. Africa, thin strips of lean meat dried in the sun.

bi-met'allism *n.* use of coins of two metals as currency, at a fixed ratio of value to each other.

bimonth'ly (bī-) *adv.* and *a.* every two months; twice a month.

bin *n.* a receptacle for storing corn, wine.

bin- *prefix.* *See* **bi-.**

bind (-ī-) *v.t.* tie fast; tie round; unite; oblige, compel; put into a cover (**bound** *p.t./p.p.*).—(**bounden** *p.p.*).—**bind'ing** *a.* —**bind'er** *n.*—**bind'ery** *n.*—**bind'ing** *n.* cover of book.—**bind'-weed** *n.*

binge *n. sl.* concerted eating and *esp.* drinking to celebrate an occasion or give vent to high spirits.

binn'acle *n.* box holding ship's compass.

binoc'ular *a.* adapted to both eyes.—*n.* field-glasses made for two eyes; (usually in *pl.*).

bio- (bī-ō) *prefix,* meaning life. Forms compounds as **biodynam'ics** *n.*—**biogen'esis** *n.*—**biom'etry** *n.*—**bi'oplasm** *n.*, etc., for which see the simple word.

biochem'istry *n.* chemistry of living things.—**biochem'ical** *a.*

biog'raphy *n.* the story of a man's life.—**biog'rapher** *n.*—**biograph'ical** *a.*—**biograph'ically** *adv.*—**biog'raphies** *pl.*

biol'ogy *n.* the science of life.—**biol'ogist** *n.*—**biolo'gical** (-oj'-) *a.* of biology. —**biolo'gically** *adv.*

biot'ics *n.* the functions or properties of living things; science dealing with these.

bi'otin (-ō-tin) *n,* basic factor in vitamin B, needed by all forms of life.

bi'ped (bī'-) *n.* a two-footed animal.

bi'plane (bī'-) *n.* aircraft with two sets of wings, one above the other.

birch *n.* a tree with smooth white bark; rod for punishment.—*v.t.* flog, cane.

bird *n.* a feathered animal.

birett'a *n.* square, stiff-sided cap with a tassel on top, worn by R.C. priests.

birth *n.* a coming to life; beginning; parentage.—**birth'day** *n.* day on which one was born; its anniversary.

bis- *prefix.* *See* **bi-.**

bis'cuit (-kit) *n.* a hard, dry bread in small cakes; *sl.* a square mattress.

bisect' (bī-) *v.t.* to cut in halves.—**bisect'ion** *n.*—**bisect'or** *n.*

bish'op *n.* clergyman in charge of a diocese.—**bish'opric** *n.* bishop's position, jurisdiction or diocese.

bis'muth *n.* a reddish-white metal.

bi'son (bī'-) *n.* the American wild ox.

bissex'tile *n.* the leap-year.—*a.*

bit *n.* a fragment; the biting part of a tool; the mouthpiece of a horse's bridle.—*v.t.* to put the bit in.

bitch *n.* female dog.

bite *v.t.* to cut into with the teeth; to corrode (**bit** *p.t.*—**bit, bit'ten** *p.p.*—**bi'ting** *pres. p.*).—*n.* act of biting; wound made by biting; a mouthful.—**bi'ter** *n.*—**bitt'en** *p.p.* imposed upon.

bitt'er *a.* sharp tasting; sharp, painful; stinging.—**bitt'erly** *adv.*—**bitt'erness** *n.*—**bitt'ers** *n.pl.* bitter medicines or essences.

bitt'ern *n.* a bird of the heron family.

bit'umen *n.* a mineral pitch, e.g. petroleum, asphalt, etc.—**bitu'minous** *a.*

bi'valve (bī'-) *a.* having a double shell.—*n.* a mollusc with such a shell.

biv'ouac *n.* a temporary resting-place of troops.—*v.i.* to pass night in the open (**biv'ouacked** *p.t./p.p.*—**acking** *pr.p.*).

bizarre' *a.* odd, quaint, fantastic.

blab' *v.i.* to tell tales, to betray confidences.—**blab'bing** *pr. p.*—**blabbed'** *p.t./p.p.*

black *a.* without light; dark; of the darkest colour.—*n.* darkest colour; black paint or fabric.—**black'en** *v.t.* and *i.*—**black'ing** *n.*—**black'bird** *n.*—**black'berry** *n.*—**black'lead** *n.*—**black'letter** *n.*

black'ball *v.t.* to vote against (by putting black balls into the ballot-box); to reject, expel.

black'board *n.* a dark surface prepared for writing with chalk.

black'guard (blag'ard) *n.* a scoundrel.

—*a.* scoundrelly.—*v.t.* to revile.—**black'guardly** *a.*—**black'guardism** *n.*
black'mail *n.* money extorted by threats of exposure.—*v.t.* to extort thus.—**blackmail'er** *n.*
black'-out *n.* a sudden cutting off of all stage-lights; complete failure of all electricity supply; a state of temporary unconsciousness; *v.t.* and *i.* obscuring all lights as a precaution against night air-attack in time of war.
black'shirt *n.* the original uniform of a fascist; a fascist.
black'smith *n.* a smith who works in iron, shoes horses, etc.
black'thorn *n.* the sloe tree; a staff made of the wood of this tree.
bladd'er *n.* a membraneous bag to contain liquid, *esp.* as part of the body.
blade *n.* a leaf; a leaf-like part of anything; a sword; a dashing fellow.
blame *v.t.* to find fault with.—*n.* censure, culpability.—**blame'able, bla'mable** *a.*—**blame'worthy** *a.*—**blame'less** *a.*
blanch' *v.t.* and *i.* to whiten, bleach; to remove the skin of almonds; to turn pale, to be drained of colour.
bland *a.* smooth in manner.—**bland'ish** *v.t.*—**bland'ishment** *n.* flattery.
Syn. soft, kind, affectionate. *Ant.* harsh, rough, rude, uncongenial.
blank *a.* without marks or writing; vacant, confused; without rhyme.—*n.* an empty space; a lottery ticket not drawing a prize.—**blank'ly** *adv.*
blank'et *n.* a woollen covering for a bed.—*v.t.* to cover with a blanket; to cover.
blare (-ėr) *v.i.* to roar; to trumpet.—*n.*
blar'ney *n.* flattery, coaxing talk; *v.t.* and *i.* to flatter, coax.
blaspheme' *v.i.* to talk profanely.—*v.t.* to speak irreverently of.—**blas'phemy** *n.*—**blasphe'mer** *n.*—**blas'phemous** *a.*—**blas'phemously** *adv.*
blast (-ȧst) *n.* a current of air; an explosion.—*v.t.* to blow up; to blight.
blast-fur'nace *n.* smelting-furnace in which heated air is driven through molten metal.
bla'tant *a.* noisy; loud; vulgar.
blaze *n.* a bright flame of fire; an outburst; display.—*v.i.* to burn fiercely.—**bla'zing** *pres. p.*
blaze *n.* white mark on horse's forehead; *v.t.* to mark a trail.
bla'zer *n.* a light flannel sports coat, often brightly coloured.
bla'zon *n.* a coat of arms; *v.t.* to describe or depict (arms); to make public.
bleach *v.t.* to whiten.—*v.i.* to become white.—**bleach'er** *n.*
bleak *a.* cold and cheerless; exposed.
Syn. chilly, raw, bare, desolate. *Ant.* warm, mild, comforting, congenial.
blear *a.* sore or inflamed.—**blear'eyed** *a.*
bleat *v.i.* and *t.* to cry, as a sheep.—*n.*
bleed *v.i.* to lose blood.—*v.t.* to draw blood from; to extort money from; in book illustration, to extend the illustration right to the edge of the page, thus leaving no margin (**bled** *p.t.* and *p.p.*).
blem'ish *v.t.* to mar.—*n.* a flaw.
blench *v.i.* to flinch, quail; he **blench'es**.
blend *v.t.* to mix (**blend'ed** or **blent** *p.t.* and *p.p.*).—*n.*—**blend'er** *n.*
bless *v.t.* to consecrate; give thanks to; make happy.—**bless'ing** *n.* **bless'edness** *n.*
blight (blīt) *n.* mildew.—*v.t.* to affect with blight; wither; spoil.—*n.* any evil which destroys hope.
blight'y (blīt'i) *n.* soldier's name for Britain, or for a wound involving a return to Britain.
blind (-ī-) *a.* lacking sight; heedless; closed at one end.—*v.t.*—*n.* a screen; a pretext.—*v.i.* (*sl.*) to drive recklessly.—**blind'ly** *adv.*—**blind'ness** *n.*—**blind flying** *n.* navigation of an aeroplane by use of instruments alone when landmarks are invisible.—**blind'fold** *v.* and *a.*—**blind'-worm** *n.*—**blind'man's buff** *n.* game in which one player is blindfolded.—**blind alley**, closed at one end.
blink *v.i.* to look with half-closed eyes; to shine unsteadily.—*v.t.* to shut the eyes to.—*n.* a gleam.—**blink'ers** *n.pl.* leather covers to prevent a horse from seeing sideways, hence to *blink the facts*
bliss *n.* perfect happiness.—**bliss'ful** *a.*—**bliss'fully** *adv.*—**bliss'fulness** *n.*
blis'ter *n.* a bubble on the skin; a plaster to produce one.—*v.t.* to raise a blister.
blithe *a.* happy, gay.—**blithe'ly** *adv.*—**blithe'ness** *n.*—**blithe'some** *a.* gay.
blitz'krieg (-krēg) *n.* a lightning attack *esp.* by air; the heavy bomber raids on Britain, 1940–41.
blizz'ard *n.* a blinding storm of wind [and snow.
bloa'ted *a.* swollen, puffy.
bloat'er *n.* a herring that has been cured by salting and smoking.
bloc *n.* a combination of two or more political or economic parties for the purpose of obstructing legislative action or fostering special interests.
block *n.* a solid piece of wood; any compact mass; an obstacle; a pulley with frame; a group of houses; a stupid person; piece of property enclosed by streets.—*v.t.* to obstruct, stop up; to shape on a block; to sketch.—**block book'ing** *n.* the booking of a large section of seats in the cinema or theatre—**blockbust'er** *n.* a heavy bomb designed to destroy a whole block of buildings.—**blockade'** *n.* shutting of a place by siege.—*v.t.*—**block'ish** *a.*—**block'head** *n.*—**block'house** *n.* small fort.
blonde *a.* light golden-brown; fair.—*n.*
blood (blud) *n.* the red fluid in the veins of men and animals; kindred; good parentage; temperament; passion.—*v.t.* to draw blood from; to harden to bloodshed (**blood'ed** *p.t.* and *p.p.*).—**bloo**

bank *n.* store of human blood in either liquid or dried plasma form, and classified according to its group, for use in transfusion.—**blood bath** *n.* (*col.*) a massacre, or scene of great bloodshed.—**blood count** *n.* the number and proportion of red and white blood corpuscles in a certain quantity of blood.—**blood'y** *a.*—**blood'ily** *adv.*—**blood'less** *a.*—**blood'-guilty** *a.*—**blood'guiltiness** *n.*—**blood'-heat** *n.*—**blood-horse** *n.*—**blood'hound** *n.* **blood'-money** *n.*—**blood'-poisoning** *n.*—**blood pres'sure,** the pressure of the blood in the arteries.—**blood'stone** *n.*—**blood'-relation***n.*—**blood'shed***n.*—**blood'-shot** *a.*—**blood sport,** sport in which animals are killed, e.g. fox hunting.—**blood'test** *n.* examination of a sample of blood.—**blood'thirsty** *a.*—**blood-transfusion** *n.* the transfer of blood from one person into the vascular system of another of the same blood group.—**blood'-vessel** *n.* vein or artery.

bloom *n.* flower of a plant; blossoming; prime, perfection; glow; powdery deposit on fruit.—*v.i.*—**bloom'er** *n.* a ludicrous blunder; a costume for ladies, consisting of a short dress with loose drawers gathered round the ankle.—*pl.* wide, loose knickerbockers.-**bloom'ing** *a.*

bloss'om *n.* a flower; a flower-bud.—*v.i.* to flower.

blot *n.* a spot; blemish; disgrace.—*v.t.* to spot; to obliterate; to dry with blotting-paper.—**blott'ing-pad** *n.*

blotch *n.* a dark spot on the skin.—*v.t.* to make spotted.—**blotch'y** *a.*

blouse (-ow-) *n.* a loose upper garment.

blow (blō) *v.i.* to make a current of air; to pant; to sound a blast; in Australia, to boast.—*v.t.* to drive air upon or into; to drive by current of air; to sound; to spout (of whales); to fan.—*v.i.* to melt under excess of electric current;—*v.t.* to cause so to melt, *e.g., to blow a fuse* (**blew** *p.t.*—**blown** *p.p.*).—*n.* a blast.—**blow'er** *n.*—**blow'fly** *n.*—**blow'hole** *n.*—**blow'pipe** *n.*—**blow job** *n. sl.* a jet-propelled aircraft.—**blow up** *v.t. sl.* to enlarge a photograph—*n.*

blow (blō) *v.i.* to blossom.

blow (blō) *n. a* stroke.

blubb'er *n.* whale-fat.—*v.i.* to weep.

bludg'eon (bluj'n) *n.* a short thick club.—*v.t.* to strike with such club.

blue *a.* of the colour of the sky or shades of that colour; livid; depressed.—*n.* the colour; paint, clothing, etc., of that colour.—*v.t.* to make blue; to dip in blue liquid.—**blu'ish** *a.*—**blue baby,** sufferer from a heart affection, characterised by blueness of the skin, due to the inability of the heart to pump the blood effectively through the body.—**blue'bell** *n.*—**blue'book** *n.*—**blue'bottle** n. blowfly. —**blue'grass** *n.*—**blue'jacket** *n.*—**blue-pen'cil** *v.t.* to correct or edit.—**blue-print** *n.* a copy of a drawing made by the action of light on sensitised paper, in which the lines are white on a blue ground.—**The Blues** *n.* the Royal Horse Guards.—**blues** *n.* a form of Amer. Negro folk song employed in jazz music. —**a blue** *n.* one chosen to represent Oxford or Cambridge University at various games or sports.

blue'y *n.* in Australia, a blue blanket in which the bushman wraps his belongings.—**to hump bluey** *v.i.* to go on tramp carrying a pack on the back.

bluff *a.* steep; abrupt; rough and hearty.—*n.* a cliff, a high steep bank.—*v.t.* to deceive by pretence.

Syn. boisterous, downright, blunt. *Ant.* gentle, tactful, considerate.

blun'der *v.i.* to flounder; make a stupid mistake, bungle.—*n.* a gross mistake.—**blun'derer** *n.*

blun'derbuss *n.* a short gun with wide bore, firing many balls.

blunt *a.* with dull edge or point; abrupt of speech.—*v.t.* to dull.—**blunt'ly** *adv.*—**blunt'ness** *n.*—**blunt'ly** *adv.*

blur *n.* a spot, stain.—*v.t.* to stain; to obscure, dim (**blur'ring** *pres. p.*—**blurred** *p.t.* and *p.p.*).

blurb *n.* a publisher's puff *esp.* on a book jacket; sentimentality.

blurt *v.t.* to utter suddenly or unadvisedly; to speak without thinking.

blush *v.i.* to become red in the face; to be ashamed.—*n.* a flush of colour.

blus'ter *v.i.* of wind, to blow boisterously; to swagger.—*n.* a blast.—**blus'terer** *n.*—**blust'ery** *a.*

bo'a *n.* large non-poisonous snake; long fur worn round the neck by ladies (**bo'as** (-az) *pl.*).

boar *n.* the male of the swine.

board *n.* a broad, flat piece of wood; a table, meals; an authorised body of men; thick, stiff paper; in Australia and N. Zealand, the floor on which sheep are shorn.—*pl.* the theatre stage. —*v.t.* to cover with planks; to supply food daily; to enter ship; to attack.—*v.i.* to take daily meals.—**board'er** *n.*—**board'ing-house** *n.*—**board'ing-pike** *n.* —**board'ing-school** *n.*—**board'-school** *n.* —**board'-wages** *n.* money allowed to servants in place of food.—**on board,** in or into a ship.

boast *n.* a brag, vaunt.—*v.i.* to brag.—*v.t.* to brag of.—**boast'er** *n.*—**boast'ful** *a.* —**boast'fully** *adv.*—**boast'fulness** *n.*

boat *n.* a small open vessel; a ship generally.—*v.i.* to sail about in a boat.—**boat'ing** *n.*—**boat'-hook** *n.*—**boat'house** *n.*—**boat'man** *n.*—**boat'swain** (bōs'n) *n.* a ship's officer in charge of boats, sails, etc.—**boat'er** *n.* a flat straw hat.

bob *n.* a pendant; a slight blow; the weight on a plumb-line, etc.; *sl.* a shilling.—*v.i.* to move up and down.—

v.t. to move jerkily; to cut (women's) hair short.—**bobbed** *a.*
bobb'in *n.* a reel or spool of thread.—**bobby pin,** *n.* a clasp used by women to hold the hair in place.—**bobbysocks** *n.pl.* short ankle socks worn by girls.—**bob'by-sox'er** *n.* an enthusiastic devotee of the fads of adolescent girls (*U.S.*).
bobb'y *n.* (*coll.*) policeman.
Boche' (bosh') *n.* (*sl.*) a German.
bode *v.t.* to portend, prophesy.
bod'ice (-is) upper part of a dress.
bod'kin *n.* a tool for piercing holes; a blunt needle.
bod'y *n.* the whole frame of a man or animal; the main part of such frame; the main part of anything; substance; a mass; a person; a number of persons united or organised; matter, opposed to spirit.—*v.t.* to give form to (**bod'ied** *p.t.* and *p.p.*—**bod'ying** *pres. p.*).—**bod'iless** *a.*—**bod'ily** *a.* and *adv.*—**bod'y-guard** *n.*—**bod'y-line** *a.* in cricket, fast bowling aimed to rise sharply at the batsman's body or head.—**bod'y-servant** *n.*—**bod'y-snatcher** *n.* a grave robber.
Boer (boor') *n.* S. African of Dutch descent, c.f. **Afrika'ner.**—*boer',* **n.** S. African farmer.
bog *n.* wet, soft ground.—*v.t.* to entangle in such ground.—**bogg'y** *a.*
bo'gey *n.* a bugbear (**bo'geys** *pl.*).
bog'gle (bog'l) *v.i.* to stop at, hesitate; make difficulties.—**bogg'ler** *n.*
bo'gie *n.* a low truck on four wheels; a revolving undercarriage.
bo'gle *n.* a spectre, goblin, evil spirit.
bo'gus *a.* sham, false.
bohem'ian *n.* a gypsy; one who lives unconventionally.
boil *n.* inflamed swelling containing pus.
boil *v.i.* to bubble up from the action of heat; to be agitated; to be cooked by boiling.—*v.t.* to cause to bubble up; cook by boiling.—**boil'er** *n.*—**boil'ing-point** *n.*
boi'sterous *a.* wild; turbulent.—**boi'sterously** *adv.*—**boi'sterousness** *n.*
Syn. stormy, tempestuous, tumultuous. *Ant.* quiet, calm, gentle, mild.
bold *a.* daring; presumptuous; well-marked.—**bold'ly** *adv.*—**bold'ness** *n.*
bole *n.* the trunk of a tree.
bole'ro (-lā-) *n.* short outside bodice as worn in dancing the Spanish bolero.
bo'lo *n.* a long one-edged knife used in the Philippines.
bolo'ney *n.* Bologna sausage; (*sl.*) senseless talk, *esp.* when intended to deceive; humbug; flattery.
bol'shevik *n.* member of Russian communist party (**bolshevi'ki** (-vē-) *pl.*).
bo'lster *n.* a long pillow; a pad.—*v.t.* to support.
bolt (bō) *n.* a bar or pin; an arrow; a running away; a discharge of lightning.—*v.t.* to fasten with a bolt; to swallow hastily.—*v.i.* to break from control.
bo'lus *n. med.* large pill (**-luses** *pl.*).
bomb (bom) *n.* an explosive projectile, a grenade.—*v.t.* to attack with bombs.—**bombard'** *v.t.* to shell.—**bombard'ment** *n.*—**bombardier'** *n.* an artillery non-commissioned officer.—**bomb'er** *n.* a soldier, aeroplane using bombs.
bom'bast *n.* inflated language.—**bombas'tic** *a.*—**bombas'tically** *adv.*
bom'bazine *n.* a twilled fabric of silk or cotton and worsted, generally used for mourning.
bon'a fi'des *adv.* or *a.* good faith.
bond *n.* that which binds; link, union; written promise to pay money or carry out a contract.—*v.t.* to bind; to store goods until duty is paid on them.
bond'age *n.* slavery.—**bond'man** *n.*
bone *n.* hard substance forming the skeleton of animals.—*v.t.* to take out bone.—**bo'ny** *a.*—**bone'less** *a.*
bon'fire *n.* an open-air fire to express joy, burn rubbish, etc.
bonn'et *n.* a hat with strings; a cap.
bonn'y *a.* beautiful, handsome, healthy.
bont *a.* in South Africa, many-coloured.
bon'te-buck *n.* a S. African antelope; the pied antelope.
bo'nus *n.* extra payment (**bo'nuses** *pl.*).
bon'zer *n. sl.* Australia, a stroke of good fortune.—*a.* excellent.
boob'y *n.* a dunce, a stupid person.—**boob'y-prize** *n.*—**boob'y-trap** *n.* a mine or other explosive, disguised as, connected to, or concealed in, a harmless looking object, so as to explode when disturbed.
boo'gie-woo'gie *n.* in jazz music, a kind of jazz piano playing, emphasising a rolling bass in syncopated eighth notes.
book *n.* a collection of sheets of paper bound together; a literary work; a main division of a work.—*v.t.* to enter in a book.—**book'ish** *a.*—**book'let** *n.* **book'binder** *n.*—**book'binding** *n.*—**book'case** *n.* **book-ends** *n.* two supports, one for each end of a row of books.—**book'maker** *n.* compiler of books for profit; a professional better on horse-races, etc.—**book'worm** *n.* a great reader.
boom *n.* a long spar; a barrier.
boom *n.* a loud deep resonant sound sudden commercial activity; prosperity —*v.i.* to become active, prosperous.—*v.t.* to push into prominence.
boo'merang *n.* a bent missile of wood used by natives in Australia, which when thrown, returns to the thrower.
boon *n.* a favour; a blessing; *a.* gay.
boor *n.* a rustic.—**boor'ish** *a.*
boost *v.t.* to push or lift from beneath praise, *esp.* in advertising.—**boost'er** *n.* in electricity an auxiliary dynamo.
boot *n.* a covering for the foot and lower leg.—**boot'ed** *a.* wearing boots.—**boot'jack** *n.* for taking off boots.—**boot'lace** *n.*—**boot'-last** *n.*—**boot'-tree** *n.*—**boots** *n. sing.* an inn servant.

boot *n.* profit.—**to boot,** in addition.
booth (-th) *n.* a stall at a fair; polling-place; any temporary erection.
boot'legger *n.* (U.S. *sl.*) a smuggler, *esp.* of alcoholic liquor into U.S.A.—**boot'leg** *v.t.* to smuggle.
boot'y *n.* plunder, spoil.
bo'rak *n.* in Australia, banter, chaff.—**to poke borak at,** to make fun of.
bo'rax *n.* (*chem.*) sodium tetraborate, or the sodium salt of pyroborac acid.—**borac'ic** *a.*—**borac'ic acid** *n.*
bord'er *n.* margin; strip of garden.—*v.t.* to put on a margin, edging; to adjoin.—*v.i.* to resemble (with *on*), to be adjacent (with *upon*).—**bord'erer** *n.* *Syn.* boundary, bounds, confines, frontier, verge, precinct, margin.
bore *v.t.* to pierce, making a hole; to weary.—*n.* a hole; the size or cavity of a gun; a wearisome person.—**bore'dom** *n.*
bore *n.* tidal wave in a river.
bore *p.t.* of **bear.**
born, borne *see* **bear.**
bo'ron *n.* a metallic element of the aluminium group, with similar properties to carbon.
bo'rough (bu'rō) *n.* a town with a corporation.
bor'row *v.t.* to obtain on loan; to adopt from abroad.—**bor'rower** *n.*
bos'cage (bosk'-ij) *n.* thick foliage; woodland.
bors'tal *a.* in *Borstal system,* a reformatory treatment for young criminals.
Bor'zoi *n.* the Russian wolfhound.
bosh' *n.* and *interj.* (*coll.*) rubbish, nonsense, empty talk.
bo'som (booz'-) *n.* human breast; *a.* close, as **a bosom friend.**
boss *n.* a knob; the head of a gang, crew, political party, etc.—*v.t.* to ornament with bosses.—*v.* to give orders.
bot'any *n.* the science of plants.—**bot'anist** *n.*—**botan'ic, botan'ical** *a.*—**bot'anize** *v.i.* to study plants.
botch *v.t.* to put together clumsily.—*n.* a bungled piece of work.
both (bō-) *a.* the two.—*adv.* and *conj.* as well; equally.
both'er (-th-) *v.t.* to pester.—*v.i.* to fuss, be troublesome.—*n.* trouble; a nuisance.
bot'tle *n.* a vessel for holding liquids; the contents of such.—*v.t.* (**bott'led** *p.t.* and *p.p.*)—**bottle'neck** *n.* a suddenly narrowing stretch of road; a hold-up in production owing to some single lack.
bott'om *n.* the lowest part of anything; the bed of a sea, river, etc.; the sitting part of the human body; a ship.—*v.t.* to put a bottom to; base (upon); get to the bottom of.—**bott'omless** *a.*—**bott'omry** *n.* a loan on the security of a ship.
bot'ulism *n.* poisoning due to a ptomaine poison sometimes found in sausages or meat kept away from air.
boud'oir (bōōd'-wah(r)) *n.* lady's private sitting-room.
bough (bow) *n.* a branch of a tree.
boul'der (bōl'-) *n.* large rock.
boul'evard (bool'-vahr) *n.* street or promenade planted with trees.
bounce *v.i.* to bound, like a ball; to throw oneself about; to boast.—*n.* a leap, rebound; boast.—**bounc'er** *n.*—**bounc'ing** *a.* large; swaggering (**bounced** *p.t.* and *p.p.*).
bound *n.* boundary.—*v.t.*—**bound'ary** *n.*—**bound'less** *a.*—**bound'ed** *a.* (**daries** *pl.*).
bound *v.i.* to spring, leap.—*n.*—**bound'er** *n.* a vulgar fellow.
bound *a.* ready to go, as *outward bound*
boundary-rider *n.* (Australia), man who rides round fences of a station, to keep them in repair.
boun'ty *n.* liberality; a premium.—**boun'teous, boun'tiful** *a.* **boun'tifully** *adv.* *Syn.* generosity, munificence, kindness, benevolence. *Ant.* parsimony, meanness, selfishness.
bouquet' (book-kā) *n.* a bunch of flowers; perfume of wine; a compliment.
bour'geois (boor-zhwah) *a.* middle-class, ordinary.
bout *n.* a turn, a round; attempt.
bo'vine *a.* of the ox, oxlike; stolid.
bow (bō) *n.* a bend, bent line; rainbow; weapon for shooting arrows; ornamental knot of ribbon, etc.; implement for playing a violin.—**bow'-window** *n.*
bow (bow) *v.i.* to bend the body in respect, assent, etc.; to submit.—*v.t.* to bend downwards; to cause to stoop.—*n.*
bow (bow) *n.* fore end of a ship.
bow'el (-ow'-) *n.* an intestine; *pl.* pity, feelings, as *bowels of compassion.*
bow'er (-ow'-) *n.* a shady retreat; an inner room.—**bower-bird** *n.* in Australia, a bird that erects a bower as a playground, and adorns it with feathers, etc.
bowie-knife *n.* a long knife used as a weapon (*-knives pl.*).
bowl (-ō-) *n.* a round vessel; a drinking-cup; the hollow part of anything.
bowl (-ō-) *n.* a wooden ball.—*v.t.* and *i.* to roll or throw a ball.—**bowls** *n.* a game.—**bowl'er** *n.*—**bowl'ing-green** *n.*
bow'sprit (-ow'-) *n.* a spar projecting from the bow of a ship.
box *n.* a tree yielding hard, smooth wood; its wood; a case, generally with a lid; the contents of such case; a small house; a driver's seat; a compartment.—*v.t.* to put in a box; to confine; in Australia, to mix together sheep that ought to be separate.—**box'-iron** *n.*—**box'-pleat** *n.*—**box'wood** *n.*—**to box the compass,** name the thirty-two points in order and backwards; make a complete turn round.
box *n.* a blow.—*v.t.* to cuff.—*v.i.* to fight with the fists, *esp.* with gloves on.—**box'er** *n.* **box'ing** *n.*

boy *n.* a male child; a young man; a native servant.—**boy'hood** *n.* **boy'ish** *a.*
boy'cott *v.t.* to refuse to deal with.—*n.* a concerted refusal to deal with.
brace *n.* a clasp, clamp; a pair; a strut; a carpenter's tool for turning boring instruments; *pl.* trouser-suspenders.—*v.t.* to stretch, string up, support, make firm.—**bra'cing** *a.* invigorating.
brace'let *n.* an ornament for the arm.
brack'en *n.* fern.
brack'et *n.* support, shelf; pipe with a gas burner; *pl.* in printing, the marks [ ] to enclose words.—*v.t.* enclose in brackets; to connect; couple together; (*artillery*) to range by dropping shells nearer and farther than a mark.
brack'ish *a.* saltish, *esp.* water.
brad *n.* a small nail.—**brad'-awl** *n.* a tool to pierce holes.
brag *v.i.* to boast.—*n.* boastful language.—**bragg'art** *n.*—**braggado'cio** (-shy-o) *n.*
braid *v.t.* to plait; to trim with braid.—*n.* plaited cord; a woven band.
braille (brāl) *n.* a system of printing books to be read by the blind; the letters used, consisting of raised dots.
brain *n.* the nervous matter in the skull; the intellect.—*v.t.* to dash out the brain.—**brain'y** *a.*—**brain'less** *a.*—**brain'storm** *n.* in N. America, an attack of madness.
brains trust *n.* a committee of experts appointed to aid in planning; *colloq.* a group of people appointed to answer spontaneously questions of general interest asked by the audience.
braise (-āz) *v.t.* to stew with vegetables, etc., and then bake (**braised** *p.t./p.p.*).
brak *n.* (S. Africa), a mongrel dog; a cur; a cad; (*brakkie,* dimin.; *-ke, pl.*); small type of dog.
brake *n.* a fern; a place overgrown with ferns; a thicket; an instrument for retarding the motion of a wheel.—*v.t.* to apply a brake to (**braked** *p.t.* and *p.p.*).—**brake'van** *n.*
bram'ble *n.* a prickly shrub; the blackberry.—**bram'bly** *a.*
bran *n.* sifted husks of corn.
branch (-å-) *n.* a limb of a tree; anything like a limb; a subdivision; a subordinate department of a business.—*v.i.* to bear branches; to diverge.—**branch'y** *a.* with many branches.
brand *n.* a burning piece of wood; a mark made by a hot iron; a trademark; a class of goods.—*v.t.* to burn with an iron; to mark.—**brand-new** *a.* absolutely new.
bran'dish *v.t.* to flourish (a weapon, etc.), he **bran'dishes.**
bran'dy *n.* a spirit distilled from wine.—**brandy-smash** *n.* in N. America, a drink made of brandy and crushed ice.—**bran'dysnap** *n.* a biscuit (**brandies** *pl.*).
brass *n.* an alloy of copper and zinc; impudence.—**brass'y** *a.*—**bra'zen** *a.*
bras'serie (-er-ē) *n.* an eating hall where alcoholic drink is also served.
bras'siere (-i-ār) *n.* a woman's undergarment to support the breasts.
brat *n.* contemptuous name for a child.
brava'do (-vå'-) *n.* a display of boldness (-does -dos (-dōz) *pl.*).
brave *a.* bold; finely dressed.—*n.* a warrior.—*v.t.* to defy, meet boldly.—**brave'ly** *adv.*—**bra'very** *n.*
Syn. fearless, valiant, valorous, intrepid, gallant, undaunted, excellent. *Ant.* cowardly, timid.
bravu'ra (*mus.*) *n.* a spirited passage.
brawl *v.i.* to quarrel noisily.—*n.* a noisy quarrel.—**brawl'er** *n.*
brawn *n.* muscle; strength; a preparation of chopped meat.—**brawn'y** *a.* strong, muscular.
bray *n.* the ass's cry.—*v.i.* to utter that cry; to give out harsh sounds.
braze *v.t.* to solder with alloy of brass.
bra'zen *a.* made from brass, resembling brass; impudently bold; resembling the sound given out by a brass instrument.
bra'zier *n.* a pan for burning charcoal.
breach *n.* a break, opening; a breaking of rule, duty, etc., as **breach of discipline;** a quarrel.—*v.t.* to make a gap in.
bread (-ed) *n.* food made of flour or meal baked; food; livelihood.
breadth (-edth) *n.* width, extent across; largeness of view, mind.
break (brāk) *v.t.* to part by force; to shatter, burst, destroy; make bankrupt; discard; dissolve; tell with care; in Australia, S. Africa, etc., to plough virgin soil.—*v.i.* to become broken, shattered, divided; open, appear; crack, give way; fall out (**broke** *p.t.*—**bro'ken** *p.p.*).—*n.* fracture; a gap; in billiards or croquet, a series of consecutive strokes, each giving the right to make the one following; in boxing, separating after a clinch; (*sl.*) a respite; an opportunity; opening; dawn, separation, interruption.—**break'able** *a.*—**break'age** *n.*—**break'away** *n.* in Australia, a bullock that separates from the herd; the panic rush of animals at the smell or sight of water.—**break'er** *n.*—**break'down** *n.*—**break'fast** *n.*—**break'water** *n.*
bream' *n.* a broad, thin fresh water [carp.
breast (brest) *n.* the human chest; a woman's mammary gland; the affections; any protuberance.—*v.t.* to face, oppose; mount.—**breast'plate** *n.*—**breast'work** *n.*
breath (breᴛʜ) *n.* air taken into and put out from lungs; life; a breeze.—**breathe** (brēth) *v.i.* to inhale and exhale air from lungs; to live; to pause.—*v.t.*—**breath'less** *a.*—**brea'ther** (-ᴛʜ-) *n.*—**brea'thing** (-ᴛʜ-) *n.* (**breathed'** *pt./p.p.*).
breech *n.* the lower part of the body behind; the hinder part of anything *esp.* of a gun.—**breech'es** *pl.* trousers.—**breech** *v.t.* to put into breeches.

breed *v.t.* to generate, bring forth; rear.—*v.i.* to be produced; to be with young (**bred** *p.t.* and *p.p.*).—*n.* offspring produced; race, kind.—**breed'ing** *n.*
breeze *n.* a gentle wind; a wind; a quarrel.—**breez'y** *a.*—**breez'ily** *adv.*
brethren (-TH-) *n.pl.* members of the same society or profession; *see* **brother.**
breve' (*mus.*) *n.* a note equal to two semi-breves.
bre'viary *n.* a book of daily prayers.
brev'ity *n.* shortness.
brew (-ōō) *v.t.* to prepare a liquor, as beer from malt, etc.; to plot.—*v.i.* to be in preparation.—**brew'age** *n.*—**brew'er** *n.*—**brew'ing** *n.*—**brew'ery** *n.*
bri'ar *n. see* **brier.**
bri'ar *a.* only in *briar pipe*, one made of a heather root.
bribe *n.* a gift to corrupt.—*v.t.*—**bri'ber** *n.*—**bri'bery** *n.* (**bri'bed,** *p.t.* and *p.p.*).
brick *n.* an oblong block of hardened clay; any oblong block.—*v.t.* to lay or pave with bricks.—**brick'layer** *n.*
bri'dal *n.* a wedding.—*a.*
bride *n.* a woman about to be, or just, married.—**bride'groom** *n.* a man about to be, or just, married.—**brides'-maid** *n.*
bridge *n.* a structure for crossing a river, etc.; a raised narrow platform on a ship; upper part of nose; part of a violin supporting the strings; a card game.—*v.t.* to make a bridge over.
bri'dle *n.* the headgear of horse-harness; a restraint.—*v.t.* to put on a bridle; to restrain.—*v.i.* to throw up the head.
brief *a.* short.—*n.* summary of a case for the use of counsel; papal letter.—**brief'less** *a.*—**brief'ly** *adv.*—**brief'ness** *n.*
brief'ie (brē'fē) *n.* in S. Africa, a note or letter.
bri'er, bri'ar *n.* the wild rose.
brig *n.* a two-masted, square-rigged ship.
brigade' *n.* an army division; two or more regiments under a general; an organised band.—*v.t.* to join units into a brigade.–**brigade'-ma'jor** *n.* **brigadier'** *n.*
brig'and *n.* robber.—**brig'andage** *n.*
brig'antine *n.* a two-masted vessel, with square-rigged foremast and fore-and-aft mainmast.
bright (brīt) *a.* shining; cheerful; clever.—**bright'en** *v.t.* and *i.*—**bright'ly** *adv.*
Syn. clear, illustrious, glorious, vivid, luminous, quick, keen, lustrous. *Ant.* dull, thick, stupid, slow.
brill'iant (-lya-) *a.* shining; sparkling; very clear; **brill'iantly** *adv.* **brill'iance** *n.*
brill'ing *n.* in S. Africa, the noise made by cattle and other animals when enraged or in pain.
brim *n.* the margin or edge.—**brim'ful** *a.*
brim'stone *n.* sulphur.
brin'dled *a.* spotted and streaked.
brine *n.* salt water.—**bri'ny** *a.*
bring *v.t.* to fetch; carry with one; to cause to come (**brought** *p.t.* and *p.p.*).
brink *n.* the edge of a steep place; verge.
briquette' *n.* block of compressed coal-dust, or ice-cream.
brisk *a.* active, lively, sharp.—*v.t.* to enliven.—*v.i.* to cheer up.—**brisk'ly** *adv.*
bris'tle (-is'l) *n.* a short, stiff hair.—*v.i.* to stand erect.—*v.t.* to erect like bristles.—**bris'tly** *a.* (**brist'led** *p.t.* and *p.p.*).
brit'tle *a.* easily broken.—**brit'tleness** *n.*
broach *n.* a boring tool; a spit.—*v.t.* to pierce (a cask); to open, begin.
broad (-awd) *a.* wide, open; outspoken; tolerant; of pronunciation, dialectal.—**broad'en** *v.t.* and *i.*—**broad'ly** *adv.*—**broad-ar'row** *n.* a Government mark (♠).—**broad'cast** *a.* scattered freely.—*v.t.* to scatter, as seed; to send out wireless messages, music, etc., for general reception.–**broad'cloth** *n.*–**broad'-gauge** *n.* and *a.*—**broad'ness** *n.*—**broad'side** *n.* a discharge of all guns on one side; a sheet printed on one side.
Syn. extensive, large, comprehensive, gross. *Ant.* narrow, intensive.
brocade' *n.* silk stuff wrought with figures.—**broca'ded** *a.*
brochure' (-shoor') *n.* a pamphlet.
bro'gan *n.* strong shoe.
brogue (-ōg) *n.* a stout shoe; a dialectal pronunciation, *esp.* the Irish pronunciation of English.
broil *n.* a noisy quarrel.—*v.t.* to cook over hot coals; to grill.
broke *p.t.*—**bro'ken** *p.p.* of **break.**
bro'ker *n.* one who buys and sells for others; a dealer; one who values goods distrained for rent.—**bro'kerage** *n.* payment to a broker.
bro'mide *n.* a photograph printed on paper which has been treated with silver bromide; a sedative drug; (*sl.*) commonplace, platitudinous matter.
bro'mine *n.* a liquid element, allied to chlorine.—**bro'mate** *n.*
bron'chi (-ngk-) *n.pl.* the branches of the windpipe.—**bronch'ial** *a.*—**bronchi'tis** *n.* inflammation in the bronchi.
bronc'o *n.* half-tamed horse (/**-os** *pl.*).
bronze *n.* alloy of copper and tin.—*a.* made of, like, bronze.—*v.t.*—**bronzed** *a.* coated with bronze, sunburnt.
brooch (-ō-) *n.* an ornamental pin.
brood (-ōō-) *n.* a family of young, *esp.* of birds; a tribe, race.—*v.t.* to sit as a hen on eggs; to meditate.—**brood'y** *a.*
brook (-oo-) *n.* a small stream; *v.t.* to put up with, tolerate.
broom (-ōō-) *n.* a yellow-flowered shrub; brush for sweeping.—**broom'-stick** *n.* handle of a broom.
broth *n.* soup of meat and vegetables.
broth'el *n.* a house of prostitutes.
broth'er (-uth-) *n.* a son of the same parents; any one closely united with another (**broth'ers, breth'ren** *pl.*).

broth'erhood *n.* relationship; a fraternity, company.—**broth'er-in-law** *n.* the brother of a husband or wife; the husband of a sister.—**broth'erly** *a.*—**broth'erliness** *n.*
brow *n.* the ridge over the eyes; the forehead; the edge of a hill.—**brow'beat** *v.t.* to bully, intimidate.
brown *a.* of a dark colour inclining to red or yellow.—*n.* the colour.—*v.t.* or *i.*
brown'ie *n.* an elf, fairy; a junior girl guide.—**brown-study** *n.* serious reverie.
browned-off *a.* (*sl.*) bored; depressed; disappointed.—**Brown Shirt,** member of a Nazi armed force of terrorists who helped Adolf Hitler in his rise to power.
browse *v.i.* to feed on shoots and leaves; to study desultorily, as books.
bruise (-ōōz) *v.t.* to injure by a blow; oppress.—*n.* a contusion, a discoloured lump raised on the body by a blow.—**bruis'er** *n.* a prize-fighter.
brum'by *n.* in Australia, a wild horse.
brum'magem *n.* anything cheap and showy; name for Birmingham.—*a.* cheap and showy.
brunch *n.* (*sl.*) late breakfast and early lunch combined.
brunette' *n.* a woman of dark complexion, hair, etc.
brunt' *n.* the shock of an attack; the chief stress of anything.
brush *n.* small shrubs; utensil for sweeping; tool of hair used by painters; a bushy tail; a skirmish; a bundle of wires, or anything like a broom.—*v.t.* to sweep or clean; to touch lightly.—*v.i.* to move lightly.—**brush'wood** *n.*—**brush-off** *n.* (*sl.*) dismissal; rebuff.
brusque (-sk) *a.* abrupt in manner.—**brus'querie** *n.* brusqueness; an abrupt expression or act.
Syn. rough, blunt. *Ant.* sensitive, polished, kind, gentle.
brute (-ōō-) *n.* one of the lower animals; a man like such animal.—*a.* animal; sensual; stupid.—**bru'tal** *a.*—**bru'tish** *a.*—**bru'tally** *adv.* **brutal'ity** *n.* **bru'talise** *v.t.*
bry (-ī) *v.t.* in S. Africa, to roast meat in hot ashes or toast it on a fork.
bub'ble *n.* a hollow globe of liquid, blown out with air; anything empty; a swindle.—*v.i.* to form bubbles, rise in bubbles.—**bubb'ly** *a.* (**bub'bling** *pres. p.*).
buccaneer' *n.* a pirate.-**buccaneer'ing** *n.*
buch'manite *n.* a member of the Oxford Group Movement, a religious body believing in public confession, founded in U.S.A. by Frank Buchman.
buck *n.* male deer, rabbit, hare, etc.; a dandy.—*v.i.* of a horse, to attempt to throw a rider by jumping upwards.—**buck'-board** *n.* in N. America, a four-wheeled vehicle in which an elastic board is used instead of springs.—**buck'jumper** *n.*—**buck'shot** *n.*—**buck'-skin** *n.*—**buck'wagon** *n.* in S. Africa, a large vehicle drawn by oxen.—**to pass the buck,** to shirk responsibility by placing it in another's hands.
buck'et *n.* vessel for water, etc.—**buck'etful** *n.* (**buck'etfuls** *pl.*).—**bucket-seat** *n.* car or theatre seat with the back shaped to fit the occupier's figure.—**bucket-shop** *n.* in N. America the office of an outside broker, *esp.* one where gambling is carried on.
buc'kle *n.* a metal instrument with a rim and tongue, for fastening straps, etc.—*v.t.* to fasten with a buckle.—*v.i.* to warp, bend.—**buck'ler** *n.* a shield.
buck'ram *n.* coarse stiffened cloth.
buckshee' *a.* and *adv.* (*sl.*) free, unexpectedly welcome.
bucol'ic (bū-) *a.* rustic.
bud *n.* the first shoot of a plant, leaf, etc.—*v.i.* to begin to grow.—*v.t.* to graft.
Buddh'ism (bood'-) the doctrines taught by the Hindu sage Gautama surnamed Buddha in the 6th century B.C.; the Buddhist religion.
bud'dy *n.* *U.S. colloq.* a close friend or comrade; a brother.
budge *v.i.* to move, stir.
bud'gerigar *n.* a small parakeet, commonly called "Lovebird."
budg'et *n.* a bag and its contents; an annual financial statement.—*v.i.* to prepare such.
buff *n.* leather from buffalo or ox hide; a light yellow colour; the bare skin.
buff'alo *n.* any of several species of large oxen, wild and domesticated (**-aloes** *pl.*).
buff'er *n.* a device to lessen the shock of collision; (*sl.*) fellow, man, as in *old buffer*.-**buff'er-state** *n.* a neutral country between two others.
buff'et *n.* a blow, slap; misfortune.—*v.t.* to strike with the fist; to contend against.—**buff'eting** *n.*
buff'et (boo'fā) *n.* refreshment bar.
buffoon' *n.* a clown.—**buffoon'ery** *n.*
bug *n.* a small blood-sucking insect.
bug'bear *n.* an object of terror.
bug'gy *n.* vehicle; gig.
bu'gle *n.* a hunting-horn; an instrument like a trumpet.—**bu'gler** *n.*—**bu'gling** *n.*
bu'gle *n.* a glass bead, usually black.
build (bild) *v.t.* to erect, as a house, bridge, etc.; to form, construct.—*v.i.* to depend (on) (**built** *p.t.* and *p.p.*).—*n.* make, form.—**build'er** *n.*—**build'ing** *n.*
bulb *n.* the rounded stem or shoot of the onion and other plants; anything resembling this.—**bulb'ous** *a.*
bulge *n.* a protuberance.—*v.i.* to swell out.—**bulg'y** *a.*—**bulg'iness** *n.*
bulk *n.* size; volume; the greater part; a cargo.—*v.i.* to be of weight or importance.—**bulk'y** *a.*—**bulk'iness** *n.*
Syn. magnitude, dimension, mass. *Ant.* part, item, dose.
bulk'head *n.* a partition in a ship.
bull (-oo-) *n.* the male of cattle or various other animals; a speculator for a rise in

stocks.—**bull's-eye'** *n.* a boss in glass; a lantern; the middle part of a target.—**bull'ock** *n.* a castrated bull.—**bull-calf** *n.*—**bull-dog** *n.*—**bull'puncher** *n. sl.* Australia, driver of a bullock team.
bull (-oo-) *n.* a Papal edict; a laughable inconsistency in language.
bull'dozer *n.* a powerful excavating and lifting machine used in road-making, etc.; *fig.* one who gains his point by overbearing argument.
bull'et (-oo-) *n.* the projectile discharged from a rifle, pistol, etc.
bull'etin (-oo-) *n.* an official report.
bull'ion (bool'yon) *n.* uncoined gold or silver, in mass.
bully (-oo-) *n.* a rough, overbearing fellow.—*v.t.* to intimidate; ill-treat (**bull'ied** *p.t.* and *p.p.*—**bull'ying** *pres.p.*).
bul'rush (-oo-) *n.* a tall, strong rush.
bult *n.* in S. Africa, a hillock or ridge (*bult'jie*, dimin.)
bul'wark (-oo-) *n.* raised side of a ship; a breakwater; any defence or means of security.—*v.t.* to protect.
bum' *v.i.* to hum loudly, boom, *n.* (*U.S. sl.*) an habitual loafer.
bum'ble-bee *n.* a large bee.
bump *n.* a heavy blow, dull in sound; a swelling caused by a blow; a protuberance.—*v.t.* to strike against.—*n.* a sudden change in air pressure which causes an airplane to move unsteadily.—**bump off** *v.t.* (*sl.*) to kill; to murder.
bump'er *n.* a full glass; a motor-car fender.—*a.* full, abundant.
bump'kin *n.* a rustic.
bump'tious (-shus) *a.* rudely assertive.
bun *n.* a small sweet cake; a round mass of hair *esp.* at nape of the neck.
bunch *n.* a number of things tied or growing together.—*v.t.* and *i.* **bunch'y** *a.*
bun'dle *n.* a package; a number of things tied together.—*v.t.* to tie in a bundle; to send (off) without ceremony.
bung *n.* a stopper for a cask; a large cork.—*v.t.* to stop up.—**bung'-hole** *n.*
bung, bong *a.* in Australia, dead; bankrupt.—**to go bung,** to die; to fail, become bankrupt.
bun'galow (bung'ga-lō) *n.* a one-storied house.—**bun'galoid** *a.*
bun'gle (bung'gl) *v.t.* to perform clumsily; to manage awkwardly.—*v.i.* to act clumsily.—*n.* a blunder, muddle.—**bun'gler** *n.*—**bun'gled** *a.*—**bun'gling** *a.*
bun'ion *n.* inflamed swelling on the foot.
bunk *n.* a sleeping berth, *esp.* in a ship's cabin.—*v.i.* (*sl.*) to run away.
bunk *n. see* **bunkum.**
bunk'er *n.* a receptacle for coal, *esp.* in a ship; a sandy hollow on a golf-course.
bunk'um *n.* claptrap oratory, bombastic speechmaking.
bunt'ing *n.* a bird allied to the lark; material for flags.
buoy (boi) *n.* a floating mark anchored in the sea; something to keep a person afloat.—*v.t.* to mark with a buoy; keep from sinking.—**buoy'ant** *a.*—**buoy'ancy** *n.*
bur, burr *n.* a prickly head of a plant; a rough edge; a north-country accent.
burd'en, burth'en (-th-) *n.* a load; cargo; anything difficult to bear.—*v.t.* to load, encumber.—**bur'densome** *a.*
burd'en *n.* the chorus of a song.
bu'reau (-rō) *n.* a writing-desk; an office, *esp.* for public business (**bu'reaux** *pl.*).—**bureau'cracy** (-ok'-) *n.* government by officials; a body of officials.—**bu'reaucrat** *n.*—**bureaucrat'ic** *a.*
bur'gess *n.* an inhabitant of a borough, *esp.* a citizen with municipal rights.
burgh'er *n.* in S. Africa, a person having the rights and privileges of citizenship.
burg'lar *n.* one who breaks into a house.—**burg'lary** *n.*—**burglar'ious** *a.*
bur'ial (ber'-) *n.* the act of burying, *esp.* a dead person; a funeral.
burgo'master *n.* the mayor of a Dutch or Flemish town.
burlesque' (-esk) *n.* a travesty, a grotesque imitation.—*v.t.* to caricature.—*a.* mocking. *Syn.* humour, sarcasm, farce, caricature, parody, lampoon.
bur'ly *a.* strudy, stout.—**bur'liness** *n.*
burn *n.* in Scotland, a small stream.
burn *v.t.* to destroy or injure by fire.—*v.i.* to be on fire, literally or figuratively; to shine; to be consumed by fire (**burned** or **burnt** *p.t.* and *p.p.*).—*n.* an injury or mark caused by fire.—**burn'ing** *a.*—**burn'er** *n.*
burn'ish *v.t.* to make bright by rubbing.
burr'ow (-rō) *n.* hole of a rabbit, etc.—*v.t.* to make holes in the ground; to bore; conceal oneself.
burs'ar *n.* a treasurer, *esp.* of a college; scholar receiving a grant or **bur'sary** *n.*
burst *v.i.* to fly asunder; break into pieces; to give vent to some expression of feeling.—*v.t.* to shatter, break violently.—*n.* an explosion; an outbreak, spurt (**burst** *p.t.* and *p.p.*).
bur'y (ber'i) *v.t.* to put underground; put in a grave, inter (**bur'ied** *p.t.* and *p.p.*—**bur'ying** *pres. p.*).
bus *n. abbrev.* of omnibus; *sl.* a motor-car, an aeroplane.
bus'by (-z-) *n.* a fur hat worn by hussars (**bus'bies** *pl.*).
bush (-oo-) *n.* a shrub; woodland, thicket; in Australia, S. Africa, etc., the backwoods.—**bushed** *a.* lost, bewildered.—**bush'man** *n.* one of a S. African or Australian tribe; woodsman.—**bush'-ranger** *n.* in Australia, an escaped convict, who turns robber.—**bush'y** *a.*
bush'el (-oo-) *n.* dry measure of 8 gallons.
busk' *n.* piece of steel or whalebone used to strengthen corsets.
bust *n.* upper part of body; statue of person's head and shoulders.
bus'tle (-sl) *v.i.* to be noisily busy; to be

active.—*n.* fuss; padding worn by ladies behind, beneath the skirt.—**bus'tler** *n.*

bus'y (biz'i) *a.* actively employed; diligent.—*v.t.* to occupy (**bus'ied** *p.t.* and *p.p.*—**bus'ying** *pres. p.*).—**bus'ily** *adv.*—**bus'ybody** *n.* a meddler.—**bus'iness** *n.*

but *prep.* and *conj.* without; except; only; yet; still; besides.

butch'er (-oo-) *n.* one who kills animals for food, or sells meat; a bloody or savage man.—*v.t.* to slaughter, murder.

but'ler *a.* head manservant in charge of wine-cellar and silver.

butt *n.* a large cask; a blow with the head, as of a sheep; a target; an object of ridicule; the thick end of anything.—*v.t.* and *i.* to strike with the head; to push.—**butt in** *sl.* to interfere.

butt'er *n.* fat obtained from cream by churning.—*v.t.* to spread with butter; to flatter grossly.—**butt'ery** *a.*

butt'ercup *n.* a plant of the genus *Ranunculus*, with yellow flowers.

butt'erfly *n.* an insect with large wings; an inconstant person.—**butt'erfly screw** *n.* a screw with finger grips.

butt'ermilk *n.* the milk that remains after churning.

butt'erscotch *n.* a toffee sweetmeat.

butt'ery *n.* a pantry; a wine-cellar.

butt'ock *n.* the rump (usually in *pl.*).

butt'on *n.* a knob or stud, *esp.* for fastening dress; a bud.—*v.t.*

butt'ress *n.* a structure to support a wall, a prop.—*v.t.* to support.

bu'tyl (-til) *n. chem.* one of the four univalent radicals.—**bu'tylene** *n.* a hydrocarbon compound gas C_4H_8.

bux'om *a.* full of health, lively, plump.

buy (bi) *v.t.* to get by payment; bribe (**bought** *p.t.* and *p.p.*).—**buy'er** *n.*

buzz *v.i.* to make a humming sound.—*n.* the sound of bees.—**buzz bomb** *sl.* a jet-propelled one-ton bomb used in the German bombardment of England and Belgium during World War 2.—**buzz-saw** *n.* circular saw.—**buzz'er** *n.* in wireless, an apparatus to test receivers.

buzz'ard *n.* a bird of falcon family.

by *prep.* near; beside; with; through; in S. Africa, at, in.—*adv.* near, close; out of the way; beyond.—**by and by,** soon.—**by and large,** on the whole; on the average; in general.

by-elec'tion *n.* an election held in circumstances other than those of a General Election.

by'law, bye'law *n.* a local law made by a subordinate authority.

by'-pass *n.* a road for diversion of traffic from crowded centres; tube in internal-combustion engine; in wireless, a diversion of undesired frequencies; *v.t.* to divert traffic.

byre *n.* a cow-shed.

by'word *n.* a common saying or proverb; an object of ridicule or contempt.

C

cab *n.* a public carriage.—**cab'man** *n.*

cabal' *n.* a secret plot; a small body of people engaged in one.—*v.i.*—**caball'er** *n.* *Syn.* conspiracy, faction, junto.

cab'aret *n.* a small tavern; a restaurant or night club entertainment.

cabb'age *n.* a green vegetable.

cab'in *n.* a hut; a small room, *esp.* in a ship.—*v.t.* to confine.—**cab'in-boy** *n.*

cab'inet *n.* a case of drawers; a small room or private apartment; a committee of politicians governing a country.

ca'ble *n.* a strong rope; a submarine telegraph line; a message sent by such line.—*v.t.* and *i.* to telegraph by cable.—**ca'blegram** *n.* a cabled message.

ca'blese (-blēz) *n.* a condensed style of writing using compound words, popular with newsmen to economise on cable charges for foreign dispatches.

caboose' *n.* (U.S.) car attached to a freight train for use of the train men.

ca'bre (kȧ'brā) *v.i.* to fly upside down.—**ca'bring** *n.*

caca'o (ka-kȧ'o) *n.* the chocolate tree.

cache' (kash') *n.* hiding-place; material hidden (in ground).

cach'et (-ā) *n.* mark of authenticity, *esp.* in matters of distinction and refinement; a gelatine capsule containing a dose of medicine.

cac'kle *v.i.* to make a chattering noise, as a hen.—*n.* cackling noise; empty chatter.—**cac'kler** *n.* (**cack'ling** *pres. p.*).

cacoph'ony *n.* a disagreeable sound, a discord of sounds.—**cacoph'onous** *a.*

cac'tus *n.* a prickly plant (**cac'tuses, cac'ti** *pl.*).—**cactac'eous** *a.*

cadav'erous *a.* corpse-like.

cadd'ie *n.* golfer's attendant; in Australia, a slouch-hat or wide-awake.

cadd'y *n.* small box for tea (**-dies** *pl.*).

ca'dence *n.* a modulation of voice, music, or verses; rhythm.

cadet' *n.* younger son or brother; student in a naval or military college.

cadge (kaj) *v.i.* and *t.* to hawk goods; to obtain by sponging or begging.—**cadg'er** *n.* a hawker, tramp; sponger.

cæsar'ean section *n.* operation in which child is removed from the uterus through the abdominal wall.

caf'e (kaf'ā) *n.* a restaurant.

cafete'ria *n.* a restaurant where the patrons serve themselves from a counter.

caff'eine *n.* an alkaloid in tea and coffee.

cage *n.* a place of confinement; a box with bars, *esp.* for keeping animals or birds.-*v.t.*-**cage'bird** *n.*-**cag'ing** *pres. p.*

cahoots' (ka-) *n.* U.S. *sl.* a combination; partnership.

cairn *n.* a heap of stones, *esp.* as a monument or landmark.

caiss'on *n.* an ammunition wagon; a box for working under water; apparatus for lifting a vessel out of water.
cai'tiff *n.* a despicable fellow.
cajole' *v.t.* to cheat by flattery.—**cajole'ment** *n.*—**cajo'ler** *n.*—**cajo'lery** *n.*
cake *n.* a piece of dough baked; fancy bread; a flattened hard mass as soap.—*v.t.* and *i.* to make into a cake.
calam'ity *n.* a great misfortune (**calam'ities** *pl.*).—**calam'itous** *a.*
calca'reous *a.* containing lime.
cal'cine *v.t.* to reduce to lime or ash.
cal'cium *n.* the metallic base of lime.
cal'culate *v.t.* to compute.—*v.i.* to make reckonings.—**cal'culating** *a.*—**calcula'tion** *n.*—**cal'culable** *a.*—**cal'culator** *n.*—**cal'culus** *n.* a stone in the body; a method of calculation (**cal'culi** *pl.*).
cal'dron *see* **cauldron.**
cal'endar *n.* a table of months, weeks and days in a year; a register.
cal'ender *n.* a machine with rollers for smoothing cloth, paper, etc.—*v.t.*
calf (kȧf) *n.* the young of the cow, elephant, whale, etc.; leather made of calf's skin (**calves** (kȧvz) *pl.*).—**calve** *v.i.* to give birth to a calf.
calf (kȧf) *n.* the fleshy hinder part of the leg below the knee (**calves** *pl.*).
cal'ibre *n.* the size of the bore of a gun; capacity, character.—**cal'ibrate** *v.t.*
cal'ico *n.* and *a.* cotton cloth (**-icoes, -icos** (-kōz) *pl.*).
ca'liph (kā-lif) *n.* title of rulers who succeeded Mohammed, *esp.* in Turkey.
calk *see* **caulk.**
call (kawl) *v.t.* to announce; summon.—*v.i.* to shout; to pay a short visit.—*n.* a shout; an animal's cry; a visit; an invitation, as to be pastor of a church, etc.; in Bridge, etc., the number of tricks (above a minimum) which a player and, or, his partner) undertakes to make, with trumps of his own choosing; bid; player's turn to bid.—*v.t.* and *i.* to bid.—**call-office** *n.* a public telephone booth.
callig'raphy *n.* penmanship.
call'ipers *n.* an instrument for measuring diameters.
callisthen'ics (kal-is-then'iks) *n.* light gymnastic exercises.—**callisthen'ic** *a.*
call'ous *a.* unfeeling.—**call'ously** *adv.*—**call'ousness** *n.*—**callos'ity** *n.* hard lump.
Syn. hard, obdurate, indurated. *Ant.* kind, susceptible, sentimental.
call'ow *a.* unfledged; inexperienced.
calm (kȧm) *n.* stillness, want of wind.—*a.* quiet.—*v.t.* and *i.* to become, make, quiet.—**calm'ly** *adv.*—**calm'ness** *n.*
cal'orie, calory *n.* unit of heat; unit of the energy obtained from foods.—**calorif'ic** *a.* heat-making.—**calorim'eter** *n.*
cal'umny *n.* a slander.—**calum'niate** *v.t.*—**calumnia'tion** *n.*—**calum'niator** *n.*
ca'lyx *n.* covering of a bud (**-lyxes, -lyces** *pl.*).—**cal'ycine** *a.*

cam *n.* a device to change a rotary motion to a reciprocating one.
cam'ber *n.* convexity upon an upper surface; curvature of aeroplane wing.
cam'bric (kā-) *n.* fine white linen.
came *p.t.* of **come.**
cam'el *n.* animal of Asia and Africa, used as a beast of burden (*Bactrian* has 2 humps, *Arabian* or *Dromedary* 1); in S. Africa, the giraffe.
cam'embert (-bār) *n.* a soft richly flavoured cheese, originally made at Camembert in Normandy.
camell'ia *n.* Asiatic evergreen shrub.
cam'eo *n.* a stone of two layers cut in ornamental relief (**-eos** *pl.*).
cam'era *n.* an apparatus used to make photographs; a judge's private room; **cam'era-man'** a photographer *esp.* for newspapers or cinematograph.
cam'ion *n.* a heavy motor vehicle used in military transport work.
cam'isole *n.* an under-bodice.
cam'omile *n.* aromatic creeping plant.
cam'ouflage (-ȧzh) *n.* disguise; means of deceiving enemy observation.—*v.t.*
camp *n.* the tents of an army; military quarters; travellers' resting-place; in S. Africa, the enclosed part of a farm.—*v.i.* to form a lodge in a camp; in S. Africa, to fence off a farm into fields.—**camp'ing** *n.*—**camp-bed** *n.*—**camp-stool** *n.*
campaign' (-pān') *n.* the time in which an army keeps the field; a series of operations.—*v.i.* to serve in a war; a planned attempt to gain public support, as a *publicity campaign.*—**campaign'er** a tried soldier.
campanol'ogy *n.* bell-lore.
cam'phor *n.* a solid essential oil with aromatic taste and smell.—**cam'phorated** *a.*—**camphor'ic** *a.*
cam'pus *n.* (U.S.) the grounds of a college or school.
cam'shaft *n.* in motoring, a rotating shaft to which cams are fixed to lift the valves.
can *v.i.* to be able; to have the power; to be allowed (**could** *p.t.*).
can *n.* a metal vessel for holding liquids.—*v.t.* to put, or preserve, in a tin.
canal' *n.* an artificial water-course; a duct in the body.—**can'alise** *v.t.*
can'ape (-a-pā) *n.* a piece of fried bread with anchovies, etc.
cana'ry (-ėr'-) *n.* a yellow singing-bird; a light wine (**cana'ries** *pl.*).
canas'ta *n.* a four-handed partnership card-game resembling rummy, played with 2 packs of cards and 4 jokers.
can'cel *v.t.* to cross out; to annul, abolish, suppress.—**cancella'tion** *n.*
Can'cer *n.* a malignant growth or tumour; the 4th sign of the Zodiac symbolised by a crab, operative June 21-July 21; constellation.

candela'bram *n.* ornamental candlestick with several branches for candles.
can'did *a.* frank, open.—**can'didly** *adv.* *Syn.* sincere, cordial, hearty, just. *Ant.* secretive, reticent, insincere.
can'didate *n.* one who seeks an appointment, privilege, etc.—**can'didature** *n.*
can'dle *n.* a stick of wax with a wick; a light.—**can'dle-stick** *n.*—**can'dlemas** *n.*
can'dour *n.* candidness, frankness.
can'dy *n.* crystallised sugar.—*v.t.* to preserve with sugar.—*v.i.* to become encrusted with sugar (**can'died** *p.t.* and *p.p.*—**can'dying** *pres. p.*).—**can'died** *a.*
cane *n.* stem of a small palm or large grass; a walking-stick.—*v.t.* to beat.
ca'nine *a.* like or pertaining to the dog.
can'ister *n.* a box or case for holding tea, etc., usually made of tin.
cank'er *n.* an eating sore, anything that eats away, destroys, corrupts.—*v.t.* to infect, corrupt.—*v.i.* to decay.—**cank'ered** *a.*—**cank'erous.**—**cank'er-worm** *n.*
cann'ibal *n.* one who eats human flesh. —**cann'ibalism** *n.*—**cannibalis'tic** *a.*
cann'on *n.* a large gun (*cann'ons*, or collectively *cannon, pl.*).—**cannonade'** *n.* and *v.*—**cann'on-ball** *n.*—**cann'on-bone** *n.* a horse's leg-bone.
cann'on *n.* in billiards, hitting both object balls with one's own.—*v.t.* to make this stroke.—*v.i.* to rebound.
cann'y *a.* shrewd; cautious; wise.—**cann'ily** *adv.*—**cann'iness** *n.*
canoe' (-nōō') *n.* a light boat rowed with a paddle (**canoes'** *pl.*).—**canoe'ist** *n.*
can'on *n.* a law or rule, *esp.* of the church; a standard; a body of books accepted as genuine; the list of saints.—**can'onise** *v.t.* to enrol in the list of saints.—**canonisa'tion** *n.*
can'on *n.* a church dignitary, a member of a cathedral chapter.—**canon'ical** *a.*
can'onise *v.t.* declare (a dead person) to be a saint; placed in the official list of saints.—**canoni'sing** *pres. p.*—**canonised'** *p.t.* and *p.p.*—**canonisa'tion** *n.*
can'opy *n.* a covering over a throne, bed, etc.—*v.t.* to cover with a canopy (**-opied** *p.t.* and *p.p.*—**opying** *pres. p.*).
cant *v.t.* and *i.* to tilt, slope.—**cant'-hook** *n.* in N. America, pole tipped with iron, used in lumber camps.
cant *n.* hypocritical speech; whining; the language of a sect; technical jargon, slang, *esp.* of thieves.—*v.i.* to use such language.
cant'aloup *n.* a variety of musk melon.
cantan'kerous *a.* quarrelsome, surly.
canta'ta' (-tah'-tah) *n.* choral work containing choruses, recitatives and arias.
canteen' *n.* small tin vessel; shop or tavern in a camp or barracks; a case of cutlery; S. Africa, a public-house.—**canteen'-keeper** *n.* S. Africa, a publican.
can'ter *n.* easy gallop.—*v.i.* move at this pace.—*v.t.* to make to canter.
can'ticle *n.* a hymn or chant.
can'to (-tō) *n.* a division of a long poem (**can'tos** *pl.*).
can'ton *n.* small division of a country.—**can'tonment** *n. pl.* quarters for troops.
can'vas *n.* coarse cloth of hemp, used for sails, painting on, etc.; the sails of a ship; a picture.—**can'vass** *v.t.* to sift, examine; to solicit votes.—*n.*
can'yon *n.* deep gorge.
caout'chouc (kout'shook, kōō'-) *n.* indiarubber.
cap *n.* a covering for the head; a lid, top, or other covering.—*v.t.* to put a cap on; to outdo; to raise the cap in respect.
ca'pable *a.* able, gifted; competent.—**capabil'ity** *n.* (**capabil'ities** *pl.*). *Syn.* fitted, efficient, qualified. *Ant.* incompetent, unfit, impotent, incapable.
capac'ity (-as'-) *n.* power of holding or grasping; room; volume; character; ability, power of mind.—**capa'cious** (-ā'-) *a.* roomy.—**capac'itate** *v.t.*
capapie (kap-à-pē-*ā*) *n.* from head to foot (*Fr.*).
capar'ison *n.* rich trappings for a horse.
cape *n.* loose, sleeveless garment.
cape *n.* a point of land running into the sea; a S. African wine.—**cape-boy** *n.* in S. Africa, a half-caste.—**cape-cart** *n.* in S. Africa, two-wheeled vehicle with a pole and hood (*cape* = hood).
ca'per *v.i.* to skip or dance.—*n.* a frolic; a pickled flower-bud of the caper-bush.
capill'ary *a.* hair-like.—*n.* tube with very small bore, *esp.* a small blood vessel.
cap'ital *n.* headpiece of a column; a chief town; a large-sized letter; money, stock, funds.—*a.* affecting life; serious; chief; excellent.—**cap'itally** *adv.*—**cap'italist** *n.* —**cap'italise** *v.t.*—**cap'italism** *n.*
capita'tion *n.* a census; a poll tax; a tax or grant per head.
capit'ulate *v.i.* to surrender on terms, yield, give in.—**capitula'tion** *n.*
ca'pon *n.* a castrated cock.—**ca'ponise** *v.t.*
caprice' (-ēs) *n.* a whim, freak.—**capri'cious** *a.*—**capri'ciousness** *n.*
Cap'ricorn *n.* the 10th sign of the Zodiac symbolised by a sea-goat, operative Dec. 21–Jan. 19.
cap'sicum *n.* genus of American plants whose fruits, chillies or red peppers are ground to produce cayenne.
capsize' *v.t.* to upset.—*v.i.* to be upset.
cap'stan *n.* a machine to wind a cable, *esp.* to hoist an anchor.
cap'sule *n.* a seed vessel of a plant; a gelatine case for a dose of medicine.
cap'tain (-tin) *n.* a leader, chief; the commander of a vessel, company of soldiers, etc.—**cap'taincy** *n.*
cap'tion *n.* title, of an article, picture; a section of the letterpress in a cinematograph film (*law*) arrest.
cap'tious (-shus) *a.* ready to find fault. —**cap'tiously** *adv.*—**cap'tiousness** *n.*

cap'tive *n.* one taken prisoner.—*a.* taken, imprisoned.—**cap'tivate** *v.t.* to fascinate.—**captiv'ity** *n.*

cap'ture *n.* seizure, taking.—*v.t.* to seize, make prisoner.—**cap'tor** *n.*

car *n.* a wheeled vehicle; a street or tram-car; a motor-car.

car-pool *n.* a group of people who pool their cars for collective use to conserve petrol, tyres, etc.

car'acul (-a-kòòl) *n.* a kind of fur like astrakhan; a fabric of similar surface.

car'amel *n.* burnt sugar; a sweet.

car'at *n.* a small weight used for gold, diamonds, etc.; a proportional measure of twenty-fourths used to state the fineness of gold.

car'avan *n.* a company of merchants, etc., travelling together, *esp.* in the East; a covered van or house on wheels.—**caravan'serai** *n.* an Eastern inn for the reception of caravans; a large hotel.

car'away *n.* plant with aromatic seeds.

carb'ide *n.* compound of carbon with an element, *esp.* calcium carbide.

carb'ine *n.* a short rifle.—**carabineer'** *n.*

carbol'ic a'cid *n.* an acid made from coal-tar and used as a disinfectant.

carb'on *n.* a non-metallic element, the substance of pure charcoal; a rod or thread of carbon used as the glowing part of an electric lamp.—**car'bon copy** *n.* a copy made by using carbon-paper.—**car'bon-paper** *n.* paper covered on one side with lamp-black, etc., which will transfer impressions to a sheet placed beneath.—**carbon'ic** *a.*—**carb'onise** *v.t.*—**carb'onate** *n.*—**carbonif'erous** *a.*

carborun'dum *n.* artificial silicate of carbon used for sharpening steel and in wireless as a crystal rectifier.

carb'oy *n.* a large glass bottle protected by a wicker casing.

carb'uncle *n.* a fiery-red precious stone; an inflamed ulcer or tumour.

carb'urettor *n.* a device for mixing oil-vapour and air in an engine.

carc'ass, carc'ase *n.* a dead body.

carcin'ogen (-ō-jen) *n.* a substance which produces cancer in the tissues.

carcino'ma (-sin-ō'-ma) *n.* a malignant cancer.—**carcinomatous** *a.*

card *n.* pasteboard; piece of stiff paper used as a **playing-card, post-card, visiting-card,** etc.; the dial of a compass.—**card'board** *n.*—**card-in'dex** *n.*

card *n.* an instrument for combing wool.

card'an-shaft *n.* in motoring, shaft carrying drive from engine to gearbox.

card'iac *a.* pertaining to the heart.

card'igan *n.* a knitted woollen jacket.

card'inal *a.* chief, principal.—*n.* a member of the Pope's council.

car'diogram (-di-ō-gram) *n.* a record showing the movements of the heart recorded by the cardiograph.

care *n.* anxiety; pains, charge.—*v.i.* to be anxious; to be disposed (to); to have regard (for).—**care'free** *a.*—**care'ful** *a.*—**care'less** *a.*—**care'fully** *adv.*—**care'lessness** *n.*—**caretak'er** *n.*—**care'worn** *a.*

Syn. solicitude, regard, management, caution, direction, attention. *Ant.* carelessness, negligence, inattention.

careen' *v.t.* to lay a ship over on her side.—*v.i.* to lie over.

career' *n.* course through life; course of action, height of activity; course, running.—*v.i.* to run or move at full speed.

caress' *v.t.* fondle, treat with affection.—*n.* act, expression of affection.

car'go *n.* a ship's load or freight (**-goes** *pl.*).—**car'go-plane** *n.* aeroplane designed to carry goods.

ca'ribou *n.* the North American reindeer.

car'icature *n.* a likeness exaggerated or distorted to appear ridiculous.—*v.t.*

car'illon *n.* a set of bells.

car'mine *n.* brilliant crimson prepared from cochineal.

carn'age *n.* slaughter.

carn'al *a.* fleshy, sensual; worldly.

carna'tion *n.* flesh colour; double-flowering pink.

carn'ival *n.* a revel; the season of revelry before Lent.

carniv'orous *a.* flesh-eating.—**carn'ivore** *n.*—**carniv'ora** *n.pl.*

car'ol *n.* song of joy or praise.—*v.i.* and *v.t.* to sing.—**car'olling** *n.*—**car'oller** *n.*

carouse' *n.* a drinking-bout.—*v.i.*—**carous'al** *n.*—**carous'er** *n.*

carp *n.* a freshwater fish.

carp *v.i.* to find fault.—**carp'er** *n.*—**carp'ing** *a.*—**carp'ingly** *adv.*

carp'enter *n.* a worker in timber as in building, etc.—**carp'entry** *n.*

carp'et *n.* thick woven cloth for covering floors.—*v.t.*—**carp'et-bag** *n.*—**carpetbagg'er** *n.* a political adventurer.—*a.* denoting a bombing raid which clears a path for ground troops;—*n.* a path cleared by carpet bombing.

car'riage *n.* act or cost of carrying; a vehicle; bearing, conduct.

car'rion *n.* rotting dead flesh.

car'ronade *n.* a ship's cannon.

car'rot *n.* a plant with a reddish, edible root.—**car'roty** *a.* red.

car'ry *v.t.* to transport; capture; effect, behave.—*v.i.* to reach, of a projectile (**car'ried** *p.t.* and *p.p.*—**car'rying** *pres.p.*).—*n.* range.—**car'rier** *n.* one that carries; a kind of pigeon; in Australia, a bag for transporting water by pack-horse, etc.

cart *n.* a two-wheeled vehicle without springs.—*v.t.* to convey in such vehicle.—**cart'age** *n.*—**cart'er** *n.*—**cart'wright** *n.*

car'tel *n.* agreement between states at war, as for exchange of prisoners, etc.; union of manufacturers to keep up prices and kill competitors.

cart'ilage *n.* firm elastic tissue in the body; gristle.—**cartila'ginous** (-aj-) *a.*

cartog'raphy *n.* map-making.
cart'on *n.* cardboard box or container. —**car'tonage** *n.* pasteboard for book-covers, etc., the casing of mummies.
cartoon' *n.* a design for a painting; an illustration in a journal, *esp.* relating to current events.—**cartoon'ist** *n.*
cart'ridge *n.* case containing the charge for a gun.
carve *v.t.* to cut; sculpture; engrave; cut up (meat).—**carv'er** *n.*—**carv'ing** *n.*
carque' *n.* helmet.
cascade' *n.* a small waterfall; anything resembling this.
case *n.* an instance; state of affairs; law-suit; grounds for a suit.—**case'-law** *n.*
case *n.* a box, sheath, covering; any receptacle.—*v.t.* to put in a case.
case'ment (-sm-) *n.* a window frame; a window opening on hinges.
cas'eous *a.* like cheese.
cash *n.* money.—*v.t.* to turn into or exchange for money.—**cash'book** *n.*—**cashier'** *n.* one in charge of money.—*v.t.* to dismiss or discharge with ignominy from the fighting services.—**cash'-register** *n.* a recording till.
cash'mere *n.* a fabric; a shawl.
casi'no (-sē'-) *n.* a public assembly-room, *esp.* one in which gambling is carried on (**casi'nos**, *-i'ni* (-nē) *pl.*).
cask *n.* a barrel.
cask'et *n.* a small case for jewels, etc.
cas'bah *n.* the native quarter of a North African town.
cass'ock *n.* a long tunic worn by priest.
cast (-á-) *v.t.* to throw or fling; to shed; to throw down; to allot, as parts in a play; to found, as metal.—*v.i.* to cast about, to look round.—*n.* a throw; the thing thrown; the distance thrown; a squint; a mould; the shape from a mould; manner; set of actors.—**cast'-away** *n.*—**cast'ing** *n.*—**cast'ing-vote.**
caste *n.* class of people, *esp.* in India; social rank.
cas'tigate *v.t.* to chastise; to correct. **cas'tigator** *n.*—**castiga'tion** *n.*
cas'tle (kás'l) *n.* a fortress; a country mansion; (*chess*) the rook.
cast'or (-á-) *n.* beaver; hat of beaver fur; small vessel with a perforated top; small wheel under furniture.
cast'or-oil (-á-) *n.* a vegetable medicinal and lubricating oil.
cas'trate *v.t.* to remove the testicles, emasculate.—**castra'tion** *n.*
cas'ual (-z-) *a.* accidental; unmethodical.—**cas'ually** *adv.*—**cas'ualty** *n.* an accident (**cas'ualties** *pl.*) losses in war or disaster. *Syn.* fortuitous, occasional, unexpected. *Ant.* expected, organised.
cas'uist *n.* one who studies and solves cases of conscience; quibbler.—**casuis'tical** *a.*—**cas'uistry** *n.*
cat *n.* a tame or wild animal of the genus *Felis*; a spiteful woman; a piece of wood tapered at both ends; a nine-lashed whip. —*v.t.* to raise an anchor to the cathead. —**cat'bird** *n.* a thrush whose call is like a kitten's mewing.—**catt'y** *a.*—**cat'gut** *n.* cord made of intestines of animals.—**cat'head** *n.* a beam at the bow of a ship. —**cat'kin** *n.* flower of willow, hazel, etc. —**cat'mint** *n.*—**cat's-paw** *n.* a dupe; a breath of wind.—**cat walk,** a narrow platform, usually high above the ground, used as a footbridge.
cata-, cat-, cath- *prefix*, down, downwards, according to, as in *cataract.*
cat'aclysm *n.* an upheaval.
cat'acomb *n.* an underground gallery or vault for burial.
cat'alogue (-og) *n.* a descriptive list, inventory.—*v.t.* to make such a list of; to enter in a catalogue.
catal'pa *n.* a shady tree with exquisite clusters of flowers, and long pods.
cat'alyse (-ạ-līz) *v.t.* to speed up a chemical or physical action by introducing a substance which itself takes no part in the chemical change.—**cat'ylist** *n.* any such substance.
catal'ysis *n.* decomposition of a substance by the presence of another which is itself unchanged.
cat'apult *n.* a small forked stick with an elastic sling; formerly an engine of war for hurling arrows, stones, etc.
cat'aract *n.* a waterfall; an eye defect.
catarrh' *n.* a discharge from the nose, a cold.—**catar'rhal** *a.*
catas'trophe (-fi) *n.* the culmination of a tragedy; a great disaster.
cataw'ba *n.* an American grape; wine from such.
catch *v.t.* to take hold of, seize, understand.—*v.i.* to be contagious; to get entangled (**caught** *p.t.* and *p.p.*).—*n.* a seizure; anything that holds, stops, etc.; what is caught; a form of musical composition; advantage taken or to be gained.—**catch'ing** *a.*—**catch'er** *n.*—**catch'ment** *n.* a surface on which water is caught and collected.—**catch'-penny** *a.* worthless, made only to sell.—**catch'word** *n.* popular phrase or idea.
Syn. to grasp, grip, arrest, charm. *Ant.* to loose, set free, disgust.
cat'echise (-k-) *v.t.* to instruct by question and answer; to question.—**cat'echism** *n.*—**cat'echist** *n.*
cat'egory *n.* class, order, type.—**categor'ical** *a.* positive; precise.—**categor'ically** *adv.* precise.—**cat'egorise** *v.t.*
catena'tion *n.* a chain or series like the links on a chain.
ca'ter *v.i.* to provide food, entertainment, etc.—**ca'terer** *n.*—**ca'tering** *n.*
cat'erpillar *n.* the grub of an insect.—**cater'pillar-wheel'** *n.* an endless band instead of a wheel for tanks, etc.
cathar'tic *n.* and *a.* purgative.

cathe'dral *n.* principal church of a diocese, containing bishop's throne.
cath'ode *n.* the negative pole of an electric current; in wireless, the filament of a thermionic valve.
cath'olic *a.* universal; including the whole body of Christians; relating to the Roman Catholic Church.—*n.* an adherent of the R.C. Church.—**cathol'icise** *v.t.*—**cathol'icism** *n.*—**catholi'city** *n.*
cat'tle *n. pl.* domestic quadrupeds, *esp.* of the ox-kind.—**cat'tleman** *n.*
cau'cus (kaw'-) *n.* an electioneering political committee.
caul'dron, cal'dron *n.* a large kettle.
cauli'flower (kol'-) *n.* a cabbage with an edible flower-head.
caulk, calk (kawk) *v.t.* to press oakum into the seams of a ship, to make it watertight.—**caulk'er** *n.*—**caulk'ing** *n.*
cause (-z) *n.* that which produces an effect; reason; motive; a lawsuit.—*v.t.* to bring about, make to exist.—**caus'al** *a.*—**causal'ity** *n.*—**causa'tion** *n.*—**cause'less** *a.*
cause'way, caus'ey (-z-) *n.* a raised road; a paved street.
cau'stic *a.* burning; bitter; sarcastic.—**cau'stically** *adv.*
cau'terise *v.t.* to burn with caustics or hot iron.—**cauterisa'tion** *n.*
cau'tion *n.* heedfulness; a warning.—*v.t.* to warn.—**cau'tious** *a.*—**cau'tiously** *adv.*—**cau'tioner** *n.*—**cau'tionary** *a.*—**cau'tiousness** *n.* *Syn.* watchfulness, circumspection, forethought. *Ant.* carelessness, imprudence, rashness.
cavalcade' *n.* a procession of persons on horseback.—**cavalier'** *n.* a horseman; a courtly gentleman; an adherent of the King in the Civil War.—*a.* disdainful.—**cav'alry** *n.* mounted troops.
cave *n.* a hollow place in the earth; a den.—**cav'ern** *n.* a deep cave.—**cav'ernous** *a.*—**cav'ernously** *adv.*—**cav'ity** *n.* a hollow.
cave in *v.i.* to fall in; to submit.
caviare', caviar' *n.* salted sturgeon roe; *fig.* too fine for the vulgar taste.
cav'il *v.i.* to find fault without sufficient reason.—**cav'illing** *n.*—**cav'iller** *n.*
caw *n.* the crow's cry.—*v.t.*
cayenne', cayenne'-pep'per *n.* a very pungent red pepper.
cayuse' (kī-us') *n.* an Indian pony; an inferior horse.
C. battery, battery which puts negative charge on grid of a vacuum tube.
cease *v.i.* to stop.—*v.t.* discontinue.—**cease'less** *a.*—**cease'lessly** *adv.*
ce'dar *n.* a large evergreen tree; its wood.
cede *v.t.* to surrender, *esp.* of territory.
cei'ling (sē'-) *n.* an inner roof; in aviation, lower level of clouds; the extreme height to which a given aeroplane can ascend.—**ceil** *v.t.*
cel'andine *n.* a yellow flower.
cel'ebrate *v.t.* to make famous; to mark by ceremony as an event.—**cel'ebrant** *n.*—**celebra'tion** *n.*—**cel'ebrated** *a.* famous.—**celeb'rity** *n.* fame; a famous person.
cel'eriac (si-ler'-i-ak) *n.* a turnip-rooted celery.
celer'ity *n.* swiftness, speed.
cel'ery *n.* vegetable with long white edible stalks.
celes'tial *a.* heavenly.
cel'ibacy *n.* unmarried state.—**cel'ibate** *n.*
cell *n.* a small room; a small cavity; a unit-mass of living matter; division of electric battery.—**cell'ular** *a.*—**cell'ule** *n.*
cell'ar *n.* underground store-room *esp.* for wine or coal.—**cell'arage** *n.*—**cell'arer** *n.*—**cell'aret** *n.* a case for bottles.
cel'lo (chel'-) *n.* short form of violoncello (**cellos** *pl.*).
cell'ophane *n.* transparent paper made from wood-pulp [protected trade name].
cell'uloid *n.* imitation ivory.—**cell'ulose** *n.* substance forming vegetable cell-wall.
cel'lulose *a.* containing cells; *n.* the substance of vegetable cells; *v.t.* to cover with varnish made from compounds of cellulose.—**cell'ulous** *a.*
cement' *n.* mortar; to join together *v.t.*
cem'etery *n.* a burial-ground.
cen'otaph *n.* a monument to some one buried elsewhere.
Cenozo'ic (sēn-ō-zō-ik) *n.* (*geol.*) Tertiary; that period of world history in which existing continents were formed;—*a.* manifesting recent life forms.
cen'ser *n.* a pan to burn incense in.
cen'sor *n.* one who examines plays, books, news, etc., before publication.—*v.t.*—**censo'rial** *a.*—**censo'rious** *a.* fault-finding.—**censo'riously** *adv.*—**censo'riousness** *n.*—**cen'sorship** *n.*
cen'sure *n.* blame; reproof, reprimand.—*v.t.*—**cen'surable** *a.*
cen'sus *n.* an official counting of the inhabitants of a country.
cent *n.* a hundred; the hundredth part of a dollar.—**per cent,** in, to, by each 100.—**centa'vo** *n.* a South American coin, the hundredth part of a peso.
cen'taur *n.* legendary being, half-man, half-horse.
cente'nary (or, **cen'-**) *n.* 100 years; a celebration of a hundredth anniversary.—*a.*—**centena'rian** *n.* one 100 years old.—**centenn'ial** *a.*—**cen'tury** *n.* 100 years; a hundred, *esp.* runs in cricket.
cent'igrade *a.* having a hundred degrees, *esp.* of centigrade thermometer.
cent'ipede *n.* a small segmented animal with many legs.
cen'tre the mid-point of anything; pivot, axis; a point of concentration.—**cen'tral** *a.*—**cen'tric** *a.*—**cent'rist** *n.* one of moderate political views, neither of the left or the right.—**cen'tralise** *v.t.* bring to a centre; concentrate under one control.—**centralisa'tion** *n.*—**central'ity** *n.*—**cen'trally** *adv.*—**centrif'ugal**

a. tending from a centre.—**centrip'etal** *a.* tending towards a centre.
centu'ple (sen-tū-p'l) *a.* hundredfold; —*v.t.* to multiply a hundredfold.
centu'rion *n.* Roman officer, commander of a hundred men.
cen'tury *see* **centenary.**
ceram'ic *a.* relating to pottery.—**ceramics** *n.* art of pottery.
ce'real *a.* pertaining to corn.—*n.* grain used as food.—**ce'reals** *n. pl.*
cer'ebral *a.* pertaining to the brain.—**cerebra'tion** *n.* brain action.
cer'emony *n.* a sacred rite; formal observance; usage of courtesy.—**ceremo'nial** *a.* and *n.*—**ceremo'nious** *a.*—**ceremo'nially, ceremo'niously** *adv.*—**ceremo'niousness** *n.*
cert'ain *a.* sure, settled, fixed, inevitable; some, one; of moderate (quantity, degree, etc.).—**cert'ainly** *adv.* —**cert'ainty** *n.*—**cert'itude** *n.*
Syn. real, regular, constant, unfailing. *Ant.* uncertain, doubtful.
cert'ify *v.t.* to make known as certain; declare formally (**-ified** *p.t./p.p.*—**-ifying** *pr. p.*).—**cert'ifier** *n.* **certif'icate** *n.* written declaration.—*v.t.*—**certifica'tion** *n.*—**cer'titude** *n.* feeling certain.
ceru'lean *a.* sky-blue.
cervic'al *a.* of, pertaining to, the neck.
cessa'tion *n.* ceasing or stopping.
cess'ion *n.* a yielding up.
cess'pool *n.* a receptacle for sewage.
chafe *v.t.* to make hot by rubbing; to wear or irritate by rubbing; to vex.—**cha'fing-gear** *n.*—**chaf'ed** *p.t.* and *p.p.*
cha'fer *n.* beetle.
chaff (-åf) *n.* husks of corn; chopped hay and straw; banter; *v.* to make fun of.
chaff'er *v.i.* to haggle, bargain.—*n.* bargaining.—**chaff'erer** *n.*
cha'fing-dish *n.* a vessel holding live charcoal to keep dishes warm.
chagrin' (sha-grin') *n.* vexation, disappointment.—*v.t.* to vex.
chain *n.* a series of links each passing through the next; a fetter; anything that binds; a connected series of things or events; a surveyor's measure.—*v.t.*—**chain-arm'our, chain'-mail, chain'-shot.**
chair *n.* movable seat; a seat of authority; a professor's office; iron support for a rail on a railway.—*v.t.* to carry in triumph.—**chair'man** *n.* one who presides.—**chair'manship** *n.*
chaise (shāz) *n.* a light carriage.
chal'dron (kawl'-) *n.* a measure for coals, 36 bushels.
cha'let (shå'lā) *n.* a Swiss cottage; a summer bungalow.
chal'ice *n.* a cup; a communion-cup.
chalk (chawk) *n.* a white substance, carbonate of lime.—*v.t.* to rub or mark with chalk.—*v.i.* to mark with chalk; to keep a reckoning.—**chalk'y** *a.*
chall'enge *v.t.* to call to fight; call to account; dispute; claim; object to.—**chall'enger** *n.*—**chall'engeable** *a.*
chalyb'eate (ka-lib'i-at) *a.* containing iron.—**chalybe'an** *a.* well tempered.
cha'mber *n.* a room; a room for an assembly; an assembly or body of men; a compartment; a cavity.—**cha'mberlain** *n.* an officer appointed by a king, etc., for domestic and ceremonial duties. —**cha'mber-maid** *n.* a servant with care of bedrooms.—**cha'mber-pot, cha'mber** *n.* vessel for urine.—**cham'ber-music** *n.*
chame'leon (ka-) *n.* a small lizard famous for its power of changing colour.
cham'fer *v.t.* to groove; to bevel.—*n.*
cham'ois (sham'wå) *n.* a goat-like mountain animal; a soft leather.
champ' *v.t.* and *i.* (of a horse) to keep biting with the teeth; to bite and chew.
champagne' (sham-pān') *n.* a light, effervescent French wine.
cham'pion *n.* one who fights for another; one who defends a cause; in sport, etc., one who excels all others; a hero.—*v.t.* to fight for, maintain.—**cham'pionship** *n.*
chance (-å-) *n.* that which happens; fortune; opportunity.—*v.t.* to risk.—*v.i.* to happen.—*a.* casual, unexpected.
Syn. hazard, probability, possibility, fate, casualty. *Ant.* cause, plan, design.
chan'cel *n.* the eastern part of a church.
chan'cellor *n.* a high officer of state; the head of a university.—**chan'cellorship** *n.* —**chan'cellery** *n.*
chan'cery *n.* a division of the High Court of Justice.
chandelier' (sh-) *n.* a frame with branches for holding lights.
chand'ler *n.* a retail dealer.
change *v.t.* to alter or make different; interchange.—*v.i.* to alter; to put on different clothes.—*n.* alteration; variety; conversion of money; small money; balance received on payment.—**change'able** *a.*—**change'ably** *adv.*—**changeabil'ity** *n.*—**change'ableness** *n.*—**change'ful** *a.* —**change'less** *a.*—**change'ling** *n.* a child substituted for another by fairies.
chann'el *n.* the bed of a stream; the deeper part of a strait; a groove; a means of passing or conveying.—*v.t.* to groove.
chant (-å-) *v.t.* and *i.* to sing.—*n.* a song; a church melody.—**chant'er** *n.*—**chant'ry** *n.* an endowment or chapel for singing masses.—**chan'ty** (sh-) *n.* a sailor's song.
chanticleer' *n.* a cock.
cha'os (kā'-) *n.* disorder, confusion.
chap *v.t.* to crack; to strike.—*v.i.* to fissure.—*n.* a crack in the skin.—**chapped** *a.*—**chap'** *n.* lad; fellow.
chap'el *n.* a subordinate place of worship, as one attached to a garrison, house, prison, etc., and not a cathedral or parish church; a division of a church with its own altar; a Dissenters' or

Nonconformists' place of worship; an association of printers.
chap'eron (sh-) *n.* one who attends a young unmarried lady in public as a protector.—*v.t.* to attend in this way.
chap'lain *n.* clergyman attached to a chapel, regiment, ship of war, institution, etc.—**chap'laincy** *n.*
chap'let *n.* a wreath or garland worn round the head; string of beads.
chaps *n.pl.* jaws, *see* **chop.**
chaps (shaps) *n.pl.* in N. America, leggings of thick leather worn by cowboys.
chap'ter *n.* a division of a book; a section; an assembly of the clergy of a cathedral, etc.; an organised branch of a society, fraternity.—**chap'ter-house** *n.*
char *v.t.* to scorch, burn, reduce to charcoal.—**charr'ed** *a.*
char' *n.* a species of fresh-water trout; a char-woman.
char'-a-banc (shar'a-bang) *n.* a long, open coach with transverse seats.
char'acter (ka-) *n.* a letter, distinctive mark; an essential feature; nature; moral qualities; the reputation of possessing them; a statement of the qualities of a person who has been in one's service; a person noted for eccentricity; a personality in a play or novel.—**characteris'tic** *a.*—**characteris'ticallyadv.**—**char'acterise** *v.t.*—**characterisa'tion** *n.* **char'acterless** *a.*
charade' (shar-råd') *n.* a riddle, often acted, on the syllables of a word.
char'coal *n.* the black residue of wood, bones, etc., by smothered burning; charred wood.—**char'coal-burner** *n.*
chare, chore *n.* a turn of work, an odd job.—*v.i.* to do odd jobs; also **char.**—**char-woman** *n.* woman who cleans house, etc.
charge *v.t.* to fill; load; lay a task on; deliver an injunction; bring an accusation against; ask as a price; fill with electricity.—*v.i.* to make an onset.—*n.* what is laid on; cost; load for a gun, etc.; command; accusation; an accumulation of electricity; *pl.* expenses.—**charge'able** *a.*—**char'ger** *n.* an officer's horse.
char'iot (cha-) *n.* a state car; a war-car.—**charioteer'** *n.* driver of a chariot.
char'ity (cha-) *n.* love; disposition to think kindly of others; practical kindliness.—**char'itable** *a.*—**char'itably** *adv.*
Syn. benevolence, affection, tenderness, indulgence, alms. *Ant.* malevolence.
charl'atan (sh-) *n.* a quack, an imposter.—**charl'atinism** *n.*—**charl'atanry** *n.*
charles'ton *n.* and *v.i.* a dance, originally American negro, with knee-bends and side-kicks.
charm *n.* a magic spell; thing worn to avert evil; attractiveness.—*v.t.* to bewitch; to delight, attract.—**charm'ed** *a.*—**charm'ing** *a.*—**charm'ingly** *adv.*—**charm'er** *n.* one who charms.
charn'el-house *n.* a place where the bones of the dead are put.
chart *n.* a map of the sea; a diagram or tabulated statement.—**chart'-house** *n.*
chart'er *n.* a writing in evidence of a grant or privileges, etc.; a patent.—*v.t.* to establish by charter; to let or hire.—**charter-party** *n.* contract between a shipowner and a merchant by which a whole vessel is hired or chartered.
char'y (-ė-) *a.* cautious, sparing.—**char'ily** *adv.*—**char'iness** *n.*
chase *v.t.* to hunt; to drive from, into, etc.—*n.* a pursuit; the thing hunted; hunting-ground.—**cha'ser** *n.* drink of beer, soda, etc., taken after neat spirit.
chase *v.t.* engrave.—**cha'sing** *n.*—**cha'ser** *n.* (*col.*) a mild drink, e.g. beer, following a hard liquor, e.g. whisky.
chasm (kazm) *n.* an abyss.
chas'sis (shas'ē) *n.* framework, wheels and machinery of a motor-car; the underframe of an aeroplane.
chaste *a.* pure; modest.—**chaste'ly** *adv.*—**chas'tity** *n.*—**cha'sten** *v.t.* to free from faults by punishment; to restrain.—**cha'stened** *a.*—**chastise'** *v.t.* to inflict punishment on.—**chas'tisement** *n.*
chat *v.i.* to talk idly, or familiarly.—*n.* familiar talk.—**chatt'y** *a.*—**chatt'ily** *adv.*
chatt'el *n.* any movable property.
chatt'er *v.i.* to talk idly or rapidly; to rattle the teeth.—*n.* idle talk.—**chatt'erer** *n.*—**chatt'ering** *n.*—**chatt'erbox** *n.*
chauffeur' (shō-fer') *n.* a motor-car driver.—**chauffeuse'** *fem.*
cheap *a.* low in price; supplying at a low price; easily obtained; mean; inferior.—**cheap'ly** *adv.* **cheap'ness** *n.* **cheap'en** *v.t.*
cheat *v.t.* to deprive of by deceit; defraud.—*v.i.* to practise deceit.—*n.*
check *v.t.* to stop; restrain; repress; control; examine; to hand over baggage to a transport company when travelling by train.—*n.* a threatening the king at chess; a repulse; stoppage; restraint; a token, ticket; an order for money (usually **cheque**).—**check'er** *n.*—**checkmate'** *n.* in chess, the final winning move; any overthrow.—*v.t.* to make the movement ending the game; to defeat.
Syn. to curb, hinder, chide. *Ant.* to help, encourage.
check'er *see* **chequer.**
chee'chee *n.* mincing in speech; Eurasian in character.
cheek *n.* the side of the face below the eye; impudence.—*v.t.* to address impudently.—**cheek'y** *a.*—**cheek'ily** *adv.*
cheer *n.* mood; mirth; food; shout of approval.—*v.t.* to comfort; gladden; encourage, *esp.* by shouts.—*v.i.* to shout applause.—**cheer'ful** *a.*—**cheer'fully** *adv.*—**cheer'fulness** *n.*—**cheer'y** *a.*—**cheer'ily** *adv.*—**cheer'less** *a.*—**cheer'lessness** *n.*
cheese *n.* curd of milk coagulated, separated from the whey and pressed.—

chees'y *a.*—**chees'iness** *n.*—**cheese'-monger** *n.*—**cheese'paring** *a.* mean.
chef' (shef') *n.* a head male cook, the chief cook in a hotel, restaurant, etc.
chemise' *n.* a woman's undergarment or underslip; (*fort.*) a wall strengthening a bastion or earthwork.
chem'istry (k-) *n.* the science which treats of the properties of substances and their combinations and reactions.—**chem'ist** *n.*—**chem'ical** *n.* and *a.*
chenille' (she-nēl') *n.* a soft cord of silk or worsted used for trimming.
cheque (-ek) *n.* an order for money from a bank.—**cheque'-book** *n.*
che'quer (-eker) *n.* marking like a chessboard; *pl.* squares like those of a chessboard.—*v.t.* to mark in squares.—**che'quered** *a.* marked in squares; uneven.
cher'ish *v.t.* to treat with affection; protect; encourage (he **cher'ishes**).
cheroot' (sh-) *n.* an open-ended cigar.
cher'ry *n.* a small stone-fruit; the tree.—*a.* ruddy (**cher'ries** *pl.*).
cher'ub *n.* a winged creature with a human face; an angel.—**cher'ubs, cher'ubim** *pl.*—**cheru'bic** *a.*
chess *n.* a game of skill played by two persons with 32 "pieces" on a board of 64 squares.—**chess'men** *n.pl.* the pieces used in chess.—**chess'board** *n.*
chest *n.* a box; the upper part of the trunk of the body.
chest'erfield *n.* a long overcoat; a sofa.
chest'nut (-sn-) *n.* a large reddish-brown nut growing in a prickly husk; the tree.—*a.* reddish-brown.
chev'ron (sh-) *a.* V-shaped band of braid or lace, a badge in the Forces.
chew (-ōō) *v.t.* to grind with the teeth, masticate.—**chew'ing-gum** *n.*
chic' (sheek') *n.* stylish, smart.
chiaroscu'ro (kya-ros-koo'rō) *n.* the light and shade in a picture.
chicane', chica'nery *n.* quibbling; trick.—**chicane'** *v.i.* to quibble.—*n.* a hand of cards containing no trumps.
chick short for **chick'en** *n.* the young of birds, *esp.* of the hen.—**chick'en-heart'ed** *a.*—**chick'en-pox** *n.* a fever.
chic'ory *n.* a salad plant of which the root is ground and mixed with coffee.
chide *v.t.* to scold (**chid** *p.t.*—**chidd'en, chid** *p.p.*—**chi'ding** *pres.p.*).
Syn. to blame, reproach, censure, reprove. *Ant.* approve, commend.
chief *n.* a principal person.—*a.* principal, foremost, leading.—**chief'ly** *adv.*
chief'tain *n.* a leader of a clan or tribe.
chignon (shayn'-yon(g)) *n.* a coil of hair, natural or artificial, worn by women at the back of the head.
chil'blain *n.* a sore due to cold.
child (-ī-) *n.* an infant; a boy or girl; a son or daughter.—**child'ren** (-i-) *pl.*—**child'ish** (-ī) *a.*—**child'ishly** *adv.*—**child'hood** *n.*—**child'birth** *a.*—**child'bed** *n.* the state of a woman giving birth to a child.—**child'like** *a.*—**child'less** *a.*
chill *n.* coldness; a cold with shivering; anything that discourages.—**chilled** *a.*—**chill'y** *a.*—**chill'iness** *n.*—**chill'ing** *a.*
chime *n.* the sound of bells in harmony; a set of bells.—*v.i.* to ring harmoniously; to agree.—*v.t.* to strike (bells).—**to chime in,** to join in a conversation (**chimed** *p.t.* and *p.p.*).
chime'ra, chimæ'ra (ki-mē'-) *n.* a fabled monster made up of parts of various animals; a wild fancy (**-ras** *pl.*).—**chime'ric, chime'rical** *a.*
chim'ney *n.* a passage for smoke.
chimpanzee' *n.* African anthropoid ape.
chin *n.* part of the face below the mouth.
chi'na *n.* fine earthenware; cups, dishes, etc., made of china.
chink *n.* a cleft; the sound of pieces of metal knocking together.—*v.i.* to make this sound.—*v.t.* to cause to do so.
chintz *n.* cotton cloth printed in coloured designs.
chip *v.t.* to chop into small pieces; to break little pieces from; to shape.—*v.i.* to break off.—*n.* small piece broken off.—**chip in** *v.i.* to intervene.—**chip-shot** *n.* in golf, short lofted shot on to the green.—**chips** *n.pl.* potatoes chipped and fried; (*sl.*) ship's carpenter.
chirog'raphy (ki-rog'ra-fi) *n.* the art of writing; hand-writing.
chirop'odist (kī-rop'-) *n.* one who treats diseases of the hands and feet.
chiroprac'tic (kī-rō-prak'-tik) *n* and *a.* a method of healing which relies upon the removal of nerve interference by manual adjustment of the spinal column.—**chiroprac'tor** *n.* one who practices chiropractic.
chirp, chirr'up *n.* a cry of a bird.—*v.i.*
chis'el (-zl) *n.* a cutting tool, with an edge at one end.—*v.t.* to cut or carve; (*sl.*) to cheat.—**chis'elling** *pres. p.*—**chis'elled** *p.t.* and *p.p.*).
chit *n.* an informal note; a child.
chi'tin (kī-tin) *n.* a hard substance present in the outer covering of insects, shellfish, etc.—**chi'tinous** *a.*
chiv'alry (sh-) *n.* bravery and courtesy; the feudal system of knighthood.—**chiv'alrous** *a.*—**chiv'alrously** *adv.*
chlo'rine (kl-) *n.* a yellowish-green gas, an element, with a suffocating action on the lungs.—**chlo'ride** *n.*—**chlo'rate** *n.*—**chlo'rinate** *v.t.* treat with chlorine.
chlo'roform (kl-) *n.* a liquid used as an anæsthetic.—*v.t.* to drug with this.
chlo'rophyll (kl-) *n.* the green colouring matter of plants.
choc'olate *n.* a sweet or drink made from cacao beans.—*a.* dark brown.
choctaw *n.* a member of an Indian tribe in Oklahoma.
choice *n.* act or power of choosing; an

alternative; something chosen.—*a.* worthy of being chosen.—**choice'ly** *adv.*
choir (kwīr) *n.* a band of singers, *esp.* in a church; the part of a church set aside for them.—**choir-or'gan** *n.*
choke *v.t.* to throttle; stop up; stifle; obstruct.—*v.i.* to suffer choking.—*n.*—**choked** *a.*—**choke'bore** *n.* a gun narrowed towards the muzzle, to concentrate the shot.—**choke-control** *n.* in wireless, a system for modulating high-frequency oscillations.—**choke'damp** *n.* carbonic gas in coal-mines.
chol'er (k-) *n.* bile; anger.—**chol'eric** *a.*
chol'era (k-) *n.* deadly infectious disease attacking the bowels.
choose *v.t.* to take one thing rather than another; select.—*v.i.* to think fit (**chose** *p.t.*—**cho'sen** *p.p.*—**choo'sing** *pres. p.*).—**choos'er** *n.*
chop *v.t.* to cut with a blow; to cut in pieces.—*n.* a hewing blow; a slice of meat containing a rib.—**chop'-house** *n.* —**chopp'er** *n.*—**chop'ping** *pres. p.*—**chopped** *p.t.* and *p.p.*
chop *v.t.* to exchange.—*v.i.* to shift, as the wind.—**chop'sticks** *n.* ivory or bamboo sticks used by the Chinese to convey food to the mouth.
chop, chap *n.* the jaw (usually in *pl.*). —**chop'-fallen** *a.* dejected.
chop-suey (-sôô-i) *n.* a Chinese stew of meat, rice, bamboo shoots, onions, etc.
chord (k-) *n.* string of a musical instrument; combination of musical notes; straight line joining the ends of an arc.
chore *see* **chare.**
choreog'raphy *n.* the art, or notation, of dancing, *esp.* ballet-dancing.—**'rapher** *n.*—**raph'ic** *a.*
cho'rus (k-) *n.* a band of singers; combination of voices singing together, a refrain.—*v.t.* to sing or say together.—**chor'ic** *a.*—**cho'ral** *a.*—**chor'ister** *n.*
chouse' *n.* swindle; and *v.t.* dupe.
Chris'tian (kris'tyan) *n.* a follower of Christ.—*a.* following Christ; relating to Christ or His religion.—**Christian name,** the name given at christening, the individual name.—**Christian Science,** a religious system founded by Mrs. Eddy, in America.—**christ'en** (kris'n) *v.t.* to baptize.—**Christian'ity** *n.*—**chris'tianise** *v.t.*—**Chris'tendom** *n.* all Christian countries.—**Chris'tmas** *n.* the festival of the birth of Christ.—**Christmas card** *n.* —**Christmas-box** *n.*
chromat'ic (k-) *a.* of colour; (*music*) of a scale proceeding by semi-tones.
chro'matin *n.* the protoplasmic substance in the nucleus of cells, the part which takes the colour in staining tests.
chro'mosome (-mō-sōm) *n.* a microscopic body formed by the chromatin of a plant or animal cell during division and carrying the genes of each species.
chron'ic (k-) *a.* lasting a long time.—**chron'icle** *n.* a record of events in order of time.—**chron'icler** *n.*—**chronol'ogy** *n.* science of dates.—**chronolo'gical** *a.*—**chronolo'gically** *adv.*—**chronol'ogist** *n.*—**chronom'eter** *n.* an instrument for measuring time.—**chronom'etry** *n.*
chrys'alis (k-) *n.* stage of an insect's life between grub and fly (**chrys'alises, chrysal'ides** (-i-dēz) *pl.*).
chub *n.* a river fish.—**chubb'y** *a.* plump.
chuck *v.t.* to tap, as *to chuck someone under the chin*; to throw.
chuc'kle *v.i.* to laugh in a quiet manner.
chukk'er *n.* one of the periods into which the game of polo is divided.
chunk' *n.* thick lump or piece.
church *n.* a building for Christian worship; the whole body of Christians; the clergy; a body or sect of Christians. —*v.t.* to give thanks on behalf of (a woman) after childbirth, etc.—**church'-man** *n.*—**churchward'en** *n.*—**church'-woman** *n.*—**church'yard** *n.*
churl *n.* a rustic; an ill-bred fellow.—**churl'ish** *a.*—**churl'ishly** *adv.*
churn *n.* a vessel for making butter.—*v.t.* to shake up, stir violently.
chute' (shoot') *n.* a slide for sending timber, etc., to a lower level; steep channel of water; toboggan-run.
chut'ney *n.* spiced sauce or relish made of fruit, vinegar, etc.
chy'ack *v.t.* in Australia, to tease, chaff.
cicero'ne (chē-chā-rō'nā) *n.* a guide (-**ni,** -**nes** *pl.*).
ci'der *n.* a drink made from apples.
cigar' *n.* a roll of tobacco-leaves for smoking. — **cigarette'** *n.* finely-cut tobacco rolled in paper for smoking.
cinch *n.* easy task; saddle-girth.—*v.t.* get a tight hold on; capture.
cinc'ture (sink-) *n.* a belt, girdle; *v.t.* to encircle, encompass.—**cinc'tured** *a.*
cin'der *n.* a piece of glowing coal; a partly-burnt coal.—**cin'der-path** *n.*
cin'ema *n.* a building used for cinematograph exhibitions.—**cin'ema-or'gan** *n.* pipe-organ fitted with many special devices to give unusual tonal effects.
cinemat'ograph *n.* an apparatus for throwing moving pictures on a screen. —**cinematograph'ic** *a.*—**cinematog'raphy** *n.* —**cine-cam'era** *n.* a camera for taking moving pictures.—**cine-film** *n.* film for a cine-camera; a moving picture.—**cine-projector** *n.* an apparatus for throwing moving pictures on to a screen.
cinerar'ium *n.* building in which are deposited urns containing the ashes of bodies which have been cremated.
cinn'amon *n.* the spicy bark of a tree; the tree.—*a.* of a light brown colour.
ci'pher, cy'pher *n.* the arithmetical symbol 0; a figure; a person of no importance; a monogram; a secret writing.—*v.i.* to work at arithmetic.
cir'cle (sẽr'kl) *n.* a perfectly round

figure; a ring; a company of persons gathered round another; a seance; a class or division of society.—*v.t.* to surround.—*v.i.* to move round.—**circ'ular** *a.* round; moving round.—*n.* a letter sent to several persons.—**circ'ulate** *v.i.* to move round; to pass from place to place; to come to readers.—*v.t.* to send round.—**circula'tion** *n.*

circ'uit (-kit) *n.* a moving round; area; a round of visitation, *esp.* of judges; a district; the path of an electric current.—**circu'itous** *a.*—**circu'itously** *adv.*

circ'umcise *v.t.* to cut off the foreskin of.—**circumcis'ion** *n.* Jewish rite.

circum'ference *n.* the boundary line, *esp.* of a circle; distance round.

circumlocu'tion *n.* roundabout speech. *Syn.* periprasis, verbosity, diffuseness. *Ant.* conciseness; terseness.

circumnav'igate *v.t.* to sail round.—**circumnaviga'tion** *n.*—**circumnav'igator** *n.*

circ'umscribe *v.t.* to confine, bound, limit, hamper.

circ'umspect *a.* watchful, cautious, prudent, careful, discreet.—**circ'umspectly** *adv.*—**circumspec'tion** *n.*

circ'umstance *n.* a detail; an event, matter of fact; *pl.* state of affairs; condition in life; the surroundings or things accompanying an action.—**circ'umstanced** *a.* situated.—**circumstan'tial** *a.* depending on details; indirect.—**circumstan'tially** *adv.*—**circumstantial'ity** *n.*—**circumstan'tiate** *v.t.* to prove by details; to describe exactly.

circumvent' *v.t.* to outwit, outmanoeuvre.—**circumven'tion** *n.*

circ'us *n.* circular building for public shows; an entertainment of horse-riding, acrobats, etc.; a group of houses built in a circle (**circ'uses** *pl.*).

cir'rus *n.* a high fleecy cloud (**cir'ri** *pl.*).

cist' (sist') *n.* prehistoric stone coffin.

cis'tern *n.* a water-tank.

cit'adel *n.* a fortress commanding a city.

cite *v.t.* to summon; quote; bring forward as proof.—**cita'tion** *n.*—**ci'ted** *p.t./p.p.*

cit'izen *n.* an inhabitant of a city; a townsman, civilian; a member of a state.—**cit'izenship** *n.*

cit'ron *n.* a fruit like a lemon; the tree.—**cit'ric** *a.* of the acid of the lemon.

cit'y *n.* a large town (**ci'ties** *pl.*).

civ'et (siv-) *n.* strong musky perfume.—**civ'et-cat** *n.* animal producing it.

civ'ic *a.* pertaining to a city or citizen.—**civ'ics** *n.* the science of municipal and national life or service.

civ'il *a.* relating to citizens or the state; refined; not military.—(*law*) not criminal.—**civ'illy** *adv.*—**civil'ity** *n.* politeness.—**civil'ian** *n.* a non-military person.—**civ'ilise** *v.t.* to bring out of barbarism.—**civilisa'tion** *n.*—**civ'ilised** *a.* *Syn.* political, civilised, urbane, courteous, well-bred, refined. *Ant.* military, rude, churlish, brusque.

civ'vies *n.pl.* (*sl.*) civilian clothes, mufti.

claim *v.t.* to call for; demand as a right.—*n.* a demand for a thing supposed due; a right; the thing claimed; in Australia, S. Africa, etc., a plot of land marked out by stakes as required by law.—**clai'mant** *n.* person claiming.

clairaud'ience *n.* the power of hearing things not present to the normal senses.—**'ient** *a.*

clairvoy'ance (klār-voi'ans) *n.* the power of seeing things not present to the normal senses.—**clairvoy'ant** *n.*

clam' *n.* an edible mollusc.

clam'ant *a.* demanding attention.

clam'ber *v.i.* to climb with hands and feet, with difficulty.

clamm'y *a.* moist and sticky.—**clamm'iness** *n.*—**mier** *comp.*—**miest** *sup.*

clam'our *n.* loud shouting, outcry.—*v.i.* to shout; to call noisily (for).—**clam'orous** *a.*—**clam'orously** *adv.*

clamp *n.* a tool for holding or compressing; a dung heap.—*v.t.* to fasten with clamps; hold very firmly.

clan *n.* group of families under a chief and common ancestry; a sect.—**clann'ish** *a.*—**clann'ishly** *adv.*—**clann'ishness** *n.*

clandes'tine *a.* secret; sly.

clang *n.* a loud ringing sound.—*v.i.* to make such sound.—*v.t.* to strike together with a clang.—**clang'our** *n.*

clank *n.* a sharp jangling sound.—*v.t.* and *i.* to cause such a sound.

clap *n.* a hard, explosive sound; a slap.—*v.i.* to strike with noise; to strike the open hands together; applaud.—*v.t.* to strike together; to applaud; thrust suddenly, impose abruptly.—**clapp'er** *n.*—**clapp'ing** *n.*—**clap'trap** *n.* empty words.

claque' (klak') *n.* an organized group of bribed applauders, or noisy vehement supporters.

clar'et *n.* red Bordeaux wine.

clar'ify *v.t.* to make clear (-**ified**) *p.t.* and *p.p.*— -**ifying** *pres. p.*).—**clarifica'tion** *n.*

clar'ion *n.* a clear-sounding trumpet.—**clarionet'**, **clar'inet** *n.* a wood-wind instrument.—**clarinett'ist** *n.*

clash *n.* a loud noise, as of weapons striking together; conflict, collision.—*v.i.* to make a clash; to come into conflict.—*v.t.* to strike together.

clasp *n.* a hook or other fastening; an embrace or hold; a military decoration.—*v.t.* to fasten; embrace; hold.

class (-à-) *n.* a rank of society; a division of pupils; a division by merit, quality.—*v.t.* to assign to the proper division.—**class'ify** *v.t.* to arrange methodically in classes (-**ified** *p.t.* and *p.p.*— -**ifying** *pres. p.*).—**classifica'tion** *n.* (he **classes**).

class'ic, class'ical *a.* of the first rank of Greek and Roman authors; of the highest rank generally, but *esp.* of

literature; resembling in style the Greek writers; refined; famous.—**class'ically** *adv.*—**class'icism** *n.*—**class'icist** *n.*
clatt'er *n.* a rattling noise; noisy conversation.—*v.i.* to make a rattling noise; to chatter.—*v.t.* to make rattle.
clause (-z) *n.* a part of a sentence; an article in a formal document.
claus'trophobia *n.* morbid fear of enclosed places.
clave *p.t.* of **cleave.**
clav'ichord (-k-) *n.* an obsolete musical instrument like a spinet.
cla'vicle *n.* a collar-bone.
claw *n.* hooked nail of a bird or beast; the foot of an animal with hooked nails; anything like a claw.—*v.t.* to tear with claws; to grip.
clay *n.* a stiff viscous earth; earth; generally, human body.—**clay'ey** *a.*—**clay'pan** *n.* Australia, hollow in surface of clay land where water collects.
clay'more *n.* a Highland sword.
clean *a.* free from dirt, or any defilement; pure; guiltless; shapely.—*adv.* so as to leave no dirt; entirely.—*v.t.* to free from dirt.–**clean'ness** *n.*–**clean'er** *n.*–**clean'ly** (klĕn-) *adv.*—**clean'liness** (klen'-) *n.*—**clean'ly** (klen'-) *a.*—**cleanse** (klenz) *v.t.* —**clean'skin** *n.* in Australia, an animal without a brand.
clear *a.* free from clouds; pure, bright; free from difficulty; plain; without defect or drawback; transparent.—*adv.* brightly; wholly, quite.—*v.t.* to make clear; acquit; pass over or through; make as profit; free from cloud, obstruction; free by payment of dues.—*v.i.* to become clear, bright, transparent.—**clear'ly** *adv.*—**clear'ance** *n.*—**clear'ness** *n.*—**clear'ing** *n.*—**clear'-ing-house** *n.* where cheques are exchanged.—**clear'ing-station** *n.* a place from which wounded are removed.—**clear-sight'ed** *a.*—**clear-starch'ing** *n.*
cleat *n.* a piece of wood or iron with two projecting ends, round which ropes are made fast; a porcelain insulator.
cleave *v.i.* to cling, adhere to; be faithful to; agree (**cleaved, clave** *p.t.*—**cleaved** *p.p.*—**cleaving** *pres. p.*).
cleave *v.t.* to split asunder.—*v.i.* to part asunder (**clove, cleft** *p.t.*—**clo'ven, cleft** *p.p.*—**clea'ving** *pres. p.*).—**clea'vage** *n.* —**clea'ver** *n.* a butcher's chopper.
cleek *n.* an iron grappling hook; a golf-club with an iron head.
clef *n.* mark to show pitch in music.
cleft *n.* an opening made by cleaving; fissure.—*p.t.* and *p.p.* of **cleave.**—**cleft'-pal'ate** *n.* malformation of the roof of the mouth in which the two halves have failed to join properly.
clem'atis *n.* a flowering, climbing perennial plant.
clem'ent *a.* merciful; gentle; kind; mild.—**clem'ently** *adv.*—**clem'ency** *n.*
clench *v.t.* to set firmly together; grasp; drive home (he **clen'ches**).
clere'story (klērs-) *n.* an upper part of a church with a row of windows.
cler'gy *n.* the appointed ministers of the Christian church.—**cler'gyman** *n.*
cler'ic *a.* belonging to the clergy.—*n.* a clergyman.—**cler'ical** *a.*—**cler'icalism** *n.*
clerk (-ark) *n.* a clergyman or priest; one who leads the responses in church; an officer in charge of records, correspondence, etc.; a subordinate in an office.—**clerk of works** one in charge of building operations.
clev'er *a.* able, skilful, adroit.—**clev'erly** *adv.*—**clev'erness** *n.*
Syn. dexterous, talented, sharp, smart. *Ant.* stupid, dull, unintelligent, clumsy.
clew *see* **clue.**
cli'che (clē'shā) *n.* a stereotyped hackneyed phrase (**cli'ches** (clē'shā) *pl.*).
click *n.* a short, sharp sound.—*v.i.*
cli'ent *n.* a customer; one who employs a professional man.—**cli'entele** *n.* a body of clients or customers.
cliff *n.* a steep rock face.—**cliff'y** *a.*
climacter'ic *n.* a critical period in human life, turning-point.
cli'mate *n.* the condition of a country with regard to weather.—**climat'ic** *a.*
cli'max *n.* a highest point, culmination; arrangement of language to rise in dignity and force; the point of greatest excitement, in a play, story, etc.
climb (klīm) *v.t.* and *i.* to mount by clutching, pulling; to creep up; ascend.
clime *n.* climate (*poetical*) q.v.
clinch *v.* clench, q.v.
cling *v.i.* to stick fast, attach; remain by (**clung** *p.t.* and *p.p.*).
clin'ic *a.* a place where medical advice and treatment are given.—*n.* a place or meeting for medical examination or teaching.—**clin'ical** *a.* medical.
clink *n.* a sharp metallic sound.—*v.t.* and *i.* to make or cause to make such sound.
clink'er *n.* hard slag.
clip *v.t.* to grip, clutch, hug.—*n.* a device for gripping papers, etc., together (**clip'ping** *pres. p.*—**clipped** *p.t.* and *p.p.*).
clip *v.t.* to cut with scissors or shears; to cut short.—*n.* wool shorn at a place or in a season.—**clipp'er** *n.*
clipp'er *n.* a fast sailing ship.
clip'ping bureau a firm which clips from newspapers, periodicals, etc., articles and reports of special interest to subscribers.
clique (-ēk) *n.* a small exclusive set.
cloak *n.* a loose outer garment; a disguise, pretext.—*v.t.* to cover with a cloak; conceal.—**cloak'-room** *n.*
cloche' (klōsh') *n.* a bell-shaped glass for cultivation of vegetables, etc.; a close-fitting bell-shaped hat.
clock *n.* an instrument for measuring time; ornament on a stocking.—**to**

clock in, out to record arrival or departure on automatic time recorder. —**clock'-work** *n.* machinery which works by means of wound-up spring.
clod *n.* a lump of earth; a blockhead.
clog *n.* an obstruction; a wooden-soled shoe.—*v.t.* choke up.—**clog'-dance** *n.*
cloisonné (klwa-zon-ā) *n.* a kind of French enamel ware in which wire divisions outline the design.
cloi'ster *n.* covered arcade in a monastery or nunnery or college.—*v.t.* to confine within walls.—**cloi'stral** *a.*—**cloi'stered** *a.* secluded.
close (-s) *a.* shut up; confined; stifling; reticent; niggardly; compact; crowded; strict, searching.—*adv.* nearly, tightly.—*n.* a shut-in place; the precinct of a cathedral.—**close'ly** *adv.*—**close'ness** *n.* —**close'-corpora'tion** *n.*—**close'-fisted** *a.* —**close'-sea'son** *n.* when it is illegal to kill certain kinds of game and fish.
close (-z) *v.t.* to shut; stop up; finish.—*v.i.* to come together; grapple.—*n.* end.
closed shop a trade in which all workers must belong to the union under contract, and new employees must join within a certain time.
clos'et (-z-) *n.* a small private room.—*v.t.* to shut up in a closet; conceal.
clo'sure (-z-) *n.* the ending of a debate by vote or other authority.
clot *n.* mass, lump.–*v.t.*–**clot'ted** *p.t./p.p.*
cloth (-th) *n.* woven fabric.—**clothes** (-th-) *n.pl.* dress; bed-coverings.—**clo'thing** *n.*—**clothe** *v.t.* to put clothes on.—**clo'thier** *n.* one who sells clothes. —**clothes-horse** *n.* U.S. (*sl.*) one who makes a fetish of wearing fine clothes.
cloud *n.* vapour floating in the air; a state of gloom; a great number or mass. —*v.t.* to overshadow.—*v.i.* to become cloudy.—**cloud'y** *a.*—**cloud'less** *a.*
clout *n.* cloth; a blow.—*v.t.* to patch.
clove *n.* a dried flower-bud of an Eastern tree, used as a spice.
clove *p.t./p.p.*—**clo'ven** *p.p.* of **cleave.**
clo'ver *n.* trefoil used as fodder.
clown *n.* a rustic; a jester.—**clown'ish** *a.*
cloy *v.t.* to weary by sweetness, sameness
club *n.* a thick stick; a bat; one of the suits at cards; an association for a common object.—*v.t.* to strike with a club; to put together.—*v.i.* to join for a common object (**clubbed** *p.t.* and *p.p.*).
cluck *n.* the noise of a hen.—*v.i.*
clue, clew (-ōō) *n.* a ball of thread; a thread used as a guidance, trail; guide *esp.* to the solution of a mystery.
clump *n.* a cluster of plants or trees.
clum'sy (-z-) *a.* awkward, unwieldy, badly made.—**clums'ily** *adv.*—**clums'iness** *n.* (**clum'sier** *comp.*; **clum'siest** *sup.*).
clus'ter *n.* a group.—*v.t.* and *i.* to gather or grow in a cluster.
clutch *v.t.* to grasp eagerly.—*v.i.* to make a snatch at.—*n.* a tight grip; a mechanical device for connecting and disconnecting; eggs laid by a bird at one sitting, the chickens hatched from these.
coach *n.* a large carriage; a railway carriage; a tutor; in Australia, a bullock used as a decoy to ensnare wild cattle.—*v.i.* to ride in a coach.—*v.t.* to tutor.—**coachbuilt** *a.*—**coach'man** *n.*
coadju'tor *n.* an assistant.
coag'ulate *v.t.* and *i.* to curdle, clot as of blood.—**coagula'tion** *n.*
coal *n.* a glowing ember; mineral used as fuel.—*v.t.* to supply with coal.—*v.i.* to take in coal.—**coal-mine** *n.*
coalesce' (-es) *v.i.* to unite.–**coales'cence** *n.*—**coali'tion** *n.* an alliance, *esp.* of political parties.
coarse *a.* rough, harsh; indecent.—**coarse'ly** *adv.*—**coarse'ness** *n.*–**coars'en** *v.*
Syn. rude, gross, unpolished, indelicate. *Ant.* fine, refined, tasteful, dainty.
coast *n.* sea-shore.—*v.i.* and *t.* to sail by the coast; to free wheel.—**coast'er** *n.* a coasting vessel; in Australia, a loafer.
coat *n.* outer garment; animal's fur or feathers; a covering; a layer.—*v.t.* to clothe; cover with a layer, e.g., of paint.
coax *v.t.* to wheedle, persuade.
coax'ial cable insulated cable for the transmission of telephone, telegraph, and television signals.
cob *n.* short-legged strong horse; lump.
cobalt' *n.* a brittle, reddish grey metal; a deep blue pigment.
cob'ble *v.t.* to patch roughly, *esp.* shoes. —*n.* a round stone.—**cob'bler** *n.* shoe-mender; clumsy workman.
cob'ra *n.* a venomous Asiatic snake.—**King co'bra** ring cobra, Hamadryad.
cob'web *n.* a spider's web.
cocaine' *n.* an alkaloid drug used as a local anæsthetic and intoxicant.
coch'ineal *n.* a scarlet dye got from a Mexican insect.
cock *n.* a male bird; a tap for liquid; the hammer of a gun; an upward turn.—*v.t.* to set or turn assertively; to draw back (gun hammer).—**cockade'** *n.* knot of ribbon, rosette, badge.
cock *n.* a conical heap, *esp.* of hay.—*v.t.* to put up in heaps.
cockatoo' *n.* a crested parrot.
cock'boat *n.* a small ship's boat.
cock'chafer *n.* a flying beetle.
cock'erel *n.* a young cock.
cock'ie, cocky *n.* in Australia, a small farmer.
coc'kle *n.* a shell-fish.
cock'ney (-ni) *n.* a native of London.
cock'pit *n.* enclosure for cock-fighting; pilot's seat in aeroplane fuselage.
cock'roach *n.* a so-called blackbeetle.
cock'tail *n.* a short drink mixture of spirits, bitters, sugar, etc.
co'coa *n.* a powder made from the seed of the cacao, a tropical tree; a drink made from the powder.—**coconut butter**

n.—**co'co-co'la** *n.* a mildly stimulating cold drink (trade name).
co'conut *n.* a tropical palm; its nut.
cocoon' *n.* the sheath of a chrysalis.
co'cotte *n.* a harlot.
cod *n.* a large sea fish (**cod** *pl.*).
cod'dle *v.t.* to nurse excessively; pamper.
code *n.* a collection of laws; a system of signals; a group of regulations; a secret alphabet or system of words representing others.—**co'dify** *v.t.* (-**ified** *p.t.* and *p.p.*—Cifying *pres. p.*).—**codifica'tion** *n.*
co'deine (-dēn) *n.* a sedative drug derived from opium.
co'dex (-deks) *n.* manuscript volume *esp.* of the scriptures (**co'dices** *pl.*).
codg'er *n.* an old man with eccentric ways; a miser.
cod'icil *n.* thing added, *esp.* to a will.
cod'ling, cod'lin *n.* a long tapering kind of apple; a small cod.
co-educa'tion *n.* education of boys and girls together.
coeffi'cient *n.* a joint agent or factor.
coerce' *v.t.* to force.—**coer'cive** *a.*—**coer'cion** *n.* restraint; government by force.
coe'val *a.* of the same age, date or time.
coexist' *v.i.* to exist together.—**coexis'tent** *a.*—**coexis'tence** *n.*
coff'ee *n.* the seeds of a shrub originally from Arabia; a drink made from these.
coff'er *n.* a chest for valuables.
coff'in *n.* a box for a dead body.—*v.t.*
cog *n.* one of a series of teeth on a wheel.
co'gent *a.* forcible, convincing.—**co'gently** *adv.*—**co'gency** *adv.*
cog'itate (koj'-) *v.i.* to think, reflect.—*v.t.* to plan.—**cogita'tion** *n.*
cogn'ac (kōn'-yak) *n.* French brandy
cog'nate *a.* of the same stock, related.
cog'nisance, cog'nizance (*or* kon'-) *n.* knowledge, awareness.—**cog'nisable** (*or* kon'-) *a.*—**cog'nisant** (*or* kon'-) *a.*
cogni'tion (-nish'un) *n.* perception; act or faculty of knowing.
cogno'men *n.* a surname (-**mens** *pl.*).
cohab'it *v.i.* to live together as husband and wife.—**cohabita'tion** *n.*
cohere' *v.i.* to stick together; to be consistent.—**cohe'rent** *a.*—**cohe'rence** *n.*—**cohe'rently** *adv.*—**coho'rer** *n.* device that becomes an electrical conductor when acted on by electric wave radiation.—**cohe'sion** *n.*—**cohe'sive** *a.*
co'hort *n.* a tenth of a Roman legion.
coiff'ure (koif-ūr) *n.* style of woman's hairdressing.—**coiff'eur** *n.* a hairdresser.
coil *v.t.* to lay in rings; to twist into a winding shape.—*v.i.* to twist, take up a winding shape—*n.* a series of rings; in motoring and aviation, a device to transform low tension current to higher voltage.
coin *n.* a piece of money; money.—*v.t.* to make into money; to invent.—**coin'age** *n.*
coincide' (kō-in-) *v.i.* to happen together; occupy same position; agree exactly.—**coin'cident** *a.*—**coin'cidence** *n.* a chance happening together.
coin'treau (kwan-trō) *n.* an orange-flavoured liqueur, once only made in Angers, France (protected trade name).
coke *n.* the residue left from the distillation of coal; *sl.* cocaine.
col'ander *n.* a sieve, strainer.
cold *a.* lacking heat; indifferent; dispiriting.—*n.* lack of heat; illness.—**cold'ly** *adv.*—**cold'ness** *n.*—**cold-storage** *n.* preserving of perishable foodstuffs at artificially reduced temperatures.
cole' *n.* a cabbage.
col'ic *n.* severe pains in the intestines.
coli'tis *n.* inflammation of the bowel.
collab'orate *v.i.* to work with another, *esp.* in literature.—**collab'orator** *n.*—**collabora'tion** *n.* (**collab'orated** *p.t.* and *p.p.*).—**collabora'tionist** *n.* a citizen of one of the occupied countries in World War 2 who worked with the fascist invaders; a quisling.
collage' (-lazh) *n.* an abstract artistic composition made up of objects with contrasting textile appeal.
collapse' *v.i.* to fall together, give way; lose strength, fail.—**collaps'ible** *a.*
coll'ar *n.* a band worn round the neck.—*v.t.* to seize, capture.
coll'ard *n.* kind of leafy greens related to the cabbage.
collate' *v.t.* to compare carefully; (of bishop) to appoint to a benefice.—**colla'tion** *n.* a light meal.
collat'eral *a.* accompanying; subordinate; of same stock but different line.—*n.* kinsman; security.
coll'eague *n.* an associate or partner, companion in an office, employment.
collect' *v.t.* to gather.—*v.i.* to come together.—**collect'ed** *a.* gathered; calm.—**collect'ive** *a.*—**collect'ively** *adv.*—**collect'ivism** *n.* the theory that the State should own all means of production.—**collec'tion** *n.* group, heap; money collected.—**collect'or** *n.*—**coll'ect** *n.* a short prayer. *Syn.* to muster, assemble aggregate, amass. *Ant.* scatter, distribute, separate.
coll'ege *n.* a society of scholars; a place of higher education; an association.—**colle'giate** *a.*—**colle'gian** *n.*
collide' *v.i.* to strike or dash together, come into conflict.—**colli'sion.**
col'lie *n.* long-haired Scottish sheep-dog.
coll'ier *n.* a coal-miner; a coal-carrying ship.—**coll'iery** *n.* a coal-mine.
collo'dion *n.* a solution of guncotton used in preparing photographic plates.
coll'oid *a.* like glue.—*n.* an inorganic gelatinous compound.
coll'op *n.* (*Scots*) coarse minced meat.
coll'oquy *n.* a conversation.—**colloquial** *a.* conversational.—**collo'quialism** *n.*
collu'sion *n.* arrangement, action in secret with another.—**collu'sive** *a.*

collyr'ium (kol-ir'-i-um) *n.* an application to the eye, usually an eyewash.
co'lon *n.* a mark (:) indicating a break in a sentence; (*med.*) the large intestine.
colonel (kur'nel) *n.* commander of a regiment, the highest regimental officer.
colonnade' *n.* a row of columns.
col'ony *n.* a body of people who settle in a new country; the country so settled (**colo'nies** *pl.*).—**colo'nial** *a.*—**col'onist** *n.* a settler.—**col'onise** *v.t.*—**colonisa'tion** *n.*
colorad'o beetle *n.* an insect hurtful to the potato.
coloss'us *n.* a huge statue; a very big man (**coloss'uses, coloss'i** *pl.*).—**coloss'al** *a.* huge, gigantic.
col'our (kul'er) *n.* hue, tint; complexion; paint; pigment; *pl.* flags.—*v.t.* to give colour to; disguise.—*v.i.* to become coloured; to blush.—**coloured** *a.* and *n.* having colour; of mixed white and African or Indian race.
colt *n.* the young of the horse.
col'umbine *a.* of, or like, a dove; dove-coloured.—*n.* a plant of the genus Aquilegia; the female companion of Harlequin in pantomime.
col'umn *n.* a long vertical cylinder, pillar; division of a page; body of troops; anything like these.—**colum'nar** *a.*
co'ma *n.* stupor, unnatural sleep.—**co'matose** *a.* drowsy.
comb (kōm) *n.* a toothed instrument for arranging hair, or ornamenting it; a cock's crest; a mass of honey-cells.—*v.t.* to apply a comb to the hair, etc.
com'bat *v.t.* to fight.—*n.* a fight.—**com'batant** *n.*—**com'bative** *a.* ready to fight; pugnacious.
combine' *v.t.* and *i.* to join together; ally.—**combina'tion** *n.*—**com'bine** *n.* a machine to harvest and thresh grain in one operation; a union of trading companies for business purposes.—**combined' operations** co-ordinated amphibious attack by land, sea and air units. *Syn.* to agree, unite, connect, coalesce, confederate. *Ant.* separate, disagree, sunder, withdraw.
combus'tion *n.* burning.—**combus'tible** *a.* easily burned.—**combustibil'ity** *n.*
come (kum) *v.i.* to approach, arrive; reach; happen (to); originate (from); become; turn out to be (**came** *p.t.*—**come** *p.p.*—**com'ing** *pres. p.*).—**come-back** *n.* (*sl.*) return to active life after retirement, *esp.* in sports.
com'edy *n.* play dealing with the lighter side of life; a play of this kind.—**come'dian** *n.* (**com'edies** *pl.*).
come'ly (kum'-) *a.* fair, pleasant to look at, pretty; seemly.—**come'liness** *n.*
comes'tible *n.* food.—*a.* edible.
com'et *n.* fast moving heavenly body with a tail of light.—**com'etary** *a.*
com'fit (kum'-) *n.* a sweetmeat.
com'fort (kum'-) *v.t.* to console, cheer.—*n.* consolation; well-being; a means of consolation, ease, or satisfaction.—**com'fortable** *a.*—**com'fortably** *adv.*
com'ic *a.* relating to comedy; funny.—**com'ical** *a.*—**com'ically** *adv.*—**com'ic strip** *n.* a series of cartoons in newspapers, etc., relating the adventures of certain stock characters.
Com'inform *n.* consultative association of Communist parties in countries influenced by Soviet political ideology.
Com'intern *n.* the *Com*munist *Inter*national or Third International.
com'ity *n.* courtesy, friendliness.
comm'a *n.* a mark (,) separating short parts of a sentence.
command' *v.t.* to order; rule; compel; have in one's power; dominate.—*v.i.* to exercise rule.—*n.* an order; rule; power of controlling; district under a commander.—**command'er** *n.*—**commandant'** *n.*—**command'ment** *n.*—**commandeer'** *v.t.* to seize for military service.
comman'do (-dō) *n.* a small body of armed S. African burghers; non-professional units of the S. African Defence Force; a small but highly mobile and efficient fighting force of special service troops; a member of such a force (**-os** (-ōz) *pl.*)
commem'orate *v.t.* to keep in memory by ceremony.—**commem'orative** *a.*—**commemora'tion** *n.*
commence' *v.t.* and *i.* to begin.—**commence'ment** *n.* (**commen'cing***pres.p.*)
commend' *v.t.* to praise; to commit, entrust.—**commend'able** *a.* praiseworthy.—**commend'ably** *adv.*—**commenda'tion** *n.*—**commen'datory** *a.* praising.
commen'surate *a.* in proportion, adequate; equal in size or length of time.
comm'ent *v.i.* to make remarks, notes, criticisms.—*n.* a note, collection of notes, criticism.-**comm'entator** *n.* (*radio*) one who broadcasts a progressive or subsequent commentary on some special happening, function, game, etc.
comm'erce *n.* buying and selling; intercourse.—**commer'cial** *a.*
commina'tion *n.* threatening with divine wrath.
commis'erate (-z-) *v.t.* to pity, condole with.—**commisera'tion** *n.*
comm'issar (-sar) *n.* one of the heads of a Soviet government department.—**com'missary** *n.* deputy; army officer dealing with food supplies.
commissar'iat *n.* the military department in charge of supplies and transport.
commis'sion *n.* a doing, committing; something entrusted to be done; payment by a percentage for doing something; delegated authority; a warrant, *esp.* a royal warrant, giving authority; a body entrusted with some special duty.—*v.t.* to give an order for; to give power to.—**commis'sioner** (-ish-) *n.* one em-

powered to act by a commission or warrant; a member of a commission or government board.

commissionaire′ *n.* a messenger or doorkeeper (usually uniformed).

commit′ *v.t.* to entrust, give in charge; to perpetrate; to compromise.—**commit′ment** *n.*—**committ′al** *n.*

Syn. to consign, confide, perform, do, post. *Ant.* redeem, ransom, release.

committ′ee *n.* a body appointed or elected for some special business.

commode′ *n.* a chest of drawers; a stool containinga chamber-pot.—**commo′dious** *a.* roomy.—**commo′diously** *adv.*—**commod′ity** *n.* an article of trade, anything meeting a need (**commod′ities** *pl.*).

comm′odore *n.* a naval officer ranking between captain and rear-admiral; the president of a yacht club.

comm′on *a.* shared by or belonging to all, or to several; general, ordinary, usual, frequent; inferior; vulgar.—*n.* unenclosed land not belonging to a private owner; *pl.* ordinary people; the lower House of Parliament; rations.—**commonly** *adv.*—**comm′onalty** *n.* the general body of people.—**comm′oner** *n.*—**comm′onwealth** *n.* a state.—**comm′onplace** *n.* anything ordinary, trivial.

commo′tion *n.* disturbance, tumult.

commune′ *v.i.* to have intimate intercourse.—**commu′nicate** *v.t.* to impart.—*v.i.* to give or exchange information; to receive Communion.—**commu′nicant** *n.* one who receives Communion.—**commu′nicable** *a.*—**communica′tion** *n.* act of giving, *esp.* information; information; passage (road, railway, etc.), or means of exchanging messages (telegraph, post, etc.) between places; connection between military base and front.—**commu′nicative** *a.*—**commu′nion** *n.* fellowship; a body with a common faith.—**Commu′nion** *n.* participation in the sacrament of the Lord's Supper; that sacrament, Eucharist.

comm′unism *n.* the doctrine that all goods, means of production, etc., should be the property of the community.—**comm′unist** *n.* a supporter of this.

commu′nity *n.* a state; a body of people with something in common; joint ownership.—**community singing** conducted but unpractised singing by large crowds.

commute′ *v.t.* to exchange; to change (a punishment, etc.) into something less; to change (a duty, etc.) for a money-payment.—**commuta′tion** *n.*—**commuta′tor** *n.* apparatus which changes alternating current into direct.

com′pact *n.* an agreement, covenant.

compact′ *a.* neatly arranged or packed; concentrated; terse—*n.* a thin flat case to hold face-powder, a powder-puff and mirror.—**compact′ly** *adv.*

compan′ion *n.* a mate, comrade, associate. — **compan′ionable** *a.* — **compan′ionship** *n.*—**native companion,** in Australia, a kind of large crane which can easily be tamed.

compan′ion *n.* staircase leading below from ship's deck; a deck skylight.

com′pany *n.* a gathering of persons; guests; an association for business; a troop under a captain (**com′panies** *pl.*).

compare′ *v.t.* to notice or point out likenesses and differences; to liken or contrast; to make the comparative and superlative of an adjective or adverb.—*v.i.* to be like; to compete with.—**com′parable** *a.*—**compar′ative** *a.* not absolute; relative.—**compar′atively** *adv.*(**compared′** *p.t.* and *p.p.*).—**compar′ison** *n.*

compara′tor (-ā-tor) *n.* in mechanical engineering, a very accurate measuring instrument used for precision examination of machined parts.

compart′ment *n.* a division or part divided off, a section.

com′pass (kum′-) *n.* instrument for showing the North; circumference; space, scope.—*v.t.* to contrive; surround; attain.—**compasses** *n. pl.* two-legged instrument for drawing circles.

compas′sion (-shn) *n.* pity, sympathy. **compas′sionate** *a.*—**compas′sionately** *adv.*

compat′ible *a.* consistent.-**compat′ibly** *adv.*—**compatibil′ity** *n.*

compat′riot *n.* a fellow-countryman.

compeer′ *n.* an equal, an associate, a companion.

compel′ *v.t.* to force, bring about by force.—**compul′sion** *n.*—**compul′sory** *a.*

compend′ium *n.* an abridgement or summary (**-diums, -dia** *pl.*).—**compend′ious** *a.*—**compend′iously** *adv.*

com′pensate *v.t.* to make up for.—**compensa′tion** *n.*—**compensa′tory** *a.*

com′père (-pār) *n.* one who explains or introduces a variety or other performance in a theatre, etc., or in a broadcast performance; *fem.* **com′mere.**

compete′ *v.i.* to strive.—**competi′tion** *n.* —**compet′itive** *a.*—**compet′itor** *n.*

com′petent *a.* able, skilful; properly qualified; proper, legitimate, sufficient. —**com′petently** *adv.*—**com′petence,** ability; sufficient money.—**com′petency** *n.*

compile′ *v.t.* to make up (e.g. a book) from various sources or materials; to put together.—**compi′ler** *n.*—**compila′tion** *n.*

compla′cent *a.* self-satisfied.—**compla′cently** *adv.*—**compla′cence, compla′cency** *n.*—**com′plaisant** (-liz-) *a.* obliging. —**com′plaisance** *n.* desire to please.

complain′ *v.t.* to grumble; bring a charge, make known a grievance.—**complaint′** *n.* a statement of a wrong, a grievance; an illness.—**complai′nant** *n.*

com′plaisance *see* **complacent.**

com′plement *n.* something making up a whole; a full allowance, equipment, etc. ; to complete.—**complemen′tary** *a.*

complete' *a.* full, finished, ended, perfect.—*v.t.* to finish; make whole, full, perfect.—**complete'ly** *adv.*—wholly. **complete'ness** *n.*—**comple'tion** *n.* finishing. *Syn.* entire, whole, total, absolute, integral. *Ant.* incomplete, imperfect, defective, faulty.
com'plex *a.* intricate, compound, involved.—*n.* a psychological abnormality, an obsession.—**complex'ity** *n.*
complex'ion (-ek'shn) *n.* colour and quality of the skin; appearance.
compli'ant *see* **comply.**
com'plicate *v.t.* to make intricate, involved, difficult.—**complica'tion** *n.*
compli'city *n.* partnership in evil.
com'pliment *n.* a remark neatly expressing praise; in *pl.* expression of courtesy, formal greetings.—*v.t.* to praise, congratulate.-**complimen'tary** *a.*
comply' *v.i.* to consent, yield, do as asked (**complied'** *p.t.* and *p.p.*—**comply'ing** *pres. p.*—he **complies'**).—**compli'ant** *a.*—**compli'ance** *n.*
compo'nent *n.* a part, element.—*a.* composing, making up.
compose' *v.t.* to make up; write, invent; arrange, put in order; settle, adjust. —**composed'** *a.* calm.—**compo'ser** *n.*—**com'posite** *a.* compound, not simple.—**composi'tion** (-zish'un) *n.*—**compo'sure** *n.* calmness.—**compos'itor** *n.* a typesetter, one who arranges type for printing. *Syn.* to confirm, form, fashion, tranquillise, soothe. *Ant.* unsettle, disarrange, irritate, excite.
com'post *n.* a fertilising mixture; a mixture for plastering exterior walls.
compound' *v.t.* to mix, make up; to compromise; make a settlement of debt by partial payment; to condone.—*v.i.* to come to an arrangement, make terms.—**com'pound** *a.* not simple; mixed.—*n.* a mixture, joining; a substance, word, etc., made up of parts.
com'pound *n.* in the East, an enclosure containing houses.
comprehend' *v.t.* to understand; to include, embrace, comprise.—**comprehen'sion** *n.* power of understanding.—**comprehen'sive** *a.* — **comprehen'sively** *adv.*—**comprehen'siveness** *n.*—**comprehen'sible** *a.* understandable.
compress' *v.t.* to squeeze together; to make smaller in size, bulk.—**com'press** *n.* a pad of wet lint, etc., applied to a wound, inflamed part, etc.—**compres'sion** (-shn) *n.* in the internal combustion engine, squeezing of the explosive charge before ignition, to give additional force; conciseness.—**compress'ible** *a.*
comprise' *v.t.* to include, contain.
com'promise (-īz) *n.* a coming to terms by giving up part of a claim.—*v.t.* to expose to suspicion.—*v.i.* to come to terms (**com'promising** *pres. p.*).
comptom'eter *n.* a machine which adds, subtracts, divides, multiplies.
comptroll'er (kon-trō'-) *n.* controller.
compul'sion *n.* act of compelling; an irresistible impulse.—**compuls'ory** *a.*
compunc'tion *n.* regret for wrongdoing.—**compunc'tious** *a.*
compute' *v.t.* to reckon, estimate.—**computa'tion** *n.* reckoning.
com'rade (kom-rid *or* kum'rid) *n.* a friend, companion.—**com'radeship** *n.*
con *v.t.* to learn, pore over; to direct the steering of a ship.—**conn'ing-tower** *n.* part of a submarine.
con- *prefix* together, with.—sometimes **co-**, **col-**, **com-**, **cor-**, **coun-**, as in *connect*, *cohere*, *collect*, *compose*, *correct.*
concat'enate *v.t.* to link together.
con'cave *a.* hollow, curved inwards.—**concav'ity** *n.*—**conca'vo-con'vex** *a.* having an in-curve on one side and a convexity on the other.
conceal' *v.t.* to hide.—**conceal'ment** *n.*
concede' *v.t.* to admit; yield.—**conces'sion** (-shn) *n.*—**concess'ive** *a.*
conceit' (-sēt) *n.* overweening opinion of oneself; a far-fetched comparison.—**conceit'ed** *a.* vain.
conceive' (-sēv) *v.t.* to become pregnant with; to take into the mind, think of; understand.—**conceiv'able** *a.*—imaginable.—**conceiv'ably** *adv.*
concen'sus *n.* a general agreement.
con'centrate *v.t.* to reduce to small space; increase in strength; gather to one point.—*v.i.* to come together; devote all attention.—**concentra'tion** *n.* —**concentra'tion camp,** a prison camp for political prisoners in a fascist or similar state.—**concen'tric(al)** *a.* having a common centre.
con'cept *n.* an abstract notion.
concep'tion *n.* act of conceiving; the thing conceived; an idea, notion.
concern' *v.t.* to be the business of.—*v.i.* *in passive*, to be interested, affected, troubled, involved.—*n.* affair, importance, business, establishment.—**concern'ing** *prep.* respecting, about.
concert' *v.t.* to plan together.—**con'cert** *n.* a musical entertainment; harmony. —**concert'ed** *a.* planned.—**concert'o** (-cher'-) *n.* a musical work for solo instrument and orchestra (**-tos** (-tōz) *pl.*).—**concerti'na** (-tē'-) *n.* a musical instrument with bellows and keys.
conces'sion *see* **concede.**
conch' *n.* a large spiral sea-shell.
conchol'ogy (kong-kol'-) *n.* the science of shells and shell-fish.
concil'iate *v.t.* to pacify, gain, friendship.—**concilia'tion** *n.*—**concil'iatory** *a.*
concise' *a.* brief.—**concise'ly** *adv.*—**concise'ness** *n.*—**conci'sion** (-sizn) *n.*
Syn. succinct, condensed, comprehensive, short. *Ant.* wordy, discursive, long-winded, diffuse, verbose.

con'clave *n.* a private meeting; the assembly for the election of a Pope.
conclude' (-ōōd') *v.t.* to end; settle.—*v.i.* to come to an end; infer, deduce; decide.—**conclu'sion** (-ōō'zhn) *n.*—**conclu'sive** *a.* final.—**conclu'sively** *adv.*
concoct' *v.t.* to make a mixture, prepare with various ingredients; make up; plan, scheme.—**concoc'tion** *n.*
concom'itant *a.* accompanying.
conc'ord *n.* agreement.—**concord'ance** *n.* agreement; an index to the words of a book.—**concord'ant** *a.*
conc'ourse *n.* a flocking together.
con'crete *a.* solid; consisting of matter, facts, practice, etc.; not abstract.—*n.* a mixture of sand, cement, etc., used in building.—**concrete'ly** *adv.*
conc'ubine *n.* a woman living with a man as his wife, but not married to him.—**concu'binage** *n.*
concu'piscence *n.* lust.
concur' *v.i.* to agree, express agreement; happen together.—**concur'rence** *n.*—**concur'rent** *a.*—**concur'rently** *adv.*
Syn. to assent, co-operate, coincide, *Ant.* disagree, dissent, oppose.
concus'sion (-shn) *n.* violent shock; injury by blow, fall, etc.
condemn' *v.t.* to blame; find guilty; find unfit for use.—**condem'natory**—**condem'ned** *a.*—**condemna'tion** *n.*
condense' *v.t.* to concentrate, make more solid; turn from gas into liquid; pack into few words.—*v.i.* to turn from gas to liquid.—**condensa'tion** *n.*—**condens'er** *n.* in electricity, an arrangement for storing electrical energy.—**condenser microphone** *n.* a microphone consisting of two plates of a condenser.
condescend' *v.i.* to stoop; be gracious; patronise.—**condescen'sion** *n.*
condign' (-īn') *a.* adequate; deserved.
con'diment *n.* seasoning for food.
condi'tion (-dish'un) *n.* a thing on which a statement or happening or existing depends; a stipulation; state or circumstances of anything.—*v.t.* to be essential to the happening or existence of; stipulate; to regulate, *esp.* health, air, etc.—**condi'tional** *a.*
condi'tioned re'flex in psychology and physiology, an automatic response induced by repeated applications of the same stimulus.
condole' *v.i.* to grieve with, offer sympathy.—**condo'lence** *n.*
condomin'ium *n.* joint rule.
condone' *v.t.* overlook, treat as not existing.—**condona'tion** *n.*
con'dor *n.* large S. American vulture; Chilean gold coin.
conduce' *v.i.* to help, to promote.
conduct' *v.t.* to lead, direct, manage.—**con'duct** *n.* behaviour.—**conduct'or** *n.* leader of a band, etc.; person in charge of bus, tram, etc.—**conduc'tion** *n.*—**conduct'ive** *a.*—**conductiv'ity** *n.*
con'duit (-dit) *n.* a passage for liquid.
cone *n.* a solid figure with a circular base and tapering to a point; the fruit of the pine, fir, etc.—**con'ic, con'ical** *a.*—**conic sections** *n.* curves formed by the intersection of the surface of a cone with planes that cut the cone in various directions.—**co'nifer** *n.* a tree bearing cones.—**conif'erous** *a.*
confec'tion *n.* prepared delicacy; made-up millinery, etc.—**confec'tioner** *n.* a dealer in cake, sweets, etc.—**confec'tionery** *n.* sweetmeats, cakes, etc.
confed'erate *n.* an ally; accomplice.—*v.t.* and *i.* to unite.—**confed'eracy** *n.*—**confedera'tion** *n.* a union, alliance.
confer' *v.t.* to grant, give.—*v.i.* talk with, take advice (**conferred** *p.t./p.p.*—**confer'ring** *pr. p.*).—**confer'ment** *n.*—**con'ference** *n.* meeting for discussion.
confess' *v.t.* to admit, acknowledge, declare; (of a priest) to hear the sins of.—*v.i.* to acknowledge; to declare one's sins orally to a priest.—**confes'sion** *n.*—**confes'sional** *n.* a confessor's stall or box.—**confess'or** *n.* a priest who hears confessions; a person who keeps his faith under persecution but without martyrdom; one who confesses.
confett'i *n.pl.* small bits of coloured paper for throwing at weddings, etc.
confide' *v.i.* trust (in).—*v.t.* entrust.—**confidant'** *n.* one entrusted with secrets.—**con'fidence** *n.* trust; boldness; intimacy.—**con'fident** *a.*—**con'fidently** *adv.*
configura'tion *n.* shape, aspect.
confine' *v.t.* to imprison; keep in house, bed.—**con'fines** *n.pl.* boundaries.—**confine'ment** *n.* *Syn.* to enclose, limit, bound, environ, restrain. *Ant.* extend, diffuse, liberate, release, unloose.
confirm' *v.t.* to make strong; settle; make valid; verify; administer confirmation to.—**confirma'tion** *n.* a making strong, valid, certain, etc.; a rite administered by a bishop to *confirm* baptized persons in the vows made for them at baptism.—**confirm'ative, confirm'atory** *a.*—**confirmed'** *a.* habitual.
con'fiscate *v.t.* to seize by authority.—**confisca'tion** *n.*—**con'fiscatory** *a.*
conflagra'tion *n.* a great fire.
con'flict *n.* a struggle, trial of strength; variance.—**conflict'** *v.t.* to be at odds with, inconsistent with; clash.
con'fluence *n.* a union of streams; a meeting place.—**con'fluent** *a.*
conform *v.t.* and *i.* to comply, adapt to rule, pattern, custom, etc.–**conform'able** *a.*—**conform'ably** *adv.*—**conforma'tion** *n.* structure; adaptation.—**conform'ity** *n.*
confound' *v.t.* to baffle, defeat; mix up.
confront' (-unt') *v.t.* to face; bring face to face with.—**confronta'tion** *n.*
confuse' *v.t.* to disorder; mix mentally.

—**confu'sion** *n.* tumult; embarrassment. *Syn.* to baffle, perplex, disconcert, astonish. *Ant.* help, clear, enlighten.
confute' *v.t.* disprove—**confuta'tion** *n.*
con'ga (kong'-gȧ) *n.* a modern ballroom dance, modelled on W. Indian rhythms.
congeal' (-j-) *v.t.* and *i.* to solidify by freezing or otherwise.—**congela'tion** *n.*
con'gener (-j-) *n.* a thing or person of the same kind.—**congener'ic** *a.*
conge'nial (-jē'-) *a.* of kindred disposition.—**conge'nially** *adv.*—**congenial'ity** *n.*
congen'ital (-je-) *a.* dating from birth.
con'ger (kong'ger) *n.* a large sea eel.
conge'ries (-jē'-) *n. sing.* and *pl.* a collection or mass.
conges'tion (-jes'chn) *n.* abnormal accumulation of blood, population, etc. —**conges'ted** *a.* overcrowded.
conglom'erate *a.* gathered into a mass.—*v.t.* to gather into a round body.
congrat'ulate (-n-g-) *v.t.* to offer expression of pleasure at another's good fortune, success, etc.—**congratula'tion** *n.* —**congrat'ulatory** *a.*
con'gregate (-ng-g-) *v.i.* to flock together; assemble.—**congrega'tion** *n.* an assembly, *esp.* for religious worship.—**congrega'tional** *a.* relating to a congregation or Congregationalism.—**Congrega'tionalism** *n.* a system in which each separate church is self-governing.—**Congrega'tionalist** *n.*
con'gress (-ng-g-) *n.* a formal assembly for discussion; a legislative body.—**congres'sional** *a.*—**con'gressman** *n.*
con'gruent (-ng-groo-) *a.* fitting together; suitable, accordant.—**con'gruence** *n.*—**con'gruous** *a.* fitting.—**congru'ity** *n.*
co'nic *a.* cone-shaped; relating to cones and their properties.—**co'nical** *a.*
co'nifer *n.* cone-bearing tree, *e.g.* pine or fir.—**conif'erous** *a.*
conjec'ture *n.* a guess.—*v.t.* and *i.* to guess.—**conjec'tural** *a.*
conjoint' *a.* united, joint, associated; in conjunction with.
con'jugal *a.* of marriage; between married persons.—**conjugal'ity** *n.*
con'jugate *v.t.* to inflect a verb in its various forms (past, present, etc.)—**conjuga'tion** *n.*—**conjuga'tional** *a.*
conjunc'tion *n.* a part of speech joining words, phrases, etc.; a union; simultaneous happening.—**conjunc'tive** *a.* joining; joint.—**conjunc'ture** *n.*
conjure' (-oor) *v.t.* to implore solemnly. —**con'jure** (kun'jer) *v.t.* and *i.* to produce magic effects by secret natural means; to invoke devils.—**conjura'tion** *n.*—**con'jurer, con'juror** *n.* magician, juggler.
conk' *v.t.* (*sl.*) to strike hard, *esp.* on the head; the head itself.—**conk out** *v.i.* of an engine, to stop suddenly through lack of fuel or mechanical defect; (*sl.*) to faint; to die.—*n.* (*sl.*) nose.
connect' *v.t.* and *i.* to join together; associate in the mind.—**connec'tion, connex'ion** (-shn) *n.*—**connect'ive** *a.*
conn'ing-tower *n. see* **con.**
connive' *v.i.* to refrain from preventing, or forbidding, an offence.—**conni'vance** *n.*
connoisseur' (kon-a-sur') *n.* a critical expert, *esp.* in matters of taste.
connote' *v.t.* to mean in addition to the chief meaning.—**connota'tion** *n.*
connu'bial *a.* connected with marriage.
con'quer (-ker) *v.t.* to win by war, overcome.—*v.i.* to be victorious.—**con'queror** (-ke-) *n.*—**con'quest** *n.*
consanguin'ity *n.* kinship, blood relationship.—**consanguin'eous** *a.*
con'science (-shens) *n.* mental sense of right and wrong.—**conscien'tious** *a.*
con'scious (-shus) *a.* aware; awake to one's surroundings and identity.—**con'sciously** *adv.*—**con'sciousness** *n.* awareness; perception.
con'script *n.* one compulsorily enlisted for military service.—**conscrip'tion** *n.*
con'secrate *v.t.* to make sacred, sanctify; to devote.—**consecra'tion** *n.* (**con'secrated** *p.t.* and *p.p.*).
consec'utive *a.* in unbroken succession. —**consec'utively** *adv.*
consen'sus *n.* joint agreement.
consent' *v.i.* to agree to.—*n.* permission.
con'sequence *n.* what follows on a cause.—**con'sequent** *a.*—**consequen'tial** *a.* self-important.—**con'sequently** *adv.*
conservatoire' *n.* a music school.
conserve' *v.t.* to keep from change or decay; to preserve, safeguard.—*n.* fruit preserved in sugar, jam.—**conser'ving** *pres. p.*—**conserved'** *p.t.* and *p.p.*—**conserva'tion** *n.*—**conserv'ative** *a.* and *n.*—**conserv'atism** *n.*—**conserv'atory** *n.* a greenhouse.
consid'er *v.t.* to think over; examine; make allowance for; esteem; be of opinion that.—**considera'tion** *n.*—**consid'erable** *a.* somewhat large.—**consid'erably** *adv.*—**consid'erate** *a.* thoughtful for others.—**consid'erately** *adv.*
consign' (-īn') *v.t.* commit, hand over; entrust to a carrier.—**consign'or** *n.*—**consignee'** *n.*—**consign'ment** *n.*
consist' *v.i.* to be composed of; to agree with.—**consist'ent** *a.*—**consist'ently** *adv.* —**consist'ency** *n.*—**consist'ence** *n.* degree of density.—**con'sistory** *n.* an ecclesiastical court or council, *esp.* held by a Pope.
console' *v.t.* to comfort in distress.—**consola'tion** *n.*—**consol'atory** *a.*
con'sole *n.* a side table with carved legs; an ornamental bracket; the keyboards, etc., of an organ.
consol'idate *v.t.* to combine into a connected whole.—**consolida'tion** *n.*
con'sols *n.pl.* funded stocks of the British National Debt.
consommé (-som-ā) *n.* a clear soup.
con'sonant *n.* a sound making a syllable

only with a vowel, a non-vowel.—*a.* agreeing with.—**con'sonance** *n.*
con'sort *n.* a ship sailing with another; a husband or wife, *esp.* of a queen or king.—**consort'** *v.i.* to keep company with.—**consort'ium** *n.* agreement between several countries to assist those of another country.
conspic'uous *a.* striking to the eye.
conspire' *v.i.* to combine for an evil purpose, to plot.—**conspir'ator** *n.*—**conspir'acy** *n.*—**conspirator'ial** *a.*
con'stable (kun'-) *n.* a policeman; an officer of the peace; the governor of a royal fortress.—**constab'ulary** *n.*–**special constable** *n.* a person sworn in as a constable on emergency.
con'stant *a.* unchanging; always duly happening or continuing.—**constancy'** *n.*
Syn. invariable, unshaken, permanent, resolute. *Ant.* inconstant, changing, fickle, impermanent.
constella'tion *n.* a group of stars.
consterna'tion *n.* a terrifying sense of disaster, dismay, terror.
constipa'tion *n.* sluggishness of bowels.—**con'stipate** *v.t.* affect with this disorder; to stop up.
con'stitute *v.t.* to set up, make into, found, give form to.—**constitu'tion** *n.* make, composition; health; character; disposition; the body of principles on which a state is governed.—**constitu'tional** *a.* relating to a constitution; in harmony with a political constitution.—*n.* a walk habitually taken for the sake of health.—**constitu'tionally** *adv.*—**constit'uent** *a.* going towards making up a whole; electing a representative.—*n.* a component part; an elector.—**constit'uency** *n.* a body of electors, a parliamentary division.
constrain' *v.t.* to force, compel.—**constraint'** *n.* compulsion, restraint.
constric'tion *n.* compression, squeezing together.—**constrict'** *v.t.*—**constrict'ive** *a.*
construct' *v.t.* to make, build, put together.—**construc'tion** *n.*—**construct'ive** *a.*—**construct'ively** *adv.*—**construe'** *v.t.* to interpret, analyse grammatically.
con'sul *n.* a state agent residing in a foreign town; in ancient Rome, one of the chief magistrates.—**con'sular** *a.*—**con'sulate** *n.*—**con'sulship** *n.*
consult' *v.t.* and *i.* to seek counsel, information (from).—**consulta'tion** *n.*
consume' *v.t.* make away with; use up; eat or drink up; destroy.—**consump'tion** *n.* using up; destruction; wasting of the body by phthisis.—**consump'tive** *a.*
consu'mer *n.* person or thing that consumes; one who buys for use or consumption.
con'summate *v.t.* to complete.—**consumm'ate** *a.* of the greatest perfection or completeness.—**consumma'tion** *n.*
con'tact *n.* a touching; a being in touch.—**conta'gion** (-jn) *n.* passing on of disease by contact.—**conta'gious** *a.*—**con'tact lens,** a very thin and barely visible lens ground to optical prescription and held against the eyeball by suction.
contain' *v.t.* to hold; have room for; restrain (oneself).—**contain'er** *n.*
contam'inate *v.t.* to sully, infect, defile, corrupt.—**contamina'tion** *n.*
contang'o *n.* the charge made by a stockbroker for carrying over a bargain to the next settling day.
contemn' *v.t.* to scorn, despise.
Syn. to disdain, spurn, slight, underrate. *Ant.* to esteem, respect, admire.
con'template *v.t.* to gaze upon; meditate on; intend.—**contempla'tion** *n.*—**contem'plative** *a.* thoughtful.
contem'porary *a.* existing at, or lasting the same time; of the same age.—*n.* one existing at the same time as another.—**contempora'neous** *a.* contemporary.
contempt' *n.* scorn; contemptible *a.* mean.—**contempt'uous** *a.*
contend' *v.i.* to strive, dispute; to argue.—**conten'tion** *n.*—**conten'tious** *a.*
content' *a.* satisfied.—*v.t.* to satisfy.—**con'tent** *n.* holding capacity; *pl.* that contained.—**content'ment** *n.* happiness.
conten'tion *n.* dispute; an opinion, argument.—**conten'tious** *a.* quarrelsome.
contest' *v.t.* to dispute, fight for.—**con'test** *n.* debate; conflict, strife; competition.—**contest'ant** *n.*—**contest'able** *a.*
con'text *n.* what comes before and after a passage, words, *esp.* as fixing meaning.
contig'uous *a.* touching.—**contigu'ity** *n.*
con'tinent *a.* self-restraining; sexually chaste.—**con'tinence** *n.* self-restraint.
con'tinent *n.* one of the main land masses of the earth.—**continent'al** *a.*
contin'gent (-j-) *a.* uncertain; depending for occurrence (on); accidental.—*n.* a body of troops, an organisation, etc.—**contin'gency** *n.* chance, possibility.
contin'ue *v.t.* and *i.* to go on, carry on, last, resume.—**contin'ual** *a.*—**contin'ually** *adv.*—**contin'uance** *n.* lasting; remaining.—**continua'tion** *n.*—**continu'ity** *n.*—**contin'uous** *a.* uninterrupted.—**contin'uously** *adv.*—**contin'uum** *n.* an unchanging and continuous factor.
Syn. to stay, remain, abide, extend, protract, endure, persist. *Ant.* to cease, desist, halt, stop, pass, vanish, suspend.
contort' *v.t.* to twist out of normal shape.—**contor'tion** *n.*—**contor'tionist** *n.*
con'tour (-oor) *n.* outline or shape of anything, *esp.* mountains, coast, etc.—**contour-line** *n.* a line on a map showing uniform elevation.
con'tra- *prefix* against, as *contradict.*
con'traband *n.* forbidden traffic; smuggled goods.—**con'trabandist** *n.*
con'tracep'tion *n.* prevention of conception by artificial means.—**con'tracep'tive** *a.* and *n.* preventing conception.

con'tract *n.* a bargain; formal writing recording an agreement; an agreement enforceable by law.—**contract'** *v.i.* to enter into an agreement; to incur, become involved in; to become smaller. —**contract'ile** *a.*—**contrac'tion** *n.*—**contract'or** *n.* one making a contract, as a builder, etc.; contracting muscle.

contradict' *v.t.* to deny; be at variance with.-**contradict'ory** *a.*-**contradic'tion** *n.*

contral'to *n.* the voice, or part, next above alto; a singer of that voice, *esp.* a female (**-tos** *pl.*).

contrap'tion *n.* a makeshift, contrivance.

contrapun'tal *a.* pertaining to counterpoint.

con'trary *a.* the opposite; perverse—*n.* the exact opposite.—*adv.* in opposition. —**con'trarily** *adv.*—**contrari'ety** *n.*— **con'trariwise** *adv.*

contrast' (-â-) *v.t.* to bring out differences; set in opposition for comparison. —*v.i.* to show great difference.—**con'trast** *n.* striking difference; something showing a marked difference; placing, to bring out difference.

contravene' *v.t.* to transgress; conflict with, infringe.—**contraven'tion** *n.*

con'tretemps (kong'-tr-tong) *n.* an unexpected and embarrassing event.

contrib'ute *v.t.* to pay to a common fund; help to a common result; subscribe.—*v.i.* to give or pay or help in a common fund or effort.—**contribu'tion** *n.* —**contrib'utor** *n.* *esp.* one who writes articles for a newspaper, etc.—**contrib'utory** *a.*—**contrib'utive** *a.*

con'trite *a.* deeply sorry for wrongdoing.—**contri'tion** *n.*—**con'tritely** *adv.*

contrive' *v.t.* to devise, design; succeed in bringing about.—**contri'ver** *n.*—**contri'vance** *n.* scheme, plan, device.

control' (-ōl) *v.t.* to command; regulate; direct; check, test.—*n.* domination; restraint; direction; check.—**controll'able** (-ōl'-) *a.*—**controll'er** (-ōl'-) *n.*— **control room** *n.* room in a wireless broadcasting station, admiralty, etc.— **control' stick,** vertical lever controlling the fore-and-aft and lateral movements of an airplane; joy stick.

con'troversy *n.* dispute, debate, *esp.* a dispute in the press.—**controvert'** *v.t.* to deny, oppose.—**controver'sial** *a.*— **controver'sialist** *n.*—**controvert'ible** *a.*

con'tumacy (-tū-) *n.* stubborn disobedience.—**contuma'cious** *a.*

con'tumely (-e-li) *n.* insulting language or treatment; disgrace.—**contume'lious** *a.* *Syn.* scorn, contempt, disrespect. *Ant.* deference, esteem, regard.

contuse' (-ūz') *v.t.* to bruise.—**contu'sion** *n.* wound without breaking skin.

conun'drum *n.* a riddle, *esp.* one with a punning answer.

convales'cent *a.* recovering from illness.—*n.* a person recovering.—**convales'cence** *n.* period of recovery.

convene' *v.t.* to call together.—**conven'tion** *n.* an assembly; a treaty, agreement; a rule or practice based on agreement; an accepted usage, *esp.* one grown quite formal, deadening.—**conven'tional** *a.*—**conven'tionally** *adv.*— **conventional'ity** *n.*—**conven'tual** *a.*— **conven'ticle** *n.* a meeting-house, *esp.* of dissenters when dissent was illegal.

conve'nient *a.* handy; well-adapted to one's purpose.—**conve'niently** *adv.*— **conve'nience** *n.* something useful or helpful; lavatory.

con'vent *n.* religious community of nuns; their building.

converge' *v.i.* to approach, tend to meet.—**conver'gent** *a.*—**conver'gence** *n.*

converse' *v.i.* to talk (with).—**con'verse** *n.* talk.—**conversa'tion** *n.*—**conversa'tional** *a.*—**con'versant** *a.* familiar with.

con'verse *a.* opposite, turned ound.— *n.* the opposite, a statement with the terms of another interchanged.

conver'sion *n.* state of being converted; a spiritual awakening; change of belief; exchange into an equivalent; act of taking and using unlawfully.

convert' *v.t.* to apply to another purpose; cause to adopt a religion, an opinion.—**con'vert** *n.* converted person. —**convert'ible** *a.*—**convertibil'ity** *n.*

Syn. to change, turn, alter, appropriate, transform, transmute. *Ant.* to maintain, keep, perpetuate.

con'vex *a.* curved outwards; opposite of concave.—**convex'ity** *n.*

convey' *v.t.* carry; communicate; make over, transfer.—**convey'ance** *n.*—**convey'ancer** *n.* lawyer dealing in forms of transfer of property.—**convey'ancing** *n.*

convict' *v.t.* to prove or declare guilty. —**con'vict** *n.* a criminal undergoing penal servitude.—**convic'tion** *n.* a convicting, verdict of guilty; firm belief, state of being sure.—**convince'** *v.t.* to bring to a belief, satisfy by evidence or argument.—**convin'cing** *a.* effective (**convinced'** *p.t.* and *p.p.*).

conviv'ial *a.* festive, jovial.—**convivial'ity** *n.* *Syn.* gay, mirthful, merry. *Ant.* sad, mournful, gloomy.

convoke' *v.t.* to call together.—**convoca'tion** *n.* an assembly, *esp.* an assembly of clergy, university graduates, etc.

convolu'tion *n.* state of being coiled; a turn of a coil or spiral.—**convolu'ted** *a.* spiral, rolled.—**convol'vulus** *n.* a genus of twining plants, *esp.* bindweed.

convoy' *v.t.* to escort for protection, as ships, war supplies, etc.—**con'voy** *n.* a party (of ships, troops, lorries, etc.) convoying or convoyed.

convulse' *v.t.* to shake violently; affect with violent involuntary contractions

of the muscles.—**convuls'ively** *adv.*—**convul'sion** *n.* violent disturbance.
co'ny, co'ney *n.* a rock-badger; rabbit.
coo *n.* cry of doves.—*v.i.* make such cry (**cooed** *p.t./p.p.*—**coo'ing** *pr. p.*).
coo'ee *n.* cry used at long distance by Australians.—*v.i.* to make this cry (**coo'eed** *p.t.* and *p.p.*—**coo'eeing** *pres. p.*)
cook *n.* one who prepares food for the table.—*v.i.* to act as cook; to undergo cooking.—*v.t.* to prepare (food) for the table, *esp.* by heat; (*sl.*) to falsify accounts, etc.—**cook'ery** *n.*—**cook'er** *n.*
cool *a.* moderately cold; unexcited; lacking friendliness or interest.—*v.t.* and *i.* to make or become cool.—*n.* cool time, place, etc.—**cool'ness** *n.*—**cool'er** *n.*
cool'ie *n.* a native labourer in the East.
coon' *n.* a racoon; (*col.*) a negro; a shrewd fellow.
coop *n.* a pen for fowls.—*n.* to shut up in a coop; to confine.—**coop'er** *n.* one who makes casks.—**coop'erage** *n.*
co-op'erate *v.i.* to work together.—**co-opera'tion** *n.* working together; production or distribution by co-operators who share the profits.—**co-op'erant** *a.* and *n.*—**co-op'erative** *a.*—**co-op'erator** *n.*
co-opt' *v.t.* to elect, as a member, by votes of the first members.
co-ord'inate *a.* equal in degree, status, etc.—*v.t.* to place in the same rank; to bring into order as parts of a whole.—*n.* a co-ordinate thing.—**co-ordina'tion** *n.*
coot *n.* a small black waterfowl.
copal' (kōpl') *n.* juice of certain tropical trees, used for varnishing.
cope *n.* an ecclesiastical vestment.—*v.t.* to cover the top of a wall.—**co'ping** *n.* the top course of a wall.
cope *v.i.* to contend, deal with.
co'per *n.* a dealer (chiefly in *horse-coper*).
co'pious *a.* plentiful, abundant.—**co'piously** *adv.*—**co'piousness** *n.*
Syn. ample, plenteous, full, diffuse. *Ant.* insufficient, scarce, rare, niggardly.
copp'er *n.* a reddish malleable ductile metal; bronze money; a large vessel for boiling clothes.—*v.t.* to cover with copper.—**copp'erplate** *n.* a plate of copper for engraving or etching; a print from such plate; copybook writing.—**copp'ersmith** *n.* one who works in copper.
copp'ice, copse *n.* a wood of small trees cut periodically.
cop'ra *n.* dried coconut kernels.
cop'ula *n.* a word acting as a connecting link in a sentence; a connection (**-ulas** *pl.*).—**cop'ulate** *v.i.* to unite sexually.—**copula'tion** *n.* **cop'ulative** *a.*
cop'y *n.* an imitation; single specimen of a book; a piece of writing for a learner to imitate; matter for printing.—*v.t.* to make a copy of, to imitate (**cop'ied** *p.t./p.p.*—**cop'ying** *pr. p.*).—**cop'y-hold** *n.* a form of land-tenure with *copy* of the manor court-roll as title.—**cop'y-right** *n.* legal exclusive right to print and publish a book, article, work of art, etc.—*a.* protected by copyright.—*v.t.* to protect by copyright.—**copy'ist** *n.*—**copy'ing-pen'cil** *n.* an indelible pencil.—**copy-wri'ter** *n.* writer of advertisements.
coquette' (-ket') *n.* a woman who plays with men's affections.—**coquett'ish** *a.*—**coquet'** *v.i.*—**co'quetry** *n.*
cor'acle *n.* a boat of wicker covered with skins.
cor'al *n.* a hard substance made by sea polyps and forming pink, red or white growths, islands, reefs; an ornament or toy of coral.—**cor'alline** *a.*
corb'el *n.* a stone or timber projection from a wall to support something.
cord *n.* thin rope or thick string; a rib on cloth, a ribbed fabric; a measure of cut wood, usually 128 cub. ft.—*v.t.* to fasten with cord.—**cord'age** *n.*
cord'ial *a.* hearty, sincere, warm.—*n.* a stimulating medicine or drink.—**cord'ially** *adv.*—**cordial'ity** *n.*
cor'dite *n.* a smokeless explosive.
cord'on *n.* a chain of troops or police; an ornamental cord or badge.
cor'duroy (-doo-) *n.* a thick cotton stuff, corded or ribbed on the surface; in N. Amer. and Australia a road of logs laid across the track.—*v.t.* to build such a road.
core *n.* the horny seed-case of the apple and other fruits; central or innermost part of anything.
co-respon'dent *n.* a person proceeded against together with the respondent in a divorce suit.
cor'gi (-gē) *n.* a small Welsh dog.
Corin'thian (-th-) *a.* of Corinth; of the Corinthian order of architecture, the most ornate Greek.—*n.* a native of Corinth; a man of fashion.
cork *n.* the bark of the cork-oak; a round piece of it used as a stopper.—*v.t.* to stop up with a cork; to stop up generally.—**cork'y** *a.* light, buoyant.—**cork'screw** *n.* a tool for pulling out corks.—**cork'age** *n.* a charge for opening bottles.—**cor'ker** *n.* (*sl.*) a superb or wonderful thing; a skilful person.
corm' *n.* an underground stem resembling a bulb, *e.g.* crocus.
cor'morant *n.* a voracious sea-bird.
corn *n.* grain, fruit of cereals; a grain; in N. Amer., maize.—*v.t.* to preserve (meat) with salt.—**corn'crake** *n.* a bird, the landrail.—**corn'flour** *n.* finely ground flour of Indian corn or other grain.—**corn'flower** *n.* a blue flower growing in cornfields.—**corn'-stalk** *n.* in Australia, a young person born in New South Wales, *esp.* if well developed.
corn *n.* a horny growth on foot or toe.
corn'ea *n.* the horny membrane covering the front of the eye.
corn'er *n.* point where two lines, walls,

streets, etc., meet; an angle, projection; a nook; buying up all the stocks of a commodity.—*v.t.* to drive into a position of difficulty; to establish a monopoly.
corn'et *n.* a trumpet with valves; (*mil.*) officer in a cavalry troop who formerly carried the colours.
corn'ice *n.* a projecting moulding near the top of a wall or pillar.
cornuco'pia *n.* a symbol of plenty, consisting of a goat's horn overflowing with fruit and flowers (**-pias** *pl.*).
coroll'a *n.* a flower's envelope of petals.
coroll'ary *n.* a proposition that follows without proof from another proved.
coro'na *n.* the flat projecting part of a cornice; a halo around a heavenly body; in wireless, blue luminous discharge from transmitting aerial at high voltage (**-nas, -næ** *pl.*).—**Coro'na Austral'is**, the Southern Crown, a constellation of twelve stars in the S. Hemisphere.
corona'tion *n.* ceremony of crowning.
cor'oner *n.* an officer who holds inquests on bodies of persons supposed killed by violence, accident, etc.—**cor'onership** *n.*
cor'onet *n.* a small crown.
corp'oral *n.* army non-commissioned officer below the rank of a sergeant.
corp'oral *a.* of the body.—**cor'porate** *a.* *Syn.* corporeal, physical, bodily. *Ant.* incorporeal, spiritual, ghostly, immaterial, mental.
cor'porate state *n.* the fascist theory of a state composed of more or less independent guilds or corporations.
corpora'tion *n.* a body of persons legally authorised to act as an individual; authorities of a town or city; (*sl.*) large paunch.—**corp'orate** *a.*
corpor'eal *a.* of the body, material.
corps (kor) *n.* a military force, body of troops (**corps** (korz) *pl.*).—**corpse** *n.* dead body of man.
corp'ulent *a.* bulky of body, very stout. —**corp'ulence** *n.* fatness.
corp'uscle (-usl) *n.* a minute organism or particle, *esp.* the red and white corpuscles of the blood.
corral' *n.* an enclosure for cattle, or for defence.—*v.t.* to drive into a corral.
correct' *v.t.* to set right; punish; neutralise.—*a.* right, exact, accurate, in accordance with facts or a standard.—**correct'ly** *adv.*—**correc'tion** *n.*—**correct'ive** *n.* and *a.*—**correct'ness** *n.*
cor'relate *v.t.* to bring into mutual relation.—*n.* either of two things or words necessarily implying the other.—**correla'tion** *n.*—**correl'ative** *a.*
correspond' *v.i.* to exchange letters; to answer or agree with in some respect.—**correspond'ence** *n.*—**correspond'ent** *n.*
cor'ridor *n.* a passage in a building, railway-train, etc.
corrigen'dum (-jen'-) *n.* a thing to be corrected (**corrigen'da** *pl.*).
corrob'orate *v.t.* to confirm, support (statement, etc.).—**corrobora-tion** *n.*—**corrob'orative** *a.*(**corrob'orated** *p.t.*/*p.p.*).
corroboree' *n.* an aboriginal Australian war-dance and festivity.
corrode' *v.t.* to eat away, eat into the surface of.—**corro'sive** *a.*—**corro'sion** *n.*
cor'rugated *a.* wrinkled, rigged, furrowed.—**corrugation** *n.*
corrupt' *v.t.* to make rotten; make evil; bribe.—*v.i.* to rot.—*a.* tainted with vice; influenced by bribery; spoilt, by mistakes, altered for the worse (of words, literary passages, etc.).—**corrupt'ly** *adv.* —**corrupt'ible** *a.*—**corruptibil'ity** *n.*—**corrup'tion** *n.* *Syn.* to defile, pollute, debase, vitiate, pervert, contaminate, deprave, spoil. *Ant.* purify, cleanse, refine.
cors'air *n.* a pirate.
cors'elet *n.* armour to cover the trunk.
cors'et *n.* a stiffened inner bodice; stays.
cortege' (-tazh') *n.* a train of attendants, a procession, *esp.* a funeral procession.
cor'tex *n.* bark of a tree; outer layers of an internal organ; layer of grey matter over most of the brain (**cor'tices** *pl.*).—**cor'tical** *a.* of bark or rind.
cor'tisone *n.* synthetic hormone, which has given promising results in the treatment of rheumatoid arthritis, etc.
corund'um *n.* a mineral aluminium oxide of great hardness, known as sapphire when blue, and ruby when red.
cor'uscate *v.i.* to sparkle, flash.—**corusca'tion** *n.*
corvette' *n.* in modern times a small warship of trawler design produced for convoy escort duties in World War 2.
cosmet'ic *n.* a preparation to beautify the complexion or the hair.
cos'mic (koz'-) *a.* relating to the universe; of the vastness of the universe.—**cosmog'ony** *n.* theory of the universe and its creation.—**cosmol'ogy** *n.* the science or study of the universe.—**cosmolo'gical** *a.*-**cosmol'ogist**-*n.*-**cosmog'raphy** *n.* the description or mapping of the universe.—**cosmog'rapher** *n.*—**cosmograph'ic** *a.*—**cos'mos** *n.* the universe; ordered system as opposed to *chaos*.
cosmopol'itan *a.* relating to all parts of the world; having the world as one's country; free from national prejudice.-*n.* —**cosmopol'itanism** *n.*—**cosmop'olite** *n.*
coss'et *v.t.* to pamper.
cost *v.t.* to entail the payment, or loss, or sacrifice of; have as price.—*n.* price; expenditure of time, labour, etc.—*pl.* expenses of a lawsuit.—**cost'ing** *n.* the system of calculating cost of production. —**cost'ly** *a.* of great price or value; involving much expenditure, loss, etc.—**cost'liness** *n.* great cost.
cos'tard *n.* a large ribbed apple.
cos'ter, cos'termonger *n.* one who sells fruit, fish, etc., from a barrow.

cos'tive *a.* constipated.
cos'tume *n.* style of dress; outer clothes for a woman; theatrical clothes.—**costu'mier** *n.* lady's tailor.
co'sy (-z-) *a.* snug, comfortable, sheltered. —*n.* a covering to keep a teapot hot.
cot *n.* a small house.—**cott'ar** *n.*
cot *n.* a child's bed; a swinging bed on board ship; a light or folding bed.
cote *n.* a shelter for animals or birds.
co'terie *n.* a set or circle of persons.
cotill'ion, cotill'on (-lyon) *n.* a dance.
cott'age *n.* a small house.—**cott'ager** *n.*
cott'on *n.* a plant; the white downy fibrous covering of its seeds; thread or cloth made of this fibre.—**cott'on-cake** *n.* compressed cotton seed, with the oil expressed, used as fodder.—**cotton'-gin** *n.* a machine for separating seeds from cotton.—**cotton'ocracy** *n.* the heads of cotton trade.—**cotton'ous** *a.* like cotton. —**cotton-wool** *n.* thick fluffy mass of hairs of cotton-plant after cleansing and extraction of seeds, used as packing and for surgical purposes.
cotyle'don *n.* primary leaf of plant embryos.—**co'tyle'donous** *a.*
couch *v.t.* to put into (words); to lower (a lance) for action; to cause to lie down. —*v.i.* to lie down, crouch.—*n.* a piece of furniture for reclining on; a bed.
cough (kof) *v.i.* to expel air from the lungs with effort and noise.—*n.* act of coughing; an ailment of coughing.
couloir' (kōōl-wor') *n.* a dredging machine; a deep gorge.
coul'omb *n.* (*elect.*) unit of quantity at the rate of one ampère in one second.
coun'cil *n.* any deliberative or administrative body; one of its meetings.—**coun'cillor** *n.* member of council.
coun'sel *n.* deliberation or debate; advice; intentions; a barrister or barristers.—*v.t.* to advise, recommend.—**coun'sellor** *n.* one who gives advice.
count *v.t.* to reckon, number; to include; to consider to be.—*v.i.* to be reckoned in; to depend (on); to be of importance. —*n.* a reckoning; an item in a list of charges or indictment; an act of counting.—**count'less** *a.*—**count'ing-house** *n.* a room or building for bookkeeping.—**count-muster** *n.* in Australia, a round-up of stock for counting.
count *n.* a foreign title corresponding to British earl.—**count'ess** *n. fem.* wife or widow of a count or earl.
count'enance *n.* the face; its expression; patronage.—*v.t.* to give support.
count'er *n.* the table of a bank, shop, etc., on which money is paid, etc.; a disc used for counting, *esp.* in card games.
count'er *n.* curved part of ship's stern.
count'er *adv.* in the opposite direction; contrary.—*v.t.* to oppose, contradict.
count'er *n.* (*fencing, etc.*) a parry.—*v.t.* and *i.* to parry; retort.
counter- *prefix* used to make compounds with meaning of reversed, opposite, rival, retaliatory.—**counteract'** *v.t.* neutralise or hinder.—**counterac'tion** *n.*—**count'er-attack** *v.t.* and *i.* and *n.* attack after an enemy's advance.—**count'erattrac'tion** *n.*—**counterbal'ance** *n.* a weight balancing another.–**count'erblast** *n.* energetic declaration in answer. —**count'erclaim** *n.*—**count'er-clockwise** *adv.* and *a.*—**count'er-irr'itant** *n.*—**count'ermarch** *v.i.*—**count'ermine** *v.i.*—**count'erplot** *n.*—**count'er-reforma'tion** *n.* —**count'er-revolut'ion** *n.* a revolt by the Right; reactionary revolution.—**count'er-revolu'tionary** *n.* and *a.*—**count'er-revolu'tionist** *n.*
count'erfeit (-fēt) *a.* forged.—*n.* an imitation, forgery.—*v.t.* to imitate with intent to deceive; forge.–**count'erfeiter** *n.*
Syn. of *a.*, false, imitated, sham, hypocritical. *Ant.* true, genuine, sincere.
count'erfoil *n.* part of a cheque, receipt, etc., kept as a record.
countermand' *v.t.* to cancel (an order).
count'erpane *n.* a coverlet or quilt.
count'erpart *n.* something so like another as to be mistaken for it; something complementary of another.
count'erpoint *n.* melody added as accompaniment to a given melody.
count'ersign (-sīn) *n.* a signal used in answer to another.—*v.t.* to sign a document already signed by another.
count'ess *n. see* **count.**
coun'try (kun'-) *n.* a region, district; the territory of a nation; land of birth, residence, etc.; rural district as opposed to town; a nation.—**coun'tryside** *n.* any rural district.—**coun'trified** *a.* rural in manner or appearance (**coun'tries** *pl.*).
count'y *n.* a division of a country.
coup (kōō) *n.* a successful stroke.
coupé' (kōō-) *n.* two-seater motor-car with enclosed body.
coup'le (kup'l) *n.* two of same kind, a pair; a leash for two hounds.—*v.t.* to tie (hounds) together; to fasten together; to connect in the mind.—*v.i.* to join, associate.—**coup'ler** *n.*—**coup'ling** *n.*—**coup'let** *n.* a pair of lines of verse, *esp.* rhyming and of equal length.
cou'pon (kōō'-) *n.* a detachable ticket entitling the holder to something.
cour'age (kur'-) *n.* bravery, boldness.—**coura'geous** *a.*—**coura'geously** *adv.*
Syn. daring, hardihood, intrepidity; of "courageous," valiant, intrepid, valorous. *Ant.* cowardice, timidity; of *a.*, cowardly, timid, faint-hearted.
cou'rier (kōō'-) *n.* an express messenger; an attendant on travellers.
course (kors) *n.* movement or run in space or time; direction of movement; successive development; line of conduct; series of lectures, etc.; any of the successive parts of a dinner; a continuous

line of masonry at a level in a building; a match between greyhounds pursuing a hare.—*v.t.* to hunt.—*v.i.* to run swiftly, gallop about.—**cours'er** *n.* a swift horse.
court (kort) *n.* a space enclosed by buildings; houses enclosing a yard opening on to a street; a section of a museum, etc.; area marked off or enclosed for playing various games; the retinue and establishment of a sovereign; an assembly held by a sovereign; a body with judicial powers, the place where they sit, one of their sittings; attention, homage. —*v.t.* to seek; woo.—**court'ier** (-yer) *n.* one who frequents a royal court.—**court'ly** *a.* ceremoniously polite; characteristic of a court.—**court'liness** *n.*—**court-mar'tial** *n.* a court of officers for trying naval or military or Air Force offences (**courts-mar'tial** *pl.*).—**court'-yard** *n.* space enclosed by buildings.
court'-card *n.* a king, queen, or knave.
courtesan' (kor-ti-zan') *n.* a prostitute, *esp.* highly-placed or refined.
cour'tesy (kur'-) *n.* politeness of manner or action.—**court'eous** (kurt'-) *a.* polite.—**court'eously** *adv.*—**courtesy title,** one to which there is no valid claim.
Syn. urbanity, affability, courteousness. *Ant.* incivility, impoliteness, disrespect.
court'ship *n.* wooing.
cous'in (kuz'-) *n.* the son or daughter of an uncle or aunt.
cove *n.* small inlet, a sheltered bay.
cov'enant (ku-) *n.* a contract, a mutual agreement; a compact.—*v.t.* to agree to by a covenant.—*v.i.* to enter into a covenant.—**cov'enanter** *n.*
cov'er (ku-) *v.t.* to place or spread over; enclose, include; shield; counter-balance. —*n.* lid, wrapper, envelope, binding, screen, anything which covers.; funds to meet possible liability or loss.—*v.t.* in journalism, to report, or be responsible for reporting, certain events. —**cov'ert** *a.* secret, veiled.—*n.* a thicket, a place sheltering game.—**cov'ertly** *adv.*
cov'erlet (ku-) *n.* top covering on a bed.
cov'et (ku-) *v.t.* to long to possess, *esp.* what belongs to another.—**cov'etous** *a.* —**cov'etousness** *n.*
cov'ey (ku-) *n.* a brood of partridges or quail, *esp.* flying together (**cov'eys** *pl.*).
cow *n.* female ox, elephant, whale, etc. (**cows, kine** *pl.*).—**cow'boy** *n.* herdsman in charge of cattle on the western plains (*sl.* **cow-pun'cher**) U.S.—**cow'-pox** *n.* a disease of cows, the source of vaccine.
cow *v.t.* to frighten into submission.
cow'ard *n.* one given to fear or fainthearted.—**cow'ardly** *a.*—**cow'ardice** *n.*
Syn. of "cowardly," timorous, mean, pusillanimous, craven. *Ant.* courageous, valiant, bold, intrepid.
cow'er *v.i.* to crouch in fear.
cowl *n.* a monk's cloak; its hood; hooded top for a chimney; front part of car carrying the windscreen and dashboard.—**cowl'ing** *n.* in aviation, casing of radiator or cylinders to direct air stream.
cow'rie *n.* a small shell used as money in parts of Africa and Asia.
cow'slip *n.* a species of primrose.
cox'comb *n.* one given to showing off.
cox'swain (kok'sn), **cox** *n.* the steersman of a boat, *esp.* one in permanent charge of a boat.—**cox** *v.t.* and *i.*
coy *a.* shy; slow to respond, *esp.* to love-making.—**coy'ly** *adv.*—**coy'ness** *n.*
coyo'te (-ō'ti) *n.* N. Amer. prairie-wolf.
coz'en (ku-) *v.t.* to cheat.—**coz'enage** *n.*
crab *n.* an edible crustacean with ten legs.—**crabb'ed** *a.* perverse; bad-tempered; of writing, hard to read, cramped.
crab' *n.* a wild apple of sour taste.—*v.t.* to criticise spitefully.
crack *v.t.* to break; to break with sharp noise; to cause to make a sharp noise, as of whip, rifle, etc.—*v.i.* to make a sharp noise; to split; of the voice, to lose clearness when changing from boy's to man's.—*n.* a sharp explosive noise; a split; a flaw.—*a.* smart, of great reputation, e.g., crack shot.—**crack'er** *n.* an explosive firework; thin dry biscuit.—**crack'ers** *n. pl.* in S. Africa, sheepskin trousers worn by settlers.—**crac'kle** *n.* sound of repeated small cracks, e.g., of distant rifle-fire, crumpled stiff paper, etc.—*v.i.* to make this sound.—**crack'-ling** *n.* the crisp skin of roast pork.—**crack'nel** *n.* a crisp biscuit.—**crack-pot** *n.* (*sl.*) an eccentric, *esp.* someone seized with a delusive mania; a crank.—*a.* impractical; crazy.—**crack-up** *n.* (*sl.*) a catastrophic accident, *esp.* of an aircraft; a nervous breakdown.
cra'dle *n.* an infant's bed on rockers; *fig.* origin or home; supporting frame. —*v.t.* to lay as in a cradle.
craft *n.* skill, cunning; a manual art; a skilled trade; the members of a trade.—**crafts'man** *n.*—**crafts'manship** *n.*—**craft'y** *a.* cunning.—**craft'ily** *adv.*
craft *n.* a vessel of any kind for carriage by water or air; ships collectively.
crag *n.* a steep rugged rock.—**cragg'y** *a.* —**crags'man** *n.* a rock-climber.
cram *v.t.* to fill quite full; pack tightly; feed to excess; prepare quickly for examination.—*n.* a close-packed state; rapid preparation for examination; information so got.—**cramm'er** *n.*
cramp *n.* painful muscular contraction; a clamp for holding masonry, timber, etc., together.—*v.t.* to hem in, to hinder, keep within too narrow limits.
cran *n*, a measure of herrings, holding about 750 fish; hence a basket, *esp.* for fish and soft fruit.
cran'berry *n.* the red berry of a dwarf shrub (**cran'berries** *pl.*).
crane *n.* large wading bird with long

legs, neck and bill; machine for moving heavy weights.—*v.i.* to stretch the neck for better seeing.

cra'nium *n.* the skull (**-niums, -nia** *pl.*).—**cra'niology** *n.* science of structure of skull as significant of race.—**craniom'etry** *n.* the study of the measurements of the human head.—**craniomet'ric** *a.*—**craniomet'rically** *adv.*—**craniom'etrist** *n.*

crank *n.* a right angled lever for turning a main shaft, etc.; a fad; a faddist.—*v.t.* and *i.* to turn, wind.—**crank'y** *a.*

crank *a.* of a ship, easily capsized.

crann'y *n.* a small opening.—**crann'ied** *a.*

crape *n.* gauzy wrinkled fabric, usually of black silk for mourning.

crash *n.* a violent fall or impact with loud noise; a burst of mixed loud sound, e.g. of thunder; sudden collapse or downfall.—*v.i.* to make a crash; fall, strike with, a crash; to collapse; of an aeroplane, to crash to earth.—**crash helmet** *n.* padded head covering worn to protect the head from accident.

crash *n.* coarse linen for towels.

crass *a.* grossly stupid; gross.

crate *n.* a large packing case.

cra'ter *n.* mouth of a volcano; a bowl-shaped cavity, *esp.* one made by the explosion of a large shell, bomb, etc.

cravat' *n.* a neckcloth; a necktie.

crave *v.t.* and *i.* to have a very strong desire for; to ask.—**cra'ving** *n.*

cra'ven *a.* cowardly.—*n.* a coward.

crawl *v.i.* to move along the ground on the belly or on hands and knees; to move very slowly; to move stealthily; to swim with the crawl-stroke.—*n.* a crawling or slow motion.—**crawl'er** *n.*

cray'fish, craw'fish *n.* a freshwater crustacean like a small lobster.

cray'on *n.* a stick of coloured chalk; a picture made with crayons.

cra'zy *a.* rickety, falling to pieces; cracked; insane, very foolish; madly eager (for).—**craze** *v.t.* make crazy.—*n.* general or individual mania.—**crazy pavement,** path surfaced with flat irregularly shaped slabs of stone.

creak *n.* a harsh grating noise.—*v.i.*

cream *n.* the oily part of milk; the best part of anything.—*v.i.* to form cream.—*v.t.* to take cream from; to take the best part from.—**cream'y** *a.*—**cream'ery** *n.* a butter and cheese factory; a dairy.

crease (-s) *n.* a line made by folding; a wrinkle.—*v.t.* and *i.* to make, develop, creases; in cricket, line showing bowler's and batsman's positions.

create' (krē-āt') *v.t.* to bring into being; give rise to; make.—**crea'tion** (-ē-ā'-) *n.*—**crea'tive** (-ē-ā'-) *a.*—**crea'tor** (-ē-ā'-) *n.*—**crea'ture** (krē'tyer) *n.* thing created, living being; dependent, tool.

creche (krāsh) *n.* a public baby nursery.

cre'dence *n.* belief, credit; side-table for elements of the eucharist before consecration.—**creden'tials** *n. pl.* letters of introduction.—**cred'ible** *a.* believable.

cred'it *n.* belief, trust; good name; reputation; influence, honour or power based on the trust of others; trust in another's ability to pay; money at one's disposal in a bank, etc.; the side of a book on which such sums are entered.—*v.t.* to believe; to put on credit side of an account; to attribute, believe that a person has.—**cred'ulous** *a.* gullible—**credit line,** a line of type acknowledging permission to reproduce a photograph, etc.; a " picture credit."—**cred'itable** *a.* bringing honour.—**cred'itably** *adv.*—**cred'itor** *n.* one to whom debt is due.

creed *n.* a system of religious belief; a summary of Christian doctrine; a system of beliefs, opinions, principles.

creek *n.* a narrow inlet on the sea-coast; in Australia, a small river, a brook.

creel *n.* an angler's basket.

creep *v.i.* to move like a snake; to move stealthily; to feel a shrinking, shivering sensation, due to fear, or repugnance (**crept** *p.t.* and *p.p.*).—**creep'er** *n.* a creeping or climbing plant.—**creep'y** *a.* uncanny, causing the flesh to creep.

crema'tion *n.* burning as a means of disposing of corpses; an act of this.—**cremate'** *v.t.*—**cremato'rium** *n.* a place for cremation; refuse-destructor.

Cremo'na (krē-) *n.* a superior kind of violin made in Cremona (Italy).

cre'ole *n.* a native of the W. Indies or Sp. America with European ancestors.

cre'osote *n.* an oily antiseptic liquid.—*v.t.* to coat or impregnate with creosote.

crêpe (krāp) *n.* a fabric with a rough surface.—**crêpe-de-chine** *n.* fine silk crape.—**crêpe rub'ber** *n.* rough-surfaced rubber for soles of shoes, etc.

crep'itate *v.i.* crackle.—**crepita'tion** *n.*

crepus'cular *a.* pertaining to twilight.

crescen'do (-sh-) *a., adv.* and *n.* increase of loudness, *esp.* in music.

cres'cent *n.* the moon as seen on the first or last quarter; any figure of this shape; a row of houses on a curve.—*a.* growing, increasing.

cress *n.* plant with edible leaves.

cress'et *n.* a fire-basket slung as a beacon and lit as a torch.

crest *n.* comb or tuft on an animal's head; plume on top of a helmet; top of mountain, ridge, wave, etc.; a badge above the shield of a coat-of-arms, also used separately on seal, plate, etc.—*v.i.* to crown.—*v.t.* to reach the top of.—**crest'fallen** *a.* cast down by failure.

creta'ceous (-shus) *a.* chalky.

cret'in *n.* a deformed idiot.—**cret'inism** *n.*—**cret'inous** *a.*

cretonne' *n.* unglazed cotton cloth printed in colours.

crev'ice (-is) *n.* a fissure.—**crevasse'** *n.* a deep open chasm in a glacier.

crew (-ōō) *n.* a ship's or boat's company, excluding passengers; a gang or set.
crib *n.* a barred rack for fodder; a manger; a child's bed with barred sides; the cards thrown out at cribbage; a plagiarism; a translation.—*v.t.* to confine in small space; to copy unfairly.—**cribb'age** *n.* a card game.
crick *n.* spasm or cramp, *esp.* in neck.
crick'et *n.* a chirping insect.
crick'et *n.* an open-air game played with bats, ball, and wickets.—**crick'eter** *n.*
crime *n.* a violation of the law (usually of a serious offence); *military*, an offence against regulations.—*v.t.* to charge (in army) with an offence against the regulations.—**crim'inal** *a.* and *n.*—**crim'inally** *adv.*—**criminal'ity** *n.*—**criminol'ogy** *n.* study of crime and criminals.
crimp *v.t.* to pinch with tiny parallel pleats; to curl the hair.
crimp *n.* an agent who procures men for service as sailors or soldiers by decoying or force.
crim'son (-z-) *a.* of rich deep red.—*n.* the colour.—*v.t.* and *i.* to turn crimson.
cringe *v.i.* to shrink; behave obsequiously (**cring'ing** *pres. p.*).
crin'gle (-g'l) *n.* a ring, loop or eyelet at the edge of a sail.
crin'kle (kring'kl) *v.t.* to wrinkle.—*v.i.* to wrinkle.—*n.* a wrinkle, winding.
crin'oline (-lēn) *n.* a hooped petticoat.
crip'ple *n.* a lame person.—*v.t.* to maim or disable (**crip'pled** *p.t.* and *p.p.*).
cri'sis *n.* turning point, decisive moment, *esp.* in illness; time of acute danger or suspense (**cri'ses** *pl.*).
crisp *a.* brittle but of firm consistence; brisk, decided; clear-cut; crackling; of hair, curly.—**crisp'ness** *n.*
crite'rion (kri-) *n.* a standard of judgment, test (**crite'ria** *pl.*).
crit'ical *a.* skilled in, or given to, judging, fault-finding; of great importance, decisive.—**crit'ic** *n.* one who passes judgment; a writer expert in judging works of literature, art, etc.—**crit'icism** *n.* judgment; fault-finding.—**crit'ically** *adv.*—**crit'icise** *v.t.*—**critique'** (-ēk) *n.* a critical essay, a carefully written criticism. *Syn.* exact, captious, censorious. *Ant.* vague, indefinite, loose, uncritical.
croak *v.i.* to utter a deep hoarse cry, as a raven, frog; to talk dismally, grumble. —*n.* such cry.—**croak'er** *n.*
cro'chet (-shā) *n.* a kind of knitting done with a hooked needle.—*v.t.* and *i.* to do such work.—**ing** *pres. p.*
crock *n.* jar or pot; broken piece of earthenware; an old broken-down horse.—**crock'ery** *n.* earthenware.
croc'odile (krok'-) *n.* a large amphibious reptile.—**croc'odile-tears,** hypocritical pretence of grief.
cro'cus *n.* a small bulbous plant with yellow or purple flowers (**cro'cuses** *pl.*).
croft *n.* small piece of arable land; a small-holding, *esp.* in Scotland.—**croft'er** *n.* one who works a croft.
crom'lech (-lek) *n.* a prehistoric structure of a flat stone resting on two upright ones.
crone *n.* a withered old woman.
cronk *a.* in Australia, of racehorse, ill, unfit to race; doped.
cro'ny *n.* an intimate friend.
crook *n.* a hooked staff; any sharp turn; criminal, swindler.—*v.t.* to bend into a hook.—**crook'ed** *a.* bent; deformed; dishonest.
croon *n.* a long continued murmuring.—*v.t.* and *i.* to sing softly.—**croon'er** *n.* one who croons songs.—**croon'ing** *n.*
crop *n.* year's produce of a farm, field, country, etc.; a harvest, *lit.* or *fig.*; a pouch in a bird's gullet; stock of a whip; a hunting whip; a cutting of the hair short, a closely-cut head of hair.—*v.t.* and *i.* to poll or clip; to bite or eat down; to raise produce or occupy land with it.—**crop'eared** *a.* with clipped ears; with hair short to show ears.—**cropp'er** *n.* a fall on the head; heavy fall.
cro'quet (-kā) *n.* a lawn game played with balls, mallets and hoops.
croquette' (-ket') *n.* a fried ball of minced meat, fish, etc.
cro'sier (-zhyer) *n.* a bishop's staff.
cross *n.* a stake with a transverse bar, used for crucifixion.—**the Cross,** that on which Christ suffered; a model or picture of this; the symbol of the Christian faith; an affliction, misfortune, annoyance; any thing or mark in the shape of a cross; an intermixture of breeds.—*v.t.* to place so as to intersect; to make the sign of the cross on or over; to pass across; to meet and pass; to mark with lines across, to thwart; oppose; to modify breed of animals or plants by intermixture.—*v.i.* to intersect; pass over.—*a.* transverse; intersecting; contrary; adverse; out of temper.—**cross'ly** *adv.*—**cross'-bill** *n.* a bird whose mandibles cross when closed.—**cross'bow** *n.* a bow fixed across a wooden shoulder-stock.—**cross cut** *v.t.* to cut across; *n.* shortened path.—**cross-exam'ine** *v.t.* to examine a witness already examined by the other side.—**cross'ing** *n.* an intersection of roads, rails, etc.; a part of street kept clear for foot passengers to cross.—**cross'ing-sweeper** *n.* a person who cleans a crossing in a street.—**cross-pollina'tion** *n.* the transfer of pollen from one flower to the stigma of another by hand, insects or wind.—**cross-section** *n.* (1) cutting across; (2) plane exposed by cutting across; (3) (*fig.*) representative sample. — **cross-stitch** *n.* type of embroidery stitch made by two stitches crossing.—**cross'wise** *adv.*—**cross'word puzzle** *n.* a puzzle built up of inter-

secting words, of which some letters are common to two or more words, the words being indicated by clues.
crotch'et *n.* musical symbol; square bracket [ ]; fad.—**crotch'ety** *a.*
crouch *v.i.* to bend low for hiding, or to spring, or servilely.
croup (-ōō-) *n.* a throat-disease of children; a horse's rump.
croup'ier (-ōō-) *n.* a raker-in of the money on a gaming-table; the vice-chairman of a dinner.
crou'ton (kroo'-) *n.* a little cube of toast used in soup.
crow (-o) *n.* a black carrion-eating bird. —**crow's nest** *n.* a cylindrical look-out shelter fixed to ship's masthead.
crow (-ō), **crow-bar** *n.* iron bar used as lever.—**crow'foot** *n.* a zinc electrode in certain batteries.
crow (-ō) *v.i.* to utter the cock's cry; to exult.—*n.* the cry of the cock.
crow (-ō) *v.t.* in S. Africa, to dig holes in the ground with a sharp-pointed stick.
crowd *v.i.* to flock together.—*v.t.* to cram, pack; fill with people.—**crowd out,** exclude by excess already in.—*n.* a throng, large number.
crown *n.* a monarch's headdress; a wreath for the head; royal power; a British coin of five shillings; various foreign coins; the top of the head; a summit or topmost part; completion or perfection of anything.—*v.t.*
cru'cial (krōō'shl) *a.* decisive, critical.
cru'cible *n.* a melting-pot.
cru'cify *v.t.* to put to death on a cross (**-ified** *p.t.* and *p.p.*—**-ifying** *pres. p.*).—**crucifix'ion** *n.*—**cru'cifix** *n.* an image of Christ on the cross (**-fixes** *pl.*).
crude (-ōō-) *a.* in the natural or raw state; rough, unfinished.—**cru'dity** *n.*
cru'el (-ōō-) *a.* delighting in or callous to others' pain.—**cru'elty** *n.*—**cru'elly** *adv.*
Syn. barbarous, severe, unmerciful. *Ant.* kind, gentle, merciful, humane.
cru'et (-ōō-) *n.* a set of containers for salt, pepper, etc.
cruise (-ōōz) *v.i.* to sail about.—*n.* a cruising voyage.—**cruis'er** *n.* a warship of light or medium displacement and high speed.
crumb (-m) *n.* a small particle, a fragment; the soft part of bread.—*v.t.* to reduce to, or cover with crumbs.
crum'ble *v.t.* and *i.* to break into small fragments; decay (**crum'bled** *p.t.*/*p.p.*).
Syn. to crush, moulder, perish. *Ant.* to consolidate, flourish, endure.
crum'pet *n.* a flat soft batter-cake.
crum'ple *v.t.* and *i.* to make or become crushed, wrinkled.—**crum'pled** *a.* crushed, creased; bent, curled.
crunch *n.* sound made by chewing crisp food, treading on gravel, etc.—*v.t.* and *i.* to chew, tread, etc., with this sound.
crupp'er *n.* a strap holding back a saddle by passing round a horse's tail; hindquarters of a horse.
cru'ral *a.* of, shaped like a leg.
crusade' *n.* a medieval Christian war to recover the Holy Land from the Turks; a campaign against evil.—*v.i.* to engage in a crusade.—**crusa'der** *n.*
cruse (-ōōz) *n.* a small earthen pôt.
crush *v.t.* to compress so as to break, bruise, crumple; break to small pieces; defeat utterly.—*n.* an act of crushing; a crowded mass of persons, etc.
crust *n.* the hard outer part of bread; a similar hard outer casing on anything.—*v.t.* and *i.* to cover with or form a crust. —**crust'y** *a.* having or like a crust; short-tempered.—**crust'ily** *adv.*—**crusta'cean** (-shn) *n.* a hard-shelled animal, e.g. crab, lobster, shrimp.—**crusta'ceous** (-shus) *a.*
crutch *n.* a staff with a cross-piece to go under the armpit for the use of cripples.
crux' *n.* hard problem; real issue.
cry *v.i.* to utter a call; shout; weep.—*v.t.* to utter loudly, proclaim (**cried** *p.t.* and *p.p.*—**cry'ing** *pres. p.*).—*n.* a loud utterance; the characteristic call of an animal; a watchword; a fit of weeping.
crypt *n.* a vault, *esp.* under a church.—**cryp'tic** *a.* secret, mysterious.—**cryp'togram** *n.* a piece of cipher-writing.
crys'tal *n.* a clear transparent mineral; very clear glass; cut-glass vessels; a form assumed by many substances with a definite internal structure and external shape of symmetrically arranged plane surfaces.—**crys'talline** *a.*—**crys'tallise** *v.t.* and *i.* to form into crystals; to become definite.—**crystallisa'tion** *n.*
cub *n.* the young of the fox and other animals.—*v.t.* and *i.* to bring forth (cubs).—**Wolf Cub,** junior Boy Scout.
cube (kū-) *n.* a regular solid figure contained by six equal squares; a cube-shaped block; the product obtained by multiplying a number by itself twice.—*v.t.* to multiply thus.—**cu'bic, cu'bical** *a.* —**cu'bism** *n.* a style of art in which objects are presented to give the appearance of an assemblage of cubes.
cu'bicle (kū'-) *n.* a small separate sleeping compartment in a dormitory.
cu'bit (kū'-) *n.* measure of 18 inches.
cuck'oo (koo'kōō) *n.* a migratory bird named from its call.
cu'cumber (kū'-) *n.* creeping plant with long fleshy green edible fruit.
cud *n.* the food which a ruminant animal brings back into its mouth to chew.
cud'dle *v.t.* to hug.—*v.i.* to lie close.
cudd'y *n.* cabin of half-decked boat.
cud'gel *n.* a short thick stick.—*v.t.*
cue (kū) *n.* a pigtail; the long tapering stick used by a billiard player.—**cue'ist** *n.*
cue (kū) *n.* last words of an actor's speech as signal to another to act or speak; a hint or example for action.
cuff *n.* a wrist-band, end of sleeve.

cuff *v.t.* to strike with the hand.—*n.*
cuirass' (kwi-) armour of breastplate and backplate; breastplate alone.
cui'sine (kwi-zeen') *n.* kitchen; cookery; style of cooking.
cul-de-sac *n.* blind alley (**culs-** *pl.*).
cul'inary *a.* of or for cooking.
cull *v.t.* to gather, select, pick.
cul'minate *v.i.* to reach the highest point; come to a climax.—**culmina'tion** *n.*
cul'pable *a.* blameworthy.—**culpabil'ity** *n.*—**cul'pably** *adv.*—**cul'prit** *n.* an offender, one guilty of an offence.
cult *n.* a system of religious worship; a pursuit of, or devotion to, some object.
cul'tivate *v.t.* to raise (crops) on land; to develop, improve, refine; devote attention to, practise, frequent.—**cultiva'tion** *n.*—**cul'tivator** *n.*—**cul'tivated** *a.* —**cul'ture** *n.* a cultivating; a state of manners, taste, and intellectual development at a time or place.—**cul'tured** *a.* showing culture.—**cul'tural** *a.*
Syn. of "cultivated," civilised, educated, refined. *Ant.* uncultivated, uncivilised, illiterate, vulgar.
cul'vert *n.* a tunnelled drain for the passage of water, under a road, etc.
cum'ber *v.t.* to block up, be in the way of, hamper.—**cum'bersome, cum'brous** *a.*
cumm'erbund *n.* waist sash.
cu'mulative (-iv) *a.* the sum of many items; of shares, entitled to arrears of interest before other shares receive current interest.
cu'mulus *n.* a cloud shaped in rounded white masses (**cu'muli** *pl.*).
cune'iform (kū-nē-i-) *a.* wedge-shaped, *esp.* of ancient Babylonian writing.
cunn'ing *n.* skill, dexterity; selfish cleverness; skill in deceit or evasion.—*a.* having such qualities.—**cunn'ingly** *adv.*
Syn. artful, wily, subtle, ingenious, clever. *Ant.* artless, frank, plain, sincere.
cup *n.* drinking vessel with handle; the contents of a cup; various cup-shaped formations, cavities, etc.; prize in the shape of a cup of gold, etc.; a portion or lot; an iced drink of wine and other ingredients.—*v.t.* to bleed surgically.—**cup'ful** *n.* (**cupfuls** *pl.*).—**cup'board** (kub'erd) *n.* a closed cabinet with shelves.
cupid'ity (kū-) *n.* greed of gain.
cup'ola (kū'-) *n.* a dome (**cu'polas** *pl.*).
cu'preous (kū'-), **cu'pric, cu'prous** *a.* of or containing copper.
cur *n.* a worthless dog; a surly, cowardly, or ill-bred person.—**curr'ish** *a.*
cura'ra (cu-ra'-rā) *n.* highly poisonous alkaloid derived from curare, now used to effect muscular relaxation in surgical operations.
cur'ate (kūr'at) *n.* a parish priest's appointed assistant.—**cur'acy** *n.*
cur'ative (kū'-) *a.* tending to cure disease; healing.—*n.* curative agent.
cura'tor *n.* person in charge, *esp.* of a museum, etc.—**cura'torship** *n.*
curb *n.* a chain or strap passing under a horse's lower jaw and giving powerful control with reins; any check or means of restraint; a stone edging to a footpath. —*v.t.* to restrain.—**curb'stone** *n.*
curd *n.* coagulated milk.—**cur'dle** *v.t.* and *i.* to coagulate; of blood, to shrink with horror, etc.—**curd'y** *a.*
cure *v.t.* to heal; to remedy; to preserve (fish, skins, etc.).—*n.* a remedy; course of medical treatment; restoration to health. —**cu'rable** *a.*—**curabil'ity** *n.*—**cure of souls,** care of a parish or congregation.
curé (koo-rā') *n.* a parish priest in France.
cur'few *n.* bell rung at fixed evening hour, originally a signal to put out fires, now, under martial law, to mark the time when inhabitants must be indoors.
cu'rie *n.* the amount of a radioactive substance that undergoes 3.70×10^{10} radioactive transformations per sec.
cu'rious (kū'-) *a.* eager to know, inquisitive; prying; puzzling, strange; minutely accurate.—**cu'riously** *adv.*—**curios'ity** *n.* eagerness to know; inquisitiveness; strange or rare thing.—**cu'rio** *n.* something odd and rare of value to collectors (**-ios** *pl.*).
cu'rium *n.* a radio-active, inert, gaseous element. Atomic No. 96, symbol Cm.
curl *v.t.* to bend into spiral or curved shape.—*v.i.* to take such shapes.—*n.* a spiral lock of hair; spiral or curved state or form or motion.—**cur'ly** *a.*—**cur'ling** *n.* a game like bowls played with large rounded stones on ice.
cur'lew *n.* a long-billed wading bird.
cur'licue (-li-kū) *n.* an ornamental twist; a flourish in handwriting.
curmudg'eon (-jn) *n.* a miser, misanthrope, churlish fellow.
curr'ach, curr'agh (kur'-ah) *n.* a coracle; a wicker boat covered with tarred canvas.
curr'ant *n.* dried fruit of a Levantine grape; the fruit of various plants allied to the gooseberry; the plants.
curr'ent *a.* in circulation or general use; going on, not yet superseded; fluent, running.—*n.* a body of water or air in motion; the flow of a river, etc.; tendency; transmission of electricity through a conductor.—**curr'ently** *adv.*—**curr'ency** *n.* time during which anything is current; money in use; state of being in use.—**curr'ency-note** *n.* a treasury note, a £1 or 10-shilling note.
curric'ulum (ku-rik'-) *n.* a specified course of study (**cur'ricula** *pl.*).
curr'y *v.t.* to rub down and groom (a horse); to dress (leather) (**cur'ried** *p.t.* and *p.p.*—**cur'rying** *pres. p.*).—**curr'ier** *n.* a leather dresser.—**curry fa'vour** to try to win favour unworthily.

curr'y *n.* a preparation of turmeric; a dish flavoured with it.—*v.t.*
curse *n.* an utterance intended to destroy a person or thing; an expletive in the form of bad language; a curse; an affliction, bane, scourge.—*v.t.* and *i.* to utter a curse, afflict.
curs'ive *a.* written in running script.
curs'ory *a.* rapid, hasty, without attention to details.—**curs'orily** *adv.*
curt *a.* short; rudely brief.—**curt'ness** *n.* —**curt'ly** *adv.*—**curtail'** *v.t.* to cut short, diminish.—**curtail'ment** *n.*
curt'ain (-tin) *n.* a cloth hung as a screen; screen between audience and stage; an end to an act or scene.—*v.t.* to provide or cover with a curtain.—**curt'ain-fire** *n.* a barrage.—**curt'ain-raiser** *n.* short play before the main one.
curt'sy *n.* a woman's bow.—*v.* to bow low (**curt'sied** *p.t.* and *p.p.*).
curve *n.* a line of which no part is straight.—*v.t.* to bend into a curve.—*v.i.* to have or assume a curved form or direction.—**curv'ature** *a.* bending; a bent shape.—**curvet'** *n.* a horse's trained movement like a short leap over nothing.—*v.i.* to make this movement. —**curvilin'ear** *a.* of bent lines.
cush'ion (koosh'n) *n.* a bag filled with soft stuffing or air; a pad; the elastic lining of the sides of a billiard-table.—*v.t.* to provide or protect with a cushion.
cush'y *a.* (*sl.*) soft, comfortable, pleasant, light and well-paid.
cus'tard *n.* a preparation of eggs and milk flavoured and cooked.
cus'tody *n.* safe-keeping, guardianship, imprisonment.–**custo'dial** *a.*–**custo'dian** *n.* a keeper, caretaker, curator.
cus'tom *n.* a usage; business patronage; *pl.* duties levied on imports.—**cus'tomary** *a.*—**cus'tomarily** *adv.*—**cus'tomer** *n.* one who enters a shop to buy, *esp.* one who deals regularly with it.
Syn. fashion, manner, habit. *Ant.* desuetude, disuse.
cut *v.t.* to sever, penetrate, wound, divide or separate with pressure of an edge or edged instrument; to pare, detach, trim or shape by cutting, to divide; abridge; to ignore (a person); to strike (with a whip, etc.); to hit a cricket ball to point's left.—*n.* an act of cutting; a blow (of knife, whip, etc.); a fashion; an incision; an engraving; a piece cut off; a division.—*n.* the curtailment of a text or programme; in a cinema film, the abrupt ending of a "shot."—*v.t.* to end a scene abruptly; to omit; in a film studio, to edit a film by cutting out portions and sticking the film together again.—**cut-back** *n.* a reduction in factory output (U.S.)—**cutting-bench** *n.* the illuminated bench at which a film is unwound so that it may be cut by the editor.—**cut-up** *n.* U.S. (*sl.*) a lively mischievous person.—**cutt'er** *n.* one who or that which cuts; a warship's rowing and sailing boat; a small sloop-rigged vessel.—**cutt'ing** *n.* an act of cutting or a thing cut off or out; *esp.* an excavation (for a road, canal, etc.) through high ground; a piece cut from a newspaper, etc.—**cut-in** *v.i.* in motoring, to overtake a vehicle in face of an oncoming one.—**cut-out** *n.* a device by which part of an electric circuit may be shut off; in motoring, a device to allow exhaust gases to escape.—**to cut one's stick**, in S. Africa, to run away, sneak off.
cuta'neous (kū-) *a.* of the skin.—**cu'ticle** *n.* the outer skin.
cute *a.* (acute) clever; sharp; fetching.
cut'lass *n.* a sailor's short broad-sword.
cut'ler *n.* one who makes, repairs or deals in knives and cutting implements. —**cut'lery** *n.* cutler's wares.
cut'let *n.* a small piece of meat broiled or fried; small chop.
cut'tle-fish *n.* ten-armed sea mollusc which ejects an inky fluid when attacked.
cy'anide *n.* a salt of hydrocyanic acid; prussic acid.
cy'clamen *n.* (*bot.*) a genus of plants related to the primrose, with fleshy root-stalks; the colour of this flower.
cy'cle (sī'-) *n.* a recurrent series or period; complete series or period; development following a course of stages; a series of poems, etc.; a bicycle.—*v.i.* to move in cycles; to use a bicycle.—**cy'clic**, **cy'clical** *a.*—**cy'clist** *n.* a bicycle-rider.—**cy'cle-car** *n.* a small light motor-car.—**cyclom'eter** *n.* an instrument for measuring circles or recording distance travelled by a wheel, *esp.* of a bicycle.—**cy'clone** *n.* a system of winds moving round a centre of low pressure.—**cyclon'ic** *a.*—**cy'clostyle** *n.* a duplicating apparatus with stencil paper.
cyclopæd'ia *see* **encyclopædia.**
cy'clotron (sī'-klō-tron) *n.* apparatus used for work in nuclear disintegration, etc.
cyg'net (sig'-) *n.* a young swan.
cyl'inder (sil'-) *n.* roller-shaped body of uniform diameter; a piston-chamber of an engine.—**cylin'drical** *a.*
cym'bals (sim'-) *n. pl.* saucer-shaped brass clappers used in orchestras.
cymom'eter *n.* instrument measuring frequency of electric waves.
cyn'ic (sin'-) *n.* one of a sect of Greek philosophers affecting bluntness of speech and contempt of luxury: a cynical person.—**cyn'ical** *a.* sceptical of or sneering at goodness; given to showing up human weakness.—**cy'nicism** *n.*
cyn'osure (sīn'o-shoor) *n.* a centre of attraction; guiding star.
cy'pher *see* **cipher.**
cy'press *n.* a coniferous tree; its wood;

its dark foliage as a symbol of mourning.
cyst (si-) *n.* a bladder or sac containing liquid secretion or morbid matter.
cy'tology (si'-) *n.* (*science*) study of the structure and functions of plant and animal cells.
czar, tzar, tsar (zȧr) *n.* emperor or king, *esp.* of Russia 1547-1917.—**czarit'sa, ts-, tz-** *n. fem.* the wife of a Russian czar.—**tsar'evitch, cz-** *n.* the heir apparent of a Russian czar.

D

dab *v.t.* to strike feebly.—*n.* a slight blow or tap; a smear; a small flat roundish mass; small flat fish.—*n.* an expert.
dab'ble *v.i.* to splash about; to be a desultory student or amateur (in).
dab'chick *n.* a small diving bird.
dace *n.* a small freshwater fish.
dachs'hund (daks'hoont) *n.* a short-legged long-bodied dog.
dacoit' *n.* a Burmese bandit.
da'daism *n.* a school of art and literature which aims at suppressing all relations between thought and expression.
da'do *n.* the lower part of a room wall when lined or painted separately (**-does** (-dōz) *pl.*).
daff'odil *n.* a yellow narcissus.
daft (-ȧ-) *a.* foolish, crazy.
dagg'er *n.* short stabbing weapon.
da'gher, da'gha (dā'ka) *n.* S. Africa, mortar (from Kaffir *u-daka*, mortar; or possibly local obsolete provinc. word, c.f. O.E. *dagh* = dough).
da'go *n.* a Spaniard, Portuguese, or other Latin (**-gos, -goes** (-gōz) *pl.*).
daguerre'otype (-gėr'o-) *n.* an early photographic process, a portrait by it.
dahl'ia (dāl'-) *n.* a garden plant.
Dail, Dail Eireann (doil ār-an) *n.* the parliament of the Irish Free State.
dail'y *a.* done, occurring, published, etc., every day.—*adv.* every day.—*n.* a daily newspaper or maid-servant.
dain'ty *a.* choice, delicate; hard to please.—*n.* delicacy, titbit.—**dain'tily** *adv.*—**dain'tiness** *n.* *Syn.* delicious, nice, fastidious, scrupulous, affected. *Ant.* coarse, nasty, common, nauseous.
dair'y (dėr'-) *n.* a place for dealing with milk and its products.—**dair'yman** *n.*
dais (dās) *n.* a low platform.
dais'y (-z-) *n.* a flower with yellow centre and white petals.
dale *n.* a valley, glen.—**dales'man** *n.* a hillsman of N. England.
dall'y *v.i.* spend time in idleness, amusement, love-making (**dall'ied** *p.t./p.p.*—**dall'ying** *pr. p.*).—**dall'iance** *n.*
Dalma'tian *n.* a large breed of dog, white with black spots.
dalmat'ic *n.* robe with wide sleeves worn by kings at their coronation and by deacons and bishops.
dam *n.* a mother, usually of animals.
dam *n.* a barrier to hold back a flow of waters; the water so collected.—*v.t.* to supply, or hold with a dam.
dam'age *n.* injury, harm; *pl.* sum claimed or adjudged in compensation for harm or injury.—*v.t.* to injure.
dam'ask *n.* figured woven material of silk or linen, *esp.* white table linen.—*a.* of damask; coloured like damask-rose.—*v.t.* to weave with figured designs.—**damaskeen', damascene'** *v.t.* to decorate (steel, etc.) with inlaid gold or silver.
dame *n.* a lady; a rank for a lady in the Order of the British Empire; Knight's wife.—**dame'-school** *n.* an elementary school run by a woman.
damn (-m) *v.t.* to condemn to hell; to be the ruin of; to give a hostile reception to.—*v.i.* to curse.—*interj.* an expression of annoyance, impatience, etc.—**dam'nable** *a.* deserving damnation, hateful.
damp *a.* moist; slightly moist.—*n.* diffused moisture; in coal-mines, a dangerous gas.—*v.t.* to make damp; to deaden, discourage.—**damp'en** *v.t.* (*radio*) to provide sound absorbance in a studio in order to eliminate echoes.—**damp'er** *n.* anything that discourages or depresses; a silencing-pad in a piano; a plate in a flue to control draught; in Australia, cake of flour and water without yeast, baked in the ashes of a wood fire.
damp'ing *n.* in wireless, rate at which an electrical oscillation dies away.
dam'sel (-z-) *n.* girl, a maiden.
dam'son (-z-) a small dark-purple plum.
dance (-ȧ-) *v.i.* to move with rhythmic steps, leaps, gestures, etc., usually to music; to be in lively movement; to bob up and down.—*v.t.* to perform (a dance); to cause to dance.—*n.* a rhythmical movement; an arrangement of such movements; a tune for them; a dancing-party.—**danc'er** *n.*—**danseuse'** (don-sėz') *n.* a female dancer (**danseuses'** (-sez') *pl.*).
dan'delion *n.* a yellow-flowered wild plant.
Dan'die Din'mont *n.* a breed of Scottish terriers.
dan'druff *n.* dead skin in small scales among the hair.
dan'dy *n.* a man who pays excessive attention to dress (**dan'dies** *pl.*).
dan'ger (dān'j-) *n.* liability or exposure to injury or harm; peril.—**dan'gerous** *a.*
dan'gle (-ng'gl) *v.t.* and *i.* to hang loosely and swaying (**dan'gled** *p.t./p.p.*).
dank *a.* oozy, unwholesomely damp.
dank'ie, *interj.* in S. Africa; literally: thank you.
dapp'er *a.* neat and precise, *esp.* in dress; small and active.
dap'ple *v.t.* and *i.* to mark with rounded

spots.—**dap'ple-grey'** *a.* grey marked with darker spots, *esp.* of a horse.

dare (dėr) *v.t.* to venture, have the courage (to); defy (**durst** or **dared** *p.t.*—**dared** *p.p.*—**da'ring** *pres. p.*).—**dar'ing** *a.* bold.—*n.* adventurous courage.—**dare'-devil** *a.* reckless.—*n.* reckless person.

dark *a.* without light; gloomy; deep in tint; secret; wicked.—*n.* absence of light or colour or knowledge.—**dark'en** *v.t.* and *i.*—**dark'ly** *adv.*—**dark'ness** *n.*—**dark'-ling** *a.* and *adv.* in the dark.—**dark'some** *a.*—**dark-room** *n.* in photography, room from which all actinic rays of light are excluded. *Syn.* obscure, mysterious, hidden, ignorant, vile. *Ant.* clear, open, light.

dar'ling *n.* one much loved or very lovable.—*a.* beloved or prized.

darn *v.t.* to mend by filling (hole, etc.) with interwoven yarn.—*n.* a place so mended.—**darn'ing** *n.*

dar'nel *n.* grass growing among corn.

dart *n.* a light pointed missile; a darting motion.—*v.t.* to throw rapidly (a dart, glance, etc.).—*v.i.* to go rapidly or abruptly, like a missile.—**darts'** *n.* an indoor game.—**dart'board** *n.*

das *n.* in South Africa, a badger.

dash *v.t.* to smash, thrust, send with violence; cast down; flavour.—*v.i.* to move or go with great speed or violence.—*n.* a rush, onset; vigour; smartness; a small quantity, a stroke (—) between words.—**dash'ing** *a.* spirited.—**dash'-board** *n.* mudscreen; in motoring, panel in front of driver with indicators, etc.

das'tard *n.* a base coward, *esp.* one who commits a brutal act without danger to himself.—**das'tardly** *a.* cowardly.

das'ymeter *n.* an instrument for testing the density of a gas.

da'ta *n. pl. see* **datum.**

date *n.* a stone-fruit of a palm; the palm.

date *n.* time of an occurrence; the period of a work of art, etc.; season, time; in N. Amer., an engagement, appointment.—*v.t.* to mark with a date.—*v.i.* to exist (from); to betray time or period of origin.—**date'less** *a.* without date; up to date, modern; up to now.

da'tive (-tiv) *n.* a noun-case indicating the indirect object, etc.

da'tum *n.* a thing given, known, or assumed as the basis for a reckoning, reasoning, etc. (**da'ta** *pl.*).

daub *v.t.* to coat, paint badly.—*n.* a smear; rough picture.—**daub'er** *n.*

daught'er (dawt'-) *n.* a female child, female descendant.—**daught'er-in-law** *n.* the wife of a son.—**daught'erly** *a.*

daunt *v.t.* to frighten, *esp.* into giving up a purpose; put off.—**daunt'less** *a.*

dau'phin (daw'fin) *n.* formerly (1349-1830) French king's eldest son.

dav'enport *n.* a small writing-table with drawers; (U.S.) large couch.

dav'it *n.* a crane, usually one of a pair, at a ship's side for lowering boats.

Da'vy Jone's's lock'er (-jōn'ziz-) *n.* the sea as a grave.

da'vy-lamp *n.* a miner's safety lamp.

daw *n.* the jackdaw.

daw'dle *v.i.* to idle, loiter, waste time.

dawn *v.i.* to begin to grow light; to appear.—*n.* daybreak, first gleam or beginning of anything.—**dawn'ing** *n.*

day *n.* the time during which the sun is above the horizon; period of 24 hours; a point or unit of time; daylight.—**dail'y** *a.*, *adv.* and *n.* (*see* in alphabet. place).—**day'-boarder** *n.* a boy fed but not lodged at school.—**day'book** *n.* a book in which the sales, etc., of a day are entered for later transfer to ledger.—**day'light** *n.* natural light, dawn, publicity, enlightenment.—**day'light-sa'ving** *n.* the system of summer-time.—**day'spring** *n.* dawn.

daze *v.t.* to stupefy, bewilder.—*n.* bewildered state.—**dazed** *a.*—**daz'zle** *v.t.* to blind or confuse with brightness, brilliant display or prospects.—*n.* a brightness that dazzles.

D-Day day on which a large-scale operation begins; June 6th, 1944, when the Allies invaded the Continent.

D.D.T. a hydrocarbon compound developed in World War 2 as a very effective insecticide.

de- *prefix* down, from, or off; as in *deject, deter, defend.*

dea'con (dē'kn) *n.* one in the lowest degree of holy orders; an official of a free church.—**dea'coness** *n. fem.* a churchwoman appointed to perform charitable works.

dead (ded) *a.* no longer alive; benumbed; obsolete; extinguished; lacking lustre or movement or vigour; sure, complete.—*n.* dead person or persons (gen. in *pl.* **the dead**).—*adv.* utterly.—**dead'en** *v.t.*—**dead'ly** *a.* fatal; death-like.—*adv.* as if dead.—**dead'-alive** *a.* dull.—**dead'-beat** *n.* in Australia, a person down on his luck.—**dead'heat** *n.* a race in which competitors finish even.—**dead'-eye** *n.* a pulley.—**dead'head** *n.* a non-paying member of audience, or passenger.—**dead let'ter** *n.* a law no longer observed; a letter which the post office cannot deliver.—**dead'lock** *n.* a standstill.—**dead-pan** *n.* a face without expression; one whose face betrays no emotion;—*a.* (U.S.).—**dead-spot,** in wireless, an area of low wave intensity caused by obstacles of great absorbing power (e.g. mountains, large buildings).—**dead-reckoning** *n.* finding of a ship's position without aid of stars.—**dead of night,** time of greatest stillness and darkness. *Syn.* lifeless, inanimate, extinct, dull, gloomy, unproductive. *Ant.* alive, lively, animated, existing, effective, useful.

deaf (def) *a.* wholly or partly without

hearing; unwilling to hear, heedless.—**deaf'ness** *n.*—**deaf'en** *v.t.*
deal *n.* a plank or wood of fir or pine.
deal *v.t.* to hand out, *esp.* cards.—*v.i.* to do business (with, in) (**dealt** *p.t.* and *p.p.*).—*n.* a share; distribution.—**deal'er** *n.* one who deals; a trader.—**deal with,** handle, act in regard to.
dean *n.* the head of a cathedral chapter; a university or college official.—**dean'ery** *n.* a dean's house or appointment.
dear *a.* beloved; costly, expensive.—*n.* beloved one.—*adv.* at a high price.—**dear'ly** *adv.*—**dear'ness** *n.*
dearth (durth) *n.* scarcity.
death (deth) *n.* dying; end of life; end; annihilation; personified power that annihilates.—**death'less** *a.* immortal.—**death'ly** *a.* and *adv.*—**death-mask** *n.* likeness made from clay, wax or plaster cast of a person's face, after death.—**death'watch** *n.* a ticking beetle.
deba'cle (di-bȧk'l) *n.* utter collapse.
debar' *v.t.* to shut out from, stop.
debase' *v.t.* to lower in value, quality or character; to adulterate the metal in coinage.—**debase'ment** *n.*
Syn. to humble, disgrace, degrade. *Ant.* exalt, elevate, dignify, honour.
debate' *v.t.* to discuss, dispute about.—*v.i.* to engage in discussion; consider; reason out (with oneself).—*n.* discussion.—**deba'table** *a.*—**deba'ter** *n.*
debauch' (-tsh) to lead away from virtue; spoil; seduce.—*n.* bout of sensual indulgence.—**debauchee'** (-osh-) *n.*—**debauch'ery** *n.* vice; drunkenness.
deben'ture *n.* a bond of a company or corporation.—**deben'tured** *a.*
debil'ity *n.* feebleness, *esp.* of health.—**debil'itate** *v.t.* to weaken.
deb'it *n.* an entry in an account of a sum owed; side of book used for this.—*v.t.* to charge, enter as due.
debonair' *a.* genial, pleasant, gay.
debouch' *v.i.* to move out from a narrow place to a wider one.—**debouch'ment** *n.*
deb'ris (-rē) *n. sing.* and *pl.* fragments, rubbish; wreckage. In S. Africa, refuse material from which gold or diamonds have been extracted.
debt (det) *n.* what is owed; state of owing.—**debt'or** *n.* person owing.
de'bunk *v.t.* to reveal sham, pretentiousness, or false sentiment.
debut' (dā-bōō') *n.* first appearance in public.—**de'butant** *n.* (**-ante** *fem.*).
dec'ade *n.* a period of ten years; a set or aggregate of ten.
dec'adent *a.* declining, falling away.—**dec'adence** *n.* decline, decay.
dec'agon *n.* a figure of ten angles.—**decag'onal** *a.*—**dec'agramme** *n.* ten grammes.—**decahe'dron** *n.* a solid of ten faces.—**decahe'dral** *a.*—**dec'alitre** *n.* ten litres.—**dec'alogue** (-log) *n.* the ten commandments.—**dec'ametre** *n.* ten metres.
decamp' *v.t.* to make off, *esp.* secretly.
dec'anal *a.* relating to a dean or deanery.
decant' *v.t.* to pour off (liquid, wine, etc.) to leave sediment behind.—**decant'er** *n.* a stoppered bottle for wine, etc.
decap'itate *v.t.* to behead.—**decapita'tion** *n.*—**decap'itator** *n.*
decarb'onise (-nīz) *v.t.* to deprive of carbon; to remove a deposit of carbon, as from a motor engine cylinder.
decasyll'able *n.* a word or line of ten syllables.—**decasyllab'ic** *a.*
decath'lon *n.* in athletics, contest consisting of 10 different events.
decay' *v.t.* and *i.* to rot, decompose; fall off.—*n.* rotting; a falling away, break up.
decease' *n.* death.—*v.t.* to die.—**deceased'** *a.* dead.—*n.* dead person.
deceive' (-sēv') *v.t.* mislead.—**deceiv'er** *n.*—**deceit'** *n.*—**deceit'ful** *a.*
decel'erate *v.i.* to slow down, *esp.* in motoring.—**decelera'tion** *n.*
Decem'ber *n.* the twelfth month.
decenn'ial *a.* of a period of ten years.
de'cent *a.* respectable; passable.—**de'cency** *n.*—**de'cently** *adv.*
Syn. proper, suitable, decorous, seemly. *Ant.* improper, indecorous, unseemly.
decep'tion *n.* deceiving; being deceived; a trick, fraud.—**decep'tive** *a.*
decide' *v.t.* to determine, bring to resolution; give judgment.—*v.i.* to determine, resolve.—**deci'ded** *a.* settled; resolute.—**deci'dedly** *adv.* certainly, undoubtedly.—**decis'ion** (-zhn) *n.*—**deci'sive** *a.*—**deci'sively** *adv.*
decid'uous *a.* of leaves, horns, etc., falling periodically; of trees, losing leaves annually, not evergreen.
dec'imal (des'-) *a.* relating to tenths; proceeding by tens.—*n.* a decimal fraction.—**dec'imal system,** system of weights, measures, money, etc., in which the value of each denomination is ten times the one below it.—**dec'igramme** *n.* tenth of a gramme.—**dec'ilitre** *n.* tenth of a litre.—**dec'imetre** *n.* tenth of a metre.—**dec'imalise** *v.t.*—**decimalisa'tion** *n.* to convert into decimal fractions.—**dec'imate** *v.t.* to kill a tenth or large proportion of.—**decima'tion** *n.*
deci'pher *v.t.* to turn from cipher into ordinary writing; to make out the meaning of; to decode.—**deci'pherable** *a.*
deck *n.* a platform covering the whole or part of a ship's hull; in N. Amer., a pack of cards; the cards left over after dealing a hand.—*v.t.* to array, decorate.
deckle *n.* the edge of a paper-making machine.—**deckle-edge** *n.* ragged edge of hand-made paper.—**deckle-edged** *a.* having a rough, uncut edge.
declaim' *v.i.* and *t.* to speak in oratorical style.—**declama'tion** *n.*—**declam'atory** *a.*
declare' (-ėr') *v.t.* to announce formally; state emphatically; name (as liable to

customs duty).—*v.i.* to take sides (for). —**declara'tion** *n.*—**declar'atory** *a.*
decline' *v.i.* to slope or bend downwards; to decay; to refuse; to make the case-endings of nouns.—*n.* a gradual decay, loss of vigour; a wasting disease.—**declen'sion** *n.* a declining; a group of nouns.—**decli'nable** *a.*—**declina'tion** *n.*
declinom'eter (dek-) *n.* a device for measuring the declination of the magnetic needle from the true north.
decliv'ity *n.* downward slope.
declutch' *v.t.* to take the clutch (e.g. of a motor car) out of engagement.
decoc'tion *n.* extraction of an essence by boiling down; an essence or whatever results from a boiling down.—**decoct'** *v.t.*
decode' *v.t.* to put in intelligible terms a message in code or secret alphabet.
décoll'eté *a.* of dress, low necked.
decompose' (dē-, -ōz') *v.t.* to separate into elements.—*v.i.* to rot.—**decomposi'tion** *n.* act or state of decomposing.
decontamin'ation *n.* removal of contaminating substances, *esp.* of poison gas.
decontrol' *v.t.* to release from state control.
décor (dā-kor) *n.* decorative background, *esp.* of a theatre scene.
dec'orate *v.t.* to adorn, beautify; to invest (with an order, medal, etc.).—**decora'tion** *n.* ornament; medal.—**dec'orative** *a.*—**dec'orator** *n. esp.* one who paints and papers houses.
deco'rum *n.* seemly behaviour, usage required by decency or good manners.—**dec'orous** *a.*—**dec'orously** *adv.*
decoy' *n.* a bird or person used to entrap others; a bait.—*v.* to entice.
decrease' *v.t.* and *i.* to make or grow less.—**de'crease** *n.* a lessening.
Syn. diminish, lessen, wane, reduce. *Ant.* increase, grow, wax, magnify.
decree' *n.* an authoritative order; an edict.—*v.t.* to order with authority (**-creed'** *p.t.* and *p.p.*—**-cree'ing** *pres. p.*).
dec'rement *n.* the act or state of decreasing; the quantity lost by decrease.
decrep'it *a.* old and feeble; worn out.—**decrep'itude** *n.* being decrepit.
decrescen'do (-kresh-) *a.* and *adv.* music, a gradually diminishing manner.
decry' *v.t.* to cry down, to belittle (**-cried'** *p.t.* and *p.p.*—**cry'ing** *pres. p.*).
ded'icate *v.t.* to devote to God's service; set aside entirely for some purpose; inscribe, address (book, etc.).—**dedica'tion** *n.*—**ded'icatory** *a.*—**ded'icator** *n.*
deduce' *v.t.* to reason from facts.
deduct' *v.t.* to subtract.—**deduc'tion** *n.* amount subtracted; deducing; conclusion deduced; an inference from general to particular.—**deduct'ive** *a.*
deed *n.* an act; action or fact, performance; a legal document.
deem *v.t.* to judge, hold to be.—**deems'ter** *n.* in the Isle of Man, a judge.
deep *a.* extending far down or in or back; at or of a given depth; far down or back; profound; heartfelt; hard to fathom; cunning; engrossed, immersed; of colour, dark and rich; of sound, low and full.—*n.* a deep place; the sea.—*adv.* far down, etc.—**deep'en** *v.t.*—**deep'ly** *adv.*—**deepsink'er** *n.* in Australia, a large tumbler; a long drink served in a large glass.
deer *n.* a family of ruminant animals with deciduous horns in the male (**deer** *pl.*).—**deer'hound** *n.* a large rough-coated greyhound.—**deer'stalker** *n.* one who stalks deer; a pattern of cloth hat.
deface' *v.t.* to mar the appearance of; blot out.—**deface'ment** *n.*
defalca'tion *n.* misappropriation of funds; the resulting shortage.—**de'falcate** *v.i.*—**de'falcator** *n.*
defame' *v.t.* speak ill of, dishonour by slander or rumour, vilify.—**defama'tion** *n.*—**defam'atory** *a.*
default' *n.* failure to act or appear or pay.—*v.t.* and *i.* to fail to pay.—**default'er** *n. esp.* a soldier punished for failure to comply with regulations.—**in default of,** in the absence of.
defeat' *n.* overthrow; lost encounter; frustration.—*v.t.* to overcome.—**defeat'ism** *n.* conduct tending to bring about acceptance of defeat.—**defeat'ist** *n.*—**defeat'ism** *n.* behaviour tending to encourage acceptance of defeat.
def'ecate *v.t.* to clear of impurities or dregs.—**defeca'tion** *n.*
defect' *n.* lack, falling short, blemish, failing.—**defec'tion** *n.* abandonment of a leader or cause.—**defect'ive** *a.* incomplete, faulty, deficient.
defend' *v.t.* to protect, guard, uphold.—**defence'** *n.*—**defend'ant** *n.* person accused.—**defend'er** *n.*—**defens'ible** *a.*—**defensibil'ity** *n.*—**defens'ive** *a.* serving for defence.—*n.* position or attitude of defence.—**defence'less** *a.*
defer' *v.t.* to put off.—*v.i.* to submit in opinion or judgment (to another).—**def'erence** *n.* respect for another.—**deferen'tial** (-shl) *a.*—**deferen'tially** *adv.* —**defer'ment** *n.* *Syn.* to procrastinate, prolong. *Ant.* expedite, quicken.
defi'ance *n.* resistance, disobedience.—**defi'ant** *a.*—**defi'antly** *adv.*
defi'cient (ish'nt) *a.* wanting or falling short in something.—**defi'ciency** *n.*—**deficiency diseases,** diseases resulting from a shortage of vitamins in diet, e.g. scurvy, rickets.
def'icit *n.* the amount short, excess of liabilities over assets, or expenditure over income.
defile' *n.* a narrow pass; a march in file. —*v.i.* to march in file.
defile' *v.t.* to pollute.—**defile'ment** *n.*
define' *v.t.* mark out; lay down clearly, fix; state contents or meaning of.—**defi'-**

nable *a.*—**defini'tion** *n.*—**def'inite** (-it) *a.* exact, precise.—**def'initely** *adv.*—**defin'itive** *a.* conclusive.—**defin'itively** *adv.*

deflate' *v.t.* to release air from (something inflated); to remove excess of paper money in circulation; to take away someone's dignity or expose his intentions.—**defla'tion** *n.*

deflect' *v.t.* and *i.* to make to turn, to turn from a straight or direct course.—**deflec'tion, deflex'ion** *n.*

defolia'tion *n.* the fall of leaves.

deform' *v.t.* to spoil the shape of.—**deform'ity** *n.*—**deforma'tion** *n.*

defraud' *v.t.* to cheat.

defray' *v.t.* to provide the money for.

defrost' *v.t.* unfreeze meat, etc., frozen for cold-storage.—**defrost'er** *n.* a heating instrument for melting ice from a part of an aircraft or car where it is an obstruction or a danger.

deft *a.* skilful, neat-handed.—**deft'ness** *n.*

defunct' *a.* dead.

defy' *v.t.* to set at naught, challenge to do, *esp.* something beyond expected power; offer insuperable difficulties (-**fied'** *p.t.* and *p.p.*—**fy'ing** *pres. p.*).—**defi'ance** *n.*—**defi'ant** *a.*—**defi'antly** *adv.*

degauss' (dē-gous) *v.t.* to counteract the magnetic attraction of ships for magnetic mines.

degen'erate *v.i.* to fall away from the qualities proper to race or kind, deteriorate.—*n.* a degenerate person.—**degenera'tion** *n.*—**degen'eracy** *n.*

degrade' *v.t.* to reduce to a lower rank; debase.—**degrada'tion** *n.*—**degra'ded** *a.*

degree' *n.* a step in a process, scale or series; relative rank, order, condition, manner; a university rank; a unit of measurement of angles or temperature; a form in the comparison of *a.* and *adv.*

dehy'drate *v.t.* extract moisture from.

de-ice *v.t.* to prevent the formation of ice on the wings of an aircraft; to remove ice.—**de-icer** *n.* device for removing ice from the wings of an aircraft.

de'ify (dē'if-ī) *v.t.* to make a god or, worship as a god.—(**de'ified** *p.t.*/*p.p.*—**ifying** *pr. p.*).—**deifica'tion** *n.*

deign (dān) *v.i.* to condescend, to grant.

de'ism *n.* belief in a god but not in revelation.—**de'ist** *n.*—**deis'tic** *a.*—**de'ity** *n.* divine status or attributes, a god.

deject' *v.t.* to dispirit.—**deject'ed** *a.*—**dejec'tion** *n.* depression, low spirits.

delay' *v.t.* to postpone, hold back.—*v.i.* be tardy, linger.—*n.* act of delaying; fact of being delayed (**delayed'** *p.t.*/*p.p.*).

de'leble *a.* capable of being blotted out.

delect'able *a.* delightful.—**delecta'tion** *n.*

del'egate *v.t.* to send as deputy; commit (authority, business, etc.) to a deputy.—**delega'tion** *n.*—**del'egate** *n.*—representative.—**del'egacy** *n.*

delete' *v.t.* to strike out.—**dele'tion** *n.*

delete'rious (-ēr'-) *a.* harmful.

Syn. hurtful, noxious, pernicious, injurious, detrimental. *Ant.* wholesome, innocuous, harmless, beneficial.

delf, delft *n.* a glazed earthenware.

delib'erate *v.t.* and *i.* to consider, debate, confer about.—*a.* done on purpose; without haste.—**delib'erately** *adv.*—**delibera'tion** *n.*—**delib'erative** *a.*

del'icate *a.* dainty; exquisite; deft; ticklish; sensitive; modest.—**del'icacy** *n.*

Syn. gentle, fastidious, refined, tender. *Ant.* rough, coarse, clumsy, healthy.

delicatess'en *n. pl.* confectionery, sweets, table delicacies; (Australia) *n.* a small-goods shop.

deli'cious (-ish'us) *a.* very delightful.

delight' (-lit') *v.t.* to please highly.—*v.i.* to take great pleasure (in).—*n.* great pleasure.—**delight'ful** *a.*—**delight'fully** *adv.*

delimita'tion *n.* fixing of boundaries.

delin'eate *v.t.* portray by drawing, describe.—**delin'eator** *n.*—**delinea'tion** *n.*

delin'quent *n.* an offender.—**delin'quency** *n.* offence, fault.

deliquesce' (-es) *v.i.* to become liquid.—**deliques'cence** *n.*—**deliques'cent** *a.*

delir'ium *n.* disorder of the mind; ecstacy.—**delir'ious** *a.*

deliv'er *v.t.* to set free; hand over; launch, deal; give forth.—**deliv'ery** *n.*—**deliv'erer** *n.*—**deliv'erance** *n.* release.

dell *n.* a wooded hollow or valley.

del'ta *n.* a tract of alluvial land at the mouth of a river (**del'tas** *pl.*).

delude' (-ōōd') *v.t.* to deceive.—**delu'sion** *n.*—**delu'sive** *a.* (**delu'ded** *p.t.* and *p.p.*).

del'uge *n.* a flood, rush, downpour.—*v.t.* to flood; overwhelm.

delve *v.t.* and *i.* to dig.

demag'netise *v.t.* to deprive of magnetic polarity.

dem'agogue (-og) *n.* a mob leader or agitator.—**demagog'ic** *a.*—**dem'agogy** *n.*

demand' (-à-) *v.t.* to ask as by right, ask as giving an order; to call for as due.—*n.* an urgent request, claim, requirement; a call for (a commodity).

demarca'tion *n.* boundary line; its marking out; separation.

démarche (dā-marsh') *n.* a step in political, *esp.* international action.

demean' (-mēn') *v.* to behave, show specified bearing.—**demean'our** (-ẹr) *n.* conduct, behaviour, bearing.

dement'ed *a.* mad; beside oneself.

démenti (dā-mān'-tē) *n.* an official denial of a rumour, *esp.* in diplomatic or political affairs.

demerar'a *n.* brown sugar from the county of this name, in British Guiana.

dement'ed *a.* mad; beside oneself.

demer'it *n.* undesirable quality.

demesne' (-ēn) *n.* an estate kept in the owner's hands; possession of land with unrestricted rights; a sovereign's or state's territory; a landed estate.

dem'i- a prefix signifying *half,* used only in composition.

dem'igod *n.* a being half-divine, half-human; inferior deity.
dem'ijohn *n.* a large wicker-cased bottle. [reputation.
dem'irep *n.* a woman of doubtful
demise' (-z) *n.* death; conveyance by will or lease;.—*v.t.* to convey to another.
demist'er *n.* apparatus for the prevention of mist forming on windscreens, etc.
demo'bilise *v.t.* to disband (troops).
democ'racy *n.* government by the people; a state so governed.—**dem'ocrat** *n.* an advocate of democracy.—**democrat'ic** *a.*—**democrat'ically** *adv.* **democ'ratise** *v.t.*—**democratisa'tion** *n.*
demol'ish *v.t.* to knock to pieces, destroy, overthrow.—**demoli'tion** *n.*
de'mon *n.* a devil; a person of preternatural cruelty or evil character.—**demo'niac** *n.* one possessed with a devil.—**demoni'acal** *a.*—**demon'ic** *a.* of the nature of a devil, or of genius.—**demonol'ogy** *n.* study of demons.
dem'onstrate *v.t.* to show by reasoning, prove; to describe or explain by specimens or experiments.—*v.i.* to make exhibition of political sympathy; make a show of armed force.—**demon'strable** *a.*—**demon'strably** *adv.*—**demonstra'tion** *n.*—**dem'onstrator** *n.*—**demon'strative** *a.* conclusive; showing emotion or feeling.
demor'alise *v.t.* to deprave morally; deprive of courage and discipline, *morale.*
demote' *v.t.* to reduce to a lower grade.
demul'cent *a.* softening; soothing.
demur' (-mĕr') *v.i.* to raise objections, make difficulties.—*n.* raising objection.
demure' *a.* reserved, staid; affecting to be grave or decorous.—**demure'ly** *adv.*
demurr'age *n.* charge for keeping a ship, truck, etc., beyond the time agreed for unloading.—**demurr'er** *n.* (*law*) an exception taken to an opponent's point.
den *n.* a hole of a wild beast; a lurking place; a small room; haunt of vice.
dena'ture *v.t.* to deprive of essential qualities.—**dena'tured al'cohol,** spirit made undrinkable.
denaz'ify (dē-natz'-i-fī) *v.t.* to rid a people or culture of Nazi philosophy and institutions.—**denaz'ification** *n.*
dene (dēn) *n.* a little valley.
deni'al *see* **deny.**
den'izen *n.* an inhabitant.
denom'inate *v.t.* to give a name to.—**denomina'tion** *n.* a name, *esp.* one applicable to each individual of a class; a distinctly named church or sect.—**denom'inational** *a.*—**denom'inator** *n.* the number written below the line in a fraction, the divisor.
denote' *v.t.* to stand for, be the name of; indicate.—**denota'tion** *n.*
denoue'ment (dā-nōō'mon) *n.* the unravelling of a dramatic plot; final solution of a mystery.
denounce' *v.t.* to speak violently against; give notice to withdraw from (a treaty, etc.), to accuse publicly.—**denuncia'tion** *n.*—**denun'ciatory** *a.*
dense *a.* thick; stupid.—**dens'ity** *n.*
Syn. close, heavy, opaque, compact. *Ant.* sparse, light, clear, quick-witted.
dent *n.* hollow or mark left by a blow or pressure.—*v.t.* to make a dent in.
dent'al *a.* relating to teeth or dentistry; pronounced by applying the tongue to the teeth.—**dent'ate** *a.* toothed.—**dent'ifrice** (-is) *n.* material for cleaning the teeth.—**dent'ist** *n.* surgeon who attends to teeth.—**dent'istry** *n.* art of a dentist.—**denti'tion** *n.* teething; arrangement of teeth.—**dent'ure** *n.* set of artificial teeth.—**dent'oid** *a.* tooth-like.
denude' *v.t.* to strip, make bare.—**denuda'tion** *n.* *esp.* removal of forest or surface soil by natural agency.
denuncia'tion *see* **denounce.**
deny' *v.t.* to declare untrue or non-existent; reject, disown; refuse to give; refuse (**deni'ed** (-nīd) *p.t.* and *p.p.*—**deny'ing** *pres. p.*).—**deni'al** *n.*—**deni'able** *a.* *Syn.* to disavow, repudiate, disclaim, abjure. *Ant.* to assert, affirm, confess, admit, grant.
deo'dorize *v.t.* to rid of smell.
depart' *v.i.* to go away; die; diverge.—**depart'ure** *n.*—**depart'ment** *n.* a division, branch, province.—**departments'al** *a.*
depend' *v.i.* to rely entirely; live (on); to be contingent, await settlement or decision (on); to hang down.—**depend'able** *a.* reliable.—**depend'ant** *n.* one for whose maintenance another is responsible.—**depend'ent** *a.*—**depend'ence** *n.*—**depend'ency** *n.* a country or province controlled by another.
depict' *v.t.* give a picture of; delineate; portray.—**depic'tion** *n.*
depil'atory *a.* removing hair.—*n.* a substance that does this.—**depila'tion** *n.*
deplete' *v.t.* to empty, exhaust, or nearly take away.—**deple'tion** *n.*
deplore' *v.t.* to regret.—**deplo'rable** *a.*
deploy' *v.i.* of troops, ships, etc., to spread out from column into line.
depo'larise *v.t.* to deprive of polarity.—**depolarisa'tion** *n.* process by which any substance loses its polarity.
depo'nent *n.* a sworn witness; a deponent verb.—*a.* of a verb, having a passive form but active meaning.
depop'ulate *v.t.* to deprive of, or reduce, population.—**depopula'tion** *n.*
deport' *v.t.* to exile, send out of a country.—**deport'ation** *n.*
deport'ment *n.* behaviour, bearing.
depose' *v.t.* to remove from high office.—*v.i.* to give evidence.—**deposi'tion** *n.* dethronement; statement.
depos'it (-z-) *v.t.* to set down; give into safe keeping; pledge for the carrying out of a contract.—*n.* act of depositing; thing deposited.—**depos'itor** *n.* person

depositing.—**depos'itory** *n.* a place for safe keeping.—**depos'itory** *n.* a person with whom a thing is deposited.
dep'ot (-ō) *n.* storehouse; military headquarters; (U.S.) (dē'pō) railway station.
deprave' *v.t.* to corrupt, pervert, make bad.—**deprav'ity** *n.* wickedness.
dep'recate *v.t.* to disapprove of; advise against. — **depreca'tion** *n.* — **dep'recatory** *a.*—**depreca'tingly** *adv.*
depre'ciate (-shi-) *v.t.* to lower the price or value or purchasing power of.—*v.i.* to fall in value.—**deprecia'tion** *n.*—**depre'ciator** *n.*—**depre'ciatory** *a.*
Syn. to detract, traduce, underestimate. *Ant.* appreciate, extol, over-estimate.
depreda'tion *n.* plundering, ravages.—**dep'redator** *n.*–**dep'redate** *v.t.* to plunder.
depress' *v.t.* to lower, in level or activity; affect with low spirits.—**depres'sion** (-s'in) *n.* a depressing; a hollow; a centre of low barometric pressure; low spirits; low state of trade.—**depress'ible** *a.*
deprive' *v.t.* to dispossess (of).—**depriva'tion** *n.* (**de'pri'ved** *p.t.* and *p.p.*).
depth *n.* deepness; degree of deepness; abyss.—**depth'-charge** *n.* a bomb for dropping on a submerged submarine, exploding at a set depth.
depute' *v.t.* to commit to (a substitute); appoint as substitute.—**dep'uty** *n.* a substitute, delegate.—**deputa'tion** *n.* persons sent to speak for others.—**dep'utise** *v.i.* to act for another.
derail' *v.t.* to make (a train) leave the rails.—**derail'ment** *n.*
derange' *v.t.* throw into confusion or disorder, disorganise; disorder the mind of.—**derange'ment** *n.*
der'by (der'-) *n.* a bowler hat; strong type of shoe; a kind of porcelain; famous horse-race run annually on Epsom Downs.
der'elict *a.* forsaken, *esp.* of a ship.—*n.* a thing forsaken, *esp.* a ship.—**derelic'tion** *n.* neglect (of duty).
deride' *v.i.* to laugh to scorn.—**deris'ion** *n.*—**deri'sive** *a.*—**deri'sory** *a.* futile.
Syn. to taunt, insult, jeer at. *Ant.* to appreciate, respect, reverence.
derive' *v.t.* to get from; deduce; show the origin of.—*v.i.* be descended (from).—**deriva'tion** *n.*—**deriv'ative** *a.* traceable back to something else.—*n.* a thing or word derived from another.
dermati'tis *n.* inflammation of skin.
der'ogate *v.i.* detract (from); degenerate.—**deroga'tion** *n.*—**derog'atory** *a.* disparaging, involving discredit.
derr'ick *n.* hoisting-machine, crane.
derr'ing-do' *n.* desperate valour.
derr'y *n.* in Australia, (*sl.*) prejudice; **to have a derry on,** to be prejudiced against.
der'vish *n.* a Mohammedan friar.
des'cant *n.* sung accompaniment to plainsong.—**descant'** *v.i.* to talk at length, dwell on, *esp.* with enthusiasm.
descend' *v.i.* to come or go down; slope down; swoop on or attack; stoop; spring from (ancestor, etc.); pass to an heir, be transmitted.—*v.t.* to go or come down.—**descend'ant** *n.* one descended from another.—**descent'** *n.* a coming down; ancestry.
describe' *v.t.* to give a detailed account of; to trace out (a geometrical figure, etc.); to pass along (a course, etc.).—**descrip'tive** *a.*—**descrip'tion** *n.* a detailed account; a kind, sort, species.
descry' *v.t.* to catch sight of, *esp.* at a distance, espy. (**-cried'** *p.t.* and *p.p.*—**-cry'ing** *pres. p.*) he **descries'.**
des'ecrate *v.t.* to violate the sanctity of, profane; convert to evil uses.—**desecra'tion** *n.*—**des'ecrator** *n.*
desert' (-z-) *n.* (usually *pl.*) conduct or qualities deserving reward or punishment; merit, virtue.
desert' (-z-) *v.t.* to abandon.—*v.i.* to run away from service, *esp.* of Army, etc.—**des'ert** (-z-) *n.* a large barren region.—*a.* barren, uninhabited.—**deser'tion** *n.*—**desert'er** *n.*
deserve' (-z-) *v.t.* show oneself worthy of; to have a claim to.—*v.i.* be worthy (of reward, etc.).—**deserv'edly** *adv.* rightly.—**deserv'ing** *a.* meritorious.
deshabille' (des-a-) *n.* undress.
des'iccate *v.t.* to dry up.—**desicca'tion** *n.*
desid'erate *v.t.* to feel as missing.—**desidera'tum** *n.*; **-ata** *pl.* a felt want.
design' (-zīn') *v.t.* to plan out; set apart for a purpose; make working drawings for; sketch.—*n.* a project, purpose, mental plan; sketch, working plan; art of making decorative patterns, etc.—**design'edly** *adv.* on purpose.—**design'ing** *a.* crafty, scheming.—**design'er** *n.*, *esp.* one who draws designs for manufacturers.—**des'ignate** (dez'-ig-) *v.t.* name, appoint to office.—*a.* appointed but not yet installed in office.—**designa'tion** *n.*
desire' (-z-) *v.t.* to wish for, long for, ask for, entreat.—*n.* longing; expressed wish; wish or felt lack; request; thing wished or requested.—**desi'rable** *a.*—**desirabil'ity** *n.*—**desi'rous** *a.*
desist' *v.i.* to cease, to stop.
desk *n.* a sloped board on which a writer rests his paper, a reader his book; a table or other piece of furniture designed for the use of a writer or reader.
des'olate *a.* solitary; neglected, barren; ruinous; dismal, forlorn.—*v.t.* to depopulate, lay waste; make unhappy; overwhelm with grief.—**desola'tion** *n.*
despair' *v.i.* to lose all hope.—*n.* loss of all hope; thing causing complete loss of hope.—**des'perate** *a.* beyond hope; hopelessly bad, difficult or dangerous.—**despera'tion** *n.*—**des'perately** *adv.*—**despera'do** (-ā-) *n.* one ready for any lawless deed (**-does, -dos** (-dōz) *pl.*).

despatch' *see* **dispatch.**
despise' (-z-) *v.t.* to look down on.—**des'picable** *a.* base, contemptible, vile.—**des'picably** *adv.*—**despite'** *n.* scorn; ill-will, spite.—*prep.* in spite of.—**despite'ful** *a.*
despoil' *v.t.* plunder, rob.—**despolia'tion** *n.*
despond' *v.i.* to lose heart or hope.—**despond'ent** *a.*—**despond'ency** *n.*
des'pot *n.* a tyrant, oppressor.—**despot'ic** *a.*–**despot'ically** *adv.*–**des'potism** *n.*
des'quamate *v.i.* to come off in scales.—**desquama'tion** *n.*—**desquam'atory** *a.*
dessert' (-z-) *n.* fruit and confections served after dinner.
des'tine (-tin) *v.t.* to ordain or fix beforehand; set apart, devote.—**des'tiny** *n.* the power which foreordains; course of events or person's fate, etc., regarded as fixed by this power.—**destina'tion** *n.* place to which a person or thing is bound.
des'titute *a.* in great need of food, clothing, etc.—**destitu'tion** *n.*
destroy' *v.t.* to make away with, put an end to, reduce to nothingness or uselessness.—**destroy'er** *n.* one who destroys; a small swift war-vessel using guns and torpedoes.—**destruct'ible** *a.*—**destruc'tion** *n.*—**destruc'tive** *a.*—**destruc'tively** *adv.*—**destruc'tor** *n.* that which destroys, *esp.* a furnace for destroying refuse. *Syn.* to ruin, overthrow, extirpate, annihilate. *Ant.* to repair, renew, recondition.
des'uetude (-swi-) *n.* state of disuse.
des'ultory *a.* off and on, flitting from one thing to another, unmethodical.
detach' (-tsh) *v.t.* to unfasten, separate.—**detach'ed** *a.* standing apart, isolated.—**detach'ment** *n.* detaching; part of a body of troops separated for a special duty; aloofness.—**detach'able** *a.*
de'tail *n.* treatment of anything item by item; a small or unimportant part; a party or man told off for a duty in the Army.—**detail'** *v.t.* to relate with full particulars; to appoint for a duty.
detain' *v.t.* to keep under restraint; to imprison; keep waiting.—**deten'tion** *n.*
detect' *v.t.* to find out or discover the existence or presence or nature or identity of.—**detect'or** *n.*—**detec'tion** *n.*—**detect'ive** *a.* employment in or apt for detection.—*n.* one employed in detecting criminals.—**detect'ophone** *n.* a telephone secretly placed for eavesdropping.
de'tente (dā'tont) *n.* improvement in political (usually international) crisis.
deter' *v.t.* to make to abstain (from); discourage, dissuade.—**deterr'ent** *a.*
deter'gent *a.* cleansing.—*n.* a purifier.
dete'riorate *v.i.* and *t.* to become or make worse.—**deteriora'tion** *n.*
deter'mine *v.t.* to make up one's mind, decide; to fix as known; to bring to decision; to be the deciding factor in; *law,* to end.—*v.i.* to come to an end; come to a decision.—**deter'minable** *a.*—**deter'minant** *a.* and *n.*—**deter'minate** *a.* fixed in scope or nature.—**determina'tion** *n.* a determining; a resolve; firm or resolute conduct or purpose.—**deter'mined** *a.* resolute.—**deter'minism** *n.* the theory that human action is settled by forces independent of the will.—**deter'minist** *n.*
detest' *v.t.* to hate, loathe.—**detest'able** *a.*—**detest'ably** *adv.*—**detesta'tion** *n.*
Syn. to execrate, abominate, abhor. *Ant.* to love, cherish, respect, like.
dethrone' *v.t.* to remove from a throne.—**dethrone'ment** *n.*
det'onate *v.i.* and *t.* to explode with a loud report; set off an explosive.—**detona'tion** *n.*—**det'onator** *n.* *esp.* a detonating apparatus as a railway fog-signal, part of a bomb, etc.
detour' (-tōōr') *n.* a course which leaves the main route to rejoin it later.
detract' *v.t.* and *i.* to take away from; belittle.—**detrac'tion** *n.*—**detract'or** *n.*
detrain' *v.i.* and *t.* to alight or make alight from a train.
det'riment *n.* harm, loss, damage.—**detriment'al** *a.*—**detriment'ally** *adv.*
detri'tus *n.* worn-down matter such as gravel, from wearing of exposed surfaces.
deuce *n.* the two at dice, cards, etc.. score of forty all at tennis.—in exclamatory phrases, the devil.—**deu'ced** *a.*
deuter'ium (dip'logen) *n.* an isotope of hydrogen having twice the atomic weight of ordinary hydrogen.
dev'astate *v.t.* to lay waste.—**devasta'tion** *n.* (**dev'astated** *p.t.* and *p.p.*).
devel'op *v.t.* to bring to maturity; bring forth; evolve.—*v.i.* to grow to a maturer state (**-oped** *p.t.* and *p.p.*—**-oping** *pres. p.*).—**devel'oper** *n.* *esp.* photographic chemical; muscle exerciser.—**devel'opment** *n.*
de'viate *v.i.* to leave the way, diverge.—**devia'tion** *n.*—**de'viator** *n.*—**de'vious** *a.*
device' *n.* a contrivance; scheme; plot; emblem, heraldic figure or design.
dev'il *n.* personified spirit of evil; superhuman evil being; vice; fierceness in fighting; person of great wickedness; one who devils for lawyer or author; dish of devilled food; S. Africa, dust storm.—*v.t.* to do work that passes for employer's, e.g. for lawyer or author; to grill with hot condiments.—**dev'ilish** *a.*—**dev'ilry** *n.*—**dev'ilment** *n.*—**dev'il-may-care** *a.* happy-go-lucky.—**dev'il's ad'vocate** *n.* one appointed to state disqualifications of one whom it is proposed to make a saint.
de'vious *a.* circuitous; indirect; *fig.* erratic; crooked, deceitful.
devis'cerate *v.t.* to disembowel.
devise' (-z) *v.t.* to plan, frame, contrive; plot; leave by will.–**devi'sor** *n.*–**devisee'** *n.*
devoid' *a.* empty of, lacking, free from.
devolve' *v.i.* to pass or fall (to, upon).—

v.t. to throw (a duty, etc.) on to another, delegate.—**devolu'tion** *n.*
devote' *v.t.* to set apart; give up exclusively (to a person, purpose, etc.).—**devo'ted** *a. esp.* very loyal or loving.—**devotee'** *n.* one devoted, a worshipper.—**devo'tion** *n.* a setting apart; dedication; religious earnestness; *pl.* prayers, religious exercises.—**devo'tional** *a.*
devour' *v.t.* to eat up, consume, ravage, destroy.—**devour'er** *n.*
devout' *a.* earnestly religious; reverent.
dew *n.* moisture from the air deposited as small drops on cool surfaces between nightfall and morning; any beaded moisture.—*v.t.* wet with, as with, dew.—**dew'y** *a.*—**dew'iness** *n.*—**dew'drop** *n.*
dew'lap *n.* fold of loose skin hanging from the neck, *esp.* of cattle.—**dew'claw** *n.* partly developed inner toe of dogs.
dew'pond *n.* means of collecting water on chalk downs in dry weather.
dexter'ity *n.* manual skill, neatness, adroitness.—**dex'terous** *a.* neat-handed, skilful.—**dex'ter** *a.* in heraldry, on the bearer's right hand of a shield.
Syn. expertness, address, cleverness, aptitude, faculty. *Ant.* clumsiness, awkwardness, unskilfulness.
dex'trose *n.* glucose; grape sugar.
dho'bi *n.* Hindu laundry man.
dhow' *n.* an Arab vessel.
dia- *prefix*, through, as in *diameter, diaphanous.*
diabe'tes (-ēz) *n.* a urinary disease.—**diabet'ic** *a.* and *n.* (victim) of this.
diabol'ic, diabol'ical *a.* devilish.—**diabol'ically** *adv.*—**diab'olism** *n.* devil-worship.—**diab'olo** *n.* a top sent spinning from string attached to two sticks.
diac'onal *a.* relating to a deacon.—**diac'onate** *n.* office or rank of deacon; body of deacons.
di'adem *n.* a crown.
diær'esis (di-ĕr'-) *n.* a mark (¨) placed over a vowel to show that it is sounded separately from a preceding one (e.g. in aërate) (**-eses** *pl.*).
diagno'sis *n.* art, act of deciding from symptoms nature of a disease (**-ses** *pl.*).—**diagnose'** *v.t.*—**diagnos'tic** *a.*—**diagnosti'cian** *n.* expert in diagnosis.
diag'onal *a.* from corner to corner.—*n.* such a line.—**diag'onally** *adv.*
di'agram *n.* a figure in lines, to illustrate something being expounded, as in a geometrical figure, a weather-chart, plan, etc.—**diagrammat'ic** *a.*
di'al *n.* a plate marked with graduations on a circle or arc on which something is recorded (e.g. dial of a clock, air speed indicator, etc.); compass used by miners, surveyors, etc.—*v.t.* to indicate on dial; work automatic telephone.
di'alect *n.* characteristic speech of a district.—**dialect'al** *a.*—**dialect'ic** *n.* the art of arguing.—**dialect'ic, dialect'ical** *a.*—**dialec'tical mater'ialism** the philosophy of Communism, formulated by Engels, Marx and Lenin.—**dialect'ically** *adv.*—**dialecti'cian** *n.*—**di'alogue** *n.* conversation; literary work representing this; conversational part of a novel, etc.
diam'eter *n.* a straight line passing from side to side of a figure or body through its centre; thickness; unit of magnifying power.—**diamet'rical** *a.*—**diamet'rically** *adv.* absolutely, exactly.
di'amond *n.* a very hard and brilliant precious stone; a lozenge-shaped figure; one of the four suits at cards.
diapa'son (-zn) *n.* one of certain organ-stops; the compass of a voice or instrument; a swelling chorus, burst of harmonious sounds.
di'aper *n.* a fabric with a small diamond pattern; a pattern of that kind; a towel, etc., made of the fabric.—**di'apered** *a.*
diaph'anous *a.* transparent. *Syn.* clear, pellucid. *Ant.* opaque, cloudy.
di'aphragm (-am) *n.* muscle dividing chest and abdomen; scientific device consisting of a vibrating sheet or plate.
diarrhoe'a (-rē'a) *n.* excessive looseness of the bowels.—**diarrhoe'al** *a.*
di'ary *n.* a daily record of events or thoughts; a book for such record.—**di'arist** *n.* one who keeps a diary.
diatherm'y *n.* curative treatment in which electric currents are applied to produce heat in deeper tissues of body.
di'atribe *n.* a bitter speech of criticism.
dib'ble *n.* an implement for making holes in the ground for seeds or plants.—*v.t.* to prepare (ground) or sow or plant with such implement.
dice, *see* **die.**
dichro'matism *n.* (*med.*) seeing only two colours.
dick'y, dick'ey *n.* a detachable false shirt-front; a seat at the back of a carriage, motor car, etc.
dictate' *v.t.* and *i.* to say or read for exact reproduction by another on paper; prescribe.—**dic'tate** *n.* bidding.—**dicta'tion** *n.*—**dicta'tor** *n.* a supreme ruler.—**dictato'rial** *a.* despotic; overbearing.—**dictato'rially** *adv.*—**dic'taphone, dic'tograph** *n.* instrument for recording speech for later writing.—**dicta'torship** *n.*
dic'tion *n.* choice and use of words.—**dic'tionary** *n.* a book setting forth in alphabetical order the words of a language with meanings, etc.
dic'tum *n.* a pronouncement, maxim, saying (**dic'ta** *pl.*).
didac'tic *a.* instructive; meant to teach.
did'dle *v.t.* to cheat.
die (dī) *v.i.* to cease to live; come to an end (**died** *p.t.* and *p.p.*—**dy'ing** *pres. p.*)—**die'hard** *n.* one who resists (reform, etc.) to the end.
die (dī) *n.* a cube with sides marked one to six for games of chance; a small cube of bread, etc.; (*pl.* **dice**); a stamp for em-

bossing, etc. (*pl.* **dies**).—**die'-sink'er** *n.* an engraver of dies.—**dice** *v.i.* to gamble with dice.—**di'cer** *n.*

die'sel (dē'zl) *a.* highly efficient internal-combustion engine, using heavy oils.

di'et *n.* kind of food lived on; regulated course of feeding; food.—**di'etary** *n.* allowance or character of food, *esp.* in an institution, etc.—*a.* relating to diet.—**dietet'ic** *a.*—*n. pl.* the science of diet.—**dieti'cian** *n.* one skilled in dietetics.

di'et *n.* a parliamentary assembly.

diff'er *v.i.* to be unlike; disagree.—**difference** *n.* unlikeness; disagreement; remainder left after subtraction.—**diff'-erent** *a.* unlike.—**diff'erently** *adv.*—**differen'tial** *a.* varying with circumstances.—*n.* the mechanism in a motor-car which allows the back wheels to revolve at different speeds when rounding a corner.—**differen'tial cal'culus** branch of higher mathematics analysing the rate of change of a variable.—**differen'tially** *adv.*—**differen'tiate** *v.t.* to make different, develop into unlikeness, —*v.i.* discriminate.—**differentia'tion** *n.*

diff'iculty *n.* hardness to be done or understood; a hindrance; an obscurity; embarrassment.—**diff'icult** *a.* not easy, hard, obscure; exacting.

diff'ident *a.* timid, shy.—**diff'idently** *adv.*—**diff'idence** *n.* lack of confidence.
Syn. bashful, distrustful, hesitating. *Ant.* confident, assured, forward.

diffuse' (-z) *v.t.* to spread abroad.—*a.* (-s) loose, verbose.—**diffu'sion** *n.*—**diffu'-sive** *a.*—**diffuse'ly** *adv.*—**diffu'sively** *adv.*

dig *v.i.* to work with a spade.—*v.t.* to turn up with a spade; hollow out; get by digging, thrust into (**dug** *p.t.* and *p.p.* —**digg'ing** *pres. p.*).—**digg'er** one who digs; a gold-miner; an Australian or New Zealand soldier.

digest' *v.t.* to prepare (food) in the stomach, etc., for assimilation; bring into handy form by sorting, tabulating; reflect on; absorb.—*v.i.* of food, to undergo digestion.—**di'gest** *n.* a methodical summary, *esp.* of laws.—**digest'ible** *a.*—**digest'ive** *a.*—**diges'tion** *n.*

dig'it (-j-) *n.* any of the numbers 0 to 9; a finger or toe.—**digita'lis** *n.* a poisonous drug made from the foxglove.

dig'nity *n.* worthiness, excellence; an honourable office or title; stateliness, gravity.—**dig'nify** *v.t.* give dignity to (**-fied** *p.t.* and *p.p.*—**-fying** *pres. p.*)—**dig'nified** *a.* stately, majestic.–**dig'nitary** *n.* a holder of high office (**dig'nitaries** *pl.*).

digress' *v.i.* to go aside from the main course, *esp.* to deviate from the subject in speaking or writing.—**digres'sion** *n.*

dike, dyke *n.* a ditch; a low wall; an embankment.—*v.t.* provide with dike.

dikk'op *n.* in S. Africa, a bird resembling a bustard; (*sl.*) a stupid person.

dilap'idated *a.* falling into ruin or decay.—**dilapida'tion** *n.*

dilate' (dī-) *v.t.* to expand.—*v.i.* to expand; to talk or write at large (on).—**dilata'tion, dila'tion** *n.* *Syn.* to amplify, swell, expatiate, descant. *Ant.* to contract, shrink, lessen, minimise.

dil'atory *a.* delaying, slow.—**dil'atorily** *adv.*—**dil'atoriness** *n.*

dilem'ma *n.* a position in fact or argument offering only choice between two or more unwelcome possibilities.

dilettan'te (-ti) *n.* a person with taste and knowledge of the fine arts (*esp.* as a pastime); an amateur (**dilettan'ti** *pl.*). —*a.* amateur, desultory.—**dilettan'tism** *n.*

dil'igent *a.* unremitting in effort, industrious.—**dil'igence** *n.* steady work.

dill *n.* a herb with medicinal seeds.

dill'y-bag *n.* an Australian native-made rush or bark bag.

dilute' *a.* to reduce (a liquid) in strength by adding water, etc.—*a.* weakened thus.—**dilu'tion** *n.* (**dilu'ted** *p.t.* and *p.p.*).

dilu'vium *n.* a surface deposit of sand, pebbles, etc., attributable to former floods (**-viums, -via** *pl.*).—**dilu'vial, dilu'-vian** *a.* pert. to a deluge.

dim *a.* indistinct, faith (**dimm'er** *comp.* —**dimm'est** *sup.*).—*v.t.* and *i.* to make or grow dim.—**dim'ly** *adv.*—**dim'ness** *n.*

dime *n.* Amer. ten-cent piece.

dimen'sion *n.* measurement, size, extent, scope.—**dimen'sional** *a.*

dimin'ish *v.t.* and *i.* to lessen.—**diminu'tion** *n.*–**dimin'utive** *a.* very small.
Syn. abate, decrease, reduce. *Ant.* increase, add to, enlarge, extend.

diminuen'do *adv.* in a gradually diminishing manner.

dim'ity *n.* a cotton fabric.

dimm'er *n.* in motoring, a device to lessen power of headlamp.

dim'ple *n.* a small hollow in the surface of the skin, *esp.* of the cheek.—*v.t.* and *i.* to mark with, or break into, dimples.

din *n.* a continuous roar of confused noises.—*v.t.* to repeat to weariness.

dine *v.i.* to take dinner.—*v.t.* to give dinner to.—**di'ning-room** *n.* a room used for meals.—**di'ner** *n.* one who dines; a restaurant-car (**dined** *p.t.* and *p.p.*).

din'ghy (-ng'gi) *n.* a small boat.

din'gle (-ng'gl) *n.* a dell.

din'go (-ng'gō) *n.* an Australian wild dog (**-goes** *pl.*).

din'gy (-j-) *a.* dirty-looking, dull, shabby.—**din'giness** *n.*

dink'um *a.* (*sl.*) in Australia, honest, genuine, trustworthy.—*n.* work.—**fair din'kum,** fair play.

din'ky *a.* (*sl.*) pert; pretty; small; neat.

dinn'er *n.* the chief meal of the day.

dint *n.* dent.—**by dint of,** by force of.

di'ocese (di'o-sēs) *n.* the district or jurisdiction of a bishop.—**dioc'esan** *a.*—*n.* a bishop, or clergyman, or the people of a diocese.

diox'ide *n.* an oxide with two parts of oxygen to one of the other constituent.
dip *v.t.* to put in and out of a liquid; to immerse; to lower and raise again; to take up in a ladle, bucket, etc.—*v.i.* to plunge partially or temporarily; go down, sink; slope downwards.—*n.* an act of dipping; a hollow.—**dipp'er** *n.*—**dip'-stick** *n.* rod inserted in sump of car engine to measure amount of oil.
diphthe'ria *n.* an infectious disease of the throat with membranous growth.
diph'thong *n.* a union of two vowel sounds in a single compound sound.
di'plex (dī-) *a.* in wireless, of or pertaining to a reception or transmission of two messages simultaneously.
dip'logen *n.* a form of hydrogen twice as heavy as the normal gas.
diplo'ma *n.* a document vouching for a person's title to some degree, honour, etc.—**diplo'macy** *n.* the management of international relations; tactful or adroit dealing.—**dip'lomat** *n.* one engaged in official diplomacy.—**diplo'matist** *n.* a diplomat; a tactful or crafty person.—**diplomat'ic** *a.*—**diplomat'ically** *adv.*
di'pole *n.* a television aerial.
dipsoma'nia *n.* inability to keep from alcohol.—**dipsoma'niac** *n.*
dip'tych (-tik) *n.* a picture on two boards hinged to close like a book.
dire, direful *a.* dread, terrible.
direct' *v.t.* to put in the straight way; address (letter, etc.); aim, turn; control, order.—*a.* straight; going straight to the point; lineal; immediate; frank.—**direc'tion** *n.* a directing; body of directors; address, instruction; aim, course of movement.—**direc'tion finder** *n.* radio equipped with directional antennae to obtain bearings for navigation, etc.—**direct'ive** *a.*—**direct'ly** *adv.* **direct'ness** *n.*—**direct'or** *n.* one who directs; a member of a board managing a company.—**direct'ress** *fem.*—**direct'orate** *n.*—**direct'orship** *n.*—**direct'ory** *n.* book of names, addresses, streets, etc.
dirge *n.* a song of mourning.
dir'igible (-ij-) *a.* that may be directed or controlled.—*n.* steerable airship.
dirk *n.* a Highland dagger.
dirt'y *a.* unclean; mean.—**dirt** *n.* filth; mud; earth.—**dirt'ily** *adv.*—**dirt'iness** *n.*
dirt'-track *n.* a loose surface track for motor-cycle racing.
dis- *prefix*, indicates negation, opposition, deprivation; in many verbs, it indicates the undoing of the action of the simple verb, e.g. **disembark'**, to come out from what one *embarked* in; many verbs, nouns and adjectives in **dis-** mean the exact opposite of the simple word, e.g. **disarra'nge, disord'er, disloy'al**; some verbs in **dis-** mean to deprive of the thing indicated by the simple word, e.g. **disbow'el.** All such words are omitted, and the meaning should be sought by looking up the simple word to which **dis-** is prefixed.
disa'ble *v.t.* to incapacitate; disqualify; cripple.—**disabil'ity** *n.* lack of power.
disabuse' (-z) *v.t.* undeceive, set right.
disaffect'ed *a.* ill-disposed, disloyal, inclined to sedition.—**disaffec'tion** *n.*
disagree'ment *n.* lack of agreement.—**disagree'** *v.i.* to be at variance.
Syn. difference, discrepancy, division, dispute, variance. *Ant.* agreement, concurrence, concord, harmony.
disappoint' *v.t.* to fail to fulfil (hope).—**disappoint'ment** *n.*—**disappoint'ing** *a.*
disarm' *v.t.* and *i.* to deprive of arms or weapons; to reduce a country's war weapons; to win over.—**disarmament** *n.*
disarray' *n.* disorder, confusion.—*v.t.* throw into disorder; undress; disrobe.
disas'ter (-á-) *n.* a sudden or great misfortune.—**disas'trous** *a.*
disband' *v.t.* and *i.* dismiss from service; disperse.—**disband'ment** *n.*
disburse' *v.t.* to pay out money.
disc *see* **disk.**
discard' *v.t.* and *i.* to reject, or play as worthless (a card); to give up; cast off.
discern' *v.t.* to make out; distinguish.—**discern'ment** *n.* insight.—**discern'ible** *a.*
discharge' *v.t.* to unload; fire off; release; dismiss; pay; emit.—*n.* a discharging; a being discharged; matter emitted; a document certifying release.
disci'ple *n.* a follower, adherent, one who takes another as teacher and model.—**disci'pleship** *n.*
dis'cipline (-in) *n.* training that produces orderliness, obedience, self-control; result of such training; a system of rules; maintenance of subordination in an army, school, etc.—*v.t.* to train; chastise.—**disciplina'rian** *n.* one who keeps order.—**dis'ciplinary** *a.*
disclaim' *v.t.* disavow.—**disclaim'er** *n.*
disclose' (-ōz') *v.t.* to unclose; to bring to light; divulge.—**disclo'sure** (-z-) *n.* act of disclosing (**disclosed'** *p.t.* and *p.p.*).
discog'rapher *n.* one who compiles information on the history of the gramophone.—**discog'raphy** *n.* encyclopedia of gramophone records.
discol'our *v.t.* to alter the colour of.
discom'fit (-um-) *v.t.* to defeat, baffle.—**discom'fiture** *n.* upsetment, annoyance.
disconcert' *v.t.* derange, ruffle, confuse.
discon'solate *a.* unhappy, downcast.
dis'cord *n.* absence of concord; difference; conflicting sounds.—**discord'ant** *a.*—**discord'antly** *adv.*—**discord'ance** *n.*
discount' *v.t.* give present value of (a bill of exchange, etc.); detract from, lessen; allow for exaggeration in.—**dis'count** *n.* a deduction made on discounting a bill, receiving payment, etc.
discour'age (-kur'-) *v.t.* to reduce the confidence of; deter from; show dis-

approval of.—**discour'agement** *n.*
Syn. dispirit, depress, dissuade, damp.
Ant. encourage, persuade, exhort.

dis'course *n.* a speech; sermon; conversation.—**discourse'** *v.i.* to speak, lecture, converse.—*v.t.* to utter.

discov'er (-kuv'-) *v.t.* to find out, light upon; exhibit, make known.—**discov'ery** *n.*—**discov'erer** *n.*—**discov'erable** *a.*

discred'it *n.* loss of credit; that which discredits; doubt, disbelief.—*v.t.* cause doubt of; decline to trust or have faith in.—**discred'itable** *a.* disgraceful.

discreet' *a.* prudent, knowing when to be silent.—**discreet'ly** *adv.*—**discre'tion** *n.*

discrep'ant *a.* not tallying.—**discrep'ancy** *n.* lack of agreement.

discrim'inate *v.t.* and *i.* to detect or draw distinctions; distinguish from or between.—**discrimina'tion** *n.*

discurs'ive *a.* passing from subject to subject, not keeping to the main thread.

dis'cus *n.* quoit, disk.

discuss' *v.t.* to exchange opinions on; debate; consume (food or drink).—**discus'sion** *n.*—**discuss'ible** *a.*

disdain' *n.* scorn, contempt.—*v.t.* to scorn.—**disdain'ful** *a.*—**disdain'fully** *adv.*

disease' *n.* illness; disorder of health.

diseuse (dē-zerz) *n.* woman who recites or acts a solo part for entertainment.

disfig'ure (-ger) *v.t.* to deface, spoil.—**disfig'urement** *n.*—**disfiguration** *n.*

disgrace' *n.* ignominy; a cause of shame; loss of favour.—*v.t.* to bring shame or discredit upon.—**disgrace'ful** *a.* shameful.—**disgrace'fully** *adv.*

disgrunt'led *a.* discontented, continually grumbling.

disguise' (-gīz) *v.t.* to change the appearance of, make unrecognisable; conceal; misrepresent.—*n.* false appearance.

disgust' *n.* violent distaste.—*v.t.* to affect with loathing.—**disgus'ting** *a.*

dish *n.* a shallow vessel for food; a portion or variety of food; the contents of a dish.—*v.t.* to put in a dish; serve up.

dishev'elled *a.* with disordered hair; ruffled, untidy.—**dishev'el** *v.*

disinfect' *v.t.* to render free from infection or germs.—**disinfec'tion** *n.*—**disinfect'ant** *n.* a germicide.

disin'tegrate *v.t.* and *i.* to break up, fall to pieces.—**disintegra'tion** *n.*

disin'terested *a.* free from selfish motives; impartial; fair.

disk, disc *n.* a thin circular plate.—**disk har'row** *n.* a farm instrument consisting of a series of revolving discs for cutting soil.—**disk'-jockey** *n.* (U.S.) (*radio sl.*) an announcer of programmes which consist chiefly of records.

dis'locate *v.t.* to put out of place, *esp.* of a bone; to put into disorder, disorganise.—**disloca'tion** *n.*

dis'mal (-z-) *a.* depressing, or depressed; cheerless, dreary.—**dis'mally** *adv.*

disman'tle *v.t.* to deprive of defences, furniture, etc.; remove equipment.

dismay' *v.t.* to dishearten, daunt.—*n.* consternation, horrified amazement.

dismem'ber *v.t.* to tear or cut limb from limb; divide, partition, e.g. a country.—**dismem'berment** *n.*

dismiss' *v.t.* to send away, disperse, disband; discharge from employment, or from the mind.—**dismiss'al** *n.*

disown' *v.t.* refuse to recognise or have anything to do with.

dispar'age *v.t.* to speak slightingly of, depreciate; to bring into disrepute.—**dispar'aging** *a.*—**dispar'agement** *n.*

dis'parate *a.* essentially different, not related.—**dispar'ity** *n.* inequality.

dispas'sionate *a.* not swayed by passion; calm, impartial.

dispatch', despatch' *v.t.* to send off; send to a destination or on an errand; kill; eat up; finish off, get done with speed.—*n.* a sending off; efficient speed; an official written message.

dispel' *v.t.* to clear away (**dispelled'** *p.t.* and *p.p.*). *Syn.* dissipate, banish, disperse. *Ant.* gather up, collect, recall.

dispense' *v.t.* to deal out; to make up (a medicine); relax, not insist on; do without.—*v.i.* to make up medicines.—**dispens'er** *n.* (**dispensed'** *p.t.* and *p.p.*).—**dispens'ary** *n.* a place where medicine is made up.—**dispensa'tion** *n.* a licence or exemption; a provision.—**dispens'able** *a.*

disperse' *v.t.* to scatter.—**dispersed'** *a.* scattered.—**disper'sion** *n.*—**disper'sal** *n.*

displace' *v.t.* take the place of; put something else in place of; remove from position of authority.—**displaced person** a native of a Nazi-occupied country who was forcibly exiled or carried off to another country for forced labour.

display' *v.t.* to spread out for show; to show, expose to view.—*n.* a displaying; exhibition; show, ostentation.

disport' *v. refl.* to gambol, move about for enjoyment, *esp.* in water, sunshine.

dispose' (-z) *v.t.* to arrange; to make inclined (to).—*v.i.* to ordain, appoint.—**dispose of,** sell, get rid of; have authority over.—**dispo'sal** *n.*—**disposi'tion** *n.* arrangement; plan; inclination towards; cast of mind or temper.

dispropor'tion *n.* want of proportion.

dispute' *v.i.* to debate, discuss.—*v.t.* to call in question; debate, argue; oppose, contest; try to debar from.—**dis'putable** *a.*—**dis'putant** *n.*—**disputa'tion** *n.*
Syn. to impugn, controvert, wrangle.
Ant. to accept, agree, acquiesce.

disqual'ify *v.t.* to make unfit, to debar or rule out.—he **disqual'ifies.**—**disqual'ifying** *pres. p.*—**disqualified** *p.t.* and *p.p.*

disquisi'tion (-zish'un) *n.* a learned or elaborate treatise or discourse.

disregard' *n.* indifference; wilful neglect.—*v.t.* to take no notice of.

disrupt' *v.t.* to shatter, break in pieces, split.—**disrup'tion** *n.*—**disrupt'ive** *a.*
dissect' *v.t.* to cut up (a body, etc.,) for detailed examination; to examine or criticise in detail, analyse.—**dissec'tion** *n.*—**dissect'or** *n.*
dissem'ble *v.t.* and *i.* to conceal or disguise (opinions, feelings, etc.); to talk or act hypocritically.—**dissem'bler** *n.*
dissem'inate *v.t.* to spread abroad.—**dissemina'tion** *n.*—**dissem'inator** *n.*
dissent' *v.i.* to differ in opinion; to express such difference; disagree with the doctrine, etc., of an established church.—*n.* such disagreement.—**dissent'er** *n.*—**dissen'tient** *a.* and *n.* one who disagrees.—**dissen'sion** *n.*
disserta'tion *n.* a learned discourse.
diss'ident *a.* not in agreement, conflicting.—**diss'idence** *n.*
dissim'ulate *v.t.* and *i.* to pretend not to have; to practise deceit.—**dissimula'tion** *n.*—**dissim'ulator** *n.*
diss'ipate *v.t.* to scatter, clear away; waste, squander.—*v.i.* to disappear; clear away.—**dissipa'tion** *n.* scattering; frivolous or dissolute way of life.—**diss'ipated** *a.* corrupted, dissolute.
disso'ciate *v.t.* to separate from, disunite, sever.—**dissocia'tion** *n.*
dissolve' *v.t.* to absorb or melt in a fluid; break up, put an end to, annul.—*v.i.* to melt in a fluid; disappear, vanish; break up, scatter.—**dissol'uble** *a.*—**dissolu'tion** *n.*—**diss'olute** *a.* lax in morals.
diss'onant *a.* jarring, discordant in sound.—**diss'onance** *n.* disharmony.
dissuade' (-sw-) *v.t.* to advise to refrain, persuade not to, discourage.—**dissua'sion** *n.*—**dissua'sive** *a.*
dissyll'able *n.* *see* **disyllable.**
dis'taff *n.* a cleft stick to hold wool, etc., for hand-spinning (**dis'taffs** *pl.*).
dis'tance *n.* amount of space between two things; remoteness; excessive dignity.—*v.t.* to leave behind, *esp.* in a race.—**dis'tant** *a.*—**dis'tantly** *adv.*
distaste' *n.* aversion; disgust; dislike.
distem'per *n.* disordered state of mind or body; a disease of dogs; a method of painting on plaster; the paint used for this.—*v.t.* to paint in distemper.
distend' *v.t.* and *i.* to swell out by pressure from within.—**disten'sion** *n.*
dis'tich (-ik) *n.* a couplet.
distil' *v.i.* to pass over or condense from a still; to trickle down.—*v.t.* to obtain (a substance or part of it) in a purified state by evaporating and then condensing it.—**distilla'tion** *n.*—**distill'er** *n.* one who distils, *esp.* a manufacturer of alcoholic spirits.—**distill'ery** *n.* (**distilled'** *p.t.* and *p.p.*).
distinct' *a.* clear, easily seen, sharp of outline; definite; separate, different.—**distinct'ly** *adv.*—**distinct'ness** *n.* clearness.—**distinc'tion** *n.* point of difference; act of distinguishing; eminence, high honour, high quality.—**distinct'ive** *a.* characteristic, peculiar.
distin'guish (-ng'gw-) *v.t.* to class; make a difference in; to recognise, make out; to honour; make prominent or honoured (usually *refl.*).—*v.i.* to draw a distinction, grasp a difference.—**disting'uishable** *a.*—he **distin'guishes.**
distort' *v.t.* misrepresent; garble; to put out of shape.—**distor'tion** *n.*
distract' *v.t.* turn aside, divert; bewilder, drive mad.—**distrac'tion** *n.*
distraint' *n.* legal seizure of goods to enforce payment.—**distrain'** *v.i.*
distrait' *a.* absent-minded.
distraught' (-awt') *a.* bewildered, crazy.
distress' *n.* severe trouble, mental pain; pressure of hunger, fatigue or want; exhaustion; (law) distraint.—*v.t.* to afflict, give mental pain.—**distress'ful** *a.*—**distress'ing** *a.*
Syn. calamity, adversity, grief, agony. *Ant.* prosperity, good fortune, benefit.
distrib'ute *v.t.* to deal out; spread, dispose at intervals; classify.—**distrib'utive** *a.*—**distribu'tion** *n.*—**distrib'utor** *n.*
dis'trict *n.* a portion of territory; a region, part of a country.
distrust' *v.t.* to put no trust in.
disturb' *v.t.* to trouble, agitate; unsettle, derange.—**disturb'ance** *n.*
disunite' *v.t.* to destroy the union of.—*v.i.* to part. *Syn.* to divide, sever, disjoin. *Ant.* to unite, join, associate.
disuse' *n.* lack of use, no longer in use.—*v.t.* to stop using.
disyll'able, dissyll'able *n.* a word or metrical foot having two syllables.—**disyllab'ic (diss-)** *a.*
ditch *n.* a long narrow hollow dug in the ground, trench.—*v.t.* and *i.* to make or repair ditches.
dith'er *v.i.* (*col.*) to shake or tremble; to vacillate, hesitate.
ditt'any *n.* (*bot.*) an aromatic plant yielding a sweet-scented oil.
ditt'o *n.* same, aforesaid; (used to avoid repetition in lists, etc.) (**ditt'os** (-ōz) *pl.*).
ditt'y *n.* a simple song (**dit'ties** *pl.*).—**ditty-bag** *n.* bag used by sailors to hold small personal necessaries.
diuret'ic (di-ūr-) *a.* promoting discharge of urine.—*n.* medicine which causes this discharge.
diur'nal *a.* daily; in or of daytime.
divaga'tion *n.* wandering, digression.—**di'vagate** *v.i.* to stray, roam.
divan' *n.* a couch without back or head; a smoking-room; an oriental council.
dive *v.i.* to plunge under the surface of water; descend suddenly; disappear, go deep down into.—*n.*—**di'ver** *n.*
diverge' *v.i.* to get farther apart, separate.—**diver'gent** *a.*—**diver'gence** *n.*
di'vers (-z) *a.* sundry.—**diverse'** *a.*

different, varied.—**divers'ify** *v.t.* (**-ified** *p.t./p.p.*— **-ifying** *pr. p.*).—**diverse'ly** *adv.*—**diversifica'tion** *n.*—**divers'ity** *n.*

divert' *v.t.* to turn aside, ward off; cause to turn; amuse, entertain.—**diver'sion** *n.* relaxation.

divest' *v.t.* to unclothe, strip, dispossess.

divide' *v.t.* to make into two or more parts, split up, separate; classify: cut off; deal out; take or have a share; part into two groups for voting.—*v.i.* to become divided.—*n.* in Canada, Australia, etc., a water-shed; ridge.—**div'idend** *n.* a number to be divided by another; a share of profits, of money divided among creditors, etc.—**divi'ders** *n.pl.* measuring compasses.

divine' *a.* of, proceeding from God; sacred; god-like, heavenly.—*n.* theologian; clergyman.—*v.t.* and *i.* to guess; predict, tell by inspiration or magic.—**divine'ly** *adv.*—**divin'ity** *n.* quality of being divine; god; theology.—**divina'tion** *n.* divining.—**divi'ner** *n.*—**divi'ning-rod** *n.* switch for detecting underground water or minerals.

divis'ion (-vizh'-) *n.* act of dividing; part of a whole; part of an army consisting of two or three brigades of infantry.—**divis'ible** *a.* able to be divided.—**divis'ional** *a.*—**divi'sor** *n.*

divorce' *n.* legal dissolution of marriage; complete separation, disunion.—*v.t.* to dissolve a marriage; separate.—**divorcee'** *n.* person divorced.

divulge' *v.t.* to reveal, let out (a secret).

dizz'y *a.* feeling dazed, unsteady, as if about to fall; causing or fit to cause dizziness, as of speed, etc.—*v.t.* to make dizzy (**dizz'ied** *p.t.* and *p.p.*—**dizz'ying** *pres. p.*).—**dizz'iness** *n.*—**dizz'ily** *adv.*

do (dōō) *v.t.* to perform, effect, transact, finish, prepare, cook.—*v.i.* to act, manage, work, fare, serve, suffice.—*v. aux.* makes negative and interrogative sentences and expresses emphasis (**did** *p.t.*—**done** *p.p.*—**do'ing** *pr. p.*).

do'cile *a.* willing to obey; easily taught or led.—**docil'ity** *n.*

dock *n.* a coarse weed.

dock *n.* the solid part of a tail; a cut end, stump.—*v.t.* to cut short, *esp.* a tail; curtail, deprive of.

dock *n.* a basin with flood-gates for loading or repairing ships.—*v.t.* to put in a dock.—*v.i.* to go into dock.—**dock'-yard** *n.* an enclosure with docks, for building or repairing ships.—**dock'er** *n.* dock labourer.—*n.* the enclosure in a criminal court for the prisoner.

dock'et *n.* an endorsement showing the contents of a document; a memorandum; a certificate of payment of customs.—*v.t.* to make a memorandum, endorse with a summary of its contents.

doc'tor *n.* one holding a University's highest degree in any faculty; medical practitioner; in Australia, cook.—*v.t.* to treat medically; to adulterate, garble.—**doc'torate** *n.*—**doc'toral** *a.*—**doc'trine** *n.* what is taught; teaching of a church school, or person; belief, opinion, dogma.—**doctri'nal** *a.*—**doctrinaire'** *n.* one who seeks to apply principles or theory without regard for circumstances.—**cape doctor,** in S. Africa, popular name for strong s.e. wind.

doc'ument *n.* written evidence or information.—*v.t.* to furnish with proofs, illustrations, certificates.—**document'ary** *a.*—**documenta'tion** *n.*

dodd'er *v.i.* to totter, tremble.

dodge *v.i.* to swerve, make zigzag movement, *esp.* to avoid a pursuer or gain an advantage; shuffle, play fast and loose.—*v.t.* to elude by dodging.—*n.* an act of dodging; a trick, artifice; shift, ingenious method.—**dodg'er** *n.*

do'do *n.* an extinct bird.

doe (dō) *n.* a female of deer, hare, rabbit.

doff *v.t.* to take off (hat, clothing).

dog *n.* a familiar domestic quadruped; a person (in contempt, abuse, or playfully).—*v.t.* to follow steadily or closely.—**dogg'ed** *a.* persistent, resolute, tenacious.—**dogg'y** *a.*—**dog'like** *a.*—**dog'cart** *n.* a light open vehicle.—**dog'-days** *n.* hot season of the rising of the dog-star.—**dog'-rose** *n.* wild rose.—**dog's'-ear** *n.* turned-down corner of a page in a book.—*v.t.* to turn down corners of pages.—**dog'-fight** a skirmish between fighter planes; any savage contest characterised by disregard of rules.—**dog'-star** *n.* the star Sirius.—**dog'-watch** *n.* in ships, a short half-watch, 4–6, 6–8 p.m.

dogg'erel *n.* slipshod, unpoetic verse.

dog'go *adv.* (*sl.*) immobile and hidden.

dog'ma *n.* an article of belief, *esp.* one laid down authoritatively by a church; a body of beliefs (**dog'mas, dog'mata** *pl.*)—**dogmat'ic** *a.* relating to dogma or dogmas; asserting opinions with arrogance.—**dogmat'ically** *adv.*—**dog'matism** *n.* arrogant assertion of opinion.—**dog'matist** *n.*—**dog'matise** *v.i.*

doi'ly *n.* a small cloth, piece of lace to place under a cake, finger-bowl, etc.

dol'drums *n. pl.* a region of light winds and calms near the equator; a state of depression, dumps.

dole *n.* a charitable gift; (*sl.*) a payment under unemployment insurance.—*v.t.* (usually **dole out**) to deal out, *esp.* in niggardly quantities.

dole *n.* woe.—**dole'ful** *a.*—**dole'fully** *adv.*

doll *n.* a child's toy image of a person.—*v.* (up) to dress up in finery.—**doll'y** *n.*

doll'ar *n.* a coin of Canada, U.S., etc., worth 100 cents.

dol'our (-er) *n.* grief, sadness.—**dol'orous** *a.*—**dol'orously** *adv.*

dol'phin *n.* a sea mammal like a porpoise; a fish that changes colour in dying.

dolt (-ō-) *n.* a stupid fellow.
domain' *n.* lands held or ruled over; sphere, field of influence, province.
dome *n.* a high rounded roof.
domes'day (dōōmz'-) *a.* in *Domesday Book*, the record of the survey of the land of England made in 1086.
domes'tic *a.* of or in the home; of the home country, not foreign; home-keeping; of animals, tamed, kept by man.—*n.* servant.—**domes'ticate** *v.t.*—**domestica'tion** *n.*—**domestic'ity** *n.* home life.
Syn. private, internal, tame. *Ant.* public, foreign, wild.
dom'icile *n.* a person's regular place of living (usually law).—**domicil'iary** *a.*
dom'inate *v.i.* to rule, control, sway; of heights, to overlook.—*v.i.* to control, be the most powerful or influential member or part of something.—**dom'inant** *a.*—**domina'tion** *n.*—**domineer'** *v.i.* to act imperiously, tyrannise.
domin'ion *n.* sovereignty, rule; territory of a government; a part of the British Empire having self-government.
dom'ino *n.* a cloak with a half-mask for masquerading.—**dom'inos** *pl.* game played with small flat pieces, marked with spots.—*sing.* one of these pieces.
don *v.t.* to put on (clothes) (**donned** *p.t.* /*p.p.*); Sp. gentleman; university tutor.
donate' (dō-) *v.t.* to give.—**dona'tion** *n.* gift.—**do'nor** *n.* giver.
don'ga (dong'-ga) *n.* South African name for water channel or gully.
donk'ey *n.* an ass; a stupid person.—**donk'ey-engine** *n.* a small hauling or hoisting engine on a ship.
doodle' *v.i.* to scribble absent-mindedly.—**doodlebug** *n.* device for locating mineral deposits; *col.* a jet-propelled one-ton bomb used in the German bombing of England and Belgium in World War 2.
doom *n.* fate, destiny; ruin; judicial sentence, condemnation; the Last Judgment.-*v.t.* to sentence, condemn; destine to destruction or suffering.—**dooms'day** *n.* the day of the Last Judgment.
door (dōr) *n.* a hinged or sliding barrier to close the entrance to a room, carriage, etc.—**door'way** *n.* an entrance.
dop *n.* the cup in which the diamond is fixed for polishing; a Cape brandy of inferior quality.
dope *n.* a kind of varnish; a drug; in N. Amer., inside information, *esp.* about horse races.—*v.i.* to drug.
Dora *n.* (*col.*) the Defence of the Realm Act, 1914, named by its initials; "grandmotherly" legislation.
Dorking *n.* a breed of fowl.
dorm'ant *a.* inactive, in a state of suspension.—**dorm'ancy** *n.*—**dorm'er** *n.* an upright window set in a sloping roof.—**dorm'itory** *n.* a sleeping-room with a number of beds.
dor'mouse *n.* a small hibernating rodent (**dor'mice** *pl.*).
dor'my *a.* in golf, as many holes up as there are holes to play.
dorp (dawp) *n.* S. Africa, village or town.
dor'sal *a.* of, or on, the back.
dose *n.* amount (of a drug, etc.) administered at one time; to give medicine.
dos'sier (dos'-yā) *n.* a set of documents, *esp.* the record of a person's antecedents and career.
dot *n.* small spot or mark.—*v.t.* mark with dot, dots; place here and there.
dote *v.t.* to be silly or weak-minded; to be passionately fond of.—**do'tage** *n.* feeble-minded old age.—**do'tard** *n.*
dotty' *a.* (*sl.*) mad, crazy.
dou'ble (dub'l) *a.* of two parts, layers, etc., folded; twice as much or many; of two kinds; ambiguous, deceitful.—*adv.* twice; to twice the amount or extent; in a pair.—*n.* a person or thing exactly like, or mistakable for, another; a quantity twice as much as another; a sharp turn; an evasion or shift.—*v.t.* and *i.* to make or become double; to increase twofold; to fold in two; to turn sharply; get round, sail round; to run.—**doub'ly** *adv.*—**double-cross** *v.t.* and *i.* to act treacherously; to betray another's trust.—**doub'let** *n.* a close-fitting body-garment formerly worn by men.—**doubloon'** *n.* a Spanish gold coin.
doubt (dowt) *v.t.* to hesitate to believe, call in question; suspect.—*v.i.* to be wavering or uncertain in belief or opinion.—*n.* a state of uncertainty, a wavering in belief; state of affairs giving cause for uncertainty.—**doubt'er** *n.*—**doubt'ful** *a.*—**doubt'fully** *adv.*—**doubt'less** *adv.*
douche (dōōsh) *n.* a jet or spray of water applied to the body or some part of it.—*v.t.* to give a douche to.
dough (dō) *n.* flour or meal kneaded with water but not baked.—**dough'y** *a.*
dought'y (dowt'i) *a.* valiant, brave.—**dought'ily** *adv.*—**dought'iness** *n.*
dour (dōōr) *a.* grim, stern, stubborn.
douse *v.t.* to thrust into water.
dove (duv) *n.* a bird of the pigeon family.—**dove'cot(e)** *n.* house for doves.—**dove'tail** *n.* a joint made with a tenon shaped as a spread dove's tail.—*v.t.* and *i.* to fit together by dovetails; to unite or combine neatly or exactly.
do'ver *n.* in Australia, a clasp knife.
dow'ager (-j-) *n.* a woman with title or property derived from her late husband.
dow'dy *a.* shabby, unfashionable.
dow'er *n.* a widow's share for life of her husband's estate; a dowry.—*v.t.* give dowry to.—**dow'ry** *n.* property which a wife brings to her husband; talent.
down *n.* an open expanse of high land; fluff or fine hair of young birds, peaches, etc.—**down'y** *a.* *sl.* knowing.

down *adv.* to, or in, or towards, a lower position; with a current or wind; from the capital, or university; of paying, on the spot; in S. Africa, describes a river swollen by rain.—*prep.* from higher to lower part of; at a lower part of; along, with.—**down'cast** *a.* looking down; dejected.—**down'pour** *n.* a heavy fall of rain.—**down'right** *a.* plain, straightforward.—*adv.* quite thoroughly.—**down'ward** *adv.* and *a.*—**down'wards** *adv.*
dow'ry *see* **dower.**
dowse *v.i.* to use a divining-rod to find water or minerals.—**dow'ser** *n.* one who uses such.—**dow'sing.**
doxol'ogy *n.* a short formula of praise.
doy'en *n.* the senior member of a body.
doy'ley *see* **doily.**
doze *v.i.* to sleep drowsily, be half-asleep. (**dozed'** *p.t.* and *p.p.*). —*n.* a nap
doz'en (duz'-) *n.* twelve, a set of twelve.
drab *a.* of dull light-brown; dull, monotonous.—*n.* drab colour; slut; prostitute.
drachm (dram) *n.* a unit of weight, 1-8 of apoth. ounce, 1–16 of avoir. ounce.
Dra'conic *a.* (*leg.*) harsh, rigorous.
draft (-à-) *n.* a detachment of men, *esp.* troops, reinforcements; in Australia, cattle, etc., separated from the herd· design, sketch; rough copy of a document; an order for money.—*v.t.* to send a detached party; in Australia, to sort cattle, etc., into different groups; to make a rough copy (of a writing, etc.). —**draft'er** *n.*—**drafts'man** *n.* one who drafts writings, etc.—**drafting-gate** *n.* in Australia, a gate in a stockyard to facilitate drafting animals.
drag *v.t.* to pull along with difficulty or friction; trail, go heavily; sweep with a net or grapnels; protract.—*v.i.* to lag, trail; be tediously protracted.—*n.* a check on progress; checked motion; iron shoe to check a wheel; a vehicle; a lure for hounds to hunt; kinds of harrow, sledge, net, grapnel, rake.—**drag'gle** *v.t.* to make limp or wet or dirty by trailing.
drag'oman *n.* an interpreter; a guide to foreigners in the East.
drag'on *n.* a fabulous fire-breathing monster, like a winged crocodile.—**drag'on-fly** *n.* a long-bodied insect with large gauzy wings.—**dragoon'** *n.* a cavalryman, usually of heavy cavalry.—*v.t.* to subject to military oppression; domineer over, persecute.
drain *v.t.* to draw off (liquid) by pipes, ditches, etc.; to dry; drink to the dregs; to empty, exhaust.—*v.i.* to flow off or away; become rid of liquid.—*n.* a channel for removing liquid; a constant outlet, expenditure, strain.—**drain'age** *n.*
drake *n.* male duck.
dram *n.* a small draught of strong drink, *esp.* whisky; a drachm.
dra'ma (drà'-) *n.* a stage-play; art or literature of plays; a play-like series of events.—**dramat'ic** *a.*—**dram'atist** *n.*—**dram'atise** *v.t.*—**dramatisa'tion** *n.*
drape *v.t.* to cover, adorn; with cloth, arrange in graceful folds.—**dra'per** *n.* a dealer in cloth, linen, etc.—**dra'pery** *n.*
dras'tic *a.* strongly effective, violent.
draught (drâft) *n.* act or action of drawing; act of drinking, quantity drunk at once; one drawing of, or fish taken in, a net; a dose; an inhaling; the depth of water needed to float a ship; a current of air between apertures in a room, etc. ; a design, sketch.—*pl.* a game played on a chess-board with flat round " men."—*a.* for drawing; drawn. —*v.t.* to make a sketch or rough design of.—**draughts'man** *n.*—**draughts'manship** *n.*—**draught'y** *a.*
draw *v.t.* pull, pull along, haul; bend (a bow); inhale; entice, attract, bring (upon, out, etc.); get by lot; of a ship, require (depth of water); take from (a well, barrel, etc.); receive (money); delineate, portray with a pencil, etc.; to frame, compose, draught, write.—*v.i.* to pull; shrink; attract; make or admit a current of air; make pictures with pencil, etc.; write orders for money; come, approach (near) (**drew** *p.t.*—**drawn** *p.p.*); *n.* an act of drawing; a casting of lots; an unfinished game, a tie.—**draw'back** *n.* a charge paid back; anything that takes away from satisfaction.—**draw'bridge** *n.* a hinged bridge to pull up.—**draw'er** *n.* one or that which draws; a sliding box in a table or chest. —*pl.* two-legged under-garment.—**draw'ing** *n.* the action of the verb; art of depicting in line; a sketch so done.—**draw'ing-room** *n.* a reception-room; a room to which ladies retire after dinner.
drawl *v.t.* and *i.* to speak slowly in indolence or affectation.—*n.* such speech.
dray *n.* a low cart without sides.
dread (dred) *v.t.* to fear greatly.—*n.* awe, terror.—*a.* feared, awful, revered. —**dread'ful** *a.*—**dread'nought** *n.* a large powerfully armed modern battleship; a thick heavy coat; a woollen cloth for such coats.
dream (drēm) *n.* a vision during sleep; a fancy, reverie, vision of something ideal.—*v.i.* to have dreams.—*v.t.* to see or imagine in dreams; think of as possible (**dreamt** or **dreamed** *p.t.* and *p.p.*).—**dream'er** *n.*—**dream'y** *a.* given to day-dreams, unpractical, vague.—**dream'land** *n.*—**dream'less** *a.*
drear'y *a.* dismal, dull.—**drear** *a.*—**drear'ily** *adv.*—**drear'iness** *n.*
dredge *n.* machinery, appliance for bringing up mud, objects, etc., from the bottom of sea or river.—*v.t.* to bring up, or clean, or deepen, with such appliance. —**dredg'er** *n.* a ship for dredging.
dredge *v.t.* to sprinkle with flour.—

dredg'er *n.* a box with holes in the lid for dredging.
dree *v.i.* to endure; to bear the penalty of (**dreed** *p.t.* and *p.p.*—**dree'ing** *pres. p.*).
dregs *n. pl.* sediment, grounds, refuse.
drench *v.t.* to wet thoroughly, soak; dose (animal) with medicine.—*n.* dose for an animal; a soaking.
dress *v.t.* to clothe; array for show, trim, smooth, prepare surface of; draw up (troops) in proper line; prepare (food) for the table; put dressing on.—*v.i.* to put on one's clothes; to form in proper line.—*n.* clothing; clothing for ceremonial evening wear; a frock.—**dress'er** *n.* one who dresses; a surgeon's assistant; a kitchen sideboard.—**dress'ing** *n.* *esp.* something applied to something else, as ointment to a wound.—**dress'y** *a.* stylish; fond of dress.—**dress-cir'cle** *n.* first gallery in a theatre.
drib'ble *v.i.* to flow in drops, trickle, run at the mouth; work a ball forward with small touches of the feet.—*v.t.* to let trickle; work (ball) forward.—*n.* a trickle, drop.—**drib'let** *n.* a small instalment; a small flow.
drift *n.* a being driven by a current; a slow current or course; deviation from a course; tendency; a speaker's meaning; a wind-heaped mass of snow, sand, etc.; material driven or carried by water; (in S. Africa) a ford.—*v.i.* to be carried as by currents of air, water; to move aimlessly or passively.—**drif'ter** *n.* one who drifts; a small fishing-vessel.
drill *n.* boring tool or machine; exercise in handling arms, etc.; routine teaching.—*v.t.* to bore; exercise in military movements, etc.—*v.i.* to practise a routine.—**drill-sergeant** *n.*
drill *n.* a small furrow for seed; a machine for sowing in drills.—*v.t.*
drill *n.* a coarse twilled fabric.
drink *v.t.* and *i.* to swallow liquid; absorb; to take intoxicating liquor, *esp.* to excess (**drank** *p.t.*—**drunk'en, drunk** *p.p.*).—*n.* liquid for drinking; a portion of this; act of drinking; intoxicating liquor; excessive use of it.—**drink'er** *n.*—**drink'able** *a.*
drip *v.t.* and *i.* to fall or let fall in drops.—*n.* a process of dripping; that which falls by dripping.—**drip'stone** *n.* projection over a window or door to stop dripping of water.—**dripp'ing** *n.* act of dripping; melted fat that drips from roasting meat.
drive *v.t.* to force to move in some direction; to make move and steer (a vehicle, animal, etc.); chase; convey in a vehicle, fix by blows, as a nail; urge, impel.—*v.i.* to keep a machine, animal, going, steer it; be conveyed in a vehicle; rush, dash, drift fast (**drove** *p.t.*—**driv'en** *p.p.*—**dri'ving** *pr. p.*).—*n.* act or action of driving; journey in a carriage; a carriage-road, *esp.* leading to a house; in N. Amer., transport of logs by river to the mill; the season's cut.—**dri'ver** *n.* one who drives; golf club.
driv'el *v.i.* to run at the mouth or nose; to talk nonsense.—*n.* silly nonsense.
driz'zle *v.i.* to rain in fine drops.—*n.*
drogue' *n.* wind-sock towed behind target aircraft.
droll (-ō-) *a.* funny, odd, queer.—*n.* a funny fellow.—**drol'ly** *adv.*—**droll'ery** *n.* *Syn.* amusing, comical, facetious. *Ant.* boring, serious, grave.
drom'edary *n.* one-humped camel.
drone *n.* male honey bee; idler; a deep humming; bass pipe of bagpipe, or its note.—*v.i.* and *t.* to hum; talk in a monotonous tone.
droop *v.i.* to hang down; languish, flag.—*v.t.* to let hang down.—*n.* drooping condition.
drop *n.* a globule of liquid; a very small quantity; a fall, descent; a round sweet; a gallows platform; distance through which a thing falls.—*v.t.* let fall; let fall in drops; utter casually; discontinue.—*v.i.* to fall; fall in drops; lapse; come or go casually.
drop'sy *n.* a disease with watery fluid collecting in the body.—**drop'sical** *a.*
dross *n.* scum of molten metal, impurity, refuse.—**dross'y** *a.* impure; worthless.
drost'dy *n.* S. Africa, official residence of a landdrost, or sheriff (obsolete).
drought (-owt) *n.* lack of rain.
drove *n.* herd, flock, *esp.* on move.—**dro'ver** *n.* driver of, dealer in, cattle.
drown *v.t.* to suffocate in water; of sound, etc., to overpower.
drow'sy (-z-) *a.* half-asleep ; lulling, soporific; dull, lacking life.—**drow'sily** *adv.*—**drow'siness** *n.*—**drowse** *v.i.*
drub *v.t.* thrash, beat.—**drubb'ing** *n.*
drudge *v.i.* to work hard at mean or distasteful tasks.—*n.* one who drudges.—**drudg'ery** *n.* toil.
drug *n.* a medical substance.—*v.t.* to mix drugs with; to administer a drug to.—**drugg'ist** *n.* a dealer in drugs.—**drug'-store** *n.* (U.S.), a pharmacy supplying ice-cream, many domestic commodities, and often a circulating library.
drugg'et *n.* a coarse woollen stuff.
dru'id (-ōō-) *n.* an ancient Celtic priest; an Eisteddfod official.—**druid'ical** *a.*
drum *n.* a musical instrument, made of skin stretched over a round hollow frame or hemisphere, and played by beating with sticks; various things shaped like a drum; a part of the ear; in Australia, a bundle wrapped in a blanket; a swag.—*v.t.* and *i.* to play a drum; to tap or thump continuously.—**drum out,** to expel from a regiment.—**drum'fire** *n.* heavy continuous rapid artillery fire.—**drum'stick** *n.* a stick for beating a drum; the lower joint of

cooked fowl's leg.—**drumm'er** *n.* one who plays a drum; (*col.*) commercial traveller.
drunk *a.* overcome by strong drink; *fig.* under the influence of strong emotion.—*p.p.* of **drink.**—**drunk'en** *a.* drunk; often drunk; caused by or showing intoxication.—**drunk'ard** *n.*—**drunk'enness** *n.*
dry *a.* without moisture; rainless; not yielding milk, or other liquid; not in, on, or under, water; cold, unfriendly; caustically witty; having prohibition of alcoholic drink; uninteresting; needing effort to study; lacking sweetness.—*v.t.* to remove water, moisture.—*v.i.* to become dry, evaporate (**dried** *p.t.* and *p.p.*—**dry'ing** *pres. p.*).—**dri'ly** *adv.*—**dry-clean** *v.t.* to clean with chemicals instead of water.—**dry-goods** *n. pl.* in Amer., drapery.—**dry'ness** *n.*—**dry'-nurse** *n.* a nurse tending but not suckling a child.—**dry'point** *n.* a needle for engraving without acid; an engraving so made.—**dry rot'** *n.* decay in wood not exposed to air.—**drysalt'er** *n.* a dealer in dyes, gums, oils.—**drysalt'ery** *n.*
dry'ad *n.* a wood-nymph.
du'al (dū'-) *a.* twofold; of two, forming a pair.—**dual'ity** *n.*—**du'alism** *n.* recognition of two independent powers or principles, as good and evil.
dub *v.t.* to confer knighthood on; give a title to; smear with grease, dubbin.—*n.* N. Amer. (*sl.*) a stupid, dull person.—**dubb'in, dubb'ing** *n.* grease for making leather supple and waterproof.
du'bious *a.* causing doubt, not clear or decided; of suspected character.
Syn. undetermined, doubtful, uncertain. *Ant.* determined, certain.
du'cal *a.* of, or relating to, a duke.
duc'at (duk'-) *n.* a former gold coin of Italy and other countries.
duch'ess *n.* the wife or widow of a duke.—**duch'y** *n.* territory of a duke.
duck *n.* wild or tame swimming bird.—**drake** *n. masc.*—**duck'ling** *n.*—**duck** *v.i.* to plunge under water; to bend or bob down.—*v.t.* to plunge some one under water.—*n.* amphibious vehicle used in World War 2 for troop and supply transport to an open beachhead.—*n.* strong linen or cotton fabric; no score (cricket).—*pl.* trousers made of it.
duct *n.* a channel or tube.—**duct'ile** *a.* capable of being drawn into wire; flexible and tough; docile.—**ductil'ity** *n.*—**duct'less** *a.* (of glands) secreting directly certain bodily substances.
dud *n.* a shell that fails to explode; a futile person or project or thing.
dude' *n.* a fop or dandy.
dudg'eon (-jn) *n.* anger, indignation.
duds *n. pl.* clothes.
due *a.* that is owing; proper to be given, inflicted, etc.; adequate, fitting, usual, ascribable; expected (to arrive).—*adv.* (with points of the compass) exactly.—*n.* a person's fair share; charge, fee, etc. (usually in *pl.*).—**du'ly** *adv.*
du'el *n.* a fight with deadly weapons between two persons; a keen two-sided contest.—*v.i.*—**du'ellist** *n.*
duenn'a *n.* a Spanish lady-in-waiting; a governess, chaperon.
duet' *n.* music for two performers.
duff'el, duf'fle *n.* coarse woollen cloth.
duff'er *n.* a stupid or inefficient person; in Australia, a mine or claim that does not pay.—**to duffer out,** to peter out.
duff'er *n.* in Australia, a cattle stealer.
dug'-out *n.* underground shelter; a hollowed-out tree canoe; a retired officer recalled for service.
duke *n.* a peer of rank next below a prince; a sovereign of a small state called a duchy.—**duch'ess** *fem.*—**duke'dom** *n.*
dul'cet (-set) *a.* (of sounds) sweet.
dul'cimer (sim-) *n.* a stringed instrument played with hammers.
dull *a.* stupid; insensible; sluggish; tedious; not keen or clear or bright or sharp or defined; lacking liveliness or variety; gloomy, overcast.—*v.t.* and *i.* to make or become dull.—**dul'ly** *adv.*—**dull'ard** *n.*—**dull'ness** *n.* *Syn.* sluggish, drowsy, gloomy. *Ant.* bright, sparkling, sunny.
du'ly *adv.* as expected.
dumb *a.* incapable of speech; silent; (*sl.*) stupid.—**dumb'-bell** *n.* a weight for exercises.—**dumbfound', dumbfound'er** *v.t.* to confound into silence.—**dumb'-show** *n.* acting without words.—**dumb'ly** *adv.*—**dumb'ness** *n.*
dum'dum *n.* a soft-nosed expanding [bullet.
dumm'y *n.* tailor's model; imaginary card-player; an imitation object; baby's rubber teat (**dum'mies** *pl.*).
dump *v.t.* to throw down in a mass; to send low-priced goods for sale abroad.—*n.* a rubbish-heap; a temporary depot of stores or munitions; a dumpy object, a small quantity.—*pl.* low spirits, dejection.—**dump'ing** *n.* the exporting and selling in a foreign country of goods at a price lower than the cost of production at home; the depositing of produce, e.g. fish and coffee, in the sea for lack of a profitable market.—**dump'ling** *n.* a small round pudding of dough, often with fruit inside.—**dump'y** *a.* short and stout.
dun *a.* of dull greyish brown.—*n.* this colour; a horse of dun colour.
dun *v.t.* to make persistent demands, *esp.* for payment of debts.—*n.* one who duns.
dunce *n.* a dullard, slow learner.
dun'derhead *n.* a blockhead.
dune *n.* a mound of dry shifting sand on a coast or desert.
dung *n.* the excrement of animals; manure.—*v.t.* to manure.
dun'garee (-ng'g-) *n.* coarse calico.—*pl.* overalls made of this.

dung'eon (dun'jn) *n.* an underground cell or vault for prisoners; formerly a tower or keep of a castle.
duode'cimo (-des'-) *n.* the size of a book in which each sheet is folded into twelve leaves; a book of this size (**-mos** *pl.*).—*a.*
du'odenum *n.* upper end of small intestine, leading out of stomach.
du'ologue (dew'-) *n.* talk between two persons; play with two actors.
dupe *n.* a victim of delusion or sharp practice.—*v.t.* to deceive.
du'plex *a.* twofold.—**du'plicate** *v.t.* to make an exact copy of; to double.—*a.* that is an exact copy.—*n.* an exact copy.—**duplica'tion** *n.*—**du'plicator** *n.*—**dupli'city** (-is'-) *n.* deceitfulness, double dealing.
du'rable *a.* lasting, resisting wear.—**durabil'ity** *n.*—**dura'tion** *n.* the time a thing lasts.—**du'rably** *adv.*
duralu'min, 'minium *n.* a strong, light alloy of aluminium.
du'rance *n.* imprisonment.
dur'bar *n.* a levee formerly held in India by King or Viceroy.
du'ress *n.* restraint, imprisonment; (*law*) illegal compulsion.
du'ring *prep.* in the time of; throughout.
durst *p.t.* of **dare.**
dusk *n.* the darker stage of twilight; partial darkness.—**dusk'y** *a.* dark; dark coloured.—**dusk'ily** *adv.*
dust *n.* fine particles, powder, of earth or other matter, lying on a surface or blown along by the wind.—*v.t.* to sprinkle with powder; to rid of dust.—**dust'er** *n.* a cloth for removing dust.—**dust'y** *a.*—**dust bowl,** an area in the U.S.A. where drought has destroyed vegetation, and dust storms have carried away the top soil.
Dutch, Dutch treat (*col.*) a treat at which everyone pays for himself.—**Dutch uncle** (*col.*) someone who critises severely but justly.
du'ty *n.* what one ought to do, moral or legal obligation; office, function, being occupied in these; tax on goods for the public revenue; deference, respect.—**du'tiful** *a.*—**du'teous** *a.*—**du'tiable** *a.* liable to customs duty.
dwarf *n.* man, animal, plant below usual size (**dwarfs** *pl.*).—*a.* stunted.—*v.t.* to make stunted; to make seem small by contrast.—**dwarf'ish** *a.*
dwell *v.i.* to live (in); write or speak at length (on) (**dwelt** *p.t.* and *p.p.*).—**dwell'ing** *n.* house.—**dwell'er** *n.*
dwin'dle *v.i.* to grow less, waste away.
dy'archy (-år-ki) government by two; a division of powers between two independent authorities.
dye (dī) *v.t.* to impregnate (cloth, etc.) with colouring matter; to colour thus (**dyed** (dīd) *p.t.* and *p.p.*—**dye'ing** *pres. p.*).—*n.* colouring matter in solution or which may be dissolved for dyeing; tinge, colour.—**dy'er** *n.*
dyke *see* **dike.**
dynam'ics (di-) *n. pl.* the branch of physics dealing with force as producing or affecting motion; physical or moral forces.—**dynam'ic** *a.* of or relating to motive force, force in operation.—**dynam'ical** *a.*—**dynam'ically** *adv.*—**dy'namite** *n.* a high explosive of nitro-glycerine.—*v.t.* to blow up with this.—**dy'namiter** *n.*—**dy'namo** *n.* a machine to convert mechanical into electrical energy, a generator of electricity (**-mos** (-mōz) *pl.*).—**dy'namo-elec'tric** *a.* used in converting mechanical energy into electric energy or vice-versa.
dyn'asty (din'-) *n.* line, family of hereditary rulers.—**dyn'ast** *n.*—**dynast'ic** *a.*
dyna'tron *n.* a three-electrode vacuum tube in which the current is decreased as the voltage increases.
dyne *n.* a unit of force which, acting for one second on a mass of one gramme, produces a velocity of one centimetre per second.
dys'entery (dis'-) *n.* a disease of the bowels.—**dysenter'ic** *a.*
dys'genic (dis-gen'-) having a bad effect on the race, *esp.* the future of the race; opposite of *eugenic.*
dyspep'sia *n.* indigestion.—**dyspep'tic** *a.* and *n.*
dyspro'sium (dis-prō-zē-um) *n.* a rare earth element which is highly magnetic.

E

each *a.* and *pron.* every one taken separately.
ea'ger (ē'ger) *a.* full of keen desire; impatient.—**eag'erly** *adv.*—**eag'erness** *n.*
ea'gle (ē'gl) *n.* a large bird of prey with keen sight and strong flight; gold coin of U.S.; in golf, hole played in two strokes under par.—**ea'glet** *n.* a young eagle.
ear *n.* the organ of hearing, *esp.* the external part of it; sensitiveness to musical sounds; attention.—**ear'mark** *n.* owner's mark on ear of sheep, etc.—*v.t.* to mark thus; to assign or reserve for a definite purpose.—**ear'shot** *n.* hearing distance.—**ear'wig** *n.* an insect formerly thought to enter the head through the ear.
ear *n.* a spike or head of corn.
earl (erl) *n.* a peer ranking between marquis and viscount.—**earl'dom** *n.*
earl'y (erl'-) *a.* and *adv.* in the first part, or near or nearer the beginning.
earn (ern) *v.t.* to get for labour, merit.
earn'est (ern'-) *a.* serious, ardent, sincere.—*n.* seriousness.—**earn'estly** *adv.*
earn'est (ern'-) *n.* money paid over to bind a bargain; foretaste.
earth (er-) *n.* the ground, soil; the dry

land; the planet we live on; mould, soil, mineral; a fox's hole.—*v.t.* to cover with earth; to connect electrically with the earth.—**earth'en** (-th-) *a.*—**earth'ly** *a.*—**earth'y** *a.*—**earth'enware** (-th-) *n.* vessels of baked clay.—**earth'quake** *n.* a volcanic convulsion of the surface of the earth.—**earth'work** *n.* a bank of earth in fortification.—**earthward** *adv.* towards the earth.

ease (ēz) *n.* comfort; freedom from constraint, awkwardness, pain, trouble; idleness; informal position or step; relief, alleviation.—*v.t.* and *i.* to relieve of pain; reduce burden; give bodily or mental ease to; slacken, relax.—**ease'ful** *a.*—**eas'y** *a.*—**eas'ily** *adv.*—**eas'y-go'ing** *a.* not fussy (**eased** *p.t./p.p.*).

eas'el (ēz'-) *n.* a frame to support a picture, blackboard, etc.

east *n.* direction of sunrise; regions towards that.—*a.* on, or in, or near, the east; coming from the east.—*adv.* from or to the east.—**east'erly** *a.* and *adv.* from or to the east.—**east'ern** *a.* of or dwelling in the east.—**east'erner** *n.*—**east'ward** *a.* and *n.*—**east'ward(s)** *adv.*

East'er *n.* festival of the Resurrection.

eas'ting *n.* distance run by a ship eastward from a given meridian.

eat *v.t./i.* chew and swallow; consume, destroy (**ate** or **eat** (et) *p.t.*—**eat'en** *p.p.*). —**eat'able** *a.*—**eat'ables** *n. pl.* food.

eaves (ēvz) *n. pl.* the overhanging edges of a roof.—**eaves'dropper** *n.* one who listens secretly.—**eaves'dropping** *n.*

ebb *n.* the flowing back of the tide; decline, decay.—*v.i.* to flow back.

eb'ony *n.* hard black wood.—*a.* of, like, ebony.—**eb'onite** *n.* vulcanite.

ebull'ient *a.* boiling; exuberant.—**ebull'ience** *n.*—**ebulli'tion** *n.* boiling; effervescence; outburst of feeling.

eccen'tric (-ks-) *a.* not placed, or not having the axis placed, centrally; not circular (in orbit); irregular; odd, whimsical.—*n.* a mechanical contrivance to change circular into to-and-fro movement; a whimsical person.—**eccen'trically** *adv.*—**eccentri'city** *n.*

Syn. singular, peculiar, strange, whimsical, abnormal. *Ant.* usual, ordinary, normal, commonplace.

ecclesias'tic(al) (-klēz-) *a.* of or belonging to the Church.—*n.* clergyman.

ech'elon (esh'-) *n.* formation of troops, etc., in steps.—*v.i.*—*a.* arranged in steps.

ech'o (ek'-) *n.* repetition of sounds by reflection; close imitation (**ech'oes** *pl.*).—*v.i.* to resound or be repeated by echo.—*v.t.* to repeat as an echo.

eclair' (āk-) *n.* a cake finger filled with cream and iced.

éclat' (-klȧ') *n.* splendour, acclamation.

eclec'tic *a.* borrowing one's philosophy from various sources; catholic in views. —*n.* an eclectic person.—**elec'ticism** *n.*

eclipse' *n.* a blotting out of the sun, moon, etc., by another heavenly body; obscurity.—*v.t.* to cause to suffer eclipse; surpass.—**eclip'tic** *a.* of an eclipse.—*n.* the apparent path of the sun.

ec'logue (-og) *n.* a short poem, *esp.* a pastoral dialogue.

e'cology *n.* branch of biology which treats of the relations between plants and animals and their environment.

econ'omy *n.* management, administration; thrift, frugal use; structure, organisation.—**econom'ic** *a.* on business lines.—**econom'ics** *n. pl.* political economy, the science of the production and distribution of wealth.—**econom'ical** *a.* saving, frugal.—**econom'ically** *adv.*—**econ'omist** *n.*—**econ'omise** *v.t.* and *i.*

écru' (āk-rōō') *n.* and *a.* colour of unbleached linen.

ec'stasy *n.* exalted state of feeling, rapture; trance; frenzy.—**ecstat'ic** *a.*

ec'toplasm *n.* in spiritualism, a semi-luminous plastic substance which exudes from the body of the medium.

ec'zema *n.* a skin disease.

Edd'a *n.* a collection of ancient Icelandic poems.

edd'y *n.* a small whirl in water, smoke, etc.—*v.i.* to move in whirls (**edd'ied** (-did) *p.t.* and *p.p.*—**-dying** *pres. p.*).

e'delweiss (ā'dl-vīs) *n.* a white Alpine plant growing at a great height.

edge *n.* the cutting side of a blade; sharpness; a border, boundary.—*v.t.* to sharpen, give an edge or border to; move gradually.—*v.i.* to advance sideways or gradually.—**edge'ways, edge'wise** *adv.*

ed'ible *a.* eatable.—**edibil'ity** *n.*

e'dict *n.* an order proclaimed by authority, a decree.

ed'ifice (-fis) *n.* a building, *esp.* a big one.—**ed'ify** *v.t.* to improve morally, instruct (**-ified** *p.t.* and *p.p.*— **-ifying** *pres. p.*).—**edifica'tion** *n.*

ed'it *v.t.* to prepare for publication.—*v.t.* to cut and title a film. *See* **cut.**—**edi'tion** *n.* the form in which a book is published; the number of copies of a book, newspaper, etc., printed at one time, an issue.—**ed'itor** *n.*—**ed'itress** *fem.* —**edito'rial** *a.* of an editor.—*n.* article written or sanctioned by editor.

ed'ucate *v.t.* to bring up; train mentally and morally; provide schooling for, train.—**educa'tion** *n.*—**educa'tional** *a.*—**educa'tionally** *adv.*—**ed'ucator** *n.*—**educa'tionalist** *n.*—**ed'ucative** *a.*

educe' *v.t.* to bring out, develop; infer.

eel *n.* a snake-like fish.

ee'rie, ee'ry *a.* weird, uncanny.

efface' *v.t.* wipe or rub out.—**efface'ment** *n.*

effect' *n.* a result, consequence; impression.—*pl.* property.—*v.t.* to bring about, accomplish.—**effect'ive** *a.*—**effect'ively** *adv.*—**effect'ual** *a.*—**effect'ually** *adv.*—**effect'uate** *v.t.* to accomplish.

effem'inate *a.* womanish, unmanly, voluptuous.—**effem'inacy** *n.*
effervesce' (-es') *v.i.* to give off bubbles. —**efferves'cent** *a.*—**efferves'cence** *n.*
effete' *a.* worn-out, feeble.
effica'cious *a.* producing or sure to produce a desired result.—**eff'icacy** *n.*
efficient (-fish'ent) *a.* capable, competent.—**effi'ciently** *adv.*—**effi'ciency** *n.* ability to do things well.
eff'igy *n.* image, likeness (**ef'figies** *pl.*).
effloresce' (-es') *v.i.* to burst into flower. —**efflores'cent** *a.*—**efflores'cence** *n.*
eff'luent *a.* flowing out.—*n.* a stream flowing from a larger stream, lake, etc.—**eff'luence** *n.*—**efflu'vium** *n.* (*pl.* **-ia**) something flowing out invisibly, *esp.* affecting lungs or sense of smell.—**eff'lux** *n.*—**efflux'ion** *n.*
eff'ort *n.* exertion, endeavour.—**effortless** *a.* easy, without effort.
effront'ery (-un-) *n.* brazen impudence. *Syn.* impudence, audacity, hardihood. *Ant.* diffidence, timidity, reserve.
efful'gent *a.* radiant, shining, brightly. —**efful'gence** *n.* splendour.
effu'sion *n.* a pouring out; a literary composition.—**effu'sive** *a.* gushing, demonstrative.—**effu'sively** *adv.*—**effu'siveness** *n.*—**effuse'** *v.t.* to pour out.
eft *n.* newt.
egg *n.* oval rounded body produced by the female of birds, etc., containing the germ of their young.—**egg'-eat'er** *n.* in Africa, a species of snake.
egg *v.t.* **to egg on,** to encourage, urge.
eg'lantine *n.* sweet briar.
eg'o *n.* the self; the conscious thinking subject.—**eg'iosm** *n.* systematic selfishness; theory that bases morality on self-interest.—**eg'oist** *n.*—**egois'tic, egois'tical** *a.*—**eg'otism** *n.* selfishness; self-conceit. —**eg'otist** *n.*—**egotis'tic, egotis'tical** *a.*
egre'gious (-jus) *a.* gross, notable (*esp.* absurdly, as egregious ass, blunder, etc.).
e'gress *n.* way out.
e'gret *n.* the lesser white heron.
ei'der (i'-) *n.* an Arctic duck.—**ei'derdown** *n.* the breast feathers of the eider; quilt stuffed with these.
eight (āt) *a.* and *n.* cardinal number one above seven.—*n.* an eight-oared boat; its crew.—**eighth** (āt-th) *a.* ordinal number.—**eighth'ly** *adv.*—**eighteen'** *a.* and *n.* eight more than ten.—**eighteenth'** *a.*—**eighteenth'ly** *adv.*—**eight'y** *a.* and *n.* ten times eight.—**eight'ieth** *a.*—**eight'-fold** *a.*—**eighteen'fold** *a.*—**eight'yfold** *a.* —**fi'gure-of-eight** *n.* a skating figure; any figure shaped as 8.
Eire (ār-e) *n.* The Irish Free State.
eistedd'fod (ās-teth'vod) *n.* a congress of Welsh bards.
eith'er (-th-) *a.* and *pron.* one or the other; one of two; each.—*adv.* or *conj.* bringing in first of alternatives or strengthening an added negation.

ejac'ulate *v.t.* and *i.* exclaim, utter suddenly.–**ejacula'tion** *n.*–**ejac'ulatory** *a.*
eject' *v.t.* to throw out; expel, drive out. —**ejec'tion** *n.*—**eject'or** *n.*—**eject'ment** *n.*
eke *v.t.* **eke out,** supply deficiencies of; make with difficulty (a living, etc.).
elab'orate *v.t.* to work out in detail; produce by labour.—*a.* highly finished; complicated.—**elabora'tion** *n.*
élan' (ā-lan) *n.* dash; ardour.
e'land *n.* a South African antelope.
elapse' *v.i.* of time, to pass by.
elas'tic *a.* resuming normal shape after distortion, springy.—**elasti'city** (-is'-) *n.*
ela'tion *n.* high spirits; pride.—**elate'** *v.t.*
el'bow *n.* the outer part of the joint between the upper arm and the forearm. —*v.t.* to thrust, jostle with the elbows.
el'der *n.* a white-flowered tree.
el'der *a.* older, senior.—*n.* person of greater age; an old person; an official of certain Churches.—**el'derly** *a.* growing old.—**el'dest** *a.* oldest.
El'dora'do (-à'-) *n.* a fictitious country rich in gold (**-does** (-dōz) *pl.*).
eld'ritch *a.* hideous; weird; haggish.
elect' *v.t.* to choose; choose by vote.—*a.* chosen; select, choice.—**elec'tion** *n.* a choosing, *esp.* by voting.—**electioneer'** to busy oneself in political elections.—**elect'ive** *a.* appointed, filled, chosen by election.—**elect'or** *n.*—**elect'oral** *a.*—**elect'orate** *n.* a body of electors.
electri'city (-is'-) *n.* active condition of the molecules of a body or of the ether round it, produced by friction, magnetism, etc.; the force which shows itself in lightning, etc.; the study of this.—**elec'tric** *a.* of, charged with, worked by, producing, electricity.—**elec'trical** *a.*—**elec'tric chair** *n.* chair in which criminals are electrocuted in U.S.A.—**elec'trically** *adv.*—**elec'trify** *v.t.* (**-fied** *p.t.* and *p.p.*—**-ing** *pres. p.*).—**electrifica'tion** *n.*—**electri'cian** *n.*—**elec'tron** *n.* a minute particle charged with electricity.
elec'tro- *prefix* makes compounds meaning of, by, caused by, electricity, as **electrodynam'ics** *n.* the dynamics of electricity.—**elec'tro-chem'istry** *n.* the science dealing with the interaction of electricity and chemical changes.—**elec'tro-chem'ical** *a.*–**elec'tro-chem'ist** *n.* —**electrode** *n.* a point at which an electric current passes from a conducting circuit into another conducting medium.—**elec'trocute** *v.t.* to execute (criminals) by electricity.—**elec'trolyse** *v.t.* to decompose by means of electricity. —**electrol'ysis** *n.*, etc.—**electrolyte** *n.* a compound which ionises in solution; a solution containing ions of such a compound.—**elect'romotive** *a.* producing current; run by electricity.—**elec'tromotive force,** the force that maintains a flow of electricity; it is measured in volts (*abbrev.* **e.m.f.**).—**elec'tromotor** *n.* an

engine using electricity to give mechanical effect; an electric generator.—**elec'tro-negative** *a.* having a negative electric charge; acidic.—*n.* (*chem.*) an acid.—**electron'ics** *n.* the physical science which studies electrons, *esp.* in instruments like radio and radar, which employ cathode-ray tubes.—**electroph'orus** *n.* a device for storing an electric charge by induction.—**elec'tro-plate** *n.* metal articles coated with another metal, e.g., silver, by means of an electric process. **elec'tropositive** *a.* possessing a positive electric charge; basic; collecting at the cathode in electrolysis.—*n.* (*chem.*) a base.—**elec'troscope** *n.* an instrument for detecting electric charges and determining whether they are positive or negative.—**elec'trostatics** *n.* the science of static electricity.—**elec'trotherapy** *n.* the treatment of diseases by the application of electricity.

eleemos'ynary *a.* charitable.

el'egant *a.* graceful, tasteful; refined.—**el'egance** *n.* good taste, refinement.
Syn. symmetrical, beautiful, handsome. *Ant.* rude, rough, coarse, indelicate, ugly, uncultured.

el'egy *n.* lament for the dead; sad poem —**elegi'ac** *a.* plaintive.—**el'egies** *n. pl.*

el'ement *n.* a component part; a substance which cannot be chemically analysed; proper abode or sphere.—*pl.* powers of the atmosphere; rudiments, first principles.—**element'al** *a.* of the powers of nature; tremendous; not compounded.—**element'ary** *a.* rudimentary.

el'ephant *n.* large four-footed animal with ivory tusks and long trunk.—**elephant'ine** *a.* unweildy, clumsy, heavily big.—**elephanti'asis** *n.* a skin disease.—**elephant's foot** *n.* in S. Africa, a food plant.

el'evate *v.t.* to raise.—**eleva'tion** *n.* raising; angle above horizon, as of a gun; a drawing of one side of a building, etc.—**el'evator** *n.* a lift; a grain-elevator.

elev'en *a.* and *n.* the number next above ten, one added to ten; a team of eleven players (football, cricket, etc.)—**elev'enth** *a.* the ordinal number.—**elev'enthly** *adv.*—**elev'enfold** *a.* and *adv.*

elf *n.* a fairy, a small elemental creature (**elves** *pl.*).—**elf'in, elf'ish, elv'ish** *a.*

elic'it (-s-) *v.t.* to draw out; to evoke.

elide' *v.t.* to omit in pronunciation (a vowel, syllable).—**elis'ion** (-izh'n) *n.*

el'igible *a.* fit or qualified to be chosen; suitable, desirable.—**eligibil'ity** *n.*

elim'inate *v.t.* to remove, get rid of, set aside.—**elimina'tion** *n.*—**elim'inator** *n.*

eli'sion *see* **elide.**

élite' (ā-lēt') *n.* the pick of.

elix'ir *n.* the preparation sought by the alchemists to change base metals into gold, or to prolong life.

elk *n.* large deer of N. Europe and Asia.

ell *n.* old measure of length.

ellipse' *n.* an oval, the figure made by a plane cutting a cone at a smaller angle with the side than the base makes; in grammar, the omission of words needed to complete the grammatical construction or full sense.—**ellip'sis** *n.*, in grammar, ellipse (**-ses** *pl.*).—**ellip'tic, ellip'tical** *a.*—**ellip'tically** *adv.*

elm *n.* a familiar tree; its wood.

elocu'tion *n.* art of public speaking or reciting; voice management.—**elocu'tionist** *n.*—**elocu'tionary** *a.*

e'longate *v.t.* to lengthen.–**elonga'tion** *n.*

elope' *v.i.* to run away with a lover; escape.—**elope'ment** *n.*

el'oquence *n.* fluent, powerful use of language.–**el'oquent** *a.*–**el'oquently** *adv.*

else *adv.* besides; otherwise.—**elsewhere** *adv.* in or to some other place.

elu'cidate *v.t.* throw light upon, explain. —**elucida'tion** *n.*—**elu'cidatory** *a.*

elude' *v.t.* escape, slip away from, dodge. —**elu'sion** *n.*—**elu'sive** *a.*—**elu'sory** *a.*

el'ver *n.* a young eel.

em *n.* in printing, the square of any size of type, used in calculating setting.

ema'ci'ate (-shi-) *v.t.* to make lean.—**emacia'tion** *n.* thinness.

em'anate *v.i.* to issue from, originate.—**emana'tion** *n.*—**em'anative** *a.*

eman'cipate *v.t.* to set free.—**emancipa'tion** *n.*—**emancipa'tionist** *n.*—**eman'cipator** *n.*—**eman'cipatory** *a.*

emas'culate *v.t.* to castrate; enfeeble, weaken.—**emascula'tion** *n.*

embalm' *v.t.* to preserve a corpse with aromatic oils and spices.

embar'go *n.* an order stopping the movement of ships; a suspension of commerce; a ban (**-goes** (-gōz) *pl.*).—*v.t.* to put under an embargo.

embark' *v.t.* and *i.* to put, go, on board ship; engage, involve (in).—**embarka'tion** *n.*—**to embark' on** to begin.

embarr'ass *v.t.* to perplex, put into difficulty; encumber, **embarr'assment** *n.*
Syn. to entangle, confuse, disconcert, trouble. *Ant.* to clear, free, put at ease.

em'bassy *n.* the office or work or residence of an ambassador; a deputation.

embed', imbed' *v.t.* to fix fast in something solid (**embed'ded** *p.t.* and *p.p.*).

embell'ish *v.t.* to adorn, make beautiful. —**embell'ishment** *n.*

em'ber *n.* a glowing cinder (**-s** *pl.*).

em'ber *a.* **Ember-days** days appointed by the Church for fasting.

embez'zle *v.t.* to divert fraudulently, misappropriate (money in trust, etc.).—**embez'zler** *n.*—**embez'zlement** *n.*

embitt'er *v.t.* to make bitter.

em'blem *n.* a symbol; an heraldic device. —**emblemat'ic** *a.*—**emblema'tically** *adv.*

embod'y *v.t.* to give body, concrete expression, to; represent, be an expres-

sion of (**-bod'ied** *p.t.* and *p.p.*—**-bod'ying** *pres. p.*).—**embod'iment** *n.*
em'bolism (-bu-) *n.* intercalation; obstruction of an artery by a blood-clot.–**embol'ic** *a.* inserted.–**em'bolise** *v.t.*
emboss' *v.t.* to mould, stamp or carve in relief.—he **emboss'es.**
embrace' *v.t.* to clasp in the arms; seize, avail oneself of, accept; include.—*n.* a clasping in the arms (**embraced'** *p.t./p.p.*).—**embrace'able** *a.*
embra'sure (-zher) *n.* an opening in a wall for a cannon; the bevelling of a wall at the sides of a window.
embroca'tion *n.* a lotion for rubbing limbs, etc.—**em'brocate** *v.t.*
embroi'der *v.t.* to ornament with needlework; to embellish.–**embroi'dery** *n.*
embroil' *v.t.* to bring into confusion; involve in hostility.—**embroil'ment** *n.*
em'bryo *n.* an unborn or undeveloped offspring, germ; an undeveloped thing (-os (-ōz) *pl.*).—**embryon'ic** *a.*—**embryol'ogy** *n.*—**embryol'ogist** *n.*
emend' *v.t.* to remove errors from, correct.—**emenda'tion** *n.*—**e'mendator** *n.*
em'erald *n.* a bright green precious stone.—*a.* of the colour of emerald.
emerge' *v.i.* to come up, out; rise to notice; come out on inquiry.—**emer'gence** *n.*—**emer'gent** *a.*—**emer'gency** *n.* sudden event needing prompt action.
emer'itus *a.* retired, honourably discharged, *esp.* of a professor.
em'ery *n.* a hard mineral used for polishing.—**em'ery paper** *n.*
emet'ic *a.* causing vomiting.—*n.* a medicine doing this.
em'igrate *v.t.* to go and settle in another country.—**emigra'tion** *n.*—**em'igrant** *n.*—**emigra'tory** *a.*
emigré' (ā-me-grā') *n.* an emigrant, *esp.* the refugees from France during the Revolution (**-grés** (-grā') *pl.*).
em'inent *a.* distinguished, notable, exalted.—**em'inently** *adv.*—**em'inence** *n.* distinction; rising ground.—**Em'inence** title of cardinal.
emit' *v.t.* to give out, put forth.—**emitt'er** *n.*—**emis'sion** *n.*—**em'issary** *n.* one sent out on a mission.
emoll'ient *a.* softening.—*n.* an ointment or other softening application.
emol'ument *n.* pay, salary, profit.
emo'tion *n.* mental agitation, excited state of feeling.—**emo'tional** *a.* given to emotion; appealing to the emotions.
empennage' (-àzh') *n.* the arrangement of planes at the tail of an aeroplane.
em'peror *n.* the sovereign of an empire.—**em'press** *fem.*
em'phasis *n.* stress on words; vigour of speech, expression; importance attached (**-ses** *pl.*).—**em'phasise** *v.t.*—**emphat'ic** *a.* forcible; stressed.—**emphat'ically** *adv.* decidedly.
em'pire *n.* a large territory, *esp.* an aggregate of states under supreme ruler.
empir'ic *a.* relying on experiment or experience, not on theory.—*n.* an empiric scientist, physician.—**empir'ically** *adv.*—**empir'icism** *n.*
emplace'ment *n.* platform for guns.
employ' *v.t.* to use; use the services of, keep in one's service (**-ployed** (-ploid) *p.t./p.p.*— **-ploy'ing** *pr. p.*).—**employ'er** *n.*—**employee'** *n.*—**employ'ment** *n.*
empo'rium *n.* a centre of commerce; a shop (**-riums, -ria** *pl.*).
empow'er *v.t.* to enable, authorise.
em'press *fem.* of **em'peror.**
emp'ty *a.* containing nothing; unoccupied; senseless; vain, foolish.—*v.t.* and *i.* to make or become empty (**-tied** *p.t.* and *p.p.*—**-tying** *pres. p.*).—*n.* an empty box, basket, etc.—**emp'tiness** *n.* *Syn.* void, devoid, vacant, unsubstantial, blank. *Ant.* full, occupied.
empyre'an *n.* the sky.
e'mu *n.* Australian bird like ostrich.
em'ulate *v.t.* to strive to equal or excel; imitate.—**em'ulator** *n.*—**emula'tion** *n.*—**em'ulative** *a.*—**em'ulous** *a.*
emul'sion *n.* a milky liquid mixture with oily or resinous particles in suspension.—**emul'sive** *a.*—**emul'sify** *v.t.* (**-fied** *p.t.* and *p.p.*—**-fying** *pres. p.*).
en- *prefix* forms verbs with sense of put in, into, on; as **engulf'** *v.t.* swallow up.—**enrage'** *v.t.* to put into a rage. Many such words are omitted and the meaning should be sought under the simple word.
ena'ble *v.t.* to make able, authorise.
enact' *v.t.* to make law; play, act.
enam'el *n.* smooth, glossy coating given to china, metals, etc.; a kind of paint; the coating of the teeth.—*v.t.* to cover with enamel; to adorn with colours.
enam'our (-er) *v.t.* to inspire with love.
encamp' *v.t.* and *i.* to settle in a camp.—**encamp'ment** *n.*
encaus'tic *a.* burnt in.—*n.* the art of ornament by burnt-in colours.
enceinte' *a.* (of a woman) pregnant.—*n.* (in fortification) an enclosure.
encephali'tis *n.* (en-sef-a-li'-tis) inflammation of the brain caused by injury, infection, etc.; sleeping sickness.—**encephal'ic** *a.* of the brain.
enchant' (-à-) *v.t.* to bewitch, delight.—**enchant'ment** *n.* a spell.—**enchant'er** *n.*—**enchant'ress** *fem.*
encir'cle *v.t.* to surround, enfold (**encir'cling** *pres. p.*—**encir'cled** *p.t.* and *p.p.*)—**encir'clement** *n.*
en'clave *n.* a portion of territory entirely surrounded by foreign land.
enclit'ic *a.* pronounced as part of (another word).—*n.* an enclitic word.
enclose' *v.t.* to shut; to place in with something else (in a letter, etc.).—**enclo-sure** (-zher) *n.*
enco'mium *n.* formal praise; eulogy.
encom'pass *v.t.* to surround, encircle.

en'core (on-kor') *interj.* again, once more.—*n.* a call for the repetition of a song, etc.; the repetition.—*v.i.* to call for repetition.
encoun'ter *v.t.* meet in hostility; meet with.—*n.* hostile or casual meeting.
encour'age (-kur'-) *v.t.* to hearten, cheer, inspirit.—**encour'agement** *n.*
encroach' *v.i.* to intrude (on) as a usurper, trespass.—**encroach'ment** *n.*
encum'ber *v.t.* to hamper; burden, hinder, block.—**encum'brance** *n.*
encyclopæ'dia (-pēd-') *n.* reference book of information on all subjects, arranged alphabetically.—**encyclopæ'dic** *a.*—**encyclopæ'dist** *n.*
end *n.* a limit; extremity; conclusion; finishing; fragment; latter part; death; event, issue; purpose, aim.—*v.t.* to put an end to.—*v.i.* to come to an end.—**end'ing** *n.*—**end'less** *a.*—**end'ways** *adv.*
endeav'our (-de'vḛr) *v.i.* try, attempt.—*n.* attempt, effort.
endem'ic *a.* regularly existing or found in a country or district.
end'ive *n.* curly-leaved chicory.
en'docrine (-īn) *n.* secreting internally; *esp.* of the ductless glands which pour secretions into the blood.—**endocrinol'ogy** *n.*
endog'amy *n.* prohibition of marriage outside one's tribe or group.—**endogam'ic** *a.*—**endogam'ous** *a.*
en'doplasm *n.* (*bot.*) the inner mass of cell material.
endorse' *v.t.* to write (*esp.* to sign one's name) on the back of.—**endorse'ment** *n.*
en'dosperm *n.* (*bot.*) the tissue around the embryo in seeds.
endow' *v.t.* to provide a permanent income for; furnish.—**endow'ment** *n.*
endue' *v.t.* to invest, furnish (with).
endure' *v.t.* to last.—*v.t.* to undergo; tolerate, put up with.—**endu'rance** *n.* power of enduring.—**endu'rable** *a.*
ene'ma *n.* an injection into the rectum.
en'emy *n.* a hostile person, opponent; armed foe; hostile force or ship.—*a.*
en'ergy *n.* vigour, force, activity.—**energet'ic** *a.*—**energet'ically** *adv.*—**en'ergise** *v.t.* give energy to.
en'ervate *v.t.* to weaken, deprive of vigour.—**enerva'tion** *n.*—**en'ervating** *a.*
enfee'ble *v.t.* to weaken, debilitate.—**enfee'blement** *n.*
enfilade' *n.* fire from artillery, etc., sweeping a line from end to end.
enfold' *v.t.* wrap up; embrace; clasp.
enforce' *v.t.* compel obedience to; impose (action) upon; drive home.—**enforce'ment** *n.*—**enforce'able** *a.*
enfran'chise *v.t.* to give the right of voting for members of parliament; to set free.—**enfran'chisement** *n.*
engage' (en-gāj') *v.t.* to bind by contract or promise; hire; order; pledge oneself, undertake; attract; occupy; bring into conflict; interlock.—*v.i.* to begin to fight; employ oneself (in); promise.—**engage'ment** *n.* (**engaged'** *p.t.* and *p.p.*).
engen'der (-jen'-) *v.t.* to give rise to, beget, produce.
en'gine (-jin) *n.* a complex machine;—*v.t.* to supply (a ship) with engines.—**engineer'** *n.* one who constructs or is in charge of engines, military or public works.—*v.t.* to construct as an engineer; to contrive.—**engineer'ing** *n.*
engraft' (-à-) *v.t.* to graft in.
engrain' *v.t.* to implant firmly, dye deeply.—**engrained** *a.*
en'gram *n.* a supposed trace of any experience preserved by the brain and forming the essence of a "memory."
engrave' *v.t.* and *i.* to cut in lines on metal for printing; carve, incise; impress deeply.—**engra'ving** *n.* a picture printed from an engraved plate.—**engra'ver** *n.* one who engraves.
engross' (-ō-) *v.t.* to write out in large letters or in legal form; to absorb (attention).—**engross'ment** *n.*
engulf' *v.t.* to swallow up; overwhelm.
enhance' *v.t.* to heighten, intensify, raise in price.—**enhance'ment** *n.*
Syn. to raise, increase, augment. ***Ant.*** decrease, deface, lower.
enig'ma *n.* a riddle; a puzzling thing or person (**-mas** *pl.*).—**enigmat'ic, enigmat'ical** *a.*—**enigmat'ically** *adv.*
enjamb'ment *n.* in verse, the continuation of a sentence beyond the end of a line or to next verse.
enjoin' *v.t.* to command, prescribe.
enjoy' *v.t.* to take pleasure in; have the use or benefit of.—*v. refl.* to be happy.—**enjoy'ment** *n.* pleasure.—**enjoy'able** *a.*
enlarge' *v.t.* to make bigger; set free.—*v.i.* to grow bigger; to talk at large; to enlarge on.—**enlarge'ment** *n.*
enlight'en (-līt'-) *v.t.* instruct, inform.—**enlight'enment** *n.*
enlist' *v.t.* and *i.* to engage as a soldier or helper; to enrol, to gain (sympathies, etc.).—**enlist'ment** *n.*
enli'ven *v.t.* to make more lively.
en'mity *n.* ill-will; hostility.
enno'ble (-n-n-) *v.t.* to make noble.
en'nui (on'wē) *n.* boredom.
enor'mous *a.* huge, vast.—**enor'mity** *n.* a gross offence; great wickedness.
enough' (i-nuf') *a.* as much or as many as need be, sufficient; stop!—*n.* a sufficient quantity.—*adv.* sufficiently.—**enow'** *a.*, *n.* and *adv.* enough.
enplane' *v.i.* to climb into an aircraft.
enrich' *v.t.* to make rich; add to.—**enrich'ment** *n.*—he **enrich'es.**
enrol', enroll' (-ō-) *v.t.* to enter in a register; engage, enlist, take in as a member; enter, record.—**enroll'ment** *n.* (**en'rolled'** *p.t.* and *p.p.*).
ensang'uine *v.t.* to stain with blood.
ensconce' *v.t.* to settle safely.

ensemble' (on-sombl') *n.* the whole, a general effect; woman's dress and coat.
enshrine' *v.t.* to place in a shrine; to preserve.
enshroud' *v.t.* to veil; conceal.
en'sign (-sīn) *n.* a naval, military or Air Force flag; a badge.
en'silage *n.* the storing of fodder in a silo; fodder so stored.
enslave' *v.t.* to make into a slave.—**enslave'ment** *n.*—**ensla'ver** *n.*
ensue' *v.i.* to follow, happen after.—*v.t.* strive for (**ensued'** *p.t.* and *p.p.*).
ensure' *v.t.* to make safe, certain.
entail' *v.t.* to settle (land, etc.) on persons in succession, none of whom can then dispose of it; to involve as result. —*n.*such settlement limiting inheritance.
entente (on-tont) *n.* a friendly understanding between nations.
en'ter *v.t.* to go or come into; to join (a society, etc.); write in, register.—*v.i.* to go or come in; join; begin; engage.—**en'trance** *n.* going or coming in; right to enter; fee paid for this; door or passage to enter.—**en'trant** *n.* one who enters, *esp.* a contest.
enter'ic *n.* typhoid fever.—*a.* typhoid; of or relating to the intestines.—**enteri'tis** *n.* bowel inflammation.
en'terprise *n.* a design, a bold or difficult undertaking; bold spirit.—**en'terprising** *a.* prompt to undertake, bold and active in spirit.
entertain' *v.t.* receive as guest; amuse; maintain; consider favourably, cherish. —**entertain'er** *n.*—**entertain'ment** *n.*
enthrall' *v.t.* to captivate, charm. (**enthral'ling** *pr. p.*—**enthral'led** *p.t./p.p.*).
enthu'siasm *n.* ardent eagerness, zeal. **enthu'siast** *n.*—**enthusias'tic** *a.*—**enthusias'tically** *adv.*—**enthuse'** *v.i.* (*sl.*) to show enthusiasm.
entice' *v.t.* to allure; attract, entrap adroitly.—**entice'ment** *n.* (**enticed'** *p.t./p.p.*).
entire' *a.* whole, complete, not broken. —**entire'ly** *adv.*—**entire'ty** *n.*
enti'tle *v.t.* to give a title or claim to.
en'tity *n.* a thing's being or existence; a thing having real existence.
entomol'ogy *n.* the study of insects.—**entomol'ogist** *n.*—**entomolo'gical** (-oj'-) *a.*
entourage' (on-tōōr-azh') *n.* surroundings; one's habitual associates.
entracte' (on-tråkt') *n.* the interval, or music played between two acts of a play.
en'trails *n. pl.* bowels, intestines.
entrance' *v.t.* to delight.—**entran'cing** *a.*
entreat' *v.t.* to ask earnestly, beg, implore.—**entreat'y** *n.* supplication.
entrée' (on-trā') *n.* right of access; a dish served between courses.
entrench' *v.t.* to establish in fortified position, with trenches; resist stoutly.—*n.* entrenchment.
entrust' *v.t.* to confide (to), commit.
en'try *n.* the action or right of entry; entrance, item entered.—(**entries** *pl.*).
entwine' *v.t.* to plait, interweave.
enu'cleate (enew'-) *v.t.* to extricate and make clear; to extract.
enu'merate *v.* to count.—**enumera'tion** *n.*—**enu'merator** *n.*
enun'ciate *v.t.* to state clearly; proclaim; pronounce.—**enuncia'tion** *n.*
envel'op *v.t.* to wrap up, enclose.—**envel'opment** *n.*—**en'velope** *n.* folded, gummed cover of a letter; a covering.
enven'om *v.t.* to put poison in.
en'viable *a.* to be envied.—**en'vious** *a.*—**en'vying** wanting something belonging to someone else.—**en'viously** *adv.*
envi'ron *v.t.* to surround.—**envi'ronment** *n.* surroundings; conditions of life or growth.—**envi'rons** *n. pl.* the districts round (a town, etc.).
envis'age (-z-) *v.t.* to view; look at.
en'voy *n.* a messenger; a diplomatic minister of rank below an ambassador; *n.* a short concluding stanza of a poem.
en'vy *n.* bitter or longing consideration of another's better fortune or success or qualities; the object of this feeling.—*v.t.* to feel envy of (**en'vied** *p.t.* and *p.p.* —**en'vying** *pres. p.*).—**en'viable** *a.*
Syn. ill-will, malevolence, jealousy, malignity, hatred. *Ant.* good-will, benevolence, kindliness.
en'zyme (en'-zim) *n.* a substance of vegetable or animal origin, capable of producing chemical transformations, as fermentation.
ep'aulette *n.* ornamental shoulder-piece of a uniform.
epergne' (-pern') *n.* an ornament for the middle of a dining-table.
ephem'eral *a.* short-lived, lasting only for a day, or few days.—**ephem'eron** *n.* (**-rons, -ra** *pl.*) an ephemeral insect or thing. Also **ephem'era** (**-ras, -ræ** *pl.*).
e'phod *n.* a Jewish priestly vestment.
ep'ic *a.* telling in continuous story the achievements of a hero or heroes.—*n.* an epic poem.—**ep'ically** *adv.*
ep'icarp *n.* outer skin of fruits.
ep'icene (-sēn) *a.* denoting either sex.
ep'icure *n.* one dainty in eating and drinking.—**epicure'an** (-ē'-) *a.* of Epicurus, who taught that pleasure was the highest good; given to refined sensuous enjoyment.—*n.* such a person or philosopher.—**epicure'anism** *n.*
epidem'ic *a.* prevalent for a time among a community, widespread.—*n.* an epidemic disease.
epider'mis *n.* the outer skin.
epiglott'is *n.* a cartilage that covers the opening of the larynx in swallowing.
ep'igram *n.* short poem with witty or satirical ending; pointed saying.—**epigrammat'ic** *a.* —**epigrammat'ically** *adv.*
ep'igraph *n.* an inscription.
ep'ilepsy *n.* a disease in which the

sufferer falls down in a fit, with foaming and spasms.—**epilep'tic** *a.* subject to epilepsy.—*n.* sufferer from epilepsy.

ep'ilogue (-og) *n.* a short speech or poem at the end of a play.

epiph'any *n.* the festival of the appearance of Christ to the Magi.

epis'copal *a.* of a bishop; ruled by bishops.—**epis'copacy** *n.* government by bishops; the body of bishops.—**episcopa'lian** *a.* of an episcopal system or church.—*n.* a member or adherent of an episcopal church.—**epis'copate** *n.* a bishop's office, see, or duration of office; the body of bishops.

ep'isode *n.* an incident; an incidental narrative or series of events; the part of a Greek tragedy between choric songs. —**episod'ic, episod'ical** *a.*

epis'tle (-sl) *n.* a letter, *esp.* one of the letters of the apostles; a poem in the form of a letter.—**epis'tolary** *a.*

ep'itaph *n.* an inscription on a tomb.

ep'ithet *n.* an adjective expressing a quality or attribute; a name full of meaning.—**epithet'ic** *a.*

epit'ome (-mē) *n.* a summary, abridgment (**-mes** *pl.*).—**epit'omize** *v.t.* condense.—**epit'omist** *n.*

e'poch (-ok) *n.* the beginning of a period; a period, era, *esp.* one marked by notable events.—**e'pochal** *a.*

epon'ymous *a.* commemorated by the adoption of the name.

eq'uable *a.* uniform, not easily disturbed.—**eq'uably** *adv.*—**equabil'ity** *n.* *Syn.* even, cool, calm. *Ant.* unsteady, irritable, excitable.

e'qual *a.* the same in number, size, merit, etc.; fit or qualified; evenly balanced.—*n.* one equal to another.—*v.t.* to be equal to.—**equal'ity** (-ol-) *n.*—**e'qually** *adv.* in equal degree.—**e'qualize** *v.t.* and *i.*—**equalisa'tion** *n.*

equanim'ity *n.* calmness, evenness of mind or temper.

equate' *v.t.* to state or assume the equality of.—**equa'tion** *n.* a statement of equality between two mathematical expressions; a balancing; a compensation for inaccuracy.—**equa'tor** *n.* a great circle of the earth equidistant from the poles.—**equato'rial** *a.*

eq'uerry *n.* a king's officer in charge of horses; an officer in attendance on an English sovereign (**eq'uerries** *pl.*).

eques'trian *a.* of, skilled in, horse-riding; mounted on a horse.—*n.* a rider or performer on a horse.

equi' *prefix* equal, at equal.—**equian'gular** (-ng-g-) *a.* having equal angles. —**equidis'tant** *a.* at equal distances.—**equilat'eral** *a.* having equal sides.—**equ'ipoise** *n.* equality of weight or force; equilibrium; counterpoise.

equilib'rium *n.* a state of balance; balanced mind (**-riums, -ria** *pl.*).—**equili'brate** *v.t.* and *i.*—**equilib'rator** *n.* in aviation, the stabilising fin of an aeroplane.—**equil'ibrist** *n.* an acrobat.

eq'uine *a.* of a horse.

e'quinox *n.* the time at which the sun crosses the equator and day and night are equal.—*pl.* the points at which the sun crosses the equator.—**equinoc'tial** *a.*

equip' *v.t.* to supply, fit out, array.—**equip'ment** *n.*—**eq'uipage** *n.* a carriage, horses and attendants; outfit.

equipoll'ent *a.* of equal force.

eq'uity *n.* fairness; the use of the principles of justice to supplement the law; a system of law so made.—**eq'uitable** *a.* fair, just.—**eq'uitably** *adv.*

equiv'alent *a.* equal in value; having the same meaning or result; corresponding.—*n.* an equivalent thing, amount, etc.—**equiv'alence, equiv'alency** *n.*

equiv'ocal *a.* of double or doubtful meaning; questionable, liable to suspicion.—**equivocal'ity** *n.*—**equiv'ocate** *v.i.* to use equivocal words to hide the truth. —**equivoca'tion** *n.*—**equiv'ocator** *n.*—**eq'uivoque, eq'uivoke** *n.* a pun.

e'ra *n.* a system of time in which years are numbered from a particular event.

erad'icate *v.t.* to root out.—**eradica'tion** *n.* destruction.—**erad'icator** *n.*

erase' *v.t.* to rub out.—**era'sure** *n.*

er'bium *n.* a rare metallic element present in gladolinite.

ere (ĕr) *prep.* and *conj.* before.

erect' *a.* upright.—*v.t.* to set up; build.—**erect'ile** *a.*—**erec'tion** *n.*—**erect'or** *n.*

e'remite *n.* a hermit.

erf *n.* in S. Africa, a house or garden-lot.

ergoster'ol *n.* a fat, produced from ergot, yielding vitamin D.

er'got *n.* a disease of rye and other plants; the diseased seed used as a drug.

er'mine *n.* an animal like a weasel with fur brown in summer and white, except for black tail-tip, in winter; its fur.

erode' *v.t.* to wear out, eat away.—**ero'sion** *n.*-**ero'sive** *a.* (**ero'ded** *p.t.*/*p.p.*).

erot'ic *a.* relating to, or treating of, sexual love.—**erot'icism, ero'tism** *n.* in psycho-analysis, love of all manifestations, direct, perverted or sublimated.

err *v.i.* to make mistakes; to be wrong; to sin.—**errat'ic** *a.*irregular in movement, conduct, etc.—**erra'tum** (-ȧ-) *n.* (**erra'ta** *pl.*) a mistake noted for correction.—**erro'neous** *a.* mistaken, wrong.—**err'or** *n.* a mistake; wrong opinion; sin.—**err'ant** *a.* wandering in search of adventure; erring.—**err'ancy** *n.* erring state or conduct.—**err'antry** *n.* state or conduct of a knight errant.

err'and *n.* a short journey for a simple business; the business; a purpose.—**err'and-boy** *n.*

ersatz' *a.* and *n.* substitute.

erst, erst'while *adv.* of old.

eructa'tion *n.* belching.

er'udite *a.* learned.—**erudi'tion** *n.*
erupt' *v.i.* to burst out.—**eruption** *n.* a bursting out, *esp.* a volcanic outbreak; a rash.—**erupt'ive** *a.*
erysip'elas *n.* a disease causing a deep red colouring of the skin.
escalade' *n.* a scaling of walls with ladders.—**es'calator** *n.* moving staircase.
escall'op *see* **scallop.**
escape' *v.i.* to get free; get off safely; go unpunished; find a way out.—*v.i.* to elude; come out unawares from.—*n.* an escaping; leakage.—**escape'ment** *n.* mechanism connecting motive power to regulator of a clock, etc.—**escap'ism** *n.* ignoring of reality; a tendency not to face the facts and to live in a world of the imagination.—**escapade'** *n.* a flighty exploit (**escaped'** *p.t./p.p.*).
escarp' *n.* the steep bank under a rampart.—*v.t.* to cut into a steep slope.—**escarp'ment** *n.*
eschatol'ogy (-k-) *n.* doctrine of death, judgment and last things.
escheat' *n.* the lapse of a property to the state, an estate so lapsing.—*v.t.* to confiscate.—*v.i.* to become an escheat.
eschew' *v.t.* to avoid, abstain from.
es'cort *n.* an armed guard of troops or warships; a person (or persons) accompanying another on a journey for protection or courtesy, attendant.—**escort'** *v.t.* to act as escort to.
es'critoire (-twår) *n.* a writing-desk.
es'culent *a.* eatable.
escutch'eon (-chun) *n.* a shield with a coat-of-arms; a family shield.
Es'kimo *n.* one of an aboriginal race inhabiting N. Amer., Greenland, etc. (**-mos** *pl.*). Also **Es'quimau** (**-aux** *pl.*).
esoter'ic (-ō-) *a.* for the initiated only.
espal'ier *n.* lattice on which trees are trained; a tree so trained.
espart'o *n.* a grass used in papermaking.
espe'cial (-esh'l) *a.* pre-eminent, more than ordinary.—**espe'cially** *adv.*
Syn. particular, essential, exclusive, specific. *Ant.* general, universal, unexacting, ordinary.
Esperan'to *n.* an artificial universal language.—**Esperan'tist** *n.*
es'pionage *n.* spying; the use of spies.
esplanade' *n.* a level space, *esp.* seafront used as a public promenade.
espouse' (-z) *v.t.* to marry; support, attach oneself to.—**espous'al** *n.*
esprit' (-prē') *n.* spirit, animation.—**esprit-de-corps** (-kōr) loyalty to the society, etc., to which one belongs.
espy' *v.t.* to catch sight of (**espied'** *p.t.* and *p.p.*—**espy'ing** *pres. p.*).—**espi'al** *n.*
esquire' *n.* a title added to a gentleman's name, *esp.* on the address of a letter (written Esq.); formerly, a squire.
essay' *v.t.* to try, attempt; test.—**ess'ay** *n.* a literary composition; an attempt.—**ess'ayist** *n.* a writer of essays.
ess'ence *n.* an existence, being; absolute being, reality; all that makes a thing what it is, an extract got by distillation, a perfume, scent.
essen'tial *a.* of, or constituting, the essence of a thing; all important.—*n.* an indispensable element; a chief point.
estab'lish *v.t.* to set up; settle; found; prove.—**estab'lishment** *n.* establishing; a permanent organised body; household; house of business; public institution.
estate' *n.* a landed property; a person's property; a class as part of a nation; rank, state, condition.
esteem' *v.t.* to think highly of; consider.—*n.* favourable opinion, regard.
es'timate *v.t.* to form an approximate idea of (amounts, measurements, etc.); form an opinion of; quote a probable price for.—*n.* an approximate judgment of amounts, etc.; the amount, etc., arrived at; an opinion; a price quoted by a contractor.—**es'timable** *a.* worthy of regard.—**estima'tion** *n.* opinion, judgment.—**es'timative** *a.*
estrange' *v.t.* to make unfriendly, put a stop to affection.—**estrange'ment** *n.*
es'tuary *n.* the tidal mouth of a river.
etch *v.t.* to make an engraving by eating away the surface of a metal plate with acids, etc.—*v.i.* to practise this art.—**etch'ing** *n.* picture so produced.—**etch'er** *n.* one who etches.
eter'nal *a.* without beginning or end; everlasting; changeless.—**eter'nally** *adv.*—**eter'nity** *n.* time without end.
ethane' *n.* a gaseous hydro-carbon present in natural gas.
e'ther (-th-) *n.* a substance or fluid supposed to fill all space; the clear sky, region above the clouds; a colourless volatile liquid used as an anæsthetic.—**ethe'real** *a.* light, airy; heavenly.
eth'ic, eth'ical *a.* relating to, or treating of, morals.—**eth'ically** *adv.*—**eth'ics** *n. pl.* the science of morals; moral principles, rules of conduct.
eth'nic *a.* of race.—**ethnog'raphy** *n.* the description of races of men.—**ethnograph'ic** *a.*—**ethnol'ogy** *n.* the science of races.—**ethnolo'gical** *a.*
eth'yl *n.* the radical of ordinary alcohol and ether.—**ethylene'** *n.* a poisonous gas used as an anæsthetic and a fuel.
e'tiolate *v.t.* to make pale by shutting out light.—**etiola'tion** *n.*
etiol'ogy (ē-ti-ol-) *n.* science of causation, *esp.* of diseases.—**etiolog'ical** *a.*—**etiolog'ically** *adv.*—**etiolo'gist** *n.*
et'iquette *n.* conventional rules of manners; court ceremonial, etc.
etymol'ogy *n.* the tracing, or an account of, a word's formation, origin, development; the science of this.—**etymolo'gical** (-oj'-) *a.*—**etymolo'gically** *adv.*—**etymol'ogist** *n.*—**et'ymon** *n.* a

primitive word from which a derivative comes (**-mons, -ma** *pl.*).

eucalypt'us *n.* the Australian gum-tree and allied plants. Also **eucalypt.**—**eucalyp'tus-oil'** *n.* a disinfectant.

eu'charist (-k-) *n.* the sacrament of the Lord's Supper; the consecrated elements, *esp.* bread.—**eucharis'tic** *a.*

eugen'ic *a.* relating to, or tending towards, the production of fine offspring. —*n. pl.* the science of this.—**eugen'ist** *n.*

eu'logy *n.* a speech or writing in praise of; praise.—**eu'logize** *v.t.*—**eu'logist** *n.*—**eulogis'tic** *a.*—**eulogis'tically** *adv.*

eu'nuch (-k) *n.* a castrated man.

eu'phemism *n.* the substitution of a mild word or expression for a blunt one; an instance of this.—**euphemis'tic** *a.*—**euphemis'tically** *adv.*—**eu'phemist** *n.*

eu'phony *n.* pleasantness of sound.—**euphon'ic** *a.*—**eupho'nious** *a.*—**eupho'nium** *n.* a bass saxhorn.

eu'phuism *n.* an affected or highflown manner of writing.—**eu'phuist** *n.*

Eura'sian *a.* of mixed European and Asiatic descent; of Europe and Asia.—*n.*

eure'ka *interj.* "I've found it" (to announce a discovery, etc.).

eurhyth'mics *n. pl.* art of rhythmical movement to music, or expression in dance movement.—**eurhyth'mic** *a.*

eu'sol *n.* an antiseptic liquid.

eusta'chian tube (ū-stā'ki-an) *n.* the passage leading from the pharynx to the middle ear.

euthana'sia *n.* gentle, easy death.

euthen'ics (ū-then) *n.* the science of the relation of environment to man.

evac'uate *v.t.* empty; withdraw from; discharge.—**evacua'tion** *n.*—**evac'uee** *n.*

evade' *v.t.* to avoid, escape from; elude, frustrate.—**eva'sion** *n.*—**eva'sive** *a.*

Syn. to equivocate, baffle, quibble. *Ant.* seek, court.

eval'uate *v.t.* to find or state the value or number of.—**evalua'tion** *n.*

evanesce' (-es') *v.i.* to fade away.—**evanes'cent** *a.*—**evanes'cence** *n.*

evan'gel (-j-) *n.* the gospel.—**evangel'ical** *a.* of, or according to, the gospel teaching; of the Protestant school which maintains salvation by faith.—**evangel'icalism** *n.*—**evan'gelist** *n.* a writer of one of the four gospels; a preacher of the gospel; a revivalist.—**evan'gelise** *v.t.* to preach to; to convert. —**evangelisa'tion** *n.*

evap'orate *v.i.* to turn into vapour; pass off in vapour.—*v.t.* to turn into vapour.—**evapora'tion** *n.*—**evap'orator** *n.*

eva'sion *see* **evade.**

eve (ēv) *n.* the evening before (a festival, etc.); the time just before evening.

e'ven *n.* evening.—**e'vensong** *n.* evening service of praise and prayer.

e'ven *a.* flat, smooth; uniform in quality; equal in amount, balanced; divisible by two; impartial.—*v.t.* to make even.—*adv.* invites comparison with something less strong; simply; notwithstanding; (*archaic*) quite.

e'vening (-vn-) *n.* the close of day.

event' *n.* the occurrence of a thing; a notable occurrence; issue; result.—**event'ful** *a.* full of exciting events.—**event'ual** *a.* that will happen under certain conditions; resulting in the end. —**event'ually** *adv.*—**eventual'ity** *n.* a possible event.—**event'uate** *v.i.* turn out.

ev'er *adv.* always; constantly; at any time; by any chance.

ev'ery (-vr-) *a.* each of all; all possible. —**ev'erybody** *n.*—**ev'eryday** *a.* usual, ordinary.—**ev'eryone** *n.*—**ev'erything** *n.* —**ev'erywhere** *adv.* in all places.

evict' *v.t.* to expel by legal process, to turn out.—**evic'tion** *n.*

ev'ident *a.* plain, obvious.—**ev'idently** *adv.*—**ev'idence** *n.* sign, indication; ground for belief, testimony.—*v.t.* indicate, prove.—**in evidence** conspicuous. —**eviden'tial** *a.* of evidence.

e'vil *a.* bad, harmful.—*n.* what is bad or harmful; sin.—**e'villy** *adv.*

evince' *v.t.* show, indicate (**evinced'** *p.t.* and *p.p.*).—**evinc'ive** *a.*

evis'cerate (-vis'er-) *v.t.* to disembowel —**eviscera'tion** *n.*

evoke' *v.t.* to call up.—**evoca'tion** *n.*

evolve' *v.t.* to develop; unfold, open out; produce.—*v.i.* to develop, *esp.* by natural process; open out.—**evolu'tion** *n.* an evolving; development of species from earlier forms; movement of troops, ships, etc.—**evolu'tional** *a.*—**evolu'tionary** *a.*

ewe (ū) a female sheep.

ew'er (ū'-) *n.* a pitcher, water-jug.

ex- *prefix*; sometimes **e-, ef-** out, from, as *exclaim, evade, effulgence*; from, out of, as *exodus*; former (as *ex-king*, etc).

exac'erbate (-as'-) *v.t.* to aggravate, embitter.—**exacerba'tion** *n.*

exact' (-gz-) *a.* precise, accurate, strictly correct.—*v.t.* to demand, extort; insist upon; enforce.—**exact'ly** *adv.*—**exac'tion** *n.*—**exact'ness** *n.*—**exact'itude** *n.*

exag'gerate (egz-aj'-) *v.t.* to magnify beyond truth, overstate.—**exaggera'tion** *n.*—**exag'gerator** *n.*—**exag'gerative** *a.*

exalt' (igz-awlt') *v.t.* to raise up; praise; make noble.—**exalta'tion** *n.* rapture.

exam'ine (-gz-) *v.t.* to investigate; ask questions of; test the knowledge or proficiency of; inquire into.—**examina'tion** *n.*—**exam'iner** *n.*—**exam'inee** *n.*

exam'ple (-gz-à-) *n.* a thing illustrating a general rule; a specimen; model.

exas'perate (-gz-) *v.t.* to irritate, enrage; intensify.—**exaspera'tion** *n.*

Syn. to anger, embitter, incense. *Ant.* soothe, calm, pacify.

ex'cavate *v.t.* to hollow out; make a hole by digging; unearth.—**excava'tion** *n.*—**ex'cavator** *n.*

exceed' *v.t.* to be greater than; do more than authorized, go beyond; surpass.—**exceed'ingly** *adv.* very.—**excess'** *n.* an exceeding; the amount by which a thing exceeds; too great an amount; intemperance or immoderate conduct.—**excess'ive** *a.*—**excess'ively** *adv.*

excel' *v.i.* to be very good, pre-eminent. —*v.t.* to surpass, be better than.—**ex'cellent** *a.* very good.—**ex'cellence** *n.*—**ex'cellency** *n.* a title of ambassadors, etc.

except' *v.t.* to leave or take out; exclude. —*v.i.* to raise objection.—*prep.* not including; but.—*conj.* unless.—**except'ing** *prep.* not including.—**excep'tion** *n.* an excepting; a thing excepted, not included in a rule; an objection.—**excep'tional** *a.*—**excep'tionally** *adv.*—**excep'tionable** *a.* open to objection.

excerpt' *v.t.* to extract, quote (passage from book).—**ex'cerpt** *n.* a quoted or extracted passage.—**excerp'tion** *n.*

excess' *see* **exceed.**

exchange' *v.t.* to give (something) in return for something else.—*v.i.* of an officer, to change posts with another.—*n.* giving one thing and receiving another; giving or receiving coin, bills, etc., of one country for those of another; a thing given for another; a building where merchants meet for business.—**exchangea'ble** *a.*—**exchangeabil'ity** *n.*—**tel'ephone exchange'** a central office where telephone connections are made.

excheq'uer (-kẹr) *n.* the government department in charge of the revenue.

excise' (-z) *n.* tax on home goods during manufacture or before sale.—**excise'man** *n.* an officer collecting and enforcing excise.—**exci'sable** *a.* liable to excise.

excise' *v.t.* to cut out.—**excis'ion** *n.*

excite' *v.t.* rouse, set in motion; stimulate, move to strong emotion; in wireless, set up oscillations in aerial.—**exci'table** *a.*—**exci'tably** *adv.*—**excitabil'ity** *n.* **excite'ment** *n.*—**excitation** *n.*

exclaim' *v.i.* and *t.* to cry out.—**exclama'tion** *n.*—**exclam'atory** *a.*

exclude' (-ōōd') *v.t.* to shut out; debar from.—**exclu'sion** *n.*—**exclu'sive** *a.* excluding; inclined to keep out (from society, etc.); sole, only; different from all others.—**exclu'sively** *adv.*

excog'itate (-koj'-) *v.t.* to think out.—**excogita'tion** *n.*—**excog'itative** *a.*

excommu'nicate *v.t.* to shut off from the sacraments of the church.—**excommunica'tion** *n.*—**excommu'nicative, excommu'nicatory** *a.*

exco'riate *v.t.* to remove skin from; attack bitterly.—**excoria'tion** *n.*

ex'crement *n.* waste matter discharged from the bowels; dung.—**excrement'al** *a.* —**excrete'** *v.t.* to discharge from the system.—**excre'tion** *n.*—**excre'tory** *a.*

excres'cent *a.* growing out of something abnormally.—**excres'cence** *n.*

excru'ciate *v.t.* to pain acutely, torture, in body or mind.—**excrucia'tion** *n.*

ex'culpate *v.t.* to free from blame, clear. —**exculpa'tion** *n.*—**excul'patory** *a.*

excur'sion *n.* a journey, ramble, trip, for pleasure.—**excur'sus** *n.* a discussion of a special point (**-suses, -sus** (rare) *pl.*).

excuse' (-z) *v.t.* to try to clear from blame; overlook, forgive; gain exemption; set free, remit.—**excuse'** (-s) *n.* that which serves to excuse; an apology.—**excu'sable** (-z-) *a.* pardonable.

Syn. exculpate, pardon, condone. *Ant.* accuse, blame, charge.

ex'ecrate *v.t.* to feel or express abhorrence, hatred for; curse.—**execra'tion** *n.*—**ex'ecrable** *a.* abominable, hateful.

ex'ecute *v.t.* to carry out, perform; sign (a document); kill (criminals).—**execu'tion** *n.*—**execu'tioner** *n.* one employed to kill those sentenced to death by law. **exec'utant** *n.* a performer, *esp.* of music. —**exec'utive** *a.* carrying into effect, *esp.* of branch of a government enforcing laws, committee carrying on the business of a society, etc.—*n.* an executive body. —**exec'utor** *n.* a person appointed by one making a will to carry out the provisions of the will.—**exec'utrix** *fem.*

exege'sis (-j-) *n.* explanation, interpretation, *esp.* of Scripture (**-ge'ses** *pl.*).—**exeget'ic, exeget'ical** *a.*

exem'plar *n.* a model type.—**exemp'lary** *a.* fit to be imitated, serving as an example.—**exemp'larily** *adv.*—**exemp'lify** *v.t.* to serve as an example of; make an attested copy of (**-fied** *p.t.* and *p.p.*—**-fying** *pres. p.*).—**exemplifica'tion** *n.*

exempt' (-gz-) *a.* freed from, not liable. —*v.t.* to free from.—**exemp'tion** *n.*

ex'equies (-kwiz) *n. pl.* funeral rites.

ex'ercise (-z) *n.* employment, use (of limbs, faculty, etc.); use of limbs for health; exertion; practice for; a task set for training.—*v.t.* to use, employ; give (training, health) exercise to; carry out, discharge; worry, harass.—*v.i.* to take exercise.—**ex'ercise-book** *n.* book of plain or ruled paper for school work.

exert' (-gz-) *v.t.* to bring into active operation.—**exer'tion** *n.* effort.

exhale' *v.t.* to breathe out; give off as vapour.—*v.i.* to breathe out; pass off as vapour.—**exhala'tion** *n.*

exhaust' (egz-awst') *v.t.* to draw off; use up; empty, treat, discuss thoroughly; tire out.—*n.* used steam or fluid from an engine; waste gases from an internal combustion engine; passage for such.— —**exhaus'tion** *n.*—**exhaust'ive** *a.*—**exhausti'ble** *a.*—**exhaustibil'ity** *n.*

Syn. weaken, spend, tire. *Ant.* revive, reanimate, replenish, refresh, fill.

exhib'it (-gz-) *v.t.* to show, display; manifest; show publicly in competition. —*n.* thing shown, *esp.* in competition or as evidence in a court.—**exhibi'tion** *n.*

display; act of displaying; public show (of art, etc.); scholarship.—**exhibi'tioner** *n.* student holding an exhibition.—**exhibi'tionism** *n.* in psycho-analysis, instinctive desire to exhibit oneself.—**exhib'itor** *n.* one who exhibits.

exhil'arate (-gz-) *v.t.* to enliven, gladden.—**exhilaration** *n.*

exhort' (-gz-) *v.t.* to urge, admonish earnestly.—**exhorta'tion** *n.*—**exhort'er** *n.*

exhume' *v.t.* to unearth; take out again what has been buried.—**exhuma'tion** *n.*

ex'igent (-j-) *a.* exacting; urgent, pressing.—**ex'igence, ex'igency** *n.* pressing need; emergency.—**ex'igible** *a.* that may be exacted.

exig'uous *a.* scanty, small.—**exigu'ity** *n.*

ex'ile *n.* banishment, expulsion or long absence from one's country; one banished.—*v.t.* to banish.

exist' (-gz-) *v.i.* to be, have being, continue to be.—**exist'ence** *n.*—**exist'ent** *a.*

existen'tialism (-ten-shal-izm) *n.* philosophy that denies objective universal values and holds that man must create his own values in a fully active existence.

ex'it *n.* an actor's departure from the stage; a going out; a way out; death.—**ex'it** *v.i. sing.* "goes out."—**ex'eunt** (-i-unt) *plur.* "go out," stage directions.

ex'odus *n.* a departure, *esp.* of a crowd.

exon'erate *v.t.* to free, declare free, from blame; exculpate.—**exoner'ation** *n.* **exon'erative** *a.* *Syn.* to clear, absolve, acquit. *Ant.* accuse, charge, blame.

exophthal'mia *n.* protrusion of eyeball due to disease.—**exophthal'mic goitre** *n.* disease characterised by exophthalmia and enlarged thyroid.

exorb'itant *a.* excessive, immoderate.—**exorb'itantly** *adv.*—**exorb'itance** *n.*

ex'orcise (-z) *v.t.* to cast out (evil spirits) by invocation; to free of evil spirits.—**ex'orcism** *n.*—**ex'orcist** *n.*

exord'ium *n.* introductory part of a speech or treatise (**-diums, -dia** *pl.*).

exoter'ic (-ō-) *a.* understandable by the many; ordinary, popular.

exot'ic *a.* brought in from abroad, not native.—*n.* an exotic plant, fashion, etc.

expand' *v.t.* and *i.* to spread out; enlarge, increase in bulk, develop.—**expan'sion** *n.*—**expan'sive** *a.* broad; effusive.—**expan'sible** *a.*—**expansibili'ty** *n.*—**expanse'** *n.* a wide space.

expa'tiate (-shi-) *v.i.* to speak or write at great length (on).

expat'riate *v.t.* to banish.—**expatria'tion** *n.* banishment, exile.

expect' *v.t.* to look on as likely to happen; to look for as due; await; anticipate.—**expect'ant** *a.*—**expect'ancy** *n.*—**expect'antly** *adv.*—**expecta'tion** *n.*

expect'orate *v.t.* and *i.* to spit out (phlegm, etc.).—**expectora'tion** *n.*

expe'dient *a.* fitting, advisable; politic.—*n.* a device, contrivance.—**expe'diently** *adv.*—**expe'diency** *n.*—**ex'pedite** (-īt) *v.t.* to help on, hasten.—**expedi'tion** *n.* promptness; a journey for a definite purpose; a war-like enterprise; a body of men sent on such.—**expedi'tionary** *a.*—**expedi'tious** *a.* prompt, speedy.

expel' *v.t.* to drive, cast out.—**expul'sion** *n.*—**expul'sive** *a.* (**expelled** *p.t.* and *p.p.*).

expend' *v.t.* to spend, pay out; use up.—**expend'iture** *n.*—**expense'** *n.* spending; cost.—*pl.* charges, outlay, incurred.—**expens'ive** *a.* costly.

expe'rience *n.* observation of facts as a source of knowledge; being affected consciously by an event; the event; knowledge, skill, gained by contact with facts and events—*v.t.* to undergo, suffer, meet with.—**experien'tial** *a.*—**exper'iment** *n.* a test, trial; something done in the hope that it may succeed, to test a theory.—*v.i.* to make an experiment.—**experiment'al** *a.*—**experiment'ally** *adv.*—**experiment'alist** *n.*

ex'pert *a.* practised, skilful.—*n.* one expert in something.

ex'piate *v.t.* to pay the penalty for; make amends for.—**expia'tion** *n.*—**ex'piator** *n.*—**ex'piatory** *a.*

expire' *v.t.* to breathe out.—*v.i.* to give out breath; die; end.—**expira'tion** *n.*—**expi'ratory** *a.*—**expi'ry** *n.* end.

explain' *v.t.* to make clear, intelligible; give details of; account for.—**explana'tion** *n.*—**explan'atory** *a.*—**ex'plicable** *a.*

ex'pletive *a.* serving only to fill out a sentence, etc.—*n.* an expletive word, *esp.* an oath.

ex'plicable *a.* explainable.—**ex'plicate** *v.t.* develop, explain.—**ex'plicative** *a.*—**ex'plicatory** *a.* explanatory.

explic'it (-s-) *a.* stated in detail; stated, not merely implied; outspoken.

explode' *v.i.* to go off with a bang; to burst violently.—*v.t.* to make explode; to discredit, expose (a theory, etc.).—**explo'sion** *n.*—**explo'sive** *a.* and *n.*

ex'ploit *n.* a brilliant feat, a deed.—*v.t.* to turn to advantage; make use of for one's own ends.—**exploita'tion** *n.*

explore' *v.t.* examine (country) by going through it; investigate.—**explora'tion** *n.*—**explor'atory** *a.*—**explo'rer** *n.*

explo'sion *see* **explode.**

ex'port *v.t.* to send (goods) out of the country.—**exports** *n.* exported articles.—**exporta'tion** *n.*—**export'er** *n.*

expose' (-z) *v.t.* to leave unprotected; to lay open (to); exhibit, put up for sale; unmask, disclose.—**expo'sure** *n.* *Syn.* reveal, divulge, publish. *Ant.* conceal, hide, cloak.

exposi'tion *see* **expound.**

expos'tulate *v.i.* remonstrate.—**expostula'tion** *n.*—**expos'tulatory** *a.*

expound' *v.t.* to explain, interpret.—**expo'nent** *n.* one who expounds; an executant; in mathematics, an index, a symbol showing the power of a factor.—**exponen'tial** *a.*—**exposi'tion** *n.* an explanation, description; exhibition of goods, etc.—**expos'itory** *a.*—**expos'itor** *n.*

express' *v.t.* to put into words; make known or understood by words, conduct, etc.; squeeze out; send by express.—*a.* definitely stated; specially designed; of a messenger, specially sent off; of a fast train.—*n.* an express train or messenger; in N. America, a rapid parcel transport service.—*adv.* specially, on purpose; with speed.—**express'ly** *adv.*—**express'ible** *a.*—**expres'sion** *n.*—**expres'sionism** *n.* theory that art depends on the expression of the artist's creative self, not on mere reproduction or obedience to accepted rules.—**express'ive** *a.* significant.

expro'priate *v.t.* to dispossess; take out of the owner's hands.—**expropria'tion** *n.*—**expro'priator** *n.*

expul'sion (shun) driving out.

expunge' *v.t.* to strike out, erase.

ex'purgate *v.t.* to remove objectionable parts (from a book, etc.).—**expurga'tion** *n.*—**ex'purgator** *n.*—**expurg'atory** *a.*

ex'quisite (-iz-it) *a.* of extreme beauty or delicacy; keen, acute; keenly sensitive.—*n.* a dandy.—**ex'quisitely** *adv.*

ex-ser'vice *a.* of or pertaining to one who has served in H.M. Forces.—**ex-ser'viceman** *n.*

extant' *a.* still existing.

extemp'ore (-rā) *a.* and *adv.* without preparation, off-hand.–**extempora'neous** *a.*—**extemp'orary** *a.*—**extemp'orise** *v.t.* to speak without preparation; devise for the occasion.—**extemporisa'tion** *n.*

extend' *v.t.* to stretch out, lengthen; prolong; widen in area, scope; accord, grant.—*v.i.* to reach; cover an area; have a range or scope; become larger or wider.—**exten'sible** *a.*—**extensibil'ity** *n.*—**exten'sion** *n.*—**extens'ive** *a.* wide, large, comprehensive.—**extent'** *n.* size, scope; a space, area; degree.—**exten'sile** *a.* that can be extended.—**exten'sor** *n.* straightening muscle.

exten'uate *v.t.* to make less blameworthy.—**extenua'tion** *n.*

exte'rior *a.* outer, outward.—*n.* the outside; outward appearance.

exterm'inate *v.t.* to root out, destroy.—**extermina'tion** *n.*—**exterm'inator** *n.*

extern'al *a.* outside.—**extern'ally** *adv.*

exterrito'rial *a.* free from the jurisdiction of the territory one lives in.—**exterritorial'ity** *n.*

extinct' *a.* quenched, no longer burning; having died out.—**extinc'tion** *n.*

exting'uish (-ng-gw) *v.t.* to put out, quench; wipe out.—**exting'uishable** *a.*—**exting'uisher** *n.* that which extinguishes; apparatus for putting out fire.

ex'tirpate *v.t.* to root out, destroy utterly.—**extirpa'tion** *n.*—**ex'tirpator** *n.*

extol' *v.t.* to praise highly (**extolled'** *p.t.* and *p.p.*). *Syn.* to laud, exalt, glorify. *Ant.* abuse, revile, vilify.

extort' *v.t.* to get by force or threats.—**extor'tion** *n.*—**extor'tionate** *a.*—**extor'tioner** *n.*—**extor'tive** *a.*

extra *a.* additional; larger, better, than usual.—*adv.* additionally; more than usually.—*n.* an extra thing.

extra- *prefix* beyond, as *extra-territorial*, *extra-mural*, situated beyond or outside the walls or boundaries of a place; of a lecturer from outside the university.

extract' *v.t.* to take out, *esp.* by force; obtain against a person's will; get by pressure, distillation, etc.; deduce, derive; copy out, quote.—**ex'tract** *n.* matter got by distillation; concentrated juice; passage from a book.—**extrac'tion** *n.* extracting; ancestry.—**extract'or** *n.*

extradi'tion *n.* delivery, under a treaty, of a foreign fugitive from justice to the authorities concerned.—**ex'tradite** (-ī-) *v.t.* to give or obtain such delivery.

extrage'neous *a.* foreign; of another kind.

extra'neous *a.* added from without; not naturally belonging.

extraord'inary (-ror-, -ra-or-) *a.* out of the usual course; additional; unusual, surprising.—**extraord'inarily** *adv.*

extrasens'ory *a.* beyond the senses.—**extrasen'sory percep'tion** *n.* psychic phenomena observed under laboratory test conditions; awareness of events not present to the normal senses.

extraterrito'rial *see* **exterritorial.**

extrav'agant *a.* wild, absurd; wasteful; exorbitant.—**extrav'agantly** *adv.*—**extrav'agance** *n.*—**extravagan'za** *n.* a fantastic composition (in music, etc.).

extrav'asate *v.t.* to force out (blood, etc.) from its vessel.—*v.i.* to flow out.

extreme' *a.* at the end, outermost; of a high or the highest degree; severe; going beyond moderation (**extre'mer** *comp.*—**extre'mest** *sup.*).—*n.* a thing at one end or the other, the first and last of a series; utmost degree.—**extreme'ly** *adv.*—**extre'mist** *n.* an advocate of extreme measures.—**extrem'ity** *n.* end.—**extrem'ities** *pl.* hands and feet; utmost distress; extreme measures.

ex'tricate *v.t.* to disentangle, set free.—**ex'tricable** *a.*—**extrica'tion** *n.*

extrin'sic *a.* accessory, not belonging, not intrinsic.—**extrin'sically** *adv.*

ex'trovert *n.* (*psych.*) one whose emotions express themselves readily in external action.—**extrover'sion** *n.* directing the mind outwards upon the world.

extrude' *v.t.* to thrust out.—**extru'sion** *n.*

exu'berant *a.* prolific, abundant, luxurious; effusive, high-flown.—**exu'berance** *n.*—**exu'berantly** *adv.*

exude' *v.i.* to ooze out.—*v.t.* to give off (moisture).—**exuda'tion** *n.*

exult' *v.i.* to rejoice, triumph.—**exulta'tion** *n.*—**exult'ant** *a.* triumphant.
eye (ī) *n.* the organ of sight; look, glance; attention; various things resembling an eye.—*v.t.* to look at; observe.—**eye'less** *a.*—**eye'ball** *n.* the ball of the eye.—**eye'brow** *n.* the fringe of hair above the eye.—**eye'glass** *n.* a glass to assist the sight; monocle.—**eye'lash** *n.* hair fringing the eyelid.—**eye'let** *n.* a small hole for a rope, etc., to pass through.—**eye'lid** *n.* the lid or cover of the eye.—**eye'opener** *n.* information that makes one understand what one had failed to see.—**eye'sore** *n.* an ugly sight.—**eye'tooth** *n.* canine tooth.—**eye'wash** *n.* (*sl.*) humbug, deception.—**eye'witness** *n.* one who saw something for himself.
ey'ot, ait *n.* a small island, *esp.* in a river.
eyr'ie *n.* an eagle's nest.

F

Fabian *a.* slow but persistent.
fa'ble *n.* legend; short story with a moral, e.g., *Æsop's Fables*.—*v.t.* to invent, tell fables about.—**fab'ulist** *n.*—**fab'ulous** *a.* told of in fables; unbelievable.
fab'ric *n.* a thing put together, building, structure; woven stuff; texture.—**fab'ricate** *v.t.* invent (lie); forge (document); build to standardised specifications.—**fab'ricator** *n.*—**fabrica'tion** *n.*
façade' (sahd') *n.* the front of a building.
face *n.* front of the head; front, surface; outward appearance; look, coolness; impudence.—*v.t.* to meet boldly; look or front towards; give a covering surface.—*v.i.* to turn.—**fa'cer** *n.* a blow in the face; a sudden difficulty.—**fac'et** (fas'-) *n.* one side of a many-sided body, *esp.* of a cut gem.—**fa'cial** (fā'shl) *a.*—**face-lift'ing** *n.* the operation of tightening the skin of the face to remove wrinkles.
face'tious (fas-ē'shus) *a.* waggish, jocose, given to jesting.—**face'tiæ** (-sē'-shē) *n. pl.* pleasantries, witticisms.
Syn. jocose, jocular, playful, jesting. *Ant.* serious, grave.
fa'cia (-sh) *n. see* **fascia.**
fac'ile (-sēl) *a.* easy; working easily; easy-going.—**facil'itate** (-sil'-) *v.t.* to make easy, help.—**facil'ity** *n.* easiness; dexterity.—*pl.* opportunities, good conditions.—**facilita'tion** *n.*—**facil'itator** *n.*
facsim'ile (fak-sim'i-li) *n.* exact copy.
fact *n.* a thing known to be true or to have occurred.—**fact'ual** *a.* concerned with fact; consisting of facts.
fac'tion *n.* a political or other party (*used always in a bad sense*); misguided party spirit.—**fac'tious** *a.* quarrelsome.
facti'tious *a.* artificial, specially got up.
fac'tor *n.* something contributing to a result; one of numbers which multiplied together give a given number; an agent, one who buys and sells for another.—**fac'tory** *n.* a building where things are manufactured; a trading station in a foreign country.—**facto'tum** *n.* a servant managing affairs, a man-of-all-work.
fac'ulty *n.* ability, aptitude; power of mind or body; department of a university; members of a profession; an authorisation.—**fac'ultative** *a.* optional.
fad *n.* a pet idea, craze, a passing fashion, crotchet.—**fadd'y** *a.*—**fadd'ist** *n.*
fade *v.i.* to wither; lose colour, grow dim; disappear gradually.—**fade'less** *a.*—**fade in, out** *v.t.* in wireless, to cause to appear or disappear gradually.
fag *n.* toil; junior schoolboy who does service to a senior; a cigarette.—*v.t.* to weary; to make act as fag.—*v.i.* to toil; to act as fag.—**fag-end'** *n.* the last part.
fagg'ot, fag'ot *n.* a bundle of sticks; bundle of steel rods; dish of baked chopped and seasoned liver, etc.—*v.t.* to bind in a faggot.
Fah'renheit (-hit) *a.* of the thermometric scale on which freezing point of water is 32° and boiling point 212°.
fai'ence (fā'-) *n.* glazed, earthenware.
fail *v.i.* to be insufficient; run short; lose power, die away; to be wanting at need; be unsuccessful; become bankrupt.—*v.t.* to disappoint, give no help to.—**fail'ure** *n.*—**fail'ing** *n.* fault, weakness.
fain *a.* glad, willing.—*adv.* gladly.
faint *a.* feeble; dim; pale, weak;—*v.i.* to swoon.—*n.* a swoon; unconscious condition.—**faint'ly** *adv.*
Syn. languid, feeble, timorous, obscure. *Ant.* energetic, strong, clear, distinct.
fair (fėr) periodical gathering for trade; an open market or entertainment.—**fair'ing** *n.* present from a fair.
fair (fėr) *a.* beautiful; ample; blonde; unblemished; of moderate quality or amount; just, honest; of weather, favourable.—*adv.* honestly.—**fair'ing** *n.* in aviation, any streamlined shape, cover or casing.—**fair'ish** *a.*—**fair'ly** *adv.* justly; rather.—**fair'ness** *n.*—**fair' isle** *a.* denoting articles made in Fair Isle in the Shetlands.—**fairway** *n.* in golf, the trimmed turf between tee and green.
fair'y (fėr'-) *n.* small elemental creature with powers of magic; enchantress.—*a.* of fairies; like a fairy, beautiful, delicate.—**fair'y-lamp** *n.* small coloured light used for outdoor illuminations.—**fair'y-land** *n.*—**fair'y-ring** *n.* a circle of darker colour in grass.—**fair'y-tale** *n.*
faith *n.* trust; belief; belief without proof; religion; promise; loyalty.—**faith'ful** *a.*—**faith'less** *a.*—**faith'fully** *adv.*
fake *v.t.* to conceal defects of, by artifice.—**fake'ment** *n.* any swindling device.—**fa'ker** *n.* one who deals in fakes; a swindler; pickpocket; a street-vendor; a hanger-on in theatres.

fa'kir (-ēr) *n.* eastern religious beggar.

Fa'lange (fa-lanj') *n.* Spanish fascist organisation which aims at the eventual reconquest of Spain's former colonies.—**Falangist** *n.* a member of the Falange.

fal'con *n.* bird of prey, *esp.* trained in hawking or fal'conry.—**fal'coner** *n.* one who keeps, trains, or hunts with, falcons.

fald'stool *n.* a folding stool, e.g., camp stool; the armless chair used by a bishop when not in his own cathedral; a small desk at which the litany is read.

fall (-aw-) *v.i.* to drop; hang down; become lower; come to the ground; cease to stand; perish; collapse; be captured; pass into a condition; become; happen (**fell** *p.t.*—**fall'en** *p.p.*).—*n.* a falling; amount that falls; amount of descent; yielding to temptation; autumn; rope of hoisting tackle.—**fall' guy** (U.S.) a scapegoat.—**to fall for** (*sl.*) to be taken in by, to fall in love with.

fall'acy (fal'a-si) *n.* a misleading argument; flaw in logic; mistaken belief.—**falla'cious** (-ā'-) *a.*—**fall'ible** *a.* liable to error.—**fall'ibly** *adv.*—**fallibil'ity** *n.*

fal'lal *n.* a piece of finery.

fall'ow (fal'ō) *a.* ploughed and harrowed but left without crop; uncultivated.—*n.* fallow land.—*v.t.* to break up (land).

fall'ow *a.* pale brown or reddish-yellow.—**fall'ow-deer** *n.* small European deer.

false (-aw-) *a.* wrong, erroneous; deceptive; faithless; sham; artificial.—**false'ly** *adv.*—**false'hood** *n.*—**false'ness** *n.*—**fal'sity** *n.*—**falsett'o** *n.* a forced voice above the natural range (**-os** *pl.*).—**fal'sify** *v.t.* to alter fraudulently; misrepresent; disappoint (hopes, etc.) (**-fied** *p.t./p.p.*— **-fying** *pres. p.*).—**falsifica'tion** *n.* *Syn.* unfaithful, feigned, spurious, forged. *Ant.* true, correct, accurate, precise, faithful, genuine.

Falstaff'ian *a.* like Shakespeare's Falstaff; corpulent; convivial; boasting.

fal'ter (-aw-) *v.i.* stumble; speak hesitatingly; waver.—*v.t.* say hesitatingly.

fame *n.* reputation; renown; rumour.—**famed** *a.*—**fa'mous** *a.*—**fa'mously** *adv.*

famil'iar *a.* intimate; closely acquainted; well-known, common; unceremonious.—*n.* a familiar friend or demon.—**famil'iarly** *adv.*—**familiar'ity** *n.*—**famil'iarise** *v.t.*—**familiarisa'tion** *n.*—**fam'ily** *n.* parents, children and near relatives; descendants of a common ancestor; a class, group of allied objects.

fam'ine (-in) *n.* extreme scarcity of food; starvation.—**fam'ish** *v.t.* to starve.—*v.i.* to be very hungry.

fa'mous *a.* well known.

fan *n.* instrument for producing a current of air; a winnowing machine; spread out as a bird's tail; a ventilating machine.—*v.t.* to winnow, blow, or cool with a fan.—**fan'light** *n.* fan-shaped window; window over door.

fan *n.* an enthusiast, *esp.* for sport.

fanat'ic(al) *a.* filled with mistaken zeal, *esp.* in religion.—*n.* fanatic person.—**fanat'ically** *adv.*—**fanat'icism** *n.*

fan'cy *n.* power of imagination; mental image; notion, whim, caprice, liking, inclination; followers of a hobby.—*a.* ornamental, not plain; of whimsical or arbitrary kind.—*v.t.* to imagine; be inclined to believe; have or take a liking for (**fan'cied** *p.t./p.p.*—**fan'cying** *pr. p.*).—**fan'cier** *n.* one with liking and expert knowledge (respecting specified thing).—**fan'ciful** *a.*—**fan'cifully** *adv.*

fandan'go *n.* a lively Spanish dance, music for it (**-gos** (-gōz) *pl.*).

fane *n.* a temple.

fan'fare *n.* a flourish of trumpets.

fang *n.* a long-pointed tooth; a snake's poison-tooth; root of a tooth.

fan'tasy *n.* power of imagination, *esp.* extravagant; mental image; a fanciful invention or design.—**fanta'sia** (-z-) *n.* a musical composition.—**fantas'tic** *a.* quaint, grotesque, extremely fanciful.—**fantas'tically** *adv.*

far *adv.* at or to a great distance, or advanced point; by very much.—*a.* distant (**far'ther, fur'ther** *comp.*—**far'thest, fur'thest** *sup.*).—*n.* a great distance or amount.

far'ad *n.* the unit of electrical capacity.

farce *n.* a play meant only to excite laughter; an absurd and futile proceeding.—**far'cical** *a.*—**far'cically** *adv.*

fare (fêr) *n.* money paid by a passenger for conveyance; a passenger; food.—*v.i.* to happen; get on; travel.—**farewell'** *interj.* good-bye.—*n.* a leave-taking.

fari'na *n.* meal; powder; starch; pollen.—**farina'ceous** *a.*—**farinose'** *a.*

farm *n.* a tract of cultivated land.—*v.t.* to pay or take a fixed sum for the proceeds of (a tax, etc.); cultivate.—**farm'stead** (-sted) *n.*—**farm'house** *n.*—**farm'yard** *n.*—**farm'er** *n.*—**intensive farming,** mixed farming; growing small areas of as many crops as possible.

farra'go *n.* a medley, hotch-potch.

farr'ier *n.* a shoeing smith; one who treats diseases of horses.—**farr'iery** *n.*

farr'ow *n.* a litter of pigs.—*v.t.* and *i.* to produce this.

far'ther (-th-) *adv.* and *a.* further; *comp.* of **far.**—**far'thest** *adv.* and *a.* furthest; *sup.* of **far.**

far'thing (-th-) *n.* quarter of a penny.

far'thingale (-th-) *n.* hooped petticoat.

fas'cia *n.* a long flat surface of wood or stone in a building; a tablet or board over a shop-front bearing the shopkeeper's name (**fas'ciæ** *pl.*).

fas'cicle (fas'-ikl) *n.* (*bot.*) small bundle; a close cluster; an instalment of a book, etc.—**fascicula'tion** *n.*

fas'cinate *v.t.* to make powerless by look or presence; to charm, attract.—**fascina'tion** *n.*—**fas'cinator** *n.*

fas'cist *n.* member of a political party aiming at the overthrow of communists, radicals, etc., by strong rule by a dictator.—**fas'cism** *n.*

fash'ion (-shun) *n.* make, style; manner; custom, mode, *esp.* in dress.—*v.t.* to shape, make.—**fash'ionable** *a.*—**fash'ionably** *adv.*—**fash'ioner** *n.*

fast (-à-) *v.i.* to go without food.—*n.* an act, or appointed time, of fasting.

fast (-à-) *a.* firm, fixed, steady, permanent; rapid; ahead of true time; dissipated.—*adv.* firmly, tightly, rapidly; in dissipated way.—**fast'en** (-sen) *v.t.* attach, fix, secure.—*v.i.* seize (upon).—**fast'ness** *n.* fast state; fortress.

fastid'ious *a.* hard to please. *Syn.* squeamish, disdainful, critical, punctilious. *Ant.* rough, unrefined, vulgar.

fat *a.* plump, thick, solid; containing much fat; fertile (**fatt'er** *comp.*—**fatt'est** *sup.*)—*n.* the oily substance of animal bodies; the fat part.—*v.t.* to feed (animals) for slaughter.—**fatt'en** *v.t.* and *i.*—**fat'ness** *n.*—**fatt'y** *a.*

fate *n.* power supposed to predetermine events; goddess of destiny; destiny; a person's appointed lot or condition; death or destruction.—*v.t.* to preordain. —**fate'ful** *a.* prophetic, fraught with destiny.—**fa'tal** *a.* deadly, ending in death; destructive; very ill-advised, disastrous; inevitable.—**fa'tally** *adv.*—**fatal'ity** *n.* rule of fate; calamity; death by accident.—**fa'talism** *n.* the belief that everything is predetermined; submission to fate.–**fa'talist** *n.*–**fatalist'ic** *a.*

fa'ther (fà'th-) *n.* a male parent; forefather, ancestor; originator, early leader; priest, confessor; oldest member of a society.—*v.i.* to beget; originate; pass as father or author of; act as father to; fix the paternity of.—**fa'therhood** *n.* —**fa'ther-in-law** *n.* the father of one's husband or wife.—**fa'therly** *a.*—**fa'therless** *a.*—**fa'therland** *n.* one's country.

fath'om (fath'-) *n.* a measure of six feet. —*v.t.* to sound (water); get to the bottom of, understand.—**fath'omless** *a.* too deep to fathom.—**fath'omable** *a.*

fatigue' (-tēg') *v.t.* to weary.—*n.* weariness; toil; a soldier's non-military duty.

fat'uous *a.* silly, foolish.—**fatu'ity** *n.*

fau'cet (faw'set) *n.* a fixture for drawing liquor from a cask or vessel.

fault *n.* defect; misdeed; blame, culpability; tennis, ball wrongly served; hunting, failure of scent; geology, break in strata.—**fault'y** *a.*—**fault'less** *a.*—**fault'ily** *adv.*—**fault'lessly** *adv.*

faun *n.* a Latin countryside god with horns and hoofs and tail.

faun'a *n.* the animals of a region or period (**-nas, -næ** *pl.*).

fauteuil (fō-te̱'ye̱) *n.* an arm-chair, usually highly ornamented; a seat, or membership, in the French Academy.

faux pas (fō pà) *n.* a false step.

fa'vour (-ve̱r) *n.* good will; approval; partiality; especial kindness; a badge or knot of ribbons.—*v.t.* to regard or treat with favour; oblige; treat with partiality; aid, support.—**fa'vourable** *a.* —**fa'vourably** *adv.*—**fa'vourite** (-it) *n.* a favoured person or thing; a horse, etc., generally expected to win a race.—*a.* chosen, preferred.—**fa'vouritism** *n.* the practice of showing undue preference.

fawn *n.* young fallow deer.—*a.* of a light yellowish-brown.

fawn *v.i.* of a dog, etc., to show affection by wagging the tail and grovelling; of a person, to cringe, court favour, grovel.

fay *n.* a fairy.

fe'alty *n.* fidelity of a vassal to his lord. *Syn.* homage, loyalty. *Ant.* disloyalty, infidelity, treachery, treason.

fear *n.* dread, alarm, unpleasant emotion caused by coming evil or danger.—*v.i.* to have this feeling, to be afraid.—*v.t.* to regard with fear; revere; hesitate, shrink from (doing something).—**fear'ful** *a.*—**fear'fully** *adv.*—**fear'some** *a.* terrible.—**fear'less** *a.*—**fear'lessly** *adv.*

fea'sible (-z-) *a.* practicable, that can be done.—**fea'sibly** *adv.*—**feasibil'ity** *n.*

feast *n.* banquet, lavish meal; religious anniversary; annual village festival.—*v.i.* partake of a banquet, fare sumptuously.—*v.t.* regale with a feast.

feat *n.* a notable deed; a surprising trick.

feath'er (feth'-) *n.* one of the barbed shafts which form the covering of birds.—*v.t.* to provide with feathers; to turn (an oar) edgeways.—*v.i.* to grow feathers; to turn an oar.—**feath'ery** *a.*—**feath'er-weight** *n.* a very light person or thing.

fea'ture *n.* a part of the face (usually *pl.*); a characteristic or notable part.—*v.t.* to portray; represent by cinematograph; to give prominence to.—**fea'tureless** *a.* uneventful.

feb'rifuge (-j-) *n.* a medicine to reduce fever.—**feb'rile** *a.* of fever.

feck'less *a.* spiritless; weak; feeble.

fec'ulent *a.* full of sediment, turbid.

fec'und *a.* fruitful, fertile.—**fecund'ity** *n.* —**fec'undate** *v.t.* to fertilise, impregnate. —**fecunda'tion** *n.*

fed *p.t.* and *p.p.* of **feed**.—**fed up**, bored, dissatisfied, sated, sick (of).

fed'eral *a.* of, or like, the government of states which are united but retain more or less independence within themselves. —**fed'eralism** *n.*—**fed'eralist** *n.*—**fed'erate** *v.i.* to enter into a league, a federal union.—**federa'tion** *n.* an act of federating; a federated society.

fee *n.* a payment for services; charge; tip.—*v.t.* to pay a fee to.

fee'ble *a.* weak.—**fee'bly** *adv.*
feed *v.t.* to give food to; supply, support. —*v.i.* to take food (**fed** *p.t.* and *p.p.*).—*n.* a feeding; fodder, pasturage; an allowance of fodder; material supplied to a machine; the part of a machine taking in material.—**feed'er** *n.*—**feeder line** (*aviation*) an auxiliary air-line which takes rural cargo and passengers to mainline airports (U.S.).—**feed'-motion** *n.*—**feed'-pipe** *n.*—**feed'-pump** *n.*
feel *v.t.* to examine, search, by touch; to perceive, have knowledge of, by touch or in emotions.—*v.i.* to use the sense of touch, grope; to be conscious of; to have, be affected by (a sentiment); sympathise (**felt** *p.t.* and *p.p.*).—*n.* the sense of touch; an impression on it.–**feel'er** *n.* the special organ of touch in some animals; a proposal put forward to test others' opinion; that which feels.—**feel'ing** *n.* sense of touch; physical sensation; emotion; sympathy, tenderness; conviction or opinion not solely based on reason.—*pl.* susceptibilities.—*a.* sensitive, sympathetic.
feign (fān) *v.t.* to pretend, simulate; imagine.—*v.i.* to pretend.
feint (fānt) *n.* sham attack or blow meant to deceive an opponent; pretence. —*v.i.* to make such.
feli'city (-is'-) *n.* great happiness, bliss; appropriateness of working.—**feli'citous** *a.* apt, well-chosen; happy.—**feli'citate** *v.t.* to congratulate.—**felicita'tion** *n.*
fe'line *a.* of cats; cat-like.—**felin'ity** *n.*
fell *n.* skin or hide with hair; mountain, stretch of moorland; *v.t.* knock down; cut down (tree); *a.* fierce, terrible.
fell'ah (fel'ah) *n.* member of the peasant or labouring class in Egypt.
fell'oe (-ō) **fell'y** *n.* the outer part of a wheel; a section of this.
fell'ow *n.* a comrade, associate; a counterpart, a like thing; member of learned society; a person.—*a.* of the same class. —**fell'owship** *n.* group; friendliness; postgraduate scholarship.
fel'on *n.* one who has committed a felony.—*a.* cruel, fierce.—**fel'ony** *n.* a crime more serious than a misdemeanour.—**felo'nious** *a.* *Syn.* malefactor, criminal, culprit, convict.
felt *n.* cloth made by rolling and pressing wool with size; a thing made of this.— *v.t.* to make into, or cover with, felt.— *p.t.* and *p.p.* of **feel.**
feluc'ca (-luk'-) *n.* a boat or vessel with oars and two masts with lateen sails, used in the Mediterranean.
fe'male *a.* of the sex which bears offspring.—*n.* one of this sex.
fem'inine (-in) *a.* of women; womanly; (*grammar*) of the gender proper to women's names.—**feminin'ity** *n.*—**fem'inism** *n.* influence of women; advocacy of women's political rights, etc.— **fem'inist** *n.*—**fem'inise** *v.t.*
fem'oral *a.* of the thigh.—**fe'mur** *n.* thigh bone; third part of an insect's leg.
fen *n.* a tract of marshy land.—**fenn'y** *a.*
fence *n.* practice of sword-play; a hedge or railing; receiver of stolen goods.— *v.t.* to put a hedge round, to enclose.— *v.i.* to practise sword-play.—**fen'cible** *n.* soldier liable only for home defence.
fend *v.t.* ward off, repel.—*v.i.* provide (for oneself, etc.).—**fend'er** *n.* buffer slung between ship's side and landing-place; a frame round a hearth; protection from collision, e.g., in a ship.
fenn'el *n.* a yellow-flowered herb.
fer'al (feer'-al) *a.* fatal, deadly.
fe'rial *a.* in the church, of a week day not a festival or a fast; of a holiday.
fer'ment *n.* leaven, substance causing a thing to ferment; excitement, tumult.— **ferment'** *v.i.* to undergo chemical change producing alcohol; process set up in dough by yeast.—*v.t.* to subject to this process; to stir up, excite.—**fermenta'tion** *n.*—**ferment'ative** *a.*
fern *n.* a plant with feathery fronds.— **fern'y** *a.* full of ferns.—**fern'ery** *n.* a place for growing ferns.—**fern'-tree** *n.* in Australia, a large fern.
fero'cious (ō'shus) *a.* fierce, savage, cruel.—**fero'city** (-s-) *n.*
ferr'et *n.* a half-tamed animal like a weasel used to catch rabbits, rats, etc.; —*v.t.* to take or clear with ferrets; to search out.—*v.i.* to search about.
ferr'ic *a.*—**ferr'ous** *a.* containing iron.— **ferrif'erous** *a.* yielding iron.—**ferru'ginous** *a.* of iron-rust; reddish-brown.— **ferr'o-con'crete** *n.* concrete strengthened by a framework of steel or iron.—**ferr'otype** *n.* a photograph on thin iron plate.
ferr'ule *n.* a metal cap or ring to strengthen the end of a stick.
ferr'y *v.t.* and *i.* to carry, pass, by boat across a river, strait, etc. (**ferr'ied** *p.t.* and *p.p.*—**ferr'ying** *pres. p.*) *n.*—a place or a boat for ferrying.—**ferr'yman** *n.*
fer'tile *a.* fruitful, producing abundantly. —**fertil'ity** *n.*—**fer'tilise** *v.t.* to make fertile.—**fer'tiliser** *n.*—**fertilisa'tion** *n.*
fer'ule *n.* a flat stick or ruler used for punishing boys.
fer'vent *a.* hot, glowing; ardent, intense. —**fer'vently** *adv.*—**fer'vency** *n.*—**fer'vour** (-er) *n.*—**fer'vid** *a.* ardent, impassioned.
fes'tal *a.* of a feast; keeping holiday; gay. —**fes'tive** *a.* of a feast; joyous, gay; jovial.—**fes'tival** *n.* a festal day; merrymaking; a periodical musical celebration. —**festiv'ity** *n.* gaiety, mirth; an occasion for rejoicing.—*pl.* festive proceedings.
fes'ter *n.* a suppurating condition, a sore.—*v.i.* to ulcerate, produce matter (in wound); rankle.—*v.t.* to cause to fester.
festoon' *n.* a chain of flowers, ribbons, etc., hung in a curve between two points —*v.t.* to adorn with festoons.
fetch *v.t.* go for and bring; draw forth;

be sold for; charm; deliver (blow).—*n.* trick.—**fetch'ing** *a.* attractive.
fête (fet') *n.* a festival, holiday or celebration; *v.t.* to feast; to honour with festive entertainment.
fet'id, foe'tid *a.* stinking.
fet'ish *n.* inanimate object worshipped by savages.—**-ism** *n.*
fet'lock *n.* tuft of hair behind horse's [hoof.
fett'er *n.* a chain or shackle for the feet; check, restraint.—*pl.* captivity.—*v.t.* to chain up; restrain, hamper.
fet'tle *n.* condition, trim, fitness.—*v.t.* to put in order.
fe'tus *see* **foetus.**
feu (fū) *n.* a fief; land held on payment of rent; perpetual possession at a stipulated rent.—*v.t.* to grant or let in feu.—**feu'ar** *n.*—**feu-duty** *n.*
feud (fūd) *n.* bitter and lasting mutual hostility, *esp.* between two families.
feud (fūd) *n.* a fief.—**feud'al** *a.* of a fief.—**feud'al system,** the mediæval political system based on the holding of land in return for service.—**feud'alism** *n.*
fe'uilleton (fe'ye-ton) *n.* a literary article or instalment of a serial, printed on the lower part of a newspaper page.—**fe'uilletonism** *n.* superficial and showy qualities in scholarship and literature.
fe'ver *n.* a condition of illness with high temperature and waste of tissue; nervous excitement.—*v.t.* to throw into fever.—**fe'verish** *a.*—**fe'verishly** *adv.*—**fe'verfew** *n.* a herb formerly used as a febrifuge.—**fever-bark** *n.*, in Australia, astringent bark used as a medicine and as bitters; the tree from which it is obtained.—**fever-tree** *n.*, in S. Africa, an acacia that grows in swampy land, thus indicating unhealthy conditions.
Syn. heat, excitement, agitation. *Ant.* tranquillity, coolness, self-possession.
few *a.* not many.—*n.* a small number.
fey *a.* doomed, fated to die; *esp.* having an unnatural gaiety of spirit.
fez *n.* a Turkish cap (**fezz'es** *pl.*).
fiancé (fē-on-sā') *n.* a betrothed man.—**fiancée** *fem.* betrothed woman.
fias'co *n.* a breakdown, ignominious failure (**-coes, -cos** (-cōz) *pl.*).
fi'at *n.* a decree; authorisation.
fib *n.* a trivial lie, falsehood.—*v.i.* to tell a fib.—**fibb'er** *n.*
fi'bre *n.* a filament forming part of animal or plant tissue; a substance that can be spun.—**fi'brous** *a.*
fi'brin *n.* organic compound of the same nature as albumen, found in animals and plants.
fich'u (fish'ōō) *n.* a triangular lace shawl for a woman's shoulders and neck.
fic'kle *a.* changeable.—**fic'kleness** *n.*
fic'tion *n.* an invented statement or narrative; novels, stories collectively; a conventionally accepted falsehood.—**ficti'tious** *a.* not genuine, imaginary.
fid'dle *n.* a violin; in a ship, a frame to stop things rolling off a table.—*v.i.* to play the fiddle; to make idle movements, to trifle.—**fid'dle-back** *n.* in Australia, a beetle.—**fid'dlestick** *n.* a bow.—*pl. interj.* nonsense.—**fid'dler** *n.*
fidel'ity *n.* faithfulness, loyalty.
fidg'et *v.t.* to move restlessly or uneasily.—*n.* restless condition; one who fidgets.—**fidg'ety** *a.*
fidu'ciary (-sh-) *a.* held or given in trust; relating to a trustee.—*n.* a trustee.
fief (fēf) *n.* an estate in land held of a superior in return for service.
field *n.* a piece of land tilled or used as pasture; an enclosed piece of land; a battleground; a tract of land rich in a specified product (e.g. *goldfield*); all the players in a game or sport; all competitors but the favourite; surface of a shield, coin, etc.; range, area of operation.—*v.i.* and *t.* at cricket, etc., to stop and return a ball.—**field'-day** *n.* a day of manœuvres; an important occasion.—**field'-glass** *n.* binoculars for outdoor use.—**Field' Marshal** *n.* a general of the highest rank.—**field'-piece** *n.* (*mil.*) a piece of field artillery, a field gun.—**field'er** *n.*
field'fare *n.* a bird related to the thrush.
fiend *n.* devil; in N. Amer., addict, as *dope fiend, crap fiend.*—**fiend'ish** *a.*
fierce *a.* savage, wild, raging; in N. America, unsatisfactory; rough; objectionable; severe; unkind; oppressive.—**fierce'ness** *n.*—**fierce'ly** *adv.*
fi'ery (fī'-) *a.* consisting of fire; blazing, glowing; flashing; irritable; spirited **fi'erier** *comp.*—**fi'eriest** *sup.*).—**fi'erily** *adv.* *Syn.* ardent, passionate, fierce, impetuous. *Ant.* cool, calm, lethargic.
fife *n.* a shrill flute played chiefly with drums in military music.—*v.i.* and *t.* to play on a fife.—**fi'fer** *n.*
fif'teen, fif'ty *see* **five.**
Fifth Col'umn *n.* body of traitors within a given area or country. (From the Spanish Civil War, 1936-9, four columns of troops threatened Madrid, and the *fifth column* consisted of the secret sympathisers inside the city.)
fig *n.* a familiar soft round many-seeded fruit; the tree bearing it.
fight (fīt) *v.i.* to contend in battle or in single combat.—*v.t.* to contend with; maintain against an opponent; settle by combat; to manœuvre (ships, troops) in battle (**fought** *p.t./p.p.*).—*n.* fighting, combat, battle; strife.—**fight'er** *n.* aircraft designed for fighting.—*a.*
fig'ment *n.* an invented statement, a purely imaginary thing.
fig'ure (-er) *n.* form, shape; bodily shape; appearance, *esp.* conspicuous appearance; a space enclosed by lines or surfaces; a diagram, illustration; likeness, image; pattern; a movement

in dancing, skating, etc.; a numerical symbol; amount, number; an abnormal form of expression for effect in speech, e.g., a metaphor.—*v.i.* to use numbers; to show, be conspicuous, be estimated.—*v.t.* to calculate, estimate; to represent by picture or diagram; to ornament.—**fig'urative** *a.* metaphorical; full of figures of speech.—**fig'uratively** *adv.*—**figure of eight** *n.* (1) knot in the form of an eight; (2) a skating figure; (3) figure in Scottish country dancing.

fil'ament *n.* a thread-like body; fine wire in electric light bulbs; electrode of thermionic valve.

fil'bert *n.* the cultivated hazel; its nut.

filch *v.t.* to steal.

file *n.* a tool for smoothing or rubbing down hard substances.—*v.t.* to apply a file to, to smooth, rub down, polish.—**fi'ling** *n.* action of using a file; a scrap of metal removed by a file.

file *n.* case, rack or wire for holding papers in order.—*v.t.* to place in a file; *n.* in formation of soldiers, a front-rank man and the man or men immediately behind him.—**single, or Indian, file,** a single line of men one behind the other. —*v.i.* to march in file.

fil'ial *a.* relating to a son or daughter.

fil'ibuster *n.* an adventurer in irregular warfare, privateer; pirate; (U.S.) political obstructionist.—*v.i.* to act as this.

fil'igree *n.* fine tracery or open-work of metal, usually gold or silver wire.

Filipi'no (-pē'-nō) *n.* a native of the Philippine Islands.—*a.*

fill *v.t.* to make full; to occupy completely; hold, discharge duties of; stop up; satisfy; fulfil.—*v.i.* to become full. —*n.* a full supply; as much as desired. —**fill'er** *n.*, in motoring, orifice of petrol or oil tank, crank-case, gearbox, etc.—**filling station,** in motoring, roadside depot for supplying oil, petrol, etc.

fill'et *n.* a head-band; a strip of meat; meat or fish boned.—*v.t.* to encircle with a fillet; to make into fillets.

fill'ip *n.* the sudden release of a finger bent against the thumb; a flip so given; a stimulus.—*v.t.* to give a fillip to, flip.

fill'y *n.* a female foal; a young girl.

film *n.* a very thin skin or layer; a thin sensitised sheet used in photography; a sensitised celluloid roll used in cinematography; a cinematographic picture; dimness on the eyes; a slight haze; a thread.—*v.t.* to photograph or represent by the cinematograph; to cover with a film.—*v.i.* to become covered with a film.—**film'y** *a.* thin.—**film pack,** a set of flat films for a photographic camera. —**film'-star** *n.* a popular actor or actress for films.—**film test,** a trial photograph of a film aspirant.

fil'ter *n.* a cloth or other apparatus for straining liquids; in wireless, a circuit passing certain frequencies only.—*v.t.* and *i.* to pass through a filter.—*v.i.* to make a way through.—**filtra'tion** *n.*—**fil'ter passer** *n.* a germ too small to be held by any filter.—**filter-press** *n.*—**fil'ter pump** *n.* an apparatus for expediting filtration.

filth (-th) *n.* loathsome dirt; garbage; vileness, obscenity.—**filth'y** *a.*—**filth'ily** *adv.*—**filth'i-ness** *n.*

fin *n.* the propelling organ of a fish.

fi'nal *a.* last; conclusive.—*n.* a game, heat, examination, etc., coming at the end of a series.—**fi'nally** *adv.* at last.—**final'ity** *n.*—**fina'le** (-åli) *n.* the closing part of a musical composition.

finance' *n.* the management of money. —*pl.* money resources.—*v.t.* to find capital for.—*v.i.* to deal with money.—**finan'cial** *a.*—**finan'cially** *adv.*—**finan'cier** *n.*

finch *n.* family of small singing birds.

find (fī-) *v.t.* to come across, light upon, obtain; recognise; experience, discover; discover by searching; ascertain; declare on inquiry; supply (**found** *p.t.* and *p.p.*). —*n.* a finding; something found.-**find'er** *n.*

fine *n.* a sum fixed as a penalty; a sum fixed in consideration of a low rent.—*v.t.* to punish by a fine.—**in fine,** to sum up.

fine *a.* choice, pure, of high quality, delicate, subtle; in small particles; slender; excellent; handsome; showy; free from rain; fastidious.—*n.* fine weather.—*adv.* in fine manner.—*v.t.* to make clear or pure; to thin.—*v.i.* to become clear or pure or thinned.—**fine'ly** *adv.*—**fine'ness** *n.*—**fi'nery** *n.* showy dress.—**finesse'** (fin-) *n.* artfulness; subtle management; at cards, the attempt to take a trick with the lower of two cards not having the intermediate one.—*v.t.* and *i.* to use or attempt finesse.

fin'ger (-ng-g-) *n.* one of the jointed branches of the hand; various things like this.—*v.t.* to touch or handle with the fingers.—**fin'gerpost** *n.* a signpost at cross-roads.—**fin'gerprint** *n.* an impression of the tip of a finger, *esp.* as used for identifying criminals.—**fin'gerstall** *n.* a cover to protect a finger.

fin'gering (ng-g-) *n.* wool for knitting stockings.

fin'icking, fin'ical, fin'iken *a.* fastidious, over-nice; too delicately wrought.

fin'ish *v.t.* to bring to an end, complete; to perfect; to kill.—*v.i.* to come to an end.—*n.* end, last stage; decisive result; completed state; anything serving to complete or perfect.—**fin'isher** *n.*,

Syn. to accomplish, cease, conclude, perfect. *Ant.* begin, commence.

fi'nite *a.* bounded, limited.

finn'an, finn'an hadd'ock *n.* haddock cured with smoke.

fiord', fjord' (fyord') *n.* a narrow inlet of the sea between steep cliffs.

fir *n.* a coniferous tree; its wood.

fire *n.* state of burning, combustion, flame, glow; a mass of burning fuel; a destructive burning, conflagration; ardour, keenness, spirit; shooting of firearms.—*v.t.* to make burn; supply with fuel; bake; to inspire; to explode; discharge (a firearm); propel from a firearm; (*sl.*) to dismiss.—*v.i.* to begin to burn; to become excited; to discharge a firearm.—**fire'arm** *n.* a weapon shooting by explosion, a gun, pistol, etc. —**fire'brand** *n.* a burning piece of wood; one who stirs up strife.—**fire'-brigade** *n.* organised body of men with appliances to put out fires and rescue those in danger from fire.—**fire'bug** *n.* in N. Amer., an incendiary.—**fire-control'** *n.* method or apparatus by which the guns of a ship, etc., are fired from a central control station.—**fire'damp** *n.* in mines, carburetted hydrogen; an explosive mixture of this with air.—**fire-engine** *n.* an engine with apparatus for extinguishing fires.—**fire'-escape** *n.* apparatus for escaping from a burning house.—**fire'-fighters** *n. pl.* men who try to subdue fires.—**fire'-float** *n.* a floating fire brigade station.—**fire'fly** *n.* an insect giving out a glow of phosphorescent light.—**fire'-irons** *n. pl.* tongs, poker, and shovel.—**fire'lock** *n.* a musket fired with a spark.—**fire'man** *n.* a member of a fire-brigade; a stoker, an assistant to a locomotive driver.—**fire'new** *a.* as if fresh from the furnace.—**fire'place** *n.* a hearth in a room.—**fire'-plug** *n.* a connection in a water-main for a hose.—**fire-raising** *n.* arson, act of setting on fire.—**fire-ranger** *n.* in N. Amer., a man whose duty is to prevent forest or prairie fires.—**fire'-ship** *n.* a burning vessel sent drifting against enemy ships.—**fire'-step** *n.* a step in a trench on which a soldier stands to fire.—**fire'-stick** *n.* in Australia, a smouldering piece of wood carried by aboriginals, when travelling, to start a new fire.—**fire'-water** *n.* strong spirits, *esp.* when supplied to savages.—**fire'-work** *n.* a device to give spectacular effects by explosions and coloured flames.

firm *n.* solid, fixed, stable; steadfast; resolute; settled.—*v.t.* to make firm, solidify.—*n.* commercial house.

firm'ament *n.* the vault of heaven.

firn *n.* accumulated snow on high mountain ranges; source of glaciers.

first *a.* earliest in time or order; foremost in rank or position.—*adv.* before others in time, order, etc.—**first-aid** *n.* help given to an injured person before the arrival of a doctor.—**first'ling** *n.* first fruits, the first product.—**first'ly** *adv.*

firth, frith *n.* an arm of the sea.

fis'cal *a.* of a state treasury; *n.* treasurer.

fish *n.* a vertebrate cold-blooded animal with gills, living in water; flesh of fish (**fish, fish'es** *pl.*).—*v.i.* to try to catch fish; to search for.—*v.t.* to try to catch fish in; to draw (up); produce.—**fish'er** *n.* —**fish'erman** *n.* one who lives by fishing. —**fish'-wife** *n.* woman who sells fish.—**fish'ery** *n.* the business of fishing; fishing-ground.—**fish'monger** *n.* one who sells fish.—**fish'y** *a.* of, or like, fish; dubious, open to suspicion.

fish *n.* a piece of wood for strengthening a mast; a metal plate for strengthening a beam.—*v.t.* to mend or join with a fish.

fis'sure (-sh-) *n.* a cleft, split.—**fis'sile** *a.* capable of splitting; tending to split.—**fis'sion** *n.* splitting; division of living cells into more cells.

fist *n.* the clenched hand; handwriting.—*v.t.* to strike with the clenched hand.—**fist'icuffs** *n. pl.* fighting with fists.

fist'ula *n.* pipe-like ulcer. (**-ulas, -æ** *pl.*).

fit *n.* a sudden passing attack of illness; seizure with convulsions, loss of consciousness, etc., as of epilepsy, hysteria, etc.; a mood.—**fit'ful** *a.* spasmodic, capricious.—**fit'fully** *adv.*

fit *a.* well-suited, worthy; proper, becoming; ready; in good condition (**fitt'er** *comp.*—**fitt'est** *sup.*).—*v.t.* to be suited to; to be properly adjusted to; to arrange, adjust, apply, insert; supply, furnish.—*v.i.* to be correctly adjusted or adapted, to be of the right size.—*n.* the way a garment fits; its style; adjustment.—**fit'ly** *adv.*—**fit'ness** *n.*—**fitt'er** *n.* —**fit'ment** *n.* a piece of furniture.—**fitt'ing** *n.* action of fitting; apparatus, fixture.—*a.* that fits; becoming, proper.
Syn. suitable, applicable, appropriate, meet, qualified. *Ant.* inapt, unsuited, improper, unseemly.

five *a.* and *n.* the cardinal number next after four.—**fifth** *a.* the ordinal number. —**five'fold** *a.* and *adv.*—**fifteen'** *a.* and *n.* ten and five.—**fifteen'th** *a.*—**fifth'ly** *adv.*—**fifteenth'ly** *adv.*—**fif'ty** *a.* and *n.* five tens.—**fif'tieth** *a.*—**fives** *n.* a ball-game.

fix *v.t.* to fasten, make firm or stable; to set, establish; appoint, assign, determine; make fast, permanent.—*v.i.* to become firm or solidified; to determine.—*n.* a difficult situation.—**fixa'tion** *n.* act of fixing; in psycho-analysis, arrest of part of psycho-sexual development.—**fix'ative** *a.*—**fix'edly** *adv.*—**fix'ings** *n. pl.* in N. Amer., apparatus, trimming.—**fix'ity** *n.*—**fix'ture** *n.* a thing fixed in position; a thing annexed to a house; a date for a sporting event; the event.

fizz *v.i.* to hiss, splutter.—*n.* hissing noise; any effervescent liquid, as soda-water.—**fiz'zle** *v.i.* to splutter weakly.—*n.* a fizzling noise; fiasco.

flabb'ergast *v.t.* to overwhelm with astonishment, dumbfound.

flabb'y *a.* hanging loose, limp; feeble.—**flabb'ily** *adv.*—**flabb'iness** *n.*

flac'cid (-ks-) *a.* flabby.—**flaccid'ity** *n.*

flag *n.* a water plant with sword-shaped leaves, *esp.* the iris.—**flagg'y** *a.*
flag *n.* a flat slab of stone.—*pl.* pavement of flags.—*v.t.* to pave with flags.
flag *n.* a banner, a piece of bunting attached to a staff or halyard as a standard or signal.—*v.t.* to inform by flag-signals.—**flag'-day** *n.* day on which small flags or emblems are sold in the streets for charity.—**flag'-off'icer** *n.* an admiral, vice-admiral or rear-admiral.—**flag'ship** *n.* ship with an admiral on board.—**flag'staff** *n.* pole on which flag is hoisted.—**flag'-station** *n.* in N. Amer., a place at which a railway train may be stopped by signalling with a flag.
flag *v.i.* to droop, fade; lose vigour.
flag'ellate (-j-) *v.t.* to scourge, flog.—**flagella'tion** *n.*—**flag'ellant** *n.* one who scourges himself in penance.
flag'eolet (-j-) *n.* a small wind-instrument with mouthpiece at the end.
flagit'ious (-jish'us) *a.* deeply criminal.
flag'on *n.* a vessel, usually with handle, spout and lid, to hold liquor for the table; a large oval bottle.
fla'grant *a.* glaring, scandalous.—**fla'grantly** *adv.*—**fla'grancy** *n.* *Syn.* blatant, notorious. *Ant.* secret, concealed.
flail *n.* a wooden instrument for threshing corn by hand.
flair' *n.* instinctive appreciation or discernment, natural aptitude.
flak' *n.* anti-aircraft gun fire.—**flak-boat** *n.*—**flak-tower** *n.*
flake *n.* a light fleecy piece, *esp.* of snow; a thin broad piece, *esp.* split or peeled off; layer.—*v.t.* to break flakes from.—*v.i.* to come off in flakes.—**fla'ky** *a.*
flam *n.* a freak; a whim.—*a.* lying, false.—*v.t.* to delude.
flamboy'ant *a.* marked by wavy lines; florid, gorgeous, showy.
flame *n.* burning gas; a tongue of light; visible burning, passion, *esp.* love; a sweetheart.—*v.i.* emit flames, blaze.
flamin'go (-ng-g-) *n.* a large bird with very long neck and legs of a vivid red colour (**-goes** (-gōz) *pl.*).
flan' *n.* a small shallow case of pastry containing fruit.
flaneur' *n.* a lounger; a saunterer.
flange (-anj) *n.* a projecting flat rim, collar, or rib.—*v.t.* provide with one.
flank *n.* the fleshy part of the side between hips and ribs; side of a building or body of troops.—*v.t.* to guard or strengthen on flank; to attack, take in flank; to be at the side of.
flann'el *n.* a woollen stuff, usually without nap.—*pl.* garments of this, *esp.* trousers for games.—*a.* made of flannel. —**flannelette'** *n.* a cotton fabric.
flap *v.t.* to strike with something broad, flat and flexible; to move (wings) up and down.—*v.i.* to sway, swing, flutter.—*n.* an act of flapping; a broad piece of anything hanging from a hinge or loosely, e.g. table-leaf.—**flapp'er** *n.* girl teen-ager.—**flapdoo'dle** *n.* nonsense.
flap'jack *n.* a flat case for face powder; a pancake, a cake containing fruit.
flare (-ėr) *v.i.* to blaze unsteadily; to burst out angrily; to spread (as a skirt). —*n.* act of flaring; a bright unsteady flame; a signal light.
flash *v.i.* to break into sudden flame; gleam; burst into view; appear suddenly.—*v.t.* to cause to gleam; to emit (light, etc.) suddenly.—*n.* a sudden burst of light or flame; sudden short access; a ribbon or badge; display.—*a.* showy; sham.—**flash'y** *a.*—**flash-back** *n.* a break in continuity of a book, play or film to introduce action which has taken place previously.—**flash-bulb,** an electric bulb giving a brilliant flash for taking a photograph.—**flash'-point** *n.* temperature at which oil vapour ignites.
flask (-ȧ-) *n.* a flat pocket-bottle; Italian wicker-covered bottle.
flat *a.* level; spread out; at full length; smooth; downright; dull, lifeless; below true pitch (**flatt'er** *comp.*—**flatt'est** *sup.*). —*n.* what is flat; a simpleton; a note half a tone below the natural pitch.—*pl.* in S. Africa, plains of the upper plateau.—**flat'ly** *adv.*—**flat'ness** *n.*—**flatt'en** *v.t.* and *i.*—**flat out** *n.* at full speed.
flat *n.* a set of rooms on one floor.
flatt'er *v.t.* to court, fawn on; to praise insincerely; inspire a belief, *esp.* an unfounded one; gratify (senses); represent too favourably.–**flatt'erer** *n.*–**flatt'ery** *n.*
flat'ulent *a.* generating gases in the intestines; caused by or attended by or troubled with such gases; vain, pretentious.—**flat'ulence** *n.*—**flat'ulency** *n.*
flaunt *v.t.* and *i.* to wave proudly.
flaut'ist *n.* a flute-player.
fla'vour (-vẹr) *n.* a mixed sensation of smell and taste; distinctive taste; an undefinable characteristic quality of anything.—*v.t.* to give a flavour to; season.
flaw *n.* a crack; defect, blemish.—*v.t.* to make a flaw in.–*v.i.* to crack.–**flaw'less** *a.*
flax *n.* a plant grown for its textile fibre and seeds; its fibres; cloth of this, linen.—**flax'seed** *n.* linseed.—**flax'en** *a.*
flay *v.t.* to strip off skin or hide.
flea (-ē) *n.* a small wingless jumping insect which feeds on human and other blood.—**flea'bane** *n.* a wild plant.—**flea'bite** *n.* the insect's bite; a trifling injury; a trifle; a small red spot on a horse.—**flea'bitten** *a.* (of a horse).
fleck *n.* a spot, freckle; a patch of colour.—*v.t.* to mark with flecks, dapple.
fledge *v.t.* to provide with feathers or down.—**fledge'ling** *n.* a young bird.
flee *v.i.* to run away.—*v.t.* to run away from; shun (**fled** *p.t.*/*p.p.*—**flee'ing** *pr. p.*).
fleece *n.* a sheep's wool.—*v.t.* to cut off fleece; to rob.—**flee'cy** *a.* woolly.

fleer *v.i.* to laugh mockingly, jeer.—*n.* a mocking laugh or look.
fleet *n.* a sea force under one command; a number of ships, cars, etc.—*a.* swift, nimble.—*v.i.* to glide away; pass quickly; flit.—**fleet'ing** *a.* transient.
flesh *n.* the soft part, muscular substance, between skin and bone; this as food; of plants, pulp; fat; sensual appetites.—**flesh'ings** *n. pl.* close-fitting flesh-coloured theatrical garments.—**flesh'-pots** *n. pl.* high living.—**flesh'ly** *a.* carnal, material.—**flesh'y** *a.* plump.
fleur-de-lis' (flur-di-lē') *n.* the iris flower; the heraldic lily; the royal arms of France (**fleurs-de-lis'** *pl.*).
flex' *n.* flexible, insulated electric cable or cord; *v.t.* to bend.—**flex'ure** *n.* a bend.
flex'ible *a.* that may be bent without breaking, pliable, manageable; supple.—**flexibil'ity** *n.*—**flex'ibly** *adv.*—**flex'ion, flec'tion** *n.* bending; bent state.
Syn. bendable, yielding, tractable. *Ant.* stiff, unyielding, inelastic, rigid.
flibb'ertigibb'et *n.* a flighty person.
flick *n.* light blow; a jerk.—*v.t.*
flick'er *v.i.* to burn or shine unsteadily; to quiver.—*n.* a flickering light.
fli'er *n.* airman; very fast vehicle.
flight (-īt) *n.* the act or manner of flying through the air; aviation; journey in aircraft; Air Force unit of command; power of flying; swift movement or passage; a sally; distance flown; the stairs between two landings; a number flying together, as birds; a running away.—**Flight-lieutenant** *n.* Air Force officer of rank equivalent to Capt., Army, or Lieut., R.N.—**flight'y** *a.* capricious, fickle, undependable.
flim'sy (-zi) *a.* frail, easily destroyed; paltry.—*n.* thin paper.—**flim'sily** *adv.*
flinch *v.i.* to shrink, draw back, recoil.
fling *v.t.* to throw.—*v.i.* to rush, go hastily; kick, plunge (**flung** *p.t./p.p.*).—*n.* a throw; a hasty attempt; a spell of self-indulgence; vigorous dance.
flint *n.* a hard stone; a piece of this.—**flint'-lock** *n.* a gun or its lock discharged by a spark struck from flint.—**flint'y** *a.*
flip *n.* a flick or fillip, a very light blow; a short trip in an aeroplane; a drink, e.g., egg-flip.—*v.t.* to strike or move with a flick.—*v.t.* to move in jerks.—**flipp'er** *n.* a limb or fin for swimming.—**flipp'ant** *a.* treating serious matters lightly.—**flipp'antly** *adv.*—**flipp'ancy** *n.*
flirt *v.t.* to throw with a jerk, give a brisk motion to.—*v.i.* to pretend to make love.—*n.* a jerk; coquette.—**flirta'tion** *n.*
flit *v.i.* to go away; change dwelling; move lightly and rapidly; make short flights.
flitch *n.* a side of bacon.
flivv'er *n.* (*sl.*) cheap or old-fashioned motor-car; (*sl.*) a failure.
float *v.i.* to rest or drift on the surface of a liquid; to be suspended freely.—*v.t.* of a liquid, to support, bear along; in commerce, to get (a company) started.—*n.* anything small that floats (*esp.* to support something else, e.g., a fishing net); a low-bodied cart.—**flota'tion** *n.*—**floating dock** *n.* dock constructed of steel compartments and capable of being submerged to admit a vessel, then raised and converted into a dry dock.—**floating kidney** *n.* a kidney liable to displacement.
flocculent (-k-) *a.* resembling flocks.
flock *n.* a lock or tuft of wool, etc.—*pl.* wool-refuse for stuffing.
flock *n.* a number of animals of one kind together; a crowd, a religious congregation; a tuft of wool.—*pl.* wool waste for stuffing.—*v.i.* to gather in a crowd.
floe (-ō) *n.* a sheet of floating ice.
flog *v.t.* to beat with a whip, stick, etc.
flood (flud) *n.* the flowing of the tide; an overflow of water, outpouring, an inundation.—*v.t.* to inundate; cover or fill with water.—**flood'-gate** *n.*
flood'lighting *n.* artificial lighting of buildings.—**flood'light** *v.t.*—**flood'lit** *a.*
floor (flōr) *n.* the lower surface of a room; a set of rooms on one level; a flat space.—*v.t.* to supply with a floor; to knock down; to confound.—**floor'walker** *n.* a section or floor supervisor in a department store.
flop *v.i.* to sway about or move clumsily; to sit or fall with a thump.—*v.t.* to throw down with a thud.—*n.* a fall, failure.—*adv.* with a flop.—**flopp'y** *a.* limp, flaccid.—**flopp'iness** *n.*—**flopp'ily** *adv.* (**flopped** *p.t.* and *p.p.*).
flo'ra (flaw'-) *n.* the plants of a region; a list of them (**ras, ræ** *pl.*).—**flo'ral** *a.* of flowers.—**flo'riculture** *n.* the cultivation of flowers.—**floricul'tural** *a.*—**floricul'turist** *n.*—**flores'cence** *n.* state or time of flowering.—**flo'ret** *n.* a small flower forming part of a composite flower.—**flor'id** *a.* flowery, ornate, ruddy, high-coloured.—**flor'ist** *n.* one who deals in flowers.
flor'in *n.* English two-shilling piece.
floss *n.* rough silk or cocoon; silk for embroidery; fluff.—**floss'y** *a.*
flota'tion *n.* act of floating; selling of shares to start a company; in mining, process of separating particles of ore according to their buoyancy.
flotill'a *n.* small fleet, *esp.* destroyers.
flot'sam *n.* floating wreckage.
flounce *v.i.* to go, or move, abruptly and impatiently.—*n.* a fling, a jerk; ornamental strip of material on a woman's garment.—*v.t.* to adorn with a flounce.
flound'er *n.* a flat-fish.
flound'er *v.i.* to plunge and struggle, *esp.* in water or mud; to proceed in a bungling or hesitating manner.
flour *n.* the sifted finer part of meal; wheat meal.—*v.t.* to sprinkle with flour.—**flour'y** *a.*—**flour'iness** *n.*

flour'ish (flur'-) *v.i.* to thrive; prosper; to use florid language.—*v.t.* brandish, display; wave about.—*n.* ornamental curve in writing; a florid expression; waving of hand, weapon, etc.; a fanfare.
flout *v.t.* to show contempt for by act or word; to mock, defy.—*n.* a jeer.
flow (flō) *v.i.* to glide along as a stream; to hang loose; move easily; move in waves; be ample in form; run full; abound.—*n.* an act or fact of flowing; quantity that flows; rise of tide.
flow'er (flow'-) *n.* the part of a plant from which the fruit is developed, a bloom, blossom; the choicest part, the pick.—*v.i.* to bloom, or blossom.—*v.t.* ornament with worked flowers.—**flow'eret** *n.* small flower.—**flow'ery** *a.* abounding in flowers; full of fine words, ornamented with figures of speech.—**flow'er-de-luce** *n.* fleur-de-lis, q.v.
flu *n. abbrev.* of **influenza.**
fluc'tuate *v.i.* to vary irregularly, rise and fall; waver.—**fluctua'tion** *n.*
flue (floo) *n.* a passage for smoke or hot air, a chimney; fluff; soft down or fur.
flu'ent *a.* flowing, copious and ready (in words); graceful (in movement).—**flu'ently** *adv.*—**flu'ency** *n.*
Syn. voluble, copious, smooth. *Ant.* halting, hesitating, forced, tongue-tied.
fluff *n.* soft feathery stuff; down.—*v.t.* to make into fluff.—**fluffy** *a.*
flu'id *a.* flowing easily, not solid.—*n.* a fluid substance, gas or liquid.—**fluid'ity** *n.*—**fluid flywheel** in motoring, unit in the transmission system whereby clutch plates are dispensed with for a "cushion" of heavy oil.
fluke *n.* a flat-fish; a parasitic worm; flat triangular point of an anchor; lucky stroke.—*v.i.* to make a fluke.—**flu'ky** *a.*
flum'mox *v.t.* to bewilder, perplex; to bring to hopeless confusion.
flunk'ey *n.* footman in livery; toady.
fluor *n.* a mineral containing fluorine.
fluores'cence *n.* luminous state produced in a transparent body by direct action of light, *esp.* violet and ultra-violet rays; the power of rendering ultra-violet rays visible.—**fluores'cent** *a.* **fluoresce'** *v.i.*—**flu'orine** *n.* non-metallic element, a pale greenish-yellow gas.
flur'ry *n.* a squall, gust; nervous haste. —*v.t.* to agitate, bewilder (**flur'ried** *p.t.* and *p.p.*—**flur'rying** *pres. p.*).
flush *v.i.* to take wing and fly away.—*v.t.* to cause to do this.—*n.* a number of birds flushed at once.—*v.i.* to flow suddenly or violently; of blood, to come with a rush; of the skin, to redden.—*v.t.* cleanse by rush of water; cause to redden; inflame with pride, etc.—*n.* a rush of water; excitement; elation; glow of colour; reddening; freshness, vigour; a set of cards all of one unit.—*a.* full, in flood; well supplied, level.
flus'ter *v.t.* to flurry, bustle; confuse with drink.—*v.i.* to be in a flurry.
flute *n.* musical instrument, a wooden pipe with holes stopped by the fingers or keys and blow-hole in the side; flute-player in a band; a groove or channel, *esp.* in pillar.—*v.i.* to play on a flute.—*v.t.* to make grooves in.
flutt'er *v.i.* to flap wings rapidly without flight or in short flights; to move, come down, quiveringly; to be excited, agitated.—*v.t.* to flap quickly; to agitate.
flu'vial *a.* of, found in, rivers.
flux *n.* a morbid discharge, as of blood; a flowing; the flow of the tide; a constant succession of changes; a substance mixed with metal to help melting.
flux *n.* in magnetism, the total number of lines of force passing through any given part of a magnetic field.
fly *n.* a two-winged insect.—**fly'blown** *a.* tainted.—**fly'catcher** *n.* a bird.
fly *v.i.* to move through the air on wings or in aircraft; float loosely, wave; spring, rush; flee, run away.—*v.t.* to cause to fly; to set flying; to run from (**flew** *p.t.*—**flown** *p.p.*).—*n.* a flying; a one-horse vehicle for hire; flap on a garment or tent; a speed-regulator in a machine; (*pl.*) place above stage of theatre from which scenery is moved.—**fly'er, fli'er** *n.* in Australia, a swift kangaroo; a fast train.—**fly'leaf** *n.* blank leaf at beginning or end of book (**-leaves** *pl.*).—**fly'wheel** *n.* heavy wheel regulating a machine.—**fly'ing-boat** *n.* aeroplane fitted with floats.—**fly'ing butt'ress** *n.* buttress to a wall at a slope with a space between its lower part and the wall.—**fly'ing-fish** *n.* fish which rises in the air by wing-like fins.—**Fly'ing Fortress,** large high-altitude four-engined monoplane precision bomber developed by the U.S.A. during World War 2, heavily armoured and with great fire-power. It was chiefly used for daylight bombing.—**fly'ing-fox** *n.* in Australia, large fruit-eating bat *n.*, wire for transporting articles across a river or chasm.—**fly'ing officer,** commissioned rank in R.A.F.—**fly'ing squad,** special detachment of police equipped with motor-cars and motor-cycles.
foal *n.* the young of the horse, ass, or other equine animal.—*v.t.* to bear (a foal).—*v.i.* to bear a foal.
foam *n.* a collection of small bubbles in a liquid; froth; froth of saliva or perspiration.—*v.i.* to give out, or form into, foam; to rage.—**foam'y** *a.*
fob *n.* small waistband pocket for watch.
fob *v.t.* to cheat; palm (off); only in **fob off** (*a thing on a person*) and **fob off** (*a person with a thing*) (**fobbed** *p.t./p.p.*).
fo'cus *n.* the point at which rays meet after being reflected or refracted; point of convergence; principal seat or centre

(fo'cuses, fo'ci *pl.*).—*v.t.* bring to a focus. —*v.i.* to come to a focus.—**fo'cal** *a.*
fodd'er *n.* dried food for cattle, etc.
foe (fō) *n.* enemy.—**foe-man** *n.*
Syn. opponent, adversary, antagonist. *Ant.* friend, comrade, ally.
foe'tus, fe'tus *n.* the fully-developed young or embryo in womb or egg.
fog *n.* thick mist; unusually dark atmosphere; aftermath.—*v.t.* to cover in fog; puzzle.—**fogg'y** *a.*—**fog'horn** *n.* instrument to warn ships in fog.—**fog'-signal** *n.* an audible signal placed on railway lines in fog.
fo'gey, fo'gy *n.* a dull old fellow. (**old fogey**) old-fashioned fellow.
foi'ble *n.* a weak point in character; a quality a person prides himself on.
foil *n.* small arc or space in window tracery; metal in a thin sheet; leaf of metal set under a gem; anything which sets off another thing to advantage; a fencing sword.—*v.t.* to baffle, defeat.
foist *v.t.* to bring in secretly or unwarrantably; palm (a thing off *on*).
fold (-ō-) *n.* enclosure for sheep, a pen; a body of believers, a church.—*v.t.* to double up; bend part of; to clasp (in the arms); to interlace (the arms); wrap up.—*v.i.* to become folded; to be or admit of being folded.—*n.* a folding; space between two thicknesses; coil; winding; line, made by folding, a crease. —**fold'er** *n.* a leaflet; a portfolio.
fo'liage *n.* leaves collectively.
fo'lio *n.* two pages numbered similarly at view; two pages, or a page, with the opposite sides of an account in a ledger; a number of words as a unit of length; a sheet of printing paper folded once into two leaves or four pages; a book of such sheets (**fo'lios** *pl.*).—**in folio,** made of folios.—*a.* made thus.
folk (fōk) *n.* nation; people; *pl.* relatives, kindred.—**folk-song** *n.* music originating among a people.—**folk'-lore** *n.* traditions, beliefs popularly held; study of these.—**folk'-dance** *n.*
foll'icle *n.* a small sac.—**follic'ular** *a.*
foll'ow *v.t.* to go or come after; to keep to (a path, etc.); accompany, attend on; take as a guide, conform to; engage in; be consequent on; grasp the meaning of. —*v.i.* to go or come after.—**foll'ower** *n.*
foll'y *n.* foolishness; a foolish action.
foment' *v.t.* to bathe with hot lotions; foster disorder, etc.—**fomenta'tion** *n.*
fond *a.* tender, loving; devoted; credulous; foolish.—**fond'ly** *adv.*—**fond'ness** *n.* —**fo'ndle** *v.t.* caress.—**fond of,** having great liking for.
fon'dant *n.* a soft sugar mixture.
fon'du *a.* dissolving one into another, *esp.* of colours.
font *n.* a vessel for baptismal water.
fontein' (-tīn, -tān) *n.* in S. Africa, a spring; a fountain.
food (-ōō-) *n.* that which is or is intended to be eaten; nourishment.
fool (-ōō-) *n.* a silly or empty-headed person; simpleton; jester; clown; dupe. —*v.i.* to act as a fool.—*v.t.* to delude; dupe; make a fool of, mock.—**fool'ish** *a.* —**fool'ishly** *adv.*—**fool'ery** *n.*—**fool'-hardy** *a.* foolishly venturesome.—**fool-hard'iness** *n.*—**fool'-proof** *a.* devised against damage from folly or clumsiness. —**fool's'cap** *n.* jester's or dunce's cap; a size of paper formerly so watermarked.
fool (-ōō-) *n.* a dish of fruit stewed, crushed and mixed with milk, etc.
foot (-ōō-) *n.* part of the leg from the ankle down; lowest part of anything, base, stand; end of a bed, etc.; infantry; a measure of length of 12 inches; a division of a verse (**feet** *pl.*).—*v.t.* to set foot to; to put a foot on (a stocking, etc.); pay (bill).—*v.i.* to step, tread, dance.—**foot'age** *n.* in films, the amount of film used in any picture.—**foot'ball** *n.* large blown-up ball; game played with it.—**foot'baller** *n.*—**foot'-bar** *n.* (*aviation*) foot-operated bar controlling the rudder. —**foot'brake** *n.* (*motoring*) brake operated by pressure on foot-pedal.—**foot'-hold** *n.*—**foot'ing** *n.* firm standing; relations, conditions.—**foot'man** *n.* a liveried servant.—**foot'pad** *n.* an unmounted highwayman.—**foot'print** *n.* the mark left by a foot.—**foot'slog** *v.i.* to walk, go on foot.—**foot'-slogger** *n.*—**foot'-stool** *n.*
foo'tle *v.i.* (*sl.*) to bungle; to be ridiculously incompetent.—**foo'tling** *a.*
foozle' *v.t.* (*sl.*) to fumble; in bowling, roll ball off alley into side gutter.
fop *n.* a dandy.—**fopp'ish** *a.*—**fopp'ishly** *adv.*—**fopp'ery** *n.*
for *prep.* because of; instead of; toward; on account of; in favour of; respecting; during; in search of; in payment of; in the character of.—*conj.* because.—**forasmuch' as** *conj.* since.
for- *prefix,* from, away, against, as *forswear, forbid.*
for'age (-ij) *n.* food for cattle and horse. —*v.i.* to collect forage; search about.
for'ay *n.* a raid.—*v.i.* to make one.
for'bear, fore'bear (-bėr) *n.* ancestor.
forbear' (-bėr') *v.i.* to refrain; be patient. —*v.t.* to refrain from; cease (**-bore'** *p.t.* —**-borne'** *p.p.*).—**forbear'ance** *n.*
forbid' *v.t.* to order not to do; refuse to allow (**-bade** (-bad) *p.t.*—**-bidd'en** *p.p.*— **-bidd'ing** *pres. p.*).—**forbidd'ing** *a.* not inviting, repellant.
force *n.* strength, power, body of troops, police, etc.; compulsion; mental or moral strength; measurable influence inclining a body to motion.—*v.t.* to constrain, compel; break open; urge, strain; drive; produce by effort; hasten the maturity of.—**for'cible** *a.*—**for'cibly** *adv.* —**force'ful** *a.*—**forced landing** *n.* in

aviation, a landing compelled by mishap. *Syn.* vigour, efficacy, coercion. *Ant.* weakness, gentleness, debility.

force'-meat *n.* meat chopped and seasoned for stuffing.

for'ceps *n.* small surgical pincers.

ford *n.* a place where a river may be crossed on foot.—**ford'able** *a.*

fore- *prefix* meaning previous, before.

fore *a.* in front (**former, further** *comp.*—**fore'most, first, fur'thest** *sup.*)—*n.* the front part.—**fore-and-aft** *a.* placed in the line from bow to stern of a ship.—**fore'arm** *n.* the arm from wrist to elbow; —**forearm'** *v.t.* to arm beforehand.—**forebode'** *v.t.* to betoken.—**forebo'ding** *n.* a presentiment.—**forecast'** *v.t.* to estimate beforehand, prophesy.—**fore'cast** *n.* a conjecture, a guess at a future event. —**fore'castle** (fō'ksl) *n.* the sailors' quarters.—**fore'father** *n.* ancestor.—**fore'finger** *n.* the finger next the thumb, —**fore'ground** *n.* the part of a view, *esp.* in a picture, nearest the spectator.—**fore'hand** *n.* the part of a horse before the rider.—*a.* of a stroke in a game, made with the inner side of the wrist leading.—**fore'head** (for'id) *n.* the part of the face above the eyebrows and between the temples.—**fore'man** *n.* one in charge of work; leader of a jury.—**fore'mast** *n.* mast nearest the bow.—**fore'noon** *n.* morning.—**fore'runner** *n.* one who goes before, a precursor.—**fore'sail** *n.* principal sail on a foremast. —**foresee'** *v.t.* to see beforehand (**-saw'** *p.t.*—**-seen'** *p.p.*).—**foreshadow'** *v.t.* to figure beforehand, be a type of.—**fore'shore** *n.* the part of the shore between high and low tide marks.—**foreshort'en** *v.t.* to draw (an object) so that it appears shortened.—**fore'sight** *n.* foreseeing; care for the future; the front sight of a gun.—**fore'skin** *n.* the skin that covers the glans penis.—**forestall'** *v.t.* to be beforehand with.—**foretell** *v.t.* to prophesy (**-told'** *p.t./p.p.*).—**fore'top** *n.* "top" of foremast.—**fore'word** *n.* preface.

foreclose', forclose' *v.t.* to take away the power of redeeming (a mortgage); to shut out, bar.—**foreclo'sure** *n.*

foregath'er *see* **forgather.**

forego' *see* **forgo.**

for'eign (-in) *a.* not of or in one's own country; introduced from outside; irrelevant.—**for'eigner** *n.*

fore'most *a.* most advanced, chief; *sup.* of **fore.**—*adv.* in the first place.

foren'sic *a.* of courts of law.

for'est *n.* large wood; the trees in it; tract of land mainly occupied by trees, brush and heather; region kept waste for hunting.—**for'ester** *n.* one in charge of a forest; in Australia, largest variety of kangaroo.—**for'estry** *n.*

forev'er *adv.* always; to eternity.

forewent', forwent' *see* **forgo.**

for'feit (-fit) *n.* a thing lost by crime or fault; penalty, fine.—*pl.* a game.—*a.* lost by crime or fault.—*v.t.* to lose, have to pay or give up.—**for'feiture** *n.*

forfend' *v.t.* avert, turn aside.

forgath'er, foregath'er (-th-) *v.i.* to meet, assemble, associate.

forge *v.t.* to shape (metal) by heating in a fire and hammering; invent; make in fraudulent imitation of a thing, to counterfeit.—*n.* a smithy; a smith's hearth; a workshop for melting or refining metal.—**for'ger** *n.*—**for'gery** *n.* a forged document; the making of it.

forge *v.i.* to advance, make headway.

forget' *v.t.* to lose memory of, not to remember (**-got'** *p.t.*—**gott'en** or **got'** *p.p.*—**gett'ing** *pres. p.*).—**forget'ful** *a.*—**forget'fully** *adv.*—**forget'-me-not** *n.* a plant with a small blue flower.

forgive' (-giv') *v.t.* to pardon, remit (**-gave'** *p.t.*—**given** *p.p.*)—**forgive'ness** *n.* *Syn.* absolve, condone, excuse, overlook. *Ant.* condemn, charge, accuse.

forgo', forego' *v.t.* go without; give up (**-went'** *p.t.*- **-gone'** *p.p.*- **-go'ing** *pr. p.*).

fork *n.* pronged farm tool for digging or lifting; pronged instrument for holding food; division into branches; the point of this division; one of the branches.—*v.i.* to branch.—*v.t.* to make fork-shaped; dig, lift, throw, with fork.

forlorn' *a.* forsaken; desperate.—**forlorn' hope** *n.* (*mil.*) body of soldiers heading desperate attack.

form *n.* shape, appearance; visible person or animal; structure; nature; species, kind; class in a school; customary way of doing a thing; set order of words; a regularly drawn up document *esp.* a printed one with blanks for particulars; behaviour according to rule; condition, good condition; long seat without a back, a bench; a hare's nest (also **forme**); a frame for type (also **forme**).—*v.t.* to shape, mould, arrange, organise; train, shape in the mind, conceive; to go to make up, make part of.—*v.i.* to come into existence or shape.—**for'mal** *a.* ceremonial, according or rule; explicit; of outward form or routine; according to a rule that does not matter; precise; stiff.—**for'mally** *adv.*—**formal'ity** *n.*—**form'alism** *n.*—**form'alist** *n.*—**forma'tion** *n.* a forming; the thing formed; structure, shape, arrangement.—**for'mative** *a.* serving or tending to form; used in forming.—**for'mat** *n.* size and shape of a book.—**for'mer** *n.* in electricity, a tube on which an inductance coil is wound.

formal'dehyde *n.* a colourless pungent gas, used in solution in water or absorbed into porous materials as an antiseptic and disinfectant.

for'mer *a.* earlier in time; of past times; first-named.—*comp.* of **fore.**—*pron.* the

first-named thing or person or fact.—**for'merly** *adv.* previously, before.
for'mic *a.* pertaining to ants.—**for'micary** *n.* an anthill.
for'midable *a.* to be feared; likely to be difficult, serious.—**for'midably** *adv.*
for'mula (-ū-) *n.* a set form of words setting forth a principle, or prescribed for an occasion; a recipe; (*science*) a rule or fact expressed in symbols and figures (**-læ, -las** *pl.*).—**for'mulary** *n.* a collection of formulas.—**for'mulate** *v.t.* to express in a formula, or systematically.—**formula'tion** *n.*–**for'mulator** *n.*
fornica'tion *n.* sexual intercourse between unmarried man and woman.—**for'nicate** *v.i.*—**fornica'tor** *n.*
forsake' *v.t.* to abandon, desert; give up (**-sook'** *p.t.*—**-sa'ken** *p.p.*—**sa'king** *pr. p.*).
forsooth' (-th) *adv.* in truth (ironic).
forswear' *v.t.* to renounce.–*refl.* perjure.
fort *n.* a fortified place.
for'te *n.* one's strong point.—*adv.* (*music*) loudly.
forth (-th) *adv.* onwards, into view; onwards in time.—**forthcom'ing** *a.* about to come; ready when wanted.—**forthwith'** *adv.* at once, immediately.
for'tify *v.t.* to strengthen; provide with defensive works (**-tified** *p.t.* and *p.p.*—**-tifying** *pres. p.*).—**fortifica'tion** *n.*
fortiss'imo *adv.* (*music*) very loud.
for'titude *n.* courage in adversity or pain, patient endurance.
fort'night (-nīt) *n.* two weeks.—**fortnight'ly** *adv.* once a fortnight.
fort'ress *n.* a fortified place; stronghold.
fortu'itous *a.* accidental, due to chance.
for'tune *n.* chance; luck; good luck, prosperity; wealth, stock of wealth.—**for'tunate** *a.* lucky, favourable.—**for'tunately** *adv.*—**for'tune-hunter** *n.* a man seeking a rich wife.—**for'tune-teller** *n.* one who predicts a person's future.
for'ty *a.* four times ten.—*n.*—**for'tieth** *adv.*—**for'tyfold** *adv.* forty times.—**for'ty-winks** *n.* short nap.
fo'rum *n.* public meeting-place in ancient Rome; tribunal (**-rums, -ra** *pl.*).
for'ward *a.* lying in front of one, onward; prompt; precocious; presumptuous, pert.—*n.* (football, etc.) a player in the first line.—*adv.* towards the future; towards the front; to the front, into view; at or in the fore part of a ship; onward, so as to make progress.—*v.t.* to help forward; to send, dispatch.—**for'wards** *adv.* forward.—**for'wardly** *adv.* pertly.—**for'wardness** *n.*
forwent' *see* **forgo.**
fosse *n.* a ditch or moat.
foss'ick *v.i.* in Australia, S. Africa, to work over waste heaps or abandoned claims in the hope of finding gold; to rummage for profit.—**foss'icker** *n.*
foss'il *a.* the hardened remains of animals or plants, *esp.* prehistoric ones; (*persons*) antiquated, old-fashioned.—*n.* a fossilised thing.—**foss'ilise** *v.t.* and *i.* to turn into a fossil.
fos'ter *v.t.* encourage; be favourable to; to rear, tend, nourish, cherish.—**fos'ter-brother** *n.* one related by upbringing, not by blood; so, **foster-father, foster-child** *ns.*
foul *a.* loathsome, offensive; dirty; charged with harmful matter; clogged, choked; unfair; wet, rough; obscene, disgustingly abusive.—*n.* a collision; an act of unfair play.—*adv.* unfairly.—*v.i.* to become foul.—*v.t.* to make foul; to jam; to collide with.—**foul'ly** *adv.*
foulard' (fōō-) *n.* a thin soft fabric.
found *v.t.* to establish, institute; lay the base of; to base, ground.—*p.t./p.p.* of **find.**—**founda'tion** *n.* a founding; base, lowest part of a building; endowed institution.–**found'er**–*n.* **found'ress** *fem.*
found *v.t.* to melt and run into a mould.—**found'er** *n.*—**found'ry** *n.* a workshop.
found'er *v.i.* of a horse, to fall lame; collapse; trip up.—*v.t.* to cause to do this.—*v.i.* of a ship, to sink.
found'ling *n.* a deserted infant.
fount *n.* fountain; a set of printer's type.
fount'ain (-in) *n.* a spring; source of water; jet of water, *esp.* ornamental.
four (fawr) *n.* and *a.* cardinal number next after three.—**on all fours,** on hands and knees.—**fourth** *a.* the ordinal number.—**fourth'ly** *adv.*—**four'teen** *n.* and *a.* four and ten.—**fourteenth** *a.*—**fourteen'fold** *adv.*—**four'-eyed** *a.* (*sl.*) in N. America, spectacled.—**four'-in-hand** *n.* a vehicle with four horses driven by one driver.—**four-post'er** (-ō-) *n.* a bed with four posts for curtains, etc.—*a.*—**four'square** *a.* firm, steady.—**four'-stroke** *n.* an internal combustion engine having cycle of four strokes.
fowl *n.* a domestic cock or hen; a bird.—*v.i.* to hunt wild birds.—**fowl'er** *n.*—**fowl'ing-piece** *n.* a light gun.
fox *n.* red bushy-tailed animal; its fur; cunning person.–*v.t.* to discolour (paper) with brown spots.—*v.i.* act craftily; sham.—**fox'y** *a.*—**fox'glove** *n.* tall flowering plant.—**fox-hole** *n.* (U.S.) (*sl.*) in World War 2, small trench position holding one or two people, giving protection against snipers and dive bombers.—**fox'hound** *n.* dog bred for hunting foxes.—**fox terr'ier** *n.* small dog.—**fox'-trot** *n.* ballroom dance.
foy'er *n.* in theatres, etc., a public room opening on to the vestibule.
fracas' (-kâ) *n.* noisy quarrel; uproar.
frac'tion *n.* a numerical quantity not an integer; a fragment, piece, small part.—**frac'tional** *a.*
frac'ture *n.* a breakage; the part broken; breaking of a bone.—*v.t.* and *i.* to break, crack (bone).
frac'tious *a.* unruly, cross, fretful.

frag'ile (-j-) *a.* breakable.—**fragil'ity** *n.* *Syn.* frail, weak, brittle, delicate. *Ant.* sturdy, stout, strong.
frag'ment *n.* a piece broken off, a small portion.—**frag'mentary** *a.*
fra'grant (-āg-) *a.* sweet-smelling.—**fra'grance** *n.*—**fra'grantly** *adv.*
frail *a.* easily broken, delicate; morally weak, unchaste.-**frail'ty** *n.*—**frail'ly** *adv.*
frame *v.t.* to put together, make; adapt; put into words; put into a frame; to shape.—*n.* that in which a thing is set, or inserted, window, picture, etc.; structure; constitution; mood.—**frame-aerial** *n.* a wireless aerial consisting of wire wound on a frame.—**frame'work** *n.* a light wooden or other structure; a structure into which completing parts can be fitted.—**frame-up** *n.* a plot, manufactured evidence.
franc *n.* French, Belgian, Swiss coin.
fran'chise *n.* the right of voting; a voting qualification; citizenship.
frank *a.* candid, outspoken; sincere.—*n.* signature on a letter of a person entitled to send it free of postage charges; a letter with this.—*v.t.* to mark a letter thus.—**frank'ly** *adv.*—**frank'incense** *n.* an aromatic gum resin.
fran'tic *a.* mad with rage, grief, joy, etc. —**fran'tically** *adv.*—**fran'ticly** *adv.*
frater'nal *a.* of a brother; brotherly.—**frater'nally** *adv.*—**frater'nity** *n.* brotherliness; a brotherhood.—**frat'ernise** *v.i.* to associate, make friends.—**fraternisa'tion** *n.*—**frat'ricide** *n.* the killing of a brother or sister; the killer.—**frat'ricidal** *a.*
fraud *n.* criminal deception; a dishonest trick.—**fraud'ulence** *n.*—**fraud'ulent** *a.*
fraught (-awt) *p.p.* and *a.*—**fraught with**, laden with, full of.
fray *n.* fight; *v.t.* and *i.* to wear through by rubbing; to try the temper.
fraz'zle *n.* the act or result of frazzling. —*v.t.* and *v.i.* to fray; reduce to tatters.
freak *n.* a caprice; prank; monstrosity.
frec'kle (frek'l) *n.* a light-brown spot on the skin.—*v.t.* and *i.* to mark or become marked with such spots.
free *a.* having liberty; not in bondage; not restricted or impeded; released from strict law, literality, tax, obligation, etc.; disengaged; spontaneous; liberal; frank; familiar.—*v.t.* to set at liberty, disengage (**freed** *p.t.* and *p.p.*—**free'ing** *pres. p.*).—**free'ly** *adv.*—**free'dom** *n.*—**free'board** *n.* that part of a ship's hull from the level of flotation to that of the upper deck.—**free'hand** *a.* of drawing, done without guiding instruments.—**free'hold** *n.* tenure of land without obligation of service or rent; land so held.—**free'-lance** (-â-) *n.* a mediæval mercenary; unattached journalist; politician independent of party. **free love'** *n.* the doctrine or practice of free choice in sexual relations unshackled by marriage.—**free'man** *n.* person not a slave; one with civil rights, admitted a citizen.—**free'mason** *n.* member of a moral and social fraternity.—**free'masonry** *n.*—**free'thinker** *n.* one who rejects authority in religion.
free'booter *n.* a pirate.
freeze *v.i.* to become ice; become rigid with cold; feel very cold.—*v.t.* to turn solid by cold; chill; affect with frost (**froze** *p.t.*—**fro'zen** *p.p.*—**free'zing** *pres. p.*).—**free'zer** *n.* in Australia and New Zealand, a sheep intended for use as frozen mutton; receptacle for holding frozen food; refrigerator.—**freez'ing-point** *n.* temperature at which a liquid becomes solid.
freight (-āt) *n.* hire of a ship; a cargo; in N. America, goods carried in a railway car.—*v.t.* to hire or load (a ship); to send goods by railway.—**freight'er** *n.* —**freight'age** *n.*-**freight-train** *n.*-**freight-car** *n.*—**freight agent** *n.*
French *n.* language of the people of France.—**french-bean** *n.* type of haricot bean.—**french-polish**, shellac varnish for furniture.
fren'zy *n.* fury, rage, mania, delirious excitement.—**fren'zied** *a.*
fre'quency *n.* occurring frequently; rate of occurrence, e.g., number of cycles per sec. of an alternating current.
fre'quent *a.* happening often; common; habitual; numerous.—**fre'quently** *adv.*—**frequent'** *v.t.* to go often or habitually to.—**frequent'ative** *a.* expressing repetition or intensity.
fres'co *n.* a method of painting in water-colour on the plaster of a wall before it dries (**-coes, -cos** (-cōz) *pl.*).
fresh *a.* new; additional; different; recent; inexperienced; pure; not pickled, salted, etc.; not stale, not faded or dimmed; not tired; of wind, strong; (*sl.*) impudent, arrogant, quarrelsome. **fresh'ly** *adv.*—**fresh'ness** *n.*—**fresh'en** *v.i.* and *t.*—**fresh'et** *n.* a rush of water at a river mouth; a flood of river water. —**fresh'man** (**fresh'er** *sl.*) *n.* member of a college in his first year.
Syn. healthy, unfaded, unimpaired, raw, unpractised, unsalted, uncured. *Ant.* old, faded, tarnished, unhealthy, weary, trained, salted, preserved.
fret *v.t.* and *i.* to chafe, worry.—*n.* irritation.—**fret'ful** *a.* easily vexed.
fret *n.* pattern of straight lines intersecting; bar to aid the fingering of a stringed instrument.—*v.t.* to ornament with carved pattern; variegate.—**fret'-saw** *n.*—**fret'work** *n.*
Freu'dian (froi'-) *a.* pertaining to the Austrian psychologist, Sigmund Freud (1856-1939) or his theories.
fri'able *a.* easily crumbled.—**friabil'ity** *n.*
fri'ar *n.* a member of a mendicant religious order.—**fri'ary** *n.* a convent.

fric'tion *n.* rubbing; resistance met with by a body moving over another; disagreement.—**fric'tional** *a.*

Fri'day *n.* the 6th day of the week.—**Good Friday** *n.* the day of the Crucifixion, the Friday before Easter.

friend (frend) *n.* one attached to another by affection and esteem; an intimate associate; a supporter; a Quaker.—**friend'less** *a.*—**friend'ly** *a.* kindly disposed.—**friend'ship** *n.*—**friend'liness** *n.*

frieze (frēz) *n.* a coarse woollen cloth; a band of decoration, *esp.* on a wall.

frig'ate *n.* small, fast warship for escort and anti-submarine duties.

fright (frit) *n.* sudden fear; a grotesque person or thing.—*v.t.* to terrify.—**fright'en** *v.t.* terrify.—**fright'ful** *a.*

fri'gid (-ij-) *a.* cold; formal; stiff, dull.—**fri'gidly** *adv.*—**frigid'ity** *n.*

frill *n.* fluted strip of fabric or paper gathered at one edge; a fringe.—*v.t.* to make into, or decorate with, a frill.

fringe *n.* ornamental border of threads, tassels, etc.; hair cut low on forehead.—*v.t.* to adorn with a fringe.

fripp'ery *n.* finery, trumpery.

frisk *v.i.* to frolic.—*n.* a frolic.—**frisk'y** *a.*

fritt'er *n.* a small pancake.

fritt'er *v.t.* **fritter away,** to throw away.

friv'olous *a.* silly, trifling; given to trifling.—**frivol'ity** *n.* foolish behaviour.

frizz *v.i.* to sputter in frying.—**friz'zle** *v.t.* and *i.* to fry with spluttering noise.

frizz *v.t.* to crisp, curl (hair).—**friz'zle** *v.t.* and *i.* to frizz.—**friz'zy** *a.*

fro *adv.* away, from (only in **to and fro**).

frock *n.* woman's dress, monk's gown.—*v.t.* to invest with the office of priest.—**frock-coat** *n.* a man's long coat.

froe'belism *n.* the kindergarten system.

frog *n.* a tailless amphibious animal.—**frog'mouth** *n.* Australia, the more-pork.

frog *n.* horny growth in the sole of a horse's hoof; waist-belt attachment for sword; military coat-fastening.

frol'ic *a.* sportive.—*v.i.* to gambol, play pranks.—*n.* a prank, merry-making (**-icked** (-ikt) *p.t.* and *p.p.*— **-icking** *pres. p.*).—**frol'icsome** *a.*

from *prep.* expressing departure, moving away, source, distance, cause, etc.

frond *n.* a plant organ consisting of stem and foliage, *esp.* in ferns.

front (-unt) *n.* the fore part; forehead.—*v.i.* to look, face.—*v.t.* to face; oppose.—*a.* of or at the front.—*n.* movement uniting diverse elements in the struggle for a common goal.—**front'age** *n.* in Australia, New Zealand, etc., land on a harbour or river bank.—**front'al** *a.*—**front'ier** *n.* boundary between two countries.—**front'ispiece** *n.* illustration facing the title-page of a book.—**front'let** *n.* a band for the forehead.

frost *n.* act or state of freezing; weather in which temperature is below freezing point; frozen dew or mist; a failure.—*v.t.* to injure by frost; cover with rime; powder with sugar, etc. ; give a slightly roughened surface; turn (hair) white.—**frost'y** *a.*—**frost'ily** *adv.*—**frost'bite** *n.*

froth (-th) *n.* a collection of small bubbles, foam; scum; idle talk.—*v.i.* and *t.* to throw up, or cause to throw up, froth.—**froth'y** *a.*—**froth'ily** *adv.*

fro'ward *a.* perverse, ungovernable.

frown *v.i.* to knit the brows.—*n.* a look of displeasure or deep thought.

frow'zy *a.* ill-smelling, dirty, slatternly.

fro'zen as'sets, assets that will not be easily sold or cashed; assets impossible to realise for the time being.

fruc'tify *v.i.* to bear fruit.—*v.t.* to make fruitful (**-tified** *p.t.* and *p.p.*— **-tifying** *pres. p.*).—**fructifica'tion** *n.*

fru'gal *a.* sparing, economical, *esp.* in use of food.—**fru'gally** *adv.*—**frugal'ity** *n.*

fruit (frōōt) *n.* a seed and its envelope, *esp.* an eatable one; vegetable products (usually in *pl.*); produce; result, benefit.—*v.i.* to bear fruit.—**fruit'erer** *n.* a dealer in fruit.—**fruit'ful** *a.*—**fruit'less** *a.*—**frui'tion** (-ōō-i'-) *n.* enjoyment; realisation of hopes.—**fruit'y** *a.*

frum'enty, fur'menty *n.* hulled wheat boiled in milk and sweetened.

frump *n.* a dowdy woman.—**frump'ish** *a.*

frustrate' *v.t.* to baffle, disappoint.—**frustra'ted** *a.*—**frustra'tion** *n.*

Syn. defeat, foil. *Ant.* help, assist.

fry *n.* young fishes.—**small fry,** young or insignificant beings.

fry *v.t.* to cook with fat in a shallow pan.—*v.i.* to be cooked thus (**fried** *p.t.* and *p.p.*—**fry'ing** *pres. p.*).—*n.* fried meat.—**frying-pan brand** *n.* in Australia, a brand that obliterates the owner's brand, used by cattle stealers.

fu'chsia (fū'sha) *n.* an ornamental shrub.

fud'dle *v.t.* to intoxicate, confuse.—*v.i.* to tipple.—*n.* drinking bout.

fudge *interj.* stuff; nonsense.—*n.* a kind of sweetmeat, soft toffee.

fu'el (fū'-) *n.* material for burning.—**fuel consumption,** the number of miles a motor vehicle, plane, etc., will travel per gallon of petrol.

fu'gitive (fū'-) *a.* that runs, or has run, away; fleeting, transient.—*n.* one who flees; an exile, refugee.

fugue (fūg) *n.* a musical composition; wandering with loss of memory.

ful'crum *n.* the point on which a lever is placed for support (**ful'cra** *pl.*).

fulfil' (fool-) *v.t.* to satisfy; carry out; obey.–**fulfil'ment** *n.* (**fulfill'ed** *p.t./p.p.*).

fuli'ginous (-ij'-) *a.* sooty.

full (fool) *a.* holding all it can; containing abundance; ample; complete; plump.—*adv.* very; quite; exactly.—**full'y** *adv.*—**ful'ness full'ness** *n.*—**ful'some** *a.* offending by excess.—**full of** in S.

Africa, covered with.—**full up of** in Australia, (*sl.*) tired of, sick of.
full'er (fool-) *n.* one who cleans and thickens cloth.—**fuller's earth** *n.* a clay used for this.—**full** *v.t.*
ful'minate (fool'-) *v.i.* to flash, explode. —*v.t.* and *i.* to thunder out (blame, etc.). —*n.* a chemical compound exploding readily.—**fulmina'tion** *n.*
fum'ble *v.i.* and *t.* to handle awkwardly, grope about.—**fum'bling** *a.*
fume *n.* smoke; vapour; exhalation.—*v.i.* to emit fumes; give way to anger, chafe.—**fu'migate** *v.t.* to apply fumes or smoke to.—**fumiga'tion** *n.*
fun *n.* sport, amusement, jest, diversion. —*v.i.* to joke.—**funn'y** *a.*—**funn'ily** *adv.*
funam'bulate *v.i.* to walk or dance on a rope.—**funam'bulist** *n.* a rope-walker.
func'tion *n.* the work a thing is designed to do; official duty; public occasion or ceremony.—*v.i.* to operate, work.—**func'tional** *a.*—**func'tionary** *n.* an official, holder of an office.
fun'ctionalism *n.* modern movement in architecture, etc., based on "fitness for purpose."—**func'tionalist** *n.*
fund *n.* a permanent stock; a stock or sum of money.—*pl.* money resources.—*v.t.* to convert (debt) into permanent form; invest money permanently.—**funda'ment** *n.* the buttocks.—**fundament'al** *a.* essential, primary; of, affecting, or serving as, the base.—*n.* a basic rule, note, etc.—**fundament'alist** *n.* one laying stress on belief in literal and verbal inspiration of the Bible and other traditional creeds.—**fundament'alism** *n.*
fu'neral *a.* of, or relating to, the burial of the dead.—*n.* the ceremonies at a burial.—**fune'real** (-ēr'-) *a.* dismal.
fun'gus (-ng-g-) *n.* mushroom, toadstool, mildew, etc.; a spongy morbid growth (**fun'gi** (-gī) **fun'guses** *pl.*).—**fun'geous** *a.*—**fun'gicide** *n.* substance used to destroy fungus.
funic'ular *a.* of or worked by a rope.
funk *n.* fear, panic; a coward.—*v.i.* to show fear.—*v.t.* to be afraid of.—**funk'y** *a.*
funn'el *n.* cone-shaped vessel ending in tube; chimney of locomotive, ship, etc.
funn'y *see* **fun.**.—**funn'y bone** *n.* part of the elbow sensitive to knocks.
fur *n.* short hair of certain animals; a lining, trimming or garment of dressed skins; a crust or coating.—*v.t.* to provide with fur.—**furr'ier** *n.* one who deals in furs.—**furr'y** *a.*
fur'below *n.* a flounce, trimming.
fur'bish *v.t.* clean up.
fur'cate, fur'cated *a.* forked.
furl *v.t.* to roll up and bind (a sail, etc.).
fur'long *n.* an eighth of a mile.
fur'lough (-lō) *n.* leave of absence.
fur'menty *see* **frumenty.**
fur'nace *n.* an apparatus for applying great heat to metals; a hot place; a closed fireplace for heating a boiler, etc.
fur'nish *v.t.* to supply, fit up with; fit up a house with furniture; yield.—**fur'niture** *n.* movable contents of a house or room, e.g. tables, chairs.
furor'e (fū-rō'-ri) *n.* a burst of enthusiastic popular admiration.
furr'ow (-ō) *n.* the trench made by a plough; a ship's track; a rut, groove.—*v.t.* to make furrows in.
fur'ther (-th-) *adv.* more; in addition; at or to a greater distance or extent.—*a.* more distant; additional; *comp.* of **fore.**—*v.t.* to help forward.—**fur'therance** *n.* advancement.—**fur'therer** *n.*—**fur'thermore** *adv.* besides, moreover.—**fur'thest** *a. sup.* of **fore.**—*adv.* (*sup.*).—**fur'thermost** *a.*
fur'tive *a.* stealthy, sly.—**fur'tively** *adv.* *Syn.* secret, clandestine. *Ant.* open, frank, undisguised.
fu'ry (fū'-) *n.* wild anger, rage, fierce passion; violence of storm, etc.—**fu'ries** *n. pl.* snake-haired avenging deities.—**fu'rious** *a.*—**fu'riously** *adv.*
furze *n.* evergreen prickly shrub.
fuse (fūz) *n.* a tube containing material for setting light to a bomb, firework, etc.—*v.t.* to fit a fuse to.—**fusee'** *n.* a conical wheel or pulley in a watch or clock; a large-headed match.—**fu'selage** *n.* the spindle-shaped body of an aeroplane.
fuse (fūz) *v.t.* and *i.* to melt with heat; blend by melting.—*n.* a wire with low melting point, used as a safety device in electric systems.—**fu'sible** *a.*—**fu'sion** *n.*
fu'sel (-ūz-) *n.* a mixture of crude alcohols (usually **fusel oil**).
fu'sil *n.* a light musket.—**fusilier'** *n.* a soldier of certain regiments formerly armed with a fusil.—**fusillade'** *n.* a continuous discharge of firearms.
fuss *n.* needless bustle or concern.—*v.i.* to make a fuss.—*v.t.* to bustle.—**fuss'y** *a.* —**fuss'ily** *adv.*—**fuss'iness** *n.*
fus'tian *n.* a thick twilled cotton cloth; inflated language.
fus'tigate *v.t.* to cudgel.—**fustiga'tion** *n.*
fus'ty *a.* mouldy; smelling of damp.
fu'tile *a.* useless, ineffectual; vain, frivolous.—**futility** *n.*
futt'er, futt'ah *n.* in New Zealand, a storehouse raised on four posts, designed to be unclimbable by rats.
fu'ture *a.* that will be; of or relating to time to come.—*n.* time to come; what will happen; tense of a verb indicating this.—**futu'rity** *n.*—**fu'turism** *n.* in art, complete abandonment of tradition.—**fu'turist** *n.* and *a.*—**futurist'ic** *a.*
fuze *see* **fuse.**
fuzz *n.* fluff.—**fuzz'y** *a.* fluffy.—**fuzz'y-wuzz'y** *n.* a Soudanese warrior.
fyl'fot (fil'fot) *n.* the swastika, 卍.

G

gab *n.* talk, chatter.—**gab'ble** *v.i.* and *t.* to talk, utter inarticulately or too fast. —*n.* such talk.—**gift of the gab,** eloquence, loquacity.

gab'erdine *n.* a fine hard-laid cloth; a loose upper garment, as of Jews.

ga'ble *n.* the triangular upper part of the wall at the end of a ridged roof.

ga'by *n.* a simpleton.

gad *v.t.* to go about idly.—**gad'about** *n.* a gadding person (**gad'ded** *p.t.* and *p.p.*).

gad'fly *n.* a cattle-biting fly.

gadg'et *n.* a small fitting or contrivance.

gaff *n.* barbed fishing spear.—*v.t.* to seize (a fish) with a gaff.—*n.* spar for extending top of sail; formerly, a public fair; a low-class theatre.

gaffe (gaf') *n.* a social blunder; a tactless remark.

gaff'er *n.* an old rustic; elderly fellow; boss; foreman.

gag *n.* a thing thrust into the mouth to prevent speech or hold it open for operation.—*v.t.* to apply a gag to.—*n.* words inserted by an actor in his part. —*v.i.* of an actor, to put in words.

gage *n.* a pledge; thing given as security; a challenge.—*v.t.* to pledge, stake.

gai'ety *n.* being gay; merriment.

gain *v.t.* to obtain, secure; obtain as profit; win; earn; persuade; reach.—*v.i.* increase, improve.—*n.* profit, increase.

gainsay' *v.t.* to deny, contradict (**-said'** *p.t.* and *p.p.*— **-say'ing** *pres. p.*).

gait *n.* manner of walking.

gait'ers *n. pl.* coverings of leather, cloth, etc., for the lower legs.

ga'la *n.* a festive occasion.

gal'antine (-ēn) *n.* boned spiced white meat (chicken, etc.) served cold.

galan'ty-show *n.* (1) a display of moving puppets silhouetted on a screen; (2) (*col.*) a lavish theatrical performance.

gal'axy *n.* the Milky Way; a brilliant company (*pl.* **gal'axies**).

gale *n.* a strong wind.

gal'ilee *n.* a porch or chapel.

gall (gawl) *n.* bile of animals; bitterness; in N. America, impudence, nerve.—**gall'sickness** *n.* in S. Africa, general term for liver disease in cattle, sheep and goats.—*n.* painful swelling, *esp.* on a horse; blister; growth caused by insects on trees.—*v.t.* to make sore by rubbing; vex, irritate.

gall'ant *a.* fine, stately, brave; chivalrous; (usually **gallant'**) very attentive to women, amatory.—*n.* a man of fashion; a lover (also **gallant'**).—**gall'antly** *adv.* (also **gallant'ly**).—**gall'antry** *n.*
Syn. heroic, courageous, brave, dignified. *Ant.* ungallant, discourteous, rude, cowardly, timid.

gall'eon *n.* a large three-decked sailing ship of war, *esp.* spanish.

gall'ery *n.* balcony overlooking hall, church, etc.; top floor of seats in a theatre; its occupants; passage in a wall; a colonnade; room for showing works of art; tunnel in mining.

gall'ey *n.* one-decked vessel with sails and oars; large rowing-boat; ship's kitchen; printer's tray for set-up type. —**gall'ey-proof** *n.* printer's first proof.

gall'igaskins *n. pl.* breeches, leggings.

gall'ipot *n.* a small earthenware pot.

gall'ium *n.* rare metallic element.

gall'on *n.* a measure of four quarts.

gall'op *v.i.* to go at a gallop.—*v.t.* to cause to move at a gallop.—*n.* horse's fastest pace with all four feet off the ground together.—**gall'oper** *n.*

gall'ows *n. pl.* structure for hanging criminals; in Australia, a framework on which slaughtered animals are cut up.

galoot' *n.* (*sl,*) clumsy, uncouth youth.

gal'op *n.* a lively dance.—*v.i.* to dance it.

galore' *adv.* in plenty.

galosh', golosh' *n.* an overshoe.

gal'vanism *n.* electricity produced by chemical action.—**galvan'ic** *a.* **gal'vanise** *v.t.* to apply galvanism to; stimulate thus; rouse by shock; coat with metal by galvanism.—**galvanisa'tion** *n.*—**galvanom'eter** *n.* instrument for measuring galvanic currents.

gam'bit *n.* a chess opening involving the sacrifice of a pawn; (*fig.*) an initial move, *esp.* one of trickery.

gam'ble *v.i.* to play games of chance for money stakes; risk much for great gain. —*n.* a risky undertaking.—**gam'bler** *n.*

gamboge' (-ōōzh) *n.* a gum-resin used as yellow pigment and purgative.

gam'bol *n.* a caper, playful leap.—*v.i.* to frisk (**gam'bolled** *p.t.* and *p.p.*).

game *n.* a diversion, sport, play, amusement; scheme, plan of action; animals or birds hunted; their flesh.—*a.* plucky.—*v.i.* to gamble.—**game'some** *a.* sportive.—**game'ster** *n.* gambler.—**game'cock** *n.* fowl bred for fighting.—**game'keeper** *n.* man employed to breed game, prevent poaching, etc.

game *a.* of arm or leg, crippled.

gam'in *n.* neglected, unruly child in the streets; city arab.—**gam'inesque'** *a.*

gamm'a-ray *n.* a penetrative X-ray.

gamm'on *n.* humbug, nonsense.—*v.t.* to humbug, deceive; bottom piece of a flitch of bacon.

gamp *n.* a large umbrella.

gam'ut *n.* the whole series of musical notes; a scale; the compass of a voice.

gan'der *n.* a male goose.

gang *n.* a company, band.—**gang'er** *n.* foreman over gang of workmen.—**gang'ster** *n.* one of a gang of violent criminals.—**gang'way** *n.* bridge from

ship to shore; anything similar; a passage between rows of seats.
gan'glion (-ng-gl-) *n.* nerve nucleus.
gan'grene (-ng-gr-) *n.* mortification, decomposition of a part of the body.—*v.t.* to affect with this.—*v.i.* to be affected with this.—**gan'grenous** *a.*
gann'et *n.* a solan goose, a sea-bird.
gan'try, gaun'try *n.* a structure to support a crane, railway signals, etc.
gaol, jail (jāl) *n.* prison.—**gaol'er, jail'er** *n.* keeper, warder in prison.
gap *n.* breach, opening; empty space. *Syn.* hiatus, chasm, interstice, vacuity.
gape *v.i.* to open the mouth wide; stare; yawn.—*n.* a yawn; a wide opening.
gar'age (-åzh, -ij) *n.* building to house motor vehicles.—*v.t.* put into a garage.
garb *n.* dress, unusual fashion of dress.—*v.t.* to dress, clothe.
garb'age (-j) *n.* offal; refuse, rubbish.
gar'ble *v.t.* to make unfair selections from; misrepresent.—**gar'bler** *n.*
garçon' *n.* a boy; a waiter.
gard'en *n.* ground for growing flowers, fruit, or vegetables.—*v.i.* to cultivate a garden.—**gard'ener** *n.*—**gard'en-city** *n.* modern planned industrial town in country surroundings.
garden'ia *n.* a tropical evergreen shrub with fragrant wax-like flowers.
gargan'tuan *a.* immense, enormous.
gar'gle *v.i.* to wash the throat with liquid kept moving by the breath.—*v.t.* to wash thus.—*n* a throat-wash.
garg'oyle *n.* a grotesque waterspout.
gar'ish *a.* showy; glaring.
garl'and *n.* a wreath of flowers worn or hung as a decoration.—*v.t.* to decorate.
garl'ic *n.* plant with strong smell and taste of onion, used in cooking.
garm'ent *n.* any article of dress.
garn'er *n.* a granary.—*v.t.* to store up.
garn'et *n.* a precious stone.
garn'ish *v.t.* to adorn, decorate (*esp.* food or literary matter).—*n.* material for this.—**garn'iture** *n.* furniture, ornament.
garr'et *n.* attic, top floor room.
garr'ison *n.* troops stationed in a town, fort, etc.—*v.t.* to occupy, with a garrison.
garrotte' *n.* Spanish capital punishment by strangling; apparatus for this; robbery by means of strangling.—**garrott'er** *n.*—**garrott'ing** *n.*
garr'ulous *a.* talkative.—**garru'lity** *n.*
gart'er *n.* a band worn near the knee to keep a stocking up.
gas *n.* an elastic fluid such as air; coal-gas, used for heating or lighting; such fluid or a mixture used as poison in warfare, found as explosive in mines, employed as anæsthetic, etc. (**gas'es** *pl.*).—*v.t.* to project gas over; poison with gas.—**gas'eous** *a.*—**gaselier'** *n.* lamp of several burners for gas.—**gasom'eter** *n.* a tank for storing gas.—**gass'y** *a.* of, like, or full of, gas.—**gas'-attack** *n.* concentrated delivery of poison gas over enemy fronts.—**gas'-filled** *a.* denotes electric light bulbs filled with nitrogen or argon.—**gas'-mask** *n.* anti-gas respirator.
gash *n.* a long deep cut or wound, a slash.—*v.t.* to make a gash in.
gasolene' *n.* petrol (American name).
gasp (-å-) *v.i.* to catch the breath with open mouth, as in exhaustion or surprise, to pant.—*n.* a convulsive catching of the breath.—**gasp'er** *n.* (*sl.*) a cheap Virginia cigarette.
gas'tric *a.* of the stomach.—**gastron'omy** *n.* the art of good eating.—**gastronomical** *a.*—**gastron'omer, gas'tronome** *n.* a judge of cooking.—**gas'teropod** *n.* a mollusc.—**gasterop'odous** *a.*
gate *n.* an opening in a wall which may be closed by a barrier; the barrier for closing it; a contrivance for regulating the flow of water; any entrance, etc.—**gate'-crash** *v.t.* and *i.* to enter a meeting, social function, etc., uninvited.
gâteau' *n.* a cake (**-teaux** *pl.*).
gath'er (-th-) *v.t.* to bring together; collect; draw together; deduce.—*v.i.* to come together; collect; form swelling of pus.—**gath'ers** *n. pl.* puckered part of a dress.—**gath'ering** *n.* assembly; inflamed swelling.
gat'-ling-gun *n.* rapid-firing American machine-gun, invented circa 1861.
gau'cherie *n.* an awkward action.
gaud (gawd) *n.* a showy ornament.—**gaud'y** *a.* showy, without taste.—**gaud'ily** *adv.*—**gaud'iness** *n.*
gauge, gage (gāj) *n.* standard measure, as of diameter of wire, thickness of sheet metal, etc.; distance between rails of a railway; capacity, extent; instruments for measuring, e.g., size of wire, rainfall, height of water in a boiler, etc.—*v.t.* to measure, test.
gaunt (gaw-) *a.* lean, haggard; grim.
gaunt'let (gaw-) *n.* an armoured glove; glove with wide cuff.—*n.* **run the gauntlet** punishment in which victim had to run between two lines of men who struck at him with sticks, etc.—usually *fig.*
gaun'try *see* **gantry.**
gauss (gous') *n.* in electricity, the unit of magnetic intensity.
gauze (gawz) *n.* thin transparent fabric of silk, wire, etc.—**gauz'y** *a.*
gav'el *n.* the mallet of a presiding officer.
gavotte' *n.* a lively dance; music for it.
gawk *n.* an awkward or bashful person.
gay *a.* light-hearted; showy; dissolute; in N. America, quarrelsome, overbearing.—**gai'ly** *adv.*—**gai'ety** *n.*
gaze *v.i.* to look fixedly.—*n.* a long intent look (**gazed** *p.t.* and *p.p.*).
gazelle' *n.* a small, soft-eyed antelope.
gazette' *n.* official newspaper for announcements of government appointments, bankruptcies, etc.—*v.t.* to publish

in the official gazette.—**gazetteer'** *n.* geographical dictionary.

gaz'ogene *n.* apparatus for making aerated waters.

gear *n.* apparatus, tackle, tools; set of wheels working together, *esp.* by engaging cogs; rigging; harness; equipment; clothing, goods, habits, utensils.—*v.t.* provide with gear; put in gear.

geez'er *n.* (*col.*) an old woman, man.

geis'ha *n.* Japanese dancing girl.

gel'atine (jel'-) *n.* a transparent substance made by stewing skin, tendons, etc.—**gelat'inise** *v.t.*—**gelat'inous** *a.*

geld (g-) *v.t.* to castrate.—**geld'ing** *n.* a castrated horse.

gel'id *a.* very cold.

gel'ignite *n.* a powerful explosive consisting of dynamite in gelatine form.

gem *n.* a precious stone, *esp.* when cut and polished; a thing of great beauty or worth.—*v.t.* to adorn with gems.

Gem'ini (gem'-in-i) *n.* the twins. 3rd sign of Zodiac operative *c.* May 21–June 20. Constellation of this name.

gems'bok *n.* in S. Africa, a species of fleet straight-horned antelope.

gendarme' (jh-ong'-darm) *n.* one of a corps of French military police.

gen'der *n.* a classification of nouns, corresponding roughly to sexes and sexlessness (in English).

gen' *n.* (*sl.*) reliable information.

gene' (jēn) *n.* a unit in the germ-plasm which controls the appearance of an hereditary character or characters.

geneal'ogy *n.* study of family history; pedigree.—**genealog'ical** *a.*—**-ogist** *n.*

gen'era *pl. of* **genus.**

gen'eral *a.* not particular or partial; including or affecting or applicable to all or most; not restricted to one department; usual, prevalent; miscellaneous; dealing with main elements only. —*n.* an officer in the army of rank above colonel.—**generaliss'imo** *n.* a supreme commander (**-mos** *pl.*).—**general'ity** *n.* —**gen'eralise** *v.t.* to reduce to general laws.—*v.i.* to draw general conclusions. —**generalisa'tion** *n.*—**gen'eralship** *n.* military skill; management.

gen'erate *v.t.* to produce.—**genera'tion** *n.* bringing into being; people born in the same period; about 30 years.—**gen'erative** *a.*—**gen'erator** *n.* a begetter; apparatus for producing electricity, etc. —**gen'erating station** *n.* power station.

gener'ic *a.* belonging to, characteristic of, a class or genus.—**gener'ically** *adv.*

gen'erous *a.* noble-minded; liberal, free in giving; copious; of wine, rich.—**gen'erously** *adv.*—**generos'ity** *n.*

gen'esis *n.* origin; mode of formation (**-eses** (sēz) *pl.*).—**Gen'esis** *n.* first book of the Old Testament (**gen'eses** *pl.*).

genet'ics *n.* scientific study of heredity and the art of breeding.—**genet'ic** *a.*

ge'nial *a.* kindly, jovial; sympathetic; mild, conducive to growth.—**ge'nially** *adv.*—**genial'ity** *n.* cordiality.

ge'nie (jee'ni) *n.* in Eastern tales, a demon (**ge'nii** *pl.*).

gen'ital *a.* pertaining to generation.—*n. pl.* **-s** the sexual organs.

ge'nius *n.* high power of mind; one with this (**gen'iuses** *pl.*); tutelary, animating, spirit (**ge'nii** *pl.*).

genre (zhon'r) *n.* genus; kind; sort; style; a painting of a homely scene.

genteel' *a.* elegant (usually ironical).

gen'tian *n.* plant with blue flowers.

gen'tile *a.* of race other than Jewish.

gen'tle *a.* mild, quiet; courteous; noble; well-born.—**gentil'ity** *n.* social superiority.—**gen'tleman** *n.* a chivalrous well-bred man.—**gen'tlemanly** *a.* like a gentleman.—**gen'tlewoman** *n.*—**gen'tleness** *n.*—**gent'ly** *adv.*—**gent'ry** *n.* people next below the nobility. *Syn.* bland, meek, soothing.—of "gentleness," mildness, suavity, meekness. *Ant.* ungentle, unkind, rude, wild.

gen'uflect *v.i.* to bend the knee, *esp.* in worship.—**genuflec'tion, genuflex'ion** *n.*

gen'uine *a.* real, true, not sham.

ge'nus *n.* a race, tribe, kind (**gen'era** *pl.*).

geog'raphy *n.* science of the earth's form, physical features, climate, population, etc.; a book on this.—**geog'rapher** *n.*-**geograph'ical** *a.*-**geograph'ically** *adv.*

geol'ogy *n.* science of the earth's crust, the rocks, their strata, etc.—**geol'ogist** *n.*—**geolog'ical** *a.*—**geolog'ically** *adv.*—**geol'ogise** *v.i.* to practise geology.

geom'etry *n.* the series of dimensions, as lines, surfaces and solids.—**geometri'cian** *n.*—**geomet'rical** *a.*

geon'omy *n.* the science of the physical laws relating to the earth.

geo'politics *n.* the study of the relationship between the geography of a nation and its political life.

georgette' (jor-jet') *n.* a fine semi-transparent fabric.

geotro'pism *n.* the determination by the force of gravity of the direction taken by an organism.—**geotropic** *a.*—**geotropically** *adv.*

gera'nium *n.* a genus of plants with fruit resembling a crane's bill.

germ *n.* the rudiment of a new organism, of animal or plant; microbe; elementary thing.—**germ'icide** *n.* substance for destroying disease-germs.—**germici'dal** *a.*—**germ'inate** *v.i.* to sprout.—*v.t.* cause to sprout.—**germina'tion** *n.*

ger'man *a.* of the same parents (only in *cousin german*, first cousin).

germane' *a.* relevant.

gerryman'der *v.t.* to manipulate a constituency to benefit one side.

Gesta'po (ges-tah'-) *n.* Nazi political secret police which maintained a spy system in Germany and abroad.

gesta'tion *n.* the carrying of young in the womb between conception and birth.
gestic'ulate *v.i.* expressive or lively movements accompanying speech.—**gesticula'tion** *n.*—**ges'ture** *n.* a movement to convey an idea or feeling.
get (g-) *v.t.* to obtain, procure, earn; cause to go or come; bring into a position or state; induce; (*in perf. tense*) to be in possession of, to have (to do).—*v.i.* to succeed in coming or going, reach, attain; become (**got** *p.t.*—**gott'en, got** *p.p.*—**gett'ing** *pres. p.*).—**get'away** *n.* (*sl.*) escape; evasion.
gew'gaw (g-) a gaudy toy, plaything.
gey'ser (gīz-, gēz-) *n.* a hot spring throwing up a spout of water from time to time; an apparatus for heating water.
ghast'ly (gȧ-) *a.* horrible, shocking; death-like, pallid; grim.—*adv.* horribly.
gher'kin (g-) *n.* a small cucumber.
ghett'o (g-) *n.* a Jews' quarter (**ghett'i** (-ē), **ghett'os** (-ōz) *pl.*).
ghil'gai (gil'-) *n.* in Australia, a depression in the land where water collects.
ghost (gō-) *n.* spirit, dead person reappearing; semblance.—**ghost'ly** *a.*—**ghost'-image** *n.* (television) a double image.
ghoul (gōōl) *n.* in Eastern tales, a spirit preying on corpses.—**ghoul'ish** *a.*
G.I. abbreviation for Government Issue, stamped on U.S. military equipment; *n.* (*sl.*) an American soldier.—*a.*
gi'ant *n.* a human being of superhuman size; a very tall person, plant, etc.—*a.* huge.—**gigant'ic** *a.* enormous, huge.
gibb'er (j-, g-) *v.i.* to make meaningless sounds with the mouth, jabber, chatter.
gibb'er (gib'-) *n.* in Australia, a stone, rock.—**gibb'er-gun'yah** *n.* aboriginal word for cave hollowed out beneath rocks; aboriginal cave dwelling.
gibb'erish (g-) *n.* meaningless speech.
gibb'et *n.* gallows on which executed criminal was hung.—*v.t.* hang on gibbet; expose to public contempt.
gibb'on (g-) *n.* a long-armed ape.
gibb'ous (g-) *a.* convex; of the moon, with bright part greater than a semicircle.—**gibbos'ity** *n.*
gibe, jibe *v.i.* to utter taunts.—*v.t.* to taunt.—*n.* a jeer, sneer.
gib'let *n.* (in *pl.*) the portion of a fowl, goose, etc., removed before cooking.
gidd'y (g-) *a.* dizzy, feeling a swimming in the head; flighty (**-ier** *comp.*—**-iest** *sup.*).—**gidd'ily** *adv.*—**gidd'iness** *n.*
Syn. light-headed, gyratory, inconstant, changeable, wild, thoughtless. *Ant.* steady, serious, sober, reliable.
gift (g-) *n.* a thing given, a present; a faculty, power.—*v.t.* to endow or present (with).—**gift'ed** *a.* talented.
gig (g-) *n.* a light two-wheeled carriage; a light ship's boat; a rowing-boat.
gigant'ic (jī-) *a.* huge.
gig'gle (g-) *v.i.* to laugh foolishly or uncontrollably.—*n.* such a laugh.
gig'olo (zhig'-) *n.* professional male dancing partner (**-los** (-lōz) *pl.*).
Gilbert'ian *a.* whimsical, like situations in a Gilbert and Sullivan opera.
gild (g-) *v.t.* to overlay with gold (**gild'ed** *p.t.*—**gilt** or **gild'ed** *p.p.*).—**gilt** *a.* gilded.—*n.* the layer of gold put on.
gill (j-) *n.* a measure, one fourth of a pint.
gill (g-) *n.* breathing organ in fishes; glen; flesh below a person's jaws and ears.-**gill-bird** *n.* Australia, wattle bird.
gill'ie, ghillie (g-) *n.* a sportsman's attendant in Scotland.
gill'yflower *n.* the clove-scented pink; other similar scented flowers.
gilt *see* **gild.**—**gilt-edged security** *n.* originally Government stock, now any stock resembling this in its soundness.
gim'bals *n. pl.* a contrivance of rings, etc., for keeping a thing level at sea.
gim'crack *a.* flimsy, trumpery.
gim'let (g-) *n.* a boring tool, usually with a screw point.
gin *n.* a snare, trap; a kind of crane; a machine for separating cotton and seeds.—*v.t.* to snare; to treat (cotton) in a gin.
gin *n.* spirit flavoured with juniper.
gin *n.* an Australian aboriginal woman.
gin'ger *n.* plant with hot-tasting root used in cooking, etc.; the root; spirit, mettle; reddish-yellow colour.—**gin'gerbread** *n.* cake flavoured with ginger.—**ginger-beer** or **wine,** beverages so flavoured.—**gin'gery** *a.*
gin'gerly *adv.* cautiously.
ging'ham (-am) *n.* patterned cotton or linen cloth made from dyed yarn.
gip'sy, gyp'sy *n.* one of a wandering race usually living by basket-making, fortune-telling, etc.
giraffe' *n.* an African ruminant animal, with spotted coat and very long neck.
gird (g-) *v.t.* to put a belt round; fasten clothes thus; belt on a sword; encircle (**girt, gird'ed** *p.t.* and *p.p.*).—**gird'er** *n.* beam supporting joists; iron or steel beam.—**gir'dle** *n.* a belt.—*v.t.* to surround.—*v.i.* to gibe.—*n.* a gibe.
girl (g-) female child; young unmarried woman.—**girl'hood** *n.*—**girl'ish** *a.*
girt *p.t.* and *p.p.* of **gird.**
girth (g-) *n.* strap fixing saddle on a horse; measurement round a thing.—*v.t.* to surround, or secure, with a girth.
gist *n.* substance, essential meaning.
give (g-) *v.t.* to bestow; confer ownership of, make a present of; deliver; impart; assign; yield, supply; make over; cause to have.—*v.i.* to yield, give way (**gave** *p.t.*—**giv'en** *p.p.*—**giv'ing** *pres. p.*).—*n.* yielding, elasticity.
gizz'ard (g-) *n.* a bird's second stomach for grinding food.
gla'brous *a.* smooth; even surface.

gla'cé *a.* iced, or with a surface like ice as confectionery; polished, glossy.
gla'cier (-ā-, -a-) *n.* slow-moving mass of ice in valleys between high mountains.—**gla'cial** *a.* of ice, or of glaciers; crystallised.—**gla'ciated** *a.* covered by ice in glacier form.—**glacia'tion** *n.*
gla'cis (-sē) *n.* the outer sloping bank of a fortification; a gentle slope.
glad *a.* pleased; happy; giving joy.—*v.t.* to make glad.—**gladd'en** *v.t.*—**glad'ly** *adv.*—**glad'ness** *n.*—**glad'some** *a.*—**glad hand'** *n.* a welcome.
glade *n.* a clear space in a wood.
glad'iator *n.* a trained fighter in the arenas of ancient Rome.
gladio'lus *n.* a flowering plant of the iris family (-**li** (lī), -**luses** *pl.*).
glad'stone *a.* in **gladstone bag** a light portmanteau.
glam'our *n.* magic, charm.—**glam'-orous** *a.* evoking enchantment.
glance *v.i.* to glide off something struck; pass quickly; allude, touch; look rapidly.—*v.t.* direct (the eyes) rapidly.—*n.* brief look; sudden oblique movement or blow.
gland *n.* an organ separating constituents of the blood, for use or ejection.—**gland'ular** *a.*—**gland'ers** *n.* a contagious disease of horses.
glare (-ār) *v.i.* to shine with oppressive brightness; look fiercely.—*n.* a dazzling brightness; a fierce look (**gla'ring** *pres. p.*).
glass (-à-) *n.* hard transparent substance made by fusing sand with soda, potash, etc.; glassware; glass drinking vessel; its contents; a lens; a telescope, barometer, or other instrument.—*pl.* spectacles.—**glass'y** *a.*—**glass'ily** *adv.*—**glass'-i-ness** *n.*—**glaze** *v.t.* to furnish with glass; cover with glassy substance or glaze.—*v.i.* to become glassy.—*n.* a transparent coating; substance used to give this; glossy surface.—**gla'zier** *n.* one who glazes windows.
glau'coma (glaw'-) *n.* a serious eye disease.
gleam *n.* a flash of light.—*v.i.* to give out gleams.
glean *v.t.* and *i.* to gather, pick up, after reapers in cornfield; pick up (facts, etc.).
glebe *n.* land forming part of a clergyman's benefice; the soil.
glee *n.* mirth, merriment; a musical composition for three or more voices.—**glee'ful** *a.*—**glee'fully** *adv.*
glen *n.* a narrow valley.
glengarr'y *n.* a woollen cap woven in one piece, with ribbons at the back.
glib *a.* fluent; more voluble than sincere; specious.—**glib'ly** *adv.*—**glib'ness** *n.*
glide *v.i.* to move smoothly and continuously; go stealthily or gradually; of an aeroplane, to move downwards with engines throttled back.—*n.* smooth, silent movement; (music) sounds made in passing from tone to tone.—**gli'der** *n.* one, that which glides; aeroplane without mechanical propulsion.
glimm'er *v.i.* to shine faintly or flickeringly—*n.* such light.—**glimpse** *n.* a momentary view; a passing flash or appearance.—*v.t.* to catch a glimpse of.
glint *v.i.* and *t.* flash, glitter.—*n.* glitter.
glissade' *n.* a slide, usually on the feet, down a slope of ice.—*v.i.* to slide thus.
glis'ten (-is'n) *v.i.* glitter, sparkle.
glitt'er *v.i.* to shine with bright quivering light, to sparkle.—*n.* such light.
gloa'ming *n.* evening twilight, dusk.
gloat *v.i.* to feast the eyes; to rejoice, exult, unpleasantly.
globe *n.* round body, sphere; a heavenly sphere, *esp.* the earth; a sphere with a map of the earth or the stars; a lamp-shade, fish-bowl, etc.—**globe'-trotter** *n.* sight-seeing traveller.—**glob'ule** *n.* small round particle; a drop.—**glob'ular** *a.* globe-shaped, spherical.
gloom *n.* darkness; melancholy, depression.—*v.i.* to look sullen, or dark.—*v.t.* to make dark or dismal.—**gloom'y** *a.*—**gloom'ily** *adv.*—**gloom'iness** *n.*
Syn. sadness, moroseness, sullenness. *Ant.* joy, happiness, brightness, light.
glo'ry *n.* renown, honour, fame; splendour; heavenly bliss; exalted state.—*v.i.* to take pride (in) (**glo'ried** *p.t.* and *p.p.*—**glo'rying** *pres. p.*).—**glo'rify** *v.t.* invest with glory (**glo'rified** *p.t.* and *p.p.*—**glo'rifying** *pres. p.*).—**glorifica'-tion** *n.*—**glo'rious** *a.*—**glo'riously** *adv.*
Syn. nobleness, honour, magnificence, fame, praise. *Ant.* insignificance, obscurity, meanness.
gloss *n.* a surface shine.—*v.t.* to put a gloss on.—**gloss'y** *a.*—**gloss'iness** *n.*
gloss *n.* marginal interpretation of a word; comment, explanation.—*v.t.* interpret; comment; explain away.—**gloss'-ary** *n.* dictionary of special words.—**glossi'tis** *n.* inflammation of tongue.
glott'is *n.* opening at top of windpipe.
glove (-uv) *n.* a covering for the hand.—**glov'er** *n.* dealer in gloves.
glow (-ō) *v.i.* to give light and heat without flames; shine; be, or look hot; burn with emotion.—*n.* shining heat; feeling of bodily heat; warmth of colour; ardour.—**glow'-worm** *n.* female insect which gives out a green light.
glow'er *v.i.* to look angrily.
gloze *v.t.* to explain away, palliate.—*v.i.* use fair words.
glu'cose *n.* a sugar obtained from fruits.
glue (-ōō) *n.* a hard substance made from horns, hoofs, etc., and used warm as a cement.—*v.t.* to fasten with glue.—**glu'ey** *a.*—**glue-pot** *n.* in Australia, bad place in road where vehicles are bogged.
glum *a.* sullen, frowning, dejected.
glut *v.t.* to feed, gratify to the full or to excess; overstock.—*n.* excessive supply.

glu'ten *n.* the viscid nitrogenous substance found in grain.—**glu'tinous** *a.*
glutt'on *n.* one who eats too much, a greedy person; one eagerly devouring. —**glutt'onous** *a.*—**glutt'ony** *n.*
gly'cerine, gly'cerin (glis'er-ēn) *n.* a colourless, sweet liquid obtained from oils and used in medicine and explosives.
gnarled (narld) *a.* knotty, twisted.
gnash (n-) *v.t.* or *i.* to grind (the teeth).
gnat (n-) *n.* small blood-sucking fly.
gnaw (n-) *v.t.* bite steadily, wear away.
gneiss (n-) *n.* a crystalline rock consisting of quartz, feldspar and mica.
gnome (n-) *n.* a subterranean goblin.
gno'mic (nō-) *a.* sententious, pithy.
gno'mon (nō-) *n.* the pin or rod which casts the shadow on a sundial.
gnos'tic (n-) *a.* of knowledge; having special knowledge; *n. pl.* an esoteric sect.
gnu (nū) *n.* a South African antelope.
go *v.i.* move; proceed; depart; elapse; be kept, put, be able to put; result, contribute to a result; tend to; become (**went** *p.t.*—**gone** *p.p.*).—*n.* a going; energy; vigour.—**go'er** *n.*—he **goes.**
goad *n.* a spiked stick for driving cattle. —*v.t.* to drive with a goad; urge on.
goal *n.* end of race; purpose, destination, object; posts between which ball is to be driven at football, hockey, etc.
goann'a *n.* in Australia, the popular name for a large Australian lizard; corruption of iguana.
go'-ashore *n.* in Australia, an iron cauldron or pot with three feet.
goat *n.* cloven-hooved animal with long hair, horns and beard.—**goat'-herd** *n.* one who tends goats.—**goat'ee** *n.* a beard like a goat's.—**to get (one's) goat**, to make (one) angry.
gob *n.* a lump, mouthful.—**gobb'et** *n.* a lump of food.—**gob'ble** *v.t.* to eat hastily. —*v.i.* of a turkey.
gob'let *n.* a drinking-cup.
gob'lin *n.* mischievous elemental.
God *n.* the Supreme Being; superhuman being having supernatural power; an object of worship, an idol.—**godd'ess** *fem.*—**god'father** *n.*, **god'mother** *fem.* a sponsor at baptism.—**god'child** *n.* one considered in relation to a godparent —**god'head** *n.* the divine nature.—**god'-fearing** *a.* religious, good.—**god'-forsaken** *a.* devoid of merit, dismal.—**god'less** *a.* —**god'ly** *a.* religious.—**god'liness** *n.*—**god'send** *n.* sudden, unexpected and welcome stroke of luck.
goff'er *v.t.* to make wavy, crimp with hot irons.—*n.* goffering iron.
gog'gle *v.i.* to roll the eyes; squint.—*a.* rolling, sticking out (only of eyes).—*n.* in *pl.* spectacles to protect the eyes from glare, dust, etc.
gold (gō-) *n.* yellow precious metal; coins of this, wealth; *fig.* beautiful or precious material or thing; the colour of gold.—*a.* of, like, or having the colour of, gold.—**gold'en** *a.*—**gold-dig'ger** *n.* (*sl.*) woman skilful in extracting money, etc., from men.—**gold'-field** *n.* place where deposits of gold are found.—**gold'finch** *n.* gold-winged song bird.—**gold'fish** *n.* red Chinese carp.—**gold'-smith** *n.* worker in gold.
golf (golf or gof) *n.* a game in which a small hard ball is struck with clubs.—*v.i.* to play this game.—**golf'er** *n.*
goll'iwog *n.* a grotesque black doll.
golosh *see* **galosh.**
gon'ad *n.* in biology, an organ that produces sex cells.
gon'dola *n.* a Venetian canal-boat; a car suspended from an airship.—**gondolier'** *n.* rower of gondola.
gong *n.* a metal disk which resounds as a bell when struck; anything so used; (*service sl.*) a decoration.
good *a.* commendable; right; proper; excellent; virtuous; kind; safe; adequate; sound; valid (**bett'er** *comp.*—**best** *sup.*).—*n.* that which is good; well-being; profit.—*pl.* property; wares.—**good'ness** *n.*—**good'ly** *a.* handsome; of considerable size.—**good-will'** *n.* kindly feeling; heartiness; right of trading as a recognised successor.—**good hu'mour** *n.* kindliness.—**good'y** *n.* a sweetmeat.—*a.* obtrusively, primly or weakly virtuous (also **good'y-good'y**).
good-bye' *interj.* farewell.
goof' *n.* (*sl.*) simpleton.
goo'gly *n.* in cricket, a ball that "breaks" in an unexpected direction.
goo'gol *n.* (*maths*) one, followed by a hundred zeros.
goose *n.* large web-footed bird; its flesh; a simpleton; a tailor's smoothing iron (**gan'der** *masc.* **geese** *pl.*).—**goose'-flesh** *n.* a bristling state of the skin due to cold or fright.—**goose'-step** *n.* a formal parade step.
goose'berry (-z-) *n.* a thorny shrub; its eatable berry; a chaperon to lovers.
go'pher *n.* N. America, popular name for various species of burrowing rodents.
gore *n.* blood.—triangular piece of cloth inserted to shape a garment. *v.t.* to pierce with horns;—**go'ry** *a.*
gorge *n.* inside of the throat; surfeit; narrow opening between hills.—*v.i.* to feed greedily.—*v.t.* to devour greedily.
gorge'ous (-jus) *a.* splendid, showy, dazzling. *Syn.* grand, imposing, magnificent. *Ant.* sordid, mean, drab, plain.
gorgonzo'la *n.* a rich cheese.
gorill'a *n.* largest anthropoid ape.
gor'mandise *v.t.* to eat like a glutton.
gorse *n.* a prickly shrub.
gory *see* **gore.**
gos'hawk *n.* a large short-winged hawk.
gos'ling (-z-) *n.* a young goose.
gos'pel *n.* the tidings preached by

Jesus; record of His life in the New Testament; guiding principle.

goss'amer *n.* a filmy substance of spiders' web floating in calm air or spread on grass; delicate gauze.—*a.* light, flimsy.—**goss'amery** *a.*

goss'ip *n.* idle talk, *esp.* regardless of fact; one who talks thus; formerly, a familiar friend.—*v.i.* talk gossip.

Goth'ic *a.* of Goths; barbarous; in architecture, pointed arch style common in Europe 12th–16th cent.; of type, German; black-letter.

gouge (gowj) *n.* a chisel with a curved cutting edge.—*v.i.* to cut with a gouge.

gou'lash (goo'-) *n.* a stew of beef or veal; in Bridge, a re-deal in which the cards are left in order of suit.

gourd (gord, gōōrd) *n.* fleshy many-seeded fruit (e.g. melon); the rind of this as a vessel.

gour'mand (gōō-) *a.* greedy.—*n.* a lover of delicate food.—**gour'met** *n.* a connoisseur of wine or food.

gout (gowt) *n.* disease, *esp.* of the smaller joints; a drop, splash.—**gout'y** *a.*

gov'ern (guv-) *v.t.* to rule, direct, guide, control; serve as a precedent for; be followed by (a grammatical case, etc.). —**gov'ernable** *a.*—**gov'ernance** *n.*—**gov'ernor** *n.* ruler.—**gov'erness** *n.* a woman teacher, *esp.* in a private household.—**gov'ernment** *n.*—**governmen'tal** *a.*

gown *n.* a woman's frock; an official robe.—*v.t.* attire in gown.

grab *v.t.* to grasp suddenly, snatch.—*n.* a sudden clutch; greedy proceedings.

grace *n.* charm, attractiveness; easy and refined motion, manners, etc.; ornament, accomplishment; favour; divine favour; short prayer before or after a meal; title of duke or archbishop.—*v.t.* to add grace to, honour.—**grace'ful** *a.*—**grace'fully** *adv.*—**grace'less** *a.* shameless, depraved.—**gra'cious** *a.* indulgent, condescending.—**gra'ciously** *adv.*

grade *n.* a step or stage; degree of rank, etc.; slope; N. America, a road, *esp.* a new one.—*v.t.* to arrange in classes.—**grada'tion** *n.* series of degrees or steps; each of them; arrangement in steps; insensible passing from one shade, etc., to another.—**gra'dient** *n.* degree of slope. —**grad'ual** *a.* taking place by degrees; moving step by step; slow and steady; not steep.—**grad'ually** *adv.*—**grad'uate** *v.i.* to take a university degree.—*v.t.* to divide into degrees, mark or arrange according to a scale.—*n.* holder of a university degree.—**gradua'tion** *n.*—**grade-crossing** *n.* America, a level crossing.—**to make the grade** to accomplish a task satisfactorily.

graft *n.* a shoot of a plant set in a stock of another plant; the process.—*v.t.* to insert (a shoot) in another stock; to transplant (living tissue in surgery).—*v.i.* to toil; swindle.—*n.* manual work; self-advancement or profit by unfair means, political influence, etc.

grail *n.* (usually Holy Grail) the platter or cup used by Jesus at the Last Supper.

grain *n.* a seed or fruit of a cereal plant; wheat and allied plants; in N. America, wheat; a small hard particle; a unit of weight, 1-7000th of the pound avoirdupois; texture; arrangement of fibres. —*v.t.* to paint in imitation of wood grain.—**grai'ny** *a.*—**grain elevator**, building in which grain is collected, sorted and prepared for shipment.

gram *see* **gramme.**

gram'arye *n.* magic.

graminiv'orous *a.* grass-eating.

gramm'ar *n.* science of the structure and usages of a language; a book on this; correct use of words.—**grammar'ian** (-ėr-) *n.*—**grammat'ical** *a.*—**grammat'ically** *adv.*-**gramm'atise** *v.t.*-**gramm'ar-school** *n.* secondary school.

gramme *n.* unit of weight in metric system, 15.432 grains troy.

gram'ophone *n.* an instrument for recording and reproducing sounds.

gram'pus *n.* a blowing and spouting sea-creature of the whale family.

granadill'a *n.* Australia and S. Africa, large fruit of a plant allied to the passion fruit; the vine itself.

gran'ary *n.* a storehouse for grain.

grand *a.* chief; splendid, magnificent; lofty; imposing; final.—*n.* (U.S.) (*sl.*) 1,000 dollars.—**grand'ly** *adv.*—**grandee'** *n.* Spanish or Portuguese nobleman.—**grand'eur** (-dyer) *n.* nobility; magnificence; dignity.—**grand'father** *n.* **grand'mother** *fem.* parents of parents.—**grand'son** *n.* **grand'daughter** *fem.* **grand'child** *n.* children of children.—**grandil'oquent** *a.* pompous in speech.—**grandil'oquently** *adv.*-**grandil'oquence** *n.*-**grand'iose** *a.* imposing; planned on a great scale.

grange *n.* a granary; a country-house.

gran'ite (-it) *n.* a hard crystalline rock.

grant *v.t.* to consent to fulfil (a request); permit; bestow, give formally; admit. —*n.* a granting; a thing granted.—**grant'or** *n.*—**grant'ee** *n.*

gran'ule *n.* a small grain.—**gran'ular** *a.* of, or like, grains.—**gran'ulate** *v.t.* to form into grains.—*v.i.* to take the form of grains; of a wound, to begin to grow in small prominences.—**granula'tion** *n.*

grape *n.* the fruit of the vine.—**grape'shot** *n.* pellets fired in clusters from gun.

grape'fruit *n.* fruit allied to orange.

graph'ic *a.* relating to writing, drawing, painting, etc.; vividly descriptive.—**graph** *n.* a graphic formula, a diagram showing symbolically a series of connections.—**graph'ically** *adv.*—**graphol'ogy** *n.* the study of handwriting.—**graph'ite** *n.* form of carbon (used in pencils).

grap'nel *n.* iron hooked instrument; for seizing; small anchor with several flukes.

grap'ple *n.* a grapnel; a grip; contest at close quarters.—*v.t.* to seize firmly.—*v.i.* contend (with), come to grips (**grap'pling** *pr. p.* **grap'pled** *p.t./p.p.*).

grasp (-å-) *v.t.* to seize firmly; understand.—*v.i.* to clutch (at).—*n.* firm hold; mastery.—**gras'ping** *a.* greedy.

grass (-å-) *n.* herbage, plants grown for cattle to eat, to cover lawns, etc.; a plant of this kind; in Australia, any fodder plant whether a true grass or not.—*v.t.* to cover with turf; to put down on grass.—**grass'hopper** *n.* a jumping, chirping insect.—**grass-wid'ow** *n.* a wife whose husband is away from her.—**grass-widower** *n.*—**grass'y** *a.*

grate *n.* a fireplace, a frame of bars for holding fuel; a framework of crossed bars (also **gra'ting** *n.*).—*v.t.* to rub into small bits with something rough.—*v.i.* to rub with harsh noise; to be irritating.—**gra'ter** *n.* (**gra'ted** *p.t.* and *p.p.*).

grate'ful *a.* thankful; pleasing.—**grate'fully** *adv.*—**grat'ify** *v.t.* to do a favour to; indulge; pay (**-ified** *p.t.* and *p.p.*—**-ifying** *pres. p.*).—**gratifica'tion** *n.*—**grat'itude** *n.* sense of thankfulness for something received.—**gra'tis** *adv.* and *a.* free, for nothing.—**gratu'itous** *a.* given free, done for nothing; uncalled for.—**gratu'ity** *n.* a gift of money, *esp.* to members of the armed forces on demobilisation.

Syn. agreeable, acceptable, delicious. *Ant.* ungrateful, thankless, harsh.

gratin' (grå-tan') *n.* a method of cooking to form a light crust; a dish so cooked.

grava'men *n.* a grievance; weightiest part (**gravam'ina, grava'mens** *pl.*).

grave *n.* hole dug for corpse; death.

grave *v.t.* to carve, engrave (**gravel** (gravd) *p.t.*—**graved** or **gra'ven** *p.p.*).

grave *a.* serious, weighty; dignified, solemn; plain, dark in colour, deep in note.—**grave'ly** *adv.*

grave *v.t.* to clean (a ship's bottom) (**graved** (gravd) *p.t.* and *p.p.*).—**gra'ving-dock** *n.* a place for this.

grav'el *n.* small stones, coarse sand; urinary crystals; a disease due to this.—*v.t.* to cover with gravel; puzzle, embarrass, vex.—**grav'elly** *a.*

grav'igrade *a.* walking with heavy steps.—*n.* an animal that walks heavily.

grav'ity *n.* importance; seriousness; heaviness; the force of attraction of one body for another, *esp.* of objects to the earth.—**grav'itate** *v.i.* move by gravity; sink, settle down.—**gravita'tion** *n.*

gra'vy *n.* juices from meat in cooking; a dressing or sauce for food (**gra'vies.** *pl.*).

gray, grey *a.* between black and white in colour, as ashes or lead; clouded; dismal; turning white; aged.—*n.* grey colour; a grey horse.—**gray'ling** *n.* a gray freshwater fish.

graze *v.i.* and *t.* to feed on grass.—**gra'zier** *n.* one who grazes cattle.

graze *v.t.* to touch lightly in passing; to abrade the skin thus.—*v.i.* to move so as to touch lightly.—*n.* a grazing (**gra'zed** *p.t.* and *p.p.*).

grease (-ēs) *n.* soft melted fat of animals; thick oil as a lubricant.—*v.t.* to apply grease to.—**grea'sy** *a.*—**grea'sily** *adv.*–**grea'siness** *n.*–**grea'ser** *n.*–**grease'-gun** *n.* appliance for injecting grease into machinery, etc.—**grea'se paint** *n.* heavy make-up used by actors.

great (-āt) *a.* large, big; important; pre-eminent, distinguished.—as *prefix*, indicates a degree further removed in relationship, e.g. **great-grand'father** *n.*—**great'ly** *adv.*—**great'ness** *n.*—**great'-coat** *n.* overcoat, *esp.* military.

Syn. numerous, superior, commanding, strong, powerful, noble, eminent, weighty. *Ant.* small, insignificant, trivial, unimportant, inconsiderable.

greave (-ēv) *n.* armour for the lower leg.

grebe *n.* fresh-water diving bird.

greed'y *a.* gluttonous, over-eager for food, wealth, etc.—**greed** *n.*—**greed'ily** *adv.*—**greed'iness** *n.*—**greed'ier** *comp.*

green *a.* colour between blue and yellow, coloured like growing grass, emerald, etc.; unripe, inexperienced; easily deceived.—*n.* the colour; a piece of grass-covered land.—*pl.* green vegetables.–**green'ery** *n.* vegetation.–**green'gage** *n.* a kind of plum.—**green'grocer** *n.* a dealer in vegetables and fruit.—**green-gro'cery** *n.*—**green'hide** *n.* in Australia, untanned hide; raw-hide.—*pl.* in S. Africa, undried, salted hides ready for export.—**green'horn** *n.* simpleton.—**green'house** *n.* a glass house for rearing plants.—**green'ish** *a.*—**green'-room** *n.* room for actors off stage.—**green'stone** *n.* a rock found in New Zealand used for making jewellery.—**green'sward** *n.* turf.—**green'wood** *n.* woodlands in summer.

greet *v.t.* to salute; hail; receive; meet.—**greet'ing** *n.* salutation.

gregar'ious (-ēr'-) *a.* living in flocks; fond of company, sociable.

grem'lin *n.* R.A.F. (*sl.*) a sportive air elemental causing faults in airplanes.

grenade' *n.* small bomb, thrown by hand or shot from a rifle.—**grenadier'** *n.* soldier of the Grenadier Guards.

grey *see* **gray.**

grey'hound *n.* swift, slender dog used in coursing and racing.—**greyhound racing** *n.* racing of greyhounds on enclosed tracks as public spectacle sport, with mechanical hare as decoy.

grid *n.* frame of bars; car's luggage bracket; in wireless, electrode in a thermionic valve.–**the grid,** in electricity, system of main transmission lines.

grid'iron *n.* a cooking utensil of metal bars for broiling.—**grid'dle** *n.* a flat round iron plate for cooking.

grief (-ēf) *n.* deep sorrow (**griefs** *pl.*).—**grie-vance** *n.* real or imaginary wrong.—**grieve** *v.i.* to feel grief.—*v.t.* to cause grief to.—**grie'vous** *a.* painful, oppressive, severe.—**grievance committee,** works committee which meets employers to discuss grievances.

griff'in, griff'on, gryph'on *n.* a fabulous monster with eagle's head and wings and lion's body.

grig *n.* a cricket; a small eel.

grill *n.* a gridiron; food cooked on one. —*v.t.* and *i.* to broil on a grill.—*v.t.* U.S. (*col.*) cross-question, *esp.* by police.—**grill'room** *n.* place where food is grilled and served.—**gril'ling** *a.* very hot.

grill'e *n.* grating, screen.

grilse *n.* a young salmon that has only been once to the sea.

grim *a.* stern; of stern or harsh aspect; joyless.—**grim'ly** *adv.*

grimace' *n.* a wry face.—*v.i.* make one.

grime *n.* soot, dirt.—**gri'my** *a.*

grin *v.i.* to smile.—*n.* an act of grinning (**grinned'** *p.t.* and *p.p.*).

grind (-ī-) *v.t.* to crush to powder between hard surfaces; oppress; make sharp or smooth; grate.—*v.i.* to perform action of grinding; to work (*esp.* study) hard; grate (**ground** *p.t./p.p.*).—*n.* action of grinding; hard work.–**grind'-stone** *n.* a revolving disk of stone for grinding knives, etc.—**grind'er** *n.*

gring'o (gring'gō) *n.* in Spanish Amer., contemptuous name for a foreigner, *esp.* Englishman (**-os** (-ōz) *pl.*).

grip *n.* a firm hold, grasp; grasping power; mastery; a handle; suit-case or travelling-bag.—*v.t.* to grasp or hold tightly (**gripped'** *p.t.* and *p.p.*).

gripe *v.t.* to grip; oppress; afflict with pains of colic.—*n.* grip.—*pl.* colic pains.
Syn. to clutch, compress, squeeze, tighten, pinch, distress. *Ant.* to relax, release, hold or touch lightly.

gris'ly (-z-) *a.* grim, causing terror.

grist *n.* corn to be ground; profit.

gris'tle (gris'l) *n.* cartilage, tough flexible tissue.—**gris'tly** *a.*

grit *n.* particles of sand; coarse sandstone; courage.—*v.i.* to make a grinding sound.—*v.t.* grind (teeth).—**gritt'y** *a.*—**gritt'iness** *n.* (**grit'ted** *p.t.* and *p.p.*).

grizz'ly *a.* grey-haired, grey.—**grizz'ly bear** *n.* a large ferocious N. American bear.—**griz'zled** *a.* grizzly.

groan *v.i.* sound of grief, pain or disapproval.—*n.* the sound.

groats *n. pl.* hulled grain, *esp.* oats.

gro'cer *n.* dealer in domestic stores.—**gro'cery** *n.* his trade, or shop.—**gro'-ceries** *n. pl.* his wares.

grog *n.* spirit (*esp.* rum) and water.—**grogg'y** *a.* unsteady, shaky, weak.

grog'ram *n.* a coarse fabric of silk, mohair, etc.

groin *n.* depression between belly and thigh; edge made by intersection of two vaults; a structure of timber, etc., to stop shifting of sand on sea beach.—*v.t.* to build with, or supply with, groins.

groom *n.* servant in charge of horses; a bridegroom; an officer in a royal household.—*v.t.* to tend, curry (a horse); make neat.—**grooms'man** *n.* friend attending a bridegroom.

groove *n.* a channel, hollow, *esp.* cut by a tool as a guide, or to receive a ridge; a rut, routine.—*v.t.* to cut a groove in.

grope *v.i.* to feel about, search blindly.

gross (-ōs) *a.* rank; overfed; flagrant; total, not net; solid; coarse; indecent. —*n.* twelve dozen.—**gross'ly** *adv.*

grot *n.* a grotto.

grotesque' (-esk) *n.* a fantastic decorative painting; a comically distorted figure.—*a.* in grotesque style; distorted; absurd.—**grotesque'ly** *adv.*

grott'o *n.* a cave (**-os, -oes** (-ōz) *pl.*).

grouch' *n.* grumble; (U.S.) (*sl.*) a person perpetually grumbling.

ground (-ow-) *n.* bottom of the sea; reason, motive; surface or coating to work on with paint; surface of the earth; position, area, on this; a special area.—*pl.* dregs; enclosed land round a house. —*v.t.* to establish; instruct (in elementary principles); place on the ground.—*v.i.* to run ashore.—**ground'less** *a.* without reason—**ground'nut** *n.* S. African earth nut.—**groundwork** *n.* foundation.

ground'sel (-ow-) *n.* a weed used as a food for cage-birds.

group (-ōōp) *n.* number of persons or things near together, or placed or classified together; a class; two or more figures forming one artistic design. —**Group Captain** *n.* commissioned rank in R.A.F. equivalent to captain in navy, colonel in army.—*v.t.* to arrange in a group.—*v.i.* to fall into a group.

grouse (-ows) *n.* a game-bird (**grouse** *pl.*).—*v.i.* to grumble.—**grous'er** *n.*

grout (-owt) *n.* thin fluid mortar; fine plaster.—*v.i.* to fill with this.

grove *n.* a small wood.

grov'el *v.i.* lie prone; abase oneself (**grov'elling** *pr. p.*—**grovelled** *p.t./p.p.*).

grow (-ō) *v.i.* to increase in size, height, etc.; flourish; be produced; become by degrees.—*v.t.* produce by cultivation.—**grow'er** *n.*—**growth** *n.* growing; increase; what has grown or is growing.
Syn. extend, thrive, swell, expand. *Ant.* diminish, shrink, wane, lessen.

growl *v.i.* to make a low guttural sound of anger; murmur.—*n.* such sound.

groyne *see* **groin.**

grub *v.t.* to dig superficially; root up.—*v.i.* to dig, rummage; plod.—*n.* insect's larva; (*sl.*) food.—**grubb'y** *a.* dirty.

grudge *v.t.* to be unwilling to give or allow.—*n.* a feeling of ill-will, resentment.—**grudg'ingly** *a.*
gru'el *n.* food of oatmeal, etc., boiled in milk or water.—*v.t.* (*sl.*) thrash.
grue'some (grōō'-) *a.* fearful, horrible.
gruff *a.* surly, rough in manner or voice.
grum'ble *v.i.* to make growling sounds; murmur, complain.—*n.* low growl; complaint.—**grum'bler** *n.*—**grumb'ling** *n.*
grump'y *a.* ill-tempered, surly.—**grump'ily** *adv.*—**grump'iness** *n.*
grunt *v.i.* of a hog, to make its characteristic sound.—*n.* a hog's sound; a noise like this.—**grunt'er** *n.*
gru'yère *n.* a Swiss cheese.
grys'bok *n.* a small S. African antelope.
gua'no (gwȧ'-) *n.* sea-fowl manure (**-nos** (nōz) *pl.*).—*v.t.* manure with it.
guarantee' (ga-) *n.* giver of guaranty or security; guaranty.—*v.t.* to answer for fulfilment, genuineness or permanence of; secure (to) a person; secure (against risk, etc.) (**-teed'** *p.t./p.p.*—**-tee'ing** *pres. p.*).–**guar'anty** *n.* a written or other undertaking to answer for performance of obligation.—**guar'antor** *n.*
guard (ga-) *n.* posture of defence; watch; protector; a sentry; soldiers protecting anything; official in charge of a train; a protection; defence.—*pl.* certain British regiments.—*v.t.* to protect, defend.—*v.i.* to be careful.—**guard'ian** *n.* keeper, protector; person having custody of an infant, etc.—**guard'ianship** *n.*—**guard'room** *n.* a room for a guard or prisoners.
gua'va (gwȧ'-) *n.* tropical tree with an acid fruit used to make jelly; the fruit.
gudge'on *n.* a small fresh-water fish.
guer'don (g-) *n.* reward.
guern'sey *n.* a knitted jumper.
guerrill'a (g-) *n.* one carrying on irregular warfare as one of a band.
guess (ges) *v.t.* to estimate without calculation; conjecture.—*v.i.* to form conjectures.—**guess'work** *n.*
guest (gest) *n.* one entertained at another's house; one living in an hotel.
guffaw' *n.* a burst of laughter.—*v.i.* to laugh loudly or boisterously.
guide (gīd) *n.* one who shows the way; an adviser; a book of instruction or information; a contrivance for directing motion.—*v.t.* to lead, act as guide to.—**guid'ance** *n.* leading, direction.
guild, gild (g-) *n.* a company of merchants or craftsmen; society with a common object.—**guild'hall** *n.*
guile (gīl) *n.* cunning, treachery.—**guile'ful** *a.*—**guile'fully** *adv.*—**guile'less** *a.*
Syn. artifice, duplicity. *Ant.* honesty, sincerity, faithfulness.
guill'emot (gil'-i-) *n.* a sea-bird.
guillotine' (gil-ō-tēn') *n.* machine for beheading; machine for cutting paper.—*v.* to behead; (*col.*) rules in parliament which may be applied to shorten the discussion of a bill.
guilt (gilt) *n.* the fact or state of having offended; culpability.—**guilt'y** *a.* deserving punishment, wicked.—**guilt'ily** *adv.*—**guilt'less** *a.* innocent.
guin'ea (gin'i) *n.* 21 shillings; formerly, a gold coin of this value.—**guin'ea-fowl** *n.* a fowl allied to the pheasant.—**guin'ea-pig** *n.* a rodent, the cavy.
guise (gīz) *n.* external appearance, *esp.* one assumed; semblance, pretence.
guitar' (git-) *n.* six-stringed musical instrument played with fingers.
gules *n.* and *a.* in heraldry, red.
gulf *n.* an enclosed portion of the sea; a chasm; abyss (**gulfs** *pl.*).
gull *n.* a long-winged web-footed seabird; a dupe, fool.—*v.t.* to dupe, cheat.—**gull'ible** *a.*—**gullibil'ity** *n.*
gull'et *n.* food-passage from mouth to stomach; throat; narrow trench.
gull'y *n.* a channel or ravine worn by water.—**gull'y-raker** *n.* Australia, long whip used by drivers of bullock-teams.
gulp *v.t.* to swallow hastily.—*v.i.* to choke.—*n.* an act of gulping.
gum *n.* the firm flesh in which the teeth are set.—**gum'boil** *n.* a boil in the gum.
gum *n.* sticky juice of trees; preparation which sticks papers, etc., together.—*v.t.* to stick with gum.—**gumm'y** *a.*—**gum'boots** *n. pl.* high rubber boots.—**gum-tree** *n.* any species of eucalyptus.—**up a gum-tree** (*sl.*) in a difficult position.—**chewing gum** *n.*
gump'tion *n.* capacity; shrewdness.
gun *n.* weapon consisting mainly of a metal tube from which missiles are thrown by explosion.—**gunn'er** *n.*—**gunn'ery** *n.* the science of using large guns.—**gun'boat** *n.* small warship.—**gun'-cotton** *n.* explosive of cotton steeped in nitric and sulphuric acids.—**gun'-man** *n.* in N. America, an armed desperado.—**gun'-metal** *n.* alloy of copper and tin or zinc.—**gun'-powder** *n.* explosive mixture of saltpetre, sulphur, and charcoal.—**gun'room** *n.* the mess-room of junior officers in a warship.—**gun'-running** *n.* the large scale smuggling of firearms, etc.—**gun'shot** *n.* the range of a gun.—*a.* caused by missile from a gun.—**gun'wale, gunn'el** *n.* the upper edge of the side of a boat or ship.
gun'yah *n.* an Australian aboriginal hut made of boughs and bark.
gur'gle *n.* a bubbling, rippling noise.—*v.i.* to make a gurgle.
gurn'et, gurn'ard *n.* a spiny sea-fish.
gu'ru (goo'-roo) *n.* a spiritual teacher, *esp.* in India; a venerable person.
gush *v.i.* to flow out suddenly and copiously.—*n.* a sudden copious flow; effusiveness.—**gush'er** *n.* an oil-well.
guss'et *n.* a triangle of material let into a garment.—**guss'eted** *a.*

gust *n.* a sudden blast of wind.—**gust'y** *a.* squally; passionate.
gust'o *n.* enjoyment in doing a thing.
gut *n.* in *pl.* entrails, intestines.—*sing.* material made from guts of animals; a narrow passage, strait.—*v.t.* to remove the guts from (fish); destroy the contents of, *esp.* by fire (**gut'ted** *p.t./p.p.*).
gutta'perch'a *n.* a horny flexible substance, the juice of a Malayan tree.
gutt'er *n.* shallow trough for carrying off water (roof, street).—*v.t.* to make channels in.—*v.i.* flow in streams (as wax from candle).—**gutt'er press** *n.* sensational newspapers.—**gutt'er-snipe** *n.* a street-arab, slum child.
gutt'ural *a.* of, relating to, or produced in, the throat.—*n.* a guttural letter.
guy (gī) *n.* a rope or chain to steady or secure something, *e.g.* crane, tent; (U.S.) chap.—*v.t.* to secure with a guy; to ridicule.—**guy'-rope** *n.*
guy (gī) *n.* an effigy of Guy Fawkes to be burnt on Nov. 5th; a ridiculously dressed person.—*v.t.* to exhibit in effigy; in N. America, to ridicule.
guz'zle *v.t.* and *i.* to eat or drink greedily.—**guz'zler** *n.*
gybe, jibe (jīb) *v.t.* and *i.* of the boom of a fore-and-aft sail, to swing over to the other side with following wind.
gymkha'na (jim-, -á-) *n.* an athletic and equestrian competitive display.
gymna'sium (jim-) *n.* a place fitted up for athletic training (**-siums, -sia** *pl.*).—**gymnas'tic** *a.* of exercise.—*n.* (in *pl.*) muscular exercises.—**gym'nast** *n.* an expert in gymnastics.
gynaecol'ogy (gin-, jin-) *n.* the part of medicine dealing with functions and diseases of women.
gyp *n.* a male attendant at Cambridge University.—*v.t.* (U.S. *sl.*) swindle.
gyp'sum (jip'-) *n.* sulphate of lime, source of plaster of Paris.
gyp'sy *see* **gipsy.**
gyrate' (jī-) *v.i.* to move in a circle, revolve.—**gyra'tion** *n.*—**gy'ratory** *a.*—**gy'roscope** *n.* a wheel spinning at great speed to preserve equilibrium.—**gyro'-compass** *n.* mariner's compass using a gyroscope.—**gyro-stab'iliser** *n.* an apparatus using two or more gyroscopes to prevent rolling of a ship or aeroplane.
gyrop'ter *n.* an aeroplane with revolving wings, a rotoplane.
gyve (jīv) *n.* (usually in *pl.*) a fetter, *esp.* for the leg or hand.—*v.t.* to shackle.

H

hab'erdasher *n.* a draper.—**hab'erdashery** *n.* small articles of dress, etc.
habil'iments *n. pl.* dress.
hab'it *n.* settled tendency or practice; constitution; dress (*esp.* **riding-habit**).—*v.t.* to dress.—**habit'ual** *a.* constant, customary.—**habit'ually** *adv.*—**habit'uate** *v.t.* accustom.—**habitua'tion** *n.*—**habit'ué** (-ū-ā) *n.* constant visitor.
hab'itable *a.* fit to live in.—**habita'tion** *n.* dwelling.—**hab'itat** *n.* natural home.
hach'ure (-sh-) *n.* shading on a map.—*v.t.* to mark with this.
hacien'da (-thē-) *n.* farm in Span. Amer.
hack *v.t.* to cut, mangle, gash.—*n.* a notch; bruise.—*n.* hired horse or carriage; a drudge.—**hack'work** *n.*
hac'kle (hak'l) *n.* a comb for flax; the neck feathers of a cock.
hack'ney *n.* horse for ordinary riding; hired carriage (**-neys** *pl.*).—*v.t.* to make trite or common, hence *a hackneyed expression.*—**hack'neyed** *a.*
hadd'ock *n.* a fish allied to a cod.
ha'des (-ēz) *n.* the abode of the dead.
haemophil'ia (hē-mō-fil'-i-á) *n.* a hereditary tendency to intensive bleeding, owing to the failure of the blood to clot.
haem'orrhage, hem'orrhage (hem'-or-ij) *n.* bleeding from blood-vessels.
haem-, hem'orrhoids *n.* piles.
haerema'i *interj.* in N.Z., welcome!
haf'nium *n.* element like zirconium.
haft *n.* handle (*esp.* of knife).
hag *n.* an ugly old woman; a witch.—**hag'-ridden** *a.* troubled with nightmares.
hagg'ard *a.* wild-looking.—*n.* untamed hawk. *Syn.* gaunt, wrinkled. *Ant.* well-conditioned, strapping, sleek.
hagg'is *n.* a Scottish dish, the pluck of a sheep, chopped with herbs, oatmeal, etc., and boiled in the maw.
hag'gle *v.i.* dispute terms, chaffer.—*n.* chaffering.—**hag'gler** *n.*
hagiol'ogy (hag-) *n.* literature of the lives of saints.—**hagiog'rapher** *n.*
ha-ha' *n.* a sunk fence.
hail *n.* frozen vapour falling in pellets.—*v.i.* **it hails,** hail falls.—*v.t.* to pour down.
hail *interj.* greeting.—*v.t.* to greet; call.—*n.* a call.—*v.i.* **hail from,** come from.
hair (hér) *n.* filament growing from the skin of an animal.—**hair'do** *n.* (*col.*) manner of arranging hair.—**hair'iness** *n.*—**hairless** *a.*—**hair'pin** *n.*—**hair'pin-bend** *n.* a v-shaped turn in road.—**hair's breadth** *n.* very small space.—**hair-split'ting** *n.* drawing of over-fine distinctions.—**hair'spring** *n.* fine spring in a watch.—**hair'-trigger** *n.* secondary trigger releasing the main one.—**hair'y** *a.*
hake *n.* a fish like a cod.
hala'tion (hạ-lā'-shun) *n.* in photography, the spreading of light in a negative through being partially reflected from the back of the plate or film, instead of passing entirely through.
hal'berd *n.* combined spear and battle-axe.—**halberdier'** *n.* man armed thus.
hal'cyon *n.* a bird fabled to calm the sea.—**halcyon days** calm, peaceful days.

hale *a.* robust, healthy, *esp.* in old age.
hale *v.t.* to drag.
half (håf) *n.* (**halves** (håvz) *pl.*) either of two equal parts of a thing.—*a.* forming a half.—*adv.* to the extent of half.—**half-back** *n.* in Association football one of 3 players placed immediately behind the forwards; in Rugby the *scrum* and stand-off halves are a link between the forwards and three-quarters.—**half-bound** *a.* (bookbinding) bound with leather on the back and corners only.—**half-breed** *n.* one of mixed parentage.—**half-brother, sister** *n.* a brother (sister) by one parent only.—**half-caste** *n.* a half-breed.—**half-crown** *n.* a British coin worth 2*s.* 6*d.*—**half-hearted** *a.* without resolution or enthusiasm.—**half-hitch** *n.* a hitch made by looping the rope and drawing the end through the loop.—**half-mast** *adv.* a flag flown lower than masthead or staff height as a sign of mourning.—**half-Nelson** *n.* a hold in wrestling with one arm held under the opponent's armpit while facing his back, and the hands pressing on the nape of his neck.—**half'penny** (hāp'ni) *n.* a British bronze coin worth half a penny.—**half-seas-over** *a.* half-drunk.—**half-tone** *n.* an illustration printed from a relief plate, showing lights or shadows by the thick or scarce distribution of minute dots, made by photographing an original through a screen etched with a network of fine lines.—**half-volley** *n.* a ball struck the instant it bounces; the striking.—*v.t.* to strike thus.—**halve** (håv) *v.t.* to divide into halves.
hal'ibut *n.* a large flat edible fish.
halito'sis (hal-i-to'-) *n.* bad breath.
hall (hawl) *n.* large room; house of landed proprietor; college; building belonging to a guild; an entrance passage.—**hall'mark** *n.* mark used (at Goldsmiths' Hall, London) to indicate standard of tested gold and silver.—*v.t.* to stamp with this.
hallelu'jah (-ya) *n.* and *interj.* an exclamation of praise to God.
hallo', hello' *interj.* exclamation of surprise; a greeting.—*v.t.* and *i.* to shout loudly to.—**halloo'** *v.* to shout.
hall'ow (-ō) *v.t.* to honour as holy.
hallu'cinate *v.t.* to produce illusion in the mind of.—**hallucina'tion** *n.* illusion.
halm *see* **haulm.**
ha'lo *n.* a circle of light round the moon, sun, etc.; disk of light round a saint's head in a picture; glory attaching to a person (**-loes, -los** (-lōz) *pl.*).
halt (hawlt) *a.* lame, crippled.—*v.i.* limp.—*n.* stoppage on march or journey.—*v.i.*/*v.t.* to make, bring to a halt.
halt'er (hawlt'-) *n.* rope with headstall to fasten horses, etc.; noose for hanging a person.—*v.t.* to fasten with a halter.
hal'yard, hall'iard *n.* rope for raising a sail, hoisting signal flags, etc.
ham *n.* back of the thigh; hog's thigh salted and dried.—**ham'string** *n.* tendon at the back of the knee.—*v.t.* to cripple by cutting this; to hinder, impede.
hamadry'ad *n.* a nymph living and dying with the tree she inhabited; an Indian snake (**-ads** (-adz), **-ades** (-a-dēz) *pl.*). also King Cobra, U.S.A.
ham'burger (-bôor-ger) *n.* steak cooked with onions; breakfast sausage.
ham'let *n.* a small village.
hamm'er *n.* tool with heavy head at end of handle, for driving nails, etc.; machine for the same purposes; contrivance for exploding the charge of a gun; an auctioneer's mallet.—*v.t.* and *i.* to beat with, or as with, a hammer.
hamm'ock *n.* a bed of canvas, netting, etc., hung on ropes.
hamp'er *n.* a large covered basket.—*v.t.* to impede, obstruct movements of.
hamstring *see* **ham.**
hand *n.* extremity of the arm beyond the wrist; side, quarter, direction; style of writing; cards dealt to a player; a measure of four inches; manual worker; person as a source.—*pl.* in S. Africa, bundles of newly gathered tobacco leaves.—*v.t.* to lead or help with the hand; deliver; pass; hold out.—**hand'-bag** *n.* bag for carrying in the hand.—**hand'bill** *n.* small printed notice.—**hand'book** *n.* a short treatise.—**hand'-cuffs** *n.* pair of fetters for the wrists.—*v.t.* to secure with these.—**hand'ful** *n.* a small quantity (**-fuls** *pl.*).—**hand'i-craft** *n.* manual occupation of skill.—**hand'iwork** *n.* thing done by any one in person.—**hand'kerchief** (hang'-ker-chif) *n.* small square of fabric carried in the pocket for wiping the nose, etc., or worn round the neck.—**hand'-maiden** *n.* female servant.—**hand'-writing** *n.* writing, script; style of writing.—**hand'y** *a.* convenient.—**at hand,** close by.
hand'icap *n.* race or contest in which the competitors' chances are equalised by starts, weights carried, etc.; a condition so imposed; a disability.—*v.t.* to impose such conditions.—**hand'icapper** *n.*
han'dle *n.* the part of a thing made to hold it by; a fact that may be taken advantage of.—*v.t.* to touch, feel, with the hands; manage, deal with; deal in (**hand'ling** *pr. p.*—**hand'led** *p.t.*/*p.p.*).
hand'sel (-ns-) *n.* gift on beginning something; earnest money; first use.—*v.t.* to give a handsel to.
hand'some (-ns-) *a.* of fine appearance; generous.—**hand'somely** *adv.*
Syn. good-looking, graceful, liberal, elegant. *Ant.* hideous, mean.
hang *v.t.* to fasten to an object above, suspend; to kill by suspending from

gallows; set up (wallpaper, doors, etc.). —*v.i.* to be suspended (**hung** or **hanged** *p.t.* and *p.p.*).—**hang'-dog** *a.* of sneaking aspect.—**hang'man** *n.* executioner.—**hang up.** *v.t.* in Australia, to tie up, *esp.* of a horse.—**hang' out** (*sl.*) to stay.
hang *n.* in S. Africa, a steep slope of a mountain, a sharp incline.
hang'ar (-ng-g-) *n.* shed for aircraft.
hang'er *n.* a short sword.
hank *n.* a coil, *esp.* as a measure of yarn.
hank'er *v.i.* to crave.
hank'y-pank'y *n.* trickery.
han'som *n.* a two-wheeled cab for two with the driver mounted up behind.
hap *n.* chance.—*v.i.* to happen.—**hap'-less** *a.* unlucky.—**haphaz'ard** *a.* random, without design.—*adv.* by chance.—**hap'ly** *adv.* perhaps.—**happ'en** *v.i.* to come about, occur.—**happ'y** *a.* glad, content; lucky, fortunate; apt (**-ier** *comp.*-**iest** *sup.*).–**happ'ily** *adv.*–**happ'i-ness** *n.*—**happ'y-go-luck'y** *a.*
ha'ra-ki'ri *n.* in Japan, ceremonious suicide by disembowelment.
harangue' (-ang') *n.* a vehement speech.—*v.t.* to speak vehemently to.
har'ass *v.t.* to worry, trouble; to attack repeatedly. *Syn.* tire, weary, perplex, annoy. *Ant.* comfort.
harb'inger (-j-) *n.* a forerunner.
harb'our (-bẹr) *n.* place of shelter for ships; a shelter.—*v.t.* to give shelter to. —*v.i.* to take shelter.
hard *a.* firm, resisting pressure; solid; difficult to understand; harsh, unfeeling; stingy; heavy; strenuous; of water, not making lather well with soap. —*adv.* vigorously; with difficulty; close. —**hard'en** *v.t.* and *i.*—**hard'ly** *adv.*—**hard'ness** *n.*—**hard'ship** *n.* ill-luck; severe toil or suffering.—**hard'ware** *n.* small ware of metal.—**hard-head'ed** *a.* shrewd.—**hard-heart'ed** *a.* pitiless.
hard'y *a.* robust, vigorous; bold; of plants, able to grow in the open all the year round (**-ier** *comp.*—**-iest** *sup.*).—**hard'ihood** *n.* extreme boldness.—**hard'-ily** *adv.*—**hard'ness** *n.*
hare (hẽr) *n.* long-eared, short-tailed, swift rodent.—**hare'bell** *n.* round-leaved bell-flower.—**hare'brained** *a.* rash, wild. —**hare'lip** *n.* fissure of upper lip.—**hare'-and-hounds'** *n.* paperchase.
ha'rem *n.* women's quarters in Mohammedan dwelling; a set of wives and concubines.
har'icot (-kō) *n.* French bean; ragout.
hark *v.i.* to listen.
harl'equin *n.* in pantomime a mute character supposed to be invisible to the clown and pantaloon.—**harlequinade'** *n.* harlequin's part.
harl'ot *n.* a prostitute.—**har'lotry** *n.*
harm *n.* damage, hurt, injury.—**harm'-ful** *a.* hurtful.—**harm'fully** *adv.*—**harm'-less** *a.*—**harm'lessly** *a.*
harm'ony *n.* agreement; combination of musical notes to make chords; melodious sound (**har'monies** *pl.*).—**har-mon'ic** *a.* of harmony.—*n.* a tone got by vibration of an aliquot part of a string, etc.—*pl.* in wireless, frequencies which are multiples of a main frequency. —**harmon'ica** *n.* various musical instruments.—**harmo'nious** *a.*—**harmo'nious-ly** *adv.*—**harm'onise** *v.t.* to bring into harmony.—*v.i.* to be in harmony.—**harm'onist** *n.*–**harmonisa'tion** *n.*–**harm-onium** *n.* small organ.
harn'ess *n.* the gear of a draught horse; armour (**har'ness, har'nesses** *pl.*). —*v.t.* to put harness on.
harp *n.* stringed musical instrument played by the hands.—*v.i.* to play on a harp; to dwell on continuously.—**harp'er** *n.*—**harp'ist** *n.*—**harp'sichord** *n.* stringed instrument with keyboard.
harpoon' *n.* barbed spear with a rope attached for catching whales, etc.—*v.t.* to strike with a harpoon.—**harpoon'er, harponeer'** *n.*—**harpoon-gun,** gun which discharges harpoons.
harp'y *n.* monster with body of woman and wings and claws of bird; a cruel, rapacious person (**harp'ies** *pl.*).
har'ridan *n.* a shrewish old woman.
har'rier *n.* hound used in hunting hares; a falcon; a runner.
har'row (-ō) *n.* frame with iron teeth for breaking up clods.—*v.t.* to draw a harrow over; to distress greatly.
har'ry *v.t.* to ravage; to keep worrying (**har'ried** *p.t.* and *p.p.*–**har'rying** *pres. p.*).
harsh *a.* rough to taste, touch or hearing; discordant; severe; unfeeling.—**harsh'ly** *adv.*—**harsh'ness** *n.*
hart *n.* male deer.—**hind** *fem.*—**harts'-horn** *n.* ammonium carbonate distilled from stags' horns.—**hart's'-tongue** *n.* fern with long tongue-like fronds.
hartal' *n.* Indian equivalent of a strike; literally, a day of mourning.
har'tebees(t) *n.* large S. African antelope.
ha'rum-sca'rum *a.* reckless, wild.
harv'est *n.* season for gathering in grain; the gathering; the crop.—*v.t.* to gather in.—**har'vester** *n.*
hash *v.t.* to cut up small.—*n.* dish of hashed meat; a muddle.
hash'ish, hash'eesh *n.* tops of Indian hemp; intoxicating infusion of this plant.
hasp *n.* clasp passing over a staple to fasten door, etc.—*v.t.* fasten thus.
hass'ock *n.* kneeling-cushion; stuffed footstool; tuft of grass.
haste (hā-) *n.* speed; hurry.—*v.i.* to hasten.—**hast'en** (-sen) *v.i.* to hurry.—*v.t.* to cause to hasten; accelerate.—**ha'sty** *a.*—**ha'stily** *adv.*
Syn. swiftness. *Ant.* slowness, delay.
hat *n.* covering for the head, usually with brim.—**hatt'er** *n.* dealer in, or

maker of, hats; in Australia, miner who works alone; one who works alone.—**hat'-trick** *n.* in cricket, the taking of three wickets with successive balls.
hatch *n.* lower half of a divided door; a hatchway; the trap-door over it.—**hatch'way** *n.* opening in ship's deck.
hatch *v.t.* to produce young from eggs; incubate.—*v.i.* to come forth from the shell.—*n.* a hatching; the brood hatched.
hatch *v.t.* to engrave or draw lines on for shading; shade with lines.
hatch'et *n.* a small axe.—**to bury the hatchet**, in N. America, to make peace.
hate *v.t.* to dislike strongly.—*n.* hatred.—**hate'ful** *a.*—**hate'fully** *adv.*—**ha'tred** *n.* emotion of extreme dislike, active ill-will.
hau'berk (how'-) *n.* long coat of mail.
haugh'ty (hawt'i) *a.* proud, arrogant.—**haught'ily** *adv.*—**haught'iness** *n.*
Syn. lofty, disdainful. *Ant.* humble, meek, submissive.
haul *v.t.* to pull, drag.—*v.i.* of wind, to shift.—*n.* a hauling; a draught of fishes.—**haul'age** *n.* carrying of loads.
haulm, halm (hawm) *n.* stalks of beans, etc.; thatch of this.
haunch (hawnsh) *n.* hip and thigh; leg and loin of venison, etc. (**haunch'es** *pl.*).
haunt *v.t.* to resort to habitually; *n.* place visited often; of ghosts.
haut'boy (hō'boi) *n.* an oboe.
hauteur' (haw-ter') *n.* haughty spirit.
havan'a, havann'ah *n.* a fine cigar.
have (hav) *v.t.* to hold or possess; to be possessed or affected with; to be obliged (to do); to engage in, carry on; obtain; (as auxiliary forms perfect and other tenses). (I **have**, thou **hast**, he **has**, we, you, they **have** *pres.*—**had** *p.t.* and *p.p.*—**hav'ing** *pres. p.*).
ha'ven *n.* a harbour; a place of rest.
hav'ersack *n.* soldier's ration-bag; similar bag for travellers.
hav'oc *n.* pillage, devastation, ruin.
haw *n.* the red berry of the hawthorn.—**haw'thorn** *n.* a thorny shrub used for hedges.—**haw'finch** *n.* a small bird.
hawk *n.* a bird of prey used in falconry.—*v.t.* and *i.* to hunt with hawks.
hawk *v.i.* to clear the throat noisily.
hawk'er *n.* one who carries wares for sale.—**hawk** *v.t.* carry about for sale.
hawse (-z) *n.* the part of a ship's bows with holes for anchor cables.
haw'ser (-z-) *n.* large rope or small cable.
hay *n.* grass mown and dried.—**hay'box** *n.* a box filled with hay in which heated food is left to finish cooking.—**hay'cock** *n.* conical heap of hay.—**hay'seed** *n.* grass seed; in N. America (*sl.*) a countryman.—**hay'stack** *n.* large pile of hay.
hay'wire *a.* (U.S.) (*sl.*) crazy.—**to go haywire**, to run riot.
haz'ard *n.* a game at dice; chance, a chance; risk, danger.—*v.t.* to expose to risk; run the risk of.—**haz'ardous** *a.*
haze *n.* misty appearance in the air, often due to heat.—**ha'zy** *a.* misty.
haze *v.t.* in N. America, to drive an animal in a direction strange to it; to punish or torment by the imposition of excessively heavy or disagreeable tasks, particularly used on sailors; to play jokes on.—**haz'ing** *n.* ragging.
ha'zel *n.* bush bearing nuts; their reddish-brown colour.—*a.* of this colour.
he *pron.* the third person masculine pronoun.
head (hed) *n.* the upper part of a man's or animal's body, containing mouth, sense organs and brain; the upper part of anything; chief part; leader; progress; section of a chapter; headland.—*v.t.* to provide with a head; get the lead of.—*v.i.* to face, front.—**head'ache** (-āk) *n.* pain in the head.—**head'er** *n.* that or who heads; plunge head foremost; brick laid with end in face of wall.—**head'land** *n.* promontory.—**head'light** *n.* bright lamp on front of car or at masthead.—**head'line** *n.* most important news in large type along the top of a newspaper.—**head'long** *adv.* head foremost, in a rush.—**head'ing** *n.* title.—**head'quarters** *n. pl.* residence of commander-in-chief; centre of operations.—**head'strong** *a.* self-willed.—**head'way** *n.* progress.—**head'y** *a.* impetuous; apt to intoxicate.
heal *v.t.* to restore to health, make well, cure.—*v.i.* become sound.—**health** (hel'th) *n.* soundness of body; condition of body; a toast drunk in a person's honour.—**health'ful** *a.* health-giving.—**health'y** *a.* having, or tending to give, health.—**health'ily** *adv.*—**health'iness** *n.*
heap *n.* a number of things lying one on another.—*v.t.* to pile up.
hear *v.t.* perceive with the ear; listen to; try (a case); get to know.—*v.i.* perceive sound; learn (**heard** *p.t.*/*p.p.*).—**hear'say** *n.* rumour.—*a.*—**hear'er** *n.*
heark'en (har-) *v.i.* to listen.
hearse (hers) *n.* a carriage for a coffin.
heart (hart) *n.* the organ which makes the blood circulate; the seat of the emotions and affections; mind, soul; courage; middle of anything; a playing-card marked with a figure of a heart, one of these marks.—**heart'en** *v.t.* to inspirit.—**heart'less** *a.* unfeeling.—**heart'y** *a.* friendly; vigorous; in good health (**-ier** *comp.*—**-iest** *sup.*).—**heart'ily** *adv.*—**heart'water** *n.* in S. Africa, a disease affecting cattle, sheep and goats.
hearth (harth) *n.* fireplace in house.
heat *n.* hotness; sensation of this; hot weather or climate; warmth of feeling, anger, etc.; sexual excitement in animals; race (of which there are several) to decide persons to compete in a deciding course.—*v.t.* to make hot.—*v.i.* to become hot.—**heat'edly** *adv.*

heath *n.* tract of waste land; shrubs found on this.—**heath'y** *a.*
hea'then (-th-) *a.* one having a primitive, or no, religious belief; a pagan.—*n.* a heathen person (**hea'thens, hea'then** *pl.*).—**hea'thenish** *a.*—**hea'thenism** *n.*
heath'er (heth'er) *n.* a shrub growing on heaths and mountains.—**heath'ery** *a.*
heave *v.t.* to lift with effort; throw (something heavy); utter (a sigh).—*v.i.* to swell, rise.—*n.* a heaving.
heav'en (hev'n) *n.* the sky; the abode of God; God; place of bliss.—**heav'enly** *a.*
heav'y (hev-) *a.* of great weight; striking or falling with force; sluggish; difficult; severe; sorrowful; serious, dull; over compact.—**heav'ily** *adv.*—**heav'iness** *n.* *Syn.* ponderous, oppressive, indolent, tedious. *Ant.* buoyant, porous, flimsy.
Heavi'side layer *n.* a layer about 60 m. up in the atmosphere, which reflects wireless waves.
heav'y water, water in which the normal hydrogen is replaced by heavy hydrogen, giving it a density about 10% greater than that of ordinary water.
hebdom'adal *a.* weekly.
heb'etude *n.* dullness.
hec'atomb *n.* a great public sacrifice.
hec'kle (hek'l) *n.* a hackle.—*v.t.* to comb with a hackle; to question severely.
hec'tic *a.* flushed, feverish, consumptive.
hec'tograph *n.* apparatus for multiplying copies of writings.—**hec'togramme** *n.* one hundred grammes.—**hec'tometre** *n.* length of 100 metres.
hec'tor *v.t.* and *i.* to bully, bluster.
hedge *n.* a fence of bushes.—*v.t.* to surround with a hedge.—*v.i.* to make or trim hedges; to bet on both sides; to secure against loss; shift, shuffle.—**hedge'hog** *n.* small animal covered with spines; a small strongly fortified defensive position.—**hedge-hop'ping** *n.* flying very low.—**hedge'row** *n.* bushes forming a hedge.—**hedge'-spar'row** *n.* small bird.
he'donism *n.* the doctrine that pleasure is the chief good.—**he'donist** *n.*
heed *v.t.* to take notice of, consider, care for, mind.—**heed'ful** *a.*—**heed'less** *a.*
heel *n.* hinder part of foot; part of a shoe supporting this.—*v.t.* to supply with a heel; touch ground, or a ball, with the heel.—*n.* (U.S.) (*sl.*) worthless, contemptible, person; a cad.
heel *v.i.* of a ship, to lean to one side.—*v.t.* to cause to do this.—*n.* a heeling.
hegem'ony (hē-g-) *n.* leadership; political domination.
heif'er (hef-) *n.* a young virgin cow.
height (hīt) *n.* measure from base to top; quality of being high; high position.—**heighten'** *v.t.* to make higher, intensify.
hei'nous (hā'-) *a.* atrocious, very bad.
heir (ėr) *n.* person legally entitled to succeed to property or rank.—**heir'ess** *fem.*—**heir-appar'ent** *n.* successor to the throne.—**heir'loom** *n.* a thing that has been in a family for generations.
held *p.t.* and *p.p.* of **hold.**
hel'ical *a.* spiral.—**helicop'ter** *n.* an aeroplane to rise vertically by the pull of an air-screw revolving horizontally.
he'liograph *n.* an apparatus to signal by reflecting the sun's rays.—**he'liotrope** *n.* plant with purple flowers; the colour of the flowers.—**heliotrop'ic** *a.* turning under the influence of light.
he'lioscope *n.* a form of telescope adapted for viewing the sun.
he'liostat *n.* an instrument for signalling by flashing the sun's rays.
he'liother'apy *n.* curative treatment by exposure to sunlight.
he'liotrope *n.* plant with small, fragrant purple or white flowers; their scent; pinkish-purple; blood stone.
he'lium *n.* a gaseous element, first discovered in the sun's atmosphere.
hell *n.* abode of the damned; place of wickedness, misery or torture; a gambling-resort.—**hell'ish** *a.*
hell'ebore *n.* a plant formerly thought to cure madness; Christmas rose.
Hellen'ic *a.* pertaining to the Hellenes or inhabitants of Greece.—**Hell'enist** *n.*
helm *n.* tiller, wheel for turning ship's rudder.—**helms'man** *n.* steersman.
helm'et, helm *n.* defensive covering for the head.—**helm'eted** *a.*
hel'ot *n.* a serf, *esp.* in Sparta.
help *v.t.* aid, assist; serve (food); remedy, prevent.—*n.* aid, assistance, an aid.—**help'er** *n.*—**help'ful** *a.*—**help'less** *a.*—**help'lessly** *adv.*—**help'mate, help'meet** *n.* companion, husband or wife.
helt'er-skel'ter *adv.* in hurry and confusion.
helve *n.* the handle of a weapon or tool.
hem *n.* border on garment made by turning over the edge and sewing it down.—*v.t.* to sew thus; confine, shut in.—**hem'stitch** *n.* an ornamental stitch.—*v.t.* sew with this.
hem'isphere *n.* a half sphere; half of the celestial sphere; half of the earth.
hem'istich (-ik) *n.* half a line of verse.
hem'lock *n.* a poisonous plant; evergreen tree of the pine family.
hem'orrhage *n. see* **haemorrhage.**
hemp *n.* Indian plant of which fibre is used to make rope; the fibre; narcotic drug.—**hemp'en** *a.*
hen *n.* female of domestic fowl and other birds.—**hen'pecked** *a.* domineered over by a wife.
hence *adv.* from this point; for this reason.—**hencefor'ward** *adv.* from this time forward.—**hence'forth** *adv.*
hench'man *n.* squire; trusty follower.
henn'a *n.* the Egyptian privet; a dye made from it, used on hair, etc.
hep'tagon *n.* figure with 7 angles.—

heptag'onal *a.*—**hep'tarchy**(-ki) *n.* rule by 7; the period of many kingdoms of Angles and Saxons.—**hep'tateuch** (-tūk) *n.* the first 7 books of Bible.

her *pron.* objective and possessive case of **she**—**hers** *pron.* of her.—**herself.**

her'ald *n.* an officer who makes royal proclamations, arranges ceremonies, etc.; a messenger, envoy.—*v.t.* to announce; proclaim the approach of.—**heral'dic** *a.*—**her'aldry** *n.* the science of dealing with coats-of-arms.

herb *n.* plant with soft stem which dies down after flowering; plant of which parts are used for medicine, food or scent.—**herba'ceous** (-shus) *a.* of or like a herb.—**herb'age** *n.* herbs; grass, pasture.—**herb'al** *a.* of herbs.—*n.* a book on herbs.—**herb'alist** *n.* one skilled in the use of medicinal herbs, dealer in herbs.—**herbar'ium** (-â-) *n.* a collection of dried plants (**-iums, -ia,** *pl.*).

herd *n.* number of animals feeding or travelling together; mass of people (*in contempt*); a herdsman.—*v.i.* to go in a herd.—*v.t.* to tend (a herd); crowd together.—**herds'man** *n.*

here *adv.* in this place; at or to this point.—**hereaf'ter** *adv.* in time to come. —*n.* a future existence.—**here'tofore** *adv.* formerly.—**herewith'** *adv.* with this.

hered'ity *n.* the tendency of an organism to transmit its nature to its descendants. —**hered'itary** *a.* descending by inheritance; holding office by inheritance; that can be transmitted from one generation to another.—**hered'itarily** *adv.*—**heredit'ament** *n.* something that can be inherited —**her'itable** *a.* that can be inherited.—**her'itage** *n.* that which may be or is inherited; portion or lot.

her'esy *n.* opinion contrary to orthodox belief (**-sies** *pl.*).—**here'siarch** (-k) *n.* originator, leader of a heresy.—**her'etic** *n.* holder of a heresy.—**heret'ical** *a.*

hermaph'rodite *n.* a person or animal with the characteristics of both sexes.

hermet'ic *a.* of alchemy; secret.—**hermetic sealing,** the airtight closing of a vessel.—**hermet'ically** *adv.*

her'mit *n.* a person living in solitude.—**her'mitage** *n.* his abode.

hern'ia *n.* rupture (**-ias, -iae** *pl.*).

he'ro *n.* an illustrious warrior; one greatly regarded for achievements or qualities; the chief man in a poem, play or story (**he'roes** *pl.*).—**hero'ic** *a.*—**hero'ically** *adv.*—**her'oism** *n.* great bravery.—**he'ro-worshipper** *n.*

her'oin *n.* trade name for a white crystalline derivative of morphine, used medicinally as a nerve sedative.

her'on *n.* a long-legged wading bird.—**her'onry** *n.* a place where herons breed.

her'pes (hėr'pēz) *n.* a skin disease; shingles.—**herpet'ic** *a.*

herr'ing *n.* familiar sea-fish.—**herr'ing-bone** *n.* a stitch or pattern of zigzag lines. —**herring-pond** *n.* (*sl.*) the N. Atlantic.

hes'itate (-z-) *v.i.* to hold back, feel or show indecision; be reluctant.—**hes'itant** *a.* undecided.—**hes'itantly** *adv.*—**hes'itancy** *n.*—**hesita'tion** *n.* (**hes'itated** *p.t./p.p.*). *Syn.* doubt, falter. *Ant.* decide, act.

hest *n.* behest, command.

het'erodox *a.* not orthodox.—**het'erodoxy** *n.*—**heteroge'nous** *a.* composed of diverse elements.—**heterogene'ity** *n.*

heterosex'ual (het-ėr-) *a.* of different sex or sexes.—**heterosexuality** *n.* tendency to be sexually attracted by persons of sex opposite to one's own.

hew *v.t.* and *i.* to chop or cut.—**hew'er** *n.*

hex'agon *n.* a figure with six angles.—**hexag'onal** *a.*—**hexam'eter** *n.* a line of verse of six feet.—**hexamet'ric** *a.*

hey'-day *n.* bloom, prime.

hia'tus (hī-ā'-) *n.* a gap in a series, etc.; break between two vowels (**hia'tuses,** *pl.*)

hi'bernate *v.i.* to pass the winter.—**hiberna'tion** *n.*—**hi'bernator** *n.*

hibis'cus *n.* kinds of mallow.

hic'cup, hic'cough (hik'up) *n.* a spasm of the breathing organs with an abrupt cough-like sound.—*v.i.* to have this.

hick *n.* a rustic; country bumpkin.

hick'ory *n.* N. Amer. tree like walnut.

hidal'go *n.* a Spanish nobleman of the lowest class (**-gos** (-gōz) *pl.*).

hide *n.* skin, raw or dressed; old measure of land.—**hide'bound** *a.* having a tight hide; bigoted.

hide *v.t.* to keep out of sight; conceal; thrash.—*v.i.* to conceal oneself.

hid'eous *a.* repulsive, revolting, frightful.—**hid'eously** *adv.*

hie *v.i.* and *refl.* to go quickly (**hied** (hīd) *p.t.* and *p.p.*—**hy'ing** or **hie'ing** *pres. p.*).

hie'laman, hee'laman *n.* in Australia, a narrow shield of bark or wood.—**hielaman-tree** *n.* the coral tree.

hi'erarch (-k) *n.* chief priest.—**hi'erarchy** *n.* graded priesthood or other organisation.—**hierarch'ical** *a.*—**hierat'ic** *a.* of the priests (*esp.* of old Egyptian writing).—**hi'eroglyph** *n.* figure of an object standing for a word or sound, as in ancient Egyptian writing.—**hieroglyph'ic** *a.*—**hieroglyph'ics** *n. pl.* **hi'erophant** *n.* one who initiates candidates into sacred mysteries.

hig'gle *v.i.* to dispute about terms; to carry wares for sale.—**hig'gler** *n.*

hig'gledy-pig'gledy *adv.* and *a.* in confusion, jumbled up.

high (hī) *a.* of great or specified extent upwards; far up; of great rank, quality, or importance; of roads, main; of meat, tainted; of a season, well advanced; of sound, acute in pitch.—*adv.* far up; strongly, to a great extent; at or to a high pitch; at a high rate.—**high'ly** *adv.* —**high'ball** *n.* N. American, whisky or brandy and soda-water, ginger-ale, etc.

—**high-brow** *a.* intellectual, *n.* an intellectual; a superior person.—**high-falut'in** *a.* (*col.*) pompous; bombastic; —*n.* affected superiority.—**high'lands** *n. pl.* mountainous country.—**Highlander'** *n.*—**high-up** *n.* (*slang*) a person in a responsible post in the Government or one of the Services.—**high'way** *n.* a main road; an ordinary route.—**high'-wayman** *n.* a robber on the road, *esp.* a mounted one.—**Highway Code,** the regulations and recommendations applying to all users of the public highways.—**high'ness** *n.* quality of being high; title of princes.

hight (hīt) *a.* named.

hi'jacker *n.* (U.S.) (*sl.*) one who robs a smuggler of his smuggled goods.

hike *v.i.* to tramp, *esp.* for pleasure.—*n.* a long journey on foot.—**hiker** *n.*

hilari'ty *n.* cheerfulness, boisterous joy, gaiety.—**hilar'ious** (-êr-) *a.*

hill *n.* a small mountain; mound.—**hill'ock** *n.* a small hill.—**hill'ocky** *a.*—**hill'y** *a.*—**hill'iness** *n.*

hilt *n.* the handle of a sword, etc.

him *pron.* objective case of **he**.—**himself**, emphatic form of **he**.

hind (hīnd) *n.* a female deer; a farm workman, bailiff.

hind (hīnd), **hind'er** *a.* at the back.

hin'der *v.t.* to obstruct, impede, delay, make difficult.—**hin'drance** *n.*

Syn. hamper, stop, restrain. *Ant.* aid, help, expedite, hasten.

Hin'du, Hindoo *n.* a native of Hindustan who is not of Mohammedan, Parsee or Christian descent.

hinge (-j) *n.* joint on which a door swings.—*v.t.* to attach with a hinge.—*v.i.* to turn on, depend on.

hint *n.* a slight indication, a covert suggestion.-*v.t.* and *i.* to suggest covertly.

hint'erland *n.* region behind coast.

hip *n.* the projecting part of the thigh; the fruit of the rose, *esp.* wild.—**hipp'ed** *a.* depressed, melancholy.

hipp'odrome *n.* course for chariot races; a circus.—**hippopot'amus** *n.* a large African animal living in rivers (**-amuses, -ami** *pl.*).—**hipp'ogriff, hipp'ogryph** *n.* griffin-like creature with horse's body.

hire *n.* payment for the use of a thing; wages; a hiring or being hired.—*v.t.* to take or give on hire.—**hire'ling** *n.* one who serves for wages.—**hi'rer** *n.*—**hire-pur'chase** *n.* a system by which a hired article becomes the property of the hirer after a stipulated number of payments.

hir'sute *a.* hairy.

his *pron.* belonging to him.

hiss *v.i.* to make a sharp sound of the letter S, *esp.* in disapproval.—*v.t.* to express disapproval of, with hissing.—*n.*

hist *interj.* hush! be silent! a word commanding silence and attention.—*v.t.* to incite by making a sibilant sound.

histol'ogy *n.* the science that treats of the minute structure of the tissues of plants, animals, etc.—**histol'ogist** *n.*

history' *n.* the study of past events; a record of these; past events; a train of events, public or private; course of life or existence; a systematic account of phenomena.—**histor'ian** *n.* a writer of history.—**histori'c** *a.* noted in history.—**histori'cal** *a.* of, or based on, history; belonging to the past.—**histor'ically** *adv.* —**histori'city** *n.* historical quality or character of an event.—**historiog'rapher** *n.* historian, *esp.* official one.

histrion'ic *a.* of acting, stagy; striving for effect.—*n. pl.* theatricals.

hit *v.t.* to strike with a blow or missile; to affect injuriously; find; suit.—*v.i.* to strike; light (upon) (**hit** *p.t.* and *p.p.*—**hitt'ing** *pres. p.*).—*n.* a blow; success.

hitch *v.t.* to raise or move with a jerk; fasten with a loop, etc.—*v.i.* to be caught or fastened.—*n.* a jerk; a fastening, a loop or knot; a difficulty, obstruction.—**hitch'hike** *v.i.* to travel by begging or stealing free rides where possible.

hith'er (-th-) *adv.* to or towards this place.—**hitherto'** *adv.* up to now.

Hit'lerite *n.* a supporter of Hitler.

hive *n.* a house for bees.—*v.t.* to place (bees) in a hive.—*v.i.* to enter a hive.

hoar (hor), **hoar'y** *a.* grey with age; greyish-white.-**hoar'-frost** *n.* white frost.

hoard (hord) *n.* a stock, store.—*v.t.* to amass and hide away; store.

Syn. accumulation, savings. *Ant.* loss.

hoard'ing (hord-) *n.* a temporary board fence round a building or piece of ground, *esp.* one used for advertisement.

hoarse (hors) *a.* rough and harsh sounding.—**hoarse'ly** *adv.*—**hoarse'ness** *n.*

hoary *see* **hoar**.

hoax *v.t.* to deceive by an amusing or mischievous story.—*n.* such deception.

hob *n.* flat-topped casing of fireplace; a peg used as a mark in some games.—**hob'nail** *n.* a large-headed nail.

hob'ble *v.i.* to walk lamely.—*v.t.* to tie the legs together of (horse, etc.).—*n.* a limping gait; a rope for hobbling.

hob'bledehoy *n.* a clumsy youth.

hobb'y *n.* formerly a small horse; a favourite occupation as a pastime.—**hobb'yhorse** *n.* a wicker horse fastened round a dancer's waist; a stick with a horse's head as a toy; a rocking-horse; a roundabout horse; a pet theme.

hob'goblin *n.* a mischievous imp.

hob'-nob *v.i.* to be familiar (with).

ho'bo *n.* N. America, a shiftless, wandering workman. (**-bos, -boes** *pl.*).

hock *n.* joint of a quadruped's hind leg between knee and fetlock.—*v.t.* to disable by cutting the tendons of the hock; *n.* a German white wine.

hock'ey *n.* a team game played with curved sticks and a hard ball.

ho'cus-po'cus *n.* jugglery, trickery; a conjuring formula.—*v.t.* to play tricks on.—**ho'cus** *v.t.* to play tricks on; to stupefy with drugs.

hod *n.* a small trough on a staff for carrying mortar.

hoe *n.* a tool for scraping up weeds, breaking ground, etc.—*v.t.* to break up or weed with a hoe (**hoed** (hōd) *p.t.* and *p.p.*—**hoe'ing** *pres. p.*).

hog *n.* a pig, *esp.* a castrated male for fattening; a young sheep before first shearing; a greedy or dirty person.—**hogs'head** *n.* a large cask; a liquid measure of 52 imperial gals.

hogmanay' *n.* in Scotland, the last day of the year, a national festival.

hoi polloi'(-pol-oi') the common mass of people; the masses.

hoist *v.t.* to raise aloft, raise with tackle, etc.—*n.* a hoisting; a lift, elevator.

hoi'ty-toi'ty *a.* touchy, arrogant.

ho'key-po'key *n.* cheap ice-cream.

ho'kum *n.* (U.S.) (*sl.*) plot of a play; hocus-pocus, nonsense.

hold (hō-) *v.t.* to keep fast, grasp; support in or with the hands, etc.; maintain in a position; have capacity for; own, occupy; carry on; detain; celebrate; keep back; believe.—*v.i.* to cling; not to give way; abide (by), keep (to); be in force; occur (**held** *p.t.*—**held** or (archaic) **hold'en** *p.p*).—*n.* grasp; a fortress.—**hold'er** *n.*—**hold'ing company** *n.* a company which controls the stock of subordinate companies.—**hold'-all** *n.* portable wrapping.—**hold'fast** *n.* a clamp.—**hold'-up** *n.* in N. Amer., robbery with violence; dishonest tradesman, swindler.

hold (hō-) *n.* the space below deck of a ship for cargo.

hole *n.* hollow place, cavity.—*v.t.* to perforate, make a hole in.

hol'iday *n.* day or period of rest from work, or of recreation; religious festival.

holl'and *n.* a linen fabric.—**holl'ands** *n.* a spirit, gin, schnapps.

holl'ow (-ō) *n.* a cavity, hole, valley.—*a.* having a cavity, not solid; empty: false; not full-toned.—*v.t.* to make a hollow in.

holl'y *n.* an evergreen shrub.

holl'yhock *n.* a tall plant bearing many flowers along the stem.

holm (hōm) *n.* an islet, *esp.* in a river; flat ground by a river.

holm (hōm), **holm-oak** *n.* evergreen oak, ilex.

hol'ocaust *n.* a sacrifice wholly burnt; wholesale slaughter.-**hol'ograph** *n.* document wholly written by signer.

hol'ophote *n.* the apparatus used in lighthouses for reflecting all the light in the required direction.—**holopho'tal** *a.*

hol'ster *n.* a leather case for a pistol.

holt *n.* a wood, or piece of woodland.

ho'ly *a.* of, devoted to, God; free from sin, divine.—**hol'ily** *adv.*—**ho'liness** *n.* quality of being holy; Pope's title.—**Holy Week** *n.* that before Easter.

ho'lystone *n.* soft sandstone for scouring ship's deck.—*v.t.* scour with this.

hom'age *n.* formal acknowledgment of allegiance; tribute, respect paid.

home *n.* dwelling-place; fixed residence; native place; institution for the infirm, etc.—*a.* of or connected with home; not foreign.—*adv.* to or at one's home; to the point aimed at.—**home'less** *a.*—**home'ly** *a.* plain.—**home'spun** *a.* spun or made at home.—*n.* cloth made of homespun yarn; anything plain or homely.—**home'stead** *n.* a house with outbuildings, a farm.—**home'steader** *n.* in N. America, one who settles on a grant of land.—**home thrust** *n.* a blow or remark which reaches its mark.—**home'ward** *a.* and *adv.*—**home'wards** *adv.*—**home'sick** *a.*

hom'icide *n.* the killing of a human being; the killer.—**hom'icidal** *a.*

hom'ily *n.* a sermon.—**homilet'ic** *a.* of sermons.—*n. pl.* the art of preaching.

hom'iny *n.* maize, hulled and ground, and boiled with water.

homo- *prefix*, same as, *homoeopathy*.

homoeop'athy (hō-mi-) *n.* the treatment of disease by small doses of what would produce the symptoms in a healthy person.—**homoeopath'ic** *a.*—**homoeopathi'cally** *adv.*—**ho'moeopath** *n.*

homoge'neous *a.* of the same nature; formed of uniform parts.—**homogene'ity** *n.*—**homogenize'** *v.t.* to make homogeneous, *esp.* to process milk so that the globules of butter-fat are broken down, thus preventing the separation of cream.—**homol'ogous** *a.* having the same relation, relative position, etc.—**hom'ologue** *n.* a homologous thing.—**hom'onym** *n.* a word of the same form as another but of different sense.

homosex'ual *a.* of the same sex.

homosexual'ity *n.* sexuality excited by an individual of the same sex.

hone *n.* whetstone.—*v.i.* sharpen on one.

hon'est (on-) *a.* upright, dealing fairly; free from fraud; unadulterated.—**hon'estly** *adv.*—**hon'esty** *n.* uprightness; a plant with semi-transparent pods.

Syn. faithful, veracious, honourable, pure. *Ant.* dishonest, disloyal, false.

hon'ey (hun'i) *n.* the sweet fluid collected by bees.—**hon'eycomb** *n.* structure of wax in hexagonal cells in which bees place honey, eggs, etc.—*v.t.* to fill with cells or perforations.—**hone'y-dew** *n.* a sweet sticky substance found on plants.—**hon'eysuckle** *n.* climbing plant, woodbine.—**hon'eymoon** *n.* the month after marriage; the holiday taken by a newly-wedded pair.

hon'eypot *n.* S. Africa, a richly-flavoured grape; corruption of Afrikaans: **han'epoot.**

hon'iton *a.* a superior kind of lace made at Honiton, in Devonshire.
honk *n.* call of goose; sound like this, *esp.* that of motor-horn.
hon'our (on'er) *n.* high respect; renown; reputation; sense of what is right or due; chastity; high rank or position; a source or cause of honour; a court-card.—*pl.* mark of respect; distinction in examination.—*v.t.* to respect highly; confer honour on; accept or pay (a bill, etc.) when due.—**hon'ourable** *a.*—**hon'ourably** *adv.*—**hon'orary** *a.* conferred for the sake of honour only; holding a position without pay; giving services without pay.—**honorif'ic** *a.* conferring honour.—**honora'rium** *n.* a fee (**-ria** *pl.*).—**hono'urs** awards by the state for services rendered, or by schools, colleges and universities for special brilliance; special favours or courtesies; the ace, king, queen, jack and ten of trumps, or four aces in no-trump, in the game of bridge.
hooch (-tch) *n.* intoxicating liquor.
hood (hood) *n.* a covering for the head and neck, often part of a cloak or gown; the adjustable top of a motor-car, perambulator, etc.; coloured cloth showing degree, worn over university graduate's gown.—*v.t.* to put a hood on.—**hood'-wink** *v.t.* to deceive.
hood'lum (U.S.)(*sl.*) *n.* a ruffian; a bully.
hoo'doo *v.t.* to bewitch; to bring bad luck to.—*n.* a person or thing which brings bad luck.
hoof (hōōf) *n.* the horny casing of the foot of a horse, etc. (**hoofs, hooves** *pl.*).
hook (hōōk) *n.* a bent piece of metal, etc., for catching hold, hanging up, etc.; a curved cutting tool; a blow delivered with a bent elbow.—*v.t.* to grasp, catch, hold as with a hook; in golf, to drive (the ball) widely to the left; in cricket, to hit an off ball to leg.
hook'-up (U.S.) (*col.*) connection; relationship; (*radio*) any series of connected stations.
hook'ah *n.* a pipe in which the smoke is drawn through water and a long tube.
hook'er *n.* a small sailing ship.
hool'igan *n.* one of a band of young street roughs.—**hool'iganism.** *n.*
hoop (hoop) *n.* a band of metal or other material for binding a cask, etc.; a circle of wood or metal for trundling as a toy; a circle of flexible material for expanding a skirt.—*v.t.* to bind with a hoop.
hoop'ing-cough *n.* a disease, *esp.* of children, in which a cough is followed by a long sonorous respiration.—**hoop** *v.i.* to make the sound heard with the cough.—*n.* the sound.
hoop'oe (-ō) *n.* a crested bird.
hoot (hōōt) *n.* the cry of an owl; a cry of disapproval.—*v.t.* to assail with hoots; to sound a motor-horn, etc.
hoot *n.* (*sl.*) in Australia, money, wage, compensation.
hop *n.* a climbing plant with bitter cones used to flavour beer, etc.—*pl.* the cones, —**hopp'ing** *n.* gathering hops.—**hop'-garden** *n.* a field of hops.
hop *v.i.* to spring (of person, on one foot); of animals, on all feet at once; in aviation, to make a single flight.—*n.* an act or the action of hopping.—**hopp'er** *n.* one who hops; a device for feeding material into a mill or machine; a boat which takes away dredged matter.—**hopp'ing-fish** *n.* in Australia, a small fish which hops about on the muddy banks of rivers; the climbing fish.—**hop'scotch** *n.* a game in which a stone is pushed in hopping.
hope *n.* expectation and desire; a thing that gives, or an object of, this feeling. —*v.i.* to feel hope.—*v.t.* expect and desire.—**hope'ful** *a.*—**hope'fully** *adv.*—**hope'less** *a.* without hope, desperate.
Syn. optimism, sanguinity, confidence, trust. *Ant.* despair, distrust, suspicion.
horde *n.* a troop of nomads; a gang.
hore'hound *n.* a plant with bitter juice.
hori'zon *n.* the boundary of the part of the earth seen from any given point; the line where earth (or sea) and sky seem to meet; boundary of mental outlook.—**horizon'tal** *a.* parallel with the horizon, level.—**horizontally** *adv.*
hor'mone *n.* a substance secreted by certain glands which stimulates the action of the organs of the body.
horn *n.* the hard projection on the heads of certain animals, e.g., cows; the substance of it; various things made of, or resembling, a horn; a wind instrument originally made of a horn.—**horn'ed** (-nd) *a.* having horns.—**horn'y** *a.*—**horn'beam** *n.* a tree like a beech.—**horn'book** *n.* a primer.—**horn'pipe** *n.* a lively dance, *esp.* with sailors.
horn'blende *n.* mineral consisting of silica, with magnesia, lime, or iron.
horn'et *n.* large insect of wasp family.
horn'swoggle *v.t.* in North America, to hoodwink, deceive, swindle.
hor'ologe *n.* a timepiece.—**horol'ogy** *n.* clock-making.—**hor'oscope** *n.* observation of, or a scheme showing, the disposition of the planets, etc., at a given moment.—**horoscop'ic** *a.*
horr'ent *a.* standing erect; bristled.
horr'or *n.* terror; intense dislike or fear of; cause of this.—**horr'ible** *a.* exciting horror, hideous, shocking.—**horr'ibly** *adv.*—**horr'id** *a.* horrible.—**horr'idly** *adv.* —**horr'ify** *v.t.* move to horror (**-ified** *p.t./p.p.*—**-ifying** *pr. p.*).—**horrif'ic** *a.*
hors' d'oeuvre (aw(r)'-) *n.* small extra dish served as an appetizer.
horse *n.* animal used for riding and draught; cavalry; a vaulting-block; a frame for support.—*v.t.* to provide with

a horse; to carry or support on the back.—**horse'back** *n. adv.*—**horse'-chestnut** *n.* tree with conical clusters of white or pink flowers and large nuts.—**horse'-power** *n.* unit of rate of work of an engine, etc.; 550 foot-pounds per second.—**horse'radish** *n.* plant with pungent root.—**horse'shoe** *n.* iron shoe for a horse; thing so shaped.—**horse'man** *n.*; **horse'woman** *fem.* rider on a horse.—**hors'y** *a.* having to do with horses.

hort'atory, hort'ative *a.* serving to exhort; to urge or encourage.

horti'culture *n.* gardening.—**horti-cult'ural** *a.*—**horticul'turist** *n.*

hosann'a *int.* a cry of adoration.

hose *n.* stockings; flexible tube for conveying water.—*v.t.* to water with a hose.—**ho'sier** *n.* a dealer in stockings, etc.—**ho'siery** *n.* his goods.

hos'pital *n.* institution for the care of the sick or wounded, infirmary; charitable institution.—**hos'pice** (-is) *n.* travellers' house of rest kept by a religious order.—**hospital'ity** *n.* friendly and liberal reception of strangers or guests.—**hos'pitable** *a.*—**hos'pitably** *adv.*

host (ho-) *n.* one who entertains another; the keeper of an inn.—**hos'tess** *fem.*

host (hō-) *n.* an army; a large crowd.

host (hō-) in R.C. Church, the bread consecrated in the Eucharist.

hos'tage *n.* a person taken or given as a pledge to the enemy; a pledge.

hos'tel *n.* a house of residence for students; an inn.—**hos'telry** *n.* an inn.

hos'tile *a.* warlike; unfriendly.—**hostil'-ity** *n.* enmity; unfriendliness (*pl.*-**ies**).

hot *a.* of high temperature, very warm, giving or feeling heat; pungent.—*a.* (U.S.)(*sl.*) denoting jazz music performed with free improvisations and vigorous variations on the score; keyed up; liable to be searched for, because fraudulently obtained.—**hot dog** (U.S.) (*sl.*) a hot sausage in a split bread roll.—**hot'-plate** *n.* a heated plate for keeping dishes, food, etc., hot.—**hot'ness** *n.*—**hot'-head** *n.* a hasty person.

hotch'potch *n.* a dish of many ingredients; a medley.

hotel' (hō-) *n.* a large or superior inn.

Hott'entot *n.* one of the native races of S. Africa; the language of this race.—**hottentot god** *n.* in S. Africa, the popular name for various kinds of mantis or praying insect.

hough *see* **hock.**

hound *n.* a hunting dog; a runner following scent in a paperchase; a despicable man; in Australia, a kind of shark.—*v.t.* to chase, hunt, pursue.

hour (owr) *n.* the twenty-fourth part of a day; the time of day; an appointed time; in S. Africa, the distance covered within sixty minutes by a man on horseback, about three and a half English miles.—*pl.* the fixed times of prayer; the prayers; a book of them.—**hour'ly** *adv.* every hour; frequently.—*a.* frequent; happening every hour.—**hour'glass** *n.* a sand-glass running an hour.

hou'ri (hōōr'i, howr'i) *n.* a nymph of the Mohammedan paradise; a beautiful woman (-**ris** *pl.*).

house *n.* a building for human habitation or for other specified purposes; an inn; a legislative or other assembly; a family; a business firm.—*v.t.* to receive, store in a house; furnish with houses.—*v.i.* to dwell, take shelter.—**house'-boat** *n.* a boat fitted for living in on a river, etc.—**house'breaker** *n.* a burglar;—**house'hold** *n.* inmates of a house collectively.—**house'holder** *n.* one who occupies a house as his dwelling; head of a household.—**house'keeper** *n.* a woman managing household affairs.—**house'maid** *n.* a maidservant who cleans rooms, etc.—**house'warming** *n.* a party to celebrate the entry into a new house.—**house'wife** *n.* mistress of a household; (**huss'if**) a case for needles, thread, etc.

housing (-z-) *n.* horse-cloth (usually *pl.*).

hov'el *n.* a mean dwelling; an open shed.

hov'er *v.i.* to hang in the air (of bird, etc.); loiter; be in a state of indecision.

how *adv.* in what way; by what means; in what condition; to what degree; (in direct or dependent question).—**how-be'it** *adv.* nevertheless.—**howev'er** *adv.* in whatever manner, to whatever extent.

how'dah *n.* a seat on an elephant's back.

how'itzer *n.* short single or multi-barrel gun firing shells at high elevation.

howl *v.i.* to utter a long, loud cry.—*n.* such cry.—**how'ler** *n.* one that howls; a S. American monkey remarkable for its strong voice; a stupid mistake.

hoy *n.* a small coasting vessel.

hoy'den *n.* a boisterous girl.

hub *n.* middle part of a wheel, from which spokes radiate; centre of activity.

hub'bub *n.* an uproar; confused din.

huck'aback *n.* rough linen for towels.

huck'leberry *n.* N. Am. shrub; its fruit.

huck'ster *n.* a hawker; a mercenary person.—*v.i.* to haggle.—*v.t.* to deal in.

hud'dle *v.t.* and *i.* heap, crowd together confusedly.—*n.* confused heap.

hue *n.* colour, complexion.—**hue and cry**, an outcry after a criminal.

huff *v.t.* to bully; offend; to remove (opponent's man) as forfeit.—*v.i.* to take offence.—*n.* a fit of petulance.—**huff'y** *a.*—**huff'ily** *adv.*

hug *v.t.* to clasp tightly in the arms; to cling; to keep close to.—*n.* a strong clasp.

huge *a.* very big, enormous.—**huge'ly** *adv.* very much.

hugg'er-mugg'er *n.* confusion; secrecy—*a.* secret; confused.—*adv.*

hulk *n.* dismantled ship; big person or mass.—**hulk'ing** *a.* clumsy, unwieldy.

hull *n.* a shell, husk; the frame or body of a ship.—*v.t.* to remove shell or husk.

hum *v.i.* to make a low continuous sound (as bee).—*v.t.* sing with closed lips.—*n.* humming sound.—**humm'ing-bird** *n.* very small bird whose wings hum.—**humm'ing-top** *n.* one spinning with a hum (**hummed'** *p.t./p.p.*).

hu'man *a.* relating to, or characteristic of, the nature of man.—**hu'manly** *adv.*—**humane'** *a.* benevolent, kind.—**hu'manism** *n.* literary culture; devotion to human interests.—**hu'manist** *n.* classical scholar.—**human'ity** *n.* human nature; the human race.—*pl.* humane studies or literature.—**humanitar'ian** *n.* a philanthropist.—*a.* of, or holding the views of, a humanitarian.—**hu'manise** *v.t.* civilise.

hum'ble *a.* not proud, lowly, modest.—*v.t.* to bring low, abase.—**hum'bly** *adv.*

hum'ble-bee *n.* a large bee.

hum'bug *n.* sham, nonsense, deception; an impostor.—*v.t.* to delude.

hum'drum *a.* commonplace, dull.

hu'meral *a.* belonging to the shoulder.—**hu'merus** *n.* the long bone of the upper arm (**hu'meri** (-ī) *pl.*).

humid *a.* moist, damp.—**humid'ity** *n.*—**humidi'fier** *n.* a device for increasing the percentage of water vapour in the atmosphere of a compartment.

humil'iate *v.t.* to lower the dignity of, abase, mortify.—**humilia'tion** *n.*—**humil'ity** *n.* humbleness, modest.

humm'ock *n.* a low knoll, a hillock.

hu'mour *n.* state of mind, mood; temperament; the faculty of saying, of perceiving what excites amusement; a transparent fluid of an animal or plant.—*v.t.* to gratify, indulge.—**hu'morist** *n.*—**hu'morous** *a.*—**hu'morously** *adv.*

hump *n.* a normal or deforming lump, *esp.* on the back.—*v.t.* to make hump-shaped; in Australia, to carry on the back; to shoulder.—the **hump** (*sl.*) depressed state of mind.—**hump'back** *n.* person with a hump.—**hump'backed** *a.*—**to hump bluey, to hump swag,** in Australia, to go on the tramp carrying one's pack on one's back.—**hump'y** *n.* in Australia, a native hut; settler's house if small and primitive.

hu'mus (hū-) *n.* vegetable mould.

hunch *v.t.* to thrust, bend into hump.—*n.* hump; in N. Amer., inspiration; premonition.—**hunch'back** *n.* humpback.

hun'dred *n.* and *a.* the cardinal number, 10 times 10; a subdivision of a county.—**hun'dredth** *a.* the ordinal number.—**hun'dredfold** *a.* and *adv.*—**hun'dredweight** *n.* 112 lb., 20th part of ton.

hun'ger (-ng-g-) *n.* discomfort or exhaustion caused by lack of food; strong desire.—**hung'ry** *a.* in Australia, of gold ore, unpromising.—**hung'rily** *adv.*

hunk *n.* a thick piece, a lump.

hunks *n.* a miser.

hunt *v.i.* to go in pursuit of wild animals or game.—*v.t.* to pursue (game, etc.); to do this over (a district); to use (dogs, horses) in hunting; to search for.—*n.* hunting; a hunting district or society.—**hunts'man** *n.* man in charge of a pack of hounds.—**hun'ter** *n.*—**hunt'ress** *fem.*

hur'dle *n.* a portable frame of bars to make temporary fences or to be jumped over in a **hurdle-race** *n.*—**hurd'ler** *n.*

hurd'y-gurd'y *n.* a barrel-organ.

hurl *v.t.* to throw with violence, to hurtle.—*n.* a violent throw.

hurl'y-burl'y *n.* bustle, commotion.

hurr'icane *n.* a violent storm, a tempest.—**hurr'icane lamp** *n.* a lamp made to be carried in wind.—**hurr'icane-deck** *n.* the upper deck of large, power-driven ships.

hurr'y *n.* undue haste; eagerness.—*v.i.* to move or act in great haste.—*v.t.* to cause to act with haste (**hurr'ied** *p.t.* and *p.p.*—**hurr'ying** *pres. p.*).—**hurr'iedly** *adv.*

hurt *v.t.* to injure, damage, give pain to, wound (**hurt** *p.t.* and *p.p.*).—*n.* wound, injury, harm.—**hurt'ful** *a.*—**hur'tle** *v.i.* to move quickly (**hurt'ling** *pres. p.*).

hus'band (-z-) *n.* a man married to a woman.—*v.t.* to economise.—**hus'bandman** *n.* a farmer.—**hus'bandry** *n.* farming.

hush *v.t.* to silence. *v.i.* to be silent.—*n.*

husk *n.* the dry covering of certain seeds and fruits; a worthless outside part.—*v.t.* to remove the husk from.—**husk'y** *a.* of, or full of, husks; dry as a husk; rough, harsh; strong, burly.

hus'ky *n.* Eskimo dog; an energetic man (**huskies** *pl.*).

hussar (-z-) *n.* a light cavalry soldier.

hus'sif *n.* *see* **house.**

huss'y *n.* pert girl; worthless woman.

hust'ings *n. pl.* platform from which parliamentary candidates were nominated; a Guildhall court.

hus'tle (hus'l) *v.t.* to push about, jostle.—*v.i.* to push, bustle.—*n.* (**hus'tling** *pres. p.*).—**hus'tler** *n.*

hut *n.* a small mean dwelling; in Australia, small building on a sheep station.—**hut'ment** *n.* camp of huts.—**to hut-keep** in Australia, to look after the hut or cottage of a shepherd or miner.

hutch *n.* a pen for rabbits, etc. (**-es** *pl.*)

hy'acinth *n.* a bulbous plant with bell-shaped flowers, *esp.* of a purple-blue; this blue; an orange precious stone.

hyae'na (hī-ē'na) wild carniverous animal related to the dog.

hy'aline *a.* crystal-clear.

hy'brid *n.* the offspring of two plants or animals of different species; a mongrel.—*a.* cross-bred.—**hy'bridise** *v.t.* and *i.*

hy'dro- *prefix* in.—**hy'drant** *n.* water-pipe with a nozzle for a hose.—**hydraul'ic** *a.* relating to the conveyance of water; worked by water-power.—*n.* (in *pl.*) the science of water conveyance or water-power.—**hydrocarb'on** *n.* a compound of hydrogen and carbon.—**hydrodynam'ics** *n.* the science that treats of the motions of a system wholly or partly fluid.—**hydroelec'tric** *a.* effecting the development of electricity by the use of water or steam.—**hy'drogen** *n.* a colourless gas which combines with oxygen to form water.—**hy'drogen bomb** *n.* atom bomb of enormous power in which hydrogen nuclei are converted into helium nuclei; first exploded by U.S. forces at Einwetok Atoll on Nov. 1, 1952.—**hydrog'raphy** *n.* the description of the waters of the earth.—**hydrog'rapher** *n.*—**hydrograph'ic** *a.*—**hydrom'eter** *n.* instrument for determining specific gravities, and thence the strength, of liquids.—**hydrop'athy** *n.* the treatment of disease by water.—**hydropath'ic** *a.*—**hy'drophone** *n.* an instrument for detecting sound through water.—**hy'droplane** *n.* a light skimming motor-boat.—**hydropho'bia** *n.* aversion to water, *esp.* as symptom of rabies in man.—**hy'drovane** *n.* the rudder of a submarine used in guiding the vessel up or down.

hydrol'ysis (-i-sis) *n.* the decomposition of a chemical compound brought about by the addition of water.—**hydroly'tic** *a.* causing decomposition by means of water.—**hydrolyse'** *v.t.*

hydrother'apy *n.* the treatment of diseases by various water baths.

hydrox'ide *n.* a chemical compound containing one or more hydiocyl groups.

hydrox'yl (-il) *n.* unit composed of one atom of hydrogen and one of oxygen.

hydrozo'an *n.* one of the class of marine animals which includes the polyp and the jellyfish.

hye'na *see* **hyæna.**

hy'giene *n.* the principles of health; sanitary science.—**hygien'ic** (-gēn) *a.*—**hygien'ically** *adv.*—**hygien'ist** *n.*

hygrom'eter *n.* instrument for measuring the amount of moisture in the air.

hymene'al *a.* of marriage.

hymn (him) *n.* a song of praise, *esp.* to God.—*v.t.* to praise in song.—**hym'nal** *a.* of hymns.—*n.* book of hymns.—**hym'nody** *n.* singing or composition of hymns. **hym'nodist** *n.*—**hymnol'ogy** *n.* study of hymns.—**hymnol'ogist** *n.*

hy'oscine *n.* poisonous alkaloid, used as sedative in cases of mania, etc.

hyper- *prefix* over, above, as *hypercritical, hyper-sensitive.*

hyper'bola *n.* a curve produced when a cone is cut by a plane making a larger angle with the base than the side makes. —**hyper'bole** (-li) *n.* rhetorical exaggeration.—**hyperbol'ical** *a.*

hyperbor'ean *a.* of the extreme north.

hypercrit'ical *a.* too critical.

hyperpla'sia (plā-zhē-ạ) *n.* excessive growth of a body organ.—**hyperpla'sic** *a.* —**hyperplas'tic** *a.*

hy'phen *n.* a short line (-) connecting two words or syllables.—**hy'phenate** *v.t.*

hy'pholin *n.* a drug like penicillin, but applicable to more diseases.

hypno'sis (hip-) *n.* a state like deep sleep in which the subject acts on external suggestion.—**hypnot'ic** *a.* of hypnosis.—*n.* person under hypnosis; thing producing it.—**hyp'notism** *n.* the production of hypnosis.—**hyp'notist** *n.*—**hyp'-notise** *v.t.* produce hypnosis.

hypo-, hyph-, hyp- *prefix* under, as *hypocrite, hyphen, hypallage;* also contraction for *hyposuplphite.*

hypochon'dria (-kon-) *n.* morbid depression.—**hypochon'driac** *n.* affected by this.—**hypochondri'acal** *a.*

hypoc'risy (hip-) *n.* the assuming of a false appearance of virtue; insincerity.—**hyp'ocrite** *n.*—**hypocriti'cal** *a.*—*adv.*

hypoderm'ic *a.* introduced beneath the skin (e.g., hypodermic injection).

hypopla'sia (-plā-zhē-ạ) *n.* in medicine, the incomplete development of a part. —**hypoplas'tic** *a.*

hyposul'phite (sul'-fīt) *n.* in photography, an acid salt (thio-sulphate) used for fixing.

hypot'enuse *n.* the side of a right-angled triangle opposite the right angle.

hypoth'ecate (-th-) *v.t.* to pledge, mortgage.—**hypotheca'tion** *n.*—**hypoth'esis** *n.* supposition as basis for reasoning, assumption (**-eses** (-esēz) *pl.*).—**hypothet'ical** *a.*—**hypothet'ically** *adv.*

hypothy'roidism (-roid-izm) *n.* deficient secretion of the thyroid gland.

hyss'op (his-) *n.* an aromatic herb.

hysteria (his-) *n.* disturbance of (a woman's) nervous system with convulsions, disturbance of mental faculties, etc.; morbid excitement.—**hyster'ical** *a.* —**hyster'ically** *adv.*—**hyster'ics** *n. pl.*

hysterec'tomy *n.* excision of the womb.

hyster'oid *a.* resembling hysteria; typified by nervous paroxysms.

hysterot'omy *n.* surgical incision of the womb.

I

I *pron.* the pronoun of the first person singular.

iamb'us, i'amb *n.* a metrical foot of a short followed by a long syllable (**iamb'uses, -bi; i'ambs** *pl.*).—**iamb'ic** *a.*

Ibe'rian *a.* pertaining to Iberia, that is Spain and Portugal.

i'bex *n.* wild goat with large horns (**i'bexes, i'bices** or **ib'ices** *pl.*).

i'bis *n.* a stork-like bird.

ice *n.* frozen water; a frozen confection.—*v.t.* to cover with ice; cool with ice; cover with sugar (**icing** *pres. p.*—**iced'** *p.t.* and *p.p.*).—**ice'berg** *n.* mass of floating ice.—**ice'blink** *n.* shining whiteness on the horizon caused by the reflection of light from ice.—**i'cicle** *n.* a long hanging spike of ice.—**i'cy** *a.*—**icily** *adv.*

i'chor *n.* in mythology, the blood of the gods; watery fluid from wound, etc.

ichthyol'ogy (ikth-) *n.* branch of zoology treating of fishes.—**ichthyo-saur'us** *n.* prehistoric marine animal (**-ri** *pl.*).

i'cicle *see* **ice.**

i'con *n.* an image (**i'cons, i'cones** (i'ko-nēz) *pl.*).—**icon'oclast** *n.* breaker of images.—**icon'oclasm** *n.*—**-oclas'tic** *a.*

id *n.* in psycho-analysis, the mind's reservoir of instinctive energies.

ide'a *n.* a notion in the mind; way of thinking; vague belief; plan, aim.—**ide'al** *a.* existing only in idea; visionary; perfect.—*n.* perfect type.—**ide'ally** *adv.*—**ide'alism** *n.* imaginative treatment; philosophy that the object of external perception consists of ideas.—**ide'alist** *n.*—**ide'alise** *v.t.* to look upon as ideal.

ident'ity *n.* absolute sameness; individuality (**-ies** *pl.*).—**ident'ical** *a.* the very same.—**ident'ically** *adv.*—**ident'ify** *v.t.* establish identity of; associate (oneself) with inseparably (**-ified** *p.t./p.p.*—**-ifying** *pr.p.*).—**identification** *n.*

id'eograph *n.* a picture symbol, figure, etc., suggesting an object without naming it. Also **id'eogram.**—**ideog'raphy** *n.* representation of things by pictures; phonetic art; shorthand writing.

ides' *n. pl.* the 15th of March, May, July and October and the 13th of other months of the ancient Roman calendar.

idiocy *see* **idiot.**

id'iom *n.* one's language; the way of expression natural to a language; an expression peculiar to it.—**idiomat'ic** *a.* characteristic of a language; marked by the use of idioms, colloquial.—**idiomat'i-cally** *adv.*—**idiosyn'crasy** *n.* feeling or view peculiar to a person.

id'iot *n.* mentally deficient person.—**id'iocy** *n.* state of being an idiot.—**idiot'ic** *a.* very stupid.—**idiot'ically** *adv.*

i'dle *a.* doing nothing; lazy; useless, vain, groundless.—*v.i.* to be idle.—*v.t.* to pass (time) in idleness.—**i'dleness** *n.*—**i'dly** *adv.*
Syn. indolent, unemployed, vacant, futile. *Ant.* hardworking, energetic.

I'do (e'-dō) *n.* an international language, an offshoot of Esperanto.

i'dol *n.* image of a deity as an object of worship; false god; object of excessive devotion.—**idol'ater** *n.* worshipper of idols.—**idol'atress** *fem.*—**idol'atry** *n.*—**idol'atrous** *a.*—**i'dolise** *v.t.* make an idol of.

i'dyll *n.* short description of a picturesque scene or incident—**idyll'ic** *a.*

if *conj.* on the condition or supposition that; whether.—*n.* supposition.

igl'oo *n.* Eskimo's snow hut.

ig'neous *a.* fiery, resulting from fire.—**ignite'** *v.t.* to set on fire, kindle.—*v.i.* to take fire.—**igni'tion** *n.*—**ig'nis fat'uus** *n.* phosphorescent light, will-o'-the-wisp (**ig'nes fat'ui** *pl.*).

igno'ble *a.* mean, base.—**igno'bly** *adv.*

ig'nominy *n.* dishonour, disgrace.—**ignomin'ious** *a.*—**ignomin'iously** *adv.*
Syn. disgrace, humiliation, degradation. *Ant.* honour, elevation.

ignore' *v.t.* disregard, leave out of account.—**ignora'mus** *n.* ignorant person (**-muses** *pl.*).—**ig'norance** *n.* lack of knowledge.—**ig'norant** *a.* **ig'norantly** *adv.*

igua'na (ĭg-wă'-) *n.* a large tree lizard of tropical America.

il- *prefix* for *in-* before "*l.*" *See* **in.**

i'lex *n.* holm-oak.

ilk *a.* same, as in *Mackintosh of that ilk*, meaning Mackintosh of Mackintosh.

ill *a.* out of health; bad, evil; faulty.—*n.* evil, harm.—*adv.* not well; faultily; unfavourably.—**ill'ness** *n.*

ille'gal *a.* unlawful.—**illegality** *n.*

illeg'ible *a.* unable to be read.

illegit'imate *a.* not lawful, born out of wedlock.—**illegit'imacy** *n.*

illib'eral *a.* mean, ungenerous; narrow-minded.—**illiberal'ity** *n.*

illic'it *a.* forbidden, contraband, illegal.

illim'itable *a.* without limit, boundless, unrestricted.—**illimitabil'ity** *n.*

illit'erate *n.* one unable to read or write; *a.* uneducated, lacking knowledge of literature.—**illit'eracy** *n.*

illog'ical *a.* not logical, unreasonable.

illu'minate *v.t.* to light up; to decorate with lights; decorate (book) with gold and colours.—**illumina'tion** *n.*—**illu'-minative** *a.*—**illu'minant** *n.* an agent of lighting.—**illu'mine, illume'** *v.t.* light up.

illu'sion *n.* a deceptive appearance, belief, or statement.—**illu'sionist** *n.* a conjuror.—**illu'sory** *a.*—**illu'sive** *a.*

ill'ustrate *v.t.* to make clear, *esp.* by examples or drawings; adorn with pictures.—**illustra'tion** *n.*—**illus'trative** *a.*—**ill'ustrator** *n.*—**illus'trious** *a.* famous.

ill-will' *n.* enmity, dislike, malice.

im- *prefix* for *in-* before "*b*," "*m*," and "*p*." *See* **in.**

im'age *n.* a statue; semblance; simile; metaphor; counterpart; optical counterpart, as in a mirror.—*v.t.* to make an image of; reflect.—**im'agery** *n.* images; use of rhetorical figures; imaginative thought of language.—**imag'ine** (-j-) *v.t.* to picture to oneself; conjecture; think.—**imag'inable** *a.*—**imag'inary** *a.* existing only in fancy.—**imagina'tion** *n.* mental faculty of making images of things not present; creative ability; fancy.—**imag'inative** *a.*

ima'go *n.* an image; the perfected state of insect life, when the pupa case is

dropped and the enclosed comes forth (ima'goes, imag'ines (i-maj'i-nēz) *pl.*).
imam, imaum (-mawm) *n.* the officer who leads the devotions in a mosque.
im'becile (-ceel) *a.* mentally weak.—*n.* person of weak mind.—**imbecil'ity** *n.*
imbibe' *v.t.* drink in (**imbibed'** *p.t./p.p.*).
im'bricated *a.* bent and hollowed like a roof or gutter tile; lying over each other in regular order, like tiles or shingles on a roof.—**imbrica'tion** *n.*
imbrogl'io (-brōl'yō) *n.* a complicated situation (**-ios** (-yōz) *pl.*).
imbue' *v.t.* to saturate, dye; inspire. (**imbu'ing** *pres.p.*—**imbued'** *p.t.* and *p.p.*)
im'itate *v.t.* to take as model; mimic, copy (**imi'tating** *pres. p.*—**im'itated** *p.t.* and *p.p.*).—**im'itable** *a.*—**imita'tion** *n.*—**im'itative** *a.*—**im'itator** *n.*
immac'ulate *a.* spotless. pure.
immana'tion *n.* entering or flowing in.
imm'anent *a.* abiding in, inherent, indwelling.—**imm'anence** *n.*
immature' *a.* not matured, unripe, undeveloped.—**immatu'rity** *n.*
imme'diate *a.* occurring at once; direct. —**imme'diately** *adv.*—**imme'diacy** *n.*
immemor'ial *a.* beyond memory; very old.—**immemor'ially** *adv.*
immense' *a.* huge ,vast.—**immen'sity** *n.* vastness.—**immense'ly** *adv.*
immerse' *v.t.* to dip, plunge, into a liquid; to absorb (in thought, etc.) (**immersed'** *p.t.* and *p.p.*).—**immer'sion** *n.*
imm'igrate *v.i.* to come or bring into a country as a settler.—**immigra'tion** *n.* —**imm'igrant** *n.* and *a.*
imm'inent *a.* close at hand.—**imm'inently** *adv.*—**imm'inence** *n.*
Syn. threatening, hanging over. *Ant.* distant, remote.
imm'olate *v.t.* to sacrifice.—**immola'tion** *n.*
immor'al *a.* not moral; lacking moral principles; licentious, wicked, vicious, unchaste.—**immorality'** *n.*
immor'tal *n.* one who is immortal or whose fame is everlasting; *a.* living for ever; imperishable, eternal.—**immortali'ty** *n.*—**immortalise'** *v.t.*
immov'able *a.* which cannot be moved; steadfast, unshakable; motionless.
immune' *a.* secure, exempt; proof (against a disease, etc.).—**immu'nity** *n.* —**im'munise** *v.* to make immune.
immure' *v.t.* to imprison.
imp *n.* a little devil; a mischievous child.
impact' *n.* collision.
impair' *v.t.* weaken, damage, diminish. —**impair'ment** *n.*
impale' *v.t.* transfix, *esp.* on a stake, to put to death; combine (two coats of arms) by placing them side by side with a line between.—**impale'ment** *n.*
impart' *v.t.* to give a share of; communicate.—**imparta'tion** *n.*
impartial *a.* just, fair, unprejudiced, disinterested.—**impartiality** *n.*
im'passe (-pas') a position from which there is no way out; a blind alley.
impas'sable *a.* which cannot be passed.
impass'ible *a.* not liable to pain or suffering.—**impassibility'** *n.*—**impass'ive** *a.* without feeling; calm.—**impassiv'ity** *n.*
impas'sioned *a.* deeply moved.
impeach' *v.t.* call in question; accuse; accuse of treason; disparage.—**impeach'able** *a.*—**impeachmen't** *n.*
impa'tience *n.* lacking patience.—**impa'tient** *a.* unwilling to bear delay, restless.—**impa'tiently** *adv.*
impecc'able *a.* incapable of sin; perfect.
impecu'nious *a.* having no money, penniless.—**impecunios'ity** *n.*
impede' *v.t.* to hinder, obstruct.—**imped'iment** *n.* obstacle.—**impediment'a** *n. pl.* baggage, *esp.* of an army.—**imped'ance** *n.* in electricity, opposition offered to an alternating current by resistance, inductance, or capacity.
impel' *v.t.* to drive, force.—**impell'er** *n.* (motoring) spindle and vanes of a rotary pump (**impelled'** *p.t.* and *p.p.*).
impend' *v.i.* be imminent; **impending** *a.* coming.—**impend'ent** *a.*
imper'ative *a.* expressing command; urgent, necessary.—*n.* the imperative mood.—**imper'atively** *adv.*
impercept'ible *a.* unable to be seen or felt.—**impercept'ibly** *adv.*
imper'fect *a.* faulty, defective; incomplete.—**imperfection** *n.*
impe'rial *a.* of an empire; of an emperor; majestic.—*n.* a small part of the beard left growing below lower lip (after Napoleon III).—**imper'ialism** *n.* extension of empire; belief in policy of empire. —**impe'rialist** *n.*—**imperialis'tic** *a.*
impe'rious *a.* domineering, dictatorial; arrogant; urgent.
imperil' *v.t.* to bring into peril.
imper'ishable *a.* undying, everlasting, eternal, indestructible.
imper'sonal *a.* having no personal significance.—**impersonally** *adv.*
impersonate *v.t.* play the part of.—**impersona'tion** *n.*—**imper'sonator** *n.*
impert'inent *a.* insolent, saucy; irrelevant.—**impert'inence** *n.* rudeness.
impertur'bable *a.* incapable of being disturbed, calm.—**impertur'bably** *adv.*
imper'vious *a.* not admitting of passage through; impenetrable.—**imper'viously** *adv.*—**imper'viousness** *n.*
im'petus *n.* force with which a body moves; impulse.—**impet'uous** *a.* ardent. vehement; acting or moving with a rush. —**impet'uously** *adv.*—**impetuos'ity** *n.*
im'pi *n.* a brigade of Kaffir warriors.
impi'ety *n.* lack of reverence, wickedness, ungodliness.—**imp'ious** *a.*
impinge' *v.i.* to dash, strike.
implac'able *a.* inexorable; not to be assuaged.—**implacabil'ity** *n.*
implant' *v.t.* to insert, fix.

im'plement *n.* a tool, instrument, utensil.—*v.t.* to carry into effect.
im'plicate *v.t.* to involve, include; entangle; imply.—**implica'tion** *n.*—**implic'it** (-s-) *a.* implied but not expressed; involved in a general principle, exclusive of individual judgment.—**implic'itly** (-s-) *adv.*—**imply'** *v.t.* involve the truth of (-**plied'** *p.t.* and *p.p.*—-**ply'ing** *pres. p.*).
implore' *v.t.* to entreat earnestly.
impolite' *a.* rude, unmannerly.
impol'itic *a.* not wise, imprudent.
import' *v.t.* to bring in, introduce (*esp.* goods from a foreign country); imply, mean; express; be of consequence to.—**im'port** *n.* a thing imported; meaning; importance.—**importa'tion** *n.*—**import'er** *n.*—**import'able** *a.*—**import'ant** *a.* of consequence; momentous; pompous.—**import'antly** *adv.*—**import'ance** *n.*
impor'tune *v.t.* to solicit pressingly.—**impor'tunate** *a.* persistent in soliciting.—**importu'nity** *n.*—**impor'tunately** *adv.*
impose' *v.t.* to lay (a tax, duty, etc.) upon.—*v.i.* to be impressive; take advantage, practise deceit (on).—**imposi'tion** *n.*-**impos'tor** *n.* a deceiver, swindler; one who assumes a false character.—**impos'ture** *n.*—**im post** *n.* duty, tax; upper course of a pillar.
imposs'ible *a.* that cannot be done; not feasible; intolerable.—**imposs'ibly** *adv.*—**impossibil'ity** *n.*
im'potent *a.* powerless, ineffective.—**im'potence** *n.*—**im'potently** *adv.*
impound' *v.t.* to shut up (cattle, etc.) in a pound; confiscate.
impoverish' *v.t.* to make poor or weak; he **impov'erishes**;—**impov'erishment** *n.*
impract'icable *a.* which cannot be done.—**impract'ical** *a.* not practical.
imprecation' *n.* an invoking of (evil); a curse.—**im'precate** *v.t.*
impreg'nable *a.* proof against attack.—**impregna'bility** *n.*—**impreg'nably** *adv.*
impreg'nate *v.t.* to make pregnant; fertilise; saturate.—**impregna'tion** *n.*
impresar'io *n.* an organiser and producer of a public entertainment; operatic manager (-**rios**, -**ri** (-rē) *pl.*).
impress' *v.t.* to imprint, stamp; fix; generate; affect deeply.—**im'press** *n.* act of impressing, mark impressed.—**impress'ible** *a.*—**impressibil'ity** *n.*—**impres'sion** *n.* impress; a printed copy; total of copies printed at once; effect produced, *esp.* on mind or feelings; notion, belief.—**impres'sionable** *a.* easily impressed.—**impressionabil'ity** *n.*—**impres'sionism** *n.* method of painting or writing to give general effect without detail.—**impres'sionist** *n.*—**impressionis'tic** *a.*—**impress'ive** *a.* solemn; making a deep impression.
impress' *v.t.* to press into, seize for service.—**impress'ment** *n.*
imprest' *v.t.* to advance on loan.—**im'prest** *n.* money advanced on loan.
imprint' *v.t.* to impress; stamp.—**im'print** *n.* impression, stamp; publisher's name on title-page of book.
imprison' (-z-) *v.t.* to put in prison, confine.—**impris'onment** *n.*
impromp'tu *adv.* and *a.* extempore.—*n.* something composed without previous preparation.
improp'er *a.* wrong; unsuitable; indecent.—**impropri'ety** *n.* improper behaviour; unfitness.
impro'priate *v.t.* to place (tithes, etc.) in hands of a layman.—**impropria'tion** *n.*
improve' (-ōōv) *v.t.* to make better. make good use of.—*v.i.* to become better, progress.-**improv'able** *a.*-**improve'ment** *n.* getting better; gain.
Syn. amend, ameliorate. *Ant.* spoil, mar.
improv'ident *a.* not provident; negligent, inconsiderate.—**improv'idence** *n.*
im'provise *v.t.* to compose (music, etc.) without preparation; arrange, perform without warning.—**improvisa'tion** *n.*
impru'dent *a.* rash, indiscreet.
im'pudent *a.* pert, insolent, saucy.—**im'pudently** *adv.*—**im'pudence** *n.*
impugn' (-ūn') *v.t.* to call in question.
im'pulse *n.* sudden application of force; motion caused by it; sudden inclination to act; incitement.-**impul'sion** *n.*—**impul'sive** *a.* given to acting without reflection.—**impul'sively** *adv.*
impu'nity *n.* freedom from punishment or hurtful consequences.
impure' *a.* not pure; mixed; defiled by sin.—**impu'rity** *n.*—(**impurities** *pl.*).
impute' *v.t.* to attribute; ascribe.—**imputabil'ity** *n.*—**imputa'tion** *n.*
in *prep.* expresses inclusion within limits.—*adv.* in or into some state, place, etc. (**inn'er** *a. comp.*—**in'most**, **inn'ermost** *a. sup.*).
in- *prefix* with its forms **il-**, **im-**, **ir-** negatives the idea of the simple word; e.g., **inac'tive** *a.* not active; also meaning in, into, upon as **inter**, **impend**, **irrigate.** Such words are omitted where the meaning may easily be inferred from the simple word.
inadvert'ent *a.* unintentional.—**inadvert'ence**, carelessness, lack of thought.—**inadvert'ency** *n.*—**inadvert'ently** *adv.*
ina'lienable *a.* that cannot be given away or taken away.
inane' *a.* empty, void; foolish, silly.—**inan'ity** *n.*—**inani'tion** *n.* a being empty.
inan'imate *a.* lifeless, dull.
in'asmuch *adv.* seeing that.
inaug'urate *v.t.* admit to office; begin, initiate the use of, *esp.* with ceremony.—**inaug'ural** *a.*—**inaug'urally** *adv.*—**inaugura'tion** *n.*—**inaug'urator** *n.*
inauspi'cious *a.* not auspicious; ill-omened; unlucky.—**inauspi'ciously** *adv.*
in'board *a.* inside the hull or bulwarks.
in'bred, in'born *a.* innate, inherent.—

inbreed'ing *n.* breeding by crossing similar types or species.
incal'culable *a.* not capable of being calculated; very great; uncertain.
incandes'cent *a.* glowing with heat, shining; of artificial light, produced by glowing filament.—**incandes'cence** *n.*—**incandesce'** *v.i.* and *t.*
incanta'tion *n.* a magic spell, a charm.
incapac'itate *v.t.* to disable, make unfit.—**incapac'ity** *n.* unfitness.
incar'cerate *v.t.* to imprison.—**incarcera'tion** *n.*—**incar'cerator** *n.*
incarn'adine *v.t.* to dye crimson.—*a.* crimson, blood-red.
incarn'ate *v.t.* to embody in flesh.—*a.* embodied in flesh.—**incarna'tion** *n.*
incen'diary *a.* of the malicious setting on fire of property; guilty of this, inflammatory.—*n.* one guilty of arson, an incendiary person.—**incen'diary bomb** *n.* fire bomb.—**incen'diarism** *n.*
incense' *v.t.* to enrage.—**in'cense** *n.* perfumes burned in religious ceremonies; their smoke.—*v.t.* to burn incense to.
incen'tive *a.* arousing, encouraging.—*n.* motive; something that arouses to feeling or action.
incep'tion *n.* beginning.—**incep'tive** *a.* beginning, commencing, initial.
incess'ant *a.* unceasing.—**incess'antly** *adv.* unceasingly.
in'cest *n.* sexual intercourse of kindred within forbidden degrees.—**incest'uous** *a.*
inch *n.* one-twelfth of a foot; a small island; by inches *adv.* gradually.
in'choate (in'kō-) *a.* just begun.
in'cident *n.* an event, occurrence.—*a.* naturally attaching to; striking, falling (upon).—**in'cidence** *n.* a falling on, or affecting.—**inciden'tal** *a.* casual, not essential.—**incident'ally** *adv.*
incin'erate *v.t.* to consume by fire.—**incin'erator** *n.*—**incinera'tion** *n.*
incip'ient *a.* beginning.
incise' *v.t.* to cut into; engrave.—**inci'sion** (-siz-) *n.*—**inci'sive** (-sī-) *a.* sharp; penetrating, pointed, trenchant.—**inci'sor** *n.* a cutting tooth.
incite' *v.t.* urge, stir up.—**incite'ment** *n.*
inclem'ent *a.* of weather, stormy, severe, cold.—**inclem'ency** *n.*
incline' *v.t.* to bend, turn from the vertical; dispose.—*v.i.* to slope; be disposed.—**in'cline** *n.*—**inclina'tion** *n.*
include' *v.t.* to reckon in; comprise, contain; shut in.—**inclu'sion** *n.*—**inclu'sive** *a.*—**inclu'sively** *adv.*
incog'nito *adv.* with identity concealed —*a.* concealing or not avowing identity. —*n.* this condition (**-tos** (-tōz) *pl.*).
incoher'ent *a.* not coherent; loose: inconsistent.-**incoher'ently** *adv.*-**incoher'ence** *n.* want of cohesion.
in'come *n.* receipts, money coming in from wages, business, etc.—**in'come tax** *n.* government tax on personal income.
incom'parable *a.* unequalled, matchless, unrivalled.—**incom'parably** *adv.*
incong'ruous (-ng'g-) *a.* not accordant, absurd.—**incongru'ity** *n.*
incon'sequent *a.* not following from the premises; illogical.
inconsid'erate *a.* not considerate.
inconsis'tent *a.* incompatible; not uniform.—**inconsistence** *n.*
inconven'ience *n.* state or quality of being inconvenient; trouble.—**inconveni'ent** *a.* troublesome.
incorporate' *v.t.* to unite into one body; form legally into a corporation; include. —**incorpora'tion** *n.*—**incorpora'tor** *n.*
increase' *v.i.* to become greater in size, number, etc.—*v.t.* to make greater.—**in'crease** *n.* growth, enlargement, multiplication.—**in'crement** *n.* increase; profit.
Syn. enlarge, expand, augment, amplify. *Ant.* decrease, diminish, contract.
incred'ible *a.* surprising, unbelievable. —**incredi'bly** *adv.*—**incredulous** *a.* sceptical.—**incredul'ity** *n.* doubt.
in'crement *n.* increase; an addition.
incrim'inate *v.t.* to charge with crime, involve in accusation.—**incrim'inatory** *a.*
incrust *see* **encrust.**
in'cubate *v.t.* to hatch (eggs).—*v.i.* to sit on eggs; of disease germs, to pass through the stage between infection and appearance of symptoms.—**incuba'tion** *n.*—**in'cubator** *n.* apparatus for artificial hatching of eggs.
in'cubus *n.* a nightmare (**-buses, -bi** *pl.*).
in'culcate *v.t.* to impress on the mind, to teach repeatedly.—**inculca'tion** *n.*
incumbent' *a.* lying, resting (on).—*n.* holder of church benefice.—**incumb'ency** *n.* office, tenure of incumbent.
incunab'ula *n.pl.* earliest phase of development; books printed in the earliest stages of printing.
incur' *v.t.* to fall into, bring upon oneself (**incurred'** *p.t.* and *p.p.*).—**incur'sion** *n.* invasion.—**incur'sive** *a.*
incur'able *a.* incapable of being cured; hopelessly bad.—**incur'ably** *adv.*
inda'ba *n.* an important council meeting of natives in S. Africa; *that is your indaba*, that is your concern.
indebt'ed (-det-) *a.* owing, in debt, obliged.—**indebt'edness** *n.*
indeed' *adv.* in truth, really.
indefat'igable *a.* untiring, unremitting. —**indefati'gably** *adv.*
indefeas'ible (-fēz'-) *a.* that cannot be lost or annulled or forfeited.
indefen'sible *a.* untenable, unjustifiable.—**indefen'sibly** *adv.*
indel'ible *a.* that cannot be blotted out, effaced or erased; permanent.—**indel'ibly** *adv.*—**indelibil'ity** *n.*
indem'nity *n.* security against loss; compensation, *esp.* exacted by a victorious country after war.—**indem'nify** *v.t.*

to give indemnity to; to compensate (-ified *p.t.* and *p.p.*—-ifying *pres. p.*).
indent' *v.t.* to make notches or holes in; draw up a document in duplicate; make an order (*upon* some one *for*); order by indent.—**in'dent** *n.* a notch; an order, requisition.—**indenta'tion** *n.*—**inden'ture** *n.* an indented document; a sealed agreement.—*v.t.* to bind by indenture.
indepen'dent *a.* not subject to others; self-directing; free; unconnected.—**independ'ently** *adv.*—**indepen'dence, indepen'dency** *n.* state or quality of being independent; self-reliance, self-support.
indescri'bable *a.* incapable of being described.—**indescri'bably** *adv.*
in'dex *n.* forefinger; anything that points out, an indicator; alphabetical list of contents of book.—*v.t.* to provide a book with an index; to insert in an index; in mathematics, a small figure indicating "power," e.g., 2^3 is $2 \times 2 \times 2$; (**in'dexes, in'dices** (-sēz) *pl.*).
indicate *v.t.* to point out, state briefly.—**indica'tion** *n.*—**indi'cative** *a.* that indicates, suggestive; in grammar, stating as a fact.—**in'dicator** *n.*
in'dia-rubber *n.* rubber, caoutchouc.
indict' (-dit) *v.t.* to accuse, *esp.* by legal process.—**indict'ment** *n.*—**indict'able** *a.*
indiff'erent *a.* impartial; careless; unimportant; neither good nor bad; having no inclination for or against.—**indiff'erently** *adv.*—**indiff'erence** *n.*
indi'genous (-dij-) *a.* born in, natural to, a country; native.—**in'digene** *n.*
in'digent (-j-) *a.* poor, needy.—**in'digence** *n.* state of poverty.
indigest'ible *a.* not easily digested.—**indiges'tion** *n.* failure to digest food.
indig'nant *a.* moved by anger and scorn; angered by injury.—**indig'nantly** *adv.*—**indigna'tion** *n.*—**indig'nity** *n.* unworthy treatment; insult.
in'digo *n.* deep blue dye obtained from plant; the plant (**-gos, -goes** (-gōz) *pl.*).
indite' *v.t.* to write, put into words.
individ'ual *a.* single; characteristic of a single person or thing.—*n.* a single person.—**individ'ually** *adv.* separately.—**individual'ity** *n.* distinctive character.—**individ'ualism** *n.* social theory of free action of individuals.—**individ'ualist** *n.*—**individualis'tic** *a.*
in'dolent *a.* lazy, slothful, inert.—**in'dolence** *n.*—**in'dolently** *adv.*
indom'itable *a.* unyielding, unconquerable, never giving up.—**indom'itably** *adv.*
in'door *a.* within a house.—**in'doors** *adv.*
indorse *see* **endorse.**
indu'bitable *a.* beyond doubt.
induce' *v.t.* to persuade; bring about, infer; produce (electricity) by induction.
inducem'ent *n.* incentive, attraction.
induct' *v.t.* to install in office.—**induc'tion** *n.* inducting; a general inference from particular instances; production of electric or magnetic state in a body by its being near (not touching) an electrified or magnetised body; internal combustion engine, that part of the piston's action which draws gas from carburettor.—**induc'tive** *a.*—**induc'tively** *adv.*
indulge' *v.t.* to gratify; give free course to; take pleasure in freely.—**indul'gent** *a.*—**indul'gence** *n.*—**indul'gently** *adv.*
indu'na *n.* S. Africa, a native councillor.
in'durate *v.t.* to harden.
in'dustry *n.* diligence; habitual hard work; a branch of manufacture or trade.—**indus'trious** *a.* diligent, hard-working.—**indus'trial** *a.* of industries, trades.—**indus'trialism** *n.* factory system.
ine'briate *v.t.* to make drunk.—*a.* drunken.—*n.* a drunkard.—**inebria'tion** *n.*—**inebri'ety** *n.* drunkenness.
ined'ible *a.* not eatable; unfit for food.
ineff'able *a.* unspeakable, too great for words.—**ineff'ably** *adv.*
ineffi'cient *a.* not efficient, incompetent.—**ineffi'ciency** *n.*
inel'igible (-ji-) *a.* incapable of being elected to an office.—**ineligibil'ity** *n.*
inept' *a.* out of place.—**inept'itude** *n.*
inert' *a.* without power of action or resistance; slow, sluggish, indolent.—**iner'tia** (-shya) *n.* the property by which matter continues in its existing state of rest or motion in a straight line unless that state is changed by external force.—**inert'ly** *adv.*—**inert'ness** *n.*
ines'timable *a.* too great to be measured; invaluable.
inev'itable *a.* unavoidable, inescapable.—**inev'itably** *adv.*—**inevitabili'ty** *n.*
inex'orable *a.* relentless, not yielding to entreaties.—**inex'orably** *adv.*
inex'plicable *n.* which cannot be explained; unaccountable.
inexpug'nable *a.* impregnable; of argument, unanswerable.
infall'ible *a.* not liable to fail.—**infall'ibly** *adv.*—**infallibil'ity** *n.*
in'famous *a.* of ill fame, shameless, bad.—**in'famy** *n.*—**in'famously** *adv.*
in'fant *n.* child under 7; person under 21, minor.—**in'fancy** *n.*—**infant'icide** *n.* murder of new-born child; one guilty of this.—**in'fantile** *a.* childish.
in'fantry *n.* foot soldiers.—**infantryman.**
infat'uate *v.t.* affect to folly or foolish passion.—**infatua'tion** *n.*
infect' *v.t.* to make noxious; affect (with disease).—**infec'tion** *n.*—**infec'tious** *a.* catching; pestilential.
infer' *v.t.* to deduce by reasoning, conclude.—**in'ference** *n.*—**inferen'tial** *a.*—**infer'able** *a.* (**inferred'** *p.t.* and *p.p.*).
infe'rior *a.* lower; of poor quality.—*n.* one lower (in rank, etc.).—**inferior'ity** *n.*—**inferiority complex** *n.* in psychoanalysis, a repressed sense of inferiority.
infern'al *a.* of the lower world; hellish.—**infern'ally** *adv.*—**infer'no** *n.* hell.

infer'tile *a.* barren.—**infertil'ity** *n.*
infest' *v.t.* haunt, swarm in.
in'fidel *n.* unbeliever.—*a.* unbelieving.—**infidel'ity** *n.* disbelief, disloyalty.
infiltrate *v.i.* to percolate, trickle through.—*v.t.* to cause to pass through pores.—**infiltra'tion** *n.*
in'finite (-it) *a.* boundless.—**infinites'imal** *a.* extremely or infinitely small.—**in'finitely** *adv.*—**infin'ity** *n.*—**infin'itive** *a.* in grammar, in the mood expressing the notion of the verb without limitation by any particular subject.—*n.* a verb in this mood; the mood.
infirm' *a.* physically or mentally weak, *esp.* through age, irresolute.—**infirm'ity** *n.*—**infirm'ary** *n.* hospital.
inflame' *v.t.* to set alight, to raise to heat or excitement.—*v.i.* to catch fire; become excited.—**inflamm'able** *a.* easily set on fire; excitable.—**inflammabil'ity** *n.*
inflamma'tion *n.* a morbid process affecting part of body with pain, redness, swelling.—**inflamm'atory** *a.*
inflate' *v.t.* to blow up with air or gas; raise (price) artificially; increase (currency) abnormally.—**infla'tion** *n.*
inflect' *v.t.* to bend; to modify (words) to show grammatical relationships.—**inflec'tion, inflex'ion** *n.*
inflex'ible *a.* incapable of being bent.—**inflex'ibility** *adv.*—**inflexibil'ity** *n.*
inflict' *v.t.* to impose, deliver forcibly, cause to be borne.—**inflic'tion** *n.*
infloresc'ence *n.* unfolding of blossoms.
in'fluence *n.* agent or action working invisibly (upon); ascendancy; moral power (over, with); thing or person exercising this.—*v.t.* to exert influence upon (**in'fluenced** *p.t.* and *p.p.*).—**influen'tial** *a.*—**influen'tially** *adv.*
influen'za *n.* contagious feverish illness.
in'flux *n.* a flowing in.
inform' *v.t.* to tell; inspire.—*v.i.* to bring a charge against.—**inform'ant** *n.* one who tells.—**informa'tion** *n.* telling; what is told, knowledge.—**inform'ative** *a.*—**inform'er** *n.* one who brings a charge.
in'fra *adv.* below; under; after.—**in'fra-red** *a.* light rays below red end of visible spectrum.—**in'fra-red photography** *n.* photography with special lens and plate giving clearer photograph.
infrac'tion *n.* violation; breach.
infre'quent *a.* seldom happening.—**infre'quently** *adv.*—**infre'quence, -ency** *n.*
infringe' *v.t.* to transgress, break.—**infringe'ment** *n.*—**infrac'tion** *n.*
infu'riate *v.t.* to enrage, fill with fury.
infuse' *v.t.* to pour in, instil; steep in order to extract soluble properties.—**infu'sion** *n.* infusing; liquid obtained.
Syn. soak, macerate, implant, inspire.
infuso'ria *n. pl.* microscopic animalcules found in fluids.—**infuso'rial** *a.*
inge'nious *a.* clever; cleverly contrived.—**ingenu'ity** *n.* skill.—**inge'niously** *adv.*
ingen'uous *a.* frank, artless, innocent, naive.—**ingen'uously** *adv.*
Syn. noble, generous, open, unreserved, plain, sincere, candid, fair. *Ant.* cunning, sly, artful, studied, insincere, artificial.
in'gle (ing'gl) *n.* a fire on a hearth.—**in'gle-nook** *n.* a chimney-corner.
in'got (ing-g-) *n.* a brick of cast metal.
ingra'tiate *v. refl.* to get oneself into favour.—**ingra'tiatingly** *adv.*
ingrain' *v.t.* to stain, dye.—**ingrained'** *a.* thoroughly inwrought.
ingre'dient *n.* one part of a mixture.
in'gress *n.* entrance, means of entrance.
inhab'it *v.t.* to dwell in.—**inhab'itable** *a.*—**inhab'itant** *n.*—**inhabita'tion** *n.*
inhale' *v.t.* to breathe in.—*v.i.* to breathe in air.—**inha'lant** *n.*—**inhala'tion** *n.*
inhere' *v.i.* of qualities, to exist (in); of rights, to be vested (in person).—**inhe'rent** *s.*—**inhe'rently** *adv.*—**inhe'rence** *n.*
inher'it *v.t.* to receive by legal descent, as heir; derive from parents.—*v.i.* to succeed as heir.—**inher'itance** *n.*—**inher'itor** *n.*—**inher'itress, inher'itrix** *fem.*
inhe'sion *n.* inherence.
inhib'it *v.t.* to repress, restrain; forbid to exercise clerical functions; hinder (action).—**inhibi'tion** *n.* morbid reluctance.—**inhib'itory** *a.*
inhu'man *a.* cruel, brutal, barbarous, savage.—**inhuman'ity** *n.*
inhume' *v.t.* to bury.—**inhuma'tion** *n.*
inimical *a.* hostile, hurtful, unfriendly.
Syn. adverse, ill-disposed, antagonistic. *Ant.* friendly, kindly-disposed.
inimitable *a.* defying imitation, excellent.—**inim'itably** *adv.*
iniq'uity *n.* wickedness.—**iniq'uitous** *a.*
ini'tial (-ish-) *a.* of the beginning, occurring at the beginning.—*n.* an initial letter.—*v.t.* to mark, sign, with one's initials.—**ini'tiate** *v.t.* to set on foot, begin; admit, *esp.* into a secret society.—*n.* an initiated person.—**initia'tion** *n.*—**ini'tiative** *n.* first step, lead, power of acting independently.—**ini'tiatory** *a.*
inject' *v.t.* to force in (fluid, medicine, etc.), as with a hypodermic syringe; fill thus.—**injec'tion** *n.*—**injec'tor** *n.*
injunc'tion *n.* a judicial order to restrain; an authoritative order.
in'jury *n.* wrong, damage, harm.—**in'jure** *v.t.* to do wrong to, damage.—**inju'rious** *a.*—**injur'iously** *adv.*
injus'tice *n.* want of equity; unfairness; wrong.—**injust'ly** *adv.*
ink *n.* fluid used for writing; paste used for printing.—*v.t.* to mark with ink; cover or smear with it.—**ink'y** *a.*—**ink'pot** *n.*—**ink'bottle** *n.*—**ink'well** *n.* vessel for ink.—**ink'stand** *n.*—**ink'er** *n.* an instrument recording with ink.
ink'ling *n.* a hint, or suspicion.
in'land *n.* the interior of a country.—*a.* in this; away from the sea; within a country.—*adv.* in or towards the inland.

in'lay *v.t.* to embed; to decorate thus (**inlaid'** *p.t.* and *p.p.*).–*n.* inlaid work.
in'let *n.* entrance; creek; a piece inserted.
in'ly *adv.* in the heart, inwardly.
in'mate *n.* an occupant, inhabitant.
inmost *a.* most inward.—*sup.* of **in**.
inn *n.* public house for lodging and refreshment.—**inn'keeper** *n.*—**Inns of Court** *n.* the four societies admitting to the English Bar, their buildings.
innate' *a.* inborn, natural.
inn'er *a.* lying within.—*comp.* of **in.**—*n.* the ring next the bull on a target. —**inner tube,** rubber air tube of pneumatic tyre.—**inner'most** *a. sup.* of **in.**
inn'ings *n. pl.* in games, the batsman's turn of play, a side's turn of batting.
inn'ocent *a.* free from guilt; guileless; harmless.—*n.* an innocent person, *esp.* a young child; an idiot.—**inn'ocence** *n.*—**inn'ocently** *adv.*—**innoc'uous** *a.* harmless.
inn'ovate *v.t.* to bring in changes, new things.—**inn'ovator** *n.*—**innova'tion** *n.*
innuen'do *n.* an allusive remark, hint; indirect accusation (**-does** (-dōz) *pl.*).
innu'merable *a.* countless, very numerous.—**innu'merably** *adv.*
inoc'ulate *v.t.* to treat with disease germs, *esp.* as a protection; implant (disease germs).—**inocula'tion** *n.*
ino'dorous *a.* having no scent.
inoffen'sive *a.* giving no offence.—**inoffen'sively** *adv.*—**inoffen'siveness** *n.*
inop'erable *a.* not able to be operated upon; not able to be carried out.
inop'erative *a.* not operative; producing no effect.
inopp'ortune *a.* unseasonable in time.
inord'inate *a.* excessive, too great.
inorgan'ic *a.* devoid of organised structure; pertaining to substances without carbon.—**inorgan'ically** *adv.*
in'-patient *n.* a patient that stays in an infirmary or hospital.
in'put *n.* in electricity, power supplied to battery, condenser, etc.
in'quest *n.* a legal or judicial inquiry.
inquire', enquire' *v.i.* to seek information.—*v.t.* to ask to be told.—**inqui'rer, enqui'rer** *n.*—**inqui'ry, enqui'ry** *n.*—**inquisi'tion** *n.* an investigation, official inquiry.—**Inquis'ition** *n.* a tribunal for the suppression of heresy.—**inquis'itor** *n.*—**inquisitor'ial** *a.*—**inquis'itive** *a.* curious; prying.—**inquis'itively** *adv.*
in'road *n.* an incursion, attack, raid.
insane' *a.* of unsound mind; lunatic.—**insane'ly** *adv.*—**insan'ity** *n.* madness.
inscribe' *v.t.* to write (*in* or *on* something); mark; trace (figure) within another; delicate.—**inscrip'tion** *n.* words inscribed on a monument, coin, etc.
inscru'table *a.* mysterious, impenetrable.–**inscru'tably** *adv.*–**inscrutabil'ity** *n.*
in'sect *n.* small invertebrate animal with 6 legs, body in 3 parts, head, thorax, abdomen, and 2 or 4 wings.—**insect'icide** *n.* preparation for killing insects.—**insectiv'orous** *a.* insect-eating.
inselec'tive *a.* in wireless, of receiver, having poor selectivity.
insem'inate *v.t.* to sow, sow in; impregnate.—**artificial insemina'tion** impregnation of female by artificial means.
insen'sate *a.* without sensibility; stupid.
insert' *v.t.* to place or put (*in, into, between*); introduce (*into* written matter, etc.).—**inser'tion** *n.*
in'set *n.* something extra inserted.
in'shore *adv.* and *a.* near the shore.
in'side *n.* the inner side, surface, or part. —*a.* of, in, or on, the inside.—*adv.* in or into the inside.—*prep.* within.
insid'ious *a.* stealthy, treacherous; working secretly or slowly (of disease, etc.).—**insid'iously** *adv.*
in'sight (-sīt) *n.* mental penetration.
insig'nia *n. pl.* badges, emblems or symbols of an honour or office.
insignif'icance *n.* unimportance.—**insignif'icant** *a.* unimpressive, unimposing; trivial, unimportant.
insin'uate *v.t.* to bring or get (something *into* something) gradually or subtly to hint.—**insinua'tion** *n.*—**insin'uating** *a.*
insip'id *a.* dull, tasteless.—**insipid'ity** *n.*
insist' *v.i.* to dwell, maintain, demand persistently.—**insist'ent** *a.* urgent—**insist'ently** *adv.*—**insist'ence** *n.*
in'solate *v.t.* to prepare by exposure to the sun.—**insola'tion** *n.*
in'solent *a.* insulting, offensively contemptuous–**in'solently** *adv.*–**in'solence** *n.*
insolv'ent *a.* bankrupt—*n.*
insom'nia *n.* sleeplessness.
inspan' *v.t.* to yoke to a vehicle.
inspect' *v.t.* to examine closely or officially.—**inspec'tion** *n.*—**inspec'tor** *n.* —**inspec'torate** *n.*—**inspector'ial** *a.*
inspect'oscope *n.* X-ray device to reveal forbidden objects in parcels.
inspire' *v.t.* to breathe in; infuse thought or feeling into; arouse, create a feeling or thought.—**inspira'tion** *n.*
inspir'it *v.t.* to animate, put spirit into.
install' *v.t.* to place (person in an office. etc.) with ceremony; establish, have put in.—**installa'tion** *n.*
instal'ment (-awl-) *n.* payment of part of a debt; any of parts of a whole delivered in succession.—**instalment plan** system of paying for goods by agreed regular instalments.
in'stance *n.* an example; particular case; request; place in a series.—*v.t.* to cite.—**in'stant** *a.* urgent; belonging to the current month; immediate.–*n.* moment, a point of time.—**in'stantly** *adv.* immediately.—**instanta'neous** *a.* happening in an instant.—**instanta'neously** *adv.*
instead' (-ed) *adv.* in place (of).
in'step *n.* the curved top of the foot between toes and ankle.

in'stigate *v.t.* to incite, bring about.—**instiga'tion** *n.*—**in'stigator** *n.*
instil' *v.t.* to put in by drops; inculcate, —**instilla'tion** *n.*—**instil'ment** *n.*
in'stinct *n.* inborn impulse or propensity; unconscious skill.—**instinct'** *a.* charged, full.—**instinct'ive** *a.*—**instinct'ively** *adv.*
instito'rial *a.* in law, pertaining to an agent or factor.
in'stitute *v.t.* to establish, found; appoint; set going.—*n.* a society for promoting some public object. *esp.* scientific; its building.—**institu'tion** *n.* instituting; an established custom or law; an institute.—**institut'ional** *a.*—**in'stitutor** *n.*
instruct' *v.t.* to teach, inform, direct.—**instruc'tion** *n.* teaching, education. —**instruc'tive** *a.*—**instruc'tively** *adv.*—**instruc'tor** *n.*—**instruc'tress** *fem.*
in'strument *n.* tool or implement; person or thing made use of; a device for producing music; a legal document.—**instrument'al** *a.*—**instrument'ally** *adv.*—**instrumental'ity** *n.*—**instrumenta'tion** *n.* arrangement of music for instruments.
insubor'dinate *a.* not submissive; mutinous.—**insubordina'tion** *n.*
insuffi'cient *a.* not sufficient, inadequate.—**insuffi'ciency** *n.*
in'sular *a.* belonging to islands; narrow-minded.—**insular'ity** *n.*—**in'sulate** *v.t.* to isolate, *esp.* by materials not conducting electricity.—**insula'tion** *n.*—**in'sulator** *n.*—**in'sulated tape** *n.* adhesive tape of indiarubber for winding round conductors of electricity.
in'sulin *n.* animal pancreatic extract used in treatment of diabetes and in mental disease.
insult' *v.t.* abuse in act or word.—**in'sult** *n.* scornful abuse, affront.—**insult'ing** *a.*
insu'perable *a.* that can not be got over.—**insu'perably** *adv.*
insure' *v.t.* to secure payment of a sum in event of loss, death, etc., by a contract and payment of sums called premiums; to make such a contract; make safe (against); make certain.—**insur'ance** *n.*—**insur'able** *a.*—**insu'rer** *n.*—**insu'rance-policy** *n.* contract of insurance.—**insu'rant** *n.*
insurg'ent *a.* in revolt.—*n.* one in revolt.—**insurrec'tion** *n.* a rising, revolt.
insuscep'tible *a.* not capable of being moved or impressed.—**insusceptibil'ity** *n.*
intact' *a.* whole, untouched, undamaged. *Syn.* undefiled, undamaged, unhurt. *Ant.* interfered with, damaged.
intagl'io (-tal-) *n.* an incised design; a gem so cut (**-ios** (-yōz), **-i** (-yē) *pl.*).
in'take *n.* that which is taken in; a point where a tube narrows; in motoring, passage for air to enter carburettor.
intan'gible *a.* not perceptible to the touch, impalpable; incapable of mental definition.—**intangibil'ity** *n.*
in'teger (-j-) *n.* a whole number.—**in'tegral** (-g-) *a.*—**in'tegrate** *v.t.* to combine into a whole.—**integra'tion** *n.*—**integ'rity** *n.* original perfect state; honesty.
integ'ument *n.* covering, skin, rind.
in'tellect *n.* the faculty of thinking and reasoning.—**intellec'tual** *a.* of or appealing to, the intellect; having good intellect. —*n.* an intellectual person.—**intellec'tual'ity** *n.*—**intell'igent** *a.* having or showing good intellect; quick at understanding.—**intell'igently** *adv.*—**intell'igence** *n.* intellect; quickness of understanding; information, news.—**intell'igencer** *n.* an informant, spy.—**intell'igible** *a.* that can be understood.—**intell'igibly** *adv.*—**intelligibil'ity** *n.*—**intelligent'zia** *n.* the part of a nation claiming power of independent thought.
intend' *v.t.* to design, purpose, mean.
intense' *a.* very strong or acute.—**intens'ify** *v.t.* (**-ified** *p.t./p.p.*—**-ifying** *pr. p.*)—**intensifica'tion** *n.*—**intens'ity** *n.*—**intens'ive** *a.* giving emphasis; aiming at increased productiveness.
intent' *n.* purpose.—*a.* eager; resolved, bent.—**intent'ly** *adv.*—**inten'tion** *n.* purpose, aim.—**inten'tional** *a.*
inter' *v.t.* to bury.—**inter'ment** *n.*
in'ter- *prefix* meaning between, among, mutually; forms compounds, e.g., **intercolo'nial** *a.* between colonies.—**in'terrela'tion** *n.* mutual relation; etc., etc. Such words are not given where the meaning may easily be inferred from the simple word.
in'teract *n.* a short performance to fill up the interval between the acts.—*v.i.* to act on each other.—**interac'tion** *n.*
intercede' *v.t.* to plead for someone.—**interces'sion** *n.*—**intercess'or** *n.*
intercept' *v.t.* cut off, seize in transit.—**intercep'tion** *n.*—**intercep'tive** *a.*
in'terchange *n.* exchange; **interchange** *v.t.* and *i.* to exchange with each other; to follow alternately (**interchanging** *pres. p.*—**interchanged** *p.t.* and *p.p.*)—**interchangeable** *a.*
in'tercourse *n.* conversation; mutual dealings; comunication; connection.
in'terdict *n.* a prohibition.—**interdict'** *v.t.* to prohibit, forbid; restrain.—**interdic'tion** *n.*—**interdict'ory** *a.*
in'terest *n.* concern, curiosity; the thing exciting this; money paid for use of borrowed money; legal concern; right; advantage; personal influence.—*v.t.* to excite interest; to cause to feel interest. —**inter'esting** *a.*—**in'terestingly** *adv.*
interfere' *v.i.* to meddle; clash; of rays, etc., to strike together.—**interfer'ence** *n.* in wireless, interruption of reception.
in'terim *n.* the meantime.—*a.* temporary, intervening between two periods.
inte'rior *a.* situated within; inland.—*n.*
interjec'tion *n.* a word thrown in; an exclamation.—**interject'** *v.t.*

interlace' *v.t.* to unite, as by lacing together.—**interlace'ment** *n.*
interleave' *v.t.* to insert between other leaves.—**in'terleaf** *n.*
inter'lock *v.i.* to lock, join together.
interloc'utor *n.* one who takes part in a conversation.—**interlocu'tion** *n.* dialogue.—**interloc'utory** *a.*
in'terloper *n.* an intruder.
in'terlude *n.* interval in a play; something filling it; an interval.
intermar'ry *v.i.* to connect families or races by a marriage.—**inter-mar'riage** *n.*
interme'diate *a.* coming between two; interposed; intervening.—**interme'diary** *n.*—**intermezz'o** (-dz-) *n.* a short performance between acts of a play or opera (**-mezz'i** (-med'zē) *pl.*).
interm'inable *a.* endless, tediously long.—**interm'inably** *adv.*
intermit' *v.t.* and *i.* to stop for a time.—**intermis'sion** *n.*—**intermitte'nt** *a.*
intern' *v.t.* to oblige to live within prescribed limits.—**intern'ment** *n.*
inter'nal *a.* inward; interior.—**inter'nally** *adv.*—**internal combustion** the process of exploding a mixture of air and fuel in a piston-fitted cylinder.
internat'ional *a.* of, common to, carried on between, different nations; belonging to all nations.—*n.* player who represents his country in any sport; organisation for propagation of socialism.
interne'cine *a.* mutually destructive.
in'ternode *n.* the space between two nodes or points of the stem from which the leaves arise.—**interno'dal** *a.*
inter'pellate *v.t.* in the French or other Chamber, to interrupt the business of the day to demand an explanation from a Minister.—**interpella'tion** *n.*
inter'polate *v.t.* to put in new matter (in a book, etc.).—**interpola'tion** *n.*
interpose *v.t.* to insert; say as an interruption; put in the way.—*v.i.* to intervene; obstruct.—**interposi'tion** *n.*
Syn. introduce, intervene, interfere, mediate, arbitrate, intercede.
inter'pret *v.t.* to explain; explain to oneself; translate.—**inter'preter** *n.* one who translates.—**interpreta'tion** *n.*
interreg'num *n.* an interval between reigns (**interreg'nums, interreg'na** *pl.*).
inter'rogate *v.t.* to question closely.—**interroga'tion** *n.* questioning.—**interrog'ative** *a.* questioning.—*n.* a word used in asking a question.—**inter'rogator** *n.*—**interrogatory** *a.* of inquiry.—*n.* question, set of questions.
interrupt' *v.t.* to break in upon; stop the course of.—**interrup'tion** *n.*
intersect' *v.t.* to cut into, or between; to divide.—*v.i.* to cut into one another; to meet and cross.—**intersec'tion** *n.*
intersperse' *v.t.* to scatter; diversify.—**intersper'sion** *n.* (**interspersed'** *p.t./p.p*).
in'terstice *n.* chink, gap.—**intersti'tial** *a.*
in'terval *n.* a pause, break, intervening time or space; (*music*) difference of pitch between two sounds.
intervene' *v.i.* to happen in the meantime; to be placed, come in, between others; interfere.—**interven'tion** *n.*
in'terview *n.* meeting, *esp.* formally arranged; visit of journalist to get person's views.—*v.t.* have interview with.—**in'terviewer** *n.*
intest'ate *a.* not having made a will.—*n.* an intestate person.—**intes'tacy** *n.*
intest'ine *a.* internal, civil.—*n.* (usually *pl.*) the lower part of the alimentary canal; the bowels.—**intest'inal** *a.*
in'timate (-āt) *a.* familiar, closely acquainted; close.—*n.* an intimate friend.—**in'timacy** *n.*—**in'timate** (-āt) *v.t.* to make known; announce.—**intima'tion** *n.*
intim'idate *v.t.* to force or deter by threats.-**intimida'tion** *n.*-**intim'idator** *n.*
in'to *prep.* expresses motion within.
intol'erable *a.* unbearable.—**intol'erance** *n.* interference with ways or opinions of others.—**intolerant** *a.*
intone '*v.t.* to recite in a singing voice.—**intona'tion** *n.* modulation of voice.
intox'icate *v.t.* to make drunk.—**intox'icant** *a.* intoxicating.—*n.* intoxicating liquor.—**intoxica'tion** *n.*
intract'able *a.* stubborn; awkward.
intrep'id *a.* fearless.—**intrepid'ity** *n.*
in'tricate *a.* involved, puzzlingly entangled.—**in'tricately** *adv.*—**in'tricacy** *n.*
intrigue' (-trēg) *n.* underhand plotting or plot; a secret love affair.—*v.i.* to carry on an intrigue.—**intri'guer** *n.*
intrin'sic *a.* inherent, essential, real, genuine.—**intrin'sically** *adv.*
intro- *prefix* into, within, as *introduce.*
introduce' *v.t.* to bring in or forward; make known formally; bring to notice; insert.—**introduc'tion** *n.*-**introductory** *a.*
introspec'tion *n.* examination of one's own thoughts.—**introspec'tive** *a.*—*adv.*
introvert' *v.t.* to turn inward.—*n.* in psycho-analysis, self-centred, introspective person, averse from action.
intrude' *v.i.* to thrust in, enter without right.—*v.t.* to force in thus.—**intru'der** *n.*—**intru'sion** *n.*—**intru'sive** *a.*
intui'tion (-ish-) *n.* immediate, instinctive, direct apprehension by the mind.—**intu'itive** *a.*—**intu'itively** *adv.*
intwine' *v.t.* to twine or twist into.
in'undate *v.t.* to flood.—**inunda'tion** *n.*
inure' *v.t.* to accustom; harden (to).
invade' *v.t.* to enter with hostile intent; encroach on.—**inva'der** *n.*—**inva'sion** *n.*
inval'id *a.* not valid, of no legal force.—**inval'idate** *v.t.*—**invalid'ity** *n.*—**invalid'** (-ēd) *a.* ill, enfeebled by sickness or injury.—*v.* remove disabled man from service.—*n.* sick person.
inval'uable *a.* above price.
in'var *n.* steel containing 36% of nickel, and with low coefficient of expansion.

inva'riable *a.* constant; always uniform.—**inva'riably** *adv.*
inva'sion *n.* attacking by entering.
inveigh' (-vā) *v.i.* to speak violently (against).—**invec'tive** *n.* abusive speech.
inveigle (-vē-, -vā-) *v.t.* to entice, coax, seduce.—**invei'glement** *n.*
invent' *v.t.* to devise, originate.—**inven'tion** *n.*—**invent'ive** *a.*—**invent'ively** *adv.*—**invento'r** *n.*—**in'ventory** *n.* (*pl.* **-ies**) a detailed list of goods, etc.—*v.t.* to enter in an inventory, catalogue.
Syn. contrive, design, fabricate, forge.
invert' *v.t.* to turn upside down; reverse the position or relations of.—*n.* person with inverted sex instincts; a homosexual.—**in'verse** *a.* inverted.—**in'versely** *adv.*—**inver'sion** *n.*
inver'tebrate *n.* animal having no vertebral column.—*a.* spineless.
invest' *v.t.* to lay out (money); to clothe; endue; cover as a garment; lay siege to.—**invest'iture** *n.* formal installation of person in office or rank.—**invest'ment** *n.* investing; money invested; stocks and shares bought.
invest'igate *v.t.* inquire into, examine.—**investiga'tion** *n.*—**invest'igator** *n.*
invet'erate *a.* deep-rooted, long established.—**invet'eracy** *n.*
invid'ious *a.* likely to arouse ill-will or envy.—**invid'iously** *adv.*
invig'orate *v.t.* to give vigour to.
invin'cible *a.* unconquerable; insuperable.—**invincibil'ity** *n.*
invi'olate *a.* unhurt; unprofaned.
invis'ible *a.* incapable of being seen, imperceptible.—**invisibil'ity** *n.*
invite' *v.t.* to request courteously to come; to ask courteously; attract, tend to call forth.—**invita'tion** *n.*
Syn. solicit, bid, call, summon, entice. *Ant.* forbid, prohibit, debar, interdict.
in'voice *n.* a list of goods sent, with prices.—*v.t.* to make an invoice of.
invoke' *v.t.* to call on.—**invoca'tion** *n.*
invol'untary *a.* not done willingly; not intentional.—**invol'untarily** *adv.*
involve' *v.t.* wrap up, entangle, implicate; imply, entail.—**in'volute** *a.* intricate; rolled spirally.—**involu'tion** *n.*
i'odine *n.* greyish non-metallic element of the chlorine group, used in medicine.—**i'odise** *v.t.* to soak in iodine.—**io'doform** *n.* an antiseptic.
i'on *n.* an electrically charged atom or group of atoms.—**i'onize** *v.t.* to divide into ions.—**ioniza'tion** *n.*
io'nium *n.* a radio-active substance that changes to radium.
io'ta (ī-ō'-) *n.* the Greek letter *i*; an atom.
I.O.U. *n.* a signed and dated paper acknowledging a debt.
ipecacuan'ha (ip-i-kak-u-an'a) *n.* the root of a S. American plant used as an emetic; the plant.
ir- *prefix* for *in-* before "r." *See* **in-**.
ire *n.* anger, wrath.—**irate'** (i-) *a.* angry.—**iras'cible** *a.* hot-tempered.—**irascibil'ity** *n.*
iren'ic *a.* peaceful, desirous of peace.
irides'cent *a.* rainbow-coloured; changing colour with position.—**irides'cence** *n.*—**irid'ium** *n.* white metal.
i'ris *n.* a genus of plants with sword-shaped leaves and showy flowers; the circular membrane of the eye containing the pupil; formerly, rainbow.
irk *v.t.* to weary, trouble.—**irk'some** *a.*
i'ron (irn) *n.* a metal, much used for tools, utensils, etc., and the raw material of steel; a tool, etc., of this metal.—*pl.* fetters.—*a.* of, or like, iron; inflexible, unyielding; robust.—*v.t.* to smooth, cover, bind, etc., with iron or an iron.—**i'ron-bark** *n.* in Australia, several species of eucalyptus with hard, solid bark.—**i'ronclad** *a.* protected with iron.—**i'ronmaster** *n.* manufacturer of iron.—**i'ronmonger** *n.* dealer in hardware.—**i'ronmongery** *n.* his wares.—**i'ron-wood** *n.* in Australia and S. Africa, a hard, heavy wood; the tree giving such wood.
i'rony *n.* speech in which the meaning is the opposite of that actually expressed; words used with an inner meaning.—**iron'ical** *a.*—**iron'ically** *adv.*
irra'diate *v.t.* to shine upon, throw light upon.—**irradia'tion** *n.* impregnation by X-rays, light-rays; illumination.
irra'tional *a.* unreasonable; illogical.
irreconcil'able *a.* who or which cannot be made to agree; quite incompatible.
irref'ragable *a.* that cannot be refuted.
irreg'ular *n. pl.* soldiers outside regular army.—*a.* not regular; uneven, not smooth; not following the rule; abnormal; unlawful.—**irregularity** *n.*
irrel'evant *a.* inapplicable, beside the point.—**irrel'evancy** *n.*
irrep'arable *a.* which cannot be rectified or regained.
irrepress'ible *a.* that cannot be repressed or restrained.
irreproach'able *a.* blameless, perfect.
irresis'tible *a.* who or which cannot be resisted; overpowering; irrefutable.
irres'olute *a.* hesitating, unsure, vacillating.—**irresolution** *n.*
irrespec'tive *a.* without taking account (of).—**irrespective'ly** *adv.*
irrespon'sible *a.* not responsible; unwilling to take responsibility; unreliable.—**irresponsibil'ity** *n.*
irretriev'able *a.* beyond recovery, irremediable, irreparable.
irrev'erent *a.* without reverence, disrespectful.—**irrev'erence** *n.*
irrev'ocable *a.* which cannot be recalled or undone, unalterable.
irr'igate *v.t.* to water by channels or streams.—**irriga'tion** *n.*—**irr'igator** *n.*
irr'itate *v.t.* to excite to anger; excite, inflame, stimulate.—**irrita'tion** *n.*—**irr'itant** *a.* causing irritation.—*n.* a thing

doing this.—**irr'itable** *a.* easily annoyed.
irrup'tion *n.* invasion; bursting in.
is third person sing. pres. indicative of **be.**
i'singlass (ī'zing-glȧs) *n.* a gelatine obtained from fish, *esp.* sturgeon.
i'sland (īl-) *n.* a piece of land surrounded by water; anything resembling this, e.g., a street-refuge.—**i'slander** *n.*—**isle** (īl) *n.* an island.—**i'slet** (īl-) *n.* a small island.
i'sobar *n.* a line on a map connecting places with the same mean barometric pressure.—**isobar'ic** *a.*
i'solate *v.t.* to place apart or alone; quarantine. (**i'solated** *p.t.* and *p.p.*).—**isola'tion** *n.*—**isola'tion hospital** *n.* hospital for infectious diseases.
isos'celes *a.* triangle, having two sides equal.
i'sotherm *n.* a line passing through points of equal mean temperature.
i'sotope (i'-sō-tōp) *n.* atom of element having a different nuclear mass and atomic weight from other atoms in same element.—**isotop'ic** *a.*
iss'ue *n.* a going or passing out; outlet; offspring, children; outcome, result; question, dispute; a sending or giving out officially or publicly; number or amount so given out.—*v.i.* go out; result in; arise (from).—*v.t.* emit; distribute. (**is'suing** *pr. p.*; **is'sued** *p.t./p.p.*—**at issue** in dispute; **join issue** (**with**) argue.
isth'mus (-th *or* is-m-) *n.* a neck of land.
it *pron.* the neuter pronoun of the third person (**they, them** *pl.*); *n.* (*sl.*) sexual attractiveness, sex appeal.—**its** the possessive case of **it.**—**itself'** emphatic form of **it.**
ital'ic *a.* of type, sloping.—**ital'ics** *n. pl.* this type, now used for emphasis, foreign words, etc.—**ital'icise** *v.t.*
itch *v.i.* to feel an irritation in the skin.—*n.* an irritation in the skin.—**itch'y** *a.*
i'tem *n.* any of a list of things, a detail, an entry in an account or list.—*adv.* also.
it'erate *v.t.* to repeat.—**itera'tion** *n.*
itin'erant *a.* travelling from place to place; travelling on circuit; of Methodists, preaching in a circuit.—**itin'eracy** *n.*—**itin'erary** *n.* a record of travel; a route, line of travel; a guide-book.
i'vory *n.* the hard white substance of the tusks of elephants, etc. (*pl.* **-ies**).—**black ivory** *n.* Negro slaves.—**ivory black** *n.* black pigment from burnt ivory.
i'vy *n.* a climbing evergreen plant. (*pl.* **-ies**).—**i'vied** *a.* overgrown with ivy.
iz'ard *n.* the wild goat of the Pyrenean mountains; the ibex.

J

jab *v.t.* to poke roughly; thrust abruptly.
jabb'er *v.i.* to chatter rapidly and indistinctly.—*n.* gabble.
jabot' (zhab-ō') *n.* a frill on a bodice, etc.
jac'inth (jas'-) *n.* reddish-orange gem.
jack *n.* a knave at cards; various mechanical appliances, e.g., machine for lifting weights; a ship's flag; various small things; added to names of animals, indicates male, as in **jack'ass,** or small, as in **jack-snipe.**—**jack'daw** *n.* British bird, the daw.—**jack-up** *v.t.* to raise with a jack.—**jack-rabbit** *n.* in N. America, a hare.—**jack the painter,** in Australia, a strong green tea.
jack *n.* a leather coat; a leather bottle.
jack'al (-awl) *n.* a wild animal like a dog.
jack'anapes *n.* pert child or fellow.
jackaroo' (-rōō) *n.* in Australia, an apprentice gaining experience on a sheep or cattle station.
jack'ass *n.* the male ass; a blockhead.
jack'boot *n.* a large riding-boot coming above the knee.
jack'et *n.* a sleeved outer garment, a short coat; an outer casing.
Jac'obean (-bē-an) *a.* of the reign of James I.—**Jac'obin** *n.* a Dominican friar; a member of a democratic club set up in 1789 in Paris in a Jacobin convent; an extreme radical.—**Jac'obite** *n.* an adherent of the Stuarts after the abdication of James II.—**ja'cob's-ladder** *n.* a plant; a rope-ladder with wooden rungs.
jade *n.* a sorry nag, a worn-out horse; in contempt, a woman.—*v.t.* to tire out.
jade *n.* ornamental stone, usually green.
jag *n.* a sharp projection.—**jagg'ed** *a.*
jag'uar *n.* large S. Amer. spotted wild animal of cat tribe, like leopard.
jail *see* **gaol.**
jal'ap *n.* a purgative drug.
jam *v.t.* to squeeze; cause to stick and become unworkable; pack together.—*v.i.* to stick and become unworkable.—*n.* fruit preserved by boiling with sugar.—**jam session** *n.* (U.S.) (*sl.*) jazz musicians gathered together to improvise freely for their own pleasure.
jamb (jam) *n.* the side post of a door.
jam'bok *n. see* **sjambok.**
jamboree' *n.* a large gathering of Boy Scouts; a spree, a celebration.
jan'gle (-ng-gl) *v.i.* to sound harshly, as a bell.—*v.t.* to make do this.—*n.* a harsh metallic sound; a wrangle.
jan'issary, jan'izary *n.* formerly soldier of bodyguard of Turkish Sultan.
jan'itor *n.* a doorkeeper, caretaker.
Jan'uary *n.* the first month.
japan' *n.* a very hard, glossy black varnish.—*v.t.* to cover with this.
jape *n.* a joke.—*v.i.* to joke.
jar *n.* a vessel of glass, earthenware, etc.
jar *v.i.* to make a grating noise; vibrate gratingly; wrangle.—*v.t.* to cause to grate, vibrate.—*n.* a jarring sound.
jar'gon *n.* barbarous or excessively technical language; gibberish.
jargonelle' *n.* an early pear.

jarr'ah *n.* a gum-tree of W. Australia.
jas'mine, jas'min, jess'amine, jess'amin *n.* a flowering shrub.
jas'per *n.* a red, yellow, or brown stone.
jaun'dice (-dis) *n.* disease which turns the skin yellow.—**jaun'diced** *a.* jealous, of soured outlook, prejudiced.
jaunt *n.* a short pleasure excursion.—*v.i.* to make one.—**jaunt'ing-car** *n.* a two-wheeled vehicle common in Ireland.
jaun'ty *a.* lively; brisk.—**jaunt'ily** *adv.*
jav'elin *n.* a light spear for throwing.
jaw *n.* one of the bones in which the teeth are set.—*pl.* mouth; part of vice.
jay *n.* noisy bird of bright plumage; chatterer.—**-walker,** careless pedestrian.
jazz *n.* discordant syncopated music and dance.—*v.i.* to indulge in jazz.—*a.*
jeal'ous (jel-) *a.* suspiciously watchful; distrustful of the faithfulness (of); envious.—**jeal'ousy** *n.*—**jeal'ously** *adv.*
jean (jān, jēn) *n.* a twilled cotton cloth. —*pl.* in N. America, overall trousers.
jeep' *n.* small open car of unusual power, used for transport of goods and men.
jeer *v.t.* and *i.* to scoff, deride.
je'hu *n.* a driver.
jejune' (-ōōn) *a.* poor, uninteresting.
jell'y *n.* semi-transparent food made with gelatine, stiffening as it cools; anything of this consistency (*pl.* **-ies**). —**jell'y-fish** *n.* jelly-like sea-animal.
jemm'y *n.* burglar's crow-bar. (*pl.* **-ies**).
jeop'ardy (jep-) *n.* danger.—**jeop'ardise** *v.t.* to endanger.—**jeop'ardous** *a.*
jeremi'ad *n.* a doleful complaint.
jerk *n.* a sharp, abruptly stopped movement, a twitch, start, sharp pull.—*v.t.* and *i.* to move, or throw with a jerk.—**jerk'y** *a.*—**jerk'ily** *adv.*—**jerk'iness** *n.*
jerked *a.* cut into long strips and dried.
jer'kin *n.* a close-fitting jacket.
jer'ry-built *a.* a flimsy construction with bad materials.—**jer'ry-builder** *n.*
jer'sey (-z-) *n.* a knitted jumper.
jest *n.* joke.—*v.i.* joke.—**jest'er** *n.* a joker, *esp.* a professional fool of a court.
Jes'uit (jez-) *n.* member of Society of Jesus in R.C. Church.—**Jesuit'ical** *a.*
jet *n.* a hard black material capable of a brilliant polish.
jet *n.* a stream of liquid, gas, etc., *esp.* shot from a small hole; the small hole; spout.—*v.t.* and *i.* spurt out in jets.—**jet-drive** *n.*—**jet-driven** *a.* driven by the backward thrust of a jet of gas, etc.—**jet-fighter** *n.* a jet-driven fighting aeroplane.—**jet-propulsion** *n.*
jet'sam *n.* goods thrown out to lighten a ship and later washed ashore.—**jett'ison** *v.t.* to throw overboard thus.
jett'y *n.* a small pier or landing-place.
jewel *n.* a precious stone; a personal ornament containing one; a precious thing.—**jew'eller** *n.* a dealer in jewels.—**jewe'lry, jew'ellery** *n.*
jib *n.* a ship's triangular staysail.—*v.t.* to pull over (a sail) to the other side; *v.i.* of a horse or person, to stop and refuse to go on, to object to proceed.—**jibboom'** *n.* a spar from the end of the bowsprit.
jibe *see* **gybe** and **gibe.**
jig *n.* a lively dance; music for it; various mechanisms or fittings; *v.i.* to dance a jig; to make jerky up-and-down movements.—**jig'saw** *n.* machine fretsaw.—**jig'saw puzz'le** *n.* picture on paper backed with wood cut into small irregular pieces, from which picture is to be completed.—**jigg'er** *n.*—**lobster-jig** *n.* in N. Amer., shift beginning in afternoon and ending at midnight.
jigg'er *n.* in S. Africa and America, a flea, the female of which burrows under human flesh to lay its eggs.
jilt *v.t.* to cast off (a lover) after encouraging.—*n.* one who does this.
jimm'y *n.* S. Africa, newly-arrived immigrant.
jin'gle (-ng-gl) *n.* mixed metallic noise, as of shaken chain; repetition of same sounds in words.—*v.i.* to make the sound.
jin'go (-ng-g-) *n.* a warmonger (**-goes** *pl.*). —**by Jingo,** a form of asseveration.
jink'er *n.* in Australia, long stout beam mounted on large wheels for transporting heavy logs.
jitter'bug *n.* young devotee of jazz who dances in a wild athletic fashion;—*v.i.* to dance thus.
jitt'ers *n. pl.* (*U.S.*) shudderings; funk.
jiu-jitsu *n. see* **ju-jutsu.**
jive' *n.* (U.S.) (*sl.*) swing music of a spectacular kind; the jargon of swing music enthusiasts.
job *n.* piece of work; occupation; an unscrupulous transaction.—*v.i.* to do odd jobs; to deal in stocks.—**job'ber** *n.*—**jobb'ery** *n.*—**job'-master** *n.* one who hires horses.—**job** *v.t.* to prod.
jockey' *n.* professional rider in horse-races.—*v.t.* to cheat; manœuvre (**-eyed** (-id) *p.t.* and *p.p.*—**-eying** *pres. p.*).
jocose' *a.* waggish, humorous.—**jocos'ity** *n.*—**joc'ular** *a.* joking, given to joking.—**jocular'ity** *n.*—**jocose'ly** *adv.*
Syn. jocular, facetious, witty, merry, pleasant, sportive. *Ant.* dismal, ponderous, serious, heavy, dull, miserable.
joc'und *a.* merry.—**jocund'ity** *n.*
jo'ey *n.* in Australia, young kangaroo; day labourer.—*v.t.* (*sl.*) to mock, chaff; to abuse.
jog *v.t.* to move or push with a jerk.—*v.i.* to walk or ride with jolting pace; to go on one's way.—*n.* a jogging.—**jog'-trot** *n.* a slow regular trot.—**jog'gle** *v.t.* and *i.* to move to and fro in jerks.
John *n.* a proper name.—**John Collins** *n.* in N. America, morning drink of gin, sugar, lemon, ice and soda-water.—**Johnn'y-cake** cake made of the meal of Indian corn; in Australia, cake of flour and water baked in hot ashes.

join *v.t.* to put together, fasten, unite.—*v.i.* to become united or connected.—*n.* a joining; place of joining.—**join'er** *n.* one who joins; a maker of furniture and light woodwork.—**join'ery** *n.* his work.

joint *n.* an arrangement by which two things fit or are joined together, rigidly or loosely; a bone with meat on, as food; in N. America (*sl.*) a gambling or opium den, a low-class public-house.—*a.* common; shared *of* or by two or more.—*v.t.* to connect by joints; to divide at the joints.—**joint'ly** *adv.*—**joint'-stock** *n.* common stock, share, capital.—**join'ture** *n.* property settled on a wife for her use after the husband's death.

joist *n.* beam stretched from wall to wall on which to fix floor or ceiling.

joke *n.* a thing said or done to cause laughter, something not in earnest.—*v.i.* make jokes.—*v.t.* banter.—**jo'ker** *n.* one who jokes; extra, distinctive, card in a pack, usually taking any value.

joll'y *a.* festive, merry.—*v.t.* N. Amer., (*sl.*) wheedle, cajole.—**joll'ity** *n.*—**jollifica'tion** *n.* marrymaking.—**jol'liest** *sup.*

joll'y-boat *n.* a small ship's boat.

Jolly Roger *n.* pirate flag, black with white skull and crossbones.

jolt (-ō-) *n.* a jerk throwing up, as from a seat; in N. America, a drink of spirits.—*v.t.* and *i.* to move or shake with jolts.

jon'quil *n.* a rush-leaved daffodil.

jor'um *n.* large drinking-bowl; its contents, *esp.* punch.

josh *v.t.* N. America, to ridicule.–*n.* hoax.

joss' *n.* Chinese idol.

jos'tle (-sl) *v.t.* and *i.* to knock or push against.—*n.* a jostling.

jot *n.* small amount.—*v.t.* to write (down) briefly.—**jot'ter** *n.* note-book.

jour'nal (jer'nl) *n.* daily record; log-book; daily newspaper or other periodical; the part of an axle or shaft resting on the bearings.—**jour'nalism** *n.* editing, or writing for press.—**jour'nalist** *n.*—**journalese'** *n.* newspaper jargon.—**journalis'tic** *a.* pert. to journalism.

jour'ney (jer-) *n.* going to a place; the distance travelled.—*v.i.* to travel.

jour'neyman *n.* fully trained workman (formerly hired by the day).

joust *n.* tournament, encounter with lances between mounted knights.

jovial *a.* cheerful, merry, good-humoured.—**jovial'ity** *n.* good-fellowship.

jowl *n.* cheek, jaw.

joy *n.* gladness, pleasure, delight; a cause of this.—**joy'ful** *a.*—**joy'less** *a.*—**joy'ous** *a.*—**joy'ride** *n.* an illicit, or pleasurable, ride in a motor-car.

Syn. happiness, felicity, transport, ecstasy, rapture, bliss, merriment, hilarity, gaiety, festivity. *Ant.* sorrow, sadness, gloom, bitterness, rue, woe, care, mourning, agony, regret.

ju'bilate *v.i.* to rejoice.—**ju'bilant** *a.*—**ju'bilantly** *adv.*—**jubila'tion** *n.* rejoicing.

ju'bilee *n.* a fiftieth anniversary; time of rejoicing, exultation.

judge (juj) *n.* officer appointed to try to decide cases in law courts; one who decides a dispute, question, contest; one fit to decide on the merits of a question or thing; an umpire; in Jewish history, a ruler.—*v.i.* to act as judge.—*v.t.* to act as a judge of; try, estimate, decide.—**judg'ment** *n.* sentence of a court; an opinion; faculty of judging; misfortune regarded as a sign of divine displeasure.—**ju'dicature** *n.* administration of justice; the body of judges.—**judi'cial** (-ish-) *a.* of, or by, a court, or judge; proper to a judge; impartial; critical.—**judi'cially** *adv.*—**judi'cious** *a.* sensible, prudent.—**judi'ciously** *adv.*—**judi'ciary** *n.* courts of law, system of courts.

ju'do *n.* scientific unarmed combat based on the Japanese jiu-jitsu.

jug *n.* deep vessel for liquids; the contents of one; (*sl.*) prison.—*v.t.* to stew (*esp.* a hare) in a jug or jar.

jug'gle *v.i.* to play conjuring tricks, amuse by sleight of hand; practise deceit.—*v.t.* to trick or cheat (out of).—*n.* a juggling.—**jug'gler** *n.*—**jug'glery** *n.*

jug'ular *a.* of or in the neck or throat.

juice (jōōs) *n.* the liquid part of vegetable, fruit, or meat; in N. America (*sl.*) electric current; petrol.—**juic'y** *a.*

ju'-ju *n.* a W. African cult; an idol to which sacrifices are made; a talisman.

ju'jube *n.* a lozenge of gelatine, sugar, etc.; a fruit; the shrub producing it.

ju-jit'su, jiu-jit'su *n.* the Japanese art of wrestling and self-defence.

juke' box U.S. (*sl.*) an automatic, coin-operated gramophone.

ju'lep *n.* sweet drink; medicated drink.

Jul'ian *a.* belonging to or derived from Julius Cæsar.— **Julian calendar,** the calendar as adjusted by Julius Cæsar.

julienne' *n.* a kind of clear soup.

July' *n.* the seventh month.

jum'bal, jum'ble *n.* varieties of thin, sweet, crisp cake.

jumble *v.t.* to mix up, confuse.—*v.i.* to disorder.—*n.* a confused heap, muddle.—**jum'ble sale** *n.* charity sale of unwanted articles, etc.

jum'buk *n.* in Australia, a sheep.

jump *v.i.* to spring from the ground; in N. America, to leave, as a job; to evade customs; neglect to complete.—*v.t.* to pass by jumping; in S. Africa, Australia and N. America, to appropriate a claim which the owner is not working.—*n.* a leap, sudden upward movement.—**jump'er** *n.*—**jump'y** *a.* nervous.

jum'per *n.* a sailor's loose jacket; a woman's loose outer garment.

junc'tion *n.* a joining; a place of joining, railway station where lines join.—

junc'ture *n.* joint; time; state of affairs. *Syn.* union, combination, coalition, connection, linking, coupling, place of meeting. *Ant.* break, split, burst.

June (jōōn) *n.* the sixth month.

jung'le (-ng-gl) *n.* tangled vegetation; land covered with it; tangled mass.—**jun'gle-hen** *n.* in Australia, mound-building bird.

jun'ior (jōōn-) *a.* younger; of lower standing.—*n.* a junior person; a son.

jun'iper (jōōn-) *n.* an evergreen shrub with berries yielding **oil of juniper,** used for medicine and gin.

junk *n.* lump; old rope; salt meat; odds and ends; rubbish.

junk *n.* Chinese sailing vessel.

junk'et *n.* curdled milk, flavoured.

junt'a *n.* a council in Spain or Italy.

Ju'piter (jōō-) *n.* the Roman chief of the gods; the largest of the planets.

jupon' (jōō-) *n.* a sleeveless jacket or coat; a petticoat.

ju'ral (jōō-) *a.* pertaining to right.

jurid'ical (joor-) *a.* relating to the administration of law, legal.—**jurisconsult'** *n.* one learned in law.—**jurisdic'tion** *n.* administration of justice; authority; territory covered by a court or authority.—**jurispru'dence** (-oo-) *n.* the science of, or skill in, law.—**ju'rist** *n.* one skilled in law.—**juris'tic** *a.*

ju'ry (joor-i) *n.* a body of persons sworn to render a verdict in a court of law; a body of judges in a competition. (*pl.* -ies).—**ju'ror** *n.* one of a jury.

ju'ry-mast (joor'i-måst) *n.* a temporary mast rigged in place of a broken one.

just *a.* upright, fair; proper, right, equitable.—*adv.* exactly, barely.—**just'ly** *adv.*—**jus'tice** (-is) *n.* quality of being just, fairness; judicial proceedings; a judge, magistrate.—**just'ify** *v.t.* to show to be right or true or innocent; to be sufficient grounds for (**-ified** *p.t.* and *p.p.*—**-fying** *pres. p.*).—**justifi'able** *a.*—**justifiably** *adv.*—**justifica'tion** *n.*

jut *v.i.* to project.—*n.* a projection.

jute (jōōt) *n.* fibre of certain plants, used in making rope, canvas, etc.

ju'venile (jōō-) *a.* young; of, or for, the youthful.—*n.* a young person, child.—*pl.* books for children.—**juvenil'ity** *n.*—**juvenes'cent** *a.* becoming young.—**juvenes'cence** *n.*—**juvenile offender,** person under sixteen indicted for criminal offence.—**juvenile court.**

juxtapose' (-z) *v.t.* to put side by side.—**juxtaposi'tion** *n.* contiguity.

K

kaa'ins, ka'ins, kai'ings (kȧ-) *n. pl.* in S. Africa, scraps from which the fat has been fried out; greaves.

kaba'ya, kaba'ai *n.* in S. Africa, a light jacket worn in hot weather.

kaff'ir, kaf'ir *n.* one of a woolly-haired race inhabiting the Eastern part of South Africa.—**kaffir piano** *n.* a xylophone made by Kaffirs.

kai (kī) *n.* in New Zealand and South Sea islands, food.—**kai'-kai,** feasting.

kaik, kain'ga (kīk, kīn-) *n.* in New Zealand, a Maori settlement or village.

ka'ka *n.* in New Zealand, a large parrot.

kale, kail *n.* cabbage, cole; in N. America (*sl.*) money, wealth.—**kail'yard** *n.* kitchen garden.

kaleid'oscope (-līd'-) *n.* rotating tube in which variety of coloured patterns are produced by means of mirrors.—**kaleidoscŏp'ic** *a.* swiftly changing.

kamika'ze (kam-i-kȧ'-zi) *n.* suicidal air attack by Japanese pilot.

kanak'a *n.* Sandwich Islander; native labourer brought from Pacific Islands to Australia.

kangaroo' (-ng-ga-) *n.* Australian marsupial with powerful hind legs for jumping.—**kangaroo'-dog** *n.* Australian dog with speed and fighting power used for hunting kangaroos.—**kangaroo'-mouse** *n.* smallest of the tribe.

ka'olin (kȧ-, kā-) *n.* fine white China clay.

ka'pok (kȧ-) *n.* vegetable fibre for stuffing cushions, etc.; a tree-cotton.

kar'ma (cur'-) *n.* physical action; the law of cause and effect; ethical causation; destiny.

karoo', karroo' *n.* in S. Africa, immense clayey tablelands, barren except in the wet season.

kaross' *n.* a skin garment worn by S. African natives; blanket made of pelts.

kar'ri, kar'i *n.* giant West Australian eucalyptus giving very durable wood.

kar'wats (-våts) *n.* in S. Africa, a whip made in one piece.

kat'ion, cat'ion *n.* electro-positive ion which seeks cathode or negative pole.

kat'ipo *n.* in New Zealand, a small venomous spider, known in Australia as the red-backed spider.

kau'ri *n.* large coniferous tree of N.Z.—**kau'ri-gum** *n.* resinous gum dug from the sites of ancient kauri forests.

ka'va (kȧ-) *n.* beverage derived from a Polynesian plant of the pepper family.

kay'ak (kī'-) *n.* skin-covered Eskimo canoe.

kea *n.* N. Zealand sheep-killing parrot.

kedge *n.* a small anchor.—*v.t.* to move (a ship) by a cable attached to a kedge.

kedg'eree *n.* a dish of rice, fish, eggs.

keel *n.* the lowest longitudinal timber, or steel substitute, on which a ship is built up.—*v.t.* to turn keel up, capsize.—**keel'less** *a.*—**keel'son** *n.* line of timbers or plates bolted to the keel.

keen *a.* sharp, vivid, acute, eager, strong.—**keenly** *adv.*

keep *v.t.* to observe, carry out; retain possession of, not lose; maintain; detain; cause to continue; reserve, manage.—*v.i.* remain good; remain; continue.—*n.* maintenance, food; central tower of a castle, a stronghold.—**keep'er** *n.*—**keep'ing** *n.* act of keeping; charge, possession; harmony, agreement.—**keep'sake** *n.* a thing treasured for the sake of the giver.
keg *n.* a small cask.
kelp *n.* a large seaweed; ashes of it for extraction of iodine.
ken *v.t.* to know.—*n.* range of knowledge.
kenn'el *n.* shelter for dogs; gutter.
kerb *see* **curb.**
ker'chief (-if) *n.* a square head-cloth.
kerm'es (-iz) *n.* female insect used for red dyestuff.
kern' *n.* an Irish peasant; (*print.*) that part of a type extended beyond the body of the type;—*v.i.* to harden, to seed.
kern'el *n.* inner soft part of nut or fruit-stone; central or essential part.
ker'osene *n.* lamp-oil from petroleum.
ker'rel, kê'rel *n.* in S. Africa, a fellow, chap.
kers'ey (-zi) *n.* coarse woollen cloth (**-seys** (-ziz) *pl.*).—**kers'eymere** (-zi-) *n.* twilled cloth of fine wool.
kes'trel *n.* a small species of falcon.
ketch *n.* small two-masted or cutter-rigged sailing vessel.
ketch'up *n.* sauce made from mushrooms, tomatoes, etc.
ket'tle *n.* metal vessel with spout and handle for boiling.—**ket'tledrum** *n.* a drum of parchment stretched over a metal hemisphere.—**to cook the kettle** in S. Africa, to boil water in a kettle.
key *n.* instrument for moving the bolt of a lock; *fig.* anything that "unlocks"; (*music,*) a set of related notes; lever to play a note of piano, etc.—**key'board** *n.* set of keys on a piano, etc.— **key'note** *n.* note on which musical key is based; a dominant idea.—**key'stone** *n.* central stone supporting arch.
kha'ki (kà-) *a.* dull yellowish-brown.—*n.* khaki cloth, military uniform.
khali'fa (-lē'-) *n.* the title assumed by the successors of Mahomet; in S. Africa, a Malay religious festival.
kham'sin *n.* hot S.E. wind that blows regularly in Egypt for about fifty days, beginning about the middle of March.
khan' *n.* title given to rulers or high officials in Central Asia.
ki'a o'ra *interj.* N. Zealand, your health!
kib'ble *v.t.* to bruise or grind closely; to clip roughly.
ki'bosh *n.* (*sl.*) nonsense, rubbish.—**to put the kibosh on** to silence, defeat.
kick *v.i.* to strike out with the foot; be recalcitrant; recoil.—*v.t.* to strike with the foot.—*n.* blow with the foot; recoil.
kid *n.* a young goat; leather of its skin; child.—*v.t.* (*sl.*) to hoax.
kid'nap *v.t.* steal (child), abduct (person) (**-napped** *p.t.*/*p.p.*).—**kid'napper** *n.*
kid'ney *n.* either of pair of organs secreting urine; nature, kind (**-neys** *pl.*).
kill *v.t.* to deprive of life, slay.—**kil'ler** *n.*
kiln *n.* a furnace, oven.
kil'ogramme *n.* a weight of 1,000 grammes.—**kil'ocycle** *n.* a frequency of 1,000 cycles or vibrations per sec.—**kil'odyne** *n.* 1,000 dynes.—**kil'ometre** *n.* 1,000 metres approx. ⅝ of a mile.—**kil'olitre** *n.*
ki'lowatt *n.* unit of electricity, 1,000 watts, about 1⅓ horse-power.
kilt *v.t.* to gather in vertical pleats; to tuck up.—*n.* short pleated skirt worn by Scottish Highlanders.
kimo'no *n.* loose, wide-sleeved Japanese robe, fastened with sash; European dressing-gown or wrap in this style.
kin *n.* family, relatives.—*a.* related by blood.—**kin'dred** *n.* relationship; relatives.—*a.* related.—**kin'ship** *n.*—**kins'man** *n.*; **kins'woman** *fem.*—**kins'folk** *n.*
kind (kīnd) *n.* genus, sort, variety, class. —*a.* having a sympathetic nature, considerate, good, benevolent.—**kind'liness** *n.*—**kind'ly** *a.* kind, genial.—*adv.*
Syn. of *a.* bounteous, beneficient, congenial, obliging, humane. *Ant.* unkind, harsh, cruel, disagreeable, severe.
kin'dergarten *n.* a school for teaching young children by games, etc.
kin'dle *v.t.* to set on fire.—*v.i.* to catch fire; to rouse.—**kind'ling** *n.* act of lighting; small wood to kindle fires.
kine' *n. pl.* cows, cattle.
kinemat'ic (ki-) *a.* relating to pure motion.—*n.* (in *pl.*) the science of this.—**kinemat'ograph** *see* **cinematograph.** —**kinet'ic** *a.* of motion in relation to force.—*n.* (in *pl.*) the science of this.
king *n.* male sovereign ruler of an independent state; piece in the game of chess; card in each suit with a picture of a king.—**king'ly** *a.*—**king'ship** *n.*—**king'dom** *n.* state ruled by a king; realm, sphere.—**king'cup** *n.* marsh marigold.—**king'fisher** *n.* small bird of bright plumage which dives for fish.—**king'pin** *n.* in skittles, the front skittle; (*col.*) the leader of an enterprise.—**king-post** *n.* beam in roof framework rising from the tie-beam to the ridge; in aviation, a strut to which bracing wires of an aeroplane are attached.—**king's evil** *n.* scrofula, which was thought to be curable by a king's touch.
kink *n.* a short twist in a rope, wire, etc. —*v.i.* and *t.* to form a kink.
kins'folk *n. pl.* relatives.—**kin'ship** *n.* relationship.—**kins'man** *n.* male relative (**kins'men** *pl.*).—**kins'woman** *fem.*
kiosk' *n.* small open pavilion.
kip *n.* the skin of a young beast. In Australia, bat for playing two-up.—

kip-skin, leather prepared from the skin of young cattle.—(*sl.*) doss-house.

kipp'er *v.t.* to cure (fish) by splitting open, rubbing with salt, and drying or smoking.—*n.* a kippered herring; salmon in spawning time; in Australia, an initiated aboriginal youth.

kir'i, kie'rie *n.* in S. Africa, a hard stick used for digging and as a weapon.

kirk *n.* Scottish word for *church.*

kiss *n.* a caress with the lips.—*v.t.* to give a kiss to.—*v.i.* to exchange kisses.

kit *n.* a wooden tub; an outfit; personal effects, *esp.* of traveller.—**kit'bag** *n.*

kitchen *n.* room used for cooking.—**kitchen -Dutch, -Kaffir,** mixture of English with Dutch or Kaffir.—**kitch'ener** *n.* cooking-range.—**kitchenette'** *n.* small room used as kitchen, pantry and scullery.—**kitchen'-garden** *n.* vegetable garden.—**kitch'enmaid** *n.*

kite *n.* bird of prey; light frame flown in wind.—**kite'-balloon** *n.* naval or military captive balloon used for observation, or defence against aircraft.

kith *n.* acquaintances (in **kith and kin**).

kitt'en *n.* a young cat.

ki'wi (kē'-) *n.* any bird of the genus *Apteryx* (found in N. Zealand).

Klax'on *n.* a loud electric horn for warning (protected trade name).

kleptoma'nia (-ā-) *n.* a morbid tendency to steal for the sake of theft.—**kleptoma'niac** *n.* one so afflicted.

klink'er *n.* in S. Africa, a brick used for paving yards; a hard biscuit.

klip *n.* in S. Africa, a rock, pebble; mountain; (*sl.*) a diamond.—**klip'springer** *n.* small S. African antelope.—*v.t.* to place a stone behind a wheel to prevent a vehicle running backwards.

klom'py *n.* S. Africa, cluster; bunch.

klooch *n.* in N. America, an Indian woman.

kloof *n.* in S. Africa, a ravine, a gulley.

knack (n-) *n.* acquired faculty for doing something adroitly; trick.

knack'er (n-) *n.* a buyer of worn-out horses for killing.—**knack'ery** *n.*

knap'sack (n-) *n.* canvas bag for kit, carried on the back.

knave (nā-) *n.* a rogue, rascal; at cards, the lowest court card, the jack.—**kna'very** *n.*—**kna'vish** *a.* dishonest.

knead (nē-) *v.t.* to work up into dough; to work with the hands, massage.

knee (n-) *n.* joint between the thigh and lower leg; part of a garment covering the knee.—**knee'-breeches** *n. pl.* breeches reaching to or just below the knee.—**knee'cap** *n.* protective covering for a knee; bone in the front of the knee, patella (also **knee'pan** *n.*).

kneel (n-) *v.i.* to fall or rest on the knees.

knell (-n) *n.* sound of a funeral bell.

knick'erbockers (n-) *n. pl.* loose-fitting breeches gathered in at the knee (also **knick'ers** (*n. pl.*) woman's undergarment of similar form); *sing.* in N. America, a person from New York state.

knick'-knack (n-, n-) *n.* a light dainty article, small ornament, a trinket.

knife (n-) *n.* a cutting blade in a handle.—*v.t.* to cut or stab with a knife.—**knife'-board** *n.* one for cleaning knives.

knight (nīt) *n.* person of rank below the baronets, having the right to prefix *Sir* to his name; a military follower, a champion; a piece in the game of chess.—*v.t.* to make (person) a knight.—**knight'hood** *n.*—**knight'ly** *a.*

knit (n-) *v.t.* to form a fabric by putting together a series of loops in wool, or other yarn.—*v.i.* to unite; to draw (brows) together.

knob (n-) *n.* a rounded lump, *esp.* at the end or on the surface of anything; door-handle.—**knobb'y** *a.*—**knobb'ly** *a.*

knob'kerry (-ki'ri) (nop'-) *n.* S. Africa, stick with large knob at end used as a club by Kaffirs.

knock (n-) *v.t.* to strike, hit.—*v.i.* in N. America, to disparage, criticise adversely.—*n.* a blow, rap.—**knock'er** *n.* who or what knocks; metal appliance for knocking on a door.—**knock'-kneed** *a.* having in-curved legs.—**knock'-out** *n.* finishing blow.

knoll (nōl) *n.* a small rounded hill.

knot (n-) *n.* a twisting together of parts of two or more strings, ropes, etc., to fasten them together; a cockade, cluster; a hard lump, *esp.* of wood where a branch joins or has joined in; a measure of speed of ships, e.g., ten knots means ten nautical miles per hour; a difficulty.—*v.t.* to tie with or in knots.—**knott'y** *a.* full of knots; puzzling, difficult.

knout (n-) *n.* a whip formerly used in Russia.—*v.t.* to flog with this.

know (nō) *v.t.* to be aware of, have information about, be acquainted with, recognise, have experience, understand.—*v.i.* to have information or understanding (**knew** *p.t.* —**known** *p.p.*).—**know'able** *a.*—**know'ing** *a.* that knows; cunning, shrewd.—**know'ingly** *adv.*

knowl'edge (nol-) *n.* knowing; what one knows; information; all that is or may be known.—**knowl'edgeable** (nol'ij-) *a.* intelligent, well informed.

knuck'le (nuc'kl) *n.* bone at a finger-joint.—*v.i.* knuckle down, to put the knuckles on the ground in playing marbles.—*v.t.* to strike with the knuckles.—**knuc'kle-dus'ter** *n.* metal appliance worn on knuckles to add force to a blow.

knur (n-) *n.* a knot on a tree-trunk; a hard hump; a wooden ball.—**knur' and spell,** game played with trap and ball.

knurl (n-) *n.* a knob or ridge.—**knurled'** (-ld) *a.* knotty, gnarled.

koal'a *n.* a pouched tree-dwelling

almost tail-less animal of Australia, protected by law, the native bear.

Ko'dak *n.* a hand photographic camera using roll films (protected trade name).

kohl (kōl) *n.* powdered antimony for darkening the eyelids.

ko'la *n.* an African tree whose seeds or nuts, having stimulating properties, are used in preparations of chocolate, aerated waters, etc.; an aerated water.

koo'doo (-ōō-) *n.* the striped antelope of Africa, with long, spiral-twisted horns.

kook'aburra *n.* in Australia, the laughing jackass, the great kingfisher.

kop'je, kop'pie (-pi) *n.* S. Africa, a hill.

Koran (korȧn') *n.* the sacred book of the Mohammedan scriptures.

korrumbur'ra *n.* Australia, aboriginal name for the common blow-fly.

ko'sher *a.* of food, etc., fulfilling the Jewish law.—*n.* kosher food or shop.

kotow' (kō-), **kowtow'** *n.* in China, touching the ground with the head in respect or submission.

kraal (krȧl) *n.* native S. African village; corral for cattle or sheep.

krantz, kranz, krans (-tz) *n.* in S. Africa, a crown of rocks on the top of a mountain, a precipice; a narrow gorge.

kryp'ton, cryp'ton *n.* one of the inert constituents of the atmosphere.

ku'dos (kū-) *n.* (*sl.*) fame; glory; credit.

kuk'ri (koo-) *n.* curved Gurkha knife.

ku'mera *n.* N. Z. sweet potato.

kum'mel (kim-) *n.* cumin-flavoured liqueur.

kursaal' (kōōr-) *n.* a public room for the use of visitors at German health resorts.

ky'a, ka'ia (kē'-) *n.* in S. Africa, a hut, house.

L

laa'ger (lȧ-) *n.* S.Africa, an encampment.

laag'te *n.* S. Africa, glen; valley; meadowland.

la'bel *n.* slip of paper, metal, etc., fixed to an object to give information about it.—*v.t.* to affix a label to.

la'bial *a.* of the lips; pronounced with the lips.—*n.* a sound so pronounced.

la'bour (-bẹr) *n.* exertion of the body or mind; a task; pains of childbirth; workmen collectively.—*v.i.* to work hard; strive; to maintain normal motion with difficulty; *esp.* of a ship, to be tossed heavily.—*v.t.* to elaborate; stress to excess.—**la'bourer** *n.* one who labours, *esp.* a man doing manual work for wages.—**labor'ious** *a.* hard-working; toilsome.—**labor'iously** *adv.*—**lab'oratory** *n.* place set apart for scientific investigations. *Syn.* work, toil, effort, industry, task. *Ant.* idleness, play, inaction, rest.

labur'num *n.* tree with yellow flowers.

lab'yrinth *n.* maze, network of winding passages.—**labyrin'thine** (-th-) *a.*

lac *n.* a dark resin.

lac, lakh *n.* 100,000 (gen. of rupees).

lace *n.* cord to draw edges together, e.g., to tighten shoes, etc.; ornamental braid; fine openwork fabric, often of elaborate pattern.—*v.t.* to fasten with laces; to flavour with spirit.—**lace'-lizard** *n.* Australia, usually the iguana.

la'cerate (las-) *v.t.* to tear, mangle; distress.—**lacera'tion** *n.*

lac'hrymal (-k-) *a.* of tears.—**lac'hrymatory** *n.* a tear bottle.—*a.* causing tears.—**lac'hrymose** *a.* tearful.

lack *n.* deficiency, want.—*v.t.* to be without, or poorly supplied with.

lackadai'sical (-dāz-) *a.* languid.

lack'ey *n.* a footman; an obsequious person.—*v.t.* to be, or play the, lackey to.

laconic' *a.* using, or expressed in, few words.—**lacon'ically** *adv.*—**lacon'icism** *n.* *Syn.* curt, terse, concise, short. *Ant.* verbose, wordy, diffuse.

lac'quer (lak'ẹr) *n.* a hard varnish.—*v.t.* to coat with lacquer.

lacrosse' (lȧ-) *n.* a team ball-game.

lac'tic *a.* of milk.—**lacta'tion** *n.* secreting of milk.—**lac'teal** *a.* of milk.

lactofla'vin *n.* a vitamin, B_2, present in whey, eggs, yeast, etc.

lacu'na *n.* gap, a missing portion, hiatus (**-nae, -nas** *pl.*).

lacus'tral, lacus'trine *a.* pertaining to lakes or swamps.

lad *n.* a boy, young fellow.—*fem.* **lass.**

ladd'er *n.* an appliance consisting of two poles connected by cross bars called rungs, used as a means of ascent; a flaw in stockings, jumpers, etc., caused by the running of a dropped or torn stitch.

lade *v.t.* to load; ship; burden, weigh down (**la'den** or **la'ded** *p.p.*).

la'dle *n.* deep, long-handled spoon.

la'dy *n.* woman of good breeding or social position; title of women of rank; formerly mistress, wife, love.—**our Lady,** the Virgin Mary.—**la'dylike** *a.*—**la'dyship** *n.*—**la'dybird** *n.* small beetle.—**La'dy-day** *n.* Feast of the Annunciation, 25th March.—**lady's-finger** *n.* in S.Africa, Australia, etc., species of small banana.

lag *v.i.* to go too slow, fall behind.—**lagg'ard** *n.* one who lags.—*a.* loitering.

lag *n.* (*sl.*) a convict; a ticket-of-leave man.—*v.t.* (*sl.*) to send to penal servitude.

la'ger (lȧ'gẹr-) *n.* light German beer.

lagoon' *n.* a salt-water lake.

la'ic *a.* secular; lay.—**la'icise** *v.t.* to render lay or laic.

lair (lẹr) *n.* resting-place of wild animal.

laird *n.* a Scottish landowner.

la'ity *n.* laymen.

lake *n.* large body of water; red pigment.

lam *v.t.* especially in N. America, to beat or hit.—**lamm'ing** *n.* a beating.

la'ma (lȧ-) *n.* Buddhist priest in Tibet.

lamb (lam) *n.* the young of the sheep; its meat; an innocent or helpless creature.—*v.i.* of a sheep, to give birth to a lamb.
lam'bent *a.* playing on a surface; shining.—**lam'bency** *n.*
lame *a.* crippled in a limb, *esp.* leg or foot; limping; of an excuse, etc., unconvincing.—*v.t.* to make lame.
lamell'a *n.* a thin plate or scale (**lamellæ** *pl.*).—**lamellar** *a.*—**lamellate** *a.*
lament' *v.* to sorrow for, weep for, mourn.—*n.* expression of grief; a song of grief.—**lamenta'tion** *n.* noisy grief.—**lamen'table** *a.* deplorable.
lam'ina *n.* a thin plate, scale, flake (**-inæ, -inas** *pl.*).—**lam'inate** *v.t.* to beat.
lam'ina *n.* a thin plate, scale, flake into, cover with, plates or layers.—*v.i.* to split into layers.
Lamm'as *n.* the 1st August.
lamp *n.* vessel holding oil to be burnt at a wick for lighting; various other appliances as sources of light.—**lamp'black** *n.* a pigment made from soot.—**lamp'ion** *n.* a fairy-light glass.
lampoon' *n.* venomous satire on individual.—*v.t.* write lampoons against.
lamp'rey *n.* a fish like an eel.
la'nary *n.* a store-place for wool.—**la'nate, la'nated** *a.* woolly.
lance (-â-) *n.* horseman's spear.—*v.t.* to pierce with a lance or lancet.—**lan'cet** *n.* pointed two-edged surgical knife.—**lan'cer** *n.* cavalry soldier (formerly) armed with a lance.—**lance-cor'poral** *n.* —**lance-ser'geant** *n.* non-commissioned officers in the army.—**lan'ceolate** *a.* lance-shaped, tapering to each end.
land *n.* the solid part of the earth's surface; ground, soil; country; property consisting of land.—*pl.* estates; in S. Africa, the cultivated parts of a farm as distinct from pasturage.—*v.i.* to come to land, disembark.—*v.t.* to bring to land.—**land'fall** *n.* a ship's approach to land at the end of a voyage.—**land'ing** *n.* act of landing; platform between flights of stairs; in N. America, a primitive port or harbour.—**land'ing-gear** *n.* apparatus which, in most modern aircraft, replaces the old fixed landing wheels. The landing wheels are retractable into either the wings or the engine cowlings of the aircraft, thus maintaining the streamlined effect of the plane when in flight.—**land'ing-stage** *n.* platform for embarkation and disembarkation.—**land'lord** *n.*; **land'lady** *fem.* a person who lets land or houses, etc.; master or mistress of an inn, boarding-house, etc.—**land'-locked** *a.* enclosed by land.—**land'lubber** *n.* a person ignorant of the sea and ships.—**land'mark** *n.* boundary-mark, conspicuous object as a guide for direction, etc.—**land'poor** *a.* in N. Amer., unable to meet payments on land.—**land'rail** *n.* corncrake.—**land'slip** *n.*—**land'slide** *n.* fall of earth from a cliff; notable collapse of a political party.—**lands'man** *n.* one who is not a sailor.—**land'ed** *a.* possessing, or consisting of, lands.—**land'ward** *a.* and *adv.*—**land'wards** *adv.* —**land'scape** *n.* a piece of inland scenery; a picture of it.—**land'scape-gard'ening** *n.* the laying out of grounds.
lan'dau (-aw) *n.* a four-wheeled carriage with a top which can be opened.
land'drost *n.* in South Africa, a sheriff.
lande (land) *n.* in France, a level sandy region unfit for cultivation and covered with heather or broom.
lane *n.* a narrow road or street.
lan'guage (-ng-gw-) *n.* speech; the words used by a people; style of speech.
lan'guish (-ng-gw-) *v.i.* to be or become weak or faint; to be in depressing or painful conditions; droop, pine.—**lan'guid** *a.* weak, faint, spiritless, dull.—**lan'guidly** *adv.*—**lan'guor** (-ger) *n.* faintness; want of energy or interest; tender mood.—**lan'guorous** *a.*
lank *a.* lean and tall.—**lank'y** *a.*
lan'olin *n.* grease from wool.
lan'tern *n.* a transparent case for a lamp or candle; an erection on a dome or roof to admit light.—**lan'tern-jaw'ed** *a.* having a square-formed jaw framing a lean, hollow-cheeked face.—**lan'thorn** *n.* lantern.
lan'yard *n.* a short cord for suspending a knife or whistle about the neck.
lap *n.* front of a woman's skirt as used to hold anything; seat made by thighs of a person seated; a single turn of wound thread, etc.; a round of a racecourse.—*v.t.* to enfold, wrap round.—**lap'dog** *n.* a small pet dog.—**lapel'** *n.* the part of the front of a coat folded back.—**lapp'et** *n.* flap or fold.
lap *v.t.* drink by scooping up with tongue; of waves, make lapping sound.
lap'idary *a.* of stones; engraved on stone.—*n.* cutter or engraver of stones. —**lap'is laz'uli** *n.* blue stone or pigment.
lapse *n.* slip; mistake; fall from virtue; passing (of time, etc).—*v.i.* fall away; come to an end (**lap'sed** *p.t./p.p.*).
lap'wing *n.* a kind of plover.
lar'board *n.* and *a.* obsolete for port or left side of ship when facing bows.
lar'ceny *n.* theft (**lar'cenies** *pl.*).
larch *n.* a coniferous tree (**larch'es** *pl.*).
lard *n.* prepared pig's fat.—*v.t.* to insert strips of bacon; to intersperse or decorate (speech with strange words, etc.).—**lard'er** *n.* storeroom for food; provisions.
large *a.* broad in range or area; great in size, number, etc.; liberal; generous.—**large'ly** *adv.*—**lar'gesse** *n.* gifts.
lar'go *adv.* (*mus.*) in broad, slow and measured time.
lar'iat *n.* a picketing-rope; a lasso.

lark *n.* a familiar singing-bird; *n.* joke, frolic, spree.—*v.i.* to indulge in one.
lar'rigan *n.* in N. America, a moccasin with a long leg made from deer-hide.
larr'ikin *n.* in Australia, a hoodlum, rough; a disorderly person.—*a.* rowdy.
lar'rup *v.t.* U.S. (*col.*) flog, whip, beat.
lar'va *n.* an insect in the grub or caterpillar stage (**lar'væ** *pl.*).—**lar'val** *a.*
lar'ynx *n.* the part of the throat containing the vocal cords (**laryn'ges** *pl.*).—**laryngi'tis** *n.* inflammation of this.
las'car *n.* a native East Indian sailor employed in European vessels.
lasciv'ious *a.* lustful.
Syn. lewd, sensual, libidinous, unchaste, licentious, prurient. *Ant.* pure, moral, chaste, clean, wholesome.
lash *n.* stroke with whip; flexible part of whip.—*v.t.* strike with whip, thong, etc. —*v.t.* bind with cord, etc.
lass *n.* girl (**lass'es** *pl.*—**lad** *masc.*).
lass'itude *n.* weariness, lack of energy.
lass'o (-ō, ōō) *n.* rope with a noose for catching cattle, etc. (**lass'os** (-ōz) *pl.*).—*v.t.* to catch with a lasso (**lass'oed** *p.t.* and *p.p.*—**lass'oing** *pres. p.*).
last (-â-) *n.* a model of a foot on which a shoemaker shapes boots, etc.
last (-â-) *n.* large measure of quantity.
last (-â-) *a.* and *adv.* after all others, coming at the end.—*n.*—**last'ly** *adv.*—*v.i.* to continue, hold out, remain.
lataki'a (-kē-) *n.* a superior quality of Turkish tobacco from *Latakia*, in Syria.
latch *v.t.* to fasten with a latch.—*n.* a fastening for a door, consisting of a bar, a catch for it, and a lever to lift it; a small spring lock (**latch'es** *pl.*).
lat'chet *n.* shoe-lace or sandal-string.
late *a.* after the proper time, backward; far on in a period of time; that was recently but now is not; recently dead; recent in date; of a late stage of development.—*adv.* after the proper time; recently; at or till a late hour.—**late'ly** *adv.* not long since, recently.
lateen' *a.* **lateen sail,** triangular sail on long yard at an angle of 45 deg. to mast.
la'tent *a.* existing but not developed.
lat'eral *a.* of or at the side.—**later'ally** *adv.*
lat'erite *n.* a brick-coloured rock found in India; a red ferruginous clay, often dried in the sun for use in building.
la'tex (lā-) *n.* the vital sap or fluid of plants.—**laticif'erous** (-sif-) *a.* in botany, bearing or containing latex or sap.
lath (lâth) *n.* a strip of wood (**laths** *pl.*).—**lath'y** *a.* like a lath; tall and thin.
lathe (lāth) *n.* a machine for spinning an object while it is being cut or shaped.
lath'er (-th-) *n.* froth of soap and water. —*v.i.* to form a lather; (*sl.*) to beat.
la'thi *n.* an iron-loaded stick used by Indian police in quelling native riots.
Lat'in *a.* of the ancient Romans; of or in their language; speaking a language descended from theirs.—*n.* the language of the ancient Romans.—**latin'ity** *n.* manner of writing Latin; Latin style.—**lat'inism** *n.* a word or idiom imitating Latin.
lat'itude *n.* freedom from restriction; scope.—(*geog.*) angular distance on a meridian reckoned N. or S. from equator. —*pl.* regions, climes.—**latitudinar'ian** (-êr-) *a.* showing latitude of thought, *esp.* in religion.–*n.*–**latitudinar'ianism** *n.*
latrine' (-ēn) *n.* in the army, hospitals, prisons, etc., a privy water closet.
latt'en *n.* a kind of brass or bronze; sheet tin; iron-plate covered with tin.
latt'er *a.* later; recent; second of two.
latt'ice *n.* a structure of laths crossing with spaces between; a window so made. —**latt'iced** *a.*—**latt'icing** *n.*
laud *n.* praise, song of praise.—*v.t.* to praise.—**laud'able** *a.*—**laud'ably** *adv.*
Syn. extol, glorify, eulogise, applaud. *Ant.* disparage, reprove, censure, blame.
laud'anum *n.* tincture of opium.
laugh (lâf) *v,i.* to make sounds expressive of amusement, merriment or scorn.—*n.* sound or act of laughing.—**laugh'able** *a.* funny.—**laugh'ably** *adv.*—**laught'er** *n.* laughing.—**laugh'ing-stock** *n.* an object of general derision.—**laugh'ing-gas** *n.* nitrous oxide as an anæsthetic.—**laughing hyæna** *Hyæna striata*, so called from its cry.—**laughing jackass** Australia, the kookaburra q.v.
launch *v.t.* to hurl; set going; set afloat. —*v.i.* to enter on a course.—*n.* the setting afloat of a vessel.—*n.* a warship's largest boat; large power-driven boat.
laun'dress *n.* woman employed in laundry.—**laun'dry** *n.* place for washing clothes.—**laun'der** *v.t.* wash and iron, etc.
lau'rel *n.* a glossy-leaved shrub, the bay tree.—*pl.* wreath of bay-leaves, emblem of victory or merit.—**lau'reate** (lawr'i-āt) *a.* crowned with laurels.—**poet laureate,** poet with an appointment to the Royal Household.—**lau'reateship** *n.*
la'va (lâ-) *n.* matter thrown out by volcanoes in fluid form.
lave *v.t.* to wash, bathe.—**lav'atory** *n.* room for washing; water-closet, etc.
lav'ender *n.* a shrub with fragrant flowers; the colour of the flowers; a pale blue tinged with red.
laverock (-vr-) the skylark.
lav'ish *a.* giving or spending profusely; very or too abundant.—*v.t.* to spend or give profusely.—**lav'ishly** *adv.*
law *n.* a rule binding on a community; the system of these rules; a branch of this system; knowledge of it, administration of it; a general principle deduced from facts, an invariable sequence of events in nature.—**law'ful** *a.* allowed by the law. —**law'giver** *n.* one who makes laws.—**law'less** *a.* regardless of the laws.—**law'fully** *adv.*—**law'lessly** *adv.*—**law'-abiding**

a. obedient to the laws.—**law'-suit** *n.* the carrying on of a claim in a court.

lawn *n.* a fine linen; stretch of carefully tended turf in garden, etc.—**lawn'-mower** *n.* machine for cutting grass.—**lawn'-tenn'is** *n.* game played by 2 or 4 players on flat court with net across it.

law'yer *n.* professional expert in law.

lax *a.* loose, slack, negligent; not strict.—**lax'ative** *a.* loosening the bowels.—*n.* a laxative drug.—**lax'ity** *n.*—**lax'ly** *adv.*

lay *v.t.* to deposit on a surface, cause to lie (**laid** *p.t.* and *p.p.*—**lay'ing** *pres. p.*). —*p.t.* of **lie.**—**lay'er** *n.* one who lays; a thickness of matter spread on a surface; one of several such; a shoot fastened down to take root.—*v.t.* to propagate plants by making layers.—**lay'-out** *n.* plan of buildings, etc.; a ground plan, to display; to expend.

lay *n.* a minstrel's song, a ballad.

lay *a.* not clerical; of or done by persons not clergymen; non-professional.—**lay'-man** *n.* one of the laity.

layette' (-et') *n.* clothes for a new-born child.

lay'-figure *n.* a jointed figure of the body used by artists.

laz'ar *n.* a leper.—**lazarett'o** *n.* a leper-hospital (**-tos** (-tōz) *pl.*).

la'zy *a.* averse to work, indolent.—**la'zily** *adv.*—**la'ziness** *n.*—**laze** *v.i.*

Syn. slothful, idle, inert, torpid. *Ant.* industrious, active, diligent, assiduous.

lea (lē) *n.* a piece of meadow, grassland.

lead (led) *n.* a soft, heavy grey metal; a plummet or lump of this used for sounding depths of water; graphite in pencil. —*pl.* piece of roof covered with lead; strips of it used to widen spaces in printing, etc.—*v.t.* to cover, weight, space with lead (**lead'ed** *p.t./p.p.*—**lead'ing** *p.p.*).—**leads'man** *n.* sailor who heaves the lead.—**lead'en** *a.*

lead (lēd) *v.t.* to guide, conduct; persuade; serve as a way, conduct people.—*v.i.* to be or go or play the first (**led** *p.t.* and *p.p.*—**lea'ding** *pres. p.*).—*n.* leading; example; front place; a wire between an electric instrument and the supply of electricity; in Australia, the old river-bed in which gold is found.—**lead'er** *n.* one who leads; an article in a newspaper expressing editorial views (also **leading article**); in S. Africa, vein of gold-bearing quartz, which is supposed to lead to the main reef.—*pl.* in Australia, the leading pair of a bullock team.—**lead'ership** *n.*—**lead'ing case** *n.* legal decision used as a precedent.—**lead'ing question** *n.* question worded to prompt the answer desired.—**to strike the lead,** in Australia, to find the river-bed containing gold; to succeed.

leaf *n.* part of a plant's foliage consisting usually of a green blade on a stem; two pages of a book, etc.; a thin sheet; a flap or movable part of a table, etc. (**leaves** *pl.*).—**leaf'let** *n.* a small leaf; a handbill.—**leaf'y** *a.*—**leaf'less** *a.*—**leaf'-insect** *n.* in Australia, an insect, the wing cases of which resemble a leaf of genus *Phasma.*

league (lēg) *n.* a measure of road distance, about three miles.

league (lēg) *n.* an agreement for mutual help; the parties to it; a federation of clubs, etc.—*v.t.* and *i.* to combine in a league.—**league-match** *n.* in football, a match between clubs in the same league. —**leag'uer** *n.* a member of a league.

lea'guer (lē-) *n.* a camp; investment of a town or fort; siege.

leak *n.* hole or defect through which a liquid passes in or out.—*v.i.* to let liquid in or out so; of liquid, to seep through a leak.—**leak'age** *n.* leaking; gradual escape or loss.—**leak'y** *a.*

leal *a.* loyal.—**le'alty** *n.*

lean *a.* lacking fat; thin.—*n.* the lean part of meat, mainly muscular tissue.

lean *v.i.* to bend or incline; tend (towards).—*v.t.* to cause to lean.—**lean'-to** *n.* a room or shed built against a house, with a separate sloping roof.

leap *v.i.* to spring from the ground.—*v.t.* to spring over.—*n.* a jump.—**leap'-frog** *n.* a game in which a player vaults over another bending down.—**leap'-year** *n.* a year with February 29th as an extra day.

learn (lern) *v.t.* to gain skill or knowledge by study, practice or being taught.—*v.i.* to gain knowledge; to be taught; to find out.—**learn'ed** *a.* having much knowledge, deeply read; showing or requiring learning.—**learn'edly** *adv.*—**learn'er** *n.*—**learn'ing** *n.* knowledge got by study.

lease *n.* a contract by which land or property is given for a stated time by an owner to a tenant, usually for a rent.—*v.t.* to take or give the use of by a lease.—**lease'hold** *n.*—**less'or** *n.*—**less'ee** *n.*

leash *n.* a thong for holding dogs; a set of three animals.—*v.t.* hold in leash.

least *a.* smallest; *sup.* of **little.**—*n.* the smallest one or amount.

leath'er (leth-) *n.* skin of an animal prepared for use.—**leath'ern** *a.*—**leath'ery** *a.* —**leather-jacket,** in Australia, a tree; a fish; a kind of pancake.—**leather-wood,** a N. American shrub, genus *Dirca.*

leave *v.t.* to go away from; deposit; allow to remain; depart without taking; bequeathe.—*v.i.* to go away, set out (**left** *p.t.* and *p.p.*—**lea'ving** *pres. p.*).

leave *n.* permission; permission to be absent from duty, furlough.

leav'en (lev-) *n.* yeast.—*v.t.* to treat with it; temper, modify.

lech'er *n.* a man given to lewdness.—*v.i.* to practise lewdness; to indulge in carnal desires.—**lech'erous** *a.* lewd; provoking lust; lascivious.—**lech'erously** *adv.*—**lech'erousness** *n.*—**lech'ery** *n.*

lec'tern *n.* a reading desk in church.

lec'tion *n.* a difference in copies of a manuscript or book; a reading.—**lec'tor** *n.* a reader.

lec'ture *n.* a discourse for the instruction of an audience; a speech of reproof.—*v.t.* to reprove, admonish.—*v.i.* to deliver a discourse.—**lec'turer** *n.*—**lect'ureship** *n.* an appointment as lecturer.

ledge *n.* a narrow flat surface sticking out from a wall, cliff, etc.; a ridge of rock.

ledg'er *n.* a book of debit and credit accounts, the chief account book of a firm.—**ledger'line** *n.* in music, a short line, added above or below the stave.

lee *n.* shelter; the side of anything, *esp.* a ship, away from the wind.—**lee'ward** *a.* on the lee side.—*adv.* towards this side.—**lee'way** *n.* the leeward drift of a ship.

leech *n.* a blood-sucking worm formerly used by doctors; (formerly) a physician.

leech *n.* the edge of a sail.

leek *n.* a herb akin to an onion.

leer *v.t.* to glance with malign, sly, or immodest expression.—*n.* such glance.

lees *n. pl.* dregs, sediment of wine, etc.

left *a.* denotes the side, limb, etc., opposite to the right; (*see* **right**).—*n.* the left hand; radical party.

leg *n.* one of the limbs on which a person or animal walks, runs, or stands; a support resembling this; part of a garment covering a leg; (*cricket*) area of field at the back of batsman.—**legg'ing** *n.* (usually *pl.*) leg covering of leather.

leg'acy *n.* anything left by a will; a thing handed down to a successor.

le'gal *a.* of, appointed or permitted by, or based on, law.—**le'gally** *adv.*—**legal'ity** *n.*—**le'galise** *v.t.* to make legal.—**legalisa'tion** *n.* *Syn.* lawful, legitimate, authorised, allowable. *Ant.* illegal, illicit, contraband, unconstitutional, lawless.

leg'ate *n.* an ambassador, *esp.* of the Pope.—**lega'tion** *n.* a diplomatic minister and his suite; his mission or residence.

legatee' *n.* one who receives a legacy.

leg'end (lej-) *n.* a traditional story or myth; traditional literature, an inscription on a coin, etc.—**leg'endary** *a.*

leg'erdemain (lej-) *n.* juggling, conjuring; sleight of hand, trickery.

leg'horn (-gorn) *n.* kind of straw used for hats; breed of fowls.

leg'ible (-j-) *a.* easily read, decipherable.—**legibil'ity** *n.*—**leg'ibly** *adv.*

le'gion (lē'jn) *n.* a body of infantry in the Roman army; various modern military bodies; an association of veterans; a large number.—**le'gionary** *a.* and *n.*

leg'islator (-j-) *n.* a maker of laws.—**leg'islate** *v.i.* to make laws.—**legisla'tion** *n.*—**leg'islative** *a.*—**leg'islature** *n.* a body that makes laws, parliament.

legit'imate (-j-) *a.* lawful, proper, regular.—**legit'imacy** *n.*—**legit'imatise, legit'imise** *v.t.* to make legitimate.—**legitimatisa'tion, legitima'tion** *n.*—**legit'imist** *n.* a supporter of an hereditary title to a monarchy.

legu'minous (-g-) *a.*—**leguminous plants.** Pod-bearing, as peas, beans.

leipo'a (lī-) *n.* a genus of Australian mound-birds, of the genus *megapodæ*.

lei'sure (lezh'er) *n.* freedom from occupation, spare time.—**leis'urely** *a.* deliberate.—**leis'urely** *adv.*—**leis'ured** *a.*

lek'ker *a.* in S. Africa, delicious; tasty; slightly intoxicated.—*n. pl.* sweets.

lemm'ing, lem'ing *n.* burrowing animal of the rat family, of N. Europe.

lem'on *n.* a pale yellow fruit with acid juice; the tree bearing it; its colour.—**lemonade'** *n.* a drink made from lemon juice.—**lem'on sole** *n.* trade name for edible fish of the family *Pleuronectes*.

le'mur (lē'-) *n.* a nocturnal animal like a monkey.—**le'murine** *a.*

lend *v.t.* to give the temporary use of; let out for hire or interest; give, bestow (**lent** *p.t.* and *p.p.*—**lend'ing** *pres. p.*).—**it lends itself to,** it is adapted to.—**lend'er** *n.*—**lend-lease** *n.* an agreement by which the U.S.A. sold, exchanged, or gave war materials to the enemies of the Axis in World War 2.

length (-th) *n.* the quality of being long; measurement from end to end; a long stretch; a piece of a certain length.—**length'en** *v.t.* and *i.*—**length'wise** *a.* and *adv.*—**length'y** *a.*—**length'ily** *adv.*

le'nient *a.* mild, being without severity—**le'nience, le'niency** *n.*—**le'niently** *adv.*—**len'ity** *n.*—**len'itive** *n.* a soothing or mildly laxative drug.

Len'inism *n.* the Soviet Marxian communism, as interpreted by Lenin.

lens (-z) *n.* a piece of glass with one or both sides curved, used for concentrating or dispersing light in cameras, spectacles, telescopes, etc.—**lenses'** *pl.*

Lent *n.* a period of fasting from Ash Wednesday to Easter-Eve.—**len'ten** *a.*

lent'il *n.* the eatable seed of a leguminous plant, a kind of bean.

lent'isk *n.* a tree yielding mastic.

Leo' *n.* the 5th sign of the Zodiac (the Lion) operative July 22–Aug. 21.

le'onine *a.* like a lion.

leopard (lep-) *n.* a large carnivorous animal of cat kind, with a spotted fawn coat.—**leop'ardess** *fem.*

lep'er *n.* one suffering from leprosy.—**lep'rosy** *n.* a disease forming silvery scales on the skin and eating away the parts affected.—**lep'rous** *a.*

lepidop'tera *n. pl.* an order of insects having four wings covered with fine scales, as moths, butterflies, etc.

les'bian *n.* a woman of homosexual nature.—**les'bianism** *n.* unnatural sexual intercourse between women.

leser'ma-jesty (lēz-) *n.* treason.

le'sion *n.* an injury, injurious change in texture or action of an organ of the body.

less *a. comp.* of **little,** not so much.—*adv.* to a similar extent or degree.—*pron.* a less amount or number.—*prep.* after deducting, minus.—**less'en** *v.t.* to diminish.—**less'er** *a.*
lessee *n.* person to whom lease is given.
less'on *n.* a portion of Scripture read in church; something to be learnt by a pupil; a part of a course of teaching.
less'or *n.* person who gives lease.
lest *conj.* in order that . . . not.
let *v.t.* to allow, enable, cause to; grant use of for rent, to leave.—*v.i.* (**let** *p.t.* and *p.p.*—**lett'ing** *pres. p.*).
let *v.t.* to hinder (**lett'ed** or **let** *p.t.* and *p.p.*—**lett'ing** *pres. p.*).—*n.* a hindrance; in games, an obstruction of a ball or player cancelling the stroke.
le'thal *a.* deadly, fatal.
leth'argy *n.* drowsiness, apathy, want of energy.—**lethar'gic** *a.*—**lethar'gically** *adv.*
lett'er *n.* one of the symbols with which words are written; a written message.—*pl.* literature, knowledge of books.—*v.t.* to mark with letters.—**lett'ered** *a.* learned.—**lett'ering** *n.*—**lett'erhead** *n.* notepaper with printed heading.—**lett'erpress** *n.* printed matter.
lett'uce (-tis) *n.* a plant for use as salad.
leu'cocyte (lū'ko-) *n.* one of the white corpuscles of the blood.
levant' *v.i.* to run away.—**levant'er** *n.*
lev'ee *n.* a sovereign's reception for men only; formerly, a great person's reception on rising; a pier or embankment.
lev'el *n.* an instrument for showing or testing a horizontal line or surface; such line or surface; a horizontal passage in a mine; a social or moral standard.—*a.* horizontal; even in surface; even in style, quality, etc.—*v.t.* to make level, bring to the same level; to lay low; to aim (a gun).—**level-head'ed** *a.* not apt to be carried away by emotion or excitement.
le'ver *n.* a bar used to apply force at one end of its length by pressure exerted at the other, a point in between resting against a fixed support.—**le'verage** *n.* the action or power of a lever.
lev'eret *n.* a young hare.
levi'athan *n.* a sea-monster.
levita'tion *n.* the power of raising a solid body into the air by unseen forces.—**lev'itate** *v.t.* and *i.*
lev'ity *n.* inclination to make a joke of serious matters, frivolity.
Syn. buoyancy, inconstancy, fickleness, unsteadiness, volatility, flightiness. *Ant.* weight, gravity, oppressiveness, sadness.
lev'y *n.* the act of collecting taxes or enrolling troops; amount or number levied.—*v.t.* to raise or impose by compulsion (**lev'ied** *p.t.* and *p.p.*—**lev'ying** *pres. p.*).
lewd *a.* indecent.—**lewd'ness** *n.*
lew'isite *n.* a peculiarly destructive explosive compound; a blister gas.
lex'icon *n.* a dictionary; word-making game.—**lexicog'raphy** *n.* art of writing dictionaries.—**lexicog'rapher** *n.*
li'able *a.* subject (to), exposed (to); answerable.—**liabil'ity** *n.*
liai'son (li-ā'zon) *n.* union; connection; an intimacy, *esp.* secret; illicit intimacy between a man and a woman.—**liaison officer,** an officer keeping troops in touch with each other.
lia'na (*bot.*) any tropical climbing plant.
liar *n.* a person who tells lies.
liba'tion *n.* drink poured out as an offering to the gods.
li'bel *n.* a published statement damaging to a person's reputation.—*v.t.* to publish a libel against.—**li'bellous** *a.*
lib'eral *a.* generous; open-minded; of a political party, favouring changes making towards democracy.—*n.* one of such a party.—**lib'eralism** *n.* the principles of a Liberal party.—**liberal'ity** *n.* munificence.—**lib'eralise** *v.t.*—**lib'erally** *adv.*—**lib'erate** *v.t.* to set free.—**libera'tion** *n.*—**lib'erator** *n.*—**lib'erty** *n.* freedom.—**Lib'erty Ship** *n.* cargo ship of about 10,000 tons with reciprocating engines, built speedily and in great numbers by the U.S.A. during World War 2.
lib'ertine (-ēn) *n.* a dissolute man.—*a.*
libid'inous *a.* lustful.
libi'do (-bē'-) *n.* in psychology, the vital urge (of general or sexual origin); sexual impulse.—**libid'inous** *a.* lustful, lewd, lascivious.
Li'bra *n.* the 7th sign of the Zodiac (the Balance) operative Sept. 22–Oct. 22.
li'brary *n.* a collection of books; a place where the books are kept; a reading or writing room in a house.—**librar'ian** (-ir-) *n.* a keeper of a library.—**librar'ianship** *n.*
librett'o *n.* the book of words of an opera (**-os** (-ōz), **-i** *pl.*).—**librett'ist** *n.*
li'cence *n.* leave, permission; formal permission; the document giving it; excessive liberty; dissoluteness; a writer's or artist's transgression of the rules of his art (often **poetic licence**).—**li'cense, li'cence** *v.t.* to grant a licence to.—**licent'iate** *n.* one licensed to practise an art or profession.—**licen'tious** *a.* sexually immoral.—**licen'tiously** *adv.*—**licensee'** *n.*
li'chen (-k-) *n.* a small flowerless plant forming a crust on rocks, trees, etc.
lich'-gate, lych'-gate *n.* the roofed gate of a churchyard.
lick *v.t.* to pass the tongue over.—*n.*
lid *n.* movable cover; cover of the eye.
li'do (lē-) *n.* a pleasure resort, usually by the sea (**-dos** (-dōz) *pl.*).
lie *v.i.* to be horizontal or at rest; to be situated; to recline (**lay** *p.t.*—**lain** *p.p.*—**lying** *pres. p.*).—*n.* direction, position; state (of affairs, etc.).
lie *v.i.* to make a false statement (**lied** *p.t.* and *p.p.*—**ly'ing** *pres. p.*).—*n.* an untrue statement.—**li'ar** *n.* one who lies.
lief (lēf) *adv.* gladly.—*a.* dear.

liege (lēj) *a.* bound to render feudal service.—*n.* a vassal; a lord.
lien (lē'en) *n.* a right to hold property until a claim is met.
lieu (lū) *n.* **in lieu of,** instead of.—**lieuten'ant** (*Army* left-, *Navy and U.S.* lōōt-) *n.* a junior navy, army or air service officer.—**lieuten'ancy** *n.*
life *n.* the active principle of the existence of animals and plants, animate existence; the time of its lasting; the history of such an existence; a manner of living; vigour, vivacity (**lives** *pl.*).—**life'less** *a.*
lift *v.t.* to raise to a higher position; in S. Africa, to steal.—*v.i.* to rise.—*n.* an apparatus to raise things; in aviation, an air force acting at right angles on an aeroplane wing, and so lifting it.
lig'ament *n.* a band of tissue joining bones.—**lig'ature** *n.* bandage; a thread for tying up an artery.
light (līt) *a.* of, or bearing, little weight; gentle; easy, requiring little effort; trivial.—*adv.* in a light manner. **light'en** *v.t.* to reduce or remove a load, etc.—**light'ly** *adv.*—**light'ness** *n.*—**lights** *n. pl.* lungs of animals.—**light'** *v.i.* to get down from a horse or vehicle; to come by chance (upon).—**light'er** *n.* a large boat used for unloading ships.—**light'-fin'gered** *a.* deft; thievish.
light (līt) *n.* the natural agent by which things are visible; a source of this; a window; mental vision; the light part of anything.—*a.* bright; pale, not dark.—*v.t.* to set burning; to give light to.—*v.i.* to take fire; to brighten (**light'ed** or **lit** *p.t.*and *p.p.*—**light'ing** *pres. p.*).—**light'-en** *v.i.* to give light to.—**light'ning** *n.* a visible discharge of electricity in the atmosphere.—**light'house** *n.* tower with a light to guide ships.—**light'some** *a.* radiant.—**light-year** (*astronomy,*) the distance light travels in a year, approx. 6 million million miles.
lig'neous *a.* of, or of the nature of, wood.
like *a.* similar, resembling.—*adv.* in the manner of.—*pron.* a similar thing.—*v.t.* to find agreeable.—*v.i.* to be pleasing. —**like'able** *a.*—**like'ly** *a.* probably true; hopeful, promising.—*adv.* probably.—**like'lihood** *n.*—**li'ken** *v.t.* to compare. —**like'ness** *n.* quality of being like; a portrait.—**like'-wise** *adv.* in like manner. *Syn.* correspondent, analogous, allied, parallel, likely, probable. *Ant.* different, distinct, dissimilar, varied, diverse.
li'lac *n.* a shrub bearing pale violet flowers; their colour.—*a.* of this colour.
lilt *v.t.* and *i.* to sing merrily.—*n.* a rhythmical effect in music.
lil'y *n.* a bulbous flowering plant.—**pig'-lily** *n.* in S. Africa, the arum lily.
limb (lim) *n.* an arm or leg; a branch of a tree; the edge of the sun or moon.
limber *n.* the detachable front part of a gun-carriage.—*a.* pliant, lithe.
lim'bo *n.* a region on the borders of Hell, assigned to the unbaptized.
lime *n.* a sticky substance used for catching birds; the alkaline earth from which mortar is made.—*v.t.* to smear, or catch with lime, to treat (land) with lime.—**lime'stone** *n.* rock which yields lime when burnt.
lime *n.* a small acid fruit like a lemon; the linden tree.
lime'light *n.* strong light showing up actors, etc., on theatre stage; public observation.
limerick *n.* self-contained, nonsensical, humorous or wittily improper stanza, rhyming *aabba.*
lim'inal *a.* on the threshold of; verging on.
lim'it *n.* boundary; utmost extent or duration.—*v.t.* to restrict, keep within limits.—**limita'tion** *n.*
limn (lim) *v.t.* to paint, depict.
lim'ousine (-zēn) *n.* a luxuriously appointed closed type of motor-car.
limp *a.* without firmness.—**limp'ly** *adv.*
limp *v.i.* to walk lamely.—*n.*
limp'et *n.* a tent-shaped shellfish which sticks tightly to rocks.
limp'id *a.* clear, transparent.—**limpid-'ity** *n.*—**limp'idly** *adv.*
linch'-pin *n.* pin to hold wheel on axle.
lind'en *n.* the lime tree.
line *n.* a linen thread; any cord or string; a wire; a stroke made with a pen, etc.; a long narrow mark; continuous length without breadth; a row; a series; course; province of activity; the 12th of an inch; electro-magnetic unit of magnetic force or flux.—*v.t.* to cover inside; to mark with a line or lines; to bring into line.—**li'ning** *n.* a covering for the inside of a garment, etc.—**lin'eage** *n.* descent from, or the descendants of, an ancestor. —**lin'eal** *a.* of lines; in direct line of descent.—**lin'eament** *n.* feature.—**lin'ear** *a.* of or in lines.—**lin'en** *a.* cloth made of flax.—**li'ner** *n.* vessel belonging to a regular line of ships; aviation, a large passenger aeroplane plying for hire.
ling *n.* a slender fish; a kind of heather.
lin'ger (-ng-g-) *v.i.* to tarry, loiter.
lin'go *n.* language, jargon; dialect; fun language, slang (**ling'oes** *pl.*).
lin'gual (-ng-gw-) *a.* of the tongue or language.—*n.* a lingual sound.—**ling'uist** *n.* one skilled in languages.—**linguist'ic** *a.* of languages or their study.
lin'iment *n.* embrocation.
link *n.* a ring of a chain; a measure, 1-100th part of a chain.—*v.t.* and *i.* to join with, or as with, a link, connect.—*n.* formerly, a torch.
links *n. pl.* ground on which gold is played; grassed sandhills.
linn'et *n.* a familiar song-bird.
li'noblock *n.* a design cut in relief, in reverse, on a linoleum-covered block.—

lino'cut *n.* a design printed from such a block; a print from it.
lino'leum *n.* floor-covering made of canvas with a surface of cork and linseed oil.—**lino'leumed** *a.*
li'notype *n.* a machine for producing lines of type cast in one piece.
lin'seed *n.* the seed of flax.
lin'sey-wool'sey *n.* coarse fabric of wool and cotton or linen; (*fig.*) confusion; jargon; gibberish.
lint *n.* soft material for dressing wounds.
lint'el *n.* the top piece of a door, etc.
li'on *n.* a large animal of the cat tribe; a person of importance.—**li'oness** *fem.*—**li'onise** *v.t.* to treat as a celebrity.
lip *n.* either edge of the mouth, an edge.—**lip'-salve** *n.* grease paint, ointment for the lips.—**lip'stick** *n.* stick of perfumed rouge for reddening lips.
liq'uid *a.* fluid, not solid or gaseous; bright, clear.—*n.* a liquid substance.—**liq'uefy** *v.t.* and *i.*—**liquefac'tion** *n.*—**liques'cent** *a.* tending to become liquid.—**liques'cence** *n.*—**liq'uidate** *v.t.* to pay (debt); to arrange affairs of, and dissolve (company); to wipe out; to eliminate opposition by killing or repressing dissenters.—**liquida'tion** *n.*—**liq'uidator** *n.*—**liq'uor** (lik'er) *n.* a liquid, *esp.* strong drink.—**liqueur'** (li-kūr') *n.* an alcoholic liquor.—**liquid air, gas,** air, or gas, reduced to the liquid form by high pressure at low temperature.—**liquid fire** liquid fuel discharged as flames against an enemy.—**liquid fuel** petrol, paraffin oil, etc., carried in liquid form and vaporised for combustion.
liq'uorice (-ker-is) *n.* a black substance used in medicine and as a sweetmeat; the plant or its root, from which the substance is obtained.
lisle (līl) *n.* a fine hand-twisted cotton thread used for making stockings.
lisp *v.t.* and *i.* to speak with faulty pronunciation of the sibilants.—*n.*
liss'om *a.* supple, lithe, agile.
list *n.* the border or edge of cloth; strips of cloth, *esp.* used as material for slippers; a roll or catalogue.—*pl.* a space for tilting.—*v.t.* to write down in a list.
list *v.i.* to desire; of a ship, to incline, lean to one side.—*n.* desire; inclination of a ship.—**list'less** *a.* indifferent, languid.
list *v.t.* and *i.* to listen.—**list'en** (lis'en) *v.i.* to try to hear; attend (advice).—**listen in** to listen to a wireless broadcast from a receiver.—**list'ener** *n.*
lit'any *n.* form of prayer (**lit'anies** *pl.*).
lit'eral *a.* of letters; exact as to words; according to the sense of actual words, not figurative.—**lit'erally** *adv.*—**lit'erary** *a.* of, or learned in, literature.—**li'terate** *a.* educated.—**lit'eracy** *n.*—**litera'tim** *adv.* letter for letter.—**lit'erature** *n.* books and writings; the profession of writers.
lithe *a.* supple.—**lithe'some** *a.*
lithog'raphy *n.* making of drawings, etc., on stone, zinc or aluminium, for printing.—**li.h'ograph** *n.* print so produced.—*v.t.* print thus.—**lithog'rapher** *n.*—**lithographic'** *a.*
lit'igate *v.i.* to go to law.—**lit'igant** *a.* and *n.*—**litiga'tion** *n.*—**liti'gious** (-j-) *a.* fond of going to law.
lit'mus *n.* a blue colouring matter turned red by acids.
li'tre (lē'ter) *n.* measure of capacity in metric system, about 1¾ pints.
litt'er *n.* portable couch; kind of stretcher for the wounded; straw, etc., as bedding for animals; fragments lying about, untidy refuse of paper, etc.; the young of an animal produced at a birth.—*v.t.* to strew with litter; to bring forth.
lit'tle *a.* small, not much; unimportant. (**less** *comp.*—**least** sup.).—*n.* a small quantity.—*adv.* slightly.
litt'oral *a.* of, or on, the seashore.—*n.*
lit'urgy *n.* a form of public worship (**lit'urgies** *pl.*).—**litur'gical** *a.*
live (liv) *v.i.* to have life; to pass one's life, continue in life; dwell; feed.—**liv'ing** *n.* the action of being in life; means of earning livelihood; a church benefice.
live (līv) *a.* living; flaming.—**live'-axle** (*motoring*) driving shaft in back axle.—**live' rail** rail carrying electric current.—**live'stock** farm animals.—**live wire** wire carrying electric current; a very energetic, able person.
live'lihood *n.* means of living.
live'long *a.* whole length of.
live'ly *a.* brisk, vivid.—**live'liness** *n.*
Syn. quick, nimble, smart, alert, sprightly, prompt, blithe, gleeful, jocund, energetic, spirited, glowing, effervescent. *Ant.* dull, slow, lethargic, vapid, inert.
liv'er *n.* the organ which secretes bile.
liv'ery *n.* allowance of food for horses; the distinctive dress of the members of a City company, or of a person's servants.—**liv'eryman** *n.* a member of a London guild.—**liv'ery-stable** *n.* a stable where horses are kept at a charge, or hired out.
liv'id *a.* of a bluish pale colour.
liz'ard *n.* a four-footed reptile.—**lace'-lizard** *n.* in Australia, the iguana or goanna.
lla'ma (lȧ-) *n.* a woolly animal used as a beast of burden in S. America; its wool; cloth made from this.
load *n.* a burden; amount usually carried at once; in motoring, vehicle's actual load; resistance against which engine has to work; in electricity, amount of electrical energy drawn from a source.—*v.t.* to put a load on or into; to charge (gun); to weigh down.—**load'stone, lode'stone** *n.* magnetic iron ore; magnet.—**load'star, lode'star** *n.* Pole Star.—**lode** *n.* vein of ore.
loaf *n.* a mass of bread baked; a cone of sugar (**loaves** *pl.*).—*v.i.* to idle.

loam *n.* a fertile soil.—**loam'y** *a.*
loan *n.* a thing lent; an act of lending.—*v.t.* to lend.—**loan'able** *a.*
loath, loth (-th) *a.* unwilling.—**loath'ly** *a.*—**loath'some** *a.* disgusting, repulsive.—**loathe** (-th) *v.t.* to hate, abhor.—**loath'ing** *n.* disgust.
lob *n.* in cricket, a slow, underhand ball; in tennis, etc., a shot pitched high in the air; slow, dull person.—*v.t.* and *i.*
lobb'y *n.* a corridor into which rooms open; entrance-hall.—**lobb'ying** *n.* in the House of Parliament or in Congress, frequenting the lobby to collect news or influence members.
lobe *n.* the soft hanging part of the ear; any similar flap.
lo'bola *n.* in S. Africa, the native practice of buying a wife.
lob'ster *n.* a shellfish with long tail and claws, which turns scarlet when boiled.
lob'worm *n.* worm used as bait.
lo'cal *a.* relating to place; of or existing in a particular place.—*n.* (*sl.*) a public house.—**local'ity** *n.* a place, situation; district.—**lo'cally** *adv.*—**lo'calise** *v.t.*—**locate'** *v.t.* attribute to a place; find the place of.—**loca'tion** *n.* a placing; situation; in S. Africa, native quarter of towns and cities.—**loc'ative** *a.* and *n.* grammatical case denoting "place where."
loch *n.* Scottish lake; an arm of the sea.
lock *n.* a tress or curl of hair.
lock *n.* an appliance for fastening a door, lid, etc.; the mechanism for discharging a firearm; an enclosure in a river or canal for moving boats from one level to another; a close crowd of vehicles.—*v.t.* to fasten with a lock; join firmly, embrace closely.—*v.i.* to become fixed or united.—**lock'er** *n.* a small cupboard with a lock.—**lock'jaw** *n.* tetanus.—**lock'out** *n.* the exclusion of workmen by employers as a means of coercion.—**lock'smith** *n.* one who makes and mends locks.—**lock'et** *n.* a small pendant.—**lock'up** *n.* a lock-up garage; private aeroplane hangar.
locomot'ive (lō-) *a.* having the power of moving from place to place.—*n.* steam engine moving from place to place by its own power.—**locomo'tion** *n.* action or power of moving from place to place.—**locomo'tor ataxy (-ia)** nervous disorder causing unsteadiness in use of limbs.
lo'cus *n.* locality, place; a geometrical line, all of whose points satisfy a certain geometrical condition to the exclusion of all other points (**lo'ci** *pl.*).
lo'cust *n.* a destructive winged insect; in Australia, common name for the cicada; a tree; its fruit resembling a bean in shape.
locu'tion *n.* a phrase.
lode *see* **load.**
lodge *n.* house for a shooting or hunting party; house at the gate of an estate; meeting-place of a branch of freemasons, etc.; the branch.—*v.t.* to house; deposit.—*v.i.* to live in another's house at a fixed charge; to become fixed after being thrown.—**lodg'er** *n.*
loft *n.* an attic; a room over a stable; a gallery in a church.—*v.t.* to send (a golf-ball) high.—**loft'y** *a.* of great height; elevated.—**loft'ily** *adv.*
log *n.* unhewn portion of a felled tree; apparatus for measuring the speed of a ship; journal kept on board ship, etc.—*v.t.* in N. America, to cut felled lumber into logs suitable for the mill.—**logg'ing** *n.* cutting and transporting logs to a river.—**log'-roll'ing** *n.* (*fig.*) mutual admiration, advertisement; practice whereby writers, etc., praise each other's work on a basis of reciprocity.
lo'gan-ap'ple *n.* an indigenous Queensland tree, with an acid fruit.
log'anberry *n.* a hybrid plant, being a cross between the blackberry and the raspberry; the fruit itself.
log'arithm *n.* one of a series of arithmetical functions tabulated for use in calculation.—**logarith'mic** *a.*
logg'erhead *n.* a blockhead.—**at loggerheads,** quarrelling, disputing.
logg'ia (loj'a) *n.* a kind of open gallery (**logg'ias** (loj'az), **log'ge** (lod'jā) *pl.*).
log'ic (loj-) *n.* the art of reasoning.—**log'ical** *a.* relating to logic; according to reason; able to reason well.—**log'ically** *adv.*—**logi'cian** *n.* one skilled in logic.
loin *n.* the part of the body on either side between ribs and hip.
loi'ter *v.i.* to waste time on the way, hang about.—**loi'terer** *n.* one who loiters.
loll *v.t.* and *i.* to sit or lie lazily; of the tongue, to hang out.
loll'ipop *n.* a sweetmeat.
lone *a.* solitary.—**lone'ly** *a.* alone; feeling sad because alone.—**lone'liness** *n.*
long *a.* having length, *esp.* great length.—*adv.* for a long time.—**long-boat** *n.*
long *v.i.* to yearn for.—**long'ing** *n.*
long'eron (lon̄-zhā-ron̄', lon'jer-on) *n.* in an aeroplane, long spar running fore and aft in the body.
longev'ity (-j-) *n.* long existence or life.—**longe'val** *a.* long-lived.
lon'gitude *n.* the distance of a place east or west from a standard meridian.—**longitu'dinal** *a.* of length or longitude.
long-suf'fering *a.* patient, *esp.* in pain and adversity; kind.
long-wind'ed *a.* capable of long effort without getting out of breath; talking or writing at great length, tiresome.
loo'fah *n.* the pod of a plant used as a sponge; the plant.
look *v.i.* to direct or use the eyes; to face; to take care; to seem; to hope.—*n.* a looking; expression; aspect.—**look'ing-**

glass *n.* a mirror.—**look'-out** *n.* a watch; a place for watching; a watchman.
loom *n.* a machine for weaving.
loom *v.i.* to appear dimly.
loon'y *a.* (*sl.*) mad, crazy.
loop *n.* figure made by a curved line crossing itself; a similar shape in cord, rope, etc., crossed on itself; in N. Amer., lariat or lasso; in aviation, an aerial manoeuvre in which aeroplane describes a complete circle, the upper side of aeroplane being always on the inside of the circle, and the lateral axis always parallel with ground.—*v.t.* to form into a loop.—*v.i.* to form a loop.—**loop'line** *n.* railway line which leaves then rejoins main line.
loop'hole *n.* a slit in a wall, *esp.* for shooting through; a means of escape, of evading a rule without infringing it.
loose *a.* not tight or fastened or fixed, or exact or tense; slack; vague; dissolute.—*v.t.* to set free; unfasten; make slack; to shoot, let fly.—**loose'ly** *adv.*—**loos'en** *v.t.* to make loose.—**loose'ness** *n.*
loot *n.* and *v.t.* plunder, booty.
lop *v.t.* to cut away twigs and branches.
lop *v.i.* to hang limply.—**lop'ear** *n.* a drooping ear; a rabbit with such ears.—**lopsi'ded** *a.* with one side lower than the other; badly balanced.
lope *n.* a steady gallop.
loqua'cious *a.* talkative.—**loquac'ity** *n.*
lo'quat (lō'kwat) *n.* a low-growing Japanese plum tree, giving yellow, slightly acid fruit, the fruit itself.
lo'ran *n.* long-range radar equipment used in navigation (from LOng and RANge).
lord *n.* a feudal superior; one ruling others; an owner; God; a title of peers.—*v.i.* to domineer.—**lord'ling** *n.* a petty lord.—**lord'ly** *a.*—**lord'liness** *n.*—**lord'-ship** *n.* rule, ownership; domain; title of peers, e.g., **your lordship,** etc.
lore *n.* learning; body of facts and traditions, e.g., **bird-lore.**
lorgnette' (lorn-yet') *n.* eye-glasses with a handle; opera-glass.
lorn *a.* abandoned.
lorr'y *n.* a long wagon, without sides.
lose (lōōz) *v.t.* to be deprived of, fail to retain; let slip; fail to get; be late for, be defeated in.—*v.i.* to suffer loss (**lost** *p.t.* and *p.p.*—**los'ing** (lōōz'ing) *pres. p.*).—**loss** *n.* a losing; what is lost; harm or damage resulting from losing.
Syn. let fall, mislay, waste, miss, be bereaved of. *Ant.* gain, win, find.
lot *n.* one of a set of objects used to decide something by chance (to cast lots); fate, destiny; an item at an auction; a collection; large quantity.—**lott'ery** *n.* a gamble in which part of the money paid for tickets is distributed to some owners of tickets selected by chance.—**lott'o** *n.* game of chance.—**in'side lot** *n.* N. America, plot of land within, or soon to be within, a town's boundaries.—**out'side lot** *n.* N. America, plot of land beyond the boundaries of a town.
lo'tion *n.* liquid for washing wounds, improving the skin, bathing eyes, etc.
lo'tus *n.* legendary plant supposed to yield a fruit causing forgetfulness when eaten; a water-lily.
loud *a.* strongly audible; noisy; (*fig.*) showy, gaudy.—*adv.*—**loud-speak'er** *n.* wireless receiver amplifying sound.
lounge *v.i.* to loll; move lazily.—*n.* comfortable rest-room; a couch.—**lounge-liz'ard** *n.* (*sl.*) gigolo who frequents hotels.—**loun'ger** *n.*
lour, lower *v.* frown, scowl; look dark.
louse *n.* parasitic insect (**lice** *pl.*).—**lous'y** *a.* having lice; (*sl.*) nasty, unpleasant; thickly populated with.
lout *n.* clumsy, ill-mannered fellow.
lou'ver, lou'vre (lōō'ver) *n.* set of slats set parallel and slanting to admit air without rain.—**lou'vered** *a.*
love (luv) *n.* warm affection; sexual passion; a sweetheart; in games, a score of nothing.—*v.t.* to have love for.—*v.i.* to be in love.—**lov'able** *a.*—**love'less** *a.*—**love'liness** *n.* beauty.—**love'lorn** *a.* forsaken by, or pining for, a lover.—**love'ly** *a.* beautiful, delightful.—**lov'er** *n.*—**love'-bird** *n.* small parrot or budgerigar.—**love'-grass** *n.* S. Africa, grass the seeds of which adhere to one's clothing.—**lov'ing-cup** *n.* bowl passed round at a banquet.—**love'-in-a-mist** *n.* blue-flowered garden plant.
low (lō) *a.* not tall or high or elevated; humble; commonplace; vulgar; dejected; not loud.—**low'er** *v.t.* to cause or allow to descend; to diminish; degrade.—**low'-land** *n.* low-lying country.—**Low'lands** *n.* the less mountainous parts of Scotland.—**low'ly** *a.* humble.—**lowli'ness** *n.*—**low'-down** *a.* (*sl.*) mean, shabby, dishonourable.—**low-fre'quency,** in electricity, any frequency of alternating current from about 30 to 10,000 cycles; one within the audible range.
low (lō) *v.i.* of cattle, to utter their cry.—*n.* the cry of cattle.
lowan *n.* in Australia, the mallee bird, the Scrub-turkey.
low'er *see* **lour.**
loy'al *a.* faithful; true to allegiance.—**loy'ally** *adv.*—**loy'alty** *n.*—**loy'alist** *n.*
loz'enge *n.* diamond-shaped figure; small sweet or tablet of medicine.
lubb'er *n.* a clumsy fellow.—**lubb'erly** *a.*
lub'ra (-ōō-) *n.* in Australia, an aboriginal woman; a **gin.**
lu'bricate *v.t.* to oil or grease; to make slippery.—**lu'bricant** *n.* substance used for this.—**lubrica'tion** *n.* motoring, aircraft, etc., the complete oiling system.—**lu'bricator** *n.*—**lubri'city** *n.* slipperiness; evasiveness; lewdness.

luce (-ōō-) *n.* a full-grown pike.
lucerne' *n.* a fodder plant like clover.
lu'cid (lōō'-) *a.* clear; easily understood.—**lucid'ity** *n.*—**lu'cidly** *adv.*—**lu'cent** *a.* bright.—**Lu'cifer** *n.* the morning star; Satan.—**lu'cifer** a match.
lu'cigen (lōō'-si-jen) *n.* a powerful light produced by burning compressed air and oil at a high temperature.
lucim'eter (-sim-) *n.* photometer.
luck *n.* good or ill fortune, chance.—**luck'y** *a.* having good luck.—**luck'less** *a.* unfortunate.—**luck'ily** *adv.*—**luck'ier** *comp.*—**luck'iest** *sup.*
lu'cre (lōō'kr) *n.* gain or profit as a motive.—**lu'crative** *a.* yielding profit.
lu'dicrous (loo'-) *a.* absurd, laughable.
luff *n.* the part of a fore-and-aft sail nearest the mast.—*v.t.* and *i.* to bring (a ship) nearer the wind.
Luftwaffe (-vȧ-fa) *n.* Nazi Germany's air force (*Ger.* "air weapon").
lug *v.t.* to drag with effort.—*v.i.* to pull hard.—*n.* act of lugging, a strong pull. (**lugged** *p.t.* and *p.p.*)—**lug'gage** (lug'ij) *n.* traveller's baggage.
luge (lōōj) *n.* toboggan without runners.
lug'sail *n.* an oblong sail fixed on a yard which hangs slanting on a mast.—**lugg'er** *n.* a vessel with such sails.
lugu'brious *a.* mournful, sad.
lug'worm *n.* lobworm, sandworm.
luke'warm (look-) *a.* moderately warm, tepid; lacking enthusiasm, indifferent.
lull *v.t.* to sing to sleep; to calm, soothe.—*v.i.* become quiet.—*n.* brief time of quiet in storm or pain.—**lull'aby** (-bī) *n.* lulling song. (**lull'abies** *pl.*).
lum'bar *a.* relating to the loins.—**lumba'go** *n.* rheumatism in the loins.
lum'ber *v.i.* to move heavily; obstruct; in N. America, to fell trees and saw them for market.—*n.* disused articles, useless rubbish; timber, *esp.* sawn in planks.—**lum'berman** *n.*—**lum'berjack** *n.* in N. America, man who fells trees and prepares logs for transport.
luminous (lōō-) *a.* bright, shedding light.—**lu'minary** *n.* heavenly body giving light; person noted for learning. (**lu'minaries** *pl.*).—**luminos'ity** *n.*
lump *n.* a shapeless piece or mass; a swelling; a sum covering various items.—*v.t.* to throw together in one mass.—**lump'ish** *a.* clumsy.—**lump'y** *a.*
lu'nar (lōō-) *a.* relating to the moon.—**lunar caustic** nitrate of silver.—**lu'natic** *a.* insane.—*n.* madman.—**lu'nacy** *n.*
lunch *n.* a meal taken in the middle of the day.—**lunch'eon** (-shn) *n.* a lunch.
lung *n.* an air-breathing organ.
lunge *v.i.* to thrust with a sword, etc.—*n.* such thrust, or thrust of the body.
lu'pin, lu'pine *n.* a leguminous plant.
lu'pine *a.* like a wolf.
lu'pus (-ōō'-) *n.* a tuberculous inflammation of the skin.—**lu'poid** *a.*
lurch *n.* **to leave in the lurch**, to leave in difficulties, abandon (comrade); sudden roll to one side.—*v.i.* make a lurch.
lurch'er *n.* a poacher's mongrel dog.
lure *n.* a falconer's apparatus for recalling a hawk; something which entices, a bait.—*v.t.* to recall (a hawk); to entice.
lu'rid *a.* ghastly, pale, glaring, fiery; sensational.—**lu'ridly** *adv.*
lurk *v.i.* to lie hidden; be latent.
lus'cious (-shus) *a.* sweet; over-rich.
Syn. honeyed, delicious, savoury, palatable. *Ant.* sour, unpalatable, nauseous.
lush *a.* of grass, etc., luxuriant and juicy.
lust *n.* sensuous desire; passionate desire. *v.i.* to have passionate desire.—**lust'ful** *a.*
lust'y *a.* healthy, vigorous.—**lust'ily** *adv.*
lus'tre *n.* gloss, shine; splendid reputation, glory; glossy material.—**lus'trous** *a.*
lus'tre, lus'trum (**lustrums, -tra** *pl.*) *n.* period of 5 years.—**lustra'tion** *n.* purification by sacrifice.—**lus'trate** *v.t.* to cleanse thus.—**lus'tral** *a.*
lute (lōōt) *n.* a stringed musical instrument played with the fingers.–**lu'tanist** *n.*
lute, lu'ting (lōōt, lōō'ting) *n.* a composition of clay or other tenacious substance, used for making joints air-tight.—*v.t.* to close or coat with lute.
lux'ury *n.* possession and use of costly things for enjoyment; something enjoyable but not necessary; comfortable surroundings. (**lux'uries** *pl.*).—**luxu'rious** *a.*—**luxu'riously** *adv.*—**luxu'riate** *v.i.* to indulge in luxury; to grow rank; to take delight (in).—**luxu'riant** *a.* growing profusely; abundant.—**luxu'riantly** *adv.*—**luxu'riance** *n.*
lychgate *see* **lichgate.**
lydd'ite *n.* powerful explosive, made from picrate of potash.
lye *n.* water made alkaline with wood ashes, for washing.
lymph *n.* colourless animal fluid; the matter from cow-pox used in vaccination.—**lymphat'ic** *a.* of lymph; flabby, sluggish; pale-skinned.—*n.* vessel in body conveying lymph.
lynch *v.t.* to put to death without proper trial.—**lynch law** *n.* mob-law.
lynx *n.* an animal of the cat tribe noted for keen sight.—**lynx-eyed** *a.*
lyre *n.* an instrument like a harp.
lyr'ic, lyr'ical (lir-) *a.* relating to the lyre; meant to be sung; of short poems, expressing the poet's own thoughts and feelings.—**lyr'ic** *n.* a lyric poem.—**lyr'ist** *n.*—**lyre'-bird** *n.* in Australia, a bird with lyre-shaped tail, the Menura Superba.
Ly'sol *n.* a disinfectant prepared from creosote and oil (protected trade name.)

M

maan'haar *n.* in S. Africa, the maned jackal; the aard-wolf; the maned lion.
maca'bre (-à-ber) *a.* grim, ghastly, gruesomely imaginative.
macad'am *n.* road surface, layers of small broken stone.—**macad'amise** *v.t.* to pave a road with broken stones.
macaro'ni *n.* Italian paste of wheat in long tubes (**-nis, -nies** (-niz) *pl.*).
macaroon' *n.* small cake.
macaw' *n.* large brilliant parrot.
mace *n.* staff caried as a sign of office; spice made of the husk of the nutmeg.
mac'erate *v.t.* to soften by steeping; to cause to waste away.—**macera'tion** *n.*
Mach number *n.* the ratio of the air speed (i.e. speed in relation to the air) of an aircraft to the velocity of sound under given conditions.
mach'iavellian (mak'-) *a.* subtle, unscrupulous, in pursuit of power.
machine' (-shēn') *n.* an apparatus combining the action of several parts, to apply mechanical force for some purpose; a person like a machine from regulation or sensibility; a controlling organisation; a bicycle, vehicle, motor-car.—*v.t.* to sew, print with a machine.
machin'ery (-ē-) *n.* parts of a machine collectively; machines.—**machin'ist** *n.* one who makes or works machines.—**machine'-gun** *n.* gun firing repeatedly and continuously by a loading and firing mechanism.—**machina'tion** (-kin-) *n.* plotting, intrigue.—**mac'hinate** *v.i.*
mack'erel *n.* edible sea-fish with blue and silver barred skin.
mack'inaw *n.* in N. America, a heavy woollen cloth; a thick blanket; a boat with sharp-pointed ends used by explorers, traders, etc.
mack'intosh *n.* cloth waterproofed with a layer of rubber; a coat of this.
mac'rocosm *n.* the universe.
mad *a.* suffering from mental disease, insane; wildly foolish; excited.—**mad'ly** *adv.*—**mad'man** *n.*—**mad'ness** *n.*—**mad'den** *v.t.*—**mad'cap** *n.* reckless person.
mad'am *n.* form of address to women.
madd'er *n.* a climbing plant; its root; a dye-stuff made from this.
madeir'a (-dēr'-) *n.* a rich sherry wine; cake to eat with wine.
Madonn'a *n.* the Virgin Mary (**madonnas** (-az) *pl.*).—picture or statue of her.
mad'rigal *n.* short love poem or song; part-song for three or more voices.
mael'strom (māl'-) *n.* whirlpool; (*fig.*) furious tumult of passions or events.
mae west *n.* an inflated jacket worn by airmen round the chest as a life-saver (Mae West—U.S. film star).
maff'ick *v.i.* to exult riotously.
magazine' (-zēn) *n.* storehouse for explosives and other military stores; cartridge-chamber in gun; periodical of miscellaneous stories and articles.
magent'a (-j-) *n.* a crimson alkaline dye. —*a.* of this colour.
magg'ot *n.* a grub, a larva.—**magg'oty** *a.*
Ma'gi *n. pl.* priests of ancient Persia; the wise men from the East.
mag'ic (-j-) *n.* art of influencing events by controlling nature or spirits, any mysterious agency of power; witchcraft, conjuring.—**magic-lant'ern** *n.* apparatus by which pictures are projected on screen in darkened room.—**mag'ical** *a.* —**mag'ically** *adv.*—**magi'cian** *n.*
mag'istrate (-j-) *n.* civil officer administering the law.—**magiste'rial** *a.* of or referring to a magistrate or master; dictatorial.—**mag'istracy** *n.* the office of a magistrate; magistrates collectively.
magnan'imous *a.* great-souled, noble, above resentment.—**magnanim'ity** *n.*
mag'nate *n.* a person of influence by wealth or high position.
magne'sium *n.* metallic chemical element.—**magne'sia** *n.* a white powder compound of this used in medicine.
mag'net *n.* a piece of iron having the properties of attracting iron and pointing north and south when suspended; loadstone.—**magnet'ic** *a.*—**magnet'ic mine** *n.* mine which is exploded by magnetic action.—**magnet'ically** *adv.*—**mag'netism** *n.* magnetic phenomena; science of this; personal charm or power of attracting others.—**mag'netise** *v.t.* to make into a magnet.—**magnetisa'tion** *n.* —**magne'to** *n.* apparatus for ignition in internal combustion engine (**-tos** (-tōz) *pl.*).—**magnetom'eter** *n.* instrument measuring magnetic intensity.
Mag'nificat *n.* song of the Virgin Mary.
magnif'icent *a.* splendid, stately, imposing, excellent.—**magnifi'cently** *a.*—**magnif'icence** *n.*—**mag'nify** (-fī) *v.t.* to exaggerate; to make greater; to praise (**-ified** *p.t.* and *p.p.*—**-ifying** *pres. p.*).
magnil'oquent *a.* speaking loftily, bombastic.—**magnil'oquence** *n.*
mag'nitude *n.* size; importance.
magno'lia *n.* flowering tree.
mag'num *n.* a two-quart wine bottle.
mag'pie *n.* a black-and-white bird.
mag'ra *n.* a contrivance used by aboriginal mothers in Australia to carry their infants on their backs.
mahat'ma *n.* a Hindu adept.
mahem' *n.* in S. Africa, the Kaffir crane, a crane with a crest.
mahog'any *n.* a reddish brown wood; in Australia, various trees resembling mahogany; their wood.
mahout' *n.* an elephant driver.
maid'en *n.* young unmarried woman. —*a.* unmarried; of, or suited to, a maiden; having a blank record.—**maid**

n. girl; a woman servant.—**maid'enhair** *n.* fern with delicate stalks and fronds.—**maid'enhead** *n.* virginity.—**maid'enhood** *n.*—**maid'enly** *a.*

mail *n.* armour made of interlaced rings or overlapping plates.—**mail'ed** *a.*

mail *n.* bag of letters; the letters conveyed at one time.—*v.t.* to send by mail.

maim *v.t.* to cripple, mutilate.

main *n.* an open ocean; chief gas or water-pipe; chief matter; strength, power.—*a.* chief, principal, leading.—**main'land** *n.* stretch of land which forms the main part of the country.—**main'ly** *a.*—**main'mast** *n.* the chief mast in a ship.—**main'sail** *n.* the lowest sail of a mainmast.—**main'spring** *n.* chief spring of a watch or clock.

maintain' *v.t.* to carry on; to preserve; to support, sustain, keep up; to keep supplied; to affirm.—**main'tenance** *n.*

Syn. to supply with, contend, uphold, assert. *Ant.* drop, neglect, abandon.

maisonette' (mā-zon-et') *n.* a small house compactly built; a flat.

maize *n.* Indian corn.

maj'esty *n.* stateliness; kingship or queenship.—**majes'tic** *a.* royal, stately, noble.—**majes'tically** *adv.*

majol'ica *n.* fine glazed Italian pottery.

maj'or *a.* greater; out of minority.—*n.* one out of minority; army officer ranking next above a captain.—**major'ity** *n.* state (or rank) of being a major; greater number; larger party voting together; excess of the vote on one side.—**major-do'mo** *n.* head-servant of large household (**-do'mos** (-ōz) *pl.*).

mak *a.* in S. Africa, of natives who have come under the influence of Europeans, domesticated, civilised; (lit. meaning: tame).

make *v.t.* to construct; produce; bring into being; establish; appoint; amount to; to cause to do something; to accomplish; to reach; to earn.—*v.i.* tend: contribute; of the tide, to rise (**made** *p.t.* and *p.p.*—**ma'king** *pres. p.*).—*n.* style of construction, form, manufacture.—**ma'ker** *n.*—**make'shift** *n.* a method, tool, etc., used for want of something better.—**make'weight** *n.* a trifle added to make something seem stronger or better.—**make-up** *n.* the arrangement of printed pages; facial painting and powdering; a person's character.

Syn. to fashion, create, effect, gain. *Ant.* break, destroy, lose, mar.

mal- *prefix* ill, badly, evil; not.—**maladjust'ment** *n.* faulty adjustment.—**maladministration** *n.* faulty administration.—**mal'content** *a.* actively discontented.—*n.* a malcontent person.—**malediction** *n.* a curse.—**mal'efactor** *n.* a criminal.—**malef'icent** *a.* hurtful.—**malef'icence** *n.*—**malev'olent** *a.* full of ill-will.—**malev'olence** *n.*—**malforma'tion** *n.* faulty formation.—**malo'dorous** *a.* evil-smelling.—**malprac'tice** *n.* wrong-doing.—**mal'treat** *v.t.* to treat ill, handle roughly.—**maltreat'ment** *a.*—**malversa'tion** *n.* corrupt handling of trust money.

malacc'a *n.* a brown cane.

mal'achite (-kīt) *n.* a green mineral.

mal'ady *n.* a disease (**mal'adies** *pl.*).

mal'aga *n.* a wine from *Malaga*, Spain.

mal'apert *a.* saucy; impudent.

malar'ia (-ėr-) *n.* a fever due to mosquito bites.—**malar'ial** *a.*—**malar'ious** *a.*

Malay *n.* in S. Africa, descendants of old East Indian slaves.

male *a.* of the begetting sex; of men or male animals;—*n.* strong, vigorous.

mal'i (-ā-) *n.* in South Africa, money.

ma'lic *a.* derived from the apple.

mal'ice *n.* action of ill-will.—**malic'ious** *a.*

malign' (-līn) *a.* hurtful.—*v.t.* to slander, misrepresent —**malig'nant** *a.* feeling extreme ill-will; of a disease, very virulent.—**'-nantly** *adv.*—**'-nancy** *n.*—**'-nity** *n.*

malin'gerer (-ng-g-) *n.* one who feigns illness to escape duty.—**malin'ger** *v.i.*

mall (mel, mal) *n.* a level, shaded walk.

mall'ard *n.* the male of the wild duck.

mall'eable *a.* capable of being hammered into shape.—**malleabil'ity** *n.*—**mall'et** *n.* hammer, usually of wood.

mall'ee *n.* in Australia, several small, scrubby species of eucalyptus.

mall'ow *n.* wild plant with purple flowers and hairy leaves.

malm'sey (mām-) *n.* strong sweet wine.

malt *n.* grain used for brewing.—*v.t.* to make into malt.—**malt'ster** *n.*

Malthu'sian (-ew'zi-) *a.* pertaining to or supporting the teaching of Malthus.—*n.* one who holds that some check is necessary to prevent overpopulation.

mamba *n.* a deadly S. African snake, usually black in colour.

mamm'al *a.* an animal that suckles its young.—**mamma'lian** *a.*

mamm'on *n.* wealth as an object of pursuit or of evil influence.

mamm'oth *n.* an extinct animal like an elephant.—*a.* enormous, gigantic.

man *n.* a human being; person; the human race; an adult human male; a man-servant; a piece used in a game, e.g., chess (**men** *pl.*).—*v.t.* to supply (a ship, etc.) with necessary men.—**man'ful** *a.* brave, resolute.—**man'fully** *adv.*—**man'handle** *v.t.* to treat roughly; to abuse; to move entirely by human strength.—**man'hole** *n.* an opening through which a man may pass.—**man'hood** *n.*—**man'ikin** *n.* a little man; a model of the human body.—**man-kind'** *n.* human beings in general.—**man'like** *a.*—**man'ly** *a.*—**man'liness** *n.*—**mann'ish** *a.* manlike.—**man'slaughter** *n.* killing of a human being unintentionally or in provocation.—**man-hour** *n.* the amount of work done by one man in one hour.

man'acle *n.* a fetter for the hand.—*v.t.* to handcuff, shackle.

man'age *v.t.* to carry on, conduct; to succeed in doing; to handle; to persuade. —*v.i.* to conduct affairs.—**man'ageable** *a.*—**man'agement** *n.*—**man'ager** *n.*

Syn. to govern, train, influence, husband. *Ant.* neglect, ignore, disregard.

manda'mus *n.* a writ from a superior court to an inferior, to a corporation, or to a person, conveying a command.

man'darin *n.* a Chinese provincial governor; figuratively, any high government official; a Chinese orange.

man'date *a.* command of, or commission to act for another; commission to govern a people not qualified for independence; an instruction from an electorate to a representative.—**man'datary** *n.* a holder of a mandate.—**man'datory** *a.*

man'dible *n.* a lower jaw bone; either part of a bird's beak.—**mandib'ular** *a.*

mando'lin(e) *n.* a stringed musical instrument like a guitar.

man'door *n.* in S. Africa, a coloured foreman.

man'drake, mandrag'ora *n.* a narcotic and emetic plant.

man'drel *n.* an axis on which material revolves in a lathe; a rod round which metal is cast or forged.

man'drill *n.* a large baboon.

mane *n.* the long hair at the back of the neck of a horse, lion, etc.

man'ganese (-ng-g-) *n.* a metallic element; a black oxide of this.

mangarco' *n.* in Australia, a small flying phalanger.

mange (-ā-) *n.* a skin disease of dogs and other animals.—**ma'ngy** *a.*

man'gel-wurz'el (-g-) **man'gold-wurzel** *n.* a variety of beet.

man'ger (mān'jer) *n.* an eating-trough for horses, cattle in a stable.

man'gle (mang'gl) *n.* a machine for rolling washed linen, etc.—*v.t.* to press thus; hack, mutilate.

man'go (-ng-gō) *n.* an excellent fruit of many varieties; the tree bearing it (**-goes, -gos** (-gōz) *pl.*).

man'gosteen *n.* fruit similar to an orange, found in the East Indies.

man'grove *n.* tropical trees which grow on the muddy banks of estuaries.

manhatt'an *n.* a cocktail containing whisky, vermouth, gin, bitters.

ma'nia *n.* madness; prevailing craze.—**ma'niac** *a.* affected by mania.—*n.*

man'icure *n.* the treatment of the finger-nails and hands; person doing this professionally.—*v.t.*—**man'icurist** *n.*

man'ifest *a.* clearly revealed, visible, undoubted.—*v.t.* to make manifest.—*n.* a list of cargo for the Customs.—**manifesta'tion** *n.*—**manifest'o** *n.* a declaration of policy by a sovereign or commander or body of persons (**-toes** *pl.*).

Syn. clear, evident, obvious;—of *v.* to show, display. *Ant.* of *a.* obscure, dim.

man'ifold *a.* numerous and varied.—*v.t.* to make copies of (a document).—*n.* in internal combustion engine, a pipe fitted with several outlets for connecting one pipe with others.

manikin *see* **man.**

manil'a, manill'a *n.* fibre used for ropes; a cheroot.

manip'ulate *v.t.* to handle; to deal with skilfully; to manage craftily.—**manip'ulator** *n.*—**manipula'tion** *n.*—**manip'ulative** *a.*—**manip'ulative surgery,** formerly known as bone-setting; use of the hands in treatment of accidents to, or diseases of, the muscles and joints.

mann'a *n.* the food of the Israelites in the wilderness; a sweet tree-juice.

mann'equin (or **-kin**) *n.* live model employed by dressmakers, etc.

mann'er *n.* the way a thing happens or is done; a sort or kind; custom; style. —*pl.* social behaviour.—**mann'erism** *n.* addiction to a literary or artistic manner; an habitual trick of style or behaviour.—**man'nerly** *a.* well-mannered.

manoeuv're (-ōō'ver) *n.* a movement of troops or ships in war.—*v.t.* to cause to perform manoeuvres.—*v.i.* to perform manoeuvres; employ stratagems.

man'or *n.* unit of land in the feudal period.—**man'or-house** *n.* the residence of the lord of the manor.—**manor'ial** *a.*

man'sion *n.* a large dwelling-house.—**manse** *n.* in Scotland, a minister's house.

man'suetude (-swit-) *n.* mild temper.

man'tel *n.* the structure enclosing a fireplace.—**man'tel-shelf** *n.* shelf at top of the mantel.—**man'telpiece** *n.*

mantill'a *n.* in Spain, a scarf worn as a head-dress; light cape.

man'tis *n.* a genus of insects including the stick-insects and leaf-insects (**man'tes** (-tēz) *pl.*). *see* **Hottentot God.**

man'tle *n.* a loose cloak; a covering; a hood fixed round a gas jet for incandescent light.—*v.t.* to cover; to conceal.—*v.i.* to become covered with scum; of the blood, to rush to the cheeks.—**mant'let** *n.* a movable bullet-proof screen.

man'ual *a.* of, or done with, the hands. —*n.* a handbook; an organ keyboard.

manufacture *n.* the making of articles or materials, *esp.* in large quantities, for sale.—*v.t.* to produce (articles), to work up (materials) into finished articles.——**manufac'tory** *n.* factory or workshop. —**manufac'turer** *n.* owner of a factory.

man'uka *n.* N.Z. shrub, the tea tree.

manumit' *v.t.* to give freedom to (a slave).—**manumis'sion** *n.*

manure' *v.t.* to enrich land.—*n.* dung or other substances used for fertilising land.

man'uscript *a.* written by hand.—*n.* a book; document, etc., written by hand

Manx *a.* of the Isle of Man.—*n.* Manx language; native of the island (**Manx** *pl.*).
man'y (men-) *a.* numerous (**more** *comp.* —**most** *sup.*).—*n.* a large number.
Mao'ri (mou'ri) *n.* an aborigine of N.Z.; Maori language (**Mao'ris** *pl.*).—*a.*
map *n.* flat representation of the earth or part of it, or of the heavens.—*v.t.* make a map of (**mapped** *p.t./p.p.*).
ma'pau (-pa-u) *n.* in New Zealand, a small tree of several kinds, sometimes corrupted into "maple."
ma'ple *n.* a tree of the sycamore family, a variety of which yields sugar.
ma'quis (ma-kē) *n.* scrubby undergrowth in Corsica; name adopted by the French underground movement in World War 2.
mar *v.t.* to spoil, impair.—**mar'plot** *n.* frustrator of plans (**marred** *p.t./p.p.*).
mar'abou *n.* a kind of stork; the soft white lower tail feathers of this bird, used to trim hats, etc.; also, a kind of silk; Mohammedan sorcerer of N. Africa.
maraschi'no (-kē'-) *n.* a liqueur distilled from cherries.
ma'rathon *n.* prolonged, gruelling sporting contest.
maraud' *v.t.* and *i.* to make a raid for plunder.—**maraud'er** *n.* robber.
marble *n.* hard limestone capable of taking a high polish; a slab of this; small ball used in a game called **marbles.**—*v.t.* to colour like veined marble.
marcel' *n.* hairdressing, special type of permanent wave.—**marcelled'** (-seld') *a.*
March *n.* the third month.
march *n.* a border or frontier (**march'es** *pl.*).—*v.i.* to border; to walk with a military step; to start on a march; to go. —*v.t.* to cause to march or go.—*n.* action of marching; distance marched in a day; tune to accompany marching.
march'ioness (-shon-) *n.* the wife or widow of a marquis.
marco'nigram *n.* a wireless telegram.
mare (mėr) *n.* female horse or other equine animal (**horse, stal'lion** *masc.*).—**mare's' nest** *n.* fancied discovery.
mar'garine (-g-) *n.* vegetable or animal fats substance imitating butter.
mar'gin (-j-) *n.* the border or edge; amount allowed beyond what is absolutely necessary; the blank space round a printed page.—**mar'ginal** *a.*
Syn. rim, brink, brim, verge, skirt, limit, confine. *Ant.* centre, middle.
mar'guerite (-ēt) *n.* ox-eye daisy.
mar'igold *n.* a plant with yellow flowers.
marine' (-ēn) *a.* of the sea or shipping; used at sea.—*n.* shipping collectively; a soldier serving on board a ship.
mari'ner *n.* a sailor.
marionette' *n.* a doll or puppet worked with strings.
mar'ital *a.* relating to marriage.
mari'time *a.* bordering on the sea; connected with seafaring or navigation.
mar'joram *n.* an aromatic herb.
mark *n.* something set up to be aimed at; a sign or token; an inscription; a line, dot, scar, or any visible trace or impression.—*v.t.* to make a mark on; to indicate, to be a distinguishing mark of; to watch. —*v.i.* to take notice.—**marked** *a.* noticeable.—**marks'man** *n.* one skilled in shooting.—**mark'er** *n.*—**a good mark** in Australia (*sl.*) trustworthy person.
mark *n.* a German coin.
mark'et *n.* assembly for buying and selling; place where goods are sold; demand for goods; place or centre for trade.—*v.t.* bring to, sell in market.—**mark'etable** *a.*—**mar'ket-place** *n.*
marl *n.* a clayey soil used as a fertiliser. —*v.t.* to fertilise with it.
marl'ine (-in) *n.* two-strand cord.—**marl'inespike** *n.* a pointed hook for unravelling rope to be spliced.
mar'malade *n.* orange jam.
mar'moset *n.* small monkey.
mar'mot *n.* rodent allied to squirrel.
mar'ocain (-kān) *n.* a dress material, usually silk with grain surface.
maroon' *n.* a brownish crimson colour; a kind of firework.—*a.* of the colour.
maroon' *n.* a fugitive slave in the West Indies; a marooned person.—*v.t.* to leave on a desert island.
marque (-k) *n.* **letters of marque,** a licence to act as a privateer.
marquee' (-kē) *n.* a large tent.
mar'quetry (-ket-) *n.* inlaid work.
mar'quis, mar'quess *n.* nobleman of rank next below a duke.—**mar'quisate** *n.*
mar'row (-rō) *n.* the fatty substance inside bones.—**vegetable marrow,** a gourd cooked as a table vegetable.—**marr'owfat** *n.* a large pea.—**mar'rowy** *a.*
mar'ry *v.t.* to join (or take) as husband and (or) wife;—*v.i.* to take a husband or wife (**mar'ried** *p.t.* and *p.p.*—**mar'rying** *pres. p.*).—**mar'riage** (-rij) *n.* wedlock.—**mar'riageable** *a.*
Mars *n.* the Roman god of war; the planet next to the earth.—**Mart'ian** *n.* a supposed inhabitant of Mars.
Marseillaise (mar-se-lāz') *n.* the French National Anthem.
marsh *n.* low-lying wet land.—**marshmall'ow** *n.* herb growing near marshes; spongy sweetmeat.—**marsh-mar'igold** *n.* plant with yellow flowers growing in wet places.—**marsh'y** *a.*
marsh'al *n.* high officer of state.—**Field Marsh'al** a military officer of the highest rank.—*v.t.* to arrange in due order.
marsu'pial (-sōō-) *n.* an animal that carries its young in a pouch.
mart *n.* market place or market hall.
mart'en *n.* weasel-like animal yielding a valuable fur.
mar'tial (-shal) *a.* relating to war.
mar'tin *n.* species of swallow.
martinet' *n.* a strict disciplinarian.

mar'tingale (-ng-g-) *n.* strap to prevent a horse from throwing up its head; system of doubling stakes at gambling.
marti'ni (-tē-) *n.* a cocktail containing vermouth, gin, bitters.
Mar'tinmas *n.* 11th November.
mart'let *n.* a martin, swift; in heraldry, a bird without feet.
mar'tyr (-ter) *n.* one put to death, or suffering greatly, for his beliefs; one in constant suffering.—*v.t.* to make a martyr of.—**mar'tyrdom** *n.*—**martyrol'ogy** *n.* a list or history of martyrs.
mar'vel *n.* a wonderful thing.—*v.i.* to wonder.—**mar'vellous** *a.* amazing.
Marx'ism *n.* the doctrine of the materialist conception of history formulated by Karl Marx.—**marx'ian** *a.*—**marx'ist** *n.* adherent of this.
mar'zipan *n.* sweetmeat, a cake of pounded almonds, sugar, etc.
mas'cot *n.* a thing supposed to bring good luck, talisman.
mas'culine (-lin) *a.* relating to males; manly, vigorous; of the grammatical gender to which names of males belong.
mash *n.* meal mixed with warm water; a warm food for horses, fowls, etc.—*v.t.*
mash'ie *n.* in golf, an iron club with a deep sloping blade, for lob shots.
mask (-à-) *n.* covering for face; disguise or pretence.—*v.t.* to cover with mask; to hide or disguise.—**masque** *n.* form of amateur theatrical performance; masquerade.—**masquerade'** *n.* a masked ball.—*v.i.* appear in disguise.
mas'ochism (-kizm) *n.* in psycho-analysis, satisfaction of sexual impulses by endurance of pain.—**mas'ochist** *n.*
ma'son *n.* a worker in stone; a freemason.—**mason'ic** *a.* of freemasonry.—**ma'sonry** *n.* stonework; freemasonry.
mass *n.* the service of the Eucharist.
mass *n.* quantity of matter; dense collection of this; large quantity.—**the mass'es,** the populace.—*v.t.* and *i.* form into a mass.—**mass'y** *a.* solid, weighty.—**mass'ive** *a.* large and heavy.
mass'acre (ker) *n.* a general slaughter; indiscriminate killing.—*v.t.*
mass'age (-àzh) *a.* rubbing and kneading the muscles, etc., as curative treatment.—*v.t.* to apply this treatment to.—**mass'eur** *n.*; **mass'euse** *fem.* one who practises massage.
masse' (-sā') *n.* in billiards, a stroke made with the cue perpendicular.
mast (-à-) *n.* a pole for supporting sails.
mast (-à-) *n.* the fruit of beech, oak, etc.
mast'er (mà-) *n.* one who employs another; head of a household; an owner; one in control; captain of a merchant ship; a male teacher; an artist of great reputation.—*v.t.* to overcome; to acquire knowledge of, or skill in.—**mast'erful** *a.* imperious, self-willed.—**mast'erly** *a.* skilfully done.—**mast'ery** *n.* victory, authority.—**mas'terpiece** *n.*
mas'tic *n.* gum got from certain trees.
mas'ticate *v.t.* chew.—**mastica'tion** *n.*
mas'tiff *n.* a large, powerful dog.
mas'toids *n.* popular name for disease of the mastoid process, below the ear.
mas'turbate *v.i.* to practise sexual self-abuse.—**masturbation** *n.*
masu'rium *n.* a chemical element.
mat *n.* small carpet made of rushes, etc.; a thick tangled mass.—*v.t.* and *i.*—**mat-house** *n.* S. Africa, a temporary hut of mats placed over a conical framework.
mat *a.* dull, unpolished, slightly rough.
mat'ador *n.* the man charged with slaying the bull in bull-fights.
match *n.* a person or thing exactly corresponding to another; one able to contend equally with another; a trial of skill; a marriage; a person regarded as eligible for marriage.—*v.t.* to join in marriage; to meet equally in contest; to place in contest with; to get something corresponding to (a colour, pattern, etc.).—*v.i.* to correspond.—**match'less** *a.* unequalled.—**match'board** *n.* boards fitted into each other by tongue and groove along the edges.
match *a.* a small stick with a head which bursts into flame when rubbed; a fuse.—**match'lock** *n.* an old musket fired by a fuse.—**match'wood** *n.* small splinters.—**match'box** *n.*—**match'box bean** *n.* Australia, climbing plant, the large, circular, flat seed of which can be made into a matchbox; the seed itself.
mate *n.* checkmate.—*v.t.* to checkmate.
mate *n.* a comrade, a husband or wife; an officer in a merchant ship immediately below the captain.—*v.t.* and *i.* to marry.
mate'rial *a.* of matter or body; unspiritual; essential, important.—*n.* the stuff from which anything is made; a stuff or fabric.—**mate'rialism** *n.* an opinion that nothing exists except matter.—**mate'rialist** *a.* and *n.*—**materialis'tic** *a.*—**mate'rialise** *v.t.* and *i.* to make material.—**mate'rially** *adv.*
mater'nal *a.* of, or related through, a mother.—**matern'ity** *n.* motherhood.
mathemat'ics *n. pl.* the science of space and number.—**mathemat'ical** *a.*—**mathemat'ically** *adv.*—**mathemati'cian** *n.*
mat'inee (-ā) *n.* a morning or afternoon performance in theatre.—**mat'ins** *n. pl.* morning prayers.
mat'ricide *n.* one who kills his mother; the crime.—**matrici'dal** *a.*
matricu'late *v.t.* to enter on a college or university register.—*v.i.* to enter one's name on such register; to pass an examination entitling one to do this.—**matricula'tion** *n.*—**matric'ular** *a.*
mat'rimony *n.* marriage.—**matrimo'-**

nial *a.* *Syn.* nuptials, wedding. *Ant.* divorce, bachelordom, spinsterhood.
ma'trix *n.* a mould for casting; in S. Africa, diamond-bearing material.
ma'tron *n.* a married woman; a woman in charge of the domestic arrangements of a hospital, school, etc.—**ma'tronly** *a.*
matt *see* **mat.**
matt'er *n.* the substance of which a thing is made up; physical or bodily substance in general; pus; the substance of a book, etc.; an affair; a reason, a cause of trouble.—*v.i.* to be of importance.
mat'ting *n.* coarse woven material; rush, fibre, etc., used for making mats.
matt'ock *n.* a tool like pickaxe for breaking up hard ground.
matt'ress *n.* flat stuffed case, used as or under a bed; frame of stretched wires supporting bed.
mature' *a.* ripe, complete in development or growth.—*v.t.* to bring to maturity.—*v.i.* to come to maturity.
maud'lin *a.* weakly sentimental; tearfully intoxicated.
maul, mawl *n.* heavy wooden hammer. —**maul** *v.t.* to handle roughly or clumsily; to beat or bruise.
maul'stick (mål'-) *n.* shaft used by painters to support the right hand.
maund (mawnd) *n.* in the East Indies, a measure of weight, varying from about 24 lb. to over 82 lb.
maund'er *v.i.* to talk or act dreamily.
Maun'dy *n.* foot-washing ceremony on Thursday before Easter (cf. John xiii. 14); royal alms given on that day.
Mau'ser (mow-) *n.* a type of repeating magazine rifle or pistol.
mausole'um *n.* stately building as a tomb (**mausole'ums, -le'a** *pl.*).
mauve (mōv) *n.* a bright purple aniline dye; the colour of this dye.—*a.*
mav'erick *n.* in N. America, an unbranded steer; a strayed cow; something dishonestly obtained by appropriation, as land, cattle, etc.— **maverick brand** brand used by dishonest cattle-raisers.
maw *n.* the stomach of animals.
mawk'ish *a.* having a sickly flavour weakly sentimental.
maxill'ary *a.* relating to the jaw or jawbone.—**maxill'a** *n.*
max'im *n.* a general truth; a rule of conduct; a machine-gun.
max'imum *n.* the greatest possible size or number (**max'ima, -imums** *pl.*).—*a.* that is a maximum.
May *n.* the fifth month; the hawthorn.
may *v. aux.* expresses possibility, permission, opportunity, etc.
mayonnaise' *n.* a sauce.
may'or *n.* head of a town corporation (Scotland, **Lord Provost** or **Provost**).—**may'oral** *a.*—**may'oral'ty** *n.* the office, or time of office, of a mayor.—**may'oress** *n.* the mayor's wife; lady mayor.
maze *n.* a labyrinth; a network of paths or lines; a confused state.—*v.t.* stupefy.
mazour'ka, mazur'ka *n.* a lively Polish dance; music for it.
me *pron.* objective case singular of the 1st personal pronoun **I.**
mead *n.* alcoholic drink made from honey; a meadow.—**mead'ow** (med'-) *n.* piece of grassland.—**mead'ow-sweet** *n.* sweet-smelling flowering plant.
mea'gre (mē'gęr) *a.* lean, thin, scanty.
meal *n.* grain ground to powder; an occasion of taking food; the food taken. —**mealy** *a.* of meal; pale.
mea'lie (mē'-) *n.* in S. Africa, an ear of maize.—**mea'lies** *n. pl.* maize.—**mealy** *a.*
mean *a.* poor; inferior; shabby; small-minded.—**mean'ly** *a.*—**mean'ness** *n.*
Syn. despicable, niggardly, spiritless. *Ant.* splendid, high, generous.
mean *a.* intermediate in time, quality, etc.—*n.* anything which is intermediate. —*pl.* that by which something is done; money resources.—**mean'time** *n.*—**mean'-while** *n.* the time between one happening and another.—*adv.* during this time.
mean *v.t.* to intend, design; signify; import (**meant** (ment) *p.t.* and *p.p.*—**mean'ing** *pres. p.*).—**mean'ing** *n.* sense, significance.—*a.* expressive.
meand'er (mē-and'-) *v.i.* to flow windingly; to wander aimlessly.—*n.* a winding.
meas'les (mēz'lz) *n. pl.* an infectious disease with red spots.—**meas'ly** *a.* relating to measles; poor, wretched.
meas'ure (mezh'ęr) *n.* a size or quantity; a vessel, rod, line, etc., for ascertaining size or quantity; a unit of size or quantity; poetical rhythm; an order or tune; musical time; a slow dance; a course or plan of action; a law.—*v.t.* to ascertain size or quantity of; to be (so much) in size or quantity; to estimate; bring into competition (with).—**meas'urable** *a.*—**meas'ured** *a.* carefully considered; regular; slow.—**mea'sureless** *a.* unlimited, immense.—**meas'urement** *n.*
meat *n.* food; the flesh of animals used as food.—**meat'y** *a.* solid, nourishing.
mechan'ic (-k-) *a.* relating to a machine. —*n.* one employed in working with machinery; a skilled workman.—*pl.* the branch of science dealing with motion and tendency of motion.—**mechan'ical** *a.* concerned with machines or manual operation; worked or produced by, or as though by, a machine; like a machine; relating to mechanics.—**mechan'ically** *adv.*—**mechani'cian** *n.*—**mech'anism** *n.* the structure of a machine.—**mechani'-sation** (mek-) *n.* change from system of animal transport or power to mechanical.—**mech'anise** *v.t.*
med'al *n.* a piece of metal, round or star-shaped with an inscription, etc., as a reward or memento.—**medall'ion** *n.* a large medal; something like this used as

a decoration or design.—med'allist *n.* winner of a medal; maker of medals.
med'dle *v.i.* to interfere, to busy oneself with unnecessarily.—**med'dlesome** *a.*
mediae'val *a.* relating to the Middle Ages.—**mediae'valism** *n.*—**mediae'valist** *n.* one who studies the Middle Ages.
me'diate *v.i.* act as go-between in a dispute to reconcile.—*v.t.* bring about, as medium.—*a.* not immediate; depending on something intermediate.—**media'tion** *a.*—**me'diator** *a.*
med'icine *n.* the art of healing; a remedy or mixture of drugs.—**med'ical** *a.*—**med'ically** *adv.*—**medic'ament** *n.* a remedy.—**med'icate** *v.t.* to impregnate with medicinal substances.—**medica'tion** *n.*—**med'icative** *a.* healing.—**medic'inal** *a.* having healing properties.
me'diocre *a.* neither bad nor good, ordinary.—**medioc'rity** *n.*
med'itate *v.t.* to think about; to plan.—*v.i.* to be occupied in thought.—**medita'tion** *n.*–**med'itative** *a.*–**med'itatively** *adv.*
me'dium *n.* a middle quality or degree; an intermediate substance conveying force; surroundings; environment; means, agency; in spiritualism, a person through whom communication with the spirit world can be held (**me'diums, me'dia** *pl.*).—*a.* between two qualities, degrees, etc.—**medium waves** in wireless, waves between 200 and 1000 metres.
med'lar *n.* a tree with a fruit like a small apple; the fruit.
med'ley *n.* a hand-to-hand fight; a miscellaneous mixture (**med'leys** *pl.*).
Médoc' *n.* a red wine from Médoc.
mee'bos *n.* in S. Africa, apricots dried with sugar and salt.
meed *n.* a reward, recompense.
meek *a.* submissive, humble.—**meek'ly** *adv.*—**meek'ness** *n.* patience; humility.
meer'kat *n.* in S. Africa, the mongoose, the suricate.
meer'schaum (-shum) *n.* a white substance resembling clay used for bowls of tobacco pipes.
meet *a.* fit, suitable.—**meet'ly** *adv.*
meet *v.t.* to come face to face with; to encounter; to satisfy, pay.—*v.i.* to come face to face; to assemble; to come into contact (**met** *p.t.* and *p.p.*—**meet'ing** *pres. p.*).—*n.* a meeting for a hunt.—**meet'ing** *n.* an assembly.
megalith'ic *a.* consisting of great stones.
megaloma'nia *n.* a passion for appearing important.—**megaloma'niac** *a.* and *n.*
meg'aphone *n.* an instrument for carrying the sound of the voice to a distance.
megg'er *n.* in electricity, an instrument for measuring resistances; trade mark distinguishing a particular make of insulation and resistance testers.
me'grims *n. pl.* depression, melancholy.
mel'ancholy (-k-) *n.* sadness, dejection, gloom.—*a.* low-spirited, dejected.—**melancholia** *n.* mental disease accompanied by depression.—**melanchol'ic** *a.*
mêlée (mā-lā') *n.* a mixed fight.
mel'inite *n.* a high explosive.
mellif'luous *a.* sweet as honey, smooth.—**mellif'luence** *n.*
mell'ow *a.* ripe; juicy; rich, delicate.—*v.t.* and *i.* to make or become mellow.
mel'odrama *n.* a play full of sensational happenings.—**melodramat'ic** *a.*
mel'ody *n.* sweet sound; series of musical notes arranged as a tune.—**melo'dious** *a.*—**mel'odist** *n.* singer; composer.
mel'on *n.* various gourds eaten as fruit.
mel'on *n. see* **paddymelon.**—**mel'onhole** *n.* in Australia, honey-combing of surface of interior plains ascribed to work of the paddy-melon.
melt *v.i.* to become liquid by heat; to be dissolved; to become softened; to waste away.—*v.t.* to cause to soften or dissolve.
mem'ber *n.* a limb; any part of a complicated structure; any of the individuals making up a body.—**mem'bership** *n.*
mem'brane *n.* thin flexible skin or tissue in a plant or animal body.
memento' *n.* a thing serving to remind (**-tos** (tōz), **-toes** *pl.*).
mem'oir (-war) *n.* record of events; an autobiography or biography.
mem'ory *n.* faculty of recollecting or recalling to mind; a recollection; length of time one can remember.—**memo'rial** *a.* of or preserving memory.—*n.* something which serves to keep in memory; statement in a petition.—**memo'rialise** *v.t.* to commemorate; to petition.—**memo'rialist** *n.*—**mem'orise** *v.t.* to commit to memory.—**mem'orable** *a.* worthy of being remembered.—**mem'orably** *adv.*—**memoran'dum** *n.* note to help memory; note of a contract; informal letter (**-dums, -da** *pl.*).
Syn. remembrance, reputation, fame. *Ant.* forgetfulness, oblivion.
mem'sahib *n.* in India, a European married lady.
men'ace *n.* a threat.—*v.t.* to threaten.
menag'erie (-j-) *n.* a collection of wild animals kept for show.
mend *v.t.* to repair, correct, put right.—*v.i.* to improve, *esp.* in health.—*n.*
menda'cious *a.* untruthful, lying, false.—**mendac'ity** *n.*
Men'delism *n.* theory of heredity based on Mendel's discovery that hybrids reproduce their parents' characteristics according to definite laws.
mendi'cant *a.* beggar.—*n.* a beggar.—**mend'icancy** *n.*—**mendic'ity** *n.*
mè'nial *a.* relating to a servant in a house; servile.—*n.* a household servant.
meningi'tis (-ji-) *n.* inflammation of the membranes of the brain.
men'opause *n.* final cessation of the menses in women (between ages 45–50).
menses' *n. pl.* monthly discharge of

blood-stained mucuous membrane from womb.—**men'strual** *a.*
men'shevik *n.* a moderate socialist in Russia.
mensura'tion *n.* measuring, *esp.* of areas.
ment'al *a.* of, done by the mind; (*col.*) insane, feeble-minded.—**ment'ally** *adv.* in the mind.—**mental'ity** *n.* quality of mind; possession of a mind.
men'thol *n.* a camphor obtained from oil of peppermint.
mention (-shn) *n.* a referring to or remark about (a person or thing).—*v.t.*
men'tor *n.* a wise and trusted adviser.
men'u *n.* a list of dishes to be served.
mep'acrine (-a-krin) *n.* one of the synthetic drugs now replacing quinine as a malaria suppressive.
mephi'tis *n.* foul, pestilential exhalations.—**mephit'ic** *a.* fetid, poisonous.
mer'cantile (-k-) *a.* relating to trade.
mer'cenary (-s-) *a.* hired; working simply for reward.—*n.* hired soldier.
mer'cer *n.* a dealer in fabrics, *esp.* silks.
mer'cerise *v.t.* to give a lustre or gloss to cotton fabrics by treating with chemicals.–**mercer'ised** *a.*–**mercer'ising** *n.*
mer'chant *n.* a wholesale trader.—**mer'chandise** *n.* his goods.—**mer'chantman** *n.* a trading ship.—**mer'chant na'vy** *n.* fleet of trading ships.
mer'cury *n.* a white metal, liquid at ordinary temperature; quicksilver.—**mercu'rial** *a.* lively, sprightly; relating to or containing mercury.
Mer'cury, the Roman god of eloquence; the planet nearest to the sun.
mer'cy *n.* the quality of compassion.—**mer'ciful** *a.*—**mer'ciless** *a.*
mere (mēr) *n.* a pool, a lake.
mere (mēr) *a.* only; not of more value or size, etc., than name implies.—**mere'ly** *adv.* only, simply.
me're (me'ri) *n.* New Zealand, a stone, wood or whalebone Maori war-club; a miniature of the war-club executed in greenstone.
me'retricious *n.* gaudy, deceitfully alluring, showy, tawdry.
merge *v.i.* to lose identity, to mix in.—*v.t.* to cause to lose identity or to be absorbed.—**mer'ger** (-j-) *n.* absorption into something greater; a business combine (**mer'ging** *pres. p.*).
merid'ian *a.* relating to noon; position of the sun at noon.—*n.* noon; the highest point reached by a star, etc.; period of greatest splendour; an imaginary circle in the sky passing through the celestial poles; a circle of the earth passing through the poles.
meringue' (mer-ang') *n.* mixture of white of eggs and sugar, slightly browned, used as icing; cake made of this.
merin'o (-ēn'-) *n.* a variety of sheep; soft material made of merino wool.
mer'it *n.* excellence, worth; a quality of deserving well.—*pl.* excellences or defects.—*v.t.* to deserve.—**meritor'ious** *a.*
mer'lin *n.* a kind of hawk.
mer'maid *n.* an imaginary sea creature, half-woman, half-fish (**mer'man** *masc.*).
mer'ry *a.* joyous, cheerful.—**merr'ily** *adv.*—**merr'iment** *n.*—**merr'ythought** *n.* forked bone between head and breast of bird.—**merr'y-go-round** *n.* revolving machine with wooden horses, etc.
mesa (*geog.*) *n.* broad, flat, high rocky tableland.
mesh *n.* one of the open spaces of a net.—*v.t.* to catch in meshes; of gearwheels, to engage.–*v.i.*– **in mesh** (of gear wheels).
mes'merism *n.* a system of inducing a hypnotic state.—**mesmer'ic** *a.*—**mes'merist** *n.*—**mes'merise** *v.t.*
mess *n.* portion of food; state of untidy confusion; group who regularly eat together; place where they do this (as *officers' mess*).—*v.i.* to eat thus; to potter untidily.—*v.t.* to make a mess of; to muddle.—**mess'mate** *n.* companion at meals.
mess'age *n.* communication from one person to another.—**mess'enger** *n.* one who carries a message.—**mess'age stick** *n.* in Australia, a piece of wood carved to represent a message.
Messi'ah *n.* the promised deliverer of the Jews; the Christian Christ.
mess'uage (-swāj) *n.* a house with outbuildings and land.
mess'y *a.* dirty, untidy.
metab'olism *n.* the chemical routine of a living body.—**metabol'ic** *a.*
met'al *n.* any of a number of chemical elements usually bright and easy to melt, e.g., gold, iron, etc.; broken stone used for macadam roads.—**metall'ic** *a.*—**met'allurgy** *n.* the art of refining metals.—**met'allurgist** *n.*
metamor'phosis *n.* change of shape, substance, character, etc. (**-phoses** (-ēz) *pl.*).—**metamor'phose** *v.t.* to transform.
meta'phor *n.* a figure of speech in which a term is transferred to something it does not literally apply to; an instance of this.—**metaphor'ical** *a.*
metaphys'ics *n. pl.* theory of being and knowing.—**metaphys'ical** *a.*—**metaphysi'cian** *n.* one versed in metaphysics.
metath'esis *n.* transposition, *esp.* of letters in a word, e.g., the movement of "r" in *bird*, O.E. *bridd* (**-theses** (-ēz) *pl.*).
mete *v.t.* to measure, share out.—**me'ter** *n.* an instrument for measuring gas, etc.
metem'psychosis *n.* the passing over of the soul after death into some other body. *See* **reincarnation.**
me'teor *n.* a shining body appearing temporarily in the sky; a shooting star.—**meteor'ic** *a.*—**me'teorite** *n.* a fallen meteor.—**meteorol'ogy** *n.* the science of weather.—**meteorolog'ical** *a.*
methinks' *v. impers.* it seems to me.

meth'od *n.* a way of doing something; orderliness, system, plan.—**method'ical** *a.*—**Meth'odist** *n.* member of any of the churches originated by John Wesley and G. Whitefield.—**Meth'odism** *n.*—**meth'odise** *v.t.* to reduce to order.

meth'yl *n.* the base of wood spirit.—**meth'ylate** *v.t.* to mix with methyl.

metic'ulous *a.* excessively particular about small details.

mét'ier (māt'yā) *n.* one's happiest profession, vocation; one's forte.

metis' (mā-tēs') *n.* a person of mixed blood, as a mulatto, etc.; in N. America, the offspring of mixed Indian and French-Canadian parents.

met'onymy *n.* figure of speech in which one word is put for another it suggests.

me'tre *n.* a verse rhythm; the unit of length in the French decimal system, 39.37 ins.—**met'rical** *a.* of measurement or of poetic metre.—**met'ric** *a.* of that system of weights and measures in which the metre is a unit.

met'ronome *n.* (*mus.*) an instrument consisting of a weighted pendulum worked by clockwork, which can be adjusted to beat time at any given rate.

metrop'olis *n.* chief city of a state (-olises *pl.*).—**metropol'itan** *a.* of a metropolis.—*n.* bishop with authority over other bishops of province.

metro'style *n.* the tone-modulating and time-changing part of a pianola.

met'tle *n.* courage, spirit.–**met'tlesome** *a.*

mew *v.i.* of a hawk, to moult.—*v.t.* to put (a hawk) into a cage for moving; to imprison, shut up.—*n.* a cage for moulting hawks.—**mews** *n. pl.* (usually treated as *sing.*) stables round an open space.

mew *n.* the cry of a cat.—*v.i.*

mez'zanine *n.* (*archit.*) an entresol; small window; room below stage.

mez'zo-sopra'no (med'so-) *n.* a voice between soprano and contralto.

mez'zotint (med'so-) *n.* the method of engraving in which lights and half-lights are made by scraping a roughened surface; a print so produced.

mi'a-mi'a *n.* in Australia, an aboriginal hut; a bed or rest.

mias'ma *n.* harmful exhalations from marshes, etc.—**miasmat'ic** *a.*

mi'ca *n.* mineral found in glittering scales or plates.—**mica'ceous** *a.*

Mich'aelmas (mik'al-) *n.* the feast of St. Michael, 29th September.

mi'crobe *n.* a minute plant or animal, *esp.* one causing disease or fermentation.—**mi'crocosm** *n.* the world of man; man as an epitome of the universe.—**microcos'mic** *a.*—**mi'crophone** *n.* an instrument for making sounds louder, e.g., as part of a telephone or of broadcasting apparatus.—**microm'eter** *n.* an instrument for measuring very small distances.—**mi'croscope** *n.* an instrument by which a very small body is magnified and made visible.—**microscop'ic** *a.* relating to a microscope; so small as to be only visible through a microscope.—**micros'copy** *n.* the use of the microscope.

mi'crocopy *n.* a minute photographic replica which is useful for storage because of its small size.

mi'crofilm *n.* a photographic recording of a manuscript or book on small film to save storage space.

mi'crowave *n.* a radiation with a frequency of under one metre.

mid *a.* intermediate, that is in the middle.—**mid'day** *n.* noon or about then.—**mid'land** *n.* the middle part of a country.—*pl.* middle counties of England.—**mid'night** *n.* 12 o'clock at night.—**mid-off'** *n.* in cricket, an in-fielder who stands to the bowler's left.—**mid'shipman** *n.* naval officer ranking below sub-lieutenant.—**mid'summer** *n.* summer solstice (June 21st, 22nd); middle part of summer.—**mid'way** *a.* and *adv.* half-way.

midd'en *n.* a dunghill.

mid'dle *a.* equidistant from two extremes; medium, intermediate.—*n.* the middle point or part.—**mid'dleman** *n.* the trader handling goods between the producer and the consumer.

midge *n.* a gnat or similar insect.—**mid'get** *n.* a very small person or thing.

midinette' *n.* a Parisian shopgirl.

mid'riff *n.* the diaphragm.

midst *n.* in the midst of, surrounded by, among.—*prep.* in the midst of.

mid'wife *n.* a woman who assists others in childbirth.—**mid'wifery** (-wif-ri) *n.*

mien (mēn) *n.* a person's bearing or look.

might (mīt) *n.* power, strength.—**might'y** *a.*—**might'ily** *adv.* powerfully.

mignonette' (min-yon-) *n.* a plant with sweet-smelling flowers.

mi'graine (mē'-) *n.* a sick headache.

mi'grate *v.i.* to move from one place to another *esp.* birds.—**mi'grant** *a.* and *n.*—**migra'tion** *n.*—**migra'tory** *a.*

Mika'do *n.* the emperor of Japan.

milch *a.* giving, or kept for, milk.

mild (-ī-) *a.* gentle, merciful, indulgent.—**mild'ly** *a.*—**mild'ness** *n.*

Syn. tender, soft, temperate. *Ant.* ungentle, rough, harsh, stormy.

mil'dew *n.* a destructive fungus on plants or things exposed to damp.—*v.i.* to become tainted with mildew.—*v.t.*

mile *n.* a measure of length, 1,760 yards.—**mi'leage** *n.* distance in miles; motoring. miles travelled per gallon of petrol.

mileom'eter (-lom-) *n.* in motoring, an instrument for measuring and recording distance travelled.

mil'itary *a.* of, or for, soldiers or armies of warfare.—*n.* soldiers.—**mil'itant** *a.* engaged in warfare; combative.—*n.* a militant person.—**mil'itancy** *n.*—**mil'itarism** *n.* enthusiasm for military force and methods.—**mil'itarist** *n.*—**mil'itate** *v.i.* to be an argument or influence (against).—**mili'tia** (-ish'a) *n.* a force of citizen soldiers for duty in an emergency.

milk *n.* white fluid with which animals feed their young; cow's milk used as food.—*v.t.* to draw milk from.—**milk-bar** *n.* shop in which milk drinks are served for immediate consumption.—**milk'-bush** *n.* a Queensland shrub used for fodder purposes.—**milk'maid** *n.* woman working with cows or in a dairy.—**milk'-sop** *n.* effeminate man or youth.—**milk'teeth** *n.* the first set of animal teeth.—**milk'y** *a.* containing or like milk.

mill *n.* machinery for grinding corn, etc.; building containing this; various manufacturing machines; factory.—*v.t.* to put through mill; to cut fine grooves across edges (e.g., sixpence).—**mill'er** *n.* —**milll'race** *n.* water driving a mill wheel.—**mill'stone** *n.* one of pair of flat circular stones used for grinding.

millenn'ium *n.* period of 1,000 years; a period of 1,000 years during which some claim Christ is to reign on earth (**-iums, -ia** *pl.*).—**millenn'ial** *a.*

mill'et *n.* the small grain of an Indian cereal plant; the plant.

milli- *prefix* one thousandth of, a **mill'igram** *n.*—**mill'imetre** *n.*

mill'iard *n.* a thousand millions.

mil'libar *n.* in meteorology, 1/1000 of a bar, the unit of atmospheric pressure; a pressure of 1/1000 dyne per sq. centimetre.

mill'iner *n.* one who makes up or deals in women's hats.—**mill'inery** *n.*

mill'ion *n.* a thousand thousands.—**millionaire** *n.* an owner of a million of money, an extremely rich person.

milt *n.* the spawn of male fish.

mime *n.* a jester; an old form of dramatic representation.—**mim'ic** *a.* imitated, feigned, *esp.* to amuse.—*n.* one skilled in amusing imitation.—*v.t.*—**mim'icry** *n.*

mim'eograph *n.* an apparatus for producing stencils of written matter, from which copies may be obtained.

mimo'sa *n.* genus of leguminous plants which includes the sensitive plant.

mi'nah, my'na, mynah *n.* an Indian bird allied to the starling.

minaret' *n.* tall tower by a mosque.

mi'natory *a.* threatening.

mince *v.t.* to cut or chop small; to utter with affected carefulness.—*v.i.* to walk in an affected manner.—*n.* minced-meat. —**mince'-meat** *n.* a mixture of chopped currants, spices, suet, etc.—**mince' pie** *n.*

mind (-ī-) *n.* the thinking faculties as distinguished from the body, the intellectual faculties; memory; attention; intention; taste.—*v.t.* to attend to; care for; keep in memory.—**mind'ful** *a.*

mine *pron.* that belonging to me.

mine *n.* a deep hole for digging out coal, metals, etc.; an underground gallery with a charge of explosive; a large shell or canister of explosive placed in the sea to destroy ships.—*v.t.* to dig from a mine; to make a mine in or under.—*v.i.* to make or work in a mine.—**mi'ner** *n.*—**min'eral** *a.* got by mining; inorganic.—*n.* a mineral substance.—**mineral'ogy** *n.* the science of minerals.—**mineral'ist** *n.*—**mineralog'ical** (-j-) *a.*—**mine'-field** *n.* an area of water sown with mines.—**mine'-layer** *n.* a ship used for laying mines.—**mine'-sweeper** *n.* a ship used to clear away mines.—**min'eral-water** *n.* water containing some mineral.

min'gle (-ng-g-) *v.t.* and *i.* to mix; unite.

min'iature *n.* small painted portrait; model on a small scale.—*a.* small-scale. —**min'iaturist** *n.* painter of miniatures.

min'im *n.* in music, a note half the length of a semibreve; the smallest fluid measure, 1-60th of a fluid dram.

min'imise *v.t.* to bring to, or estimate at, the smallest possible amount.—**min'imum** *n.* the lowest size or quantity (**min'ima, -mums** *pl.*).—*a.*

min'ion *n.* favourite; servile dependant.

min'ister *n.* person in charge of a state department; a diplomatic representative; a clergyman.—*v.t.* to supply.—*v.i.* to serve; to contribute; to be serviceable or helpful.—**ministe'rial** *a.*—**min'istry** *n.* office of clergymen; the body of ministers forming a government; agency; action of ministering.—**ministe'rialist** *n.* supporter of the government.—**min'istrant** *a.* ministering.—*n.* an officiating clergyman.—**ministra'tion** *n.* rendering help, *esp.* to the sick.

min'iver *n.* a kind of white fur with occasional black markings, used for ceremonial robes, ermine.

mink *n.* a variety of the weasel tribe, valuable for its fur.

minn'ow (-ō) *n.* small freshwater fish.

mi'nor *a.* lesser; under age.—*n.* person under 21.—**minor'ity** *n.* state of being a minor; lesser number; smaller party voting together.—*pl.* ethnical or religious groups in a minority.

min'otaur *n.* a fabled monster, half-bull, half-man.

min'ster *n.* monastery church; cathedral.

min'strel *n.* mediaeval singer or musician.—*pl.* performers of Negro songs.—**min'strelsy** *n.* art or poetry of minstrels.

mint *n.* a place where money is coined. —*v.t.* coin.—*n.* an aromatic plant.

minuet' *n.* a stately dance; music for it.

mi'nus *prep.* less, with the deduction of. —*a.* of quantities, negative.

minute' (mī-nūt') *a.* very small; very precise.—**min'ute** (min'it) *n.* 60th part of an hour, degree or angle; a moment; a memorandum.—*pl.* record of the proceedings of a meeting, etc.—*v.i.* to

make a minute of; to record in minutes. —**minute'ly** (mī-nū-) *adv.*—**minu'tiæ** (-shi-ē) *n. pl.* precise details.
minx *n.* a pert girl, a hussy.
mio'cene (mī-ō'sēn) *a.* a term denoting the geological period in which can be observed a minority of living species.
mir'acle *n.* supernatural event; a marvel.—**mirac'ulous** *a.*—**mirac'ulously** *adv.*—**mir'acle-play** *n.* drama (*esp.* mediaeval) based on life of Christ.
mirage' (-ȧzh) *n.* deceptive image in the atmosphere having semblance of reality.
mire *n.* swampy ground, mud.—*v.t.* to stick in, or dirty with, mud.—**mi'ry** *a.*
mirr'or *n.* a polished surface for reflecting images of objects.—*v.t.* to reflect.
mirth *n.* merriment.—**mirth'ful** *a.*
Syn. jollity, laughter, hilarity, glee, cheerfulness. *Ant.* sadness, sorrow.
Mir'za (mēr'za) *n.* a Persian title.
mis *n.*, in S. Africa, dried cow-dung; a species of light, fibrous peat formed from the soil, refuse, etc.
mis- *prefix* meaning amiss, wrongly; makes compounds, e.g., **misapply'** *v.t.* to apply wrongly.—**misman'agement** *n.* bad management. Such words are not given where the meaning may easily be found from the simple word.
misalli'ance *n.* an improper, unsuitable or degrading marriage.
mis'anthrope *n.* a hater of mankind.—**misanthrop'ic** *a.*—**misan'thropy** *n.*
miscast' *v.t.* and *i.* to reckon erroneously; to distribute unsuitably, as the parts of a play.—*n.* an erroneous reckoning.
miscella'neous *a.* mixed, assorted.—**mis'cellany** *n.* a collection of assorted writings in one book, a literary medley.
mis'chief (-chif) *n.* harm, a source of harm or annoyance; annoying conduct.
mis'chievous *a.* having harmful effect; disposed to or full of mischief.
mis'creant *n.* a wicked person.
misdemea'nour *n.* offence less grave than a felony.—**misdemea'nant** *n.*
mi'ser (-z-) *n.* one who hoards instead of using money; a stingy fellow.—**mi'serly** *a.*—**mis'erable** *a.* very unhappy, wretched; mean.—**mis'ery** *n.*
mis'ericorde (-kord) *n.* mercy; dagger of mercy.
misgive' *v.t.* to cause fear, suspicion, [doubt.
misno'mer *n.* a wrong name.
misog'amy *n.* hatred of marriage.—**misog'amist** *n.*
misog'yny (-j-) *n.* hatred of women.—**misog'ynist** *n.*
Miss *n.* title of unmarried woman, girl.
miss *v.t.* fail to hit, reach, find, catch, or notice; not to be in time for; to omit, to notice or regret absence of.—*n.*
miss'al *n.* a mass-book.
miss'el-thrush *n.* a large thrush.
miss'ile (-īl) *n.* that which may be thrown or shot to do damage.
mis'sion (mish'n) *n.* sending or being sent on some service; party of persons sent; a person's calling in life.—**mis'sionary** *a.* of religious missions.—*n.* one who goes on religious missions.—**miss'ive** *n.* a letter, *esp.* official.
mist *n.* water vapour in fine drops.—*v.* to dim.—**mist'y** *a.*—**mist'ily** *adv.*
mistake' *v.t.* not to understand; to form a wrong opinion about; to take (a person or thing) for another.—*v.i.* to be in error.—*n.* error in thought or action. (**mista'king** *p.p.*)—**mista'ken** *a.* wrong.
mis'tletoe (-sl-) *n.* evergreen parasitic plant with white berries.
mis'tral *n.* a violent north-west wind that blows over the Gulf of Lyons.
mis'tress *n.* a woman who employs other persons; a woman teacher; the object of a man's illicit love.
mite *n.* a very small insect; a very small coin; a very small child or person.
mit'igate *v.t.* to relieve, make less severe.—**mitiga'tion** *n.* (**mit'igating** *pres. p.*). *Syn.* of *n.* relief, decrease. *Ant.* aggravation, increase.
mi'tre (-tẹr) *n.* bishop's headdress; joint between two pieces of wood, etc., meeting at right angles.—*v.t.* put mitre on; join with, shape for mitre-joint.
mitt'en *n.* a glove with one compartment for the four fingers; a glove leaving the fingers and end of the thumb bare.
mix *v.t.* to put together or to combine or blend, to mingle.—*v.i.* to be mixed; to associate.—**mix'ture** *n.*
mizz'en, miz'en *n.* lowest fore and aft sail on mizzenmast.—**miz'(z)enmast** *n.* aftermost mast on full-rigged ship.
mnemon'ic (n-) *a.* helping memory.—*n.* something to help memory.
mo'a *n.* an extinct New Zealand bird.
moan *n.* a low murmur, usually indicating pain.—*v.t.* to bewail.—*v.i.*
moat *n.* deep wide ditch round town or building.—*v.t.* surround with moat.
mob *n.* a disorderly crowd of people; in Australia, a large number, *esp.* of cattle or sheep.—*v.t.* to attack in a mob, to hustle (**mobbed** *p.t.* and *p.p.*).
mob'-cap *n.* woman's indoor cap.
mo'bile (-bīl) *a.* capable of movement; easily moved or changed.—**mobil'ity** *n.* —**mo'bilise** *v.t.* to prepare (forces) for active service.—*v.i.* of an army, to prepare for active service.—**mobilisa'tion** *n.*
mocc'asin *n.* an American Indian soft shoe, usually of deerskin.
mock *v.t.* to make fun of, to hold up to ridicule; to disappoint.—*v.i.* to scoff.—*n.* act of mocking; a laughing stock.—*a.* sham, imitation.—**mock'er** *n.*—**mock'ery** *n.* *Syn.* to deride, taunt, scoff at. *Ant.* respect, revere, take seriously.
mode *n.* method, manner, style, fashion. —**mo'dish** *a.* in the fashion.
mod'el *n.* representation of an object

made to scale; a pattern; a person or thing worthy of imitation; person employed by an artist to pose, or by a dressmaker to show off clothes.—*v.t.* to work into shape; to make to a model.
mod'erate (-it) *a.* not going to extremes, not excessive, medium.—*n.* a person of moderate views.—(-āt) *v.t.* and *i.* to make or become less violent or excessive.—**mod'erately** *adv.* fairly.—**modera'tion** *n.* restraint.—**mod'erator** *n.* mediator; president of a Presbyterian body.
mod'ern *a.* of present or recent times; new fashioned.—*n.* a person living in modern times.—**mod'ernism** *n.* any movement which aims at expressing the mind or the emotions of the present day.—**mod'ernist** *n.*—**modern'ity** *n.*—**mod'ernise** *v.t.* to adapt to modern ways or views.—**modernisa'tion** *n.*
mod'est *a.* unassuming, shy, retiring, not vain or boastful, moderate, unpretentious.—**mod'esty** *n.*
mod'icum *n.* a small quantity.
mod'ify (-fī) *v.t.* to make small changes in; to tone down (-ified *p.t.* and *p.p.*—-ifying *pres. p.*).—**modifica'tion** *n.*
modiste' (mō-dēst') *n.* a fashionable milliner or dressmaker.
mod'ulate *v.t.* to regulate; vary in tone.—*v.i.* change key of music.—**modula'tion** *n.*—**mod'ulator** *n.* one who, that which, modulates; wireless transmitter valve superimposing microphone signals on to high frequency carrier.
mo'dus *n.* a way or mode; a compensation in lieu of tithes.
mo'hair *n.* a fine cloth of goat's hair.
Mohamm'edan *a.* of Mohammed or his religion.—*n.* a believer in Mohammed.—**Mohamm'edanism** *n.*
moi'ety *n.* a half, one of two parts.
moil *v.i.* to drudge.
moir'é (-rā) *a.* watered.—*n.* a watered fabric, usually of silk.
moist *a.* damp, slightly wet.—**moist'en** *v.t.*—**moist'ure** *n.* liquid, especially diffused or in small drops.
moke *n.* (*sl.*) a donkey; in Australia and S. Africa (*sl.*) an inferior horse.
mo'kihi, moki *n.* in New Zealand, a raft made of dried bulrushes.
mo'ko *n.* in New Zealand, tattooing as practised by the Maoris.
mo'ko-mo'ko *n.* N.Z., the bell-bird.
mo'lar *a.* of teeth, serving to grind.—*n.*
molass'es (-ez) *n.* syrup drained from raw sugar, treacle, syrup.
mole *n.* a small dark growth on the skin.
mole *n.* a small burrowing animal.—**mole'skin** *n.* its fur; a kind of fustian.
mole *n.* a stone pier or breakwater.
mol'ecule *n.* one of the uniform small particles, composed of atoms, of which a homogeneous substance is made up.—**molec'ular** *a.*—**molec'ular film** *n.* a layer one molecule thick.—**molecular** rays, a stream of molecules forced to move in a single direction.
molest' *v.t.* to interfere with, meddle with so as to annoy or injure.—**molesta'tion** *n.* hostile interference.
moll'ify *v.t.* to calm down (-ified *p.t.* and *p.p.*—-ifying *pres. p.*).—**mollifica'tion** *a.*
moll'usc *n.* a soft-bodied and (usually) hard-shelled animal, e.g., snail, oyster.
moll'y-codd'le *v.t.* to pamper.
Mo'loch *n.* the deity of the Ammonites, to whom human sacrifices were offered.
molyb'denum *n.* a rare metal.
mo'ment *n.* a very short space of time.—**mo'mentary** *a.* only a moment.—**mo'mentarily** *adv.*—**moment'ous** *a.* important.—**moment'um** *n.* force of a moving body (**moment'a, -tums** *pl.*).
mon'arch (-k) *n.* the sovereign ruler of a state.—**mon'archy** *n.* a state ruled by a sovereign; his rule.—**monarch'ic** *a.*—**mon'archist** *n.* a supporter of monarchy.
mon'astery *n.* a house occupied by a religious order.—**monas'tic** *a.* relating to monks, nuns, or monasteries.—**monas'ticism** *n.* the monastic system.
Mon'day *n.* second day of week.
mon'ey (mun'-) *n.* current coin and paper money; a medium of exchange.—**mon'etary** *a.*—**mon'etise** *v.t.* make into money.—**monetisa'tion** *n.*
mon'eywort *n.* an evergreen trailing plant, named from its round leaves.
mon'goose (-ng-g-) *n.* small Indian animal which kills snakes (**-gooses** *pl.*).
mon'grel (mung-g-) *n.* an animal, *esp.* a dog, of mixed breed.—*a.*
mon'itor *n.* one who warns or advises; senior pupil in school given special duties and authority; small warship with heavy guns.—*n.* one who listens to radio broadcasts to determine whether transmitting apparatus is on calibration or deviating from its allotted frequency; one who listens to and records foreign broadcasts.—**mon'itress** *fem.*—**mon'itory** *a.*—**moni'tion** *n.*
monk (munk) *n.* one of a religious community of men living apart under vows.—**monk'ish** *a.*—**monk's-hood** *n.* a herbaceous plant, extremely poisonous.
monk'ey (munk'i) *n.* mammal of group ranging from apes to marmosets; an imitative or mischievous child; (**-keys** *pl.*).—*v.i.* to play tricks.—**monk'ey-nut** *n.* pea-nut.—**monkey-puzzle** *n.* a kind of prickly tree.—**monkey suit** (U.S.) (*sl.*) men's formal attire; military or naval dress uniform; airman's overall.
mono- *prefix*, single, as *monograph*.
mon'ochrome *n.* representation in one colour.—*a.* of only one colour.—**monochromat'ic** *a.*—**mon'ochord** *n.* musical instrument with one string.—**mon'ocle** *n.* eyeglass for one eye.—**mon'ody** *n.* a lament.—**monog'amy** *n.* custom

of being married to only one person at a time.—**mon'ogram** *n.* two or more letters interwoven.—**mon'ograph** *n.* short book on a single subject.—**mon'olith** *n.* monument consisting of a single stone. —**mon'ologue** *n.* dramatic composition with only one speaker.—**monoma'nia** *n.* madness on a single subject.—**monoma'niac** *n.*—**mon'omark** *n.* (trade name) a combination of letters and numbers used instead of the name of the owner to identify property.—**mon'oplane** *n.* aeroplane with single wings.—**monop'oly** *n.* exclusive possession of a trade, privilege, etc.-**monop'olise** *v.t.*—**monop'olist** *n.*—**mon'orail** *n.* railway having cars running on or suspended from a single rail.—**mon'osyllable** *n.* word of one syllable.—**monosyllab'ic** *a.*—**mon'otheism** *n.* belief that there is only one God.—**mon'otheist** *n.*—**mon'otone** *n.* continuing on one note.—**monot'onous** *a.* lacking in variety, wearisome.—**monot'ony** *n.*—**mon'otype** *n.* machine for casting and setting printing type in individual letters.

monsoon' *n.* seasonal wind of Indian Ocean blowing from S.W. in summer, N.E. in winter; rainy season.

mon'ster *n.* misshapen animal or plant; a person of great wickedness; a huge animal or thing; S. Africa, a sample of goods, such as those carried by commercial travellers.—*a.* huge.—**mon'strous** *a.*—**mon'strously** *adv.*—**monstros'ity** *n.* a monstrous being; a monster.

montage (-tàzh') *n.* elements of two or more pictures imposed upon a single background to give a unified effect; the editing of a cinema film.

month (munth) *n.* one of the 12 periods into which a year is divided; period of the revolution of the moon.—**month'ly** *a.* happening, payable, etc., once a month.—*adv.* once a month.—*n.* a monthly magazine.

mon'ument *n.* anything that commemorates; a written record.—**monument'al** *a.* of or serving as a monument; vast, stupendous, colossal.

moo'cha, mu'tya *n.* in S. Africa, apron or short skirt worn by native men.

mood *n.* state of mind and feelings.—**mood'y** *a.* changeable in mood; gloomy.

mood *n.* in grammar, a group of forms indicating function of a verb.

moo'i (mōō'i) *a.* S. Africa, fine; handsome; pretty.—**moo'ipraat** *v.t.* to fawn.

moon *n.* satellite of the earth; a satellite of a planet.—*v.i.* to go about dreamily; Australia, to hunt opossum at night by sighting through tree branches against the moon.—**moon'-bird** *n. see* **dikkop.**—**moon'light** *n.*—**moon'shine** *n.* nonsense. —**moon'stone** *n.* precious stone.-**moon'struck** *a.* crazy.

Moor *n.* member of mixed Arab and Berber race inhabiting Morocco and adjoining parts of N.W. Africa.

moor *n.* a tract of waste land, often hilly and covered with heather, land preserved for grouse shooting.—**moor'cock** *n.* red grouse.—**moor'hen** *n.* water-hen.

moor *v.t.* to fasten (a ship) with chains or ropes.—*v.i.* to secure a ship thus.—**mooring mast** *n.* in aviation, steel-girder structure fitted at head with receiving arm for holding airship while allowing its free movement in any direction.

moose *n.* the largest of the deer tribe.

moot *n.* a meeting.—*v.t.* to bring for discussion.—*a.* that is open to argument, a moot point, a doubtful point.

mop *n.* a bundle of yarn, cloth, etc., fastened to the end of a handle for cleaning floors.—*v.t.* to clean or wipe with a mop (**mopped'** *p.t.* and *p.p.*).

mope *v.i.* to be depressed.—**mo'pish** *a.*

mo'poke *n.* the morepork q.v.

mor'al *a.* concerned with right and wrong conduct; of good conduct.—*n.* a practical lesson, e.g., of a fable.—*pl.* habits with respect to right and wrong, *esp.* in matters of sex.—**morale'** (-àl) *n.* discipline and spirit of an army or other body of persons.—**mor'alist** *n.* a teacher of morals.—**moral'ity** *n.* good moral conduct; moral goodness or badness; a kind of mediæval drama, containing a moral lesson.—**mor'alise** *v.t.* to interpret morally.—*v.i.*—**mor'ally** *adv.*—**moral victory,** a failure or defeat that inspirits instead of crushing the loser.—**moral certainty,** a thing that can hardly fail.

Syn. ethical, virtuous, just, honourable, blameless. *Ant.* wicked, sinful, vicious.

morass' *n.* a marsh (**morass'es** *pl.*).

morato'rium (-tō-) *n.* act of authorising the suspension of payments by a bank or a debtor (**-ria** *pl.*).

mor'bid *a.* unwholesome, sickly.

mord'ant *a.* biting; acute.—*n.* any substance that fixes dyes.

more *a.* greater in quantity or number; *comp.* of **many** and of **much.**—*adv.* to a greater extent, in addition.—*pron.* greater or additional amount or number. —**moreo'ver** *adv.* besides.

more'pork *n.* aboriginal name for Australian bird, from its note; the boobook owl; the mopoke; in New Zealand, a kind of owl.

morganat'ic *a.* **morganat'ic marriage,** of king or prince in which wife does not share husband's rank.

mor'gen *n.* in S. Africa, an area of land.

mor'ibund *a.* dying.

Mor'mon *n.* member of religious sect founded by Joseph Smith (U.S.A.) in 1830.—**mor'monism** *n.*

morn *n.* the morning.—**morn'ing** *n.* early part of the day, before noon.

morocc'o *n.* goatskin leather (**-os**) *pl.*).

mo'ron *n.* mentally deficient person.—*a.*
morose' *a.* sullen, unsociable.
morph'ia, morph'ine *n.* narcotic part of opium; drug to relieve pain.
morphol'ogy *n.* the science of the structure of organisms and of linguistic forms.—**morpholog'ical** *a.*
morr'is *n.* dance by persons represent ing characters in Robin Hood stories.
morr'is tube *n.* a small-bore barrel for fixing in rifle for practice at short range.
morr'ow *n.* the following day.
Morse *a.* **Morse-code** system of sound or visual signalling in which letters of alphabet are represented by combinations of dots and dashes.
mor'sel *n.* mouthful; fragment.
mort *n.* a salmon in the third year.
mort'al *a.* subject to death; causing death.—*n.* a mortal creature.—**mortal'-ity** *n.* condition of being mortal; death rate.—**mort'ally** *adv.* fatally; bitterly.
mort'ar *n.* vessel in which substances are pounded; short gun throwing at high angles; a mixture of lime, sand, and water for holding bricks and stones together.
mort'gage (morg'ij) *n.* a conveyance of property as security for debt with provision that the property be reconveyed at payment within an agreed time.—*v.t.* to convey by mortgage.—**mort'gagor** (morg'a-jẹr) *n.*—**mortgagee'** *n.*
mortic'ian *n.* (U.S.) funeral undertaker.
mort'ify *v.t.* to subdue by self-denial; to humiliate.—*v.i.* of a part of the body, to be affected with gangrene (**mort'ified** *p.t.* and *p.p.*—**-ifying** *pres. p.*).—**mortifica'tion** *n.* shame; decay.
mort'ise (-is) *n.* hole made in a piece of wood, etc., to receive the tongue at the end of another piece, called a tenon.—*v.t.* make mortise in; fasten thus.
mort'uary *a.* of, or for, burial.—*n.* a building where dead bodies are kept.
mosa'ic *n.* a picture or pattern made by fixing side by side small bits of coloured stone, glass, etc.; this process.
moselle' *n.* a light wine.
Mos'lem *n.* a Mohammedan.—*a.* pertaining to the Mohammedans.
mosque (mosk) *n.* Mohammedan place of worship, temple.
mosquito' (-kē'tō) *n.* various kinds of gnat (**-toes** *pl.*).
moss *n.* a swamp; a small plant growing in masses on a surface.—*v.t.*—**moss'y** *a.*
moss'ie *n.* S. Africa, the cape sparrow.
most (mō-) *a.* greatest in size, number, or degree.—*sup.* of **much** and of **many.**—*n.* the greatest amount or degree.—*adv.* in the greatest degree.—**most'ly** *adv.*
mot (mō) *n.* a pithy or witty saying or remark (**mots** (mōz) *pl.*).
mote *n.* a particle of dust, a speck.
moth *n.* a nocturnal insect like the butterfly.—**moth-ball** *n.* a white ball containing naphthalene used to repel clothes moths.—**moth'-eaten** *a.* eaten or damaged by the grub of the moth.
moth'er (muth-) *n.* female parent; head of a religious community of women.—*a.* inborn.—*v.t.* to act as a mother to.—**moth'erhood** *n.*—**moth'erly** *a.*—**moth'er-in-law** *n.* the mother of one's wife or husband.—**moth'er-of-pearl'** *n.* an iridescent substance.
mo'tif *n.* a subject; a dominating theme.
mo'tion *n.* process or action or way of moving; proposal in a meeting; an application to a judge.—*v.t.* to direct by a sign.—**mo'tionless** *a.*—**mo'tive** *a.* causing motion.—*n.* that which makes a person act in a particular way; the chief idea in a work of art.—**mo'tor** *n.* that which imparts movement; machine to supply motive power; *abbrev.* of **motor-car.**—*v.* to travel by motor-car.—**mo'tor-car** *n.* an automobile.—**mo'torist** *n.* user of a motor-car.—**motor-boat** *n.*—**motorcade'** *n.* a convoy of motor vehicles.—**motor-cycle** *n.*—**motorise** *v.t.* to provide with a motor or motor vehicles.
Syn. movement, impulse. *Ant.* rest.
mot'ley *a.* checkered.—*n.* a motley colour; a jester's dress (**-leys** *pl.*).—**mot'tle** *n.* a blotch on a surface.—*v.t.*
mott'o *n.* saying adopted as a rule of conduct; short inscribed sentence or quotation; word or sentence in heraldic crest (**-oes** *pl.*).
moujik' (mōō-zhik') *n.* Russian peasant.
mould (mōld) *n.* loose or surface earth.
mould (mōld) *n.* a pattern for shaping; hollow object in which metal is cast; character, form.—*v.t.* to shape.—**mould'-ing** *n.* moulded object; decoration.
mould (mōld) *n.* mildew, a growth caused by dampness.—**mould'y** *a.*—**mould'er** *v.* to rot, decay.
moult (mōlt) *v.i.* to change feathers.—*v.t.* to shed (feathers).—*n.*
mound *n.* a heap of earth or stones; a small hill.—**mound'bird** *n.* Australia, bird which leaves its eggs to hatch under a mound of decomposing matter, the jungle hen.
mount *n.* a hill; that on which anything is supported or fitted; a horse.—*v.i.* to go up; get on horseback; to rise.—*v.t.* to go up; to get on the back of; to set on a mount; to furnish with a horse.—**mount'-ain** *n.* a hill of great size.—**mountaineer'** *n.* one who lives among or climbs mountains.—**mount'ainous** *a.*
moun'tebank *n.* a quack; a market-place entertainer; flamboyant person.
mourn (mōrn) *v.i.* to feel sorrow.—*v.t.* to grieve for.—**mourn'er** *n.*—**mourn'ful** *a.*-**mourn'fully** *adv.*-**mourn'-ing** *n.* grief; clothes of a mourner.
Syn. lament, bewail. *Ant.* rejoice.
mouse *n.* **mice** *pl.* a small rodent animal.—*v.i.* to catch mice.—**mous'er** *n.* a cat good at catching mice.

mousse' (-mōōs') *n.* sweet dish made with whipped cream, variously flavoured.
moustache' (mus-tâsh') *n.* hair on (a man's) upper lip.
mouth (-th; *pl.* -thz) *n.* opening in the head, for eating, speaking, etc.; opening into anything hollow; out-fall of a river, entrance to harbour, etc.—(-th) *v.t.* to take into the mouth; to declaim.—*v.i.* to declaim.—**mouth'piece** *n.* end of anything intended to be put between lips; one who speaks for others.
move (mōōv) *v.t.* to change the position of; to stir; to propose.—*v.i.* to change places; to take action.—*n.* a moving; a motion making towards some goal.—**mov'able** *a.* and *n.*—**move'ment** *n.* the process or action of moving; the moving parts of a machine; a division in music.—**mo'ving** *a.* stirring, touching.
mo'vies (mōō-) *n.* (*sl.*) cinematograph.
mow (mō) *v.t.* to cut (grass, etc.).—*v.i.*
much *a.* existing in quantity (more, *comp.*—most *sup.*).—*n.* a large amount—*adv.* in a great degree.
mu'cilage *n.* in N. America, gum.
muck *n.* cattle dung; refuse.–**muck'y** *a.*
mud *n.* wet and soft earth; in N. America (*sl.*) land.—**mud'dle** *v.t.* to confuse; bewilder, mismanage.—*v.i.* to be busy in a fumbling way.—**mudd'y** *a.*
mud'guard *n.* a guard over a wheel to prevent mud, water, etc., being splashed.
mud'lark *n.* a street arab.
mud'-pack *n.* a treatment with impregnated mud beneficial to skin.
muff *n.* covering to keep the hands warm; one with no practical sense; a duffer.—*v.* to miss a catch, a chance etc.
muff'in *n.* a light round flat cake.
muf'fle *v.t.* wrap up, *esp.* to deaden sound.—**muf'fler** *n.* a scarf to cover the neck and throat; in motoring, a silencer.
muf'ti *n.* a Mohammedan priest; plain clothes as distinguished from uniform.
mug *n.* a drinking cup; (*sl.*) one easily imposed upon, simpleton.
mugg'y *a.* damp and stifling.
muid *n.* in S. Africa, a measure of capacity, slightly under three bushels.
muis'hond *n.* in S. Africa, a kind of skunk.
mulatt'o (mū-) *n.* person with one white and one Negro parent (-oes *pl.*).
mul'berry *n.* a tree of which the leaves are much used to feed silkworms; its fruit.
mulch *n.* straw, leaves, etc., spread as a protection for the roots of plants.—*v.t.*
mulct *n.* a fine.—*v.t.* to fine.
mule *n.* animal which is a cross between a horse and an ass; a stupid, obstinate person.—**muleteer'** *n.* a mule driver.—**mu'lish** *a.* stubborn, sullen.
mul'ga *n.* Australia, several species of *acacia*.—**mul'ga-down** *n.*—**mul'ga-grass** *n.* fodder grass growing among mulga.—**mul'ga scrub** *n.* thickets of mulga trees.
mull *v.t.* to heat (wine) with sugar and spices; to muddle.—*n.* a mess; failure.
mull'et *n.* a sea fish sought after as food.
mulligataw'ny *n.* soup with curry.
mull'igrubs *n.* (*col.*) stomach-ache; fit of depression, the dumps.
mull'ion *n.* an upright dividing bar in a window or screen.
mull'ock *n.* rubbish from a mine; in Australia, rock containing no gold, or from which the gold has been extracted.
multi-, mult- *prefix* many.
mul'tiple *a.* having many parts.—*n.* a quantity which contains another an exact number of times.—**multipli'city** a variety, greatness in number.—**mul'tiply** *v.t.* to make many; to find the sum of a given number taken a stated number of times.—*v.i.* to increase in number or amount (**multiplied** *p.t.* and *p.p.*—**-plying** *pres. p.*).—**multiplica'tion** *n.*
mul'titude *n.* great number.—**multitu'dinous** *a.* very numerous.
mul'tiphase *a.* in electricity, having components of various phase.
mul'tiplex *a.* manifold; multiple; in telegraphy, equipped to carry numerous messages over the same wire.
mul'tivalve *a.* having many valves; in wireless, consisting of several thermionic valves.—*n.* a mollusc with a shell of many valves or pieces.
mum'ble *v.i.* and *t.* to speak indistinctly.
mum'bo-jum'bo *n.* grotesque Negro idol worshipped by certain African tribes; (*fig.*) a foolish fetish.
mumm'er *n.* one who acts in a dumb-show.—**mumm'ery** *n.* dumb-show acting.
mumm'y *n.* an embalmed body.—**mumm'ify** *v.t.* (**mumm'ified** *p.t.*/*p.p.*—**-ifying** *pr. p.*).—**mummifica'tion** *n.*
mumps *n. pl.* contagious disease marked by swelling in the neck glands.
munch *v.t.* to chew noisily.
mun'dane *a.* belonging to this world.
muni'cipal (-is'-) *a.* belonging to the affairs of a city or town.—**municipal'ity** *n.* a city or town with local self-government.
munif'icent *a.* magnificently generous.—**munif'icence** *n.* great generosity.
muni'tions (-ish-) *n. pl.* military stores, *e.g.*, shells, guns, aircraft, etc.
mu'ral *a.* of or on a wall.—**mu'ral paint'ing** *n.* a painting executed upon the wall of a building.
mur'der *n.* the unlawful and deliberate killing of a human being.—*v.t.* to kill thus.—**mur'derer** *n.*—**mur'deress** *fem.*
murk *n.* thick darkness.—**murk'y** *a.*
mur'mur *v.i.* making a low continuous sound; to complain.—*v.t.* to utter in a low voice.—*n.* a sound of murmuring.
murr'ain *n.* cattle plague.
murr'nong *n.* in Australia, a plant with edible tubers, a kind of yam, eaten by the aborigines.
mus'cat *n.* a musk-flavoured grape; a

strong wine made from it.—**muscatel'** *n.*
mus'cle (mus'l) *n.* a part of the body which produces movement by contracting; system of muscles.—**mus'cular** *a.*
muse (-z) *v.i.* to be lost in thought.—*n.*
muses (-z) *n.* goddesses inspiring learning and the arts.—**muse'um** *n.* building containing collection of objects illustrating the arts, history, etc.
mush *n.* in N. America, porridge of maize meal; in wireless, interference from high-power arc transmitting stations.—**mush-area** *n.*
mush'room *n.* an eatable fungus.
mu'sic (-z-) *n.* the art of expressing or causing an emotion by melodious and harmonious combination of notes; the laws of this; composition in this art. —**mu'sical** *a.*—**mu'sically** *adv.*—**musi'cian** (-zish'en) n.—**mu'sic-hall** *n.*
musk *n.* a scent obtained from a gland of the musk-deer; various plants with a similar scent.—**musk'y** *a.*—**musk'-ox** *n.* an ox of arctic America.—**musk'-rat** *n.* a N. American rodent taken for its fur.
mus'keg *n.* in N. America, marshy land.
musk'et *n.* an infantryman's gun, *esp.* unrifled (now obsolete)—**musketeer'** *n.* —**musk'etry** *n.* use of firearms.
Mus'lim *see* **Moslem.**
mus'lin (-z-) *n.* a fine cotton fabric.
mus'quash *n.* the musk-rat; its fur.
muss' *v.t.* (U.S.) mix-up, muddle.
muss'el *n.* a bivalve shellfish.
Mus'sulman *n.* Mohammedan (*-s pl.*).
must *n.* new or unfermented wine.
must *v. aux.* to be obliged to.
mus'tang *n.* the wild prairie horse.
must'ard *n.* plant; powder made from its seeds, used as a condiment.
must'er *v.t.* and *i.* to assemble; in Australia, *esp.* of sheep, cattle, etc.—*n.* an assembly, *esp.* for exercise, inspection.—**count-muster** *n.* in Australia, a round-up of stock for counting.
must'y *a.* mouldy, stale.
mu'table *a.* liable to change.—**muta'tion** *n.* alteration; umlaut.
mute *a.* dumb; silent, soundless.—*n.* a dumb person; a hired mourner; a slip placed on a stringed instrument to soften the tone.—**mute'ly** *a.*
mu'tilate *v.t.* to deprive of a limb or other part; to damage.—**mutila'tion** *n.*
mu'tiny *n.* rebellion against authority, *esp.* against the officers of a disciplined body.—*v.i.* (**mu'tinied** *p.t.* and *p.p.*—**-tinying** *pres. p.*).—**mu'tinous** *a.* rebellious.—**mutineer'** *n.* a rebel.
mutt *n.* (*sl.*) a stupid person.
mutt'er *v.i.* and *t.* to speak with the mouth nearly closed, indistinctly.—*n.*
mutt'on *n.* flesh of sheep used as food. —**mutt'on-bag** *n.* N. Zealand, cloth used to protect frozen mutton.—**mutt'on-bird** *n.* Australia, migratory sea-bird of petrel kind inhabiting islands of Bass Strait.—**mutt'on-wood** *n.* Australian shrub found in coastal areas visited by mutton-birds.
mu'tual *a.* done, possessed, etc., by each of two with respect to the other; common to both.—**mu'tually** *adv.*
Syn. reciprocal, interchangeable, common. *Ant.* separate, distinct, unrelated.
mutya *see* **moocha.**
muz'zle *n.* projecting mouth and nose of an animal; a thing put over these to prevent biting; the end of a firearm by which the projectile leaves.—*v.t.* to put a muzzle on, to prevent from speaking.
muz'zy *a.* bewildered; tipsy.
my *pron.* belonging to me.—**myself** *pron.* emphatic or reflective form of **I** or **me.**
myal'gia *n.* cramp in a muscle.
my'all *n.* in Australia, an acacia tree; a wild native; wild cattle.
myasthe'nia *n.* muscular debility.
mycol'ogy *n.* the study of fungi.
my'na, my'nah *see* **minah.**
mynheer', meneer' (-hār, hēr) *n.* in South Africa, a term of respect, used to a superior or stranger.
myo'pia *n.* short-sightedness.
myosi'tis *n.* inflammation of muscles.
myr'iad (mir-) *n.* ten thousand; an endless number.—*a.* innumerable.
myr'midon (mẹr-) *n.* a servile follower.
myrrh (mẹr) *n.* an aromatic gum.
myr'tle (mẹr-) *n.* an evergreen shrub.
mys'tery (mis-) *n.* an obscure or secret thing; a state of being obscure; a religious rite; a Biblical play.—**myste'rious** *a.*—**myste'riously** *adv.*—**myst'ic** *a.* of hidden meaning, *esp.* in a religious sense. —*n.* one who seeks direct communication with God by self-surrender or contemplation.—**myst'ical** *a.*—**myst'icism** *n.* **myst'ify** *v.t.* to bewilder (**-ified** *p.t.* and *p.p.*—**-ifying** *pres. p.*).—**mystifica'tion** *n.*
myth (mith) *n.* a tale, often with secret meaning, with supernatural characters or events; an imaginary person or object.—**myth'ical** *a.*—**mythol'ogy** *n.* myths collectively; the study of them.—**mytholog'ical** (-j-) *a.*—**myth'ologies** *n.*

N

naart'ie (nart'i) *n.* a tangerine orange.
nab *v.t.* to catch suddenly.
na'bob *n.* an Indian prince or deputy governor; a rich retired Anglo-Indian.
nacelle' *n.* a small boat; in aviation, that part of aeroplane which houses engine, pilot, passengers and goods.
nacht'slang, nag'slang (nàht-) *n.* in South Africa, a nocturnal snake; adder.
na'cre (-ker) *n.* mother-of-pearl.
na'dir *n.* the point opposite the zenith.
nag *n.* a small horse for riding; a horse.
nag *v.t.* and *i.* to worry, be worrying by constant fault-finding (**nag'ging** *pres. p.*)

naga'na *n.* in S. Africa, a cattle disease caused by the tsetse fly.
nai'ad (nī-) a river nymph.
nail (nāl) *n.* the horny shield of the ends of the fingers; a claw; a small metal spike for fixing wood, etc.—*v.t.* to fix with a nail.—**nail'rod** *n.* in Australia, a dark, coarse tobacco smoked by bushmen.
nain'sook *n.* a thin, fine cotton material.
naive (nȧ-ēv') *a.* simple, unaffected.
Syn. frank, candid, ingenuous. *Ant.* disingenuous, sophisticated, insincere.
na'ked *a.* without clothes; exposed, bare. —**na'kedness** *n.*—**na'kedly** *adv.*
nakong' *n.* an African antelope, the water koodoo.
na'loop *n.* in S. Africa, the weak spirit obtained at the end of a charge in distilling brandy.
nam'by-pam'by *a.* weakly sentimental; ineffectual, insipid.
name *n.* the word by which a person, thing, etc., is denoted; reputation.—*v.t.* to give a name to; to call by a name; appoint; mention.–**name'less** *a.*–**name'ly** *adv.* that is to say.—**name'sake** *n.* a person having the same name as another.
namm'a hole *n.* Australia, native well.
nan'du (-dōō) *n.* the S. American ostrich.
nankeen' *n.* yellow cotton cloth.
nap *n.* woolly surface on cloth.
nap *v.i.* to take a short sleep, doze.—*n.* —*n.* a card game.
na'palm (nȧ'-) *n.* a highly inflammable petroleum jelly, used in bombs.
nape *n.* the back of the neck.
na'pery *n.* household (table) linen
naph'tha *n.* an inflammable oil distilled from coal, etc.—**naph'thalene** *n.*
nap'kin *n.* a square piece of linen used for wiping fingers or lips at table; a small towel, *esp.* for use with babies.
napoo' *interj.* (*sl.*) no more, finished.
narciss'us *n.* bulbous plant with white scented flower (-**ciss'uses**, -**ciss'i** (-ī) *pl.*).
nar'colepsy *n.* a condition marked by short attacks of irresistible drowsiness.
narco'sis *n.* the effect of a narcotic.
narcot'ic *n.* a drug causing sleep or insensibility.—*a.* inducing sleep.
nardoo' *n.* an Australian plant, whose spores are used as food by the aborigines.
nar'ghile (-gi-lā) *n.* an Eastern hookah or tobacco-pipe in which the smoke is drawn through water.
nark' *n.* (*sl.*) informer, police spy.—*v.t.*
narrate' *v.t.* to relate, tell (story).—**narra'tion** *n.*—**narr'ative** *n.* an account or story.—*a.* relating.—**narra'tor** *n.*
narr'ow (-ō) *a.* of little breadth.—*n.* a narrow part of a strait.—*v.t.* to make narrow.—*v.i.* to become narrow.—**narro'wly** *adv.*—**narr'owness** *n.*
nar'whal *n.* a sea animal with a tusk or tusks developed from teeth.
na'sal (-z-) *a.* relating to the nose.—*n.* sound partly produced in the nose.—**na'salise** *v.t.* to make nasal in sound.
nas'cent *a.* just coming into existence.
nastur'tium (-shum) *n.* a genus of plants which includes the watercress and a garden plant with red or orange flowers.
nas'ty (nȧ-) *a.* foul, disagreeable.—**nast'ily** *adv.*–**nas'tiness** *n.*–**nas'tiest** *sup.*
na'tal *a.* of birth.—**natal'ity** *n.*
na'tant *a.* floating, *n.* swimming.
nata'tion *n.* act or art of swimming.
natato'res (-tō'rēz) *n. pl.* birds that swim.—**natato'rial** *a.*
na'tion (-shn) *n.* a people or race organised as a state.—**na'tional** (nash-) *a.*—**nat'ionally** *adv.*—**nationali'ty** *n.* national quality or feeling; the fact of belonging to a particular nation.—**nat'ionalism** *n.*—**nat'ionalist** *n.* one who supports national rights.—**nat'ionalise** *v.t.*—**nationalisa'tion** *n.* the taking over and management by the state of trades and industries, land, etc., with or without compensation; change from private to state ownership.
Nation'al So'cialism *n.* the theories, policies and organisation of the former German National Sozialistische Arbeiter-partei (Nazi).
na'tive *a.* inborn; born in a particular place; found in a pure state; that was the place of one's birth.—*n.* one born in a place; member of non-European race; oyster reared in artificial bed.—**nativ'ity** *n.* birth, horoscope.—**The Nativity'**, birth of Christ; representation of this; Christmas, December 25th.
natt'erjack *n.* a kind of toad.
natt'y *a.* neat and smart.—**natt'ily** *adv.*
nat'ural *a.* of, according to, occurring in, provided by, nature.—*n.* a half-witted person; in music, a note neither sharp nor flat.—**nat'urally** *adv.*—**nat'uralist** *n.* one who studies plants and animals.—**nat'uralise** *v.t.* to admit to citizenship; to accustom to a new climate.—**naturalisa'tion** *n.*
nature *n.* innate, essential qualities of thing; class, sort; life force; power underlying all phenomena in material world; material world as a whole.
naught (nawt) *n.* nothing, zero.—*a.* bad, useless.—**naught'y** *a.* not behaving well. —**naught'ily** *adv.*—**naught'iness** *n.*
nau'sea (-si-a) *n.* sickness.—**nau'seate** *v.t.* to affect with sickness; to disgust.—**nau'seous** *a.* sickening, loathsome.
nautch (nawch) *n.* in India, a ballet dance by women called nautch-girls.
naut'ical *a.* of seamen or ships.
nau'tilus (naw-) *n.* a univalvular shell-fish; a form of diving-bell which requires no suspension (-**tiluses**, -**tili** *pl.*).
naval *see* **navy.**
nave *n.* a hub of a wheel; the body of a church from the W. door to the choir.
na'vel *n.* the small pit on the belly.

nav'igate *v.i.* to sail.—*v.t.* to sail over; to direct the steering of a ship.—**nav'igator** *n.* one who navigates; a worker employed in digging a canal.—**nav'igable** *a.*—**naviga'tion** *n.*
navv'y *n.* a person employed at heavy, unskilled labour on roads, etc.
na'vy *n.* a fleet; the warships of a country with their crews and organisation.—**na'val** *a.*—**na'vies** *pl.*
nawab' (-wawb') *n.* in India, a viceroy; [a nabob.
nay *adv.* no.
Na'zi (nát'-) member of the National Socialist Party in Germany.
ne- *prefix* not, as *nefarious*, *neuter*.
Nean'derthal *a.* to denote man of the earliest long-headed race in Europe.
neap *a.* neap tide, the low tide at the first and third quarters of the moon.
near *adv.* at or to a short distance.—*prep.* close to.—*a.* close at hand, close; closely related; stingy; of horses, vehicles, etc., left.—*v.t.* and *i.* to approach.—**near'ly** *adv.* closely; almost.—**near-sight'ed** *a.* unable to see far.—**near miss**, almost a hit.
neat *n.* ox, cow; cattle.—**neat'herd** *n.*
neat *a.* pure, undiluted; simple and elegant; deft.—**neat'ly** *adv.*—**neat'ness** *n.*
neb'ula *n.* cluster of stars (**-ulae** *pl.*).—**neb'ular** *a.*—**neb'ulous** *a.* vague.
nec'essary (nes-) *a.* needful, requisite, that must be done.—*n.* a needful thing.—**nec'essarily** *adv.*—**necess'ity** *n.* a constraining power or state of affairs; a being needful; a needful thing; poverty. (**-ies** *pl.*).—**necess'itate** *v.t.* to make necessary.—**necess'itous** *a.* poor, needy. *Syn.* essential, needful, requisite. *Ant.* unnecessary, inessential, needless.
neck *n.* part of body joining head to shoulders; narrower part of bottle, etc.; narrow piece of anything between wider parts.—*v.t.* (*sl.*) to swallow; (U.S.) (*sl.*) to hug and kiss.—**neck'erchief** (-chif) *n.* kerchief for the neck.—**neck'lace** *n.* ornament round neck.—**neck'let** *n.* ornament, piece of fur, etc., to go round neck.—**neck'tie** *n.*
necrol'atry *n.* ancestor worship.
nec'romancy *n.* magic, *esp.* by supposed communication with the dead.—**nec'romancer** *n.* wizard, magician.
necropo'lis *n.* a cemetery (**-olises** (-lis-ez), **-oleis** (-lis) *pl.*).
necrosis *n.* gangrene, *esp.* of a bone.
nec'tar *n.* the drink of the gods; the honey of flowers.—**nect'arine** *a.*—*n.* variety of smooth-skinned peach.
nec'tary *n.* the honey-gland of a flower.
née (nā) *a.* born; used to indicate a woman's maiden name.
need *n.* a want, requirement; necessity; poverty.—*v.t.* to want, require.—**need'ful** *a.* necessary.—**need'less** *a.*—**needs** *adv.* of necessity (only in **needs must** or **must needs**).—**need'y** *a.* poor.
need'fire *n.* a fire produced by friction; phosphorescent light; a beacon.
nee'dle *n.* thin, pointed tool with a hole for thread, used in sewing; a knitting pin; magnetised bar of a compass; an obelisk; a leaf of fir or pine.—**nee'dle-bush** *n.* Australia, two trees armed with sharp, thin spines.—**nee'dle-gun** *n.* firearm in which cartridge is exploded by slender pin.—**needle'-valve** *n.* valve with very small opening controlled by slender needle-shaped rod.
nefar'ious (-ér-) *a.* wicked.
negate' *v.t.* to deny, nullify.—**nega'tion** *n.* denial; opposite.
neg'ative *a.* expressing denial or refusal; wanting in positive qualities; not positive.—*n.* a negative word or statement; in photography, a picture made by the action of light on chemicals in which the lights and shapes are reversed.—*v.t.* to disprove, reject, contradict.
neglect' *v.t.* to disregard, take no care of; fail to do; omit through carelessness—*n.* the fact of neglecting or being neglected.—**neglect'ful** *a.*—**neg'ligence** *n.*—**neg'ligent** *a.* careless.—**neg'ligible** *a.* which can be overlooked.—**neg'ligently** *adv.* *Syn.* omit, overlook, slight. *Ant.* care for, cherish, regard.
neg'ligee (-zhā) *n.* an easy, unceremonious attire, loose gown.
nego'tiate *v.i.* to discuss with a view to finding terms of agreement.—*v.t.* to arrange by conference; transfer (a bill, cheque, etc.); get over (an obstacle).—**nego'tiable** *a.*—**negotia'tion** *n.*
ne'gro *n.* man of the black, woolly-haired African race (**ne'groes** *pl.*).—**ne'gress** *fem.*—**ne'groid** *a.*
ne'gus *n.* hot wine and water flavoured.
neigh (nā) *v.i.* of a horse, to utter its cry.
neigh'bour (nā'ber) *n.* one who lives near another.—**neigh'bouring** *a.* situated near by.—**neigh'bourhood** *n.* district; people of a district; region round about.—**neigh'bourly** *a.* friendly.
nei'ther *a.* and *pron.* not the one or the other.—*adv.* not either.—*conj.* nor yet.
nek *n.* in South Africa, a narrow ridge of land joining together two mountains.
nem'esis *n.* retribution.
nen'ta *n.* in S. Africa, a disease contracted by animals while grazing.
neolith'ic *a.* of later stone age.—**neol'ogism** *n.* new coined word or phrase.
ne'ophyte *n.* new convert; a beginner.
ne'on *n.* one of the inert constituent gases of the atmosphere.—**neon'-light** *n.* a brilliant, fog-penetrating form of electric light produced by high voltage discharge through rarefied neon.
neo-so'cialist *n.* a member of a political organisation (in France) which separated from the Socialist Party to combat fascism.—**neo-so'cialism** *n.*
ne'oteric *a.* new; newfangled.

neph'ew *n.* a brother's or sister's son.
ne'potism *n.* favouritism.
Nep'tune *n.* the god of the sea; the planet farthest from the sun.
neptun'ium (tūn-i-um) *n.* a radio-active element obtained by the bombardment of uranium with neutrons, used in the atom bomb.
nereid (nē'-rē-id) *n.* a sea-nymph.
nerve *n.* sinew, tendon; a fibre or bundle of fibres conveying feeling, impulses to motion, etc., to and from the brain and other parts of the body; assurance, coolness in danger.—*pl.* irritability, unusual sensitiveness to fear, annoyance, etc.—*v.t.* to give courage or strength to.—**nerve'less** *a.*—**ner'vous** *a.* of the nerves; vigorous; excitable, timid.—**nerv'ously** *adv.*—**nerv'ousness** *n.*—**nerv'y** *a.*
nes'cient (nesh'yent) *a.* ignorant, agnostic.—**nes'cience** *n.*
ness *n.* a headland, cape.
nest *n.* the place in which a bird lays and hatches its eggs; an animal's breeding place; any snug retreat.—*v.i.* to make or have a nest.—**nes'tle** (-sl) *v.i.* to settle comfortably.—**nest'ling** *n.* a bird too young to leave the nest.
net *n.* an open-work fabric or meshes of cord, etc.; a piece of it used to catch fish, etc.—*v.t.* and *i.* to cover with, or catch in, a net.—**net'ting** *n.* string or wire net.
net *a.* left after all deductions; free from deduction.—*v.t.* to gain as clear profit.
neth'er (-th-) *a.* lower.—**nether'most** *a.*
net'suke (-sū-kā) *n.* carved wooden or ivory toggle or button worn by Japanese.
net'tle *n.* a plant with stinging hairs on the leaves.—*v.t.* to irritate, provoke.—**ne'ttle-rash** *n.* a disorder of the skin.—**net'tle-tree** *n.* in Australia, one of several trees, the leaves of which possess rigid stinging hairs.
neural'gia (nū-) *n.* pain in the nerves, *esp.* in the face and head.—**neural'gic** *a.*
neurasthe'nia *n.* nervous debility.—**neurasthe'nic** *a.*—**neuri'tis** *n.* inflammation of nerves.
neuro'sis *n.* nervous disease without lesion of parts.—**neurot'ic** *a.* suffering from nervous disorder; abnormally sensitive.—*n.* a neurotic person.
neut'er *a.* neither masculine nor feminine.—*n.* a neuter word; the neuter gender.—**neut'ral** *a.* taking neither side in a war, dispute, etc.; without marked qualities; belonging to neither of two classes.—*n.* a neutral state, or a subject of one.—**neutral'ity** *n.*—**neut'ralise** *v.t.* to make ineffective; to counterbalance.
neu'trodyne *a.* in wireless, a form of valve control to prevent interference and gain clearness of sound.
neu'tron *n.* a minute particle, part of the atom, electrically neutral, and consisting of an electron and proton closely associated.
névé' (nā-vā') *n.* a mass of snow-ice, not yet converted into a glacier.
nev'er *adv.* at no time; not at all.—**nevertheless'** *adv.* for all that.
nev'er-nev'er *n.* the thinly-populated country, *esp.* in W. Queensland, Central and N. Australia.
new *a.* not existing before, fresh; that has lately come into some state or existence.—*adv.* (usually **new-**) recently, fresh.—**newfang'led** (-ng-gld) *a.* of new fashion.—**new'ly** *adv.*—**new'ness** *n.*—**news'paper** *n.* a periodical publication containing news.—**news** *n.* report of recent happenings; fresh information.—**newsvend'or** *n.* a newspaper seller.—**news'monger** *n.* a gossip.—**news'-reel** *n.* short cinema film illustrating current news.—**news theatre** *n.* *Syn.* novel, recent, modern. *Ant.* old, stale, worn, antiquated.
newel *n.* the central pillar of a winding staircase; the post at the top or bottom of a staircase rail.
Newfound'land *n.* a kind of large dog.
newt *n.* a small amphibious creature.
next *a.* nearest (as *next house*); immediately following.—*sup.* of **nigh.**—*adv.* on the first future occasion.
nex'us *n.* tie; connection (nex'us *pl.*).
ni'acin (-a-sin) *n.* vitamin B_5, deficiency in which results in pellagra and other deficiency diseases.
nib *n.* split pen-point; bird's bill.—*pl.* crushed cocoa beans.
nib'ble *v.t.* to take little bites of.—*v.i.* to take little bites.—*n.* a little bite.
nib'lick *n.* golf-club with deep, iron head, for high angle shots.
nice *a.* hard to please; careful, exact; difficult to decide; minute; subtle, fine; (*sl.*) pleasant, friendly, kind, agreeable, etc.—**nice'ly** *adv.*—**ni'cety** *n.* precision; minute distinction or detail.—**-ies** *pl.*
niche (-tsh) *n.* a recess in a wall.
nick *v.t.* to make a notch in, indent; just catch in time.—*n.* a notch, score; the exact point of time.
nick'el *n.* silver-white metal used in alloys and plating; Amer., 5-cent coin.
nick'name *n.* a name added to or replacing an ordinary name, e.g. *William the Silent*, *Boney* (for Napoleon).—*v.t.*
nic'otine (ēn) *n.* a poisonous oily liquid extracted from tobacco.—**nic'otinism** *n.* tobacco poisoning.
nic'tate *v.i.* to wink.
niece *n.* a brother's or sister's daughter.
nif'ty *a.* (*sl.*) in N. America, neat; smart.
nigg'ard *n.* a stingy person, miser.—**nigg'ardly** *a.* and *adv.*
nigge'r *n.* a negro; dark brown colour.
nigg'ling *a.* fussy; petty and over-elaborate, finicking.
nigh (nī) *a.*, *adv.* and *prep.* near.
night (nīt) *n.* the time of darkness between day and day; end of daylight; dark.—**night'ly** *a.* happening or done

every night; of the night.—**night'ly** *adv.* every night, by night.—**night'-club** *n.* establishment for dancing, music, etc., remaining open till morning.—**night'-effect** *n.* in wireless, transmission phenomena occurring after sunset, e.g., fading.—**night'ingale** (-ng-g-) *n.* a small bird which sings usually at night.—**night'-mare** *n.* a bad dream.—**night'shade** *n.* various plants of the potato family, some of them with very poisonous berries.

ni'hilism *n.* rejection of all religious and moral principles; opposition to all constituted authority.—**ni'hilist** *n.*

niks. *See* **nix.**

nil *n.* nothing, zero.

nim'ble *a.* active, quick.—**nim'bly** *adv.*

nim'bus *n.* a cloud of glory, a halo; a rain-cloud or storm-cloud (**-bi, -buses** *pl.*).

nim'rod *n.* a hunting enthusiast, *esp.* big game hunting.

nin'compoop *n.* feeble character, fool.

nine *a.* and *n.* the cardinal number next above eight.—**ninth** (-ī-) *a.*—**ninth'ly** *adv.*—**ninet'y** *a./n.* nine tens.—**nine'tieth** *a.*—**nine'pins** *n. pl.* skittles.

ninn'y *n.* a fool; a simpleton; a doll.

nio'bium *n.* a rare metal found in the mineral tantalite.

nip *v.t.* to pinch sharply; detach by pinching; check growth (of plants) thus.—*n.* a pinch; a check to growth; sharp coldness of weather; a sip, small drop of liquid.—**nipper'** *n.* (*sl.*) a small boy.—**nipp'ers** *n. pl.* pincers.

nip'ple *n.* the point of a breast, a teat.

nirva'na (-vȧ-) *n.* in Buddhism, extinction of desire in affinity with the divine.

ni'si *conj.* in law, if not, unless.—**decree' ni'si** a decree (*esp.* divorce) that takes effect after a certain period, provided no cause is shown for rescinding it.

Niss'en hut *n.* a long portable hut, semi-circular in section.

nit *n.* egg of a louse or other parasite.

ni'ton *n.* former name for radon.

ni'tre *n.* potassium nitrate, saltpetre.—**ni'trate** *n.* a compound of nitric acid and an alkali.—**ni'trogen** *n.* one of the gases making up the air.—**nitrog'enous** (-j-) *a.* of or containing nitrogen.—**ni'tric** *a.*—**ni'trous** *a.*—**nitrogly'cerine** (-s-) *n.* an explosive liquid.

nit'wit *n.* (*sl.*) a blockhead, fool.

nix, niks *n.* in S. Africa and Australia, nothing.—**nix'-nie** *n.* absolutely nothing.—**nix'nuts** *n.* a stupid and incapable person; a rogue.

no *a.* not any.—*adv.* expresses a negative reply to question or request.—*n.* a refusal; a denial; a voter against a motion (**noes** *pl.*).—**no'body** *n.* no person; a person of no importance.—**noth'ing** (nuth'-) *n.* not anything.

nob' *n.* (*sl.*) head; a swell, an upper-class gentleman; (*cribbage*) the knave.

nob'bler *n.* in Australia, a glass of spirits.—**nob'blerise** *v.i.* to drink heavily.

no'ble *a.* distinguished by deeds, character, rank or birth; of lofty character; impressive; excellent.—*n.* a member of the nobility.—**nobil'ity** *n.* class holding special rank, usually hereditary, a being noble.—**no'bly** *adv.*—**no'bleman** *n.*

noctur'nal *a.* of, in, or by, night; active by night.—**noc'turne** *n.* a dreamy piece of music; a night scene.

nod *v.i.* to bow the head slightly and quickly in assent, command, etc.; to let the head droop with sleep.—*v.t.* to incline (the head) thus.—*n.*

nod'dle *n.* the head.

node *n.* a knot or knob; a point at which a curve crosses itself.—**no'dal** *a.*

nod'ule *n.* a little knot; a rounded irregular mineral mass.

noet'ic *a.* in psychology, relating to, or originating in, the intellect.—**noet'ical** *a.*

nog *n.* a tree-nail; a timber-brick.—**nogg'ing** *n.* a wall of scantling and bricks.

nogg'in *n.* a small mug; a gill.

noise *n.* clamour, din; any sound.—*v.t.* to rumour.—**noise'less** *a.*—**nois'y** *a.*—**nois'ily** *adv.*—**nois'iness** *n.* being noisy.

noi'some *a.* disgusting.

nomad *a.* roaming from pasture to pasture.—*n.* a member of a nomad tribe; a wanderer.—**nomad'ic** *a.*

no-man's-land *n.* the ground between trenches occupied by hostile armies.

no'menclature *n.* a system of names.

nom'inal *a.* of a name or names; existing only in name.—**nom'inally** *adv.*—**nom'inate** *v.t.* to propose as a candidate; appoint to an office.—**nom'inator** *n.*—**nomina'tion** *n.*—**nominee'** *n.*

non- *prefix* makes compounds which negative the idea of the simple word, e.g., **non-com'batant** *n.* one who does not fight; **non-commiss'ioned** *a.* not commissioned. The meaning of those not given should be sought by reference to the simple word.

non'age *n.* minority; period of youth.

nonagenar'ian (-ê-) *a.* between 90 and 100 years old.—*n.* one of such age.

non'agon *n.* a nine-sided figure.

nonce *n.* **for the-** for the occasion only.

non'chalant (-sh-) *a.* unconcerned.—**non'chalantly** *adv.*—**non'chalance** *n.*

non-comm'ittal *a.* remaining neutral.

nonconform'ist *n.* one who does not conform to the established church, a dissenter.—**nonconform'ity** *n.*

non'da *n.* in Australia, an indigenous tree; its edible fruit resembling a plum.

non'descript *a.* not easily described, indeterminate, indefinite.

none (nun) *pron.* no one.—*a.* no (none other than).—*adv.* in no way.

nonen'tity *n.* non-existence; a non-existent thing; a person of no importance.

nonil'ion (nō-nil'-yon) *n.* a number represented by 1 and 30 noughts.

nonpareil' (-rel) *a.* unequalled.—*n.*
nonplus' *n.* a state of perplexity, a deadlock.—*v.t.* to bring to a nonplus.
non'sense *n.* lack of sense; language without meaning.—**nonsen'sical** *a.*
non'such *n.* person without equal.
noo'dle *n.* a simpleton, a foolish person.—**noo'dles** *n. pl.* strips of rolled dough, used in soup, etc.
nook (-ōō-) *n.* a sheltered corner.
noon (-ōō-) *n.* midday.—**noon'day, noon'tide** *n.* the time about noon.
noose (-ōō-) *n.* a running loop; snare.—*v.t.* to catch in a noose.
nor *conj.* and not.
nor'dic *a.* pertaining to one of the fundamental racial types of mankind, distributed over Scandinavia, Britain and N.W. Europe.
norm *n.* a rule, standard; model.
nor'mal *a.* perpendicular; conforming to type, natural, regular, ordinary.—**nor'mally** *adv.*—**normal'ity** *n.*
north (-th) *n.* to people in the N. Temperate Zone, the region or cardinal point opposite to the midday sun; the part of the world, of a country, etc., towards this point.—*adv.* towards or in the north.—*a.* to, from, or in, the north.—**nor'therly** (-th-) *a.*—**nor'thern** *a.*
nose *n.* the organ of smell, used also in breathing; prow.—*v.t.* to detect by smell.—*v.i.* to smell—**nose'dive** *n.* a swift downward plunge by aircraft.—**nose'-gay** *n.* a bunch of flowers.
nosol'ogy *n.* the branch of medicine treating generally of diseases; classification of the phases of disease.
nostal'gia *n.* home-sickness.
nos'tril *n.* one of two openings of nose.
nos'trum *n.* a quack medicine; a pet scheme (**-trums** *pl.*).
not *adv.* expressing negation.
no'table *a.* worthy of note, remarkable.—**no'tably** *adv.*—**notabil'ity** *n.* eminent person.—**no'tary** *n.* one authorised to draw up deeds, etc.—**nota'tion** *n.* representing of numbers, quantities, etc., by symbols; set of these; in N. Amer., foot-note, memorandum.
notch *n.* a V-shaped cut or indentation.—*v.t.* to make notches in; to score.
note *n.* a symbol standing for a musical sound; a single tone; a mark, sign; a brief written message, memorandum, letter; fame, regard.—*v.t.* to observe; to set down.—**no'ted** *a.* well known.—**note'-worthy** *a.* worth noting, remarkable.
noth'ing (nuth-) *n.* no thing; not anything, naught.—*adv.* not at all.
no'tice (-tis) *n.* warning, intimation, announcement, a bill, etc., with an announcement.—*v.t.* to mention; observe; give attention to.—**no'ticeable** *a.*
no'tify (-ī) *v.t.* to report, give notice of or to (**-ified** *p.t.* and *p.p.*—**-ifying** *pres. p.*).—**notifi'able** *a.*—**notifica'tion** *n.*
no'tion *n.* an idea, opinion, belief; fancy.
notor'ious *a.* known for something bad; well known.—**notori'ety** *n.*
notwithstand'ing *prep.* in spite of.—*adv.* all the same.—*conj.* although.
nou'gat (nōō'gȧ) *n.* a soft kind of toffee.
nought (nawt) *n.* nothing; a cipher (0).
noum'enon *n.* a thing as discerned by the understanding (**noum'ena** *pl.*).
noun (nown) *n.* a word used as a name of person, idea, or thing.
nour'ish (nur'-) *v.t.* to supply with food; keep up.—**nour'ishment** *n.*
nous (nows) *n.* mind; sense; talent.
nov'el *a.* new, strange.—*n.* a fictitious tale published as a whole book.—**nov'elist** *n.* a writer of novels.—**nov'elty** *n.*—**novelette'** *n.* a short novel.
Novem'ber *n.* the eleventh month.
nov'ice *n.* a candidate for admission to a religious order; one new to anything.—**novi'tiate, novi'ciate** (-vish-) *n.*
no'vocaine (nō'-) *n.* a harmless form of cocaine used as a local anæsthetic in dentistry (protected trade name).
now *adv.* at the present time.—**now'a-days** *adv.* in these times.
nowel (nou-, nō-) *n.* the inner part of a large mould used for castings.
Now'el, No'el *n.* Christmas.
no'where *adv.* not in any place or state; in N. America (*sl.*) not in the reckoning; far behind; utterly defeated.
no'wise *adv.* in no way or degree.
nox'ious (-kshus) *a.* hurtful.
Syn. harmful, dangerous, insalubrious. *Ant.* innocuous, harmless, safe.
noz'zle *n.* a spout, *esp.* at end of hose.
nu'ance (nū'áns) *n.* a shade of difference.
nub' *n.* (*sl.*) knob; point, gist.
nu'bile *a.* marriageable.—**nubil'ity** *n.*
nu'clear *a.* forming a nucleus; having to do with nuclei.
nu'cleus *n.* a centre, kernel; the central unit of an atom (**nu'cleuses, nu'clei** *pl.*).
nude *a.* naked, unclothed.—**nu'dity** *n.*—**nu'dism** *n.* cult of living nude for health's sake.—**nu'dist** *n.*
nudge *v.t.* to touch with the elbow.
nu'gatory *a.* trifling.
nugg'et *n.* a rough lump of native gold.
nui'sance (nū-) *n.* something harmful, offensive, troublesome, or annoying.
null *a.* of no effect, invalid, void.—**null'ity** *n.* being null.—**null'ify** *v.t.* (**-ified** *p.t.* and *p.p.*—**-ifying** *pres. p.*).
null'ah *n.* in India, a water-course.
null'a-null'a (nōōl-) *n.* in Australia, a club used in battle by the aborigines.
numb (num) *a.* deprived of feeling.—*v.t.*
num'ber *n.* sum or aggregate; word or symbol saying how many; a single issue of a paper, etc., issued in regular series; classification as to singular or plural;

rhythm; metrical feet or verse; a company or collection.—*v.t.* to count; to class, reckon; give a number to; amount to.—**num'berless** *a.* countless.
num'bles *n. pl.* the entrails of a deer.
nu'meral *a.* of or expressing number. —*n.* a sign or word denoting a number. —**nu'merate** *v.t.* to count.—**numera'tion** *n.*—**nu'merator** *n.* the top part of a fraction, the figure showing how many of the fractional units are taken.—**numer'ical** *a.* of, or in respect of, number.—**nu'merous** *a.* many.
numismat'ic *a.* of coins.—*n.* in *pl.* the study of coins.—**numis'matist** *n.*
num'nah, num'dah *n.* a thick cloth placed under a saddle.
num'skull *n.* a dolt, a stupid person.
nun *n.* a woman living in a convent under religious vows.—**nunn'ery** *n.* a convent.
nun'cio (-shi-) *n.* a representative of the Pope at a foreign court (-**cios** (ōz) *pl.*).
nuncu'pate *v.t.* to vow publicly; to dedicate.—**nuncupative** *a.*
nup'tial *a.* of or relating to marriage or a marriage.—*n.* in *pl.* a marriage.
nurse *n.* one trained for care of sick or injured; woman tending another's child. —*v.t.* to act as nurse to.—**nurs'ery** *n.* room for children; rearing place for plants.—-**man** *n.* owner of nursery garden.—**nurs'ling** *n.* infant.
nur'ture *n.* bringing-up.—*v.t.* bring up.
nut *n.* fruit consisting of a hard shell and a kernel; a small block with a hole to be screwed on a bolt.—*v.i.* to gather nuts.—**nut-grass** *n.* Australia, S. Africa, etc., troublesome weed with bulb-like roots.—**nut'meg** *n.*the aromatic seed of an Indian tree.—**bon'duc nut, nick'er nut** *n.* Australia, fruit of an indigenous leguminous tree; the Molucca bean.
nu'tant *a.* nodding; bent downwards, of flowers.—**nuta'tion** *n.* a slight declination of the earth's axis.
nu'tria *n.* fur of a S. American rodent about the size and shape of a beaver.
nu'trient *a.* nourishing.—*n.*
nu'triment *n.* food.—**nutri'tion** (-trishn) *n.* the receiving or supply of food; food. —**nutri'tious** *a.* good in effects as food.
nux vom'ica *n.* the seed of an Eastern tree which yields strychnine.
nuz'zle *v.i.* to burrow or press with the nose; nestle (**nuz'zling** *pres. p.*).
nyctalo'pia (nik-ta-lō-) *n.* night blindness.—**nyc'talops** *n.* one afflicted with nyctalopia.
nyl'ghau (-gaw) *n* large Indian antelope.
Ny'lon *n.* a synthetic silk used for fabrics, bristles, etc. (protected trade name).
nymph *n.* a legendary semi-divine maiden living in the sea, woods, etc.
nym'pha *n.* pupa or chrysalis (-**phæ** *pl.*).
nym'phomania *n.* excessive and morbid sexual desire in women.

O

oaf *n.* a changeling; a dolt (**oafs, oaves** *pl.*).
oak *n.* a familiar forest tree.—**oak'en** *a.*
oak'um *n.* loose fibre got by picking old rope and used for caulking.
oar *n.* a wooden lever with a broad blade worked by the hands to propel a boat.—**oars'man** *n.*—**oars'manship** *n.*
oa'sis (ō-ā'-) *n.* a fertile spot in the desert (**oa'ses** (-sēz) *pl.*).
oast *n.* a kiln for drying hops.
oat *n.* a grain of a common cereal plant (usually *pl.*), the plant.—**oat'en** *a.*—**oat'meal** *n.* ground or rolled oats.
oath *n.* the confirmation of the truth of a statement by the naming of something sacred; an act of swearing (**oaths** *pl.*).
ob-, with its forms **o-, oc-, of-, op-, os-**, *prefix* against, in front, in or on, as *obloquy, omit, occur, oppose, ostensible.*
ob'durate *a.* stubborn.—**ob'duracy** *n.*
Syn. hard, callous, impenitent, inflexible. *Ant.* yielding, flexible, obedient.
obeah', obi' (ōbay'a) *n.* native West African magic; a fetish.
obedient *a.* doing what one is told to do.
obeis'ance (-bās-, or -bēs-) *n.* a bow, a curtsey; homage, respect.
ob'elisk *n.* tapering stone shaft of rectangular section with pyramid top.
obese' *a.* very fat.—**obe'sity** *n.*
obey' (-bā') *v.t.* do bidding of.—**obe'dience** *n.*—**obe'dient** *a.*—**obe'diently** *adv.*
ob'fuscate *v.t.* to stupefy.
ob'iter *adv.* incidentally.—**o'biter dic'tum** an incidental opinion (**dic'ta** *pl.*).
obit'uary *n.* a notice or record of a death.
ob'ject *n.* a material thing; that to which feeling or action is directed; an end or aim; a word dependent on a verb or preposition.—**object'** *v.t.* to state in opposition.—*v.i.* to feel dislike or reluctance to something.—**objec'tion** *n.*—**objec'tionable** *a.*—**object'ive** *a.* external to the mind.—*n.* a thing or place aimed at.—**objectiv'ity** *n.*—**objec'tor** *n.*
ob'jurgate *v.t.* to scold.—**objurga'tion** *n.*
oblate' *a.* of sphere, flattened at poles.
obla'tion *n.* an offering.—**ob'late** *n.* a person dedicated to religious work.
obliga'to *a.* in music, of an accompaniment, necessary to the effect.
oblige' *v.t.* to bind morally or legally to do a service; to compel.—**obliga'tion** *n.* a binding promise; a debt of gratitude; a favour; duty.—**oblig'atory** *a.* required; binding.—**ob'ligate** *v.t.*—**obli'ging** *a.* ready to serve others.
oblique' (-lēk) *a.* slanting; indirect.—**obliq'uity** *n.* indirectness; dishonesty.—**oblique'ly** (-lēk'li) *adv.*
oblit'erate *v.t.* to blot out.
obliv'ion *n.* forgetting.—**obliv'ious** *a.*

ob'long *a.* rectangular with adjacent sides unequal.—*n.* an oblong figure.
ob'loquy *n.* abuse, disgrace, reproach. *Syn.* disgrace, odium, infamy. *Ant.* favour, respect, esteem.
obnox'ious (-ok'shus) *a.* offensive.
o'boe (-boi) *n.* a wood-wind instrument.
ob'ole *n.* a weight of 10 grains; a small coin of ancient Greece.
obscene' *a.* indecent.—**obscen'ity** *n.*
obscure' *a.* dark, dim; indistinct; unexplained; humble.—*v.t.* to dim; conceal; make unintelligible.—**obscu'rant** *n.* one who opposes enlightenment or reform.—**obscu'rantism** *n.*—**obscu'rity** *n.*
ob'secrate *v.t.* to beseech; to entreat.—**obsecra'tion** *n.* act of imploring.
ob'sequies (-iz) *n. pl.* funeral rites.
obse'quious *a.* servile, fawning.
observe' (-z-) *v.t.* to keep, follow; watch; note systematically; notice; remark.—*v.i.* make a remark.—**observ'able** *a.*—**observ'ably** *adv.*—**observ'ant** *a.* quick to notice.—**observ'ance** *n.* paying attention; keeping.—**observa'tion** *n.* action or habit of observing; noticing; a remark.—**observ'atory** *n.* a place for watching stars, etc.—**observ'er** *n.*
obsess' *v.t.* to haunt, fill the mind.—**obses'sion** *n.*—a fixed, haunting idea.
obsid'ian *n.* a fused volcanic rock.
ob'solete *a.* no longer in use, out of date.—**obsoles'cent** *a.* going out of use.
ob'stacle *n.* a thing in the way.
obstet'ric *a.* of midwifery.—*n.* in *pl.* the science of midwifery.—**obstetri'cian** *n.* one skilled in obstetrics.
ob'stinate *a.* stubborn.—**ob'stinacy** *n.*
obstrep'erous *a.* unruly, noisy.
obstruct' *v.t.* to hinder; block up.—**obstruc'tion** *n.*—**obstruc'tionist** *n.*
obtain' *v.t.* to get.—*v.i.* to be customary.—**obtain'able** *a.* procurable.
obtem'per *v.t.* Scots law, to obey.
obtrude' *v.t.* to thrust forward unduly, to push in where unwanted.—**obtru'sion** *n.*—**obtru'sive** *a.*—**obtru'sively** *adv.*
obtuse' *a.* not sharp or pointed; greater than a right angle; stupid.—**obtuse'ly** *adv.*
ob'verse *n.* the side of a coin or medal opposite the side with the chief design.
ob'viate *v.t.* to prevent, to clear away.
ob'vious *a.* clear, plain, evident. *Syn.* plain, manifest, open. *Ant.* hidden, obscure, doubtful.
ocari'na (-rē-) *n.* a small wind instrument of music made of terra-cotta.
occa'sion *n.* opportunity; reason, need; immediate but subsidiary cause; time when a thing happens.—*v.t.* to cause.—**occa'sional** *a.* happening or found now and then.—**occa'sionally** *adv.* sometimes.
oc'cident(-ks-)*n.* the West.—**occident'al** *a.*
oc'ciput (ok'si-) *n.* the hind part of the head.—**occip'ital** *a.* pertaining to this.
occult' *a.* secret, mysterious.—*v.t.* to hide from view.—**occulta'tion** *n.*
occ'upy *v.t.* to take possession of; inhabit; fill; employ (**occ'upied** *p.t.* and *p.p.* —**-pying** *pres. p.*).—**occu'pancy** *n.* fact of occupying; residing.—**occ'upant** *n.*—**occupa'tion** *n.* seizure; possession; employment.—**occupa'tional** *a.* to do with an occupation, *esp.* of diseases arising from a particular occupation.—**occupa'tional ther'apy,** the treatment of mental and physical defects by the teaching of occupational skills.—**occ'upier** *n.* (he **oc'cupies**).
occur' *v.i.* to happen; come to mind; to be found.—**occurr'ence** *n.* event.
o'cean (ō'shn) *n.* the great body of water surrounding the land of the globe; a large division of this; the sea.—**ocean'ic** *a.*
oceanol'ogy (ō-shē-a-nol'o-ji) *n.* branch of science which relates to the ocean.
o'celot *n.* the leopard cat of America.
o'chre (ō'kẹr) *n.* various earths used as yellow or brown pigments.
oct-, oc'ta-, oc'to- *prefix* eight.—**oc'tagon** *n.* a figure with eight angles.—**octag'onal** *a.*—**oc'tave** *n.* a group of eight days; eight lines of verse; a note eight degrees above or below a given note; this space.—**octa'vo** *n.* a size of book in which each sheet is folded into eight leaves.—**Octo'ber** *n.* the tenth month (Roman eighth).—**octogena'rian** *a.* of an age between eighty and ninety.—*n.* a person of such age.—**oc'topus** *n.* a mollusc with eight arms covered with suckers (**-puses, -pi** *pl.*).—**octosyll'able** *n.* a word of eight syllables.—**octet', octette'** *n.* a group of eight.
oc'tant *n.* the eighth part of a circle; an instrument for measuring angles; having an arc of 45°.
octenn'ial *a.* happening every eighth year; lasting eight years.
oc'topod *a.* having 8 feet.—*n.* an animal with 8 feet.
oc'troi (-trwa) *n.* a duty paid on goods entering French cities.
oc'ular *a.* of the eye or sight.—**oc'ularly** *adv.*—**oc'ulist** *n.* an eye surgeon.
oc'ulomotor *a.* in anatomy, connected with movement of eye.
od *n.* a natural power supposed to produce the phenomena of mesmerism.
odd *a.* that is one in addition when divided by two; not even; not part of a set; strange, queer.—**odd'ity** *n.* quality of being odd; an odd person or thing.—**Odd'fellow** *n.* member of mutual aid society so named.—**odd'ments** *n. pl.* odd things.—**odds** *n. pl.* difference, balance; advantage to one of two competitors; advantage conceded in betting; likelihood.—**odds and ends,** odd fragments or left-over things.
ode *n.* a lyric poem of lofty style.
o'dium *n.* hatred, widespread dislike, blame.—**o'dious** *a.* hateful.
o'dour *n.* smell.—**o'dorise** *v.t.* to fil with

scent. — **o'dorous** *a.* — **o'dourless** *a.* — **odorif'erous** *a.* spreading an odour.

of *prep.* denotes removal, separation, ownership, attribute, material, etc.

off *adv.* away.—*prep.* away from; in traffic directions, farthest from pavement; (*cricket*) side of the field to right of batsman as he faces bowler; outside.—*a.* distant; of horses, vehicles, etc., right. —*prefix* off, from, away, as in offal, offset.—**off-chance** *n.* a slight chance.—**off-hand'** *a.* and *adv.* without previous thought or preparation, curt, aloof.—**off'-licence** *n.* permission to sell alcoholic liquors for consumption off the premises. —**off'-scourings** *n. pl.* worst part, dregs. —**off'set** *n.* side branch; in printing, smudges on back of one sheet taken from the still wet underlying sheets.—**offset process** in lithography, method of reproduction by which impressions are rolled on to paper by means of a rubber roller which took impressions off an inked plate.—**offside** *a.* and *adv.* in football, between the ball in play and the opponent's goal.—**off'spring** *n.* children, issue. —**off-white** *n.* and *a.* a greyish or yellowish white; impure white.—**off the beam** (*sl.*) incorrect (**on the beam** (*sl.*) right, correct).—**off'ing** *n.* more distant part of the sea visible to an observer.

off'al *n.* parts cut out in preparing a carcass for food; refuse, scraps.

offend' *v.t.* to displease.—*v.i.* to do wrong.—**offence'** *n.*—**offender'** *n.*—**offen'sive** *a.* causing displeasure.—*n.* position or movement of attack.

Syn. to annoy, shock, insult. *Ant.* please, humour, delight.

off'er *v.t.* to present for acceptance or refusal; propose; attempt.—*v.i.* present itself.—*n.* an offering, bid.—**off'ertory** *n.* collection in a church service.

off'ice *n.* a service; a duty; official position; form of worship; a place for doing business; a corporation carrying on business.—*pl.* the parts of a house in which the domestic work is done.—**off'icer** *n.* one in command in an army, navy, ship, etc.—*v.t.* to supply with officers.—**offi'cial** (-fish'-) *a.* having or by authority.—*n.* one holding an office, *esp.* in a public body.—**offi'cialism** *n.* undue official authority or routine.—**offi'cialdom** *n.* officials collectively; their work, usually in a contemptuous sense.—**offi'ciate** *v.i.* to perform the duties of an office; perform a service.—**offi'cious** (-ishus) *a.* meddlesome, interfering.

off'ing, off'set, etc., *see* **off.**

off'ward *adv.* (*naut.*), away from land.

oft, of'ten (of'n) *adv.* many times.

o'gee *n.* a moulding of two members, the one concave the other convex, somewhat like an S.

ogive' (-i-) *n.* a pointed arch.

o'gle *v.i.* and *t.* to make eyes.—*n.*

o'gre (-gẽr) *n.* a man-eating giant; hideous person.—**o'gress** *fem.*

oh *interj.* an exclamation of surprise, pain, anxiety.

ohm *n.* the unit of electrical resistance.

oil *n.* a light inflammable viscous liquid, obtained from various plants, animal substances, and minerals.—*v.t.* to apply oil to.—**oil'y** *n.*—**oil'cloth** *n.*—**oil'skin** *n.*

oint'ment *n.* a greasy preparation for healing or beautifying the skin.

oka'pi (-kà'-) *n.* an African animal allied to the giraffe.

O.K., okay' *inter.* (U.S.) (*sl.*) all right.

old (ōld) *a.* aged, long-lived; belonging to an earlier period (**old'er, eld'er** *comp.*—**old'est, eld'est** *sup.*).—**old'en** *a.* old.—**old-fash'ioned** *a.* in the style of an earlier period; out of date; fond of old ways.—**old man** *n.* in Australia, full-grown male kangaroo; hence **old-man** *a.* unusually large.

oleag'inous (ō-lē-aj'-) *a.* oily, producing oil; unctuous.—**oleag'inousness** *n.*

olean'der (ō-lē-an'-) *n.* poisonous, evergreen flowering shrub.

o'leograph *n.* lithograph in oil-colours.

oleom'eter *n.* an instrument for ascertaining the weight and purity of oils.

olfac'tory *a.* of smell.

ol'igarchy (-ki) *n.* government by a few.—**ol'igarch** *n.*—**oligarch'ic** *a.*

ol'ive (-iv) *n.* an evergreen tree; its oil-yielding fruit.—*a.* grey-green in colour.

om'elot, om'elette *n.* a dish of fried eggs with seasoning, etc.

omen *n.* a prophetic object or happening.—**om'inous** *a.* portending evil.

omit' *v.i.* to leave out, neglect.—**omis'sion** *n.* something left out.

om'nibus *n.* vehicle travelling on fixed route and taking passengers at any stage; volume containing several works. —*a.* serving or containing several objects.

om'ni-direc'tional *a.* in wireless, denotes transmission in which the waves are radiated in all directions.

omnip'otent *a.* all-powerful, almighty. —**omnip'otence** *n.*—**omnipres'ent** *a.* everywhere at the same time.—**omnipres'ence** *n.*—**omnis'cient** (-shi-ent) *a.* knowing everything.—**omnis'cience** *n.* —**omniv'orous** *a.* devouring all foods.

on *prep.* above and touching, at, near, towards, etc.—*adv.* so as to be on, forwards, etc.—*prefix* on, as **on'looker.** —**on'ward** *a.* and adv.

once (wuns) *adv.* one time; ever; formerly. —**at once** immediately.

on dit' (ōn dē') *n.* a rumour; gossip.

one (wun) *a.* lowest cardinal number; a single; a united; only, without others; identical.—*n.* number, figure 1; unity; single specimen.—*pron.* particular but not stated person; any person.—**oneself** *pron.*—**one'ness** *n.*—**one'-shot** in motoring, system of chassis lubrication.—

one'-step *n.* ballroom dance.—**one'-way** restricted to one direction only.
on'erous *a.* burdensome.
on'ion (un'yun) *n.* plant with a bulb of pungent flavour, used for flavouring.
on'ly (ō-) *a.* that is the one specimen.—*adv.* solely, merely, exclusively.—*conj.* but then, excepting that.
onomatopoeia (-pē'ya) *n.* formation of a word by using sounds that resemble or suggest the object or action to be named.—**onomatopoet'ic** (-po-et'-) *a.*
on'set *n.* a violent attack; an assault.
on'slaught (-slawt) *n.* a fierce attack.
on'to *prep.* on top of.
o'nus *n.* the burden; responsibility.
on'ward *a.* advanced or advancing.
on'weer *n.* in S. Africa, bad weather.
on'yx *n.* variety of quartz (on'yxes *pl.*).
oodles' *n. pl.* (*sl.*) an abundance.
o'olite (ō'o-līt) *n.* a limestone grained loosely like fish roe.
ool'ogy (ō-ol-) *n.* study of eggs, and of birds during the nesting season.
oom *n.* in South Africa, uncle; a term of affection and respect.
ooze *n.* wet mud, slime; sluggish flow.—*v.i.* to pass slowly through, exude.
o'pal *n.* a white or bluish stone with iridescent reflections.—**opales'cent** *a.* showing changing colours.
opaque' (ō-pāk') *a.* not allowing the passage of light.—**opa'city** (ō-pas'-) *n.*
ope *a.* and *v.* open (used poetically).
o'pen *a.* not shut or blocked up; without lid or door; bare; undisguised; not enclosed or covered or limited or exclusive.—*v.t.* to set open, uncover, give access to; disclose, lay bare; begin; make a hole in.—*v.i.* to become open.—*n.* clear space, unenclosed country.—**o'penly** *adv.* without concealment.—**o'pener** *n.*—**o'penness** *n.* frankness.—**o'pen-mind'ed** *a.* fair, not deciding beforehand.—**o'pening** *n.* a hole, gap; beginning.
op'era *n.* musical drama.—**operat'ic** *a.*—**op'eretta** *n.* short, light musical play.
operam'eter *n.* an instrument for recording the number of movements made by a part of a machine.
opera'tion *n.* working, way a thing works; scope; an act of surgery.—**op'erate** *v.i.*—**op'erative** *a.* working.—*n.* a mechanic.—**op'erator** *n.*
oper'culum (ō-per-) *n.* lid, cover (-culums, -cula *pl.*).—**oper'cular** *a.*
ophthal'mia *n.* inflammation of the eye.—**ophthal'mic** *a.*
opiate *see* **opium.**
opin'ion *n.* what one thinks about something; belief, judgment.—**opine'** *v.t.* to think; utter an opinion.—**opin'ionated** *a.* stubborn in holding an opinion.
o'pium *n.* a sedative and narcotic drug made from the poppy.—**o'piate** *v.t.* to mix with opium.—*n.* an opiated drug.
opop'anax (ō-pop-) *n.* a gum resin.
oposs'um *n.* small American marsupial animal which lives in trees; in Australia, term applied to the phalanger, usually shortened to **possum.**
oppo'nent *n.* adversary.—*a.* opposing.
opp'ortune *a.* seasonable, well-timed; —**opportu'nity** *n.* a favourable time or condition (-ies *pl.*).—**opp'ortunism** *n.* the policy of doing what is expedient at the time regardless of principle.
Syn. timely, welcome, seasonable. *Ant.* inopportune, unseasonable, untimely.
oppose' (-z) *v.t.* to set against; contrast; resist, withstand.—*past p.* adverse.—**oppo'ser** *n.*—**opp'osite** (-zit) *a.* contrary, facing, diametrically different.—**opposi'tion** (-ish-) *n.* a being opposite; resistance; a party opposed to that in power.
oppress' *v.t.* to govern with tyranny; weigh down.—**oppress'ive** *a.*—**oppress'ively** *adv.*—**oppres'sion** *n.*—**oppress'or** *n.*
oppro'brium *n.* disgrace; infamy; insult; scorn; abuse.—**oppro'brious** *a.*
oppugn' (o-pūn') *v.t.* to fight against; to oppose.—**oppug'nant** *a.* opposing.—*n.*
op'slag *n.* in S. Africa, a new growth of plants deriving from seed left in the ground at harvest time, *esp.* potatoes, sweet potatoes, etc.
opsoma'nia *n.* a morbid liking for some particular kind of food.
opson'in *n.* substance in blood which affects germs so that they can be destroyed by white corpuscles.—**opson'ic index** standard by which power of resistance to disease is estimated.
op'tative *n.* a mood of the verb expressing desire.
op'tic *a.* of the eye or sight.—*n.* the eye; in *pl.* the science of sight or light.—**op'tical** *a.*—**opti'cian** (-ish'-) *n.* a maker of or dealer in optical instruments.
op'timism *n.* disposition to look on the bright side; doctrine that good must prevail in the end.—**op'timist** *n.*—**optimis'tic** *a.*—**optimis'tically** *adv.*
op'tion *n.* choice; thing chosen.—**op'tional** *a.* not compulsory.
op'ulent *a.* rich.—**op'ulence** *n.* wealth.
o'pus *n.* a work; a musical composition (op'era *pl.*).—**mag'num o'pus,** supreme work. [treatise.
opus'cule (ō-pus'-) *n.* a little work or
or *conj.* introduces alternatives; if not.
or'acle *n.* place where the gods were consulted; an answer there given; very wise person.—**orac'ular** *a.* wise and mysterious; dogmatic; doubtful.
or'al *a.* by mouth.—**or'ally** *adv.*
or'ange (-inj) *n.* a familiar bright reddish-yellow round fruit; the tree bearing it; the colour of the fruit.—*a.*
orang'-outang', orang'-utan' *n.* a large, long-armed ape.
or'ator *n.* a maker of a speech, a skilful speaker.—**ora'tion** *n.* a formal speech.—**orator'ical** *a.* of orator or oration,

rhetorical.—**or'atory** *n.* speeches; eloquent language; small chapel.—**orato'rio** *n.* a semi-dramatic composition of sacred music (**-rios** (-ōz) *pl.*).

orb *n.* a globe,sphere; eye.—**orb'it** *n.* eye-socket; track of heavenly body.

orch'ard *n.* an enclosure containing fruit-trees.—**orch'ardist** *n.*

or'chestra (-k-) *n.* a band of musicians; the place they occupy in a theatre, etc.—**orches'tral** *a.*—**or'chestrate** *v.t.* to compose or arrange music for an orchestra.—**orchestra'tion** *n.*

or'chid, or'chis (-k-) *n.* various exotic plants with showy flowers.

ordain' *v.t.* to admit to the Christian ministry; confer holy orders upon; decree, destine, fix.—**ordina'tion** *n.*

or'deal *n.* a method of trial by requiring the accused to undergo a dangerous physical test; a trying experience.

or'der *n.* rank, class, group; monastic society, sequence, succession, arrangement; command, pass, instruction.—*v.t.* to arrange; command; require.—**or'derly** *a.* methodical.—*n.* soldier following an officer to carry orders; soldier in a military hospital acting as attendant.—**or'derliness** *n.*—**or'dinal** *a.* showing position in a series.—**or'dinary** *a.* usual, commonplace.—*n.* a bishop in his province; a public meal supplied at a fixed time and price.—**or'dinarily** *adv.* usually.
Syn. regularity, rule, system, injunction. *Ant.* chaos, confusion, rebellion.

ordin'ance *n.* an established rule, rite.

ord'nance *n.* guns, cannon; military stores.—**ord'nance sur'vey** the official survey of Great Britain.

or'dure *n.* dung; filth.

ore *n.* native mineral yielding metal.

o'read (ō're-ad) *n.* a mountain nymph.

or'gan *n.* a musical instrument of pipes worked by bellows and played by keys; a member of an animal or plant carrying out a particular function; a means of action; a newspaper.—**organ'ic** *a.* of the bodily organs; affecting bodily organs; having vital organs; organised, systematic.—**organ'ic chemistry** the chemistry of the carbon compounds.—**organ'ically** *adv.*—**or'ganism** *n.* an organised body or system.—**or'ganist** *n.* one who plays an organ.—**or'ganise** *v.t.* to give a definite structure; to get up, arrange, put into working order.—**organisa'tion** *n.*

or'gandie *n.* a muslin of great transparency and lightness.

or'gasm *n.* paroxysm of desire, rage or other passion.—**orgas'tic** *a.*

or'geat (or'zhat) *n.* a flavouring liquor extracted from barley and almonds.

or'gy (-ji) *n.* a drunken or licentious revel (**or'gies** *pl.*).—**orgias'tic** *a.*

or'ibi *n. see* **ourbei.**

or'iel *n.* a projecting part of an upper room with a window.

or'ient *n.* the East; the lustre of the best pearls.—*a.* rising; Eastern; of pearls, from Indian seas. —*v.t.* to place so as to face east; to find one's bearings.—**orien'tal** *a./n.*—**or'ientate** *v.t.* and *refl.* to orient; bring into clearly understood relations; to see how one stands.—**orienta'tion** *n.*—**orien'talist** *n.* expert in Eastern languages and history.

or'ifice *n.* opening, mouth of a cavity.

or'igin *n.* beginning, source, parentage.

ori'ginal (-ij-) *a.* primitive, earliest; new, not copied or derived; thinking or acting for oneself, eccentric.—*n.* a pattern, thing from which another is copied; an eccentric person.—**ori'ginally** *adv.*—**original'ity** *n.*—**ori'ginate** *v.t.* to bring into existence (**orig'inating** *pres. p.*).—**origina'tion** *n.*—**ori'ginator** *n.*
Syn. commencement, foundation, derivation. *Ant.* end, finish, culmination.

o'riole (ō'ri-ōl) *n.* a tropical bird.

Ori'on *n.* a bright constellation.

or'ison *n.* a prayer.

or'lop *n.* the lowest deck in a ship that has three or more decks.

or'molu (-lōō) *n.* gilded bronze; a gold-coloured alloy; articles of these.

or'nament *n.* decoration.—*v.t.* to adorn. —**ornament'al** *a.*—**ornamenta'tion** *n.*—

ornate' *a.* elaborately decorated.

ornithol'ogy *n.* the science of birds.—**ornitholo'gical** *a.*—**ornithol'ogist** *n.*

o'rotund *a.* resonant, clear; pompous.

or'phan *n.* a child bereaved of one or both of its parents.—**or'phanage** *n.* an institution for the care of orphans.

or'piment *n.* a yellow mineral of the arsenic group, used as colouring.

Or'pington *n.* a breed of poultry, white, black or buff, of general utility.

or'rery *n.* an instrument constructed to show the revolutions of the planets, their relative sizes, distances, etc.

or'ris *n.* the plant iris.—**or'ris root** violet-scented perfume from the dried roots of some kinds of iris.

ort *n.* a scrap of food; a fragment.

ortho- *prefix* makes combinations with the meaning of "straight," "correct," as in **or'thodox** *a.* holding accepted views; conventional.—**or'thodoxy** *n.*—**orthog'raphy** *n.* correct spelling.—**orthopaed'ic** *a.* for curing deformity.—**orthopae'dics** (-pē-) *n.* the science of correcting body deformities *esp.* in children.

orthop'tics *n.* the science of correcting ocular deviation, e.g. squint, by exercising the eye muscles.—**orthop'tist** *n.*

ort'olan *n.* a small bird, a bunting.

os'cillate *v.i.* swing to and fro; waver; in wireless, to set up wave motion.—**oscilla'tion** *n.*—**os'cillator** *n.* one that oscillates, *esp.* one setting up unauthorised wireless waves from a radio receiving set.—**oscill'ograph** *n.* device for recording electrical vibrations.

os'culate *v.t.* and *i.* to kiss.–**oscula'tion** *n.*
o'sier (-z-) *n.* a species of willow.
os'mium *n.* blue-white metallic element. —**os'mic, os'mious** *a.*
osmo'sis *n.* penetration of fluids through porous partitions.—Also **os'-mose.**—**osmo'tic** *a.*
os'prey *n.* the fishing eagle; egret plume.
oss'eous *n.* of or like bone.—**oss'ify** *v.t.* and *i.* to turn into bone.—**ossifica'tion** *n.*
osten'sible *a.* professed, used as a blind.—**osten'sibly** *adv.*—**ostenta'tion** *n.* show, display.—**ostenta'tious** *a.* showing off.
osteop'athy *n.* art of treating diseases by removing structural derangement by manipulation, *esp.* of spine.—**os'teopath** *n.* one skilled in this art.
os'tler, hos'tler (-sl-) *n.* man who attends to horses at inns.
os'tracise *v.t.* to exclude from society, exile.—**os'tracism** *n.* social exclusion.
os'trich *n.* a large swift-running bird.
oth'er (uth-) *a.* not this, not the same; alternative, different.–*pron.* other person or thing.–**oth'erwise** (-iz) *adv.* differently.
o'tiose (ō'shi-ōz) *a.* lazy, futile.
ott'er *n.* a furry aquatic animal.
Ott'oman *a.* Turkish.—*n.* a Turk; a cushioned seat without back or arms.
ought (awt) *v. aux.* expressing duty or obligation or advisability.
ounce *n.* a weight, the 12th of the troy pound, 16th of the avoirdupois pound; a lynx; a snow-leopard.
our *pron.* belonging to us.—**ourself'** *pron.* myself, used only in the regal or formal style.—**ourselves'** *pron. pl.* emphatic or reflexive form.
ou'rebi, o'ribi *n.* a yellowish, S. African antelope with straight horns.
ou'sel (ōō'zl) *n.* the blackbird; applied to others of the thrush family.
oust *v.t.* to put out, drive out.
ous'titi (wis-) *n.* a marmoset.
out *adv.* from within, from among, away, not in the usual or right state.—**out'ing** *n.* a pleasure, excursion.—**out'ward** *a.* and *adv.*–**out'wards** *adv.*–**out'wardly** *adv.*
out- as *prefix* makes many compounds with sense of "beyond," "in excess," etc., e.g., **outflank'** *v.t.* to get beyond the flank.—**out'put** *n.* quantity put out, etc. These are not given where the meaning may easily be found from simple word.
out'back *n.* in Australia, remote, sparsely populated country.—*a.*
out'balance *v.t.* to outweigh; to exceed.
out'board *a.* (*naut.*) away from the keel; outside a boat.—**outboard motor,** a small motor engine attached to the stern of a racing or rowing boat.
out'cast *n.* a vagabond; a pariah; a homeless, friendless person.—*a.* cast out.
outclass' *v.t.* to excel; to surpass.
out'crop *n.* in geology, the coming out of a stratum to the surface.—*v.i.* to come out to the surface (**out'cropped** or **out'-cropt** (-kropt) *p.t.* and *p.p.*).
out'door *a.* out of doors.
out'fit *n.* a fitting-out; equipment.—**out'fitter** *n.* seller of outfits.
outflank' *v.t.* to go round the flank of.
outgrow' *v.t.* to surpass in growth (**out-grew'** *p.t.* **-grown'.** *p.p.* **-grow'ing** *pr. p.*).
out'house *n.* a building connected with and beside a main house.
out'land *n.* foreign country.—**out-land'ish** *a.* queer, extravagantly strange.
out'law *n.* one placed beyond the protection of the law, an exile.—**out'lawry** *n.*
out'lay *n.* expenditure, expenses.
out'rage *n.* violation of others' rights; gross or violent offence or indignity.—*v.t.* to injure, violate, ravish, insult.—**outra'geous** *a.* atrocious.
ou'tré (ōō'trā) *a.* extravagantly odd.
out'rigger *n.* a frame outside a ship's gunwale; a frame on the side of a rowing boat with a rowlock at the outer edge; a boat with one.
out'right *a.* downright.—*adv.* frankly.
outspan' *n.* S. Africa, reserved space, where animals are unyoked to graze.—*v.t.* to unyoke, unsaddle.—*v.i.* to unyoke; to encamp.
o'val *a.* egg-shaped, elliptical.—*n.* an oval figure or thing.
o'vary *n.* an egg-producing organ.
ova'tion *n.* enthusiastic applause.
ov'en (uv'-) *n.* a heated iron box or other receptacle for baking in.
o'ver *adv.* above, above and beyond, going beyond, in excess, too much, past, finished, in repetition, across, etc.—*prep.* above, on, more than.—*a.* upper, outer.—*n.* in cricket, a series of 6 balls.
o'ver- as *prefix* makes compounds with meaning of "too," "too much," "in excess," "above," e.g., **o'verdo** *v.t.* to do too much.—**overdraw'** *v.t.* to draw in excess of what is in credit, etc. These are not given where the meaning may easily be found from the simple word.
overhaul' *v.t.* to come up with in pursuit; to examine and set in order.—*n.* a thorough examination, *esp.* for repairs.
o'verland *a.* made or performed by land.—*adv.* across the land.—**o'ver-lander** *n.* Australia, a person who drives stock long distances.
overlay' *v.t.* to spread over, to smother (**-laid'** *p.t.* and *p.p.*—**-lay'ing** *pres. p.*).
overproduc'tion *n.* production in excess of demand.
o'vert *a.* open, unconcealed.–**o'vertly** *adv.*
overtake' *v.t.* to come up with in pursuit; to catch up (**-took'** *p.t.*—**-ta'ken** *p.p.*—**-taking** *pres. p.*).
overthrow' *v.t.* to upset or overturn; to defeat (**overthrew'** *p.t.*—**-thrown'** *p.p.*—**-throw'ing** *pres. p.*).—*n.* ruin; defeat; in cricket, baseball, etc., a fielder's return

missed by wicket-keeper or bowler, for which runs may be scored.
o'verture *n.* an opening of negotiations; a proposal; opening piece played by an orchestra, introducing an opera, etc.
overturn' *v.t.* and *i.* to upset, throw over, tip over; to overthrow.
overween'ing *a.* thinking too much of oneself, presumptuous.
overwhelm' (-hwelm') *v.t.* to crush utterly; to submerge and bear down, engulf (**-ing** *a.* irresistible.)
overwrought' *a.* over-excited; under an unusual nervous strain.
o'vine (-ī-) *a.* of, or like, sheep.
owe (ō) *v.t.* to be bound to repay, be indebted for.—**ow'ing** *a.* owed, due.—**owing to,** caused by.
owl *n.* a night bird of prey.—**owl'et** *n.* a young owl.—**owl'ish** *a.* solemn and dull.
own (ōn) *a.* emphasises possession.—*v.t.* to possess; acknowledge.—*v.i.* to confess.—**own'er** *n.*—**own'ership** *n.*
ox *n.* a large cloven-footed and usually horned animal used for draft, milk, and meat, a bull or cow (**oxen** *pl.*).—**ox'-eye** *n.* a large daisy.—**ox'-lip** *n.* a hybrid between cowslip and primrose.
oxal'ic *a.* acid from wood-sorrel.
ox'ygen *n.* the gas in the atmosphere which is essential to life, burning, etc.
ox'ide *n.* a compound of oxygen.
ox'idise *v.t.* to cause to combine with oxygen; to cover with oxide, make rusty.—*v.i.* to combine with oxygen, to rust.
ox'y-acet'ylene *a.* denoting a very hot blowpipe flame.
o'yez (ō'yes) *n.* a call, usually uttered three times, by a public crier.
oy'ster *n.* a bivalve mollusc or shellfish.
o'zone *n.* a condensed form of oxygen with a pungent odour.

P

pa', pah' *n.* N.Z., native settlement surrounded by stockade; fortified village.
pab'ulin *n.* an albuminous substance in blood just after digestion.
pab'ulum *n.* nourishment.
pace *n.* a step; length of a step; walk or speed of stepping; speed.—*v.i.* to step.—*v.t.* to cross, measure with steps; to set the speed for.—**pa'cer** *n.* (**pa'cing** *pr. p.*).
pach'yderm (-k-) *n.* thick-skinned animal, e.g., an elephant.—**pachyderm'atous** *a.*
Pacif'ic *n.* ocean lying between the Americas and Asia.—*a.* peaceful, mild, permitting peace; pertaining to the Pacific.
pac'ify *v.t.* to calm, quiet, still; establish peace (**pac'ified** *p.t./p.p.*—**-ifying** *pr. p.*).—**pacifica'tion** *n.*—**pacif'icatory** *a.*—**pa'cifist** *n.* advocate of abolition of war.—**pacif'icism** *n.*
pack *n.* a bundle; company of animals; large set of people or things; a set of playing cards; a mass of floating ice.—*v.t.* to make into a bundle; to put together in a box, etc.; to fill with things; to order off.—**pack'age** *n.* a parcel.—**pack'er** *n.* Australia, a pack-horse; person who transports goods on pack-horses.—**pack'et** *n.* small parcel.—**pack'-horse** *n.* a horse for carrying bundles of goods.—**pack'-ox** *n.* in S. Africa, an ox used for riding or for bearing a load.—**pack'-saddle** *n.* a saddle to carry goods.—**pack'-thread** *n.* coarse, strong thread for sewing up packages.—**pack'-train** *n.* N. America, a string of animals carrying supplies.—**pack'ing-ring** *n.* in internal combustion engine, the piston ring.
pact *n.* a covenant or agreement.
pad *v.i.* to travel on foot.—*n.* an easy-paced horse; piece of soft stuff used as a cushion; shin-guard; sheets of paper fastened together in a block; foot or sole of various animals.—*v.t.* to make soft, fill in, protect, etc., with a pad or padding.—**padd'ing** *n.* material used for stuffing (**pad'ded** *p.t.* and *p.p.*).
padd'a *n.* in S. Africa, a frog; toad.
pad'dle *n.* short oar with a broad blade at one or each end; blade of a paddle-wheel.—*v.i.* to move by paddles; to roll gently.—*v.t.* to propel by paddles; to walk with bare feet in shallow water.
pad'dle-wheel *n.* wheel with cross-wise blades which strike the water successively to propel a ship.—**pad'dle-box** *n.* upper casing of a paddle wheel.
padd'ock *n.* small field or enclosure; Australia, fenced-in area of land
Padd'y *n.* an Irishman; (*coll.*) a rage.
padd'y *n.* rice in the husk.—**padd'y-field** *n.* the field where rice is grown.
padd'ymelon *n.* Australia, a species of small wallaby.
pad'kos *n.* S. Africa, food for a journey.
pad'lock *n.* a detachable lock with a hinged hoop to go through a staple or ring.—*v.t.* to fasten with padlock.
pa'dre (pȧ'drā) *n.* chaplain to H.M. Forces; a parson.
pae'an *n.* song of praise or triumph.
paediat'rics *n.* study and care of children in sickness and in health.
pa'gan *a.* heathen.—*n.* a heathen.—**pa'ganism** *n.* heathen beliefs etc.
page *n.* a boy servant or attendant; one side of a leaf of a book.—*v.t.* or **pa'ginate** to number the pages of.—**pagina'tion** *n.*—**pag'inal** *a.*
pa'geant (paj'ent) *n.* a show or procession of persons in costume, dramatic scenes from history, etc.; a brilliant show.—**pa'geantry** *n.*

pago'da *n.* a temple or sacred tower of Chinese or Indian type.
pag'ter *n.* S. Africa, a tenant farmer.
pah *interj.* an exclamation of disgust.
pail *n.* a bucket.—**pail'ful** *n.* (**pail'fuls** *pl.*).
paillasse'. *See* **palliasse'.**
pain *n.* bodily or mental suffering; penalty or punishment.—*v.t.* to inflict pain upon.—**pain'ful** *a.*—**pain'fully** *adv.* —**pain'less** *a.*—**pain'lessly** *adv.*—**pains'-taking** *a.* diligent, careful.
Syn. anguish, agony, distress, torment. *Ant.* ease, comfort, solace.
paint *n.* colouring matter prepared for putting on a surface with brushes.—*v.t.* and *i.* to portray, colour, coat, or make a picture of, with paint; to describe.—**paint'er** *n.*—**paint'ing** *n.*
paint'er *n.* a rope for fastening the bow of a boat to a ship, etc.; (U.S.) panther.
pair (pār) *n.* a set of two, *esp.* existing or generally used together.—*v.t.* and *i.* to arrange in a pair or pairs.
pal *n.* (*sl.*) a close friend, mate or partner.
pal'ace *n.* official residence of a king, bishop, etc.; stately mansion.—**pala'-tial** *a.*—**pal'atine** *a.* having royal privileges and rights.
pal'adin *n.* a chivalrous person (originally one of the 12 peers of Charlemagne).
pa'laeography *n.* study of ancient writing and inscriptions.
pal'ate *n.* roof of the mouth; the sense of taste.—**pal'atable** *a.* agreeable to eat.—**pal'atal** *a.* of the palate; made by placing the tongue against the palate.—*n.*
pal'atial *a.* grand, like a palace.
pala'ver (-ȧ-) *n.* a conference; empty talk.—*v.i.* to use many words.
pale *a.* faint in colour, dim, whitish.—*v.i.* to grow white.—**pale'ness** *n.*
pale *n.* a stake, boundary.—**pa'ling** *n.* (usually in *pl.*) a fence.
pal'ette *n.* thin board on which an artist mixes his colours.
pal'frey *n.* a small saddle-horse.
palisade' *n.* a fence of stakes or railings. —*v.t.* to enclose with one.
pall (pawl) *n.* a cloth spread over a coffin. —*v.i.* to become tasteless or tiresome.
pall'et *n.* a straw bed; a mean bed.
palliasse' (pal-yas') *n.* a hard straw under-mattress.
pall'iate *v.t.* to relieve without curing; to excuse.—**pallia'tion** *n.*—**pall'iative** *a.* giving temporary or partial relief.—*n.*
pall'id *a.* pale.—**pall'or** *n.* paleness.
palm (pȧm) *n.* the flat of the hand; a tropical tree; leaf of this tree as a symbol of victory.—*v.t.* to conceal in the palm of the hand; to pass off by trickery.—**palm'istry** *n.* fortune-telling from the lines on the palm of the hand.—**palm'ist** *n.*—**palm'ary** *a.* worthy of a palm of victory, distinguished.—**palm'er** *n.* pilgrim from the Holy Land.—**Palm Sunday** *n.* Sunday before Easter.—**palm'y** *a.* flourishing.
palm'er worm *n.* hairy caterpillar.
pal'miped, pal'mipedede *a.* web-footed.—*n.* a swimming bird.
pal'pable *a.* that may be touched or felt; certain, obvious.—**pal'pably** *adv.*—**pal'pitate** *v.i.* to throb.—**palpita'tion** *n.*
pal'sy (pawl'-) *n.* paralysis.—**pal'sied** *a.*
pal'ter *v.t.* to shuffle, deal evasively.
pal'try *a.* worthless, contemptible.
pam'pas *n. pl.* vast grassy, treeless plains in South America.
pam'per *v.t.* to over-indulge.
pamph'let *n.* a thin book, stitched but not bound.—**pamphleteer'** *n.* writer of (political) pamphlets.
pan *n.* broad, shallow vessel; S. Africa, a depression holding water in the wet season.—*v.t.* S. Africa, Australia, to wash gold ore in a pan.
pan-, panto- *prefix* all, as **panacea, pantomime, pantology.**
panace'a *n.* a universal remedy.
panache' (-ash') *n.* plume of feathers used as a headdress; glory.
pana'da *n.* bread boiled to a pulp in water and sweetened.
Pan'ama (-mȧ) *n.* a hat made of fine straw-like material.
pan'atrope *n.* gramophone magnifying sound through loud-speaker.
pan'cake *n.* thin cake of batter fried in pan.—*v.i.* aviation, land clumsily.
panchromat'ic (-krō-mat'-ik) *a.* in photography, sensitive to all colours.
pan'creas *n.* digestive gland discharging into the duodenum; the sweetbread.
pan'da *n.* a racoon-like animal of India.
pandemo'nium *n.* confusion and uproar; abode of evil spirits.
pan'der *n.* a go-between in illicit love affairs; procurer.—*v.t.* to minister basely.
pane *n.* a piece of glass in a window, etc.
panegyr'ic (-i-jir'-) *n.* a speech of praise. —**panegyr'ical** *a.* —**panegyr'ist** *n.*
pan'el *n.* a compartment of a surface, usually raised or sunk, e.g., in a door; a strip of different material in a dress; a thin board with a picture on it; a list of jurors, doctors, etc.; Australia, a section between two posts in a fence, a movable fence.—*v.t.* decorate with panels.—**pan'elling** *n.* panelled work.
pang *n.* a sudden pain, twinge.
pang'olin *n.* the scaly ant-eater.
pan'ic *n.* sudden and infectious fear.—*a.* (of fear) unreasoning.—**pan'ic-strick'-en** *a.* terrified.
pann'ier *n.* basket carried by a beast of burden or on a person's shoulders; part of a skirt looped up.
pann'ikin *n.* small metal drinking-cup. —**pann'ikin boss** *n.* Australia, an overseer on a station, *esp.* one of restricted power.
pan'oply *n.* a full suit of armour.

panoram'a (-am-a) *n.* a picture unrolled before spectator; a wide or complete view.—**panoram'ic** *a.*
pan'sy (-zi) *n.* a flowering plant; a species of violet (**pan'sies** *pl.*); an effeminate man.
pant *v.i.* to gasp for breath.—*n.* a gasp.
pantaloon' *n.* in pantomime, a foolish old man who is the butt of the clown.—*pl.* long, tight-fitting trousers.
pantech'nicon (-k-) *n.* storehouse, or large closed van for moving furniture.
pan'theism *n.* identification of God with the universe.—**pan'theist** *n.*—**pan'theon** *n.* temple of all the gods; a system of deities; building for memorials of a nation's great dead.
pan'ther *n.* a variety of leopard.
pan'tile *n.* a tile with a cross-section like the letter S.
pan'tograph *n.* instrument for copying diagrams, maps, etc., to any scale.
pantom'eter *n.* an instrument for measuring angles or determining perpendiculars.
pan'tomime *n.* a dramatic entertainment in dumb show; Christmas-time dramatic entertainment.—**pantomim'ic** *a.*
pan'try *n.* a room for storing food.
pants *n. pl.* trousers; long tight or short loose drawers worn by men.
Pan'zer (pant'ser) *a.* armoured.—*n.* an armoured vehicle or tank (*Ger.*).
pap *n.* soft food for infants, etc.
pa'pacy *n.* the office of the Pope; the papal system.—**pa'pal** *a.* of, or relating to, the Pope.—**pa'pist** *n.*—**papist'ic** *a.*
papaw' *n.* a tropical tree bearing melon-shaped fruit; the fruit.
pa'per *n.* a material made by pressing pulp of rags, straw, wood, etc., into thin flat sheets; a sheet of paper written or printed on; a newspaper; an article or essay.—*pl.* documents, etc.—**pa'per-chase** *n.* hare and hounds.—*v.t.* to cover with paper.—*a.* made of paper.
pap'ier-mâché (pap'yā-mash-ā) *n.* pulp from rags or paper mixed with size, shaped by moulding and dried hard.
pa'pies *n. pl.* in S. Africa, larvae of the bot fly; ailment of horses.
papoose' *n.* a N. American Indian child.
papri'ka (-rē-) *n.* Hungarian red pepper.
papy'rus *n.* a species of reed; a manuscript (*esp.* ancient Egyptian) written on papyrus (**papy'ri** (rī) *pl.*).
par *n.* equality of value or standing; equality between market and nominal value.—**par'ity** *n.* equality.
par'a-, par-, pa- *prefix* beside, beyond, as **paradigm, parody, palsy.**
par'able *n.* an allegory, story told to point out a moral.
parab'ola *n.* a section of a cone made by a plane parallel to surface of cone.
parachute' (-sh-) *n.* an apparatus extending like an umbrella to enable a person to come safely to earth from a great height.—**parachut'ist** *n.*
parade' *n.* display; a muster of troops; a parade ground.—*v.t.* to muster; display.—*v.i.* to march with display.
par'adigm *n.* an example; a model.
par'adise *n.* the Garden of Eden; Heaven; state of bliss.
pa'rados *n.* the back wall of a firing trench in warfare.
par'adox *n.* statement that seems absurd but may be true.—**paradox'ical** *a.*
Syn. enigma, riddle. *Ant.* platitude, commonplace, truism.
par'affin *n.* a wax or oil distilled from shale, wood, etc.
par'agon *n.* a pattern of excellence.
par'agraph *n.* a section of a chapter or book; a short news item in a newspaper.—*v.t.* to arrange in paragraphs.
par'akeet, par'oquet *n.* a small parrot.
paral'dehyde *n.* a narcotic.
par'allel *a.* continuously at equal distances; precisely corresponding.—*n.* a line of latitude; a thing exactly like another; a comparison.—*v.t.* to represent as similar, compare.—**par'allelism** *n.*
parallel'logram *n.* four-sided plane figure with opposite sides parallel.
paral'ysis *n.* an incapacity to move or feel, due to damage to the nerve system (**paral'yses** (-sēz) *pl.*).—**paralyt'ic** *a.*—*n.*
paramatt'a *n.* fabric of wool and cotton.
par'amount *a.* supreme, greatest.
Syn. eminent, pre-eminent, chief. *Ant.* unimportant, insignificant, small.
par'amour (-ōōr) *n.* one for whom a married person has illicit love.
par'ang *n.* a large, heavy Malay knife used in felling trees, etc.
par'apet *n.* a low wall; a defensive wall on a fort or earth-wall on a trench.
paraphernа'lia *n. pl.* personal belongings, odds and ends of equipment.
par'aphrase *n.* an expression of a meaning of a passage in other words.—*v.t.* to put the meaning of in other words.
paraple'gia *n.* paralysis of the lower part of the body.
para-psychology *n.* psychical research; the study of subjects pert. to extra sensory perception, i.e. telepathy, clairvoyance, etc.—**parapsycho'sis** *n.* an abnormal psychosis.
par'asite *n.* a self-interested hanger-on; an animal or plant living in or on another.—*pl.* in wireless, atmospherics.—**parasit'ic** *a.*—**parasit'ically** *adv.*
parasol' *n.* a light umbrella for protection against the sun.
par'atroops *n. pl.* troops trained to descend by parachute.
paraty'phoid *n.* an infectious disease like, but distinct from, typhoid fever.
par'avane *n.* a contrivance for cutting the moorings of submerged mines.
par'boil *v.t.* to scald the surface in

boiling water, to boil partly; to scorch.
par'buckle *n.* a rope for raising or lowering round objects.—*v.t.*
par'cel *n.* things packed in a box or paper; a quantity dealt with at one time; a piece of land.—*v.t.* to divide into parts; to make up in a parcel (**par'celling** *pres. p.*—**parcel'led** *p.t.* and *p.p.*).
parch *v.t.* and *i.* dry by exposure to heat, to make or become hot and dry.
parch'ment *n.* skin prepared for writing; a manuscript of this.
pard *n.* leopard; **pard'ed** *a.* spotted.
pard *n.* (*sl.*) in N. Amer., partner, friend.
par'don *v.t.* to forgive.—*n.* forgiveness. —**par'donable** *a.*—**par'donably** *adv.*
Syn. to absolve, remit, condone. *Ant.* to grudge, resent, to be implacable.
pare (pėr) *v.t.* to trim by cutting away edge or surface of, remove skin from.—**par'ing** *n.* a piece pared off.
paregor'ic *a.* soothing.—*n.* a soothing medicine; a tincture of opium.
par'ent (pėr-) *n.* a father or mother.—**parent'al** *a.*—**par'enthood** *n.*—**par'entage** *n.* descent, ancestry, family.
paren'thesis *n.* a word or sentence inserted in a passage independently of the grammatical sequence and usually marked off by brackets, dashes, or commas (**paren'theses** *pl.*).—*pl.* round brackets, ( ), used for this.–**parenthe'tic** *a.*
par'get *v.t.* to cover with plaster.—*n.* gypsum; rough plaster; pargeting.
par'iah *n.* an Indian of lowest Hindu caste; a social outcast.—**pariah dog** a yellow roaming dog in India.
par'i-mutuel' (-mē-tē-el') *n.* the French form of the totalisator.
par'ish *n.* a district under a priest; a sub-division of a county.—**parish'ioner** *n.* an inhabitant of a parish.
parity *see* **par.**
park *n.* a large enclosed piece of ground, usually with grass or woodland, attached to a country house or set aside for public use; a recreation ground in a town; the artillery of a military force; its space in a camp; a place set aside for storing motor-cars, aeroplanes, etc.—*v.t.* to put or leave a car, aeroplane, etc., in a place reserved for it; to leave for a short time. —**park' country** *n.* in N. America, prairie dotted with clusters of trees.
par'ka *n.* an Eskimo outer garment of undressed skin; a hooded overcoat worn by troops, etc.
par'ky *a.* (*sl.*) cold; chilly.
parl'ance *n.* a way of speaking.
parl'ey *n.* a meeting between leaders or representatives of opposing forces to discuss terms (**parleys** *pl.*).—*v.i.* to hold a discussion about terms.
parl'iament *n.* legislature of United Kingdom; any legislative assembly.—**parliament'ary** *a.*—**parliamenta'rian** *n.*
parl'our *n.* a sitting-room.—**parl'our-car** *n.* in N. America, a luxuriously fitted railway car, with revolving seats.
parman'tig *a.* in S. Africa, overbearing; impertinent; haughty.
paro'chial (-k-) *a.* of a parish; narrow, provincial.—**paro'chialism** *n.* concentration on the local interests.
par'ody *n.* a composition in which the author's characteristics are made fun of by imitation; burlesque; feeble imitation.—*v.t.* to write parody of (**paro'died** *p.t./p.p.*—**odying** *pr. p.*).—**par'odist** *n.*
parole' *n.* a promise given by a prisoner of war not to attempt to escape or to abstain from taking up arms again.
paroquet *see* **parakeet.**
par'oxysm *n.* a sudden violent attack of pain, rage, laughter, etc.
par'quet (-ket) *n.* flooring of wooden blocks.—*v.t.* to lay a parquet.—**par'quetry** *n.* parquet work.
parr *n.* a young salmon.
parr'icide *n.* murder or murderer of a parent.
parr'ot *n.* bird with short hooked beak; some varieties can be taught to imitate speaking; an unintelligent imitator.
parr'y *v.t.* to ward off (**parr'ied** *p.t.* and *p.p.*—**parr'ying** *pres p.*).—*n.* an act of parrying, *esp.* in fencing.
parse (-z) *v.t.* to describe (a word) or analyse (a sentence) in terms of grammar.
par'sec *n.* a unit of length used in expressing the distance of the stars.
par'simony *n.* stinginess, undue economy.—**parsimo'nious** *a.*
par'sley *n.* a herb used for seasoning.
par'snip *n.* a plant with a yellow root cooked as a vegetable.
par'son *n.* a clergyman of a parish or church.–**parson'age** *n.* the parson's house.
part *n.* a portion, section, share; duty; actor's role; interest.—*v.t.* to divided separate; distribute.—*v.i.* to divide; separate from.—**part'ly** *adv.*
parta'ker *n.* one taking a share.—**partake'** *v.t.* to have a share in.—*v.i.* to take or have a share (**partook'** *p.t.*—**parta'ken** *p.p.*—**parta'king** *pres. p.*).
par'tial *a.* prejudiced; fond of; being only in part.–**partial'ity** *n.*–**par'tially** *adv.*
par'terre *n.* ornamental arrangement of flower beds; pit of theatre.
partic'ipate (-is-) *v.t.* and *i.* to share in. —**partic'ipant** *n.*—**partic'ipator** *n.*—**participa'tion** *n.* (**parti'cipating** *pres. p.*).
part'iciple *n.* adjective made by inflection from verb and keeping verb's relation to dependent words, verbal adjective.—**particip'ial** *a.*
part'icle *n.* a minute portion of matter; minor part of speech.
par'ticoloured *a.* differently coloured in different parts, variegated.
partic'ular *a.* relating to one, not general; considered apart from others; minute; very exact, fastidious.—*n.* a detail or item.—*pl.* a detailed account.—

particular'ity *n.*—partic'ularly *adv.*—partic'ularise *v.t.* to mention in detail.
partisan' (-z-) *n.* an adherent of a party; military weapon like a halberd.—*a.* adherent to a faction.
parti'tion *n.* division; dividing wall.—*v.t.* to divide into parts.
part'ner *n.* a member of a partnership; one that dances with another; a husband or wife.—**part'nership** *n.* association of persons for business, etc.
part'ridge *n.* a small game bird.
parturi'tion *n.* bringing forth young.
part'y *n.* a group of people with the same political opinions; persons working, travelling or being entertained together; a social assembly.—*a.* of, or belonging to, a faction (**par'ties** *pl.*).
par'venu *n.* an upstart; one newly risen into notice or power.
pas'chal (-sk-) *a.* of the Passover, of Easter or Easter celebrations.
pash'a *n.* Turkish title bestowed on high-ranking officials.
pas op' *interj.* in S. Africa, a cry of warning, with meaning "take care!"
pass (-â-) *v.t.* to go by, beyond, through, etc.; to exceed; to be accepted by.—*v.i.* to go; to be transferred from one state to another; to elapse; to undergo examination successfully (**passed** (past), (rare) **past** *p.t.*—**passed** or **past** *p.p.*—**pass'ing** *pres. p.*).—*n.* a way, *esp.* a narrow and difficult way; a passport; condition; successful result from a test.—**pass'able** *a.* which can be crossed; fairly good.—**pass'age** *n.* journey; voyage; fare; part of a book, etc.; an encounter.
passade' *n.* a thrust; a turn or course of a horse backward or forward.
pass'enger (-jer) *n.* a traveller by airplane, ship, train, bus, etc.
passe-partout' *n.* a master-key; a mount or light frame for a picture.
pas'sion *n.* suffering; strong feeling; wrath; object of ardent desire.—**pas'sionate** *a.* moved by strong emotions.—**The Passion**, the sufferings of Christ.—**pas'sion fruit** *n.* a small, round, hard-shelled fruit; the vine producing it.
passim'eter (-i-mē-) *n.* an automatic machine for printing, dating and delivering tickets.
pass'ive *a.* suffering, submissive; the grammatical mood of a verb in which the action is suffered by the subject.
Syn. inactive, unresisting, quiescent. *Ant.* active, energetic, vigorous.
Pass'over (-â-) *n.* a feast of the Jews to commemorate the time when God, smiting the firstborn of the Egyptians, *passed over* the houses of the Israelites.
pass'port *n.* document or book giving official permission to travel in a certain country, under the protection of one's own government; that which gives admission or acceptance.
pass'word *n.* secret word allowing one to pass a sentinel; countersign.
past *a.* ended.—*n.* bygone times.—*adv.* by; along.—*prep.* beyond; after.
paste *n.* a soft composition, as of flour and water; a fine glass to imitate gems.—*v.t.* to fasten with paste.—**past'y** *n.* a pie enclosed in paste.—*a.* like paste. (**pa'sting** *pres. p.*).—**paste'board** *n.* a stiff, thick paper.—*a.* flimsy.
pas'tel *n.* coloured crayon; woad, dye from this.—*a.* soft and pale.
by series of inoculations.
pasteur'ism (-ter-) *n.* cure of diseases by series of inoculation.
pas'teurized (-ter-izd) *a.* heated to a sufficient temperature to kill germs, *esp.* milk.—**pasteuriza'tion** *n.*
pastich'e (past-eech) *n.* a jumble; a work in another's style and manner.
pastille' (pas-tēl') *n.* a lozenge; aromatic substance burnt as a fumigator.
pas'time (-â-) *n.* that which serves to make time pass agreeably.
pas'tor (-â-) *n.* minister of the gospel.—**past'oral** *a.* of shepherds or rural life; of the office of pastor.—*n.* poem of rural life.—**past'orate** *n.* office or jurisdiction of spiritual pastor.
pas'toralist *n.* Australia, a sheep or cattle farmer.
pa'stry *n.* articles of food made chiefly of paste, e.g. cakes, tarts.
past'ure (-â-) *n.* grass for food of cattle; ground on which cattle graze.—*v.t.* to feed on grass.—*v.i.* to graze.—**past'urage** *n.* pasturing; pasture.
pat *n.* a small mass, as of butter, beaten into shape; a light, quick blow.—*v.t.* to tap (**pat'ting** *pr. p.*—**pat'ted** *p.t./p.p.*)
patch *n.* a piece of cloth sewed on a garment; a spot or plot; a plot of ground.—*v.t.* to men; to repair clumsily (**patch'es** *pl.*).—**patch'work** *n.* odd pieces sewn together; jumble.—**patch'y** *a.* full of patches; irregular.
patchou'li *n.* a herb furnishing perfume; the perfume itself.
pate *n.* the head; the top of the head.
patell'a *n.* a small vase; the knee-cap; a limpet (**patell'ae** *pl.*).
pa'tent *a.* open; evident; manifest; open to public perusal, as letters *patent*.—*n.* a deed securing to a person the exclusive right to an invention.—*v.t.* to secure a patent.–**patentee'** (pā-ten-tē', pat-en-tē') *n.* one that has a patent.
paterfamil'ias *n.* the father of a family (**patersfamil'ias** *pl.*).
pater'nal *a.* of a father; fatherly; related on the father's side.—**patern'ity** *n.* fatherhood; authorship.
path (-â-) *n.* a way or track.
pathol'ogy *n.* the science of disease.
pa'thos *n.* power of exciting tender emotions.—**pathet'ic, pathet'ical** *a.* affecting or moving the tender emotions.

pa'tient (-shent) *a.* bearing trials without murmuring.—*n.* a person under medical treatment.—**pa'tience** *n.* the quality of enduring; a card game.

Syn. passive, submissive, enduring. *Ant.* impatient, rebellious, restive.

pati'na *n.* a bowl; bloom on antique bronze (**pati'næ** *pl.*).

pat'io *n.* an uncovered enclosure connected with a house.

pat'ois (-waw) *n.* a rustic or provincial form of speech or dialect.

pa'triarch (-k) *n.* the father and ruler of a family, *esp.* in Biblical history.

patri'cian (-shn) *n.* a noble of ancient Rome; a person of noble birth.—*a.* of noble birth (cf. **plebeian**).

pat'rimony *n.* right or estate inherited from ancestors, heritage.

pat'riot *n.* one who loves and supports his country.—**patriot'ic** *a.*—**pat'riotism** *n.*

patrol' (-ōl) *n.* a marching round of a guard; troops, aircraft or warships patrolling; a unit of Boy Scouts; in N. America, a policeman on street duty.—*v.i.* to reconnoitre or keep guard.

pa'tron *n.* person who protects and supports another; a guardian saint; one having the disposition of a church-living, etc.—**pat'ronage** *n.* special countenance or support; right of presentation to a church-living, etc.—**pat'ronise** *v.t.* to assume the air of a superior towards; to frequent as a customer.

patronym'ic *n.* a name derived from that of a father or an ancestor.

patt'en *n.* a raised wooden shoe or sole; the base of a column.

patt'er *v.i.* to tap in quick succession; to make a noise, as the sound of quick, short steps; to pray or talk rapidly.—*n.* a quick succession of small sounds.

patt'ern *n.* model for imitation; a specimen; a paper shape from which to cut cloth, etc.; a design.

patt'y *n.* a little pie.

pau'city *n.* scarcity; fewness.

paunch *n.* the belly.

pau'per *n.* a poor person.–**pau'perism** *n.* destitution.—**pau'perise** *v.t.* to reduce to pauperism.

pause *n.* stop, rest.–*v.i.*(**paus'ing** *pr. p.*).

pav'an, pav'en *n.* a Spanish dance; its music.

pave *v.t.* to form a surface with stone or brick; to prepare (*the way*).–**pave'ment** *n.* a paved floor or footpath; material for paving; in N. America, the traffic way.

pavil'ion *n.* a large tent; a club-house on a playing-field, etc.

paw *n.* the foot of an animal having claws; *sl.* hand.—*v.i.* to scrape with the fore foot.—*v.t.* to touch.

paw'ky *a.* Scotland, cunning; sly, arch.

pawn *n.* goods deposited as security for money borrowed.—*v.t.* to pledge.—**in pawn**, left as security.—**pawn'broker** *n.* one that lends money on goods pledged.–**pawn'shop** *n.* pawnbroker's shop.

pawn *n.* a piece in a game, *esp.* chess.

pax *interj* (*sl.*) peace! leave me alone.

pay *v.t.* to give money, etc., for goods received or services rendered; to compensate.—*v.i.* to be remunerative (**paid** *p.t.* and *p.p.*—**pay'ing** *pres. p.*).—*n.* wages.–**pay'able** *a.* justly due; Australia, of a mine, claim, etc., able to give a higher return than the working cost.—**pay'ment** *n.* discharge of a debt.—**pay'-streak** *n.* N. America, a rich part of a seam of gold-bearing ore; a paying proposition of any kind.—**pay'ing-guest'** *n.* a euphemism for a boarder or lodger.

pay *v.t.* to pitch the seams of a ship (**payed** (pād) *p.t.* and *p.p.*—**-ing** *pres. p.*).

pay'nim *n.* a pagan; a heathen.

pea *n.* fruit growing in pods, of a leguminous plant; the plant.—**pea'nut** *n.* the ground nut.

peace *n.* calm; repose; freedom from war; quietness of mind.—**peace'able** *a.* disposed to peace.—**peace'ful** *a.*—**peace'fully** *adv.*—**peace'maker** *n.*

Syn. quiet, tranquillity, concord. *Ant.* war, strife, uproar, turmoil.

peach *n.* a stone fruit of delicate flavour.

peach *v.i.* to inform against (**-es** *pl.*).

pea'cock *n.* a bird with brilliant plumage and fan-like tail.—**pea'hen** *fem.*—*v.t.* Australia, to pick out the best portions of an area so that the remainder is useless to anyone else.

pea'-jacket *n.* thick woollen jacket worn by seamen.

peak *n.* the sharp top of a mountain; maximum point in a cure, record, etc.; front brim of a cap.—**peak'y** *a.*

peak'ish *a.* looking thin and sickly from illness.

peal *n.* a loud sound of bells, laughter, thunder, etc.; chime.—*v.i.*

pear (pėr) *n.* tree yielding delicious fruit; the fruit.—**prick'ly pear** *n.* Australia, S. Africa, a cactus; the spiny edible fruit of the plant.—**native pear'** *n.* tree found on east coast of Australia, with tough fibrous fruit; its fruit.

pearl (purl) *n.* a hard, smooth, lustrous substance, found in several molluscs, particularly the pearl oyster; a jewel.—**pear'ly** *a.* clear; pure.—**pearl'-shell** *n.* Australia, the shell of a large marine bivalve, used for making buttons, etc.

pearl'-barley *n.* barley tapioca, with the skin ground off.

peas'ant (pez'-) *n.* a rural labourer; a rustic.—*a.* rural.—**peas'antry** *n.* peasants collectively.

peat *n.* a decomposed vegetable substance, used for fuel.

pea'vey *n.* in N. America, a lumberman's cant-hook; a pick.

peb'ble *n.* a small, roundish stone; transparent and colourless rock-crystal.

pecc'able *a.* liable to sin.
peccadill'o *n.* a slight offence; a petty crime (**-los** (lōz), **-loes** *pl.*).
pecc'ary *n.* a vicious American animal allied to the hog.
peck *n.* the 4th part of a bushel.—*v.t.* and *i.* to pick or strike with a beak.
pec'tin *n.* a gelatinising substance obtained from ripe fruits.—**pec'tic** *a.* congealing; denoting pectin.
pec'toral *a.* of the breast.—*n.* ornament hung there; lung medicine.
pec'ulate (pek'ū-) *v.t.* and *i.* to embezzle.—**pecula'tion** *n.*—**pec'ulator** *n.*
pecu'liar *a.* one's own; particular; strange, odd.— **peculiar'ity** *n.* something that belongs to, or is found in, one person or thing; strangeness (**peculiar'ities** *pl.* *Syn.* special, exceptional, unique. *Ant.* normal, ordinary, usual.
pecu'niary *a.* relating to money.
ped'agogue (-gog) *n.* schoolmaster; pedantic teacher.—**pedagog'ic** *a.*
ped'al *a.* of a foot.—*n.* something to transmit motion from the foot.—*v.i.* to use a pedal (**ped'alling** *p.t.* and *p.p.*).
ped'ant *n.* one who overvalues, or insists out of season on, petty details of book-learning, grammatical rules, etc.—**pedant'ic** *a.* —**ped'antry** *n.*
ped'dle *v.t.* to retail, as a hawker.
ped'estal *n.* the base of a column, pillar.
pedes'trian *a.* going on foot; dull, prosaic, commonplace.—*n.* one that walks on foot.—**pedes'trianism** *n.*
pediat'rics. *See* **paediatrics.**
ped'icure *n.* care of feet; chiropodist.
ped'igree *n.* register of ancestors, human and animal; genealogy.
ped'im nt *n.* the triangular space over a Greek portico, etc.
ped'lar, -ler *n.* one who travels about hawking small commodities.
pedom'eter *n.* an instrument resembling a watch, which measures the distance walked in a given time.
ped'rail *n.* a device which provides a traction engine with its own rail for use over rough ground; a car or vehicle provided with pedrails.
peel *n.* an old, square fortified tower.
peel *v.t.* to strip off the skin or rind.—*v.i.* to come off, as the skin or rind.—*n.* rind. —**peeled** (pēld) *a.* in N. America (*sl.*) of eyes, on the watch, alert.
peep *v.i.* to cry, as a chick; to chirp.—*n.*
peep *v.i.* to look slyly or momentarily.—*n.*
peer *n.* one of the same rank; a nobleman.—**peer'age** *n.* the rank of a peer; the body of peers.—**peer'ess** *fem.*
peer *v.i.* to peep; to look narrowly.
peer'less *a.* without equal.
peev'ish *a.* fretful; querulous; complaining.—**peev'ishly** *adv.*—**peev'ishness** *n.*
pee'wit *n.* the lapwing.
peg *n.* a wooden nail or pin.—*v.t.* to fasten with pegs.—*v.i.* to persevere.—**peg out** *v.t.* Australia, to mark out a gold mining, or other, claim as required by law.
peg *n.* a drink of whisky and soda-water.
Pekinese' (-ēz') *n.* a breed of small Chinese dog.—**peke** *n.* *abbrev.*
pelf *n.* money (in contempt).
pel'ican *n.* a large fish-eating waterfowl, remarkable for its enormous bill.
pell'et *n.* a little ball; a pill.
pell-mell' *adv.* in utter confusion.
pellu'cid *a.* translucent; clear.
pel'met *n.* a canopy, or valance, for a window frame, to hide the curtain rods.
pelt *v.t.* to strike with missiles.—*v.i.* to throw missiles; to fall persistently.
pelt *n.* a hide or skin before tanning.
pel'vis *n.* the bony cavity at the base of the human trunk (**pel'ves** (-vēz) *pl.*).
pemm'ican *n* .meat dried, pounded and pressed into cakes.
pen *n.* an instrument for writing.—*v.t.* to compose and commit to paper; write.
pen *n.* a small enclosure, as for sheep.—*v.t.* to put or keep in an enclosure.
pe'nal *a.* of, incurring, inflicting punishment.—**pen'alty** *n.* punishment for crime or offence.—**pe'nalise** *v.* to make thing punishable; to punish.
pen'ance *n.* suffering submitted to as an expression of penitence.
pena'tes *n. pl.* the household gods of the ancient Romans.
pence *n.*; *pl.* of **penny.**
pen'chant (pon̄'shon) *n.* inclination.
pen'cil *n.* a small brush used by painters; an instrument, as of graphite, for writing, etc.; (*opt.*) collection of rays of light.—*v.t.* to paint or draw; to mark with a pencil.—**pen'cilled** *p.t.* and *p.p.*
pend'ant *n.* a hanging ornament.—*a.* suspended; hanging; projecting.—**pend'ing** *prep.* during.—**pend'ulous** *a.* hanging loosely; swinging.—**pend'ulum** *n.* a suspended weight swinging to and fro, *esp.* as a regulator for a clock (**-lums** *pl.*).
pen'etrate *v.t.* to enter into; to pierce; to arrive at the meaning of.—**pen'etrable** *a.* capable of being pierced.—**penetrabil'ity** *n.* quality of being penetrable. —**penetra'tion** *n.* insight; acuteness.—**pen'etrative** *a.* piercing; discerning.
pen'guin *n.* a swimming sea bird with flippers, unable to fly.
penicill'in (-sil'-in) *n.* a substance for killing germs, formed from the bacterial mould *penicillium notatum.*
penin'sula *n.* a portion of land nearly surrounded by water.—**penin'sular** *a.*
pe'nis *n.* the male organ of generation (**pe'nises, pe'nes** (-ēz) *pl.*).
pen'itent *a.* affected by a sense of guilt. —*n.* one that repents of sin.—**pen'itence** *n.* sorrow for sin; repentance.—**peniten'tial** *a.* of, or expressing, penitence.—**peniten'tiary** *a.* of penance, or the rules of penance.—*n.* a prison.

Syn. repentant, contrite, remorseful. *Ant.* unrepentant, impenitent, obdurate.

pen'-knife *n.* folding pocket-knife, with one or more blades (**-knives** *pl.*).

penn'ant *n.* a narrow piece of bunting, *esp.* a long narrow flag borne at the mast-head of a ship at war (also **pennon**).

penn'on *n.* a small pointed or swallow-tailed flag.

penn'y *n.* **penn'ies** *pl.* (denoting the number of coins).—**pence** *pl.* (amount of pennies in value), a copper coin; the twelfth part of a shilling.—**penn'iless** *a.* having no money.—**penn'yweight** *n.* a troy weight of 24 grains.–**pen'nyworth** *n.*

pennyroy'al *n.* an aromatic herb.

pen'sile *a.* hanging; suspended; pendulous.—**pen'sileness** *n.*

pen'sion *n.* an allowance for past services; an annuity paid to retired public officers, soldiers, etc.—*v.t.* to grant a pension to.—**pen'sioner** *n.*

pen'sive *a.* thoughtful with sadness.

pent', pent-up' *a.* closely shut up.

pent'agon *n.* a plane figure having five angles.—**pentag'onal** *a.*

pent'ateuch (-k) *n.* the first five books of the Old Testament.

pentath'lon *n.* at the modern Olympic Games, a contest of 5 events, namely, long jump, javelin and discus throwing, and 200 and 1,500 metres races.

pentam'eter *n.* a verse of five feet.

Pent'ecost *n.* Jewish festival on 50th day after Passover; Whitsuntide.

pent'house *n.* a shed standing with its roof sloping against a higher wall.

pen'tode *n.* in wireless, a five-electrode thermionic valve which contains filament, plate and three grids.

pe'nult *n.* last syllable but one of a word.—**penul'timate** *a.* next before the last.

pen'ury *n.* want; extreme poverty.—**penu'rious** *a.* miserly; niggardly.

pe'on *n.* India, a native constable, or soldier; Mexico, a labourer or serf.

pe'ony *n.* a plant with showy flowers.

peo'ple (pē'pl) *n.* the body of persons that compose a community, nation; persons generally.—*v.t.* to inhabit; to stock with inhabitants.

pep *n.* (*sl.*) vigour; energy.—*v.t.* to impart energy to; speed up.—**pep-talk** *n.* (*sl.*) verbal urge to greater effort.

pepp'er *n.* the fruit of a climbing plant, which yields a pungent aromatic spice.—*v.t.* to sprinkle with pepper; to pelt with shot.—**pepp'ery** *a.* having the qualities of pepper; irritable.—**pepp'ermint** *n.* a plant noted for the aromatic pungent liquor distilled from it.

pep'sin *n.* a ferment in gastric juice (used as a drug).—**pep'tone** *n.* one of the soluble compounds due to the action on food of pepsin and hydrochloric acid.

per-, par-, pel-, *prefix,* through, thoroughly, as **perfect, parson, pellucid.**

peradven'ture *adv.* perhaps.

peram'bulate *v.t.* to walk through or over.—*v.i.* to walk about.—**peram'bulator** *n.* a small carriage for a child.

perceive' *v.t.* to know by seeing, hearing, feeling, etc.; to observe; to understand.—**perceiv'able** *a.* (**perceiv'ing** *pres. p.*).

percent'age *n.* proportion or rate per hundred.—**per cent** in each hundred.

percep'tible *a.* discernible.–**perceptibil'ity** *n.*—**percep'tion** *n.* the faculty of perceiving.—**percep'tibly** *adv.*

perch *n.* a fresh-water fish.

perch *n.* a pole or rod; a measure of 5½ yards; a roost.—*v.t.* to place, as on a perch.—*v.i.* to alight or settle on a fixed body; to roost.

perchance' *adv.* perhaps.

percip'ient *a.* having the faculty of perception; perceiving.

per'colate *v.t.* and *i.* to pass through small interstices, as a liquor; to filter.—**percola'tion** *n.*—**per'colator** *n.*

percus'sion *n.* a collision; vibratory shock; instruments played by striking.

perdi'tion (-ish-) *n.* ruin; future misery; death; hell, damnation.

per'egrinate *v.i.* to travel from place to place.—**peregrina'tion** *n.*—**per'egrine** *a.* foreign.—*n.* blue falcon.

perempt'ory *a.* authoritative; final; forbidding debate; allowing of no refusal.

perenn'ial *a.* lasting through the years; perpetual, continual; in botany, continuing more than two years.

per'fect *a.* complete; finished.—*n.* a tense denoting a complete act.—*v.t.* to finish; to make skilful.—**perfect'able** *a.* capable of becoming perfect.—**perfec'tion** *n.* state of being perfect.—**per'fectly** *adv.* in a perfect manner; quite.

per'fidy *n.* treachery.—**perfid'ious** *a.*

per'forate *v.t.* to pierce.—**perfora'tion** *n.* a hole bored through anything.

perforce' *adv.* of necessity.

perform' *v.t.* to bring to completion; to fulfil; to represent on the stage.—*v.i.* to act a part; to play, as on a musical instrument.—**perform'ance** *n.* doing; a single show.—**perform'er** *n.*

per'fume *n.* an agreeable scent; fragrance.—*v.t.* to scent.—**perfu'mer** *n.*—**perfu'mery** *n.* perfumes in general.

perfunct'ory *a.* done indifferently.

per'gola *n.* an arbour, or covered walk, formed of growing plants.

perhaps' *adv.* it may be; possibly.

pe'ri *n.* a fairy (or elemental) in Eastern mythology (**pe'ris** (-īz) *pl.*).

peri- *prefix* round, near, about, as **perimeter, periphrasis, period.**

perihe'lion *n.* point in orbit of a planet or comet nearest to sun (**-lia** *pl.*).

per'il *n.* danger; exposure to injury.—**per'ilous** *a.* full of peril, dangerous.

perim'eter *n.* the outer boundary of a plane figure; length of this.
pe'riod *n.* the time in which a heavenly body makes a revolution; a particular portion of time; a complete sentence; a full stop (.).—**period'ic** *a.* recurring at regular intervals.—**period'ical** *a.* relating to a period; periodic.—*n.* a publication issued at regular intervals.
periph'ery *n.* circumference; surface.
per'iphrase *v.i.* to use circumlocution.
per'iscope *n.* an instrument with mirrors used *esp.* in submarines, for giving a view of what is going on above.
per'ish *v.i.* to die, to waste away.—*n.* Australia (*sl.*) any hardship in the bush.—**per'ishable** *a.* liable to decay.
peritone'um *n.* the membrane investing the internal surface of the abdomen (**-ne'a** *pl.*).—**peritoni'tis** *n.* inflammation of the peritoneum.—**peritone'al** *a.*
per'iwig *n.* a peruke; a wig.
per'iwinkle *n.* trailing plant with a blue flower; common mollusc.
per'jure (-jer) *v.t.* to forswear.—*v.i.* to bear false witness.—**per'jury** *n.* false swearing; false testimony on oath.
perm' *n.* (*col.*) for permanent wave, a treatment of the hair inducing a wave lasting for several months.
per'manent *a.* continuing in the same state; lasting.—**per'manence, per'manency** *n.* fixedness.—**per'manently** *adv.*
perman'ganate *n.* a salt of an acid of manganese, *esp.* permanganate of potash salt used as disinfectant.
per'meate *v t.* pass through pores of; saturate (**per'meating** *pr. p.*)-**per'meable** *a.* admitting passage of fluids.
permit *v.t.* to allow; to give leave to; to give leave.—(per'-) *n.* a written permission.—**permis'sion** *n.* leave, liberty.—**permiss'ible** *a.* allowable.—**permiss'ive** *a.*
permute' *v.t.* to interchange.—**permuta'tion** *n.* mutual transference; in algebra, change in the arrangement of a number of quantities.
perni'cious (-nish'-) *a.* having the quality of destroying or injuring; hurtful.
Syn. injurious, noxious, deadly. *Ant.* salutary, wholesome, beneficial.
pernick'ety *a.* (*sl.*) fussy; fastidious about trifles; punctilious.
perora'tion *n.* conclusion of oration.
perox'ide (-ok'sīd) *n.* that oxide of a given base which contains the greatest quantity of oxygen.—**perox'ide of hy'drogen** *n.* a mild bleaching compound.
perpendic'ular *a.* exactly upright; at right angles to the plane of the horizon; at right angles to a given line or surface. —*n.* a line at right angles to the plane of the horizon; a line falling at right angles on another line or plane.
per'petrate *v.t.* to commit (something bad).—**perpetra'tion** *n.*—**per'petrator** *n.*
perpet'ual *a.* continuous, lasting for ever.—**perpet'ually** *adv.*—**perpet'uate** *v.t.* to make perpetual; not to allow to be forgotten.—**perpetua'tion** *n.*—**perpetu'ity** *n.*
perplex' *v.t.* to puzzle; complicate.—**perplex'ity** *n.* a puzzled or tangled state.
per'quisite (-it) *n.* a casual payment in money or kind, in addition to salary belonging to an employment.
per'ry *n.* fermented cider-like drink made from pears.
per'secute *v.t.* to oppress for holding opinion; subject to persistent illtreatment.—**persecu'tion** *n.*—**per'secutor** *n.*
persevere' *v.i.* persist, maintain effort. —**perseve'rance** *n.* (**perseve'ring** *pr. p.*).
per'siflage (-flázh) *n.* idle talk, frivolous style of treating a subject.
persist' *v.i.* to continue in a state or action in spite of obstacles or objections. —**persist'ent** *a.*—**persist'ence** *n.*
per'son *n.* a human being; a divine being; a character in a play, etc.; in grammar, a classification, or one of the classes, of pronouns and verb-forms according to the person speaking, spoken to, or spoken of.—**per'sonable** *a.* goodlooking.—**per'sonage** *n.* a notable person.
per'sonal *a.* individual, private, of one's own; of or relating to grammatical person.—**personal property** or **estate**, all property except land and interests in land that pass to an heir.—**personal'ity** *n.* distinctive character.—*pl.* offensive personal remarks.—**per'sonally** *adv.* in person.—**per'sonalty** *n.* personal property.—**per'sonate** *v.t.* to pass oneself off as.—**persona'tion** *n.*—**person'ify** *v.t.* to represent as a person; to typify (**-ified** *p.t.* and *p.p.*—**-ifying** *pres. p.*).—**personifica'tion** *n.*—**personnel'** *n.* staff employed in a service or institution.
perspect'ive (-iv) *n.* the art of drawing on a flat surface to give the effect of solidity and relative distances and sizes; drawing in perspective; mental view.
Per'spex *n.* an unbreakable plastic substitute for glass (trade name).
perspic'uous *a.* clearly expressed.—**perspicu'ity** *n.*—**perspica'cious** *a.* having quick insight.—**perspica'city** (-kas'-) *n.*
perspire' *v.i.* to sweat.—**perspira'tion** *n.*
persuade' (-sw-) *v.t.* to convince; to bring (any one to do something) by argument, etc.—**persua'sion** *n.* persuading; belief.—**persua'sive** *a.*
Syn. to influence, urge, entreat. *Ant.* to dissuade, discourage, deter.
pert *a.* forward, saucy.
pertain' *v.i.* to belong, to relate.
pert'inent *a.* to the point.—**pert'inence** *n.*—**pertina'cious** *a.* obstinate, persistent, dogged.—**pertina'city** (-as-) *n.*
perturb' *v.t.* to make uneasy; to alarm. —**perturb'able** *a.*—**perturba'tion** *n.*
peruke' (-ōōk') *n.* a wig.
peruse' (-ōōz') *v.t.* to read, *esp.* in a slow or careful manner.—**peru'sal** *n.* reading.

pervade' *v.t.* to spread through.—**perva'sion** *n.*—**perva'sive** *a.*
perverse' *a.* obstinately or unreasonably wrong, wayward, etc.-**perver'sity** *n.*
pervert' *v.t.* to turn to a wrong use; to lead astray.—**per'vert** *a.* one who has turned to error, *esp.* in religion; one who expresses abnormality, *esp.* in sexual matters.—**perver'sion** *n.*—**perver'sive** *a.*
per'vious *a.* permeable; penetrable.
pes'ky *a.* in N. America, (*sl.*) annoying; vexatious, troublesome.
pess'imism *n.* theory that everything turns to evil; tendency to see the worst side of things.—**pess'imist** *n.*
pest *n.* troublesome or harmful thing or person; a plague.—**pestif'erous** *a.* bringing plague; harmful, deadly.-**pest'ilent** *a.*
pest'er *v.t.* to trouble or vex persistently.
pes'tilence *n.* disease; the plague; any epidemic disease.—**pestilen'tial** *n.* infectious, bringing disease.
pes'tle (-tl) *n.* an instrument with which things are pounded in a mortar.
pet *n.* a favourite animal; person regarded with affection; fit of ill-temper or sulking.—*v.t.* to make a pet of (**pet'ting** *pres. p.*—**pet'ted** *p.t.* and *p.p.*).
pet'al *n.* coloured flower leaf.
petard' *n.* explosive bomb, firework.
pe'ter *v.i.* (usually with "out") to become exhausted, come to an end.
pe'tersham *n.* a heavy overcoat; also breeches; heavy woollen cloth; strong kind of corded silk ribbon.
peti'tion (-ish'-) *n.* a request, *esp.* one presented to a sovereign or parliament; a prayer.—*v.t.* to present a petition to.—**peti'tionary** *a.*—**peti'tioner** *n.*
pet'rel *n.* (**stormy-petrel**) small sea-bird.
pet'rify *v.t.* to turn into stone; to strike with terror (**-rified** *p.t.* and *p.p.*—**-rifying** *pres. p.*).—**petrifac'tion** *n.*
pet'rol *n.* refined petroleum.
petro'leum *n.* a mineral oil.
pe'trous *a.* like stone; stony.
pett'icoat *n.* a woman's underskirt.
pett'ifogger *n.* a low-class lawyer; one given to mean dealing in small matters.—**pett'ifog** *v.i.* be, act like pettifogger.
pet'tish *a.* peevish, petulant.
pett'y *a.* unimportant, trivial; small-minded, ungenerous, mean; on a small scale.—**petty officer** (*Navy*) non-commissioned officer.—**pet'tiness** *n.*
pet'ulant *a.* being cross and peevish.—**pet'ulance** *n.* *Syn.* hasty, cross, fretful. *Ant.* contented, placid, serene.
petun'ia *n.* a genus of herbaceous plants allied to the nightshade, bearing white or purple flowers; a purple colour.
pew *n.* a fixed seat in a church.
pe'wit *see* **peewit.**
pew'ter *n.* an alloy of tin and lead; ware made of this, *sl.* prize-money.
phae'ton (fā'-) *n.* a light, horse-drawn, four-wheeled open carriage.
phag'ocyte *n.* a white blood-corpuscle which devours germs.
phalan'ger *n.* a group of small furry marsupials, some having flying membranes, as the flying squirrels.
phal'anx (fal'angks) *n.* body of infantry soldiers, or people, in close formation (**phal'anxes, phalan'ges** *pl.*).
phal'lus *n.* image of the penis, venerated in religious systems as a symbol of generative power in nature (**-li** *pl.*).—**phal'lic** *a.*—**phal'licism** *n.*
phan'tasm *n.* an illusion; a vision of an absent person.—**phantas'mal** *a.*—**phantasmagor'ia** *n.* an exhibition of illusions, a crowd of dim or unreal figures.—**phan'tasy** *n. see* **fantasy**
phan'tom *n.* an apparition; a spectre; a fancied vision.—**phantom aerial** *n.* in wireless, a special form of non-rigid aerial; a cage aerial.
Phar'isee *n.* member of Jewish sect; hypocrite.—**pharisa'ic, pharisa'ical** *a.*
pharmaceut'ic *a.* relating to pharmacy.—*n.* in *pl.* the science of pharmacy.—**pharmaceut'ical** *a.*—**pharmacopœ'ia** *n.* official book with a list and directions for the use of drugs.—**phar'macy** *n.* the preparation and dispensing of drugs; drugstore (**phar'macies** *pl.*).
pha'ros *n.* a lighthouse; a beacon.
phar'ynx (-ingks) *n.* cavity forming the back part of the mouth and terminating in the gullet (**pharyn'ges** *pl.*).
phase (-z) *n.* an aspect of the moon or a planet; a stage of development.
pheasa'nt (fez-) *n.* a game-bird.
phenac'etin (-nas'-) *n.* an antipyretic medicine obtained from coal-tar, used for headache etc. (trade name).
phenobarb'ital (fēn-ō-barb'-i-tal) *n.* a drug inducing sleep.
phe'nol *n.* carbolic acid.
phenom'enon *n.* anything appearing or observed; a remarkable person or thing (**phenom'ena** *pl.*).—**phenom'enal** *a.* recognisable or evidenced by the senses; relating to phenomena; remarkable.
phi'al *n.* a small glass bottle.
phil- *prefix* forms compounds with the meaning of "loving," as in **philan'der** *v.i.* to amuse oneself with love-making.—**philan'thropy** *n.* love of mankind; practice of doing good to one's fellow-men.—**philanthrop'ic** *a.*—**philan'thropist** *n.*—**phila'tely** *n.* stamp collecting.—**philat'elist** *n.*—**philatel'ic** *a.*—**phil'harmon'ic** *a.* musical (only for titles of societies).—**philol'ogy** *n.* science of structure and development of languages.—**philolo'gical** *a.*—**philol'ogist** *n.*—**philos'ophy** *n.* pursuit of wisdom; study of realities and general principles; system of theories on nature of things or on conduct; calmness of mind expected of a philosopher.—**philos'opher** *n.* one who studies, possesses, or originates, philo-

sophy.—**philosoph'ic, philosoph'ical** *a.* —**philos'ophise** *v.i.*
philan'der *v.i.* to flirt.
philo'gyny (fil-oj'-i-ni) *n.* fondness for women.–**philo'gynist** *n.*–**philo'gynous** *a.*
phil'omel *n.* the nightingale.
phil'tre (-tẹr) *n.* a love-potion.
phlebi'tis *n.* inflammation of a vein.
phlegm (flem) *n.* viscid substance formed by mucous membrane ejected by coughing; calmness; apathy.—**phlegmat'-ic** (-eg-) *a.* not excitable.
phlox *n.* a flowering plant.
pho'bia *n.* morbid fear or aversion.
phoe'nix *n.* a fabulous bird; a genus of tropical plants including the date palm.
phonau'tograph (fōn-aw'tu-) *n.* a device for recording sound vibrations in a visible form.
phone *n., a.,* and *v.i.* an abbreviated form of **telephone.**
phonet'ic *a.* of, or relating to, vocal sounds.—**phonet'ics** *n. pl.* the science of vocal sounds.—**phoneti'cian** *n.*
pho'ney, pho'ny *a.* (U.S.) (*sl.*) counterfeit, false, suspect, bogus.
phono- *prefix* forms compounds with the meaning of "sound" as in **pho'no-graph** *n.* a character representing a sound; (*U.S.*) an instrument recording and reproducing sounds.—**phono-graphic'** *a.*
phor'mium *n.* genus of plants including New Zealand flax.
phos'phorus *n.* a non-metallic element which appears luminous in the dark.—**phos'phate** *n.*—**phos'phide** *n.*—**phos'phite** *n.* compounds of phosphorus.—**phos-phores'cence** *n.* a faint glow in the dark.
pho'to- *prefix* forms compounds or makes combinations with the meaning of "light" as in **photo-chem'istry** *n.* the study of the chemical action of light. —**pho'to-electri'city** *n.* electricity produced or affected by action of light. —**photo-elec'tric cell,** a device worked by electrical changes caused by light, and used in various automatic controls.—**pho'to-elec'tron** *n.* an electron liberated from a metallic surface by action of light. —**photo-engrav'ing** *n.* method of preparing printing plates in relief from photographs by subjecting them to action of a corrosive agent.—**photogen'ic** *a.* capable of being photographed attractively.—**pho'tograph** *n.* picture made by chemical action of light on a sensitive film.—*v.t.* to take a photograph of.—**photog'rapher** *n.*—**photograph'ic** *a.*—**photog'raphy** *n.*—**photogravure'** *n.* process of etching a product of photography. —*n.* a picture so reproduced.—**photom'-eter** *n.* instrument for measuring intensity of light.—**photom'etry** *n.*—**pho'-toplay** *n.* film drama.—**pho'to-ther'apy** *n.* healing by means of light.
phrase (-z) *n.* a mode of expression; a small group of words; a pithy expression. —*v.t.* to express in words.—**phraseol'ogy** (-i-ol'-) *n.* manner of expression, wording (**phra'sing** *pres. p.*).
phrenol'ogy *n.* the study of the shape of the skull; the theory that mental powers are indicated by the shape of the skull.—**phrenol'ogist** *n.*
phthi'sis (th-) *n.* consumption of the lungs.—**phthi'sical** *a.*
phut *n.* the sound of a bullet passing, of a bladder collapsing, etc.—*adv.* **to go phut,** to collapse.
phylac'tery *n.* an amulet.
phys'ic (-iz'-) *n.* medicine.—*pl.* the science of the properties of matter and energy.—*v.t.* dose with medicine.
phys'ical *a.* relating to physic, or physics, or the body.—**phys'ically** *adv.*—**physi'cian** *n.* a qualified medical practitioner.—**phys'icist** *n.* a student of physics. — **physiog'nomy** *n.* judging character by face; the face.—**physiog'-raphy** *n.* science of the earth's surface.—**physiog'rapher** *n.*—**physiol'ogy** *n.* the science of the normal function of living things.—**physiol'ogist** *n.*—**physique'** (-ēk) *n.* bodily structure and development.
pi (pī) *n.* (*math.*) symbol π (Greek P) of the ratio of the circumference to the diameter of a circle.
pian'o *a.* and *adv.* in a low tone or voice. —*n.* a pianoforte (**pian'os** (-ōz) *pl.*).—**pian'oforte** (-ti) *n.* a musical instrument with strings which are struck by hammers worked by a keyboard.—**pi'anist** (pē'-) *n.* performer on the pianoforte.—**piano'la** *n.* a mechanical device for playing on the piano (protected trade name).
piazz'a *n.* square, open space surrounded by buildings, *esp.* in Italy.
pi'ca *n.* a printing type having 6 lines in an inch, now called 12 point.
picaresque' (-esk') *a.* of fiction, dealing with the adventures of rogues.
picc'olo *n.* a small flute (**-olos** (-ōz) *pl.*).
pick *n.* tool consisting of a curved iron crossbar and a wooden shaft for breaking up hard ground.—**pick'axe** *n.* a pick.—**pick on** *v.t.* (U.S.) (*col.*) to find fault with constantly.—**pick-up** *n.* a casual acquaintance; an instrument for directly converting the vibrations of a gramophone record, while it is being played, into electrical currents to be amplified through a loud-speaker.
pick *v.t.* to break the surface of; to skin with something pointed; to gather; to choose, select carefully; to find an occasion for.—*n.* an act of picking; the choicest part.—**pick'ings** *n. pl.* odds and ends of profit.—**pick'pocket** *n.*
pick'-a-back *n.* a ride on the back of a man or animal, given to a child.
pick'et *n.* a prong or pointed stake; a small body of soldiers on police duty; a party of trade unionists posted to deter

would-be workers during a strike.—*v.t.* to tether to a peg; to post as a picket; to beset with pickets.

pic'kle (pik'l) *n.* a brine or other liquid for preserving food; a sorry plight; a troublesome child.—*pl.* pickled vegetables.—*v.t.* to preserve in pickle.

pic'nic *n.* a pleasure excursion including a meal out of doors; in Australia (*sl.*) a troublesome job, an awkward experience. —*v.i.* to take part in a picnic (**pic'nicked** (-nikt) *p.t.* and *p.p.*—**-nicking** *pres. p.*).

pic'ric *a.*—**picric acid** *n.* a powerful acid used in dyeing, medicine, and as an ingredient in certain explosives.

pic'ture *n.* a drawing or painting.—*pl.* the cinema.—*v.t.* to represent in, or as in, a picture.—**pictor'ial** *a.* of, in, with, painting or pictures; graphic.—*n.* newspaper with many pictures.—**picto'rially** *adv.*—**picturesque'** (-esk) *a.* making an effective picture; striking, vivid.—**pic'ture-go'er** *n.* cinema habitué.—**pic'ture-pal'ace** *n.* a cinema.

pidg'in *a.* — **pidg'in English** jargon used in conversation between natives and Europeans in the Far East.

pie *n.* a magpie, woodpecker; a dish of meat, fruit, etc., covered with paste; a mass of printer's type in confusion, etc.

pie'bald *a.* irregularly marked with black and white; motley.—*n.* a piebald horse or other animal.—**pied** *a.* piebald.

piece (pēs) *n.* a separate part or fragment; a single object; a coin; a literary or musical composition, etc.—*v.t.* to mend, put together.—**piece'meal** *adv.* by, in, or into pieces; bit by bit.—**piece'work** *n.*

pier (pēr) *n.* a piece of solid upright masonry, *esp.* supporting a bridge; a stone wall to break the force of the sea; a structure running into the sea as a landing-stage, etc.

pierce (pērs) *v.t.* to make a hole in; to make a way through (**pier'cing** *pres. p.* —*a.* sharp; shrill (sound)).

pier'rot (pēr'ō) *n.* traditional pantomime character; member of troupe of entertainers, usually in white costume trimmed with black pom-pons.

pi'ety *n.* godliness, devoutness.
Syn. holiness, sanctity, devotion. *Ant.* impiety, ungodliness, wickedness.

pif'fle *n.* (*sl.*) rubbish, twaddle.

pig *n.* a swine; an oblong mass of smelted metal.—*v.i.* of a sow, to produce a litter; to herd together in a dirty untidy way.—**pigg'ery** *n.* a place for keeping pigs.—**pigg'ish** *a.*—**pig'-dog** *n.* Australia, a dog used in hunting wild pig.—**pig'-face** *n.* Australia, a kind of cactus.—**pig'sty** *n.* enclosed place for pigs.—**pig'tail** *n.* a plait of hair hanging down back.

pi'geon (pij'en) *n.* a bird of many wild and domesticated varieties, often trained to carry messages.—**pi'geon'hole** *n.* compartment for papers.—*v.t.* put away.

pig'ment *n.* colouring matter.

pig'my *see* **pygmy.**

pike *n.* spear formerly used by infantry; a peaked hill; a large fresh-water fish.—**pike'-pole** *n.* N. America, pole used by lumbermen to control floating logs.

pike'let, pike'lin *n.* a light round tea-cake; a crumpet.

pike'staff *n.*—**plain as a pikestaff** easy to see or understand.

pilas'ter *n.* a rectangular column, usually set in a wall.

pilau' (pi-lō') *n.* meat or fowl boiled with rice, raisins and spice.

pil'chard *n.* a small sea fish.

pile *n.* a beam driven into the ground, *esp.* as a foundation for building in water or wet ground.—**pile'-driver** *n.* a machine for driving down piles; a heap; a huge building; an electric battery.—*v.t.* to heap up.—*n.* a nap of velvet, plush, etc.

piles *n. pl.* tumours of veins of rectum.

pil'fer *v.t.* to steal in small quantities.—**pil'ferage** *n.*—**pil'ferer** *n.*

pil'grim *n.* one who journeys to a sacred place; a wanderer.—**pil'grimage** *n.*

pill *n.* a small ball of medicine.

pill'age *n.* seizure of goods by force, *esp.* in war; plunder.—*v.t./i.* plunder.

pill'ar *n.* a column; support.—**pillar-box** *n.* hollow, short pillar with slit in which letters may be posted.

pill'ion (-yun) *n.* a cushion or seat for a person to ride behind a horseman, motor-cyclist, etc.; luggage-bracket.

pill'ory *n.* a frame with holes for head and hands in which an offender was exposed to pelting and ridicule.—*v.t.* set in pillory; expose to ridicule and abuse (**pill'oried** *p.t./p.p.*—**-orying** *pr. p.*).

pill'ow *n.* a cushion for the head, specially in bed.—*v.t.* to lay on a pillow.

pi'lot *n.* person who takes charge of a ship entering or leaving harbour, or where knowledge of local waters is needed; a steersman; one who flies an aeroplane; a guide.—*v.t.* to act as pilot to.—**pi'lotage** *n.* work or payment of a pilot.—**pi'lot jet** *n.* in motoring, a carburettor jet for starting and slow running.—**pilot-officer** *n.* junior commissioned rank in the R.A.F., equivalent to 2nd Lieut. Army and Midshipman Navy.—**pilot tube** *n.* in aviation, an air-speed indicator.

pil'ule *n.* a small pill.

pimen'to *n.* allspice, or the tree producing it (**-tos** (-tōz) *pl.*).

pimp *n.* a pander.—*v.i.* to pander.

pim'pernel *n.* a plant with small scarlet or blue or white flowers.

pim'ple *n.* a small tumour of the skin.—**pim'ply** *a.* covered with pimples.

pin *n.* a short thin piece of wire with a head and a point for fastening soft materials together; a wooden or metal peg or rivet.—*v.t.* to fasten with a pin or pins; to seize and hold fast (**pinned'** *p.t.* and *p.p.*).—**pin-money** *n.* an allowance made to a woman for her private expenditure.—**pinpoint** *v.t.* to locate with great precision.—**pin-table** *n.* a game in which balls, released on the insertion of a coin, are to be shot into various holes round obstacles originally formed by the pins.—**pin-up (girl)** *n.* (*sl.*) a picture of a woman hung up for admiration; a very attractive girl.

pin'afore *n.* a child's apron or overall.

pince'-nez (pans'nā) *n.* eyeglasses kept on the nose by a spring.

pin'cers *n. pl.* a tool for gripping, composed of two limbs crossed and pivoted.

pinch *v.t.* to nip or squeeze; N. America (*sl.*) to steal.—*n.* a nip; stress; as much as can be taken up between finger and thumb.—**pinch' out** *v.i.* Australia, in mining, of a seam, to thin out and disappear.

pinch'beck *n.* a zinc and copper alloy; cheap jewellery.—*a.* counterfeit, flashy.

pine *n.* an evergreen coniferous tree.—*v.i.* to waste away, *esp.* with grief.

pine'apple *n.* tropical plant bearing a large edible fruit; the fruit itself.

pin'fold *n.* a pound for cattle.

ping'-pong *n.* table tennis.

pin'ion *n.* a wing.—*v.t.* to disable by binding wings, arms, etc., to confine thus.—*n.* small cog-wheel.

pink *n.* a garden plant; height or excellence.—*a.* pale red in colour.—*v.t.* to pierce; to ornament with perforations.

pink'ing *n.* the metallic noise of an engine similar to knocking.

pinn'ace *n.* a warship's boat; formerly a small ship attending on a larger one.

pinn'acle *n.* pointed turret on a buttress or roof; a slender mountain peak; highest pitch or point, climax.

pint (pīnt) *n.* liquid measure, half a quart.

pin'tle *n.* a pivot-pin; *esp.* of rudder.

pin'to *a.* multicoloured; dappled.—*n.* an animal with a motley coat.

pi'oneer (pī'on-) *n.* one of an advanced body preparing a road for troops; explorer; one who first originates.—*v.i.* to act as pioneer or leader.

pi'ous *n.* devout, godly, religious.

pip *n.* disease of fowls; seed in fruit; spot on playing cards, dice, etc.; (*sl.*) star on army officer's shoulder.—**have the pip** (*sl.*) be depressed, irritable.

pipe *n.* tube of metal or other materials, a musical instrument, a whistle; a shrill voice or bird's note; tube with a small bowl at the end for smoking tobacco; a wine cask; in S. Africa, soft, volcanic rock in which diamonds are found.—*v.i.* and *t.* to play on a pipe.—**pipe'clay** *n.* clay used for tobacco pipes and for whitening military equipment, etc.—*v.t.* to whiten with pipeclay.—**pi'per** *n.* a player on a pipe or bagpipes.—**pipeline** *n.* an overland pipe through which petrol is pumped over long distances.

pipette' *n.* a small tube to transfer fluids from one vessel to another.

pip'it *n.* a bird of many species.

pip'kin *n.* a small earthenware jar.

pipp'in *n.* various sorts of apple.

pi'quant (pēk'ant) *a.* pungent; stimulating.—**pi'quancy** *n.*—**pique** (pēk) *v.t.* to irritate; hurt the pride of; stimulate.—*n.* feeling of injury or baffled curiosity.

pi'qué (pē'kā) *n.* stiff ribbed or ridged cotton fabric.

piquet' (-ket') *n.* a card game for two.

pi'rate *n.* a sea-robber; publisher, etc., who infringes copyright; in wireless, a person using a receiver without a licence; a privately owned omnibus or coach competing against an established company.—*v.t.* to publish or reproduce regardless of copyright.—**pi'racy** *n.*—**pirat'ical** *a.*—**pirat'ically** *adv.*

pirouette' *n.* a spinning round on the toe.—*v.i.* to do this.

Pi'sces (pī'cēz) *n. pl.* the Fishes, 12th sign of Zodiac, operative Feb. 19–Mar. 20.

pista'chio *n.* the nut of a turpentine tree (**-chios** (-ōz) *pl.*).

pist'il *n.* the female organ of a flower.

pist'ol *n.* small firearm used with one hand.—*v.t.* to shoot with a pistol.

pist'on *n.* a plug fitting a cylinder and working up and down, e.g., as in a steam engine, etc.—**piston-slap** *n.* noise in an engine occurring when the piston is too loose a fit in the cylinder, as when cold.

pit *n.* a deep hole in the ground; a coal mine or its shaft; a depression in any surface; the part of a theatre behind the stalls; an enclosure in which animals were set to fight.—*v.t.* to set to fight; to put to the test; to mark with small scars.—**pit'fall** *n.* a covered pit for catching animals or men.—**pit'head** *n.* entrance to a coal-mine.—**pit'head price** price of coal at pithead.—**pit' prop** *n.* (*mining*) prop of wood temporarily to support coal seams when undercut.—**pit'saw** *n.* long saw with double handle for dividing timber, worked by top sawer on log and pitsawer in pit below.—**pitt'ing** *n.* in motoring, uneven wearing of surfaces, e.g. valve seatings (**pit'ted** *p.t./p.p.*).

pit *n.* in South Africa, the name for a fruit kernel, as a plum-stone.

pit'-a-pat *adv.* in a flutter; with palpitation; with light quick steps.

pitch *n.* a dark sticky substance obtained from tar or turpentine.—*v.t.* to coat with this.—**pitch'-blende** *n.* a black ore, an oxide of uranium yielding radium, uraninite.—**pitch'-pine** *n.* resinous kind of pine.—**pitch'y** *a.* covered with pitch; black as pitch.

pitch *v.t.* to set up; to cast or throw.—*v.i.* to fix upon; to fall headlong; of a ship, to plunge lengthwise.—*n.* an act of pitching; degree, height, station; a slope; distance an airscrew advances during one revolution; distance between threads of a screw, teeth of a saw, etc.; part of ground where wickets are set up; acuteness of tone.—**pitch'fork** *n.* a fork for lifting and pitching hay, etc.—*v.t.* to throw with, or as with, a pitchfork.

pitch'er *n.* large jug.

pitch'ery, pitch'eri, pit'uri in Australia, narcotic leaves of a shrub, used by the natives.

pith *n.* the tissue in the stems and branches of certain plants; essential substance, most important part.—**pith'less** *a.*—**pith'y** *a.* consisting of pith; terse concise.—**pith'ily** *adv.* concisely.

pitt'ance *n.* scanty allowance, wages.

pitu'itary body *n.* a ductless gland at the base of the brain, affecting growth.

pit'y *n.* sympathy or sorrow for others, suffering; a regrettable fact.—*v.t.* to feel pity for (**pit'ied** *p.t.* and *p.p.*—**pit'ying** *pres. p.*).—**pit'eous** *a.* deserving pity.—**pit'iable** *a.*—**pit'iably** *adv.*—**pit'iful** *a.* full of pity; contemptible.—**pit'iless** *a.*

piv'ot *n.* a shaft or pin on which something turns.—*v.t.* to furnish with a pivot. —*v.i.* to turn on a pivot.

pix'y, pix'ie *n.* a fairy (**pix'ies** *pl.*).

pizzica'to (pitz'-ik-ah'-tō) *adv.* (*mus.*) with the fingertips instead of the bow.

plac'ard *n.* a paper with a notice on one side for posting up.—*v.t.* to post placards on; to advertise or display on placards.

placat'e *v.t.* to conciliate, pacify, appease, soothe.—**plac'able** *a.*

place *n.* a particular part of space, spot; position; town, village, residence, buildings; office or employment.—*v.t.* to put in a particular place.—**pla'cing** *pres. p.*

placen'ta (-sen-) *n.* the soft disc which connects the fetus with the mother; the after-birth (**placen'tas, -tæ** *pl.*).

pla'cid (-as-) *a.* calm.—**placid'ity** *n.*
Syn. unruffled, serene, tranquil. *Ant.* ruffled, troubled, tempestuous.

pla'giary *n.* stealing and using as one's own another's ideas, writings, inventions.—**pla'giarism** *n.*—**pla'giarist** *n.*—**pla'giarise** *v.t.* and *i.*

plague (plāg) *n.* pestilence; affliction.—*v.t.* to pester or annoy.—**pla'guy** *a.*

plaice *n.* a flat fish used for food.

plaid (plad) *n.* a long Highland shawl; a checkered or tartan pattern.

plain *a.* flat, level; unobstructed, not intricate; easily understood; simple, ordinary; unadorned; ugly.—*n.* tract of level country; in Australia, unwooded country, even if undulating.—*adv.* clearly.—**plain'ly** *adv.*—**plain-bearings** *n. pl.* in motoring, bearings offering sliding contact.—**plain'clothes man** *n.* a policeman, detective who wears ordinary clothes on duty.—**plain' dealing** *n.* frank honest dealing.—**plain'sailing** *n.* (1) untroubled sailing on a clear course; (2) Straightforward action.—**plain-song,** vocal music in churches, resting upon a system of octaves.

plaint *n.* a statement of complaint in a law court; a lament.—**plaint'iff** *n.* one who sues in a law court.—**plaint'ive** *a.* sad.

plait (plat) *n.* a fold; a braid of hair, straw, etc.—*v.t.* to form into plaits.

plan *n.* drawing of a thing's horizontal section; diagram, map; project, design; scheme.—*v.t.* make a plan of; design; arrange beforehand.

plan'chet *n.* a disc of metal for a coin.

planchette (plon-shet') *n.* a small board used in spiritualistic experiments.

plane *n.* a tree with broad leaves; a carpenter's tool for smoothing wood.—*v.t.* to make smooth with one.

plane *a.* perfect, flat, or level.—*n.* a smooth surface; a level.—*v.t.* to glide in an aeroplane.—*n.* one of the supporting surfaces of an aeroplane.

plan'et *n.* a heavenly body revolving round the sun.—**plan'etary** *a.*

planetar'ium *n.* an apparatus that shows the movement of sun, moon, planets, and stars by projecting lights on the inside of a dome; building in which the apparatus is housed.

plank *n.* a long flat piece of sawn timber.—*v.t.* to cover, to build a floor.

plank'ton *n.* the minute animal and vegetable organisms floating in the ocean, on which many fish live.

plant (-å-) *n.* a member of the vegetable kingdom, a living organism feeding on inorganic substances and without power of locomotion; building and equipment used for manufacturing purposes; (*sl.*) a swindle; Australia, something hidden away.—*v.t.* set in the ground to grow; to fix firmly; to support or establish; to stock with plants; to hide.—**planta'tion** *n.* a wood of planted trees; an estate for cultivation of tea, tobacco, etc.; formerly, a colony.—**plant'er** *n.* one who plants; a grower of tropical produce; Australia, a cattle-thief.

plant'ain *n.* low-growing herb with broad leaves; tropical plant like a banana; its fruit.

plaque (plak) *n.* the plate of a clasp or brooch; a plate of metal on which enamels are painted.

plash *n.* a puddle; a splash.—*v.i.*

plas'ma *n.* formless matter; protoplasm.

plast'er *n.* a piece of fabric spread with a medicinal or adhesive substance for application to the body; a mixture of lime, sand, etc., to spread on walls, etc.—*v.t.* to apply plaster to.—**plast'erer** *n.*—**plast'ic** *a.* produced by moulding; easily moulded; giving form to shapeless matter, as clay, wax, etc.—**plastic surgery** *n.* the art of restoring lost or damaged parts of the body by grafting on sound tissue.—

Plast'icene (-ȧ-) (trade name) *n.* a kind of modelling clay.—**plasti'city** *n.*
plas'tics *n.* the science of connecting several resins by moulding into durable materials to be used in industry; the articles or materials so made.
plas'tron *n.* breast-plate worn by fencers for protection.
plat *n.* a plot of ground.—*v.t.*, *n.* plait.
plate *n.* a flat thin sheet of metal, glass, etc.; utensils of gold or silver; shallow round dish from which food is eaten.—*v.t.* to cover with a thin coating of gold, silver, or other metal.—*n.* (*col.*)—dental plate.—**plate'ful** *n.*—**platt'er** *n.* a flat dish or plate.
plat'eau (-ō) *n.* a tract of level high land (**-teaus, -teaux** (-tōz) *pl.*).
plat'en *n.* in a printing-press, a plate by which paper is pressed against type; the roller in a typewriter.
plat'form *n.* raised level surface or floor.
plat'inum *n.* a white heavy malleable metal.—**plat'inum blonde'** (*col.*) a woman with hair of a white-gold colour, either natural or bleached.—**plat'inotype** *n.* a photographic process in which platinum is used.
plat'itude *n.* commonplace remark, dull truism.—**platitu'dinous** *a.*
Platon'ic *a.* pertaining to Plato or Platonism.—**Platon'ic love** pure spiritual affection between the sexes.—**Pla'tonism** *n.* philosophy of Plato or his followers.
platoon' *n.* a small body of soldiers employed as a unit; sub-division of an infantry company.
platy'pus *n.* the ornithorhynchus, a duck-billed aquatic mammal of Australia.
plau'sible *a.* something fair or reasonable; fair-spoken.—**plau'sibility** *n.*
plau'dit *n.* an act of applause.
Syn. specious, superficial, ostensible. *Ant.* real, authentic, positive.
play (plā) *v.i.* to move with light or irregular motion, to flicker, etc.; amuse oneself; to take part in a game; to perform on a musical instrument.—*v.t.* to use or work (an instrument); to take part in (a game); to contend with in a game; to perform (music), perform on (an instrument); to act; to act the part of.—*n.* brisk or free movement; activity; sport; amusement; gambling; a dramatic piece or performance.—**play'er** *n.*—**play'er-piano** *n.* a mechanically played piano.—**play'boy** *n.* a man devoted to expensive dissipations.—**play'ful** *a.* frolicsome.—**play'thing** *n.* a toy.—**play'wright** *n.* an author of plays; a dramatist.
plea (plē) *n.* excuse; statement of a prisoner or defendant; request.
plead *v.i.* to address a court of law; to make an earnest appeal.—*v.t.* to bring forward as an excuse or plea.
please *v.t.* to be agreeable to.—*v.i.* to like; to be willing.—**pleas'ance** (plez-) *n.* delight; a pleasure-ground.—**pleas'ure** *n.* enjoyment; satisfaction, will, choice.—**pleas'urable** *a.* giving pleasure.—**pleas'ant** *a.* pleasing, agreeable.—**pleas'antly** *adv.*—**pleas'antry** *n.* a joke.
pleat *n.* a three-fold band on a garment, etc., made by folding the material on itself.—*v.t.* to make a pleat in.
plebe'ian *a.* belonging to the common people; low or rough.—*n.* one of the common people.–**pleb'iscite** *n.* a decision by direct voting of a whole people.
plec'trum *n.* a small rod for plucking the strings of a lyre (**-tra** *pl.*).
pledge *n.* a thing given over as security; a toast; promise.—*v.t.* to give over as security; to engage; drink the health of.
pledg'et *n.* a small plug; a flat mass of lint laid over a wound.
ple'nary *a.* complete, unlimited.—**plenipoten'tiary** *a.* with full powers.—*n.* envoy, ambassador with full powers.—**plen'itude** *n.* completeness.
plent'y *n.* quite enough; abundance.—**plent'eous** *a.*—**plent'iful** *a.* abundant.
ple'onasm *n.* the use of more words than are needed for the sense.
pleth'ora *n.* an excess of red corpuscles in the blood; oversupply.—**plethor'ic** *a.*
pleur'isy (plōō-) *n.* inflammation of membrane round the lungs.
Plexiglas *n.* a tough transparent plastic used in aeroplanes, etc. (trade name).
plex'us *n.* network of nerves, or fibres; collection of related parts (**plex'us** *pl.*).
pli'able *a.* easily bent or influenced.—**pliabil'ity** *n.*–**pli'ant** *a.* pliable.–**pli'ancy** *n.*
pli'ers *n. pl.* small pincers.
plight (plit) *n.* promise.—*v.t.* to promise, betroth.—*n.* state; predicament.
Plim'soll (mark) *n.* mark on British merchant ships indicating maximum draught permitted when loaded.
plim'solls *n. pl.* rubber-soled shoes with fabric uppers for physical drill, etc.
plinth *n.* a square slab as the base of a column, etc.
pli'ocene *n.* the most recent tertiary [deposits.
plod *v.i.* to walk or work doggedly.
plot *n.* a small piece of land; the plan or essential facts of a story, play, etc.; a secret design, a conspiracy.—*v.t.* to make a map of; to devise secretly; to divide into plots.—*v.i.* to conspire.
plough (plow) *n.* an implement for turning up the soil.—*v.t.* to turn up with a plough, to furrow.—*v.t.* to reject, as a candidate in an examination; to fail.
plo'ver (pluv-) *n.* various birds, including the lapwing.
pluck *v.i.* to pull or pick off; to strip the feathers from; to reject in an examination.—*n.* a plucking; a beast's heart, lungs, etc.; courage.—**pluck'y** *a.* brave.
plug *n.* something fitting into and filling a hole; tobacco pressed hard; a piece of

this for chewing.—*v.t.* to stop with a plug; in N. America (*sl.*) to hit or strike with the fist; to shoot; (*sl.*) to advertise a dance tune, etc., by having bands to play it (**plug'ging** *pres p.*).

plum *n.* a stone fruit; the tree bearing it.

plumb (-m) *n.* weight on a line used for sounding, finding the perpendicular, etc.—*a.* perpendicular.—*adv.* perpendicularly; exactly.—*v.t.* to find the depth of; to set exactly upright.—**plumb'er** (-mer) *n.* one who works in lead, etc.—**plumb'ing** *n.* plumber's work.—**plumm'et** *n.* plumb.—**plumb'line** *n.* cord with a plumb attached.—**plumba'go** (-m-bā-) *n.* black lead, graphite.

plume (-ōōm) *n.* a feather; ornament consisting of feathers or horse-hair.—*v.t.* to furnish with plumes; to strip of feathers; to boast, pride oneself.

plu'mage *n.* the feathers of a bird.

plump *a.* of rounded form.—*v.i.* to sit or fall abruptly; vote only for.—*v.t.* to drop or throw abruptly.—*adv.* abruptly, bluntly.

plun'der *v.t.* to rob systematically; to take by open force.—*v.i.* to rob.—*n.* a violent robbery; property so obtained.

plunge *v.t.* to put forcibly (into).—*v.i.* to throw oneself (into); to enter or move forward with violence.—*n.* a plunge, dive.—**plun'ger** *n.* (**plun'ging** *pres. p.*).

pluper'fect (plōō-) *a.* of a tense, expressing action completed before a past point of time.

plu'ral *a.* more than one; denoting more than one person or thing.—*n.* a word in its plural form.—**plu'ralism** *n.* holding more than one appointment, vote, etc.—**plu'ralist** *n.*—**plural'ity** *n.*

plus *prep.* with addition of (usually indicated by the sign +); to be added; positive.—**plus'-fours** *n. pl.* (*sl.*) wide knickerbockers worn by golfers.

plush *n.* a fabric with a long soft nap.

plutoc'racy *n.* government by the rich, the wealthy class.—**plu'tocrat** *n.* a wealthy person.—**plutocrat'ic** *a.*

Pluton'ian *a.* pertaining to the god Pluto, or his home; dark; subterranean.

Pluton'ium (-tōn'-i-um) *n.* a radio-active element produced when neptunium releases an electron.

plu'vial *a.* of or caused by rain.

ply *n.* fold, thickness.—*v.t.* wield, work at; supply pressingly.—*v.i.* go to and fro (**plied** *p.t./p.p.*—**ply'ing** *pr. p.*).

ply'wood *n.* boards made by glueing together several thin layers of wood under pressure, the grain of each layer being at right angles to that of the adjoining layer.

pneumat'ic (nū-) *a.* worked by or filled with air; inflated with air.

pneumo'nia *n.* inflammation of lungs.

poach *v.i.* to cook (an egg) by dropping without the shell into boiling water.

poach *v.t.* to take (game) illegally.—*v.i.* to trespass for this purpose.—**poach'er** *n.*

pock *n.* a pustule, as in smallpox.

pock'et *n.* a small bag inserted in a garment; a cavity filled with ore, etc.; a mass of water or air differing in some way from that surrounding it.—*v.t.* to put into one's pocket; appropriate.

pod *n.* a long seed-vessel, as of peas, beans, etc.—*v.i.* form pods.—*v.t.* to shell.

pod'gy *a.* short and fat; thick.

po'e *n.* early name for N. Zealand bird, the tui or parson bird.

po'em *n.* an imaginative composition in verse.—**po'et** *n.* a writer of poems.—**po'etess** *fem.*—**po'etry** *n.* the art or work of a poet.—**po'esy** *n.* poetry.—**poet'ic, poet'ical** *a.*—**poet'ically** *adv.*—**po'etaster** *n.* an inferior or paltry verse-writer.

pog'rom *n.* organised plunder and massacre of opponents, *esp.* Jews.

poign'ant (poin-) *a.* pungent, stinging; moving, vivid.—**poign'ancy** *n.*

poilu' (pwā-lōō') *n.* French soldier.

point *n.* a dot or mark; a punctuation mark; an item, detail; a unit of value; position, degree, stage; moment; the essential object or thing; a sharp end; the headland; a movable rail changing a train to other rails; one of the direction marks of a compass; striking or effective part or quality; an act of pointing.—*v.t.* to sharpen; to give value to (words, etc.); to fill up joints with mortar; to aim or direct.—*v.i.* to show direction or position by extending a finger, stick, etc.; to direct attention; of a dog, to indicate the position of game by standing facing it.—**point'ed** *a.*—**point'edly** *adv.*—**point'er** *n.* an index, indicating rod, etc., used for pointing; a dog trained to point.—*pl.* Australia, in a bullock team, the pair ahead of the pole pair.—**point'less** *a.*—**point'-blank'** *a.* aimed horizontally.—*adv.* with level aim; at short range; uncompromisingly, flatly.

points rat'ioning *n.* a system by which certain foods were valued in points and obtained by the individual according to his free choice of allocation of the total number issued to him.

poise *v.t.* to place or hold in a balanced or steady position.—*v.i.* to be so held; to hover.—*n.* balance, equilibrium, carriage (of body, etc.).

poi'son (-z-) *n.* substance which kills or injures when introduced into living organism.—*v.t.* to give poison to; to infect; to pervert (the mind or intention), spoil.—**poi'soner** *n.*—**poi'sonous** *a.*

poke *v.t.* to push or thrust with a finger, stick, etc.; to thrust forward.—*v.i.* to make thrusts; to pry.—*n.* act of poking.—**po'ker** *n.* a metal rod for poking a fire; a game of cards.—**po'ker-face** *n.* (*fig.*) a countenance giving no signs of emotion.—**po'ky** *a.* small, confined.

pole *n.* a long rounded piece of wood; a measure of length, 5½ yards; a measure of area; 30¼ square yards.—*v.t.* to propel with a pole.—**polar'ograph** *n.* an instrument for recording the amount of dissociation or polarisation in an electrolytic solution.—**Po'laroid** *n.* a light polarising substance used in glass to reduce the light glare (trade name).—**po'lers** *n. pl.* in Australia, in a bullock team, the pair at the pole.

pole *n.* each of the two points about which the stars appear to revolve; each of the ends of the axis of the earth; each of the opposite ends of a magnet, electric cell, etc.—**po'lar** *a.*—**polar'ity** *n.*—**po'larise** *v.t.* to give magnetic polarity to; to affect light so that its vibrations are kept to one plane.—**polarisa'tion** *n.*

pole'-axe *n.* a butcher's axe.

pole'cat *n.* small evil-smelling animal of weasel family.

polem'ic *a.* controversial.—*n.* a war of words.—**polem'ical** *a.*

polen'ta *n.* a porridge made of maize.

police' (-ēs) *n.* public order; the civil force which maintains public order.—*v.t.* to keep in order.—**police'man** *n.* a member of the police.—**police'woman** a woman member of a police force.

pol'icy *n.* political wisdom; a course of action adopted, *esp.* in state affairs; prudent procedure; a contract of insurance; in Scotland, the grounds about a gentleman's country house.

pol'ish *v.t.* to make smooth and glossy; to refine.—*n.* act of polishing; smoothness; substance used in polishing.
Syn. to burnish, brighten, furbish. *Ant.* to tarnish, sully, stain.

polite' *a.* refined; well-mannered, courteous.—**polite'ly** *adv.*—**polite'ness** *n.*

pol'itic *a.* wise, shrewd, expedient, cunning.—*n.* in *pl.* the art of government; political affairs of life.—**politi'cal** *a.* of the state or its affairs.—**politi'cian** *n.* one engaged in politics.—**polit'ical econ'omy** *n.* science dealing with the nature and distribution of wealth.—**pol'ity** *n.* civil government; form of government; a state.

pol'ka *n.* a dance; music for it.

poll (pōl) *n.* the head or top of the head; a counting of voters; voting; the number of votes recorded.—*v.t.* to cut off the top of; to take the votes of; to receive (votes).—*v.i.* to vote.—**poll'ard** *n.* a tree on which a close head of young branches has been made by polling; a hornless animal of a normally horned variety.—*v.t.* to make a pollard of (a tree).

poll'en *n.* fertilising dust of a flower.

pollina'tion *n.* fertilisation of flowers, etc., by carrying of pollen from anther to stigma.—**poll'inate** *v.t.*

poll'iwog, poll'ywog *n.* a tadpole.

pollute' (-ōōt) *v.t.* to make foul; to desecrate.—**pollu'tion** *n.*

po'lo *n.* a game like hockey played by men mounted on ponies.

polonaise' *n.* a Polish dance; the music for it; a kind of woman's dress.

polo'ny *n.* a kind of sausage.

poltroon' *n.* a coward.—**poltroon'ery** *n.*

poly- *prefix* makes combinations with the meaning of "many" as in **polyan'dry** *n.* practice by which one woman has more than one husband.—**polyan'thus** *n.* a cultivated primrose.—**pol'ychrome** *a.* many colours.—*n.* a work of art in many colours.—**polychromat'ic** *a.*—**polyg'amy** *n.* the practice of being married to several wives at a time.—**polyg'amist** *n.*—**pol'yglot** *a.* speaking, writing, or written in several languages.—**pol'ygon** *n.* a figure with many angles or sides.—**polyg'onal** *a.*—**polyg'yny** *n.* polygamy in which one man has more than one wife.—**polyhe'dron** *n.* a solid figure contained by many faces.—**poly-syll'able** *n.* a word of many syllables.—**polysyllab'ic** *a.*—**polytech'nic** *a.* dealing with various arts and crafts.—*n.* a school doing this.—**pol'ytheism** *n.* the belief in many gods.

pol'yp *n.* a coral insect or other creature of low organisation.

pol'ypus *n.* (*pl.* **pol'ypi** (-pī)) a polyp; a kind of branched tumour.

pomade' *n.* a scented ointment for the head or hair.—**poma'tum** *n.* pomade.

pom'egranate *n.* a large fruit with thick rind containing many seeds.

Pomera'nian *n.* a breed of small dogs.

pomm'el *n.* the knob of a sword hilt; the front of a saddle.—*v.t.* to strike repeatedly, to strike with a sword-pommel.

pomm'y *n.* in Australia, a newly arrived person from Great Britain.

pomp *n.* splendid display or ceremony.

pomp'ous *a.* self-important; puffed up; of language, inflated.—**pompos'ity** *n.*

pom'padour *n.* a style of hair-dressing in which the hair is brushed back and upwards from the forehead.

pom'-pom *n.* a quick-firing gun.

pom'-pon *n.* a tuft of ribbon, wool, etc., decorating a hat, shoe, etc.

pon'cho *n.* a loose garment or cloak worn in South America (**-chos** *pl.*).

pond *n.* pool, small lake.

pon'der *v.t.* and *i.* to meditate, think over.—**pond'erable** *a.* capable of being weighed.—**pond'erous** *a.* heavy, dull.

pondok' *n.* in S. Africa, a native hut.

pon'iard *n.* a dagger.—*v.t.* stab with one.

pont *n.* in South Africa, a large ferry-boat worked by a cable.

pon'tac *n.* in South Africa, wine resembling port.

pon'tiff *n.* the Pope; a high priest.—**pontif'ical** *a.*—**pontif'icate** *n.*

pontoon' *n.* flat-bottomed boat or metal drum used in supporting bridge.

po'ny *n.* a horse of a small breed; (*sl.*) a bet of £25; a very small glass.
poo'dle *n.* a variety of pet dog.
pooh *interj.* an exclamation of scorn.
pooh'-bah *n.* person holding many offices at the one time.
pool (-ōō-) *n.* a small body of still water; a deep place in a river.
pool (-ōō-) *n.* the collective stakes in various games; a variety of billiards; a combination of capitalists to fix prices and divide business; the common fund. —*v.t.* to throw into a common fund.
poop (-ōō-) *n.* a stern of a ship; South Africa, porridge made from mealie flour.
poor *a.* having little money; feeble; unproductive, inadequate, insignificant, unfortunate; to be pitied; S. Africa, thin. —**poor'ly** *adv.*—**poor'ly** *a.* not in good health.—**poor'ness** *n.*
poort *n.* S. Africa, a mountain-pass.
pop *n.* an abrupt small explosive sound. —*v.i.* to make such sound; to go or come unexpectedly or suddenly.—*v.t.* to put or place suddenly; (*sl.*) pawn.—**popping** *n.* in an internal combustion engine, noise in the carburettor due to weak mixture of gas and air.—**pop'corn** *n.* in N. America, any maize that contains sufficient oil to cause explosion when roasted; the roasted product.
pope *n.* the bishop of Rome as head of the Roman Catholic Church.—**po'pery** *a.* the papal system.—**po'pish** *a.*
pop'injay *n.* a parrot; a fop.
pop'lar *n.* a tree noted for slender tallness and tremulous leaves.
pop'lin *n.* a corded fabric of silk and worsted; imitation of this.
popp'et *n.* timber to support a vessel while being launched; one of the heads of a lathe; control valve; darling.
popp'y *n.* a bright red-flowered plant.
pop'ulace *n.* the common people.
pop'ular *a.* of or by the people; finding general favour.—**pop'ular front**, a union of democratic parties against fascism.—**popular'ity** *n.* being generally liked.—**pop'ularise** *v.t.* to make popular.—**popularisa'tion** *n.*—**pop'ularly** *adv.*—**pop'ulate** *v.t.* to fill with inhabitants.—**popula'tion** *n.* inhabitants; the number of them.—**pop'ulous** *a.* thickly populated.
poran'gi *n.* in New Zealand, foolishness; silliness.—*a.* silly, crazy.
por'celain *n.* fine earthenware, china.
porch *n.* a covered approach to the entrance of a building (**porch'es** *pl.*).
por'cine (-sīn) *a.* of or like a pig or pigs.
porc'upine *n.* a rodent animal covered with long pointed quills.
pore *n.* a minute opening, *esp.* in the skin.
por'ous *a.* full of pores; allowing a liquid to soak through.—**poros'ity** *n.*
pore *v.i.* to fix the eyes or mind upon.
pork *n.* pig's flesh as food.—**pork'er** *n.* a pig raised for food.—**pork-pie hat** *n.* a soft felt hat with a round flat crown.—**pork'y** *a.* fleshy; fat, paunchy.
pornog'raphy *n.* indecent literature or pictures.—**pornograph'ic** *a.*
porph'yry *n.* a reddish stone with embedded crystals.
por'poise (-pus) *n.* a blunt-nosed sea-animal about five feet long.
porr'idge *n.* a soft food of oatmeal or other meal boiled in water.—**porr'inger** *n.* a small basin for porridge, etc.
port *n.* a harbour or haven; town with a harbour; a city gate; an opening in the side of a ship.—**port'-hole** *n.* a small opening in the side of a ship for light and air; the larboard or left side of a ship looking towards the bows.—*v.t.* to turn (a ship) to the left.
port *n.* a strong red wine.
port *n.* bearing.—*v.t.* to carry (a rifle) slanting upwards in front of the body.—**port'able** *a.* easily carried.
port'age *n.* carrying or transporting; in N. America, carrying goods, boats, etc., overland between rivers.
portend' *v.t.* to foretell; to be an omen of.—**port'ent** *n.* an omen, a marvel.—**portent'ous** *a.* threatening, solemn.
port'er *n.* a door-keeper; man employed to carry luggage, etc.; a dark beer.
por'tal *n.* a large door or gate.
portcull'is *n.* a grating to raise or lower in front of a gateway.
portfo'lio *n.* a portable case for loose papers, drawings; the office of a minister of state (**-lios** (-oz) *pl.*).
port'ico *n.* colonnade; porch, covered walk (**-icoes, -icos** (-ōz) *pl.*).
portière' (-tyār) *n.* a door curtain.
por'tion *n.* a part or share; destiny, lot; dowry.—*v.t.* to divide into shares; to give a dowry to.—**por'tionless** *a.*
port'ly *a.* having a dignified mien; bulky. *Syn.* stately, grand, corpulent. *Ant.* undignified, puny, slim.
portman'teau *n.* a bag for carrying apparel (**-teaus, -teaux** (-tōz-) *pl.*).
portray' *v.t.* to make a picture of, describe.—**port'rait** *n.* a likeness.—**port'raiture** *n.*—**portray'al** *n.*
pose *v.t.* to lay down; place in an attitude.—*v.i.* to assume an attitude, to give oneself out as.—*n.* an attitude, *esp.* one assumed for effect; affectation, pretence.
pose *v.t.* to puzzle.—**po'ser** *n.* a puzzling question (**po'sing** *pres. p.*).
poseur' (-zer) *n.* an affected, attitudinising person.—**poseuse** *fem.*
pos'it (poz'-) *v.t.* to place; to lay down as a principle; to affirm.
posi'tion *n.* place; situation, attitude; posture; state of affairs; rank, office, employment; strategic point.
positive *a.* firmly laid down; definite, absolute, unquestionable; confident; overconfident; greater than zero.—*n.* positive degree; in photography, print in

which lights and shadows are not reversed.—**pos'itively** *adv.*—**pos'itivism** *n.* philosophy recognising only matters of fact and experience.

pos'itron (-i-tron) *n.* the smallest charge of positive electricity known. An essential ingredient of the atom.

poss'e *n.* a body of men.

possess' (-zes) *v.t.* to own; of an evil spirit, to have the mastery of.—**posses'sion** *n.*—**possess'ive** *a.* of or indicating possession.—*n.* the possessive case in grammar.—**possess'or** *n.* owner.
Syn. to have, occupy, hold. *Ant.* disown, renounce, dispossess.

poss'et *n.* hot milk curdled as by wine.

poss'ible *a.* that can or may be, exist, happen, be done.—**possibil'ity** *n.* possible event (**-ities** *pl.*)—**poss'ibly** *adv.*

poss'um *n.* Australia, the opossum.

post (pōst) *n.* an upright pole fixed firmly, usually as a support.—*v.t.* to display; stick up (on a post, notice board, etc.).—**post'er** *n.* a placard.

post (pōst) *n.* official carrying of letters or parcels; mail; collection or delivery of these; a point, station, or place of duty; a place where a soldier is stationed, a place held by a body of troops, a fort; an office or situation.—*v.t.* to put into the official box for carriage by post; to transfer (entries) to a ledger; to supply with latest information; to station (soldiers, etc.) in a particular spot.—*v.i.* to travel with posthorses.—*adv.* in haste.—**post'age** *n.* the charge for carrying a letter.—**post'card** *n.* card sent by post.—**post'al** *a.*—**post-haste** *adv.* very quickly.—**post'master** *n.* official in charge of a post office.—**posthorse** *n.* a horse (formerly) kept for hire at intervals on main roads for use in relays.—**post'-chaise** *n.* travelling carriage hired and drawn from stage to stage by post-horses.—**post'er-col'ours** *n. pl.* such lustreless colours as are peculiarly suited for posters.—**post'man** *n.* man who collects or delivers the post.—**post'-mark** *n.* an official mark with the name of the office, etc., stamped on letters.

post- *prefix* "after," "behind," as in **postdate'** (pōst-) *v.t.* to give a date later than the actual date.—**post-grad'uate** *a.* carried on after graduation.-**post-prand'-ial** *a.* after-dinner.—**poste'rior** (post-) *a.* later; hinder.—**poster'ity** *n.* descendants; future generations.—**post'ern** *n.* back or private door.—**post-mor'tem** (pōst-) *a.* taking place after death.—*n.* a medical examination of a dead body.—**postpone'** *v.t.* to put off to a later time.—**postpone'ment** *n.*—**post'script** *n.* an addition to a letter or book.

pos'thumous (-tū-) *a.* born after the death of the father; published after the death of author.—**post'humously** *adv.*

postiche' *n.* false hair made up into a coil, braid, etc.—*a.* artificial.

postil'lion *n.* a man who rides one of a pair of horses drawing a carriage.

postmerid'ian *a.* belonging to the afternoon.—*n.* the afternoon, *contr.* **p.m.**

pos'tulate *v.t.* claim, demand, take for granted.—*n.* thing taken for granted.

pos'ture *n.* attitude, position.—*v.* pose.

po'sy *n.* a bunch of flowers; motto inscribed on a ring (**po'sies** *pl.*).

pot *n.* a round vessel; a cooking vessel.—*v.t.* to put into or preserve in a pot (**pot'-ting** *pres. p.*—**pot'ted** *p.p.*).

pott'er *n.* a maker of earthenware.

pott'ery *n.* a place where earthenware is made; earthenware; the art of making it.—**pot'brood** *n.* in S. Africa, bread baked in a pot.—**pot-hole** *n.* a hole or hollow in the road worn out by traffic.—**pot-pie** *n.* a meat pie; a fricassee with dumplings.

po'table *a.* drinkable.—**pota'tion** *n.* a drink or drinking.

pot'ash *n.* an alkali made from wood ashes used in soap, etc.; crude potassium carbonate.—**potass'ium** *n.* a white metal.

pota'to *n.* a plant with tubers grown for food (**-toes** *pl.*).—**sweet potato** *n.* in S. Africa, Australia, etc., a trailing plant; its sweetish starchy tubers.

poteen', potheen' *n.* Irish whisky *esp.* illicitly distilled.

po'tent *a.* powerful.—**po'tency** *n.*

po'tentate *n.* prince, ruler.

poten'tial *a.* latent, that may or might but does not now exist or act.—*n.* amount of potential energy or work; level of electric pressure.— **-ial'ity** *n.*

poth'er (**-th-**) *n.* disturbance, fuss.

po'tion *n.* a dose of medicine or poison.

potoroo' *n.* Australia, aboriginal name for the kangaroo rat.

pot-pourri' (pō-pōō-rē') *n.* a mixture of dried rose petals, spices, etc.; a musical or literary medley.

pott'age *n.* oatmeal porridge; thick or thin soup or stew.

pott'er *v.i.* to work or act in a feeble way.

pot'tle (-l) *n.* a liquid measure of 4 pints; a little pot; a small fruit basket.

pott'y *a.* (*sl.*) of a person, mad or markedly eccentric; of a thing, silly, contemptible, trivial, petty.

pouch *n.* a small bag.—*v.t.* put into one.

poult (pōlt) *n.* chicken.—**poult'erer** *n.* dealer in poultry.—**poult'ry** *n.* fowls, etc.

poultice' (pōl'-tis) *n.* a mass of bread, linseed, or other substance mixed with hot water, spread on a cloth, and applied to the skin.—*v.t.* to put a poultice on.

pounce *v.i.* to spring upon suddenly, swoop.—*n.* a swoop upon something.

pounce *n.* fine powder used to prevent ink from spreading on unsized paper, etc.

pound *n.* weight, 12 oz. troy, 16 oz. avoirdupois; a unit of money, 20 shillings.—**pound'age** *n.* payment or commission of so much per pound (money); charge per pound (weight).

pound *n.* an enclosure for stray cattle.

pound *v.t.* to crush to pieces or powder; to thump; cannonade; to beat heavily.

pound'al *n.* a unit of force; the amount of force which generates a velocity of 1 ft. per sec. when acting for 1 sec. on a weight of 1 lb.

pour (pawr) *v.i.* to come out in a stream, crowd, etc.—*v.t.* to cause to flow.

pourpar'ler (pōōr-pár'lā) *n.* a preliminary consultation or conference.

pout *v.i.* and *t.* to thrust out the lips.—*n.* an act of pouting.

pout'er *n.* a pigeon with the power of inflating its crop.

pov'erty *n.* the condition of being poor; poorness, deficiency, lack.—**pov'erty-stricken** *a.* very poor.

pow'der *n.* solid matter in fine dry particles; a medicine in this form; gunpowder.—*v.t.* to apply powder to, to reduce to powder.—**pow'dery** *a.*

pow'er *n.* ability to do or act; authority; person or thing having authority; a mighty nation.—**pow'erful** *a.* strong, mighty.—**pow'erless** *a.*—**pow'er-house, -sta'tion** *n.* building where electrical power is generated and distributed.

pow'-wow (pou'wou) *n.* in N. America, a conjurer; a medicine man; (*sl.*) conference, *esp.* a noisy or futile one.

prac'tice *n.* habitual doing; action as distinguished from theory; a habit; exercise in an art or profession.

prac'tise *v.t.* to do habitually; to put into action; to work at; to exercise oneself in.—*v.i.* to exercise oneself; to exercise a profession (**prac'tising** *pres. p.*)—**prac'tised** *a.* skilled, expert.

prac'tical *a.* relating to action or real existence; given to action rather than theory; that is (something) in effect though not in name.—**prac'tically** *adv.*—**pract'icable** *a.* that can be done or used or passed over.—**practicability'** *n.*

practi'tioner *n.* one engaged in a profession, *esp.* medicine, law.

pragmat'ic *a.* of affairs of state; concerned with practical consequence; dogmatic.–**pragmat'ical** *a.*–**prag'matism** *n.*

prair'ie *n.* a large tract of grassland without trees.—**prair'ie-chicken** *n.* N. America, a species of grouse.—**prair'ie-dog** *n.* N. America, a small rodent, allied to the marmot.—**prair'ie-oyster** *n.* N. America, a cocktail.—**prair'ie-schooner** *n.* in N. America, a large covered wagon.—**prair'ie-value** *n.* the value of land in its unimproved state.

praise *v.t.* to express approval or admiration of; to glorify.—*n.* commendation; the fact or state of being praised (**prais'ing** *pres. p.*).—**praise'worthy** *a.*

pram *n.* abbrev. for **perambulator.**

prance (-á-) *v.i.* to walk with bounds; to strut about (**pran'cing** *pres. p.*).

pran'dial *a. pert.* to dinner.

prank *n.* a trick or escapade; frolic.

prank *v.t.* to adorn or rig out showily.

prase *n.* a leek-green quartz.

prate *v.i.* to talk idly, chatter.—*n.* chatter (**pra'ting** *pres. p.*).—**prat'tle** *v.i.* and *t.* to utter childishly.—*n.* childish chatter.—**prat'tler** *n.*

prawn *n.* edible shell-fish like shrimp.

pray *v.t.* to ask earnestly.—*v.i.* to offer prayers, especially to God.—**pray'er** (prĕr) *n.* an earnest entreaty; an action or practice of praying to God.—**pray'erful** *a.*–**pray'ing insect** *n.* a mantis, known in S. Africa as the Hottentot god.

pre- *prefix* makes compounds with the meaning of before or beforehand; e.g. **predeter'mine** *v.t.* to determine beforehand.—**pre-exist'** (-eg-zist') *v.i.* to exist beforehand or before something else. These are not given where the meaning can easily be found from the simple word.

preach *v.i.* to deliver a sermon.—*v.t.* to set forth in religious discourse.—**preach'er** *n.* (he **preaches'**).

pream'ble *n.* the introductory part.

preb'end *n.* the stipend of a canon or member of a cathedral chapter.—**preb'endary** *n.* holder of a prebend.

precar'ious (-kĕr-) *a.* unsecure, unstable, perilous, dangerous, dubious.

precau'tion *n.* previous caution; care taken beforehand.—**precau'tionary** *a.*

precede' *v.t.* to go or come before in rank, order, time, etc.—*v.i.* to go or come before.—**prec'edence** (pres-) *n.* a higher or more honourable place; the right to this.—**prece'dent** (pres-) *n.* a previous case or occurrence taken as a rule.—**prece'ding** *a.* antecedent.

precent'or *n.* a leader of singing.

pre'cept *n.* a rule for conduct; a maxim.

precept'or *n.* a teacher.

precess'ion (-sesh-) *n.* the act of going before or forward.

pre'cinct *n.* ground attached to a sacred or official building.—*pl.* environs.

prec'ious (presh-us) *a.* of great value, highly valued; affected, over-refined.—**prec'iously** *adv.*—**prec'iousness** *n.*—**precios'ity** *n.* over-refinement in art.

Syn. valuable, rare, beloved. *Ant.* cheap, common, valueless.

pre'cipice (pres-) *n.* a very steep cliff or rockface.—**precip'itance, precip'itancy** *n.* rashness, speed, hastiness.—**precip'itate** *v.t.* to throw headlong; hasten the happening of; in chemistry, to cause to be deposited in solid form from a solution.—*a.* oversudden, rash.—*n.* a substance chemically precipitated.—**precip'itately** *adv.*—**precipita'tion** *n.*—**precip'itous** *a.*

pré'cis (prā'sē) *n.* abstract summary.

precise' *a.* exact, strictly worded; particular; careful in observance.—pre-

cise'ly *adv.*—**preci'sian** *n.* punctilious or formal person.—**preci'sion** *n.*
preclude' *v.t.* to shut out, prevent.
preco'cious (-ō-) *a.* developed or mature too soon.—**precoc'ity** (-os-) *n.*
precur'sor *n.* a forerunner.
pred'atory *a.* relating to plunder; given to plundering.—**preda'cious** *a.* of animals living by capturing prey.
predecease' (-sēs) *v.t.* and *v.i.* to die before.—*n.* death before another.
pre'decessor *n.* one who precedes another in an office or position.
predes'tine (-tin) *v.t.* to decree beforehand; to foreordain.—**predes'tinate** *v.t.* to ordain beforehand by an unchangeable purpose.—**predestina'tion** *n.*
predic'ament *n.* a state or situation, usually an unpleasant one.
pred'icant, predikant' *n.* in S. Africa, a clergyman.
pred'icate *v.t.* to affirm or assert.—*n.* what is predicated; in grammar, statement made about a subject.—**pred'icable** *a.*—**predica'tion** *n.*—**predic'ative** *a.*
predict' *v.t.* to foretell.—**predic'tion** *n.*
predilec'tion *n.* a preference or liking.
predispose' *v.t.* to incline beforehand.
predom'inate *v.i.* to be the main or controlling element.—**predom'inance** *n.* -**predom'inant** *a.* (**predom'inating** *pr. p.*).
pre-em'inent *a.* excelling all others.—**pre-em'inently** *adv.*—**pre'em'inence** *n.*
pre-emp'tion *n.* buying, or the right to buy, before opportunity is given to others.—**pre-emp'tive** *a.*
preen *v.t.* (of birds) to trim (feathers) with the beak; smarten oneself; to strut.
pre-fab'ricate *v.t.* to make houses, etc., in shaped sections, ready to be assembled on the site.—**pre-fab'ricated** *a.*
pref'ace *n.* an introduction to a book, etc.—*v.t.* to introduce.—**pref'atory** *a.*
pre'fect *n.* a person put in authority; Roman official; a head of a French department; senior scholar maintaining discipline.—**pre'fecture** *n.* office, residence, district of a prefect.
prefer' *v.t.* to like better; to promote.—**pref'erable** *a.* better.—**pref'erably** *adv.*—**pref'erence** *n.* liking better, choice.—**preferen'tial** *a.* giving or receiving a preference.—**prefer'ment** *n.* promotion.
prefig'ure *v.t.* to exhibit, or suggest, by previous types; to foreshadow.
pre'fix *n.* a proposition or particle put at the beginning of a word or title.—**prefix'** *v.t.* to put as introduction; put before a word to make a compound.
preg'nant *a.* full of meaning; with child, fertile.—**preg'nancy** *n.*
prehen'sile *a.* capable of grasping.
prehistor'ic *a.* prior to the period in which history begins.
prejudge' *v.t.* to judge before hearing.
prej'udice (-is) *n.* judgment or bias decided beforehand; harm likely to happen to a person or his rights as a result of others' action or judgment; prepossession (usually unfavourable).—*v.t.* to injure.—**prejudi'cial** *a.*
prel'ate *n.* bishop or other church dignitary of equal or higher rank.
prelim'inary *a.* preparatory, introductory.—*n.* an introductory or preparatory statement or action.
prel'ude *n.* a performance, event, etc., serving as an introduction; preface; in music, an introductory movement.—*v.i.* and *t.* to serve as prelude.
premature' *a.* happening or done before the proper time.—**prem'aturely** *adv.*
premed'itate *v.t.* to plan beforehand.—**premedita'ting** *pr. p.*—**premedita'tion** *n.*
prem'ier *a.* chief, foremost.—*n.* a prime minister.—**prem'iership** *n.*
première' (-mē-yār') *n.* a first performance of a play.
prem'ise (prem'is) *n.* in logic, a proposition from which an inference is drawn.—*pl.* in law, beginning of a deed; house or building with its belongings.—**premise'** (-īz) *v.t.* to state by way of introduction.—**prem'iss** *n.* a (logical) premise.
pre'mium *n.* a reward, bounty; sum paid for insurance; bonus; excess over nominal value (**premiums** *pl.*).
premoni'tion *n.* forewarning; presentiment of coming evil.
preocc'upy (-pī) *v.t.* to occupy to the exclusion of other things (**-pied** *p.t.* and *p.p.*—**-pying** *pres. p.*).—**preoccupa'tion** *n.* mental concentration with the appearance of absentmindedness.
prepare' *v.t.* make ready; make.—*v.i.* get ready.—**prepara'tion** *n.*—**prepar'atory** *a.* introductory, preparing for.
prepay' *v.t.* to pay in advance (**prepaid'** *p.t.* and *p.p.*—**prepay'ing** *pres. p.*).
prepense' (-pens) *a.* deliberate; premeditated.—**prepen'sely** *adv.*
prepond'erate *v.i.* to be of greater weight or power.—**prepond'erance** *n.*
preposi'tion *n.* a part of speech, a word marking the relation between two other words.—**preposi'tional** *a.*
prepossess' (prē-) *v.t.* to impress, *esp.* favourably beforehand.-**prepossess'ion** *n.*
prepos'terous *a.* utterly absurd.
pre-Raph'aelite *n.* one of group of artists centred round Holman Hunt and Rossetti who admired and imitated Italian painting before Raphael.—*a.*
prerog'ative *n.* a peculiar power or right, *esp.* as vested in a sovereign.
pres'age *n.* omen, indication of something to come.—**presage'** *v.t.* foretell.
presbyo'pia *n.* indistinct vision of near objects in old age.
pres'byter (-z-) *n.* an elder in a church; a priest.—**pres'bytery** *n.* a priest's house (in the R.C. Church); the eastern part of the chancel; in certain churches, a

court composed of ministers and elders. —**presbyte'rian** *a.*—**presbyte'rianism** *n.*
pres'cience (presh'yens) *n.* foreknowledge.—**pres'cient** (presh'yent) *a.*
prescribe' *v.t.* and *i.* to order, point; to order the use of (a medicine).—**prescrip'tion** *n.* prescribing; the thing prescribed; a written statement of it; in law, uninterrupted use as the basis of a right or title; such title.—**prescrip'tive** *a.*
preselec'tive *a.* motoring, of a gear-box in which change-speed lever can be moved before change is actually desired.
pres'ence *n.* a being present; personal appearance.—**pre'sence of mind** *n.* ability to think and act quickly.
pres'ent *a.* that is here, now existing or happening.—*n.* the present time.—**pres'ently** *adv.* soon, shortly.
present' *v.t.* to introduce formally; to show; to point or aim; to give, offer.—**pres'ent** *n.* a gift.—**present'able** *a.* fit to be seen.–**presenta'tion** *n.*–**present'ment** *n.*
present'iment (-z-) *n.* a foreboding.
preserve' (-z-) *v.t.* to keep from harm or injury or decay.—*n.* jam; a place where game is kept for shooting.—**preserva'tion** *n.*—**preserv'ative** *a.* and *n.*
Syn. to hold, secure, shield. *Ant.* endanger, expose, imperil.
preside' (-z-) *v.i.* to be chairman; to superintend (**presi'ding** *pres. p.*).—**pres'ident** *n.* the head of a society, company, college, republic.—**pres'idency** *n.*—**presiden'tial** *a.*
press *v.t.* to push or squeeze; to urge steadily or earnestly.—*v.i.* to bring weight to bear.—*n.* a crowd; a machine for pressing, *esp.* a printing machine; the printing house; its work or art; newspapers collectively; a large cupboard.—**press agent** *n.* one employed to advertise and secure press publicity for any person, enterprise, etc.—**press-clipping** *n.*–**press-cutting** *n.*–**pres'sure** *n.*
press *v.t.* to force to serve in the navy or army; to take for royal or public use. —**press'gang** *n.* a body of men formerly employed in pressing men for the navy.
prestidig'itator (-j-) *n.* a conjurer, juggler.—**prestidigita'tion** *n.*
prestige' (-ēzh) *n.* reputation, or influence depending on it.
pres'to *adv.* in music, quick.
presume' (-z-) *v.t.* to take for granted. —*v.i.* to take liberties.—**presu'mable** *a.* —**presu'mably** *adv.*—**presump'tion** *n.* something very probable; impudent behaviour.—**presump'tive** *a.* that may be assumed as true or valid until the contrary is proved.—**presump'tuous** *a.* forward, taking liberties, over-confident. —**presump'tuously** *adv.*
presuppose' (-su-pōz') *v.t.* to take for granted.—**presupposi'tion** *n.* previous supposition.—**presuppo'sal** *n.*
pretend' *v.t.* to feign, make believe.—*v.i.* to lay claim, to feign.—**pretence'** *n.*—**pretend'er** *n.*—**preten'sion** *n.*—**preten'tious** *a.* making claim to special merit.
pret'erite (-it) *a.* past (of tense, expressing past state or action).—*n.*
pretermit' *v.t.* to pass by; to omit.
preternat'ural (prē-) *a.* out of the ordinary way of nature, abnormal.
pre'text *n.* excuse, false reason.
prett'y (prit'i) *a.* having beauty that is attractive rather than imposing; charming, etc.—*adv.* fairly, moderately.—**prett'ily** *adv.* in a pretty manner.
pret'zel *n.* a biscuit of wheaten flour baked crisp, cracknel.
prevail' *v.i.* to gain the mastery; to be in fashion, be general.—**prevail'ing** *a.* —**prev'alence** *n.*—**prev'alent** *a.*
prevar'icate *v.i.* make evasive or misleading statements.—**prevarica'tion** *n.*–**prevar'icator** *n.* (**prevaricating** *pr. p.*).
preve'nient *a.* going before; preceding.
prevent' *v.t.* to stop from happening.—**preven'tion** *n.*—**prevent'ive** *a.* and *n.*
pre'view *n.* advance showing of film or of scenes from forthcoming film.
pre'vious *a.* preceding; happening before.—**pre'viously** *adv.* before.
Syn. antecedent, foregoing, former. *Ant.* subsequent, succeeding, later.
pre'war *a.* before the war; old-fashioned.
prey *n.* that is hunted and killed by carnivorous animals; victim.–*v.i.* to prey upon; to treat as prey, to afflict; to vex.
price *n.* that for which a thing is bought or sold.—*v.t.* to fix or ask a price of.—**price'less** *a.* invaluable, beyond price.
prick *n.* a slight hole made by pricking; pricking or being pricked.—*v.t.* to pierce slightly with a sharp point; to mark by a prick; to erect (the ears).—**prickle** *n.* a thorn or spike.—*v.i.* to feel a tingling or pricking sensation.–**prick'ly** *a.*–**prick'ly heat'** *n.* tropical skin disease accompanied with stinging pains.—**prick'ly pear'** *n.* a cactus; its spiny, edible fruit.
pride *n.* too high an opinion of oneself; feeling of elation or great satisfaction; something causing this.— **London pride** the flower.—*v. refl.* to take pride.
prie-dieu' (prē-di-e') *n.* a praying desk.
priest *n.* an official minister of a religion; a clergyman.—**priest'ess** *fem.*—**priest'hood** *n.*—**priest'-like** *a.*--**priest'ly** *a.*
prig *n.* self-righteous person who professes superior culture, morality, etc.—**prig'gish** *a.*—*v.t.* (*sl.*) to steal.
prim *a.* very restrained, stiff, prudish.
pri'ma (prē-) *n.* first.—**pri'ma-donna,** the first female singer in an opera (**pri'ma donn'as** *pl.*).
pri'mal *a.* of the earliest age.—**pri'mary** *a.* chief; of the first stage, decision, etc.—**pri'marily** *adv.*–**prim'er** *n.* an elementary school book.—**pri'mate** *n.* an archbishop. —**pri'macy** *n.* pre-eminence; the office of archbishop.—**prime** *a.* first in time,

quality, etc.—*n.* an office for the first hour of the day; first or best part of anything.—**Prime Minister** the leader of the government.—**prime'val** *a.* of the earliest age of the world.—**prim'itive** *a.* of an early, undeveloped kind.—**primogen'iture** *n.* the rule by which real estate passes to the firstborn.—**primor'dial** *a.* existing at or from the beginning.

prime *v.t.* to prepare for paint with preliminary coating of oil, etc.; to fill up, e.g., with information; to prepare (gun, explosive, etc.) for firing.—**pri'ming** *n.* powder mixture used for this.—**pri'mer** *n.* textbook for beginners.

prim'rose *n.* a plant bearing pale-yellow flowers in spring; the colour of the flowers.—*a.* of this colour.

primula *n.* a genus of plants, including primrose, cowslip, etc.

pri'mus *n.* in the Scottish Episcopal Church, the head bishop.

pri'mus *n.* an oil stove in which the fuel is supplied by air pressure created by a force pump (**-muses** *pl.*) (trade name).

prince *n.* a ruler, chief; son of a king or queen.—**prin'cess** *fem.*—**prince'ly** *a.*—**prince'ling** *n.* a young prince; a petty ruler.—**prin'cipal** *a.* chief in importance.—*n.* the head of certain institutes, *esp.* schools, colleges, etc.; person for whom another is agent or second; a sum of money lent and yielding interest.—**principal'ity** *n.* territory or dignity of a prince.—**prin'ciple** *n.* a fundamental truth or element; a moral rule.—**prin'cipally** *adv.* mainly, chiefly.

prink *v.t.* to smarten, dress to ostentation.—*v.i.* to strut; to preen.

print *v.t.* to impress; to reproduce (words, pictures, etc.), by pressing inked types or blocks to paper, etc.; to produce in this way; to stamp (a fabric) with a coloured design.—*n.* an impression, mark left on a surface by something that has pressed against it; printed cotton fabric; printed lettering; a photograph; written imitation of printed type.—**print'er** *n.* one engaged in printing.

pri'or *a.* earlier.—*adv.* **prior to** before. —*n.* chief of a religious house or order.—**pri'oress** *fem.*—**prior'ity** *n.* precedence. —**pri'ory** *n.* monastery, nunnery under prior or prioress (**-ies'** *pl.*).

prise *n.* lever.—*v.t.* to raise, force open as by means of a lever.

prism (-zm) *n.* a solid whose two ends are similar, equal, of parallel rectilineal figures and whose sides are parallelograms; a transparent body of this form usually with triangular ends by which light can be refracted.—**prismat'ic** *a.* of prism shape; of colour, such as is produced by refraction through a prism.

pris'on (-z-) *n.* a jail.—**pris'oner** *n.* one kept in prison; one captured in war.

prist'ine *a.* original, primitive, unspoiled, undiminished.

prith'ee a corruption of I *pray thee.*

pri'vate *a.* not public; personal, confidential; of a soldier, not holding any rank.—*n.* a private soldier.—**pri'vacy** *n.* seclusion.—**pri'vately** *adv.* secretly.—**priva'tion** *n.* an act of depriving; want of comforts or necessaries; hardship.—**priv'ative** *a.* denoting privation or negation.

priv'et *n.* a bushy evergreen shrub much used for hedges.

priv'ilege *n.* a right or advantage belonging to a person or class; an advantage or favour that only a few obtain.—*v.t.* to give an advantage to.—**priv'ileged** *a.*

priv'y *a.* private, confidential—*n.* water closet.— **Privy Council** a body of persons appointed by the sovereign, *esp.* in recognition of great public services.—**priv'ily** *adv.*

prize *n.* a reward given for success in competition; a thing striven for; a thing that is won, e.g., in a lottery, etc.—*v.t.* to value highly.—**prize'-fight** *n.* a boxing-match for money.—**prize'-fighter** *n.* a professional pugilist.—**prize-ring** *n.*

prize *n.* a ship or property captured in naval warfare.—**prize'-money** *n.* money from the sale of such prizes.

pro- *prefix* before; in favour of.

pro'a *n.* fast, long narrow sail canoe.

prob'able *a.* likely.—**probabil'ity** *n.*—**prob'ably** *adv.*—**pro'bate** *n.* a proving of a will; a certificate of this.—**proba'tion** *n.* testing of a candidate before admission to full membership of some body; a system of releasing offenders, *esp.* juveniles, that their punishment may be cancelled by a period of good behaviour. —**proba'tioner** *n.* candidate on trial.

probe *n.* an instrument for examining a wound.—*v.t.* to examine thoroughly into.

pro'bity *n.* honesty, uprightness.

prob'lem *n.* a question or difficulty set for or needing a solution.–**problemat'ic** *a.*

probos'cis (-sis) *n.* elephant's trunk, a long snout; sucking tube of insects.

proceed' *v.i.* to go forward; to begin; to be carried on; to go to law.—**proce'dure** *n.* act or manner of proceeding; conduct. —**pro'ceeds** *n. pl.* price or profit.—**pro'cess** *n.* a state of going on, a series of actions or changes; method of operation; an action of law; an outgrowth.—*v.t.* to print from a block by a photographic or other process.—**pro'cess-block** *n.* a block used for printing illustrations, and prepared by photographic method. —**pro'cess engra'ver** *n.* one who prepares a process block.—**proces'sion** *n.* persons marching in a fixed or formal order; orderly progress.—**proces'sional** *a.*

Syn. to advance, emanate, progress. *Ant.* to stop, retreat, recede.

proclaim' *v.t.* to announce, make public. —**proclama'tion** *n.* an official notice.
procliv'ity *n.* inclination.
procon'sul *n.* Roman officer who discharged the duties of a consul; the governor of a province.
procrast'inate *v.i.* to put off, delay.—**procrastina'tion** *n.*—**procrast'inator** *n.*
pro'create *v.t.* to beget.—**procrea'tion** *n.*
proc'tor *n.* a university official with disciplinary powers; an attorney in an ecclesiastical court.
procure' *v.t.* to obtain; bring about.—**procu'rable** *a.* (**procur'ing** *pres. p.*).—**proc'urator** *n.* Roman official in province; manager of another's affairs.—**procura'tion** *n.* appointment, authority of procurator.—**procure'ment** *n.*—**procu'-rer** *n.*—**procu'ress** *fem.*
prod *n.* a pointed instrument; goad; awl. —*v.t.* to poke with something pointed. —*n.* a prodding (**prod'ded** *p.t.* and *p.p.*).
prod'igal *a.* wasteful; lavish.—*n.* a spendthrift.—**prodigal'ity** *n.* extravagance, open-handedness.
prod'igy (-ji) *n.* a marvel; a person with some marvellous gift.—**prodi'gious** *a.*
produce' *v.t.* bring forward; to bring into existence, make; to extend in length.—**prod'uce** *n.* that which is yielded or made.—**produ'cer** *n.*—**prod'uct** *n.* the result of a process of manufacture; a number resulting from a multiplication.—**produc'tion** *n.* producing; things produced.—**produc'tive** *a.*—**productiv'ity** *n.*
pro'em *n.* preface; introduction.
profane' *a.* not sacred; blasphemous, irreverent.—*v.t.* to pollute, desecrate.—**profana'tion** *n.*—**profan'ity** *n.* irreverence; profane talk or behaviour.
Syn. impious, wicked, irreligious. *Ant.* pious, devout, holy.
profess' *v.t.* to assert; to lay claim to; to have as one's profession or business; to teach as a professor.—**profess'edly** *adv.* avowedly.—**profes'sion** *n.* a professing, a vow of religious faith; entering a religious order; calling or occupation, *esp.* learned or scientific or artistic.—**profes'sional** *a.* of a profession.—*n.* a paid player.—**profess'or** *n.* a teacher of the highest rank in a university.—**professo'rial** *adj.*—**profess'orship** *n.*—**profess'orate** *n.* a professorship.—**professor'iate** *n.* a body of professors of a university.
proff'er *v.t.* to offer.—*n.*
profi'cient (-ish-) *a.* skilled.—*n.* one who is skilled.—**profi'ciency** *n.* ability.
pro'file (-fēl, -fīl) *n.* an outline of anything as seen from the side, e.g., of face; a brief, vivid biographical sketch.
prof'it *n.* benefit obtained; money gains. —*v.t.* and *i.* to benefit.—**prof'itable** *a.* yielding profit.—**prof'itless** *a.*—**profiteer'** *n.* one who makes excessive profits at the expense of the public.—*v.i.*

prof'ligate *a.* dissolute; reckless.—*n.* a dissolute man.—**prof'ligacy** *n.*
profound' *a.* deep; very learned, hard to understand.—**profun'dity** *n.*
profuse' *a.* abundant, prodigal, lavish. —**profus'ion** *n.* great abundance.
prog *n.* (*sl.*) food, grub.
pro'geny (-oj-) *n.* offspring, descendants; race.—**pro'gen'itor** (prō) *n.* forefather, ancestor.
prognath'ic *a.* having projecting jaws.
progno'sis *n.* forecast.—**prognost'ic** *n.* a prediction.—**prognost'icate** *v.t.* to foretell.—**prognostica'tion** *n.*
pro'gramme *n.* a plan or detailed notes of intended proceedings.
pro'gress *n.* onward movement; development; a state journey.—**progress'** *v.i.* to go forward.—**progres'sion** *n.*—**progress'ive** *a.* advancing; favouring progress, aiming at reforms.
prohib'it *v.t.* to forbid.—**prohibi'tion** *n.* —**prohib'itive** *a.*—**prohib'itory** *a.*
proj'ect *n.* a plan.—**project'** *v.t.* to throw; to plan; to cause to appear on a distant background.—*v.i.* to stick out.—**project'ile** *a.* capable of being thrown.—*n.* a heavy missile, *esp.* a shell or rocket. —**projec'tion** *n.*—**project'or** *n.*
projet' (-zhā) *n.* a draft of a proposed treaty in international law.
prolap'sus *n.* the falling down of a part of the body from its normal position.
prolegom'ena *n. pl.* preliminary observations; preface of a book.
prolep'sis *n.* a figure by which objections are anticipated and answered; an error in chronology when an event is antedated (**-ses** (-sēz) *pl.*).—**prolep'tic** *a.* anticipating the usual time.
proletar'iat, proletar'iate (-tēr-) *n.* the lowest class of a community, the common people.—**proletar'ian** *a.*
prolif'ic *a.* fruitful; producing much.
pro'lix *a.* wordy, long-winded, tedious, wearisome.—**prolix'ity** *n.*
proloc'utor *n.* the speaker or chairman of a convocation, spokesman.
pro'logue *n.* a preface, *esp.* a speech, poem recited before a play.
prolong' *v.t.* to lengthen out.—**prolonga'tion** *n.* extension.
promenade' (-ád) *n.* a leisurely walk; a place made or used for this.—*v.i.* to take a leisurely walk; to go up and down.—**prom** *n.* (*col.*) a promenade concert; a musical entertainment at which part of the audience walks or stands about the floor of the hall.
prom'inent *a.* sticking out; distinguished.—**prom'inence** *n.*
promis'cuous *a.* mixed without distinction, indiscriminate.-**promiscu'ity** *n.*
prom'ise (-is) *n.* an undertaking to do or not to do something.—*v.t.* to make a promise of.—*v.i.* to make a promise.—**prom'issory** *a.* containing a promise.

prom'ontory *n.* a point of high land jutting into sea (**prom'ontories** *pl.*).

promote' *v.t.* to move up to a higher rank or position; to help forward; to begin the process of forming or making. —**promo'ter** *n.*—**promo'tion** *n.*

prompt *a.* done at once; ready.—*v.t.* and *i.* to suggest, help out (an actor or speaker) by reading his next words or suggesting words.—**prompt'er** *n.*—**prompt'itude** *n.*—**prompt'ly** *adv.*

prom'ulgate *v.t.* to proclaim or publish.—**promulga'tion** *n.*

prone *a.* lying face or front downward; inclined (to), disposed.

prong *n.* one spike of a fork.

prong'buck *n.* the American antelope; pronghorn.

pro'noun *n.* word representing noun, e.g., *he, she, it,* etc.—**pronom'inal** *a.*

pronounce' *v.t.* to utter formally; to form with the organs of speech.—*v.i.* to give an opinion or decision.–**pronounce'albe** *a.*—**pronounced'** *a.* strongly marked, decided.—**pronounce'ment** *n.* declaration.—**pronuncia'tion** *n.* the way a word, etc., is pronounced.

proof *n.* something which proves; test or demonstration; a standard of strength of spirits; a trial impression from type or an engraved plate.—*a.* of proved strength; giving impenetrable defence. —**proof-plane** *n.* a small insulated metal disc for carrying electricity.—**proof-sheet** printer's proof.—**proof-reading** *n.*

prop *n.* a pole, beam, etc., used as a support.—*v.t.* to support, hold up; in Australia, to halt suddenly, *esp.* of a horse.–*n.* aviation, *abbrev.* for propeller.

propagand'a *n.* any organisation for propagating a doctrine, etc.; an attempt, or material used, to propagate ideas, facts, etc.—**propagand'ist** *n.* one who spreads propaganda.

prop'agate *v.t.* to reproduce or breed; to spread by sowing, breeding, example, instruction, persuasion, etc.—*v.i.* to breed or multiply.—**propaga'tion** *n.*

propel' *v.t.* to cause to move forward (**propel'ling** *pr. p.*—**propelled'** *p.t./p.p.*). **propell'er** *n.* a revolving shaft with blades driving ship or aeroplane.

propen'sity *n.* inclination or bent.

prop'er *a.* own, peculiar, individual; of a noun, denoting an individual person or place; fit, suitable; strict; conforming to etiquette, decorous.—**prop'erly** *adv.*

prop'erty *n.* owning; being owned; that which is owned; a quality or attribute belonging to something; article used on the stage in a play, etc. (**prop'erties** *pl.*).

proph'et *n.* an inspired teacher or revealer of the Divine Will; one who foretells future events.—**proph'etess** *fem.*—**proph'ecy** (-si) *n.* a prediction or prophetic utterance.—**proph'esy** (-sī) *v.i.* to utter predictions.—*v.t.* to foretell.—**propheti'c** *a.*—**prophet'ically** *adv.*

prophylact'ic (prō-) *a.* done or used to ward off disease.—*n.* a prophylactic medicine or measure (**-lax'is** *n.*).

propin'quity *n.* nearness.

propi'tiate (-ish-) *v.t.* to appease, gain the favour of.—**propitia'tion** *n.*—**propi'tiatory** *a.*—**propi'tious** *a.* favourable.

Syn. to conciliate, reconcile. *Ant.* to antagonise, incite, render unfavourable.

propor'tion *n.* a share; relation; comparison; relative size or number; due relation between connected things or parts.—*v.t.* to arrange proportions of.—**propor'tional** *a.*—**propor'tionable** *a.* in due proportion.—**propor'tionally** *adv.*

propose' *v.t.* to put forward for consideration.—*v.i.* to offer marriage.—**propo'sal** *n.*—**propo'ser** *n.*—**proposi'tion** *n.* a statement or assertion; a suggestion of terms.—**propound'** *v.t.* to put forward for consideration or solution.

propri'etor *n.* an owner.—**propri'etress (etrix)** *fem.*—propri'etorship *n.* ownership.—**propri'etary** *a.* holding or held as property.—**propri'ety** *n.* properness, correct conduct.

props *n. pl.* theatrical, *abbrev.* for properties, *pl.* of **property** q.v.

propul'sion *n.* driving forward.

prorogue' (-rōg') *v.t.* to dismiss at the end of a session without dissolution.

prosa'ic *a.* commonplace.—**prosa'ical** *a.*

prosce'nium *n.* the part of the stage in front of the drop-scene (**-nia** *pl.*).

proscribe' *v.t.* outlaw, banish; condemn. —**proscrip'tion** *n.* (**prosori'bing** *pr. pt.*).

prose *n.* speech or writing not verse.—*v.t.* talk, write prosily.—**pro'sy** *a.* tedious, dull.—**pro'sily** *adv.*—**pro'siness** *n.*

pros'ecute *v.t.* to carry on, to bring legal proceedings against.—**prosecu'tion** *n.*—**pros'ecutor** *n.*—**pros'ecutrix** *fem.*

pros'elyte *n.* a convert.—**proselytise'** *v.t.*

pros'ody *n.* science or theory of verse composition, scansion.—**pros'odist** *n.*

pros'pect *n.* a view; mental view; that is to be expected.—(pros-pekt') *v.t.* and *i.* to explore, *esp.* for gold.–**prospect'ive** *a.* future, awaited, expected.—**prospect'ively** *adv.*—**prospect'or** *n.*—**prospect'us** *n.* circular describing company, school, etc.

pros'per *v.i.* to do well, succeed.—*v.t.* to cause to do well.—**prosper'ity** *n.* good fortune, well-being.—**pros'perous** *a.* fortunate, wealthy.—**pros'perously** *adv.*

pros'tate *n.* gland accessory to the male generative organs in mammals.

pros'titute *n.* a woman who hires herself for sexual intercourse.—*v.t.* to make a prostitute of; to sell basely, put to an infamous use.—**prostitu'tion** *n.*

pros'trate *a.* lying flat on the ground; overcome by physical or moral exhaustion, helpless.—**prostrate'** *v.t.* to throw down flat; to overcome; to make a

low, submissive bow; to fall flat in worship, adoration or servility.—**prostra'ting** *pres. p.*—**prostra'tion** *n.*
protag'onist *n.* leading character; active supporter; principal actor.
pro'tean (-ti-an) *a.* variable.
protect' *v.i.* to defend or guard.—**protec'tion** *n.*—**protec'tive** *a.*—**protec'tionist** *n.* one who advocates protecting industries by taxing competing imports.—**protect'or** *n.* one who protects; a regent. —**protect'orate** *n.* an office or period of a protector of a state, regency; relation of a state to a territory that it protects and controls; such territory.
prot'égé (-e-zhā) *n.*—**pro'tégée** *fem.* a person who is under the care, protection or patronage of another.
pro'teid *n.* a constituent of food.
pro'tein (-tēn) *n.* kinds of organic compound which form the most essential part of the food of living creatures.
protest' *v.i.* to assert formally; to make a declaration against.—**pro'test** *n.* a declaration of objection.—**prot'estant** *a.* belonging to any branch of the Western Church outside the Roman communion. —*n.* a member of such church.—**prot'estantism** *n.*—**protesta'tion** *n.*
proto-, prot- *prefix*, first, as **prototype.**
pro'tocol *n.* a draft of terms signed by parties as basis of formal treaty.
pro'ton *n.* the positively charged nucleus of the hydrogen and other atoms.
pro'toplasm *n.* a soft, inelastic substance, from which the primitive tissue of animal and vegetable life is formed.
pro'totype *n.* primary type of a series; a model; a pattern.
protozo'an *n.* an animal of the lowest and simplest class.—**protozo'ic** *a.*
protract' *v.t.* to lengthen; to draw to scale.—**protrac'tion** *n.*—**protract'or** *n.* an instrument for measuring angles.
protrude' *v.i.* and *t.* to stick out, project, obtrude.—**protru'sion** *n.*—**protru'sive** *a.* thrusting forward.—**protru'sively** *adv.*—**protru'siveness** *n.*
protu'berant *a.* bulging out.—**protu'berance** *n.* a bulge or swelling.—**protu'berate** *v.i.* to bulge out.—**protubera'tion** *n.* act, condition of swelling beyond the surrounding surface.
proud *a.* feeling or displaying pride; that is the cause of pride; arrogant; stately.—**proud'ly** *adv.*—**proud flesh** *n.* an excessive granulation in wounds or ulcers.
prove (prōōv) *v.t.* to demonstrate, test; to establish the validity of (a will, etc.). —*v.i.* to turn out (to be, etc.) (**pro'ving** *pres. p.*).—**prov'en** *a.* proved.
Syn. to verify, justify, test, confirm, establish. *Ant.* disprove, confute, refute.
prov'ender *n.* fodder, provisions.
prov'erb *n.* short pithy saying in common use.—**proverb'ial** *a.* like a proverb; well known.
provide' *v.i.* to make preparation.—*v.t.* supply, equip, furnish (**provi'ding** *pr. p.*). —**provided** *conj.* on condition.—**prov'ident** *a.* thrifty; far-seeing.
prov'idence *n.* foresight, economy; kindly care of God or nature.—**providen'tial** *a.* strikingly fortunate or opportune.—**providen'tially** *adv.*
provi'sion *n.* a providing; a thing provided.—*pl.* food.—*v.t.* to supply with food.—**provi'sional** *a.* temporary.—**provi'so** *n.* a condition (**-sos** (-sōz) *pl.*).—**provi'sor** *n.* one appointed, *esp.* by the Pope, to a benefice before the death of the incumbent; the steward of a religious house; a vicar-general.
prov'ince *n.* division of a country; a sphere of action.—*pl.* any part of the country outside the capital.—**provin'cial** *a.* and *n.*—**provin'cialism** *n.* an idiom peculiar to a province; narrowness of outlook; lack of refinement.
provoke' *v.t.* to bring about, irritate, excite.—**provoca'tion** *n.*—**provoc'ative** *a.*
prov'ost *n.* the head of certain colleges; in Scotland, an official corresponding to a mayor.—**prov'ost-mar'shal** (prov'ō) *n.* the head of a body of military police.
prow *n.* of a ship, part round the stem.
prow'ess *n.* bravery, fighting capacity.
prowl *v.i.* to roam stealthily, *esp.* of animal in search of prey, etc.
prox'imate *a.* nearest, next, immediate. —**proxim'ity** *n.* nearness.—**prox'imo** *adv.* in the next month.
prox'y *n.* an authorised agent or substitute; a writing authorising a substitute.
prude *n.* a woman who affects excessive propriety.—**pru'dish** *a.*—**pru'dery** *n.*
pru'dent *a.* careful, discreet.—**pru'dence** *n.*—**pruden'tial** *a.* showing prudence.
prune *n.* a dried plum.—*v.t.* to cut out dead parts, excessive branches, etc.—**prun'ing-hook** *n.* knife with curved blade for pruning trees.
pru'rient *a.* given to or springing from lewd thoughts.—**pru'rience** *n.*
Prus'sian *a.* of Prussia.—**Prus'sian blue** a blue pigment.—**pruss'ic acid** *n.* a poison, orig. got from Prussian blue.
pry *v.i.* to look curiously; make furtive inquiries; in N. America, to force open (**pried** *p.t.* and *p.p.*—**pry'ing** *pres. p.*).
psalm (sàm) *n.* a sacred song.—**psalm'ist** *n.* a writer of psalms.—**psalm'ody** *n.* the art or practice of singing sacred music.—**psal'ter** *n.* the book of psalms; a copy of the psalms as a separate book.—**psal'tery** *n.* obsolete stringed instrument.
pseu'donym (sū-) *n.* a false, fictitious name.—**pseudon'ymous** *a.*
pshaw (shaw) *interj.* an exclamation expressing contempt or dislike.
psitt'acid (sit'-) *n.* a parrot.—**psitt'acine** *a.* of, like parrots.—**psittaco'sis** *n.* dangerous infectious disease, germ of which is carried by parrots.

psychi'atrist (sī-kī'-at-rist) *n.* a doctor skilled in psychiatry.—**psychi'atry** *n.* the treatment of mental diseases.

psy'chic (sī'kik) *a.* of the soul or mind; that appears to be outside the region of physical law.—**psy'chical** *a.* psychic.—**psy'cho-anal'ysis** *n.* theory that the mind can be divided into conscious and unconscious or subconscious elements; medical practice based on this.—**psy'cho-an'alyst** *n.*—**psychol'ogy** *n.* the study of the mind.—**psycholo'gical** *a.*—**psychol'-ogist** *n.*—**psychom'etry** *n.* the measurement of the duration of the mental processes; occult power of divination from mere contact with objects.—**psychoneuro'sis** *n.* a slight mental disorder which has physical manifestations.—**psy'chother'apy** *n.* the treatment of disease by mental influence.

psy'cho-galvanom'eter *n.* (sī'-ko-) so-called "lie-detector" machine that shows a change of electrical skin conductivity in relation to emotional reaction.

psychosomat'ic *a.* pert. to physical diseases having an emotional origin.

ptar'migan (t-) *n.* bird of the grouse family, which turns white in winter.

pto'maine (t-) *n.* a poisonous alkaloid found in putrefying matter.

pu'berty *n.* sexual maturity.

pub'lic *a.* of or concerning the public as a whole; not private; open to general observation or knowledge.—*n.* the community or its members.—**pub'licly** *adv.* —**pub'lic-house** *n.* house licensed to sell alcoholic liquors to be drunk on the premises.—**pub'lican** *n.* one who keeps such.—**public-spirited** active on behalf of the public good.

publi'city *n.* advertisement; notoriety; the business of advertising.—*a.* pertaining to advertisement.—**pub'licist** *n.* one skilled in international law; a writer on public concerns; a journalist.—**publicise** *v.t.* to bring to the notice of the public.—**publicity agent** a person employed to obtain publicity, advertisement, etc., for a person, enterprise, article, etc.

pub'lish *v.t.* to make generally known; to prepare and issue for sale (books, music, etc.).–**pub'lisher** *n.*–**publica'tion** *n.* *Syn.* announce, divulge, advertise, proclaim, declare, disclose.

puce *a./n.* flea colour, purplish brown.

puck *n.* a rubber disc used instead of a ball in ice hockey.

puck'a, pukk'a *a.* of full weight; substantial; real; superior.

puc'ker *v.t* and *i.* to gather into wrinkles or creases.—*n.* wrinkle.

pudd'ing (pood-) *n.* a form of cooked food usually in a soft sweetened mass.

pu'dding-ball *n.* in Australia, a fish resembling a mullet.

pud'dle *n.* a small muddy pool; a rough cement for lining ponds, etc.—*v.t.* to line with puddle-clay; to stir molten iron; to dabble, wallow.—**puddler** *n.*

pudic'ity *n.* modesty; chastity.

pu'erile *a.* childish, trivial.

puer'peral *a.* pertaining to childbirth.

puff *n.* a short blast of breath or wind, etc.; its sound; a piece of pastry; a laudatory notice, a piece of advertisement.—*v.i.* to blow abruptly; to breathe hard.—*v.t.* to send out in a puff; to blow up; to advertise; to smoke hard.—**puff'-ball** *n.* a ball-shaped fungus.—**puff'-ad'der** *n.* a venomous S. African snake.—**puff'y** *a.* swollen; short-winded.

puff'in *n.* a sea bird of auk family with a large parrot-like beak.

pug *n.* a small snub-nosed dog.—**pug'-nose** *n.* a snub nose.

pu'gilist *n.* a boxer.—**pu'gilism** *n.* boxing.—**pugilist'ic** *a.*

pugna'cious *a.* given to fighting; quarrelsome.—**pugna'city** *n.*

pug'ree (-rē) *n.* a scarf round the hat to keep off the sun's rays.

puis'ne (pū'nē) *a.* younger or inferior in rank.—**puis'ne judge** *n.*

puiss'ant (pwi-) *a.* powerful and mighty. —**puiss'antly** *adv.*—**puiss'ance** *n.* power, armed strength, might.

puke *v.i.* to vomit.—*n.* vomiting.

pu'keko *n.* in New Zealand, Maori name for a handsome rail that lives in swamps; the swamp hen.

pule' (pewl) *v.i.* to whimper.

pull (pool) *v.t.* to pluck or tug at; to draw or haul; to propel by rowing.—*n.* an act of pulling; force exerted by it; draught of liquor; (*sl.*) power, influence, *esp.* improperly acquired.—**pull'over** *n.* buttonless jersey or sweater pulled over head.—**to pull off** to carry through to successful issue.

pull'et (pool-) *n.* a young hen.

pull'ey (poo-) *n.* a wheel with a groove in the rim for a cord, used to raise weights by a downward pull (**pul'leys** *pl.*)

pull'man-car *n.* railway sleeping or saloon car with luxurious equipment.

pul'monary *a.* of the lungs.

pulp *n.* soft moist vegetable or animal matter.—*v.t.* to reduce to pulp.

pul'pit (poo-) *n.* platform for a preacher.

pulse *n.* throbbing of the arteries, *esp.* in wrist; vibration.—**pulsate'** *v.i.* throb, quiver (**pulsa'ting** *pr. p.*).—**pulsa'tion** *n.*

pulse *n.* eatable seeds of such plants as peas, beans, lentils, etc.

pul'verise *v.t.* to reduce to powder, to grind.—**pulverisa'tion** *n.* *Syn.* to crush. *Ant.* to build up, amalgamate.

pu'ma *n.* a large S. American carnivorous feline quadruped, the cougar.

pum'ice (-is) *n.* a light porous variety of lava used for cleaning and polishing.

pumm'el *v.t.* to beat with the fists.

pump *n.* an appliance for raising water,

or putting in or taking out air or liquid, etc.—*v.t.* to raise, put in, take out, etc., with a pump.—*v.i.* to work a pump; (*fig.*) to try to elicit information.
pump *n.* a light dancing shoe.
pump'kin *n.* a large gourd used as food.
pun *n.* a play on words.—*v.i.* to make one.—**pun'ster** *n.* one who makes puns.
punch *n.* a tool for perforating or stamping; a blow with the fist.—*v.t.* to stamp or perforate with a punch; to strike with the fist (he **punch'es**).
punch *n.* a drink made of spirit or wine with water or milk, lemon, spice, etc.
punch'-drunk *a.* of a pugilist, suffering from concussion as the result of repeated blows.
punctil'io *n.* a minute detail of conduct; a mere form (**-ios** *pl.*).—**punctil'ious** *a.* making much of punctilios.
punc'tual *a.* in good time, not late.—**punctual'ity** *n.*—**punc'tually** *adv.*
punc'tuate *v.t.* to put in punctuation marks.—**punctua'tion** *n.* marks, e.g., commas, etc., put in writing or printing to assist in making the sense clear.
punc'ture *n.* an act of pricking; a hole made by pricking.—*v.t.* to prick a hole in.
pun'dit *n.* a learned Brahmin; an expounder of the Sanskrit language, literature and laws; very learned man.
pu'nga-pu'nga *n.* in New Zealand, the pollen of a plant, used by the Maoris for making a kind of cake; the cake so made.
pun'gent *a.* biting; caustic; sharp, full-flavoured.—**pun'gency** *n.*
Pu'nic *a.* pertaining to the Carthaginians; faithless; treacherous, deceitful.
pun'ish *v.t.* to cause to suffer for an offence, to inflict a penalty on; to hurt.—**pun'ishable** *a.*—**pun'ishment** *n.*—**pu'nitive** *a.* intended to punish; **cap'ital pun'ishment** *n.* execution, death.
punk *n.* fungus, decayed wood used as tinder; in N. Amer., idle, empty talk; worthless object or person.—*a.* worthless, bad, poor, stale.
punt *n.* a flat-bottomed, square-ended boat, propelled by pole; (*football*) volleying kick.—*v.t.* to propel with pole ; in gambling, to stake against the bank; to back horse.—**punt'er** *n.*
pu'ny *a.* small and feeble.
pu'pa *n.* case or cocoon stage in an insect's life, chrysalis (**pu'pae** *pl.*).
pu'pil *n.* person who is taught; the opening in the middle of the eye.
pupp'et *n.* a figure with jointed limbs controlled by wires, a marionette.—**pupp'et-show** *n.* a show with puppets, worked by a hidden showman.
pupp'y *n.* a young dog; conceited young man.—**pup** *n.* puppy.
pur'blind *n.* dim-sighted; (*fig.*) obtuse.
pur'chase *v.t.* to buy.—*n.* buying; what is bought; leverage, grip, good position for applying force.—**pur'chaser** *n.* buyer.
purdah' *n.* a curtain; a curtain serving to screen women of high rank from the sight of men; a mark of caste.
pure *a.* unmixed, untainted; simple; spotless; faultless; innocent.—**pure'ly** *adv.*—**pu'rify** *v.t.* and *i.* (**-ified** *p.t.* and *p.p.*—**-ifying** *pres. p.*).—**puri'fica'tion** *n.*—**purifica'tory** *a.*—**pu'rism** *n.* excessive insistence on correctness of language.—**pu'rist** *n.*—**pu'rity** *n.* state of being pure.—**pu'ritan** *n.* member of the extreme Protestant party, who desired further *purification* of the church after the Elizabethan reformation; person of extreme strictness in morals or religion.—**pu'ritanism** *n.*—**puritan'ical** *a.*
purge *v.t.* to make clean, clear out.—*n.* an aperient; *n.* forcible elimination of enemies of régime.—*v.t.* to liquidate political enemies.—**purga'tion** *n.*—**purg'ative** *a.* and *n.* purging (medicine).—**purg'atory** *n.* place where souls are cleansed of sin; state of pain or distress.—**purgator'ial** *a.*
purl *n.* an edging of gold or silver wire or of small loops; a stitch that forms a rib in knitting.—*v.t.* to ornament with purls.—*v.i.* to knit in purl.
purl *v.i.* to flow with a burbling sound.
pur'lieu (-lyōō) *n.* formerly tract of land on the edge of a royal forest.—(*pl.*) ground bordering on something, outskirts.
purloin' *v.t.* to steal, filch.
pur'ple *n.* a colour between crimson and violet.—*a.* of this colour.—*v.t.* to make purple.—**Purple Heart** *n.* an honour awarded to U.S. service personnel wounded by enemy action.
purport' *v.t.* to mean; be intended to seem.—**pur'port** *n.* meaning, apparent meaning; significance.
pur'pose (-pus) *n.* intention, design, aim.—*v.i.* intend, plan.—**pur'posely** *adv.*
pur'purin *n.* red dye found in madder.
purr *n.* a noise which a cat makes when pleased.—*v.i.* to make this sound.
purse *n.* small bag for money.—*v.t.* to contract in wrinkles.—*v.i.* to become wrinkled up.—**pur'ser** *n.* officer who keeps accounts, etc., on ship.
pursue' (-sū) *v.t.* to run after, trail; aim at; engage in.—*v.i.* to go in pursuit; to continue. **pursu'ance** *n.* carrying out.—**pursu'ant** *adv.* accordingly.—**pursu'er** *n.*—**pursuit'** (-sūt) *n.* a running after, attempt to catch; occupation.—**pur'suivant** *n.* an officer of the College of Arms ranking below a herald.
pur'sy *a.* short-winded, fat.
pu'rulent *a.* containing and discharging pus.—**pur'ulence** *n.*
purvey' *v.t.* to supply.—**purvey'or** *n.*
pur'view *n.* scope or range.
pus *n.* matter formed or discharged in a wound, sore or inflammation.
push (poosh) *v.t.* to move or try to move away by pressure.—*v.i.* to make one's

way.—*n.* an act of pushing; persevering self-assertion; a big military adv..nce; in Australia, a band of toughs, a clique, a set, a political party.—**push'ful, push'ing** *a.* given to pushing oneself.
pusillan'imous (pū-) *a.* cowardly.—**pusillanim'ity** *n.* cowardice.
puss (poos) *n.* a cat; a hare.—**puss'y** *n.*
puss'yfoot *n.* (*sl.*) an advocate of total liquor-prohibition.
put (poot) *v.t.* to place or set; to express.
puta'tive *a.* reputed; supposed.—**puta'tively** *adv.* supposedly.
pu'trid *a.* rotten.—**pu'trefy** *v.t.* and *i.* to make or become rotten (**-efied** *p.t.* and *p.p.*—**-efying** *pres. p.*).—**putrefac'tion** *n.*—**putres'cent** *a.* becoming rotten. —**putres'cence** *n.*—**putrid'ity** *n.*
putsch (pootch) *n.* a surprise attempt to overthrow the existing power.
putt (put) *v.t.* to throw (a weight or shot) from the shoulder; to strike (a golf ball) along the ground in the direction of the hole.—**putt'er** *n.* a golf club for putting.
putt'ee *n.* strip of cloth wound round the leg, serving as a gaiter.
putt'y *n.* a paste of whiting and oil used in glazing windows; polishing powder of calcined tin used by jewellers.—*v.t.* to fix or fill with putty.
puz'zle *n.* a bewildering or perplexing question, problem or toy.—*v.t.* to perplex.—*v.i.* to think in perplexity.
Syn. a riddle, enigma, bewilderment.
pye'mia *n.* a disease caused by the absorption of pus or fetid matter; blood poisoning.—**pyem'ic** *a.*
pyg'my, pig'my *n.* a dwarf.—*a.* dwarf.
pyja'mas (-â-) *n. pl.* sleeping suit of loose trousers and jacket. Also **pajamas.**
py'lon *n.* a tower for suspension of electric cables; tower erected as a landmark for aircraft; a temple gateway.
pyorrhoe'a (-rē-a) *n.* an affection of the gums accompanied by discharge of pus.
pyr'amid *n.* solid figure with sloping sides meeting at an apex; a structure of this shape, *esp.* the ancient Egyptian; a group of persons or things highest in the middle.—**pyram'idal** *a.*
pyre *n.* pile of wood for burning a dead body.—**pyrotech'nics** (-k-) *n.* art of making or using fireworks; firework display.—**pyrotech'nic** *a.*
py'rene *n.* a hydrocarbon obtained from dry distillation of coal.
Py'rex *n.* glassware resistant to heat [protected trade name].
pyr'idine *n.* a liquid of pungent smell obtained from coal-tar, etc.
py'roscope *n.* an instrument for ascertaining the intensity of radiant heat.
pyrox'ylin *n.* an explosive substance.
Pyrr'hic *a.* — **Pyrr'hic-foot** (*verse*) foot consisting of two short syllables.—**Pyrr'hic victory,** one won at high cost.
py'thon (-th-) *n.* a large non-poisonous snake that crushes its prey.
pyx (piks) *n.* a vessel in which the Host is reserved; a box in which specimen coins are placed to be tested at the Mint.

Q

quack *n.* the harsh cry of the duck; a pretender to medical or other skill.—*v.i.* of a duck, to utter its cry.
Quadrages'ima *n.* the forty days of fast preceding Easter; Lent.—**quadrages'imal** *a.* belonging to Lent.
quad'rangle (-ng-gl) *n.* a four-sided figure; a four-sided court in a building.—**quadrang'ular** *a.*—**quad'rant** *n.* a quarter of a circle; an instrument for taking angular measurements; in motoring, a metal arc forming a combined rack and index for operation of control levers.—**quadrate** *v.t.* to make square.—**quad'rate** *a.* square.—**quadrat'ic** *a.* of an equation, involving the square of an unknown quantity.—**quadri'ga** *n.* a four-horsed chariot (**-gæ** *pl.*).—**quadrilat'eral** *a.* 4-sided.—*n.* a 4-sided figure.—**quadrille'** *n.* a square dance.—**quad'roon** *n.* the offspring of a mulatto and a white.—**quad'ruped** *n.* a 4-footed animal.—**quad'ruple** *a.* fourfold.—*v.t.* and *i.* to make or become 4 times as much.
quaff *v.i.* to drink deeply.—*v.t.* to drink.
quag, quag'mire *n.* a marshy tract with insecure surface; a bog.
quagg'a *n.* an extinct S. African animal related to the zebra.
quail *n.* small bird of partridge family.
quail *v.i.* to flinch, show fear.
quaint *a.* interestingly old-fashioned or odd, eccentric.—**quaint'ly** *adv.*
quake *v.i.* to shake or tremble.—**qua'ky** *a.*
Qua'ker *n.* a member of the Society of Friends.—**Qua'keress** *fem.*
qual'ify (kwol-) *v.t.* to ascribe a quality to, describe; to make competent; to moderate.—*v.i.* to make oneself competent, *esp.* by passing an examination (**qual'ified** *p.t.* and *p.p.*—**-ifying** *pres. p.*). —**qualifica'tion** *n.* qualifying, thing that qualifies.—**qual'ity** *n.* attribute, characteristic, property; degree of excellence; rank.—**qual'itative** *a.* relating to quality.
Syn. to fit, adapt, capacitate, equip, prepare, enable, dilute, assuage, restrict.
Ant. unfit, incapacitate, disable.
qualm (kwâm) *n.* a sudden feeling of sickness; misgiving; doubt; scruple.
quandary (kwon'- or kwon-dėr'-) *n.* a state of perplexity, a puzzling situation.
quan'tity (kwon-) *n.* size, number, amount; specified or considerable amount.—**quan'titative** *a.*
quan'tum *n.* a desired or required amount (*pl.* **quan'ta**).—**quan'tum theory**

n. in physics, one theory that energy transferences take place not continuously, but in bursts of a minimum amount or *quantum*.

quar'antine (kwor'-, -ēn) *n.* isolation of person, ship, etc., to prevent the spread of infection.—*v.t.* to put in quarantine.

quarr'el (kwor-) *n.* an angry dispute; break-up of friendship.—*v.i.* to fall out with; find fault with (**quar'relling** *pr. p.*—**quar'relled** *p.t./p.p.*).—**quarr'elsome** *a.* inclined to quarrel.

quarr'y (kwor'i) *n.* the object of a hunt.

quarr'y (kwor'i) *n.* a place where stone is got from the ground for building, etc. —*v.t.* and *i.* to get from a quarry (**-ied** *p.t./p.p.*—**-ying** *pr. p.*—(**quar'ries** *pl.*).

quart (kwort) *n.* a quarter of a gn. allo

quart'er *n.* a fourth part; region, district; mercy.—*pl.* lodgings.—*v.t.* to divide into quarters.—**quart'erdeck** *n.* part of the upper deck used by officers. —**quart'erday** *n.* day on which payments are due for the preceding quarter of the year.—**quart'ermaster** *n.* a naval, military or air force rank.—**quart'erstaff** *n.* a long staff for fighting.— **quart'erly** *a.* happening, due, etc., each quarter of the year.—*n.* a quarterly periodical.—**quart'ern-loaf** *n.* a four-pound loaf.—**quartet'** *n.* music for 4 performers; a group of 4 musicians.—**quart'o** *n.* a size of book in which each sheet is folded into 4 leaves.—*a.* of this size (**-tos** *pl.*).

quartz (kworts) *n.* a stone of silica, often containing gold.

quash (kwosh) *v.t.* to annul, *esp.* by legal procedure; crush (revolt); make void.

quat'rain (kwot'-) *n.* a stanza of 4 lines, sometimes rhyming alternately.

qua'ver *v.i.* to tremble, shake.—*v.t.* to say or sing in quavering tones.—*n.* a trill; a musical note half the length of a crotchet.—**qua'very** *a.*

quay (kē) *n.* a solid, fixed landing-stage.

quean' *n.* a saucy girl, a hussy; (*Scots.*) **queyn** *n.* (kwin) a girl.

quea'sy *a.* inclined to, or causing, sickness.

queen *n.* the wife of a king; a female sovereign; a piece in the game of chess; a perfect female bee, wasp, etc.; a court card.—*v.* to act as queen.—**queen'ly** *adv.*

queer *a.* odd, strange.—**queer'ly** *adv.*

quell *v.t.* to crush, put down, subdue.

quench *v.t.* to extinguish, put out; slake.

quern *n.* hand-mill for grinding grain.

quer'ulous (-roo-) *a.* full of complaints.

que'ry *n.* a question; a mark of interrogation.—*v.t.* to question, ask (**que'ried** *p.t.* and *p.p.*–**que'rying** *pres.p.*).–**que'rent** *n.*

quest *n.* a search.—*v.i.* to search.

ques'tion (-chn) *n.* a sentence seeking for an answer; a problem; debate, strife.—*v.t.* to ask questions of, to interrogate; to dispute.—**ques'tionable** *a.* doubtful, *esp.* not clearly true or honest.

questionnaire' (kes-ti-on-nār') *n.* questions drawn up for formal answer.

queue (kū) *n.* a plait of hair; a line of waiting persons, cars, etc.

quib'ble *n.* a play on words; an evasion, a merely verbal point in argument.—*v.i.* to evade a point by a quibble.

quick *a.* rapid, swift, keen, brisk; living. —*n.* sensitive flesh.—*adv.* rapidly.—**quick'ly** *adv.*—**quick'en** *v.t.* to give life to; make speedier, stir up.—*v.i.* to become living; to become faster.—**quick'lime** *n.* unslaked lime.—**quick'sand** *n.* loose wet sand which swallows up animals, people, etc.—**quick'set** *a.* of a hedge, made of living plants.—**quick'silver** *n.* mercury. —**quick-time** *n.* speed of military quick march, 120–140 steps or yards per min.; dance music based on this speed of step. *Syn.* speedy, nimble, hasty, pregnant. *Ant.* slow, tardy, dilatory, inactive, stupid.

quid *n.* a lump of tobacco for chewing; (*sl.*) one pound sterling.

quid'nunc *n.* one that is curious, pretends to know everything that passes.

quies'cent *a.* at rest.—**quies'cence** *n.*

qui'et *a.* undisturbed; with little or no motion or noise.—*n.* a state of peacefulness, absence of noise or disturbance.—*v.t.* and *i.* to make or become quiet.

qui'etly *adv.*—**qui'etude** *n.*—**qui'etism** *n.* a passive attitude to life, *esp.* as a matter of religion.—**qui'etist** *n.*—**quie'tus** (kwī-ē-) *n.* death; being got rid of.

quill *n.* the hollow stem of a large feather; the spine of a porcupine; a pen, fishing-float, etc., made of a feather-quill.—**quill'-driver** *n.* a writer.

quilt *n.* a padded coverlet.—*v.t.* to stitch (two pieces of cloth) with padding of down, wool, etc., between.

quince *n.* an acid, yellowish, pear-shaped fruit; the tree bearing it.

quinine' (-ēn) *n.* bitter drug obtained from cinchona bark; its sulphate used to cure fever, etc.

quin'sy (-zi) *n.* inflammation of throat, suppurative tonsilitis.

quintess'ence *n.* the purest form or essential feature.—**quintessen'tial** *a.*

quintet', quintette' *n.* composition for 5 voices or instruments; a company of 5 singers or players.

quin'tuplet (-tū-plet) *n.* one of 5 children born at one birth.

quip *n.* a smart saying, an epigram.

quire *n.* 24 sheets of writing paper.

quirk *n.* a quibble; clever or witty saying; flourish in writing.

quirt *n.* in N. America, a riding whip.

quis'ling *n.* a traitor; a collaborationist (from Vidkun Quisling, puppet premier of Norway under the Nazis).

quit *a.* free, rid.—*v.t.* to leave, go away from (**quit** or **quitt'ed** *p.t.* and *p.p.*—**quitt'ing** *pres. p.*).—*v. refl.* to bear oneself.—**quits** *a.* on equal or even terms by repayment, etc.—**quitt'ance** *n.* receipt, discharge.—**quit'rent** *n.* a rent reserved in grants of land, by the payment of which the tenant is quit from all other service.—**quitt'er** *n.* in N. America, one who lacks perseverance; (*sl.*) a coward.

quite *a.* wholly, entirely, completely.—*interj.* just so.

quiv'er *v.i.* to shake or tremble.—*n.* an act of quivering; case for carrying arrows.

qui vive (kē vēv) *interj.* Who goes there?—**on the qui vive,** on the alert.

quixot'ic *a.* showing enthusiasm for visionary ideals, neglecting own interests for honour or generosity.

quiz *v.t.* to make fun of; look at curiously or critically.—*n.* one given to quizzing; unprepared examination, in which examinee gives spontaneous answers to questions.—**quizz'ical** *a.* odd, mocking.

quoit (k-) *n.* heavy ring for throwing at a mark in the game of quoits.

quon'dam *a.* former, that was once.

quor'um *n.* the number that must be present in a meeting to make its transactions valid.

quo'ta *n.* a share to be contributed or received (**quo'tas** (-taz) *pl.*).

quote *v.t.* to copy or repeat passages from; refer to, *esp.* to confirm a view; state a price for.—**quota'tion** *n.*—**quo'table** *a.* (**quo'ting** *pres. p.*).

quoth (-ō-) *v.t.* said.

quotid'ian *a.* daily; every day.

quo'tient (-shent) *n.* number resulting from dividing one number by another.

R

raad (rât) *n.* in S. Africa, a council or board.

rabb'i *n.* Jewish title of respect for a teacher, minister, or doctor of the law.

rabb'it *n.* a small rodent animal which resembles the hare.—*v.i.* to hunt rabbits.—*v.t.* in Australia, to render an area free from rabbits.—**rabb'iter** *n.* one employed to kill rabbits. –**rabb'it-proof** *a.* denoting, in Australia, a fence that rabbits cannot pass, even by burrowing.

rab'ble *n.* a crowd of vulgar, noisy people; a mob, common herd.

Rabelai'sian (-z-) *a.* as of Rabelais; exuberantly and coarsely humorous.

rab'id *a.* raging; mad.—**rab'idly** *adv.*—**rab'idness** *n.*—**ra'bies** *n.* canine madness.

race *n.* the descendants of a common ancestor; one of the distinct varieties of mankind; a peculiar breed, as of horses, etc.—**ra'cy** *a.* having a strong flavour; spicy; spirited; piquant.—**ra'cily** *adv.*—**ra'ciness** *n.*—**ra'cial** *a.* of race.

race *n.* running; act of running in competition for a prize; strong current of water, *esp.* leading to a water-wheel.—*pl.* meeting for the sport of horse-racing.—*v.t.* to cause to run rapidly.—*v.i.* to run swiftly; of an engine, etc., to move rapidly and erratically, *esp.* on removal of resistance.—**ra'cer** *n.*—**race'track** *n.*

ra'ceme *n.* a flower-cluster with short and equal flowered pedicels as in the currant.—**rac'emose** *a.*

racial'ism (-shal-izm) *n.* hatred or opposition between different races of men; the assumption that some races are superior to others.

rack *v.t.* to stretch or strain; to stretch on the rack or wheel; to torture.—*n.* an instrument for stretching anything—hence, torture; a wooden frame in which hay is laid; a framework on which earthenware, bottles, or other articles are arranged; in mechanics, a straight bar with teeth on its edge, to work with a pinion.—**rack'-rent** *n.* the highest rent that can be exacted.

rack *n.* thin, flying clouds.

rack'et *n.* the bat used in tennis.—*pl.* a ball game played in a paved court surrounded by four walls.—**rack'et-court** *n.*

rack'et *n.* loud noise, uproar; in N. Amer., occupation by which money is made, usually illegally.—*v.i.* to make a noise.—**racketeer'** (-e-tēr') *n.* (*sl.*) gangster; one who blackmails traders.

racoon' *n.* small, carnivorous, N. American mammal, taken for its fur.

ra'dar (rā'dår) *n.* a device for finding range and direction by ultra-high frequency point-to-point radio waves which reflect back to their source and reveal the position and nature of the objects sought.

ra'dial *a.* relating to a ray or radius; radiating, having radiations.

ra'diate *v.i.* to emit rays.—*v.t.* to emit in rays (**ra'diating** *pres. p.*).—**radia'tion** *n.*—**ra'diance** *n.* brightness.—**ra'diant** *a.*—**ra'diator** *n.* that which radiates, *esp.* heating apparatus for a room; part of an engine for cooling it.

rad'ical *a.* of a root; fundamental; thorough.—*n.* a politician desiring thorough reforms.—**rad'icalism** *n.*

rad'icle *n.* embryonic root; beginning of a vein.—**radic'ulose** *a.*

radio- *prefix* of rays, of radiation, of radium.—**ra'dio-act'ive** *a.* emitting invisible rays that penetrate matter.—**ra'dio-activ'ity** *n.*—**radiol'ogy** *n.* science of use of rays in medicine.—**radios'copy** *n.* examination by X-rays.

ra'dio *n.* wireless telegraphy or telephony; broadcast wireless programmes; domestic receiving sets for such (**ra'dios** *pl.*).—**ra'dio-drama** *n.* drama for broadcast production.—**ra'diogram** *n.* telegram sent by radio; apparatus combining wireless receiving set and gramophone.—**radiog'raphy** *n.* the practice of producing an image on a sensitive plate by X-rays.—**radiolocation** *n.* a system of detecting the presence of aircraft, etc., by electro-magnetic waves of very high frequency.—**radiol'ogist** *n.* one skilled in the interpretation of radiographs.—**radiometeor'ograph** *n.* a radio apparatus which, sent high into the atmosphere, records weather data and transmits it to a receiving station below by ultra-high frequency.—**radionics** *n.* the branch of electronics dealing with radio.—**radiotellur'ium** *n.* a radio-active element, polonium.—**radiothal'lium** *n.* a radio-active product of the disintegration of thallium.—**radiother'apy** *n.* employment of radio-activity in the treatment of disease.—**radiotherm'y** *n.* treatment of diseases of the body by a localised fever brought about by radio-active radiation.—**radiothor'ium** (-ium) *n.* a radio-active element produced by atomic disintegration of thorium.—**radio tube** electron tube which picks up or amplifies a radio-signal; vacuum tube.

rad'ish *n.* a pungent root (**rad'ishes** *pl.*).

ra'dium *n.* a rare metal named from its radio-active power.

ra'dius *n.* a straight line from the centre to the circumference of a circle or sphere (**ra'dii, ra'diuses** *pl.*).—**ra'dial** *a.* of a ray or rays; of a radius; of radium; in aviation, of an aero-engine, having cylinders placed like spokes of a wheel.

ra'don *n.* a gaseous, radio-active emanation of radium.

raff'ia *n.* a prepared palm fibre used for making mats, etc.

raff'ish *a.* rakish, disreputable.

raf'fle *n.* a lottery in which an article is assigned by lot to one of those buying tickets.—*v.t.* to dispose of by raffle.

raft (-à-) *n.* a floating platform of logs or planks, etc., of wood fastened together —**rafts'man** *n.* lumberman.

raft'er (-à-) *n.* one of roof's main beams.

rag *n.* a fragment of cloth; a torn piece; a rowdy practical joke.—**ra'ger** *n.* in Australia, an old, bad-tempered bullock or cow.—**ragg'ed** *a.* shaggy; torn; clothed in frayed or torn clothes; wanting smoothness.—**rag'man** *n.* dealer in rags; a coward; the devil.—**rag'stone** *n.* a rough sandy limestone, so named from its rag-like fracture.—**rag'time** *n.* music with much syncopation.

rag'amuffin *n.* a ragged person or boy.

rage *n.* violent anger or passion; fury.—*v.i.* to speak or act with fury; to be widely and violently prevalent (**ra'ging** *pres. p.*).—**all the rage** very popular.

Syn. anger, choler, frenzy. *Ant.* calm, equity, sang-froid, phlegm, self-control.

rag'lan *n.* an overcoat with wide sleeves running up to the neck.—*a.*

ragou't (rag-oo') *n.* a highly seasoned dish of chopped meat and vegetables.

raid *n.* a rush, attack; a foray.—*v.t.* to make a raid on.—**raid'er** *n.* person, ship, aircraft, etc., briefed for raiding.

rail *n.* a horizontal bar, *esp.* as part of a fence, railway line, etc.; a bird.—*v.t.* to enclose with rails.—**rail'ing** *n.* fence of rails.—**rail'way** *n.* a road with lines of steel rails on which trains run.—**rail'road** *n.* railway.—**rail-car** *n.* a railway motor-car.—**rail-chairs** grooved pieces of cast-iron bolted to sleeper.

rail *v.i.* utter abuse.—**raill'ery** *n.* banter. —**rail'ling** *n.* complaints, jeers.

rai'ment *n.* clothing, dress.

rain *n.* moisture falling in drops from the clouds; the fall of such drops.—*v.i.* to fall as rain.—*v.t.* to pour down like rain.

rain'y *a.*—**rain'bow** *n.* an arch of prismatic colours formed in the sky by the sun's rays.—**rain'coat** *n.* a light rainproof overcoat.—**rain-gauge** *n.* instrument for measuring rainfall.

raise (-z) *v.t.* to set up, rear; lift up; breed, bring into existence; levy, collect; end (siege). (**rai'sing** *pr. p.*).—**to raise Cain** (*sl.*) make a scene, be angry.

rai'sin (-z-) *n.* a dried grape.

raj (ràj) *n.* sovereignty; rule, *esp.* in India.

ra'jah *n.* Indian prince or ruler.—**ra'nee** *fem.*

rake *n.* long-handled, pronged tool for drawing together hay, etc., or breaking the ground.—*v.t.* to draw or break with a rake; to sweep or search over; sweep with shot (**ra'king** *pres. p.*).—**rake-off** *n.* (*sl.*) monetary "consideration"; commission; back-hander.

rake *n.* a dissolute man.—**ra'kish** *a.*

rake *n.* inclination from vertical, as ship's funnels and masts—*v.t.* and *i.*

rall'y *v.t.* to bring together, *esp.* what has been scattered, as a routed army or dispersed troops; to tease.—*v.i.* to come together; regain health or strength (**rall'ied** *p.t.* and *p.p.*—**rall'ying** *pres. p.*). —*n.* an act of rallying; (in tennis, etc.) quick exchange of strokes; (in Boy Scouting) a competitive meeting of troops in scouting activities.

ram *n.* a male sheep (**ewe** *fem.*); a swinging beam with a metal head for battering; a hydraulic machine.—*v.t.* to beat down; stuff; strike with a ram (**ram'ming** *pres. p.*—**rammed** *p.t.* and *p.p.*).—**ram'rod** *n.* a rod for pressing down the charge of a muzzle-loading gun.

Ramadan', Ra'madhan *n.* the ninth Mohammedan month; the great annual fast or Lent of the Mohammedans.

ram'ble *v.i.* walk without definite route; wander; talk incoherently.—*n.* a rambling walk (**ram'bling** *pr. p.*).—**ram'bler** *n.* one who rambles; climbing rose.

ram'ify (-fī) *v.t.* and *i.* to spread in branches (**-ified** *p.t.* and *p.p.*—**-ifying** *pres. p.*).—**ramifica'tion** *n.* development.
ram'kie *n.* in S. Africa, a primitive stringed musical instrument.
ramp *v.i.* to stand on hind legs.—*n.* slope; (*sl.*) swindle, plot.—**ramp'ant** *a.* rearing; violent; prevalent.-**rampage'** *v.i.* dash about violently.—**rampa'geous** *a.*
ramp'art *n.* a mound for defence.
ram'shackle *a.* tumbledown, rickety.
ranch *n.* a cattle farm in America.—*v.i.* to conduct one.—**ranch'er** *n.*
ran'cid *a.* smelling or tasting like stale fat, sour.—**rancid'ity** *n.*
ran'cour (-ker) *n.* bitter and inveterate ill-feeling.—**ran'corous** *a.* spiteful.
Syn. malice, malevolence, ill-will, grudge, venom. *Ant.* benevolence, friendliness, sweetness, good-will.
rand *n.* a border; in S. Africa, high land above a river valley.
ran'dom *n.* **at ran'dom** haphazard.—*a.* made or done at random; by chance.
rangati'ra *n.* in N. Zealand, a chief of either sex; a person of rank, an employer.
range *n.* a rank; area, scope, sphere; distance a gun can reach; distance of a mark shot at; place for practising shooting; cooking-stove; in Australia, a line of mountains.—*v.t.* to set in a row, to roam.—*v.t.* to extend, roam.—**rang'er** *n.* forest keeper; senior Girl Guide.—**rang'y** (rānj'i) *a.* in Australia, hilly.
rank *n.* a row or line; order; social position; high social position; relative place or position.—*v.t.* to draw up in a rank, classify.—*v.i.* to have rank, or place.—**rank'er** *n.* commissioned officer promoted from the ranks.
rank *a.* growing too thickly or coarsely; offensively strong; vile; flagrant.—**rank'ly** *adv.*—**rank'ness** *n.*
rank'le (rang'kl) *v.i.* to fester, continue to cause anger (**rank'ling** *pres. p.*).
ran'sack *v.t.* to search thoroughly.
ran'som *n.* release from captivity by payment; the amount paid, blackmail.—*v.t.* pay ransom for.
rant *v.i.* to rave in violent, high-sounding language.—*n.* boisterous speech; wild gaiety.—*a.* boisterous.—**ran'ter** *n.*
rap *n.* a smart slight blow; a counterfeit Irish halfpenny; worthless thing.—*v.t.* tap (**rap'ping** *pr. p.*—**rapped** *p.t.*/*p.p.*).
rapa'cious *a.* greedy, hungry, grasping.—**rapa'city** (-pas-) *n.*
rape *n.* a plant with oil-yielding seeds; a plant used to feed sheep.
rape *v.t.* to violate.—*n.* an act of raping.
rap'id *a.* quick, swift, steep, sudden.—**rapid'ity** *n.*—**rap'idly** *adv.*—**rap'ids** *n. pl.* swift running waters.
ra'pier *n.* a light sword for thrusting.
rap'ine *n.* plunder, pillage.
rapt *a.* snatched away; lost in thought; intent.—**rap'ture** *n.* delight, ecstasy.—**rap'turous** *a.* enthusiastic, joyful.
rare (rėr) *a.* uncommon; of uncommon quality.—**rare'bit** *n.* Welsh rabbit.—**rare'ly** *adv.*—**rar'ity** *n.*
rar'efy *v.t.* to lessen the density of; spiritualize. (**rar'efied** *p.t.* and *p.p.*—**-efying** *pres. p.*).—**rarefac'tion** *n.*
rare *a.* imperfectly cooked, underdone.
ras'cal *n.* a rogue, knave.—**ras'cally** *a.*
rascal'ity *n.* dishonest behaviour.
rash *n.* a skin eruption.
rash *a.* hasty, reckless.—**rash'ly** *adv.*
Syn. headstrong, foolhardy, incautious, venturesome, daring, indiscreet. *Ant.* cautious, careful, discreet, timid, guarded.
rash'er *n.* a thin slice of bacon or ham.
rasp (-ȧ-) *n.* a coarse file.—*v.t.* to scrape with one.—*v.i.* to scrape; make a scraping noise; to irritate.
rasp'berry (rȧzb-) *n.* a familiar soft fruit; the plant (**-berr'ies** *pl.*).
rat *n.* a small rodent animal; one who deserts his party; in N. America (*sl.*). a workman who works during a strike, or for less than union wages.—*v.i.* to hunt rats; to desert one's party.—**rats'bane** *n.* poison for rats.—**ratt'y** *a.* (*sl.*) ill-tempered.—**rat-catch'er** *n.*—**rat'-tail** *b.* in wireless, a bunch of wires connecting a multi-wire aerial to its lead-in.
ratafi'a *n.* a spirituous liquor flavoured with fruit kernels and sweetened with sugar; biscuit so flavoured.
rat'chet *n.* a set of teeth on a bar or wheel allowing motion in one direction.
rate *n.* proportion between two things; charge; local taxation; speed.—*v.t.* estimate value of; assess for local taxation.—**rate'able** *a.* that can be rated; liable to pay rates.—**rate'payer** *n.*—**rated horse-power** in motoring, horse-power according to R.A.C. formula.
rate *v.t.* to scold.
rat'el *n.* in S. Africa, an animal allied to the glutton.
ra'ther (rȧth-er) *adv.* to some extent; in preference; more readily.
rat'ify *v.t.* to confirm (**-ified** *p.t.* and *p.p.*—**-ifying** *pres. p.*).—**ratifica'tion** *n.*
ra'ting *n.* valuing or assessing; fixing a rate; classification, *esp.* of ship; sailor (**naval rating**); angry rebuke.
ra'tio (-shi-ō) *n.* proportion; fixed relation of one thing to another (**-s** *pl.*).
ratio'cinate *v.i.* to reason.—**ratiocina'tion** *n.* the process of reasoning.
ra'tion (rash'un) *n.* a fixed daily allowance.—*v.t.* to supply with, or limit to, rations.—**ra'tion-book** *n.* booklet containing coupons by which the permitted ration can be obtained.
ra'tional *a.* reasonable.—**ra'tionalism** *n.* the philosophy which regards reason as the only guide or authority.—**ra'tionalist** *n.*—**ra'tionalise** *v.t.* to explain away by reasoning.—**rationalisa'tion** *n.* in indus-

try, reorganisation, *esp.* in the larger units, to meet changed or adverse conditions.—**rational'ity** *n.*—**ra'tionally** *adv.*

rat'lines (-inz) *n. pl.* cords fixed across ship's shrouds forming steps.

rattan' *n.* a palm with long thin jointed stems; a cane of this.

ratteen' *n.* thick twilled woollen material, used for lining.

rat'tle *v.i.* to give out a succession of short sharp sounds, as of shaking small stones in a box.—*v.t.* to cause to sound thus; to confuse, fluster.—*n.* the sound; an instrument for making it; the set of horny rings in a rattlesnake's tail.—**rat'tlesnake** *n.* a poisonous snake.

rauc'ous *a.* hoarse, harsh.

rav'age *v.t.* to lay waste.

rave *v.i.* to talk in delirium or with great enthusiasm; to rage, storm.

rav'el *v.t.* to entangle or disentangle; fray out; make complicated (**rav'elling** *pr. p.*—**rav'elled** *p.t./p.p.*).

rave'lin *n.* a detached work with two faces meeting in a salient angle at the front and open at the rear.

ra'ven *n.* a black bird of the crow family.

rav'en *v.i.* and *t.* to seek prey or plunder.—**rav'enous** *a.* very hungry; greedy.

ravine' (-ēn') *n.* a narrow gorge.

rav'ish *v.t.* to carry off, sweep away; commit rape upon (a woman); to enrapture.—**rav'ishing** *a.*—**ravish'ment** *n.*

raw *a.* uncooked; not manufactured; crude; stripped of skin; sensitive; chilly; unpractised, inexperienced; N. Amer., annoyed, angry.—**raw deal** *n.* unfair or dishonest treatment.—**raw'hide** *n.* untanned hide; whip from this.

ray *n.* a single line or narrow beam of light, heat, etc.; any of a set of radiating lines.—*v.i.* to come out in rays.

ray *n.* various kinds of flat-fish.

ray'on *n.* a radius.—*n.* artificial silk.

raze *v.t.* to destroy completely; level to the ground (**ra'zing, ra'sing** *pres. p.*).

ra'zor *n.* an instrument for shaving.

razz' *v.t.* (U.S.) (*sl.*) to tease, taunt.—**raz'zer** *n.*—**razz'ing** *n.*

re, in re *prep.* in the matter of.

re-, red-, ren- *prefix* makes compounds with meaning of "again," e.g., **re-address'** *v.t.* to address afresh.—**recap'ture** *v.t.* to capture again. These are not given where the meaning may easily be found from the simple word.

reach *v.t.* succeed in touching; arrive at.—*v.i.* to stretch out the hand; extend; to obtain and pass on.—*n.* act of reaching; power of touching, grasp, scope; stretch of river between two bends.

react' *v.i.* to act in return or opposition or towards a former state.—**reac'tance** *n.* in electricity, resistance in a coil, apart from ohmic resistance, due to current reacting on itself.—**reac'tion** *n.* any action resisting another action; in wireless, arrangement feeding back energy to grid circuit.—**reac'tionary** *n.* one advocating backward movement, in politics, etc.—*a.* of or inclined to such reaction.—**reac'tion coil** *n.* in wireless, coil by which energy is fed back in reaction.—**reac'tion formation** *n.* in psycho-analysis, a habit contracted as protection against repressed impulse.—**rea'gent** *n.* a chemical substance that reacts with another and is used to detect the presence of the other.

read *v.t.* to look at and understand written or printed matter; to interpret mentally; learn by reading; read and utter.—*v.i.* to be occupied in reading; to find mentioned in reading.—**read'able** *a.* that can be read, or read with pleasure.—**readabil'ity** *n.*—**read'er** *n.*

read'iness *n.*—**read'ily** *adv.*—**to ready up** *v.t.* in Australia, to prepare for a dishonest purpose; to tamper with.

read'y (red'i) *a.* prepared, prompt.—**read'y-made** *a.* not made to order.

rea'gent *see* **react.**

re'al *a.* existing in fact; happening; actual; of property, consisting of land and houses.—**re'alism** *n.* regarding things as they are; artistic treatment with this outlook.—**re'alist** *n.*—**realist'ic** *a.* life-like; practical.—**real'ity** *n.* real existence.—**re'alise** *v.t.* to make real; to convert into money; to understand.—**realisa'tion** *n.* understanding; making real; fulfilment.—**re'ally** *adv.* truly, positively, in fact.—**re'alty** *n.* real estate.

Syn. substantial, absolute, positive, veritable, genuine, authentic, intrinsic, essential, internal. *Ant.* unreal, negative, spurious, counterfeit, adventitious.

realm (relm) *n.* kingdom; province, region, sphere, domain.

real'tor (-al-tor) *n.* in U.S., one who deals in real-estate.

ream *n.* twenty quires of paper.

reap *v.i.* to cut grain.—*v.t.* to cut (grain).

rear *n.* the back part.—**rear'guard** *n.* troops protecting the rear of an army.

rear *v.t.* to set on end; build up; breed, bring up.—*v.i.* to rise on the hind feet.

reason (-z-) *n.* ground or motive; faculty of thinking; sensible or logical thought or view.—*v.i.* to think logically in forming conclusions.—*v.t.* to persuade by logical argument (*into* doing, etc.).

reason'able *a.* sensible, not excessive; fair, moderate; suitable; marked by logic.

reassure' *v.t.* to banish fears, restore confidence, reinsure (**reassur'ing** *pr. p.*).

reave *v.t.* and *i.* to plunder.—**reav'er** *n.*

re'bate *n.* a discount.—*v.t.* to diminish.

re'bec, re'beck *n.* a musical instrument akin to the violin, with three strings.

rebel' *v.i.* to revolt, take arms against the ruling power.—**reb'el** *n.* one who rebels; one resisting authority.—*a.* in rebellion.—**rebell'ion** *n.* organised open resistance to authority.—**rebell'ious** *a.*

rebor'ing *n.* boring of cylinder to regain true shape (internal combustion engine).
rebound' *v.t.* to drive back; to reverberate.—*v.i.* to spring back; to re-echo.—*n.* act of flying back upon collision with another object; recoil.
rebuff' *n.* a blunt refusal; check.—*v.t.* to repulse, snub, refuse to accept.
rebuke' *v.t.* to reprove, reprimand, find fault with.—*n.* an act of rebuking.
re'bus *n.* riddle in which the names of things, etc., are represented by pictures standing for syllables, etc. (**rebuses** *pl.*).
rebut' *v.t.* to force back, refute; to disprove.—**rebutt'al** *n.* (**rebut'ting** *pres. p.*).
recal'citrant *a.* refractory, rebellious.
recall' *v.t.* to call back; to remember; to withdraw.—*n.* order, message or signal to return; power of remembering, etc.
recant' *v.t.* to withdraw a statement, opinion, etc.—**recanta'tion** *n.*
recapit'ulate (rē-) *v.t.* to state again briefly, to sum up.—**recapitula'tion** *n.*
recede' *v.i.* to go back; to slope backwards; decline in value.
receipt' (-sēt) *n.* written acknowledgment of money received; fact of receiving or being received; a recipe.
receive' (-sēv) *v.t.* to take, accept, get; experience.—**receiv'er** *n.* person who takes stolen goods; officer appointed to take public money; apparatus for receiving wireless messages; telephone earpiece.—**receiv'able** *a.*
re'cent *a.* that has lately happened, new, modern.—**re'cently** *adv.*
recep'tacle *n.* a containing bag or vessel, place or space.—**recep'tion** *n.* receiving; manner of receiving; in broadcasting, the quality of the signals received.—**recep'tionist** *n.* one whose business is to receive guests, customers and visitors.—**recep'tive** *a.* able or quick to receive, *esp.* impressions or ideas.—**receptiv'ity** *n.*
recess' *n.* a vacation or holiday; niche or alcove; secret hidden place.—**reces'sion** *n.* withdrawal.—**reces'sional** *n.* hymn sung while the clergy are retiring.—**recess'ive** *a.* receding.—*n.* an inheritable characteristic, which may show itself only if derived from both parents.
réchauffé' (rā-shō'fā) *n.* a warmed-up dish; a literary rehash.
recher'ché (re-sher'shā) *a.* of studied elegance; exquisite, choice.
recid'ivist *n.* one who relapses into crime.—**recid'ivism** *n.*
re'cipe (res'i-pi) *n.* directions for cooking a dish; a prescription; expedient.
recip'ient *a.* that can or does receive.—*n.* that which receives.
recip'rocal *a.* in return, mutual.—**recip'rocally** *adv.*—**recip'rocate** *v.i.* to move backwards and forwards.—*v.t.* to give in return, give and receive mutually.—**reciproca'tion** *n.*—**recipro'city** *n.*
Syn. alternate, correlative, convertible, interchangeable. *Ant.* individual, personal, peculiar, uninterchangeable.
recite' *v.t.* to repeat aloud, *esp.* to an audience.—**reci'tal** *n.*—**recita'tion** *n.*—**recitative'** (-ē-) *n.* musical declamation.
reck *v.i.* to care, heed.—**reck'less** *a.*
reck'on *v.t.* to count; include; consider.—*v.i.* to make calculations, cast accounts—**recko'ner** *n.*—**reck'oning** *n.* calculation; account, settlement of bill.
reclaim' *v.t.* to bring back (from wrong); to make fit for cultivation.—**reclaim'able** *a.*—**reclama'tion** *n.*
recline' *v.i.* to sit or lie with back supported on a slope; repose; depend, rely (**recli'ning** *pres. p.*).
recluse' *a.* living in complete retirement.—*n.* a hermit.—**reclu'sive** *a.*
rec'ognise *v.t.* to know again; treat as valid; notice.—**recognition'** *n.*—**recogni'sable** *a.*—**recog'nisance** (or -kon'-) *n.* a bond by which a person undertakes before a court to observe some condition.
recoil' *v.i.* rebound, *esp.* of a gun when fired; retreat.—*n.* draw or spring back; an act of recoiling.
recollect' *v.t.* to call back to mind.—**recollec'tion** *n.* memory, remembrance.
recommend' *v.t.* to entrust; present as worthy of favour or trial; make acceptable.—**recommenda'tion** *n.*
rec'ompense *v.t.* reward or punish; make up for.—*n.* reward, compensation.
rec'oncile *v.t.* to bring back into friendship; adjust, settle, harmonise.—**reconcilia'tion** *n.*—**reconcile'ment** *n.*—**reconci'lable** *a.*—**rec'onciling** *pres. p.*
rec'ondite *a.* (of subjects) obscure, abstruse, little known; (of authors) difficult, very learned.
reconn'aissance *n.* survey of enemy positions, spying out the land.
reconnoi'tre (-ter) *v.i.* to survey the position of an enemy, a strange district, etc.—*v.i.* to make a reconnaissance.
record' *v.t.* to put down in writing.
rec'ord *n.* a being recorded; document or other thing that records; of a gramophone, a disc on which are cut impressions which a gramophone transforms into sound; the best recorded achievement.—**record'er** *n.* one who records; a city or borough chief magistrate; formerly a large flute; the instrument which records sound for a sound film.—**record'ing** *n.* the process of making records from sound; the reproduction of sound by mechanical means.
recount' *v.t.* to tell in detail.
recoup' *v.t.* to recompense; recover what has been expended or lost.
recourse' *n.* a resorting to; thing resorted to for aid; expedient.
recov'er (-kuv-) *v.t.* to get back, regain, retrieve.—*v.i.* to get back health.—**recov'erable** *a.*—**recov'ery** *n.*

rec'reant *a.* craven, cowardly; apostate —*n.* a recreant person, traitor, coward.
rec'reate *v.t.* to restore.—*v.i.* to take recreation.—**recrea'tion** *n.* agreeable or refreshing occupation.—**rec'reative** *a.*
recrim'inate *v.i.* to make a counter charg. or mutual accusation.—**recrimina'tion** *n.*—**recrim'inatory** *a.*
recrudesce' (-es) *v.i.* to break out again.—**recrudes'cence** *n.*
recruit' (-ōōt) *n.* a newly-enlisted soldier; one newly joining a society.—*v.i.* to enlist.—*v.t.* to enlist fresh soldiers, etc.; to recover health.—**recruit'ment** *n.*
rect'angle *n.* a 4-sided figure with 4 right-angles.—**rectang'ular** *a.*—**rectilin'eal, rectilin'ear** *a.* in a straight line, of or characterised by straight lines.
rect'ify (-fī) *v.t.* to put right, purify (**-ified** *p.t.* and *p.p.*—**-ifying** *pres. p.*).
rectifica'tion *n.* act of setting right; process of refining by repeated distillation; in wireless, conversion of alternating current into direct current.—**rec'tifying detector** *n.* in wireless, detector which performs rectification.
rect'itude *n.* moral uprightness.
rec'to *n.* right-hand page, front of a leaf.
rec'tor *n.* clergyman in charge of a parish; head of various English and Scottish colleges.—**rec'tory** *n.* rector's house or benefice.
rect'um *n.* the final section of the large intestine (**-ta** *pl.*).
recum'bent *a.* lying down.
recu'perate *v.t.* and *i.* to restore, be restored from illness, losses, etc.—**recupera'tion** *n.*—**recup'erative** *a.*
recur' *v.i.* to go or come back in mind; happen again; be repeated.—**recurr'ent** *a.*—**recurr'ence** *n.*
rec'usant *a.* obstinate in refusal, specifically, refusing to conform to the rites of the Established Church.
red *a.* of a colour varying from crimson to orange and seen in blood, rubies, glowing fire, etc.—*n.* the colour; a communist.—**red en'sign** *n.* flag of British merchant navy.—**red flag** *n.* the emblem of the U.S.S.R.; their song.—**red'shirt** *n.* member of a Pathan nationalist movement on N.W. frontier of India.—**red'-breast** *n.* the robin.—**redd'en** *v.t.* and *i.*—**redd'ish** *a.*—**red'start** *n.* a song-bird. —**red'skin** *n.* a N. American Indian.
redeem' *v.t.* to buy back; set free; free from sin; make up for.—**redemp'tion** *n.* —**redeem'able** *a.*—**redeem'er** *n.*
red'olent *a.* smelling strongly (of); bringing to one's mind.—**red'olence** *n.*
redou'ble (-dub'l) *v.t.* and *i.* to increase, multiply (**redoub'ling** *pres. p.*).
redoubt' (-dowt) *n.* a detached outwork in fortifications.
redoubt'able (-dowt-) *a.* dreaded, formidable.—**redoubt'ed** *a.*
redound' *v.i.* to contribute or turn to.
redress' *v.t.* to set right.—*n.* relief, compensation; reparation.
reduce' *v.t.* to bring down, lower, lessen; bring by force or necessity to some state or action; in chemistry, to separate a substance from other substances with which it is combined; in Scots law, to set aside, as a deed, etc.—**redu'cible** *a.* which can be reduced.—**reduc'tion** *n.*—**reducing agent,** a substance used for deoxidizing.—**redu'cing-box,** in motoring, a gear-box to reduce speed and increase turning power.
Syn. to humble, degrade, diminish, curtail, shorten, depreciate. *Ant.* enlarge, increase, lengthen, enhance, exalt.
redund'ant *a.* superfluous, unnecessary. —**redund'ancy** *n.*
reed *n.* various marsh or water plants; the tall straight stem of one; the vibrating part of certain musical instruments; powerful organ stop.—**reed'y** *a.* full of reeds; like reed instrument in tone; long and slender.
reef *n.* a part of a sail which can be rolled up to reduce the area; a ridge of rock near the surface of the sea; a lode of auriferous quartz.—*v.t.* to take in a reef of; in Australia, to work at a reef for gold.
reek *n.* strong smell or smoke.—*v.i.* to smoke, emit fumes.
reel *n.* a winding apparatus; cylinder for winding cotton, etc., on; a lively Scottish dance; music for it; an act of staggering; in cinematography, a spool on which a film is wound; a portion of film, usually 1,000 ft.—*v.t.* to wind on a reel.—*v.i.* to stagger, sway.
reeve *v.t.* to pass (a rope) through a hole, in a block, etc.
refec'tory *n.* a room for meals, *esp.* in a monastery.—**refec'tion** *n.* a meal.
refer' *v.t.* to trace or ascribe to; to submit for decision; to send to for information.—*v.i.* to have relation, allude (**referred'** *p.t.* and *p.p.*).—**ref'erable** *a.* —**referee'** *n.* an umpire.
ref'erence *n.* the act of referring; the act of directing attention to some information; mention, allusion; one who can give information on another's ability, etc.; a certificate of character, etc. —**referen'dum** *n.* the submitting of a question to a whole body of voters, plebiscite (**-dums, -da** *pl.*).
refine' *v.t.* to purify.—**refined'** *a.* pure; polite, genteel.—**refine'ment** *n.* fineness of feeling or manners or taste.—**refi'ner** *n.*—**refi'nery** *n.* a place where sugar, etc., is refined.
reflect' *v.t.* to throw back, *esp.* rays of light; to cast (discredit, etc.) upon.—*v.i.* to meditate.—**reflec'tion, reflex'ion** *n.*—**reflect'ive** *a.*—**reflect'or** *n.* a polished surface for reflecting light, etc.
re'flex *a.* reflected, bent back; of muscle, involuntary.—**re'flex camera** *n.* camera

with a mirror in which subject of a photograph can be seen and focused.—**reflex'ive** *a.* in grammar, describes a verb denoting the agent's action on himself. —**condi'tional re'flex** reflex action due to associative attachment as shrinking from something because of some previous unpleasant association.—**re'flex cir'cuit** in wireless, thermionic valve circuit giving dual amplification, high and low frequency.

re'flux *n.* a flowing back.

reform' *v.t.* and *i.* to form again; to amend, improve.—*n.* amendment, improvement.—**reforma'tion** *n.* a change for the better. —**reform'atory, reform school** *n.* an institution for reforming juvenile offenders.—*a.* reforming.—**reform'er** *n.*—**reform'ist** *n.*

refract' *v.t.* to break the course of (light, etc.).—**refrac'tion** *n.*—**refrac'tive** *a.*—**refract'ory** *a.* unmanageable, difficult to treat or work; stubborn.—**refran'gible** *a.*

refrain' *n.* chorus in a poem or song.

refrain' *v.i.* abstain from.—*v.t.* to check.

Syn. curb, govern, forbear, withhold. *Ant.* indulge, gratify, yield to, proceed.

refresh' *v.t.* to cheer, revive, make fresh.

refresh'er *n.* one that, or that which, refreshes; an extra fee to counsel in addition to the retaining fee.—**refresh'ment** *n.* that which refreshes, *esp.* food, etc.

refrig'erate (-j-) *v.t.* to freeze; cool.

refrigera'tion *n.*—**refrig'erator** *n.* an apparatus for cooling or freezing.

ref'uge *n.* shelter, protection.—**refugee'** *n.* one who seeks refuge (*esp.* in a foreign country) from persecution or war.

reful'gent (-j-) *a.* shining.—**reful'gence** *n.* brilliance, splendour.—**reful'gency** *n.*

refund' *v.t.* to pay back.

refur'bish *v.t.* to furbish or polish anew, to restore to its former condition.

refuse' (-z) *v.t.* and *i.* to decline.—**refu'sal** *n.* (**refu'sing** *pres. p.*).

Syn. to reject, repel, rebuff, repudiate. *Ant.* accept, receive, welcome, embrace.

ref'use (-s) *a.* discarded.—*n.* rubbish, useless matter, garbage.

refute' *v.t.* to disprove (**refu'ting** *pres. p.*).—**refu'table** *a.*—**refuta'tion** *n.*

re'gal *a.* of, or like, a king.—**rega'lia** *n. pl.* the insignia of royalty, as used at a coronation, etc.–**re'gally** *adv.*–**regal'ity** *n.*

regale' *v.t.* to feast.—**regale'ment** *n.*

regard' *v.t.* to look at; consider (as); heed; relate to.—*n.* a look; particular respect; esteem.—*pl.* an expression of goodwill.—**regard'ful** *a.*—**regard'less** *a.*

Syn. mark, watch, remark, contemplate, mind, value, respect, admire.

regatt'a *n.* boat or yacht race.

regen'erate *v.t.* to give new and better life to, re-create; to reform spiritually–*a.* reformed, born anew.—**regenera'tion** *n.*

re'gent *a.* ruling.—*n.* one who rules a kingdom during the absence, minority, etc., of its king.—**re'gency** *n.*

re'gicide *n.* one who kills a king; his crime.—**regicid'al** *a.*

régime' (rā-zhēm') *n.* system of government or management.—**reg'imen** (-j-) *n.* a prescribed system of diet.

reg'iment *n.* an organised body of troops as a unit of an army.—**regiment'al** *a.* of a regiment.—*n.* in *pl.* uniform.

re'gion (-jn) *n.* an area, district, place.

reg'ister (-j-) *n.* a written record; compass of a voice; a device for registering. —*v.t.* to set down in writing, to enter in a register.—**registrar'** *n.* the keeper of a register.—**registra'tion** *n.*—**reg'istry** *n.* a place where registers are kept (**-ies** *pl.*).

re'gius *a.* appointed by the crown.

reg'nal *a.* pertaining to a reign.—**reg'nant** *a.* reigning.—**reg'nancy** (reg'nạn-si) *n.* rule; predominance.

re'gress *n.* passage back; the power of passing back.—**regres'sive** *a.* passing back.—**regres'sively** *adv.*—**regres'sion** *n.* returning; retrogression; in psychology, diversion of physic energy, owing to obstacles encountered, into channels of fantasy instead of reality.

regret' *v.t.* to grieve for the loss of, or on account of.—*n.* grief for something done or left undone or lost.—**regret'ful** *a.* sorry.—**regrett'able** *a.*

reg'ular *a.* done according to rule; habitual; living under rule; belonging to the standing army.—*n.* a regular soldier. —**regular'ity** *n.*—**reg'ulate** *v.t.* to adjust. —**regula'tion** *n.* a rule.—**reg'ulator** *n.*

regur'gitate *v.t.* and *i.* to throw or pour back; vomit, eject from stomach.

rehabil'itate (rē-) *v.t.* to restore to reputation or former position, reinstate.—**rehabilita'tion** *n.* restoration of former rights, position, etc.

rehears'al *n.* practice for a performance

rehearse' (-hẹrs) *v.t.* to repeat aloud; say over again; to practise (a play, etc.).

Reich (rīh) *n.* the German State (*Ger. reich*—kingdom).—**Reichsbank** *n.* the national bank of Germany under the Nazis.—**Reichs'tag** *n.* one of the houses of the supreme legislature of Germany.

reign (rān) *n.* royal power; period of a sovereign's rule.—*v.i.* to rule.

reimburse' (rē-im-) *v.t.* to pay back.—**reimburse'ment** *n.* (**reimburs'ing** *pres. p.*).

rein (rān) *n.* narrow strap attached to the bit to check or guide a horse.—*v.t.* to check or manage with reins; to control.

reincarna'tion *n.* progressive rebirth of the soul in successive physical bodies. —**reincar'nate** *v.t.*—**reincarna'tionist** *n.* believer in reincarnation.

rein'deer (rān-) *n.* a deer of cold regions.

reinforce' (rē-in-) *v.t.* to strengthen, *esp.* by sending fresh men.—**reinforce'ment** *n.*

reins (rānz) *n. pl.* the kidneys; the lower

part of the back over the kidneys; the affections and passions.
reinstate' (rē-in-) *v.t.* to replace, restore to a former position.—**reinstate'ment** *n.*
reit'erate *v.t.* to repeat again and again.
reit'erative *n.* a word, or part of a word, repeated so as to form a reduplicated word.—**reitera'tion** *n.* repetition.
reject' *v.t.* to refuse to have, decline, put aside; cast up.—**rejec'tion** *n.*
rejoice' *v.t.* and *i.* to make or be joyful.
rejoin' *v.t.* to join again; to say in answer.—**rejoin'der** *n.* answer, retort.
reju'venate *v.t.* to restore to youth.—**rejuvena'tion** *n.*—**rejuvenes'cence** *n.*—**rejuvenes'cent** *a*—**reju'venise** *v.t./i.*
relapse' *v.i.* to fall back, into evil, illness, etc. (**relap'sing** *pres. p.*)—*n.*
relate' *v.t.* to narrate, recount; establish relation between; to have reference or relation to.—**rela'tion** *n.* narration; a narrative; correspondence, connection; connection by blood or marriage.
rel'ative *a.* dependent on relation to something else, not absolute; having reference or relation to.—*n.* a relative word or thing; one connected by blood or marriage.—**rel'atively** *adv.*
relativ'ity *n.* the doctrine in philosophy that knowledge is not absolute but conditioned by standpoint and circumstance; in physics, that measurement is conditioned by the choice of co-ordinate axes.
relax' *v.t.* to make loose or slack.—*v.i.* to become loosened or slack; become more friendly.—**relaxa'tion** *n.* recreation.
re'lay *n.* fresh set of horses to replace tired ones; gang of men, supply of material, etc., used similarly; in electricity, a device for making or breaking a local circuit; in wireless, a broadcast relayed from another station.—**relay'** *v.t.* to pass on, as a message, broadcast, etc. (**relayed** (relād') *p.t.* and *p.p.*—**relay'ing** *pres. p.*).—**re'lay-race** *n.* a race between teams of which each runner does part of the distance.
release' *v.t.* give up, surrender, set free; (cinema) permit on specified date, private or public exhibition of film.—*n.* a releasing; written discharge.
rel'egate *v.t.* to banish, consign (**rel'egating** *pres. p.*).—**relega'tion** *n.*
relent' *v.i.* to give up harsh intention, become less severe.—**relent'less** *a.* cruel.
rel'evant *a.* bearing upon the matter in hand.—**rel'evance** *n.*—**rel'evancy** *n.*
rel'ic *n.* something remaining, *esp.* as a memorial of a saint; a thing kept as a memento.—*pl.* dead body; remains, surviving traces.—**rel'ict** *n.* a widow.
relief' *n.* alleviation or end of pain, distress, etc.; money or food given to victims of a disaster, poverty, etc.; release from duty; one who relieves another; projection of a carved design from a surface; distinctness, prominence.—**relieve'** *v.t.* to bring or give relief to.
reli'gion (-ijn) *n.* a system of faith and worship.—**reli'gious** *a.*—**reli'giously** *adv.*
relin'quish (-inkw-) *v.t.* to give up.—**relin'quishment** *n.* (he **relin'quishes**).
rel'iquary *n.* a case or shrine for relics.
rel'ish *n.* taste or flavour; a savoury taste; a liking.—*v.t.* to enjoy, like.
reluct'ant *a.* unwilling.—**reluct'ance** *n.*
rely *v.i.* to depend (on) (**relied'** *p.t.* and *p.p.*—**rely'ing** *pres. p.*).—**reli'able** *a.* trustworthy.—**reliabil'ity** *n.*—**reli'ance** *n.* trust, confidence.—**reli'ant** *a.* confident.
remain' *v.i.* to stay or be left behind; continue.—**remains** *n. pl.* a dead body.—**remain'der** *n.* rest, what is left after subtraction.—**rem'anence** *n.* magnetic flux remaining in iron parts of electro-magnet after the current is switched off.
Syn. to tarry, sojourn, wait, dwell, endure. *Ant.* to go, depart, leave, quit.
remand' (-ȧ-) *v.t.* to send back, *esp.* into custody for further evidence.
remark' *v.t.* to take notice of; to say.—*v.i.* to make a remark (on).—*n.* an observation, comment.—**remark'able** *a.* noteworthy, unusual.—**remark'ably** *adv.*
rem'edy *n.* a means of curing, counteracting or relieving a disease, trouble, etc.—*v.t.* to put right (**-edied** *p.t.* and *p.p.*—**-edying** *pres. p.*).—**reme'dial** *a.*—**reme'diable** *a.* (**rem'edies** *pl.*).
remem'ber *v.t.* to retain in or recall to the memory.—*v.i.* to have in mind.—**remem'brance** *n.* memory; keepsake.—**remem'brancer** *n.* one who reminds.
remind' (-mīnd) *v.t.* to put in mind (of).—**remind'er** *n.* thing that reminds.
reminis'cence *n.* remembering; thing recollected.—**reminis'cent** *a.* reminding.
remiss' *a.* negligent.—**remiss'ly** *adv.*
remit' *v.t.* to forgive, not to exact, give up; slacken.—*v.i.* to slacken, give up.—**remiss'ible** *a.*—**remis'sion** *n.* forgiveness; pardon; release.—**remitt'ance** *n.* money sent.—**remittance man** idler, living in colonies on money sent from home.
rem'nant *n.* a fragment remaining.
remon'etise (re-mun'e-tīz) *v.t.* to make legal tender again; to make basis of credit again, e.g., remonetise silver, to make a silver standard alongside, or instead of, the gold standard.
remon'strate *v.i.* to protest, expostulate, argue.—**remon'strance** *n.*
remorse' *n.* regret and repentance.—**remorse'ful** *a.*—**remorse'fully** *adv.*—**remorse'less** *a.* pitiless, unforgiving.
remote' *a.* far away; slight, *e.g.*, remote chance.—**remote'ly** *adv.*
remove' (-mōōv) *v.t.* to take away or off, withdraw.—*v.i.* to go away; change residence; to dismiss from a post.—**remo'val** (-ōō-) *n.*—**remo'vable** *a.*
remu'nerate *v.t.* to reward, pay.—**remunera'tion** *n.*—**remu'nerative** *a.*

renais'sance (-nā'sans) *n.* a revival of learning, *esp.* in 14th to 16th centuries.
re'nal *a.* pertaining to the kidneys.
renas'cence *n.* revival, *esp.* of learning.
renas'cent *a.* springing up again.
rend *v.t.* and *i.* to tear, wrench apart (**rent** *p.t.* and *p.p.*—**rending** *pr. p.*).
ren'der *v.t.* to give in return, deliver up; submit, present; portray, represent; melt down; translate.—**rendering** *n.* translation; interpretation.
rend'ezvous (rond'i-vōō) *n.* meeting-place (**-vous** (-vōōz) *pl.*).—*v.i.* to meet by appointment, come together.
rendi'tion *n.* surrender; translation.
ren'egade *n.* a deserter, apostate.
renew' *v.t.* to make new; to revive; to restore to a former state, renovate; to re-establish; to grant, or to accept, a new bill or note for the amount of a former one; to begin again; to implant holy affections in the heart.—*v.i.* to be made new; to grow again.—**renew'al** *n.* revival; restoration; regeneration; a reloan on a new note given in place of a former note.—**renew'able** *a.*—**renew-abil'ity** *n.* quality of being renewable.
renn'et *n.* an artificial preparation for curdling milk.
renn'et *n.* a species of French apple.
renounce' *v.t.* to give up, cast off.—*v.i.* at cards, to fail to follow suit.—**re-nuncia'tion** *n.* act of renouncing, self-denial.—**renun'ciative** *a.*
ren'ovate *v.t.* to restore, repair (**reno'-vating** *pres. p.*).—**renova'tion** *n.*
renown' *n.* fame.—**renowned'** *a.* famous.
rent *n.* payment for the use of land or buildings.—*v.t.* to hold as a tenant; to let.—**rent'al** *n.* sum payable as rent.—**rent'er** *n.* one who rents films.
rent *n.* a tear.—*p.t.* and *p.p.* of **rend**.
rente (rȁnt) *n.* interest; *esp.* in *pl.*, that paid by a government on public loans.
rentier' (rȁn-tyā') *n.* a person whose income is derived from invested capital.
renuncia'tion *see* **renounce**.
rep *n.* a fabric with corded surface.
repair' *v.i.* to resort, betake oneself (to).
repair' *v.t.* to mend.—*n.* a mend.—**re-pair'able** *a.*—**repara'tion** *n.* a repairing; amends, compensation for injury done.
repartee' *n.* a witty retort.
repast' *n.* a meal, food.
repat'riate *v.t.* to restore to his own country.—**repatria'tion** *n.*
repay' *v.t.* to pay back; make return for (**repaid'** *p.t.* and *p.p.*—**repay'ing** *pres. p.*).—**repay'ment** *n.*—**repay'able** *a.*
repeal' *v.t.* to annul, cancel.—*n.*
repeat' *v.t.* to say or do again, reproduce.—**repeat'edly** *adv.*—**repeat'er** *n.* watch that strikes the hours; quick-firing rifle.—**repeti'tion** *n.* act of repeating.
repel' *v.t.* to drive back, ward off, refuse,—**repell'ent** *a.* revolting; unpleasant. *Syn.* resist, withstand, check, confront, parry, rebuff, reject, decline. *Ant.* invite, welcome, accept, attract, entice.
repent' *v.i.* to wish one had not done something, feel regret for a deed or omission.—*v.t.* to feel regret for.—**re-pent'ant** *a.*—**repent'ance** *n.*
repercus'sion (rē-) *n.* recoil; echo; indirect effect; reverberation.
rep'ertoire (-twar) *n.* a stock of plays, songs, etc., that a player or company is prepared to give.
rep'ertory *n.* a store; a repertoire.—**repertory' theatre** *n.* a theatre in which a succession of plays is produced by the same company.
repetend' *n.* that part of a repeating decimal which recurs continually.
repine' *v.i.* to fret (**repi'ning** *pres. p.*).
replace' *v.t.* to put back; find or be a substitute for.—**replace'ment** *n.*
replen'ish *v.t.* to fill up again.
replete' *a.* filled.—**reple'tion** *n.* fullness.
replev'y *v.t.* to take or get back goods wrongfully taken or detained, upon giving security to try the right to them in a suit at law (**-plev'ied** *p.t.* and *p.p.*—**-plev'ying** *pres. p.*).—**replev'in** *n.* a personal action to recover possession of goods.—**replev'iable, replev'isable** *a.*
rep'lica *n.* exact copy of a work of art.
reply' *v.i.* and *t.* to answer (**-plied'** *p.t.* and *p.p.*—**-ply'ing** *pres. p.*).—*n.*
report' *v.t.* to relate; take down in writing; make or give an account of; name as an offender.—*v.i.* to make a report.—*n.* a rumour; account or statement; repute; a bang.—**report'er** *n.* one who reports, *esp.* for a newspaper.
repose' *v.i.* to take rest.—*v.t.* to give rest to; put (trust, etc.).—*n.* rest.
repos'itory *n.* a store or shop.
repouss'é (rē-pōōs'ā) *a.* embossed; hammered into relief from the reverse side.—*n.* metal work so produced.—**re-poussage** (re-pōō-sazh', re-pōōs'ij) *n.* art of this, or the work itself.
reprehend' *v.t.* to find fault with.—**reprehen'sible** *a.*—**reprehen'sion** *n.*
represent' *v.t.* to describe or portray; make out to be; act, play, symbolise; act as deputy for; stand for.—**represent-a'tion** *n.*—**represent'ative** *n.* and *a.*
repress' *v.t.* to keep down or under.—**repress'ive** *a.*—**repres'sion** *n.* restraint; in psychology, active exclusion of thoughts and tendencies from consciousness.
reprieve' *v.t.* to suspend execution of (condemned person).—*n.* warrant for it.
rep'rimand *n.* a sharp rebuke.—*v.t.* to rebuke sharply.
repri'sal *n.* retaliation.
reproach' *v.t.* to scold, rebuke.—*n.* a scolding or upbraiding; expression of this; a thing bringing discredit.—**re-proach'ful** *a.* (he **reproach'es**).

rep'robate *v.t.* to disapprove of, reject, condemn, censure.—*a.* depraved—*n.* a wicked person.—**reproba'tion** *n.* blame, disapproval.
reproduce' (rē-) *v.t.* to produce anew; make a copy of; bring new individuals into existence.—**reprodu'cible** *a.*—**reproduc'tion** *n.*—**reproduct'ive** *a.*
reproof' *n.* blame, reproach.
reprove' (-ōōv) *v t.* to blame, rebuke.
rep'tile *n.* a crawling animal such as a snake, lizard, tortoise, etc.—**reptil'ian** *a.*
repub'lic *n.* a state in which the supremacy of the people or its elected representatives is formally acknowledged.—**repub'lican** *a.* and *n.*—**repub'licanism** *n.* republican principles.
repu'diate *v.t.* to cast off, disown (**repu'diating** *pres. p.*).—**repudia'tion** *n.*
repug'nant *a.* contrary; distasteful.—**repug'nance** *n.* aversion, strong dislike.
repulse' *v.t.* to drive back; rebuff.—*n.* a driving back, rejection, rebuff.—**repul'sion** *n.* repulsing; distaste, aversion.—**repul'sive** *a.* loathsome, disgusting.
Syn. to repel, disagree, revolt. *Ant.* to attract, entice, charm, invite, allure.
repute' *v.t.* to reckon, consider.—*n.* reputation, credit.—**reputa'tion** *n.* what is generally thought or believed about a character; good fame.—**reputable** *a.* of good repute.—**repu'ted** *a.*
request' *n.* act of asking; thing asked for.—*v.i.* to ask, invite.
req'uiem (-kwi-em) *n.* a mass for the dead; music for this service.
require' *v.t.* to demand; want, need.—**require'ment** *n.*—**req'uisite** (-zit) *a.* needed.—*n.* something necessary.—**requisi'tion** *n.* a formal demand, *esp.* written; list of things required.—*v.t.* to demand by an order of requisition.
requite' *v.t.* to repay; reward or avenge, return (**requi'ting** *pres. p.*)—**requi'tal** *n.*
rere'dos (rēr'dos) *n.* an ornamental screen on a wall behind an altar.
rescind' (-s-) *v.t.* to cancel, annul (a law, decree, etc.).—**rescis'sion** *n.*
re'script (rē'skript) *n.* among the Romans, the answer of an emperor consulted on some question—hence, an edict or decree.—**rescribe'** *v.t.* to write back.
res'cue *v.t.* to save, deliver.—**res'cuer** *n.*
research' *n.* investigation, *esp.* scientific study to try to discover facts.
resem'ble (-z-) *v.t.* to be like, similar.—**resem'blance** *n.* likeness, similarity (**resem'bling** *pres. p.*).
resent' (-z-) *v.t.* to show or feel indignation at, retain bitterness about.—**resent'ment** *n.*—**resent'ful** *a.* bitter.
reserve' (-z-) *v.t.* hold back, set apart, keep for future use.—*n.* something reserved; part of an army only called out in emergency; reticence, concealment of feelings or friendliness; in S. Africa, an area of land for a particular purpose, as for a road, for the use of natives, etc.—*pl.* troops in support.—**reserva'tion** *n.* a reserving or thing reserved; an exception or limitation.—**reserved'** *a.* not showing feelings, lacking cordiality.—**reserv'ist** *n.* one serving in the reserve.
res'ervoir *n.* a receptacle for liquid, *esp.* a large one built for storing water; store.
reside' (-z-) *v.i.* dwell.—**res'idence** *n.* dwelling; house.—**res'idency** *n.* official residence of a British agent at an Indian court.—**res'ident** *a.* and *n.*—**residen'tial** *a.*
res'idue (-z-) *n.* what is left.—**resid'ual** *a.*—**resid'uary** *a.*—**resid'uum** *n.*
resign' (-zīn) *v.t.* to give up.—*v.i.* to give up an office, employment, etc.—**resigned'** *a.* uncomplaining, patient.—**resigna'tion** (-zig-nā'-) *n.* resigning; being resigned.
resil'ient (-z-) *a.* rebounding.—**resil'ience** *n.* elasticity.—**resil'iency** *n.*
res'in (-z-) *n.* a sticky substance formed in and oozing from plants, *esp.* firs and pines.—**res'inous** *a.*—**ros'in** *n.* resin.
resist' (-z-) *v.t.* to withstand.—*v.i.* to oppose.—**resist'ance** *n.* in electricity, the opposition offered by a circuit to the passage of a current through it.—**resist'ances** *n. pl.* in psycho-analysis, mental forces opposed to self-knowledge.—**resist'ant** *a.*—**resist'ible** *a.*—**resist'less** *a.*
res'olute *a.* determined, firm, bold.—**res'olutely** *adv.*—**resolu'tion** *n.* analysis, firmness, resolve; the decision of a court, the vote of an assembly.
resolve' *n.* fixed purpose; resolution.—*v.t.* to separate the component parts of; to make clear; to form by vote or resolution.—**resolv'able** *a.*—**resolved'** *a.* determined, decided.—**resol'ver** *n.*—**resol'vent** *a.* and *n.*
res'onant (-z-) *a.* echoing, resounding.—**res'onance** *n.*—**res'onator** *n.*
resort' (-z-) *v.i.* to have recourse to; frequent.—*n.* recourse; a holiday centre.
resound' (-z-) *v.i.* to echo, ring, go on sounding (his fame **resound'ed**).
resource' (-sors) *n.* skill in devising means.—*pl.* means of supplying a want; stock that can be drawn on, means of support.—**resource'ful** *a.*—**resource'fully** *adv.*
respect' *v.t.* to refer to, to treat with esteem.—*n.* reference, relation; deference, esteem; point or aspect.—**respect'able** *a.* worthy of respect.—**respectabil'ity** *n.*—**respect'ful** *a.*—**respect'ive** *a.* several, separate.—**respect'ively** *adv.*
respire' *v.i.* and *t.* to breathe.—**respi'rable** *a.*—**respira'tion** *n.*—**res'pirator** *n.* an apparatus worn over the mouth as a protection against dust, poison-gas, etc.—**res'piratory** *a.*—**respirom'eter** *n.* an apparatus for supplying air to a diver under water.
res'pite *n.* a delay; period of rest or relief; suspension of the execution of a capital sentence; reprieve.—*v.t.* to grant a respite to; to reprieve.

resplend'ent *a.* brilliant, shining, dazzling.—**resplend'ence** *n.*
Syn. radiant, lustrous, effulgent, beaming, glorious. *Ant.* dull, grey, dismal, gloomy, drab, plain, ordinary, dowdy.
respond' *v.i.* to answer; act in answer.
respond'ent *a.* replying.—*n.* one who answers; a defendant.—**response'** *n.* an answer.—**respon'sions** (re-spon'shuns) *n.* at Oxford, first examination undergone by candidates for the B.A. degree.
respon'sible *a.* liable to answer for something; of good credit or position.—**responsibil'ity** *n.*—**respon'sive** *a.*—**responden'tia** *n.* loan on a ship and cargo, payment depending on safe arrival.
ressaldar' *n.* a native captain in an Indian cavalry regiment.
rest *n.* repose; freedom from exertion or activity; a pause; a supporting appliance.—*v.i.* to take rest; be supported.—*v.t.* to give rest to; to place on a support.—**rest'ful** *a.*—**rest'less** *a.*—**rest'lessness** *n.*
rest *n.* remainder.—*v.i.* to be left over.
rest'aurant (-ãn) *n.* an eating-house.—**restaurateur'** *n.* keeper of one.
restitu'tion *n.* act of giving back or making up; reparation.
rest'ive *a.* stubborn, resisting control.
restore' *v.t.* to build up again, repair, renew; re-establish; give back.—**restora'tion** *n.* (*hist.*) return to English throne of Charles II.—**restor'ative** *a.* restoring.—*n.* a medicine to strengthen, etc.
restrain' *v.t.* to check, hold back.
restraint' *n.* restraining; being restrained; self-control.
restrict' *v.t.* to limit, bound.—**restric'ted** *a.*—**restric'tion** *n.*—**restric'tive** *a.*
result' (-z-) *v.i.* to follow as a consequence; end.—*n.* effect, outcome, final score in a game.—**result'ant** *a.*
resume' (-z-) *v.t.* to begin again; to summarise.—**résumé'** *n.* a summary.—**resump'tion** *n.* a resuming.—**resump'tive** *a.*
resurge' *v.i.* to rise again.—**resur'gent** *a.*
resurrect' *v.t.* to restore to life.
resurrec'tion *n.* rising again; revival.
resus'citate *v.t.* to revive, bring back from being nearly dead.—**resuscita'tion** *n.*
ret *v.t.* to expose to moisture.—**rett'ing** *n.* the process of soaking flax.
re'tail *n.* sale in small quantities.—*v.t.* to sell in small quantities; to recount.—*adv.* by retail.—**re'tailer** *n.*
retain' *v.t.* to keep; engage services of.
retain'er *n.* fee to retain a barrister; a follower of a nobleman, etc.—**reten'tion** *n.*
retal'iate *v.t.* and *i.* to repay in kind.—**retalia'tion** *n.*—**retal'iatory** *a.*
retard' *v.t.* to make slow or late; in internal combustion engine, to time spark to take place later in engine cycle.
retent'ive *a.* capable of retaining.
retch *v.i.* to make effort to vomit.
ret'icent *a.* reserved in speech, not communicative.—**ret'icence** *n.*
retic'ulate, retic'ulated *a.* made like a net.—**retic'ulate** *v.t.* and *i.*
ret'icule *n.* lady's handbag.
ret'ina *n.* the sensitive layer at the back of the eye (**ret'inas, ret'inae** (-nee) *pl.*).
ret'inue *n.* attendants, followers.
retire' *v.i.* to withdraw; give up office or work; go away; go to bed.—*v.t.* to cause to retire.—**retired'** *a.* that has retired from office, etc. **retire'ment** *n.*—**reti'ring** *a.* unobtrusive, shy.
retort' *v.t.* to repay in kind; reply; hurl back (a charge, etc.).—*n.* a thing done or said as vigorous reply or repartee; a vessel with a bent neck used for distilling.
retouch' *v.t.* to improve by new touches.—*n.*—**retouch'ing** *n.* process of correcting defects in photographic negatives.
retrace' *v.t.* to go over again; to renew the outline of, as drawing; to return by same way.—**retrac'ing** *pres. p.*
retract' *v.t.* to draw back, recant.—*v.i.* to recant.—**retracta'tion** *n.*
retreat' *n.* act of retiring, withdrawal; a sunset call on a bugle, etc.; a place of seclusion; retirement for prayer and contemplation.—*v.i.* to retire.
retrench' *v.t.* to cut down, reduce amount of.—**retrench'ment** *n.*
retribu'tion *n.* recompense, *esp.* for evil deeds; vengeance.—**retribu'tive** *a.*
retrieve' *v.t.* to bring in; regain; restore; rescue from a bad state.—**retriev'al** *n.*—**retriev'er** *n.* dog trained to find and bring in shot game.—**retriev'able** *a.*
ret'rograde *a.* going backwards, reversed, reverting; reactionary.—**retrogres'sion** *n.*— **retrogress'ive** *a.*
ret'rospect *n.* looking back, survey of the past.—**retrospect'ive** *a.*—**retrospec'tion** *n.*—meditation on past.—**retroces'sion** *n.* ceding back again.
retroussé' (re-trōō-sā') *a.* turned up, as the end of a nose, pug.
return' *v.i.* to go or come back.—*v.t.* to give or send back; to report officially; report as being elected; elect.—*n.* returning; being returned; profit; official report.
rev' *v.t.* (*of an engine*) to increase the number of revolutions per minute.
reveal' *v.t.* to make known; disclose.
Syn. divulge, unveil, uncover, open, discover, impart, communicate, publish. *Ant.* conceal, hide, secrete.
reveill'é, revell'y (-val'i) *n.* a morning bugle-call to waken soldiers, etc.
rev'el *v.i.* to make merry.—*n.* a merry-making.—**rev'eller** *n.*—**rev'elry** *n.*
revela'tion *n.* act of disclosing, making known; a surprising disclosure.
revenge' *v. refl.* to avenge oneself.—*v.t.* to make retaliation for; avenge.—*n.* a revenging, desire for vengeance; act that satisfies this.—**revenge'ful** *a.*
rev'enue *n.* income, *esp.* of a state or institution.—**inland revenue** *n.* public money derived from income tax, etc.

reverb'erate *v.t.* and *i.* to echo or throw back (sound, etc.).—**reverbera'tion** *n.*
revere' *v.t.* to respect deeply, to honour.
rev'erence *n.* revering; capacity for revering.—**reverend** *a.* worthy of reverence, *esp.* as a prefix to a clergyman's name.—**reverant** *a.* showing reverence.—**reveren'tial** *a.* marked by reverence.
rev'erie *n.* a day-dream, fit of musing.
revers' (rē'vār', rē-vēr') *n.* that part of a garment which is turned back.
reverse' *v.t.* to turn upside down or the other way round; change completely—*n.* the opposite or contrary; the side opposite the obverse; a defeat; in motoring, abbrev. for **reverse gear.**—*a.* opposite, contrary—**revers'al** *n.*—**revers'ible** *a.*—**revers'ion** *n.* the return of an estate at the expiry of a grant to the person granting it; the right to succeed to an estate, etc., on a death or other condition; a returning to a state or condition.—**rever'sionary** *a.*—**rever'sioner** *n.* one holding a reversionary right.—**reverse' gear** *n.* mechanism to enable a vehicle to move backwards.
revert *v.i.* to return to a former state; come back to a subject.
revet' *v.t.* to face a wall with masonry, sand-bags, etc.—**revet'ment** *n.*
review' (-vū') *n.* revision; survey, inspection, *esp.* of massed military forces; a critical notice of a book, etc.; a periodical with critical articles, discussion of current events, etc.—*v.t.* to hold, make, or write, a review of.—**review'er** *n.*
revile' *v.t.* to call by ill names, abuse.
revise' *v.t.* to look over and correct.—**revi'ser** *n.*—**revi'sion** (-vizh-) *n.*
revive' *v.i.* to come back to life, vigour, etc.—*v.t.* to bring back to life, vigour, use, etc.—**revi'val** *n.* a reviving, *esp.* of religious fervour.—**revi'valist** *n.* an organiser of religious revival.
revoke' *v.t.* to annul.—*v.i.* at cards, to fail to follow suit though able to.—*n.* at cards, an act of revoking.—**rev'ocable** *a.*—**revoca'tion** *n.* act of cancelling.
revolt' (-ō-) *v.i.* to rise in rebellion; to feel disgust.—*v.t.* to affect with disgust.—*n.* a rebellion.—**revolt'ing** *a.* disgusting.
revolve' *v.i.* to turn round, rotate.—*v.t.* to rotate; meditate upon.—**revolu'tion** *n.* a complete rotation; turning or spinning round; a great change; the violent overthrow of a system of government.—**revolu'tionary** *a.* and *n.*—**revolu'tionise** *v.t.*
revol'ver *n.* a repeating pistol with a revolving cartridge-magazine.
revue *n.* theatrical entertainment, partly burlesque, partly musical comedy.
revul'sion *n.* sudden violent change of feeling.—**revul'sive** *a.* *i.*
reward' (-word) *v.t.* to pay, or make return, for service, conduct, etc.—*n.* a recompense or return.
rhab'domancy (rab'do-man-si) *n.* divination by means of rods.—**rhab'doid** (rab'doid) *n.* a small rod-like body found in certain vegetable cells.—**rhabdoid'al** (rab-doi'dal) *a.* rod-like.—**rhab'dosphere** (rab'do-sfēr) *n.* microscopic spherical body found in abysmal muds and believed to be an alga, or seaweed.
Rhadaman'thine (rad-a-man'thin,—tin) *a.* judicially strict; severe.
rhap'sody *n.* an enthusiastic or high-flown composition or utterance.—**rhapsod'ic** *a.*—**rhap'sodist** *n.*
rheol'ogy *n.* the science of the study of the deformation and flow of matter.—**rheol'ogist** *n.*—**rheom'eter** *n.* an instrument for measuring a current of fluid.
rheo'stat *n.* instrument for varying an electric resistance.
rhe'toric *n.* the art of effective speaking or writing; artificial or exaggerated language.—**rhetor'ical** *a.*—**rhetori'cian** *n.*
rheum (rōōm) *n.* watery discharge.
rheum'atism *n.* painful inflammation of joints or muscles.—**rheumat'ic** *a.*
rhino' *n.* (*sl.*) money ; rhinoceros *a.*
rhino'ceros (-os-) *n.* a large thick-skinned animal with one or two horns on its snout. **rhinocerot'ic** *a.*
rhododen'dron *n.* a flowering shrub.
rhom'bus, rhomb *n.* an equilateral but not right-angled parallelogram, a diamond or lozenge.
rhu'barb *n.* plant with fleshy leaf stalks used as food; a purgative from the root of a Chinese plant.
rhyme, rime' *n.* identity of sound of the ends of verse lines from the last accented syllable; verse marked by rhyme.—*v.t.* to make rhymes.—**rhy'mer, rimer, rhym'ester** *n.* a maker of rhymes.
rhythm (rithm) *n.* measured beat or flow, *esp.* of words, music, movement, etc.—**rhyth'mic** *a.*—**rhyth'mical** *a.* having rhythm.—**rhyth'mically** *adv.*
rib *n.* one of curved bones springing from spine and making framework of upper part of body; curved timber in boat's framework; strengthening ridge on cloth etc.—*v.t.* furnish mark with ribs; (U.S.) chaff, tease.
rib'ald *a.* irreverent, scurrilous; indecent.—*n.* a ribald person.—**rib'aldry** *n.*
ribb'on, rib'and *n.* a narrow band of fine material; anything resembling this.—**ribbon building** ribbon development, the erection of buildings outwards from a town, along main roads, leaving land on either side undeveloped.
riboflav'in (ri-bō-) *n.* vitamin B_2, necessary for growth, and present in green vegetables, eggs, etc.
rice *n.* the white seeds of an Eastern plant, used as food; the plant.—**rice'-paper** *n.* fine Chinese paper.
rich *a.* wealthy; fertile; abounding in some product or material; valuable; of

food, containing much fat or sugar; mellow; amusing.—**rich'es** *n. pl.* wealth. —**rich'ly** *adv.*—**rich'ness** *n.* rich quality.
Syn. opulent, plentiful, splendid, affluent, abundant, golden. *Ant.* poor, needy, unfertile, barren, skimpy, mean.
rick *n.* a stack of hay, etc.—**rick-stand,** a basement on which a rick may be built.
rick'ets *n.* a disease of children marked by softening of bones, bow-legs, etc.—**rick'ety** *a.* suffering from rickets; shaky.
ric'ochet (-shā) *n.* a skipping on water or ground of a bullet or other projectile; a hit made after it.—*v.i.* to skip thus.—*v.t.* to hit or aim at with a ricochet.
rid *v.t.* to clear, relieve of (**rid** or **ridd'ed** *p.t.* and *p.p.*—**ridd'ing** *pres. p.*).
ridd'ance *n.* clearing away.
rid'dle *n.* a question, puzzle, enigma; a puzzling fact, thing, or person.—*v.i.* to speak in or make riddles.
rid'dle *n.* a coarse sieve.—*v.t.* to pass through a sieve; to pierce with many holes like those of a sieve.
rid'dlings *n. pl.* siftings.
ride *v.i.* to go on horseback or in a vehicle; lie at anchor; float lightly (**rode** *p.t.*—**ridd'en** *p.p.*—**ri'ding** *pres. p.*).—*n.* a journey on a horse or other animal or in any vehicle; road for riding on horseback.—**ri'der** *n.* one who rides; a supplementary clause; a mathematical problem on a given proposition; an addition made to a verdict.—**ri'derless** *n.*
ridge *n.* the line of meeting of two sloping surfaces; a long narrow hill; a long and narrow elevation on a surface.—*v.t.* to form into ridges.—**ridged** *a.*
ridic'ulous *a.* deserving to be laughed at, absurd, foolish.—**rid'icule** *v.t.* to laugh at, hold up as ridiculous (**rid'iculing** *pres. p.*)—*n.* treatment of a person or thing as ridiculous; mockery.
ri'ding *n.* an administrative division of Yorkshire or New Zealand.
riem (rēm) *n.* S. Africa, rawhide thong.
riet'bok (rēt'bok) *n.* African antelope.
rife *a.* prevalent, common, numerous.
riff'-raff *n.* rabble, disreputable people.
ri'fle *v.t.* to search and rob; to make spiral grooves in (gun-barrel, etc.).—*n.* a rifled musket.—**ri'fling** *n.* the arrangement of grooves in a gun barrel.
rift *n.* a crack, split, break.
rig *v.t.* to provide (a ship) with spars, ropes, etc.; to equip; to set up, *esp.* as a makeshift.—*n.* the way a ship's masts and sails are arranged; costume; style of dress; in N. America, a vehicle for light work, a horse and trap or sleigh.
rigg'ing *n.* the spars and ropes of a ship; in aviation, assembly or alignment of aeroplane.—**rigg'er** *n.* fitter employed on ship or aircraft.
rigadoon' *n.* a lively dance for one couple; the music for such a dance.
right (rīt) *a.* straight; just; proper; true; correct; genuine.—*v.t.* to bring back to a vertical position; to do justice to.—*v.i.* to come back to a vertical position.—*n.* what is right, just, or due.—*adv.* straight; properly; very; on or to the right side.—**right'eous** (rī'chus) *a.* just, upright.—**right'eousness** *n.*—**right'ful** *a.* —**right'ly** *adv.*—**right-of-way** *n.* in law, the right to pass through a field, etc.; in Australia, a lane.—**right side,** the side of a person which is to the east when he faces north, the opposite of left.—**right angle** *n.* an angle of 90°.
right, right'ist *n.* (*col.*) a political conservative; a reactionary.—**right wing,** the conservative element in a government, nation, organisation, etc.
ri'gid (rij'-) *a.* stiff; harsh.—**rigid'ity** *n.*
rig'marole *n.* a meaningless string of words; rambling statement.
ri'gor *n.* a sudden coldness attended by shivering.—**ri'gor mor'tis,** *n.* the stiffening of the body, caused by the contraction of the muscles after death.
rig'our *n.* harshness, severity, strictness.—**rig'orous** *a.*—**rig'orously** *adv.*
rile *v.t.* (U.S. and *col.*) to stir up, make muddy; (*fig.*) to make angry.
rill *n.* small stream, brook.
rim *n.* the outer ring of a wheel; edge, margin, border.—**rim'less** *a.*
rime *see* **rhyme.**
rime *n.* hoar-frost.—**ri'my** *a.*
rind (-ī-) *n.* the outer coating of trees, fruits, etc.; bark, peel, outer crust.
rind'erpest *n.* cattle-plague.
ring *n.* a small circle of gold, etc., *esp.* as worn on the finger; any circular appliance, band, coil, rim, etc.; a circle of persons.—*v.t.* to put a ring round; in S. Africa, to tie horses together by passing a rope through their snaffles and fastening the ends together; in Australia, to kill a tree by cutting bark round the trunk; to make cattle move in a circle.—**ring'er** *n.* in Australia, the man who shears most sheep in a day.—**ring'-let** *n.* a curly lock of hair.—**ring'leader** *n.* the instigator of a mutiny, riot, etc.—**ring'-dove** *n.* wood-pigeon.—**ring'worm** *n.* a skin disease in circular patches.
ring *v.i.* to give out a clear resonant sound, as a bell; to resound.—*v.t.* to cause (a bell) to sound (**rang** *p.t.*—**rung** *p.p.*—**ring'ing** *pres. p.*).—*n.* a ringing.
rink *n.* a sheet of ice for skating, curling; a floor for roller-skating.
rinse (-s) *v.t.* to clean by putting in and emptying out water; to wash lightly.—*n.*
ri'ot *n.* tumult, disorder; loud revelry; unrestrained indulgence or display.—*v.i.* to make or engage in a riot.—**ri'otous** *a.*
rip *n.* worthless horse; dissipated person. —*v.t.* to cut or tear away, slash, rend.—*n.* a rent or tear; wicker basket in which to carry fish.—**rip'ping** *a.* (*sl.*) splendid

capital.—**rip-cord** *n.* the cord which is pulled to open a parachute.—**rip-roaring** *a.* (*sl.*) noisy, boisterous.

ripa'rian *a.* of or on the banks of a river.

ripe *a.* matured, ready to be reaped, eaten, etc.—**ri'pen** *v.i.* and *t.*—**ripe'ness** *n.* *Syn.* mature, full, mellow, complete, finished, perfect. *Ant.* unripe, immature, sour, imperfect, callow.

rip'ple *v.i.* to flow or form into little waves.—*v.t.* to form ripples on.—*n.* a slight wave or ruffling of surface.

rip'saw *n.* a hand-saw with coarse but narrow-set teeth (used for cutting wood in the direction of the fibre).

rise *v.i.* to get up; to move upwards; to reach a higher level; appear above the horizon; adjourn; rebel (**rose** *p.t.*—**ris'en** *p.p.*—**ri'sing** *pres. p.*).—*n.* rising; upslope; increase; beginning.

ris'ible (-z-) *a.* laughable; inclined to laugh.—**risibil'ity** *n.*—**ris'ibly** *adv.*

risk *n.* danger.—*v.t.* to venture.—**risk'y** *a.* dangerous.—**risk'ily** *adv.*

risqué (rēs-kā) *a.* suggestive; slightly indecent or immoral, indelicate.

riss'ole *n.* fried cake of minced meat, etc. rolled in bread-crumbs.

rite *n.* a formal practice or custom, *esp.* religious.–**rit'ual** *a.* concerning rites.–*n.* a prescribed order or book of rites.—**rit'ualism** *n.*–practice of ritual.–**rit'ualist** *n.* one who practises ritual.

ri'val *n.* one that competes with another for favour, success, etc.—*v.t.* to vie with.—*a.* in the position of a rival.—**ri'valry** *n.*

rive *v.t.* and *i.* to split (**rived** (rīvd) *p.t.*—**riv'en** *p.p.*—**ri'ving** *pres. p.*).

riv'er *n.* a large stream of water.—**river-horse** *n.* the hippopotamus.

riv'et *n.* bolt for fastening plates of metal together, the end being put through the holes and then beaten flat.—*v.t.* to fasten with rivets; clinch.

riv'ulet *n.* a small stream.

roach *n.* a fresh-water fish.

road *n.* track or way prepared for passengers, vehicles, etc.; direction, way; roadstead.—**road'-hog** *n.* one who drives to the danger of the public.—**road'house** *n.* modern semi-rural restaurant, *esp.* within motoring distance of large town.—**road'sense** *n.* capacity for sound judgment in driving road vehicles.—**road'-stead** *n.* sheet of water near shore where ships may lie at anchor.—**road'ster** *n.* horse, bicycle, etc., for the road; type of open touring car.

roam *v.t.* and *i.* to wander about, rove.

roan *a.* bay or dark colour mixed with grey or white.—*n.* a roan horse; a soft sheep-skin leather.—*n.* an animal.

roan'-tree *n.* native British tree; the mountain ash; wild service-tree producing clusters of berries of a bright red colour and acid taste; also **row'an-tree.**

roar (rawr) *n.* a loud deep hoarse sound, as of a lion, thunder, voice in anger, etc.—*v.i.* to make such sound.—*v.t.* to utter in roaring voice, shout out.

roast *v.t./i.* cook before open fire; in N. Amer. (*sl.*), to abuse; expose; reprimand.—*n.* roasted joint.—*a.* roasted.

rob *v.t.* plunder, steal from (**robb'ed** *p.t./p.p.*).—**robb'er** *n.* thief. swindler—**robb'ery** *n.*

rob, *pl.* **robbe** *n.* in S. Africa, a fur seal.

robe *n.* a long outer garment.—*v.t.* to dress.—*v.i.* to put on robes or vestments.

rob'in *n.* small bird with red breast.

ro'bot *n.* a mechanical slave.

robust' *a.* sturdy, strong and healthy.

roc (rok) *n.* the monstrous bird well known in the mythology of the Arabians.

roch'et *n.* a garment like a surplice, with tight sleeves, worn by bishops.

rock *n.* stone; a large rugged mass of stone; a hard toffee.—**rock'ery** *n.* a mound of stones for plants in a garden.—**rock'y** *a.*—**rock'-rabbit** *n.* S. Africa, the hyrax.—**rock-shelter** *n.* Australia, aboriginal cave-dwelling.—**rock-snake** *n.* S. Africa, the Natal python.

rock *v.i.* to sway to and fro.—*v.t.* to cause to do this.—**rock'er** *n.* a curved piece of wood, etc., on which a thing may rock, *e.g.* a cradle.

rock'et *n.* firework on stick that can be shot up in the air by igniting (used for display, signalling, etc.); deadly self-propelled missile of war fired from sites, aircraft, landing craft, etc.

roco'co *a.* of furniture, architecture, etc., having much conventional decoration, tastelessly florid; antiquated.—*n.*

rod *n.* a slender straight round bar, wand, stick or switch; a birch or cane; a measure (= a pole, 5½ yards).

ro'dent *a.* gnawing.—*n.* gnawing animal.

rode'o (-dā-o) *n.* a round-up of cattle to be branded or marked; an exhibition and contest in steer-wrestling and buck-jumping by cowboys.

rodomontade' *n.* boastful language.

roe *n.* small deer. **-'buck** *masc.*

roe *n.* a mass of eggs in a fish.

Roent'gen ray (rent'-g'n) X-ray; high-frequency radiation, capable of penetrating solids, discovered by the German physicist, W. K. Roentgen.

roer *n.* in S. Africa, a long-barrelled gun.

rog'er (roj'-er) *interj.* understood; O.K. (from the radio-telephone signal for receipt of a message).

rogue (rōg) *n.* a rascal, knave; mischievous person or child; wild beast of savage temper living apart from its herd.—**ro'guish** (-gish) *a.*—**ro'guery** *n.*
Syn. scamp, villain, caitiff, scoundrel.

rois'ter *v.i.* to bluster, to swagger.—**rois'terer** *n.* noisy reveller.

rôle *n.* actor's part; task, function.

roll (rōl) *n.* a piece of paper, etc., rolled up; a list or catalogue; a small loaf; in

N. America, a bundle of paper money carried by a person.—*v.t.* to move by turning over and over; to wind round; to smooth out with a roller.—*v.i.* to move by turning over and over; to move or sweep along; of a ship, to swing from side to side; of an aeroplane, to turn about a line from nose to tail in flight.—**roll'-call** *n.* calling over names from a list.—**roll'er** *n.* a cylinder used for pressing or smoothing, supporting something to be moved, winding something on, etc.—**roll'er-skate** *n.* skate mounted on rollers.—**roll'ing-pin** *n.* roller for smoothing out dough.—**roll-up** *n.* in Australia, a meeting.—**roller-bearings,** bearings consisting of hardened steel rollers to give a line of contact.—**roll'ing stock** *n.* locomotives, carriages, etc., of a railway.

roll'icking *a.* boisterously jovial.

ro'ly-po'ly *n.* a pudding of paste covered with jam and rolled up.

Ro'man *a.* of Rome or the Church of Rome.—**Ro'man type,** plain upright letters, the ordinary script of printing.—**Roman fig'ures,** the letters I, V, X, L, C, D, M, used to represent numbers in the manner of the Romans.

Romance' *n.* vernacular language of certain countries, developed from Latin and developing into French, Spanish, etc.—**romance'** *n.* a tale of chivalry; a tale with scenes remote from ordinary life; literature like this; an event or love-affair or atmosphere suggesting it; sympathetic imagination; exaggeration; picturesque falsehood.—**romanc'er** *n.*—**Roman'ic** *a.* evolved from Latin.—**roman'tic** *a.* characterised by romance; of literature, etc., preferring passion and imagination to proportion and finish.—**romant'icism** *n.*—**romant'icist** *n.*

Romany *n.* a gipsy; the gipsy language or race.—*a.* gipsy.

romp *v.i.* to frolic.—*n.* a frolic.

rond'avel *n.* S. Africa, a circular hut.

ron'deau (-dō) *n.* a short, rhymed poem, with refrain (**-deaux** (-dōz) *pl.*).

ron'del *n.* a kind of short poem.—**ron'delet** *n.* a poem of seven lines, of which two are refrains.—**ron'do** *n.* (*mus.*) a rondeau, a jig.

rond'loper *n.* in S. Africa, a tramp.

Ro'neophone *n.* a variation of the dictaphone (trade name).

roo *n.* in Australia, kangaroo.

rood (-ōō-) *n.* the Cross of Christ; a crucifix; a quarter of an acre.

roof (-ōō-) *n.* the outside top covering of a building; something resembling this.—*v.t.* to put a roof on, be a roof over.

roo'inek *n.* in S. Africa, an Englishman, *esp.* a new arrival.

rook (-ōō-) *n.* a bird of the crow family; a piece at chess, also called a castle.

rook'ery *n.* a colony of rooks; a collection of tumbledown houses.

rook'ie *n.* recruit; novice.

room (-ōō-) *n.* space; space enough; a division of a house.—**room'er** *n.* in N. America (*sl.*) a person in a lodging house who takes a room only, arranging for meals elsewhere.—**room'y** *a.* spacious.

roor'back *n.* N. America, untrue story spread in political intrigue.

roost (-ōō-) *n.* a perch for fowls; a hen-house.—*v.i.* to perch.—**roost'er** *n.*

root (-ōō-) *n.* part of plant growing down into earth and conveying nourishment to plant; source, origin; original, vital part.—*v.t.* to cause to take root.—*v.i.* to take root; N. Amer., (*sl.*) cheer; applaud.—**root'er** *n.*

rope *n.* a thick cord.—*v.t.* to secure or mark off with a rope; in Australia, to lasso.—**rope'able** *a.* in Australia, of cattle, wild and intractable and, by extension to human beings, angry, infuriated.—**ro'per** *n.* in N. America, a cowboy, *esp.* an expert with the lasso.—**ro'ping pole** *n.* in Australia, a pole with a noose of rope at its end, used in roping individual cattle in a mob.—**ro'py** *a.* sticky and stringy.

Roque'fort (rōk'fōr) *n.* French cheese made of ewes' and goats' milk.

roquet' (rō-kā) *v.t.* in croquet, to strike one ball with another.—*n.* the stroke.

rose *n.* a beautiful flower of many varieties; a rose-bush; a perforated flat nozzle for a hose, etc.; a pink colour.—*a.* of this colour.—**ro'sary** *n.* a string of beads for keeping count of prayers; a form of prayer, a rose-garden.—**ros'eate** *a.* rose-coloured, rosy.—**rosette'** *n.* a rose-shaped bunch of ribbon; a rose-shaped architectural ornament.—**rose'wood** *n.* a reddish wood.—**ro'sy** *a.* rose-coloured.

rose'mary *n.* evergreen fragrant shrub.

ros'in *see* **resin.**

ros'ter *n.* a list showing turns of duty.

ros'trum *n.* platform for public speaking (**-trums, -tra** *pl.*).

rot *v.t.* and *i.* to decompose naturally.—*n.* decay; a disease of sheep; nonsense.

rott'en *a.* decomposed; corrupt.

ro'ta *n.* a wheel; a course; a roster; an ecclesiastical tribunal in the R.C. church.

rotam'eter *n.* an opisometer, *i.e.,* an instrument that, with a small wheel, measures the curved lines of a map.

ro'ttang *n.* in S. Africa, the name of several species of E. Indian climbing plants; a walking-stick cut from the strong stem of the plant.

ro'tary *a.* of movement, circular.—**ro'tary** *n.* of an international system of clubs, in which each member of club is of different occupation.

rotate' *v.i.* to move round a centre or on a pivot.—*v.t.* to cause to do this.

rota'tion *n.*—**rota'tory** *a.*—**rotary club** *n.*

one of an international association of business men's clubs for mutual service. —**rotar'ian** *n.*—**rotary engine** *n.* in aviation, an aero engine in which cylinders and crank-case rotate with air-screw.—**rotor** *n.* revolving part of a machine, *esp.* electrical machine.

rote *n.* **by rote** by memory, by heart.

ro'togravure (-grav-ūr) *n.* a method of reproduction by a photographic screen process in which prints are obtained from a chemically etched cylinder; an illustrated newspaper printed thus.

rotund' *a.* round, plump.—**rotund'ity** *n.*

rouge (rōōzh) *n.* red powder used to colour the cheeks or lips.—*v.t.* and *i.* to colour with rouge.

rough (ruf) *a.* not smooth, of irregular surface; violent, boisterous; lacking refinement; approximate; in a preliminary form.—*v.t.* to make rough; to plan out approximately.—*n.* a disorderly ruffian; a rough state.—*n.* in golf, the untrimmed parts of the course.—**rough'age** *n.* the bulky, unassimilated portion of food necessary to promote proper intestinal action.—**rough'en** *v.t.*—**rough'cast** *a.* coated with a mixture of lime and gravel. —*n.* such mixture.—*v.t.* to coat with it.— **rough'hew'** *v.t.* to shape roughly.— **rough'ly** *adv.*—**rough and ready,** crude; serviceable; unpolished but straightforward; bluff.

Syn. unpolished, harsh, discordant, stormy, brutal, terrible. *Ant.* polished, level, smooth, gentle, courteous, polite.

roulade' *n.* in music, an embellishment.

rouleau' (rōō-lō') *n.* a cylindrical packet of coins (-**leaux'**, -**leaus'** (-lō',-lōz') *pl.*).

roulette' (rōō-) *n.* a game of chance played on a table with a revolving centre; a small toothed wheel used by engravers to roll over the surface of a plate to produce dots; a hair-curling roller; in geometry, a kind of curve.

round (rownd) *a.* spherical or cylindrical or circular, or nearly so; roughly correct; large; plain.—*adv.* with a circular or circuitous course.—*n.* something round in shape; a rung; movement in a circle; recurrent duties; customary course, as of a postman or military patrol; a cartridge for a firearm; a 3 min. bout in pugilism.— *prep.* about; on all sides of.—*v.t.* to make round; to get round.—*v.i.* to become round.—**round'about** *n.* a merry-go-round.—*a.* to denote extension of one-way traffic round a central point; indirect.—**Round'head** *n.* a supporter of the Parliament in the Civil War.— **round'ly** *adv.*—**round'ers** *n.* (*pl.*) a ball game.—**round'-rob'in** *n.* a petition signed with names in a circle.—**round-table con'ference,** a meeting of opposing parties on an equal footing, to try to reach agreement.—**round'-up** *n.* in N. America and Australia, the collecting of cattle into large herds for branding, etc.—*v.t.* to gather animals into herds.

roup *v.t.* in Scotland and N. Amer., sell by auction.—*n.* sale by auction.

rouse (rowz) *v.t.* to wake up, stir up, cause to rise.—*v.i.* to waken (**rous'ing** *pres. p.*).—**rouse'about** *n.* Australia, man doing odd jobs on a sheep or cattle station, *esp.* in a shearing shed.

rout (rowt) *n.* a troop; a disorderly crowd; a large evening party; a disorderly retreat.—*v.t.* to put to rout.

route (rōōt) *n.* a road, way; (rowt) military, written marching orders.

route march *n.* military, a long march undertaken for training purposes.

routine' (-ēn) *n.* regular course or practice; regularity of procedure.

rove *v.i.* to wander without fixed destination.—*v.t.* to wander over.—**ro'ver** *n.*— **Ro'ver Scout** *n.* elder Boy Scout.—**ro'ver ticket** *n.* ticket entitling holder to make unlimited journeys, during one day, over tram or bus system.

row (rō) *n.* a number of things in a straight line.—*v.i.* to propel a boat by oars.—*v.t.* to propel by oars.—*n.*

row *n.* a disturbance or dispute.

row'an *n.* the mountain ash.

rowd'y *n.* a rough.—*a.* disorderly.

row'el *n.* small pointed wheel on a horseman's spur.

row'lock (rol'ok) *n.* an appliance serving as point of leverage for an oar.

roy'al *a.* of, worthy of, befitting, patronised by, a king or queen; splendid.

Syn. regal, noble, illustrious, august, majestic. *Ant.* plebeian, ignoble, vulgar.

roy'alist *n.* a supporter of monarchy.

roy'alty *n.* royal dignity or power; royal persons; payment to an owner of land for the right to work minerals, or to an inventor for use of his invention; payment to an author depending on sales.

ru'a *n.* in New Zealand, Maori word for a storage pit for edible roots.

rub *v.t.* to subject to friction; pass the hand over; abrade, chafe; remove by friction.—*v.i.* to come into contact accompanied by friction; become frayed or worn with friction.—*n.* a rubbing; an impediment.—**rubb'er** *n.* one who rubs; a thing for rubbing; indiarubber.—*a.* made of indiarubber.—*v.i.* in N. America, to stare inquisitively, hence **rubber'neck** *n.*—**rubb'ers** *n. pl.* goloshes.

rubb'er *n.* a series of three games at various card games; a series of an odd number of games or contests at various games; two out of three games won.

rubb'ish *n.* refuse, waste material; trash, nonsense.—**rubb'ishy** *a.*—**rub'ble** *n.* fragments of stone, broken bricks, etc.

rube *n.* N. America, a rustic.

rub'eroid *n.* roofing felt soaked in bitumen (protected trade name).

ru'bicund (rōō-) *a.* ruddy.—**ru'bric** *n.* a

chapter-heading; a direction in a liturgy (properly one printed in red).—**ru'bricate** *v.t.* to mark, write, or print in red; supply with rubrics.—**rubrica'tion** *n.*—**ru'by** *n.* a red precious stone; its colour.—*a.* of this colour (**ru'bies** *pl.*).

ruche *n.* a kind of plaited or goffered trimming, *esp.* for the edges of dresses.

ruck *n.* crowd; band.

ruck *n.* a crease; main body (of competitors in a race, etc.).—*v.t.* and *i.* to make or become wrinkled.

ruck'sack (rŏŏk-) *n.* pack carried on the back of walker, climber, etc.

rudd'er *n.* a flat piece hinged to the stern of a ship or boat to steer by; in aviation, hinged vertical surface at rear of aeroplane.—**rudd'er-wheel** *n.* a small wheel on a plough, to help in guiding it.

rudd'y *a.* of a fresh or healthy red.

rude *a.* primitive; roughly made; uneducated; uncivil.—**rude'ly** *adv.*

ru'diment *n.* beginning, germ (*pl.* elements, first principles).—**rudimen'tary** *a.* elementary, undeveloped.

rue (rōō) *n.* a plant with strong-smelling bitter leaves.—*v.t.* and *i.* to repent.—*n.* repentance.—**rue'ful** *a.* sorrowful, dejected.—**rue'fully** *adv.*

ruff *n.* a starched and frilled collar; a bird allied to the woodcock and sand-piper; a species of pigeon.—**ruf'fle** *n.* a frilled cuff.—*v.t.* to crumple, disorder; frill or pleat; annoy, put out.

ruff *n.* at cards, an act of trumping.—*v.t.* and *i.* to trump.

ruff'ian *n.* a rough lawless fellow.

rug *n.* a thick woollen wrap; a mat for the floor, of shaggy or thick-piled surface.

rugg'ed *a.* rough, broken; furrowed.

Rug'by *n.* a form of football in which the ball may be seized and run with.

rugg'ens *n. pl.* in South Africa, undulating hills or slopes.

ru'in *n.* downfall; fallen or broken state; decay, destruction (*pl.* ruined buildings, etc.)—*v.t.* to reduce to ruins; bring to decay or destruction, spoil; cause loss of fortune to.—**ruina'tion** *n.*—**ru'inous** *a.*

rule *n.* a principle or precept; what is usual; government; a strip of wood, etc., for measuring length.—*v.t.* to govern; decide.—**ru'ler** *n.* one who governs; a strip of wood, etc., for measuring or drawing lines (**ru'ling** *pres. p.*).

rum *n.* a spirit distilled from sugar-cane.

rum *a.* (*sl.*) odd; queer.

rum'ba (-oo-) *n.* a native dance of Spanish-American negroes with syncopated rhythm, now a modern ballroom dance in many countries.

rum'ble *v.i.* to make a noise as of distant thunder.—*n.* such noise.—*v.t.* (*sl.*) to detect or see through, find out.

ru'minate *v.i.* to chew cud; meditate.—**ru'minant** *a.* cud-chewing.—*n.* cud-chewing animal.—**rumina'tion** *n.* chewing cud; reflection.—**ru'minative** *a.*

rumm'age *v.t.* and *i.* to search thoroughly.—*n.* a ransacking; discarded odds and ends, old clothing.

rumm'er *n.* a large drinking-glass.

rumm'y *n.* a simple card game.

ru'mour *n.* hearsay, common talk; current but unproved statement.—*v.t.* to put round as a rumour.

rump *n.* tail-end; buttocks.

rum'ple *v.t.* to crease or wrinkle.—*n.*

rum'pus *n.* a disturbance; row.

run *v.i.* to move rapidly on the legs; to go quickly; flow; flee; compete in a race; revolve; continue; have a certain meaning.—*v.t.* to cross by running; expose oneself, be exposed; cause to run; land and dispose of (smuggled goods); to manage (**ran** *p.t.*—**run** *p.p.*—**runn'ing** *pres. p.*).—*n.* an act or spell of running; a rush; tendency, course.—**run'ning-board** *n.* the footboard at the side of a vehicle; in Australia, a range of pasture for feeding stock.—**run'about** *n.* a small motor-car.—**run'-abouts** *n. pl.* in Australia, cattle free to wander about to feed.—**run'way** *n.* a prepared way for aircraft to take off and land; a trail, track, animal pathway, etc.

run'agate *n.* a deserter, renegade.

rune *n.* a character of the earliest Teutonic alphabet.—**ru'nic** *a.*

rung *n.* a cross-bar or spoke, *esp.* in a ladder; crossbar joining legs of a chair.

runn'el *n.* a gutter; a small stream.

runn'er *n.* a messenger, a racer; a curved piece of wood or metal on which a sleigh slides; a slender stem coming from the main stem and taking root.

runt *n.* any animal small below the usual size of the species; a variety of pigeon; stem of a cabbage.

rupee' *n.* the Indian unit of money; a silver coin worth about 1*s.* 4*d.*

rup'ture *n.* a breaking or breach; a hernia.—*v.t.* and *i.* to break or burst.

Syn. fracture, disruption, quarrel, contention. *Ant.* union, junction, harmony.

ru'ral *a.* of the country, rustic.

rus'bank *n.* S. Africa, a wooden couch or bed.

ruse (-z-) *n.* a stratagem, trick, device.

rush *n.* marsh plant with slender pithy stem used in basket-making, etc. (**rush'es** *pl.*).—**rush'y** *a.*

rush *v.t.* to mpel or carry along violently and rapidly; to take by sudden assault.—*v.i.* to move violently or rapidly.—*n.* a rushing; Australia, stampede of cattle.

rusk *n.* a piece of bread rebaked; biscuits prepared for children and invalids.

rus'per *n.* in S. Africa, small very destructive caterpillar.

russ'et *a.* of reddish-brown colour.—*n.* the colour; a variety of apple.

rust *n.* reddish coating formed on iron by oxidation and corroding it; plant disease.—*v.i./t.* to contract, affect with

rust.—**rust'y** *a.*—**rust'less steel** steel containing chromium used in manufacture of stainless cutlery, etc.
rust'ic *a.* of, or as of, country people; rural; of rude manufacture; made of untrimmed branches.—*n.* a countryman, peasant.—**rusticity** *n.*—**rust'icate** *v.t.* to banish from a university.—*v.i.* to live a country life.—**rustica'tion** *n.*
rus'tle (-sl) *v.i.* to make a sound as of blown dead leaves, etc.—*n.* the sound.
rus'tle *v.t.* (U.S.) (*col.*) to steal, *esp.* cattle.—**rus'tler** *n.* a cattle thief.
rut *n.* the periodical sexual excitement of the male of deer and certain other animals.—*v.i.* to experience this.
rut *n.* a furrow made by a wheel; a settled habit or way of living.—**rutt'y** *a.*
rutaba'ga (ròò-tạ-bā'-gạ) *n.* a large yellow turnip with a long fibrous root.
ruth (rōōth) *n.* pity.—**ruth'less** *a.* pitiless, cruel.—**ruth'lessly** *adv.*
ruthen'ium (rooth-ēn'-i-um) *n.* a greyish-white metal similar to platinum and usually associated with it.
rye *n.* a grain used for fodder and in some places for bread; the plant bearing it.
rye-grass *n.* kinds of fodder grass.
ry'ot *n.* an Indian peasant.

S

saam *prep.* in S. Africa, too; as well.
Sabb'ath *n.* the Jewish Sunday or seventh day.—**Sabbata'rian** *n.* a strict observer of Sunday.—**Sabbatar'ianism** *n.*—**Sabbat'ical** *a.* of, like sabbath.
sa'ble *n.* a small Arctic animal; its fur; black.—*a.* black, gloomy.
sab'ot (-ō) *n.* wooden shoe worn by poorer classes in parts of Europe.
sab'otage *n.* intentional damage done by malcontents or enemies to machinery, etc.—**saboteur'** *n.* one who commits acts of sabotage.
sa'bre (-bẹr) *n.* a cavalry sword.
sac *n.* cavity in animal or vegetable.
sacc'harin(e) *a.* pertaining to sugar.—*n.* sweet substance from coal-tar.
sacerdo'tal (sas-) *a.* of priests or priesthood.—**sacerdo'talism** *n.*
sa'chem *n.* a chief of a tribe of the American Indians; a sagamore.
sach'et (sash'ā) *n.* a scent-bag.
sack *n.* a large bag, usually of some coarse textile material; (*sl.*) dismissal.—*v.t.* to pillage (a captured town, etc.); (*sl.*) to dismiss.—**sack'cloth** *n.* a coarse fabric used for sacks.—**sack'ing** *n.* material used for sacks.
sack *n.* unsweetened white wine.
sack'but *n.* a wind instrument of music; old name for trombone.
sac'rament *n.* a solemn religious ceremony, *esp.* the Eucharist.—**sacrament'al** *a.*—**sa'cred** *a.* dedicated, regarded as holy.—**sacred'ly** *adv.*
sac'rifice *n.* making of an offering to a god; the thing offered; a giving up for sake of something else; the thing so given up as a sacrifice.—*v.t.* to offer as sacrifice.—**sacrifi'cial** *a.*
sac'ristan *n.* an official in charge of the vestments and vessels of a church.
sac'rosanct *a.* secure by religious fear against desecration or violence.
sac'rilege *n.* violation of something sacred.—**sacrile'gious** *a.*
sa'crum (-krum) *n.* five vertebræ forming a compound bone at the base of the spinal column.
sad *a.* sorrowful; deplorably bad; of colour, dull, sober.—**sad'ly** *adv.*—**sadd'en** *v.t.* *Syn.* dejected, downcast, distressing, dark-coloured, sombre, heavy. *Ant.* happy, joyous, gay, bright, light.
sad'dle *n.* rider's seat to fasten on a horse, or form part of a bicycle, etc.; a part of a shaft; a joint of mutton or venison; a ridge of a hill.—*v.t.* to put a saddle on.—**sadd'ler** *n.* a maker of saddles, etc.—**sadd'lery** *n.*
Sadd'ucee *n.* one of a sect among the ancient Jews who denied the resurrection, a future state, and the existence of angels.—**Sadduce'an** *a.* pertaining to the Sadducees; sceptical; irreligious.
sad'ism *n.* a form of sexual perversion marked by love of cruelty.—**sad'ist** *n.*
safa'ri (-fà-) *n.* a hunting expedition in E. Africa; a caravan, its carriers, or its day's journey.—**on safa'ri.**
safe *a.* uninjured, out of danger; not involving risk; cautious; trustworthy.—*n.* a strong box; a ventilated cupboard for meat, etc.—**safe'ly** *adv.*—**safe'ty** *n.*—**safe-con'duct** *n.* a passport or permit to pass somewhere.—**safe'guard** *n.* a protection.—*v.t.* to protect.—**safe'ty-cur'tain** *n.* in theatre, fireproof curtain on stage.—**safety-glass** *n.* unsplinterable glass.—**safe'ty-valve** *n.* automatic valve letting off steam when pressure exceeds safety margin.
saff'ron *n.* the orange-red colouring matter obtained from the autumn crocus.—*a.* of this colour.
sag *v.t.* to sink in the middle, to hang sideways or curve downwards (**sag'ging** *pres. p.*—**sagged** *p.t.* and *p.p.*).
sa'ga (sà'ga) *n.* a mediaeval tale of Norse heroes; tale of heroism.
saga'cious *a.* shrewd, mentally acute; (of animals) unusually intelligent.—**saga'ciously** *adv.*—**saga'city** *n.*
sage *n.* an aromatic herb.
sage *a.* wise, discreet, shrewd.—*n.* a very wise man.—**sage'ly** *adv.*
Sagitta'rius *n.* the Archer, the 9th sign of the zodiac, operative Nov. 22nd–Dec. 20th; constellation of this name.
sa'go *n.* a starch; foodstuff made from it, obtained from the pith of palms.
sah'ib (sà'ib) *n.* term of respect used

by natives of India and Persia in addressing Europeans; a true gentleman.

sail *n.* a piece of canvas stretched to catch the wind for propelling a ship; the arm of a windmill; in S. Africa, the heavy canvas cover of an ox-wagon; ships collectively; the act of sailing.—*v.i.* to travel by water; to begin a voyage.—*v.t.* to navigate.—**sail'or** *n.*

saint *a.* holy; title of a canonised person.—*n.* one who has been canonised.—**saint'ly** *a.*—**saint'ed** *a.* canonised; sacred.—**saint'hood** *n.*—**saint'liness** *n.*

sake *n.* **for the sake of** on behalf of, to please or benefit, or get, or keep.

salaam' (-lâm') *n.* a salutation or mark of respect in the East.—*v.t.* to salute.

sala'cious *a.* lustful.—**sala'city** *n.*

sal'ad *n.* uncooked vegetables or fruit served cold with a dressing.

sal'amander *n.* an elemental creature living in fire; a variety of lizard.

sala'me (-à-) *n.* variety of sausage; strongly seasoned meat delicacy shaped like sausage (**-mi** *pl.*).

sal'ary *n.* fixed payment of persons employed in non-manual or non-mechanical work (**sal'aries** *pl.*).—**sal'aried** *a.*

sale *n.* a selling; a special disposal of stock at low prices.—**sales'man** *n.* a shop assistant or traveller.—**sales'manship** *n.*—**sale of work**, a sale of articles made by voluntary labour to raise funds.—**sales resist'ance** in commerce, disinclination to buy.

Sal'ic *a.* designating a law by which only males can inherit the throne.

sal'icin *n.* a bitter substance obtained from the bark and leaves of willows and poplars.—**salicyl'ic** *a.* derived from the willow.—**salicyl'ic acid** an antiseptic acid.—**salic'ylate** *n.* a salt, *esp.* the sodium salt, of salicylic acid.

sa'lient *a.* jutting out.—*n.* a salient angle, *esp.* in fortification.—**sa'lience** *n.*

sa'line *n.* a fruit salt.—*a.* salty.

sali'va *n.* a liquid which forms in the mouth, spittle.—**sali'vary** *a.*

sall'ow *a.* of a sickly yellow colour.—*n.* a tree or low shrub allied to the willow.

sall'y *v.i.* to rush; to set out (**sall'ied** *p.t.* and *p.p.*—**sall'ying** *pres. p.*).—*n.* a rushing out, *esp.* from a fort; an outburst; witty remark.—**sall'ies** *pl.*

salm'on (sam-) *n.* a large food fish with orange-pink flesh; the colour of its flesh.—*a.* of this colour.

saloon' *n.* a large reception room; a public dining-room; the principal cabin or sitting-room in a passenger ship; a drawing-room car on a railway; a public room for specified use, such as billiards; in motoring, a car with all seats enclosed; in N. America, a tavern.—**saloon' bar** *n.* first-class bar.

sal'picon *n.* stuffing; chopped meat or bread used to stuff legs of veal.

salt (solt) *n.* sodium chloride, a substance which gives sea-water its taste; a chemical compound of an acid and a metal.—*a.* preserved with, or full of, or tasting like, salt.—*v.t.* preserve with salt; to put salt on; S. Africa, to fake, as a gold mine, by adding gold; S. Africa, to become immune from disease.—**salt'y** *a.*—**salt'ness** *n.*—**salt'-cellar** *n.* small vessel for salt on the table.—**salt'-lick** *n.* S. Africa, salt left on certain land during dry weather; the land where such incrustations occur.—**salt'-pan** *n.* S. Africa and Australia, a depression where water collects during the rains and leaves an incrustration of salt on drying.—**salt'petre** *n.* potassium nitrate used in gun-powder.

sal'tant *a.* leaping; dancing.—**sal'tatory** *a.*—**salta'tion** *n.*

saltarell'o *n.* a very animated Italian and Spanish dance for a single couple; music for such a dance (**-os** (-ōz) *pl.*).

sal'tire *n.* in heraldry, an ordinary in form of St. Andrew's cross, formed by two bends crossing each other.

salu'brious *a.* favourable to health, health-giving.—**salu'brity** *n.*

Syn. healthful, beneficial, good. *Ant.* unhealthy, bad.

sal'utary *a.* wholesome, resulting in good.—**salute'** *v.t.* to greet with words or sign; to kiss.—*v.i.* to perform a military salute.—*n.* a word or sign by which one greets another; a kiss; a prescribed motion of the arm as a mark of respect to a superior, etc., in military usage.—**saluta'tion** *n.* a greeting.

sal'vage *n.* payment for, or the act of, saving a ship or other property from danger; property so saved.

sal'varsan *n.* a preparation of arsenic used by injection for the cure of anthrax and syphilis (protected trade name).

salva'tion *n.* fact or state of being saved; act of saving the soul from sin.

salve (salv *or* sâlv) *n.* healing ointment.—*v.i.* to anoint with such; to heal.

sal'ver *n.* a tray for refreshments, etc.

sal'vo *n.* simultaneous discharge of guns as a salute, or in battle (**-vos** (-vōz) *pl.*).

sal'-volat'ile (-i-li) *n.* a preparation of ammonia used for faintness, etc.

Samar'itan *a.* pertaining to *Samaria*, in Palestine.—*n.* native or inhabitant of Samaria; a benevolent person.

sama'rium *n.* a rare-earths metal discovered in *Samarskite*; the latter is notable as containing uranium.

sam'bal *n.* in S. Africa, a hot sauce containing chillies, spices, etc., used with curries.

sam'bo *n.* offspring of black person and mulatto; nickname for negro.

sambok, *see* **sjambok.**

Sam Browne *n.* leather belt, part of British officer's service uniform.

same *a.* identical, not different, unchanged, unvarying.—**same'ness** *n.*
sa'miel (sā'mi-el) *n.* a hot wind that blows in Arabia from the desert.
sam'isen *n.* a guitar or banjo of three strings used in Japan.
sa'mite *n.* medieval fabric of silk woven with gold thread.
sam'pan *n.* Chinese boat, 12–15 ft. long.
sam'phire *n.* herb growing on rocks by the sea; St. Peter's wort; sea-fennel.
sam'ple *n.* a specimen.—*v.i.* to take or give a sample of.—**sam'pler** *a.* beginner's exercise in embroidery.
san'ative *a.* curative, healing.
sanator'ium *n.* an establishment for the treatment of invalids, *esp.* tuberculosis; a health resort (**-ria, -riums** *pl.*).
sanc'tify *v.t.* to set apart as holy; to free from sin (**-ified** *p.t.* and *p.p.*—**-ifying** *pres. p.*).—**sanctifica'tion** *n.*—**sanctimo'nious** *a.* making a show of piety.—**sanct'imony, sanctimo'niousness** *n.* assumed outward holiness.—**sanc'tity** *n.* saintliness, sacredness; inviolability.
sanc'tuary *n.* a holy place; a place where a fugitive was safe from arrest or violence.—**sanc'tum** *n.* a sacred place or shrine; a person's private room.
sanc'tion *n.* a penalty or reward following breaking or observing law; express permission; countenance given by custom.—*v.t.* allow, authorise.
sand *n.* a powdery substance made by the wearing down of rock.—*pl.* stretches or banks of this, e.g., a seashore.—*v.t.* to cover or mix with sand.—**sand'y** *a.*
sand'stone *n.* rock composed of sand.
sand'bag *n.* bag filled with sand or earth as a weapon and used in fortification.—*v.t.* hit, beat with sandbag.
sand'paper *n.* paper with sand stuck on it for scraping or polishing wood, etc.—**sand'-river** *n.* S. Africa, a river running beneath sand and which can be reached by digging.—**sand'shoe** *n.* a canvas shoe for beach wear, etc.—**sand'-veld** *n.* S. Africa, arid, sandy plain, e.g., the Kalahari desert.
san'dal *n.* a shoe consisting of a sole attached by straps; an openwork shoe.
san'dalwood *n.* a scented wood.
sand'wich *n.* two slices of bread with meat or other substance between.—*v.t.* to insert between two things.—**sandwich'man** man carrying through streets, notice boards front and back.
sandy'blight *n.* in Australia, a form of ophthalmia.
sane *a.* of sound mind, sensible.—**san'ity** *n.*
sang-froid' (-frwa') *n.* freedom from agitation; coolness; indifference.
san'guine (-ng'gwin) *a.* hopeful or confident; florid.—**san'guinary** *a.* bloodthirsty; accompanied by bloodshed.
Syn. plethoric, full-blooded, cheerful. *Ant.* hopeless, diffident, dejected.

san'itary *a.* helping or not hindering the protection of health against dirt, etc.
sanita'tion *n.* the apparatus, etc., for making and keeping houses healthy.
san'serif *n.* a type face without ornamentation or serifs.
sap *n.* life-giving juice of plants.—**sap'less** *a.*—**sap'ling** *n.* a young tree.
sap *n.* the covered trench approaching a besieged place or enemy trench.—*v.t.* to construct such trenches.—*v.i.* to undermine; to destroy insidiously.—**sapp'er** *n.*
sa'pient *a.* wise (usually ironical).—**sa'pience** *n.*—**sapien'tial** *a.*
sapona'ceous *a.* of or containing soap.
Sapph'ic *a.* pertaining to Sappho, a Grecian poetess; noting a kind of verse.—*n.* a Sapphic verse.
sapph'ire (saf-) *n.* a blue precious stone.
sar'aband, sar'abande *n.* a stately Spanish dance; the music for it.
Sar'acen *n.* an Arabian; a Mussulman; an adherent of Mohammedanism in countries farther west than Arabia.
sar'casm *n.* a bitter or wounding ironic remark; such remarks; use of them.—**sarcast'ic** *a.*—**sarcast'ically** *adv.*
sarcoph'agus *n.* a stone coffin.
sard *n.* precious stone; yellow cornelian; a variety of chalcedony.
sardine' (-dēn') *n.* a small food fish of herring family, usually packed in oil.
sardon'ic *a.* of a smile or laughter, bitter, scornful.—**sardon'ically** *adv.*
sardon'yx *n.* onyx in which layers of chalcedony alternate with sand.
sargass'um *n.* a genus of seaweeds.—**sargass'o** *n.* the gulf-weed.—**Sargasso sea**, part of the Atlantic covered by this.
sark *n.* a shirt; a chemise; the body garment.—**sar'king** *n.* thin boards for lining, to be used under slates; linen for shirts.
sarong' *n.* garment worn in the E. Indies.
sass'afras *n.* laurel-like tree; its aromatic bark used medicinally.
sarto'rial *a.* of tailors or tailoring.
sash *n.* frame forming a window, sliding up or down; a scarf wound around body.
sas'katoon *n.* in N. America, the service tree; its edible berry.
sass'aby *n.* in S. Africa, a large, red antelope with curved horns.
Sa'tan *n.* the devil.—**satan'ic** *a.* devilish.—**satan'ically** *adv.*—**satanism** *n.*
sat'chel *n.* small bag; school-bag.
sate *v.t.* to gratify to the full.
sateen' *see* **satin.**
sat'ellite *n.* a hanger-on; a planet revolving round another; a moon.—*a.* subsidiary, e.g., a satellite company.
sa'tiate (sāsh'i-āt) *v.t.* to satisfy to the full; surfeit.—**sa'tiable** *a.*—**satia'tion** *n.*
sati'ety *n.* overfed feeling, disgust.
sat'in *n.* silk fabric with a glossy surface on one side.—**sateen'** *n.* glossy cotton or woollen fabric.—**sat'inwood** *n.* ornamental wood of tropical tree.—**sat'iny** *a.*

sat'ire (-ir) *n.* a composition in which vice or folly, or a foolish person, is held up to ridicule; use of ridicule or sarcasm to expose vice and folly.—**satir'ic, satir'ical** *a.*—**sat'irist** *n.*—**sati'rise** *v.t.*

sat'isfy *v.t.* content, to meet the wishes of; to pay, fulfil, supply adequately; convince; to have sufficient (**-fied** *p.t.* and *p.p.*—**-fying** *pres. p.*).—**satisfac'tion** *n.* —**satisfac'tory** *a.*—**satisfac'torily** *adv.*

sat'urate *v.t.* to soak thoroughly; to cause to dissolve a maximum amount. (**sat'urating** *pres.p.*).—**satura'tion** *n.*

Sat'urday *n.* seventh day of the week.

Sat'urn *n.* a Latin god; one of the planets.—**sat'urnine** *a.* gloomy.

sat'yr (-er) *n.* a woodland god, part man and part beast.—**satyr'ic** *a.*

sauce *n.* liquid added to food to give relish.—*v.t.* to add sauce to.—**sauce'pan** *n.* a cooking-pot.—**sau'cer** *n.* a curved plate under a cup, etc.—**sau'cy** *a.* impudent, cheeky.—**sau'cily** *adv.*

sauer'kraut (sour'krout) *n.* a German dish of chopped cabbage pressed with salt till it ferments.

saun'ter *v.i.* to walk in leisurely manner, to stroll.—*n.* a leisurely walk or stroll. *Syn.* ramble, dawdle, linger, loiter. *Ant.* speed, hasten, hurry, run.

saus'age (sos-) *n.* minced meat enclosed in a tube of thin membrane.

sauter' (sō-tā') *v.i.* to fry quickly and lightly with little grease.

Sauterne' (sō-tern') *n.* a kind of French wine, from *Sauterne,* in the Gironde.

sav'age *a.* uncivilised, primitive; cruel. —*n.* a member of a savage tribe, a barbarian.—*v.t.* to attack with trampling and biting.—**sav'agery** *n.*—**sav'agely** *adv.*

savann'ah *n.* an extensive open plain covered with grass, prairie.

save *v.t.* to rescue, preserve; keep for the future, lay by; to prevent the need of.— *v.i.* to lay by money.—*prep.* except.— *conj.* but.—**sa'viour** *n.* a deliverer.

sav'eloy *n.* highly-seasoned dried sausage.

sav'ing *a.* frugal, economical, avoiding waste; redeeming.—*n.* something saved. —*pl.* money saved.—*prep.* except.

sa'vour (-ver) *n.* characteristic taste.— *v.i.* to smack of.—**sa'voury** *a.* having an appetising taste or smell.—*n.* a savoury dish at the beginning or end of a dinner.

savoy' *n.* a variety of cabbage.

saw *n.* old saying, maxim.

saw *n.* a tool with sharp teeth for cutting wood, etc.—*v.t.* to cut with a saw.— *v.i.* to make the movements of sawing (**sawed** (sawd) *p.t.*—**sawn** *p.p.*—**saw'ing** *pres. p.*).—**saw'dust** *n.* fine wood fragments made in sawing.—**saw'fish** *n.* a fish armed with a toothed snout.— **saw'yer** *n.* a workman who saws timber; in New Zealand, a large grasshopper.

saxe *n.* a shade of blue.

sax'horn *n.* an instrument of the trumpet class.—**sax'ophone** *n.* a large wide-mouthed instrument like a clarinet.

sax'ifrage *n.* an Alpine or rock plant.

say *v.t.* to utter or deliver with the speaking voice; state; express; take as an example or as near enough; form and deliver an opinion: to try; to assay (**said** *p.t.* and *p.p.*—**say'ing** *pres. p.*—**says** 3rd *pers. sing. pres. indicative*).—*n.* what one has to say; chance of saying it; share in a decision.—**say'ing** *n.* a maxim.—**I say** (*interj.*) listen.

scab' *n.* a crust formed over a wound; a skin disease in animals; a disease of plants; a blackleg.—**scabb'y** *a.*

scabb'ard *n.* sheath for sword or dagger.

sca'bies *n.* the itch, a troublesome contagious skin disease.

scaff'old *n.* a temporary platform for workmen; a gallows.—**scaff'olding** *n.* a framework of poles and platforms for workmen erecting building, etc.

scal'awag *n.* an undersized animal; a rogue or worthless fellow.

scald (skawld) *v.t.* to injure with boiling liquid or steam; to clean with boiling water.—*n.* injury by scalding.

scale *n.* a pan of balance; a weighing instrument.—*v.t.* to weigh in scales.— **sca'ler** *n.* in N. America, in logging, the person who measures logs and records the amount of lumber cut.

scale *n.* one of the plates forming the outer covering of fishes and reptiles; a thin flake.—*v.t.* to remove the scales from.—*v.i.* to come off in scales.— **scale'-insect** *n.* an insect-pest of plants which lives under a scale.

scale *n.* a series of musical notes, degrees, or graduations; the steps of graduated measuring instrument; relative size, ratio of enlarging or reduction (e.g. in a map, etc.).—*v.t.* to climb or attack with ladders.—**scale up,** make larger.—**scale down,** make smaller.

sca'lene *a.* of a triangle, having its three sides and angles unequal.

scall'op *n.* an eatable shellfish; edging in small curves as in scallop shell.— *v.t.* to shape thus; to cook in a scallop shell or a dish resembling one.

scalp *n.* the skin and hair of the top of the head.—*v.t.* to cut off the scalp of.

scal'pel *n.* a small surgical knife.

scamp *n.* rascal a lazy fellow—*v.t.* to do hastily or negligently.

scamp'er *v.i.* to run about; to run hastily from place to place.—*n.*

scan *v.t.* to look at carefully; to measure or read (verse) by its metrical feet.

scan'sion *n.* the metre, or ordered rhythm, of poetry; the study of this.

scan'dal *n.* malicious gossip; disgrace, action offending public opinion; the thing causing such feeling.—**scan'dalise** *v.t.* to shock.—**scan'dalous** *a.* outrageous;

disgraceful.—**scan'dalmonger** *n.* person who spreads malicious gossip.
Syn. opprobrium, defamation, rumour. *Ant.* praise, commendation, reticence.
scanso'res *n. pl.* birds having the toes arranged to facilitate climbing, as the woodpeckers, parrots, etc.—**scanso'rial** *a.* climbing, or adapted for climbing.
scant *a.* barely sufficient; not sufficient. —*v.t.* to put on short allowance; to supply grudgingly.–**scant'y** *a.*–**scant'ily** *adv.*
scant'ling *n.* a size to which stone or wood is to be cut; a small beam, *esp.* one under five inches square.–**scan'tle** *v.t.* to cut into small pieces.
scape *n.* and *v.t.* to escape.–**scape'goat** *n.* a person bearing blame due to others.—**scape'grace** *n.* an incorrigible fellow.
scaphan'der *n.* diver's water-tight suit.
scap'ula *n.* the shoulder-blade (**-lae**, **-las** *pl.*).—**scap'ular** *a.* pertaining to the scapula.—*n.* a part of the habit of certain religious orders in the R.C. church, consisting of two bands of woollen stuff, of which one crosses the back and the other the stomach.
scar *n.* the mark left by a healed wound, burn or sore.—*v.t.* to mark with a scar.—*v.i.* to heal with a scar (**scarred'** *p.t.*/*p.p.*).
scar'ab *n.* the sacred beetle of ancient Egypt; a gem cut in the shape of this.
scar'amouch *n.* an idler; a buffoon in motley dress; a personage in the old Italian comedy characterised by boastfulness and poltroonery.
scarce (skėrs) *a.* hard to find; existing or available in insufficient quantity.—**scarce'ly** *adv.* only just; not quite.—**scarce'ness** *n.*—**scarcity** *n.* lack.
scare (skėr) *v.t.* to frighten.—*n.* fright; unreasoning terror; commercial panic.—**scare'crow** *n.* anything set up to frighten birds from crops; a badly dressed or miserable-looking person.—**scare'monger** *n.* one who raises scares, as of war, *esp.* by spreading unfounded reports.
scarf *n.* a long narrow strip of material to put round neck; (*carp.*) special form of joint keeping two ends of timber firmly clamped together (**scarfs, scarves** *pl.*).
scar'ify *v.t.* to scratch or cut slightly all over; criticise mercilessly (**-ified** *p.t.*/*p.p.* —**-ifying** *pr. p.*).—**scarification** *n.*
scar'let *n.* a brilliant red colour; cloth or clothing of this colour, *esp.* military uniform.—*a.* of this colour.—**scar'let fe'ver** *n.* highly infectious fever with a scarlet rash.—**scar'let runn'er** *n.* a trailing bean with scarlet flowers.—**scarlati'na** (-tē-) *n.* scarlet fever.
scarp *n.* the inside slope of a ditch in fortifications.—*v.t.* to make steep.
scathe (-th) *n.* injury.—*v.t.* to injure, especially by withering up.—**scathe'less** *a.* unharmed.—**scath'ing** *a.*
scatol'ogy *a.* study of obscene literature; of body wastes, excrements, etc.
scatt'er *v.t.* to throw or put here and there; to sprinkle.—*v.i.* to disperse.
scav'enger *n.* one employed in cleaning streets, removing refuse, etc.—**scav'enge** *v.t.* to clean (streets).—*v.i.* to work as a scavenger.
scene (sēn) *n.* place of action of novel, play, etc.; place of any action; subdivision of play; view; episode; stormy conversation, *esp.* with display of temper.—**sce'nery** *n.* stage scenes; natural features of a district.—**sce'nic** *a.* picturesque; of, on, the stage.—**scenar'io** *n.* skeleton libretto of dramatic work; plot of play; written version of play to be produced by cinematograph.—**scenar'ist** *n.* writer, editor of scenario (**-arios, -ari** (-rē) *pl.*).
scent (s-) *v.t.* to track by smell; to detect, get wind of; to make fragrant.—*n.* a smell; liquid perfume.
scep'tic (sk-) *n.* one who maintains doubt.—**scep'tical** *a.*—**scep'ticism** *n.*
Syn. unbeliever, infidel, atheist, heretic, deist. *Ant.* believer, Christian, theist.
scep'tre (s-) *n.* an ornamental staff as a symbol of royal power.
sched'ule (sh-; in U.S. sk-) *n.* an appendix to an Act of Parliament; a tabulated statement; in N. America, a time-table.—*v.t.* to enter in a schedule.
schelm, shell'um, skell'um *n.* in Scotland and S. Africa, a thief; pest; ne'er-do-well; bad-tempered animal.
schemat'ic (skē-mat'-) *n.* in electronics, a diagram showing the connections and component parts of a radio circuit; also called schematic diagram.—*a.*
scheme (sk-) *n.* plan, design, project; list, table; outline, syllabus.—*v.i.* to make plans, esp. as secret intrigue.—*v.t.* to plan, to bring about.—**sche'mer** *n.* —**sche'ming** *a.* crafty.
schipp'erke (-er-ki) *n.* a small black dog related to the Pomeranian.
schism (sizm) *n.* a division in a church or party.—**schismat'ic** *n.* and *a.* causing discord.—**schismat'ical** *a.*
schizophre'nia (skiz-ō-frēn'-i-a) *n.* (*psych.*) the state of dissociated personality, or of living in a morbid dream.—**schiz'ophrene, schiz'oid** *n.* one suffering from schizophrenia.
schlen'ter, slenter' *a.* S. Africa (*sl.*) false, unreliable.
schnapps, schnaps *n.* Hollands gin.
scho'liast *n.* commentator, annotator.
scholias'tic *a.* pertaining to a scholiast or his pursuits.
scho'lium (sk-) *n.* a marginal annotation; note; comment; usually a grammatical or philological note; in mathematics a remark or observation subjoined to a demonstration (**-lia, -liums** *pl.*).
school (skōōl) *n.* institution for teaching boys or girls or both, or for giving instruction in any subject; buildings of

such institution; time of lesson; group of thinkers, writers, artists, etc., with principles or methods in common.—*v.t.* to educate; to bring under control; to train.—**school'man** *n.* medieval philosopher.—**schol'ar** *n.* one taught in a school; one quick to learn; learned person one holding scholarship.—**schol'arly** *a.* —**schol'arship** *n.* learning; a prize or grant to student for payment of school or college fees.—**scholast'ic** *a.* of schools or school children.

school (sk-) *n.* a shoal (of fish, etc.).

schoon'er (sk-) *n.* a ship with fore and aft sails on two or more masts; in N. America, a prairie-schooner; a long drink; a tall drinking-glass.

schottische' (shot-ēsh') *n.* a dance like polka; music for this.

sciat'ica (sī-) *n.* pain in the sciatic nerve. —**sciat'ic** *a.* of the hip.

sci'ence (sī-) *n.* systematic knowledge; the investigation of this; any branch of study concerned with a body of observed material facts.—**scientif'ic** *a.*—**scientif'ically** *adv.*—**sci'entist** *n.*

scim'itar (s-) *n.* a short curved sword.

scintill'a (s-) *n.* a spark.—**scin'tillate** *v.i.* to sparkle.—**scintilla'tion** *n.*

sci'on (s-) *n.* a shoot, twig for grafting; a descendant or heir.

sciss'ors (siz-) *n. pl.* a cutting instrument of two blades pivoted together so that the edges slip over each other.

sclero'sis *n.* a hardening (**-ses** (-sēz) *pl.*).

scoff (sk-) *n.* taunt; mocking words.—*v.t.* to jeer or mock.—**scoff'er** *n.* scorner.

scoff *v.t.* in Australia (*sl.*) to eat; to eat greedily.

scold (sk-) *n.* a nagging woman.—*v.i.* to find fault noisily.—*v.t.* to rebuke.

sconce (sk-) *n.* wall bracket for candle, etc.; small fort.

sconce (sk-) *n.* the top of the head.

scone (skōn) *n.* a small flat, plain cake baked on a griddle.

scoop *n.* an article for ladling; a kind of shovel; a tool for hollowing out; (*sl.*) a profitable deal; in journalism, an exclusive news item.—*v.t.* to ladle out; to hollow out or rake in with a scoop.

scoot *v.i.* (*sl.*) to move off quickly.

scooter *n.* small vehicle with two wheels and a guiding handle, to carry one.

scope *n.* range of activity or application; room, play; opportunity.

scorbu'tic *a.* of, affected with, scurvy.

scorch *v.t.* to burn the surface of.—*v.i.* to dry up, wither (he **scor'ches**).

score *n.* a group or set of twenty; a cut, notch, stroke, or mark; a written or printed piece of orchestral music; a tally; reason; sake; debt; number of points made in a game.—*v.t.* to notch or mark; to cross out; to record; to make (points) in a game.—*v.i.* to achieve a success.—**scor'er** *n.* (**sco'ring** *pr. p.*).

scorn *n.* contempt, derision.—*v.t.* to despise.—**scorn'er** *n.*—**scorn'fully** *adv.*—**scorn'ful** *a.* contemptuous.

Scorpio *n.* a scorpion; 8th sign of Zodiac, operative Oct. 23 to Nov. 21st; constellation of this name.

scorp'ion *n.* small lobster-shaped animal with a sting in its jointed tail.

scot *n.* tax, rate.—**scot-free'** *a.* free from payment, punishment, etc.

Scot *n.* a native of Scotland.—**Scott'ish** *a.* (also **Scotch, Scots**).—**Scots'man** *n.*—**scott'icism** *n.* a Scottish turn of speech.

scotch *v.t.* to disable or wound; to put an end to; *n.* whisky made in Scotland.

scoto'ma, scot'omy *n.* dimness of sight, accompanied by giddiness.

scoun'drel *n.* a villain.—**scoun'drelly** *a.*

scour *v.t.* to clear or polish by rubbing. move rapidly along or over in search of, to range (e.g., scour the country).

scourge (skurj) *n.* whip, or lash; punishment; evil, calamity. —*v.t.* flog.

scout *n.* a man sent out to reconnoitre; a ship used for reconnoitring; a boy scout. —*v.i.* to go out or act as a scout.

scout *v.t.* to reject scornfully.

scow *n.* a large, flat-bottomed boat.—*v.t.* to transport in a scow.

scowl *v.t.* to frown gloomily.—*n.* frown.

scrag *n.* a lean person or animal; the lean end of a neck of mutton.—**scragg'y** *a.*

scram *interj.* (*sl.*) get out!, clear off!

scram'ble *v.i.* to move by crawling, climbing, etc.; to struggle with others for; to cook (eggs) by stirring them in the pan.—*n.* a scrambling, rough climb; a disorderly proceeding.

scran *n.* scraps; broken victuals.

scrap *n.* a small detached piece or fragment.—*v.t.* and *i.* to discard as useless; fight (**scrap'ping** *pres. p.*—**scrapped** *p.t.* and *p.p.*)—**scrap'book** *n.* book in which pictures, cuttings, etc., are kept.

scrape *v.t.* to rub with something sharp; to clean or smooth in this way; to rub with harsh noise.—*v.i.* to make an awkward bow.—*n.* an act or sound of scraping; an awkward situation, *esp.* one resulting from an escapade.—**scra'per** *n.*

scra'per-board *n.* prepared cardboard for artists which may be scraped away or left to be inked or coloured and indicate light and shade (grained scraper board).

scrapp'y *a.* unfinished, full of gaps.

scratch *v.t.* to score or mark, a narrow surface wound with claws, nails, or anything pointed; to make marks on with pointed instruments; to remove from a list.—*v.i.* to use claws or nails.—*n.* a wound or mark or sound made by scratching; a line or starting point.—*a.* got together at short notice; impromptu.

scrawl *v.t.* to write or draw untidily.—*n.* something scrawled; careless writing.

scream *v.i.* to utter a piercing cry; to speak, whistle or hoot shrilly.—*n.*

screech *v.i.* to scream, shriek.—*n.* harsh, piercing scream.
screed *n.* a long tedious letter or passage; list of grievances, etc.
screen *n.* piece of furniture to shelter from heat, light, draught or observation; anything used for such purpose; sheet to display lantern pictures, etc.; in the cinema, sheet on which films are exhibited and from which sound is reflected; in motoring, the wind-screen; a wooden or stone partition in a church. —*v.t.* to shelter or hide; to film; to make a film of (a story, book or play); in electricity, to protect from stray electric or magnetic fields.—**the screen** the cinema generally.—**screen-wiper** *n.* in motoring, an appliance to keep part of the wind-screen free from dust, rain, etc.
screw (-ōō) *n.* a cylinder with a spiral ridge running round it, outside or inside; a ship's propeller; a turn of a screw; a twist; a miser; a worn-out horse; (*sl.*) salary.—*v.t.* to fasten with a screw; to press or stretch with a screw; to obtain by pressure, to extort, force; to work by turning, to twist round; distort.—**screw'-ball** *n.* (U.S.) (*sl.*) odd, daft person.—*a.* eccentric, unpredictable.—**screw'-driver** *n.* tool for turning screws.
scribe *n.* a writer; a copyist; an author; a Jewish doctor of the law.
scrib'ble *v.t.* and *i.* to write or draw carelessly; to make meaningless marks with a pen or pencil.—*n.* something scribbled.—**scrib'bler** *n.*
scrim *n.* thin, strong cotton or woollen cloth, used in upholstery for linings, etc.
scrimm'age *n.* a tussle; a confused struggle, rough and tumble.
scrimp *v.t.* to make too small or short; to stint.—**scrim'py** *a.* scanty.
scrim'shank *v.i.* to avoid doing one's duty.—**scrim'shanker** *n.*
scrip *n.* a small wallet; a certificate of holding stocks or shares.
script *n.* handwriting; written characters; the written text of a film or wireless programme.—**script'writer** *n.*
scrip'ture *n.* sacred writings; the Bible.—**script'ural** *adv.*
scriv'ener *n.* a copyist.
scrof'ula *n.* tuberculosis, *esp.* of the lymphatic glands of the neck; king's-evil.—**scrof'ulous** *a.* diseased with scrofula.
scroll (-ō-) *n.* a roll of parchment or paper; a list; an ornament shaped thus.
scrounge *v.t.* and *i.* (*sl.*) to pilfer.
scrub *n.* a stunted tree; brushwood.—**scrubb'y** *a.* covered with scrub; insignificant.—**scrubb'er** *n.* Australia, a bullock which has escaped into scrub.—**scrub'-cattle** *n. pl.* animals which have escaped into scrub.—**scrub dan'gler** *n.* a wild bullock.—**scrub'-ri'der** *n.* one employed to retrieve cattle from scrub.
scrub *v.t.* to clean with a hard brush and water.—*n.* a scrubbing.—**scrub'by** *a.* stunted; paltry; unkempt.
scruff *n.* nape (of neck).
scrump'tious *a.* (*sl.*) pleasant, delightful.
scru'ple *n.* a small weight; a feeling of doubt about a proposed action; a conscientious objection.—*v.i.* to hesitate.
scru'pulous *a.* extremely conscientious, thorough; attentive to small points of conscience.—**scrupulos'ity** *n.*
scrutineer' an examiner of votes.
scru'tinise *v.t.* to examine closely.
scru'tiny *n.* close inspection; an official examination of votes; a searching look.
scry'ing *n.* foretelling the future by gazing steadily into a crystal ball.
scud *v.i.* to run quickly; to run before the wind.—*n.* the act of scudding; flying clouds or spray; in Scotland, slap.
scuf'fle *v.i.* to struggle at close quarters. —*n.* confused struggle (**scuf'fling** *pr. p.*).
scull *n.* an oar used at the stern of a boat; short oar used in pairs.—*v.t.* and *i.* to propel or move by means of a scull.
scull'ery *n.* a place for washing dishes.
scull'ion *n.* a kitchen underservant.
sculp'ture *n.* art of forming figures in relief or solid; product of this art.—*v.t.* to represent, by sculpture.—**sculp'tural** *a.*—**sculp'tor** *n.*—**sculp'tress** *fem.*
scum *n.* froth, etc., on the surface of a liquid; the waste part; worthless people.
scunn'er *v.i.* to feel disgust at; to loathe. —*v.t.* to disgust.—*n.* loathing; disgust.
scupp'er *n.* a hole in the side of a ship level with the deck.
scurf *n.* dried flakes detached from the skin; dandruff.—**scurf'y** *a.*
scurr'ilous *a.* coarse or indecent language.—**scurril'ity** *n.*
scurr'y *v.i.* to run hastily, scamper (**scurr'ied** *p.t./p.p.*—**scurr'ying** *pr. p.*). —*n.* bustling haste (he **scur'ries**).
scur'vy *n.* a disease characterised by spots, debility, etc., due to vitamin C. deficiency.—*a.* afflicted with the disease; mean, low, contemptible.
scut *n.* the tail of a hare, or other animal whose tail is short.
scu'tage *n.* in feudal law, a tax on a knight's fee; a commutation for personal service.
scutch'eon *n.* a shield with a coat of arms, escutcheon.
scut'tle *n.* a coal-bucket; a large open basket.—*v.i.* to rush away.
scut'tle *n.* hole with lid in ship's side or deck.—*v.i.* to make hole in, sink ship (**scut'tling** *pr. p.*).
scythe (sīth) *n.* a mowing implement consisting of a long curved blade swung by a bent handle held in both hands.—*v.t.* to cut with a scythe.
sea *n.* the mass of salt water covering most of the earth; a broad tract of this; waves; swell.—**sea'board** *n.* coast.—**sea'-**

faring *a.* occupied in sea voyages.—**sea'horse** *n.* small fish with head shaped like that of a horse.—**sea-lord** a high-ranking naval officer on the Board of Admiralty.—**sea'man** *n.* a sailor.—**sea'-manship** *n.* skill in navigating.—**sea'-plane** *n.* form of aircraft which can take off from and land on water.—**sea'weed** *n.* a plant growing in the sea.—**sea'worthy** *a.* in a fit condition to put to sea.

seal *n.* amphibious, carnivorous mammal with flippers, as limbs, hunted for its fur.—*v.i.* to hunt seals.—**seal'skin** *n.* the skin or fur of seals.—**seal'er** *n.* man or ship engaged in sealing.

seal *n.* a piece of metal or stone engraved with a device for impression on wax, etc.; the impression made by this (on letters, documents, etc.).—*v.t.* to affix a seal to; to ratify; to mark with a stamp as evidence of some quality; to keep close, or secret; to settle, as doom.—**Great Seal** *n.* official seal of the United Kingdom.—**seal'ing wax** *n.* wax which, when heated, becomes soft and takes impression.

Seal'yham *n.* a breed of Welsh terrier.

seam *n.* a line or junction of two edges of cloth, etc.; a thin layer or stratum.—*v.t.* to mark with furrows or wrinkles.—*v.* to join by sewing.—**seam'less** *a.*—**seam'stress, semp'stress** *n.* a sewing woman.—**seam'y** *a.* marked with seams; unpleasant, sordid.

se'ance (sā'ans) *n.* a session of a public body; a meeting of Spiritualists.

sear *v.t.* to scorch or brand with a hot iron; to deaden; to wither, dry up.

search *v.t.* to look over or through in order to find something; to probe into.—*v.i.* to explore, to look for something.—*n.* the act of searching; a quest.—**search'-ing** *a.* piercing, sharp.—**search'light** *n.* electric arc-light which sends a concentrated beam in any desired direction.
Syn. to examine, scrutinise, investigate.
Ant. overlook, neglect, disregard, find.

seas'on (sēz-) *n.* one of the four divisions of the year associated with a type of weather and a stage of agriculture; a proper time; a period during which something happens, grows, is active, etc.—*v.t.* to bring into sound condition; to flavour with salt or condiments, etc.—**seas'onable** *a.* suitable for the season, timely.—**seas'onal** *a.* of, varying with seasons.—**seas'oning** *n.* flavouring.

seat *n.* a thing made or used for sitting on; manner of sitting (of riding, etc.); a right to sit (e.g. in a council, etc.); the sitting part of the body, the locality of a disease, trouble, etc.; a country house.—*v.t.* to make to sit; to provide seats.

seba'ceous *a.* made of, or pertaining to, tallow or fat, secreting oil.

sebun'dy *n.* in East Indies, a native soldier or policeman.

sec *a.* dry (said of wines).

sec'ateurs *n. pl.* small pruning shears with hooked blades.

Sec'cotine *n.* a quick-drying cold liquid glue (protected trade name).

secede' *v.i.* to withdraw, *esp.* from a church.—**seces'sion** *n.*—**seces'sionist** *n.*

seck'el *n.* small, delicious variety of pear.

seclude' *v.t.* to guard from, remove from sight or resort.—**seclu'sion** *n.* solitude.

sec'ond *a.* next after the first.—*n.* a person or thing coming second; one giving aid, *esp.* assisting a principal in a duel: the sixtieth part of a minute; in motoring, second gear.—*v.t.* to support; further; to support (a motion in a meeting) so that discussion may be in order; (si-kond') military, to detach an officer from his regiment on special duty.—**sec'ondly** *adv.*

sec'ondary *a.* subsidiary, of less importance; of education, between primary and university stages.—**sec'ondarily** *adv.*—**sec'onder** *n.*—**sec'ond-hand** *a.* bought after use by previous owner, not original.—**sec'ond-sight** *n.* faculty of psychic or supernatural vision.

se'cret *a.* kept from general knowledge; hidden.—*n.* something kept secret.—**Secret Service** *n.* espionage and counter espionage services.—**se'cretly** *adv.*—**se'crecy** *n.* a keeping or being kept secret; an ability to keep secrets.

sec'retary *n.* one employed by another or appointed by a society to deal with papers and correspondence, keep records, prepare business, etc.—**secreta'-rial** *a.*—**secretar'iat** *n.* a body of secretaries; a building occupied by a secretarial staff.—**sec'retaryship** *n.*

secrete' *v.t.* to hide; of a gland, etc., to collect and supply a particular substance in the body.—**secre'tion** *n.*—**secre'tory** *a.*—**secre'tive** *a.* uncommunicative, reticent.—**secre'tiveness** *n.*

sec'retary bird *n.* a snake-eating bird of S. Africa, with an aquiline head and beak and the legs of a crane.

sect *n.* a party within a church; a religious denomination.—**sect'ary** *n.*—**secta'rian** *a.* belonging to a sect, denominational; narrow-minded.

sec'tion *n.* a cutting; a part cut off; a drawing of anything as if cut through.—**sec'tional** *a.*—**sec'tor** *n.* a part of a circle enclosed by two radii and the arc which they cut off; division of battle front.

sec'ular *a.* worldly; lay; not monastic; lasting for, or occurring once in, an age.

sec'ularist *n.* one who would exclude religion from schools.—**sec'ularism** *n.*—**sec'ularise** *v.t.* to transfer from religious to lay possession or use.—**secularisa'tion** *n.*

secure' *a.* safe; free from care; stable.—*v.t.* make safe; free (creditor) from risk of loss; make firm; gain possession of.—**secure'ly** *adv.*—**secu'rity** *n.* condition of

being secure; protection; thing given as bond, pledge.
sedan' *n.* a small covered chair for one, carried on poles by two men; kind of car.
sedate' *a.* calm, collected, serious.—**sedate'ly** *adv.*—**sed'ative** *a.* soothing.—*n.* soothing drug.
sed'entary *a.* sitting much, done in a chair. *Syn.* quiet, tranquil, serene, undisturbed, sober, serious. *Ant.* restless, disturbed, indiscreet, rash.
sedge *n.* a grass-like plant growing in swampy places.—**sedge'-flat,** sedgy land below high-water mark.—**sedge'-war'bler,** British summer bird.
sedil'ia *n. pl.* stone seats on the south side of the altar in churches for the priest, deacon, and sub-deacon.
sed'iment *n.* a matter which settles to the bottom of liquid.—**sediment'ary** *a.*
sedi'tion *n.* talk or action exciting discontent or rebellion.—**sedi'tious** *a.*
seduce' *v.t.* to lead astray, to persuade to commit some sin or folly; to induce (a woman) to surrender her chastity.—**seduc'tion** *n.*—**seduc'tive** *a.* alluring.
sed'ulous *a.* persevering.—**sedu'lity** *n.*
see *v.t.* perceive with eyes or mentally; find out, reflect; come to know; interview.—*v.i.* perceive; understand (**saw** *p.t.*—**seen** *p.p.*—**see'ing** *pr. p.*).
see *n.* the diocese and work of a bishop.
see'cawk *n.* the skunk.
seed *n.* the reproductive germs of flowering plants; one grain of this; such grains saved or used for sowing; offspring.—*v.i.* to produce seed.—*v.t.* to sow with seed; to arrange the draw, for tennis or other tournament, so that the best players, or those of same nationality, should not be drawn against each other in the early rounds.—**seed'ling** *n.* a young plant raised from seed.—**seeds'man** *n.* dealer in seeds.—**seed'y** *a.* full of seeds; run to seed; shabby; feeling ill.
seek *v.t.* to make search or inquiry for (**sought** *p.t.* and *p.p.*—**seek'ing** *pres p.*).—*v.i.* to search; endeavour.
seem *v.i.* to appear (to be or to do).—**seem'ingly** *adv.*—**seem'ly** *a.* becoming and proper.—**seem'liness** *n.* fitness.
seep' *v.i.* to ooze, percolate.
seer *n.* prophet, one who has visions.
see'-saw *n.* up and down movement; a plank supported in the middle and moving up and down; vacillation.—*v.i.* to move up and down.
seethe *v.t.* to boil, cook or soak in hot liquid.—*v.i.* to be violently agitated (**seethed** (sēthd) *p.t.*—**sodd'en, seethed** *p.p.*—**see'thing** *pres. p.*).
seg'ment *n.* a piece cut off; a section.
seg'regate *v.t.* set apart from the rest.—**segrega'tion** *n.* (**seg'regating** *pr. p.*).
Seid'litz-powders (sēd'-, sīd'-, sed'-litz-) *n. pl.* aperient powders.
seine (sēn, sān) *n.* a large net for catching fish.—*v.t.* to catch fish with a seine.
seis'mic (sīz'-) *a.* pertaining to earthquakes.—**seis'mograph** *n.* an instrument to record earthquakes.—**seis'mogram** *n.* the record made by a seismometer.—**seismol'ogy** *n.* doctrine of earthquakes.—**seismol'ogist** *n.* one versed in seismology.—**seismom'eter** *n.* an instrument for measuring the time of occurrence, duration, direction, and intensity of earthquakes.—**seis'moscope** *n.* an instrument for showing movements of the ground in an earthquake.
seize (sēz) *v.t.* grasp, clutch; perceive.—*v.i.* take possession; in internal combustion engine, of a bearing or piston, to jam in seating or cylinder, through overheating.—**seiz'ure** *n.* seizing; sudden attack of illness.
sel'dom *adv.* rarely, not often.
select' *v.t.* to pick out, choose.—*a.* choice, picked; exclusive.—**selec'tion** *n.*—**select'or** *n.*—**selec'tive** *a.* having power to select.—**selectiv'ity** *n.*
sel'enite *n.* a variety of gypsum.
sele'nium *n.* an elementary substance, allied to sulphur and tellurium.—**selen'ium cell** primary cell used for the transmission of pictures.
selenog'raphy *n.* a description of the surface of the moon.
self *pron., n.* one's own person or individuality (**selves** *pl.*).—*a.* of a colour, uniform, the same throughout.—**self'ish** *a.* concerned unduly over personal profit or pleasure, lacking consideration for others.—**self'ishly** *adv.*—**self'less** *a.*
self- *prefix* forms combinations with a reflexive meaning or to express emphasis, as in **self-adjusting** *a.* requiring no adjustment, used *esp.* of motor vehicle components.—**self-determination** *n.* the right of every subject people to decide its own form of government.—**self-possessed'** *a.* calm, composed.—**self-posses'sion** *n.*—**self'-same** *a.* very same.—**self-star'ter,** automatic contrivance for starting a motor-car.
sell *v.t.* to hand over for a price; to betray or cheat.—*v.i.* to find purchasers (**sold** *p.t.* and *p.p.*—**sell'ing** *pres. p.*).—*n.* a disappointment.—**sell'er** *n.*
sel'vedge, sel'vage *n.* an edge of cloth finished to prevent ravelling out.
seman'tics *n.* the science of the origin and evolution of language.
sem'aphore *n.* a post with movable arms for signalling; a system of signalling with arms, flags, etc.
sem'blance *n.* appearance; image.
semels *n.* in S. Africa, bran.
se'men *n.* seed, *esp.* the male generative product of animals; sperm.
semes'ter *n.* a college half-year in some American and other universities.
semi- *prefix* half, as in **sem'ibreve** *n.* a musical note half length of a breve.—

sem'icircle *n.* half of a circle.—semicir'cular *a.*—semico'lon *n.* a punctuation mark (;).—sem'iquaver *n.* musical note half length of quaver.—sem'itone *n.* musical half-tone.—sem'i-detached *a.* of house, joined to another on one side.
sem'inary *n.* a school or college.
semolin'a (-ēn-a) *n.* hard grains left after the sifting of flour, used for puddings.
semp'stress *see* **seamstress.**
sen'ate *n.* the upper council of a state, university, etc.-sen'ator *n.*-senator'ial *a.*
send *v.t.* to cause to go or be conveyed (sent *p.t.* and *p.p.*—sending *pres. p.*).
se'nile *a.* showing the weakness of old age, doting.—senil'ity *n.*
se'nior *a.* older; superior in rank or standing.—*n.* an elder person; a superior.—senior'ity *n.*
sen'night *n.* a week.
sense *n.* any of the bodily faculties of perception or feeling; sensitiveness of any or all of these faculties; ability to perceive, mental alertness; consciousness; meaning; coherence, intelligible meaning.—sensa'tion *n.* an operation of a sense, feeling; excited feeling or state of excitement; an exciting event.—sensa'tional *a.*—sensa'tionalism *n.*—sense'less *a.* stupid; unconscious.—sense'lessly *adv.*—sen'sible *a.* that can be perceived by the senses; aware, mindful; considerable; appreciable; reasonable, wise.—sensibly *adv.*—sensibil'ity *n.*—sen'sitive *a.* open to or acutely affected by external impressions; easily affected or altered; responsive to slight changes.—sen'sitively *adv.*—sen'sitiveness *n.*—sensitise' *v.t.* to make sensitive, *esp.* to make (photographic film, etc.) sensitive to light.—sen'sual *a.* depending on the senses only and not on the mind; given to the pursuit of pleasures of sense, self-indulgent; licentious.—sensual'ity *n.*—sen'sualist *n.*—sen'sualism *n.*—sen'suous *a.* stimulating, or apprehended by, the senses.—sensitive plant *n.* a leguminous plant of the genus *mimosa*, the leaves of which close up at the lightest touch. *Syn.* of **sensational,** startling, exciting. *Ant.* unexciting, commonplace, ordinary, everyday, humdrum.
sen'tence *n.* judgment passed on a criminal by a court or judge; combination of words which is complete as expressing thought.—*v.t.* to condemn.—senten'tial *a.*—senten'tious *a.* abounding with axioms; short and pithy; bombastic.—senten'tiously *adv.*—senten'tiousness *n.*
sen'tient *a.* feeling or capable of feeling.
sen'timent *n.* a mental feeling; an emotion; a tendency to be moved by feeling rather than reason; a verbal expression of feeling.—sentiment'al *a.*—sentiment'alist *n.*—sentimental'ity *n.*
sent'inel *n.* sentry; one placed on guard.
sent'ry *n.* a soldier on watch.
sep'al *n.* a leaf of flower's calyx.
sep'arate *v.t.* to put apart; to occupy a place between.—*v.i.* to withdraw, to become parted from.—*a.* disconnected, apart.—sep'arately *adv.* one at a time.—sep'arable *a.*—separa'tion *n.*—sep'aratists *n. pl.* those in any country who take their orders from an outside government.—sep'aratism *n.*—sep'arator *n.* that which separates, *esp.* an apparatus for separating cream from milk.
se'pia *n.* a brown pigment made from a fluid secreted by the cuttlefish. — *a.*
se'poy *n.* an Indian soldier in European service.
Septem'ber *n.* the ninth month (seventh in the Roman reckoning).—septenn'ial *a.* occurring every seven years.—septet(te) *n.* music for seven instruments or voices.
sep'tic *a.* poisoned, infected.—sep'sis *n.* septic state or agency.—septice'mia *n.* blood-poisoning.
Septuages'ima (sep-tū-ạ-jes'i-mȧ) *n.* the third Sunday before Lent.
sep'tuagint *n.* a Greek version of the Old Testament.
sep'tum *n.* a partition; e.g., in anatomy, a partition that separates two cavities, as of the nostrils (sep'ta *pl.*).
sep'tuple *a.* seven times as much; sevenfold.—*v.t.* to multiply by seven.
sep'ulchre (-kẹr) *n.* a tomb.—sepul'chral *a.*—sep'ulture *n.* burial.
se'quel *n.* a consequence or continuation.—se'quent *a.* following.—se'quence *n.* a connected series, a succession; a chapter of a film or film script.
sequest'er *v.t.* to seclude.—sequest'rate *v.t.* to confiscate; to divert to satisfy claims against its owner.-sequestra'tion *n.*
se'quin *n.* an ornamental metal disc on dresses; formerly, a Venetian gold coin.
seragl'io (se-rȧl'yō) *n.* the palace of the Grand Seignior or Turkish sultan, in which were confined the females of the harem; a harem; a house of debauchery (-ragli (-yē), -raglios (-yōz) *pl.*).
serai' (-rī) *n.* a place for the accommodation of travellers in India.
serang' *n.* boatswain of a Lascar crew.
ser'aph *n.* one of the highest of the order of angels.-seraph'ic *a.*-seraphim *n.*
sere *a.* dried up, withered.
serenade' *n.* music sung or played at night below a person's window, *esp.* by a lover.—*v.t.* to entertain with a serenade.
serene' *a* calm, tranquil, clear.—serene'ly *a.*—seren'ity *n.* peace, calmness.
Syn. peaceful, undisturbed, unruffled, placid. *Ant.* agitated, troubled, unsettled.
serf *n.* one of a class of labourers bound to, and transferred with, land.—serf'dom *n.*
serge *n.* a strong twilled worsted fabric.
serg'eant, serj'eant (sarj'ant) *n.* a non-commissioned officer; a police officer; a member of the highest rank of English

barristers.—**sergeant-ma'jor** *n.* highest non-commissioned officer in a regiment.
se'rial *a.* of and forming a series; published in instalments.—*n.* a serial story or publication.—**seria'tim** *adv.* one after another; point by point.
ser'ies (sēr'ēz) *n.* a sequence, succession, set (**ser'ies** *pl.*).
ser'ious (sēr-) *a.* earnest; thoughtful; sedate, not jesting or frivolous; of importance; dangerous.—**se'riously** *adv.* —**se'riousness** *n.*
ser'mon *n.* a discourse of religious instruction or exhortation spoken or read from a pulpit; any similar discourse.—**ser'monise** *v.i.* to talk like a preacher.
serp'ent *n.* a snake; a kind of firework; an obsolete wind instrument.—**serp'entine** *a.* shaped like a serpent; treacherous.
serra'ted *a.* notched like the teeth of a saw.—**serra'tion** *n.*
ser'ried *a.* in close order.
ser'um (sēr-) *n.* a watery animal fluid, *esp.* a thin part of blood as used for inoculation (**-rums, -ra** *pl.*).—**ser'ous** *a.*—**serum therapy** *n.* prevention or cure of disease by inoculation with serum.
serve *v.i.* to work under another; to carry out duties; to be a member of a military unit; to be useful or suitable or enough; in tennis, to start play by striking ball. —*v.t.* to work for, attend on, help to food; supply something; be useful to; contribute to; to deliver formally; to treat in specified way.—**ser'vant** *n.* personal or domestic attendant.—**ser'vice** *n.* state of being a servant; work done for and benefit conferred on another; department of State employ; employment of persons engaged in this, i.e., **civil servants**; set of dishes, public vehicles run to scheduled times.—*v.t.* repair; keep in running order; attend to.—**ser'viceable** *a.* useful, profitable (**ser'ving** *pr. p.*). —**ser'ver** *n.* tray for plates: priest's assistant at Eucharist.
ser'vice *n.* a tree like a mountain ash with a pear-shaped fruit.
serv'iette *n.* table napkin.
ser'vile *a.* slavish, without independence. —**servil'ity** *n.*—**ser'vitor** *n.* a servant; a student assisted out of college funds in certain colleges.—**ser'vitude** *n.* bondage. —**service-flat** *n.* self-contained flat with full hotel service.—**ser'vice hatch** *n.* a hatch through which dishes can be passed from kitchen or passage to dining-room.
ses'ame *n.* annual herbaceous plant, from seeds of which oil is expressed.—**open ses'ame** magic password.
ses'sion *n.* meeting of a court, etc.: series of such meetings.—**ses'sional** *a.*
set *v.t.* to cause to sit, to put in place; to fix, point, to put up; to make ready; to put to music; to put in position, etc.—*v.i.* of the sun, to go down; to become firm or fixed; to have a direction (**set** *p.t.* and *p.p.*—**sett'ing** *pres. p.*).—*a.* deliberate; formal, arranged beforehand; unvarying.—*n.* a setting; a tendency.—*v.t.* of hair, to arrange in curls, waves, etc., while wet, so that it dries in position. — **sett'ing lotion** a fixative to assist hair to set well.—**set'back** *n.* check.
set *n.* a number of things or persons associated as being similar or complementary or used together, etc.; in wireless, complete apparatus for reception (or transmission); in cinematography and stage, organised settings and equipment to form the ensemble of a scene; at games (also **sett**) a match.
seta'ceous *a.* consisting of bristles.
sett *n.* a match; a number of mines taken on lease; stone block for paving.
settee' *n.* a couch with a back.
set'ter *n.* a person who sets, e.g., printing type, jewels, etc.; breeds of dog trained to mark game.
set'tle *n.* bench with a back and arms.—*v.t.* to put in order; arrange; to establish, make firm or secure or quiet; to decide upon; to bring (a dispute, etc.) to an end; to pay.—*v.i.* to come to rest; subside; to become clear; to take up an abode; to come to an agreement.—**set'tlement** *n.* conditions of settling property; payment; a colony.—**sett'ler** *n.* a colonist.—**sett'ler's clock** *n.* Australia, the laughing jackass.—**sett'ler's matches** *n.pl.* Australia, strips of dry bark from certain eucalyptus trees.
sev'en *a.* and *n.* cardinal number, next after six.—**sev'enth** *a.* the ordinal number.
sev'er *v.t.* separate, divide: cut off.—*v.i.* to divide.—**sev'erance** *n.*
sev'eral *a.* separate; individual; some, a few.—*pron.* a few.—**sev'erally** *adv.*
severe' (-ēr) *a.* strict, rigorous; hard to do or undo.—**severe'ly** *adv.*—**sever'ity** *n.*
sew (sō) *v.t.* to join with thread.—*v.i.* to be occupied in sewing (**sewed** (sōd) *p.t.*—**sewed, sewn** (sōn) *p.p.*—**sew'ing** *pres. p.*).
sew'er (sū-) *n.* an underground drain to remove waste water and refuse.—**sew'age** *n.* refuse so carried off.—**sew'erage** *n.*
sex *n.* the state of being male or female. males or females collectively.—**sex'ual** *a.* —**sex'ually** *adv.*—**sex'-appeal** *n.* all that goes to make a member of one sex desirable to a member of the other.
sexag'enary *a.* pertaining to the number sixty; proceeding by sixties.—**sexagena'rian** *n.* a person of the age of sixty years.—*a.* sixty years old.
Sexages'ima *n.* the second Sunday before Lent, the next to Shrove Tuesday.
sexenn'ial *a.* lasting six years, or happening once in six years.
sex'tain *n.* a stanza of six lines.
sext'ant *n.* instrument with a graduated arc of a sixth of a circle to measure angles, altitudes of a heavenly body, etc.

sex'ton *n.* an official in charge of a church, often acting as gravedigger.

shabb'y *a.* poorly dressed; faded, worn; dishonourable, mean, ungenerous.—**shabb'ily** *adv.*—**shabb'iness** *n.*

shack *n.* a shanty, hut, cabin.

shac'kle *n.* a fetter; a link to join two pieces of chain, etc.; anything that hampers.—*v.t.* to fetter or hamper.

shad *n.* a fish of the herring tribe.

shadd'ock *n.* tree of orange genus; a fruit of this tree, grapefruit.

shade *n.* partial darkness; darker part of anything; depth of colour; tinge; shelter or a place sheltered from light, heat, etc.; ghost.—*v.t.* to screen from light, to darken; to represent shades in drawing.—**shad'ow** *n.* patch of shade; dark figure projected by anything that intercepts rays of light.—*v.t.* to cast shadow over; to follow and watch.—**shad'owy** *a.*—**sha'dy** *a.* dim, protected from light; of doubtful honesty.

shadoof', shaduf' (-dōōf) *n.* a contrivance, used in Egypt and the East generally, for raising water, *esp.* for the irrigation of small areas of land.

shaft *n.* straight rod, stem, shaft; one of the bars between which horse is harnessed; entrance boring of mine; revolving rod for transmitting power; main part of column; arrow.

shag *n.* matted wool or hair; cloth with long nap; fine cut tobacco; the green cormorant.—**shagg'y** *a.* rough, hairy, untidy; unkempt; villous.

shagreen' *n.* a rough untanned leather.

shagroon' *n.* N. Zealand, a settler from some country other than England.

Shah (shȧ) *n.* the king of Persia.

shake *v.i.* to tremble, totter, vibrate.—*v.t.* to cause to shake; in Australia, to steal (**shook** *p.t.*—**shaken** *p.p.*—**shaking** *pr. p.*).—*n.* act of shaking; vibration; jolt; in motoring, slackness in bearings, etc.—**sha'ker** *n.* one who or that which shakes; cocktail mixer.—**sha'ky** *a.* trembling; weak.—**sha'kily** *adv.*-**shake'-down** *n.* any temporary bed.

shak'o *n.* a military cap with a peak (**-oes, -os** (-ōz) *pl.*).

shale *n.* a clay rock like slate but softer.

shall *v. aux.* makes compound tenses or moods to express obligation, command, condition or intention (**should** *p.t.*).

shall'op *n.* a sort of large boat with two masts; a small boat with lug-sails.

shallot' *n.* a variety of onion.

shall'ow (-ō) *a.* not deep; not profound.—*n.* a shallow place; a shoal.

sham *n.* an imitation, a counterfeit.—*a.* imitation.—*v.t.* and *i.* to pretend.

sham'ble *v.i.* to walk with shuffling gait (**shamb'ling** *pres. p.*).

shamb'les *n. pl.* a slaughter-house.

shame *n.* the emotion caused by consciousness of something wrong or dishonouring in one's conduct or state; a cause of disgrace.—*v.t.* to cause to feel shame; to disgrace.—**shame'faced** *a.* shy.—**shame'ful** *a.*—**shame'fully** *adv.*—**shame'less** *a.* impudent.

Syn. of *shameful* infamous, disgraceful, scandalous, indecent, degrading. *Ant.* proper, becoming, honourable.

shampoo' *v.t.* to wash (the scalp) with something forming a lather in rubbing.—*n.* act of shampooing (**-poos** *pl.*).

sham'rock *n.* a trefoil plant taken as the emblem of Ireland.

shan'dry *n.* a light two-wheeled cart or gig; any old, rickety conveyance. Also **shan'drydan.**

shan'dygaff *n.* a mixture of bitter ale or beer with ginger-beer or lemonade.

shanghai' *n.* a long-legged hen; in Australia, a catapult.—*v.t.* to drug and ship as a sailor.—**shanghai-shot** *n.* in Australia, a short distance.

shank *n.* the lower leg; the shinbone.

shantung' *n.* lightweight rough-textured material, usually silk.

shant'y *n.* a hut; in Australia, a public-house, *esp.* an unlicensed one.

shant'y *n.* a sailor's song with chorus.

shape *n.* external form or appearance; a mould or pattern.—*v.t.* to give shape to, mould, fashion, devise, make (**shaped** (shāpt) *p.t.*—**shaped, sha'pen** *p.p.*—**sha'ping** *pres. p.*).—**shape'less** *a.*—**shape'ly** *a.* well-proportioned.

shard *n.* a broken fragment.

share (shėr) *n.* the blade of a plough.

share (shėr) *n.* a portion.—*v.t.* to give or allot a share.—*v.i.* to take a share; to have in common (**sha'ring** *pres. p.*).

shark *n.* large sea-fish, of which some varieties are man-eaters; a grasping person; a sharper, a swindler.

sharp *a.* having a keen edge or fine point; apt, keen; brisk; harsh; dealing cleverly but unfairly; shrill; strongly marked, *esp.* in outline.—*n.* in music, a note half a tone above the natural pitch.—**sharp'ly** *adv.*—**sharp'en** *v.t.* to make sharp.—**sharp'er** *n.* a swindler.—**sharp'ness** *n.*—**sharp'-shooter** *n.* a marksman.

shatt'er *v.t.* to break in pieces, smash; to destroy.—*v.i.* to fly in pieces.

shave *v.t.* to pare away; to cut close, *esp.* the hair of the face or head; to graze.—*v.i.* to shave oneself (**shaved** (shāvd) *p.t.*—**sha'ven** *p.p.*—**sha'ving** *pres. p.*).—*n.* a shaving; a narrow escape.—**sha'vings** *n.pl.* thin slices of wood planed off.

Sha'vian *a.* in the manner of George Bernard Shaw; (loosely) paradoxical.

shawl *n.* a square of fabric mainly used to cover the shoulders of women.

shawm *n.* a musical instrument like an oboe, used in Middle Ages.

she *pron.* the third person singular feminine pronoun.

she'a *n.* a tree of tropical Africa and Asia, yielding an edible fat.
sheaf *n.* bundle, *esp.* corn (**sheaves** *pl.*).
shear *v.t.* to cut through; to clip, cut; to clip hair, wool from (**sheared** (shērd) *p.t.*—**shorn, sheared** *p.p.*—**shear'ing** *pr. p.*).—*n.* in *pl.* large pair of scissors; scissor-shaped erection of beams used as crane.—**shear'er** *n.*
sheath *n.* a close-fitting cover, *esp.* for a knife or sword; a scabbard (**sheaths** (-thz) *pl.*).—**sheathe** *v.t.* to put into a sheath.
she'bang *n.* in N. America, a hut, a shanty, a shack; contrivance.
shed *n.* roofed shelter, store, workshop.
shed *v.t.* to cast off, scatter, throw off (**shed** *p.t.* and *p.p.*—**shedd'ing** *pres. p.*).—*n.* a dividing ridge.—**water'shed** *n.*
sheen *n.* gloss, brightness.—**sheen'y** *a.*
sheep *n.* a ruminant animal with a heavy coat of wool (**sheep** *pl.*).—**sheep'ish** *a.* bashful, shy.—**sheep'cote** *n.* a shelter for sheep.—**sheep'-dip** *n.* tank containing an insecticide through which sheep are passed to free them from ticks; the insecticide used.—**sheep'-sick** *a.* in Australia, pastureland incapable of supporting sheep owing to long use.
sheer *a.* complete, absolute; perpendicular, steep; pure; transparent.
sheer *v.i.* to deviate from a course; sheer off (*naut.*), go away; upward slope of a ship's hull fore and aft.
sheet *n.* a large piece of linen, etc., to cover a bed; a broad piece of any thin material; a large expanse *esp.* of water.—*v.t.* to cover with a sheet.
sheet *n.* a rope fastened in the corner of a sail.—**sheet'-anchor** *n.* a large anchor used only in an emergency.
sheikh (-āk, -ēk) *n.* an Arab chief.
shek'el *n.* a Jewish weight and coin.
shelf *n.* a board fixed horizontally (on a wall, etc.), on which to put things (**shelves** *pl.*).—**shelve** *v.t.* to put on a shelf; to put off (**shel'ving** *pres. p.*).
shell *n.* a hard outer case of an animal, fruit, etc.; an explosive projectile; an inner coffin; the outer part of a structure left when the interior is removed or destroyed.—*v.t.* to take a shell from, or out of a shell; to fire at with shells.—**shell'-back** *n.* an old sailor; a barnacle.—**shell'fish** *n.* shelled water-animal, e.g. oyster, lobster, etc.—**shell'-proof** *a.* proof against bombshells.—**shell-shock** *n.* a nervous disorder caused by bursting of shells or bombs.
shellac' *n.* lac in scales.
shelt'er *n.* a place or structure giving protection from danger, weather, attack; protection; refuge.—*v.t.* to give protection to, to screen.—*v.i.* to take shelter.—**shelt'ered industry** an industry which is not subject to competition with goods from abroad.
shelve *v.i.* to slope gradually.
shenan'igan *n.* in N. America, frolicking; playing tricks, jokes, etc.
she'-oak *n.* in Australia, a species of *casuarina.*
She'ol *n.* the place, or state, of the dead.
shep'herd (shep'ērd) *n.* a man who tends sheep.—**shep'herdess** *fem.*—*v.* to drive sheep; to guide, conduct.
sher'bet *n.* cooling drink of water and fruit juices; effervescent drink.
sher'iff *n.* a county or city officer.
sherr'y *n.* a Spanish wine.
shew (shō) old form of **show.**
shibb'oleth *n.* a test word.
shi'cer *n.* in Australia, a welsher; in mining, an unproductive claim.
shield *n.* a plate of armour carried on the left arm; a protective covering.—*v.t.* to cover, screen, protect, defend.
shift *v.t.* to move, remove.—*v.i.* to remove; change position.—*n.* an evasion; an expedient; a relay of workmen; the time of their working; a removal; woman's undergarment.—**shift'less** *a.* lacking in resource or character.—**shift'y** *a.* shuffling, full of evasions.–**shift'iness** *n.*
shikar' *n.* in India, hunting, sport.—**shikar'i** *n.* in India, a hunter.
shille'lagh (-ā'la) *n.* a cudgel.
shill'ing *n.* a silver coin=twelve pence.
shill'y-shally *v.i.* to waver.—*n.*
shimm'er *v.i.* to shine with faint quivering light.—*n.* such light.
shimm'y *n.* a kind of jazz dance.
shin *n.* the front of the lower leg.
shin'dig *n.* (U.S. (*sl.*) a noisy party.
shin'dy *n.* a row; disturbance.
shine *v.i.* to give out or reflect light; to polish (**shone** *p.t.* and *p.p.*—**shi'ning** *pres. p.*).—*n.* brightness.—**shi'ny** *a.*
shin'gle (-ng-gl) *n.* a flat piece of wood used as a tile.—*v.t.* to cover with shingles; to cut (a woman's hair) close.
shin'gle (-ng-gl) *n.* pebbles on the shore.
shin'gles (-ng-gl-) *n.* disease with eruptions often forming a belt round the body.
Shin'to *n.* system of nature- and hero-worship formerly prevailing in Japan.
shin'ty *n.* a game similar to hockey.
ship *n.* large sea-going vessel.—*v.t.* to put on or send in a ship.—*v.i.* to embark; to take service in a ship.—**ship'ment** *n.* act of shipping; goods shipped.—**shipp'ing** *n.* ships collectively.—**ship'-lap** *n.* N. America, quality of timber used for general purposes.—**ship'mate** *n.* fellow sailor.—**ship'shape** *a.* orderly, trim.—**ship'yard** *n.* place where ships are built or repaired.
shir'allee *n.* Australia (*sl.*) a bundle of blankets; clothes, provisions, etc., tied up in a blanket.
shire *n.* a county.
shirk *v.t.* to evade, try to avoid (a duty, danger, etc.).—**shirk'er** *n.*
shirt *n.* an undergarment for the upper part of the body.

shiv'er *n.* a splinter.—*v.t.* to splinter, break in pieces.—*v.i.* to split into pieces.

shiv'er *v.i.* to tremble, usually with cold or fear.—*n.* an act or state of shivering.

shoal *n.* a sandbank or bar, a shallow; a school of fish; crowd.—*v.i.* to become shallow; to collect in a shoal.

shock *n.* a group of corn-sheaves placed standing together in a field.

shock *v.t.* to horrify, scandalise.—*n.* a violent or damaging blow; a collision.—**shock'-bri'gade, shock'-work'ers** *n.* in Soviet Russia, workers undertaking unusually severe or long tasks.—**shock'-troops'** *n.* troops selected for some specially arduous and dangerous duty.

shock *n.* a mass of hair.—*a.* shaggy.

shodd'y *n.* cloth made of mixed old and new wool.—*a.* worthless, second-rate.

shoe (shōō) *n.* covering for foot; curved bar put on horse's hoof; various protective plates or under-coverings; in N. Amer., both shoes (**low shoes**) and boots (**high shoes**).—*v.t.* to furnish, protect with a shoe, or shoes (**shod** *p.t./p.p.*—**shoe'ing** *pr. p.*).—**shoe'maker** *n.*—**shoe-packs** *n. pl.* Canada, shoes of tanned leather like moccasins.

shooldarr'y *n.* in India, a small tent.

shoot *v.i.* to move swiftly and suddenly; to let off a gun, etc.; to go after game with a gun; to sprout.—*v.t.* to pass quickly under or along; to dump; to discharge; to kill or wound with a missile; in cinematography, to photograph a film (**shot** *p.t.* and *p.p.*—**shoo'ting** *pres. p.*).—*n.* an act of shooting; an expedition to shoot; a young branch or stem. — **shoot'ing-iron** *n.* in N. America (*sl.*) a firearm, *esp.* a revolver.

shop *n.* place where goods are bought and sold.—*v.i.* to visit shops (**shop'-ping** *pr. p.*).—**shop'-lifter** *n.* one who steals from shops. — **shop-steward** *n.* trade union representative of workers, in negotiations with employers.

shore *n.* the edge of the sea, or large lake.

shore *n.* a prop.—*v.t.* to prop.

short *a.* having little length; brief; hasty; friable.—*n.* in *pl.* breeches coming to, and open at, the knee.—*adv.* abruptly. —**short'age** *n.* deficiency.—**short'bread** *n.* a brittle kind of cake made of butter, flour and sugar.—**short'-cir'cuit** *n.* in electricity, a connection, often accidental, of very low resistance between two parts of a circuit.—**short'en** *v.t.* and *i.*—**short'hand** *n.* a method of rapid writing by signs or contractions.—**short'ly** *adv.* soon; briefly.—**short head,** in horse racing, a distance less than the length of a horse's head.— **short time** working less than the usual number of hours.—**short waves** *n.* in wireless, waves between 10 and 50 metres.

Syn. of **shorten,** abridge, diminish, reduce, curtail. *Ant.* expand, lengthen, increase, magnify.

shot *n.* an act of shooting; a shooter; a missile; try, attempt, *esp.* at hitting; lead in small pellets; a bill at a tavern.—in the cinema, a photograph of one scene taken from one position or during one movement of the camera.—*a.* woven so that the colour is different according to the angle of the light.—**shot, shots** *pl.*

shot *p.t.* and *p.p.* of **shoot.**

shoul'der (-ōl-) *n.* the part of a body to which an arm or foreleg is attached; a support or bracket.—*v.t.* to put on one's shoulder.—*v.i.* to make a way by pushing.—**shoulder'-blade** *n.* shoulder bone.

shout *n.* a loud cry.—*v.i.* to utter one.—*v.t.* to utter with a very loud voice; in Australia, to stand some one a drink.

shove (-uv) *v.t./n.* push (**shov'ing** *pr. p.*).

shov'el (-uv-) *n.* a broad spade.—*v.t.* to lift or move with a shovel (**shov'elling** *pres. p.*—**shov'elled** *p.t.* and *p.p.*).

show (-ō) *v.t.* to expose to view, point out; guide; accord (favour, etc.).—*v.i.* to appear, be visible (**showed** (shōd) *p.t.*—**shown** *p.p.*—**show'ing** *pres. p.*).—*n.* something shown; a display, spectacle.—**show'y** *a.* bright; too bright, conspicuous.

show'-down *n.* (*col.*) the final test, disclosure of plans and possibilities.—**show'-boat** *n.* a boat on which entertainments are given.—**show'-girl** *n.* a girl whose part in an entertainment is to exhibit looks, figure and dresses.

show'er *n.* a short fall of rain; anything coming down like rain; in N. America, a number of presents of a similar kind for a prospective bride, as a **linen shower.**—*v.t.* and *i.* to rain.—**show'ery** *a.*

shrap'nel *n.* a shell filled with bullets which explode in a shower; (loosely) shell or bomb splinters.

shred *n.* a fragment, torn strip.—*v.t.* to break, tear to shreds (**shred** or **shredd'ed** *p.t./p.p.*—**shredd'ing** *pr. p.*).

shrew *n.* an animal like a mouse; a malicious person; a scold.—**shrew'-mouse** *n.* shrew.—**shrew'ish** *a.*—**shrewd** *a.* intelligent; crafty; coming near the truth.—**shrewd'ly** *adv.*—**shrewd'ness** *n.*

shriek *v.t.* and *i.* and *n.* screech, scream.

shriev'alty *n.* the office of sheriff.

shrift *n. see* **shrive.**

shrike *n.* butcher-bird.

shrill *a.* piercing, sharp.—**shril'ly** *adv.*

shrimp *n.* a small crustacean of lobster shape.—*v.i.* to go catching shrimps.

shrine *n.* a case with relics of a saint; a chapel for this; sacred place, temple.

shrink *v.i.* to become smaller; to retire, flinch.—*v.t.* to make shrink (**shrank** *p.t.*—**shrunk'en, shrunk** *p.p.*—**shrink'ing** *pres p.*).—**shrink'age** *n.*

shrive *v.t.* to give absolution to (**shrived** (shrīvd), **shrove** *p.t.*—**shriv'en** *p.p.*—**shri'ving** *pres. p.*).—**shrift** *n.*

shriv'el *v.i.* to shrink and wrinkle (**shriv'elling** *pr. p.*—**shriv'elled** *p.t.*/*p.p.*).
shroff *n.* in India, a banker or money-changer.—*v.t.* to ascertain the quality of coins.—**shroff'age** *n.* the examination of coins by an expert.
shroud *n.* sheet for corpse; covering.—*pl.* set of ropes to masthead.—*v.t.* put a shroud on; wrap up; hide.
Shrove'tide *n.* the days just before Lent.—**Shrove Tues'day.**
shrub *n.* a bush, low tree.—**shrubb'y** *a.* —**shrubb'ery** *n.* plantation of shrubs.
shrug *v.i.* to raise shoulders, as sign of disdain, etc.—*v.t.* move (shoulders) thus (**shrugged'** *p.t.*/*p.p.*)—*n.*
shudd'er *v.i.* to tremble violently.—*n.*
shuf'fle *v.i.* to move the feet without lifting them; to act evasively.—*v.t.* to mix (cards); (with off) to evade.—*n.*
shun *v.t.* to avoid, abstain from.
shunt *v.t.* to move (a train) from one line to another, to push aside.
shut *v.t.* and *i.* to close (**shut** *p.t.* and *p.p.*—**shutt'ing** *pres. p.*).—**shutt'er** *n.* a movable screen for a window.
shut'tle *n.* instrument which threads woof between threads of warp in weaving; similar appliance in sewing machine.—**shut'tlecock** *n.* cork with cup-shaped fan of feathers stuck in it for use with battledore.—**shuttle ser'vice** *n.* transport service worked over short distance by same vehicle running to and fro.—**shuttle train** *n.*
shy *a.* timid, bashful, awkward in company; reluctant; in N. America (*sl.*) not having contributed to the pool; short; scarce; lacking.—*v.i.* to start back in sudden fear; to show sudden reluctance (**shied** *p.t.* and *p.p.*—**shy'ing** *pres. p.*).–*n.* a sudden start of fear by a horse.—**shy'ly** *adv.* timidly.—**shy'ness** *n.*
shy *v.t.* and *i.* throw (**shied** *p.t.* and *p.p.*—**shy'ing** *pres. p.*).
sib'ilant *a.* having a hissing sound.—*n.* a speech sound with a hissing effect.
sib'yl *n.* woman possessing the gift of prophecy and divination.—**sib'ylline** *a.*
sic *adv.* so, thus.
sick *a.* ill; inclined to vomit, vomiting.—**sick'en** *v.t.* and *i.*—**sick'ly** *a.*—**sick'ness** *n.*—**sick'-bay** *n.* a place set aside for treating the sick, *esp.* in ships.
sic'kle *n.* curved reaping hook.
side *n.* one of the surfaces of an object, *esp.* an upright inner or outer surface; either surface of a thing having only two; part of the body that is to the right or left; the region nearer or farther than, or right or left of, a dividing line, etc.; one of two parties or sets of opponents; (*sl.*) conceit; swagger.—*v.t.* to take up the cause of.—**side'arms** *n. pl.* weapons worn at the side.—**side'board** *n.* piece of furniture for holding dishes, etc., in a dining-room.—**side-car** *n.* in motoring, a small canoe-shaped body attached to a motor-cycle; a kind of cocktail.—**side'long** *adv.* obliquely.—**sides'man** *n.* assistant to churchwardens.—**side'-step** *n.* in boxing, a step to the side.—*v.i.*—**side'-track** *v.t.* to postpone treatment or consideration of.—**side'walk** *n.* N. America, the footpath, pavement.—**side'ways** *adv.*—**si'ding** *n.* a track added at the side of a railway.—**side'slip** *n.* a skid.—**to put on side,** to be conceited.
sider'eal (-dēr'-) *a.* relating to the stars.
si'dle *v.i.* to edge along, move sideways.
siege *n.* a besieging of a town or fort.
sienn'a *n.* an earthy pigment of a brownish-yellow colour.
sierr'a *n.* a chain of mountains.
siest'a (sē-est'a) *n.* a rest or sleep in the afternoon, *esp.* in hot countries.
sieve (siv) *n.* utensil with network or a perforated bottom for sifting.
sift *v.t.* to separate coarser portion from finer, good from bad; to analyse.
sigh (sī) *v.i.* to utter a long audible breath of relief, etc.—*n.* such a breath.
sight (sīt) *n.* act, faculty of seeing; something seen; a device for guiding the eye; (*sl.*) a large number; a great deal.—*v.t.* catch sight of; to adjust the sights of rifles, big guns, etc., according to the range.—**sight'er** *n.* a trial shot.—**sight'less** *a.* blind.—**sight'ly** *a.* comely,
sign (sīn) *n.* a movement, mark, or indication to convey some meaning.—*v.t.* to put one's signature to.—*v.i.* to make a sign or gesture; to affix a signature.
sig'nature *n.* a person's name written by himself; the act of writing it.—**sig'nature tune** tune associated with a particular band, comedian, etc.—**sig'natory** *n.* one of those who sign a document.—**sign' manual** (sīn-) *n.* autograph signature, *esp.* of a sovereign.—**sign'-post** (sīn-) *n.* post supporting a sign-board, *esp.* to show the way at cross roads.—**sign'board** (sīn-) *n.* board with some device or inscription.—**sig'nal** *n.* sign to convey an order, etc.; a semaphore, *esp.* on a railway.—*v.t.* to make signals to.—*v.i.* to give orders, etc., thus. —*a.* remarkable, striking.—**sig'nally** *adv.* —**sig'nalise** *v.t.* make notable.
sig'net *n.* a small seal.
sig'nify *v.t.* to mean; to imitate; partend. —*v.i.* to be of importance (**-nified** *p.t.*/*p.p.*— **-nifyin** g*pres.p.*).—**signif'icant** *a.* expressing the importance.—**signif'icantly** *adv.*—**signif'icance** *n.*—**significa'tion** *n.* the meaning.
si'lage (-lij) *n.* stored, cured fodder.
si'lence *n.* stillness, absence of noise; a refraining from speech.—*v.t.* to make silent.—**si'lent** *a.*—**si'lencer** *n.* in internal combustion engine, firearm, expansion chamber deadening sound of exhaust.—**si'lently** *adv.*
silhouette' *n.* portrait cut from black

paper or done in solid black on white; outline seen against the light; profile.

sil'ica *n.* silicic acid in a state of purity.—**sil'icate** *n.* a salt of silicic acid.—**sil'icon, silic'ium** *n.* a dark, nut-brown, elementary substance, destitute of metallic lustre, which communicates valuable properties when incorporated in steel.—**silic'eous, silic'ious** *a.* containing silica, or partaking of its qualities.—**silic'ic** *a.* pert. to flint or quartz.

silk *n.* fibre made by the larvæ of certain moths; thread or fabric made from this.—**silk'screen** *n.* a method of reproducing a design by means of a pattern made on a screen of silk or nylon.—*v.t.*—**silk'en** *a.* of silk.—**silk'y** *a.*—**silk'iness** *adv.*—**silk'ily** *a.*—**silk'-worm** *n.* caterpillar that produces silk.

sill *n.* slab of wood or stone at bottom of a door or window.

sill'y *a.* foolish; weak in intellect (**sil'lier** *comp.*—**sil'liest** *sup.*—*n.*)—**sill'iness** *n.*

si'lo *n.* a pit or tower for storing fodder or grain (**si'los** (-lōz) *pl.*).

silt *n.* mud, sand, etc., deposited by water.—*v.t.* and *i.* to fill with silt.

sil'van *a.* of the woods; wooded; rural.

sil'ver *n.* a white precious metal; things made of it; silver coins.—*v.t.* to coat with silver.—**sil'very** *a.*—**sil'versmith** *n.*

sil'verside *n.* a silver-fish; the lower and choicer part of the round of beef.

sim'ian *a.* of apes; ape-like.

sim'ilar *a.* resembling, like.—**sim'ilarly** *adv.*—**similar'ity** *n.* likeness.—**sim'ile** (sim'i-li) *n.* a comparison of one thing with another, *esp.* in poetry.—**simil'itude** *n.* outward appearance; guise.

simm'er *v.t.* and *i.* to keep or be just bubbling or just below boiling-point; to be on the point of bursting out into anger, laughter, etc.

si'mony *n.* the crime of buying or selling of church preferment.

simoom' *n.* a hot, dry wind that blows from the Arabian desert.

sim'per *v.i.* to smile in a silly way.

sim'ple *a.* plain; straightforward; ordinary, mere.—**sim'ply** *adv.*—**sim'pleton** *n.* a foolish person.—**simpli'city** *n.*

Syn. uncomplicated, elementary, artless, easy. *Ant.* intricate, artful, involved, difficult.

sim'plify (-fī) *v.t.* (**-ified** *p.t.* and *p.p.*—**-ifying** *pres. p.*).—**simplifica'tion** *n.*

sim'ulate *v.t.* to pretend to be.—**simulac'rum** *n.* a shadowy likeness; an unreal thing (**simulac'ra** *pl.*).—**simula'tion** *n.* pretence; imitation.

simulta'neous *a.* existing or occurring at the same time.—**simulta'neously** *adv.*—**simul'taneity** *n.*–**simulta'neous broadcasting** *n.* broadcasting of programme transmitted by one station by others connected by telephone.

sin *n.* a transgression against divine or moral law, *esp.* one committed consciously; conduct or state of mind of a habitual or unrepentant sinner.—*v.i.* to commit sin.—**sin'ful** *a.* of the nature of sin; guilty of sin.—**sin'fully** *a.*—**sinn'er** *n.*

since *adv.* from then till now; subsequently; ago.—*prep.* at some time subsequent to.—*conj.* from the time that; seeing that; because.

sincere' *a.* not assumed or merely professed; true, genuine, honest, straightforward.—**sincere'ly** *adv.*—**sincer'ity** *n.*

si'necure *n.* an office with pay but few or no duties.—**sin'ecurist** *n.*

sin'ew *n.* a tendon.—*pl.* muscles, strength; mainstay.—**sin'ewy** *a.* strong.

sing *v.i.* to utter musical sounds.—*v.t.* to utter (words) with musical modulation; to celebrate in song or poetry (**sang** *p.t.*—**sung** *p.p.*—**sing'ing** *pres. p.*).—**sing'er** *n.*

singe (-nj) *v.t.* to burn the surface (**singed** (-nj-) *p.t.*/*p.p.*—**singe'ing** (-nj-) *pr. p.*).—*n.* an act, effect of singeing.

sin'gle (-ng-gl) *a.* one only; alone, separate; unmarried; formed of only one part, fold, etc.—*v.t.* to pick (out).—**sing'let** (-ng-gl-) *n.* an unlined woollen undergarment.—**sin'gleton** *n.* a single thing; the only card of a suit in a hand.—**sing'ly** *adv.*—**single-hand'ed** *a.* without help.—**single-heart'ed** *a.* sincere.—**single-mind'ed** *a.* true to one purpose.—**sin'gle-stick** *n.* fencing with a basket-hilted stick; the stick.

sin'gular *a.* unique; remarkable; odd; unusual; denoting one person or thing.—*n.* a word in singular.—**sin'gularly** *adv.*—**singular'ity** *n.*

sin'ister *a.* evil-looking; wicked; in heraldry, on the left-hand side.

Syn. unlucky, inauspicious, unfortunate, evil. *Ant.* lucky, auspicious, fortunate.

sink *v.i.* to become submerged in water; to drop, give way, decline.—*v.t.* to cause to sink; to make by digging out; to invest (**sank** *p.t.*—**sunk'en, sunk** *p.p.*—**sink'ing** *pres. p.*).—*n.* a receptacle with a pipe for carrying away waste water.—**sink'er** *n.*—**sink'ing fund** *n.* money set aside at intervals to provide for payment of a particular liability at a future date.

sink'ings *n.* in S. Africa, toothache; neuralgia; rheumatism.

Sinn Fein' (shin fān') *n.* Irish policy and movement which led to establishment of Irish Free State (Eire), 1921.

sin'uous *a.* curving, winding.—**sin'uously** *adv.*—**sinuos'ity** *n.*

si'nus *n.* an opening; a hollow; a recess in the shore; a bay; (*surg.*) a cavity in a bone or other part; an abscess with a small orifice (**si'nuses, si'nusi** *pl.*).

sip *v.t.* and *i.* to drink in very small draughts.—(**sip'ping** *pr. p.*—**sipped** *p.t.*/*p.p.*—*n.* portion of liquid sipped.

si'phon *n.* bent tube for drawing off

liquids; a bottle with a tap through which liquid is forced by pressure of gas inside.—**si'phonal** *a.*—**'ic** *a.*
sir *n.* the title of a knight or baronet; a public or respectful form of address.
sir'dar *n.* a military commander in India; the British commander-in-chief of the Egyptian army.
sire *n.* a term of address to a king; a father; animal's male parent.
si'ren *n.* legendary maiden who enticed men to their doom by sweet singing; long, piercing whistle used as a signal or warning; hooter.
sir'loin *n.* upper part of a loin of beef.
siroco'o *n.* a hot, dry Mediterranean wind (**sirocc'os** (-ōz) *pl.*).
sis'al, si'sal *n.* fibre of the S. Amer. aloe.
sis'sy *n.* (*sl.*) a term of derision for a weak or timid person; an effeminate man; a sister, a girl.
sis'ter *n.* daughter of same parents or having common parent.—*a.* closely related, exactly similar.—**sis'terly** *a.*—**sis'terhood** *n.* relation of sister; order, band of women.—**sis'ter-in-law** *n.* sister of husband or wife; brother's wife.
sit *v.i.* to rest, e.g., on a chair, to seat oneself; to hold a session; to incubate; pose.—*v.t.* to sit upon (horse) (**sat** *p.t.* and *p.p.*—**sitt'ing** *pres. p.*).—**sit-down strike** *n.* an industrial strike, *esp.* among shop assistants, in which the workers refuse to leave their shop, etc., until their demands are granted.
site *n.* a place, situation, a plot of ground for, or with, a building.
sit'uate, sit'uated *a.* placed.—**situa'tion** *n.* place or position; employment, post; case, state of affairs.
si'wash *n.* in N. America, an adult male Indian; a contemptible, useless person.
six *a.* and *n.* cardinal number, one more than five.—**sixth** *a.* the ordinal number.—*n.* a sixth part.—**six'pence** *n.* the sum of six pence; silver coin of this value.—**six'penny** *a.*
si'zar *n.* a student at Cambridge or Dublin admitted at lower fees.—**si'zarship** *n.* the station of a sizar.
size *n.* bigness, dimensions; substance resembling glue.—*v.t.* to coat or treat with size; to sort or estimate by size.
siz'zle *v.i.* to make a hissing or sputtering sound; to dry and shrivel up with hissing by the action of the fire.—*n.* a hissing sound; extreme heat.
sjam'bok (syàm-) *n.* in S. Africa, a whip.—*v.t.* to beat with such a whip.
skaai *v.t.* in S. Africa, to steal.
skaap'steker *n.* in S. Africa, the night-adder, erroneously believed to kill sheep.
skaf (skof) *n.* in S. Africa, food (*sl.*) *v.t.* to eat.
skans *n.* in S. Africa, a defensive protection made of earth, stones, etc.
skate *n.* a flat fish; a steel blade with a framework to attach it to a boot, used for gliding over ice.—*v.i.* to glide on skates (**skat'ing** *pres. p.*—**skat'er** *n.*).
skedadd'le *v.i.* (*sl.*) to rush off; bolt.
skee'ter *n.* (*sl.*) a mosquito.
skein (-ā-) *n.* a quantity of yarn, wool, etc., in a loose knot.
skel'eton *n.* bones of an animal; frame, outline; **skel'eton-key** *n.* key made to fit most locks.—**skel'etal** *a.*
skelm *see* **schelm.**
skerm (sh-) *n.* in S. Africa, a barricade to protect cattle.
sketch *n.* a rough drawing; a brief account; essay, play, story, etc.—*v.t.* to make a sketch of.—*v.i.* to practise sketching.—**sketch'y** *a.* unfinished.
skew *v.i.* to move obliquely.—*a.* slanting.—**skew'gear,** a gear wheel with teeth at an angle to the axis.
skew'bald *a.* bay and white in patches.
skew'er *n.* a pin to fasten meat together.—*v.i.* to pierce or fasten with a skewer.
ski (shē) *n.* a long wooden runner fastened to the foot for sliding over snow (**skis** (shēz), **ski** *pl.*).—*v.i.* to glide on skis.
skid *n.* a drag for a wheel.—*v.t.* to apply a skid to; in N. America, to slide lumber down an incline.—*v.i.* of a wheel, to slip without revolving or to slip sideways; of aeroplane, to slip sideways in turning.
skiff *n.* small light row-boat.
skill *n.* practical ability, cleverness.—**skilled** *a.*—**skil'ful** *a.*—**skil'fully** *adv.*
Syn. dexterity, aptitude. *Ant.* awkwardness, clumsiness, inaptitude.
skill'et *n.* a small vessel with a handle, used for heating water, etc.
skill'y *n.* watery broth or soup.
skil'pad *n.* in S. Africa, a tortoise; a lazy, idle person.
skim *v.t.* to rid of floating matter; to remove from the surface of a liquid; to glide over lightly and rapidly; to read carelessly.—*v.i.* to move thus.
skimmel (sh-) *n.* S. Africa, grey horse.
skimp *v.t.* to give short measure, to be saving; to do a thing imperfectly.
skin *n.* outer covering of the body; peel, rind.—*v.t.* to remove the skin of.—**skinn'y** *a.* thin.—**skin'less** *a.*—**skin'-deep** *a.* superficial; slight.—**skin-flint** *n.* mean person.—**skin'-grafting,** transplanting a piece of healthy skin to a wound to form a new skin.—**skin-tight** *a.* fitting close to the skin.
skip *v.i.* to leap lightly; to jump a rope as it is swung under one.—*v.t.* to pass over.—*n.* an act of skipping.—**skip'-dis'tance** *n.* (*television*) the distance from a transmitter to any large object over which the beam bounces.
skipp'er *n.* the captain of a ship.
skirm'ish *n.* a fight between small groups.—*v.i.* to engage in such.
skirt *n.* lower part of a woman's dress,

coat, etc., an outlying part.—*v.t.* to border; to go round.—**skirt'ings** *n. pl.* in Australia, the parts of a fleece containing the poorer grades of wool.
skit *n.* a satire or caricature.
skitt'ish *a.* frisky, frivolous.
skit'tles *n. pl.* game like ninepins.
skoff *see* **skaf.**
skof'fel *v.t.* in S. Africa, to clear land [by hoeing.
skrik *n.* in S. Africa, a fright; a start.
skuldug'gery *n.* (*sl.*) plotting; sinister activity, nefarious deeds.
skulk *v.i.* to hide, to lurk, to sneak.
skull *n.* the bony case that encloses the brain.—**skull'cap** *n.* a close-fitting cap.
skunk *n.* small striped N. American animal valued for its fur. It defends itself by emitting an evil-smelling fluid; a mean fellow.
skut *n.* S. Africa, a pound (for cattle).
sky *n.* the apparent canopy of the heavens; the heavenly regions.—**sky'-light** *n.* window in a roof.—**sky'-pilot** *n.* in N. America (*sl.*) a clergyman.—**sky-scra'per** *n.* a very tall building.—**sky'-writing** *n.* smoke writing executed in the sky by an aeroplane.
slab *n.* thick, broad piece.
slack *a.* loose; sluggish; not busy.—*n.* loose part, as of rope.—*n. pl.* loose trousers.—*v.t.* to slake (lime).—*v.i.* be idle or lazy.—**slack off** become less intense or active.—**slack'ly** *adv.*—**slack'en** *v.t./i.* become slower; loosen.
slack *n.* small coal.—**slag** *n.* refuse of smelted metal.—*v.i.* form slag.
slake *v.i.* to moderate.—*v.t.* to quench; to slack (lime) (**sla'king** *pres. p.*).
slam *v.t.* to shut noisily; to dash down.—*v.i.* to shut with a bang.—*n.* a noisy shutting or other bang.—**slam (grand or little)** 13 or 12 tricks taken in one deal in cards (**slammed'** *p.t.* and *p.p.*).
slan'der (-à-) *n.* a false or malicious statement about a person.—*v.t.* to utter such.—**slan'derer** *n.*—**slan'derous** *a.*
slang *n.* a colloquial language.—*v.t.* to scold violently.—**slang'y** *a.*
slang'vreter *n.* S. Africa, secretary bird.
slant (-à-) *v.t.* and *i.* and *n.* slope.—*adv.* obliquely, slanting.—*n.* **slant'wise.**—*a.* sloping, in slanting direction.
slap *n.* a blow with the open hand or a flat instrument.—*v.t.* to strike thus.—**slap'-dash** *a.* careless, random.—**slap'-stick** *n.* the lath used by a harlequin in old comedy; hence, rough, low fun.
slash *v.t.* to gash; to lash; to cut into long strips.—*n.* a gash; a cutting stroke.
slat *n.* a narrow strip of wood or metal; a thin, flat stone, lath.
slate *n.* a kind of stone that splits into smooth layers; piece of this for covering roof or writing on.—*v.t.* to cover with slates; to abuse.—**sla'ting** *n.* severe reprimand.—**slate club** *n.* society for providing Christmas gifts by members' small weekly payments.
slatt'ern *n.* a slut.—**slatt'ernly** *a.*
slaught'er (slawt'-) *n.* killing.—*v.t.* to kill.—**slaught'erous** *a.*—**slaught'er-house** *n.* a place for killing animals for food.
slave *n.* a captive, a person without freedom or personal rights.—*v.i.* to work like a slave.—**sla'very** *n.*—**sla'vish** *a.*—**sla'ver** *n.* person or ship engaged in slave traffic.—**sla'vey** *n.* (*sl.*) maidservant.
slav'er *v.i.* to let saliva run from the mouth.—*n.* saliva running from mouth.
slay *v.t.* to kill (**slew** *p.t.*—**slain** *p.p.*—**slay'ing** *pres. p.*).—**slay'er** *n.*
sledge *n.* a carriage on runners for sliding on snow; a toboggan (also **sled, sleigh**).
sledge, sledge'-hammer *n.* heavy blacksmith's hammer.
sleek *a.* glossy and smooth.
sleep *n.* an unconscious state regularly occurring in man and animals.—*v.i.* to take rest in sleep, to slumber (**slept** *p.t.* and *p.p.*—**sleep'ing** *pres. p.*).—**sleep'er** *n.* one who sleeps; a beam supporting a rail of a railway; a sleeping-car.—**sleep'less** *a.*—**sleep'iness** *n.*—**sleep'y** *a.*—**sleep'ily** *adv.*—**sleeping sickness** a deadly Central African endemic disease.—**sleepy sickness** an epidemic European disease, marked by great drowsiness.
sleet *n.* partly-thawed snow.
sleeve *n.* the part of a garment which covers the arm; in motoring, case surrounding shaft; in aviation, wind indicator at aerodrome.—*v.t.* to furnish with sleeves; to put sleeves into.—**sleeved** *a.*—**sleeve'less** *a.*—**sleeve'-band** the wrist-band or cuff.—**sleeve'-link** two buttons linked together, and securing the edges of a cuff or wrist-band.—**sleeve valve** sliding-valve.—**to have up one's sleeve** to have something in readiness for an emergency, unknown to others.
sleight (slīt) *n.* dexterity.—**sleight'-of-hand'** *n.* conjuring, juggling.
slen'der *a.* slim, slight; small.
slenter *see* **schlenter.**
sleuth *n.* a track; a bloodhound; a relentless tracker; a detective.
slew, slue *v.t.* and *i.* to swing round.
slice *n.* thin flat piece cut off.—*v.t.* to cut into slices (**sli'cing** *pres. p.*).
slick *a.* smooth; smooth-tongued; smart.—*adv.* deftly.—*v.t.* to make glossy.
slide *v.i.* to slip smoothly along.—*v.t.* to cause to slide (**slid** *p.t.*— **slidd'en, slid** *p.t.*—**sli'ding** *pr. p.*).—*n.* sliding; track on ice made for or by sliding; sliding part of mechanism.—**sliding-roof**, roof of saloon car which is designed to open by sliding.
slight (-īt) *a.* slim, slender, not substantial; trifling.—*v.t.* to disregard; to neglect or offend.—*n.* indifference; an act of discourtesy.—**slight'ly** *adv.*
Syn. weak, fragile, thin, faint, transient, silly, soft, gentle, cursory, superficial. *Ant.* important, serious, strong, sturdy.

slim *a.* thin, slender, slight; crafty; in S. Africa, clever, sharp.—*v.i.* to scamp one's work; to reduce one's weight and bulk by diet and exercise.—**slimm'ing** *n.*
slime *n.* sticky mud.—**sli'my** *a.*
sling *n.* strap with a string attached at each end for hurling a stone; hanging bandage for a wounded limb; any rope, belt, etc., for hoisting or carrying.—*v.t.* to throw; to hoist, swing (**slung** *p.t.* and *p.p.*—**sling'ing** *pres. p.*).
slink *v.i.* to move stealthily (**slunk** *p.t.* and *p.p.*—**slink'ing** *pres. p.*).
slip *n.* a twig cut for grafting or planting; a long narrow slip; a landing place; a slope on which ships are built; a leash; a mistake; an act of slipping; in cricket, a position on the offside, a few yards behind the wicket; the fieldsman in this position; in motoring, revolution of wheels without movement along the surface of the road; in aviation, pitch of an airscrew, less distance it actually travels in one revolution; woman's undergarment.—*v.i.* to lose one's foothold.—*v.t.* to cause to slip; to put on or off easily or gently; to release (a dog) (**slip'ping** *pres. p.*—**slipped** *p.t.* and *p.p.*).
slipp'er *n.* light indoor shoe.—**slipp'ery** *a.* so smooth as to cause slipping, difficult to hold or catch; unreliable.—**slip'-shod** *a.* slovenly, careless.—**slip stream** *n.* aviation, stream of air driven astern by airscrews or jets.
slips *n. pl.* upper side-boxes in theatre; wings; frame on which ships are built; man's abbreviated bathing costume tying round middle.
slit *v.t.* to cut open, to sever (**slit** or **slitt'ed** *p.t.* and *p.p.*—**slitt'ing** *pres. p.*).—*a.* cut, torn.—*n.* a straight narrow cut.
slith'er (-th-) *v.i.* to slide and bump.
slobb'er *v.i.* to slaver.—*v.t.* to wet with saliva.—*n.* running saliva.—**slobb'ery** *a.*
sloe *n.* the blackthorn; its blue-black fruit.—**sloe-gin** *n.* liqueur made from sloes.
slog *v.t.* and *i.* to hit hard; to work hard, plod.—*n.* wild, violent hit at ball.—**slog'ging** *pr. p.*—**slog'ged** *p.t./p.p.*
slo'gan *n.* Highland war-cry; catch-word or phrase, motto.
sloop *n.* a one-masted cutter-rigged vessel; a small warship designed for escort and general duties.
sloot *see* **sluit.**
slop *n.* dirty liquid; semi-liquid food; an overall.—*pl.* ready-made clothing, dirty water.—*v.t.* spill, splash.—*v.i.* spill.—**slopp'y** *a.* watery; slovenly.
slope *n.* a slant, an upward or downward inclination.—*v.i.* to move obliquely.—*v.t.* to place slanting (**slo'ping** *pres. p.*).
slot *n.* slit; groove; trail of animal. (skin).—**slough'y** *a.*
sloth (-ō-) *n.* sluggishness; a sluggish S. American animal.—**sloth'fully** *adv.*
slouch *n.* a stooping, careless, shambling walk.—*v.i.* to walk thus.—*v.t.* to pull down (a hat).—**slouch'ing** *a.*
slough (-ow) *n.* muddy place, a bog; in N. America, depression in the prairie where rain collects enabling good hay to be obtained later on.
slough (-uf) *n.* skin shed by a snake.—*v.i.* of such tissue, to be shed.—*v.t.* to shed (skin).—**slough'y** *a.*
slov'en (-uv-) *n.* a dirty, untidy person.—**slov'enly** *a.* untidy.—**slov'enliness** *n.*
slow (-ō) *a.* moving at a low rate of speed; behindhand, dull.—*v.i.* to slacken speed.—**slow'ly** *adv.*—**slow'ness** *n.*—**slow-motion** film photography using high speed camera to enable motion to be shown in exaggeratedly slow time.
slow'worm (slō-) *n.* a harmless small lizard, the blind-worm.
slug *n.* land snail with no shell; lazy fellow; a cylindrical bullet.—**slugg'ard** *n.*—**slugg'ish** *a.* slowmoving.—**slugg'ishness** *n.*
sluice (-ōōs) *n.* a gate or door to control a flow of water.—*v.t.* to pour water over.
sluit, sloot (-oo-) *n.* in S. Africa, a crack in the veld caused by water action.
slum *n.* squalid street or neighbourhood.
slum'ber *v.i.* to sleep.—*n.* sleep.
slump *v.i.* of prices, etc., to fall suddenly or heavily.—*n.* such fall.
slur *v.t.* to pass over lightly; to depreciate (**slurred'** *p.t.* and *p.p.*)—*n.* a slight.
slush *n.* liquid mud; half-melted snow.—**slush'y** *a.*—**slush'er, slush'y** *n.* in Australia, a cook, *esp.* for shearers.
slut *n.* a dirty, untidy woman.—**slut'tish** *a.*—**slut'ishness** *n.*
sly *a.* cunning, wily; done with artful dexterity.—**sly'ly** *adv.*—**sly'ness** *n.*
smack *n.* a taste, characteristic flavour.—*v.i.* to taste (of)—*v.t.* to open (the lips) with a loud sound; to slap.—*n.* a smacking or slap.
smack *n.* a small sailing vessel.
small (-awl) *a.* little.—**small'ness** *n.*—**small'clothes** *n. pl.* breeches.—**small'pox** *n.* contagious disease.—**small-arms** rifles, pistols, etc.—**small debts** debts that are in England under £20; in Scotland £12.—**small end** in internal-combustion engine, bearing of a connecting rod connecting it to piston.—**small holding** an allotment.—**small' hours** early morning.—**small' talk** light or trivial conversation.
Syn. diminutive, tiny, insufficient, inadequate. *Ant*, large, considerable, big.
smalt *n.* common glass tinged deep blue by protoxide of cobalt, ground fine, and used as a pigment in various arts.
smart *a.* brisk; clever; trim, well dressed; fashionable.—*v.i.* to be very painful; to suffer acutely.—*n.* a sharp pain.—**smart'en** *v.t.*—**smart'ly** *adv.*
smash *v.t.* to shatter; to dash.—*v.i.* to break.—*n.* a heavy blow; wrecked state; an accident wrecking vehicles.—**smash'er** *n.* a coiner.

smatt'ering *n.* a superficial knowledge.—**smatt'er** *v.i.* to have a smattering.
smear *v.t.* to rub with grease, etc.—*n.* a mark made thus, daub, blur.
smeer, smeer'goed *n.* in S. Africa, a salve, ointment.—**smeer'lap** *n.* a rogue.
smell *v.t.* to perceive by the nose.—*v.i.* to use the nose; to give out an odour (**smelt, smelled** *p.t.* and *p.p.*—**smell'ing** *pres. p.*).—*n.* an odour; the faculty of perceiving odours by the nose.—**smel'ly** *a.*
smelt *n.* a small salmon-like fish.
smelt *v.t.* to extract metal from ore.
smew *n.* a diving bird, visiting Britain in the winter.
smi'lax *n.* a climbing shrub.
smile *v.i.* to assume a pleased or amused expression.—*n.* an act of smiling.
smirch *v.t.* to make dirty; to disgrace.
smirk *v.i.* to smile affectedly.—*n.*
smite *v.t.* to strike; attack; affect (**smote** *p.t.*-**smitt'en, smit** *p.p.*-**smi'ting** *pr. p.*).
smith *n.* a worker in iron, gold, etc. blacksmith.—**smith'y (-th-)** *n.* forge, blacksmith's workshop.
smithereens' *n. pl.* small fragments.
smock *n.* loose outer garment with the upper part gathered.—*v.t.* to gather by diagonal lines of sewing.—**smock'-frock** *n.* a farm-labourer's smock.
smoke *n.* the cloudy mass of suspended particles that rises from fire or anything burning; a spell of tobacco smoking.—*v.i.* to give off smoke; to inhale and expel the smoke of burning tobacco; in Australia, (*sl.*) to escape.—**to go into smoke,** to go into hiding—(of a criminal).—*v.t.* to expose to smoke (*esp.* in curing fish, etc.); to consume (tobacco) by smoking.—**smo'ker** *n.*—**smo'ky** *a.*—**smo'kily** *adv.*—**smoke-bomb** *n.*—**smoke'-screen** *n.*
smooth (**-th**) *a.* not rough, even of surface; plausible.—*v.t.* to make smooth; to quieten.—**smooth'ly** *adv.*—**smooth'-ness** *n.*—**smoothing circuit** in electricity, a device used for eliminating a pulsating component from an unidirectional current, such as that obtained from a rectifier. *Syn.* flat, polished, sleek, bland. fluent, deceptive. *Ant.* rough, uneven, unpolished, rude, blunt, tempestuous.
smoth'er (-uth-) *n.* dense smoke, spray, foam, etc.—*v.t.* to suffocate, stifle, choke; suppress, keep down.—*v.i.* to be suffocated.—**ed** *a.*—**ing** *a.*
smoul'der *v.i.* to burn without flame.
smudge *n.* a smear, stain, dirty mark, in N. America, a smoky fire made to drive off mosquitoes.—*v.t.* to make a dirty mark on.—**smud'gy** *a.*
smug *a.* self-satisfied, complacent.
smug'gle *v.t.* to bring into a country without payment of customs duties payable (**smug'gling** *pres. p.*).—**smugg'ler** *n.*
smut *n.* soot, particle of dirt; a disease of grain; lewd or obscene talk.—*v.t.* to blacken, smudge.—**smutt'y** *a.*
snack *n.* a light meal.—**snack'-bar** *n.*—**snack'-counter** *n.* counter for light meals.
snaf'fle *n.* a light bit for a horse.—*v.t.* to put one on.—(*sl.*) to steal.
snag *n.* a stump, *esp.* a tree-trunk in a river; (*col.*) a difficulty, obstacle, catch.
snail *n.* a slow-moving mollusc with a shell.—**snail'y** *a.* resembling a snail, or its motion.—**snail'ey** *n.* in Australia, a bullock or cow with a slightly-crumpled horn.
snake *n.* a long scaly limbless reptile; malevolent person.—**sna'ky** *a.*
snake'stone *n.* a fossil ammonite; any specific for snake-bites.
snap *v.i.* to make a quick bite or snatch.—*v.t.* to snatch or bite; break abruptly.—*n.* a quick sharp sound; a bite; a break; in N. America (*sl.*) an easy duty, a sinecure.—**snapp'y** *a.* ill tempered; (*col.*) speedy, smart, quick.—**snapp'ish** *a.*—**snap'-dragon** *n.* a plant with flowers resembling a mouth; a game of snatching raisins from burning brandy.—**snap'shot** *n.* instantaneous photograph.
snare *n.* a noose used as a trap.—*v.t.* to catch with one; to entangle.
snarl *n.* a growl with bared teeth; an entanglement.—*v.i.* to make this sound; to growl in a savage tone.
snatch *v.i.* to make a quick grab or bite (at).—*v.t.* to seize, catch.—*n.* a grab; a short spell, small amount (**snatch'es** *pl.*).
sneak *v.i.* to move secretly, to slink.—*n.* a mean or treacherous person; (U.S.) a light, soft-soled shoe.
sneer *v.i.* to smile, speak or write scornfully.—*n.* a sneering.
sneeze *v.i.* to emit breath with a sudden convulsive spasm and noise.—*n.*—**sneeze'wood** *n.* a S. African tree, the dust of which causes sneezing.
snib *v.t.* to fasten; to bolt.—*n.* a fastening of a door; latch; bolt.
snick *n.* a small cut or mark; notch; nick.—*v.t.* to cut; to clip; to nick.—**snick'ersnee** *n.* a kind of knife.
sniff *v.i.* to draw in breath through the nose with a sharp hiss; to express disapproval, etc., by sniffing.—*v.t.* to take up through the nose, to smell.—*n.*
snig'ger *v.i.* to laugh slyly; to laugh with half-suppressed catches of voice.—*n.*
snip *v.t.* to cut, cut bits off (**snip'ping** *pr. p.*—**snip'ped** *p.t./p.p.*).—*n.* bit cut off; a small cut.—**snipp'et** *n.* shred.
snipe *n.* a long-billed marsh bird.—*v.i.* to shoot at enemy individuals from cover.—*v.t.* to hit by so shooting.—**sni'per** *n.*
sniv'el *v.i.* to make a sniffing to show real or sham emotion, *esp.* sorrow.
snob *n.* a cobbler; one who judges by rank or wealth rather than merit.—**snobb'ery** *n.*-**snobb'ish** *a.*-**snobb'ishly** *adv.*
snoo'ker *n.* a game resembling pool or pyramids played on a billiard table.

snoop' *v.i.* (*col.*) to investigate with stealth, pry into others' affairs.
snoot'y *a.* (*col.*) uppish; snobbish.
snooze *v.i.* to take a short sleep, to be half-asleep.—*n.* a nap.
snore *v.i.* to make noises with the breath when asleep.—*n.* an act of snoring.
snort *v.i.* to make a noise by driving breath through the nostrils.—*n.* **-ing** *n.* and *a.*—**snort'-mast** *n.* a ventilating device which enables a submarine to remain under water for long periods.
snout *n.* nose and mouth of an animal.
snow *n.* frozen vapour which falls in flakes.—(*sl.*) cocaine, heroin, or other narcotic drug in dry, powdered form.—*v.i.* **it snows** snow is falling.—*v.t.* to let fall or throw down like snow; to cover with snow.—**snow'y** *a.*—**snow'-blink** *n.* the reflection of snow or ice in the sky.—**snow'-drop** *n.* bulbous plant with white flowers in early spring.—**snow'-fence** *n.* N. Amer., protective embankment of snow on windward side of railways or roads.—**snow'-line** *n.* elevation above which snow does not melt.
snub *v.t.* to mortify or repress intentionally; to rebuke.—*n.* a snubbing.—**snub'-nose** *n.* a turned-up stumpy nose.
snuff *n.* charred candle-wick; powdered tobacco for inhaling through the nose; an act of snuffing.—*v.t.* to clean a candle-wick; to put out; draw up or through the nostrils.—*v.i.* to draw air or snuff into the nose.—**snuff'box** *n.*
snuf'fle *v.i.* sniff, snivel; speak nasally.—*n.* act, sound of snuffling.
snug *a.* cosy; trim.—**snug'gle** *v.* nestle.—**snug'ly** *adv.*—**snugg'ery** *n.* cosy room.
so *adv.* in such manner; very; the case being such.—*conj.* therefore; in case that.
soak *v.i.* to lie in a liquid.—*v.t.* to steep, make thoroughly wet.—*n.* a soaking, in Australia, a damp or swampy spot round base of granite rocks; aboriginal watering place.—**soak'-hole** *n.* in Australia, a sheep-dip constructed in the middle of a stream.
soap *n.* a compound of alkali and oil used in washing.—*v.t.* to apply soap to.
soar *v.i.* to fly high; hover.—**soar'ing** *n.* act of mounting on the wings, as a bird; lofty flight; also, act of rising high in thought; intellectual flight.
sob *v.i.* to catch the breath, *esp.* in weeping.—*n.* a sobbing.—**sob'stuff** *n.* (*sl.*) talk, writing, drama, etc., provoking or displaying extreme sentimentality.
so'ber *a.* temperate; subdued; not drunk.—*v.t.* and *i.* to make or become sober.—**so'berly** *adv.*—**sobri'ety** *n.* soberness.
Syn. abstemious, moderate, dispassionate, serious. *Ant.* intemperate, extreme, passionate, careless.
so'briquet (-kā) *n.* a nickname.
so'cial *a.* living in communities; relating to society; sociable.—**so'cially** *adv.*—**so'ciable** *a.* inclined to be friendly, of ready companionship.—**sociabil'ity** *n.*—**so'ciably** *adv.*—**soci'ety** *n.* companionship; living associated with others; those so living; fashionable people collectively; an association or club.—**sociol'ogy** *n.* social science.—**so'cialism** *n.* policy aiming at ownership of means of production, transport, etc., by the community.—**so'cialist** *n.*—**socialist'ic** *a.*
sock *n.* a short stocking; an inner sole.
sock *v.t.* (*sl.*) to hit, thrash.
sock'et *n.* a hole for something to fit into.
sod *n.* a flat piece of earth with grass.
sod *n.* *abbrev.* of sodomite.
so'da *n.* an alkali.—**so'da-water** *n.* water charged with gas under pressure.—**so'dium** *n.* a metallic element.
sodd'en *a.* soaked, wet through; like dough (old *p.t.* and *p.p.* of **seethe**).
sod'omy *n.* unnatural sexual intercourse.
so'fa *n.* a long padded seat with back.
soft *a.* yielding easily to pressure, not hard; smooth; mild; easy; subdued; over-sentimental; kind, as *soft-hearted*; weak, silly.—**soft'ly** *adv.*—**soft'en** (sof'n) *v.t.* and *i.*—**soft' drink** *n.* one that is non-alcoholic.—**soft'-soap** *n.* (*col.*) ingratiating flattery.—**soft'-valve** *n.* in wireless, a thermionic valve not completely exhausted of gas.
sogg'y *a.* damp and heavy.
soigné' (swan'-yā) *a.* carefully groomed or finished.
soil *n.* earth, ground.—*v.t.* and *i.* to make or become dirty.—*n.* dirt; sewage.
soir'ee (swȧ-rā') *n.* an evening party; a public meeting of a society, congregation, etc., where refreshments are served.
soj'ourn (suj'ərn) *v.i.* to stay for a time.—**soj'ourner** *n.*—**soj'ournment** *n.*
so'lace *n.* and *v.t.* comfort.—**sola'tium** *n.* money compensation (**-tia** *pl.*).
so'lan *n.* a large sea-bird like a goose; a gannet (Also **so'lan goose.**)
so'lar *a.* of the sun.—**so'lar sys'tem** *n.* the sun and planets.
sol'der (sōl-, sol-, sod-) *n.* an easily-melted alloy used for joining metal.—*v.t.* to join with it.—**sol'dering-iron** *n.*
sol'dier (sō-) *n.* one serving in an army.—*v.i.* to serve in the army.—**sol'dierly** *a.*—**sol'diery** *n.* troops.
sole *n.* the flat of the foot; the under part of a boot or shoe, etc.; a flat-fish.—*v.t.* to supply with a sole (**so'ling** *pres. p.*).
sole *a.* only, unique.—**sole'ly** *adv.*
sol'ecism *n.* a breach of the rules of grammar or etiquette.
sol'emn (-em) *a.* serious; formal; impressive.—**sol'emnly** *adv.*—**solem'nity** *n.*—**sol'emnise** *v.t.* to celebrate, perform; make solemn.—**solemnisa'tion** *n.*
so'lenoid *n.* cylindrical coil of wire (without fixed iron core) forming an electro-magnet.
soli'cit (-lis'-) *v.t.* to urge; request, en-

tice.—**solicita'tion** *n.*—**soli'citor** *n.* one who solicits; a lawyer; in N. America, a commercial traveller.—**soli'citous** *a.* anxious.—**soli'citude** *n.* concern, anxiety.
sol'id *a.* not hollow; compact.—*n.* a body of three dimensions.—**sol'idly** *adv.*—**solid'ity** *n.*—**solid'ify** *v.t.* and *i.* (**-ified** *p.t.* and *p.p.*—**-ifying** *pres. p.*).—**solidifica'tion** *n.*—**solidar'ity** *n.* united state.
solil'oquy *n.* a talking with oneself; discourse not addressed to any one (**solil'oquies** *pl.*).—**solil'oquise** *v.i.*
sol'itary *a.* alone, single.—*n.* a hermit.
sol'itude *n.* condition of being alone.—**solitaire'** *n.* a single precious stone set by itself; a game for one.—**so'lo** *n.* music for one performer; (**solos, soli** (-lē) *pl.*).—*a.* not concerted; driving car, or piloting aeroplane, alone.—**so'loist** *n.*
sol'stice *n.* a period of the year when the sun is overhead at one of the tropics.—**solsti'tial** *a.* appertaining to solstice.
solve *v.t.* to work out, clear up, find the answer of.—**sol'uble** *a.* capable of solution.—**solubil'ity** *n.*—**solu'tion** *n.* the answer to a problem; a dissolving; a liquid with something dissolved in it.—**sol'vable** *a.*—**sol'vent** *a.* able to pay debts, having more assets than liabilities.—*n.* a substance, liquid with a power of dissolving.—**sol'vency** *n.*
som'bre *a.* dark or gloomy.
sombre'ro *n.* wide-brimmed hat.
some (sum) *pron.* a portion, a quantity.—*a.* one or other; an amount of; certain; approximately.—**some'body** *n.* some person.—**some'how** *adv.* in some way.—**some'thing** *n.*—**some'time** *a.* former.—*adv.* formerly; at some (past or future) time.—**some'times** *adv.* on occasion.—**some'what** *n.* something.—*adv.* to some extent, rather.—**some'where** *adv.*
som'ersault (sum-) *n.* a tumbling head over heels.—*v.* perform this.
somnam'bulist *n.* a sleep-walker.—**somnam'bulism** *n.*
som'nolent *a.* sleepy.—**som'nolence** *n.*
son *n.* a male child.—**son'-in-law** *n.* a daughter's husband.
sona'ta (-à-) *n.* a piece of music in several movements.—**sonati'na** (-tē-) *n.* a short and simple sonata (**-ne** (-nā) *pl.*).
song *n.* singing; a poem for singing.—**song'ster** *n.*—**song'stress** *fem.*
son'ifer *n.* an acoustic instrument for collecting sound, and conveying it to the ear of a particularly deaf person.
sonn'et *n.* a fourteen-line poem with a rhyme system.—**sonneteer'** *n.*
sonor'ous *a.* giving out deep sound, resonant.—**son'orously** *adv.*—**sonor'ity** *n.*
son'sy, son'cy *a.* in Scotland, plump.
sool *v.t.* in Australia (*sl.*) to incite a dog; to worry, tease, torment.
soon (-ōō-) *adv.* before long; early.
soot (-oo-) *n.* a black substance formed by the burning of coal, etc.—**soot'y** *a.*
sooth (-ōō-) *n.* truth.—**sooth'sayer** *n.* a person professing to foretell the future.
soothe (-ōōth) *v.t.* to calm, soften; please. *Syn.* quiet, pacify, assuage, mollify. *Ant.* excite, irritate, inflame.
sop *n.* a piece of bread, etc., soaked in liquid; a bribe.—*v.t.* to steep.
soph'ist *n.* a captious reasoner.—**soph'ism** *n.* a specious argument.—**sophist'ical** *a.*—**soph'istry** *n.*—**sophist'icate** *v.t.* to make artificial, spoil, falsify, corrupt.—**sophistica'tion** *n.*
soph'omore *n.* in N. America, a student in the second year of his college course.
soporif'ic (sop- or sō-) *a.* causing sleep.
sopra'no (-rà-) *n.* the highest voice in women and boys; a singer with this voice, musical part written for it (**-nos** (-nōz), **-ni** (-nē) *pl.*).
sor'cerer *n.* a wizard.—**sor'ceress** *fem.*
sor'cery *n.* witchcraft, magic.
sor'did *a.* mean, squalid; base.—**sor'didly** *adv.*—**sor'didness** *n.*
sore *a.* painful; distressed.—*adv.* grievously.—*n.* a sore place, an ulcer or boil, etc.—**sore'ness** *n.*—**sore'ly** *adv.*
sorop'timist (sor-op'-tim-ist) *n.* a member of a women's Rotary Club.
sorr'el *n.* a plant; a reddish-brown colour; a horse of this colour.—*a.* of reddish-brown colour.
sorr'ow (-ō) *n.* pain of mind, grief.—*v.i.* grieve.—**sorr'owful** *a.*—**sorr'owfully** *adv.*
sorr'y *a.* distressed, feeling regret; mean, poor (**sor'rier** *comp.*).—**sorr'ily** *adv.*
sort *n.* a kind or class.—*v.t.* to classify.—**sort'er** *n.*—**out of sorts** not well.
sortie (-ē) *n.* a sally by besieged forces.
S.O.S. *n.* the wireless signal sent out by a ship or plane in distress; any desperate appeal, *esp.* a broadcast message to trace relatives of a dying person.
sosa'tie *n.* in S. Africa, meat cooked on skewers round a fire.
sot *n.* drunkard.—**sott'ish** *a.* stupid.
sott'o *adv.* under.—**sott'o vo'ce** (vō'chā) under one's breath; in an aside.
sough' (sōō, sow, suf) *n.* a sound such as a sighing of the wind.—*v.i.*
soul (sōl) *n.* the spiritual part of a human being; a person.—**soul'ful** *a.* expressing elevated feeling.—**soul'less** *a.* mean, prosaic, lacking in spiritual awareness.
sound *n.* that which is heard.—*v.i.* to make a sound.—*v.t.* to cause to sound.—**sound'er** *n.* telegraphic device, for transmission of messages by clicking sounds.—**sound-box** *n.* in a gramophone, diaphragm which makes vibrations of needle audible.—**sound-screen** *n.* screen for reproducing sound-film.—**sound track** strip on one side of cinema film which records sound vibrations.
sound *a.* in good condition; solid; of good judgment.—**sound'ly** *adv.* thoroughly.
Syn. healthy, perfect, strong, correct,

well-founded, trustworthy. *Ant.* unsound, unhealthy, imperfect, fallacious.
sound *n.* a channel or strait.
sound *v.t.* to find the depth of.—*v.i.* to find the depth of water; to test, examine.
soup (sōōp) *n.* a liquid food made by boiling meat or vegetables.
sour *a.* acid; peevish, bad-tempered.—*v.t.* and *i.* to make or become sour.—**sour'ly** *adv.*—**sour'ness** *n.*
source (*sors*) *n.* a spring; origin.
souse *v.t.* to pickle; soak.—*v.i.* to soak; to fall into water, etc.—*n.* act of sousing.
soutane' (sōō) *n.* a cassock; the outer garment worn by R.C. ecclesiastics.
south *n.* cardinal point opposite the north; the region, or part of a country, etc. lying, to that side.—*a.* that is towards the south.—*adv.* towards the south.—**south'erly** (suth-) *a.*—**south'ern** (suth-) *a.*—**south'wards** *a.* and *adv.*—**sou'wester** *n.* waterproof hat.—**South'-down** *a.* of, or pert. to, the Hampshire or Sussex Downs.—*n.* sheep bred on the Hampshire or Sussex Downs.
sou'venir (sōō'ven-ēr) *n.* keepsake.
sov'ereign (sov'ran) *n.* a king; British gold coin worth 20 shillings.—*a.* supreme; efficacious; independent.—**sov'ereignty** *n.*
soviet' *n.* council, assembly forming part of Russian government.
sow *n.* female of the swine.
sow (sō) *v.i.* to scatter seed.—*v.t.* to scatter or deposit (seed); to spread abroad (**sowed** (sōd) *p.t.*—**sown** or **sowed** *p.p.*—**sow'ing** *pres. p.*).—**sow'er** *n.*
soy *n.* a kind of sauce for fish or meat, prepared from a bean; the plant.
soy'a, soy' (a) bean *n.* an edible bean used in many food stuffs.
spa (spȧ) *n.* a medicinal spring; a health-resort with one
space *n.* extent; period; area; expanse; the expanse of the universe; an empty place.—*v.t.* to place at intervals.
spa'cious *a.* vast, ample, roomy.
spade *n.* a tool for digging.—**spade'-press** *n.* in Australia, a primitive wool press in which wool is compressed with a spade.—**spade-work** *n.* arduous work preparatory to the main task.
spade *n. pl.* one of the suits at cards.—*sing.* a card of this suit.
spaghett'i *n.* a kind of macaroni.
span *n.* the space from the thumb to little finger as a measure (9 inches); an extent or space; the stretch of an arch, etc.; a team of oxen; of an aeroplane, distance across an arch or from wing-tip to wing-tip.—*v.t.* to stretch over; to measure with the hand; to harness or yoke.
spann'er *n.* tool for gripping nut of a screw, a wrench.
span'gle (-ng-gl) *n.* small piece of glittering metal on dress, etc., as an ornament.—*v.* to glitter.
spaniel *n.* breed of dog with long drooping ears and silky hair.
spank *v.i.* to move with vigour or spirit.—*v.t.* to slap with the hand.—**spank'ing** *a.* brisk; fine, big.
spar *n.* a pole, *esp.* as part of a ship's rigging; a crystalline mineral.
spar *v.i.* to box; dispute, *esp.* in fun.
spare (ėr) *a.* additional, in reserve; not in use; meagre, scanty.—*v.t.* to leave unhurt; abstain from using; do without, give away.—**spa'ring** *a.* saving economical.—**spa'ringly** *adv.*
spark *n.* a small glowing or burning particle; a trace; in internal combustion engines, electric spark which ignites explosive mixture in cylinder.—*v.i.* to emit sparks.—**spar'kle** *v.i.* to glitter, to flash.—**spark'ler** *n.*—**spark'less** *a.*—**spark'-lessly** *a.*—**spark'let** *n.* a small spark.—**spark-arrester** in electricity, a contrivance to prevent sparking where undesirable.—**sparking-plug** in internal combustion engines, plug screwed into cylinder head to carry electric current from outside to inside of cylinder.
spark *n.* a gay, lively, showy man; a lover.—*v.i.* to play the spark; to court.
sparr'ow (-ō) *n.* small brown bird.
sparse *a.* thinly scattered.
Spar'tan *a.* hardy; frugal.
spasm (-zm) *n.* a convulsive muscular contraction; a short spell of pain, energy, temper, etc.—**spasmod'ic** *a.* of the nature of a spasm; jerky; intermittent.
spat *n.* a short cloth gaiter.
spatch'cock *n.* a cock killed and cooked hastily on some sudden demand.—*v.t.* to thrust hastily into the middle of, as some additional matter in a written or telegraphed communication.
spate *n.* a sudden flood in a river.
spa'tial *a.* of space; existing in space.
spatt'er *v.t.* to splash, cast drops over.—*n.* a slight splash.—**spatt'erdash** *n.* a protection against splashes.
spat'ula *n.* tool with a broad blade, used for mixing paint, ointment, etc.
spav'in *n.* a tumour on a horse's leg.
spawn *n.* eggs of frogs, fishes, etc.—*v.i.* of fish, to cast eggs.
speak *v.i.* to utter words; to converse; to deliver a discourse.—*v.t.* to utter; communicate with (a passing ship) (**spoke** *p.t.*—**spo'ken** *p.p.*—**speak'ing** *pres. p.*).—**speak'er** *n.*—**speak'easy** *n.* (U.S.) a bar where illicit liquor is sold.
spear *n.* a long pointed weapon, a pike.—*v.t.* to pierce with a spear.—**spear'head** *n.* sharp, pointed head of spear; the forces in the van of an attack.—**spear'-mint** *n.* an aromatic garden mint much used for flavouring.
spe'cial (spesh'l) *a.* beyond the usual; particular, individual; distinct; limited.—**spe'cially** *adv.*—**spe'cialist** *n.* one who devotes himself to a special subject or branch of a subject.—**spe'cialism** *n.*—

spe'cialise *v.i.* to be a specialist.—*v.t.* to make special.—**special'ity** *n.* a special product, characteristic, etc.

Syn. peculiar, exceptional, unique, specific. *Ant.* general, usual, common.

spe'cie (spē'shi) *n.* coined money.

spe'cies *n.* a class of animals, plants, etc.; a subdivision (*sing.* and *pl.*).

specif'ic *a.* characteristic of a thing or kind; definite; specially efficacious for something.—*n.* a remedy for a particular ailment.—**specif'ically** *adv.*—**spe'cify** (-fī) *v.t.* to state definitely or in detail (**-ified** *p.t.* and *p.p.*—**-ifying** *pres. p.*).—**specifica'tion** *n.* detailed description.

spe'cimen *n.* an individual example; a part used to typify a whole.

spe'cious (spē-) *a.* having a fair appearance: plausible.—**spe'ciously** *adv.*

speck *n.* a small spot, particle.—*v.t.* to spot.—**spec'kle** *n.* and *v.t.* speck.

spec'tacle *n.* a show; a thing exhibited.—*pl.* an arrangement of lenses to help defective sight.—**spectac'ular** *a.* showy.—**specta'tor** *n.* one who looks on.

spec'tre *n.* a ghost.—**spec'tral** *a.*

spec'trum *n.* the coloured band into which a beam of light can be decomposed (**spec'tra** *pl.*).—**spec'troscope** *n.* an instrument for decomposing light and examining spectra.

spec'ulate *v.i.* make theories, guess; engage in risky commercial transactions (**spec'ulating** *pr. p.*).—**spec'ulator** *n.*—**spec'ulative** *a.*—**specula'tion** *n.*

spec'ulum *n.* a mirror; a reflector of polished metal, *esp.* as used in reflecting telescopes (**-la, -lums** *pl.*).—**spec'ular** *a.* having the qualities of a speculum; having a smooth, reflecting surface.

speech *n.* act or faculty of speaking; words; language; conversation; a discourse.—**speech'ify** *v.i.* to make a speech (**-ified** *p.t.* and *p.p.*—**-ifying** *pres. p.*).

speed *n.* swiftness; rate of progress.—*v.i.* to move quickly; to succeed.—*v.t.* to further; expedite; bid farewell to; to drive at high speed (**sped** or **speed'ed** *p.t.* and *p.p.*—**speed'ing** *pres. p.*).—**speedom'eter** *n.* instrument to show speed of moving vehicle.—**speed'y** *a.*—**speed'ily** *adv.*—**speeding** *n.* driving a motor-car at high speed, *esp.* on a road.—**speed cop** *n.* (*sl.*) policeman who patrols the highways on look out for dangerous driving.—**speed-boat** *n.* motor-boat built for high speeds.—**speed-up** *v.t.* and *i.* to increase one's speed.—*n.* an increase in a rate of work or production.—**speed'way** *n.* road reserved for fast motor traffic; a dirt-track for motor-cycle racing.—**speed'well** *n.* plant with blue flowers.

spek *n.* in S. Africa, bacon, fat.—**spek'-boom** *n.* a large shrub used as cattle food.—**spek'-vet** *a.* very fat, of a man, animal.

spell *n.* a magic formula; an enchantment.—**spell-bind'er** *n.* public speaker who entrances his audience.

spell *n.* a turn of work, etc.; a bout; in Australia, a rest during work.

spell *v.t.* to read letter by letter (**spelled** (speld) or **spelt** *p.t.* and *p.p.*—**spell'ing** *pres. p.*).—**spell'bound** *a.* fascinated.

spelt'er *n.* an alloy of zinc.

spen'cer *n.* a short woollen jacket.

spend *v.t.* to lay out; disburse; employ (**spent** *p.t.* and *p.p.*—**spend'ing** *pres. p.*).—**spend'thrift** *n.* a wasteful person.

spermacet'i *n.* fatty substance obtained from head of the sperm whale and used for making candles, ointment, etc.—**sperm' whale** *n.* the cachalot.

spew *v.t.* to vomit.

sphere *n.* a globe, ball; scope, range, province.—**spher'ical** *a.* round.—**sphe'roid** *n.* a body nearly a sphere in shape.—**spher'ics** *n.* branch of meteorology dealing with long-range electronic detection of atmospheric changes.

sphinx *n.* a symbolic figure, half-woman, half-lion, *esp.* Egyptian; an enigmatic person (**sphinx'es, sphin'ges** (-jēz) *pl.*).

spice *n.* an aromatic or pungent vegetable substance; spices collectively; a trace.—*v.t.* to season with spices.—**spi'cy** *a.*—**spi'cily** *adv.*

spick and span *a.* new and neat.

spi'der *n.* animal which spins a web to catch its prey.—**spi'der-line** *n.* the spider's web that, in a telescope, is used to gauge the exact position.

spiff'ing *a.* (*col.*) excellent.

spig'ot *n.* a peg for a hole in a cask.

spike *n.* an ear (of corn, etc.), a sharp-pointed piece of metal or wood, a nail.—*v.t.* to drive a spike into, supply with spikes, fasten with spikes.—**spi'ky** *a.*

spike'nard *n.* an aromatic substance got from an Eastern plant; the plant.

spill *n.* a splinter or twist of paper for use as a taper.

spill *v.t.* to shed; pour out; throw off.—*v.i.* to flow over (**spilled** (spild) or **spilt** *p.t.* and *p.p.*—**spill'ing** *pres. p.*).—*n.* a fall, accident, mishap.

spin *v.t.* to twist into thread; to revolve rapidly.—*v.i.* to make thread; to revolve rapidly (**spun** (archaic) **span** *p.t.*—**spun** *p.p.*—**spinn'ing** *pres. p.*).—*n.* a rapid run or ride; a spinning.—**spind'le** *n.* a rod or axis for spinning.—**spinn'er** *n.*

spin'ach (-ij) *n.* a vegetable.

spin'dle *n.* the rod on which spun thread is wound; axles, shafts, etc.

spin'drift *n.* spray blown along the surface of the sea.

spine *n.* a thorn; various things like this; a backbone.—**spi'nal** *a.*—**spine'less** *a.* having no spine; weak. [sichord.

spin'et *n.* musical instrument like a harp-

spin'ifex *n.* a kind of pointed grass, common in Australia.

spinn'aker *n.* a large triangular yacht sail spread by a boom.

spinn'ekop *n.* in S. Africa, a spider.
spinn'ey *n.* a small wood, copse.
spinn'ing *n.* the act or process of drawing out and twisting into threads, as wool, cotton, flax, etc.—**spinn'ing-jenny** a machine for spinning wool or cotton.—**spinn'ing-wheel** a machine for spinning wool, cotton, or flax into threads.
spin'ster *n.* an unmarried woman.
spi'ral *n.* a continuous curve round a cylinder, like the thread of a screw.—*a.* of this form.—**spi'rally** *adv.*
spire *n.* the pointed part of a steeple; a peak; a pointed stem; a coil.
spir'it *n.* vital principle; soul; a ghost; essential character or meaning; courage, liveliness; a frame of mind; a liquid got by distillation, *esp.* an alcoholic one.—*v.t.* to carry away mysteriously.—**spirit'less** *a.* without spirit.
spir'itual *a.* of the soul or spirit; caring for things spiritual; sacred, religious.—*n.* a negro sacred song or hymn.—**spir'itually** *adv.*—**spir'ituality** *n.*—**spir'itualism, spir'itism** *n.* belief that the spirits of the dead can communicate with living people.—**spir'itualist, spi'ritist** *n.*—**spir'ituous** *a.* alcoholic.
spirt *v.t.* and *i.* to send or come out in a jet.—*n.* a jet, violent gush.
spit *n.* a sharp rod to put through meat for roasting; a sandy point projecting into the sea.—*v.t.* to thrust through.
spit *v.i.* to eject saliva.—*v.t.* to eject from the mouth (**spit** (archaic) **spat** *p.t.* and *p.p.*—**spitt'ing** *pres. p.*).—*n.* a spitting; saliva.—**spit'fire** *n.* a shrewish, spiteful person; type of British fighter plane, used in World War II.—**spit'tle** *n.* saliva.—**spittoon'** *n.* a vessel to spit into.
spite *n.* malice, ill will.—*v.t.* to thwart spitefully.—**spite'ful** *a.*—**spite'fully** *adv.*
spiv' *n.* (*sl.*) a man who lives by his wits, within the law; a black-market hawker.
splash *v.t.* to spatter liquid over.—*v.i.* to dash, scatter (of liquids).—*n.* the sound or result of splashing; patch, spot.—(**splash'es** *pl.*).—**splash'-board** *n.* mudguard.
splay *v.t.* to spread out; make slanting.—*n.* slanting surface; spread.—*a.*
spleen *n.* an organ in the abdomen; irritable or morose temper.—**splenet'ic** *a.*
splen'did *a.* magnificent, gorgeous; excellent.–**splen'didly** *adv.*–**splen'dour** *n.*
Syn. shining, bright, effulgent, glorious. *Ant.* dull, insignificant, inglorious.
splice *v.t.* to join by interweaving strands; to join (wood) by overlapping; (*sl.*) to join in marriage (**spli'cing** *pres. p.*).—*n.* a spliced joint.
splint *n.* a rigid strip of material for holding a broken limb in position.
splin'ter *n.* split-off fragment, a chip.—*v.i.* to break into fragments.
split *v.t.* and *i.* to break asunder (**split** (rare) **splitt'ed** *p.t.* and *p.p.*—**splitt'ing** *pres. p.*).—*n.* a crack or fissure.—**split-stuff** *n.* in Australia, in the timber trade, material obtained by splitting as opposed to sawing, as rails, shingles, etc.
splutt'er *v.t.* to utter incoherently with spitting sounds.—*v.i.* to emit such sounds.—*n.* such sounds or speech.
Spode' *n.* a kind of chinaware.
spoil *v.t.* to damage or injure; to pillage; to damage the manners or behaviour of by indulgence.—*v.i.* to go bad (**spoiled** (spoild) or **spoilt** *p.t.* and *p.p.*—**spoil'ing** *pres. p.*).—*n.* booty.—**spolia'tion** *n.*—**spoil-sport** *n.* a person who likes to prevent others from enjoying themselves.
spoke *n.* a radial bar of a wheel.—**spoke'shave** *n.* a tool for shaping wood.
spokes'man *n.* one deputed to speak for others, representative.
spondu'lics *n.* (*sl.*) money; notes.
sponge (-unj) *n.* a marine growth used to absorb liquids.—*v.t.* to wipe with a sponge.—*v.i.* to live craftily at the expense of others.—**spon'gy** *a.*
spon'sor *n.* one who answers for an infant at baptism; a surety, a guarantor.
sponta'neous *a.* voluntary (said of persons); acting from its own energy, or by the law of its being produced without external force (said of physical effects, as growth, combustion, etc.).—**sponta'neously** *adv.*—**sponta'neousness** *n.*—**spontane'ity** *n.* voluntariness.
spoof *n.* humbug.—*v.t.* to fool.
spook *n.* a ghost.—*v.i.* in S. Africa, to haunt, as a ghost.—**spook'y** *a.*
spool *n.* bobbin, reel.
spoon *n.* implement with a shallow bowl at the end of a handle; golf club with a sloping wooden head.—*v.t.* and *i.* to transfer with a spoon; to make love with.
spoon'erism *n.* amusing transposition of initial consonants of phrase, e.g. "half-warmed fish" for "half-formed wish."
spoor *n.* the trail of wild animals; scent.—*v.i.* to follow a spoor.
spore' *n.* a single cell capable of growing into a new plant or animal; germ; seed.
sporad'ic *a.* occurring at intervals or in small numbers.—**sporad'ically** *adv.*
sporr'an *n.* a pouch worn in front of the kilt by Highlanders.
sport *n.* pastime; merriment.—*v.i.* to amuse oneself, take part in a game, etc.—**sport'ive** *a.* playful.—**sports'man** *n.* one who hunts, etc.; a good fellow.
sports *a.* suitable for, designed for, or connected with outdoor occupations of a recreational, athletic, or informal nature, e.g., sports clothes.—**sports mod'el** a fast open car.
spot *n.* a small mark or stain; a place.—*v.t.* to mark with spots, detect; in Australia, to select the best parts of an area.—**spot'less** *a.*—**spott'ed dog** *n.* a form of plum or raisin pudding.—**spot'light** *n.* circle of intense light; the

apparatus used.—**spot'ty** *a.* spotted.—**spot cash,** payment of cash on purchase or delivery.— **spot dance** a dance competition in which prizes are awarded to dancers stopping at a prearranged spot. —**in a spot** (U.S.) (*sl.*) in difficulties.—**on the spot** (U.S.) (*sl.*) in a difficult position or marked for assassination.

spouse *n.* a husband or wife.

spout *v.t.* and *i.* to pour out.—*n.* a projecting tube for pouring a liquid; a copious discharge, gush, jet.

sprain *n.* and *v.t.* twist (of a muscle, etc.).

sprat *n.* a small sea fish.

sprawl *v.i.* to lie with limbs spread out.

spray *n.* twig; a graceful branch or twig; flung drops of water; instrument for spraying.—*v.t.* to sprinkle.—**spray'er** *n.*

spread (-ed) *v.t.* to stretch out; scatter; to smear, put a layer on a surface.—*v.i.* to become spread (**spread** *p.t.* and *p.p.*—**spread'ing** *pres. p.*).—*n.* extent.—**spread'-eagle** *a.* (U.S.) bombastic.—*v.t.* to tie up with arms and legs spread out.—**spread'er** *n.* a bar to stretch.—**spread-over'** *n.* a system of compensation in an industry so that those who necessarily work irregular periods shall not be penalised in regard to total hours of work.

spree' *n.* lively frolic; drinking bout.

sprig *n.* a small twig; a small nail.

spright'ly (-rīt-) *a.* lively, brisk, vivacious.—**spright'liness** *n.*

spring *v.i.* to leap; appear; crack.—*v.t.* to produce unexpectedly (**sprang** *p.t.*—**sprung** *p.p.*—**spring'ing** *pres. p.*).—*n.* a flow of water from the earth; the first season of the year; a leap, recoil; a piece of coiled or bent metal with much resilience.—**spring'board** *n.*—**spring' drive** in motoring, transmission of engine power through springs.—**spring'-tide** *n.* a high tide at new or full moon.—**spring'-time** *n.*—**spring'y** (-g-) having elasticity.

spring'bok *n.* a S. African antelope, gazelle; a S. African international sportsman, *esp.* footballer.

springe *n.* a snare.

sprin'kle (-ng-kl) *v.t.* to scatter small drops on (**sprink'ling** *pres. p.*). *n.* small quantity.—**sprink'ler** *n.*

sprint *v.i.* to tun a short distance at great speed.—*n.* such run or race.

sprit *n.* a small spar crossing the sail of a boat, to extend and elevate it.—**sprit'-sail** *n.* a sail so extended.

sprite *n.* an elf, fairy.—**sprite'ly** *a.*

sprout *v.i.* to put forth shoots.—*n.*

spruce *n.* variety of fir.—*a.* neat, spry.

spru'it (sprōō-) *n.* in S. Africa, a small stream, feeder of a large one, *esp.* one dry in the hot weather.

spry' *a.* active, lively, nimble.

spud *n.* a small spade-like implement for weeding; (*sl.*) a potato.

spume *n.* and *v.i.* spray, foam.

spunk' *n.* touchwood; (*col.*) courage.

spur *n.* pricking instrument attached to a horseman's heel; projection on the leg of a cock; a projecting mountain range; a stimulus.—*v.t.* to apply spurs to; urge. —*v.i.* to ride hard.—**spur'-track** *n.* in N. America, a branch railway line to a factory, etc. (**spurred'** *p.t.* and *p.p.*).

spu'rious *a.* sham, not genuine.
Syn. illegitimate, false, fictitious, counterfeit. *Ant.* genuine, true, authentic.

spurn *v.t.* to reject with scorn.

spurt *n.* a short sudden effort; a jet, stream.—*v.* to rush out, squirt.

sputt'er *v.t.* and *i.* and *n.* splutter.

spu'tum *n.* spittle (**-ta** *pl.*).

spy *n.* one who enters hostile territory to observe and report.—*v.i.* to act as a spy.—*v.t.* to catch sight of (**spied** *p.t.* and *p.p.*—**spy'ing** *pres. p.*).

squab (-ob) *n.* an unfledged bird.

squab'ble (-ob-) *n.* a noisy quarrel.—*v.i.* to engage in one (**squab'bling** *pres. p.*).

squad (-od) *n.* a small party, *esp.* of soldiers.—**squad'ron** *n.* a division of a cavalry regiment, fleet, or air force.

squal'id (-ol-) *a.* mean and dirty.—**squal'or** *n.* filth, misery.

squall (-awl) *n.* a scream; a sudden gust of wind.—*v.i.* to scream.—**squal'ly** *a.*

squan'der (-on-) *v.t.* to spend wastefully.—**squan'derma'nia** *n.* passion for reckless spending, particularly of public money, without promise of profitable return.—**squan'dermaniac** *n.*

square (-ėr) *n.* an equilateral rectangle; an area of this shape; the product of a number multiplied by itself; an instrument for drawing right angles.—*a.* square in form; honest.—*v.t.* to make square; to find the square of; to pay; bribe.—*v.i.* to fit, suit.—**square'ly** *adv.* —**square'face** *n.* (*sl.*) gin.—**a square deal** a fair transaction.

squash (-osh) *v.t.* to crush flat or to pulp. —*n.* a crowd; a game played with rackets and soft balls on a court (*abbrev.* for **squash rackets**).

squat (-ot) *v.i.* to sit on the heels (**squatt'ed** or **squat** *p.t.* and *p.p.*—**squatt'ing** *pres. p.*).—*a.* short and thick.

squatt'er *n.* one who settles on land without title, or occupies vacant premises without leave; in Australia, a well-to-do pastoralist.

squaw *n.* a Red Indian wife or woman. —**squaw'man** *n.* in N. America, a white man with an Indian wife.

squawk' *n.* a short, shrill, harsh cry.—*v.i.* to utter a squawk.

squeak *v.i.* to make a short high-pitched sound.—*n.* such sound.

squeal *n.* a long, piercing squeak.—*v.i.* to make one.

squeam'ish *a.* easily made sick; over-scrupulous; easily shocked.

squee'gee (-jė) *n.* a piece of gutta-percha or rubber, fixed to a handle, for cleaning windows, pavements, etc.; a rubber roller used in photography, printing, etc. —*v.i.* to use as a squeegee on.

squeeze *v.t.* to press; subject to extortion.—*n.* an act of squeezing.

squelch (skwelch) *v.i.* to make a splashing, smacking sound as of watery suction or walking through mud.

squib *n.* a small firework; a short satire.

squid *n.* a cuttle-fish; **anti-submarine squid,** apparatus carried by escort and patrol warships for hurling depth-charges.

squint *v.i.* to have the eyes turned in different directions.—*n.* this affection of the eyes; *sl.* a glance, a peep.

squire *n.* a country gentleman; a lady's escort.—*v.t.* to escort (a lady).

squirm *v.i.* and *n.* wriggle.

squirr'el *n.* a small rodent living in trees and having a large bushy tail.

squirt *v.t.* and *i.* to eject, be ejected, in a jet.—*n.* an instrument for squirting.

stab *v.t.* to pierce with a pointed weapon. —*v.i.* to strike with such weapon.—*n.* a blow or wound so inflicted.

stabi'lity *n.* firmness, being likely to last. —**sta'bilise** *v.t.* to make steady, restore to equilibrium, *esp.* of money values, prices and wages.—**stabilisa'tion** *n.*

sta'ble *n.* a building for horses.—*v.t.* to put into one (**sta'bling** *pres. p.*).

sta'ble *a.* firmly fixed; resolute, steady. —**sta'bly** *adv.*—**stabil'ity** *n.*–**stabili'ser** *n.* a person or mechanism which gives steadiness, firmness or balance.

stacca'to *a.* disconnected; distinct (direction to play notes of passage in short, distinct and pointed manner).

stack *n.* a pile or heap, *esp.* of hay, etc.; a tall chimney.—*v.t.* to pile in a stack.

sta'dium *n.* a big open-air arena with spectator accommodation for public sporting events; a Greek measure equal to 606 ft. 9 in. (**sta'dia, -diums** *pl.*).

staff *n.* a pole; a body of officers or workers; the five lines on which music is written (**staffs, staves** *pl.*).

stag *n.* a male deer.—*a.* in N. America, (*sl.*) for men only, as in **stag hotel.**

stage *n.* raised floor or platform; the platform of a theatre; dramatic art or literature, scene of action; point of development; a stopping-place on a road, distance between stops.—*v.t.* to put (a play) on the stage.—**sta'gy** *a.* theatrical.

stagg'er *v.i.* to walk unsteadily, to sway, reel, totter.—*v.t.* to shock.—*n.* an act of staggering.—*v.t.* to arrange holidays, lunch-hours, etc., of workers so that they do not coincide for all at the same time.

stag'nate *v.i.* to cease to flow, be motionless.–**stag'nant** *a.*–**stagna'tion** *n.*

staid *a.* of sober and quiet character.— **staid'ness** *n.*—**staid'ly** *adv.*

stain *v.t.* and *i.* to discolour, blemish, soil; to spoil by disgrace.—*n.* a spot or mark.—**stain'less** *a.*—**stain'less cutlery** table knives having blades of rustless chromium steel.

stair *n.* a set of steps, *esp.* as part of a house.—**stair'case** *n.*–**stair'way** *n.* stairs.

stake *n.* a sharpened stick or post; money wagered or contended for.—*v.t.* to secure or mark out with stakes; to wager.

Stakhan'ovism (-kan'-ov-izm) *n.* a Russian system for increasing production by utilising the workers' initiative. —**stakhan'ovist -vite** *n.*

stal'actite *n.* a deposit of lime like an icicle on the roof of a cave.—**stal'agmite** *n.* a similar deposit on the floor.

stale *a.* old, lacking freshness.—*n.* urine of horses.—*v.i.* of horses, to make water. —**stale'mate** *n.* in chess, a draw through one player being unable to move.

Syn. insipid, musty, commonplace, hackneyed. *Ant.* sparkling, fresh, new.

Sta'linism *n.* the principles of the former Russian leader Josef *Stalin.*

stalk (-awk) *n.* stem of plant or flower.

stalk (-awk) *v.i.* to steal up to game; to walk in a stiff and stately manner.—*v.t.* to steal up to (game, etc.).—*n.* a stalking.

stall (-awl) *n.* compartment in a stable; an erection for the display and sale of goods; seat in the chancel of a church; front seat in a theatre, etc.—*v.t.* to put in a stall.—*v.i.* to stick fast; of an aeroplane, to lose flying speed; to give up working, *esp.* of an engine; (U.S.), to fence in conversation.—**stalling speed** that speed of an aeroplane below which steady flight becomes impossible.

stall *n.* an ambush; a stale; a stalking-horse; pretext; a thief's assistant.

stall'ion *n.* a horse not castrated.

stal'loy *n.* a silicon steel; used in wireless for cores of low-frequency transformers.

stal'wart *a.* strong, sturdy, brave.—*n.*

sta'men *n.* male or pollen-bearing organ of a flowering plant.

stam'ina *n.* strength, endurance.

stamm'er *v.i.* to speak with repetitions of syllables.—*v.t.* to utter thus.—*n.* the habit of so speaking.—**stamm'erer** *n.*

stamp *v.i.* to put down a foot with force. —*v.t.* to impress a mark on; to affix a postage stamp.—*n.* a stamping with the foot; an imprinted mark; an appliance for marking; a piece of gummed paper printed with a device as evidence of postage, etc.; character.

stampede' *n.* a sudden rush, *esp.* of terrified people or animals.—*v.t.* and *i.* to put into, take part in, a stampede.

stance *n.* a site; an area for building; a stand or stall in a market; position of the feet in certain games.

stanch *see* **staunch.**

stanch'ion (-un) *n.* a post or prop.

stand *v.i.* to have an upright position; to be situated; to become or remain firm or stationary; to be a symbol of, etc.—

v.t. to set upright; to endure; pay for drinks (**stood** *p.t.* and *p.p.*—**stand'ing** *pres. p.*).—*n.* stoppage; a holding firm; resistance; something on which thing may be placed, e.g. pedestal; structure for spectators, *esp.* **grand-stand**; growth of standing timber.

stand'ard *n.* a flag; weight or measure to which others must conform; degree, quality; an upright support.—**stan'dardise** *v.t.* to regulate by a standard.

stand'point *n.* point of view, opinion; moral or mental attitude.

stan'za *n.* group of lines of verse **zas** (*pl.*).

sta'ple *n.* a U-shaped piece of metal with pointed ends to drive into wood; a main commodity; the thread or pile of wool, cotton or flax.—*a.* pertaining to commodities; regularly produced or made for market; chief.—*v.t.* to sort or classify according to the length of fibre.—**sta'pler** *n.* a dealer in staple commodities.

star *n.* celestial body, seen as a twinkling point of light; an asterisk (*); a celebrated player; a medal or jewel, etc., of the shape of a star(*).—*v.i.* to take chief part (in film, play, etc.).—*v.t.* to mark with an asterisk.—**starry** *a.* full of stars; shining.—**star'-shell** *n.* a shell that on exploding sheds a powerful, lingering light.

star'board *n.* right-hand side of a ship, looking forward.—*a.* of, or on, this side. —*v.t.* to put (the helm) to starboard.

starch *n.* substance forming the main food element in bread, potatoes, etc., and used for stiffening linen, etc.—*v.t.* to stiffen with it.—**starch'y** *a.*

stare *v.t.* to look fixedly at; to be prominent or obvious.—*n.* a staring.

stark *a.* stiff; downright: absolute.—*adv.* quite, completely (e.g., in **stark mad**).

star'ling *n.* a speckled bird.

start *v.i.* twitch suddenly; to begin, *esp.* a journey.—*v.t.* to begin; set going.—*n.* an abrupt movement; an advantage of less distance to run in a race.—**start'er** *n.* person giving signal for start.

star'tle *v.t.* to surprise, give a fright to.

starve *v.i.* to suffer from cold or hunger; to die of hunger.—*v.t.* to kill or distress with lack of food, warmth, or other necessary thing.—**starve'ling** *n.* a starving person.—**starva'tion** *n.* starving.

state *n.* condition; a politically organised people; rank; pomp.—*v.t.* to express in words; fix.—**state'ly** *a.* dignified.—**state'ment** *n.* an expression in words; an account.-**states'man** *n.* one who is able in managing the affairs of a state.—**states'manship** *n.* his art.—**state'room** *n.* a separate cabin in a ship.

stat'ic, stat'ical *a.* pert. to bodies at rest, or in equilibrium, still.—*n.* in *pl.* the branch of physics studying such forces. —**statically** *adv.*

sta'tion *n.* place where a thing stops or is placed; position in life; post for firemen, soldiers, police, etc.; a stopping place for railway trains; in Australia, the homestead of a sheep or cattle farmer.—*v.t.* to put in a position.—**sta'tionary** *a.* not moving, fixed.—**cat'tle-station, sheep-station.**—**sta'tion-jack** *n.* in Australia, meat boiled in dough.

sta'tioner *n.* one who deals in writing materials, etc.—**sta'tionery** *n.* his wares.

statist'ics *n. pl.* numerical facts collected systematically and arranged; the study of them.—**statisti'cian, stat'ist** *n.* one who deals with statistics.—**statist'ic** *a.*—**statist'ically** *adv.*

stat'ue *n.* a solid carved or cast image of a person, etc.—**stat'uary** *n.* statues collectively.—**statuesque'** *a.* like a statue. —**statuette'** *n.* a small statue.

stat'ure *n.* height (of a person).

sta'tus *n.* position; rank, standing.

stat'ute *n.* a written law.—**stat'utory** *a.*

staunch, stanch *v.t.* to stop a flow (of blood) from.—*a.* trustworthy, loyal.

stave *n.* one of the pieces forming a cask; verse, stanza; cudgel, staff.—*v.t.* to break a hole in; to ward (off) (**stove, staved** (stāvd) *p.t.*/*p.p.*—**sta'ving** *pr. p.*).

stay *v.t.* to stop.—*v.i.* to remain; sojourn; reside for a time; pause (**stayed** (stād) or **staid** *p.t.* and *p.p.*—**stay'ing** *pres. p.*).—*n.* a remaining or sojourning.—**stay-in-strike** an industrial strike in which the workers refuse to leave the factory, etc., until their demands are granted.

stay *n.* a support, prop; a rope supporting a mast, etc.—*pl.* corsets.—*v.t.* to prop or support; satisfy.

stead (-ed) *n.* **in stead** in place; **in good stead** of service.—**stead'y** *a.* firm; regular; temperate.—**stead'ily** *adv.*—**stead'fast** *a.* firm, unyielding.—**stead'fastly** *adv.*—**stead'iness** *n.* being steady.
Syn. of "steadfast," fixed, established, resolute. *Ant.* unsteady, vacillating, irresolute, wavering.

steak (stāk) *n.* a slice of meat for broiling.

steal *v.i.* to rob; to move silently.—*v.t.* to take without right or leave (**stole** *p.t.* —**sto'len** *p.p.*—**steal'ing** *pres. p.*).-**stealth** (stelth) *n.* secrecy, slinking way.—**stealth'y** *a.*—**stealth'ily** *adv.*

steam *n.* vapour of boiling water.—*v.t.* to cook or treat with steam.—*v.i.* to give off steam; to rise in vapour; to move by steam power.—**steamboat** *n.*—**steam'-roller** *n.* a large roller moved by steam, for flattening or compressing road-surfaces, etc.; any great power used to over-ride opposition.—*v.t.* to flatten with a steam-roller; to over-ride all opposition. —**steam'er** *n.* a vessel for cooking or treating with steam; a steam-propelled ship.—**steam'y** *a.* of, like steam.

steed *n.* a spirited horse, war-horse.

steel *n.* a hard and malleable metal made by mixing carbon in iron; a tool or

weapon of steel.—*v.t.* to harden.—**steel'iness** *n.*—**steel'y** *a.*
steel'yard *n.* balance with unequal arms.
steen'bok *n.* a small African antelope.
steen'bras *n.* in S. Africa, a large, common sea fish.
steep *v.t.* to soak; saturate.
steep *a.* having an abrupt or decided slope.—*n.* a steep place.—**steep'ly** *adv.*
stee'ple *n.* a church tower with a spire. —**stee'plechase** *n.* cross-country horse-race.—**stee'plejack** *n.* man who repairs steeples and tall chimneys.
steer *v.t.* to guide, direct the course of.—*v.i.* to direct one's course.—**steer'age** *n.* the effect of a helm; part of ship allotted to passengers paying lowest fare.—**steers'man** *n.* one who steers a ship.—**steering column** in motor-car, hollow column carrying steering-wheel at top.—**steering-lock** maximum angular amount wheels can swivel from side to side.
steer *n.* a young male ox.
stel *n.* in S. Africa, a stand; a place; a spring-gun.
stell'ar *a.* of stars.
stell'enbosch *v.t.* in S. Africa, to supersede (a person), to remove an incompetent officer.
stem *n.* a stalk or trunk; the part of a word to which inflectional endings are added; the foremost part of a ship.
stem *v.t.* to check (**stemmed** *p.t.* and *p.p.*).
stench *n.* a bad smell.
sten'cil *v.t.* to paint with figures, etc., by passing a brush over a pierced plate.—*n.* the plate; the pattern made.
stenog'raphy *n.* shorthand writing.—**stenog'rapher** *n.*—**stenograph'ic** *a.*
stentor'ian *a.* very loud (of voice).
step *v.i.* to move and set down a foot.—*v.t.* to measure in paces; to set up (a mast).—*n.* an act of stepping; the mark made by the foot; a measure, an act, a stage in a proceeding; a stair, rung, etc.; action; to put the foot on; a degree in a scale; a mast socket.—**to step on it, the gas** *v.* (*sl.*) to hurry.
step'child *n.* the child of a husband or wife by a former marriage.—so **step'father** *n.*—**step'mother** *n.*—**step'brother** *n.*—**step'sister** *n.*—**step'daughter** *n.*—**step'son** *n.*—**step'parent** *n.*
steppe *n.* an extensive treeless plain in European and Asiatic Russia.
stereochem'istry *n.* the part of physical chemistry dealing with the geometrical structure of molecules and of atoms in relation to their optical or chemical properties.
ster'eoscope *n.* an instrument in which two pictures taken at different view-points are combined into one image with an effect of solidity.—**stereoscop'ic** *a.*
ster'eotype *n.* a plate for printing cast from set-up type.—*v.t.* to make a stereotype from; to make into an empty formula.—**stereotyped** *a.* fixed, unchanging; reduced to formula.
ster'ile *a.* barren; free from disease germs.—**steril'ity** *n.*—**ster'ilise** *v.t.*
sterilisa'tion *n.* the act of making sterile; the process of freeing from living germs; rendering incapable of procreating children, *esp.* the unfit.
ster'ling *a.* of standard value or purity; of solid worth; in English coin.
stern *a.* severe, strict; determined.—**stern'ly** *adv.*—**stern'ness** *n.*
Syn. harsh, unrelenting, hard, afflictive, cruel, immovable, dark, gloomy. *Ant.* lax, gentle, mild, yielding, irresolute.
stern *n.* the after part of a ship.
ster'torous *a.* characterised by a deep snoring; hoarsely breathing.
stet "let it stand" (a proof-reader's direction to cancel a correction).
steth'oscope *n.* instrument for listening to the action of the heart or lungs.
Stet'son *n.* in N. America, felt hat of finest quality (trade name).
ste'vedore *n.* skilled dock-worker who loads or unloads ships.
stew *v.t.* and *i.* to cook slowly in a closed vessel; *sl.* study hard.—*n.* food so cooked; a state of excitement.
stew'ard *n.* one who manages another's property; an attendant on a ship's passengers; an official managing a race-meeting, an assembly.—**stew'ardess** *fem.*
stick *v.t.* to jab, stab, fix, transfix, fasten. —*v.i.* to adhere; project, come to a stop, etc.; in S. Africa, to jib (**stuck** *p.t.* and *p.p.*—**stick'ing** *pres. p.*).—*n.* a rod.—**stick'y** *a.* adhesive, viscous.—**stick'-insect** *n.* an insect the body and legs of which resemble twigs.—**stick'er-up** *n.* in Australia, a bushranger.—**to stick away** to hide.—**to stick up** to hold up and rob; to rob; to bring a kangaroo to bay; to puzzle; perplex (**stick'ier** *comp.*—**stick'iest** *sup.*).
stic'kleback (-klb-) *n.* small spiny fish.
stick'ler *n.* one who insists on trifles.
stiff *a.* rigid; awkward.—**stiff'ly** *adv.*—**stiff'en** *v.t.* and *i.* —**stiff'ness** *n.*—**stiff'ly** *adv.*—**stiff'necked** *a.* obstinate.
stiff *n.* (*sl.*) a stupid or rough or hopeless or familiar person; (U.S.) (*sl.*) a corpse.—*a.* (*sl.*) excessive; high in price.
sti'fle *v.t.* to smother.—**sti'fling** *pres. p.*
stig'ma *n.* a brand, a mark (**stigmas** (-maz), **-mata** *pl.*).—**stig'matise** *v.t.* to mark out, describe (as something bad).
stile *n.* an arrangement of steps for climbing a fence or wall.
stilett'o *n.* a small dagger (**-os** (-ōz) *pl.*); pointed tool for making eyelet-holes.
still *a.* motionless, at rest, noiseless.—*v.t.* to quiet.—*adv.* to this time; yet; even. —**still'ness** *n.*—**still'y** *a.* quiet.—**still'born** *a.* born dead.—**still life** *n.* painting of inanimate objects.

still *n.* an apparatus for distilling.—**still'-room** *n.* a housekeeper's store-room.
still *n.* cinema photograph taken during the production of a film; enlargement of one unit of a film.
stilt *n.* one of a pair of poles with foot-rests for walking raised from the ground. —**stilt'ed** *a.* stiff in manner, pompous.
Stil'ton *n.* a fine cheese, originally popular at *Stilton*, in Huntingdonshire.
stim'ulus *n.* something that rouses to activity, incentive (**-uli** *pl.*).—**stim'ulate** *v.t.* to rouse up, spur.—**stim'ulant** *a.* producing a temporary increase of energy.—*n.* a drug, etc., doing this.—**stim'ulative** *a.*—**stimula'tion** *n.*
sting *v.t.* to thrust a sting into; to cause sharp pain to.—*v.i.* to be affected with sharp pain (**stung** *p.t.* and *p.p.*—**sting'ing** *pres. p.*).—*n.* a pointed weapon, often poisoned, of certain insects and animals; the thrust, wound, or pain of one.
stin'gy (-ji) *a.* mean; avaricious; niggardly.—**stin'gily** *adv.*—**stin'giness** *n.*
stink *v.i.* to give out a strongly offensive smell (**stank** or **stunk** *p.t.*—**stunk** *p.p.*—**stink'ing** *pres. p.*).—*n.* such smell.
stink'-hout *n.* a S. African tree; its useful but unpleasantly smelling wood.
stint *v.t.* to keep on short allowance.—*n.* limitation of supply or effort.
sti'pend *n.* salary, *esp.* of a clergyman.—**stipend'iary** *a.* receiving a stipend.—*n.* a stipendiary magistrate.
stip'ple *v.t.* to engrave in dots.—*n.*
stip'ulate *v.i.* to insist on, mention in making a bargain.—**stipula'tion** *n.*
stir *v.t.* to set or keep in motion.—*v.i.* to begin to move.—*n.* commotion.
stirr'up *n.* rider's foot-rest hung from saddle.—**stirr'up-cup** *n.* a drink given to a departing rider.
stitch *n.* a movement of the needle in sewing; its result in the work (**stitch'es** *pl.*); a sharp pain in the side.—*v.t.* and *i.* to sew.—**stitch-bird** *n.* a beautiful, rare, flightless bird of New Zealand.
sti'ver *n.* a Dutch coin.
stoat *n.* kind of weasel, ermine.
stock *n.* stump or post; a stem; a handle or piece to hold by; lineage; animals, materials, etc., requisite for farming, trade; a supply; the liquor used as a foundation of soup; various sweet-smelling flowers; money invested in a concern.—*pl.* a frame of timber supporting a ship while building; a frame with holes to confine the feet of offenders. —*v.t.* to supply with, or keep, a stock.—**stock'broker** *n.* an agent for buying and selling shares in companies.—**stock company** a theatrical company playing for a long season of different plays at one theatre.—**stock'ist** *n.* one who keeps a stock of certain goods.—**stock'-holder** *n.* in Australia, a grazier of cattle or sheep. —**stock'-horse** *n.* in Australia, a horse trained in working cattle or sheep.—**stock'-jobber** *n.* a dealer in stocks and shares.—**stock'man** *n.* in Australia, an experienced hand on a cattle or sheep station.—**stock'-riding** *n.* in Australia, art and practice of handling cattle, sheep, etc., on horseback.—**stock-route** *n.* in Australia, a fenced-in track in occupied land for the passage of cattle, etc.—**stock-size** a size of ready-made clothing to fit the average build.—**stock'-still** *a.* motionless.—**stock'-whip** *n.* a short-handled whip with a long lash used in working cattle, etc.
stockade' *n.* an enclosure of stakes.
stock'ing *n.* a close-fitting covering for the leg and foot; a wind indicator at an aerodrome.—**stockinet'** *n.* an elastic-knit textile fabric of which stockings, *v.t.* and *i.* to tend (a fire) (**sto'king** *pres.p.*). undergarments, etc., are made.
stocky' *a.* thick-set, sturdy.
stod'gy *a.* heavy, dull, indigestible.—**stodge** *n.* heavy solid food.
stoep *n.* in S. Africa, a covered verandah at the door of a house.
sto'gie *n.* N. America, a cheap, bad cigar.
sto'ic *n.* philosopher holding virtue to be the highest good and teaching indifference to pleasure and pain; a person of great self-control.—**sto'ic, sto'ical** *a.*—**sto'ically** *adv.*—**sto'icism** *n.*
sto'ker *n.* one who tends a fire.—**stoke** *v.t.* and *i.* to tend (a fire) **stoking** *pres. p.*).
stole *n.* a long, loose garment, reaching to the feet; a narrow band of silk or stuff, worn by deacons, bishops, and priests.
stol'id *a.* hard to excite.—**stol'idly** *adv.* —**stolid'ity** *n.* *Syn.* heavy, obtuse, slow. *Ant.* acute, active, susceptible.
stom'ach (-um'ak) *n.* the bag forming the chief digestive organ; appetite; inclination.—*v.t.* to put up with.—**stomach'ic** *a.*—**stom'achal** *a.*
stone *n.* a piece of rock; a gem; the hard seed of a fruit; a weight=14 lb.; a concretion formed in the bladder.—*v.t.* to throw stones at; to free (fruit) from stones.—**stone'-blind** *a.* quite blind.—**stone'-deaf** *a.*—**stone'chat** *n.* a variety of small bird.—**stone'ware** *n.* heavy common pottery.—**sto'ny** *a.*—**sto'nily** *adv.*
stonewall' *v.i* to obstruct business; to play a slow game, *esp.* in cricket.
stooge' *n.* (U.S.) (*sl.*) a person who is used by another to boost his position, or to impress others, scapegoat; (*theatre*) performer who always becomes the butt of another's jokes.
stook *n.* a collection of sheaves, usually twelve, set up in the field.—*v.t.* to set up, as sheaves of grain, in stooks.
stool *n.* a chair with no back; a place for evacuating the bowels; what is evacuated. —**stool pigeon** (*sl.*) a spy, an informer.
stoop *v.i.* to lean forward or down.—*n.* a stooping carriage of the body.

stop *v.t.* to fill up; to check, bring to a halt.—*v.i.* to cease, stay.—*n.* a stopping or being stopped; a punctuation mark; a set of organ pipes; the lever for putting it in action.—**stopp'age** *n.*—**stopp'er** *n.* a plug for closing a bottle.—**stop'gap** *n.* substitute in an emergency.—**stop-light** red light at rear of motor-car automatically switched on by application of brakes.—**stop'-off, stop'-over** in N. America, permission to break a railway journey temporarily.—**stop-press** *n.* news put into a newspaper at latest possible moment.—**stop'-watch** *n.* watch used for timing sporting events.

store *n.* abundance; stock; a place for keeping goods; in Australia, a bullock, cow, sheep, etc., bought to be fattened. —*pl.* stocks of goods, etc.—*v.t.* to stock, furnish, keep.—**stor'age** n.—**stor'age battery,** an accumulator.—**store-clothes** *n.pl.* in S. Africa, ready-made clothing.—**store'house** *n.*

stor'ey, story *n.* a horizontal division of a house (**stor'eys, stor'ies** *pl.*).

stork *n.* a large wading bird.

storm *n.* a violent wind or disturbance of the atmosphere; an assault on a fortress.—*v.t.* to take by storm.—*v.i.* to rage; to attack.—**storm'y** *a.*

storm' troop'er *n.* a member of the Nazi Party, trained to promote ruthlessly Hitler's ideology and system.

stor'y *n.* a tale; an account; *see* **storey.**

stout *a.* sturdy; fat; bold, vigorous, strong.—*n.* a kind of beer.—**stout'ly** *a.*—**stout'ness** *n.*—**stout-hearted** *a.*

stove *n.* apparatus for cooking or heating.

stove *p.t.* and *p.p.* of **stave.**

stow *v.t.* to pack away.—**stow'age** *n.*—**stow'away** *n.* one who hides himself in a ship to obtain passage.

strad'dle *v.i.* to spread the legs wide; (of bombs from aircraft or a salvo from guns) to fall in a line across the target.

strafe (-ȧ-) *v.t.* punish; bomb, attack.

strag'gle *v.i.* to stray, get dispersed; fall or lag behind.—**strag'gler** *n.*

straight (strāt) *a.* without bend; honest; level; in order; in N. America, undiluted, neat (of spirits).—*n.* straight state or part.—*adv.* direct.—**straight'en** *v.t.* and *i.* to make straight; to tidy.—**straight-for'ward** *a.* open, frank, candid, simple. —**straightfor'wardly** *adv.*

strain *v.t.* to stretch tightly; stretch to the full or to excess; filter.—*v.i.* to make great effort.—*n.* stretching force; violent effort; injury from being strained; a burst of music or poetry; tone of speaking or writing.—**strain'er** *n.* a filter.

strain *n.* a breed or race; streak, trace.

strait *a.* narrow, strict.—*n.* a channel of water connecting two larger areas.—*pl.* a position of difficulty or distress.—**strait'en** *v.t.* to make strait; to narrow; to press with poverty.—**strait'laced** *a.* puritanical.—**strait'-jacket, waistcoat** *n.* a jacket to confine the arms.

strake *n.* a continuous section of wood or plating along a ship's side.

strand *n.* shore.—*v.t./i.* run aground.—**strand'loper** *n.* S. Africa, ring plover; bushman living near shore.

strand *n.* one of the strings, threads or wires making up a rope.

strange (-ānj) *a.* unaccustomed, singular.—**strange'ly** *adv.*—**strange'ness** *n.*—**stra'nger** *n.* an unknown person; a foreigner; one unaccustomed (to).

Syn. unusual, peculiar, foreign, alien. *Ant.* usual, familiar, customary, native.

stran'gle (-ng-gl) *v.t.* to kill by squeezing the windpipe; to suppress (**strang'ling** *pres. p.*).—**strangula'tion** *n.*

strap *n.* a strip of leather or metal.—*v.t.* to fasten with a strap; to beat with one. —**strapp'ing** *a.* tall and well-made.—**strap'-hanger** *n.* traveller in a bus, etc., who has to stand, steadying himself by a strap provided for the purpose.

strat'agem *n.* an artifice in war; a trick, device.—**strat'egy** *n.*—**strat'egist** *n.*—**strate'gic** *a.* important in strategy.

stra'tosphere *n.* upper part of the atmosphere, in which temperature does not decrease with height.

stra'to-vision *n.* the broadcasting of television from the stratosphere to secure greater range of transmission.

stra'tum (strȧ-) *n.* a layer; a social level. (**-ta, -tums** *pl.*).—**stra'tify** *v.t.* to arrange thus (**-ified** *p.t./p.p.*—**-ifying** *pres. p.*).—**stratifica'tion** *n.*

straw *n.* dry, cut stalks of corn.—**straw'-berry** *n.* a creeping plant producing a red fruit; the fruit (**-ber'ries** *pl.*).—**straw'-board** *n.* cardboard made of straw.

stray *v.i.* to wander, get lost.—*a.* strayed; occasional.—*n.* a stray animal.

strays *n. pl.* in wireless, atmospherics.

streak *n.* a line, stripe, layer; a strain in the character.—*v.t.* to mark with streaks. —**streakiness** *n.*—**streak'y** *a.*

stream *n.* a flowing body of water, or other liquid; a moving crowd.—*v.i.* to flow; to run with liquid; to float or wave in the air. — **stream'er** *n.* a ribbon, pennon.—**stream'let** *n.* a small stream.

stream'line *n.* that shape of a body (e.g. motor-car, aeroplane) calculated to present the smallest amount of resistance to the air when passing through it.—*v.t.* to design a body streamline.—**stream'-lined** *a.*—**stream'lining** *n.*

street *n.* a road in a town or village with houses at the side.—**street-railway** *n.* in N. America, tram lines.—**street car** *n.* in N. America, a tram-car.

strength *n.* power, being strong.—**strength'en** *v.t.* and *i.* to make stronger.

stren'uous *a.* energetic, earnest; requiring much effort.—**stren'uously** *adv.*

streptococ'cus (-kok'-us) *n.* spherical microbe found in chain-like groups. —**streptococ'ci** *pl.*
streptomy'cin (mi'sin) *n.* a germ-killing substance (antibiotic) got from fission-fungi.
stress *n.* strain; impelling force; effort; emphasis.—*v.t.* to emphasise; to put mechanical stress on (he **stress'es**).
stretch *v.t.* to tighten, pull out; to reach out; to exert to the utmost.—*v.i.* to reach; to have elasticity.—*n.* a stretching or being stretched; an expanse; a spell.
stretch'er *n.* a person or thing that stretches; a bar in a boat for a rower's feet; an appliance on which a sick or disabled person can be carried.
strew (-ōō) *v.t.* to scatter over a surface (**strewed** (strewd) *p.t.*—**strewn** (strōōn, strōn), **strewed** *p.p.*—**strew'ing** *pres. p.*).
stri'a *n.* a small channel or thread-like line in the surface of a shell or other object (**stri'ae** *pl.*).—**stri'ate** *a.* streaked. —**striate** *v.t.* to streak.—**stria'tion** *n.*
strict *a.* defined; without exception; stern, not lax or indulgent.—**strict'ly** *adv.* —**strict'ness** *n.*—**stric'ture** *n.* a critical remark; a morbid contraction.
stride *v.i.* to walk with long steps.—*v.t.* to pass over with one step (**strode** *p.t.*— **stridd'en** *p.p.*—**strid'ing** *pr. p.*).—*n.* step.
stri'dent *a.* harsh in tone, shrill.
strife *n.* conflict, fighting; striving.
strike *v.t.* to hit.—*v.i.* to hit; to cease work in order to enforce a demand; to make a coin, etc.; to find gold, etc. (**struck** *p.t.*—**strick'en, struck** *p.p.*— **stri'king** *pres. p.*).—*n.* such stoppage of work.—**stri'ker** *n.* one that, or that which, strikes.—**stri'king** *a.* noteworthy.
string *n.* fine cord; a row or series.—*v.t.* to tie with or thread on string; gut or wire used in musical instruments (**strung** *p.t.* and *p.p.*—**string'ing** *pres. p.*).— **string'y** *a.* fibrous.—**string'y-bark** *n.* in Australia, eucalyptus having fibrous bark used as rope, etc.
strin'gent *a.* strict.—**strin'gency** *n.*
strip *v.i.* to lay bare, take the covering off.—*v.i.* undress; (of machinery, etc.) take to pieces.—*n.* long narrow piece.— **strip'ling** *n.* youth.—**strip'tease,** form of entertainment in which actress disrobes garment by garment.
stripe *n.* a narrow mark or band; a blow with a scourge.—*v.t.* to mark with stripes.
strive *v.i.* to try hard, struggle (**strove** *p.t.*—**striv'en** *p.p.*—**stri'ving** *pres. p.*).
stroke *n.* a blow; an attack of paralysis; a mark of a pen; a completed movement in a series; the rower sitting nearest the stern; in an internal combustion engine, the travel of piston during half a revolution.—*v.t.* to set the time in rowing; to pass the hand lightly over.
stroll (-ō-) *v.i.* to walk in a leisurely or idle manner.—*n.* a leisurely walk.
strong *a.* powerful; able to resist, firm (**strong'er** *comp.*—**strong'est** *sup.*)— **strong'hold** *n.* a fortress.—**strong'ly** *adv.*
stron'tium *n.* a metallic element.— **stron'tia** *n.* oxide of strontium.
strop *n.* piece of leather for sharpening a razor.—*v.t.* to sharpen on one.
structure *n.* make, construction.—*n.* a building, something made of various pieces.—**struc'tural** *a.*—**struc'turally** *adv.*
strug'gle *v.i.* to contend, fight; proceed or work with difficulty and effort.—*n.* a contest, effort.—**strug'gling** *pres. p.*
strum *v.i.* strike notes of stringed instrument unskilfully.—**strum'ming** *pr. p.*
strut *v.i.* to walk affectedly or pompously.—*v.t.* to support with struts.—*n.* such gait; a brace; rigid support, usually set obliquely; any short spar on an aeroplane.
strych'nine (-ik'nēn) *n.* a poison got from nux vomica seeds.
stub *n.* stump of a tree; a remnant of anything.—*v.t.* to strike, as the toes against a fixed object.—**stub-ax'le** motoring, a short swivelling axle on which the steering rod wheels run.
stub'ble *n.* stumps of cut grain.
stubb'orn *a.* unyielding, obstinate.— **stubb'ornly** *adv.*—**stubb'ornness** *n.*
Syn. refractory, unbending, obdurate. *Ant.* yielding, manageable, docile.
stucc'o *n.* plaster (**-coes, -cos** (-cōz) *pl.*).
stud *n.* a movable double button; nail with large head sticking out; a boss.—*v.t.* to set with studs;—*n.* a set of horses kept for breeding.—**stud'-farm** *n.*
stu'dio *n.* workroom of an artist, etc.; room or building where film plays are produced and photographed; room from which a broadcast is made. (**-dios** *pl.*).
stud'y *n.* effort to acquire knowledge; a subject of this; a room to study in; artistic composition, *esp.* in music or painting.—*v.t.* to make a study of; to try constantly to do.—*v.i.* to be engaged in learning (**stud'ied** *p.t.* and *p.p.*-**stud'ying** *pres. p.*).—**stu'dent** *n.* one who studies.— **stu'dious** *a.*—**stu'diously** *adv.*
stuff *n.* material, fabric.—*v.t.* to stop or fill up.—*v.i.* to eat greedily.—**stuf'fing** *n.* padding; seasoning for stuffing a fowl.— **stuff'y** *a.* lacking fresh air.
stult'ify *v.t.* to make look ridiculous, make of no effect (**-ified** *p.t.* and *p.p.*— **-ifying** *pres. p.*).—**stultifica'tion** *n.*
stum'ble *v.i.* to trip and nearly fall.— **stum'bling-block** *n.* obstacle, hindrance.
stump *n.* remnant of a tree, etc., when main part has been cut away; one of the uprights of the wicket at cricket.—*v.i.* walk noisily.—*v.t.* tour making speeches; break wicket of (batsman out of his ground in playing the ball).—**stump'y** *a.* —**stump orator** *n.* travelling speaker.— **to be stumped** be at a loss, at wits' end.
stun *v.t.* to knock senseless, to shock.— **stun'ning** *pres. p.*—**stunned'** *p.t.* and *p.p.*

stung (*sl.*) tricked, imposed upon.
stunt *n.* (*sl.*) a spectacular effort or feat.
stunt *v.t.* to check the growth of.—**stunt'ed** *a.* small, undersized.
stu'pefy *v.t.* to make stupid, deprive of full consciousness (**-efied** *p.t.* and *p.p.*—**-efying** *pres. p.*).—**stupefac'tion** *n.*
stupen'dous *a.* amazing; vast.
stupid *a.* slow-witted, dull, unintelligent.—**stupid'ity** *n.*—**stu'pidly** *adv.*
stu'por *n.* dazed state; torpor.
stur'dy *a.* robust, strongly built.—**stur'dily** *adv.*—**stur'diness** *n.* strength.
stur'geon *n.* a large fish valued as food.
stutt'er *v.i.* and *t,* to speak with difficulty, to stammer.—*n.* an act or habit of stuttering.
sty *n.* a place to keep pigs in (**sties** *pl.*).
sty, stye *n.* inflammation on eyelid.
style *n.* manner of writing, doing, etc.; designation; sort; superior manner or quality; pointed tool for writing on waxed tablets.—*v.i.* to designate, give title to.—**sty'lish** *a.* fashionable.—**sty'lishly** *adv.*—**sty'list** *n.* master of style.—**stylise'** *v.t.* to make or alter according to conventional style.
sty'mie *n.* formerly in golf; position in which a player had to putt for the hole with his opponent's ball directly in the line of approach; any difficult situation.—*v.t.* to place obstacle in the way.
styp'tic *a.* stopping bleeding.—*n.*
suave *a.* smoothly polite.—**sua'vity** *n.*
sub- *prefix* forms combinations with meaning of "under," "in lower position," etc., as in **sub-human** *a.* under or beneath the human.—**sub-normal** *a.* below normal. These words are omitted where the meaning may easily be inferred from the simple word.
subac'id *a.* moderately acid.
suba'gent *n.* a deputy-agent.
sub'altern *a.* of inferior rank.—*n.* an army officer below the rank of captain.
subcon'scious *a.* partially or feebly conscious.—*n.* in psycho-analysis, the unapprehended; that part of the human mind unknown to the possessor.
subdivide' *v.t.* to divide again.—**subdivis'ible** *a.*—**sub-divis'ion** *n.*
subdue' *v.t.* overcome(**subdu'ing** *pres.p.*).
sub'ject *a.* liable to, owning allegiance;—*n.* one owing allegiance; that about which something is predicated; conscious self; topic, theme.—**subject'** *v.t.* to make liable, or cause to undergo.—**subjec'tion** *n.* conquering; being controlled.—**subjec'tive** *a.* relating to self.—**subjectiv'ity** *n.*—**subject to,** conditional upon.
subjoin' *v.t.* to add at the end.
sub'jugate *v.t.* conquer.-**subjuga'tion** *n.*
subjunc'tive *n.* mood used mainly in subordinate clauses expressing wish, etc.—*a.* in or of that mood.
sublet' *v.t.* of a tenant, to let the whole or part of what he has rented to another (**sublet'** *p.t.* and *p.p.*—**sublett'ing** *pres.p.*).
sublime *a.* noble, grand, awe-inspiring.—**sub'limate** *v.t.* to purify; to heat into vapour and allow to solidify again.—*n.* a sublimated substance.—**sublima'tion** *n.* act of sublimating; in psycho-analysis, an unconscious process by which the repressed energy is directed into ways of cultural and social development.—**sublime'ly** *adv.*—**sublim'ity** *n.*
Syn. lofty, stately, dignified, glorious, grand. *Ant.* lowly, abject, ignominious.
sublu'nary (-ōō-) *a.* earthly.
sub'marine *a.* below the surface of the sea.—*n.* a submersible vessel, *esp.* warship carrying torpedoes, which can remain submerged for long periods.
submerge' *v.t.* to place under water.—*v.i.* to go under.—**submer'sion** *n.*
submit' *v.t.* to put forward for consideration, suggest; surrender.—*v.i.* surrender; urge.—**submiss'ive** *a.* humble, obedient.—**submis'sion** *n.* surrender, obedience; presentation for consideration or examination.
submul'tiple *n.* number that divides another without a remainder.
subord'inate *a.* of lower rank or importance.—*n.* one under the orders of another.—*v.t.* to make or treat as subordinate.—**subord'inately** *adv.*—**subordina'tion** *n.*—**subord'inative** *a.*
suborn' *v.t.* to bribe to do evil, *esp.* perjury.—**suborna'tion** *n.*
subox'ide *n.* an oxide containing one equivalent of oxygen and two of another element.
subpoen'a (-pēn'a) *n.* a writ requiring attendance at a court of law.—*v.t.* to summon by subpoena (**-naed** (-nad) *p.t.* and *p.p.*—**-naing** *pres. p.*).
subscribe' *v.t.* to write one's name at the end of a document; to pay or promise to pay (a contribution); express agreement.—**subscri'ber** *n.*—**subscrip'tion** *n.*
subsec'tion *n.* a division of a section.
sub'sequent *a.* later.—**sub'sequence** *n.*—**sub'sequently** *adv.* afterwards.
sub'serve *v.t.* to be useful to.—**subserv'ient** *a.* servile; serving a purpose.—**subserv'iently** *adv.*—**subserv'ience** *n.*
subside' *v.i.* to sink, settle; come to an end.—**sub'sidence** *n.*—**sub'sidy** *n.* money granted.—**sub'sidise** *v.t.* to pay a grant to.—**sub'sidiary** *a.* supplementing.
subsist' *v.i.* to exist.—**subsist'ence** *n.*
sub'soil *n.* soil beneath the surface soil.
subson'ic *a.* concerning speeds less than that of sound; below 700–750 m.p.h.
sub'stance *n.* matter; a particular kind of matter; chief part, essence; wealth.—**substan'tial** *a.* solid, big, important.—**substan'tially** *adv.*—**substantial'ity** *n.*—**substan'tiate** *v.t.* to bring evidence for.—**substantia'tion** *n.*-**sub'stantive** *a.* having independent existence.—*n.* a noun.
substa'tion *n.* a subordinate station.

sub'stitute *n.* thing, person in place of another.—*v.t.* put in exchange for (**sub'stituting** *pr. p.*).—**substitu'tion** *n.*
substra'tum *n.* that which is laid or spread under; a layer of earth, rock, etc., lying under another (**substra'ta** *pl.*).
subsume' *v.t.* to classify; to range with the particular included in the general.
subtend' *v.t.* to be opposite to.
sub'terfuge *n.* an evasion, lying excuse.
subterra'nean *a.* underground.
subtle (sut'l) *a.* ingenious, clever; acute; fine, faint.—**subt'ly** *adv.*—**subt'lety** *n.*
subtract' *v.t.* to take away.—**subtrac'tion** *n.*—**subtrac'tive** *a.*
sub'urb *n.* an outlying part of a city.—**suburb'an** *a.*—**subur'banite** *n.*
subven'tion *n.* a subsidy.
subvert' *v.t.* to overthrow, corrupt, destroy.—**subver'sive** *a.* causing overthrow.—**subver'sion** *n.* ruin.
sub'way *n.* an underground passage; electric railway below the ground.
succeed' (-ks-) *v.t.* to follow, take the place of.—*v.i.* to follow; to accomplish a purpose.—**success'** *n.* accomplishment, attainment; issue, outcome.—**success'ful** *a.*—**success'fully** *adv.*
succes'sion *n.* a following; a series.—**success'ive** *a.*—**success'ively** *adv.*—**success'or** *n.* one who succeeds another.
succinct' (-ks-) *a.* terse, concise.—**succinct'ly** *adv.*—**succinct'ness** *n.*
Syn. brief, short, compendious. *Ant.* rambling, loose, discursive.
succ'otash *n.* (*Amer.*) a mixture of boiled Indian corn and beans.
succ'our *v.t.* and *n.* help.
succ'ulent *a.* juicy.—**succ'ulence** *n.*
succumb' (-kum) *v.i.* to yield; to die.
such *a.* of the kind or degree mentioned; so made, etc.; of the same kind.
suck *v.t.* to draw into the mouth; to roll in the mouth.—*n.* a sucking.—**suck'er** *n.* a person or thing that sucks; an organ or appliance which adheres by suction; underground stem which makes new plant; (*sl.*) a person easily deceived; a toady, sponger, a hanger-on.
suc'kle *v.t.* to feed from the breast.—**suck'ling** *n.* an unweaned child.—**suc'tion** *n.* drawing in or sucking, *esp.* of air.
sudd *n.* a mass of floating water-plants, interlaced with trunks of trees, etc., forming islands on the White Nile.
sudd'en *a.* quick, unexpected, abrupt.—**sudd'enly** *adv.*—**sudd'enness** *n.*
su'dorific *a.* producing sweating.—*n.*
suds *n. pl.* froth of soap and water.
sue *v.t.* to seek justice from.—*v.i.* to make application or entreaty (**su'ing** *pres. p.*—**sued** *p.t.* and *p.p.*)
suède (swād) *n.* soft kid leather.
su'et (sōō'it) *n.* hard animal fat.
suff'er *v.t.* to undergo; permit.—*v.i.* to undergo pain, hurt, etc.—**suff'erable** *a.*—**suff'erance** *n.* toleration.—**suff'erer** *n.*
suffice' *v.i.* to be enough.—*v.t.* to meet the needs of (**suf'fi'cing** *pres. p.*).—**suffi'cient** *a.* enough.—**suffi'ciency** *n.*
suff'ix *n.* a letter or word added to the end of a word.—(-fiks') *v.t.* to add thus.
suff'ocate *v.t.* to kill by stopping breathing, stifle.—*v.i.* to feel suffocated.—**suffoca'tion** *n.*
suff'ragan *n.* an assistant bishop.
suff'rage *n.* a vote or right of voting.—**suff'ragist** *n.* one claiming a right of voting.—**suffragette'** *n. fem.*
suffuse' *v.t.* to well up and spread over.—**suffu'sion** *n.* suffusing; flush.
su'gar (shoog'-) *n.* a sweet crystalline vegetable substance.—**su'gary** *a.*
suggest' (suj-) to propose; call up the idea of.—**suggest'ive** *a.* full of ideas.—**suggest'ively** *adv.*—**sugges'tion** *n.*
su'icide *n.* one who kills himself intentionally; the act.—**suici'dal** *a.* causing suicide, disastrous.—**suici'dally** *adv.*
su'int *n.* the natural grease of wool.
suit (sūt) *n.* an action at law; a set, *esp.* of man's outer clothes; one of the four sets in a pack of cards.—*v.t.* to go with, be adapted to; meet the desires of; make fitting, etc.; to be convenient.
suit'able *a.* fitting, convenient.—**suit'ably** *adv.*—**suitabil'ity** *n.*—**suite** (swēt) *n.* a set of things going, or used, together, *esp.* furniture; a retinue.—**suit'or** (sūt-) *n.* one who sues; a wooer.—**suit'-case** *n.* flat rectangular travelling case.
sul'fa drugs, sul'pha drugs *a.* group of powerful synthetic drugs used to combat bacterial-infection.
sul'ky *a.* sullen.—**sulk** *n.* sulky mood.—*v.i.* to be sulky.—**sulk'ily** *adv.*
sull'en *a.* resentful, ill-humoured.
sull'y *v.t.* to stain, tarnish; he sullies (**sull'ied** *p.t.* and *p.p.*—**sull'ying** *pres. p.*).
sulphanil'amide (sulf-an-il'-a-mīd) *n.* one of the group of sulphonamides used to fight bacteria.
sul'phonal *n.* a heavy crystalline compound, a sedative, hypnotic, drug.
sulphon'amide *n.* the amide of a sulphonic acid; any of a group of drugs with antibacterial action.
sul'phur *n.* a pale-yellow non-metallic element.—**sul'phurous** *a.*—**sulphu'ric** *a.*—**sulphu'reous** *a.*—**sul'phate** *n.* a salt formed by sulphuric acid in combination with any base.—**sulpha'ting** *n.* a deposit of white lead sulphate on the plates of an electric accumulator left uncharged.
sul'tan *n.* ruler of a Mohammedan country; breed of hen.- **sulta'na** *n.* sultan's wife; kind of raisin.
sul'try *a.* hot and close.—**sul'triness** *n.*
sum *n.* amount, total.—*v.t.* to add up.
summ'ary *a.* done quickly.—*n.* an abridgement or statement of the chief points of a longer document, speech, etc.—**summ'arily** *adv.*—**summ'arise** *v.t.*
summa'tion *n.* an adding up.

summ'er *n.* second season.—**summ'er country** *n.* in N. Z., grazing land, etc., that can only be used during summer. —**summer-time** time shown by clocks advanced 1 hour during a part of the year fixed by law.
summ'it *n.* top, highest point.
summ'on *v.t.* to demand the attendance of; to call on or gather (e.g. strength).—**summ'ons** *n.* a call, authoritative demand, order.
sump *n.* the bottom of a shaft in which water collects; in motoring, a well in the crank-case containing lubricating oil.
sump'tuary *a.* regulating expenditure.
sump'tuous *a.* lavish, magnificent.—**sump'tuously** *adv.*—**sump'tuousness***n.*
sun *n.* luminous body round which the earth revolves; its rays.—*v.i.* to expose to sun's rays.—**sun'day** *n.* first day of the week.—**sun'flower** *n.* a plant with large golden flowers.—**sunn'y** *a.* —**sun'less** *a.*—**sun'bathing** *n.* exposure of the whole or part of the body to sunshine.—**sun'down** *n.* sunset.—**sun'-downer** *n.* in Australia, etc., a tramp who times his arrival at a station at sunset in order to obtain free food and lodging.— **sun'rays** *n. pl.* ultra-violet rays produced artificially and used in medicine.—**sun'shine roof** *n.* a roof for a saloon car which can be slid back.
sun'dae (-dā) *n.* an ice-cream decked with fragments of fruit and nuts.
sund'er *v.t.* to separate.—**sund'ry** *a.* several, divers.—*n. pl.* odd items.
sup *v.t.* to take by sips.—*v.i.* to take supper.—*n.* a mouthful of liquid.
su'per- *prefix* makes compounds with meaning of above, in excess, e.g., **super-hu'man** *a.* more than human.—**super-abund'ant** *a.* excessively abundant, etc. These are not given where the meaning may be found from the simple word.
su'perable *a.* that can be overcome.
superann'uate *v.t.* to pension off, or discharge as too old.-**superannua'tion** *n.*
superb' *a.* splendid, grand, impressive.
su'percar'go *n.* one in charge of the commercial affairs of a ship (**-goes** *pl.*).
supercharge' *v.t.* to charge or fill to excess.—**superchar'ger** *n.* in the internal combustion engine, a device to ensure complete filling of the cylinder with explosive mixture when running at high speed.—**supercharged** *a.*
supercil'ious *a.* indifferent and haughty.—**supercil'iously** *adv.*—**supercil'iousness** *n.* lofty superiority.
super-cin'ema *n.* a de luxe cinema theatre, *esp.* one with dance hall, café.
super-eg'o *n.* in psycho-analysis, that unconscious morality within the mind which directs the action of the censor.
superoga'tion *n.* a doing more than duty requires.—**supererog'atory** *a.*
superfi'cies (-fish'i-ēz) *n.* surface, area.
superfi'cial *a.* of or on a surface; without depth.—**superficial'ity** *n.*
super'fluous *a.* extra, unnecessary.—**superflu'ity** *n.*—**super'fluously** *adv.*
superfort'ress *n.* largest U.S. long-range bomber, in World War 2.
super-gear' *n.* in motoring, a type of gear giving 8 forward speeds.
superintend' *v.t.* to have charge of, overlook, manage, direct.—**superintend'-ent** *n.*—**superintend'ence** *n.*
supe'rior *a.* upper, higher in position or rank or quality; proud.—**superior'ity** *n.*—**superiority complex** *n.* in psycho-analysis, a sense of superiority, repressed below consciousness.
super'lative *a.* of or in the highest degree.—*n.* the superlative degree of an adjective or adverb, e.g. tallest.
super'man *n.* one superior to humans in intellect and morality.
supernat'ural *a.* being beyond the powers or laws of nature; miraculous.—**supernat'urally** *adv.*
supernu'merary *a.* in excess of the normal or necessary number.—*n. a* supernumerary person or thing.
superphos'phate *n.* manure made of bones treated with sulphuric acid.
supersede *v.t.* to set aside; supplant; take the place of.—**superses'sion** *n.*
superson'ic *a.* above the audible limit; concerning speeds greater than that of sound; more than 780 miles per hour.
supersti'tion *n.* unreasonable fear of the unknown; religion, opinion, practice based on belief in luck or magic.—**supersti'tious** *a.*—**supersti'tiously** *adv.*
su'per-tax *n.* a tax on large incomes in addition to income tax, now **sur'tax.**
super-tuned' (-tūnd) *a.* in motoring and aviation, tuned to racing pitch.
supervene' *v.i.* to happen as an interruption or change.—**superven'tion** *n.*
su'pervise *v.t.* to superintend, oversee. —**supervi'sion** *n.*—**supervi'sor** *n.*
su'pine *a.* indolent; lying on the back.—*n.* a Latin verbal noun.
Syn. sluggish, torpid, careless. *Ant.* alert, brisk, quick, industrious, careful.
supp'er *n.* the last meal of the day.
supplant *v.t.* to take the place of, *esp.* unfairly.—**supplant'er** *n.*
sup'ple *a.* pliable.—**sup'ply** *adv.*—**sup'ple-jack** *n.* a strong pliant cane; a walking-stick made from the cane.
sup'plement *n.* something added to fill up, supply a deficiency.—(**-ment'**) *v.t.* to add to.—**supplement'ary** *a.* additional.
supp'licate *v.t.* and *i.* to beg humbly.—**supplica'tion** *n.*—**supp'licatory** *a.*-**supp'-liant** *a.* petitioning.—*n.* a petitioner.
supply' *v.t.* to furnish; substitute for (**-plied'** *p.t./p.p.*—**ply'ing** *pr. p.*).—*n.* a supplying, substitute; stock, store.
support' *v.t.* to hold up; assist; sustain.

—*n.* a supporting or being supported, or means of support.—**support'able** *a.*—**support'er** *n.* person who supports.
suppose' *v.t.* to assume as a theory; take for granted; accept as likely.—**suppo'sedly** *adv.*—**suppo'sable** *a.*—**supposition** *n.*—**suppositi'tious** *a.* sham.
suppress' *v.t.* to crush, put down; restrain, keep back, check.—**suppres'sion** *n.*—he **suppress'es.**—**suppres'sive** *n.* a drug which removes the symptoms of a disease without curing it.
supp'urate *v.i.* to fester, become septic.—**suppura'tion** *n.*
supra- *prefix* over, above, as **supramundane** *a.* above the world.
supralat'eral *a.* situated on the upper part of the side.
supralu'nar (-lōō-) *a.* beyond the moon.
supreme' *a.* highest.—**supreme'ly** *adv.* —**suprem'acy** *n.* highest authority; power or domination.
surcease' *v.t.* to cause to cease.—*v.i.* to cease.—*n.* cessation.
sur'charge *n.* an additional charge; a charge against a responsible official.—*v.t.* to exact such charge; to overload.
surd *a.* not capable of being expressed in rational numbers, e.g. square root of 2; radical; not sonant.—*n.* such a quantity.
sure (shōōr) *a.* certain; trustworthy.— —*adv.* in N. America, surely, doubtless, certainly.—**sure'ly** *adv.*
sure'ty *n.* certainty; security against loss, etc.; one making himself responsible for obligations of another. (**'ties** *pl.*).
surf *n.* foam of breaking waves.
sur'face (-fis) *n.* outside face of a body exterior; a plane; top visible side; outward appearance.
sur'feit (-fit) *n.* excess, *esp.* of food.—*v.t.* and *i.* to feed to excess.
surge *v.i.* to move in large waves, swell. —*n.* wave; in electricity, a sudden rush of current in a circuit.
sur'geon (-jn) *n.* medical expert who performs operations.—**sur'gery** *n.* treatment by operation; doctor's consulting room.—**sur'gical** *a.*—**sur'gically** *adv.*
sur'icate *n. see* **meercat.**
sur'ly *a.* gloomily morose; ill-natured; cross and rude.—**surlily** *adv.*—**surliness** *n.*
surmise' *v.t.* and *i.* and *n.* guess.
surmount' *v.t.* to get over, overcome; to be on top of.—**surmount'able** *a.*
sur'name *n.* family name.—*v.* to give a name.—**surnom'inal** *a.*
surpass' *v.t.* to outdo, to excel.
surp'lice (-plis) *n.* a loose white vestment worn by clergy and choristers.
sur'plus *n.* what remains over.
surprise' *n.* what takes unawares; the emotion roused by being taken unawares.—*v.t.* to cause surprise to.
surre'alism (sur-rē'-a-lizm) *n.* a movement in art and literature for the liberation and expression of the unconscious.—**surrealist** *n.*
surren'der *v.t.* to hand over.—*v.i.* to yield.—*n.* an act of surrendering.
surrepti'tious *a.* done secretly or stealthily.—**surrepti'tiously** *adv.*
surr'ogate *n.* deputy, *esp.* of a bishop.
surround *v.t.* to be or come all round, hem in.—**surround'ings** *n. pl.* neighbourhood, scenery, environment.
sur'tax *n.* an additional tax.—*v.t.* to impose a surtax on.
surveill'ance (ser-vāl'-) *n.* close watch.
survey' *v.t.* to view; to measure or map (land).—**sur'vey** *n.*—**survey'or** *n.*
survive' *v.t.* to outlive; to come alive through.—*v.i.* to continue to live or exist.—**survi'val** *n.*—**survi'vor** *n.*
suscep'tible *a.* sensitive; impressionable; (of) admitting of.—**susceptibil'ity** *n.*
suspect' *v.t.* to have an impression of the existence or presence of; to be inclined to believe, to doubt the innocence of.—*a.* of suspected character.—*n.* a suspected person.—**suspi'cion** *n.* a suspecting.–**suspi'cious** *a.*–**suspi'ciously** *adv.*
suspend' *v.t.* to hang up; to sustain in fluid; to cause to cease for a time, keep inoperative.—**suspend'er** *n. pl.* straps for supporting stockings or, in Amer., braces. —**suspense'** *n.* state of uncertainty.—**suspen'sion** *n.* a state of being hung up, or debarred; being suspended; in motoring, duty of springs to support frame and body of motor-vehicle on axles.—**suspen'sory** *a.*
sustain' *v.t.* to keep or hold up; endure; confirm.—**sustain'able** *a.*—**sus'tenance** *n.* food.—**sustenta'tion** *n.* maintenance.
Syn. nourish, aid, support, approve, justify. *Ant.* let down, abandon, lose.
sut'ler *n.* campfollowerselling provisions.
su'zerain *n.* a feudal lord; a sovereign with rights over an autonomous state.—**suz'erainty** *n.* authority of suzerain.
svelte *a.* lightly built; supple; graceful.
swab (-ob) *n.* a mop; a pad of surgical wool.—*v.t.* to clean with a swab.
swad'dle (-od-) *v.t.* to swathe.—**swaddling-bands** (**-clothes**) *n. pl.* clothes in which an infant is swathed.
swag *v.i.* to sway, sag; in Australia, to tramp the bush carrying a swag.—*n.* a bundle; baggage; stolen property.—**swagg'ie, swag'man, swag'sman, swagg'erer** *n.* Australia, a tramp who carries his belongings in a bundle, wrapped up in a blanket called a bluey (q.v.).
swagg'er *v.i.* to strut; to talk boastfully. —*n.* a strutting gait; a boastful manner.
swain *n.* a rustic; a lover.
swall'ow (-ol'ō) *n.* a migratory bird with a skimming manner of flight.
swall'ow (-ol'ō) *v.t.* to cause or allow to pass down the gullet; to engulf.
swamp (-omp) *n.* a marsh, bog.—*v.t.* to entangle in a swamp; to overwhelm; flood, soak.—**swamp'y** *a.*

swan (-on) large water bird with graceful curved neck (the young are **cyg'nets**).
swank *a.* pliant, agile; active.—*v.i.* (*sl.*) to swagger; to boast, bounce; to show off.—*n.* (*sl.*) bluster, swagger.—**swank'y** *a.* (*sl.*) smart; showy; swaggering.
swap, swop *v.t.* to exchange; to barter.
swaraj' *n.* political party in India which worked for home rule.—**swara'jist** *n.*
sward (-ord) *n.* turf, short grass.
swarm (-orm) *n.* large number of animals or insects; a vast crowd.—*v.i.* of bees, to emigrate in a swarm; to crowd.
swarm (-orm) *v.i.* to climb, clamber by gripping with hands and knees.
swart (-ort) *a.* dark in colour.—**swar'thy** *a.* dark-complexioned.
swas'tika *n.* a form of cross (卍); ancient religious symbol adopted by the German National Socialist Party as its emblem.
swat (swot) *v.t.* to hit smartly.
swath *n.* a line of grass or grain cut and thrown together by the scythe; the whole sweep of a scythe.
swathe *v.t.* to cover with wraps or bandages.—*n.* a bandage.
sway *v.i.* to swing unsteadily.—*v.t.* to make to do this; to influence, govern.
swear *v.t.* to promise on oath; to cause to take an oath.—*v.i.* to curse (**swore** *p.t.* —**sworn** *p.p.*— **swear'ing** *pres. p.*).
sweat (swet) *n.* moisture oozing from the skin.—*v.i.* to exude sweat; to toil.—*v.t.* to cause to sweat; to employ at wrongfully low wages (**sweat** or **sweat'ed** *p.t.* and *p.p.* —**sweat'ing** *pres. p.*).—**sweat'er** *n.* an athlete's woollen jersey.
swede *n.* a variety of turnip.
sweep *v.i.* to pass quickly or magnificently; to extend in a continuous curve. —*v.t.* to clean with a broom; to carry impetuously (**swept** *p.t./p.p.*—**sweep'ing** *pr. p.*).—*n.* a sweeping motion; a wide curve; range; an act of cleaning with a broom; a long oar; one who cleans chimneys; *abbrev.* of "sweepstake."—**sweep'stake** *n.* gamble in which winner takes stakes contributed by all.
sweet *a.* tasting like sugar; agreeable; tuneful; in good condition.—*n.* the sweet part; a sweetmeat.—*pl.* sweet dishes at table; delights.—**sweet'en** *v.t.* and *i.*—**sweet'ly** *adv.*—**sweet'ish** *a.*—**sweet'bread** *n.* an animal's pancreas as food.—**sweet'-brier** *n.* a wild rose.—**sweet'meat** *n.* a piece of confectionery.—**sweet'heart** *n.* a lover.—**sweetpea'** *n.* garden plant with bright, scented flowers.—**sweet pota'to** *n.* S. Africa, etc., a trailing plant; its sweetish, starchy, edible tubers.
Syn. luscious, redolent, soft, harmonious, dulcet, lovely, delightful, charming, mild, tender. *Ant.* bitter, acid, sour.
swell *v.i.* to expand.—*v.t.* to cause to expand (**swelled** (**sweld**) *p.t.*-**swo'llen** *p.p.* —**swell'ing** *pres. p.*).—*n.* an act of swelling or being swollen; the heave of the sea after a storm; a mechanism in an organ to vary the volume of sound; (*col.*) *n.* fashionable, well-dressed person. —*a.* (*col.*) smart, first rate, high class.—**swell'ing** *n.* painful, swollen spot.
swelt'er *v.i.* to sweat profusely, or be oppressed with heat.
swer'noot *n.* S. Africa, term of abuse.
swerve *v.i.* to swing round, change direction during motion; a swerving.
swift *a.* rapid, quick, ready.—*n.* bird like a swallow.—**swift'ly** *adv.*—**swift'ness** *n.*
swill *v.t.* to pour water over or through; to drink greedily.—*v.i.* to drink greedily. —*n.* a rinsing; liquid food for pigs.
swim *v.i.* to support and move oneself in water; to float; to be flooded.—*v.t.* to cross by swimming (**swam** *p.t.*—**swum** *p.p.*—**swimm'ing** *pres. p.*).—**swimm'er** *n.*
swim *v.i.* to have a feeling of dizziness, to be giddy (**swam** *p.t.*—**swum** *p.p.*—**swimm'ing** *pres. p.*).
swind'ler *n.* a cheat.—**swin'dle** *v.t.* and *i.* and *n.* cheat (**swind'ling** *pres. p.*).
swine *n.* pig, hog; coarse brutal person. (**swine** *pl.*).—**swine'herd** *n.*—**swi'nish** *a.*
swing *v.i.* to move to and fro, *esp.* as a suspended body; to revolve.—*v.t.* to cause to swing; to suspend (**swung** *p.t.* and *p.p.*—**swing'ing** *pres. p.*).—*n.* an act of swinging; a seat hung to swing on; syncopated music, jazz.—**swing'-boat** *n.* —**swing'-gate** *n.* Australia, gate used in drafting sheep.—**to swing the lead** fighting services (*sl.*) to malinger.
swipe *v.t.* and *i.* to hit with a sweeping stroke; (*sl.*) to steal.—*n.*
swirl *v.i.* to move with an eddying motion; to whirl, move round swiftly.
swish *v.i.* to swing a rod, etc., with a hissing sound; to move with a similar sound.—*v.t.* to swing thus; to cane.—*n.* hissing sound; stroke of cane.
switch *n.* flexible stick or twig; a device for making and breaking an electric circuit, etc., a movable rail at junctions. —*v.t.* to strike with a switch; to affect (current, etc.) with a switch; to swing round abruptly; to turn from one railway line to another.—**switch'board** *n.* a device by means of which connections can be established readily between the many circuits employed in electrical systems.
swiv'el *n.* a mechanism of two parts which can revolve the one on the other. —*v.t.* and *i.* to turn on a swivel.
swiz'zle *n.* (*col.*) a drink compounded of rum, sugar and bitters, poured over crushed ice.—**swiz'zle stick** *n.* an instrument, frequently of silver, used to de-aerate alcoholic or soft drinks.
swoon *v.i./n.* faint, lose consciousness.
swoop *v.i.* to come down like a hawk.—*n.* a swift downward sweep; attack.
sword (sord) *n.* a weapon, a long blade for cutting or thrusting.—**sword'-fish** *n.* a fish with a long sharp upper jaw.

swot *v.t.* and *i.* (*sl.*) to study hard.
syb'arite *n.* a luxurious person.
syc'amore *n.* tree resembling the plane.
syc'ophant *n.* a toady, flatterer.—**sycophant'ic** *n.*—**syc'ophancy** *n.*
syll'able *n.* a division of a word as a unit for pronunciation.—**syllab'ic** *a.*
syll'abus *n.* a programme, outline of a course of study (**-buses** (-ēz), **-bi** (-bī) *pl.*).
syll'ogism (-j-) *n.* a form of logical reasoning consisting of two premises and a conclusion.—**syllogist'ic** *a.*
sylph *n.* an air spirit or elemental.
syl'van *a.* wooded, rustic (also **silvan**).
sym'bol *n.* a sign; a thing representing or typifying something.—**symbol'ic** *a.*—**symbol'ically** *adv.*—**sym'bolise** *v.t.*—**sym'bolism** *n.* representation (of abstract ideas) by means of symbols; in psycho-analysis, indirect manifestation of repressed tendencies.
symm'etry *n.* proportion between parts; balance of arrangement between sides.—**symmet'rical** *a.*—**symmet'rically** *adv.* *Syn.* shapeliness, harmony, order. *Ant.* disparity, incongruity.
sym'pathy *n.* feeling for another in pain, etc.; sharing of emotion, interest, desire, etc.—**sympathet'ic** *a.*—**sympathet'ically** *adv.*—**sym'pathise** *v.i.*
sym'phony *n.* a harmony of sounds; a composition for a full orchestra.—**symphon'ic** *a.*—**sympho'nious** *a.* harmonious.
sympo'sium *n.* a drinking party, a friendly discussion; a set of articles or broadcast talks by various authors on the same subject (**sympo'sia** *pl.*).
symp'tom *n.* a sign or token; a change in the body indicating its state of health or disease.—**symptomat'ic** *a.*
syn- with its forms **sy-**, **syl-**, **sym-** *prefix* together, with; as **syntax, system, syllogism, sympathy, symphony.**
syn'agogue *n.* a Jewish congregation or its meeting-place for worship.
syn'chronise *v.t.* to make agree in time.—*v.i.* to happen at the same time.—**syn'chronism** *n.*—**synchronisa'tion** *n.*
syn'chrotron *n.* (sing'-kro-) a machine, using a combination of electrical and magnetic forces, for accelerating electrons.
syn'cope (-pi) *n.* fainting; a syncopated spelling, etc.—**syn'copate** *v.t.* to shorten by the omission of an interior element (in words, music, etc.).—**syncopa'tion** *n.*
syn'dic *n.* a chief magistrate; one chosen to transact business for others.—**syn'dicalism** *n.* an economic movement, combination of workers in all trades to enforce the demands of labour by strikes.
syn'dicate *n.* a body of persons associated for some enterprise.—*v.t.* to publish news, articles, etc., simultaneously in several periodicals owned by one syndicate.—**syndica'tion** *n.*
synec'doche (-nek'-do-kē) *n.* a figure or trope by which the whole of a thing is put for a part, or a part for the whole.
syn'od *n.* a church assembly, council.
syn'onym *n.* a word having the same meaning as another.—**synon'ymous** *a.* meaning the same.—**synonym'ity** *n.*
synop'sis *n.* a summary (**synop'ses** *pl.*).
synop'tic *a.* having the same viewpoint.
syn'tax *n.* the part of grammar treating of the arrangement of words in sentences.—**syntact'ic** *a.*—**syntact'ically** *adv.*
syn'thesis *n.* a putting together, combination (**-theses**) (-ēz) *pl.*).—**synthet'ic** *a.*—**synthet'ically** *adv.*—**syn'thetist** *n.*
syn'tony *n.* in wireless, state in which natural frequencies of oscillations of two tuned circuits are equal.
syph'ilis *n.* a venereal disease.
sy'ren *n.* *see* **siren.**
syr'inge *n.* an instrument for drawing in liquid by a piston and forcing it out in a fine stream.—*v.t.* to spray with a syringe.
syr'up *n.* a thick solution of sugar and water; treacle.—**syr'upy** *a.*
sys'tem *n.* a complex whole; an organisation; method; classification.—**systemat'ic** *a.*—methodical.—**systemat'ically** *adv.* **sys'tematise** *v.t.* to arrange into, reduce to a system
sys'tole (-to-lē) *n.* the shortening of a long syllable; the contraction of the heart and arteries for expelling the blood and carrying on the circulation.—**systol'ic** *a.* contracting.

T

Taal (tál) *n.* "Cape Dutch," **Afrikaans.** (Obsolete name.)
tab *n.* a tag, label, short strap or loop.
tab'ard *n.* a herald's short, loose coat.
tabb'y *n.* a brindled cat; a she-cat.
tab'ernacle *n.* a tent or booth; a non-conformist place of worship.
ta'ble *n.* a piece of furniture with a flat top supported by legs, brackets, etc.; a tablet; food; a set of facts or figures arranged in lines or columns.—*v.t.* to lay on a table.—**ta'ble-land** *n.* a plateau.
tab'leau (-lō) *n.* a dramatic scene; representation of a scene by a group of persons.—**tab'leaux** (-lō) *pl.*—**tableau-vivant** (tab'lō vē'vaṅ) *n.* a group of persons, silent and motionless, arranged to represent some scene.
tab'let *n.* a small flat slab.—**tabloid** *a.* concentrated, brief.—*n.* a tablet containing a specified portion of a drug (protected trade name); an illustrated, popular newspaper with terse, sensational headlines, *esp.* in New York.
taboo' *n.* a setting apart of a thing as sacred or accursed; a ban or prohibition (**-boos** *pl.*).—*a.* put under a taboo.

ta'bor *n.* a small drum.—**tab'ouret** *a.* a low stool; embroidery frame.
tab'ular *a.* shaped or arranged like a table.—**tab'ulate** *v.t.* to arrange (figures, facts, etc.) in tables.
tac'it (tas'-) *a.* implied but not spoken.—**tac'itly** *adv.*—**tac'iturn** *a.* talking little, habitually silent.—**taciturn'ity** *n.*
Syn. inferred, understood, secret, quiet, still, taciturn. *Ant.* overt, manifest, spoken, express, explicit.
tack *n.* a small nail; a long loose stitch; a rope at the corner of a sail; the course of a ship obliquely to windward.—*v.t.* to nail with tacks; to stitch lightly; to beat to windward on a zig-zag course.—**tack'y** *a.* sticky (of varnish, etc.).
tack'ies *n. pl.* S. Africa, rubber-soled shoes.
tac'kle *n.* equipment, apparatus, *esp.* lifting appliances with ropes.—*v.t.* to take in hand; to seize *esp.* as in Rugby football (**tack'ling** *pres. p.*).
tact *n.* skill in dealing with people or situations.—**tact'ful** *a.*—**tact'less** *a.*—**tact'fully** *adv.*—**tact'lessly** *adv.*—**tact'ile** *a.* of or relating to the sense of touch.
tact'ics *n. pl.* art of handling troops, ships, planes in battle.—**tact'ical** *a.*—**tacti'cian** *n.* one skilled in tactics.
tad'pole *n.* young frog in the tailed stage.
tae'po, tai'po *n.* in New Zealand, the devil; a vicious dog or horse.
taff'erel, taff'rail *n.* the rail at the stern of a ship.
taff'eta *n.* a smooth, lustrous, silk fabric.
tag *n.* a ragged end; pointed end of lace, etc.; a trite quotation; an address label.—**tag-on** to fasten on.
tail *n.* projecting continuation of backbone at hinder end of animal; any hind part.—*v.* (off) to get smaller; in aviation, group of stabilising planes or fins at rear of aeroplane to which are attached elevator and rudder controls.—*v.t.* Australia, to herd and tend cattle, sheep, etc.—**tailed** *a.*—**tail'less** *a.*—**tail'-plane** *n.* aviation, stabilising surface at rear of aeroplane, function of which is to secure steady motion in vertical plane.—**tail'-skid** *n.* aviation, metal rod, situated below fin, with foot, along which aeroplane slides in taxying.—**tail'spin** *n.* aviation, vertical dive by aeroplane, nose foremost and describing a spiral, tail descending in straight line.—**tail-light** *n.* rear light of vehicle.
tail'or *n.* a maker of outer clothing.
taint *n.* stain, corruption, disgrace; an infection.—*v.t.* to stain slightly; corrupt.—*v.i.* to become corrupted.—**taint'ed** *a.*
take *v.t.* to grasp, get hold of, capture; get; receive, assume, adopt; accept, understand.—*n.* in a film studio, one photographic record of one short scene (**took** *p.t.*—**ta'ken** *p.p.*—**ta'king** *pres. p.*).—**take'-off** *n.* in aviation, the instant an aeroplane leaves land (or water).—*v.i.*
talc *n.* a soft magnesian mineral.—**tal'cum pow'der** *n.* toilet powder containing talc.
tale *n.* a story; number, count.
talegall'a *n.* aboriginal name for the Australian brush turkey.
tal'ent *n.* special skill, ability; an ancient weight or money.—**tal'ented** *a.* gifted.
tal'isman *n.* an object supposed to have magic powers; a charm (**-mans** *pl.*).
talk (tawk) *v.i.* to speak or converse.—*v.t.* to express in speech; to use (a language); to discuss.—*n.* speech; conversation; rumour.—**talk'ative** *a.*—**talk'er** *n.*—**talkies** *n.* (*sl.*) "talking films."
tall *a.* high; of great stature; in N. America (*sl.*) incredible, untrue, as a *tall story*.—**tall'er** *comp.*—**tall'est** *sup.*
tall'ow (tal'ō) *n.* melted and clarified animal fat.—*v.t.* to smear with tallow.—*a.* made of tallow, *esp.* candles.
tall'y *n.* a notched rod for keeping accounts; an account so kept; a reckoning.—*v.t.* to record by a tally.—*v.i.* to fit, agree, correspond with (**tall'ied** *p.t.* and *p.p.*—**tall'ying** *pres. p.*).
tal'on *n.* claw of a bird of prey.
tam'bour (-ōōr) *n.* a large drum; a round frame for embroidery.—**tambourine'** *n.* a flat half-drum with jingling discs of metal attached.
tame *a.* not wild; domesticated; without excitement, uninteresting.—*v.t.* to make tame.—**tame'ly** *adv.*—**ta'mer** *n.*
tam o' shanter *n.* a large circular tight-fitting cap of woollen stuff.
tam'pan *n.* a S. African tick, remarkable for the venom of its bite.
tamp'er *v.i.* to interfere (with); to corrupt, to influence improperly.
tan *n.* crushed oak-bark; the colour of this; sunburn.—*v.t.* to make hide into leather; to make brown (**tan'ning** *pres. p.*—**tanned'** *p.t.* and *p.p.*).
tan'dem *adv.* one behind the other.—*n.* a vehicle with two horses one behind the other; a bicycle for two riders.
tang *n.* penetrating smell; harsh clanging sound.—*v.t.* to clang.
tan'gent (-j-) *a.* touching, meeting without cutting.—*n.* a line tangent to a curve.—**tangen'tial** *a.*—**tangen'tially** *adv.*
tan'gible *a.* that can be touched; definite.—**tangibil'ity** *n.*
tangerine' *n.* a variety of orange.
tan'gle (-ng-gl) *v.t.* to twist together in a muddle.—*n.* a tangled mass.—**tan'gle-foot** *n.* N. America, spirits, *esp.* whisky.
tang'o *n.* a dance originating in S. America (**tango's** (-gōz) *pl.*).
tank *n.* storage vessel for liquids, *esp.* a large one; armoured vehicle with caterpillar wheels used in warfare.—**tank'er** *n.* a ship fitted with tanks for carrying oil; a motor-vehicle or railway container-wagon for carrying liquid fuel.

tank'ard *n.* a large drinking-cup of metal, *esp.* for beer; its contents.
tan'talise *v.t.* to torment by presenting and then taking away something desired (**tan'talising** *pr. p.*).—**tan'talus** *n.* appliance for keeping decanters locked up.
tan'tamount *a.* equivalent in value or signification; equal.
tante *n.* in S. Africa, a courtesy title given to an elderly lady.
tan'trum *n.* an outburst of temper.
tap *n.* a hollow plug for drawing off liquid; a valve with a handle to regulate or stop the flow of a fluid in a pipe, etc. —*v.t.* to put a tap in; to draw off.—**tap'root** *n.* a long tapering root growing directly downwards.—**tap'ster** *n.* one who draws beer in an inn.
tap *v.t.* to strike lightly, to knock gently. —**tap'-dancing** *n.* a kind of exhibition dancing with much tapping of the feet.—*n.* a slight blow or rap.
tape *n.* a narrow long strip of fabric, paper, etc.—**tape-meas'ure** *n.* tape marked for measuring.—**tape'worm** *n.* a flat worm parasitic in animals and man.
ta'per *n.* a long wick covered with wax; a thin candle.—*v.t.* to become gradually thinner towards one end.
tap'estry *n.* fabric decorated with woven designs in colours (**tap'estries** *pl.*).
tapio'ca *n.* a granular food made from the cassava-root.
ta'pir (-er) *n.* an American animal, with flexible proboscis, allied to the pig.
tapp'et *n.* in an internal combustion engine, a short steel rod or lever conveying to the valve stem movement imparted by the lift of a cam.
tar *n.* a thick black liquid distilled from coal, etc.—*v.t.* to coat with tar.
taran'tula *n.* a large, poisonous spider found in Southern Europe.
tard'y *a.* slow, behindhand.-**tard'ily** *adv.*
tare (tĕr) *n.* a weed; the vetch.
tare (tĕr) *n.* allowance made for the weight of box, cart, etc., when goods are weighed in such container.
tar'get (-g-) *n.* a mark to aim at in shooting; an objective in air offensive; a standard of quantity set for output; a small shield; butt.
tar'iff *n.* duty to be paid on goods; a list of charges *esp.* at a hotel.
tar'mac *n.* mixture of tar and road metal or macadam used for giving a smooth, non-friable road surface.
tarn *n.* a small mountain lake.
tar'nish *v.t.* to discolour by oxidation (*esp.* metal).—*v.i.* to become stained, lose brightness.—*n.* discoloration, dullness.—it **tar'nishes.**
ta'ro (tä'-) *n.* a plant grown in S. Pacific islands for its edible roots (**-os** *pl.*).
tarpaul'in *n.* canvas treated with tar or oil to make it waterproof.
tar'pon *n.* a large edible fish.
tarr'y *v.i.* to linger, delay (**tarr'ied** *p.t.* and *p.p.*—**tarr'ying** *pres. p.*).—he **tarries.**
tart *n.* an open pie of fruit, etc.; a small covered fruit pie; a prostitute.—*a.* sour.
Syn. bitter, pungent, biting, harsh, testy, snappish. *Ant.* agreeable, mild.
tart'an *n.* a woollen cloth woven in a pattern of stripes crossing at right angles; a pattern used in this cloth.
tar'tar *n.* a crust deposited on the teeth; deposit on wine-casks, etc.
Tar'tar *n.* a native of Tartary; a person of an irritable temper.
tas'al *n.* in S. Africa, pickled meat.
task (-ȧ-) *n.* a piece of work set or undertaken.—*v.t.* to put a task on, to take to task, to reprove.—**task'master** *n.* overseer.—**task'-force** *n.* a naval or military unit dispatched to carry out a specific undertaking.
tass'el *n.* ornament consisting of a bunch of threads on a knob.—**tass'elled** *a.*
taste *v.t.* to perceive or try the flavour of; to eat or drink; to experience.—*v.i.* to have a flavour.—*n.* a small quantity; flavour; sense of tasting; appreciation and judgment in matters of beauty, style, etc.; style or manner; preference. —**taste'ful** *a.* showing good taste.—**taste'fully** *adv.*—**taste'less** *a.* insipid.—**ta'sty** *a.* pleasantly flavoured.
tat *v.t.* to make trimming by tatting.—*v.i.* to make tatting.—**tatt'ing** *n.* lace-edging, woven or knit from common sewing thread, with a peculiar stitch.
tatt'er *n.* a rag.—*v.* to tear into rags.
tatterdema'lion *n.* a ragged fellow.
tat'tle *v.i.* to gossip.—*n.* foolish talk.
tattoo' *n.* a beat of drum and bugle-call; a military spectacle or pageant.
tattoo' *v.t.* to mark the skin in patterns, etc., by pricking and filling the punctures with colouring matter (**tattooed'** (-tōōd) *p.t.* and *p.p.*—**tattoo'ing** *pres. p.*).
tau (taw) *n.* the toad-fish.
taunt *n.* a reproach, insulting words.—*v.t.* to insult, reproach bitterly, mock.
Tau'rus (taw-) *n.* the Bull, a constellation; 2nd sign of the Zodiac operative *c.* Apr. 21–May 20.
taut *a.* drawn tight; in good condition.—**taut'en** *v.* to make tense.
tautol'ogy *n.* repetition of the same thing in other words.—**tautolo'gical** *a.*
tav'ern *n.* an inn or ale-house.
taw'dry *a.* showy but cheap and without taste.—**taw'drily** *adv.*
tawn'y *a.* yellowish-brown.—*n.*
tawse *n.pl.* a leather strap, fringed at the end, for whipping children.
tax *v.t.* to exact a contribution to the cost of government; to examine accounts; to put a burden or strain on; to accuse. —*n.* the charge imposed; a burden.—**taxa'tion** *n.*—**tax'able** *a.*—**tax'-payer** *n.*
tax'i- (**cab**) *n.* a motor-car for hire with

driver (**tax'is** *pl.*).— **tax'i** *v.i.* to go in a taxi; (of an aeroplane) to run along the ground under its own power (**tax'ied** *p.t.* and *p.p.*—**tax'ying** *pres. p.*).—**taxim'eter** *n.* an automatic fare-indicator.

tax'idermy *n.* the art of stuffing dead animals.—**tax'idermist** *n.*

tea *n.* the dried leaves of a plant cultivated in China, India, etc.; an infusion of it as a beverage; various herbal infusions; an afternoon meal with tea.

teach *v.t.* to instruct; to impart knowledge of.— *v.i.* to act as teacher (**taught** *p.t.* and *p.p.*—**teach'ing** *pres. p.*).
Syn. train, school, educate, preach, discipline, direct, advise. *Ant.* misdirect, mislead, deceive, misguide.

teak *n.* an East Indian tree; the very hard wood obtained from it.

teal *n.* a small water-fowl.

team *n.* a set of animals, players of a game, etc., associated in an activity.—**team'ster** *n.* one who drives a team.

tear *n.* a drop of fluid in, or falling from, the eye.—**tear'ful** *a.*—**tear'less** *a.*—**tear' gas,** a gas which causes temporary blindness by affecting the lachrymal glands, inducing a profuse flow of tears.

tear (tėr) *v.t.* to pull apart, rend.—*v.i.* to become torn; to rush (**tore** *p.t.*—**torn** *p.p.* —**tear'ing** *pres. p.*).—*n.* a rent.

tease *v.t.* to pull apart the fibres of; to torment, irritate.—*n.* one who torments.

tea'sel *n.* a plant of which one species bears a large prickly burr.

teat *n.* the nipple of a female breast; an artificial substitute for this.

tech'nical (tek-) *a.* of or used in an art, craft or science; belonging to such.—**technical'ity** *n.* state of being technical; that which is technical.—**tech'nically** *adv.*—**technique'** (tek-nēk') *n.* method of performance in an art.—**techni'cian** *n.*—**technol'ogy** *n.* systematic knowledge of industrial arts.—**technol'ogist** *n.*

technoc'racy (-nok'-) *n.* a movement founded in America in 1920 for scientific and technical study of factors, *esp.* economic, affecting modern life.

te'dium *n.* boredom or quality of boring. —**te'dious** *a.* wearisome.

tee *n.* mark aimed at in quoits, etc.; small heap of sand, etc., on which golfer's ball is placed for a drive.

teem *v.i.* to abound with, swarm, be prolific; to pour, to rain heavily.

teens' *n. pl.* years of life between 12–20. —**teen'-age** *n.*—**-ager** *n.*

tee'pee *n. see* **tepee.**

tee'ter *v.i.* in N. America, to see-saw, or make similar movements; to vacillate.

teethe (-th) *v.t.* to cut teeth.

teeto'tal *a.* abstaining or pledged to abstain from intoxicating drink.—**teeto'taller** *n.*—**teeto'talism** *n.*

teeto'tum *n.* a top.

teg' *n.* sheep or doe in its 2nd year.

teg'ument *n.* a covering; the covering of the living body.—**tegumen'tal** *a.*

telau'tograph *n.* a form of telegraph that transmits messages as set out by hand, whether writing or drawing.

teleg'ony (-leg-) *n.* theory of the supposed influence exercised by a male on the children begotten on his mate by a later cohabitor.

tel'egraph *n.* an apparatus for sending messages mechanically to a distance, as by semaphore, electricity, etc.—*v.t.* and *i.* to communicate by telegraph.—**teleg'raphist** *n.* one who works a telegraph. —**telegraph'ic** *a.*—**telegraph'ically** *adv.*—**teleg'raphy** *n.*—**tel'egram** *n.* a message sent by telegraph.—**telep'athy** *n.* the action of one mind on another at a distance.—**telepath'ic** *a.*—**telepath'ically** *adv.*—**tel'ephone** *n.* an apparatus for communicating sound to a distance.—*v.t.* and *i.* to communicate or speak by telephone.—**telephon'ic** *a.*—**teleph'ony** *n.* —**teleph'onist** *n.*—**tel'eprinter** *n.* an apparatus resembling a typewriter, by means of which a subscriber can call up on the telephone another subscriber and send and receive typed messages.—**tel'eran** *n.* radio device for sending pilot charts, together with radio-obtained course and altitude information by television to planes in flight.—**tel'escope** *n.* an instrument of lenses to see things more clearly at a distance; in N. America, an expanding travelling case.–**telescop'ic** *a.*—**tel'evise** *v.t.* to transmit by television. —**tel'evision** *n.* the viewing of distant objects and events by means of electrical transmission to a televisor; the transmission of such programmes.—**tel'evise** *a.* to transmit by television.

tell *v.t.* to narrate, make known; count.—*v.i.* to give account; be of weight or importance (**told** *p.t.*/*p.p.*—**tell'ing** *pr. p.*).—**tell'er** *n.*—**tell'ing** *a.* effective.—**tell'-tale** *n.* gossip, sneak; indicator; index.

tellu'rium *n.* a substance of a silver-white colour like sulphur, sometimes reckoned among the metals.

tel'otype *n.* an electric telegraph which prints the messages.

temer'ity *n.* rashness, boldness.—**temera'rious** *a.* foolhardy.

temp'er *v.t.* to harden; to bring to proper condition; to restrain, moderate.—*n.* degree of hardness of steel, etc.; mental constitution; frame of mind; anger, *esp.* in noisy outburst.—**temp'erament** *n.* mental constitution.—**temperament'al** *a.* due to temperament; moody, capricious, sensitive. — **temperament'ally** *adv.* —**temp'erate** *a.* showing or practising moderation; moderate (as climate).—**temp'erance** *n.* moderation, self-restraint.—**temp'erately** *adv.*—**temp'erature** *n.* degree of heat or coldness.

temp'est *n.* a violent storm.—**tempest'uous** *a.*—**tempest'uously** *adv.*
tem'ple *n.* a building for worship.
tem'ple *n.* the flat part on either side of the head above the cheekbone.
tem'po *n.* in music, time, rate; rhythm (*n. pl.* **-pos, -pi.**).
tem'plet, tem'plate *n.* a mould used by bricklayers, masons, machinists, etc.
temp'oral *a.* relating to time, of this life or world; secular.—**temporal'ity** *n.*
temp'orary *a.* lasting or used only for a time.—**temp'orarily** *adv.*—**temp'orise** *v.t.* to gain time by negotiation, etc.; to conform to circumstances.—**temp'oriser** *n.* *Syn.* transitory, fleeting, impermanent, worldly, earthy. *Ant.* permanent, lasting, spiritual.
tempt *v.t.* to try; to try to persuade, *esp.* to evil.—**tempt'er** *n.*—**tempta'tion** *n.*
ten *n.* and *a.* the cardinal number next after nine.—**tenth, ten'fold** *a.* and *n.*
ten'able *a.* that may be held or defended.—**tena'cious** *a.* holding fast.—**tenac'ity** *n.*—**ten'ant** *n.* one who holds lands or house, etc., on a rent, or lease.—**ten'ancy** *n.*—**ten'antry** *n.* tenants.
te'nakoe (tē-na'kwi) *interj.* in New Zealand, a Maori greeting, good-morning! how do you do?
tench *n.* a fresh-water fish.
tend *v.t.* to take care of.—**tend'ance** *n.*—**tend'er** *n.* a vessel attending a larger one; a carriage for fuel and water attached to a locomotive.
tend *v.i.* to incline; make in direction of.—**tend'ency** *n.* inclination, bent.
tenden'cious, tenden'tious *a.* directed to some special end or purpose, propagandist, not impartial.
tend'er *v.t.* to offer.—*n.* an offer; what may legally be offered in payment.
tend'er *a.* delicate, soft; easily injured; gentle.—**tend'erly** *adv.*—**tend'erness** *n.*—**tend'erfoot** *n.* in N. America and Australia, a newcomer on the plains or in the bush; a novice; a Boy Scout until he has passed his third test.
tend'on *n.* a sinew attaching a muscle to a bone, etc. —**tend'inous** *a.*
tend'ril *n.* a slender curling stem by which a climbing plant attaches itself.
ten'ebrous, ten'ebrose *a.* dark; obscure.—**ten'ebrousness** *n.*–**tenebros'ity** *n.*
ten'ement *n.* a piece of land or a house; a part of a house forming a separate dwelling.—**ten'ement-house** *n.*
ten'et *n.* a doctrine, belief held to be true.
ten'nis *n.* a game in which a ball is struck between players on opposite sides of a net in a covered court; a variation of this played on a grass or other court (also called **lawn-tennis**).—**tennis arm**, a lameness of tennis players.
ten'on *n.* a tongue cut on the end of a piece of wood, etc., to fit into a mortise.
ten'or *n.* meaning; general course; a male voice between alto and bass; a singer with music for, this voice.
tense *n.* a modification of a verb to show time of action, etc.
tense *a.* stretched tight, taut; strained.
ten'sile *a.* capable of being stretched.
ten'sion *n.* stretching or strain when stretched; suppressed excitement; in electricity, voltage.
tent *n.* a portable shelter of canvas.
tent'acle *n.* organ on certain animals' heads for feeling, holding, etc.
tent'ative *a.* done as a trial.—*n.* an attempt.—**tent'atively** *adv.*
tent'er *n.* a frame for stretching cloth.—**tent'er-hook** *n.* a hook for holding the cloth.— **on tent'er-hooks** in painful suspense, keyed up.
ten'uous *a.* thin, rare, fine.—**tenu'ity** *n.*
ten'ure *n.* conditions or period of holding land, an office, etc.—**tenu'rial** *a.*
te'pee, tep'ee *n.* a N. American Indian wigwam or tent, also **tee'pee.**
tep'id *a.* lukewarm.—**tepid'ity** *n.*
ter'bium *n.* a rare metal.
tercente'nary *n.* a three-hundredth anniversary.—*a.* pertaining to one.
ter'ebine *n.* a disinfectant derived from oil of turpentine.—**ter'ebinth** *n.* a tree or shrub yielding a limpid, balsamic resin; the turpentine tree.
tere'do *n.* a genus of worm-like molluscs (**-dos** (-dōz), **-dines** (-di-nēz) *pl.*).
tergiversa'tion (-j-) *n.* shuffling; evasion; desertion of party.
term *n.* limit, end; fixed day for regular payment, e.g., rent; period during which courts sit, schools are open, etc.; word, expression.—*pl.* conditions, mutual relationship.—*v.t.* to name.
term'inal *a.* at or forming an end.—*n.* a terminal part or structure.—**term'inate** *v.t.* to bring to an end.—*v.i.* to come to an end.—**termina'tion** *n.*—**ter'minable** *a.*—**terminol'ogy** *n.* the study of terms; a set of technical terms or vocabulary.—**terminolo'gical** (-j-) *a.*—**term'inus** *n.* a finishing point; a station at the end of a railway (**-ini** (-nī) *pl.*).
term'agant *n.* a brawling woman.
ter'mite *n.* the so-called white ant.
ter'race *n.* a raised level place; shelf cut out of a hill; a row of houses.
ter'ra-cott'a *n.* a hard unglazed pottery; its colour, a brownish-red.
ter'rain (-ān) *n.* in geology, any rock, or series of rocks; in military affairs, an extent of ground or country.
ter'rapin *n.* a water tortoise.
terrest'rial *a.* of the earth; of land.
ter'rible *a.* causing fear; excessive.—**terr'ibly** *adv.*—**terrif'ic** *a.* terrible, awe-inspiring.—**terrif'ically** *adv.*—**ter'rify** *v.t.* to frighten (**-ified** *p.t./p.p.*—**-ifying** *pr. p.*).—**ter'ror** *n.* state of great fear.—**ter'rorise** *v.t.* to force, oppress by fear.—

ter'rorism *n.* *Syn.* of **terror, fright,** dismay. *Ant.* courage, assurance.
ter'rier *n.* a small dog of various breeds, orig. for following a quarry into a burrow.
ter'ritory *n.* a region; the land subject to a ruler.—**territor'ial** *a.* relating, confined to a territory.—*n.* volunteer soldier for home defence.
ter'ry *n.* fabric of wool or silk, woven like velvet, but with the loops uncut.
terse *a.* expressed in few words, pithy.
ter'tiary *a.* third degree, order, etc.
tess'ellate *v.t.* to form into squares or checkers; to lay with checkered work.—**tess'ellated, tess'ellar** *a.*—**tessella'tion** *n.*
test *n.* examination to decide fitness or quality.—*v.t.* to try, put to the proof.—**test'-case** *n.* in law, a lawsuit viewed as a means of establishing a precedent.—**test'-match** *n.* one of a series of international sports contests, *esp.* cricket.
test'ament *n.* a will; one of the two divisions of the Bible.—**testament'ary** *a.*
test'ate *a.* that has left a will.—**test'acy** *n.* being testate.—**testa'tor** *n.* one who makes a will.—**-trix** *fem.*
test'icle *n.* a male genital organ.
test'ify *v.i.* to bear witness.—*v.t.* to bear witness to (**-ified** *p.t.* and *p.p.*—**-ifying** *pres. p.*).—**test'imony** *n.* evidence.
testimo'nial *n.* a certificate of character, ability, etc.; a gift by a number of persons to express their regard.
test'y *a.* irritable, short-tempered.
tête-à-tête (tāt-à-tāt) *n.* private conversation between two persons.—*a.*—*adv.*
tet'anus *n.* lockjaw, rigidity of muscles.
teth'er (-th) *v.t.* to tie up (a horse, etc.) with a rope.—*n.* a rope or chain for fastening a grazing animal; limit of endurance (*at the end of his tether*).
tet'ragon *n.* a figure with 4 angles and 4 sides.—**tetrag'onal** *a.*—**tetrahe'dron** *n.* solid contained by four plane faces.
tet'rode *n.* in wireless, a four-electrode thermionic valve.
tex'as *n.* in N. America, a structure on a river steamboat containing the officers' quarters, pilot house, etc.
text *n.* the actual words of a book, passage, etc.; the main body of a literary work; letterpress; a passage from the Scriptures, etc., *esp.* as the subject of a discourse.—**text'-book** *n.* a manual of instruction.—**text'ual** *a.* of or in a text.
text'ile *a.* woven; capable of being woven; relating to weaving.—**text'ure** *n.* the character or structure of a fabric.
thall'ium *n.* a bluish-white soft metal.
than (th-) *conj.* and *prep.* introduces second part of a comparison.
thank *v.t.* to give thanks, to express gratitude to.—**thanks** *n. pl.* words of gratitude.—**thank'ful** *a.* feeling grateful.—**thank'less** *a.* having or bringing no thanks.—**thanks-giv'ing** *a.*
that (th-) *a.* demonstrates or particularises.—*dem. pron.* the particular thing meant.—*adv.* as.—*rel. pron.* which, who.—*conj.* introduces noun clauses.
thatch *v.t.* to roof (a house) with straw or similar material.—*n.* the material.
thaum'aturge *n.* a wonder-worker.—**thaum'aturgy** *n.* magic, miracle-working.
thaw *v.t.* and *i.* to melt.—*n.* a melting (of frost, ice, snow, etc.).
the (th-) is the definite article.
the'atre (-ter) *n.* a place where plays are performed; the drama or dramatic works generally; a surgical operating room; (of war) field of operations.
theat'rical *a.* of or for the theatre; showy, spectacular.—**theat'rically** *adv.*—**theat'ricals** *n. pl.* amateur dramatics.
thé' dansant' (tā' dan͡-san͡') *n.* afternoon tea with dancing.
thee *pron.* obj. and dative case of **thou.**
theft *n.* the act of stealing.
their *a.* theirs.—*pron.* belonging to them.—**theirs** *pron.* possessive case of **they.**
the'ism *see* **theology.**
them *pron.* objective case of **they**; those persons or things.—**themselves'** *pron.* emphatic and reflexive form of **they**
theme *n.* subject of a composition.
then (th-) *adv.* at that time; next; that being so; now and then occasionally.
thence (th-) *adv.* from that place, point of reasoning, etc.; elsewhere.
theod'olite *n.* a surveying instrument for measuring angles, etc.
theol'ogy *n.* the science treating of God (**theologies** *pl.*).—**theolo'gical** *a.*—**theolo'gically** *adv.*—**theolo'gian** (-lōj-) *n.*—**theoc'racy** *n.* government by God.—**theocrat'ic** *a.*—**the'ism** *n.* belief in divine creation of the universe without denial of revelation.—**the'ist** *n.*—**theos'ophy** *n.* any of various ancient and modern systems of esoteric philosophy by which the soul may attain knowledge of, and ultimate union with, the universal spirit.—**theos'ophist** *n.*
the'orem *n.* a proposition which can be demonstrated by argument.—**the'ory** *n.* a supposition to account for something; a system of rules and principles; rules and reasoning, etc., as distinguished from practice.—**theoret'ical** *a.*-**theoret'ically** *adv.*—**the'orist** *n.*—**the'orise** *v.i.*
therapeut'ic *a.* relating to healing.—*n.* in *pl.* the art of healing.
ther'apy *n.* in medicine, curative treatment; usually in compound words as **radio-therapy.**
there (th-) *adv.* in that place, to that point.—**there'fore** *adv.* in consequence.
therm' *n.* the amount of heat needed to raise one gramme of water one degree centigrade; the British thermal unit; the unit of cost for gas, equivalent to 100,000 such units.
ther'mal *a.* of or pertaining to heat.—

ther'mic *a.* thermal.—**thermom'eter** *n.* an instrument to measure temperature.—**thermomet'ric** *a.*—**ther'mostat** *n.* device for keeping temperature even.

ther'mion *n.* a positively or negatively charged particle or ion, emitted by an incandescent body.—**thermion'ic** *a.* pertaining to a thermion.—**thermion'ic valve** a vacuum tube with incandescent filament and auxiliary electrodes, used as generator, detector or amplifier of wireless signals.

ther'mit, ther'mite (-mīt) *n.* aluminium powder mixed with a metal oxide, which, when ignited, emits tremendous heat, used *esp.* for welding.

thermodynam'ics *n.* the science that deals with the conversion of heat into mechanical energy.

thermo-electric'ity *n.* electricity developed by the action of heat.

ther'mos flask *n.* a double-walled container with vacuum interspace, for keeping liquids at one temperature (protected trade name.)

these *pron. pl.* of **this,** opposed to **those.**

the'sis *n.* proposition; dissertation; essay in support of a statement (**-ses** (-sēz) *pl.*).

thes'pian *a.* pert. to tragedy; *n.* a tragedian.

thews *n. pl.* muscular strength.

they (thā) *pron.* the third person plural pronoun.

thi'amin (-ạ-min) *n.* vitamin B_1, a complex compound, deficiency in which causes beri-beri.

thick *a.* having great thickness, not thin; dense, crowded; viscous; foggy.—**thick'ly** *adv.*—**thick'en** *v.t.* and *i.*—**thick'ness** *n.* the dimension of anything measured through it, at right angles to the length and breadth.—**thick'et** *n.* a thick growth of small trees.—**thick'set** *a.* set cl sely together; sturdy and solid in limbs.

thief *n.* one who steals (**thieves** *pl.*).

thieve *v.t.* and *i.* to steal.—**thiev'ish** *a.*

thigh (thī) *n.* the upper part of the leg.

thim'ble *n.* a metal cover for the end of the finger in sewing.

thin *a.* of little thickness; of little density; loose, not closely packed.—*v.t.* and *i.* to make or become thin.

Syn. spare, slender, scanty, lean, dilute, slight, flimsy, insufficient. *Ant.* thick, bulky, dense, close, compact, numerous.

thine (thīn) *pron.* and *a.* belonging to thee.—**your, yours** *pl.*

thing *n.* a material object.

think *v.i.* to use one's mind; to reflect; hold an opinion.—*v.t.* to conceive or consider in the mind (**thought** *p.t.* and *p.p.*—**think'ing** *pres. p.*).—**think'er** *n.*

third *a.* ordinal number corresponding to *three.*—*n.* third part.—**third degree** severe and lengthy examination, *esp.* by police, to extract information or confession.—**Third Reich** German fascist dictatorship founded 1933, and brought to an end 1945, after World War 2.

thirst *n.* the feeling caused by lack of drink; strong desire.—*v.i.* to feel the lack of drink.—**thirst'y** *a.*—**thirst'ily** *adv.*

thirteen' *a.* and *n.* a number, three and ten.—**-th** *a.* the last of thirteen.—**thirt'y** *n. a.* three times ten.

this (th-) *dem. a.* and *pron.* denotes a thing or person near, or just mentioned.

this'tle (-sl) *n.* a prickly plant with a purple flower.—**thistle-down** *n.*

thith'er (thith'-) *adv.* to or toward that place, there.—**thith'erward(s)** *adv.*

thole'-pin *n.* one of two pegs between which an oar works.

thong *n.* a narrow strip of leather.

tho'rax *n.* the chest; the second section (legs and wings) of an insect's body.

tho'rium *n.* a grey metallic element, used in the manufacture of incandescent gas mantles, filaments, etc.

thorn *n.* a prickle on a plant; a bush.—**thor'ny** *a.* full of thorns; troublesome.

thor'ough (thur'a) *a.* complete, entire; accurate, careful.—**thor'oughly** *adv.*—**thor'oughbred** *a.* of pure breed.—*n.* a pure-bred animal, *esp.* a horse.—**thor'oughfare** *n.* road, passage open at both ends; right of way.

those *pron. pl.* of **that**; noting, as a correlative of **these,** the former, as distinguished from the latter.

thou (th-) *pron.* the second person singular pronoun (**ye, you** *pl.*).

though (thō) *conj.* in spite of the fact that.—*adv.* for all that; as though, as if.

thought (thawt) *n.* the process of thinking; what one thinks; a product of thinking; meditation.—*p.t.* and *p.p.* of **think.**—**thought'ful** *a.* engaged in meditation; considerate.—**thought'less** *a.* careless, heedless, inconsiderate.

thou'sand (-z-) *a.* and *n.* a cardinal number, ten hundreds.—**thou'sand-jacket** *n.* New Zealand tree from which the bark may be removed layer by layer, ribbonwood.

thrall (-awl) *n.* a slave; slavery.—*v.t.* to enslave.—**thral'dom** *n.* bondage.

thrash, thresh *v.t.* to beat out the grains of.—**thrash** *v.t.* to beat, whip.

thread (-ed) *n.* a fine cord; yarn; the ridge cut spirally on a screw.—*v.t.* to put a thread into; to put on a thread; to pick (one's way, etc.).—**thread'bare** *a.* worn.

threat (-et) *n.* an announcement of what the speaker intends to do if his orders or wishes are not complied with.—**threat'en** *v.t.* to utter threats; to menace.

three *n.* and *a.* a cardinal number, one more than two.—**three'fold** *a.*—**three'-score** *a.* sixty.—**three'-ply** in weaving, three distinct webs in-wrought together, as cloth or carpeting; three thin layers

of wood glued together with the grain crossing.—*a.* of three strands.
thresh *v.t. see* **thrash.**
thresh'old (-ōld) *n.* bar of stone or wood forming the bottom of a doorway; entrance; beginning.
thrice *adv.* three times.
thrift *n.* saving, economy; the sea-pink. —thrift'y *a.*—**thrift'ily** *adv.*—**thrift'less** *a.* *Syn.* frugality, parsimony, carefulness. *Ant.* extravagance, waste, prodigality.
thrill *v.t.* to send a nervous tremor of emotion through.—*v.i.* to feel one.—*n.* such emotional tremor.—**thrill'ing** *a.*
thrive *v.i.* to grow well; flourish, prosper (**throve, thrived** (thrīvd) *p.t.*—**thriv'en, thrived** *p.p.*—**thri'ving** *pres. p.*).
throat *n.* the front of the neck; either or both of the passages through it.—**throat'y** *a.* of voice, hoarse.
throb *v.i.* to beat or quiver strongly.—*n.*
throe *n.* a spasm or pang; agony.
thrombo'sis *n.* the coagulation of the blood in a blood-vessel, or in the heart.
throne *n.* a seat of state, *esp.* of a king.
throng *n., v.t.* and *i.* a crowd.
thros'tle (-sl) *n.* a thrush.
throt'tle *n.* the wind-pipe; in the internal combustion engine, abbrev. for throttle-valve; in motoring, aircraft, etc., a lever controlling the throttle-valve.—*v.t.* to choke.—*v.i.* to suffocate; to open or close the throttle.—**throttle down** to slow down by closing the throttle.
through (thrōō) *prep.* from end to end or from side to side of; between the sides of; in consequence of; by means or fault of. —*adv.* from end to end; to the end; N. America (*sl.*) finished.—**throughout'** *adv.* in every part.—*prep.*—**through-ticket** *n.* ticket for the whole of a journey.—**through-train** *n.* train which travels the whole length of a long route.—**to go through the hoop** *v.i.* (*sl.*) to go bankrupt.
throw *v.t.* to fling; bring down (**threw** *p.t.*—**thrown** *p.p.*—**throw'ing** *pr. p.*).—*n.* act or distance of throwing.—**throw'back** *n.* living creature or organism reverting to ancestral type.
thrum *n.* the fringe of threads remaining attached to a loom when the web has been cut off; any loose thread.—*pl.* coarse yarn; waste yarn.—*a.*
thrush *n.* a song-bird; a throat disease of children; a foot disease of horses.
thrust *v.t.* to push, stab, drive.—*v.i.* to lunge, stab; push one's way (**thrust** *p.t.* and *p.p.*—**thrust'ing** *pres. p.*).—*n.*
thud *n.* a dull, heavy sound.—*v.i.*
thug *n.* one of a band of professional robbers and assassins.
thu'lium *n.* a rare-earth metal.
thumb (-m) *n.* the short thick finger, the one which can be opposed to the others. —*v.t.* to handle or dirty with the thumb.
thump *v.t.* to strike heavily.—*n.* a dull heavy blow; the sound of one.
thun'der *n.* the loud noise accompanying lightning.—*v.i.* of thunder, to sound. —*v.t.* to utter loudly.—**thun'derbolt** *n.* a destructive lightning flash.—**thun'der clap** *n.* crash of thunder.—**thun'der-struck** *a.* amazed.—**thun'dery** *a.* close, sultry.—**thun'derous** *a.*
Thurs'day *n.* the fifth day of the week.
thus (th-) *adv.* in this way; therefore.
thwack *v.t.* and *n.* whack, hit hard.
thwart *v.t.* to foil, frustrate.—*adv.* across. —*n.* seat for a rower across a boat.
thy (thī) *pron.* or *a.* belonging to thee.—**thyself'** *pron.* emphatic and reflexive form of **thou.**—**your** *pl.*
thyme (tīm) *n.* an aromatic herb.
thy'mus *n.* a small ductless gland in the upper part of the chest.
thy'roid (thi-) *a.* shield-shaped; *n.* the thyroid gland (in neck) or the thyroid cartilage; the principal cartilage of throat, forming the Adam's apple.
tiar'a *n.* a jewelled head-ornament.
tib'ia *n.* the shin-bone (**tibiae** (-i-ē), —**tibias** (-az) *pl.*).—**tib'ial** *a.*
tic *n.* a spasmodic nervous twitch in the muscles of the face.
tick *n.* a mite in hair or fur; mattress case. **tick'-bird** *n.* S. Africa, the ox-pecker, which eats ticks infesting animals.
tick *n.* a slight tap, as of a watch-movement; a small mark (✓).—*v.t.* to mark with a tick.—*v.i.* to make the sound.—**tick'-tack** *n.* a code of hand and arm signals used by bookmakers' assistants.
tick *n.* (*sl.*) credit; trust.—*v.t.* to buy or sell on tick; to live on credit.
tick'et *n.* card or paper entitling to admission, travel, etc.; a label; in N. America, a list of candidates of one party for an election.—*v.t.* to attach a label to. —**ticket-of-leave** *n.* permission to be at large, under certain conditions, granted to a convict for good conduct.
tick'ey *n.* in S. Africa, a threepenny bit.
tickle *v.i.* to itch.—*v.t.* to make itch with light touches, etc.—**tick'lish** *a.* sensitive to tickling; requiring care.
tide *n.* season or time; rise and fall of the sea happening twice each lunar day; stream.—**ti'dal** *a.* of, like a tide.—**ti'dal wave** *n.* great ocean wave usually caused by earthquake.—**ti'dings** *n.* news. —**ti'dy** *a.* orderly, neat.—*v.t.* to put in order (**-died** (-did) *p.t./p.p.*—**-dying** *pr. p.*).—**to tide over** *v.i.* get over, surmount.—*v.t.* to enable one to do this.
tie *v.t.* to fasten, bind; restrict (**tied** *p.t.* and *p.p.*—**ty'ing** *pres. p.*).—*n.* that with which anything is bound; a necktie; a bond; a drawn game with equal points; a match; in N. America, a railway sleeper.—**tie'up** *n.* in N. America, a blockade, obstruction; stoppage of work or progress; in business, co-operation in marketing, etc. *Syn.* unite join, secure,

attach, knot, connect, link. *Ant.* untie, loosen, separate.
ti'er (tē'er) *n.* a row, rank, layer.—*pl.* in Tasmania, mountains.—**tier'sman** *n.* in Tasmania, a mountaineer.
tiff' *n.* trifling quarrel; huff; small draught of liquor.—*v.i.*
tiff'in *n.* in India, a lunch, or slight repast, between breakfast and dinner.
ti'ger *n.* a large carnivorous animal with striped coat; **ti'gress** *fem.*
tight (tīt) *a.* firm; tense, taut; fitting close; not allowing the passage of water, etc.; (*sl.*) drunk.—**tights** *n. pl.* tight-fitting elastic garments worn by acrobats, etc.—**tight'en** *v.t.* and *i.*—**tight'ly** *adv.*
tile *n.* slab of stone or baked clay; (*sl.*) a tall hat.—*v.t.* to cover with tiles.
till *n.* a drawer for money in a shop; a stiff clay containing boulders.
till *v.t.* to cultivate.—**till'er** *n.* one who digs the soil.—**till'age** *n.* husbandry.—**tilth** *n.* tilled land; cultivation.
till *prep.* up to the time of, as late as.—*conj.* to the time that.
till'er *n.* a lever to move a rudder.
tilt *n.* a cover for a wagon.—*v.t.* and *i.* to slope, slant, heel over.—*n.* slope.—*v.i.* to take part in a medieval combat with lances.—*n.* a thrust.
tim'bale (-b'l) *n.* a pastry case with a savoury filling; mould used for cooking.
tim'ber *n.* wood for building, etc.; trees suitable for felling.—**tim'bered** *a.* made or partly made of wood.
tim'bre (tam'br) *n.* quality of sound distinguishing voices or instruments.
time *n.* existence as a succession of states; hour; duration; period; a point in duration; occasion; rhythm, speed.—*v.t.* to choose or note time of.—**time'ly** *a.* seasonable.—**time'-honoured** *a.* respected because old.—**time'piece** *n.* watch, clock.—**time-server** *n.* opportunist.—**time'-table** *n.* plan showing hours of work, times of arrival and departure, etc.—**Greenwich time,** time as settled by passage of sun over meridian at Greenwich.—**mean'time** an average of apparent time.—**on time** punctual.
tim'id *a.* lacking courage.—**timid'ity** *n.*—**tim'idly** *adv.*—**tim'orous** *a.* timid, shy.
tim'othy *n.* in N. America, a tall grass making good hay but poor pasture.
tin *n.* a malleable white metal; a vessel of tin or tinned iron; (*sl.*) money.—*v.t.* to coat with tin: preserve (food) in a tin (**tinned'** *p.t./p.p.*).—**tinn'y** *a.* of sound, harsh or cracked.—**tin'-hat** (*sl.*) shrapnel-proof steel-helmet.
tinc'ture *n.* colour, stain; solution of a medical substance.—*v.t.* tinge, imbue.
tin'der *n.* dry easily-burning material used to catch a spark from flint and steel.
tine *n.* tooth or spike of a fork, point of an antler, a harrow, etc.
ting *n.* a sharp sound, as of a bell.
tinge *v.t.* to colour or flavour slightly.—*n.* a slight trace (**ting(e)'-ing** *pres. p.*).
tin'gle (-ng-gl) *v.i.* to vibrate; thrill.
tink'er *n.* a mender of pots and pans.—*v.i.* to work in clumsy fashion.
tin'kle (-ng-kl) *v.i.* to give out a series of light sounds like a small bell.—*v.t.* to cause to do this.—*n.* the sound or action.
tin'sel *n.* glittering metal foil, etc., used for decoration; sham splendour.
tint *n.* a colour; a tinge.—*v.t.* to dye.
tintinnabula'tion *n.* the sound of bells.
tintom'eter *n.* a contrivance for measuring intensity of colour.
ti'ny *a.* very small (**tiniest** *sup.*).
tip *n.* the slender or pointed end of anything; a piece of metal, leather, etc., protecting or softening a tip.—*v.t.* to put tip on.—**tip'staff** *n.* a sheriff's officer, who carries a tipped staff.—**tiptop'** *a.* of the best quality or highest degree.
tip *n.* a small present of money; a piece of useful private information.—*v.t.* give tip to (**tipped'** *p.t./p.p.*).—**tip'ster** *n.* one who sells racing tips.—**tip'-toe** *n.*
tip *v.t.* to upset.—*v.i.* to topple over.—*n.* a place for tipping carts, emptying out rubbish, etc.—**tip'-cat** *n.* a game in which a spindle of wood is struck into the air by hitting one of the pointed ends with a stick; the piece of wood struck.
tip *v.t.* to touch lightly.
tipp'et *n.* covering for the shoulders.
tip'ple *v.i.* to take strong drink habitually in considerable quantity.—*v.t.* to drink.—*n.* drink.—**tipp'ler** *n.*
tip'sy *a.* drunk or partly drunk.
tirade' *n.* a long, ranting speech.
tire *n.* and *v.* attire; (also **tyre**) a rim of metal, rubber, etc., round a wheel.—*v.t.* to put one on.
tire *v.i.* to become weary or fatigued.—*v.t.* to fatigue.—**tire'less** *a.* of great energy.—**tire'some** *a.* wearisome.
Syn. harass, bore, fag, exhaust.
tiro *n.* (also **tyro**) a beginner, novice (**tiros** (-rōz) *pl.*).
'tis contraction of *it is.*
tiss'ue *n.* a fine woven fabric; the substance of an animal body, a plant, etc.—**tiss'ue-paper** *n.* a very thin paper.
tit *n.* a small horse; varieties of small birds.—**tit'bit** *n.* a toothsome morsel.
titan'ic (tī-) *a.* huge, gigantic.
tita'nium *n.* a metallic element; light metal of great strength and with exceptional corrosive-resistant powers.
tithe (-th) *n.* a tenth part, *esp.* of agricultural produce paid as a tax.—*v.t.* to exact tithes from; to put a tax on.
tit'illate *v.t.* to tickle, stimulate agreeably.—**titilla'tion** *n.*
titi'vate *v.t.* and *i.* dress or smarten up.
ti'tle *n.* a heading, name of a book; name, appellation; legal document.—**ti'tle-page** *n.* page of book showing title and author.—**ti'tled** *a.* of noble rank.

tit'mouse *n.* a small bird (**tit'mice** *pl.*).
titt'er *v.i.* to giggle or laugh in a suppressed way.—*n.* such laugh.
tit'tle *n.* a small mark; a whit, detail.
tit'tle-tat'tle *n.* gossip.—*v.i.* to gossip.
tit'ular *a.* so in name or title only; held by virtue of a title.—**tit'ularly** *adv.*
to *prep.* towards, in the direction of; as far as; *used* to introduce a comparison, ratio, indirect object, infinite mood, etc. —*adv.* to the required or normal state or position; dosed.
toad *n.* an animal like a frog.—**toad'stool** *n.* poisonous mushroom.—**toad'y** *n.* one who fawns or curries favour unworthily. —*v.i.* to do this (**toad'ied** *p.t.* and *p.p.*— **toad'ying** *pres. p.*).— **toad-in-the-hole** beef, sausage, baked in batter.
toast *v.t.* to brown at the fire; to warm; to drink the health of.—*n.* slice of bread browned at the fire; a health; a person toasted.—**toast'master** *n.* one who announces toasts at a banquet.
tobacc'o *n.* a plant of which the leaves are dried and used for smoking; the prepared leaves (**-os** (-ōz) *pl.*).—**tobacc'onist** *n.* dealer in tobacco.
tobog'gan *n.* a sledge for sliding down a slope of snow or ice.—*v.i.* to slide on one.
tob'y *n.* a small jug in the form of an old man with a three-cornered hat.
toc'sin *n.* an alarm rung on a bell.
to-day' n. this day.—*adv.* on this day.
tod'dle *v.i.* to walk with unsteady short steps (**tod'dling** *pres. p.*).—*n.* **tod'dler**—*n.*
todd'y *n.* drink made of mixture of whisky, hot water, sugar, etc.
toe *n.* a digit of the foot.—*v.t.* to reach or touch with the toe (**toed** *p.t.* and *p.p.*— **toe'ing** *pres. p.*).—**toe'-ragger** *n.* in Australia and New Zealand, a term of abuse.
toff' *n.* (*sl.*) a swell; a gentleman.
toff'ee *n.* a sweetmeat made of boiled sugar, etc.—**toff'ee apple** *n.*
to'ga *n.* loose outer garment worn by the ancient Roman citizens (**to'gas** (-gaz), **to'gae** (-jē) *pl.*).
togeth'er (-th-) *adv.* with each other, in company; simultaneously.
togg'ery *n.* clothes; garments.–**togs** *n.pl.*
tog'gle *n.* a small wooden pin, tapering toward both ends, with a groove round its centre; the cross-piece at the free end of a watch-chain.—**tog'gle-iron** *n.* harpoon with blade instead of flukes.
toil *v.i.* labour.—*n.* heavy work, task.— **toil'er** *n.*—**toil'some** *a.*—**toil'worn** *a.*
Syn. of *n.* struggle, effort, travail, plans. *Ant.* ease, idleness, repose.
toil'et *n.* process of dressing; dress, style of dress.—*a.* used for the toilet.
toils *n. pl.* nets for catching game.
Tokay' *n.* a kind of wine produced at *Tokay* in Hungary, made of white grapes.
to'ken *n.* sign, symbol, keepsake, or guarantee.—**to'ken pay'ment** *n.* a payment of a small part of a debt, as a token that the whole is not repudiated.
tol'erate *v.t.* to put up with.—**tolera'tion** *n.*—**tol'erable** *a.*—**tol'erably** *adv.*—**tol'erant** *a.* disinclined to interfere with others. —**tol'erance** *n.*—**tol'erantly** *adv.*
toll (tōl) *n.* a charge or tax, *esp.* for the use of a bridge or road.
toll (tōl) *v.t.* to make (a bell) ring slowly at regular intervals; to announce a death thus.—*v.i.* to ring in this way.—*n.* the action or sound of tolling.
tom'ahawk *n.* Red Indian war-axe.— *v.t.* strike, kill with one; in Australia, to cut sheep when shearing.
toma'to (-à-) *n.* a plant bearing a bright red fruit; the fruit (**-toes** *pl.*).
tomb (tōōm) *n.* a grave or monument.
tom'boy *n.* a romping boyish girl.
tom'-cat *n.* a male cat.
tome *n.* a volume or large book.
tomm'y-axe *n.* in Australia, corruption of tomahawk.
to-mor'row (-ō) *n.* the day after to-day.
ton (tun) *n.* a measure of weight, 20 cwt.; a unit of a ship's carrying capacity.— **tonn'age** *n.* displacement (warships); carrying capacity; charge per ton; ships.
tone *n.* quality of musical sound; quality of voice, colour, etc.; healthy condition. —*v.t.* to give a tone to.—**tone'arm** *n.* in a gramophone, the tubular arm conveying sound from the sound-box to the horn.—**ton'ic** *a.* relating to tone; improving bodily tone or condition.—*n.* a medicine to do this (**to'ning** *pres. p.*).— **to tone down** to soften.
tongs (-z) *n. pl.* large pincers.
tongue (tung) *n.* the muscular organ inside the mouth, used for speech, taste, etc.; things shaped like this; language.— **tongue-tied** *a.* slow in speech, shy.
to-night' (-nīt) *n.* this night; the coming night.—*adv.* on this night.
ton'ite (ton'īt) *n.* an explosive of gun-cotton and barium nitrate.
tonneau' (ton-ō') *n.* back part of a motor-car (orig. with back entrance.).
ton'sil *n.* a gland at the side of the throat.
ton'sure *n.* the shaving of part of the head as a religious or monastic practice; the part shaved.—*v.t.* to shave thus.
ton'tine (-ēen) *n.* an annuity paid to subscribers or the survivor(s).
too *adv.* in addition; in excess.— **too right** in Australia (*sl.*) very good, satisfactory. —**too true** in Australia, correct.
tool *n.* an implement, utensil or appliance for mechanical operations.—*v.t.* to work on with a tool.
toot *n.* sound of horn.—*v.t./i.* to make it. —*n.* in N.Z., shrub with a stringent bark, of which the berries can be made into wine, but the seeds are poisonous; also **tutu**.—**toot'ed** *a.* poisoned by toot.
tooth *n.* an ivory process of the jaw,

various pointed things like this (**teeth** *pl.*).—**tooth'ache** *n.*—**tooth'-brush** *n.*—**:ooth'some** *a.* pleasant to eat.

op *n.* highest part or rank; platform on ship's mast.—*v.t.* to cut off, put on, pass, reach, a top.—**topp'ing** *a.* (*sl.*) excellent, splendid.—**top'most** *a.*—**top'notch** *a.* in N. Amer., very proficient in work.—**topp'ing up** in electricity, addition of distilled water to make up for loss in accumulator acid by evaporation.—**top-gear, top** *n.* in motor-car, gear giving highest speed.—**top kick** (U.S. Army) (*sl.*) First Sergeant; highest-ranking sergeant of platoon.

op *n.* a toy which spins on a point.

o'paz *n.* precious stone, usually yellow.

ope *v.i.* to drink to excess habitually.—**to'per** *n.* a drunkard.

opee', topi *n.* the cork or pith helmet worn in the tropics.

o'piary *a.* shaped by cutting or pruning; made ornamental by trimming.

op'ic *n.* a subject of a discourse or conversation.—**top'ical** *a.* of a topic; up-to-date, having news value.—*n.* in the cinema, a film of current events; in wireless, broadcast reading of topical interest.—**topog'raphy** *n.* the description of a place, its features.—**topograph'ic** *a.*—**topograph'ically** *adv.*

op'ple *v.i.* to fall over (**top'pling** *pres. p.*).

opsy-tur'vy *a.* upside down.

oque' (tōk) *n.* woman's brimless hat.

or *n.* a prominent hill; a rocky height.

orch *n.* a twist of hemp, etc., soaked in tar or oil to burn as a portable light (-es *pl.*).—**torch'light** *n.*—**torch'bearer** *n.*

oreador' *n.* Spanish bull-fighter.

or'ment *n.* suffering or agony of body or mind.—**torment'** *v.t.* to afflict; to tease.—**torment'or** *n.* one who torments.
Syn. torture, pang, throe.

orna'do *n.* violent storm (**-does** *pl.*).

orpe'do *n.* fish which gives out electric discharge; cigar-shaped, explosive, self-propelling underwater missile discharged from ship (**-does** (-dōz) *pl.*).—*v.t.* strike, sink with torpedo (**-doed** (-dōd) *p.t./p.p.*—**-doing** *pr. p.*).—**torpe'do-boat-destroy'er** *n.* (now **destroyer**) fast warship armed with guns and deck torpedo-tubes, used in battle and for anit-submarine and escort duties.

or'pid *a.* sluggish, dormant.—**torpid'ity** *n.*—**tor'por** *n.* apathy, lack of feeling.

orque' *n.* collar, necklet of twisted metal; in mechanics, rotating or twisting forces.—**torque'-rod** (motoring) rod fitted to live axle to prevent its twisting round with drive.—**torque'-tube** tube enclosing propellor shaft, and acting as torque-rod.

orr'ent *n.* a rushing stream; violent outburst.—**torren'tial** *a.*

orr'id *a.* parched; dried with heat.—**torr'idness** *n.*—**torrid'ity** *n.*

tor'sion *n.* twist.—**tor'sional** *a.*

tor'so *n.* the trunk of a statue mutilated of head and limbs; the human trunk (**-sos** (-sōz), **-si** (-sē) *pl.*).

tort *n.* a wrong; a twist or wrench.

tor'tile *a.* twisted; coiled.—**tor'tive** *a.* twisted, distorted; wreathed.

tort'oise (-us) *n.* a four-footed reptile covered with a shell of horny plates.—**tor'toise-shell** *n.* substance used for making combs, etc.—*a.*

tort'uous *a.* winding, twisting; not straightforward, deceitful.

tort'ure *n.* the infliction of severe pain.—*v.t.* to subject to torture.—**tort'urer** *n.*

Tor'y *n.* a political conservative.

tosh *n.* (*sl.*) nonsense; bosh.

toss *v.t.* to throw up or about.—*v.i.* to be thrown, or fling oneself, about.—*n.* an act of tossing.—**toss'pot** *n.* a toper.

tot *n.* a very small thing; a small quantity, *esp.* of a drink; a tiny child.

tot *v.t.* to add up.—*v.i.* (with *up*) to amount to.—*n.* an addition sum.

to'tal *n.* whole amount.—*a.* complete, entire.—*v.t.* add up; amount to. (**to'talling** *pr. p.*—**to'talled** *p.t./p.p.*).—**total'ity** *n.*—**totalisa'tor** *n.* machine to operate mutual betting on racecourse.

totalitar'ian *a.* applied to a state such as Nazi Germany where no representation is allowed to any political opinion except that of the ruling party.

tote *v.t.* in N. America, to haul.

tote *n.* abbreviation from **totalisator.**

to'tem *n.* a tribal badge or emblem.

tott'er *v.i.* to walk unsteadily, begin to fall.—**tott'eringly** *adv.*—**tott'ery** *a.*

tou'can (tou'kan) *n.* a bird of tropical America remarkable for its large bill.

touch (tuch) *v.t.* to put the hand on, come into contact with; reach; move the feelings of; in N. America (*sl.*) to try to borrow from—*v.i.* to call; (with *on*) to refer to.—*n.* touching; being touched; sense of feeling; style; a slight blow, stroke, contact, amount, etc.—**touched** *a.* (*sl.*) somewhat insane.—**touch'ing** *a.* moving (to the emotions).—*prep.* about.—**touch'line** *n.* side-line on football-field. **touch'-wood** *n.* tinder.—**touch'stone** *n.*—a stone for testing gold or silver.—**touch'-paper** *n.* fuse for firing a charge.—**touch'y** *a.* irritable, sensitive.

tough (tuf) *a.* strong and pliable, not brittle; sturdy; difficult; needing effort to bite.—*n.* (*sl.*) a ruffian.—**tough'ness** *n.*—**tough'en** *v.t.* and *i.* make tough.

toupee', toupet' (-pē, -pā) *n.* a curl, or artificial lock of hair.

tour (tōōr) *n.* a travelling round.—*v.t.* to travel through.—*v.i.* to travel.—**tour'ist** *n.* one who travels for pleasure.

tour'nament *n.* meeting for knightly contests; meeting for games or athletic contests.—**tour'ney** *n.*

tour'niquet (-nē-kā) *n.* device for stopping bleeding by pressure on artery.
tou'sle *v.t.* disorder.—**tou'sled** *a.* untidy.
tout *v.i.* to solicit custom (usually in an undesirable fashion) (**tout** *for*).—*n.*
tow (tō) *n.* hemp or flax fibre.
tow (tō) *v.t.* to drag at the end of a rope or hawser.—*n.* a towing or being towed; a vessel in tow.—**tow'age** *n.*
tow'ard (tō'ard) *a.* docile (also **tow'ardly**).—**towards'** (tordz, to-wordz') *prep.* in the direction of (also **toward'**).
tow'el *n.* a cloth for wiping off moisture after washing.—**tow'elling** *n.* material used for making towels.
tow'er *n.* a tall square or round building or part of a building; a fortress.—*v.i.* to rise aloft, to stand very high.—**tow'ering** *a.* very tall; very fierce (rage, anger).
town *n.* collection of dwellings, etc., larger than a village.—**town-coun'cil** *n.* citizens elected to govern town.—**town-hall** *n.* place where town business is transacted.—**town'ship** *n.* division of a large parish containing a village or town.
tox'ic *a.* poisonous, due to poison.—**toxicol'ogy** *n.* the science of poisons.—**tox'in** *n.* a poisonous ptomaine.
toxoph'ilite *n.* a devotee of archery.
toy *n.* a plaything.—*v.i.* to act idly, trifle.
trace *n.* the chain or strap by which a horse pulls a vehicle, a track left by anything; an indication; a minute quantity. —*v.t.* to follow the course or track of; to find out; to make a plan of, to draw (**tra'cing** *pres. p.*—*n.* a drawing).—**tra'cery** *n.* interlaced ornament.
trache'a (-kē-) *n.* the windpipe (**trache'ae** *pl.*).—**trache'al** *a.*
track *n.* a mark, or line of marks, left by the passage of anything; a path; a course prepared for racing; railway line; (motoring) distance between two road wheels on one axle.—*v.t.* to follow up the track of.—**trackless** *a.* pathless.
tract *n.* a space of land, water, sky, etc., an area; a pamphlet, *esp.* a religious one. —**tract'ate** *n.* a treatise.
tract'able *a.* easy to manage, docile.
trac'tion *n.* action of drawing.—**trac'tion-engine** *n.*-**tract'or** *n.* machine, *esp.* motor-driven, for ploughing, etc.
trade *n.* commerce, traffic; the practice of buying and selling; any profitable pursuit; those engaged in a trade.—*v.i.* to engage in trade.—*v.t.* to buy and sell; to barter.—**trade'-mark** *n.* a distinctive mark on a maker's goods.—**tra'der** *n.*—**trades'-man** *n.*—**trade-u'nion** *n.* society of workmen for protection of their interests.—**trade'-wind** *n.* wind blowing constantly towards the equator.
tradi'tion *n.* a body of beliefs, facts, etc., handed down from generation to generation; the process of handing down. —**tradi'tional** *a.*—**tradi'tionally** *adv.*
traduce' *v.t.* to slander, to speak ill of. *Syn.* calumniate, vilify, disparage.
traff'ic *n.* the passing to and fro of people, vehicles, etc.; trade.—*v.i.* to trade (**traff'icked** *p.t.* and *p.p.*— **-icking** *pres. p.*).—**traff'icker** *n.* a trader.
traff'icator *n.* a movable pointer by which the driver of a vehicle can indicate a coming change of direction.
trag'edy (-j-) *n.* a serious play with an unhappy ending, e.g., *Hamlet*; this type of drama; terrible event, disaster.—**trag'ic** *a.* of, or in the manner of, tragedy; disastrous; appalling.—**trag'ically** *adv.*—**trage'dian** *n.* a player in tragedy.—**-dienne'** *fem.*—**tragi-com'edy** *n.* a play with tragic and comic elements.
trail *v.t.* to drag behind one, to follow, track down.—*v.i.* to be drawn behind; to hang loosely.—*n.* a thing that trails; the back end of a gun-carriage; a track or trace; in N. America, a rough ill-defined road in wild country.
trai'ler *n.* person or animal following a trail; a creeper; a vehicle attached to another vehicle; a trailing plant; a weight-carrying engineless vehicle designed to be towed by a heavy motor-car.—*n.* in cinema, an advertisement of a forthcoming film, itself a short film. —**trailing-axle** in motoring, usually rear-axle of flexible six-wheeler.
train *v.t.* to cause to grow in a particular way; to educate, instruct, exercise; to aim (a gun).—*v.i.* to follow a course of training, *esp.* to achieve physical fitness for athletics.—*n.* trailing part of a dress; body of attendants; fuse or trail of powder to a mine; a line of railway vehicles joined to a locomotive; a collection of vehicles, etc., *esp.* in military use. —**train'ing** *n.* process of educating; education; the act of forming young trees or shrubs to grow in a particular way; the art of preparing men for athletic exercises, or horses for the race-course.
train'-oil *n.* oil from whale blubber.
trait (trā) *n.* a characteristic.
trait'or *n.* one who betrays or is guilty of treason.—**trait'ress** *fem.*—**trait'orous** *a.* disloyal.—**trait'orously** *adv.*
trajec'tory *n.* line of flight of projectile.
tram *n.* a mining wagon-road; a line of rails; truck running on rails; a car for passengers running on rails laid through streets.—**tram'car** *n.*—**tram'way** *n.*
tramm'el *n.* net; thing that restrains or checks; beam compass.—*v.t.* restrain (**tram'elled** *p.t./p.p.*).
tramp *v.i.* to walk heavily; to travel on foot, *esp.* as a vagabond or for pleasure —*n.* sound of heavy steps; homeless vagrant.—**tramp-steamer** *n.* ship that takes cargo wherever wanted.
tram'ple *v.t.* to tread under foot.
trance (-à-) *n.* a state of suspended consciousness, *esp.* of rapture or ecstasy.
tran'quil (-ng-kw-) *a.* calm, quiet.—

tran'quilly *adv.*—**tranquill'ity** *n.*—**tran'quillise** *v.t.* to make calm.

Syn. still, serene, unruffled, placed. *Ant.* restless, uneasy, nervy.

trans- *prefix* across, through, beyond. —**transact'** *v.t.* to carry on through; conduct (an affair, etc.).—**transac'tion** *n.* the performing of any business; that which is performed; a single sale or purchase. —*pl.* proceedings; reports of scientific or philosophical associations.—**transcend'** *v.t.* to exceed, surpass.—**transcend'ent** *a.*—**transcend'ence** *n.*—**transcendent'al** *a.* surpassing experience; supernatural; abstruse.–**transcendent'alism** *n.*—**transcribe'** *v.t.* to copy out.—**trans'cript** *n.* a copy.—**transcrip'tion** *n.* an electrical sound recording, *esp.* one used for radio broadcasts.—**trans'ept** *n.* the transverse part of a cruciform church; either of its arms.—**transfer'** *v.t.* to make over; move from one place to another.—**trans'fer** *n.* a transferring or being transferred.—**trans'ferable** *a.*—**trans'ference** *n.* transfer; in psycho-analysis, redirection of emotion when under analysis, towards, usually, the analyst.—**transfig'ure** *v.t.* to alter the appearance of; glorify.—**transfigura'tion** *n.*—**transfix'** *v.t.* to pierce.—**transform'** *v.t.* to change the shape or character of.—**transforma'tion** *n.*—**transform'er** *n.* in electricity, apparatus for changing the voltage of an alternating current without the use of moving parts.—**transfuse'** *v.t.* to convey from one vessel to another, *esp.* of blood from a healthy person to an ill one.—**transfu'sion** *n.*—**transgress'** *v.t.* to break (a law); to sin.—**transgres'sion** *n.*—**transgress'or** *n.*—**tranship'** *v.t.* to move from one ship, train, etc., to another.—**tranship'ment** *n.*—**tran'sient** *a.* passing away.—**tran'sience** *n.*—**tran'sit** *n.* passage, crossing.—**transi'tion** *n.* change from one state to another.—**transi'tional** *a.*—**tran'sitory** *a.* transient.—**tran'sitive** *a.* in grammar, a transitive verb is one which takes a direct object (e.g., *raise your glasses*). When the verb does not take a direct object (e.g., *he runs well*) it is intransitive.—**translate'** *v.t.* to move (a bishop) from one see to another; to turn from one language into another. —**transla'tion** *n.*—**transla'tor** *n.*—**translit'erate** *v.t.* to write in the letters of another alphabet.—**translitera'tion** *n.*—**translu'cent** *a.* letting light pass, semi-transparent.—**translu'cence** *n.*—**trans'migrate** *v.i.* of the soul, to pass into another body.—**transmigra'tion** *n.*—**transmit'** *v.t.* to send or cause to pass to another place, person, etc.—**transmis'sion** *n.* transference; in motoring, gear by which power is communicated from engine to road-wheels; in wireless, the radiation of waves by transmitting station.—**transmute'** *v.t.* to change in form, properties, or nature.–**transmuta'tion** *n.*—**tran'som** *n.* a cross-piece; a lintel.—**trans-so'nic** *a.* pert. to a narrow zone of speed just greater than that of sound.—**transpar'ent** *a.* letting light pass without distortion, that can be seen through distinctly; obvious. —**transpar'ence** *n.*—**transpar'ency** *n.* transparence; a picture made visible by a light behind it.—**transpar'ently** *adv.*—**transpire'** *v.t.* to exhale.—*v.i.* to exhale; to come to be known.—**transpira'tion** *n.* **transplant'** *v.t.* to move and plant again in another place.—**transplanta'tion** *n.*—**transpon'tine** *a.* situated across a bridge, as the Surrey side of London.—**transport'** *v.t.* to convey from one place to another; to carry into banishment; to enrapture. —**trans'port** *n.* means of conveyance, ships; vehicles, etc., used in transporting stores; a ship so used.—**transpose'** *v.t.* to change the order of, interchange; put music into a different key.—**transpo'sal** *n.*—**transposi'tion** *n.*—**transubstantia'tion** *n.* change in essence or substance.—**transude'** *v.i.* to pass through the pores of a substance.—**trans'verse** *a.* lying across.

trap *n.* a snare, a contrivance for catching game, etc.; a movable covering for an opening, *esp.* through a ceiling, etc. a two-wheeled carriage; an arrangement of pipes to prevent escape of gas, etc.—*v.t.* to catch, entrap; to run down (a person, etc.).—**trap'ping** *pr. p.*—**trapped** *p.t./p.p.*—**trap'door** *n.* horizontal door in floor or roof.—**trapp'er** *n.*

trap *v.t.* to caparison.—**trapp'ings** *n. pl.* caparison; equipment, ornaments.

Syn. of "trappings," decorations, accoutrements, equipments, paraphernalia.

trape'zium *n.* a quadrilateral figure with two sides only parallel (**-ziums, -zia** *pl.*).—**trape'zoid** *n.* a quadrilateral figure with no parallel sides.–**trapeze'** *n.* a horizontal bar suspended from two ropes.

trash *n.* rubbish, refuse; nonsense; loppings of trees.—**trash'y** *a.*

trau'ma (traw'-ma) an abnormal state of the body due to external injury.

trav'ail *v.i.* to labour or be in labour.—*n.* toil; the pains of childbirth.

trav'el *v.i.* to journey.—*v.t.* to journey through.—*n.* journeying; in machinery, distance a component is permitted to move.—*pl.* an account of travelling.—**trave'ller** *n.* one who travels; salesman travelling for firm; in Australia, a swagman.—**trav'elling** *pres. p.*—**trav'elled** *p.t.* and *p.p.*—**trav'eller's cheque** *n.* a cheque, *esp.* for tourists, payable at any branch or by any agent of the bank that issues it.—**trav'elogue** *n.* travel talk; a geographical film.

trav'erse *v.t.* to cross, go through or over; oppose.—**trav'erse-table** a table of differences of latitude and departure; a movable platform for shifting carriages, etc., from one line to another.

trav'esty *n.* a comic imitation, a parody. —*v.t.* to ridicule by a travesty (**-estied** *p.t.* and *p.p.*— **-estying** *pres. p.*).

trawl *n.* a net dragged along the bottom of the sea.—*v.i.* to fish with one.

trawl'er *n.* a trawling vessel.

tray *n.* a flat board, usually with a rim, for carrying things; any similar utensil.

treach'ery (trech-) *n.* deceit, betrayal. —**treach'erous** *a.*—**treach'erously** *adv.*

trea'cle *n.* unrefined molasses, a thick syrup.—**treac'ly** *a.* like treacle, sticky.

tread (tred) *v.t.* to set foot on.—*v.i.* to walk (**trod** *p.t.*—**trodd'en, trod** *p.p.*— **tread'ing** *pr. p.*).—*n.* sound, fashion of walking; upper surface of step.

trea'dle *n.* a lever worked by the foot to turn a wheel, a pedal.

trea'son *n.* offence of attempting to overthrow government to which offender owes allegiance; treachery.—**trea'sonable** *a.* constituting treason.—**high treason,** treason against the crown.

treas'ure (trezh-) *n.* riches, stored wealth, valuables.—*v.t.* to prize; to store up.—**treas'urer** *n.* an official in charge of funds.—**treas'ury** *n.* a place for funds or treasure; government department controlling public money (**treas'uries** *pl.*).— **treas'ure-trove** *n.* treasure found hidden with no evidence of the ownership.

treat *v.t.* to deal with, act towards.—*v.i.* to negotiate.—*n.* an entertainment, a pleasure given.—**treat'ise** *n.* a book discussing a subject.—**treat'ment** *n.*

treat'y *n.* a contract between states.

treb'le (treb'l) *a.* threefold.—*n.* a soprano voice; part of music for it; a singer with such a voice.—*v.t.* and *i.* to increase threefold.—**treb'ly** *adv.*

tree *n.* a large perennial plant with a woody trunk; piece of wood, a beam.

tre'foil *n.* a plant with leaves in three parts, like the clover.

trek *v.i.* in S. Africa, to draw a vehicle, as oxen; to migrate, shift.—*n.*

trell'is *n.* a lattice of light bars fixed crosswise; to supply with a trellis.

trem'ble *v.i.* to quiver, shake; be terrified.—*n.* a trembling.

tremen'dous *a.* causing fear or awe; vast, immense, huge.

trem'or *n.* a trembling.—**trem'ulous** *a.* timorous, frightened, shy.

trench *v.t.* to cut grooves or ditches in.— *v.i.* to infringe.—*n.* a long narrow ditch, *esp.* as a shelter in war.

trench'ant *a.* cutting, sharp.

trench'er *n.* a wooden plate, *esp.* for cutting bread on.— **tren'cherman** *n.* person who eats huge meals.

trend *v.i.* to have a general direction.—*n.* direction, tendency; inclination.

trepan' *n.* a cylindrical saw for perforating the skull.—*v.t.* to perforate the skull with a trepan; *v.t.* to ensnare, to trap.

trepang' *n.* a sea-slug or bêche-de-mer.

trepida'tion *n.* fear, alarm.

tres'pass *n.* wrong-doing; wrongful entering on another's land (**-es** *pl.*).— —*v.i.* to commit trespass.—**tres'passer** *n.* *Syn.* of *v.* transgress, encroach, infringe, trench, offend, sin; of *n.* misdemeanour, misdeed, sin, infringement.

tress' *n.* a lock of hair (**-es** *pl.*).

tres'tle (-sl) *n.* a bar fixed on pairs of spreading legs and used as a support.

trews (trōōz) *n. pl.* (tartan) trousers of soldiers in Highland regiments.

tri- *prefix* three.— **tri'car** *n.* a 3-wheeled motor-car with the single wheel behind. —**tri'colour** *a.* three coloured.—*n.* a tricolour flag, *esp.* the French one. — **tri'cycle** *n.* a vehicle like a bicycle, but with three wheels.—**tri'dent** *n.* a three-pronged fork.—**trienn'ial** *a.* happening every, or lasting, three years.

trial' *n.* test, trying; hardship; judicial examination in court.

tri'angle *n.* a figure with three angles; musical instrument made of triangular steel rod.—**triang'ular** *a.* three-cornered.

tribe *n.* a race or subdivision of a race of people, animals, etc.—**tri'bal** *a.*

tribula'tion *n.* misery, trouble.

tribu'nal *n.* a law-court.

trib'une *n.* a popular leader; a speaker's platform; a bishop's throne.

trib'ute *n.* a tax paid by one state to another.—**trib'utary** *a.* paying tribute; auxiliary.—*n.* a stream flowing into another (**trib'utaries** *pl.*).

trice *v.t.* to pull up and secure with a rope.—*n.* **in a trice** in an instant.

trick *n.* a stratagem; a feat of skill or cunning; the cards played in one round. —*v.t.* to cheat; to attire.—**trick'ery** *n.*— **trick'ster** *n.*—**trick'sy** *a.* sportive; deceptive; crafty.—**trick'y** *a.* crafty.

tric'kle *v.i.* to flow slowly or in drops.

tri'dent *n.* a three-pronged fork, sceptre or spear borne by Neptune.

tri'fle *n.* an insignificant thing or matter; a pudding of sponge-cake, whipped cream, etc.—*v.i.* to act or speak idly.

trigg'er *n.* a catch which releases a spring, *esp.* to fire a gun, etc.

trigonom'etry *n.* the branch of mathematics dealing with the relations of the sides and angles of triangles.—**trigonomet'rical** *a.* of trigonometry.

trilat'eral *a.* having three sides.

tril'by *n.* a kind of soft felt hat.

trill *v.i.* to sing with quavering voice; to sing lightly.—*n.* such singing.

tril'ogy (-j-) *n.* a series of three related dramas or novels (**tril'ogies** *pl.*).

trim *v.t.* to prune; to make tidy by cutting, to clip; to decorate; to adjust, (*esp.* sails), put in good order; in aviation, to balance aeroplane against air forces. —*v.i.* to shuffle, act as a time-server.—

n. order, state of being trimmed.—*a.* neat, smart; in good order.
trinitrotol'uene *n.* a high explosive derived from toluene; (T.N.T.).
trin'ity *n.* the state of being threefold; the three persons of the Godhead.—**trinitar'ian** (-ér-) *n.* and *a.*
trink'et *n.* small personal ornament.
tri'o (-ē-) *n.* a group of three; music for three performers, etc. (**tri'os** *pl.*).
tri'ode *n.* in wireless, a three-electrode thermionic valve.
trip *v.i.* to run lightly, skip; to stumble.—*v.t.* to cause to stumble.—*n.* a light step; a stumble; a journey, an excursion.
tri'partite *a.* having three parts.
tripe *n.* stomach of ruminant animal as food; (*sl.*) nonsense, rubbish.
trip'le *a.* threefold.—*n.* S. Africa, of a horse, shuffling canter on three legs.—*v.t./i.* to treble; S. Africa, of horses, to amble.—**trip'ly** *adv.*—**trip'lets** *n. pl.* three children born at one birth.—**trip'licate** *a.* threefold.—*v.t.* to make threefold or three copies.
trip'lex *a.* threefold.—**Triplex glass** a three-ply safety glass, consisting of two layers of glass and one of micaceous substance (protected trade name).
tri'pod *n.* a stool or stand, table, mast, etc., with three feet.
tri'pos *n.* an honours examination at Cambridge; list of the successful candidates in it.
trip'per *n.* one who makes a popular trip or excursion, excursionist.
trip'tych (-tik) *n.* a carving or picture in three compartments.
tri'reme *n.* a three-banked galley.
trite *a.* hackneyed, stale, commonplace.
trit'urate *v.t.* to rub to powder, pulverise.—**tritura'tion** *n.*
tri'umph *n.* great success, victory; exultation.—*v.i.* to achieve great success or victory; to exult.—**triumph'ant** *a.* victorious.—**triumph'al** *a.* of triumph.
tri'umvir *n.* one of three men joined equally in an office.—**trium'virate** *n.*
tri'une *a.* three in one.—**triun'ity** *n.*
triv'et *n.* an iron bracket or stand for putting a pot or kettle on.
triv'ial *a.* commonplace, trifling.—**trivial'ity** *n.* trifle (**trivial'ities** *pl.*).
tro'chee (trō'kē) *n.* in verse, a foot of two syllables, long-short.
trog'lodyte *n.* a cave-dweller.
troll (-ō-) *v.t.* to pass (cup) round; to sing heartily; to fish for by dragging a hook through the water.
troll (-ō-) *n.* a diminutive supernatural being in Scandinavian mythology.
troll'ey *n.* truck; pole by which tramcar, trolley-bus draws electric power from overhead wire.—**trolley-bus** *n.* a street omnibus deriving power from overhead electric wires, but not running on rails; in N. Amer., electric street car.
troll'op *n.* a loose woman; a slattern.
trom'bone *n.* a large trumpet.
tronk *n.* in S. Africa, a prison.
troop *n.* a group of persons or animals; a unit of cavalry.—*pl.* soldiers.—*v.i.* to move in a troop.—**troop'er** *n.* a cavalry soldier; troop-horse; troop-ship.
trope *n.* a figure of speech.
tro'pism *n.* the response of living tissue to any kind of stimulus.
tro'phy *n.* a memorial of a victory, hunt.
trop'ic *n.* either of two circles in heavens or round earth where sun seems to turn at solstice.—*pl.* hot regions between tropics.—**trop'ical** *a.* of tropics; sultry.
trot *v.i.* of a horse, to move at a medium pace, lifting the feet in diagonal pairs; of a person, etc., to run easily.—*n.*
troth (-ō-) *n.* faith; promise.
trou'badour *n.* one of a class of early poets that first appeared in Provence.
trou'ble (trub'l) *v.t.* to disturb, afflict.—*v.i.* to be agitated or disturbed.—*n.* disturbance, agitation; inconvenience; distress.—**troub'lous** *a.*—**troub'lesome** *a.*
Syn. of *n.* affliction, suffering, calamity, misfortune, adversity, sorrow, misery.
trough (trof) *n.* a long open vessel; the hollow between two waves; a channel.
trounce *v.t.* to beat thoroughly.
troupe' *n.* troop; band; company, *esp.* a group of actors, singers or acrobats.
trou'sers *n. pl.* a two-legged outer garment with legs reaching to the ankles.
trou'sseau (trōō-) *n.* an outfit of clothing, *esp.* for a bride.
trout *n.* a fresh-water fish.
trow' *v.i.* to think, believe, suppose.
trow'el *n.* small tool for lifting plants, spreading mortar, etc.—*v.t.*
troy-weight *n.* a system of weights used for gold and silver, etc.
tru'ant *n.* one absent from school or duty without leave; idler.
truce *n.* a temporary cessation of fighting, an armistice; respite.
truck *v.t.* and *i.* to barter.—*n.* barter; payment of workmen in goods; garden produce; (*sl.*) worthless articles collectively; rubbish.—**truck farm** *n.* in N. America, a market garden.
truck *n.* open vehicle for heavy goods; motor-lorry; a kind of barrow; a disc at a masthead.—**truc'kle-bed** *n.* small bed on castors (to go under a larger bed).—**truc'kle** *v.i.* to cringe, fawn.
truc'ulent *a.* ferocious, inclined to fight.
trudge *v.i.* to walk laboriously.—*n.*
trudge'n (truj-) *n.* racing stroke in swimming in hand over hand style.
true (trōō) *a.* in accordance with facts; faithful; exact, correct.—**truth** (-ōō-) *n.* state of being true; something that is true.—**tru'ism** *n.* a self-evident truth.—**tru'ly** *adv.*—**truth'ful** *a.*—**truth'fully** *adv.*
truf'fle *n.* round edible fungus growing underground.

trull *n.* a drab; a trollop.
trump *n.* trumpet.—*v.i.* blow, make sound like one.—*v.t.* proclaim.
trump *n.* a card of a suit temporarily ranking above the other.—*v.t.* to play the trump card, to take with a trump.—*v.i.* **to trump up** to get up, fabricate.
trum'pery *a.* showy but worthless.—*n.* worthless finery; trash, nonsense.
trum'pet *n.* metal wind-instrument with loud, clear tone; something shaped like one.—*v.t.* and *i.* to sound on a trumpet; to announce loudly, to acclaim. —**trum'peter** *n.* player of trumpet.
trunc'ate *v.t.* to cut short.
trun'cheon *n.* a short thick club or baton; a staff of office.
trun'dle *n.* any round, rolling thing; a low cart, with small wooden wheels; a wheel or pinion having its teeth formed of cylinders or spindles, as in mill-work. —*v.t.* to roll, as a thing on little wheels. —*v.i.* to roll, as on little wheels.
trunk *n.* the main stem of a tree; person's body without or excluding the head and limbs; box for clothes, etc.; an elephant's or other proboscis.—**trunk-call** *n.* telephone call over a main or trunk line.—**trunk-line** *n.* main line of a railway, canal, telephone system.
truss *v.t.* to fasten up, tie (up).—*n.* a support; bundle (of hay, etc.) (**-es** *pl.*).
trust *n.* confidence, firm belief; property held for another; state of being relied on; a combination of producers to do away with competition and keep up prices.—*v.t.* to rely on, believe in.—**trustee'** *n.* one legally holding property on another's behalf.—**trustee'ship** *n.*—**trust'ful** *a.* trusting.—**trust'worthy** *a.*—**trust'y** *a.* faithful. —*n.* in N. America, a convict with special privileges.
truth *see* **true.**
try *v.t.* test; investigate (case); attempt (**tried** *p.t./p.p.*—**try'ing** *pr. p.*).—*v.i.* attempt thing, endeavour.
tryst *n.* an appointment to meet; a place of meeting, rendezvous.
tset'se *n.* S. African fly with a bite often fatal to horses and cattle; small flies that transmit trypanosome parasites and cause sleeping-sickness.
tub *n.* an open wooden vessel like the bottom half of a barrel; a bath.
tu'ba *n.* a brass wind instrument of low pitch; organ stop of reed family.
tube *n.* a pipe, a long narrow hollow cylinder; an underground railway running in a tubular tunnel.—**tu'bular** *a.*
tu'ber *n.* a swelling on the roots of certain plants, e.g., a potato.—**tu'bercle** *n.* a granular small tumour in consumptive lungs, etc.—**tuber'cular** *a.*—**tuber'culin** *n.* a preparation of tuberculosis bacilli; used as a test for the disease, etc.—**tuberculo'sis** *n.* a disease marked by the presence of tubercles and a characteristic bacillus, *esp.* consumption of the lungs.
tuck *v.t.* to gather or stitch in folds; to draw or roll together.—*n.* a stitched fold; food, *esp.* dainties eaten by school-boys. —**tuck'er** *n.* (*sl.*) food.—**tuck'-box** *n.* —**tuck'-shop** *n.*—**tucker out** *v.t.* in N. America, to exhaust, weary completely.
Tues'day *n.* the third day of the week.
tuft *n.* a bunch of feathers, threads, etc.
tug *v.t.* to pull hard or violently.—*n.* a violent pull; steamship used to tow other vessels.—**tug-of-war'** *n.* contest between two teams pulling against each other on a rope; laborious contest.
tui'tion *n.* teaching, instruction.
tu'lip *n.* bulbous spring plant with bright bell-shaped flowers.
tulle (tôôl) *n.* a kind of fine thin silk.
tum'ble *v.i.* to fall; turn somersaults.—*v.t.* throw down, upset, overturn; rumple. —*n.* fall; somersault.—**tum'bler** *n.* acrobat; flat-bottomed drinking-glass; kind of pigeon.
tum'bril, tum'brel *n.* farmer's cart; cart that carried persons to be executed.
tu'mid *a.* swollen; pompous.
tu'mour *n.* diseased growth; morbid swelling in any part of body.
tu'mult *n.* uproar, commotion.—**tumult'uous** *a.* noisy, rough.
tu'mulus *n.* ancient burial mound, barrow. (**-li** *pl.*).—**tu'mular** *n.*
tun *n.* a large cask.
tu'na *n.* game and food fish; a kind of tunny of N. Amer. Pacific coast.
tun'dra *n.* vast mossy plains in the north of Russia and Siberia.
tune *n.* music of a song, air, melody; concord; adjustment of a musical instrument.—*v.t.* to put in tune.—**tune'ful** *a.*—**tune'fully** *adv.*—**tu'ner** *n.*
tung'sten *n.* a rare metal, chiefly got from wolframite, used in the manufacture of steel and for electric lamp filaments.—**tung'stic** *a.*
tu'nic *n.* short military coat; child's sleeveless outer garment.
tunn'el *n.* an artificial underground passage.—*v.t.* to make a tunnel through.
tunn'y *n.* large sea fish used for food.
tu'puna *n.* in New Zealand, Maori for an ancestor, a progenitor, male or female.
tur'ban *n.* Oriental man's head-dress.
tur'bid *a.* muddy.—**turbid'ity** *n.*
tur'bine *n.* a rotary engine driven by water, steam, air, gas, in which a shaft or drum fitted with curved vanes is driven by impact or reaction, or both.
tur'bot *n.* a large flat-fish used for food.
tur'bulence *n.* disorder, commotion.
tur'bulent *a.* riotous, in commotion.
tureen' *n.* a covered dish for soup.
turf *n.* short grass with the earth bound to it by the matted roots; a sod (**turfs, turves** *pl.*).—**the turf** *n.* horse-racing; the race-course.—*v.t.* to lay with turf.

tur'gid *a.* bombastic.—**turgid'ity** *n.*
Syn. swollen, inflated, tumid, pompous.
tur'key *n.* a large bird reared for food; in N. America, a lumberman's outfit of clothing, blankets, etc., in a bag.
tur'moil *n.* confusion and bustle.
turn *v.t.* to make move round or rotate; to shape on a lathe; to change, reverse, alter position of, etc.—*v.i.* to move round; to change; to become, etc.—*n.* act of turning; road, walk, rotation, part of a rotation; a performance; an inclination, etc.—**turn'er** *n.*—**turn'back** *n.* a coward; something turned back.—**turn'-coat** *n.* one that forsakes his party or principles.—**turn'cock** *n.* person in charge of public taps, etc.—**turn'key** *n.* a gaoler. —**turn'out** *n.* act of coming forth; short side track on a railroad; an equipage; a strike, as of workmen; a crowd of spectators; quantity of produce yielded. —**turn'over** *n.* act of turning over; the amount of money drawn in a business.—**turn'pike** *n.* gate across a road where tolls are paid.—**turn'stile** *n.* revolving gate for controlling admission of people. —**turn'table** *n.* revolving platform, *esp.* to turn locomotives.—**turning circle,** (motoring) circle described by vehicle driven on full steering lock.
turn'ip *n.* plant with a large round root used as a vegetable or fodder.
turp'entine *n.* a resin got from certain trees; oil or spirit made from this.
turp'itude *n.* baseness, wickedness.
tur'quoise *n.* a blue precious stone.
tur'ret *n.* a small tower; a revolving tower for a gun on a ship, tank, etc.
tur'tle *n.* a dove; a sea-tortoise.
tusk *n.* a long pointed tooth sticking out from animal's mouth.—**tusk'er** *n.* fully grown elephant or boar.
tus'sle *n.* a scuffle, struggle.—*v.*
tuss'ock *n.* a clump of grass.
tu'tor *n.* a person giving lessons, privately, or to individuals in a college; a guardian.—**tutor'ial** *a.*—**tu'telage** *n.* guardianship.—**tu'telary** *a.*
tu'tu *n. see* **toot.**
tuxe'do *n.* (U.S.) a dinner jacket.
twad'dle *n.* idle talk, nonsense.—*v.*
twain *a.* two.—*n.* two persons or things.
twang *n.* a ringing metallic sound; nasal tone of voice.—*v.i.* and *t.* to make, or cause to make, such sound.
tweak *v.t.* to seize and twist sharply.—*n.*
tweed *n.* rough-surfaced cloth.
tweez'ers *n. pl.* small forceps or pincers.
twelve *n.* and *a.* cardinal number, two more than ten.—**twelfth** *a.* the ordinal number.—*n.* **twelve'month** *n.* one year.
twent'y *n.* and *a.* a cardinal number, twice ten (**-ies** *pl.*).—**twent'ieth** *a.* the ordinal number.—*n.*
twice *adv.* two times.
twid'dle *v.t.* to twirl (**twid'dling** *pres. p.*).
twig *n.* a small branch.—*v.t.* (*sl.*) to detect, understand.
twi'light *n.* the half-light after sunset or before dawn; faint light.—**twilight sleep** partial insensibility induced to lessen the pains of childbirth.
twill *n.* fabric woven to give surface of parallel ridges.—*v.t.* to weave thus.
twin *n.* one of a pair, *esp.* of children born together.—*a.* being a twin.
twine *v.t.* and *i.* to twist or coil round; tangle.—*n.* string; a twist.
twinge *n.* a momentary sharp pain.
twin'kle *v.i.* to shine with dancing or quivering light.—*n.* a twinkling; a flash.
twirl *v.t.* to turn, spin, twist.
twist *v.t.* and *i.* to make or become spiral; to curve; to distort, make crooked.—*n.* an act of twisting; something twisted; tobacco, etc.—**twist'er** in Australia, a cigarette; (*sl.*) crook, dodger.
twit *v.t.* to taunt.
twitch *v.i.* to give a momentary sharp pull; to jerk.—*v.t.* to pull at thus.—*n.*
twitt'er *v.i.* of birds, to utter a succession of tremulous sounds.—*n.*
two (tōō) *n.* and *a.* a cardinal number one more than one.—**two'fold** *adv.* and *a.* double.—**two'-decker** a bus having two decks for passengers.—**two-seat'er** *n.* motor-car designed to accommodate two persons.—**two'-stroke** internal combustion engine making one explosion to every two strokes of piston.—**two-up'** *n.* in Australia, an illegal gambling game resembling pitch and toss played with two pennies; also called **swy-up.**
ty'coon (tī-) *n.* the chief of the Japanese army; shogun; a powerful business leader.
type *n.* a class; characteristic build; a specimen; a wooden or metal block bearing a letter used for printing, such pieces collectively; state of being set up for printing.—*v.t.* to print with a typewriter.—**type'script** *n.* typewritten document or copy.—**type'writer** *n.* a keyed writing machine.—**ty'pist** *n.*
typ'ical *a.* true to type, serving as a type, characteristic.—**typ'ically** *adv.*
typ'ify *v.t.* to serve as a type or model of (**-ified** *p.t.* and *p.p.*— **-ifying** *pres. p.*).
typog'raphy *n.* the art of printing; style of printing.—**typograph'ical** *a.*
ty'phoid *n.* a fever attacking the intestines.—**ty'phus** *n.* a contagious fever.
typhoon' *n.* a violent hurricane.
ty'rant *n.* an oppressive or cruel ruler.—**tyrann'ical** *a.*—**tyrann'ically** *adv.*—**tyrann'icide** *n.* the slayer of a tyrant, his deed.—**tyr'annise** *v.i.*—**tyr'annous** *a.*—**tyr'anny** *n.* cruel and harsh use of power.
tyre *n. see* **tire.**
tyro, ti'ro *n.* a beginner (**ty'ros** *pl.*).

U

ubiq'uity (ū-bik'w-) *n.* a being everywhere.—**ubiq'uitous** *a.*
udd'er *n.* milk-bag of a cow, goat, etc.
ug'ly *a.* unpleasing or repulsive to the sight; threatening.—**ug'liness** *n.*
u'itlander (ōō'it-) *n.* an outlander or incomer in S. Africa, *esp.* in the Transvaal.
ukele'le (ū-ke-lā'li) *n.* a small four-stringed instrument of Hawaiian origin.
ul'cer *n.* an open sore.—**ul'cerate** *v.i.* to form an ulcer.—*v.t.* to make ulcerous.—**ul'cerous** *a.*—**ulcera'tion** *n.*
ull'age *n.* that quantity which a cask wants of being full; (*sl.*) dregs.
ul'na *n.* the larger of the two bones of the forearm (**ulnae** *pl.*).
ul'ster *n.* a long, loose overcoat.
ulte'rior *a.* situated beyond; beyond what appears, e.g., *an ulterior motive.*
ult'imate *a.* last, furthest.—**ult'imately** *adv.*—**ultima'tum** *n.* a final proposal the rejection of which causes war (**-tums**,**-ta** *pl.*).—**ult'imo** *adv.* in last month.
ultra- *prefix* beyond, as *ultramarine*; excessively, as *ultra-modern.*
ultramarine' (-ēn) *a.* beyond the sea.—*n.* a blue pigment.—**ultramont'ane** *a.* south of or beyond the Alps; favourable to the absolute authority of the Pope.—**ul'tra-modern** *a.* very up-to-date.—**ul'tra-short waves** in wireless, by international definition, waves below ten metres.—**ultravi'olet** *a.* beyond the violet (of rays of the spectrum).
um'ber *n.* a dark-brown pigment.
umbili'cal *a.* of the navel.
um'brage *n.* sense of injury, offence.
umbrage'ous *a.* shady.
umbrell'a *n.* a light folding circular cover of silk, etc., on a stick, carried in the hand to protect against rain.
um'pire *n.* person chosen to decide a question; one chosen to decide disputes and enforce rules in game.—*v.t.* act as umpire in.—*v.i.* act as umpire.
ump'teen *a.* (*sl.*) many; any number.
u'mu *n.* in New Zealand, Maori for a native oven.
un- *prefix* makes compounds negativing the idea of the simple word, e.g., **unarmed'** *a.* not armed.—**unfast'en** *v.t.* to loosen or remove the fastening.—**untruth'** *n.* a lie. These are not given except where the meaning cannot easily be found from the simple word.
unan'imous (ū-) *a.* of one mind, agreeing.—**unan'imously** *adv.*—**unanim'ity** *n.*
unassu'ming (-sū-) *a.* modest, not bold.
unavai'ling *a.* of no avail; ineffectual.
unbi'ased *a.* free from bias; impartial.
uncann'y *a.* weird, strange, mysterious; not canny.—**uncann'iness** *n.*
un'cate *a.* hooked.
unc'le (ung'kl) *n.* the brother of a father or mother; the husband of an aunt.
uncouth' (-ōōth) *a.* clumsy, awkward, without ease or polish.—**uncouth'ly** *adv.*
unc'tion *n.* anointing; soothing words or thought; fervour of words or tone; imitation of this; affected enthusiasm.
unc'tuous *a.* full of unction; greasy.
undamped' (-dampt) *a.* not moistened or wet; not depressed.—**undamped oscillations** in electricity, continuous waves.
un'der *prep.* below, beneath; bound by, included in; in the time of.—*adv.* in a lower place or condition.—*a.* lower.—**underbred'** *a.* ill-bred.—**under-carriage** *n.* landing gear of an aeroplane.—**undercharge'** *v.t.* to charge less than the proper amount.—*n.* too low a charge.—**underhand'** *a.* unfair, sly.—**underhung'** *a.* with the lower part projecting beyond the upper.—**un'derling** *n.* a subordinate.—**underneath'** *adv.* below.—*prep.* under.—**un'dershot** *a.* moved by water passing under.—**un'dertow** *n.* a current beneath the surface moving in a different direction from the surface current; backwash.
undergrad'uate *n.* a student who has not taken his first degree.
un'derground *n.* secret but organised resistance to the government in power, *esp.* resistance movements in fascist-ruled countries during World War 2.
und'erslung *a.* in motoring, of a car having frame or chassis below the axles.
understand' *v.t.* to see the meaning of; infer; take for granted.—*v.i.* to be informed (**-stood'** *p.t.* and *p.p.*— **-stand'ing** *pres. p.*).—**understand'ing** *n.* intelligence.
undertake' *v.t.* to make oneself responsible for; enter upon (**-took'** *p.t.*— **-ta'ken** *p.p.*— **-ta'king** *pres. p.*).–**un'dertaker** *n.* one who undertakes; one who manages funerals.—**underta'king** *n.* enterprise; promise; obligation; management of funerals.
un'derwrite *v.t.* to agree to pay, to take up shares in, e.g., in marine insurance (**-wrote** *p.t.*— **-written** *p.p.*— **-writing** *pres. p.*).—**un'derwriter** *n.* an agent in marine insurance, etc.
undo' *v.t.* to reverse what has been done; to annul; to unfasten (**undid'** *p.t.*—**undone'** *p.p.*—**undo'ing** *pres. p.*).—**undo'ing** *n.* ruin, destruction.—**undone'** *a.* not performed; ruined.
un'dulate (-dū-) *v.i.* to move in waves or like waves (**un'dulating** *pres. p.*).—**undula'tion** *n.*—**un'dulatory** *a.*
ungain'ly *a.* clumsy, awkward, uncouth.
un'guent *n.* an ointment.
uni- *prefix* one.
u'nicorn *n.* fabulous animal resembling horse with a single horn on forehead.
u'niform *a.* not changing, unvarying; conforming to the same standard or rule.

—*n.* uniform dress worn by members of the same body, e.g., soldiers, nurses, etc. —u'niformly *adv.*—uniform'ity *n.*

u'nify *v.t.* to bring to unity or uniformity (-ified *p.t.* and *p.p.*— -ifying *pres. p.*).—unifica'tion *n.* unifying.

u'nion *n.* joining into one; state of being joined; the result of being joined; alliance; harmony; federation, combination of societies, etc.; a trade-union.—u'nionist *n.* a supporter of union.—Union Jack *n.* national flag of Britain.—u'nionism *n.*

unique' (-ēk) *a.* the only one of its kind.

u'nison *n.* agreement, harmony; in music, sounding at the same pitch.

u'nit *n.* a single thing or person; a standard quantity.—u'nitary *a.*

unitar'ian (-ėr-) *n.* member of a Christian body that denies the doctrine of the Trinity.—unitar'ianism *n.*

unite' *v.t.* to join into one, connect.—*v.i.* to become one, combine.—u'nity *n.* the state of being one; harmony.—Uni'ted Na'tions a union, developed during World War 2, of 32 nations who had declared war on one or more of the three Axis powers.—Uni'ted Na'tions Organisa'tion (U.N.O.) an organisation formed in 1945 for maintaining international peace and settling international difficulties by arbitration.

u'niverse *n.* the whole of creation, all existing things.—univer'sal *a.* relating to all things or all men; applying to all members of a community.—*n.* (motoring) universal joint.—univer'sally *adv* —universal'ity *n.*—univer'sity *n.* an educational institution for study, examination and conferment of degrees in the important branches of learning.

univ'ocal *a.* having but one meaning; having unison in sounds; sure; certain.

unkempt' *a.* of uncared-for appearance.

unless' *conj.* if not, except when.

unru'ly *a.* badly behaved, ungovernable.

unshel'tered *a.* not protected; of industry, exposed to foreign competition.

until' *prep.* up to the time of.—*conj.* to the time that; with a negative, before.

un'to *prep.* to (archaic).

untouch'able *n.* a Hindu without caste.

up *adv.* in or to a higher position, a source, an activity, etc.; quite (upp'er (*a.*) *comp.*—upp'ermost (*a.*) *sup.*).—*prep.* to or towards the source, etc.—up'ward *a.* and *adv.*—up'wards *adv.*

up- as *prefix* makes compounds mostly of obvious meaning, e.g., up'bringing *n.* bringing up.—uphold' *v.t.* to hold up, support, etc. (upheld' *p.t.* and *p.p.*— -holding *pres. p.*).

upbraid' *v.t.* to scold, reproach.

upholst'erer (-ō-) *n.* one who provides carpets, hangings, or covers chairs, etc. —upholst'er *v.t.*—upholst'ery *n.*

up'land *n.* high land; ground elevated above meadows and valleys.—*a.* rustic.

uplift' *v.t.* to raise aloft.—(up'-) *n.* an upheaval; exaltation of any kind.

upon' *prep.* on.

upp'er *a.* higher, situated above; *comp.* of **up.**—*n.* the upper part of a boot or shoe.—upp'ish *a.* self-assertive.—upp'ermost *a. sup.* of **up.**

up'right *a.* erect; honest, just.—*n.* a thing standing upright, e.g. a post in a framework.—up'rightness *n.*

up'roar *n.* a tumult, disturbance.—uproar'ious *a.*—uproar'iously *adv.*

uproot' *v.t.* to tear up by the roots; (*fig.*) to exterminate, destroy.

upset' *v.t.* to overturn (upset' *p.t.* and *p.p.*).—*a.* overturned.—*n.* an upsetting; trouble.—up'set *n.* trouble.

up'shot *n.* result, outcome, end.

up'start *n.* one suddenly raised to wealth, power, etc., parvenu.

up'swept *a.* in motoring, to denote upward sweep of frame.

ur'aemia, ure'mia (ūr-ē'mi-a) *n.* a morbid condition of the blood.

u'ranite *n.* term for a number of uranium-phosphate ores.

ura'nium *n.* white radioactive metallic element.—ura'nium 235 isotopic form of uranium important to fissure of atom.

urbane' *a.* polished, courteous.—urban'ity *n.*—ur'ban *a.* relating to a town.

urch'in *n.* hedgehog; ragged or untidy mischievous boy; boy or youngster.

urge *v.t.* to drive on; entreat or exhort earnestly.—ur'gent *a.* pressing; needing attention at once; importunate.—ur'gently *adv.*—ur'gency *n.* pressing need.

u'rine *n.* the fluid secreted by the kidneys.—u'ric *a.*—u'rinate *v.t.* to discharge urine.—u'rinal *n.* a place for urinating.

urn *n.* ornamental vase with a foot or pedestal; large vessel with tap, for tea, etc.; vase for ashes of dead.

us *pron. pl.* objective case of **we.**

use (ūs) *n.* employment, application to a purpose; profit, serviceableness; need to employ; habit.—use (ūz) *v.t.* to employ, avail oneself of; accustom.—u'sable (-z-) *a.*—u'sage (-z-) *n.* act of using; custom; customary way of using.—use'ful (-s-) *a.* —use'fully *adv.*—use'fulness *n.*—use'less *a.*—use'lessly *adv.*—use'lessness *n.*

ush'er *n.* a doorkeeper, one showing people to seats, etc.; formerly an under-teacher.—*v.t.* to introduce, announce.

u'sual *a.* ordinary; customary.—usually, commonly, generally *adv.*

u'sufruct *n.* right of using the property of another, without alienating.

usurp' (ū-) *v.t.* to seize wrongfully.—usurp'er *n.*—usurpa'tion *n.*

u'sury (-z-) *n.* lending of money at excessive interest; such interest.—u'surer *n.*—usu'rious *a.*

uten'sil (ū-) *n.* a vessel or implement, *esp.* in domestic use in the kitchen.

util'ity (ū-) *n.* usefulness; a useful thing

—**utilita'rianism** *n.* doctrine that the morality of actions is to be tested by their utility, *esp.* that the greatest good of the greatest number should be sole end of public action.—**utilita'rian** (-ĕr-) *a.*—**u'tilise** *v.t.* make use of.—**utilisa'tion** *n.* *Syn.* advantageousness, benefit, profit.
ut'most, uttermost *a.* extreme, furthest (*sup.* of **out**).
Uto'pia (ū-) *n.* an imaginary state with perfect political, social conditions or constitution.—**Uto'pian** *a.* visionary.
utt'er *a.* complete, total, absolute, unqualified (*comp.* of **out**).—**utter'most** *sup.*—**utt'erly** *adv.*
utt'er *v.t.* express, emit audibly; put in circulation.—**utt'erance** *n.* uttering; expression in words; spoken words.
u'tu *n.* in New Zealand, payment for services, compensation.
u'vula *n.* the pendent fleshy part of the soft palate.—**u'vular** *a.*
uxor'ious *a.* excessively or submissively fond of one's wife.

V

va'cant *a.* unoccupied; without thought, empty.—**va'cantly** *adv.*—**va'cancy** *n.*
vacate' *v.t.* to quit, leave empty.—**vaca'tion** *n.* act of vacating; holidays.
vac'cinate (-ks-) *v.t.* to inoculate with vaccine as a protection against smallpox. —**vaccina'tion** *n.*—**vac'cinator** *n.*—**vac'cine** *n.* a virus of cowpox.
va'cillate (vas'-) *v.i.* to be undecided, to waver.—**vacilla'tion** *n.* hesitation.
vac'uous *a.* vacant.—**vacu'ity** *n.*
vac'uum *n.* a place devoid of matter; a place from which air has been practically exhausted (**vac'uums, vac'ua** *pl.*).—**vacuum cleaner** *n.* a machine for removing dust, etc., by suction.
va'de-me'cum *n.* a manual for ready reference; a pocket companion.
vag'abond *a.* having no fixed dwelling; wandering.—*n.* a wanderer; an idle scamp; a rogue.—**vag'abondage** *n.*
vagar'y (-ĕr-) *n.* a freak; an unaccountable proceeding (**vagar'ies** *pl.*).
va'grant *n.* a tramp.—*a.* on tramp; wandering idly.—**va'grancy** *n.*
vague *a.* of indefinite or uncertain character or meaning.—**vague'ly** *adv.*
vain *a.* worthless, useless; conceited; foolish.—**vainglor'ious** *a.* boastful.—**vain'glory** *n.*—**vain'ly** *adv.*
val'ance *n.* a short curtain round a bedstead, etc.—**val'anced** *a.*
vale *n.* valley.
valedic'tion *n.* a farewell.—**valedic'tory** *a.*
va'lence, va'lency *n.* in chemistry, the combining power of an element.
Valenci'ennes (-sē'enz) *n.* a rich kind of lace made at *Valenciennes.*
val'entine *n.* a picture, set of verses, etc., sent to a sweetheart on Feb. 14th.
valer'ian (-ėr-) *n.* a flowering herb.
val'et (-ā, or -et) *n.* a manservant.
valetu'dinary *a.* sickly.—**valetudina'rian** *n.* a person obliged or disposed to live the life of an invalid.
Valhall'a *n.* in Scandinavian mythology, the place of immortality.
val'iant *a.* brave, courageous.
val'id *a.* sound; of binding force in law.—**valid'ity** *n.*—**val'idate** *v.t.*
val'ise (-ēs) *n.* a travelling bag.
vall'ey *n.* low area between hills.
val'orize *v.t.* to establish the value of a country's currency by government control.—**valoriza'tion** *n.*
val'our (-er) *n.* bravery.—**val'orous** *a.*
val'ue *n.* worth, price; equivalent.—*v.t.* to estimate a value of; to care for.—**val'uable** *a.* capable of being valued; of great value.—*n.* a valuable thing.—**valua'tion** *n.*—**val'ueless** *a.*—**val'uer** *n.*
valve *n.* a device to control the passage of fluid, steam, gas, etc., through a pipe; in wireless, *abbrev.* for **thermionic valve**—**val'vular** *a.* of, affecting valves.
vamoose' *v.t.* and *i.* in N. America, to depart quickly; leave; decamp.
vamp *n.* the upper leather of a shoe; a woman who indulges in the art of attracting men.—*v.t.* and *i.* to patch; to improvise (accompaniment).
vamp'ire *n.* a blood-sucking ghost; (*sl.*) a person who preys on others, extortioner.—**vamp** *n.* (*sl.*) vampire.
van *n.* covered vehicle, *esp.* for goods; leading division of army or fleet.—**van'guard** *n.* advance guard.
vana'dium *n.* a metallic element used in the manufacture of hard steel.
van'dalism *n.* barbarous destruction of works of art.—**van'dal** *n.*
vane *n.* a weather-cock; a fin on a bomb, etc.; blade of a ship's propeller.
vanill'a *n.* plant of the orchid kind; extract of the bean of this for flavouring.
van'ish *v.i.* to disappear.—he **vanishes.**
van'ity *n.* empty display; vain pride.
van'quish *v.t.* to subdue in battle; to conquer; to refute.—**van'quishable** *a.*
van'tage (vȧ-) *n.* advantage.
vap'id *a.* flat, dull.—**vapid'ity** *n.*
va'pour (-er) *n.* a gaseous form of a substance more familiar as liquid or solid; steam or mist; invisible moisture in the air.—**va'porise** *v.t.*—**va'porous** *a.*—**va'poriser** *n.* in internal combustion engine, device for reducing liquid to vapour.
var'icose *a.* of a vein, morbidly dilated.
var'iegate *v.t.* to diversify by patches of different colours.—**variega'tion** *n.*
vari'ety *n.* state of being varied or various; a varied assortment; a sort or kind (**vari'eties** *pl.*).—**var'ious** *a.* manifold, diverse, of several kinds.
var'nish *n.* a resinous solution put on a

surface to make it hard and shiny.—*v.t.* to apply, coat with varnish.
var'y (vėr'-i) *v.t.* to change.—*v.i.* to be changed; to become different (**var'ied** *p.t.* and *p.p.*—**var'ying** *pres. p.*).—**var'iable** *a.*—**variabil'ity** *n.*—**var'iance** *n.* state of discord.—**var'iant** *a.* different.—*n.* a difference in form.—**varia'tion** *n.* *Syn.* modify, transform, metamorphose, variegate, deviate, depart, alternate.
vas'cular *a.* of, or having, vessels for conveying sap, blood, etc.
vase (vāz) *n.* a vessel, a jar.
Vas'eline (vas'-e-lin) *n.* protected trade name applied to a brand of petrolatum which is a translucent yellowish semi-solid substance used in ointments, pomades, as a lubricant, etc.
vass'al *n.* a holder of land by feudal tenure; a dependant.—**vass'alage** *n.*
vast (-â-) *a.* very large.—**vast'ly** *adv.*
vat *n.* a large tub, tank.
vaude'ville (vōd'vil) *n.* a light gay song with a refrain; theatrical performance with light satirical songs, etc.
vault (volt) *n.* an arched roof or apartment; a cellar, underground tomb.—*v.t.* to build with an arched roof.
vault (volt) *v.i.* to spring or jump with the hands resting on something.—*v.t.* to jump over in this way.—*n.* such jump.
vaunt *v.i.* to boast.—*v.t.* to boast of.—*n.*
veal *n.* calf flesh as food.
vedette' *n.* a mounted sentinel.
veer *v.i.* of wind etc., to change direction; to change one's opinion.
veg'etable (-j-) *a.* of, from, or concerned with, plants.—*n.* a plant, *esp.* one used for food —**vegeta'rian** *n.* one who does not eat meat.—**vegeta'rianism** *n.*
veg'etate *v.i.* to live the life of a plant.
vegeta'tion *n.* plants collectively; the plants growing in a place.
ve'hement (vē'im-) *a.* vigorous, impetuous.–**ve'hemently** *adv.*— **-mence** *n.*
ve'hicle (vē'ikl) *n.* carriage, car, truck or other land conveyance; a means of expression.—**vehic'ular** *a.*
veil (vāl) *n.* a piece of material to cover face or head (e.g., nun's veil); pretext. —*v.t.* cover with, as with veil.
vein (vān) *n.* tube in the body taking blood to the heart; rib of a leaf or insect's wing; fissure in rock filled with ore; a streak; a mood, manner, style.—*v.t.* to mark with streaks.—**vein'y** *a.*
veld (velt) *n.* in S. Africa, a grassland.—**bush'veld** *n.* wooded country.—**high'-veld** *n.* elevated grass country.—**on'der-veld** *n.* up country, inland areas.
vel'kombers *n.* S. Africa, a skin rug.
vell'um *n.* parchment of calf skin prepared for writing on or bookbinding.
velo'city (-os'-) *n.* rate of motion, *esp.* of inanimate things; speed.
vel'skoen *n.* home made shoe.
vel'vet *n.* silk fabric with a thick, short pile.—**vel'vety** *a.* like velvet, soft and smooth.—**velveteen'** *n.* cotton fabric resembling velvet.
ve'nal *a.* guilty of taking, prepared to take, bribes; corrupt.—**venal'ity** *n.*
vend *v.t.* to sell.—**vend'or** *n.*–**vend'ible** *a.*
vendett'a *n.* a blood-feud.
veneer' *v.t.* to cover with a thin layer of finer wood.—*n.* such covering.
ven'erable *a.* worthy of reverence, very old.—**ven'erate** *v.t.*—**venera'tion** *n.*
vene'real *a.* from, connected with, communicated by, sexual intercourse.—**V D.** venereal disease.
ven'geance *n.* revenge, retribution for a wrong.—**venge'ful** *a.*—**venge'fully** *adv.*
ve'nial *a.* pardonable excusable.
ven'ison *n.* the flesh of deer.
ven'om *n.* poison; spite.—**ven'omous** *a.*
vent *n.* a small hole or outlet.—*v.t.* to give outlet to, to pour out, express.
vent'ilate *v.t.* to supply with fresh air; to bring into discussion.—**vent'ilator** *n.* —**ventila'tion** *n.*—**ven'tilating** *pres. p.*
ven'tral *a.* abdominal.
ven'tricle *n.* a cavity or hollow in the body, *esp.* in the heart or brain.
ventril'oquist *n.* one who can make his voice seem to come from some other person or place.—**ventril'oquism** *n.*
ven'ture *n.* a risky undertaking; a speculation.—*v.t.* to risk.—*v.i.* to dare; have courage to do something.—**ven'turesome** *a.*—**ven'turous** *a.* bold.
ven'ue *n.* district in which lawsuit must be tried; meeting place.
vera'cious (-ā-) *a.* truthful.—**vera'city** (-as'-) *n.* truth. *Syn.* of credibility, honesty, consistency. accuracy. *Ant.* falseness, dishonesty, untruth.
veran'dah *n.* an open gallery or portico along the side of a house.
verb *n.* the part of speech which asserts or declares.—**verb'al** *a.* of, by, or relating to, words.—**verb'ally** *adv.*–**verba'tim** *adv.* word for word.—**verb'iage** *n.* excess of words.—**verbose'** *a.* wordy.–**verbos'ity** *n.*
verd'ant *a.* green.—**verd'ure** *n.* greenery.
ver'dict *n.* decision of a jury; judgment after examination of facts, etc.
ver'digris *n.* green rust on copper.
verd'ure *n.* fresh green growth.
verge *n.* edge, brink.—*v.i.* to be on the border of.—**ver'ging** *pres. p.*
ver'ger *n.* bearer of a wand of office; an usher in, or custodian of, a church.
ver'ify (-fī) *v.t.* to prove or confirm the truth of (**-ified** *p.t.* and *p.p.*—**-ifying** *pres. p.*).—**verifi'able** *a.*—**verifica'tion** *n.*
ver'itable *a.* true, genuine.—**ver'itably** *adv.*—**ver'ity** *n.* truth.—**ver'ily** *adv.* truly.—**verisimil'itude** *n.* appearance of truth, likelihood.—**verisim'ilar** *a.*
ver'juice *n.* sour fruit juice.
vermicell'i *n.* an Italian paste of flour made in long thin strings.
verm'icide *n.* a substance to destroy

worms.—**verm'ifuge** *n.* a substance to drive out worms.
vermil'ion *n.* a bright red colour or pigment.—*a.* of this colour.
ver'min *n. sing.* and *pl.* injurious animals, parasites, etc.—**ver'minous** *a.*
ver'mouth (-mōōth) *n.* liqueur of wormwood made in Italy and France.
vernac'ular *a.* of language, of one's own country.—*n.* mother tongue.
vern'al *a.* of spring; fresh.—**ver'nal eq'uinox** equinox occurring March 21–22
verneu'ker *n.* in S. Africa, a swindler.
vern'ier *n.* a small sliding scale for obtaining fractional parts of the subdivisions of a graduated scale.
Ver'onal *n.* protected trade name of a colourless crystalline compound of malic acid, used extensively as hypnotic.
veron'ica *n.* a genus of plants including the speedwell.
ver'satile *a.* able to do many different things well.—**versatil'ity** *n.*
verse *n.* poetry; a line of poetry; a short division of a poem or other composition.
ver'sify *v.t.* to turn into verse.—*v.i.* to write verses (**-ified** *p.t. and p.p.*— **-ifying** *pres. p.*).—**versifica'tion** *n.*— **versed** (in) *a.* skilled, familiar with.
ver'sion *n.* a translation from another language; an account or description.
vers libre (vār lēbr) *n.* free verse.
ver'so *n.* the back of an object; a left-hand page; reverse of coin.
ver'sus *prep.* against.
vert'ebra *n.* a single section of a backbone (**-brae** *pl.*).—**vert'ebrate** *a.* having a backbone.—**vert'ebral** *a.*
vert'ex *n.* summit (**vert'ices** *pl.*).
vert'ical *a.* upright; overhead.
verti'go *n.* giddiness, dizziness (**-goes** (-gōz), **vertig'ines** (-ij'-) *pl.*—**verti'ginous** (-ij'-) *a.* dizzy.
ver'vain *n.* a plant of the genus *Verbena.*
verve *n.* enthusiasm; spirit; energy.
ver'vet *n.* a South African monkey.
ver'y *a.* true, real; identical, actual.—*adv.* extremely, to a great extent.
Véry light (ver'-i) *n.* a brilliant light produced by the explosion of a small shell from a Véry light pistol.
ves'icle *n.* a small blister, bubble, or cavity.—**vesic'ular** *a.*
ves'pers *n. pl.* evening church service.
vess'el *n.* any utensil or appliance for containing, *esp.* for liquids; a ship.
vest *n.* a waistcoat; an under-garment for the trunk.—*v.t.* to endow (with authority, property, etc.).—*v.i.* to be in a person's authority.—**vest'ed** *a.* robed in church garments; concerned with wealth, property, etc. (**vest'ed interests**).
ves'ta *n.* a small wax lucifer match; a small planet.—**ves'tal** *a.* pure; chaste.
vest'ibule *n.* an entrance hall, passage.
vest'ige (-j) *n.* trace or mark.
vest'ment *n.* a robe or official garment.
vest'ry *n.* room in a church for keeping vestments, holding meetings, etc.; a parish meeting.—**vest'ries** *pl.*
vest'ure *n.* dress, garments.
vetch ... a plant of the bean family.
vet'eran *n.* a person who has served a long time, *esp.* an old soldier.
vet'erinary *a.* of, or for, the diseases of domestic animals.—**vet'erinary sur'geon** *n.*—**vet** *v.t.* (*sl.*) examine; check; audit.
ve'to *n.* the power of rejecting a piece of legislation, or preventing it from coming into effect; any prohibition (**vetoes** *pl.*).—*v.t.* to enforce a veto against; forbid.
vex *v.t.* to annoy, distress, imitate.—**vexa'tion** *n.*—**vexa'tious** *a.*—**vexed** *a.* much discussed; cross, angry.
vi'aduct *n.* a bridge over a valley for road or rail.—**via** *prep.* by way of.
vi'al, phi'al *n.* a small glass bottle.
vi'ands *n. pl.* food.
vi'brate *v.i.* to move to and fro rapidly and continuously, to oscillate, quiver.—*v.t.* to cause to do this.—**vibra'tion** *n.*— **vibra'tory** *a.*—**vi'brant** *a.* resonant.
vic'ar *n.* clergyman in charge of a parish; a deputy.—**vic'arage** *n.* a vicar's house.—**vicar'ial** (-ėr-) *a.*—**vicar'ious** *a.* done or suffered by one person on behalf of another.—**vicar'iously** *adv.*
vice *n.* a fault or blemish; an evil or immoral habit or practice.—**vi'cious** (vish'us) *a.*—**vi'ciously** *adv.*
vice *n.* an appliance with a screw jaw for holding things while working on them.
vice- *prefix, see* **vis-.**
viceger'ent (visj-) *n.* holder of delegated authority.—**vice'roy** *n.* ruler acting for king in province or dependency.—**vicere'gal** *a.*—**vice'reine** *n. fem.* viceroy's wife.—**vicercy'alty** *n.*—**vi'ce** (-sē) **ver'sa** *adv.* other way round.
vicin'ity *n.* neighbourhood; nearness.
viciss'itude *n.* change of fortune.
vic'tim *n.* a person or animal killed as a sacrifice; one killed or injured as an accident or so that an object may be gained by another.—**vic'timise** *v.t.* to persecute.—**victimisa'tion** *n.*
vic'tor *n.* a conqueror or winner.
vic'tory *n.* winning of a battle, etc. —(**-ies** *pl.*)—**victor'ious** *a.*— **-iously** *adv.*
victual (vit'l) *n.* (usually in *pl.*) food.—*v.t.* to supply with food.—*v.i.* to obtain supplies.—**vic'tual'ler** *n.* inn-keeper.
vicu'na (-kōō-) *n.* a S. American llama; its wool or an imitation.
vi'de *v.* see; refer to.
videl'icet (-set) *adv.* to wit; namely.
vid'eo *n.* in television, the process of image transmission or reception.—*a.*
vie (vī) *v.i.* to contend, compete with (**vied** *p.t. p.p.*—**vy'ing** *pr. p.*).
view (vū) *n.* a survey by eyes or mind; a picture; a scene; opinion; purpose.—*v.t.* to look at, examine, survey.

view'er *n.* one who views; (cinema) one who visits trade shows of films with view to renting; one who receives a television programme.—**view'less** *a.* invisible.—**view'point** *n.* place of vantage; attitude, outlook.

vig'il (-j-) *n.* a keeping awake, a watch. —**vig'ilant** *a.* alert.—**vig'ilance** *n.*

vignette' (vin-yet') *n.* ornament of leaves, etc., in architecture; illustration in a book not enclosed in a definite border; portrait showing only head and shoulders with the background shaded off; a slight word-sketch.

vig'our (gėr) *n.* force, strength, activity. —**vig'orous** *a.*—**vig'orously** *adv.*

vi'king, vik'ing *n.* a Northern sea-rover of the eighth to tenth centuries.

vile *a.* base, mean, bad.—**vile'ness** *n.*—**vile'ly** *adv.*—**vil'ify** *v.t.* to speak ill of (**-ified** *p.t.* and *p.p.*—**-ifying** *pres. p.*).

vill'a *n.* a country or suburban house.

vill'age *n.* an assemblage of dwellings in the country.—**vill'ager** *n.* one who dwells in a village.

vill'ain *n.* a scoundrel.—**vill'ainous** *a.*—**vill'ainy** *n.* wickedness, crime.

vill'ein (-en), **vill'ain** (-en) *n.* serf under feudal system.—**vill'einage** *n.*

vim *n.* (*sl.*) force, energy; vigour.

vinaigrette' *n.* a bottle of smelling salts or aromatic vinegar.

vin'dicate *v.t.* to establish the truth or merit of, to clear of charges.—**vindica'tion** *n.*—**vin'dicator** *n.*—**vin'dicatory** *a.*

vindic'tive *a.* revengeful; inspired by resentment.—**vindic'tiveness** *n.*

Syn. define, justify, excuse, exonerate. *Ant.* condemn, accuse, incriminate.

vine *n.* climbing plant which bears grapes.—**vine'yard** (vin'-) *n.* vine farm, or plantation of vines.—**vi'nery** *n.* greenhouse for grapes.—**vi'nous** *a.* of, due to, wine.—**vin'tage** *n.* gathering of grapes; the yield; wine of particular year.—**vint'ner** *n.* dealer in wine.

vine'gar *n.* an acid liquid got from wine and other alcoholic liquors.

vi'ol *n.* mediæval instrument like a violin.—**violin'** *n.* a fiddle.—**vi'ola** *n.* tenor or alto fiddle; single-coloured pansy, violet.—**violoncell'o** (-chel'-) *n.* large bass violin (**-os** *pl.*).—**violin'ist** *n.* —**violoncell'ist** *n.*

vi'olate *v.t.* to outrage, desecrate; infringe.—**viola'tion** *n.*—**vi'olator** *n.*

vi'olent *a.* of great force; marked by, or due to, extreme force or passion or fierceness.—**vi'olence** *n.*—**vi'olently** *adv.*

vi'olet *n.* a plant with a small bluish-purple flower; the flower; the colour.—*a.*

vi'per *n.* a venomous snake.

vira'go *n.* an abusive woman (**-goes** *pl.*).

vir'gin *n.* a girl or woman who has not had sexual intercourse with a man.—*a.* pure, unsullied; fresh, untilled (of land). —**vir'ginal** *a.*—**virgin'ity** *n.* maidenhood.

Virgin'ia (-jin-) *n.* tobacco from *Virginia, U.S.*—**virginia creeper,** climbing vine.—**virgin'ium** *n.* element related to alkali metals, atomic number 87.

Vir'go *n.* the Virgin, 6th sign of the zodiac operative *c.* Aug. 22–Sept. 21. Constellation of this name.

vir'ile *a.* manly; strong.—**viril'ity** *n.*

vir'tue *n.* moral goodness; a good quality; inherent power.—**vir'tual** *a.* so in effect though not in name.—**vir'tually** *adv.*—**vir'tuous** *a.* morally good; chaste. —**vir'tuously** *adv.*—**virtu'** *n.* artistic excellence; objects of art taken collectively.

virtuo'so *n.* one with special skill in a fine art (**-sos** (-sōz), **-si** (-sē) *pl.*).

vir'ulent *a.* poisonous; bitter, malignant. —**vir'ulently** *adv.*—**vir'ulence** *n.*

vi'rus *n.* poison; a disease infection.

vis *n.* force; power; energy.—**vis iner'tiae** inertia; sluggishness.

vis-, vice- *prefix* in place of, as **viscount, viceregent, viceroy**

vi'sa (vē) *n.* endorsement on passport to show it has been examined.—*v.t.* mark with visa (**visaed** (-zad) *p.t./p.p.*—**visaing** *pr. p.*).

vis'age (-z-) *n.* the face.

visc'era (vis-) *n. pl.* the contents of the great cavities of the body as of the abdomen, etc.—**visc'eral** *a.*

vis'cid *a.* sticky, of a consistency like treacle.—**vis'cous** *a.* viscid.—**viscid'ity** *n.*

vis'cose *n.* fibre used in the manufacture of rayon.

vis'count (vī'kownt) *n.* a peer of rank above baron and below earl.

vis'ion (vizh'n) *n.* sight; imagination, foresight; dream, apparition.—**vis'ionary** *a.* unpractical, dreamy.—*n.* one full of fancies.—**vis'ible** *a.* that can be seen.—**visibil'ity** *n.* degree of clarity of atmosphere, *esp.* for flying.—**vis'ibly** *adv.*

Syn. of *a.* discernible, perceptible, clear, conspicuous. *Ant.* indiscernible, imperceptible, obscure, inconspicuous.

vis'it *v.t.* to go or come and see; to stay with; to punish, afflict, bless (with).—*n.* visiting.—**vis'itor** *n.*—**vis'itant** *n.* visitor.—**visita'tion** *n.* formal visit or inspection; affliction, plague.

vi'sor, vi'sard *n.* the front part of a helmet made to move up and down before the face; peak of cap, eyeshade.

vis'ta *n.* a view, *esp.* between trees, etc.

vis'ual *a.* of sight.—**vis'ualise** *v.t.* to make visible; to form a mental image of. —**visualisa'tion** *n.*

Vi'ta-glass *n.* protected trade name for a kind of glass which ultra-violet rays can penetrate.

vi'tal *a.* necessary to, or affecting life.—**vi'tally** *adv.*—**vital'ity** *n.* life, vigour.—**vi'talise** *v.t.* give life to.—**vi'tals** *n. pl.* vital organs of the body.

vi'talism *n.* modern theory that life

cannot be explained as resulting entirely from physico-chemical processes.
vi'tamin *n.* factor in certain foodstuffs regarded as essential to life and health.
vi'tiate (vish'-) *v.t.* spoil; make ineffective.—**vi'tiating** *pr. p.*—**vitia'tion** *n.*
vit'iculture *n.* the culture of vines.
vit'reous *a.* of glass; glassy.—**vit'rify** *v.t.* and *i.* (-**ified** *p.t.* and *p.p.*—**-ifying** *pres. p.*).—**vitrifac'tion, vitrifica'tion** *n.*
vit'riol *n.* sulphuric acid; caustic speech. —**vitriol'ic** *a.* bitter, burning.
vitu'perate (vī-) *v.t.* to abuse in words, revile.—**vitupera'tion** *n.*—**vitu'perative** *a.*
viva'cious (vī-) *a.* lively, gay, sprightly, animated.—**viva'city** (-as'-) *n.*
viva'rium *n.* a place to keep living creatures (-**riums, -ria** *pl.*).
vi'va vo'ce (vī'va vō'sē) *adv.* by word of mouth, orally.
viv'id *a.* bright, intense; clear, lively, graphic.—**viv'idly** *adv.*
viv'ify *v.t.* to give life to, animate, inspire (-**ified** *p.t.* and *p.p.*— **-ifying** *pres. p.*).
vivip'arous *a.* bringing forth young alive.—**vivipar'ity** *n.*
viv'isection *n.* dissection or experiment on living animals, etc.—**viv'isector** *n.*
vix'en *n.* a female fox; a spiteful woman.
viz *adv.* namely, that is.
viz'ard *n.* a mask.
viz'ier *n.* a minister of state in a Mohammedan country.
vlei (vlē) *n.* in S. Africa, a valley; a marshy place; small lake.
voc'able *n.* a word.—**vocab'ulary** *n.* a list of words; a stock of words used.
vo'cal *a.* of, with, or giving out, voice.—**vo'calist** *n.* a singer.—**vo'cally** *adv.*—**vo'calise** *v.t.* to utter with the voice.
voca'tion *n.* calling; feeling that one has calling for special kind of life or work (e.g., nun).—**voca'tional** *a.* for an occupation.—**voc'ative** *n.* case of nouns used in addressing person.
vocif'erate *v.t.* to shout.—**vocif'erous** *a.* shouting, noisy.—**vocifera'tion** *n.*
vod'ka *n.* a Russian alcoholic spirit.
voer'sies *n.* in S. Africa, a kind of printed calico.
voet'ganger (fut'-) *n.* in S. Africa, a locust before it begins to fly; an infantryman; a pedestrian.
voet'sek (fut'-) *interj.* in S. Africa, go away! get out! be off!
vogue (vōg) *n.* fashion.
voice *n.* the sound given out by a person in speaking or singing, etc.; the quality of the sound; expressed opinion; share in a discussion; the verbal forms proper to relation of subject and action.—*v.t.* to give utterance to.—**voice'less** *a.*
void *a.* empty; without force or effect.—*n.* empty space.—*v.t.* to empty out.
voile *n.* thin woollen or silk material.
vol'atile *a.* evaporating quickly; lively. —**volatil'ity** *n.*—**volat'ilise** *v.t.* and *i.*
volca'no *n.* a mountain with a hole through which lava, ashes, smoke, etc., are discharged (-**noes, -nos** (-nōz) *pl.*).—**volcan'ic** *a.*—**vol'canism** *n.*
vole' *n.* a kind of field-mouse.
voli'tion (-ish'-) *n.* act or power of willing.—**voli'tional** *a.*
volks'raad (folks'råd) *n.* in S. Africa, a legislative assembly.
vol'ley *n.* simultaneous discharge of weapons or missiles; rush of oaths, questions, etc.; in tennis, hard return of ball before it touches ground.—*v.t./i.* to discharge, utter, fly in volley.
vol'plane *v.i.* and *n.* descent of an aeroplane by gravity at an angle.
volt *n.* unit of electromotive force.—**volt'age** *n.* electrical potential difference expressed in volts.—**volt'meter** *n.* instrument for measuring force in volts.
vol'uble *a.* with incessant or abundant speech.—**volubil'ity** *n.*—**vol'ubly** *adv.* *Syn.* fluent, glib, loquacious. *Ant.* hesitant, slow of speech, taciturn.
vol'ume *n.* a book, or part of a book, bound ; a mass; bulk, space occupied.—**volu'minous** *a.* bulky, over ample.
vol'untary *a.* acting, done by, choice. —*n.* organ solo in church service.—**vol'untarily** *adv.* freely, from choice.—**volunteer'** *n.* one who offers service, joins force, etc., of his own free will.
volup'tuous *a.* of or contributing to the pleasures of the senses.—**volup'tuary** *n.* one given to sensual pleasures.
vom'it *v.t.* to eject from the stomach through the mouth.—*v.i.* to be sick.—*n.*
voo'doo *n.* among the negroes of America, one who practises witchcraft, enchantments.—*v.t.* to put a spell on.
voor- (fōr-) *prefix* in S. Africa, front, foremost. —**voor'loper** *n.* the man who leads the animals at the head of a bullock team.—**voor'-kamer** *n.* front room.—**voor'trekker** *n.* a pioneer.
vora'cious *a.* greedy, ravenous.—**vora'city** (-as'-) *n.*—**vora'ciously** *adv.*
vor'tex *n.* a whirlpool (**vor'tices** *pl.*).
vor'ticism *n.* modern movement in painting, which holds that the artist's aim is to create new realities, not copy nature.—**vor'ticist** *n.*
vo'tary *n.* one vowed to a service or pursuit.—**vo'taress** *fem.*
vote *n.* the formal expression of a choice; an individual pronouncement, or right to give it, in a question or election; the result of voting; that which is given or allowed by vote.—*v.i.* to give a vote.—*v.t.* to grant or enact by vote.—**vo'ter** *n.*
vo'tive *a.* given or consecrated by vow.
vouch *v.i.* to vouch for, to guarantee, make oneself responsible for.—**vouch'er** *n.* a document proving the correctness of an item in accounts.—**vouchsafe'** *v.i.* to condescend to grant or do something.

vow *n.* a solemn promise.—*v.t.* to promise by vow, to declare earnestly.
vow'el *n.* any of the sounds pronounced without stoppage or friction of the breath; a letter standing for such sound.
voy'age *n.* a journey, *esp.* a long one, by water.—*v.i.* to make a voyage.
voyageur' (vwo-ya-zher') *n.* a Canadian boatman or trapper.
vul'canise *v.t.* to treat (rubber) with sulphur at a high temperature.—**vul'canite** *n.* rubber so hardened.–**vulcanisa'tion** *n.*—**vulcanol'ogy** *n.* the science of igneous phenomena, volcanoes, geysers.
vul'gar *a.* of the common people; common; coarse, not refined; offending against good taste.—**vulgar'ian** (-èr-) *n.* a vulgar fellow, *esp.* a rich one.—**vul'garly** *adv.*—**vul'garism** *n.* a word or construction used only by the uneducated.—**vulgar'ity** *n.*—**vul'garise** *v.t.* to make vulgar or too common.–**vulgarisa'tion** *n.*—**vul'gar fract'ion** *n.* fraction expressed by numerator above and denominator below the line, e.g. ⅜.
Vul'gate *n.* the fourth century Latin version of the Bible.
vul'nerable *a.* not proof against wounds or damage; sensitive to ridicule, etc.; in contract bridge, denoting a side which has won its first game in the rubber and is subject to increased honours and penalties.—**vulnerabil'ity** *n.*
vul'pine *a.* of foxes; foxy.
vul'ture *n.* large bird of prey which feeds chiefly on carrion.
vy'ing *pres. p.* of **vie.**

W

wab'ble *see* **wobble.**
wack *n.* (*sl.*) one who acts irrationally or eccentrically; screw-ball.—**wac'ky, wack'** *a.* (*sl.*) eccentric; bemused.
wad (wod) *n.* a small pad of fibrous material; in N. America and Australia, a sum of money.—*v.t.* to line, pad, stuff, etc., with a wad.—**wadd'ing** *n.* stuffing.
wad'dle (wod'l) *v.i.* to walk like a duck.—*n.*—**wad'dling** *pres. p.*
wadd'y *n.* in Australia, an aboriginal wooden war-club.
wade *v.i.* to walk through something that hampers movement, *esp.* water.—**wa'der** *n.* a person or bird that wades; a high waterproof boot.
wad'y, wad'i (wod-) *n.* in the East, the channel of a water-course which is dry, except in the wet season; river valley.
wa'fer *n.* a thin cake or biscuit; a disc of gummed paper used as a seal.
waf'fle *n.* a kind of pancake.
waft (wȧ-) *v.t.* to convey through the air or over water.—*n.* whiff.
wag *v.t.* to cause to move to and fro.—*v.i.* to shake, swing.—*n.* a merry fellow.—**wag'ging** *pres. p.*—**wagged** *p.t.* and *p.p.*—**wagg'ery** *n.*—**wagg'ish** *a.*—**wagtail** *n.* a small bird with a wagging tail.
wage *n.* payment for work done (usually in *pl.*).—*v.t.* to carry on.
wa'ger *n.* and *v.t.* and *i.* a bet; to bet.
wag'gle *v.t.* to wag.
wagg'on, wag'on *n.* a four-wheeled vehicle for heavy loads.—**wagg'oner, wag'oner** *n.*—**waggonette', wagonette'** *n.* a horse-drawn four-wheeled carriage with lengthwise seats.—**wagon lit'** (vagoṉ lē') *n.* sleeping car on a train.
wahi'ne (-hē'-) *n.* Maori woman.
waif *n.* a homeless person, *esp.* a child.
wail *n., v.t.* and *i.* cry of pain; lament.
wain *n.* a wagon, *esp.* in farm use.
wains'cot *n.* wooden lining of the walls of a room.—*v.t.* to line thus.
waipi'ro *n.* in New Zealand, Maori name for alcoholic drinks in general.
waist *n.* the part of the body between hips and ribs; various central parts.—**waist'coat** *n.* a sleeveless garment worn under a coat.—**waist'line** *n.*
wait *v.t.* to await, defer action.—*v.i.* be expecting, attend; serve at table.—*n.* act of waiting; **waits** *n. pl.* carol-singers.—**wait'er** *n.*—**wait'ress** *fem.*—**wait'-a-bit, -awhile** *n.* in Australia, mass of tangled vegetation.
waive *v.t.* to forgo.—**waiv'ing** *pres. p.*
wa'ka *n.* New Zealand, a Maori canoe.
wake *v.i.* to rouse from sleep.—*v.t.* to rouse from sleep; to stir up.—*n.* a watch by a dead person; a holiday.—**wa'ken** *v.t.* to wake.—**wake'ful** *a.*
wake *n.* the track left by a ship; a track; air disturbance to rear of (in the wake of) an aeroplane in flight.
wale, weal *n.* mark left on flesh by the blow of a stick or whip.
wa'ler *n.* a cavalry horse imported into India from New South Wales.
walk (wawk) *v.i.* to move on the feet at an ordinary pace; to cross by walking; to cause to walk.—*n.* the slowest gait of animals; occupation or career; a path or other place for walking; a spell of walking for pleasure, etc.—**walk'er** *n.*—**walk'ing stick** *n.*—**walk'-over** *n.* easy victory.—**walkie-talkie** *n. col.* a portable radio set containing both transmission and receiver units.
wall (wawl) *n.* structure of brick, stone, etc., serving as fence, side of building, etc.; surface of one.—*v.t.* supply, block up with a wall.—**wall'flower** *n.* garden flower.—**wall'paper** *n.*
wall'a, wall'ah (wol'-) *n.* a merchant, an agent, human or animal; a worker.
wall'aby (wol-) *n.* a small kangaroo.—**on the wallaby track,** in Australia (*sl.*) tramping about on foot, usually of a sundowner (q.v.)
wallaroo' *n.* a large kangaroo.

wall'et (wol-) *n.* small bag; pocket-book.
wall'-eyed (wawl'-īd) *a.* having eyes with pale irises due to disease.
wall'op *v.t.* to beat soundly; to flog.—*n.* (*sl.*) inferior beer.
wall'ow (wol'-ō) *v.i.* to roll (in a liquid).
wal'nut (wawl-) *n.* large nut with a crinkled shell; the tree, wood of tree.
wal'rus (wol-) *n.* a large sea-animal like seal with long tusks.
waltz (wawlts) *n.* a dance for partners, in three-four time.—*v.i.* to dance it.
wa'mmerah, woomera *n.* Australia, aboriginal name for a throwing stick.
wam'pum *n.* small beads made of shells, used by North American Indians as money and for ornament.
wan (won) *a.* pale, sickly-complexioned.
wand (wond) *n.* slender, straight stick.
wand'er (won-) *v.i.* to roam; ramble.
wander'lust *n.* a great desire, urge or fondness for travel.
wane *v.i.* and *n.* decline.—**wa'ning** *pres.p.*
wan'gan (-ng-g-) *n.* a flat boat used by lumbermen in N. America.
wan'gle (-ng-g-) *v.t.* to manipulate, manage in a skilful way.
wan'igan *n.* in N. America, a store place; lumberman's clothes chest.
want (wont) *n.* and *v.t.* and *i.* lack; poverty; things needed (*pl.*); to need, to be without; to wish for, desire.—**wan'ting** *a.* lacking.—*prep.* without.
want'on (won-) *a.* unrestrained; playful; dissolute; without motive.—*v.i.* to frolic, run riot.—*n.* a wanton person.
Syn. loose, luxuriant, lewd. *Ant.* restrained, controlled, reserved, austere.
wap'iti (wop-) *n.* a North American stag.
war (wor) *n.* fighting between nations; state of hostility.—*v.i.* to make war. **war'fare** *n.* hostilities.—**war'like** *a.*—**warr'ior** *n.* a fighter.—**war'paint** *n.* special adornments of Red Indians when on the warpath; (*sl.*) ceremonial attire.
war'atah *n.* an Australian shrub, with large, bright crimson flowers; emblematic of Australia.
war'ble (wor-) *v.i.* to sing with trills or quavers, carol.—*n.*—**warb'ling** *pres. p.*—**warb'ler** *n.* a song bird.
ward (word) *n.* guardianship; a minor under care of a guardian; a division of a city, or hospital, etc.—*pl.* indentations of head of key or lock.—*v.t.* to guard.—**ward'er** *n.* a prison keeper.—**ward'ress** *fem.*—**ward'ship** *n.*—**ward'robe** *n.* a piece of furniture for hanging clothes in; stock of clothes.—**ward'room** *n.* senior officers' mess on a warship.—**ward'en** *n.* a president or governor; watchman.
ware *n.* goods; articles collectively, *esp.* in pottery or metal.—**ware'house** *n.* a store-house, repository; a large commercial establishment.
ware *a.* on guard.—*v.t.* to beware.
warm (worm) *a.* moderately hot; giving warmth; hearty, enthusiastic; ardent.—*v.t.* and *i.* to heat.—**warm'ly** *adv.*—**warm'th** *n.* being warm.
warn (worn) *a.* to caution, put on guard.—**war'ning** *n.* notice of danger, of intention to leave, etc.; caution, something said or done to warn.
warp (worp) *n.* the lengthwise threads in a loom; a rope.—*v.t.* to twist; to move by a rope fastened to a buoy, etc.—*v.i.* to become twisted.
warr'ant (wor-) *a.* authority; a document giving authority.—*v.t.* to authorise; to guarantee.—**war'rant off'icer** *n.* officer senior to N.C.O.'s but below commissioned rank.—**warr'anty** *n.*
warr'en (wor-) *n.* ground occupied by rabbits, rabbit colony.
warr'igal *n.* in Australia, a wild dog; wild horse; wild native; (*sl.*) a worthless person.
wart (wort) *n.* a hard growth on the skin.
war'y (wėr'i) *a.* cautious.—**war'ily** *adv.*
wash (wosh) *v.t.* to clean with liquid; to carry along with a rush of water; to colour lightly.—*v.i.* to wash oneself; to stand washing.—*n.* an act of washing; clothes washed at one time; sweep of water, *esp.* set up by moving ship; a thin coat of colour.—**wash'er** *n.* one who or that which washes; a ring put under a nut.—**wash'y** *a.* diluted.—**wash'-dirt** *n.* in Australia, alluvial deposit that can be profitably worked for gold by washing.—**wash'-out** *n.* (*sl.*) failure; unsuccessful business, person; in N. Amer. hole, in road, railway, etc., made by flood.
wasp (wosp) *n.* a striped stinging insect resembling a bee.—**wasp'ish** *a.* irritable.
wass'ail (wos'l, was'l) *n.* a drinking-bout; liquor for it.—*v.i.* to carouse.
waste (wāst) *v.t.* to expend uselessly, use extravagantly; lay desolate.—*v.i.* to dwindle; pine away.—*a.* wasted; desert.—*n.* what is wasted; act of wasting; a desert.—**wast'age** *n.*—**waste'ful** *a.*—**waste'fully** *adv.*—**wast'er** *n.*
watch (wotsh) *n.* state of being on the look-out; spell of duty, *esp.* on board ship; a pocket clock.—*v.t.* to observe closely; guard.—*v.i.* to be on watch, be wakeful.—**watch'ful** *a.*—**watch'fully** *adv.*—**watch committee** *n.*—**watch'man** *n.*—**watch'keeper** *n.* officer of the watch.—**watch'maker** *n.*—**watch'tower** *n.*—**watch'word** *n.* a rallying cry.
wat'er (wawt'er) *n.* a transparent liquid, the substance of rain, rivers, the sea, etc.; the transparency of a gem.—*v.t.* to put water on or into; to cause to drink.—*v.i.* to take in or obtain water.—**wat'ery** *a.*—**wa'ter-bok** *n.* in S. Africa, water back (a species of antelope).—**wa'ter-chute** *n. pl.* an artificial slide leading down to water, to be descended for amusement.—**wa'ter-colour** *n.* paint to be mixed with water; painting with

water-colours.—**wa'ter-fowl** *n.*—**water-glass** *n.* soluble silicates of soda and potash used for preserving eggs.—**water-jacket** *n.* space round an internal combustion engine cylinder for water.—**wa'ter-logged** *a.*—**wat'ermark** *n.* a mark in paper made during manufacture and visible on holding the paper to the light.—**wat'erproof** *a.* not letting water through.—*n.* waterproof garment.—**wa'ter-shed** *n.* ridge separating two river systems.—**water-spout** *n.* column of water sucked up from the sea by whirlwind.—**wat'ertight** *a.*—**water wings** *n. pl.* a kind of double balloon used for buoying up persons learning to swim.

watt (wot) *n.* the unit of electric power.

wat'tle (wot-) *n.* a hurdle of wicker; in Australia, numerous species of acacia.—*v.t.* to make into basket-work.

waul, wawl *v.i.* cry, as cat; squall.

wave *v.i.* to move to and fro; to beckon; to have an undulating shape.—*v.t.* to move to and fro; to give the shape of waves; to express by waves.—*n.* an act or gesture of waving; a ridge and trough on water, etc.; a vibration, as in wireless waves, of electric and magnetic forces alternating in direction.—**wa'vy** *a.*—**wa'vily** *adv.*—**wave'length** *n.* distance between maximum positive points of two successive waves.

wa'ver *v.i.* to hesitate, be irresolute, falter, flutter.—**wa'verer** *n.*

Syn. vacillate, fluctuate. *Ant.* decide, determine, remain steady.

wax *v.i.* to grow, increase.—he **wax'es.**

wax *n.* yellow plastic material made by bees; similar substance used for sealing, making candles, etc.—*v.t.* to put wax on.—**wax'en** *a.*—**waxy** *a.* like wax.

wax *n.* (*sl.*) a fit of anger or annoyance.—**waxy** *a.* (*sl.*) angry.

way *n.* track; direction; method; habit; manner.—**way'farer** *n.* a traveller, *esp.* on loot.—**waylay'** *v.t.* to lie in wait for.—**way'ward** *a.* disobedient, wilful, capricious, perverse.—**way'wardly** *adv.*—**way'wardness** *n.*

wayz'goose *n.* a fat goose; a printers' annual feast or picnic.

we *pron.* the first person plural pronoun.

weak *a.* lacking strength, flavour, etc.—**weak'ly** *a.* weak; sickly.—*adv.*—**weak'en** *v.t.* and *i.*—**weak'ling** *n.* a feeble creature.—**weak'ness** *n.* being weak, frailty; infirmity, fault; fondness for.

weal *n.* well-being.—**wealth** (welth) *n.* riches; abundance.—**wealth'y** *a.*

weal *see* **wale.**

weald (wēld) *n.* a forest; wold; any open country; a district in Kent.—**weald'en** *a.*

wean *v.t.* to accustom a baby or animal to food other than mother's milk.—**wean'-ling** *n.* a newly weaned child.

weap'on (wep'n) *n.* an implement to fight with, means of attack.

wear (wėr) *v.t.* to carry on the body; show; consume.—*v.i.* to last; to become impaired by use (**wore** *p.t.*—**worn** *p.p.*—**wear'ing** *pres. p.*).—*n.* act of wearing; impairment; things to wear.—**wear'er** *n.*

wear *v.t.* to turn, veer (a ship).

wear'y *a.* tired.—*v.t./i.* tire (**wear'ied** *p.t./p.p.*—**wear'ying** *pr. p.*).—**wear'ily** *adv.*—**wear'iness** *n.*—**wear'isome** *a.*

weas'el (-z-) *n.* small animal like a ferret which preys on other animals.

weath'er (weth-) *n.* atmospheric conditions.—*a.* towards the wind.—*v.t.* to expose to the air, to season; to sail to windward of; to come safely through.—**weath'er-cock** *n.* a revolving vane to show which way the wind blows.—**weather report** *n.* daily report of meteorological elements.—**weath'er ship** *n.* a unit of the marine branch of the Meteorological Office of the Air Ministry, stationed in the N. Atlantic, to assist in the compilation of official weather forecasts.—**weath'erly** *a.*

weave *v.t.* to form in texture or fabric by interlacing (**wove** *p.t.*—**wo'ven** *p.p.*—**weav'ing** *pres. p.*).—**weav'er** *n.*

web *n.* woven fabric; net spun by spider; membrane between toes of waterfowl.—**webbed'** *a.*—**web'bing** *n.* strong, coarse material used for straps, etc.

wed *v.t.* to marry; to unite closely.—**wedd'ing** *n.* a marriage.—**wed'lock** *n.* marriage.—**wed'ded** *p.t.* and *p.p.*

wedge *n.* a piece of material sloping to an edge.—*v.t.* to fasten or split with a wedge; to stick by compression or crowding.—**wedg'ing** *pres. p.*

Wed'nesday (wenz'di) *n.* the fourth day of the week.

wee *a.* very small; little, tiny.

weed *n.* a plant growing where it is not desired.—*v.t.* to free from weeds.—**weed'y** *a.* full of weeds; ill-grown.

weeds *n.pl.* widow's mourning garments.

week *n.* a period of seven days.—**week'ly** *a.* happening, done, etc., once a week.—**week'ly** *adv.* once a week.—**week-end** *n.*

ween *v.i.* to think, trow.

weep *v.i.* to shed tears.—*v.t.* to lament (**wept** *p.t.* and *p.p.*—**weep'ing** *pres. p.*).

wee'vil *n.* beetle harmful to grain, etc.

weft *n.* cross threads in weaving; woof.

weigh (wā) *v.t.* to find the weight of; ponder; estimate; raise.—*v.i.* to have weight.—**weigh'bridge** *n.* platform on which loaded vehicles are weighed.—to **weigh' an'chor,** raise anchor prior to sailing.—**weight** *n.* gravity as a property of bodies; a heavy mass; an object of known mass for weighing; importance; value.—*v.t.* to add a weight to.—**weight'y** *a.*—**weight'ily** *adv.*

weir *n.* a dam across a river.

weird *a.* unearthly, queer, uncanny.

wel'come *a.* received gladly.—*n.* kindly greeting.—*v.t.* to receive gladly.

weld *v.t.* to unite (hot metal) by hammering; to unite closely.—*n.* a welded joint.
wel'fare *n.* well-being, happiness.
wel'kin *n.* the sky.
well *adv.* in good manner or degree.—*a.* in good health; suitable; satisfactory.
Syn. healthy, hearty, sound, expedient. *Ant.* unhealthy, cold, unsound.
well *n.* a deep hole for water or oil; a spring.—*v.i.* to flow out or up.
Well'ington *n.* a rubber boot reaching to below the knee.
Welsh *a.* of Wales.—*n.* the language of Wales, or the people.
welsh, welch *v.t.* and *i.* to cheat, by running off from a racecourse without paying one's debts.–**welsh'er, welch'er** *n.*
welt *n.* a seam; leather rim put on a boot-upper for the sole to be attached to; a wale.—*v.t.* to provide a shoe with a welt; to thrash; to fit with a welt.
welt'er *v.i.* to roll or tumble, wallow.—*n.* turmoil (racing) for heavy riders; (boxing) above light weight and below heavy weight.
wen *n.* a tumour forming a permanent swelling beneath the skin.
wench *n.* young woman.—**wench'es** *pl.*
wend *v.i.* go, direct one's way.
werf *n.* in S. Africa, a farmyard.
wer'wolf, were'wolf *n.* human being with power to become a wolf.
Wes'leyan (wes'-) *a.* of Wesley or the Church founded by him.—*n.* a member of that church.
west *n.* the part of the sky where the sun sets, a part of a country, etc., lying to this side.—*a.* that is toward this region. —*adv.* to the west.—**wes'terly** *a.*—**west'ward** *a.* and *adv.*—**west'wards** *adv.*
wet *a.* having water or other liquid on a surface or being soaked in it; rainy.—*v.t.* to make wet.—*n.* moisture, rain.—**wet'blanket** *n.* (*fig.*) a killjoy.
weth'er (-th-) *n.* a castrated ram.
whack *v.t.* to hit, *esp.* with a stick.—*n.* such a blow; (*sl.*) a share.
whale *n.* large fish-shaped sea animal. —**whale'bone** *n.* a springy substance from jaw of some whales.—**wha'ler** *n.* man, ship employed in hunting whales; Australia (*sl.*) sundowner.—**whale'-back,** vessel with covered-in and rounded deck.—*v.t.* (*sl.*) beat.
wha're (hwo'ri) *n.* N.Z. Maori for house.
wharf (worf) *n.* a quay for loading and unloading ships.—**wharf'age** *n.* accommodation or dues at a wharf.—**wharf'inger** *n.* wharf owner (**wharves'** *pl.*)
what (hwot) *pron.* which thing; that which.—*a.* which.—**whatev'er** *pron.* anything which; of what kind it may be.
what'a *n.* *see* **futtah.**
what'not *n.* a piece of furniture having shelves for books, ornaments, etc.
wheat *n.* cereal plant the grain of which is made into bread.—**wheat'en** *a.*—**wheat'-belt** *n.* in Canada, the plains of Manitoba, Saskatchewan, and Alberta.
wheat'ear *n.* a small bird.
whee'dle *v.t.* coax (**whee'dling** *pr. p.*).
wheel *n.* circular frame or disc with spokes revolving on axle.—*v.t.* to convey on wheels; cause to turn or change direction.—*v.i.* revolve; change direction.—**wheel'barrow** *n.* a barrow with one wheel.—**wheel'wright** *n.* maker, repairer of wheels.—**wheel'-—base,** distance between front and rear hubs of vehicle.
wheeze *v.i.* to breathe with difficulty and whistling noise.—*n.* (*sl.*) joke; anecdote; dodge.—**wheez'y** *a.*
whe'kau *n.* N. Zealand,the laughing owl.
whelk *n.* a sheelfish used for food.
whelm *v.t.* to submerge; to destroy.
whelp *n.* pup or cub, young of dog, lion, etc.—*v.i.* and *t.* to produce whelps.
when *adv.* at what time.—*conj.* at the time that.—**whenev'er** *adv.* and *conj.* at whatever time; every time that.
whence *adv.* from what place; from which.
where *adv.* and *conj.* at what place.—**whereas'** *conj.* considering that, while on the contrary.—**where'fore** *adv.* why. —*conj.* consequently.—**wherev'er** *adv.* at whatever place.—**where'with** *adv.* with which, with what.
wherr'y *n.* a light boat.—**wher'ries** *pl.*
whet *v.t.* to sharpen.—**whet'stone** *n.* a stone for sharpening tools.
Syn. incite, stimulate, provoke. *Ant.* make blunt, restrain, check, allay.
wheth'er (-th-) *a.* and *pron.* which of the two. -*conj.* introduces the first of two alternatives, of which the second may be expressed or implied.
whey *n.* the watery part of milk.
which *a.* asks for a selection from alternatives.—*pron.* which person or thing; the thing "who."—**whichev'er** *pron.* whether one or the other.—**whichsoev'er** *pron.* whichever.
whiff *v.t.* and *i.* and *n.* puff, blow lightly.
Whig *n.* a member of the political party out of which grew the Liberal Party.
while *n.* a space of time.—*conj.* in the time that.—*v.t.* to pass (time, usually idly).—**whilst** *adv.* whereas, although.
whim *n.* a caprice, fancy.—**whim'sical** *a.* full of whims.—**whimsical'ity** *n.*
whim'per *v.i.* to cry or whine softly or plaintively.—*n.* such cry.
whin *n.* a plant with yellow flowers.—**whin'-chat,** a small singing-bird.
whine *n.* a long-drawn wail.—*v.i.*
whinn'y *v.i.* to neigh joyfully (**whinn'ied** *p.t.* and *p.p.*—**whinn'ying** *pres. p.*).—*n.* such neigh; the cry of a horse.
whip *v.t.* to apply a whip to; thrash; lash.—*v.i.* to dart.—*n.* lash with handle for urging or punishing; one who enforces attendance of political party; call made

on members of Parliament to be in their places against important divisions; in motoring, excessive bending or twisting of parts intended to be rigid.—**whip'cord** *n.* thin hard cord.—**whip'hand** *n.* advantage, control over another.—**whipp'er-snapper** *n.* small child; insignificant person.—**whip'ping** *n.* act of punishing; the punishment; a severe defeat.

whipp'et *n.* a coursing dog like a small greyhound; fast light tank.

whip'-poor-will *n.* an American bird.

whir *v.i.* to fly with a buzzing or whizzing sound.—*n.* a buzzing or whizzing sound.

whirl *v.t.* and *i.* swing rapidly round.—*n.* a whirling movement.—**whirl'igig** *n.* a spinning toy.—**whirl'pool** *n.* a circular current.—**whirl'wind** *n.* violent wind whirling round a forward-moving axis.

whist *v.t.* and *i.* brandish, sweep, or beat lightly.—*n.* a light brush; a flapper; an egg-beating implement.

whisk'er *n.* hair of man's face; bristles on cat's face.—**whisk'ered** *a.*

whisk'y *n.* spirit mainly distilled from barley.—**whisk'y-jack** *n.* Canadian jay.

whisp'er *v.t.* and *i.* to speak with rustling breath instead of voice; to tell secretly.—*n.* such speech.

whist *n.* card game for four persons.

whis'tle (-sl) *n.* the sound made by forcing the breath through rounded and nearly closed lips; any similar sound; an instrument to make it.—*v.i.* to make such sound.—*v.t.* to utter or summon, etc., by whistle.—**whis'tler** *n.*

whit *n.* a very little bit, a jot.

white *a.* of the colour of snow; pale; light in colour; N. America (*sl.*) honest, just, decent.—*n.* the colour of snow; white pigment; a white part; S. Africa, a plume from the wing of a male ostrich.—**whi'ten** *v.t.* and *i.* to make white.—**white'ness** *n.*—**whi'tish** *a.*—**white'-ant** *n.* incorrect name for the termite, an insect that destroys wood.—**white'-bait** *n.* a small edible fish.—**white lie** *n.* a small, harmless lie.—**white-line** *n.* a traffic sign; a safety line at a bend or corner of a road.—**white'-smith** *n.* a tinsmith.—**white-wash** *n.* liquid mixture for whitening.—*v.t.* to apply this; to clear of imputations.—**white drugs,** harmful narcotics; dope.—**whi'ting** *n.* dried chalk; a fish.

whith'er (-th-) *adv.* to what place.

whit'low *n.* an extremely painful inflamed swelling on a finger.

whit'tle *v.t.* to cut or carve with a knife; to pare away (down) reduce.

whiz *n.* a violent hissing sound.—*v.i.* to move with such sound, or make it.

whizz'bang *n.* (*sl.*) light, high velocity shell, the sound of which is heard before the gun's report.

who (hōō) *pron.* relative and interrogative pronoun, always referring to persons.—**whoev'er** *pron.* any one or every one that.—**whom** (hōōm) *pron.* objective case of **who.**—**whom'soever** *pron.* the objective of **whosoever.**—**whosoev'er** *pron.* any person whatever that.

whole (h-) *a.* complete; healthy; all.—*n.* a complete thing or system.—**who'lly** *adv.*—**whole'meal** *a.* of or pertaining to flour which contains the whole of the grain.—**whole'sale** *n.* sale of goods by large quantities.—*a.* dealing by wholesale; extensive.—**whole'saler** *n.*—**whole'-some** *a.* sound; healthy, beneficial.

whoop (hōōp) *v.t.* and *i.* and *n.* shout.—**whoop'ing-cough** *n.* an infectious disease marked by a whooping breath.

whoo'pee *n.* (U.S. *sl.*) gay time.

whop *v.t.* to beat severely.—**whopp'er** *n.* anything unusually large.

whore (h-) *n.* a prostitute.

whorl *n.* a turn of a spiral; a ring of leaves round the stem.

whor'tleberry *n.* bilberry.

whose *pron.* the possessive case of **who** or **which.**

why *adv.* and *conj.* for what cause.

wick *n.* the strip or thread feeding the flame of a lamp or candle.

wick'ed *a.* evil, sinful; playful, mischievous.—**wick'edly** *adv.*—**wick'edness** *n.*

wick'er *n.* plait osiers, etc., used for baskets.—**wick'er work** *n.*

wick'et *n.* small gate; cricket, set of 3 stumps and bails; the playing pitch.

wick'iup, wik'iup *n.* in N. America, a roughly made hut.

wide *a.* broad; far from the mark.—*n.* in cricket, a ball bowled wide of the wicket out of the batsman's reach.—**wi'den** *v.t.* and *i.*—**wide'ly** *adv.*—**wide'spread** *a.*

wid'geon *n.* a wild duck.

wid'ow (-ō) *n.* woman whose husband is dead and who has not married again.—*v.t.* to make a widow of.—**wid'ower** *n.* man whose wife has died and who has not married again.—**wid'owhood** *n.*

wield *v.t.* to hold and use.

wife *n.* a woman married to a man (**wives** *pl.*).—**wife'ly** *a.*

wig *n.* artificial hair for the head.

wight (wīt) *n.* formerly, a person.

wig'wam *n.* Red Indian's tent.

wild (wīld) *a.* not tamed, domesticated or civilised; not cultivated; savage; excited, rash.—**wild'ly** *adv.*—**wild'ness** *n.*—**wil'derness** *a.* desert.—**the wilds** *n.* uninhabited country.

wil'debeest (wēl'de-bāst) *n.* the gnu.

wile *n.* a trick.—**wi'ly** *a.* cunning, sly.

will *v. aux.* forms moods and tenses indicating intention or conditional result (**would** *p.t.*).—*v.i.* to have a wish.—*v.t.* to wish; to intend, purpose; to leave as a legacy.—*n.* the faculty of deciding what one will do; purpose, wish; directions written for disposal or property after death.—**will'ing** *a.* ready or given cheer, fully.—**will'ingly** *adv.*—**will'ingness** *n.*—**will'y-nill'y** *adv.* willing or unwilling.—**wil'ful** *a.* obstinate, refractory.

Syn. of "wilful," perverse, stubborn, wayward, dogged, headstrong. *Ant.* obedient, submissive, unintentional.

will'-o'-the-wisp' *n.* light flitting over marshes; elusive person or hope.

will'ow(-ō) *n.* a tree yielding osiers and wood for cricket-bats, etc.—**will'owy** *a.* lithe and slender, graceful.

will'y-nill'y *adv.* inevitably.

wi'lly-wi'lly *n.* in Australia, aboriginal name for a heavy gale on the north-west coast.

wilt *v.t.* to make flaccid, as a plant; to depress.—*v.i.* to fade; to droop.

win *v.t.* to get by labour or effort; to reach; to allure; be successful in.—*v.i.* to be successful (**won** *p.t.* and *p.p.*—**winn'ing** *pres. p.*).—**winn'er** *n.*

wince *v.i.* to flinch; to draw back from pain, etc.–*n.* a flinching.–**win'cing** *pres. p.*

win'cey *n.* a cotton and woollen cloth.—**winceyette'** *n. a.* plain, light weight cotton cloth, raised slightly on both sides.

winch *n.* a crank or pulley; a windlass.

wind *n.* air in motion; breath.—(wind) *v.t.* to sound by blowing.—**wind'age** *n.* difference between diameter of bore of a gun and that of ball or shell.—**wind' breaker** *n.* light-weight wind-resisting jacket.—**wind'fall** (-awl) *n.* fallen fruit; piece of good luck.—**wind'jammer** *n.* large sailing vessel; (*coll.*) type of lumber jacket.—**wind'mill** *n.* mill worked by sails.—**wind'pipe** *n.* passage from throat to lungs.—**wind'row** *n.* N. Amer., long row of hay, maize, etc., left to dry in wind.—**wind'-shakes** *n. pl.* N. Amer., concentric cracks in timber.—**wind'-screen** *n.*—**windshield** *n.* in motoring and flying, glass screen in front of car driver as protection.—**wind'y** *a.* condition of strong wind; flatulent; (*sl.*) nervous, apprehensive.—**wind'ward** (-ord) *n.* side towards the wind.

wind (wīnd) *v.i.* to twine; to vary from a direct course.—*v.t.* to twist round, wrap; to make ready for working by tightening a spring (**wound** (wownd) *p.t.* and *p.p.*—**wind'ing** *pres. p.*).—**wind'lass** *n.* a machine which hauls or hoists by wrapping rope round an axle.

win'dow (-ō) *n.* a hole, opening in a wall to admit light or air.—**window-dressing** *n.* effective arrangement of goods in a window; deceptive display.

wine *n.* the fermented juice of the grape.—**wine'press** *n.*—**wine'bibber** *n.* tippler.

wing *n.* a limb a bird uses in flying; flight; a lateral extension; one of the sides of a stage; the flank position in football, etc., or in an army on either side; in aviation, that portion of a main supporting plane on one side of the body.—*pl.* front wheel mudguards of a motor-car; in the R.A.F., division composed of two or more squadrons; pilot's chevron.—**wing'-command'er** *n.* officer ranking next below Group Captain.—*v.t.* to cross by flight; supply with wings; wound in wing, disable.—*v.i.* to fly.

wink *v.i.* to close and open an eye; to blink.—*n.* act of winking.

win'kel, win'kle *n.* in S. Africa, a retail shop.—**win'kler** *n.* petty trader.

win'kle *n.* a periwinkle (mollusc).

winn'ow (-ō) *v.t.* to separate the grain from the chaff by blowing; to sift (e.g. truth from falsehood).

win'some *a.* sweet and charming.

win'ter *n.* the fourth and coldest season.—*v.i.* to pass the winter.—*v.t.* to tend during winter.—**win'try** *a.*

wipe *v.t.* to rub so as to clean or dry.—*n.* a wiping.—**wi'per** *n.* one that wipes; an automatic wiping apparatus.

wire *n.* metallic thread, cord; telegram.—*v.t.* to provide, catch, fasten with wire; send by telegraph.—**wi'ry** *a.* like wire, tough.—**wire'less** *n. a.* and *v.t.* telegraphy or telephony without connecting wires; radio; radio receiving set.—**wire'-less sta'tion,** place used for radio transmitting and receiving.—**wire'-drawn** *a.* of argument, spun out into needless fine distinctions.—**wire-haired** *a.* of various breeds of terriers, with short stiff hair.—**wire-pho'to** *n.* photograph sent by telegraph; telephotograph.–**wire-pulling,** political intrigue.

wise *a.* sagacious; having intelligence and knowledge.—**wis'dom** *n.* superior knowledge of truth and beauty; wise and good judgment; sagacity; prudence, experience.—**wise'ly** *adv.*

Syn. sensible, judicious, sage, erudite, politic, crafty, prudent, sound. *Ant.* foolish, irrational, senseless, idiotic, unwise, absurd, indiscreet, preposterous.

wise *n.* manner (e.g. thus wise).

wise'acre *n.* a foolish pretender to great knowledge and wisdom.

wise'crack *n.* a smart remark.—*v.i.* to make smart remarks.

wish *v.i.* to have a desire.—*v.t.* to desire.—*n.* a desire or thing desired.–**wish'es** *pl.*—**wish'ful** *a.* desirous.

wisp *n.* a twisted handful, usually of straw, etc; a twist of hair.

wist'ful *a.* longing.—**wist'fully** *adv.*

wit *n.* sense; mind, intellect; ingenuity in connecting amusingly incongruous ideas; a person gifted with this power.—**witt'y** *a.*—**witt'ily** *adv.*—**witt'icism** *n.* a witty remark.—**witt'ingly** *adv.* on purpose.—**to wit** *adv.* namely.

witch *n.* woman capable of using black magic.—**witch'craft** *n.*—**witch'-ery** *n.*

witch'-elm, wych'-elm *n.* a variety of elm.—**witch'-hazel** *n.*—**witch'-alder** *n.*

witch'etty *n.* in Australia, a beetle

grub, found in decayed timber, etc., and eaten by the natives.

with *prep.* in company or possession of; against; in relation to; through.—**withal'** (-awl) *adv.* also, likewise.—**withdraw'** *v.t.* and *i.* to draw back, retire.—**withdraw'al** *n.*—**within'** *prep.* and *adv.* in, inside.—**without'** *adv.* outside.—*prep.* lacking.—**withstand'** *v.t.* to oppose.

withe *n.* a tough, flexible twig.

with'er *v.i.* to fade, to shrivel.—*v.t.* to cause to fade; to blight; to rebuff.

with'ers *n. pl.* ridge between a horse's shoulder-blades.

withhold' *v.t.* to restrain; to keep back. —**withheld'** *p.t.* and *p.p.*

with'y *n.* a willow; a withe.

wit'ness *n.* testimony; one who sees something; one who gives evidence in a law court.—*v.i.* to give testimony.—*v.t.* to see; to attest; to see and sign as having seen.—**wit'nesses** *pl.*

wiz'ard *n.* a sorcerer, magician.

wiz'ened *a.* shrivelled, withered.

woad *n.* plant; blue dye got from this.

wobb'egong *n.* Australia, carpet shark.

wobble *v.i.* to rock unsteadily, to sway from side to side (*fig.*) to be hesitant, to waver, to vacillate.—**wobb'ler** *n.*—**wobb'ling** *pres. p.*—**wobb'ly** *a.*

wob'bles *n.* Australia; disease of horses caused by eating palm leaves.

woe *n.* grief, distress.—**woe'begone** *a.* sorrowful.—**woe'ful** *a.*—**woe'fully** *adv.*

wold *n.* a down; a treeless moor.

wolf (woolf) *n.* wild beast allied to the dog; S. Africa, the spotted hyena (**wolves** *pl.*).—**wolf' pack,** a group of submarines acting together in attack, *esp.* against merchant shipping.—**wolverine'** *n.* a carnivorous mammal inhabiting the Arctic.

wolwe'boon *n.* in S. Africa, a poisonous fruit used to destroy hyenas, etc.

wom'an (woo-) *n.* an adult human female; the female sex (**women** *pl.*).—**woman'hood** *n.*-**wom'anly** *a.*-**wom'anish** *a.* weak.—**wom'ankind** *n.*

womb (wōōm) *n.* the female organ of conception and gestation.

wom'bat *n.* a mammal with a pouch.

womm'era, *see* **wammerah.**

won'der (wun-) *n.* a marvel; the emotion excited by an amazing or unusual thing.—*v.i.* to feel this emotion.—**won'derful** *a.*—**won'derfully** *adv.*—**won'drous** *a.*—**won'drously** *adv.*

wong'a-wong'a *n.* an Australian pigeon valued for its flesh.

won'ky *a.* (*sl.*) wobbly; out of order; hesitant; unreliable.

wont (-ō-) *n.* custom, habit; accustomed. —**wont'ed** *a.* habitual.

woo *v.t.* to court, seek to marry.—**woo'er** *n.* a suitor, lover.

wood *n.* a tract of land with growing trees; the substance of trees, timber.—**wood'en** *a.*—**wood'y** *a.*—**wood'bine** *n.* honeysuckle.—**wood'cock** *n.* a bird like a snipe.—**wood'chuck** *n.* in N. America, a burrowing marmot.—**wood'cut** *n.* engraving on wood; an impression from such an engraving.—**wood'land** *n.* woods, forest.—**wood'pecker** *n.* a bird which searches tree-trunks for insects.—**wood'man** *n.* a forester.—**wood'craft** *n.* knowledge of woodland conditions.

woof *n.* weft, the threads that cross the warp in weaving.

wool *n.* soft hair of the sheep and certain other animals.—**wooll'en** *a.* made of wool.—**wooll'y** *a.*—**wool'-gathering** *n.* absentmindedness.—*a.*—**wool'sack** *n.* a cushion stuffed with wool, *esp.* the Lord Chancellor's seat in the House of Lords.

word (wurd) *n.* a single symbol used in speaking or writing, a unit of speech; information; promise.—*v.t.* to express in words.—**word'y** *a.*—**word'ily** *adv.*

work (wurk) *n.* labour; task; something made or accomplished.—*pl.* a factory.—*v.t.* to cause to operate; make, shape.—*v.i.* to apply effort; labour; operate; ferment; to be engaged in a trade, profession, etc. (**wrought, worked** (wurkd) *p.t.*/*p.p.*—**work'ing** *pr. p.*).—**work'able** *a.*—**work'er** *n.*—**work'house** *n.* institution for paupers.—**work'man** *n.* manual worker.—**work'man's ticket** *n.* cheap ticket issued in early morning, for journey by workman's train.—**work'manship** *n.* skill of a workman; way thing is made, style.—**work'shop** *n.* place where things are made.

world (wurld) *n.* the universe; the earth; sphere of existence; mankind; society.—**world'ling** *n.* one given up to affairs of this world.—**world'ly** *a.* engrossed in temporal pursuits.

worm (wurm) *n.* a small limbless creeping creature, shaped like a snake; the thread of a screw; a gear-wheel with teeth forming part of screw threads.—*v.i.* to crawl.—*v.t.* to work (oneself) in insidiously; to extract (a secret) craftily. —**worm'wheel,** a gear wheel with teeth cut to be driven by a worm.

worm'wood (wurm-) *n.* a bitter herb.

worn *p.p.* of wear.—*a.* used until damaged; tired, weary.—**worn-out** *a.* unfit for further use; exhausted.

worr'y (wur'i) *v.t.* to seize and shake with teeth; to trouble, harass.—*v.i.* to be unduly concerned (**worr'ied** *p.t.* and *p.p.*—**worr'ying** *pres. p.*).—*n.* useless care or anxiety; cause of this.

worse (wurs) *a.* and *adv. comp.* of bad or badly.—**worst** *a.* and *adv. sup.* of bad or badly.—**wors'en** *v.t.* and *i.*

wor'ship (wur-) *n.* reverence, adoration. —*v.t.* to adore; love and admire.—**wor'shipful** *a.*—**wor'shipper** *n.*

wor'sted (wur-) *n.* woollen yarn.—*a.* made of woollen yarn; spun from wool.

worth (wurth) *a.* having value specified; meriting.—*n.* merit, value.—**wor'thy** (-th-) *a.*—**wor'thily** *adv.* in a worthy manner.—**wor'thiness** *n.*—**worth'less** *a.*

wot' *v.i.* in literature, to know.

wound (wōōnd) *n.* an injury, hurt by cut, stab, etc.; hurt to reputation or feelings.—*v.t.* injure; to pain.

wrack *n.* sea-weed; wreckage, ruin.

wraith *n.* an apparition of a person seen shortly before or after death.

wran'gle (-ng-gl) *v.i.* to quarrel noisily.

wrap *v.t.* to cover, *esp.* by putting something round; to put round.—*n.* a loose garment; a covering.—**wrapp'er** *n.*

wrath (roth, rawth) *n.* anger.—**wrath'ful** *a.* furious.—**wrath'fully** *adv.*

wreak *v.t.* to inflict (vengeance, etc.)

wreath *n.* something twisted into ring form; a garland.—**wreathe** *v.t.* to surround, encircle; to curl, twist.

wreck *n.* destruction of a ship by accident; a wrecked ship; ruin; something ruined.—*v.i.* to cause the wreck of.—**wreck'age** *n.*—**wreck'er** *n.* person who wrecks (or) who plunders wrecked ships.

wren *n.* a very small song bird.

Wren *n.* a member of the Women's Royal Naval Service.

wrench *n.* a violent twist; a tool for twisting or screwing.—*v.t.* to twist; distort; seize forcibly.—he **wrench'es.**

wrest *v.t.* to take by force; to twist violently.—*n.* a tool for tuning a harp, etc.—**wres'tle** (-sl) *v.i.* to contend by grappling and trying to throw down.—**wres'tler** *n.*—**wrest'ling** *pres. p.*—*n.*

wretch *n.* a miserable creature.—**wretch'ed** *a.* miserable; worthless.—**wretch'edness** *n.*—**wretch'edly** *adv.*

Syn. of *a.* distressed, afflicted, forlorn, dejected, pitiable, contemptible. *Ant.* happy, prosperous, flourishing, worthy.

wrig'gle *v.t.* and *i.* to move sinuously. like a worm.—*n.* a quick twisting movement.—**wrig'gling** *pres. p.*

wright (rīt) *n.* a workman, a maker, *esp.* playwright, wheelwright, shipwright.

wring *v.t.* to twist; to extort; to pain (**wrung** *p.t.* and *p.p.*—**wring'ing** *pres. p.*).—**wring'er** *n.* machine for squeezing moisture from clothes.

wrin'kle (-ng-kl) *n.* a slight ridge or furrow on a surface; hint, a clever idea.—*v.t.* to make wrinkles in.—*v.i.* to become wrinkled.

wrist *n.* the joint between hand and arm.—**wrist'band** *n.* the band of a shirt sleeve which covers the wrist; a cuff.—**wrist'let** *n.* band worn on the wrist.—**wrist'-watch** *n.* a watch attached to a band, for wearing on the wrist.

writ *n.* a formal or legal document; written order from a law-court.—**ho'ly writ** *n.* the Bible.

write *v.i.* to mark paper, etc., with the symbols which are used to represent words or sounds; compose; to send a letter.—*v.t.* to set down in words; to compose; to communicate in writing (**wrote** *p.t.*—**writt'en** *p.p.*—**wri'ting** *pres. p.*).—**wri'ter** *n.*—**write up** *n.* N. America, favourable or partial criticism; advertisement copy.—*v.t.* to praise.

writhe *v.i.* to twist or roll about, *esp.* in pain (**writhed** (rīthd) *p.t.*—**writhed** (in poetry) **writh'en** *p.p.*—**wri'thing** *pres. p.*).

wrong *a.* not right or good or suitable; out of order, mistaken.—*n.* that which is wrong; harm; evil, wickedness.—*v.t.* to do wrong to.—**wrong'ly** *adv.*—**wrong'ful** *a.*—**wrong'fully** *adv.*

wroth *a.* angry; in commotion.

wrought (rawt) *p.t.* and *p.p.* of **work.**—**wrought-iron,** iron wrought by forging.

wry *a.* turned to one side, distorted.

wry'neck *n.* genus of small birds allied to woodpecker.

wur'ley *n.* in Australia, aboriginal name for a native hut.

wy'andotte *n.* a breed of fowls.

wych'-elm *n.* a common wild elm; the witch-hazel.

X

xan'thein (zan'-the-in) *n.* yellow colouring matter of flowers that is soluble in water.—**xan'thin** *n.* yellow, insoluble, colouring matter in flowers.

X chromosome, in biology, factor deciding the sex of an offspring. When there are two X chromosomes in the germ cell the offspring is female, if one X and one Y, the offspring is male.

xen'on *n.* an inert constituent of air.

xenopho'bia (zen-o-fōb'i-a) *n.* dislike, hatred, fear, of strangers or aliens.

X-rays (eks-) *n.* electro-magnetic rays that can penetrate opaque substances, used to locate breaks in bones and to diagnose certain diseases.—**X-ray** *n.* a picture made by means of X-rays.—*v.t.* examine, treat, or photograph with X-rays.

xy'lograph (zī'lō-graf) *n.* a wood, engraving; impression from a wood-block.—**xylo'graphy** *n.* wood-engraving.—**xylog'rapher** *n.* an engraver on wood.

xy'lonite (zī) *n.* celluloid.

xy'lophone (zī) *n.* a musical instrument of wooden bars which vibrate when struck by small wooden hammers.

xy'lose (zī-lōs) *n.* wood sugar, a white crystalline substance prepared from wood pulp.

Y

yabb'er *n.* in Australia, used by whites for the speech of the aborigines.

yacht (yot) *n.* a light vessel for racing or pleasure.—*v.i.* to cruise or race in a yacht.—**yachts'man** *n.*
yahoo' *n.* a brute in human form.
yak *n.* the wild ox of Central Asia.
yam *n.* a large, esculent tuber.
Yank'ee *n.* an inhabitant of U.S.A., *esp.* of the New England states.—*a.* belonging to U.S.A.; smart.
yap *n.* and *v.i.* bark (of small dog).
yapp *n.* bookbinding with limp leather, etc.; case projecting over the edges.
yar'borough *n.* a whist or bridge hand containing no card higher than a 9.
yard *n.* a unit of measure, 36 inches; that length of anything; a spar slung across a ship's mast to extend sails.—**yard'arm** *n.*
yard *n.* piece of enclosed ground near building, usually with hard floor.
yarn *n.* spun thread, *esp.* for weaving or knitting; a tale.—*v.i.* to tell a tale.
yar'rah *n.* in Australia, the river gum; its hard, durable timber.
yar'raman *n.* in Australia, aboriginal name for a horse.
yar'ran *n.* Australia, kind of acacia.
yaw *v.i.* to fall off from a course in steering a ship, steer unsteadily.
yawl *n.* a small yacht or boat.
yawn *v.i.* to gape; to open the mouth wide, *esp.* in sleepiness.—*n.* a yawning.
ye *pron.* you.—*pl.* of **thou.**
yea (yā) *interj.* yes (U.S.) Oh yea!
year *n.* time taken by one revolution of earth round sun, about 365½ days; 12 months.—**year'ling** *n.* animal one year old.—**year'ly** *adv.* every year, once a yeai.—*a.* happening, etc., once a year.
yearn (yern) *v.i.* to fell a longing for, to desire; to feel compassion, tenderness etc.
yeast *n.* a substance used as a fermenting agent, *esp.* in raising bread.—**yeast'y** *a.* frothy, fermenting; restless.
yegg *n.* in N. America, (*sl.*) a safe-robber; a tough, *esp.* a criminal; hobo.
yell *v.i.* to cry out in a loud shrill tone.—*n.* loud, shrill cry: in N. Amer., students' cry of prearranged words.
yell'ow (-ō) *a.* of the colour of lemons, gold, etc.; cowardly, spiritless.—*n.* this colour; *a. coll.* cowardly.
yell'ow-hammer *n.* a yellow bunting.
yelp *n.* dog's quick, shrill cry.—*v.i.*
yen *n.* a gold or silver coin of Japan.
yen *n.* (*U.S. sl.*) an urge, craving.
yeo'man (yō) *n.* a man owning and farming a small estate.—**yeo'manry** *n.* yeomen collectively; a volunteer or territorial cavalry force.
yes *interj.* affirms or consents, gives an affirmative answer.
yes'terday *n.* the day before to-day.
yet *adv.* now, still; hitherto; nevertheless. —*conj.* but, at the same time.
yew *n.* evergreen coniferous tree with dark leaves, its wood.
Yid'dish *n.* dialect of mixed German and Hebrew spoken by Jews.—**Yid'** *n.* **Yid'disher** *n.* a Jew.
yield *v.t.* to give or return as food, profit, or result; to give up, surrender.—*v.i.* to produce; to surrender, give way.—*n.* an amount produced, return.
Syn. give way, assent, relinquish, resign, furnish, afford, allow, admit, relax. *Ant.* resist, retain, keep.
yo'del, yo'dle *v.i.* to warble in a falsetto tone.—*n.* falsetto warbling as do Swiss mountaineers.—**yo'delling** *pres. p.*
yo'ga (yō-) *n.* Hindu system of philosophic meditation and asceticism aiming at union of devotee's soul with that of the universal spirit.—**yo'gism** *n.*
yoke *n.* a wooden bar put across the necks of two animals working together various objects like a yoke in shape or use; part of a garment round the neck and shoulders; a bond or tie.—*v.t.* to put a yoke on; couple, unite.
yo'kel *n.* a rustic, a country fellow.
yolk (yōk) *n.* the yellow part of an egg.
yon *a.* that or those over there.—**yon'der** *a.* yon.—*adv.* over there.
yore *n.* the past, long ago.
york'er *n.* a ball (*cricket*) pitching directly under the bat and a little inside the crease.
you (ū) *pron.* the plural of the second person pronoun, but used also in the singular instead of *thee* and *thou.*
young (yung) *a.* not far advanced in growth, life or existence, not yet old; vigorous.—*n.* offspring.—**young'ster** *n.* a child, *esp.* an active or lively boy.
your (yawr) *pron.* belonging to you.—**yours** *pron.* (*sing.* thine).—**yourself'** *pron.* (**yourselves'** *pl.*).
youth (ūth) *n.* the state or time of being young; the state before adult age; a young person; young people.–**youth'ful** *a.*
Yo'yo *n.* a child's toy, a kind of top on a string (protected trade name).
yule (ūl) *n.* Christmas festival.—**yule'log** *n.*—**yule'tide** *n.* Christmas time.

Z

za'ny *n.* a clown; a simpleton.
zare'ba, zaree'ba *n.* Sudan, an enclosure against enemies or wild animals.
zarp *n.* in S. Africa, a Boer police official of the former S. African Republic.
zeal *n.* fervour, keenness.—**zeal'ous** (zel-us) eager, conscientious *a.*—**zeal'-ously** *adv.*—**zeal'ot** *n.* a fanatic.
Syn. intensity, energy, ardour. *Ant.* apathy, indifference, unconcern.
ze'bra *n.* any of a group of horselike striped animals of the genus Equus; **ze'bra cross'ing** *n.* black and white striped street crossing on which pedestrians have right of way.

ze'bu (-boo) *n.* the humped Indian ox.
zena'na (-å-) *n.* the women's quarters in high-caste Indian homes.
zen'ith *n.* a point of the heavens directly above an observer; the highest point.
zeph'yr (zef'er) *n.* west wind; gentle breeze; thin woollen fabric.
Zepp'elin *n.* a German airship.
ze'ro *n.* nothing; figure 0; point on graduated instrument (thermometer) from which positive and negative quantities are reckoned (**zeros, zeroes** *pl.*)—**ze'ro hour,** military, moment at which attack is planned to begin.
zest *n.* relish; enthusiasm, enjoyment.
zig'zag *n.* a line bent by a series of angles, thus VVVV.—*a.* forming a zigzag *adv.*—with a zigzag course.—*v.i.* (*esp.* ships) to move along in a zigzag course.
zinc *n.* a white metal.—*v.t.* to coat with it.
zing'aro *n.* a gipsy (**zing'ari** *pl.*).
Zion'ist *n.* an advocate of the colonisation of Palestine by modern Jews.—**Zion'ism** *a.* this movement.
zip' *n.* a whizzing sound, as of a flying bullet; energy, force.—**zip'-fastener zipper** *n.* device for fastening, worked by a tongue sliding backwards and forwards between two flexible metal stringers.
zith'er, zith'ern *n.* a flat stringed instrument with 29 to 42 strings.
zo'diac *n.* an imaginary belt of the heavens outside which the sun, moon, and planets do not pass and divided crosswise into twelve equal areas, called **signs of the zodiac,** each named after a constellation.—**zo'diacal** *a.*
zo'el *n.* in S. Africa, hot, moist weather.
zom'bi, zom'bie (-bē) *n.* a corpse that has been revived by black magic; in voodoo, the snake god.
zone *n.* a girdle; an encircling band; any of the five belts into which the tropics and the arctic and antarctic circles divide the earth.—**zo'nal** *a.*
zool'ogy (zō-ol'-) *n.* the natural history of animals.—**zoolo'gical** *a.*—**zool'ogist** *n.* one who studies animal life.—**zoo** (zōō) *n.* short for **zoolo'gical gardens,** place where wild animals are kept for show.
zo'ophyte *n.* a plant-like animal, e.g. a sponge.—**zoophyt'ic** *a.*
zo'osperm *n.* a spermatozoid; a zoospore.
zoom *n.i.* in aviation, turn suddenly upwards at a sharp angle.—**zoom'ing** *n.*
zouve (zwav, zōō-åv') *n.* a soldier of French-Algerian infantry.
zy'gote (zī'-got) *n.* a body formed from the coalescence of two gametes; a fertilised ovum.
zymot'ic *a.* of or caused by fermentation; of a disease, due to multiplication of germs introduced into the body from outside.—**zymo'sis** *n.*

CLASSICAL AND FOREIGN WORDS AND PHRASES

Abbreviations—*L.* Latin; *G.* Greek; *F.* French; *It.* Italian; *Ger.* German.

à bas [F.] down with.
ab extra [L.] from without.
ab initio [L.] from the beginning.
ab intra [L.] from within.
abonnement [F.] subscription.
ab ovo [L.] from the beginning.
abrégé [F.] abridgement.
absit invidia [L.] let there be no ill-will.
absit omen [L.] may there be no ill omen.
à cheval [F.] on horseback, astride.
ad finem [L.] to the end.
ad hoc [L.] for this special object.
ad hominem [L.] to the man.
ad infinitum [L.] to infinity.
ad interim [L.] in the meanwhile.
ad libitum (ad lib.) at pleasure.
ad majorem Dei gloriam [L.] for the greater glory of God.
ad nauseam [L.] to the point of disgust.
ad referendum [L.] for consideration.
ad rem [L.] to the point.
adsum [L.] I am here; present!
ad unum omnes [L.] to a man, all.
ad valorem [L.] according to value.
affaire d'amour [F.] a love affair.
affaire d'honneur [F.] an affair of honour, a duel.
affaire du cœur [F.] an affair of the heart.
a fortiori [L]. with stronger reason.
agent provocateur [F.] a police or secret service spy.
à la belle étoile [F.] in the open air.
à la bonne heure [F.] well and good; that's good.
à la carte [F.] picking from the bill of fare, *see* **table d'hôte.**
à la française [F.] in the French style.
à la mode [F.] in the fashion.
al fresco [It.] in the open air.
alma mater [L.] benign mother; the term is used by former students in referring to their university.
alter ego [L.] another self, a close friend.
alter idem [L.] another exactly the same.
alto relievo [It.] high relief.
amende honorable [F.] apology.
amor patriæ [L.] love of country.
amour propre [F.] self-esteem.
ancien régime [F.] the old order.
anglice [L.] in English.
anno ætatis suæ [L.] in the year of his (or her) age.
anno Domini [L.] in the year of our Lord.
anno urbis conditæ [L.] **(A.U.C.)** in the year from the time of the building of the City (Rome).
annus mirabilis [L.] year of wonder.
ante meridiem [L.] before noon.
à outrance [F.] to the utmost, to excess.
à propos [F.] to the point.
arbiter elegantiarum (or elegantiæ) [L.] a judge in matters of taste.
arrière-pensée [F.] mental reservation.
ars longa, vita brevis [L.] art is long, life is short.
à tort et à travers [F.] at random.
au courant [F.] fully acquainted (with).
au revoir [F.] good-bye, till we meet again.
auf Wiedersehen [Ger.] good-bye, till we meet again.
auto da fé [Portuguese] act of faith, the public burning of heretics.
aut vincere aut mori [L.] death or victory.
avant-propos [F.] preliminary matter, preface.
avant-coureur [F.] forerunner.
a vostra salute [It.] } Your health!
à votre santé [F.] }

beatæ memoriæ [L.] of blessed memory.
beau idéal [F.] ideal excellence, imagined state of perfection.
beau monde [F.] fashionable world.
bel esprit [F.] a man of wit.
bête noire [F.] an object of special detestation, pet aversion.
billet doux [F.] a love-letter.
bis dat, qui cito dat [L.] he gives twice who gives promptly.
blitzkrieg [Ger.] lightning war.
bona fide [L.] in good faith.
bonhomie [F.] good nature.
bonjour [F.] good-morning, good-day.
bon marché [F.] cheaply.
bonsoir [F.] good-evening, good-night.
bon ton [F.] good breeding.
breveté [F.] patented.

campo santo [It.] a burial-ground.
carpe diem [L.] enjoy the present day.
carte blanche [F.] full powers.
casus belli [L.] something which involves war.
ça va sans dire [F.] that is a matter of course.
chacun à son goût [F.] every one to his taste.
cetera desunt [L.] the rest is wanting.
ceteris paribus [L.] other things being equal.
chef-d'œuvre [F.] masterpiece.
cherchez la femme [F.] look for the woman; there is a woman at the bottom of the business.
che sarà, sarà [It.] what will be, will be.
chevalier d'industrie [F.] literally, a "knight of industry"; a professional swindler.
ci-devant [F.] former.
comme il faut [F.] as it should be.
compos mentis [L.] sane.

compte rendu [F.] a report.
con amore [It.] with love, earnestly.
concierge [F.] a porter or doorkeeper.
coram populo [L.] in the presence of the people, openly.
corpus delicti [L.] the substance of the offence; the body of the victim of murder.
corrigenda [L.] things to be corrected.
coup d'état [F.] a stroke of policy, a sudden decisive political move, an abuse of authority.
coup de grâce [F.] a finishing blow.
coup de théâtre [F.] a theatrical effect, a sudden change in a situation.
coûte que coûte [F.] at any price.
cui bono? [L.] for whose benefit is it? (i.e. the crime—in a law-case).
cum grano salis [L.] with a grain of salt, with reservation.

de die in diem [L.] from day to day.
de facto [L.] actually, in fact.
de gustibus non est disputandum [L.] there is no arguing about tastes.
Dei gratia [L.] by the grace of God.
de jure [L.] in law, by right.
de mortuis nil nisi bonum [L.] say nothing but good about the dead.
de novo [L.] anew.
Deo gratias [L.] thanks to God.
Deo volente [L.] **(D.V.)** God willing.
de profundis [L.] out of the depths. (The first words of the Latin version of Psalm 130.)
de rigueur [F.] indispensable, obligatory.
de trop [F.] superfluous, intrusive.
deus ex machina [L.] literally, a god out of the (theatrical) machine, i.e. a too obvious device in the plot of a play or story.
dies non [L.] a day on which judges do not sit.
Dieu et mon droit [F.] God and my right; motto of the British crown.
disjecta membra [L.] the scattered remains.
distingué [F.] of distinguished appearance.
distrait [F.] absent-minded.
dolce far niente [It.] pleasant idleness.
double entente [F.] double meaning. (Often **double entendre.**)
douceur [F.] a tip, a bribe.
dramatis personæ [L.] the characters in a drama.

ecce homo! [L.] behold the man! (Spoken by Pilate; St. John, c. 19, v. 5.
embarras de richesses [F.] perplexing wealth.
emeritus [L.] retired from office.
enfants perdus [F.] a forlorn hope.
enfant terrible [F.] literally, a terrible child.
en fête [F.] on holiday, in a state of festivity.
en grande tenue [F.] in full dress.
en masse [F.] in a body.
en passant [F.] in passing, by the way.
en rapport [F.] in sympathy with.
en règle [F.] in due order.
en route [F.] on the way; march!
entente cordiale [F.] friendly understanding between two nations.
entre nous [F.] between ourselves.
e pluribus unum [L.] one out of many. (Motto of the U.S.A.)
errare est humanum [L.] to err is human.
erratum (*pl.* **errata**) [L.] error.
esprit de corps [F.] team-spirit.
et cetera (etc.) [L.] and the rest.
et sequentes (abbreviated as **et seq.**) [L.] and those that follow.
eureka! (heureka) [G.] I have found it! (The exclamation of Archimedes).
ex cathedra [L.] from the chair of office, hence, authoritatively.
exeat [L.] literally, "let him go out"; formal leave of absence.
exempli gratia [L.] **(e.g.)** for example.
exeunt omnes [L.] all go out.
exit [L.] goes out.
ex libris [L.] from the books . . . (followed by the name of the owner).
ex officio [L.] by virtue of his office.
ex parte [L.] on one side, partisan.

facile princeps [L.] an easy first.
fait accompli [F.] a thing done.
faux pas [F.] a false step, a mistake.
felo de se [L.] a suicide, literally, a "felon of himself."
festina lente [L.] hasten slowly.
fête champêtre [F.] a rural festival.
feu de joie [F.] a bonfire.
fiat lux [L.] let there be light.
fidei defensor [L.] defender of the faith.
fin de siècle [F.] end of the 19th century; decadent.
finis [L.] the end.
flagrante delicto [L.] in the very act, red-handed.
fons et origo [L.] the source and origin.

gaudeamus igitur [L.] let us then rejoice.
gendarme [F.] one of the *gendarmerie*, a body of armed police in France.
guerre à outrance [F.] war to the uttermost.

hic jacet [L.] here lies.
hinc illæ lacrimæ [L.] hence these tears.
Hoch! [Ger.] Your health!
honi soit qui mal y pense [Old F.] shame to him who thinks ill of it.
horrible dictu [L.] horrible to relate.
hors de combat [F.] out of condition to fight.

ibidem (abbreviated as **ib.** or **ibid.**) [L.] in the same place.
ich dien [Ger.] I serve.
ici on parle français [F.] here French is spoken.
idée fixe [F.] an obsession, monomania.
id est [L.] (usually **i.e.**) that is.
idem [L.] the same.

ignis fatuus [L.] a will-o'-the-wisp.
impasse [F.] a dead end, an insoluble difficulty.
impedimenta [L.] baggage.
imprimatur [L.] literally, "let it be printed," a licence to print, sanction.
in articulo mortis [L.] at the point of death.
in camera [L.] in a (judge's private) room.
in esse [L.] in being.
in extremis [L.] at the point of death.
in forma pauperis [L.] as a poor man.
infra dignitatem [L.] below one's dignity.
in loco parentis [L.] in the place of a parent.
in medias res [L.] into the midst of things.
in memoriam [L.] to the memory of.
in posse [L.] in possibility.
in propria persona [L.] in one's own person.
in puris naturalibus [L.] quite naked.
in re [L.] in the matter of.
in situ [L.] in its original position.
in statu pupillari [L.] in the state of wardship.
in statu quo [L.] in the former state.
inter alia [L.] among other things.
inter alios [L.] among other people.
in toto [L.] entirely. [(comes out).
in vino veritas [L.] in wine the truth
ipse dixit [L.] "he himself said it"; his unsupported word.
ipsissima verba [L.] the very words.
ipso facto [L.] by the fact itself.

je ne sais quoi [F.] "I don't know what," a something or other.
jeu d'esprit [F.] a witticism.
Jupiter Pluvius [L.] rain-bringing Jupiter, wet weather.

laissez faire [F.] policy of inaction.
lapsus linguæ [L.] a slip of the tongue.
lares et penates [L.] household gods.
leitmotif [Ger.] a theme used to indicate a person, idea, etc., in opera, etc.
lèse-majesté [F.] high treason.
l'état, c'est moi [F.] the state? I am the state. (Saying of Louis XIV.)
lettre de cachet [F.] a sealed letter; a royal warrant for imprisonment.
lex non scripta [L.] unwritten law, i.e. common law.
lex scripta [L.] written, i.e. statute law.
locum tenens [L.] "one occupying the place," a deputy or substitute.
locus classicus [L.] a classical passage.
locus standi [L.] recognised position, right to interfere.

magnum opus [L.] a great work.
mal à propos [F.] ill-timed.
mal de mer [F.] sea-sickness.
malentendu [F.] a misunderstanding.
mariage de convenance [F.] a marriage from motives of interest rather than love.
mauvaise honte [F.] false modesty, bashfulness.
mauvais sujet [F.] a worthless fellow.
mea culpa [L.] by my fault.
memento mori [L.] remember death.
mens sana in corpore sano [L.] a sound mind in a sound body.
mésalliance [F.] marriage with some one of lower social status.
meum et tuum [L.] mine and thine.
mirabile dictu [L.] wonderful to relate.
mise en scène [F.] scenic setting.
modus operandi [L.] manner of working.
mot juste [F.] the exact right word.
multum in parvo [L.] much in little.
mutatis mutandis [L.] with the necessary changes.

née [F.] "born," her maiden name being; e.g. *Mrs. Brown, née Smith.*
nemine contradicente [L.] (often as **nem. con.**) without opposition.
nemo me impune lacessit [L.] no one hurts me with impunity.
ne plus ultra [L.] nothing further; the uttermost point.
nil admirari [L.] to admire nothing, to be superior.
nil desperandum [L.] despair of nothing.
noblesse oblige [F.] nobility imposes obligations.
nolens volens [L.] whether he will or not.
noli me tangere [L.] don't touch me.
nom de guerre [F.] an assumed name. (**nom de plume** is hardly used in French).
non compos mentis [L.] insane.
non omnis moriar [L.] I shall not wholly die.
non sequitur [L.] it does not follow.
nota bene [L.] (N.B.) note well.
nous avons changé tout cela [F.] we have changed all that.
nouveau riche [F.] one newly enriched, an upstart.
nuance [F.] shade, slight difference of meaning or tone.
nulli secundus [L.] second to none.

obiit [L.] he (or she) died.
obiter dictum [L.] (*pl.* **obiter dicta**) something said by the way.
on dit [F.] they say; a rumour.
ora pro nobis [L.] pray for us.
O tempora! O mores! [L.] literally, "O the times! O the manners!"; what dreadful times and doings. [retirement.
otium cum dignitate [L.] dignified
outre [F.] extravagant, eccentric.

pace [L.] by leave of.
par excellence [F.] pre-eminently.
pari passu [L.] with equal pace; together.
passim [L.] here and there, everywhere.
pax vobiscum [L.] peace be with you.
peccavi [L.] I have sinned.
pied-à-terre [F.] temporary lodging.
pinxit [L.] (name of artist) painted this.

poste restante [F.] department of a post office where travellers' letters are kept till called for.
post hoc, ergo propter hoc [L.] after this, therefore because of this. (A fallacy in reasoning.)
post mortem [L.] after death.
prima facie [L.] at a first view.
pro patria [L.] for one's country.
pro tempore [L.] for the time being.
proxim accessit [L.] "he came next." (The "runner-up.")
quantum sufficit [L.] (quant. suff.) as much as suffices.
quis custodiet ipsos custodes? [L.] who will guard the guards?
qui vive? [F.] who goes there?
quod erat demonstrandum [L.] which was to be proved. (Q.E.D.)
quod erat faciendum [L.] (Q.E.F.) which was to be done.
quot homines, tot sententiæ [L.] as many men, so many opinions.
quo vadis? [L.] whither goest thou?
rara avis [L.] a rare bird, something prodigious.
réchauffé [F.] warmed-up dish, stale.
recherché [F.] sought after, exquisite.
reductio ad absurdum [L.] a reducing to the absurd.
répondez, s'il vous plait [F.] (R.S.V.P.) please reply.
requiescat in pace [L.] (R.I.P.) may he (or she) rest in peace.
résumé [F.] a summary or abstract.
resurgam [L.] I shall rise again.
revenons à nos moutons [F.] let us return to our subject. (Literally, "let us return to our sheep.")
rus in urbe [L.] the country in the town.
sang-froid [F.] cold blood; calmness.
sans peur et sans reproche [F.] without fear and without reproach.
sans souci [F.] without care.
sartor resartus [L.] the tailor patched.
sauve qui peut [F.] save himself who can—the cry of disorderly retreat.
savoir faire [F.] knowledge of what to do; skill; tact.
semper fidelis [L.] always faithful.
semper idem [L.] always the same.
se non è vera, è ben trovato [It.] it's not true, it's well invented.
seriatim [L.] in order.
sic [L.] thus. Often used to call attention to some quoted mistake.
sic itur ad astra [L.] such is the way to the stars, to fame or immortality.
sic transit gloria mundi [L.] so passes the glory of the world.
sine die [L.] without date, indefinitely postponed.
si momentum requiris, circumspice [L.] if you seek (his) monument, look around you. (The inscription on the architect Wren's tomb in St. Paul's.)
sine qua non [L.] an indispensable condition.
status quo [L.] "the state in which," the pre-existing state of affairs.
stet [L.] let it stand.
Sturm und Drang [Ger.] storm and stress.
suaviter in modo, fortiter in re [L.] gentle in manner, firm in deed; an iron hand in a velvet glove.
sub judice [L.] under consideration.
sub pœna [L.] under a penalty.
sub rosa [L.] "under the rose," secretly.
sub voce [L.] under that head.
sui generis [L.] of its own kind, peculiar.
sursum corda [L.] lift up your hearts (to God).
table-d'hôte [F.] general guest-table, meal at a fixed price.
tempus fugit [L.] time flies.
terra firma [L.] solid earth.
tertium quid [L.] a third something.
tour de force [F.] a feat of strength or skill.
tout ensemble [F.] the whole taken together, the general effect.
ubique [L.] everywhere.
ultima Thule [L.] the utmost boundary or limit.
ultra vires [L.] beyond one's powers.
ut infra [L.] as below.
ut supra [L.] as above.
vade mecum [L.] go with me; a constant companion, work of reference.
væ victis [L.] woe to the conquered.
vale [L.] farewell.
veni, vidi, vici [L.] I came, I saw, I conquered.
verbum sapienti sat [L.] (verb. sap.) a word is enough for a wise man.
versus [L.] (often v.) against.
via [L.] by way of.
via media [L.] a middle course.
vice [L.] in the place of.
vice versa [L.] the other way round.
videlicet [L.] (viz.) namely, to wit.
virginibus puerisque [L.] for maidens and youths.
vis-à-vis [F.] facing, opposite.
vis inertiæ [L.] the power of inertia.
viva voce [L.] by the living voice; oral.
vive l'empereur! [F.] long live the emperor!
voilà [F.] there! behold!
voilà tout [F.] that's all.
vox et præterea nihil [L.] a voice and nothing more.
vox populi, vox Dei [L.] the voice of the people is the voice of God.
Wanderjahre [Ger.] years of journeymanship, of wandering before settling down.
Weltschmerz [Ger.] world weariness; sentimental pessimism.
Zeitgeist [Ger.] the spirit of the times.

ABBREVIATIONS IN COMMON USE

A

A.A., Automobile Association.
A.A.A., Amateur Athletic Association.
A.A.C.C.A., *Associate* of Association of Certified and Corporate Accountants.
A.A.I.—of the Auctioneers' Institute.
A.A.I.A.—of the Association of International Accountants.
A.B., Able-bodied Seaman.
A.C. (*Ante Christum*) = B.C.
A.C.A., *Associate* of Inst. of Chartered Accountants.
A.C.G.I.—of City and Guilds Institute.
A.C.I.B.—of Corpn. of Insurance Brokers.
A.C.I.I.—of Chartered Insurance Inst.
A.C.I.S.—of the Chartered Institute of Secretaries.
A.C.W.A.—of Inst. of Cost and Works Accountants.
A.D. (*Anno Domini*), In the year of our Lord.
A.D.A., Atomic Development Authority.
A.D.C., Aide-de-Camp.
A.E.A., Air Efficiency Award.
A.F.A.S., *Associate* of Faculty of Architects and Surveyors.
A.F.C., Air Force Cross.
A.F.M., Air Force Medal.
A.I.A.—of the Institute of Actuaries.
A.I.A.A., Architect (A.I.A.S. = Surveyor) Member of Incorp. Assn. of Architects and Surveyors.
A.I.A.C., *Associate* of the Institute of Company Accountants.
A.I.C.—of Institute of Chemistry.
A.I.C.S.—of Institute of Chartered Shipbrokers.
A.Inst.P.—of Institute of Physics.
A.M. (*Ante meridiem*), Before noon.
A.M.G., Allied Military Government.
A.M.I.C.E.—*Associate Member* of Institution of Civil Engineers.
A.M.I.E.E.—Do. Electrical Engineers.
A.M.I.Mech.E.—Do. Mechanical.
A.M.Inst.T.—Do. of Transport.
A.R.A., *Associate* of Royal Academy.
A.R.A.M.—of Royal Academy of Music.
A.R.C.A.—of Royal College of Arts.
A.R.C.M.—Do. Music.
A.R.C.O.—Do. Organists.
A.R.C.S.—Do. Science.
A.R.I.B.A.—of Royal Institute of British Architects.
A.R.I.C.—of Royal Institute of Chem.
A.R.I.C.S.—of Royal Institute of Chartered Surveyors.
A.R.P.S., *Associate* of Royal Photographic Society.
A.R.R.C.—of Royal Red Cross.
A.R.S.M.—of the Royal School of Mines.
A.R.W.S.—of Royal Society of Painters in Water Colours.
A.S.A., Amateur Swimming Association.
A.T.A., Air Transport Auxiliary.
A.T.C., Air Training Corps.
A.T.I., *Associate* of Textile Institute.

B

B.A., *Bachelor* of Arts.
B.Ch. (or Ch.B.)—of Surgery.
B.C.L.—of Civil Law.
B.D.—of Divinity.
B.D.S. (or B.Ch.D).—of Dental Surgery.
B.Eng.—of Engineering.
B.Litt.—of Literature.
B.Phil.—of Philosophy.
B.Sc.—of Science.
B.B.C., British Broadcasting Corporation.
B.C., Before Christ.
B.D.A., British Dental Association.
B.E.M., British Empire Medal.
B.M.A., British Medical Association.
B.O.A.C., British Overseas Airways Corporation.
B.S.T., British Summer Time.
B.Th.U., British Thermal Unit.
B.V.M., Blessed Virgin Mary.

C

C.A., Chartered Accountant (*Scotland*).
Cantab., Cambridge.
Cantuar., Canterbury.
C.B., Companion of the Bath.
C.B.E., Commander of Order of British Empire.
C.E., Civil Engineer.
C. of E., Church of England.
C.F., Chaplain to the Forces.
C.G.M., Conspicuous Gallantry Medal.
C.G.S., Centimetre-gramme-second (system).
C.H., Companion of Honour.
C.I.D., Criminal Investigation Dept.
C.I.E., Companion, Order of Indian Empire.
C.I.F. (usually cif.), Cost, Insurance and Freight.
C.I.G.S., Chief of Imperial General Staff.
C.-in-C., Commander-in-Chief.
C.L.B., Church Lads' Brigade.
C.L.B., Central Land Board.
C.M. (*Chirurgiae Magister*), Master of Surgery.
C.M.G., Companion, Order of St. Michael and St. George.
C.M.S., Church Missionary Society.
C.O., Commanding Officer.
C.S.I., Companion of Order of Star of India.
C.S.C., Civil Service Commission.
C.V.O., Commander of Royal Victorian Order.

D

D.B.E., Dame Commander of Order of British Empire.
D.C.L., *Doctor* of Civil Law.
D.D.—of Divinity.
D.D.S.—of Dental Surgery.

D.Litt. (Camb.)—of Letters.
D.Litt. (Oxon.)—of Literature.
D.Sc.—of Science.
D.C.M., Distinguished Conduct Medal.
D.D.T., dichlorodiphenyltrichloroethane (insecticide).
D.F.C., Distinguished Flying Cross.
D.F.M., Distinguished Flying Medal.
D.I.C., *Diploma* of the Imperial College.
D.P.H.—in Public Health.
D.L., Deputy-Lieutenant.
D.P., Displaced Person(s).
D.S.C., Distinguished Service Cross.
D.S.M., Distinguished Service Medal.
D.S.O., Companion of Distinguished Service Order.

E

E. and O.E., Errors and omissions excepted.
Ebor, York.
E.C.O., European Coal Organization.
E.N.S.A., Entertainments National Services Association.
E.R.P., European Recovery Plan.
E.V.W., European Voluntary Workers.

F

F.A., Football Association.
F.A.C.C.A., *Fellow* of Association of Certified and Corporate Accountants.
F.A.I.A.—of Assoc. of International Accountants.
F.B.A.—of the British Academy.
F.B.A.A.—of Brit. Assoc. of Accountants and Auditors.
F.B.O.A.—of British Optical Association.
F.C.A. — of Institute of Chartered Accountants.
F.C.C.S.—of Corporation of Certified Secretaries.
F.C.I.A.—of Corporation of Insurance Agents.
F.C.I.B.—of Corporation of Insurance Brokers.
F.C.I.I.—of the Chartered Insurance Insitute.
F.C.S.—of the Chemical Society.
F.G.S.—of the Geological Society.
F.H.A.S.—of Highland and Agricultural Society of Scotland.
F.I.A.—of the Institute of Actuaries.
F.I.A.A.—Architect Member of Inc. Assoc. of Architects.
F.I.A.C.—of the Institute of Company Accountants.
F.I.A.S.—Surveyor Member of Inc. Assoc. of Architects.
F.I.C.S.—of Chartered Shipbrokers.
F.Inst.P.—of Physics.
F.I.O.B.—of Builders.
F.I.O.—of Ophthalmic Opticians.
F.J.I.—of Journalists.
F.M.S.—of the Medical Society.
F.R.A.I. — of Royal Anthropological Institute.
F.R.A.M.—of Royal Academy of Music.
F.R.A.S.—of the Royal Astronomical Society.
F.R.Ae.S—of Royal Aeronautical Society.
F.R.C.M.—of the Royal College of Music.
F.R.C.O.—of Royal College of Organists.
F.R.C.P., F.R.C.P.Ed., and F.R.C.P.I.—of the Royal College of Physicians of London, of Edinburgh, and of Ireland respectively.
F.R.C.S.—of Royal College of Surgeons.
F.R.C.S.I., ditto of Ireland.
F.R.C.V.S.—of Royal College of Veterinary Surgeons.
F.R.F.P.S.G.—of the Royal Faculty of Physicians and Surgeons of Glasgow.
F.R.G.S.—of the Royal Geographical Society.
F.R.H.S.—of the Royal Horticultural Society.
F.R.I.B.A.—of the Royal Institute of British Architects.
F.R.I.C.—of the Royal Institute of Chemistry.
F.R.Met.S.—of Royal Meteorological Society.
F.R.P.S. — of Royal Photographic Society.
F.R.S.—of the Royal Society.
F.R.S.E., ditto of Edinburgh.
F.R.S.A.—of the Royal Society of Arts.
F.R.S.L.—Do. Literature.
F.S.A.—of the Society of Antiquaries.
F.T.I.—of Textile Institute.
F.A.N.Y., First Aid Nursing Yeomanry.
F.A.O., Food and Agriculture Organization.
F.B.I., Federation of British Industries.
F.O., Foreign Office.
FOB (*usually* f.o.b.), Free on board.

G

G.B.E., Knight or Dame Grand Cross of British Empire.
G.C., George Cross.
G.C.B., Knight Grand Cross of the Bath.
G.C.M.G., Knight Grand Cross of St. Michael and St. George.
G.C.V.O., Knight Grand Cross of Royal Victorian Order.
G.M., George Medal.
G.M.T., Greenwich Mean Time.
G.O.C., General Officer Commanding.
G.R.C.M., Graduate of the Royal College of Music.
G.R.S.M., Graduate of the Royal Schools of Music (Royal Academy and Royal College).
G.S.O., General Staff Officer.

H

H.A.C., Honourable Artillery Company.
H.E.H., His [Her] Exalted Highness (British India).
H.H., His [Her] Highness.

H.I.H., His [Her] Imperial Highness.
H.I.M., His [Her] Imperial Majesty.
H.J.S. (*Hic. jacet sepultus*), Here lies buried. *cf.* H.S.E.
H.M., His, or Her, Majesty.
H.M.A.S., Her Majesty's Australian Ship.
H.M.O.W., Her Majesty's Office of Works.
H.M.S., Her Majesty's Ship.
H.M.S.O., Her Majesty's Stationery Office.
H.Q., Headquarters.
H.R.H., His [Her] Royal Highness.
H.S.H., His [Her] Serene Highness.

I

I.C.S., Indian Civil Service.
I.C.A.O., International Civil Aviation Organization.
I.H.S. (*Iesus Hominum Salvator*), Jesus the Saviour of Mankind; originally, these were the Greek Capital letters ΙΗΣ.
I.L.O., International Labour Organization.
I.L.P., Independent Labour Party.
I.M.S., Indian Medical Service.
I.N.R.I. (*Iesus Nazarenus Rex Judaeorum*), Jesus of Nazareth King of the Jews.
Inst. (instant), current month.
I.O.O.F., Independent Order of Odd Fellows.
I.Q., Intelligence Quotient.
I.R.O., International Refugee Organization.
I.S.O., Imperial Service Order.

J

J.P., Justice of the Peace.

K

K.B.E., Knight Commander of British Empire.
K.C.B., Do. the Bath.
K.C.I.E., Do. Indian Empire.
K.C.M.G., Do. of St. Michael and St. George.
K.C.S.I., Do. the Star of India.
K.C.V.O., Do. Royal Victorian Order.
K.G., Knight of the Garter.
K.P., Knight of St. Patrick.
K.T., Knight of the Thistle.
Kt., Knight Bachelor.

L

L.A.H., *Licentiate* of Apothecaries' Hall, Dublin.
L.C.P.—of College of Preceptors.
L.D.S.—in Dental Surgery.
L.M.—in Midwifery.
L.M.S.S.A.—in Medicine and Surgery, Soc. of Apothecaries.
L.R.A.M.—of Royal Acad. of Music.
L.R.C.P.—of the Royal College of Physicians.
L.R.C.P.Ed., ditto Edinburgh.
L.R.C.P.I., ditto Ireland.
L.R.C.S.Ed.—of Royal College Surgery, Edinburgh.
L.R.C.S.I., ditto Ireland.
L.R.F.P.S.G.—of the Royal Faculty of Physicians and Surgeons of Glasgow.
L.S.A.—of Society of Apothecaries.
L.C.C., London County Council.
Litt.D., Doctor of Literature.
LL.B., Bachelor of Laws.
LL.D., Doctor of Laws.
L.L.M., Master of Laws.
L.T.A., Lawn Tennis Association.

M

M.A., *Master* of Arts.
M.Ch.—of Surgery.
M.Ch.D.—of Dental Surgery.
M.S.—of Surgery.
M.Sc.—of Science.
M.B., Bachelor of Medicine.
M.D., Doctor of Medicine.
M.B.E., *Member* of British Empire Order.
M.E.C.—of Executive Council.
M.I.Chem.E.—of Institute of Chemical Engineers.
M.I.E.E., M.I.Mar.E., M.I.Mech.E., ditto of Electrical, Marine, and Mechanical Engineers.
M.I.Loco.E.—of Locomotive Engineers.
M.I.Min.E.—of Mining Engineers.
M.Inst.C.E.—of Institution of Civil Engineers.
M.Inst.N.A.—of Naval Architects.
M.Inst.T.—of Transport.
M.L.A.—*Member* of Legislative Assembly.
M.L.C., ditto Council.
M.P.—of Parliament (also Military Police).
M.P.S.—of Pharmaceutical Society.
M.R.A.C.—of Royal Agricultural Coll., Cirencester.
M.R.C.P. — of Royal College of Physicians.
M.R.C.S.—of Royal College of Surgeons.
M.R.C.V.S.—of Royal College of Veterinary Surgeons.
M.R.I.—of the Royal Institution.
M.R.S.T.—of the Royal Society of Teachers.
M.V.O.—of Royal Victorian Order.
M.C., Military Cross.
M.C.C., Marylebone Cricket Club.
Mgr., Monsignor.
M.M., Military Medal.
M.O.H., Medical Officer of Health.
m.p.h., Miles per hour.
MS., manuscript (pl. MSS).
Mus.D.[B.], Doctor, [Bachelor], of Music.

N

N.A.A.F.I., Naval, Army and Air Force Institutes.
N.C.B., National Coal Board.
N.C.O., Non-commissioned Officer.
N.P., Notary Public.

N.R.A., National Rifle Association.
N.S.P.C.C., National Society for the Prevention of Cruelty to Children.
N.S.W., New South Wales.
N.T., New Testament.
N.U.J., *National Union* of Journalists.
N.U.R.—of Railwaymen.

O

O.B.E., Officer of British Empire Order.
O.C., Officer Commanding.
O.E.E.C., Organization for European Economic Co-operation.
O.H.M.S., On Her Majesty's Service.
O.M., Order of Merit (and member of).
O.T., Old Testament.
Oxon., Oxford.

P

P.C., Privy Counsellor.
P.E.N. (*Club*), Poets, Essayists, Novelists.
Ph.D., Doctor of Philosophy.
P.M. (*post meridiem*), Afternoon (also *post mortem*).
P.M.G., Postmaster-General.
P.S. (*Post scriptum*), Postscript.
P.T., Physical Training.
P.T.O., Please turn over.
P.W.D., Public Works Dept.

Q

Q.C., Queen's Council.
Q.M.G., Quartermaster-General.
Q.S., Quarter Sessions.

R

R.A., *Royal* Artillery or Royal Academy.
R.A.C.—Armoured Corps (also Royal Automobile Club).
R.A.E.C.—Army Educational Corps.
R.A.F., — Air Force.
R.A.M., — Academy of Music.
R.A.M.C., — Army Medical Corps.
R.A.N., — Australian Navy.
R.A.P.C., — Army Pay Corps.
R.A.O.C., — Army Ordnance Corps.
R.A.S.C., — Army Service Corps.
R.A.V.C., — Army Veterinary Corps.
R.B.A., — Society of British Artists.
R.C.N., — Canadian Navy.
R.C.N.C., — Corps of Naval Constructors.
R.D., — Naval Reserve Decoration, or Rural Dean.
R.E., — Engineers.
R.E.M.E., — Electrical and Mechanical Engineers.
R.H.A., — Horse Artillery, or— Hibernian Academy.
R.I.A., — Irish Academy.
R.L.S.S., — Life Saving Society.
R.M., — Marines.
R.M.A., — Military Academy.
R.N., — Navy; R.N.R.—Naval Reserve; R.N.V.R.—Naval Volunteer Reserve.
R.O.I., — Institute of Oil Painters.
R.S.A., — Scottish Academician.
R.S.P.C.A., — Society for the Prevention of Cruelty to Animals.
R.W.S., — Water Colour Society.
R.C., Roman Catholic.
R.I.P. (*Requiescat in pace*), May he rest in peace.
R.R.C., Lady of Royal Red Cross.
R.S.V.P. (*Répondez, s'il vous plaît*), Answer, if you please.
R.V., Revised Version (of Bible).

S

Sc.D., Doctor of Science.
S.J., Society of Jesus.
S.O.S. ("Save Our Souls") Distress Signal.
S.P.C.K., Society for the Promotion of Christian Knowledge.
S.R.N., State Registered Nurse.
S.S.A.F.A., Soldiers', Sailors, and Airmen's Families Association.
S.S.C., Solicitor in the Supreme Court (Scotland.)

T

T.D., Territorial Decoration.
T.C.D., Trinity College, Dublin.
T.N.T., Trinitrotoluene (explosive).
T.U.C., Trades Union Congress.

U

U.C.D., University College, Dublin.
Ult. (*ultimo*), in the preceding month.
U.K., United Kingdom.
U.N.A., United Nations Association.
U.N.A.C., United Nations Appeal for Children.
U.N.E.S.C.O., United Nations Educ. Scientific and Cultural Organization.
U.N.O., United Nations Organization.
U.P., United Press.
U.P.U., Universal Postal Union.
U.S.A. or U.S., United States of America.
U.S.C.L., United Society for Christian Literature.
U.S.S.R., Union of Socialist Soviet Republics.

V

V.A.D., Voluntary Aid Detachment.
V.C., Victoria Cross.
V.D., Volunteer Officers' Decoration.
Viz. (*videlicet*), Namely.

W

W.H.O., (United Nations) World Health Organization.
W.O., War Office.
W.R.A.C., Women's Royal Army Corps.
W.R.A.F., Women's Royal Air Force.
W.R.N.S., Women's Royal Naval Service.
W.V.S., Women's Voluntary Services.

Y

Y.M.C.A., Young Men's Christian Assoc.
Y.W.C.A., Young Women's ditto.

WEIGHTS AND MEASURES

TROY WEIGHT

grains = 1 pennyweight.
pennyweights = 1 ounce (480 grains).
ounces = 1 pound (5760 grains).

Diamonds and Pearls are weighed by rats, of 4 grains each (equal only to Troy grains). The Troy ounce is equal 150 Diamond Carats. Gold, when re, is said to be 24 carats fine; if it tains one part alloy it is said to be carats fine, and so on.

AVOIRDUPOIS WEIGHT

Used for all General Merchandise

drams =1 ounce (437½ grains Troy).
ounces =1 pound (7000 grains Troy).
pounds =1 stone.
pounds =1 quarter.
quarters =1 hundredweight (112 pounds).
hundredweights =1 ton (2240 pounds).

Avoirdupois Pounds exceed Troy in proportion of 17 to 14 nearly; Troy nces are greater than Avoirdupois in proportion of 79 to 72 nearly.

APOTHECARIES' WEIGHT

Used for Dispensing Drugs, etc.

20 grains = 1 scruple.
3 scruples = 1 dram.
8 drams = 1 ounce.
12 ounces = 1 pound.

MEASURES OF LENGTH

Linear Measure

12 inches = 1 foot.
3 feet = 1 yard.
5½ yards = 1 pole, rod, or perch.
4 poles = 1 chain.
10 chains = 1 furlong.
8 furlongs = 1 mile (1760 yds)..
3 miles = 1 league.

Surveyors' Measure

7·92 inches = 1 link.
100 links = 1 chain.
80 chains = 1 mile.
10 sq. chains = 1 acre.

SQUARE MEASURE

144 square inches = 1 square foot.
9 square feet = 1 square yard.
30¼ square yards = 1 square pole.
40 square poles = 1 rood.
4 roods = 1 acre.
640 acres = 1 square mile.

SOLID OR CUBIC MEASURE

1728 cubic inches = 1 cubic foot.
27 cubic feet = 1 cubic yard.
5 cubic feet = 1 barrel bulk. shipping.
40 cubic feet = 1 ton shipping.
40 cubic feet = 1 load hard timber.
50 cubic feet = 1 load foreign fir.

MEASURE OF CAPACITY

Used for Liquids and Dry Goods

4 gills = 1 pint.
2 pints = 1 quart.
4 quarts = 1 gallon.
2 gallons = 1 peck.
4 pecks = 1 bushel.
8 bushels = 1 quarter.
5 quarters = 1 load.
36 bushels = 1 chaldron.

A bushel of wheat on an average weighs 60 pounds; of barley 47 pounds; of oats, 40 pounds. The gallon contains 10 pounds avoirdupois of distilled water.

DECIMAL MEASURE OF CAPACITY

Pints		*Gall.*		*Cub. Ft.*		*Litres*
1	=	0·125	=	·02	=	0·567
8	=	1·000	=	·1604	=	4·541
16	=	2·000	=	·3208	=	9·082

APOTHECARIES' FLUID MEASURE

60 minims = 1 dram.
8 drams = 1 ounce.
20 ounces = 1 pint.
8 pints = 1 gallon.

THE METRIC SYSTEM MEASURE OF LENGTH

10 Millimetres = 1 Centimetre.
10 Centimetres = 1 Decimetre.
10 Decimetres = 1 Metre.
10 Metres = 1 Dekametre.
10 Dekametres = 1 Hectometre.
10 Hectometres = 1 Kilometre.
10 Kilometres = 1 Myriametre.
One Metre = 1·094 yards = 39·371 ins.

MEASURE OF SURFACE

10 Centiares	=	1 Deciare.
10 Deciares	=	1 Are (100 sq. metres).
10 Ares	=	1 Dekare.
10 Dekares	=	1 Hectare.
100 Hectares	=	1 Sq. Kilometre.

One Hectare = 2 acres, 1 rood, 35 poles.

MEASURE OF WEIGHT

10 Milligrams	=	1 Centigram.
10 Centigrams	=	1 Decigram.
10 Decigrams	=	1 Gram.
10 Grams	=	1 Dekagram.
10 Dekagrams	=	1 Hectogram.
10 Hectograms	=	1 Kilogram.
10 Kilograms	=	1 Myriagram.
1 Kilogram	=	2 lb. 3¼ oz.
1 Pound Avoir.	=	·4535 Kilogs.

MEASURE OF CAPACITY

10 Millitres	=	1 Centilitre.
10 Centilitres	=	1 Decilitre.
10 Decilitres	=	1 Litre.
10 Litres	=	1 Dekalitre.
10 Dekalitres	=	1 Hectolitre.
10 Hectolitres	=	1 Kilolitre.
1 Litre	=	1¾ pints.

USEFUL DATA

1 Kilogramme (Kilo.)	=	2·204 Lbs.
1 Hectolitre	=	22 Imperial Gallons.
1 Pood	=	36 Lbs.
1 Ton (2240 lbs.)	=	62·22 Poods.
U.S. Gallon	=	0·883 Imperial Gallons.
6 U.S. Gallons	=	5 Imperial Gallons.
1 Metric Ton (1000 Kilos)	=	2204 Lbs.
1 Metre	=	3 Feet 3¼ Inches.
1 Kilometre	=	0·621 Mile.

ROMAN NUMERALS

I.	=	1	XX.	=	20
II.	=	2	XXX.	=	30
III.	=	3	XL.	=	40
IV. or IIII.	=	4	L.	=	50
V.	=	5	LX.	=	60
VI.	=	6	LXX.	=	70
VII.	=	7	LXXX.	=	80
VIII.	=	8	XC.	=	90
IX.	=	9	C.	=	100
X.	=	10	CC.	=	200
XI.	=	11	CCC.	=	300
XII.	=	12	CCCC. or CD.	=	400
XIII.	=	13	D.	=	500
XIV.	=	14	DC.	=	600
XV.	=	15	DCC.	=	700
XVI.	=	16	DCCC.	=	800
XVII.	=	17	CM.	=	900
XVIII.	=	18	M.	=	1000
XIX.	=	19	MM.	=	2000

CIRCULAR OR ANGULAR MEASURE

60 seconds (sec. or ″)	=	1 minute (min. or ′).
60 minutes	=	1 degree (deg. or °).
45 degrees	=	1 octant.
60 degrees	=	1 sextant.
90 degrees	=	1 quadrant or right ang (rt. ang. or L).
360 degrees	=	1 circle, or circumferen (cir.).

The diameter of a circle is a straigl line passing through its centre. Tl radius is half the diameter. The circun ference is almost exactly 3⅐ times tl diameter. Given the diameter, to fin the circumference, multiply by 22 an divide by 7.

NAUTICAL MEASURE

6 feet	=	1 fathom.
100 fathoms	=	1 cable's length.
1000 fathoms	=	1 nautical mile c knot.
3 naut. miles	=	1 sea league.
60 naut. miles	=	1 degree.
360 degrees	=	1 circle.

PAPER MEASURE

24 sheets	=	1 quire.
20 quires	=	1 ream.
21½ quires or 516 sheets	=	1 printer's ream.
2 reams	=	1 bundle.
10 reams	=	1 bale.
60 skins of parchment	=	1 roll.

In a ream of paper there are two out side or damaged quires. An outsid quire of paper contains only 20 sheet

SIZES OF BOOKS

Fo.	=	Folio. Sheet folded into 2 leave or 4 pages.
4to	=	Quarto. Sheet folded int 4 leaves or 8 pages.
8vo	=	Octavo. Sheet folded int 8 leaves or 16 pages.
12mo	=	Duodecimo. Sheet folded int 12 leaves or 24 pages.
16mo	=	Sextodecimo. Sheet folded int 16 leaves or 32 pages.
18mo	=	Octodecimo. Sheet folded int 18 leaves or 36 pages.

Foolscap 8vo	=	6¾	×	4¼	inche
Crown 8vo	=	7½	×	5	,,
Demy 8vo	=	8⅜	×	5⅝	,,
Royal 8vo	=	10	×	6¼	,,
Imperial 8vo	=	11	×	7½	,,
Crown 4to	=	10	×	7½	,,
Demy 4to	=	11¼	×	8¾	,,
Crown Folio	=	15	×	10	,,
Royal Folio	=	20	×	12½	,,